DK SMITHSONIAN

TIMELINES *of* HISTORY

SMITHSONIAN

TIMELINES *of* HISTORY

Penguin
Random
House

SECOND EDITON

Senior Art Editor
Mahua Mandal

Senior Editor
Bharti Bedi

Designers
Anjali Sachhar, Devika Khosla,
Jomin Johny

Editors
Rishi Bryan, Priyadarshini Gogoi,
Arani Sinha, Isha Sharma

Managing Art Editor
Sudakshina Basu, Michael Duffy

US Executive Editor
Lori Hand

Jacket Designer
Suhita Dharamjit

Managing Editors
Angeles Gavira, Rohan Sinha

Jacket Design Development Manager
Sophia MTT

Jacket Editor
Priyanka Sharma

Senior DTP Designer
Harish Aggarwal, Vishal Bhatia

Managing Jackets Editor
Saloni Singh

Producer, Pre-production
Gillian Reid

Senior Producer
Alex Bell

Art Director
Karen Self

Associate Publishing Director
Liz Wheeler

Publishing Director
Jonathan Metcalf

First American Edition, 2011
This edition published in the United States in 2018 by DK Publishing,
345 Hudson Street, New York, New York 10014

Copyright © 2011, 2018 Dorling Kindersley Limited
DK, a Division of Penguin Random House LLC

18 19 20 21 22 10 9 8 7 6 5 4 3 2 1
001–308512–April/2018

A catalog record for this book
is available from the Library of Congress.
ISBN 978-1-4654-7002-7

DK books are available at special discounts when purchased
in bulk for sales promotions, premiums, fund-raising, or educational use. For details, contact:
DK Publishing Special Markets, 345 Hudson Street, New York, New York 10014
SpecialSales@dk.com

Printed and bound in China

A WORLD OF IDEAS:
SEE ALL THERE IS TO KNOW

www.dk.com

FIRST EDITION

Senior Art Editor
Sudakshina Basu, Balwant Singh,
Ina Stradins

Senior Editors
Soma B. Chowdhury, Peter Frances,
Angeles Gavira Guerrero, Janet Mohun

Project Art Editors
Paul Drislane, Alison Gardner, Anna Hall,
Francis Wong

Project Editors
Lara Maiklem, Ruth O'Rourke-Jones,
Peter Preston, David Summers

Designers
Mini Dhawan, Riccie Janus, Fiona
Macdonald, Anjana Nair, Pallavi Narain,
Duncan Turner

Editors
Rahul Ganguly, Corinne Masciocchi, Lizzie
Munsey, Martyn Page, Laura Palosuo, Gill
Pitts, Steve Setford, Nikki Simms, Alison
Sturgeon, Miezan van Zyl, Laura Wheadon,
Victoria Wiggins

Design Assistants
Showmik Chakraborty, Arushi Nayar, Neha
Sharma, Pooja Verma

Editorial Assistants
Sudeshna Dasgupta, Sam Priddy,
Himanshi Sharma

Senior Production Controller
Mandy Inness

Production Editor
Ben Marcus

Creative Technical Support
Adam Brackenbury

Indexer
Hilary Bird

Picture Researchers
Ria Jones, Liz Moore

Managing Art Editor
Michelle Baxter, Arunesh Talapatra

Jacket Designer
Mark Cavanagh

DTP Manager
Balwant Singh

US Editors
Jill Hamilton, Christine Heilman, Margaret
Parrish

Production Manager
Pankaj Sharma

DTP Designers
Rajesh Singh Adhikari, Shankar Prasad,
Arjinder Singh, Tanveer Abbas Zaidi

Cartographer
Encompass Graphics Limited

Managing Editors
Sarah Larter, Rohan Sinha

Senior DTP Designers
Dheeraj Arora, Jagtar Singh

Art Director
Phil Ormerod

Publisher
Jonathan Metcalf

SMITHSONIAN INSTITUTION

Project Co-ordinator
Ellen Nanney

CONTRIBUTORS

HUMAN ORIGINS
Dr. Fiona Coward
Research Fellow at Royal Holloway University of London; contributed to DK's *Prehistoric*.
Additional text by Dr. Jane McIntosh

EARLY CIVILIZATIONS
Dr. Jen Green
Author of over 250 books on a range of subjects from history to nature.
Additional text by Dr. Jane McIntosh

THE CLASSICAL AGE
Philip Parker
Historian and writer; books include *The Empire Stops Here* and *DK Eyewitness Companion to World History*.

TRADE AND INVENTION
Joel Levy
Writer specializing in history and scientific history; books include *Lost Cities* and *Lost Histories*.

REFORMATION AND EXPLORATION
Thomas Cussans
Author and contributor to *The Times* newspaper; previous titles for DK include *Timelines of World History* and *History*.
Additional text by Frank Ritter

THE AGE OF REVOLUTION
Dr. Carrie Gibson
Writer who has contributed to *The Guardian* and *Observer* newspapers; doctorate in 18th- and 19th-century history from the University of Cambridge, UK.

TECHNOLOGY AND SUPERPOWERS
R.G. Grant
History writer who has published more than 20 books, including *Battle*, *Soldier*, *Flight*, and *History* for DK.

Sally Regan
Contributor to several books for DK including *History*, *World War II*, and *Science*; award-winning documentary maker whose films include *Shell Shock* and *Bomber Command* for the UK's Channel 4.

GLOSSARY
Richard Beatty

CONSULTANTS

Dr. Jane McIntosh
8MYA–700BCE
Senior Research Associate, Faculty of Asian and Middle Eastern Studies, University of Cambridge, UK

Professor Neville Morley
700BCE–599CE
Professor of Ancient History, School of Humanities, University of Bristol, UK

Dr. Roger Collins
600–1449
Honorary Fellow, School of History, Classics and Archaeology, University of Edinburgh, UK

Dr. David Parrott
1450–1749
Fellow in History and University Lecturer, New College, University of Oxford, UK

Dr. Michael Broers
1750–1913
Fellow and Tutor, Lady Margaret Hall, University of Oxford, UK

Professor Richard Overy
1914–present
Professor of History, University of Exeter, UK

SMITHSONIAN

Smithsonian contributors include historians and museum specialists from:

National Air and Space Museum
The Smithsonian's National Air and Space Museum is one of the world's most popular museums. Its mission is to educate and inspire visitors by preserving and displaying aeronautical and space flight artifacts.

National Museum of American History
The Smithsonian's National Museum of American History dedicates its collections and scholarship to inspiring a broader understanding of the American nation and its many peoples.

National Museum of Natural History
The Smithsonian's National Museum of Natural History is the most visited natural history museum in the world and the most visited museum in the Smithsonian complex.

1
8MYA–3000BCE

2
3000–700BCE

3
700BCE–599CE

4
600–1449

CONTENTS

5
1450–1749

6
1750–1913

7
1914–2017

8

Foreword

Like many people, my early enthusiasm for history focused on particular dates and events: 1588 and the defeat of the Spanish Armada; the battle of Waterloo in 1815; the fall of Constantinople in 1453. Some had personal connections: July 1, 1916, when my grandfather, serving as an artilleryman, lost several of his closest friends on the first day of the Somme offensive.

From the earliest times, history was cast as a grand chronicle of events and actions, the work of often larger-than-life protagonists, and was intended to enthrall and capture the imagination in the same way as a great novel. But during the 20th century, academic historians grew skeptical about the "history of the event." Most often the events were battles, treaties, and political struggles, a narrative that excluded the lives of the great majority of men, women, and children. In reaction to this, historians focused on cultural, social, and economic continuities, looking for their evidence in everyday objects, trading records, accounts of childhood and old age. The result was certainly a richer and more diverse account of human experience, but one that often left little sense of change over time.

As the present book shows, history constructed on a timeline does not have to be a narrow account of war and conquest, treaties and treason. All of these feature here, but so do the dates of intellectual and technological innovations, the creation of key works of art, crucial shifts in patterns of agriculture,

exploration, and commerce. This is an exhilarating and comprehensive account of human creativity as much as its destructiveness, of discovery and understanding as well as natural disasters and human folly. Spectacularly illustrated and succinctly explained, key events in history from the first beginnings of agriculture to the most recent astrophysical discoveries are laid out along what is probably the most comprehensive timeline ever assembled.

No less exciting for me in helping to compose this book and to choose from all facets of human history to build up the timeline, is the contribution that *Timelines of History* makes to an understanding of global history. Throughout the book, events, discoveries, and achievements occurring in Europe and North America are set against the equally momentous and significant events in the Mideast and East Asia, India, Africa, or South America and the Pacific Rim. This is a history that stimulates awareness of a wider world by placing events from across that world side by side and reminding us that progress and discovery, feats of social organization, and challenges to a political status quo are no monopoly of the Western world, but as likely to originate in India or Egypt as in France and Spain.

The design of this book offers a unique opportunity to appreciate a global history of mankind in all its facets. I hope that you enjoy reading *Timelines of History* and using it as a reference as much as we enjoyed planning and writing it

DAVID PARROTT
University of Oxford

Lost city of the Incas
Perched 7,970 ft (2,430 m) above sea level, in the Peruvian Andes, the Inca citadel of Machu Picchu was probably constructed in the 15th century, and abandoned in the 16th.

HUMAN ORIGINS

8 MYA–3000 BCE

Our earliest ancestors lived in Africa almost eight million years ago. Over seven million years later, we appeared and developed the skills—including sophisticated toolmaking and agriculture—that allowed us to colonize the world.

Olduvai Gorge in Tanzania is an area of great archaeological significance and is sometimes referred to as the "Cradle of Mankind." At least two species of early hominins are associated with this area.

THE DIFFERENCES BETWEEN HUMANS AND OTHER APES' DNA and blood proteins suggest that our lineage separated from that of the chimpanzees between 8 and 6 million years ago (MYA). Only a few fossil specimens are known from this time: *Sahelanthropus tchadensis* (7.1–6.8 MYA), *Orrorin*

7 MYA
THE TIME WHEN **THE FIRST** HUMAN **ANCESTOR** APPEARS

tugenensis (6.1–5 MYA), and two species of *Ardipithecus*, *kadabba* (5.8–5.2 MYA) and *ramidus* (4.4 MYA). While all of these species seem to have **walked on two legs** like us, it is not certain whether any were actual ancestors of humans. Because species are **constantly evolving**, and individuals of those species can vary, it is difficult to tell from isolated and often fragmented fossils which species they should be assigned to, or how these are related to one another. However, these fossils do tell us a great deal about what the **last common ancestor** we shared with chimpanzees was like.

SEVERAL DIFFERENT AUSTRALOPITHECINE species lived in Africa between 4.2 and 2 MYA. Although they walked on two legs most of the time, they were rather **small and apelike**

Lucy
This unusually complete skeleton of Australopithecus afarensis, discovered in Kenya in 1974, was named after the Beatles' song "Lucy in the Sky with Diamonds."

and still lived partially in trees. Their brains were about the size of those of modern chimpanzees, but some australopithecines seem to have **used tools**. The earliest stone tools come from Kenya and date to 3.3 MYA, but bones with cut marks made by stone tools have been found associated with *Australopithecus afarensis* nearby, and date to 3.4 MYA. The australopithecines' descendants followed two distinct modes of life: members of the genus *Paranthropus* had huge jaws and big teeth for eating tough vegetable foods; meanwhile, *Homo rudolfensis* and *H. habilis* seem to have eaten **more protein**, using tools to get at the protein-rich marrow inside long bones by scavenging from carnivore kills.

OLDOWAN TOOL

ACHEULEAN TOOL

TOOLS

Many animal species use natural objects as tools, but only the hominins are known to have manufactured stone tools. The earliest are simply sharp flakes broken off stone cobbles by striking them with a "hammerstone." These are known as "Oldowan" tools, after Olduvai Gorge, where they were first found. Later tools, such as Acheulean handaxes, required more skill. Our manufacture of tools might be one explanation for the evolution of the human brain.

ULTIMATELY, THE PARANTHROPINES' WAY OF LIFE was unsuccessful and they became **extinct** after about **1.2 MYA**, while their cousins *Homo habilis* and *H. rudolfensis* survived. These early *Homo* species were not very different from australopithecines.

It was with *Homo ergaster* (1.8 MYA) that our ancestors started to **look much more familiar**. *H. ergaster* was tall and slender, and may have been the first hominin (a term used to describe humans and their ancestors) without much body hair. Their **brains were larger** than those of their ancestors, and they lost the last of their adaptations to tree-climbing to become fully adapted to walking and running.

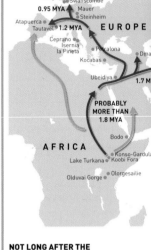

NOT LONG AFTER THE APPEARANCE of *Homo ergaster*, hominins expanded their range **beyond Africa** for the first time. A species called *H. georgicus* appeared in Dmanisi, Georgia, by 1.7 MYA. Another close relative of *Homo ergaster*, *Homo erectus*, lived in East Asia about the same time. Some archaeologists believe that earlier groups of hominins may also have left Africa, as some of the skulls from Dmanisi and from the much later site of Liang Bua in Flores, Indonesia (currently known as *Homo floresiensis*), resemble those of *Homo habilis* and *Homo rudolfensis*.

Living farther north would have required a **different way of life** than life in the African savanna.

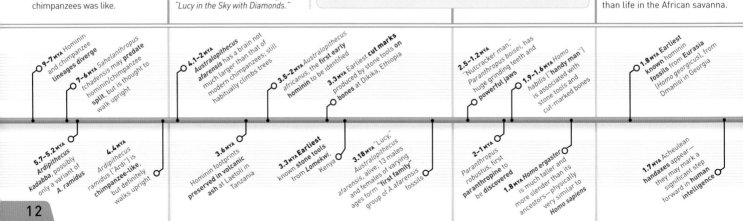

9–7 MYA Hominin and chimpanzee **lineages diverge**

7–6 MYA *Sahelanthropus tchadensis* may **predate** hominin/chimpanzee **split**, but is thought to walk upright

5.7–5.2 MYA *Ardipithecus kadabba*, possibly only a variant of *A. ramidus*

4.4 MYA *Ardipithecus ramidus* ("Ardi") is **chimpanzee-like**, but definitely walks upright

4.1–2 MYA *Australopithecus afarensis* has a brain not much larger than that of modern chimpanzees; still habitually climbs trees

3.6 MYA Hominin footprints **preserved in volcanic ash** at Laetoli in Tanzania

3.5–2 MYA *Australopithecus africanus*, the **first early hominin** to be identified

3.3 MYA **Earliest stone tools** from Lomekwi, Kenya

3.3 MYA Earliest **cut marks** produced by stone tools on **bones** at Dikika, Ethiopia

3.18 MYA "Lucy," *Australopithecus afarensis*, alive; 13 males and females of varying ages form **"first family"** group of A afarensis fossils

2.5–1.2 MYA "Nutcracker man," *Paranthropus boisei*, has huge grinding teeth and **powerful jaws**

2–1 MYA *Paranthropus robustus*, first **paranthropine** to be **discovered**

1.9–1.6 MYA *Homo habilis* ("**handy man**") is associated with stone tools and cut-marked bones

1.8 MYA *Homo ergaster* is much taller and more slender than its ancestors—physically very similar to *Homo sapiens*

1.8 MYA **Earliest known** hominin **fossils** from Eurasia (*Homo georgicus*), from Dmanisi in Georgia

1.7 MYA Acheulean **handaxes** appear— they may mark a significant step forward in **human intelligence**

> ALL LIVING HUMANS **DESCENDED FROM COMMON ANCESTORS** WHO LIVED IN AFRICA LESS THAN 200,000 YEARS AGO.

Stephen Jay Gould, American paleontologist, from *I Have Landed: The End of a Beginning in Natural History*, 2002

Hominins beyond Africa

KEY
- Site of fossil finds
- → Likely route
- ⇢ Other possible routes

Our earliest ancestors evolved in Africa. Possible dispersal routes from Africa are shown on this map, with dates referring to the earliest fossils known from each region.

The climate was cooler and environments were more seasonal, with significant variation in food resources over the course of a year. Fewer edible plants meant that hominins would have had to rely more on harder-to-find and fiercely competed-for **animal protein** for food. They needed to move over greater distances and **work together** to share resources and information to **survive** in these regions.

ACHEULEAN HANDAXES made by *Homo ergaster* and *H. erectus* were produced across most of Africa and Eurasia, but were less common in Asia. They demonstrate the ability to learn **complex skills** from one another and pass them down over generations. To make these tools, knappers had to think several steps ahead in order to select a suitable stone and to prepare and place each strike. Handaxes were used for a wide range of activities, especially butchery, but they might also have been important for **personal or group identity**, demonstrating their makers' strength and skill.

While *Homo erectus* continued to thrive in Asia, **Homo antecessor** had appeared as far west as northern Spain and Italy by 1.2 MYA. Marks on their bones at the site of **Atapuerca** in Spain suggest **cannibalism** sometimes happened. However, these early colonists may not have thrived in these unfamiliar landscapes, as very few sites are known, perhaps because they did not yet habitually make fire. By 600,000 years ago, a new hominin species, **Homo heidelbergensis**, had spread much more widely across Europe. *H. heidelbergensis* seems to have been a good hunter, probably alongside some scavenging.

HOMININ BRAIN SIZES

 Australopithecines 28 cubic inches (461 cubic cm)

 Paranthropines 32 cubic inches (517 cubic cm)

 Homo habilis Homo rudolfensis 40 cubic inches (648 cubic cm)

Homo erectus Homo ergaster 59 cubic inches (969 cubic cm)

 Homo heidelbergensis 73 cubic inches (1,204 cubic cm)

 Homo neanderthalensis 95–101 cubic inches (1,550–1,600 cubic cm)

Homo sapiens 90 cubic inches (1,480 cubic cm)

Humans have a disproportionately large brain for a primate of their size, but archaeologists disagree about how and why this expansion happened. Switching to fatty and calorific foods such as bone marrow and meat may have "powered" brain growth, and also demanded more complex tools and effective hunting and foraging skills. Social skills were also a part of this process, as increasing group cooperation and pair-bonding were necessary to sustain the longer periods of childhood that infants needed for their larger brains to develop.

Burying the dead
Neanderthals often disposed of their dead with care. Some were buried in graves, as here at Kebara Cave in Israel, which dates to 60,000 BCE.

BY AROUND 350,000 YEARS AGO, while *Homo erectus* evolved locally in eastern Asia, *Homo heidelbergensis* in Europe and Western Asia had evolved into *Homo neanderthalensis*.

Neanderthals were **stockier and stronger** than modern humans, and their brains were as large or even larger, although shaped slightly differently. Neanderthals were hunters at the top of the food chain. They were also **highly skilled** at making stone tools and heavy spears with which they tackled even large and dangerous animal prey, such as horses and bison.

However, despite treating some of their dead in special ways, including burial, Neanderthals do not seem to have created any **representative art**, or repeated symbols, as all modern humans do. Whether or not they spoke in a similar way to modern humans is also difficult to establish. Although minor anatomical differences did exist in the voice box and throat, **Neanderthals** could produce most sounds humans can. Gestures probably were as important to them as they are to humans.

In Africa, hominin fossils gradually began to reveal the characteristic skeletal traits of *Homo sapiens* from around 300,000 YA: smaller brow ridges, higher and rounder skulls, and chins. New dating of the fossils from Jebel Irhoud, Morocco, show that North Africa was also an important region for these early *Homo sapiens*. DNA analysis of living humans suggests that the **common ancestors** of all living humans (known as **Mitochondrial Eve**) lived in Africa around 300,000–200,000 YA.

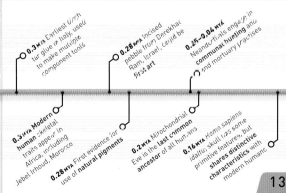

1.65–1 MYA Finds of *Homo erectus* from Java dated as early as 1.5 MYA, but more likely to date from around 1 MYA

1.5 MYA Tanzania 'boy' is an almost complete skeleton of an adolescent *Homo ergaster* from Tanzania

0.79 MYA First reliable evidence for control of fire at Gesher Benot Ya'aqov, Israel

0.78 MYA Earth's magnetic field assumes current polarity

0.3 MYA Earliest birch tar glue in Italy, used to make multiple component tools

0.28 MYA Incised pebble from Berekhat Ram, Israel, could be first art

0.25–0.04 MYA Neanderthals engage in communal hunting and mortuary practises

1.6 MYA Earliest known artifacts in China thought to have been made by *Homo erectus*, although fossils from region currently date to only 0.8 MYA

1.5–1.4 MYA Evidence of fire at sites in South Africa, but may be natural

1.2 MYA Appearance of first Europeans—*Homo antecessor*

0.4 MYA *Homo heidelbergensis* now widespread

0.4 MYA Distinctive Neanderthal anatomy appearing across Europe

0.4 MYA Fire-hardened wooden spears in use

0.3 MYA Modern human skeletal traits appear in Africa, including Jebel Irhoud, Morocco

0.28 MYA First evidence for use of natural pigments

0.2 MYA Mitochondrial Eve is the last common ancestor of all humans

0.16 MYA *Homo sapiens idaltu*: skull has some primitive features, but shares distinctive characteristics with modern humans

COLONIZING THE
PLANET

THE SPREAD OF MODERN HUMANS AROUND THE WORLD

Skeletal and DNA evidence suggests that our species, *Homo sapiens*, evolved in Africa and then spread around the globe. The first traces of modern humans beyond Africa come from fossils in Israel and possibly from stone tools found in Arabia. They date to before 100,000 years ago.

Homo sapiens' colonization of the globe involved many stops, starts, and sometimes retreats, as well as waves of different groups of people in some areas. *Homo sapiens* may have moved into Eurasia via the Mediterranean coast of western Asia, spreading into Western Europe more than 40,000 years ago (YA). Archaeological evidence suggests that people may also have taken a "southern route" across Arabia into southern Asia. New archaeological finds suggest movement toward China around 120,000–80,000 YA and the Sumatra region around 73,000–63,000 YA. Together this suggests a date before 120,000 YA for leaving Africa. In Australia, widespread colonization did not occur until 50,000 YA, although some sites have been dated to as early as 65,000 YA. Farther north, *Homo sapiens* first spread across northern Eurasia before 40,000 YA. However, different dispersals took place, and earlier populations were replaced over time. Genetically, the North American peoples are likely to have originated in East Asia. They probably traveled across the plain of "Beringia"—now beneath the Bering Straits between Siberia and Alaska, but exposed by low sea levels at the height of the last Ice Age. Distinctive "Clovis" spear points (flaked on both sides) are found across North America around 12,000 YA, so modern humans were widespread at that point, but earlier sites are also known, including South American sites such as Monte Verde (15,000 YA).

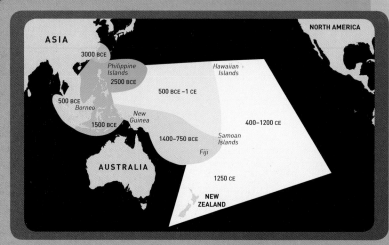

LATE ARRIVALS
The islands of Oceania were some of the last parts of the globe to be colonized, via the Philippines, by Austronesian-speaking early farmers from Taiwan. The more remote northern and eastern islands of Micronesia and Polynesia remained uninhabited until after 700 CE, and New Zealand was populated as late as 1250 CE.

Tracking language
The spread of languages can often be tracked to reflect the movement of people. This map shows the spread of Austronesian speakers across Oceania. Earlier settlers were already present in some western areas.

KEY

→ General direction of *Homo sapiens* around the world

● Site of early *Homo sapiens*

18,000 YEARS AGO

Bering Straits

14,000 YEARS AGO

quet and

● Swan Point

● Bluefish Caves

Tuluaq Hill (Sluiceway-Tuluaq complex)

● Ushki Lake

● Derelekh

● Yana

Ust-Mil ● Diuktai

35,000 YEARS AGO

EUROPE

31,000 YEARS AGO

● Kara-Bom

● Tianyuan

32,000 YEARS AGO

42,000 YEARS AGO

● Mal'ta

ASIA

● Yamashita-Cho

Paviland Cave

Kent's Cavern

Trou Magrite

Höhlenstein-Stadel

● Kostienki

45,000 YEARS AGO

Vindija Cave

Arcy-sur-Cure

Korolevo I

Istállóskö

120,000–80,000 YEARS AGO

El Castillo

Saint Césaire

Le Piage

Pestera cu Oase

● Fuyan Cave

ueva Morín

Riparo Mochi

41,000 YEARS AGO

Gato Preto

El Pendo

Bacho Kiro

77,000–45,000 YEARS AGO

Liujiang ●

Abric Romaní

Temnata Cave

Uçagizli Magara

Zhirendong

Cova Beneito

Ksar Akil

Skhul ● Qafzeh

Jebel Irhoud

300,000 YEARS AGO

140,000–130,000 YEARS AGO

● Jebel Faya

PACIFIC OCEAN

AFRICA

● Herto

INDIAN OCEAN

● Jwalapuram

Matenkupkum, Balof 2, and Panakiwuk

190,000 YEARS AGO

● Omo Kibish

Kota Tampan ●

● Niah Caves

Huon Peninsula

Lida Ajer, Sumatra ●

73,000–63,000 YEARS AGO

65,000 YEARS AGO

120,000 YEARS AGO

Diepkloof Shelter ●

● Malakunanja

Nawalabila I

Dlumbos Cave ●

Klasies River Mouth

Riwi and Carpenter's Gap

Ngarrabulgan

Puritjarra

AUSTRALIA

45,000 YEARS AGO

Upper Swan ●

Going global

Skeletal and genetic evidence suggests that modern humans originated in Africa and spread around the globe from there, as reflected on this map. This is called the "Out of Africa" theory. Dispersals of humans encountered and interbred with other archaic hominins at different times and places.

Devil's Lair

Allen's Cave

Cuddie Springs

Lake Mungo

Kow Swamp

Willandra Lakes

These cave paintings from Lascaux, France, date to around 17,000 years ago. Many cave paintings are from a similar period, though some were created by early *Homo sapiens* around 39,000 years ago in Asia.

A FOSSIL SKULL FROM 160,000 YA discovered in the Middle Awash region of Ethiopia in 1997 is almost modern in shape; this has been identified as a subspecies of modern humans, *Homo sapiens idaltu*. Humans moved north into Western Asia sometime before 100,000 YA, but this may not have resulted in permanent occupation.

It is debated whether uniquely human behaviors such as **language and the ability to use symbols** evolved before or after modern human anatomy. One theory is that such behaviors became vital only after 74,000 YA, when the massive eruption of **Mount Toba** in Indonesia triggered a global "volcanic winter." DNA

Prepared core and flake
Neanderthals and other hominins prepared a stone core before striking off a sharp flake to use. In Europe this technology is known as Levallois.

which could have made the difference between survival and extinction. However, others argue that the impact of the eruption of Mount Toba has been exaggerated, and that archaeology in Africa shows complex hunting practices and the development of symbolism many millennia before the eruption.

There were probably multiple dispersals of modern humans into Eurasia after 120,000 YA, using different routes. Archaeological and genetic data support migration into north and east Asia before 74,000 YA. Their population expansion was probably supported by flexible stone tool technology, including long, thin flint "blades," which formed parts of composite tools, as well as extended social networks.

300,000
THE NUMBER OF YEARS THE **NEANDERTHAL DOMINATED** EUROPE AND WESTERN ASIA

analysis suggests that many human groups died out at this time and, in such harsh conditions, complex modern language and symbolism would have allowed groups to **exchange resources and information** with one another,

The earliest modern humans in Asia may have encountered groups of *Home erectus*, who survided in China until at least 60,000 YA.

Excavations in Indonesia in 2003, revealed that specialized, extremely small hominins, perhaps descendants of *Homo erectus*, were living on the island of Flores. The first fossils were initially dated to just 18,000 YA but have been re-dated to 100,000-60,0000 YA. Fragments of jaw and teeth at another site on the island indicate that this species, *Homo floresiensis*, was living on Flores from around 700,000 YA.

HOMO SAPIENS   NEANDERTHAL

MODERN HUMANS AND NEANDERTHALS

Neanderthal skulls (right) were slightly larger than anatomically modern human skulls (left), but they had lower, more sloping foreheads and a double arch of bone over their eyes that created heavy brow ridges. Their lower faces jutted out and they did not have chins. Overall, Neanderthal skeletons reveal that they were much more muscular than modern humans, as well as being extremely physically active, but they were not cold-climate specialists, as once believed.

HUMANS SPREAD RAPIDLY across Europe and Asia. In **Europe**, modern humans had reached **Central Europe** by 45,000 YA. In Asia, they had reached **Central Asia** by 42,000 YA. Settlement in **Australia** increased after 45,000 YA. More evidence comes from **Denisova Cave** in Russia – analysis of bones reveals DNA distinct from both modern humans and Neanderthals, from a hominin that lived here between 150,000 and 40,000 YA. It seems likely that several groups descended from hominins who left Africa before *Homo sapiens* may have **coexisted in Eurasia** at this time.

> THE NEANDERTHALS **WERE NOT APE-MEN**… THEY WERE **AS HUMAN AS US**, BUT THEY REPRESENTED A **DIFFERENT BRAND OF HUMANITY.**

Chris Stringer and Clive Gamble, from *In Search of the Neanderthals*, 1993

IN EUROPE, MODERN HUMANS overlapped with Neanderthals, who survived, in some places, until 30,000 YA. How and why **Neanderthals disappeared** is one of the most intensely debated topics in archaeology. There is little evidence of violent interactions between the species, and comparison of DNA shows that **interbreeding between the groups** occurred in many places and times.

Early humans may have **outcompeted** their relatives for **food and raw materials** in the rapidly changing environmental conditions. Environments at the time were highly unstable, so even a slight increase in competition could have been significant. However, populations were small and spread out, and coexisted for up to 10,000 years in Europe, and more than 30,000 in Indonesia. Alternatively, the **exchange of**

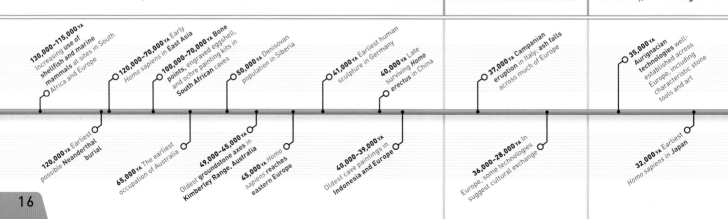

130,000–115,000 YA Increasing use of shellfish and marine mammals at sites in South Africa and Europe

120,000–70,000 YA Early *Homo sapiens* in East Asia

100,000–70,000 YA Bone points, engraved eggshell, and ochre painting kits in South African caves

50,000 YA Denisovan population in Siberia

41,000 YA Earliest human sculpture in Germany

40,000 YA Late surviving *Homo erectus* in China

37,000 YA Campanian eruption in Italy; ash falls across much of Europe

35,000 YA Aurignacian technologies well-established across Europe, including characteristic stone tools and art

120,000 YA Earliest possible Neanderthal burial

65,000 YA The earliest occupation of Australia

49,000–45,000 YA Oldest groundstone axes in Kimberley Range, Australia

45,000 YA *Homo sapiens* reaches eastern Europe

40,000–39,000 YA Oldest cave paintings in Indonesia and Europe

36,000–28,000 YA In Europe, some technologies suggest cultural exchange

32,000 YA Earliest *Homo sapiens* in Japan

resources and information allowed by modern humans' language and symbol use, and their planned and flexible technologies, made *Homo sapiens* better able to withstand climatic downturns than Neanderthals.

Others believe that these behaviors were not unique to modern humans. Hominins would have needed to **use rafts or boats** to reach the island of Flores in Indonesia by 800,000 YA. Some late Neanderthal sites also contain elements of technologies normally associated with *Homo sapiens*, and cultural exchange as well as biological reproduction may have taken place.

A combination of environmental unrest and slower reproduction is currently considered to be the most likely explanation for **Neanderthal extinction**.

EUROPE

ATLANTIC OCEAN

Mediterranean Sea

KEY
- Neanderthal sites
- Modern human sites

Neanderthal and human ranges
Modern humans and Neanderthals coexisted for several thousand years. This map shows some of the interaction sites in Europe.

THE MAXIMUM EXTENT OF THE LAST ICE AGE

European climates after 23,000 BCE grew steadily cooler, and during the "Last Glacial Maximum" (21,000–18,000 YA), ice caps covered most of northern Europe. Farther south, huge areas of grassland with few trees offered good hunting for groups of humans able to survive the cold.

THE "GRAVETTIAN" CULTURE OF Europe and Russia (28,000–21,000 YA) is known for its elaborate sites, which often have complex structures and burials, jewelery, sculpted ivory and antler, and impressions of woven material. Also found at Gravettian sites are some of the earliest known ceramic objects, including some of the famous **"Venus" figurines**. These may have been fertility or religious charms, or part of a system of exchange between social networks across the region as the **Ice Age intensified**.

"Venus" statuette
This figurine from Willendorf, Austria, depicts a stylized pregnant or post-partum female figure.

emphasized belly

AT THE HEIGHT OF THE GLACIAL Maximum, when the ice caps were at their greatest extent, people living in more northerly and mountainous areas retreated to **"refuge" areas** such as—in Europe—northern Spain and southwest France, where this period is known as the "Solutrean." Globally, **many groups probably died out**, but some held on in more sheltered regions. To survive the harsh conditions, much time and effort was invested in hunting. Weapons include beautifully worked points known as "leaf-points." Although little evidence survives beyond finely worked bone needles, people probably relied on **close-fitting clothing** to keep them warm.

Perhaps more importantly, hunters would have worked hard to predict and intercept the movements of herds of large animals, ensuring the **hunting success** that was the difference between life and death.

IN EUROPE, SOPHISTICATED BONE and antler points, needles, and harpoons characterize the **"Magdalenian"** technologies that were used to hunt a wide range of species, especially reindeer.

The Magdalenian (18,000–12,000 YA) is famous for its beautiful art objects, engravings, and cave paintings. There are many theories about what these mean and why they were produced. As most depict animals that were hunted, the paintings may represent a magical means of ensuring hunting success, or show information about the best ways to hunt different species. Paintings of imaginary half-human, half-animal creatures and the inaccessibility of some cave art suggest that painting may have been a magical or ritual activity, but footprints and finger marks show children were also in these spaces. Alternatively, paintings and art objects may have helped establish group identities and territories, as the number of archaeological sites in this period suggests that populations were growing, and competition for rich and localized resources may have been intensifying.

A rise in temperature led to the **retreat of the ice sheets** that had covered northern Europe, and these areas were rapidly recolonized, with **groups expanding** as far north as Siberia by around 14,000–13,000 YA. Some groups had already entered North America via Alaska by this time. Farther east, in China and in the Jomon culture of Japan, some of the first pots manufactured from clay appeared between 20,000 and 18,000 YA.

Altamira cave paintings
This Paleolithic cave painting of bison was discovered at the Altamira cave site in Spain.

32,000 YA Chauvet cave paintings, France

30,003 YA Youngest known Neanderthal sites

28–21,000 YA Height of Gravettian culture with ceramic sculptures

27,000 YA Complex hunter-gatherer sites on the Russian plains

21,000 YA Solutrean technologies appear

21–18,000 YA Last glacial maximum

18,000 YA Magdalenian technologies appear

18,000 YA Latest known date of the controversial *Homo floresiensis* specimen, "the hobbit"

17,000 YA Earliest known atlatl, or spear-thrower, from Combe Saunière, France

16–15,000 YA Beginning of recolonization of areas of northern Europe abandoned during worst climatic conditions

17,000 YA Lascaux cave paintings, France

15,000 YA Monte Verde, Chile, a South American site with controversially early dates

14,000 YA Increased hunting of fish using antler harpoons

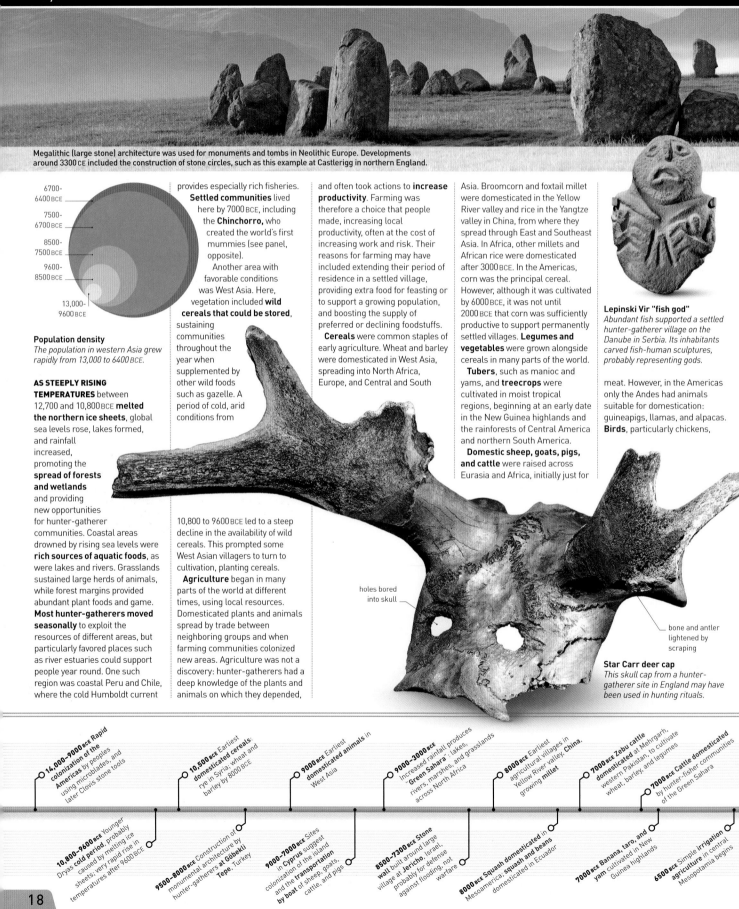

Megalithic (large stone) architecture was used for monuments and tombs in Neolithic Europe. Developments around 3300 CE included the construction of stone circles, such as this example at Castlerigg in northern England.

Population density
The population in western Asia grew rapidly from 13,000 to 6400 BCE.

6700–6400 BCE
7500–6700 BCE
8500–7500 BCE
9600–8500 BCE
13,000–9600 BCE

AS STEEPLY RISING TEMPERATURES between 12,700 and 10,800 BCE **melted the northern ice sheets**, global sea levels rose, lakes formed, and rainfall increased, promoting the **spread of forests and wetlands** and providing new opportunities for hunter-gatherer communities. Coastal areas drowned by rising sea levels were **rich sources of aquatic foods**, as were lakes and rivers. Grasslands sustained large herds of animals, while forest margins provided abundant plant foods and game. **Most hunter-gatherers moved seasonally** to exploit the resources of different areas, but particularly favored places such as river estuaries could support people year round. One such region was coastal Peru and Chile, where the cold Humboldt current

provides especially rich fisheries. **Settled communities** lived here by 7000 BCE, including the **Chinchorro,** who created the world's first mummies (see panel, opposite).

Another area with favorable conditions was West Asia. Here, vegetation included **wild cereals that could be stored**, sustaining communities throughout the year when supplemented by other wild foods such as gazelle. A period of cold, arid conditions from

10,800 to 9600 BCE led to a steep decline in the availability of wild cereals. This prompted some West Asian villagers to turn to cultivation, planting cereals.

Agriculture began in many parts of the world at different times, using local resources. Domesticated plants and animals spread by trade between neighboring groups and when farming communities colonized new areas. Agriculture was not a discovery: hunter-gatherers had a deep knowledge of the plants and animals on which they depended,

and often took actions to **increase productivity**. Farming was therefore a choice that people made, increasing local productivity, often at the cost of increasing work and risk. Their reasons for farming may have included extending their period of residence in a settled village, providing extra food for feasting or to support a growing population, and boosting the supply of preferred or declining foodstuffs.

Cereals were common staples of early agriculture. Wheat and barley were domesticated in West Asia, spreading into North Africa, Europe, and Central and South

Asia. Broomcorn and foxtail millet were domesticated in the Yellow River valley and rice in the Yangtze valley in China, from where they spread through East and Southeast Asia. In Africa, other millets and African rice were domesticated after 3000 BCE. In the Americas, corn was the principal cereal. However, although it was cultivated by 6000 BCE, it was not until 2000 BCE that corn was sufficiently productive to support permanently settled villages. **Legumes and vegetables** were grown alongside cereals in many parts of the world.

Tubers, such as manioc and yams, and **treecrops** were cultivated in moist tropical regions, beginning at an early date in the New Guinea highlands and the rainforests of Central America and northern South America.

Domestic sheep, goats, pigs, and cattle were raised across Eurasia and Africa, initially just for

Lepinski Vir "fish god"
Abundant fish supported a settled hunter-gatherer village on the Danube in Serbia. Its inhabitants carved fish-human sculptures, probably representing gods.

meat. However, in the Americas only the Andes had animals suitable for domestication: guineapigs, llamas, and alpacas. **Birds**, particularly chickens,

holes bored into skull

bone and antler lightened by scraping

Star Carr deer cap
This skull cap from a hunter-gatherer site in England may have been used in hunting rituals.

14,000–9000 BCE Rapid colonization of the Americas by peoples using microblades, and later Clovis stone tools

10,800–9600 BCE Younger Dryas cold period, probably caused by melting ice sheets; very rapid rise in temperatures after 9600 BCE

10,500 BCE Earliest domesticated cereals: wheat and rye in Syria; wheat and barley by 8000 BCE

9500–8000 BCE Construction of monumental architecture by hunter-gatherers at **Göbekli Tepe**, Turkey

9000 BCE Earliest domesticated animals in West Asia

9000–7000 BCE Sites in Cyprus suggest colonization of the island and the **transportation by boat** of sheep, goats, cattle, and pigs

9000–3000 BCE Increased rainfall produces "Green Sahara": lakes, rivers, marshes, and grasslands across North Africa

8500–7300 BCE Stone wall built around large village at **Jericho, Israel**, probably for defense against flooding, not warfare

8000 BCE Earliest agricultural villages in Yellow River valley, China, growing **millet**

8000 BCE Squash domesticated in Mesoamerica; **squash and beans** domesticated in Ecuador

7000 BCE Zebu cattle domesticated at Mehrgarh, western Pakistan, to cultivate wheat, barley, and legumes

7000 BCE Banana, taro, and yam cultivated in New Guinea highlands

7000 BCE Cattle domesticated by hunter-fisher communities of the Green Sahara

6500 BCE Simple irrigation agriculture in central Mesopotamia begins ducks, and turkeys, were also kept by Old and New World farmers. By 5000 BCE cattle, sheep, and goats were **raised for milk** as well as meat, while cattle were used to pull **plows**, enabling people to cultivate much larger areas. **Wool-bearing sheep** were bred in West Asia in the 4th millennium BCE, and rapidly spread into Europe and Central Asia. The use of **pack animals** such as llamas and donkeys allowed long-distance transport.

Agriculture was more productive than foraging and could support **larger communities**. Settled life also encouraged **population growth**. Many early farming villages in West Asia grew to a considerable size. Most remarkable was **Çatalhöyük** in Turkey, occupied around 7400–6200 BCE, which housed as many as 8,000 people. Its tightly packed houses were entered from the roof by ladders, and were

> ❝ THE **NEOLITHIC** WAS… A POINT IN A CONTINUOUS STORY OF **GREATER ECONOMIC CONTROL** OVER RESOURCES… FROM **SCAVENGING** TO… **FARMING.** ❞

Clive Gamble, from *Origins and revolutions: human identity in earliest prehistory*, 2007

decorated with paintings and modeled animal heads.

After 7000 BCE **farmers spread** from Turkey into southeast and central Europe, while Mediterranean hunter-gatherers gradually turned to agriculture, using imported West Asian crops and animals. By 3500 BCE most of Europe had adopted farming.

Megalithic chambered tombs, of which a wide variety were built, often with earthen mounds—were constructed in western and northern Europe from the early 5th millennium BCE. Most housed the

bones of a number of individuals. Native (naturally occurring pure) **copper and gold** were being shaped into small objects by cold hammering before 8000 BCE in West Asia. Around 7000 BCE, **ores were smelted** here to extract metal and by 6000 BCE copper and lead were also cast. Metals were initially made into small personal objects that could enhance prestige and status. Later, however, copper began to be used for **tools**, and by 4200 BCE copper ores containing arsenic were deliberately selected to produce a harder metal. The addition of tin created a stronger alloy, **bronze**, which was in use in West Asia by 3200 BCE.

The development of **water-control techniques** enabled West Asian farmers to colonize the southern **Mesopotamian plains**, where agriculture depended entirely on irrigation but was highly productive. By the mid 4th millennium BCE, this region was densely populated, and villages were developing into **towns**, with craft specialists. There was a growing demand for raw materials, including metal ores, which often came from

distant sources. A **trading network** developed that stretched from Egypt through West Asia to the mountainous borderlands of South Asia, with towns controlling sources of materials and strategic points along the routes. **Sumer** (southern Mesopotamia) was at the forefront of this development, but social, religious, economic,

and political complexity was also emerging in **Elam** (southwest Iran) and **Egypt**. Before 3000 BCE all three regions developed **writing systems**, used to record and manage economic transactions and the ownership of property. The earliest known pictographic writing, around 3300 BCE, comes from **Uruk** in Sumer, a huge and complex settlement that is deservedly known as the **world's first city**.

Copper ax heads
Gold and copper were the first metals to be worked. They became widespread in Europe around 2500 BCE.

CHINCHORRO MUMMIES

The earliest mummies come not from Egypt, but from coastal northern Chile, an arid region where natural mummies occur from 7000 BCE. After 5000 BCE the Chinchorro began artificial mummification. They removed the flesh, reassembled and reinforced the skeleton, stuffed the skin with plant material, coated it in clay, and painted it with black manganese or red ocher. Only some individuals, particularly children, were mummified.

The spread of agriculture
Humans began to cultivate plants and manage animals independently, in different areas at different times, across the world.

KEY
▲ Livestock   ▲ Other
△ Cereals   ▪ Areas with agriculture

6200 BCE First farming communities established in Euphrates valley of southern Mesopotamia

6000 BCE Villages in Yangtze valley (China) fish, grow rice, and raise pigs and chickens

6000 BCE Domestic corn develops from wild teosinte in Mexico

5500 BCE Independent development of copper metallurgy in the Balkans

5100 BCE Copper mining at Aibunar, Bulgaria

5000–1000 CE Old Copper Culture, a major industry and trade network based on locally mined, cold-hammered native copper, flourishes in Great Lakes region of North America

5000 BCE Domestic animals kept for milk and pulling plows, as well as for meat, in West Asia, North Africa, and Europe

5000 BCE Domesticated llamas, alpacas, and probably guinea pigs grown in the Andes; range of crops grown in Andean coast and tropical lowlands of northeast South America

4000 BCE Wet-rice cultivation in plowed, flooded paddy fields in China begins

4000 BCE Domestication of vine and olive in eastern Mediterranean

3500 BCE Stamp seals begin to be used in West Asia for administrative and economic purposes

3300 BCE Writing invented in southern Mesopotamia

2500 BCE Wheeled transport emerges, spreads rapidly through Eurasia—used for local transport and military purposes

3200 BCE Uruk emerges as first city

3200 BCE Beginning of Egyptian writing

3200 BCE First bronze manufactured in West Asia

3100–2900 BCE Proto-Elamite script (early Bronze Age writing system) across the Iranian plateau

3000 BCE Metallurgy reaches western China

Pottery shard
4000 BCE • ROMANIA
Different cultures can be identified
by their unique ways of decorating
objects—this shard is typical of the
Cucuteni-Tripolye culture.

colorful geometric design

Human figurine
6750–6500 BCE • JORDAN
This large statue from Ain Ghazal
is one of several from sites in
the Near East that may have
represented ancestors or gods.

minerals define facial features

reed framework coated in thick plaster

Schist plaque
4000 BCE • PORTUGAL
It is unclear what Neolithic engraved
plaques, like this one from Alentejo,
symbolized, but they seem to have
been made for burial with the dead.

hole for cord

geometric, abstract pattern

Engraved bone
13,000–8000 BCE • FRANCE
Paleolithic artists often carved as well
as painted their depictions of animals,
as with this scene of a bison being
chased, from Laugerie-Basse.

finely detailed engraving

PREHISTORIC PEOPLES

EARLY HUMANS ARE DEFINED BY THE RAW MATERIALS THEY USED TO FASHION TOOLS, WEAPONS, AND ORNAMENTS

Prehistory is traditionally divided into the Stone, Bronze,
and Iron ages, but many other kinds of raw materials
such as wood, hide, and plant fibers were also used in
early technologies. Rare evidence of these survives.

In addition to being functional aids to survival and subsistence, the objects
made by prehistoric peoples would also have been important in their social
lives. Different groups develop their own ways of manufacturing and
decorating objects, and distinctive designs may become badges of identity
or status symbols. The trade and exchange of objects is another vital way in
which individuals and groups establish social relationships and hierarchies.

carefully sharpened tip

carved antler setting

leather or sinew binding

flint head set into wooden sleeve

reproduced wooden handle

thick base is easy to hold

Oldowan tool
3.3 MYA • LOMEKWI, KENYA
The earliest stone tools were
simple, sharp-edged flakes of
stone, made by striking a stone
cobble with a hard "hammerstone."

remains of flaked cobble

Blades and core
500,000–400,000 BCE ONWARD • WIDESPREAD
Various hominins, including Neanderthals,
produced uniform, narrow blades that
could be attached to wooden and antler
handles or held in the hand. They were
useful for many different purposes.

scars where blades chipped from core

long, thin blade

Flint handax
1.8 MYA • UK
Handaxes, such as this one from
Swanscombe, were skillfully made
and used for a wide range of activities,
especially woodworking and butchery.

Tools with ax heads
11,660–4000 BCE • EUROPE
These Mesolithic axes were used for
cutting and working with wood in the
forests that spread across Europe
after the last Ice Age ended.

Antler harpoon
8000 BCE • UK
This harpoon head is attached to a long
handle for spearing fish—a key source of food
when sea levels rose as the last Ice Age ended.

barbed head made from antler

Clay burial chest
4000 BCE • NEAR EAST
One Chalcolithic ("copper age") burial practice involved allowing the dead to decay, then collecting the bones and placing them in clay chests like this one.

excavation damage

Carved spear-thrower
12,500 BCE • FRANCE
Spear-throwers, such as this one from Montastruc, were often carved into animal shapes—here, a woolly mammoth made from antler. They enabled hunters to throw spears farther and with greater force.

stylized features

Neolithic flint blade set in reproduction handle

Lespugue Venus
24,000–22,000 BCE • FRANCE
This ivory figurine from Lespugue in the Pyrenees is one of many "Venus" figurines—depicting women who appear pregnant or have had many children, and highlighting their figures.

Mummified head
7000–3000 BCE • PERU
In very dry climates, bodies can become mummified. Some of the earliest mummies have been found in Peruvian deserts.

Bronze Age sickle

Gold jewelry
4700–4200 BCE • BULGARIA
At the cemetery of Varna in Bulgaria, more than 3,000 pieces of some of the earliest gold jewelry have been found, mainly buried with elite males.

gold easily worked into decorative animal shapes

loom weight

bone shuttle

iron sickle blade

soft clay was baked to preserve design

Agricultural tools
9500 BCE ONWARD • WIDESPREAD
Ph si wild and later domestic and cereals were harvested using sickles like these, until they were superseded in most places by the invention of the combine harvester.

Neolithic seal
7500–5700 BCE • ANATOLIA
Seals such as this one from the settlement of Çatal Hoyuk were used during the Neolithic to stamp decorative designs onto skin or cloth.

Cloth-making tools
6500 BCE • ORIGIN UNKNOWN
Though woven materials existed as early as 20,000 BCE, large looms appeared during the mid-Neolithic period. Loom weights held vertical threads taut; bone shuttles were used to weave horizontal threads in and out.

EARLY
CIVILIZATIONS

Stonehenge in western Britain was a ceremonial site by 2900 BCE. An outer ring of bluestones within an early earthen enclosure was later rearranged within the cirlce of sarsen stones seen here.

DURING THE LAST HALF OF THE FOURTH MILLENNIUM BCE, the world's first civilizations arose, first in Western Asia, then North Africa and South Asia. Civilization also appeared in China in the early second millennium BCE. By 3000 BCE the **first cities** had emerged in southern **Mesopotamia**, in what is now Iraq. This region, the lower Euphrates River plain, had been settled by 6200 BCE by farmers practising simple irrigation. During the fourth millennium it saw major advances in agricultural technology and resultant productivity. Increasingly **sophisticated irrigation systems** supplied fields cultivated with the recently developed plow, drawn by cattle and newly domesticated donkeys, which also pulled wheeled carts, invented around 3500 BCE. The resulting food surplus freed some people from the farming life, allowing specialization into professions such as priesthood, crafts, trade, and administration. The world's first tiered society

60 THOUSAND
THE **POPULATION** OF THE CITY OF **URUK** *c.* 2800 BCE

developed, headed at first by priests. Woolly sheep, first bred at this time, supplied a **growing industry** producing textiles for domestic use and foreign trade. Many towns developed and by 3400 BCE Uruk had become a city. Other cities, including Ur and Nippur, emerged by 3000 BCE, each dominating its surrounding area, and over the subsequent centuries **Sumer** (the southern part of the region) became a patchwork of competing city-states, ruled by kings. While **metalworking** had begun in West Asia during the 9th millennium BCE, by 3000 BCE Sumerian smiths had begun to manufacture bronze, alloying copper with tin imported from distant Afghanistan.

In **Egypt**, one of the world's **most complex ancient civilizations** was forming along the banks of the Nile River by 3100 BCE. The Nile formed a narrow strip of cultivatable land, floodplain, as the river's annual flood (known as the inundation) spread black silt along its banks. The Egyptian farming year began in the fall when the inundation subsided, and farmers cultivated wheat, barley, beans, and lentils in the fertile soil.

By the end of the 4th millennium BCE, farming communities had evolved into two kingdoms: **Upper Egypt** in the south and **Lower Egypt** in the north. **King Narmer** united the two kingdoms *c.* 3100 BCE. After Narmer came **Menes**, although historians are unsure whether Menes was Narmer's successor or a different name for Narmer himself. Menes is credited with founding the Egyptian capital at Memphis and Egypt's first dynasty.

As in Mesopotamia, efficient agriculture produced prosperity and specialism, allowing **arts, crafts, engineering, and early medicine** to develop. The Early Dynastic Period (*c.* 3100–2686 BCE) was already characterized by many of the celebrated aspects of Egyptian culture: **hieroglyphic** writing, a sophisticated **religion** (including belief in an afterlife), and preserving the dead using **mummification**. A complex hierarchical society developed, with the king at the apex accorded semi-divine status. Egyptian kings—later known as **pharaohs**—ruled with the help of a chief minister, or vizier, regional governors (nomarchs), and a huge staff of lesser officials including priests, tax collectors, and scribes.

In China, civilization originated in the valleys of eastern rivers such as the Huang He (Yellow River), where the rich loess soil made the land fertile. The introduction of **wet-rice** agriculture to this region around 3000 BCE supplemented its long-established cultivation of sorghum and foxtail millet, bringing high productivity to the **Longshan culture**. This developed from the Yangshao and Dawenkou cultures in the central plains of northern China around this time. As in other early civilizations, agricultural success allowed the development of an elaborate society. Chinese craftsmen were making **bronze tools** *c.* 3000 BCE, **jade vessels** *c.* 2700 BCE, and **silk weaving** had begun by 3500 BCE.

The **Bronze Age** was underway in western Asia by 3000 BCE, and possibly considerably earlier. The Bronze Age in Europe seems to have developed separately from around 2500 BCE, using ore sources from the Carpathian Mountains in Central Europe. This era also saw the beginnings of the **Minoan civilization** on the Greek island of Crete around 2000 BCE, with trading links to the nearby Cyclades Islands and the wider Mediterranean. In Western Europe, the earlier tradition of megalithic tomb building and a growing interest in astronomical observation gave rise to a new **megalithic tradition** of erecting stone circles, stone rows, standing stones, and tombs including astronomical features. **These include** Newgrange in Ireland, Stonehenge in England, and Carnac in France.

Ancient cities of Mesopotamia
Sumer in southern Mesopotamia was the location of the world's first urban civilization from c. 3000 BCE as high agricultural productivity supported the development of a complex society.

KEY
■ Extent of Early Dynastic city-states
····· Ancient coastline

Narmer Palette
This carved piece of green siltstone records the triumph of the legendary King Narmer of Upper Egypt over his enemies.

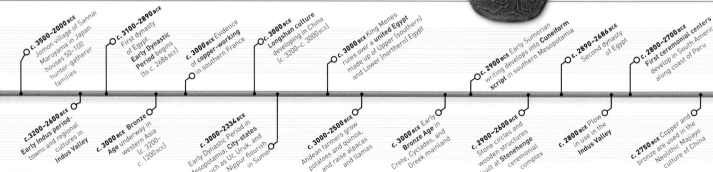

c. 3500–2000 BCE Jomon village of Sannai Maruyama in Japan houses 50–100 hunter-gatherer families

c. 3200–2600 BCE Early Indus period—towns and regional cultures in **Indus Valley**

c. 3100–2890 BCE First dynasty of Egypt. **Early Dynastic Period** begins (to c. 2686 BCE)

c. 3000 BCE Bronze Age underway in western Asia (c. 3200–c. 1200 BCE)

c. 3000 BCE Evidence of copper-working in southern France

c. 3000 BCE Longshan culture developing in China (c. 3200–c. 3000 BCE)

c. 3000–2334 BCE Early Dynastic Period in Mesopotamia. **City-states** such as Ur, Uruk, and Nippur flourish in Sumer

c. 3000 BCE King Menes rules over a **united Egypt**, made up of Upper (southern) and Lower (northern) Egypt

c. 3000–2500 BCE Andean farmers grow potatoes and quinoa, and raise alpacas and llamas

c. 3000 BCE Early **Bronze Age** in Crete, Cyclades, and Greek mainland

c. 2900 BCE Early Sumerian writing develops into **Cuneiform** script in southern Mesopotamia

c. 2900–2600 BCE Stone circles and wooden structures built at **Stonehenge** ceremonial complex

c. 2890–2686 BCE Second dynasty of Egypt

c. 2800 BCE Plow in use in the **Indus Valley**

c. 2800–2700 BCE First ceremonial centers develop in South America, along coast of Peru

c. 2750 BCE Copper and bronze are used in the Neolithic Majiayo culture of China

2.3 MILLION THE NUMBER OF **BLOCKS** USED TO BUILD THE GREAT **PYRAMID** OF GIZA

The three pyramids at Giza were built for the pharaohs Khufu, Khafra, and Menkaura between 2575 and 2465 BCE. They are guarded by the statue of the Sphinx, which may bear the features of King Khafra.

Standard of Ur
This boxlike object has two side panels—one depicting war, the other (shown here) times of peace.

SOUTHERN MESOPOTAMIA was a patchwork of over 40 city-states, among which Ur, Uruk, Nippur, and Kish were the most important. **Trade flourished** using a network of rivers and canals, and trade links extended to Anatolia (modern-day Turkey), Iran, and Afghanistan, with grain, minerals, lumber, tools, and vessels traded. The **Sumerian** population was unique in being **predominantly urban**. In Ur, Uruk, and other centers, people lived in clustered mud-brick houses. The temple at the city's heart was its religious focus, the home of its patron deity. The surrounding precinct housed priests who managed substantial temple estates and industries. Between 2600 and 2450 BCE, 16 important people—perhaps royalty—were buried in the huge **cemetery at Ur**, accompanied by

Cuneiform tablet
Over time, the inventory of signs regularly used in cuneiform script was greatly reduced.

human sacrifices and treasures such as the **Standard of Ur**. This object was decorated with intricate designs in precious materials.

Arising from the need to keep economic and administrative records, the **first pictographic writing** developed in **Sumer** (c. 3300 BCE). Pictographs (pictorial writing representing a word or idea) evolved into a script called **cuneiform** c. 2900 BCE, in which scribes pressed sharpened reeds into soft clay to leave wedge-shaped impressions.

Southern Mesopotamia became densely populated, putting pressure on natural resources. This led to **conflicts** over land and water, and alliances between cities were forged and broken.

The first signs of **civilization in the Americas** appeared along the coast of Peru and in the Andes c. 3000 BCE. **Andean farmers** grew potatoes and the cereal quinoa, and raised alpacas and llamas. There were fishing communities on the coast, while inland towns became ceremonial centers, built around mud-brick temple platforms. An exceptional example is **Caral**, about 125 miles (200 km) from Lima and dating from c. 2800 BCE. Another, **Aspero**, had six platform mounds topped by temples. Cotton was grown in the region, as well as corn, beans, guava, avocado, and sweet potato.

Farmers settled in the **Indus plains** in the 4th millennium, developing **flood-control technology** and establishing towns. Major changes around 2600 BCE marked the emergence of the **Indus Valley civilization**. **Mohenjo-daro** on the Indus River, and **Harappa**, to the northeast, were preeminent cities, with populations of around 100,000 and 60,000, respectively.

In **Egypt**, King Sanakht acceded to the throne in the year 2686 BCE, marking the beginning of the Third dynasty and the **Old Kingdom** era—a time of strong, centralized rule and **pyramid-building**. These magnificent monuments were built as **royal tombs**. In Early Dynastic times, kings had been buried beneath rectangular mud-brick platforms called mastabas. Around 2650 BCE, the first pyramid, the **Step Pyramid of Saqqara**, was completed for King Djoser. Designed by the architect Imhotep, it resembled six stone mastabas on top of one another.

Straight-sided pyramids appeared soon after, the greatest of which were the **three pyramids at Giza**. These feats of engineering were constructed not by slaves as was once thought, but by a staff of full-time craftsmen and masons supported by farmers performing a type of national service during the Nile floods. Enormous blocks of stone (lower stones of 6–10 tons; higher ones of 1–2 tons) were cut from local quarries, hauled on site using sleds, and then heaved up ramps, which grew higher as construction progressed.

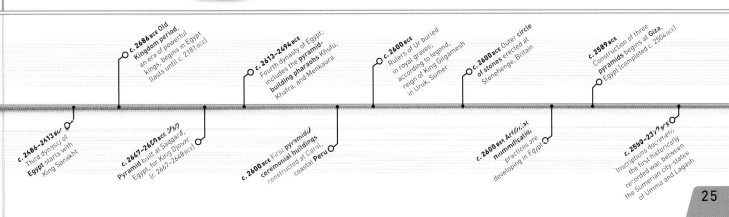

c. 2686–2413 BCE Third dynasty of Egypt starts with **King Sanakht**

c. 2686 BCE **Old Kingdom period**, an era of powerful kings, begins in Egypt (lasts until c. 2181 BCE)

c. 2667–2648 BCE **Pyramid** built at Saqqara, Egypt, for King Djoser (r. 2667–2648 BCE)

c. 2613–2494 BCE Fourth dynasty of Egypt; includes the **pyramid-building pharaohs** Khufu, Khafra, and Menkaura

c. 2600 BCE **First pyramidal ceremonial buildings** constructed at Caral, coastal **Peru**

c. 2600 BCE Rulers of Ur buried in royal graves; according to legend, reign of King Gilgamesh in Uruk, Sumer

c. 2600 BCE **Artificial mummification** practices are developing in Egypt

c. 2600 BCE **Outer circle of stones** erected at Stonehenge, Britain

c. 2589 BCE Construction of three **pyramids begins at Giza**, Egypt (completed c. 2504 BCE)

c. 2550–2370 BCE Inscriptions document the first historically recorded war, between the Sumerian city-states of Umma and Lagash

The ruined citadel of Mohenjo-daro was made up of various buildings. It was built on a platform to guard against flooding of the Indus River.

IN THE SECOND HALF OF THE 3RD MILLENNIUM BCE, civilizations continued to develop in western Asia, Egypt, and and southern Asia, and complex societies were emerging in China, Europe, and South America.

In southern Asia, the **Indus civilization** (see 2700–2500BCE) emerged in its mature form around 2500BCE, stretching 1,060 miles (1,700 km) from east to west and 800 miles (1,300 km) from north to south. The region's prosperity was based on farming, mining, crafts, and trade. More than 100 sites have been excavated, including the cities of Mohenjo-daro, Harappa, and Dholavira.

Mohenjo-daro and **Harappa** were **well-planned** cities laid out on a grid system. Each city was protected by brick walls and dominated by a **citadel** overlooking a "lower town" of public buildings and residential **town houses** of one or two stories. The residential areas were seemingly divided

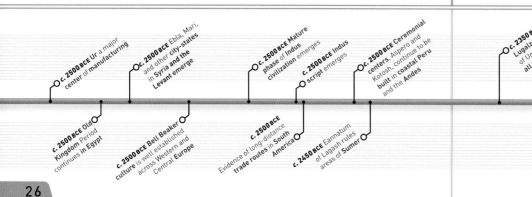

one-piece cart wheel

Indus civilization
Excavations suggest that the Indus civilization covered an area far larger than Mesopotamia and Egypt combined.

KEY
■ Zone of urban civilization
• Urban centers
····· Ancient coastline

by industry, such as pottery, bead-making, and metalworking.

Indus cities and towns had the most **advanced plumbing** system in the ancient world, with enclosed wells and covered drains. Latrines emptied waste into drains, which ran below the streets.

These urban centers were also connected by extensive **trade links**. Merchants supplied craft products from the valleys to

Agrarian lives
A clay model of a bullock cart found at Mohenjo-daro, dating back to c. 2500–1900 BCE, gives an insight into farming life in the Indus civilization.

the surrounding regions in return for metal ores, precious stones, and timber. Long-distance trade routes reached as far as Mesopotamia and Afghanistan.

By around 2500 BCE, an **Indus script** of hundreds of signs appeared on seals and pottery. Attempts to decipher the script have failed; hence, many aspects of this culture remain a mystery.

In western Asia, **Mesopotamia** (see 2700–2500BCE) remained a patchwork of small but **powerful city-states**, each controlling the surrounding farmlands where barley, legumes, and date palms were grown. To the west, city-states were developing in Syria and the Levant. A **trade network** linking Mesopotamian towns suggests cooperation between states, but there was **frequent warfare** as well.

The vast chalk mound of Silbury Hill in Wiltshire, England, is the largest man-made mound in Europe. Its purpose, however, is unknown.

A NEW POWER AROSE IN MESOPOTAMIA c. 2334BCE, **King Sargon** (c. 2334–2215 BCE) from the northern region of **Akkad** defeated Lugalzagesi of Umma to become the ruler of Sumer. Through subsequent campaigns to the Levant, Syria, and Anatolia, Sargon carved out the **world's first empire**—the Akkadian Empire— stretching from the eastern Mediterranean to the Gulf.

Sargon and his successors recorded their conquests and other achievements in many inscriptions. His name means "legitimate king," which led some scholars to believe that he took power through force. Sargon spoke Akkadian, a Semitic language that replaced Sumerian as the

> ❝ UNDER HIM **ALL COUNTRIES** LAY [CONTENTED] IN THEIR MEADOWS, AND THE **LAND REJOICED.** ❞
>
> **Inscription of Lugalzagesi, king of Sumer**, describing his reign

official language of the empire.

Akkadian rule was enforced through regional governors who collected tributes and taxes. The **empire's weakness** lay in its lack of defensible **borders**, and it came under regular **attacks** from

BRONZE AGE EUROPE

Bronze-working had begun in West Asia c. 3200BCE (see 10,000–3000BCE). It was developed by the Únětice culture of Bohemia and Poland c.2300 BCE, and by 2100 BCE separately in Atlantic Europe, spreading rapidly. Bronze provided a hard metal for forging armor, weapons, and tools such as this ax. The bronze industry also increased trade, making Europe more interconnected than ever before.

neighboring **hill tribes**. Sargon's grandson, Naram-Sin, extended the empire, but it lasted for only four generations before falling to attacks. Sargon's rule established a practice of statewide bureaucratic controls and standardization in many aspects of economic life.

In **Egypt**, this period saw a **weakening** of the power of the **Old Kingdom** rulers (see 2700–2500BCE), in favor of regional governors called **nomarchs**, who administered different parts of the Nile valley and delta. To the south of the first cataract on the Nile, the kingdom of Nubia also grew **more powerful**. Nubia was centered around the city of Kerma at the third cataract. By the end of the Sixth dynasty (c. 2184 BCE),

Timeline

c. **2500 BCE** Ur a major center of manufacturing

c. **2500 BCE** Ebla, Mari, and other **city-states** in **Syria and the Levant** emerge

c. **2500 BCE** Mature phase of Indus civilization emerges

c. **2500 BCE** Indus script emerges

c. **2500 BCE** Ceremonial centers, Aspero and Kotosh, continue to be **built** in coastal Peru and the Andes

c. **2350 BCE** Lugalzagesi of Umma unites all Sumer

c. **2345–2181 BCE** Sixth dynasty of Egypt founded

c. **2500 BCE** Old Kingdom Period continues in Egypt

c. **2500 BCE** Bell Beaker culture is well established across Western and Central Europe

c. **2500 BCE** Evidence of long-distance trade routes in South America

c. **2450 BCE** Eannatum of Lagash rules areas of Sumer

c. **2334–2316 BCE** Sargon of Akkad conquers Sumer to create world's first empire

Relief sculptures in Egyptian tombs represented everyday life and religious rituals. This carving from the Sixth dynasty shows boys with sticks, on the left, and youths wrestling, on the right.

the authority of the Egyptian rulers had steadily eroded.

In **Western Europe**, the **Bell Beaker culture** flourished. Named after the distinctive shape of **pottery vessels** found in graves, this culture emerged around 2900 BCE, probably in Iberia, spreading first by sea to France. By around 2500 BCE it was widespread in Western and Central Europe. Around 2300 BCE, **bronze technology** from Mediterranean regions and from Central Europe started to **spread** northward **along the Rhine** and **Danube**. The increasingly militaristic societies used bronze to create weapons, triggering the appearance of **small chiefdoms** across Europe.

As populations grew, **competition** over **land** and **resources** intensified. Fields were enclosed, farming expanded, and boundary walls built. Imposing structures such as **funerary mounds** were constructed in many areas.

In **South America**, societies continued to develop in two distinct regions: the upland **valleys** and **high plains** of the **Andes**,

and along the **Pacific coast** and inland valleys. Andean cultures were based on **farming** and **herding**. **Coastal settlements** such as Aspero (Peru) were unique in their dependence on **fishing** rather than on agriculture. The coastal people grew cotton for textiles, and gourds, which were used as fishing floats.

Akkadian warrior king
This bronze cast of an Akkadian ruler may depict Sargon I or his grandson, Naram-Sin, who extended Sargon's empire.

WEAK LATER KINGS ENABLED many **Sumerian city-states** such as **Uruk**, **Ur**, and **Lagash** to break away from the Akkadian empire by 2193 BCE. **Gutian tribesmen** from the eastern mountains frequently raided the shrinking empire, conquering it in 2154 BCE. A coalition of Sumerian city-states eventually drove out the Guti. Under **Ur-Nammu of Ur** (r. 2112–2095 BCE, Sumerian armies conquered **Elam** and eastern regions and created a vast new empire.

Ur-Nammu founded the **Third dynasty of Ur**, which witnessed a **revival of Sumerian power**, as well as an artistic and cultural **renaissance**. Sumerian scholars devised a method of counting, based on units of 60. This system is reflected in our modern division of hours into 60 minutes, minutes into 60 seconds, and a circle into 360 degrees.

Ur-Nammu also commissioned the **first ziggurat** in Ur—an imposing stepped platform topped with a temple. The ziggurats later became a characteristic of ancient western Asian architecture.

In c. 2181 BCE, Egypt's **Old Kingdom collapsed** following a series of natural disasters, including famine. This undermined the authority of the king, who was believed to secure the annual floods that

brought fertility to the Nile valley. The rule of Memphis, the capital city of the Old Kingdom, was overthrown as nomarchs and nobles seized control of the provinces. This ushered in a time of **unrest** called the **First Intermediate Period**, the first of the three eras of uncertainty in Egyptian history. For 140 years, kingdoms such as Herakleopolis in central Egypt vied for control with Thebes in the south. In c. 2040 BCE, the Theban ruler Nebhepetre **Mentuhotep** defeated his rivals and **united Egypt** once more, beginning the start of what came to be known as the **Middle Kingdom**.

In China, the Neolithic **Longshan culture** (see 3200 BCE) continued to develop along the Yellow River on the central plains of northern China. According to Chinese historical tradition, the **first dynasty**, **Xia** (Hsia), was **founded** by Yu the Great. However, **no archaeological**

Longshan pottery
This elegant pottery tripod pitcher has tapering legs and swirling patterns, characteristic of the Longshan culture.

evidence has been found to confirm the existence of **a centralized state** in China at this time.

By the end of the 3rd millennium, **Europe's first civilization** was emerging on the Mediterranean island of **Crete**, which lay at the heart of Mediterranean trade routes. Known as the **Minoan civilization**, it grew prosperous through **trade** and **farming**. Cretan farmlands produced wheat, olives, wine, and wool, which could be easily transported by sea. The Minoans also made bronzework, pottery, and dyes for export. By 2000 BCE, Crete was home to several small kingdoms centred on palaces at Knossos, Mallia, and Phaistos.

100
THOUSAND
THE LIKELY **POPULATION** OF **UR** c.2100

c. 2300 BCE Bronze Age begins in **Central Europe**

2278–2184 BCE Reign of **Pepy II** of the Sixth dynasty in **Egypt**

c. 2200 BCE Stones erected in final positions at **Stonehenge** ceremonial complex

c. 2181 BCE Sixth dynasty and Old Kingdom period **ends in Egypt** after natural disasters weaken authority of ruler

c. 2181 BCE First **Intermediate Period** begins in Egypt (to 2040 BCE)

2119 BCE A coalition of **Sumerian city-states** led by **Utu-hegal** of Uruk expel the Guti and regain control of Akkad

2112 BCE Third Dynasty of Ur, founded by Ur-Nammu (to 2004 BCE)

c. 2040 BCE Nebhepetre **Mentuhotep** of Thebes defeats rivals to **unite Egypt**

c. 2300 BCE Bronze Age begins in southern Europe, in Italy and the Balkans

c.2205 BCE Xia dynasty founded in eastern China by Yu the Great, according to Chinese tradition; said to have ruled until 1766

c. 2150 BCE Nubian kingdom emerges south of Egypt, based at Kerma on Third Cataract of Nile

2112–2095 BCE Reign of Ur-Nammu of Ur reunites much of Mesopotamia; builds the first **ziggurat** at Ur

c.2050 Emergence of the **Minoan palace** civilization, Crete

c.2040 BCE Mentuhotep founds a new capital at Itj-Tawy near Memphis; **Middle Kingdom begins**

2004 BCE City of **Ur falls** to Elamites, ending the Third dynasty of Ur

27

hieroglyphs are picture signs

hieratic script reads from right to left

papyrus, made by pressing together layers of strips of reed

illustration shows a priest making an offering to the god Osiris

Egyptian hieroglyphic and hieratic script
This ancient Egyptian papyrus manuscript shows two forms of Egyptian writing: hieratic script (left) and hieroglyphic script (right) above the two figures. Hieroglyphic is an elaborate script in which signs take a highly pictorial form, while hieratic is a simplified version of hieroglyphic for ease of speed and writing.

Prehistory
Pictograms
Pictures painted on walls of caves up to 25,000 years ago are considered a precursor to writing, recording information that could then be understood by others.

Cave images by Anasazi Indians

c. 3200 BCE
Egyptian hieroglyphs
Egyptian writing develops 100 years after cuneiform. This script begins as a form of picture writing, and includes signs for words and also sounds. It remains in use until the 4th century CE.

8th century BCE
The Greek alphabet
The first alphabets, using only consonants, develop in the Levant by c. 1150 BCE. They include the Phoenician alphabet, which spreads to the Greeks through trade, who add vowels.

Greek wax tablet

100
The Roman alphabet
The Romans adapt the Greek script to write Latin. Through the Roman Empire, this alphabet spreads across Europe and is used for personal as well as official correspondence.

3300 BCE
Cuneiform
The first true written script is developed by the Sumerians of Mesopotamia. Writing with a reed stylus creates a wedge-shaped impression on tablets of wet clay, which then dry hard.

Mesopotamian tablet

c. 1900 BCE
Chinese writing
The first surviving Chinese writing appears on oracle bones, used in divination. This ancient script is still in use today. Chinese script involves 50,000 characters that stand for words.

Chinese paper scroll

c. 6th century BCE
Parchment
Made from dried and processed animal skins, parchment becomes a popular medium for writing around the 6th century BCE, taking over from papyrus, a paper made from reeds.

Chinese parchment scroll

THE STORY OF
WRITING

FROM CAVE PAINTINGS TO THE DIGITAL AGE, WRITING IN ITS VARIOUS FORMS HAS ALWAYS BEEN AN IMPORTANT PART OF OUR CIVILIZATION

The development of writing was an amazing breakthrough, as it allowed people to communicate over distance and record information for posterity. Writing evolved separately in different cultures: in Mesopotamia, Egypt, and the Indus Valley before 2500 BCE and later in Crete, China, and Mesoamerica.

Some scholars think that prehistoric cave paintings featuring images and symbols constitute a form of writing. The first true script was developed by the Sumerians of Mesopotamia (now Iraq) around 3300 BCE. Soon, a number of different ancient cultures had developed writing, usually to keep economic records or keep track of time. As writing developed, it was commonly used to reinforce the authority of rulers. Many early texts, including monumental ones in stone, glorify the deeds of kings and attribute their success to divine approval.

Writing systems can be divided into three types, according to the function of the signs used: logographic, syllabic, and alphabetic. However, many scripts make use of two types of signs. In logographic scripts, each sign stands for a whole word; Chinese writing is an example, although it also uses syllabic signs. The drawback is that a very large number of symbols are needed (Chinese has 50,000 characters). In syllabic scripts, signs stand for syllables. A smaller but still large number of signs are needed—700 in Babylonian cuneiform. In alphabetic scripts, each sign stands for a sound. Far fewer symbols are needed—usually around 26. The first alphabets developed in the Levant between 1450 and 1150 BCE. For years, the spread of writing was limited by the labor involved in hand-copying texts, but this changed with the invention of printing. In the late 20th century, writing became electronic with the invention of word processors. In the 1990s, the spread of information was again revolutionized by the arrival of the Internet.

Ancient texts in the digital world
Nowadays, ancient texts can be viewed digitally. Here, a student examines a digitized page of the Codex Sinaiticus, *handwritten in Greek over 1,600 years ago.*

Roman mosaic   Modern sign

PICTOGRAPHIC SIGNS

Pictograms, or picture signs, are an ancient form of communication. Some scholars do not consider pictograms to be "true" writing, since the symbols do not convey the sounds of words in any language. For example, the pictures above—from a house in Roman Pompeii dating to 79 CE, and a modern sign—convey the same warning. The symbol can be read in any language—for instance, as *canis*, *chien*, *Hund*, or dog. Those words convey the same idea but reproduce the sounds of different languages—Latin, French, German, and English. Pictograms have limited use but remain widespread, appearing, for example, on street signs, maps, and clothes labels.

7th century
Arabic script
The Arabic alphabet is used to write down the Qu'ran, the holy book of Islam. Its use spreads with the Islamic faith to become one of the world's most widely used scripts.

Medieval Qu'ran

c.1450
Invention of the printing press
The laboriousness of copying by hand limits the spread of writing. Invention of moveable type in China by Pi Sheng in *c.*1040 CE ultimately leads to Gutenberg's printing press that makes writing far more accessible in Europe.

1884
The fountain pen
The first practical fountain pen is produced by American inventor L. E. Waterman, and quickly replaces the quill pen. Ballpoints, invented by László Bíró, are in use by the 1940s.

Waterman fountain pen

1990–present
Text messaging
In the 1990s, the first text messages are sent via mobile phones. Texting becomes very popular in the 2000s. In 2009, more than 1.5 trillion text messages are sent.

Smartphone

4th century
The codex
The codex, or manuscript in book form, gradually supersedes the roll of parchment. Originally developed by the Romans, the use of codices spreads with the Christian religion.

7th–9th centuries
Illuminated manuscripts
In early medieval times, the use of writing spreads through the copying of Christian texts. Illuminated manuscripts are highly heautiful, with ornate capital letters and marginal illustrations.

Book of Durrow

1867–1868
The typewriter
American inventor Christopher Latham Sholes helps to build the first practical typewriter. The patent is sold to Remington, and the first typewriters on sale in 1874.

The Remington Model I

1965
Writing enters the digital age
In the mid-1960s, the first electronic messages (emails) are sent from one computer to another. Emails become popular with the spread of personal computers in the 1980s.

Egyptian hieroglyphics involved the use of pictorial signs. This example is from a coffin from the Middle Kingdom period.

THE MINOAN CIVILIZATION, named after the legendary King Minos, **flourished** on the **Aegean island** of **Crete** in the early 2nd millennium, reaching its peak between 2000 and 1600 BCE. It is thought that Crete's **prosperity** was based on productive agriculture and the **export** of **pottery, textiles, food products,** and **luxury goods** to Egypt, Cyprus, the Levant, and the Aegean. The Minoans established colonies in many parts of the Aegean, including the islands of Kythera, Thera, Melos, and Rhodes, and at Miletos on the Turkish mainland.

The farmlands of Crete were ruled from cities with **central** **palaces** that housed workshops, the administration, religious facilities, and state storerooms. Those at Knossos, Phaestos, Mallia, and Zakros were particularly impressive, judging by their remains. Around 1700 BCE, these palaces were destroyed by an earthquake. **Knossos** was **rebuilt** on a more magnificent scale than before, suggesting its dominance over the entire island. The palace was five stories high, with rooms opening onto inner courtyards. This mazelike complex is thought to have given rise to the labyrinth in the **legend** of the **Minotaur,** a bull-headed monster. Bulls certainly featured in Minoan ceremonies. The **deities** worshipped in Minoan shrines seem to have been **female,** with a **goddess of nature** being the most popular. However, details of Minoan culture remain obscure, since the Minoan scripts, known as Cretan hieroglyphic and Linear A, have yet to be deciphered.

In Egypt, King Mentuhotep had reunited the country at the end of the 3rd millennium. Yet the second of Egypt's eras of strong, centralized rule only **began with** the reign of **Amenemhet I,** from about 1985 BCE, during the Middle Kingdom. In 1965 BCE, his successor **Senwosret I** conquered the land of **Nubia** to the south,

40
THE NUMBER OF **DAYS** IT TOOK **TO MUMMIFY** A **BODY**

extending Egypt's borders as far as the second cataract of the Nile. Nubia yielded gold, copper, and slaves. The Egyptian army also employed some Nubian mercenaries. Around a century later, **Senwosret III** conducted a successful campaign in the **Levant**.

Middle-Kingdom Egypt was **more democratic** than it was during the Old Kingdom period. Rulers presented themselves as shepherds of the state rather than absolute monarchs. The process of **mummification,** once confined to kings, was now **permitted for ordinary citizens**. In order to preserve it as a permanent home for the spirit, the body was dried in natron salt, its vital organs were removed, and it was stuffed with linen and wrapped in bandages.

Shang bronze
This bronze plate was found at Erlitou, and is of the Xia period. It is inlaid with turquoise mosaic, believed to represent a dragon's scales.

TRADITIONALLY, CHINA'S FIRST DYNASTY was the **Xia,** who came to power after a great flood in the the **Yellow River** valley. Recent discoveries suggest a massive flood did occur around 1920 BCE. Erlitou in Henan province is now believed to have been the Xia capital. Here, archaeologists have uncovered a **palace complex** built

20,000
THE NUMBER OF **CLAY TABLETS** SO FAR FOUND AT **MARI**

Charging bull
Minoan rituals included a bull-leaping ceremony. This Knossos fresco dates back to c.1500 BCE.

c.2000–1750 BCE After fall of Ur III empire, rival **Mesopotamian states** compete for power: Isin then Larsa are dominant in the south

c. 2000 BCE Corn, beans, and squash cultivated in southwestern North America; long-distance trade routes in place

c.2000–1600 BCE **Minoan** civilization of Crete reaches height

c. 1985–1955 BCE King Amenemhet I brings stability to Egypt during **Middle Kingdom** period

c.1920 BCE **Lajja settlement** on the Yellow River is destroyed by earthquake and flooding

1960 BCE **Senwosret I** of Egypt defeats Nubia and extends his kingdom as far as second cataract on Nile

c. 1900 BCE City of **Erlitou** constructed around Yellow River, China

c.1900 BCE Towns and small kingdoms developing in **Anatolia**

c.1900 BCE Emergence of **Xia dynasty** in China

c.1900–1700 BCE **Indus civilization declines**, its cities gradually abandoned

c.1894 BCE Founding of first dynasty of **Babylon**

c.1830 BCE Ashur merchants' trading station at Kanesh in Anatolia is **destroyed** by fire, ironically **preserving** their archives of more than **25,000 clay tablets**

KEY

▨ Area of Shang influence
• Shang city

Shang China

The middle course of the Yellow River was the heartland of the Shang civilization c. 1800–1100 BCE. From here, Shang influence, such as bronze-working, spread elsewhere.

ASIA

Yellow River
Bo Hai
• Taixicun
Xi'ang • Xingtai
Shang capital
1400–1300 BCE
Shandong
Anyang
Shang capital
1300–1027 BCE
Huixian
Zhengzhou
Shang capital
1600–1400 BCE
Luoyang
Erlitou
Yellow Sea
Huai River
Henan
Yangtze River
• Panlongcheng
East China Sea
Wucheng •

on a platform of compressed earth around 1900 BCE. They have also unearthed bronze vessels. The Xia was succeeded by the **Shang** around 1600 BCE. Many features that were to characterize Chinese society later, such as a strong **bureaucracy** and the **worship of ancestors**, date back to this time.

In southern Asia, the **Indus civilization**, which had thrived during the 3rd millennium (see 2500–2350 BCE), went into a **decline** by around 1800 BCE. Scholars believe that this was partly caused by the changes in the regimes of the rivers that provided water for irrigation. Cities seem to have been **ravaged by diseases** such as cholera and malaria. Trade with Mesopotamia also declined. The growing importance of crops such as millet and rice changed agricultural practices. All these factors seem to have led to a **decline in urban culture**, characterized by writing and a centralized bureaucracy, in favor of a **rural-based culture**.

In South America, large-scale cultivation was taking place along the Pacific coast by about 1800 BCE. Substantial settlements such as **El Paraíso** and **Sechin Alto** in Peru

were dominated by **massive temple complexes**. Long-distance trade routes linked coastal towns with communities in Andean valleys to the east and beyond. This allowed for the **spread of pottery** from Colombia to Peru by 1800 BCE. Meanwhile, in North America, crops such as sunflowers and gourds began to be cultivated in the east.

After the Ur III Empire fell, rival West Asian city-states vied for power. **Ashur** on the Tigris operated a lucrative trade network in the 19th century BCE, trading Mesopotamian textiles and Afghan

Sumerian hero
Tablets and stone carvings from the Old Babylonian period provide a record of the Epic of Gilgamesh, originally passed down in the oral tradition.

tin for Anatolian silver. Amorite kings ruled many states, including Larsa, which dominated southern Mesopotamia; Babylon, whose first dynasty was established in 1894 BCE; and Mari in the middle Euphrates. In 1813–1781 BCE Shamshi-Adad, another Amorite king, conquered all the north and central regions, creating the Kingdom of Upper Mesopotamia. Clay tablets from Mari record administrative and political details of life under Shamshi-Adad. Many literary texts also survive from this period, including one of the earliest surviving works of literature, *The Epic of Gilgamesh.*

> ❝ IF A MAN **PUTS OUT** THE **EYE** OF AN **EQUAL, HIS EYE** SHALL BE **PUT OUT.** ❞

Law Code of Hammurabi, king of Babylon

BABYLON CITY-STATE EMERGED AND GREW in importance between 2000 and 1800 BCE. Ruled by **Hammurabi** from 1790 BCE, it became a vassal state of **Shamshi-Adad**. However, after Shamshi-Adad's death, his weak successor **Ishme-Dagan** became a vassal of Hammurabi, who led a coalition against the most powerful states of the time. In 1764 BCE, Hammurabi and his allies drove the Elamites back east and in 1762 BCE conquered Eshnunna farther to the north. His greatest achievement, in 1763 BCE, was defeating Larsa, which controlled southern Mesopotamia. In 1757–1755 BCE, Hammurabi turned on his main ally, Mari, sacking its city, thus completing his control of the empire that encompassed all southern and central Mesopotamia.

Hammurabi introduced the Babylonian law code in the region under his control. Its 282 laws covered property, family, trade, and business practices. The **Law Code of Hammurabi** is famous for punitive laws that meted out punishments in the same measure as the crime committed ("an eye for an eye"). However, it is thought that the law code was more of a moral statement of principle than an enforced judicial system. As such, the code bound the powerful and wealthy as well as ordinary people; the strong were exhorted to refrain from oppressing the weak.

Set in stone
Hammurabi's code was inscribed on stone pillars called stele. This stele shows the god of justice Shamash (right) dictating laws to the king.

1813–1781 BCE Reign of Shamshi-Adad; conquers northern Mesopotamia to establish **Kingdom of Upper Mesopotamia**, with its capital at Shubat-Enlil

c.1800 BCE Major ceremonial **center of Caral** in Peru is abandoned

c.1800 BCE Potter's wheel is introduced into Minoan Crete, beginning the **mass production** of high-quality pottery

1792–1750 BCE Reign of **Hammurabi** of Babylon; establishes **Babylonian Empire** in Mesopotamia and promulgates a law code for use throughout his empire

1766 BCE Traditional date for founding of **Shang dynasty** by King Tang, according to Chinese history

c.1725 BCE Middle Kingdom in Egypt torn by unrest; start of **Second Intermediate Period** (to c.1540)

c.1800 BCE Elite burials appear in Central Europe, placed under barrows with rich grave goods

c.1800 BCE Regular production of iron objects at Kaman-Kalehöyük in Anatolia

c.1800 BCE Ceremonial center of **La Florida** built in Peru; **first pottery in Peru** is found here

c.1800 BCE Settlement begins at San Lorenzo, later a major Olmec ceremonial center in Mesoamerica

c.1750 BCE Linear A script comes into use in Crete

c.1700 BCE Votive offerings placed in a sacred spring at Manatí in Mesoamerica's Gulf region show the **beginnings of Olmec culture**

to Central and
Northern Europe

**MYCENAEAN
GREECE**

*Ionian
Sea*

Orchomenos

Gla

Thebes

Mycenae

Athens

Pylos

Menelaion

Tiryns

Knossos

Crete

WILUSA
Troy
*SEHA
RIVER M
LAND*
Apasa
ARZA
Miletu

Sardinia

Sicily

Mediterranean Sea

A F R I C A

S A H A R A

The importance of trade
*Trade was essential to supply societies with the raw
materials and manufactured goods needed for daily life
(such as metals and lumber), for displaying status (such as
fine weaponry), or for embellishing religious monuments
and royal palaces (such as lapis lazuli). Trade also promoted
the spread of knowledge, technology, and ideas.*

KEY

Mycenaean Greece	Elam
Hittite Empire	New Kingdom Egypt
Mitanni	Arzawa
Assyria	— Trade routes *c.*1350 BCE
Kassite Babylonia	

TRADE COMMODITIES

gold	timber	glass
silver	grain	faience objects
tin	ivory	turquoise
copper	ivory objects	murex dye
fine metalwork	perfumed oils	seashells
fine pottery	olive oil	horses
textiles	wine	weapons

ANCIENT EMPIRES
THE BIRTH OF ADVANCED SOCIETIES

to sub-Saharan Afr

**In the 3rd millennium BCE, states emerged in Egypt, Mesopotamia, and the
Indus. Urban society was consolidated in Western Asia in the 2nd millennium,
and powerful states vied for control of lands; in contrast, in South Asia, towns
disappeared. Complex societies emerged in China and the Americas.**

The exceptional agricultural productivity of the
Nile, Euphrates, Indus (see p.26), and Yellow (see
p.31) river valleys undoubtedly played a part in the
precocious emergence of civilizations in these
regions. So did international trade, which was also
important in the development of the first New
World civilizations. Trade also enabled many
neighboring societies to achieve prosperity:
through time they developed complex cultures

increasingly focused on urban centers, and came
into competition for resources and markets.
High-level diplomacy was essential to the smooth
operation of international trading networks and
to success in inter-state power struggles. Royal
letters found in the Egyptian capital, Akhetaten
(Amarna), provide a fascinating picture of relations
between the 14th-century BCE rulers of the rival
great states of the eastern Mediterranean.

> ❝ FOR A **LONG TIME** WE HAVE
> HAD GOOD RELATIONS BETWEEN
> US **KINGS…** ❞

Babylonian king Burnaburiash II to Egyptian pharaoh Akhenaten,
from the Amarna letters, 14th century BCE

THE WORLD PICTURE

Urbanism and complex societies became mor
widespread during the 2nd millennium BCE.
While they shared many features such as
trade, high agricultural productivity, dense
populations, and their managerial needs, urba
societies took many different forms. In the
Americas, large ceremonial complexes with
residential suburbs provided the focus for the
communities of the wider region, strongly
connected by shared religion and trade.

Advanced centers
*This map shows
established and
emerging civilizations
in the later 2nd
millennium BCE.
Societies of farmers
and hunter-gatherers
occupied other
regions.*

KEY

Chavín	Assyria
Olmec	Hittites
Shang	Mitanni
Mycenaeans	Elam
Egypt	
Babylonia	

KINGDOMS OF ANCIENT EGYPT

The Nile Valley's exceptional agricultural fertility promoted the early development of urbanism in Egypt. Settlements clung to the Nile delta and riverbanks, beyond which lay arid desert. The great mineral resources of the flanking desert regions and Nubia, which included gold, were important both for domestic use and to support international trade.

KEY

—— Trade routes   ● Capital cities

Black Sea

TUMMANNA
PALA
KASKAS
Hattusas
UPPERLAND

HITTITE EMPIRE
PALLA
ARHUNTASSA
KIZZUWATNA
Carchemish
ISUWA
URUADRI (URARTU)
MUKISH
Harran
Washshukanni
Nineveh
Arbil
Alalah
Aleppo
Emar
MITANNI
ASSYRIA
Ugarit
NIYA
Ashur
Arwad
[orus shiya]
Tunip
Qatna
Qadesh
Labwe
Euphrates
Tigris
to Afghanistan
Simurru
Byblos
Kumida
Hazor
Dur-Kurigalzu
Sidon
Shechem
BABYLONIA
Tyre
Jerusalem
Babylon
SEALAND
Susa
ELAM
Gaza
Lachish
Nippur
Sharuhen
Uruk
Ur
Anshan
Memphis
Liyan

Persian Gulf

khetaten
EGYPT
Red Sea
DILMUN
ebes

Arabian Peninsula

to Punt

Siberia
Hattusas
Mycenae
Anyang
Xi'ang
PACIFIC OCEAN
Babylon
Ashur
Susa
Memphis
Zhengzhou
ATLANTIC OCEAN
SAHARA
San Lorenzo
Chavín de Huántar
ATLANTIC OCEAN
INDIAN OCEAN
PACIFIC OCEAN

Cyprus
Mediterranean Sea
Nile Delta
LOWER Giza Memphis
Saqqara Sinai
EGYPT
Eastern Desert
Abydos
WESTERN DESERT
UPPER EGYPT
Elephantine
NUBIA
SATJU
YAM
NUBIAN DESERT
SAHARA
Red Sea
MEDJA

Old Kingdom *c.* 2686–2181 BCE
Rulers exercised centralized control and commanded impressive resources, as shown by the pyramids at Giza.

Cyprus
Mediterranean Sea
Avaris (Tell el-Dab'a)
capital 1650–1550 BCE
LOWER Memphis
EGYPT
Itjtawy
capital c.1985–1650 BCE
Sinai
Eastern Desert
Waset Thebes
Karnak
capital c.2055–1985 BCE and c.1650–1550 BCE
WESTERN DESERT
UPPER EGYPT
NUBIA
WAWAT
SAHARA
NUBIAN DESERT
KUSH
Red Sea

Middle Kingdom *c.* 2040–1640 BCE
Decorated tombs record prosperous life under the stable 12th dynasty, but the state disintegrated under later rulers.

Cyprus
Mediterranean Sea
Per-Ramesse (Qantir)
capital c.1279–1069 BCE
LOWER EGYPT
Memphis
Sinai
capital c.1333–1279 BCE
Eastern Desert
Akhetaten (Amarna)
capital c.1349–1333 BCE
Waset Thebes
WESTERN DESERT
UPPER EGYPT
capital c.1550–1344 BCE
NUBIA
SAHARA
NUBIAN DESERT
KUSH
Red Sea

New Kingdom *c.* 1550–1069 BCE
Egypt reached its greatest power and prosperity, conquering Nubia and the Levant, and building several temples.

Hattusas, the Hittite capital, was founded by Hattusalis I in 1650 BCE and destroyed in 1180 BCE.

Built over 300 years, the temple complex at Karnak, Egypt, includes the world's largest temple, dedicated to Amun-Re, the patron deity of the pharaohs.

AFTER HAMMURABI'S DEATH in 1750 BCE, the Babylonian Empire (see 1850–1790 BCE) declined. At the same time, other powers were on the rise, such as the **Hurrians** of Mitanni in Syria, and the **Hittites** of Anatolia in Turkey. By 1650 BCE, the Hittites had built an extensive kingdom in central Anatolia, with its capital at Hattusas. The Hittites had developed advanced bronze- and **ironworking** skills, and they were also known to be **fierce fighters**. In 1595 BCE, the Hittite king **Mursilis** (r. 1620–1590 BCE) **raided Babylon** and expanded his empire. However, he was killed soon after, and the empire shrank back for about a century.

In Egypt, the **Middle Kingdom** (see 2000–1850 BCE) was **waning** by 1670 BCE, partly due to erratic floods

IRON-WORKING

By 2000 BCE, iron was being produced in Anatolia and used in luxury objects, such as decoration on this box from Acemhöyük. The Hittites exported iron as an expensive prestige material, apparently monopolizing its manufacture. From around 1200 BCE, low-carbon began to be regularly produced, turning iron into a hard metal of practical use for producing tools and weapons. Its use spread widely, reaching Greece around 1200 BCE and central Europe by 800 BCE.

in the Nile. As regional governors became more powerful, **civil war** broke out. Outsiders soon took advantage of the unrest.

The **Nubians** won back lands that the Egyptians had taken earlier (see 2000–1850 BCE). In 1650 BCE, the **Hyksos**, settlers originally from the Levant, seized Lower Egypt, but Upper Egypt remained under the control of Egyptian kings.

Man and beast
The Hittite Empire was known for its bronze craftsmanship. Bronze weapons and artifacts fetched a high price. This statuette of a man and a horse was probably a commission.

IN *c.* **1550 BCE, THE THEBAN KING Ahmose I** (r. 1550–1525 BCE) **drove** the Hyksos from Lower Egypt, ushering in the third period of settled rule in Egypt, known as the **New Kingdom** (*c.* 1550–1070 BCE). During this time, **Egyptian rulers** assumed

2,000
THE NUMBER OF **NAMES** FOR **GODS** AND **GODDESSES** IN **ANCIENT EGYPT**

the **title "pharaoh,"** meaning "great house." A succession of warrior kings campaigned to expand Egypt's boundaries once more. **Tuthmosis I** (r. 1504–1492 BCE) **drove** the **Nubians** back in the south and recaptured Sinai and parts of Syria and Palestine. Under **Tuthmosis III** (r. 1479–1425 BCE), Egypt controlled a strip along the Mediterranean coast and north of the Euphrates (see p.33). The conquered states paid huge annual tributes to Egypt, a part of which was spent building one of the world's largest **religious sites at Karnak** and the impressive mortuary temple **of Queen Hatshepsut** (r. 1473–1458 BCE).

Egyptian religion was very **complex**. Every village, town, and district had its own patron deity. In paintings and sculptures, many **deities** were shown with **animal heads**, representing their most important attributes. For example, the falcon god Horus protected the king, while the ibis-headed Thoth was the patron god of scribes.

By 1600 BCE, a new civilization emerged on the Greek mainland. Its people are now known as the **Mycenaeans**, after the fortress-palace of Mycenae, believed to be the home of the mythical king Agamemnon from Homer's *Iliad*.

Mask of gold
German archaeologist Heinrich Schliemann found this funerary mask at a grave in Mycenae, and claimed it belonged to King Agamemnon.

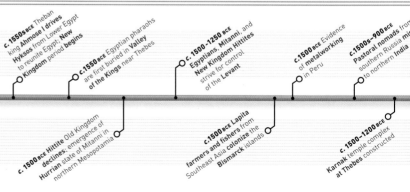

c. 1650 BCE Hittites establish Old Kingdom in central Anatolia, with Hattusas as its capital

c. 1628 BCE A volcano on the Greek island of Thera erupts violently, burying Minoan settlements on the island with ash

c. 1595 BCE Hittite king Mursilis raids Babylon, ending the empire founded by Hammurabi

c.1650–1550 BCE The Hyksos, settlers from the Levant, become kings of Lower Egypt

c. 1600 BCE Mycenaean civilization emerges on the Greek mainland

c. 1570 BCE Kassites of Iran begin creation of new empire in Babylonia, uniting the region

c. 1550s BCE Theban king Ahmose I drives Hyksos from Lower Egypt to reunite Egypt; New Kingdom period begins

c.1550 BCE Egyptian pharaohs are first buried in Valley of the Kings near Thebes

c. 1500–1250 BCE Egyptians, Mitanni, and New Kingdom Hittites strive for control of the Levant

c.1500 BCE Evidence of metalworking in Peru

c.1500s–900 BCE Pastoral nomads from southern Russia migrate to northern India

c. 1500 BCE Hittite Old Kingdom declines; emergence of Hurrian state of Mitanni in northern Mesopotamia

c.1500 BCE Lapita farmers and fishers from Southeast Asia colonize the Bismarck islands

c. 1500–1200 BCE Karnak temple complex at Thebes constructed

Tutankhamun was buried with fabulous treasure. This detail from the pharaoh's throne shows him being anointed by his wife Ankhesenamun.

However, the Mycenaeans probably called themselves Ahhiyawa. Richly furnished burials such as those in the Shaft Graves at Mycenae reflect a warrior aristocracy. Their **lands** were a **patchwork of small kingdoms**, each later dominated by a palace-citadel such as the ones at Mycenae, Tiryns, and Pylos. They spread their influence through trade. After the collapse of the Minoans in 1450 BCE, the Mycenaeans took over several sites formerly under Minoan control, including Knossos. After c. 1400 BCE, they also took over Minoan trade networks and **established settlements** on Rhodes, Kos, and the Anatolian mainland. The Mycenaeans inherited Minoan arts and crafts, adapting the **Linear A script** to write an early form of Greek known as the **Linear B script**. They were **great traders**, and ventured out to Sicily and Italy. A ship believed to be of Canaanite origin, wrecked off Uluburun on the coast of Turkey, was found to contain tin from Iran or Afghanistan, copper and pottery from Cyprus, ivory and jewelry from Egypt, and Mycenaean swords.

In **West Asia** the **Kassites** seized power in Babylonia and by 1475 BCE created a stable empire that endured until 1155 BCE. They

Aegean civilizations
Around 1450 BCE Mycenaean influence spread throughout the Aegean, including taking control of many formerly Minoan sites.

KEY
♦ Mycenaean site
■ Mycenaean major palace

enjoyed generally good relations with their neighbors, **Elam** to the east and **Mitanni**, which by 1500 BCE ruled all northern Mesopotamia. Egypt controlled much of the Levant, bringing it into frequent conflict with Mitanni. In Anatolia, the **Hittite New Kingdom** emerged around 1400 BCE, growing in power. As Mitanni declined after 1380 BCE, the Hittites and the **rising Assyrian state** gradually carved up its territory, bringing Hittites into conflict with Egypt in the Levant.

In China, the **Shang civilization** (see 1850–1790 BCE) **flourished** around 1500 BCE, with its rulers dominating a large area of central China. However, the Shang had to regularly fend off threats to their kingdom from nomadic tribes to the north. **Shang capitals** were surrounded by **defensive walls**. Kings and nobles were buried in tombs, which held fabulous grave goods. The Shang capital moved several times during this period. Shang society was believed to be well organized and extremely hierarchical. Writing began around 1900 BCE. Most examples of **early writing** took the form of **oracle bones**, attesting to the Shang rulers' practice of consulting their ancestors on important decisions. Questions concerning the future were inscribed on the bone of an ox or on a turtle shell, which was then struck with a hot metal tool. The way the bone cracked was believed to provide the answer.

IN *c.* **1352 BCE, AMENHOTEP IV**, a religious reformer, became **Egypt's pharaoh**. He broke with the traditional religion, with its pantheon of gods, and **initiated** the **worship of a single god, Aten**, or sun-disk. He changed his name to Akhenaten, meaning "living spirit of Aten," and founded a **new capital** between Thebes and Memphis. He named it Akhetaten, meaning "horizon of Aten."

Akhenaten's religious reforms were believed to have been unpopular, especially with the influential priestly elite. After his death in *c.* 1336 BCE, his son **Tutankhamun** ascended the throne at the age of nine. He restored the old gods and abandoned the new capital. Tutankhamun is believed to have died under mysterious circumstances at 18, and was hastily buried in a minor tomb. It was thought for years that Tutankhamun died of a blow to the head; latest evidence suggests he died of an infection after breaking his leg, combined with poor health including malaria and congenital

defects due to his incestuous parentage. Since the 1570s BCE, Egypt's pharaohs had been buried in rock-cut tombs in the **Valley of the Kings**, on the west bank of the Nile. Rulers hoped their tombs would be safe from robbers, but almost all the **tombs** were **robbed** of their rich goods. However, in 1922, British archaeologist Howard Carter found **Tutankhamun's tomb** virtually **intact**. The shrine room had four gilded shrines, holding the king's **nested coffins and mummy** with a solid gold mask. The other rooms contained jewelry, furniture, golden statues, and musical instruments.

Sun worship
Akhenaten instituted the worship of the sun-disk Aten. In this relief carving found at Akhetaten (modern el-Amarna), he is seen worshipping the sun with his wife Nefertiti.

c. 1400s BCE Bronze-working spreads to Vietnam and Thailand

c. 1450 BCE Mycenaean trading network stretches from Sicily to the Levant

c. 1450 BCE Mariana Islands in Micronesia are settled from Luzon in the Philippines, a sea crossing of 1,125 miles (1,810 km)

c. 1300s BCE Hittite king Suppluliumas I (r. 1380–1334 BCE) defeats Mitanni, beginning Hittite conquest of their western territories

mid-1300s BCE City of Ashur breaks free from Mitannian rule: rise of Assyrian power

mid-1400s BCE Lapita people migrate eastward from Melanesia to colonize Pacific islands

c. 1450 BCE Minoan palaces on Crete destroyed, Mycenaeans take control of the island

c. 1400 BCE Shang capital moves from Zhengzhou to Xi'ang in China

c. 1352–1336 BCE Reign of Amenhotep IV, breaks with Egypt's old religion to worship the sun-disk Aten and takes the name Akhenaten

c. 1336–1327 BCE Brief reign of the boy king Tutankhamun; old Egyptian religion restored and Akhetaten abandoned

The facade of the temple of Ramesses II at Abu Simbel features four colossal seated statues of the pharaoh, but the statue second from left has crumbled.

TOWARD THE END OF THE 2ND MILLENNIUM BCE, the eastern Mediterranean and Western Asia were a **mosaic of empires**, which comprised Egypt, Babylonia, Elam, Assyria, and the Hittites in Anatolia. Borders fluctuated as each kingdom strove to gain ascendancy over its neighbors through conquest or diplomacy. In war and peace, **vital trade routes**, through which tin and copper for **bronze** reached the region, remained intact.

A frequent flashpoint for conflict was the northern **Levant** (coastal Syria and Lebanon), where Egypt had lost territory to the Hittites who had conquered western Mitanni (see 1550–1400 BCE). In the 13th century BCE, Pharaoh Seti I and his son **Ramesses II** campaigned to win it back. Ramesses' 67-year

> ## YOU ARE A **GREAT WARRIOR** WITHOUT EQUAL, **VICTORIOUS** IN SIGHT OF THE WHOLE WORLD.

Inscription commemorating the victory of Ramesses II at Qadesh

reign (r. 1279–1213 BCE) was a time of **stability and prosperity** for Egypt. Through a combination of war, diplomacy, and strategic marriage, Ramesses sought to extend Egyptian influence to Western Asia. In the 1270s BCE, he fought a series of wars with the Hittite king, Muwattalis II, of which

Ancient propaganda
A detail from the temple of Ramesses II at Abu Simbel shows the king firing an arrow, taking on the Hittite army single-handedly at the Battle of Qadesh.

the most famous was the **Battle of Qadesh** (c. 1274 BCE). Although Ramesses claimed victory at Qadesh, the battle is believed to have been inconclusive, and the Hittites held on to the region.

In 1259 BCE, after further campaigns in Syria, Ramesses tried a different tactic, and negotiated a **pioneering peace treaty** with the new Hittite king, **Hattusilis III**. Ramesses also took two Hittite princesses in marriage (he had eight wives in total). Following the treaty, Ramesses kept up a friendly correspondence with the Hittite ruler, which was recorded on clay tablets in Akkadian cuneiform script.

Ramesses also embarked on an extensive program of **monument-building**. On Egypt's southern border with Nubia, he constructed the magnificent temple of **Abu Simbel**. He founded a new capital at **Per-Ramesse** in Lower Egypt, although Thebes in Upper Egypt remained an important center. West of Thebes he built a vast mortuary temple, which doubled as a palace, court, and center of learning.

The late 2nd millennium BCE saw the resurgence of Ashur, in what is now called the **Middle Assyrian Empire** (1350–1000 BCE). Following the collapse of the Kingdom of Upper Mesopotamia, Ashur had regained its independence but later became a vassal of Mitanni. A revival of Ashur's fortunes began under **Ashur-uballit I** (r. 1363–1328 BCE), who broke free of Mitannian rule and carved out a kingdom in northern Iraq. His later successors, Shalmaneser I and Tukulti-Ninurta I, continued to gain territory, expanding the kingdom's borders west to conquer eastern Mitanni and briefly, from 1225–1216 BCE, southeast to Babylonia.

In the Aegean, the **Mycenaean** palace-kingdoms of the Greek mainland **continued to thrive**.

The boulders used to make these walls, now in ruins, at Mycenae on the Greek mainland were so huge, later civilizations believed they were built by giants.

BETWEEN 1250 AND ABOUT 1050 BCE, many of the **powers** that had dominated Western Asia for centuries **went into decline**, and some disappeared altogether. The eastern Mediterranean entered a **time of turmoil**, and many coastal cities were laid waste by unknown invaders—written records of the period give few clues as to their identity. First to succumb were the Hittites, whose capital **Hattusas** was **sacked** and abandoned c.1200 BCE. By c.1180 BCE, Hittite possessions in the Levant were lost and the **empire fragmented**.

These conflicts were most likely instigated by the waves of migrants known collectively as the **Sea Peoples**. These warlike peoples came from many different areas, including Sicily, Sardinia, Greece, Libya, and Anatolia. Whatever their origins, their movements through the eastern Mediterranean in c.1200–1100 BCE led to attacks on Cyprus, Egypt, Anatolia, and Canaan and Syria in the Levant. In 1178 BCE, the Egyptian pharaoh **Ramesses III** drove the Sea Peoples from Lower Egypt, but could not prevent them from colonizing the Levant.

Around 1200 BCE, the **Mycenaean kingdoms** entered a time of upheaval, a result of both internal disintegration and external threats. The defenses of many Mycenae palaces were strengthened. Records at Pylos show the inhabitants feared attack from the sea. By 1100 BCE, most of the Mycenaean palaces had been sacked and abandoned. This triggered the so-called **Dark Age of Greece**, when writing fell out of use, not to be reintroduced until the Homeric age (see 800 BCE).

In the late Bronze Age, parts of Europe came to be dominated by the **Urnfield Culture**—named after the practice of cremating the dead and burying the remains in funerary urns, sometimes accompanied by rich grave goods. This culture originated in the **Danube region** in 1300 BCE, and spread to Italy and central and eastern Europe in the following centuries.

Between 1200 and 700 BCE **iron technology** spread northward from Greece to Central Europe. Iron rapidly replaced bronze in tools and weapons, signaling the end of the **Bronze Age**.

> ## THEY CAME **BOLDLY SAILING** IN THEIR WARSHIPS FROM THE **MIDST OF THE SEA,** NONE BEING ABLE TO WITHSTAND THEM…

An inscription by **Ramesses II** (r. 1279–1213), referring to the Sea Peoples

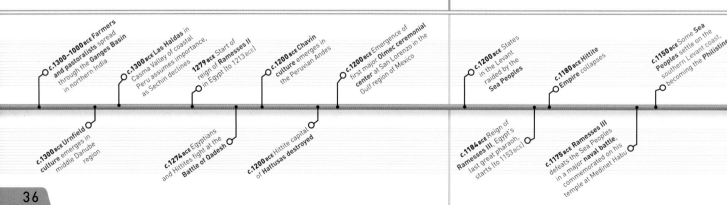

c.1300–1000 BCE Farmers and pastoralists spread through the Ganges Basin in northern India

c.1300–1000 BCE Las Haldas in Casma Valley of coastal Peru assumes importance, as Sechin declines

1279 BCE Start of reign of **Ramesses II** in Egypt (to 1213 BCE)

c.1200 BCE Chavín culture emerges in the Peruvian Andes

c.1200 BCE Emergence of first major **Olmec ceremonial center** at San Lorenzo in the Gulf region of Mexico

c.1200 BCE States in the Levant raided by the **Sea Peoples**

c.1180 BCE Hittite Empire collapses

c.1150 BCE Some Sea Peoples settle on the southern Levant coast, becoming the **Philistines**

c.1300 BCE Urnfield culture emerges in middle Danube region

c.1274 BCE Egyptians and Hittites fight at the **Battle of Qadesh**

c.1200 BCE Hittite capital of **Hattusas destroyed**

c.1184 BCE Reign of Ramesses III, Egypt's last great pharaoh, starts (to 1153 BCE)

c.1175 BCE Ramesses III defeats the Sea Peoples in a major **naval battle**, commemorated on his temple at Medinet Habu

> **WHEN ALL LONGINGS** THAT ARE IN THE HEART **VANISH,** THEN **A MORTAL BECOMES IMMORTAL…**

Krishna Yajur Veda

In Mesoamerica, the region's first great civilization, the **Olmec**, was emerging in the lowlands of Mexico's southern Gulf coast. The Olmecs built ceremonial centers, including San Lorenzo, constructed temples and houses on earthen mounds, and carved huge stone heads clad in helmets. They also established long-distance trade routes. In contemporary Peru, the highland ceremonial center of Chavín de Huántar was founded (see 900–800 BCE), while some coastal centers such as Cerro Sechin were now in decline.

Stone warrior
Monumental carvings from temples at Cerro Sechin on the Peruvian coast show warriors, torture victims, and human sacrifices.

THE CLOSE OF THE 2ND MILLENNIUM SAW MAJOR CHANGES in the power politics of West Asia. In 1070 BCE, the Egyptian New Kingdom ended and Egypt entered a time of unrest called the **Third Intermediate Period**, which lasted until 747 BCE (see 800–700 BCE). Historians believe that the power of the pharaohs had been eroded by a priestly elite who had gained control of many areas. By 1000 BCE, all of the territories won by New Kingdom pharaohs had been lost.

In **Mesopotamia**, there were **frequent wars** between the Babylonians, Assyrians, and Elamites; the region was also subjected to devastating raids by Aramaean nomads from the west. Meanwhile, other powers were rising in the region. A Semitic-speaking people, known as **Canaanites**, had inhabited the Levant for centuries, living in coastal city-states that controlled the surrounding territory. They were skilled seafarers and played a major role in international trade. From 1100 BCE, Canaanite port cities such as Arwad, Byblos, Tyre, and Sidon were expanding their operations, establishing trading posts and colonies throughout the eastern Mediterranean. They traded cedarwood from Lebanon, glass- and ivory-ware, metal ores, and, most important, an expensive purple dye made from murex shellfish. It was this luxury commodity that caused them to be known by their more familiar Greek name, the **Phoenicians**, after *phoinix*, Greek for "purple."

In China, a new dynasty replaced the Shang in 1027 BCE, when King Wu of the Zhou defeated the last Shang ruler, Di-Xin. The **Zhou dynasty** was to **rule China for 700 years**. This long era is usually divided into two periods: the Western and Eastern Zhou. During the first era, the Zhou capital was Zongzhou. This was a **time of prosperity** and strong central control. Zhou territory was divided into fiefs held by trusted noblemen, in return for military allegiance. But many aspects of Chinese tradition already present in the Shang period continued in the Zhou, including ancestor worship and the use of oracle bones for divination.

Meanwhile in Japan, the **Jomon people** were still hunter-gatherers, albeit prosperous and sedentary. The Jomon culture got its name from the cord patterns (jomon) that decorate its pottery.

After the decline of the Indus civilization's towns and cities (see 1850–1790 BCE), smaller farming and herding communities flourished in **northern India**. By 1200 BCE they were spreading into the **Ganges basin**, establishing mixed farming settlements growing rice and raising

Mark of a culture
In this example of late-Jomon pottery, the bowl and stand bear the distinctive rope patterns that give the Jomon period its name.

animals including cattle and horses. The earliest Indian sacred texts, the **Vedas**, which were transmitted orally for many centuries, reflect this period. They were composed in **Sanskrit**, an **Indo-European** language related to Iranian and almost all European languages, which is ancestral to many languages now spoken in South Asia, such as Hindi and Urdu.

Although the Vedas are largely religious writings and hymns, the geographical information that they contain not only describes the gradual spread of farmers and pastoralists from the Punjab to the Ganges basin, but also gives some information about conflicts with other groups, and local life at the time. For example, the **division of society** into **varnas** or **castes** is described in the Vedas, first appearing in Book X of *Rigveda*, although there is nothing in the text to suggest that the system was hereditary at at the time.

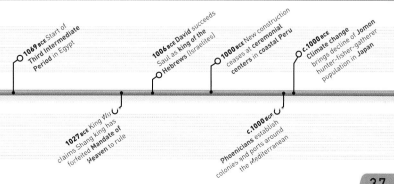

c.1150 BCE Mycenaean defenses strengthened, indicating fear of attack

c.1100 BCE Mycenaean period ends and **Dark Age of Greece** begins

c.1100 BCE Traditional date of foundation of Gadir (modern Cadiz) by Phoenician colonists from Tyre

c.1100 BCE Continuing colonization of the **Pacific islands** sees settlers established on **Fiji**

1069 BCE Start of **Third Intermediate Period** in Egypt

1027 BCE King Wu claims Shang king has forfeited **Mandate of Heaven** to rule

1006 BCE David succeeds Saul as **king of the Hebrews** (Israelites)

1000 BCE New construction ceases at ceremonial centers in coastal Peru

c.1000 BCE **Phoenicians** establish colonies and ports around the Mediterranean

c.1000 BCE Climate change brings decline of **Jomon** hunter-fisher-gatherer population in **Japan**

neck is circled
by a collar

knob is part of
locking device

Decorated box of Perpauty
c. 1370 BCE
This sycamore box belonging
to a man called Perpauty may
have held linen. All four sides
are painted with scenes. This
side shows Perpauty and his
wife being offered gifts by their
son and three daughters.

Perpauty and
his wife

children bringing
offerings

Duck-shaped flask
c. 1700 BCE
This jar is carved in the shape of a
duck, which appears to be trussed
and plucked. It probably held cosmetic
paste, such as eye-paint, which was
likely removed and applied using a
stopper/applicator, now lost.

Cat figurine
c. 600 BCE
This copper alloy figurine sits on a
wooden base. Cats were linked with
the goddess Bastet, who protected
the pharaoh. A hole through the
nose originally held a ring.

Statue with stele
c. 1360 BCE
A carved figure representing a high priest
of Amun holds a stele, or carved slab. These
slabs were used as grave or commemorative
markers. The inscription is a hymn to the Sun
god and lists local dignitaries.

material is the rare
blue stone anhydrite

ANCIENT EGYPT

A REMARKABLE CIVILIZATION REVEALED THROUGH EVERYDAY ITEMS AND TREASURES

**Artifacts manufactured over some 2,000 years bear
witness to the skills of Egyptian craft workers. They also
reflect Egypt's wealth and its trade network, through
which ebony, lapis lazuli, and turquoise were imported.**

Many of the objects shown here were used in daily life by well-to-do
Egyptians. They reflect belief in the afterlife and the practice of burying
possessions that it was believed would be used by the dead person's
spirit in the afterlife. The ruling classes were buried with great wealth,
but almost all of their tombs were stripped of their riches either in
antiquity or more recently.

Mummiform shabti
c. 1300 BCE
This large shabti figure
was carved from wood.
The tools the figure carries
are traditional symbols of
kingship, while the scarab
represents the god Khepri.

scarab ornament
on chest

mask of cartonnage—a combination
of plaster and linen

details such
as eyes are
modeled
in paler
wrappings

lapis lazuli
inlay

Shabtis
1292–1190 BCE
Statuettes of servant-figures called shabtis
were commonly placed in tombs. The Egyptians
believed they would come alive to serve the
dead person's spirit in the life to come.

Funerary mask
c. 1500 BCE
This mask would have been placed over the head
of a mummy. The Egyptians mummified bodies
because the deceased spirit could not survive
unless there was a body for it to return to.

Mummified jackal or dog
c. 600 BCE
Jackals and, from the 8th century BCE
onward, also dogs were mummified in
honor of the jackal-headed god Anubis,
who presided over funerals and embalmings.

Necklaces
c. 1550–1069 BCE
Egyptian craftsmen had access to many semiprecious stones and precious metals. Necklaces were worn in daily life and also buried with the dead.

gold band

purple amethyst

Ear studs and earring
c. 1550–1069 BCE
Once the basic shapes for these studs and earring were made, strands of glass in a contrasting color were wound around them. The studs required large perforations in the wearer's lobes.

backing for mirror

Wooden comb
c. 300 BCE
This double-sided comb has a row of longer and shorter teeth. Many Egyptians had short hair and wore wigs. Combs were used to keep both natural hair and wigs tidy.

handle and backing made of ebony

ibex symbolizes grace and mastery over the natural world

Cosmetic spoon
c. 1360 BCE
This spoon for cosmetic paste was carved from schist in the shape of an ibex, with its head bent over its back, so that its straight horns touch the bowl.

Amulet
912–343 BCE
The wedjat eye symbolizes the eye of the god Horus. This charm was placed on mummies to protect the dead person's spirit in the afterlife. It also symbolized regeneration.

Mirror handle
c. 1360 BCE
This hardwood mirror setting originally held a polished bronze mirror disk. The handle is carved in the shape of a papyrus column topped with the god Bes—a popular deity.

disk representing sun

Male figure amulet
c. 2200 BCE
This golden charm shows a kneeling male god clasping two palm ribs. He is probably the god Heh, who symbolized eternity. The palm ribs are notched, representing years.

Frog amulets
c. 1360 BCE
Frogs were a symbol of life and fertility. Women wore frog amulets for luck. These charms are made of blue faience with details picked out in gold.

inlay held within cells of gold

Scarab pectoral
c. 1361–52 BCE
This magnificent chest ornament represents the scarab god Khepri rolling the red sun-disk. It was found in the tomb of King Tutankhamun.

charm may have been part of a necklace

Winged scarab
644–322 BCE
Scarabs were common lucky charms. The scarab beetle was a symbol for rebirth and was worn as jewelry in ancient Egypt.

In the mid-10th century BCE, during the reign of King Solomon, Megiddo (in modern Israel) was an important Israelite fortress and administrative center.

The jaguar featured in many Mesoamerican and South American religions. Here it is depicted in a stone carving from Chavín de Huántar.

IN THE 10TH CENTURY BCE, THE PERIOD OF DECLINE in the major powers of Western Asia continued. Egypt and Assyria had loosened their grip on the Levant, enabling the rise of the short-lived but historically significant **Kingdom of Israel**. The Israelites were Semitic-speaking pastoralists who, according to the Bible, migrated into the land of Canaan in the 1200s BCE. There, they came into conflict with the local Philistines and Canaanites. Around 1000 BCE **King David** (r. 1006–965 BCE) **united the Israelite tribes** and established his capital at **Jerusalem**. David's son **Solomon** (r. c. 965–928 BCE) increased Israelite territory and built a magnificent palace and temple in the capital, but on his death the kingdom split in two. Eventually

Etched in gold
This golden plaque showing the protective wedjat eye symbol dates from the reign of Psusennes I of the 21st dynasty, when Egypt was divided.

SHALMANESER III (858–824 BCE)

In the 9th century BCE, King Shalmaneser III of Assyria consolidated and protected his empire, with campaigns against Mesopotamian tribes, Israel and Judah, Syria, Urartu, and Anatolia. This black limestone obelisk commemorates his deeds and those of his commander-in-chief, Dayyan-Assur. It details, in cuneiform, the enforced tributes paid by the people he conquered.

Israel and, later, Judah became part of the Assyrian Empire.
Meanwhile, **Assyria** began to reemerge as a **major power in Mesopotamia**. King Ashur-dan II (r. 934–912 BCE) boosted agriculture, bringing prosperity. His successor Adad-nirari II increased Assyria's territory, regaining lands that had been held by the Middle Assyrian Empire in the 13th century BCE.

THE OLMEC CULTURE CONTINUED TO DEVELOP IN MESOAMERICA in the 9th century BCE. After San Lorenzo was destroyed in c. 900 BCE, **La Venta** to the northeast became the **main Olmec center**. This larger settlement was dominated by a 111ft (34m) high pyramid, the forerunner of Mayan temples. The Olmecs also devised a script of **glyphs**—the first in the region. Their influence spread across Mesoamerica, impacting on other cultures that were starting to emerge at this time—the **Zapotecs** and the **Maya**.
In eastern North America, the **Adena culture** was developing in the Ohio Valley. It was characterized by ritual earthworks and burial mounds containing objects of fine craftsmanship.
Far to the south, the **Chavín culture** had appeared in the Peruvian Andes by c. 1200 BCE and spread to the coast. The Chavín

were **skilled engineers** and **architects** who built canals and leveled slopes for farming and construction. The main settlement, **Chavín de Huántar**, was high in the Andes, and seems to have been a pilgrimage center for a cult of supernatural beings that were part-human, part-animal. The main god, the "Staff God," is usually depicted with fangs.
In **Europe**, iron was gradually **replacing bronze** as the metal of choice for tools and weapons. The area around **Hallstatt** in Austria became a center for an early Iron Age culture that developed from the Urnfield culture (see 1200 BCE). Hallstatt chieftains dominated local salt mining and ironworking. They lived in hilltop forts and were buried with rich grave goods.
During the 9th century BCE, the **Phoenicians** were becoming a major power in the Mediterranean. They had developed the navigational skills to make direct long-distance

Grave goods
This Iron Age brooch was discovered in a grave at Hallstatt in Austria. The type of jewelry found suggests that a woman was buried there.

sea crossings, enabling them to ply the entire Mediterranean Sea. Colonies were set up in Cadiz in Spain, Sicily, Sardinia, and on the North African coast at Carthage (in modern Tunisia). Through this trading network, the Phoenician **alphabet** became known throughout the Mediterranean.
In Western Asia, the **Neo-Assyrian Empire** began to expand, and, one by one, Israel, Judah, and the small states of nearby Syria and Phoenicia were brought under Assyrian control.

KEY
- Assyria
- Egypt
- Phoenician colonies
- Phoenician city-states
- Greek colonies
- Greek city-states
- Emerging Etruscan city-states

EUROPE

Black Sea

Caere
Pithekoussai
Athens
Corinth
Gadir
Syracuse
Sparta
Carthage
Mediterranean Sea
Miletus
Khorsabad
Nimrud
Al Mina
Byblos
Babylon
Jerusalem
Tanis
Bast

AFRICA

Mediterranean region
This map of the Mediterranean region in the 8th century BCE shows the colonies established by the dominant civilizations of the period, including the Phoenicians and Greeks.

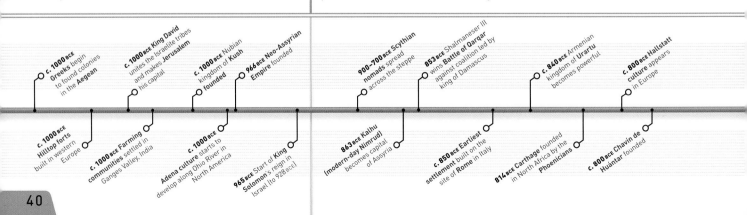

c. **1000** BCE **Greeks** begin to found colonies in the **Aegean**

c. **1000** BCE **King David** unites the Israelite tribes and makes **Jerusalem** his capital

c. **1000** BCE Nubian kingdom of **Kush** founded

966 BCE Neo-Assyrian Empire founded

900–700 BCE **Scythian** nomads spread across the steppe

853 BCE Shalmaneser III wins **Battle of Qarqar** against coalition led by king of Damascus

c. **840** BCE Armenian kingdom of **Urartu** becomes powerful

c. **800** BCE **Hallstatt culture** appears in Europe

c. **1000** BCE **Hilltop forts** built in western Europe

c. **1000** BCE **Farming communities** settled in Ganges Valley, India

c. **1000** BCE **Adena culture** starts to develop along Ohio River in North America

965 BCE Start of **King Solomon's** reign in Israel (to 928 BCE)

863 BCE **Kalhu (modern-day Nimrud)** becomes capital of Assyria

c. **850** BCE Earliest settlement built on the site of **Rome** in Italy

814 BCE **Carthage** founded in North Africa by the **Phoenicians**

c. **800** BCE **Chavín de Huántar** founded

In 705 BCE, the Assyrian capital moved to Nineveh. This stone relief shows the Assyrian king and his queen feasting in the gardens of the royal palace there.

ASSYRIA CONTINUED ITS POLICY OF AGGRESSION through the 8th century BCE, conquering rival states in Western Asia and reducing them to provinces. Assyrian success was based on a **disciplined**, technically advanced **army** and an **efficient bureaucracy**. Conquered peoples had to pay costly tributes, and revolts were ruthlessly crushed. Especially troublesome nations suffered forced deportations—large numbers of people were resettled in other regions of the empire.

Following a period of weak rule in the first half of the 8th century BCE, Tiglath-Pileser III (r. 744–727 BCE) recouped Assyria's losses. **Sargon II** (r. 722–704 BCE) campaigned in

Ritual container
Zhou smiths were highly skilled metalworkers. This bronze vessel dates from the 8th century BCE, the time of the Eastern Zhou dynasty.

Iran and Anatolia, conquering Babylon and, in 14 BCE, defeating the Armenian state of Urartu. He also defeated the Israelites and transported the "ten lost tribes" of Israel to northern Mesopotamia.

In **China**, the Zhou capital moved east to Luoyang in 770 BCE, marking the start of the earlier part of the **Eastern Zhou era**, which lasted until about 480 BCE (see 500 BCE). Royal control had weakened, as the lords who held large fiefdoms had grown more powerful. Now central control disintegrated, and **rival warlords** fought one another. Despite the chaos, this era was a time of technical and cultural advancement. Iron tools increased efficiency in agriculture and food production. Populations and cities grew, and **philosophy**, **the arts**, and **literature** began to **develop**.

In Egypt, the unrest of the Third Intermediate Period continued. Since 850 BCE, the country had

been embroiled in a destructive civil war and was now divided into small states. In the 8th century BCE, the Kushite ruler of Nubia to the south, **Piye** (r. 747–716 BCE), **conquered** both Upper and Lower **Egypt**, and united them under **Kushite rule**.

In the Mediterranean, Phoenician influence continued to spread, as the city of **Carthage** in North Africa **grew powerful**. Greece, by then, was starting to emerge from the Dark Age that had followed the Mycenaeans' downfall. City-states or *poleis* were forming on the Greek mainland, centered on hilltop citadels. To increase their territory, the *poleis* founded colonies around the shores of the Aegean. Although rivalry between cities was often intense, a **distinct Greek identity and culture** was emerging. All Greeks were identified as "Hellenes." In 776 BCE the first pan-Hellenic games were held in honor of Zeus at **Olympia**. By the mid-700s BCE the Greeks had adapted the Phoenician alphabet for their own language,

Twin discovery
This painting by Charles de La Fosse depicts the legend of Romulus and Remus, who were abandoned as babies and suckled by a she-wolf, before being rescued by shepherds.

Kushite statue
This alabaster statue dates from the period of Kushite rule in Egypt. Amenirdis I, sister of Shabaka (r. c. 716–702 BCE), is shown holding a flail—a traditional symbol of Egyptian rule.

and not long after, Homer's epic poems the *Iliad* and the *Odyssey*—hitherto transmitted orally—were probably written down.

In the 8th century BCE, **central Italy** was a mosaic of small states ruled by the dominant **Etruscans**—Italy's first indigenous civilization—and Italic tribes such as the Latins, Umbrians, and Sabines. **Rome** is thought to have been founded by the Latin chief **Romulus** in 753 BCE. In its early days, the city, built on seven hills, was ruled by various peoples, including Etruscans, Latins, and Sabines.

> **SUCH A GREAT TASK IT WAS TO FOUND THE ROMAN RACE.**
>
> **Virgil**, from *Aeneid* 1:33

Timeline:

776 BCE First pan-Hellenic games held at Olympia in Greece, and every four years thereafter

c. 775 BCE Start of Greek colonization of Mediterranean

771 BCE Zhou capital moves east to Luoyang, marking beginning of Eastern Zhou period

753 BCE Traditional date for founding of Rome by Romulus

c. 750 BCE Kushite rulers of Nubia send armies into Egypt, conquering it by 747 BCE

c. 750 BCE Homer's *Iliad* and *Odyssey* written down

c. 750 BCE Major construction completed at Chavín de Huántar, the main cultural center in Peru

c. 744 BCE Tiglath-Pileser III of Assyria's reign begins (to 727 BCE)

c. 722 BCE Sargon II takes Assyrian throne (to 705 BCE)

714 BCE Sargon II defeats Urartu and sacks its major sacred site of Musasir

722–700 BCE Marduk-apla-iddina of Babylonia expels the Assyrians and opposes their attempts to reconquer Babylonia

705 BCE Assyrian capital moves to Nineveh

701 BCE Assyrians mount punitive expedition against revolt in Judah

THE
CLASSICAL AGE
700 BCE–599 CE

Culturally dynamic civilizations emerged in Greece, Rome, Persia, India, and China, marking the beginning of the Classical Age. The impact of Classical developments in science, art, and politics is still felt to this day.

"HE EVERYWHERE SOUGHT EXCUSES FOR STIRRING UP WAR."

Livy, from *Histories* book I, xxi, on Tullus Hostilius, third King of Rome

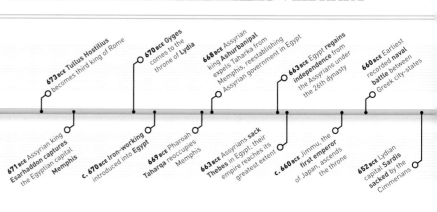

Pyramids from the cemetery at Nuri, Sudan, which was the burial site of the Napatan and Meroitic kings from around 650 BCE.

IN CHINA, THE CITY OF LUOYANG HAD FALLEN TO THE SHEN in 771 BCE, and the Western Zhou capital was transferred east to Chengzhou. From there, the Eastern Zhou dynasty presided over the **fragmentation of China** into as many as 148 states. From around 700 BCE the Zhou were ruled by puppet-emperors, while real power lay with the **ba** ("senior one") among nearby states. Under **Qi Huan Gong** (r. 685–643 BCE), the state of Qi had supremacy. After Huan Gong's death the **competition for power** between his five sons weakened Qi, and **Jin Wen Gong** (r. 636–628 BCE), the ruler of Jin, rose to become ba. By the end of the century, power in China alternated among the **states of Qi, Jin, Qin, and Chu**.

Nubian Pharoah
Taharqa ruled Egypt for 19 years before an Assyrian invasion forced him to return to Nubia in 671 BCE.

7 THE NUMBER OF KINGS OF ROME

In Italy, the **city-state of Rome** was beginning to acquire an urban heart, and the **first forum** was constructed. The second king of Rome, **Numa Pompilius** (r. 715–674 BCE) is believed to have established the main Roman priesthoods and a calendar.

In the Near East, the **Assyrians continued their expansion**, confronting Egypt, whose intermittent support for rebels against Assyrian rule in Syria had long been a source of tension. In 671 BCE, the Assyrian ruler Esarhaddon invaded, **capturing the Egyptian royal capital** of Memphis. However, Assyrian control over Egypt was weak, and the Nubian pharaoh **Taharqa** drove the invaders out.

The **Etruscans** expanded southward from modern Tuscany and Umbria around 700 BCE. Their language remains undeciphered, but lavish tombs indicate a **rich material culture**. During their expansion, the Etruscans founded cities such as Capua, but came into **conflict** with Greek colonies and with Rome. Although more powerful at first, the Etruscans were **politically disunited**, and a **long series of wars** with the Romans turned against them.

IT TOOK A CONCERTED CAMPAIGN BY ASHURBANIPAL (r. 668–627 BCE) in 664–663 BCE to defeat the Egyptians who had rebelled against Assyrian rule, and to push Assyrian control as far south as Thebes (modern Luxor). This was not the last rebellion against the Assyrians—only ten years later, the vassal king of Saïs, **Psammetichus I** (r. 664–610 BCE), revolted against his Assyrian masters, driving them out and founding the 26th Dynasty, under which **Egypt's independence was restored**. After the final collapse of Assyrian power, in 609 BCE, Egypt was able to establish a foothold in Palestine under **Pharaoh Necho II** (610–595 BCE).

In Greece, the **rise** to preeminence of a number of **city states**, notably **Athens**, **Sparta**, and **Corinth**, began. In Corinth, a new type of ruler, the "tyrant," emerged with the overthrow of the Bacchiadae kings in 658 BCE.

ASHURBANIPAL (r. 668–627 BCE)

Ashurbanipal initially shared rule over Assyria with his brother, Shamash-shuma-ukin. After defeating his brother's revolt in 648 BCE he greatly expanded the Assyrian domains. As well as annexing Egypt, he attacked Elam, sacking its capital, Susa, in 647 BCE. His latter years saw none of the military successes of his early reign. At his death a dispute between his two sons further weakened the Assyrian Empire.

"TAHARQA THE GODLESS CAME OUT TO TAKE EGYPT."

Ashurbanipal's account of the conquest of Egypt, 664 BCE

The new ruler, **Cypselus** (reign c. 657–627 BCE) relied on force of personality rather than divine sanction, and established a dynasty under which Corinth enjoyed a **seven-decade period of dominance**, creating colonies throughout the western Mediterranean.

On the fringes of the Greek world, in western Asia Minor, the **kingdom of Lydia** was increasing in power under **Gyges** (685–647 BCE), its first great king. He allied with Ashurbanipal of Assyria to see off a joint threat to their two lands by Cimmerian raiders in 668–665 BCE, but then

assisted Psammetichus I of Egypt in his revolt against the Assyrians. He also adopted an aggressive stance towards his neighbors, the Ionian Greeks of Miletus and Smyrna.

According to Japanese tradition, the first emperor, **Jimmu Tenno**, a descendant of the sun goddess **Amaterasu**, ascended to the throne in 660 BCE. The stories of his migration from southern Honshu eastward to establish his kingdom near Nara are legendary, but may echo real events of the Japanese **Yayoi** period after 100 BCE, when tribal chieftains began to **consolidate their territories**.

The third king of Rome, **Tullus Hostilius** (r. 673–642 BCE) was more martially inclined than his precedessor Numa Pompilius, and

30,000 THE NUMBER OF CLAY TABLETS UNCOVERED IN ASHURBANIPAL'S LIBRARY

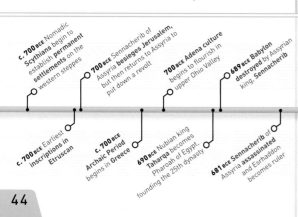

c. 700 BCE Nomadic Scythians begin to establish **permanent settlements** on the western steppes

c. 700 BCE Sennacherib of Assyria **besieges Jerusalem**, but then returns to Assyria to put down a revolt

700 BCE Adena culture begins to flourish in upper Ohio Valley

689 BCE Babylon destroyed by Assyrian king, Sennacherib

c. 700 BCE Earliest inscriptions in Etruscan

c. 700 BCE Archaic Period begins in Greece

690 BCE Nubian king **Taharqa** becomes Pharoah of Egypt, founding the 25th dynasty

681 BCE Sennacherib of Assyria **assassinated** and Esarhaddon becomes ruler

673 BCE Tullus Hostilius becomes third king of Rome

670 BCE Gyges comes to the throne of **Lydia**

668 BCE Assyrian king **Ashurbanipal** expels Taharka from Memphis, reestablishing Assyrian government in Egypt

663 BCE Egypt **regains independence** from the Assyrians under the 26th dynasty

660 BCE Earliest recorded **naval battle** between Greek city-states

671 BCE Assyrian king **Esarhaddon captures** the Egyptian capital **Memphis**

c. 670 BCE Iron-working introduced into Egypt

669 BCE Pharoah **Taharqa reoccupies** Memphis

663 BCE Assyrians **sack Thebes** in Egypt; their empire reaches its greatest extent

c. 660 BCE Jimmu, the **first emperor** of Japan, ascends the throne

652 BCE Lydian capital **Sardis sacked** by the Cimmerians

A lion frieze from the Processional Way in Babylon, which was built around 600 BCE and ran through the heart of the city to the Ishtar Gate.

The Assyrian Empire
From its core around Assur and Nineveh, the Assyrian empire grew to encompass Babylonia, Media, Elam, Urartu, Syria, and Egypt.

led the war against neighboring Alba Longa, which ultimately led to that city's destruction and the deportation of its population to Rome, in the **first major Roman expansion**. The fourth king, **Ancus Marcius** (r. 642–617 BCE), expanded Roman territory toward the coast, and founded Rome's great port of Ostia at the mouth of the Tiber. His successor, **Tarquinius Priscus** (616–578 BCE) was the fifth king of Rome and one of the city's greatest kings. He came from an Etruscan background, a sign of the high level of Etruscan influence over the early city of Rome. Tarquinius Priscus won a series of victories over the Sabines, the Latins, and the Etruscans, who all competed with Rome for dominance over central Italy. He is also said to have established the public games in Rome.

THE ASSYRIANS HAD FINALLY CONQUERED BABYLON in 691 BCE, partially destroying the city. Reconstruction work began under Esarhaddon (680–669 BCE), and by 652 BCE Babylon had recovered its importance and became the center for a **major revolt** led by Shamash-shuma-ukin against his younger brother Ashurbanipal. It took **four years of war** to suppress the Babylonians and their Elamite allies, and the fighting drained Assyria's ability to hold on to its empire. By 630 BCE, Assyria had lost Egypt and Palestine, and in 626 BCE the **Babylonians regained their independence**. By 616 BCE Babylon was strong enough to invade Assyria, aided by the Medes (whose base was in northwestern Iran). In 612 BCE the Babylonians, Medes, and Scythians sacked the Assyrian capital of Nineveh. The **Assyrian empire crumbled**. A remnant of the Assyrian army regrouped and established a small kingdom around Harran, but by 609 BCE this, too, had fallen.

The **Scythians** formed part of a culture of **nomadic horsemen** which held a large territory on the steppes north of the Caucasus from around 800 BCE. In 652 BCE they forced the Medes to submit to them and the Scythian King Bartatua was even sufficiently influential to be given an Assyrian princess as his wife. The **alliance with Assyria** survived into the reign of his son Madyes, but around 615 BCE the Scythians switched sides and played a **key role in Assyria's destruction**. Their Median subjects soon turned on them and around 590 BCE the Scythians retreated north.

In the Greek world, there was a growing movement to **establish colonies** in the Mediterranean. Among the earliest were in Italy, including **Syracuse**, founded around 733 BCE. In North Africa, Greek settlers founded **Cyrene** (in Libya) in about 630 BCE, and **Massilia** (Marseilles) around 600 BCE. New cities were established as far west as Spain, and around the Black Sea coast.

In Greece itself, the **city-state of Sparta** was establishing its dominance in the Peloponnese. A defeat by the city-state of Argos, in 669 BCE, was followed by military reforms and victory against the Messenians (660–650 BCE). By 600 BCE, **Sparta had conquered** almost all the southern Peloponnese and established a stratified social system.

Sparta's future rival, **Athens**, gradually united the area surrounding Attica under its rule in the 8th century BCE. The hereditary monarchy was replaced by nine "archons," chosen annually. Shortly after a damaging popular uprising by Cylon in 632 BCE, Athens received its first law code, drafted by Draco in 621 BCE. The **Draconian law** was later known for the severity of the punishments it prescribed.

To the south of Egypt the **state of Napata** became a power of the first order, conquering Egypt under Piankhy (r. 747–716 BCE) and controlling it under after the death of Taharqa (690–664 BCE).

stylized body

Scythian stag
The flowing lines and realistic depiction of the stag's muscled flanks in this late 7th century shield ornament are typical of the art of the Scythians.

652 BCE Babylonian rebellion threatens Assyrian rule, but is put down (ends 649 BCE)

c. 650 BCE Age of "tyrants" begins in many Greek states

c. 650 BCE Iron technology reaches Zhou China

650 BCE First coins minted in Lydia

648 BCE Babylon surrenders to Ashurbanipal

647 BCE Ashurbanipal sacks Susa

630 BCE Sparta wages war against the Messenians

630 BCE Greek colony of Cyrene founded (in modern Libya)

631 BCE Ashurbanipal dies

626 BCE Nabopolassar becomes ruler of Babylon, founding Neo-Babylonian Dynasty

625 BCE Periander takes power as tyrant in Corinth

621 BCE First Athenian law code, Code of Draco

620 BCE Foundation of Greek colony of Tartessus in Spain

616 BCE Tarquin, an Etruscan, becomes king of Rome

615 BCE The Medes, an emerging power, defeat the Scythians

612 BCE Assyrian empire collapses in face of attacks from Medes and Babylonians

609 BCE Residual Assyrian state, Harran, captured by Babylonians and Medes; Assyrian state disappears forever

608 BCE Necho II of Egypt invades Judah

605 BCE Nebuchadnezzar II succeeds to the throne of Babylon

604 BCE Traditional date for the birth of Laozi, the founder of Taoism

A medieval view of the city of Jerusalem, which was captured by the Babylonians in 597 BCE. It was taken again, and largely destroyed, 10 years later. After both sieges many of its inhabitants were deported to Babylon.

Central Asia became a stronghold of Buddhist beliefs. These cave paintings in Dunhuang, China, illustrate a variety of Buddhist parables.

HAVING HELPED DESTROY THE ASSYRIAN EMPIRE, Nabopolassar (r. 626–605 BCE), first king of the **neo-Babylonian dynasty**, embellished the city of Babylon. His son Nebuchadnezzar (r. 605–562 BCE) defeated the Egyptians in 605 BCE, repaired Babylon's main ziggurat, and ordered the building of the famous "Hanging Gardens." The last neo-Babylonian king, **Nabonidus** (r. 556–539 BCE), moved his royal court to the Arabian oasis of Tema, but **discontent rose** among the Babylonians during his reign.

The **Medes** of northwest Persia (Iran), consolidated their kingdom under **Cyaxares** (r. 624–585 BCE) and took part in the destruction of the Assyrian Empire in 612 BCE.

Under the last Median king, Astyages (r. 584–550 BCE), Median armies campaigned in Azerbaijan and controlled land as far west as Lydia (Turkey). But by the 550s BCE, Media was under pressure from the Babylonians to the south and the new power of Persia.

The kingdom of Judah had long acted as a block to Assyrian and Babylonian expansion to the west. In **597 BCE**, Nebuchadnezzar **took Jerusalem** and deposed King Jehoiakim. The king they installed in his place, Zedekiah, turned against the Babylonians, and in **587 BCE** there was **another siege**. Much of the city was burned, the Jewish Temple destroyed, and many of its inhabitants deported to a **life of exile** in Babylon.

The powerful city-state of **Athens** experienced reforms under **Solon** about 594 BCE, notably a **law code** that protected the property rights of the poor, forbade debt-slavery, and moderated the more extreme parts of the **Draconian laws** (see 650–601). Around 560 BCE, Pisistratus seized power and began to rule as a **tyrant** (dictator). Driven out once, he returned in 547 BCE and established a stable regime.

The **Greek city** of Miletus saw the beginnings of **philosophical thought** from about 600 BCE. Thales (born c. 624 BCE) tried to understand the basic nature of the universe and thought its fundamental element was water.

Lawgiver and reformer
This image shows the Greek statesman and lawgiver Solon teaching. His reforms began to undermine the power of the aristocracy in Athens.

CYRUS, RULER OF THE SMALL KINGDOM OF PERSIS (also called Pars) in the west of Persia (Iran), **revolted** against his Median overlords in 559 BCE. By 550 BCE he had conquered the Median capital of Ecbatana and overthrown their ruler, King Astyages. Afraid of the **increasing power of Persia**, the Lydians under **King Croesus** opposed Cyrus, but he struck west and in 547 BCE, on the Halys River, defeated the Lydian army and annexed western Asia Minor.

In 539 BCE **Cyrus captured Babylon**, acquiring most of Mesopotamia and making the **Persian Empire** the greatest in the Middle East. **Cyrus died in** 530 BCE while fighting in what is today Turkmenistan, and was succeeded by his son **Cambyses**.

In 526 BCE Cambyses sent his **armies south into Egypt**. The Pharaoh Amasis had just died and his successor Psammetichus III

Darius the Great
King Darius is shown enthroned and bearing symbols of power in this frieze. His son Xerxes succeeded him.

Cambyses died in 522 BCE and after the brief rebellion of Bardiya, who was either the younger brother of Cambyses or someone impersonating him, **Darius**, a Persian noble, took over as king. Widespread revolts broke out, including in Media, but Darius put

> **“ I HAVE FOUGHT 19 BATTLES IN ONE YEAR… I HAVE WON THEM. ”**

The Behistun inscription of **Darius**

was not well established. Cambyses defeated the Egyptian army at Pelusium in 525 BCE and then **captured the royal capital at Memphis**. He installed himself as the pharaoh and then subdued southern Egypt. Persian rule in Egypt lasted until 401 BCE.

them all down. He then **expanded the Persian Empire** by annexing lands in central Asia and on the borders of India from 519 to 515 BCE. In **India**, the political power had coalesced around the **Mahajapanadas**, a group of around 16 powerful

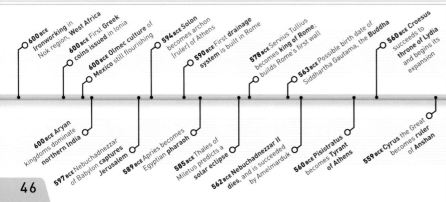

600 BCE Ironworking in Nok region, **West Africa**

600 BCE First Greek **coins** issued in Ionia

600 BCE Olmec culture of **Mexico** still flourishing

594 BCE Solon becomes archon (ruler) of Athens

590 BCE First drainage system is built in Rome

578 BCE Servius Tullius becomes **king of Rome**; builds Rome's first wall

563 BCE Possible birth date of Siddhartha Gautama, the **Buddha**

560 BCE Croesus succeeds to **throne of Lydia** and begins its expansion

600 BCE Aryan kingdoms dominate **northern India**

597 BCE Nebuchadnezzar of Babylon captures **Jerusalem**

589 BCE Apries becomes **Egyptian pharaoh**

585 BCE Thales of Miletus predicts a **solar eclipse**

562 BCE Nebuchadnezzar II **dies**, and is succeeded by Amelmarduk

560 BCE Pisistratus becomes **Tyrant of Athens**

559 BCE Cyrus the Great becomes **ruler of Anshan**

550 BCE Birth of **Confucius**, author of the *Analects*, which provide the **central philosophy** of **Chinese** way of life

550 BCE Servius Tullius establishes **Latin League** with Rome's neighbors, beginning slow rise to political ascendancy of city

547 BCE Pisistratus **returns to Athens** and rules again as tyrant

550 BCE Rich states arise around **Red Sea** and **Gulf of Aden**

550 BCE Cyrus wins **Median throne**

547 BCE Cyrus invades Sardis, **Lydia**, capturing Sardis the next year and deposing Croesus

545 BCE The Ionian **Greek cities of Asia Minor** are forced to accept Persian **overlordship**

482

THE NUMBER OF **YEARS** OF THE **ROMAN REPUBLIC**

kingdoms. Of these, Magadha was the most important state. Afterward, Darius subdued most of the Greek city-states of Ionia, before he **crossed into Europe** in 513 BCE to conquer Thrace.

In Italy, Servius Tullius (r. 578–535 BCE), the **sixth king of Rome** and said to be a former slave, had succeeded Tarquinius Priscus in 578 BCE. During his reign he implemented **important reforms**, fixing the formal boundaries of the city by dividing the Romans into four "tribes," a system that would be extended as Roman territory grew, and also into classes that were **graded by wealth**. The population was divided by what equipment they could afford and what role they played in the Roman army. The wealthiest class fought as cavalry, the higher classes as heavy infantry, and the poor as light auxiliary troops. The votes of the richer classes carried much greater weight in the popular assembly. **The last king of Rome**, Tarquinius Superbus (r. 534–509 BCE) was an Etruscan. Concerned at the **growing tyranny** of his rule, a group of

Roman aristocrats led by Lucius Junius Brutus and Lucius Tarquinius Collatinus (the king's cousin) won over the army and barred the gates of the city to the king, who was deposed. The coup leaders then **established a republic** in which supreme authority was held by two magistrates called **consuls**. The power of the consuls was limited by the fact that **new**

CYRUS THE GREAT
(r. 559–530 BCE)

Little is known about the early life of Cyrus. He was the ruler of the kingdom of Pars when he led a revolt against his Median overlord Astyages. By defeating Astyages, Cyrus became king of the Medes. He then continued to expand Persian influence with the conquest of Lydia. Cyrus adapted local ideas about kingship to cast himself as an ideal ruler in the cities he conquered. Cyrus died in 530 BCE.

consuls were elected by the popular assembly each year.

Some time around 530 BCE, **Siddhartha Gautama**, a Hindu prince of Kapilvastu (now in Nepal), had a religious revelation and rejected his noble upbringing to embark on a quest for "enlightenment." Six years later he received it and began to preach a way of moderate asceticism to gain release from the suffering of material life. He is known as the Buddha (which means the "awakened one" in Sanskrit), and his followers, who became known as **Buddhists**, spread his ideas throughout South Asia and, in the late 3rd century CE, into China and thence to Korea, Japan, and Southeast Asia.

Confucius (or Kong Fuzi) was born around 551 BCE, in a period of political instability during China's **Spring and Autumn period**. From the age of 15 he devoted himself to scholarship, and the **political philosophy** he developed reflects the turbulent times. He taught that the righteous man (or junzi) must have regard to others and **inflict no unnecessary harm**. His philosophy, as developed by his disciples, taught respect for elders and became a cornerstone of the later imperial system.

Persian elite
These archers from the palace of Darius at Susa were the elite of the Persian army, which included representatives from provinces as far off as Ethiopia and Afghanistan.

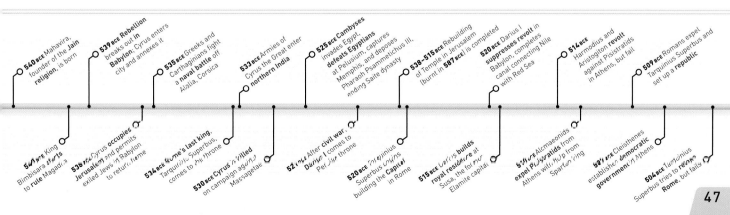

- **540 BCE** Mahavira, founder of the **Jain religion**, is born
- **540 BCE** King Bimbisara starts to **rule** Magadha
- **539 BCE Rebellion** breaks out **in Babylon**; Cyrus enters city and annexes it
- **538 BCE** Cyrus **occupies Jerusalem** and permits exiled Jews in Babylon to return home
- **535 BCE** Greeks and Carthaginians fight a **naval battle** off Alalia, Corsica
- **534 BCE Rome's last king**, Tarquinius Superbus, comes to the throne
- **533 BCE** Armies of Cyrus the Great enter **northern India**
- **530 BCE** Cyrus is killed on campaign against Massagetae
- **525 BCE Cambyses** invades Egypt, **defeats Egyptians** at Pelusium, captures Memphis, and deposes Pharaoh Psammetichus III, ending Saite dynasty
- **522 BCE** After **civil war**, Darius I comes to Persian throne
- **520 BCE** Tarquinius Superbus begins building the **Capitol** in Rome
- **538–515 BCE** Rebuilding of Temple in Jerusalem (burnt in 587 BCE) is completed
- **515 BCE** Darius **builds royal residence** at Susa, the former Elamite capital
- **520 BCE** Darius I **suppresses revolt** in Babylon, completes canal connecting Nile with Red Sea
- **514 BCE** Harmodius and Aristogiton **revolt** against Pisistratids in Athens, but fail
- **510 BCE** Alcmaeonids **expel Pisistratids** from Athens with help from Sparta
- **507 BCE** Cleisthenes establishes **democratic government** in Athens
- **504 BCE** Tarquinius tries to **retake Rome**, but fails
- **509 BCE** Romans expel Tarquinius Superbus and set up a **republic**

snake-haired Medusa figure

Medusa antefix
DATE UNKNOWN
This terra-cotta antefix—an ornament placed at the cornice of buildings or at roof eaves—is in the form of Medusa, the mythical creature whose gaze turned people to stone.

swept-forward cheek piece

leaf-shaped blade

Corinthian helmet
600–500 BCE
The Corinthian helmet, made from a single bronze sheet, was the most common type in Greece, from around 750–300 BCE.

Spearhead
600–400 BCE
Greek hoplites (armed infantry soldiers) carried a large thrusting spear, of which this is the tip.

Aphrodite, the goddess of love

ANCIENT GREECE
FROM THE FUNCTIONAL TO THE DECORATIVE, THE GREEKS PRODUCED ART OF GREAT BEAUTY

While the Greeks created magnificent monumental art, smaller items such as jewelry, musical instruments, weaponry, and vases show the Greek love of intricate forms and decorative adornment throughout all periods of their history.

Greek art underwent a series of phases that were reflected in all aspects of artistic production, but particularly on vases. In the Geometric phase (c. 850–700 BCE), decoration was mainly composed of geometric forms, replaced in the Orientalizing phase (c. 700–600 BCE) with floral and animal themes, followed by the more naturalistic representations of the Classical phase (from 600 BCE).

fastening chain

Bronze mirror
490–460 BCE
This mirror is richly adorned with an image of Aphrodite flanked by cupids.

Gold earrings
420–400 BCE
These delicate gold filigree earrings depict boats containing sirens, mythical creatures whose beautiful voices lured unwary seafarers to their doom.

Bronze cymbals
500–400 BCE
Greek cymbals are bell- or cup-shaped, and are often depicted on vases being held by fauns or satyrs, or by women in Bacchanalian revels.

cup-shaped form

Mirror lid and fibula
420–400 BCE
This silver fibula (brooch) and chain may have fastened together a cloak. The ornate mirror-back shows Aphrodite with the half-goat god Pan.

Gold brooch
650–600 BCE
This hawk-shaped brooch dates from a period in which Oriental (and particularly Egyptian) influences were strong in Greece.

Aulos
400 BCE
This wind instrument was originally a double one (one wooden pipe has been lost), played through a reed.

silver mouthpiece

finger hole

Boeotian horse and rider figurine
550 BCE
The depiction of this horse and rider has an archaic feel about it, in contrast to the production of Boeotian terra-cotta workshops over 200 years later (see right).

Boeotian figurine
400–200 BCE
This terra-cotta figurine of a woman holding a jar comes from Boeotia, where a tradition of such sculptures began as early as the 8th century BCE.

Ostrakon
c. 475–470 BCE
In Athens, influential politicians could be ostracized (exiled) by public vote. The name of the politician each voter wished to be banished was inscribed on a piece of pottery.

retrograde (right-to-left) inscription

Discus
600–500 BCE
This fine bronze discus belonged to an athlete named Exoidas. After he won a victory in a sporting contest using it, he dedicated the discus to the gods Castor and Pollux.

Attic askos
425–400 BCE
The askos was a type of vessel for pouring liquids such as oil, shaped in the form of a traditional wine sack. The design is in the red-figure style that became popular around 530 BCE.

lotus and honeysuckle pattern

Attic skyphos
525–500 BCE
This drinking vessel shows a couple at their wedding standing in a chariot. The vase is painted in the black-figure style.

Apulian pyxis
500–400 BCE
A pyxis was often used for storing small items of jewelry and cosmetics. This south-Italian example is decorated with geometrical shapes.

hero Hercules carrying Erymanthean boar

lotus bud pattern

Athenian amphora
540–530 BCE
An amphora was a type of vessel used for storing wine. This one is decorated using the black-figure technique, which predates the red-figure method.

checkerboard pattern

cylindrical neck

double band of meanders

top of foot and lower base painted black

Attic lekythos
480–470 BCE
Greek vases were often painted with mythological scenes. This black-figure vase shows the goddess Athena beating a giant to his knees.

Epichysis
375–340 BCE
The long-spouted epichysis was a vessel used for pouring wine. This south-Italian vase has its base decorated with a pattern of white chevrons.

> ## " THIS IS **GOOD NEWS** ... IF THE PERSIANS **HIDE THE SUN,** WE SHALL DO BATTLE **IN THE SHADE.** "

Herodotus, ancient Greek historian, quoting words attributed to Dieneces, a Spartan, on being told that the Persian archers shot so many arrows they would conceal the Sun; from *Histories*

This 19th-century painting shows the Spartan king Leonidas I (center, facing) and his men at the Battle of Thermopylae in 480 BCE. Thermopylae became a byword for heroic defiance against overwhelming odds.

Plebeians withdraw from Rome
The departure of the plebeians (on the left in this engraving) threatened to split Rome irreparably, so the patricians (right) ceded some political power.

THE GREEK CITY-STATES OF IONIA
in western Anatolia had been subjects of the Persian Empire since Cyrus conquered Lydia, their previous overlord, in 547 BCE (see 550–501 BCE). In 499 BCE, **Aristagoras,** the ruler of Miletus, set out to mainland Greece to recruit allies for a **planned**

600
PERSIA

353
IONIA

The Battle of Lade
The Ionian Greek navy fought hard at Lade, but the prearranged defection of the Samians to the Persians led to its utter defeat.

uprising against the Persians. Sparta rejected his pleas, but only Athens and Eretria sent forces. A failed attack on Sardis led the Athenian forces to return home. The Ionians gradually lost ground to a **Persian land offensive** from 497 BCE. The death of Aristagoras that year undermined Ionian unity, and after a naval defeat at the **Battle of Lade** in 494 BCE the revolt fell apart. The next year witnessed the fall of Miletus to the Persians.
In Italy, the **young Roman Republic** was rocked by **social dissent** in 494 BCE when the plebeians (the lower social groups) withdrew from Rome en masse in protest at their treatment by the patricians (the higher social groups); they threatened to set up an alternative state. They were persuaded back only by official recognition of their own representatives (tribunes).

THE KINGDOM OF MAGADHA
emerged as an important state in northern India under the rule of **Bimbisara** (r. 543–491 BCE), friend and protector of Gautama **Buddha** (c. 563–c. 486 BCE), who founded Buddhism (see 550–501 BCE). Bimbisara's son Ajatashastru (r. 491–461 BCE) strengthened the royal capital at Rajagirha and **built a center at Pataligrama** on the Ganges River, which later became **Pataliputra, the Mauryan royal capital.** By conquering Kosala and Kashi, and annexing the Vrijji confederacy, Ajatashastru turned Magadha into the **dominant power** on the Ganges Plain.
In China, the political system of the Spring and Autumn period evolved into the **Warring States period** (481–221 BCE), in which seven main states engaged in a constant round of diplomatic

maneuvers to weaken each other, periodically interrupted by outbreaks of war.
In 490 BCE, **Darius I** (548–486 BCE) of Persia decided to take revenge on the mainland Greeks for their support of the Ionian revolt. Darius despatched a **huge naval expedition** under Artaphernes and Datis, which sailed from Cilicia, landing first at Naxos

before seizing Eretria, which had aided the Ionians in 499 BCE. Although the **Athenians** appealed to Sparta for aid, the only help they received came from Plataea, which sent 1,000 reinforcements. The Athenians opted to march out to meet the **Persians** rather than wait for a siege, on the advice of their general, Miltiades (550–489 BCE). In 490 BCE at

Persian winged-lion rhyton
The Persian Empire enjoyed vast wealth, as illustrated by everyday items such as this golden drinking vessel. They directed huge resources toward the conquest of Greece.

7
THE **NUMBER** OF **WARRING STATES**

animals were often the inspiration for a rhyton's shape

Marathon, the Greek hoplite (heavy infantry) formation advanced head-on against a far more numerous Persian force to win **an unlikely victory**.

Chastened, the Persian expeditionary force withdrew from Greece after Marathon, but in 481 BCE **Xerxes I** (519–465 BCE) dispatched another huge Persian army, which crossed over the Hellespont (near modern-day Istanbul) and proceeded south toward Athens. Many northern Greek states chose to submit, but Athens and Sparta patched together a league of southern states. In 480 BCE, a **heroic defense** of the pass at **Thermopylae** by the Spartan king Leonidas I, in which he and 300 Spartans died in a last stand, bought time for the Athenians to evacuate. The Persians burned the city, but soon after, under the command of **Themistocles** (see panel below), the Athenian fleet inflicted a serious defeat on Xerxes's naval force at **Salamis**. Further Greek

The Greco–Persian wars
Although the Persians possessed vastly superior numbers, the Greek forces were motivated to win crucial land and sea engagements.

KEY

- ⬛ Annexed by Persia
- → Persian campaigns against Greece 490–479 BCE
- ✕ Greek victory
- ✕ Persian victory
- ✕ Indecisive battles

victories followed in June 479 BCE, on land at Plataea in Boeotia and at sea at Mycale off the Ionian coast. The Greeks then took the offensive, and during 478–477 BCE won a string of victories in Ionia and Cyprus, which **reversed most of the Persians' gains.**

After the initial defeats of the Persians in 480–479 BCE, Athens sought to formalize the **league of anti-Persian allies**. A treasury was set up on the island of Delos in around 477 BCE. The league's funds were to be deposited here and regular meetings were to take place. But this **Delian League** soon became little more than an Athenian empire, and Sparta and its allies refused to take part.

> ❝ THE **GREAT STRUGGLE** HAS COME. ❞

Herodotus, ancient Greek historian, quoting Pausanias, the Spartan commander, before the Battle of Plataea in 479 BCE; from *Histories*

THEMISTOCLES (c. 524–460 BCE)

A clever politician and strategist, Themistocles persuaded the Athenians to use the wealth of a silver mine discovered at Laurium in 483/2 BCE to double their fleet. However, after the naval victory at Salamis, he became the object of increasing jealousy from political rivals. In about 470 BCE Themistocles was ostracized from Athens (exiled by public vote).

THE ATHENIANS ENJOYED EARLY SUCCESS under the direction of Cimon (510–450 BCE), wresting Eion on the Strymon River (in Anatolia) from the Persians in 476 BCE and then attacking Carystos on Euboea (which had submitted to the Persians) in 470 BCE. An attempt by the island of Naxos to leave the Delian League around the same time led to an Athenian expeditionary force that powerfully suppressed the breakaway movement. In 466 BCE, Athenian forces won a great **victory over the Persians** at the Eurymedon River on the south coast of Anatolia, establishing Athenian supremacy in the Aegean.

Pericles (c. 495–429 BCE), the Athenian statesman largely responsible for making Athens the political and cultural focus of Greece, tried but failed to prosecute Cimon in 463 BCE, on a charge of having neglected a chance to conquer Macedonia. From this maneuver, **Pericles' vision** and ideas of expansion for Athens were already evident. When the leading figure among the democrats, Ephialtes, was assassinated in 461 BCE, Pericles, his protégé, swiftly took his place.

Periodically, the Persians had tried to bribe the Spartans into diversionary attacks on Athens, initially to little effect. In 464 BCE, a **revolt of the Messenian Helots** (unfree men) in the western Peloponnese further distracted the Spartans from any attempt to stem the rising power of the Delian League. The Messenians received little outside assistance,

Athenian treasury at Delos
All members of the Delian League had to deposit funds at treasuries on Delos, but the contribution of Athens was the most important.

and by 462 BCE their last stronghold at Ithome had been reduced. Soon after, open conflict broke out between Sparta and Athens and their respective allies. The **First Peloponnesian War** was inconclusive. It ended in 451 BCE with a five-year truce, extended in 446 BCE to a **Thirty Years' Peace** between the two sides.

Meanwhile, the western part of the Greek world was becoming increasingly important, marked by the **rise of** the Sicilian city-state of **Syracuse**. Under a series of able rulers (tyrants) that began with **Gelon** (r. 485–478 BCE) and his brother **Hieron** (r. 478–467 BCE), Syracusan forces subdued the neighboring city of Acragas and expanded territory around Catana. Although Hieron's younger brother **Thrasybulus** was driven out in 466 BCE, the Syracusans retained their dominant position in Sicily beyond the 450s BCE.

In the late 5th century, the Mexican city of Monte Albán began to build its public buildings—the ancestors of its later magnificent pyramids, shown here.

IN THE ROMAN REPUBLIC, the two social classes—the patricians and the plebeians (see 500–491 BCE)—were still divided. The two sides came to an agreement in 451 BCE, appointing a group of ten men (**the decemviri**) to govern Rome outside the normal constitution. In 449 BCE, the decemviri produced the **Laws of the Twelve Tables**, which formed the basis for all Roman law codes.

Around 450 BCE in Central Europe, a **new Celtic culture emerged,** called La Tène, which supplanted the earlier dominant

villages. Monte Albán's center housed **large-scale public buildings**—including truncated pyramids, great plazas, and ballgame courts—as well as elaborate burial tombs. Within 150 years, the population of Monte Albán would swell to around 17,000, making it the **largest city in Mesoamerica.**

Zapotec figure from Monte Albán
This elaborate ceramic deity is typical of the production of Monte Albán, which became Mexico's premier site in the 5th century BCE.

12

THE NUMBER OF **TABLES** OF **ROMAN** LAW

Halstatt culture. Ruled over by a warrior aristocracy that buried its dead with swords, spears, and funerary chariots, **La Tène** had important centers in Bohemia (in what is now the Czech Republic) and around the Marne and Moselle rivers (in modern France).

In Oaxaca on Mexico's Pacific Coast, a new center arose shortly before 450 BCE at **Monte Albán**. This proto-city, on a hilltop above the Oaxaca Valley, drew people from the surrounding agricultural

ATHENS AND SPARTA HAD FOUGHT EACH OTHER BEFORE (see 451 BCE). The Athenian Empire had the **naval advantage** as it included most of the island and coastal states around the northern and eastern shores of the Aegean Sea. Meanwhile, the city-state of Sparta led an alliance of independent states from the Peloponnese and central Greece, as well as Corinth, and had the **strongest army**. Despite the Thirty Years' Peace of 446 BCE, tensions remained high between Athens and Sparta. The events that led to **renewed**

> ## " THE **EMPIRE** YOU POSSESS IS BY NOW **LIKE A TYRANNY**—PERHAPS WRONG TO ACQUIRE IT, BUT CERTAINLY **DANGEROUS** TO LET IT GO. "

Thucydides, ancient Greek historian, relating a speech by Pericles to the Athenians; from *History of the Peloponnesian War*, II.63

hostilities in 430 BCE began three years earlier, when Athens had intervened on behalf of Corcyra in a dispute with Corinth; the Spartans took it as a sign that Athens had breached the peace. An attack by Thebes, a Spartan ally, on Plataea, which supported Athens, was similarly taken by the Athenians to indicate Sparta was fixed on war. Athens, led by Pericles, achieved early success in the **Peloponnesian War** (431–404 BCE). In 426 BCE, **the Athenians invaded the Peloponnese**, and the following year landed a large

force at Pylos southwest of Sparta. Yet neither side could land a fatal blow and in 421 BCE they agreed the **Peace of Nicias**, which was supposed to last for 50 years.

The truce soon began to unravel. Corinth refused to recognize its authority, a pro-war leadership emerged in Sparta, and a complex set of political maneuvers by **Alcibiades** (450–404 BCE), the newly dominant politician in Athens, led to the **renewal of the war** in 419 BCE. The following year, Sparta's allies won a **key victory at Mantinea**. Athens struck back

SOCRATES (469–399 BCE)

One of the greatest Greek philosophers, Socrates served on the Athenian Council in 406 BCE, but his challenges to conventional morality at a time of political uncertainty gained him powerful enemies. He refused to mount a conventional defense against charges of corrupting the Athenian youth and was sentenced to die by drinking the poison hemlock.

c. 450 BCE La Tène culture emerges in Central Europe

c. 450 BCE Construction begins on Zapotec city of Monte Albán in Mexico

449 BCE Peace of Callias struck between Greeks and Persians

449 BCE Pericles begins building the Long Wall between Athens and its port, Piraeus

433 BCE Athens intervenes for Corcyra in its quarrel with Corinth, inviting Spartan retaliation

430 BCE Sparta invades Attica; Athens stricken with plague, killing many thousands

427 BCE City of Plataea, an Athenian ally, surrenders to Sparta

423 BCE One-year truce in the war between Athens and Sparta (extended in 422 BCE)

421 BCE Peace of Nicias between Athens and Sparta puts temporary halt to Peloponnesian War

c. 450 BCE Steppe nomad burials at Pazyryk and Noin-Ula in Siberia

449 BCE The Twelve Tables of the Law officially adopted in Rome

447 BCE Construction of a new Parthenon begins (finished 432 BCE)

431 BCE Quarrel between Plataea and Thebes leads to another Peloponnesian War between Athens and Sparta

c. 428 BCE Birth of Greek philosopher Plato (d. c. 347 BCE)

423 BCE Darius II becomes Persian king after assassination of Artaxerxes I

The Great Peloponnesian War

The period of 431–404 BCE saw the destruction of the Athenian Empire at the hands of a coalition of Sparta and its allies.

KEY

- ▓ Athenian Empire
- ▓ Athenian ally
- ▓ Sparta and allied states
- ░ neutral territory
- ✕ Athenian victory
- ✕ Spartan victory

2,800 ATHENIANS — Spartans **420**

BATTLE OF SPHACTERIA 425 BCE

7,000 ATHENIANS **18,500** BOEOTIANS

BATTLE OF DELIUM 424 BCE

30,000 ATHENIANS — Spartans **3,000**

SIEGE OF SYRACUSE 415–413 BCE

in 416 BCE by capturing Melos—the only main Aegean island not in its possession—but fatally overreached itself in 415 BCE with an expedition to Sicily, ending in the **total destruction** of the Athenian force by **the Syracusans** in 413 BCE. The Spartans, meanwhile, established a fort at Decelea in Attica that denied the Athenians access to the rich silver mines. An alliance with Persia further strengthened Sparta's position in 412 BCE, and a year later the democratic regime in Athens

was briefly overthrown. Democracy was restored the following year, and, although the Athenians won victories at Cyzicus in 410 BCE and Arginusae in 406 BCE, the **total destruction of their fleet at Aegospotami** off Ionia in 405 BCE left Athens defenseless. The Spartans blockaded the city, and, despite a determined resistance, the **Athenians were forced to surrender**. Athens was deprived of its fleet and in 404 BCE a pro-Spartan Council of Thirty was installed to govern it.

In Magadha in **India** the Haryanka dynasty founded by Bimbisara was replaced c. 413 BCE after the death of Ajatashatru (c. 459 BCE) and a series of ineffectual rulers. **Shishunaga founded a new dynasty**, which was responsible for overseeing the final transfer of the Magadha royal capital to **Pataliputra**. The Shishunaga dynasty lasted only 60 years.

AFTER ITS VICTORY IN THE PELOPONNESIAN WAR, Sparta found itself embroiled in a quarrel with Persia over whether the Ionian Greek cities should regain their autonomy. Through the 390s BCE, sporadic fighting and abortive peace talks diverted Sparta from a weakening position in mainland Greece. The "**King's Peace**," a definitive treaty with Persia in 386 BCE, deprived the Ionians of autonomy but allowed the Spartans to quash any threats to its supremacy. In 385 BCE, they attacked Mantinea in the central Peloponnese and in 383 BCE occupied Thebes. Spartan power seemed unassailable.

In Persia, the **death of Darius II** (r. 423–404 BCE) was followed by a **brief civil war**, when Cyrus the Younger tried to overthrow his older brother **Artaxerxes II** (r. 404–358 BCE). Cyrus was defeated and killed at the **Battle of Cunaxa** in 401 BCE, but in its aftermath some 10,000 Greek mercenaries were left trapped in northern Mesopotamia. Under **Xenophon**, the Greeks marched to the Black Sea coast and safety near Trapezus (Trabzon in modern-day Turkey), a feat their commander immortalized in his book *Anabasis*.

In Italy, the **Romans widened their territory** and annexed the city of Veii in 396 BCE, whose submission represented the **end of any Etruscan threat**. However, c. 390 BCE, an army of Celts, who had been attacking the Etruscan city of Clusium, turned south, defeated a Roman army at the Battle of the Allia, and then **took Rome** itself. This disaster haunted the Romans for centuries.

Etruscan tomb painting
The Etruscan language has never been deciphered, so it is through the frescoes in their tombs that much has been learned of their culture.

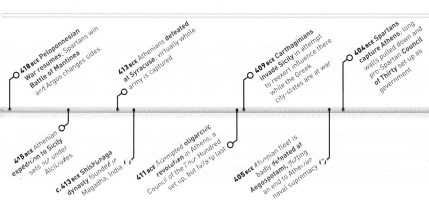

418 BCE Peloponnesian War resumes; Spartans win **Battle of Mantinea** and Argos changes sides

415 BCE Athenian expedition to Sicily sets out under Alcibiades

413 BCE Athenians **defeated at Syracuse**; virtually whole army is captured

c. 413 BCE Shishunaga dynasty founded in Magadha, India

411 BCE Attempted oligarchic revolution in Athens; a Council of the Four Hundred set up, but fails to last

409 BCE Carthaginians **invade Sicily** in attempt to reextert influence there while the Greek city-states are at war

405 BCE Athenian fleet is badly **defeated at Aegospotami**, putting an end to Athenian naval supremacy

404 BCE Spartans **capture Athens**; long walls pulled down and pro-Spartan **Council of Thirty** set up as government

403 BCE Council of Thirty in Athens dissolved; **democracy restored**

401 BCE Xenophon leads 10,000 Greek mercenaries supporting a Persian rebellion from Babylon to the Black Sea

399 BCE Greek philosopher **Socrates** executed

399 BCE Egypt breaks away from Persia and begins its 29th dynasty

398–397 BCE Dionysius of Syracuse wages war against Carthaginians

396 BCE Romans capture Etruscan **city of Veii**

386 BCE Sparta and Persia sign the "**King's Peace**"

384 BCE Plato completes his *Symposium* and founds his Academy

367 BCE War restarts between Carthage and Dionysius of Syracuse

Sutton Hoo buckle

animal interlace
picked out in circles

plain boss connected
with sliding catch
on backplate

circular plate at base
of buckle tongue

Sutton Hoo buckle
Made of solid gold and decorated with an interlaced animal pattern, the Anglo-Saxon Sutton Hoo belt buckle was found in a 7th-century ship burial in East Anglia, England.

bird's head
in profile

central interlace
pattern

animal interlace with
a biting head and tail

Prehistory
Use of copper ore
In western Iran and Anatolia, copper ore is ground or beaten into shape to make small objects such as beads.

Copper ore

c. 1500–1200 BCE
Refinement of bronze casting
New techniques are developed for casting and adorning bronze vessels, such as decorating them by beating on the inside.

Shang
cauldron

c. 900 BCE–100 CE
Using iron
Ironworking spreads from western Anatolia, reaching Greece around 900 BCE and West Africa about 400 BCE, enabling stronger tools and weapons to be made.

Weapon heads

c. 100–700
Anglo-Saxon metalworking
The Anglo-Saxons bring a new level of sophistication to metalworking, often using animal forms as decoration.

2600–2400 BCE
Use of beaten copper plate
Early copper smelting methods are refined, allowing the beating of copper while still hot into more complex shapes.

Sumerian copper bull

c. 1500–30 BCE
Purifying gold
The ancient Egyptians learn how to separate pure gold from silver in around 1500 BCE and begin to use it more extensively for decorative purposes.

Funeral mask of
Tutankhamun

c. 640–500 BCE
Metal as money
Metal coins (made of an alloy of gold and silver) are first used in Lydia (in present-day Turkey) around 640 BCE. The ancient Greeks adopt the idea and spread it around the Mediterranean.

Greek coin

THE STORY OF
METALWORKING

FROM EVERYDAY OBJECTS TO COMPLEX MACHINES, METALS ARE VITAL FOR OUR CIVILIZATION

Since their earliest known use in the 8th millennium BCE, metals have played a crucial role in the production of a vast range of objects, and even today, with the availability of sophisticated polymers and composites, they still permeate every aspect of modern civilization.

Around 7000 BCE, naturally occurring metals, notably copper, began to be used for small items such as pins in western Iran and eastern Anatolia. These were made by simply grinding or beating the metal into shape. Heating copper to make it more malleable was probably discovered by accidentally dropping the metal in fire, but it was the introduction of smelting in a crucible around 3800 BCE that led to the large-scale use of metals.

THE DEVELOPMENT OF ALLOYS

About 3000 BCE, the first alloy—bronze—was produced. Made by smelting tin and copper together in a crucible, bronze is stronger and more easily worked than either of its individual constituents, and it remained the principal metal for tools and weapons until the invention of ironworking around 1250 BCE. The technology to melt pure iron was not invented until the 19th century, so early iron objects were made by first smelting iron ore to an impure iron "bloom," then separating out the iron pieces and welding them

together in a furnace. This method of production continued until the introduction of blast furnaces in Europe in the 15th century. The Industrial Revolution in the 18th century brought new techniques and the use of coking coal in blast furnaces, but it was English inventor Henry Bessemer's invention of the Bessemer converter in 1856 that permitted the large-scale production of steel, a strong, high-quality, iron–carbon alloy. Later in the Industrial Revolution, further advances made it possible to produce other metals, such as aluminum, magnesium, and titanium, whose light weight and strength played a vital role in the development of the aviation and space industries.

HOW ALLOYS ARE MADE

An alloy is a mixture of metals or of a metal with a nonmetal (such as iron with carbon in steel). Many metals occur naturally in alloyed form, but synthetic alloys were not produced until around 3000 BCE, when copper was melted with tin to produce bronze. The technique spread, reaching Mesopotamia soon after 3000 BCE and Egypt by 2000 BCE or possibly earlier.

1,981°F

THE **MELTING POINT** OF **COPPER.** WHEN COPPER IS **ALLOYED** WITH **TIN**, THIS **DROPS** TO **1,742°F**

700–800
Sword-making
In Europe, sword-makers develop stronger swords by welding together successive layers of iron with carbon added, or by beating out thin iron strips then welding them together.

Viking sword

c. 15th century
Weapons from cast metal
Cast iron is developed. Because it is strong and can be used to make shapes such as tubes, it finds an immediate use in making artillery.

Medieval cannon

1950s
Titanium aircraft
Because of its high strength-to-weight ratio, titanium starts to be used extensively in military aircraft. It is now also widely used in commercial aircraft.

Lockheed Blackbird

800–1300/1450
Christian objects in precious metals
Medieval Christians make sacred objects, such as crucifixes and reliquaries, from gold and other precious metals, sometimes encrusted with gemstones.

The Verdun Altar

1810
Tin can
English inventor Peter Durand patents the tin can for preserving food. His patent was for a can made of iron and coated with tin to inhibit rusting of the iron.

1856
Bessemer converter
Englishman Henry Bessemer invents a converter that enables large-scale production of high-quality steel.

Bessemer converter

1910
Aluminum foil
The first aluminum foil is produced. It was made possible by the invention in 1886 of a method of mass-producing the metal by passing an electric current through molten ore.

A carving showing the pharaoh Nectanebo I, founder of the 30th Dynasty, making offerings to gods, including the crocodile-headed Sobek.

The ruins of Thebes, Greece's dominant city-state in the 360s BCE.

EGYPT HAD BROKEN AWAY FROM Persian control after the revolt of Amyrtaeus, who founded the 28th Dynasty in 404 BCE. However, the **Persians** had not given up on Egypt. **Nectanebo I** established the 30th Egyptian Dynasty in 380 BCE. He was able to repel a force sent by the Persians and their Greek allies in 373 BCE. Persia was diverted from further attempts to bring Egypt to heel by the **Great Rebellion of the Satraps** in the 360s BCE. This rebellion was partially aggravated by the campaigns of Tachos, son of Nectanebo I, in Persian-ruled Palestine from 361–360 BCE. **Nectanebo II** (r. 360–343 BCE) succeeded Nectanebo I, and continued to meddle in the Persian civil wars. In an ill-judged intervention in 346 BCE, he sent troops to aid an uprising in Sidon (Lebanon). In response, **Artaxerxes III of Persia** marched

150 COUPLES FORMED THE ELITE MILITARY UNIT THE **SACRED BAND OF THEBES**

into the Nile Delta region in 343 BCE, and Egypt was defeated within two years. Now under Persian rule, Egypt was never again ruled by a native dynasty.

In Greece, the **Spartan occupation of Thebes,** which had begun in 383 BCE, was short-lived. In 379 BCE, the Spartan **polemarch** (governor) of Thebes was assassinated, and the Thebans drove out the Spartan garrison with the aid of two Athenian generals who arrived on their own initiative to help. In retaliation, the **Spartans mounted an expedition** under King Cleombrotus (r. 380–371 BCE). This expedition failed to retake Thebes, but it so alarmed the Athenians that they executed one general and exiled the other, and temporarily abandoned the alliance with Thebes. The **Spartans invaded the region of Boeotia** in 378–377 BCE but made little headway, although the Athenians were

alarmed enough to revive the Theban alliance and try to establish a **Second Athenian Confederacy** in opposition to Sparta. In 375 BCE the Thebans, Athenians, and Spartans signed a "Common Peace," but it broke down almost immediately. The Thebans then took the offensive, aided by a new elite force of citizen soldiers, the **Sacred Band**, which consisted of 150 male couples. The Sacred Band supplemented the mercenaries who largely fought Greek city-states' wars by this period. Theban attempts to conquer the region of Phocis and retain dominance in Boeotia rankled with Sparta, and scuppered Athenian attempts to broker a peace in 372 BCE. At **Leuctra** in 371 BCE, the Theban army under the general **Epaminondas** fought a tactically brilliant battle to smash the Spartan phalanx. At Sparta's mercy just eight years before, **Thebes** was now the **dominant power in Greece**.

In Sicily, **Syracuse** continued to flourish under the strong rule of

Temple of Thoth
Situated at Hermopolis in Upper Egypt, the temple of Thoth dates from the New Kingdom but was renovated in the 4th century BCE.

Dionysius I (r. 405–367 BCE), who fought the third in a series of wars against the Carthaginians from 383 to 375 BCE. At first, the war went badly for Dionysius, whose fleet was wrecked in a storm. Carthaginian efforts to mount an expedition to Sicily were hampered by plague in 379 BCE and a revolt by subject cities in Libya, so that it was only in 377 BCE that an army was landed. Dionysius, who had been campaigning against Carthage's allies in southern Italy, returned to Sicily and **crushed Mago's force**—10,000 are said to have died. Dionysius allowed the remnants to slip away, and they regrouped and returned the following year under Mago's son Himilco to deliver a stinging defeat to the Syracusans. Both sides were war-weary and in 375 BCE **made peace**, leaving Dionysius in possession of most of eastern Sicily and parts of southern Italy.

ALTHOUGH THE ATHENIANS brokered a **general peace** in Greece in 371 BCE, the Thebans did not participate. Thebes built up a coalition of allies and invaded **Sparta** in 370–369 BCE. As a result, Messenia was finally detached from Spartan control, but further Theban success was hampered by the temporary deposition of **Epaminondas**, who was tried for allegedly sparing the city of Sparta in exchange for a bribe. Once Epaminondas was back in control, the Thebans won Persian backing for their anti-Spartan alliance in 367 BCE, and a further **invasion of the Peloponnese** in 366 BCE gained recruits for the Theban coalition. However, Theban successes relied too narrowly on the personality of one man, and when Epaminondas

Ancient theater
The Odeon was a temple built in the town of Messene, which was founded by Epaminondas of Thebes in 367 BCE.

Battle of Leuctra

11,000 SPARTANS

9,000 THEBANS AND ALLIES

Battle of Leuctra
At Leuctra in central Greece, the Thebans exploited the tendency of the Spartans to shift right by concentrating their attack on the left, enabling them to defeat an enemy with larger numbers than theirs.

c. 380 BCE Farming and **iron metallurgy** is spread by Bantu-speaking people in the **Western Zambezi** region of Africa

380 BCE The Servian Wall is built around Rome

380 BCE Nectanebo becomes the first pharaoh of Egypt's 30th Dynasty

378 BCE Exiled Theban democrats under **Epaminondas** lead an uprising against the pro-Spartan ruling party. The Spartan garrison abandons the city of Thebes

373 BCE Artaxerxes II is defeated after invading Egypt in attempt to bring it back under Persian control

371 BCE Athens and Sparta make peace, ending an eight-year conflict

371 BCE Theban general Epaminondas wins the **Battle of Leuctra** against Sparta, and the Arcadians revolt against Spartan rule

369 BCE Epaminondas invades **Messenia**

360 BCE Revolt of the satraps (governors) begins in the Persian empire

362 BCE Battle of Mantinea marks final eclipse of Spartan power

> **AN ARMY OF DEER LED BY A LION IS MORE TO BE FEARED THAN AN ARMY OF LIONS LED BY A DEER.**

Attributed to **Philip II, king of Macedonia**, 4th century BCE

was killed in battle in 362 BCE, Theban power was rapidly eclipsed.

In India, the **Nanda dynasty** began its **expansion** in the 370s BCE, and continued to expand until it was able to take power from the Shishunaga in 345 BCE. The dynasty's founder **Mahapadma Nanda** conquered much of north India, building up a huge army. He operated an efficient administrative system with centrally appointed tax collectors and undertook irrigation works. However, the deposition of Dhana Nanda in 321 BCE was followed by the **absorption of the Nanda empire into the Mauryan empire.**

The **state of Chu** was the most southerly of China's **Warring States**, centered on the Middle Yangtze River. Throughout the 5th century BCE it annexed a number of states, becoming the dominant power by 380 BCE. In 366 BCE a resounding victory by the state of **Qin** against the armies of **Hann** and

88

THE AGE OF **MAHAPADMA NANDA** AT HIS DEATH

Wei, followed by another defeat of Wei at the **battle of Shimen** in 364 BCE led to Chu's decline and the shift eastward of Wei's royal center to Daliang. A rejuvenated Wei was strong enough to force the rulers of four other Warring States to attend its court in 356 BCE. Wei's supremacy was short-lived, and defeats inflicted on it by Qi armies at Guiling in 353 BCE and Maling in 341 BCE reduced it to a Qi vassal.

IN 359 BCE PERDICCAS III OF Macedonia died and his successor, **Philip II** (r. 359–336 BCE) began to transform the position of what had been regarded by other Greeks as a very minor kingdom. In 357 BCE, he made his first major conquest, Amphipolis in Thrace. He became involved in the **Third Sacred War** (356–346 BCE), which was fought over perceived violations by Sparta and Phocis of the sacred oracle at Delphi, using this to cement his position as an important player in the power politics of central Greece and the Peloponnese. In the 340s, Philip strengthened his position in Thessaly and became involved in petty disputes between the city-states, as rival factions turned either to him or to Athens for support. In 340 BCE **open war** broke out between Philip and the Athenian-Theban alliance. Just two years later, at Chaeronea in Boeotia, **Philip defeated the Athenians** and annihilated the

Mausoleum of Halicarnassus
Mausolus was the Persian satrap (governor) of a region of south-western Turkey. After his death in 353 BCE his wife built a tomb for him, which became one of the Seven Wonders of the Ancient World.

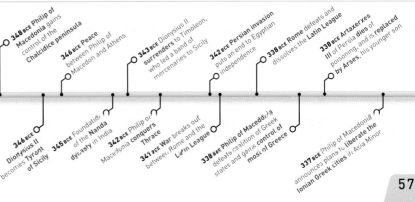

PHILIP OF MACEDONIA (382–336 BCE)

Philip II reformed the Macedonian army and forced the Greek states to join a League of Corinth under Macedonian control. After his return to Macedonia, he took a new wife, Cleopatra, but was stabbed to death at his wedding feast, possibly on the orders of his son, Alexander the Great, who stood to lose his position if Cleopatra bore another heir.

Theban Sacred Band (see 380–371 BCE). Macedonian power in Greece was now unchallenged.

Rome's steady expansion in central Italy had caused alarm among its neighbors. This led to a bitter six-year struggle with the town of Tibur from 360 BCE, among other conflicts. In 341 BCE, a general **war broke out between Rome and the Latins**, who inhabited the modern region of Lazio around Rome. The Romans had just emerged from a war with the Samnites, a people who inhabited the central Apennines, and the Latins took advantage of Rome's exhausted

state to launch an attack. During the first year of the war, at a battle near Vesuvius, the consul Publius Decius Mus is said to have dedicated his body to the gods of the underworld and then undertaken a suicidal charge against the Latin ranks that turned the tide of battle in the Romans' favor. By 338 BCE, the **Romans had defeated the Latin League.** The peace terms were favorable, with many Latins being granted Roman citizenship. The League was then dissolved, and many of the former Latin cities were absorbed into the Roman state, moving Rome further toward complete dominance of central Italy.

By 350 BCE the **Chavín culture** of southern Peru was at its height. It expanded to cover neighboring coastal areas and highland valleys, spreading its characteristic iconography of part-human, part-feline beings, which were portrayed in stone on textiles and ceramics.

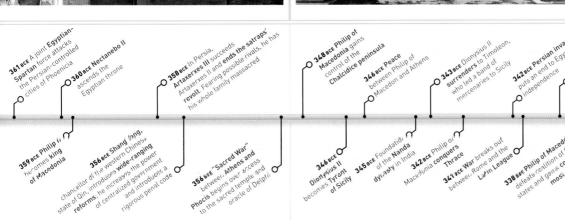

361 BCE A joint Egyptian-Spartan force attacks the Persian-controlled cities of Phoenicia

360 BCE Nectanebo II ascends the Egyptian throne

358 BCE In Persia, Artaxerxes III succeeds Artaxerxes II and **ends the satraps' revolt.** Fearing possible rivals, he has his whole family massacred

348 BCE Philip of Macedonia gains control of the **Chalcidice peninsula**

346 BCE Peace between Philip of Macedon and Athens

343 BCE Dionysius II **surrenders** to Timoleon, who led a band of mercenaries to Sicily

342 BCE Persian invasion puts an end to Egyptian independence

338 BCE Rome defeats and dissolves the Latin League

338 BCE Artaxerxes III of Persia **dies** of poisoning, and is **replaced by Arses**, his younger son

359 BCE Philip becomes king of Macedonia

356 BCE Shang Yang, chancellor of the western Chinese state of Qin, introduces **wide-ranging reforms**; he increases the power of centralized government and introduces a rigorous penal code

356 BCE "Sacred War" between Athens and Phocis begins over access to the sacred temple and oracle of Delphi

346 BCE Dionysius II becomes Tyrant of Sicily

345 BCE Foundation of the **Nanda** dynasty in India

342 BCE Philip of Macedonia conquers Thrace

341 BCE War breaks out between Rome and the Latin League

338 BCE Philip of Macedonia defeats coalition of Greek states and gains control of most of Greece

337 BCE Philip of Macedonia announces plans to liberate the Ionian Greek cities in Asia Minor

Despite being heavily outnumbered at Issus, Alexander the Great, depicted here on his horse Bucephalus, made brilliant use of his cavalry to win a stunning victory over King Darius III.

Ruins of Persepolis
The Persian ceremonial capital of Persepolis was burned to the ground by Alexander's troops in 330 BCE.

AFTER THE ASSASSINATION OF PHILIP OF MACEDONIA in 336 BCE (see 355–337 BCE), his 20-year-old son Alexander (often referred to as Alexander the Great) became commander of the major Greek city states. The next year Alexander invaded Thrace, but a rumor that he had been killed caused a major revolt centered on the Greek city of Thebes, supported by **Darius III of Persia** (r. 336–330 BCE). Alexander reacted swiftly; the Thebans were defeated and their city razed. The other states soon submitted. In 334 BCE, Alexander hurried to Anatolia, where a Macedonian army was already established, totaling perhaps 43,000 infantry and 6,000 cavalry. Although this figure was dwarfed by the forces of the local Persian satraps (governors), Alexander's cavalry smashed the lines of the **satrap Arsamenes** at the Granicus River in northwest Turkey. He pushed on toward the heart of the Persian Empire. In 333 BCE, at Issus, northern Syria, he routed an army

led by Darius III himself. In 331 BCE, the Macedonians defeated Darius III again at **Gaugamela** (in modern Iraq). The next year Darius was stabbed to death by **Bessus**, one of his generals. Alexander now seemed to have acquired the whole of the vast Persian Empire.

Aristotle
The philosopher Aristotle was employed by Philip of Macedonia as Alexander the Great's tutor.

AFTER HIS MURDER OF DARIUS, Bessus declared himself the new king of Persia (as **Artaxerxes V**), but some of the Persian satraps submitted to Alexander instead of Bessus. During 330–329 BCE, Alexander pursued Bessus into the easternmost regions of the Persian Empire, beyond the Hindu Kush and into Bactria. Finally, in Sogdiana, north of the Oxus River, the local nobles, led by the Sogdian warlord **Spitamenes**, betrayed Bessus and handed him over to Alexander. Once Alexander had continued his march north, however, Spitamenes revolted. It took Alexander a year of bitter campaigning to relieve the **siege**

Alexander the Great's conquests
Alexander penetrated the farthest corners of the Persian empire. To cement his rule, he founded a series of new cities, almost all named after himself, notably Alexandria in Egypt.

CONQUEST OF ALEXANDER
■ Macedonian Empire 336–323 BCE
→ Route taken by Alexander's forces

of Macaranda (Samarkand) and pacify Sogdiana, although the fortress of the "Sogdian Rock" managed to hold out against the Macedonian forces until 327 BCE. Alexander then crossed into the Kabul Valley, and the following year, at the Hydaspes River, he overcame the local ruler **Porus**. His plans to push further into India were stymied by his soldiers who, demoralized and disease-ridden, mutinied and demanded to go home. Part of the army returned home by sea under Nearchus, but a detachment under Alexander marched through the harsh Gedrosian desert, suffering heavy losses. His army reached central Persia early in 324 BCE, but Alexander, still planning new expeditions into Arabia, died of a fever at Babylon in June 323 BCE, at age 33.

In central Italy, the Samnites of the central-southern Apennines, who had lost a war against the Romans in 342–340 BCE, fought them once more in the **Second Samnite War** (326–304 BCE). The

30
THE AGE OF ALEXANDER'S **FAVORITE HORSE, BUCEPHALUS,** WHEN IT DIED

advance of the Romans into Campania after their abolition of the **Latin League** in 338 BCE alarmed the Samnites, and the Roman placing of a colony in their land in 328 BCE and tensions over the control of Neapolis (Naples) led to the **outbreak of war** in 326 BCE. In 321 BCE, the Samnites defeated a Roman army at the Caudine Forks. The **Romans humiliated** by being forced to bow down and "pass under the yoke" (an arch made from their captured spears). Four years of peace followed before the Romans renewed the war and, despite dogged resistance by the Samnites, finally emerged victorious in 304 BCE.

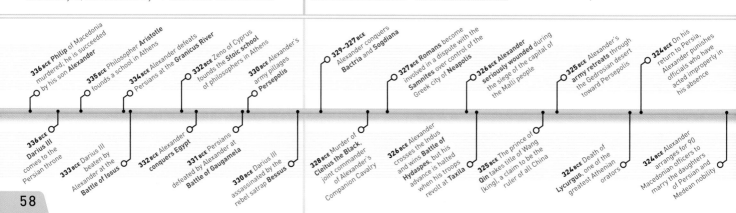

336 BCE Philip of Macedonia murdered; he is succeeded by his son **Alexander**

335 BCE Philosopher **Aristotle** founds a school in Athens

334 BCE Alexander defeats Persians at the **Granicus River**

332 BCE Zeno of Cyprus founds the **Stoic school** of philosophers in Athens

330 BCE Alexander's army pillages **Persepolis**

336 BCE Darius III comes to the Persian throne

333 BCE Darius III beaten by Alexander at the **Battle of Issus**

332 BCE Alexander **conquers Egypt**

331 BCE Persians defeated by Alexander at **Battle of Gaugamela**

330 BCE Darius III assassinated by rebel satrap **Bessus**

329–327 BCE Alexander conquers **Bactria and Sogdiana**

327 BCE **Romans** become involved in a dispute with the **Samnites** over control of the Greek city of **Neapolis**

326 BCE Alexander **seriously wounded** during the siege of the capital of the Malli people

325 BCE Alexander's **army retreats** through the Gedrosian desert toward Persepolis

324 BCE On his return to Persia, Alexander punishes officials who have acted improperly in his absence

328 BCE Murder of **Cleitus the Black,** joint commander of Alexander's Companion Cavalry

326 BCE Alexander crosses the Indus and wins **Battle of Hydaspes,** but his advance is halted when his troops revolt at **Taxila**

325 BCE The prince of **Wang Qin** takes title of (king), a claim to be the ruler of all China

324 BCE Death of **Lycurgus,** one of the greatest Athenian orators

324 BCE Alexander arranges for 90 Macedonian officers to marry the daughters of Persian and Medean nobility

" TO THE STRONGEST! "

Alexander the Great, on his deathbed in reply to a question about who would succeed him

ALEXANDER THE GREAT had not provided for an orderly succession after his death in 323 BCE, and his most experienced generals were also dead—except for Antipater, who had been left as regent in Macedonia. Alexander's wife Roxane was pregnant, and he had a half-brother Arrhidaeus, who was, unfortunately, mentally unstable. **A clique of generals** who were present at Alexander's deathbed— **Ptolemy, Cassander, Seleucus,** and **Lysimachus**— engineered a solution by which Roxane's newborn son Alexander IV (r. 323–311 BCE) notionally shared power with Arrhidaeus, who became **Philip III**. In reality, this military clique carved up the empire between themselves and four other generals. **Perdiccas** emerged as the main power in the center; **Antipater** and **Craterus** took Europe; **Antigonus Monopthalmus** ("the one-eyed") was given Phrygia; **Ptolemy** got Egypt; and **Seleucus** and **Cassander** were promoted to senior military commands.

These generals, who became known as the **Diadochoi** ("successors"), then fought a long series of wars for dominance in Alexander's former empire, at first pitting the others against Perdiccas, who was assassinated in 320 BCE. Antipater rose to power next, but he died of natural causes in 319 BCE, leaving Antigonus to make a bid for

80,000
ANTIGONUS

75,000
LYSIMACHUS

Battle of Ipsus
Although slightly outnumbered, Lysimachus deployed his archers against his enemy's flank, causing Antigonus's infantry to flee in panic.

power against the four remaining principal players: Cassander in Macedonia, Ptolemy in Egypt, Lysimachus in Thrace, and Seleucus in Babylon. War between the parties raged inconclusively until 311 BCE. But when it was renewed again in 307 BCE, it looked as if Antigonus might overcome all the others. Then, in 301 BCE, **Lysimachus crushed the Antigonid army** at Ipsus, and annexed most of Antigonus's former territories, so cementing a **tripartite division** of Alexander's empire between himself, Ptolemy, and Seleucus.

In India, in around 320 BCE, **Chandragupta Maurya** (r. c. 320–297 BCE) overthrew the last of the Nandas (see 370–356 BCE) to become ruler of Magadha and the Ganges plain. An energetic ruler, he then gradually absorbed the

outlying regions of the Nanda Empire, pushing his control as far as Gujarat and the Punjab. In 305 BCE, he began a campaign against one of Alexander's successors, **Seleucus**, which ended in a treaty in 303 BCE, under which the Greeks ceded control of eastern Afghanistan and Baluchistan to Chandragupta. Having established the **Mauryan Empire** in 307 BCE, Chandragupta decided to abdicate in favor of his son **Bindusara** (r. 297–272 BCE). He then retired to become a Jain monk, ultimately starving himself to death.

In China, **Meng Zi** (or Mencius) (c. 372–289 BCE) arrived at the Wei court around 320 BCE and rapidly earned himself a reputation as the "second sage" of the

Confucian tradition. Most of what is known of Meng Zi comes from the *Shiji*, a history written in the form of dialogues with several contemporary kings. Meng Zi stresses the value of *de* (virtue) for a king and, more practically, recommends lower taxes, less harsh punishments, and ensuring that the people have enough to eat. He believed that if a king acted benevolently, everyone would want to be ruled by him, and he would have no need of conquest. Meng Zi's benevolent view of human nature had a widespread appeal, and politically his views were most influential in the time of the **Song dynasty** (960–1279 CE).

ALEXANDER THE GREAT (356–323 BCE)

At age 20, Alexander inherited much of Greece from his father; by his death just 13 years later, he had extended this to cover a vast area from the Indus River in the east to Illyria in the west. He was a brilliant general but prone to acts of impetuous violence. His adoption of Persian court ritual alienated many native Macedonians, and his not naming an heir proved catastrophic.

Samnite-style helmet
The Romans admired the Samnites as fighters. This gladiator helmet is based on the Samnite style of armor.

323 BCE Alexander **dies** in Babylon; his empire begins to disintegrate among warring factions

323 BCE Outbreak of the **Lamian or Hellenic War** between Athens and her allies and the Macedonians in Thessaly

321 BCE Roman army defeated by Samnites at the **Caudine Forks**

321 BCE Athens defeated by Antipater; peace terms entail the end of **Athenian democracy**

320 BCE Ptolemy annexes Judaea and Syria

315 BCE Olympias, the mother of Alexander, murdered

312 BCE Rome's first aqueduct built by **Appius Claudius**

311 BCE Alexander's successors agree on **division of the empire**

311 BCE Alexander IV, son of Alexander the Great, dies

308 BCE Last royal burial of a **Kushite king**, Natasen, takes place at Napata

307 BCE Athens falls under Macedonian control

306 BCE Ptolemy I of Egypt defeated off Salamis (Cyprus) by Greeks under Demetrius

305 BCE Seleucus establishes himself in Persia and Anatolia, founding the **Seleucid Dynasty**

304 BCE Second Samnite War ends; Rome wins but gains no territory

303 BCE Chandragupta Maurya signs a **peace treaty** with Seleucus

301 BCE At the **Battle of Ipsus**, Lysimachus and Seleucus defeat **Antigonus**, who is killed

The Pharos lighthouse was built under Ptolemy II in around 280 BCE. It guided ships into Alexandria harbor at night.

> ## " ANOTHER SUCH VICTORY AND **WE ARE UNDONE.** "

Pyrrhus, king of the Greek state of Epirus, 279 BCE

At the Battle of Mylae, in 260 BCE, Rome defeated the Carthaginian navy.

IN ITALY, A THIRD WAR broke out between the **Romans and Samnites** in 298 BCE, apparently provoked by Samnite harassment of their neighbors, the Lucanians. Despite two Roman victories in 297 BCE, the Samnites, this time allied with the Gauls, could still field a huge army against the Romans at **Sentinum** in 295 BCE.

275
THE NUMBER OF YEARS THE **PTOLEMAIC DYNASTY** RULED EGYPT

The equally vast Roman army—at 45,000, the largest they had ever fielded—was threatened with defeat until the Roman consul **Publius Decius Mus** dedicated himself and the enemy army as sacrificial victims to the gods of the underworld and led a **suicidal charge** that shattered the Samnite line. A string of **Roman successes** followed in 293 and 292 BCE, and two years later the Samnites finally surrendered and their lands were annexed. Roman territory now stretched across the Italian peninsula to the Adriatic Sea.

Demetrius Poliorcetes (c.337–283 BCE), the son of Antigonus (see 322–301 BCE), was now rebuilding his strength from bases in the Aegean islands and in Cyprus. He was able to exploit the need of **Seleucus**, in Babylon, for allies against the now overmighty **Lysimachus**. In 294 BCE, Demetrius **invaded Macedon**, whose ruler Cassander had died three years before, leaving his two young sons to engage in a **bitter civil war**. Demetrius then attacked Lysimachus's Asian territories, but in 292 BCE he was brought back to Greece by a revolt in Aetolia. By 289 BCE, Demetrius had suppressed the revolt, but he had lost most of his island bases to Ptolemy's Egyptian fleet. He retreated to Asia, and died in 283 BCE, a captive of Seleucus.

Of Alexander's successors, Ptolemy inherited the weakest position. A naval defeat in 306 BCE by Demetrius Poliorcetes confined his ambitions temporarily to Egypt. Yet here he shrewdly chose to exploit the existing mechanisms of power, establishing himself as a pharaoh in the old style and setting up an administration that melded the best of Greek and Egyptian traditions. By 295 BCE, Ptolemy's naval forces had recovered and conquered much of the Aegean. In Egypt, Ptolemy's position was sufficiently secure that, at his death in 283 BCE, aged 84, he passed the kingdom on to his son Ptolemy II Philadelphos (r. 283–245 BCE), the second king of a Ptolemaic dynasty that would rule Egypt until 30 BCE.

IN 281 BCE, THE APPEAL by envoys from the southern Italian city of Tarentum for protection against the Romans provided **Pyrrhus**, the king of the Greek state of Epirus, with a perfect excuse for fulfilling his ambitions and intervening there. He arrived with an army more than 25,000 strong, including war elephants. He beat the Romans at the **River Siris** in 280 BCE, but the Roman senate refused to make peace. Pyrrhus vanquished another Roman army at **Asculum** the next year, but his losses were so severe that it seemed more like a defeat. After invading Sicily, Pyrrhus retreated back to **Epirus** in 275 BCE, nursing huge losses in troops and having made no territorial gains.

The defeat and **death of Lysimachus** in 281 BCE in battle

500 | 20
3,000 | 2,000
20,000

KEY
- Infantry
- Cavalry
- Archers
- Slingers
- War elephants

Pyrrhus's army
The army that Pyrrhus took over to Italy included a small number of war elephants, whose presence caused the Roman cavalry to panic and flee.

Pyrrhus of Epirus
Despite his many campaigns, when Pyrrhus died he ruled little more than the kingdom he had inherited.

against Seleucus, and the latter's assassination, soon led to instability on the frontier between the **Seleucid Empire** (now ruled by his son Antiochus I) and the Egyptian ruler **Ptolemy II Philadelphos**. Finally, in 274 BCE the **First Syrian War** broke out between them. The Egyptians emerged victorious, annexing parts of the Syrian coast and southern Anatolia. This position was in part reversed by Egyptian losses in the **Second Syrian War** (260–253 BCE) and then renewed in the **Third Syrian War** (246–241 BCE), which was fought between the Seleucid **Antiochus II** and **Ptolemy III**. These three debilitating wars left the Seleucids particularly vulnerable to the now growing power of **Parthia**.

IN INDIA, the accession of **Ashoka** (c. 294–232 BCE) to the throne in 268 BCE had marked a watershed for the **Mauryan Empire**. On his father Bindusara's death (see 322–301 BCE), Ashoka had to fight a four-year **civil war** with his brothers before he was enthroned. Around eight years later, he launched a campaign against **Kalinga** (modern Orissa), which was so bloody that around 100,000 people are said to have died. So struck with remorse was Ashoka at this slaughter, that he ever after rejected war and promoted the Buddhist concept of **dharma**, meaning mercy or piety. He set up a series of edicts carved in rock throughout the empire—many of them on pillars topped with a lion—promoting his adherence to dharma. Under his patronage the **Third Buddhist Council** met at Pataliputra around 250 BCE, and Ashoka sought to export his ideas abroad, exchanging diplomatic missions with foreign rulers, such as **Antiochus II of Syria** and **Ptolemy II of Egypt**. At his death in 232 BCE, the Mauryan Empire had reached its greatest extent and seemed securely established.

In China, **Zhao Zheng** succeeded his father to the throne of Qin in 246 BCE. From 228 BCE, ably advised by **chancellor Li Si**, Zhao Zheng unleashed a final war of conquest against the remaining **Warring States** (see 370–356 BCE). Zhao and Yan soon fell to his forces, the Qin armies captured Wei and, in 223 BCE, overcame Chu. Only Qi still held out but, in 221 BCE, Zhao Zheng finally annexed it, leaving

---

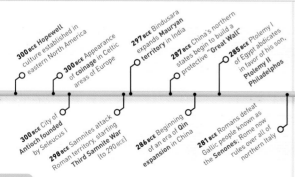

300 BCE Hopewell culture established in eastern North America

300 BCE Appearance of **coinage** in Celtic areas of Europe

300 BCE City of **Antioch founded** by Seleucus I

298 BCE Samnites attack Roman territory; starting **Third Samnite War** (to 290 BCE)

297 BCE Bindusara expands **Mauryan territory** in India

288 BCE Beginning of an era of Qin **expansion** in China

287 BCE China's northern states begin to build a protective "**Great Wall**"

285 BCE Ptolemy I of Egypt abdicates in favor of his son, **Ptolemy II Philadelphos**

281 BCE Romans defeat Gallic people known as the **Senones**; Rome now rules over all of northern Italy

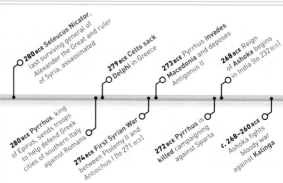

280 BCE Seleucus Nicator, last surviving general of Alexander the Great and ruler of Syria, assassinated

280 BCE Pyrrhus, king of Epirus, sends troops to help defend Greek cities of southern Italy against Romans

279 BCE Celts sack **Delphi** in Greece

274 BCE First Syrian War between Ptolemy II and Antiochus I (to 271 BCE)

273 BCE Pyrrhus invades **Macedonia** and deposes Antigonus II

272 BCE Pyrrhus is killed campaigning against Sparta

268 BCE Reign of **Ashoka** begins in India (to 232 BCE)

c. 268–260 BCE Ashoka fights bloody war against **Kalinga**

264 BCE Outbreak of **First Punic War** between Rome and Carthage (to 241)

263 BCE Eumenes I establishes **Pergamum** as independent kingdom

262 BCE After long siege, **Athens falls** to the Macedonians

262 BCE Ashoka converts to **Buddhism**

ROMAN RELIGION

Early Roman religion combined the worship of the great gods, such as Neptune (shown here), with that of more local deities. There were several different types of priest: *haruspices* made predictions from the entrails of sacrificed animals; *augures* determined the divine will from signs, such as the flight of birds; and *pontifices* controlled the complex calendar of religious festivals. In their homes, Romans had shrines to household gods and the spirits of their ancestors.

little headway. However, after they had built their first-ever fleet, the Romans' fortunes changed. In 260 BCE, they won an important victory over the Carthaginians at **Mylae**. A Roman invasion of North Africa in 256 BCE failed to capture Carthage only through the ineptitude of the consul, Regulus. On land, the Romans took the Carthaginian strongholds in Sicily one by one until, by 249 BCE, only **Drepana**, in western Sicily, held out against them. A massive **Carthaginian naval victory** there set back the Roman cause, but in 242 BCE, a new Roman fleet appeared off Drepana, took it, and the next year smashed a Carthaginian fleet at the **Aegades Islands**. This defeat caused **Hamilcar Barca**, the Carthaginian general, to sue for peace. The peace terms involved the Carthaginians leaving Sicily. The two sides' spheres of influence remained uncomfortably overlapping, creating the seeds of two future conflicts.

> **IF THEY WILL NOT EAT, LET THEM DRINK!**
>
> **Publius Claudius Pulcher, Roman consul and general**, ordering the drowning of the sacred chickens when they refused to eat grain before the Battle of Drepana, 249 BCE

him the master of all China. The same year he proclaimed himself the "First Emperor" as Qin Shi Huangdi, and the first ruler of the new **Qin dynasty**.

In Persia, the Greek Seleucid dynasty, which had inherited the region after Alexander the Great's death in 323 BCE, faced a series of nomad incursions after 280 BCE. **Antiochus I** (reign c. 280–261 BCE)

expelled the nomads, but wars with Egypt (280–272 BCE and 260–253 BCE) overstretched the kingdom's resources. On the death of **Antiochus II** (r. 261–246 BCE), civil war broke out between the king's widow Berenice and his former wife Laodice. This led to the **breakaway of Bactria under Diodotus and Parthia under Andragoras**. Taking advantage of this instability,

the nomadic Parni, led by **Arsaces**, entered Parthia in the mid-240s BCE.

Rivalry over Sicily, where the Carthaginians had possessed colonies since the 8th century BCE, was at the root of the **First Punic War** (264–241 BCE), a conflict between Rome and the North African power of Carthage. In 264 BCE, the Romans sent an army to help the **Mamertines**—a group of south-Italian mercenaries occupying the Sicilian city of Messana—in their conflict with the city of Syracuse, which was in turn aided by Carthage. The Carthaginian's resistance was so stubborn that the Romans made

Great Stupa at Sanchi
This Buddhist stupa in central India was begun by the Mauryan ruler Ashoka in the 3rd century BCE.

KEY
- ▦ Carthaginian Empire in 264 BCE
- ▦ Roman territory in 264 BCE
- ▦ Roman gains by 238 BCE
- ✕ Roman victory

The First Punic War
The two decades of fighting was concentrated around Sicily, but also saw Roman invasions of North Africa and Sardinia.

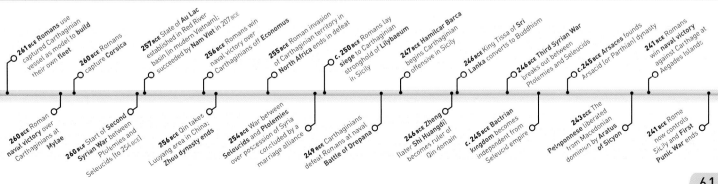

261 BCE Romans use captured Carthaginian vessel as model to **build their own fleet**

260 BCE Roman **naval victory** over Carthaginians at **Mylae**

260 BCE Romans capture Corsica

260 BCE Start of **Second Syrian War** between Ptolemies and Seleucids (to 254 BCE)

257 BCE State of **Au Lac** established in Red River basin (in modern Vietnam); succeeded by **Nam Viet** in 207 BCE

256 BCE Romans win naval victory over Carthaginians off **Economus**

256 BCE Qin takes Luoyang area in China; **Zhou dynasty ends**

255 BCE Roman invasion of Carthaginian territory in **North Africa** ends in defeat

254 BCE War between Seleucids and Ptolemies over possession of Syria concluded by a marriage alliance

c. 250 BCE Romans lay **siege** to Carthaginian stronghold of **Lilybaeum** in Sicily

249 BCE Carthaginians defeat Romans at naval **Battle of Drepana**

247 BCE **Hamilcar Barca** begins Carthaginian offensive in Sicily

246 BCE Zheng (later **Shi Huangdi**) becomes ruler of Qin domain

246 BCE King **Tissa** of **Sri Lanka** converts to Buddhism

246 BCE Third Syrian War breaks out between Ptolemies and Seleucids

c. 245 BCE Bactrian kingdom becomes independent from Seleucid empire

c. 245 BCE Arsaces founds **Arsacid (or Parthian) dynasty**

243 BCE The **Peloponnese** liberated from Macedonian dominion by **Aratus of Sicyon**

241 BCE Romans win **naval victory** against Carthage at **Aegades Islands**

241 BCE Rome now controls **Sicily** and **First Punic War** ends

36

THE NUMBER OF **COMMANDERIES** (REGIONS) SET UP BY EMPEROR **QIN SHI HUANGDI**

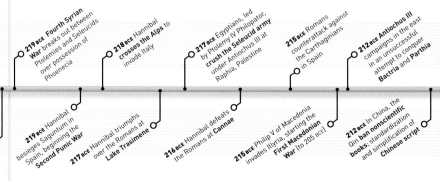

This rendition of Hannibal's crossing of the Alps is attributed to Italian artist Jacopo Ripanda. Amazingly, all 37 elephants survived the mountain passage.

IN 221 BCE, QIN SHI HUANGDI, the first emperor of China, divided his empire into 36 commanderies on the advice of his minister **Li Ssu**. The dispossessed aristocrats and nobles of Qin's former enemies were moved to the capital Xianyang to keep them under close control. To further encourage a sense of unity, Li Ssu commissioned a single script and a standardized system of weights and measures for China. Further conquests were made to the north and south in 219 and 214 BCE, and thousands of colonists were sent to the new territories. Shi Huangdi dealt firmly with opposition. In 213 BCE, he ordered the "**burning of the books**," by which the writings of philosophers opposed to the Qin state were burned, and in 212 BCE he had many intellectuals who opposed him brutally killed.

Suppressing opposition
This watercolor-on-silk painting shows Shi Huangdi, China's first emperor, overseeing the burning of books and the execution of scholars.

In the aftermath of the **First Punic War** (see 264–241 BCE), which Sicily and Sardinia lost, Carthage turned its attention to **Spain**. In 237 BCE, **Hamilcar** was sent there, and he conquered almost all of southern Spain. He died in battle against the **Oretani**, a Celtic tribe, in 229 BCE, but by then he had won a **new empire** for Carthage and a strong power base for his family, the **Barcids**.

Despite their victory in the First Punic War, the Romans' position in northern Italy was still weak. In 226 BCE, the Celtic **Insubres and Boii tribes** tried to drive them out. At the **Battle of Telamon** the next year, the Celts were trapped between two Roman armies and routed. Although the Boii accepted defeat in 224 BCE and the Insubres sued for peace two years later, the Romans rebuffed them and pushed for total victory. The king of the Boii was killed in single combat against a Roman consul, and their capital **Mediolanum** (Milan) captured. The Romans established colonies in the Celtic territories in 218 BCE, including at Piacenza.

A revolt led by **Arsaces** (see 265–241 BCE) in Parthava, a former satrapy in the northeast of the Seleucid Empire, could not be quelled by Seleucus II (r. 246–225 BCE), and a separate **Parthian kingdom emerged** in the region of modern Iran. The Parthians gradually annexed more territory to the west, especially under **Mithridates I** (r. 171–138 BCE). By the early 1st century BCE, only a small area of Syria was under Seleucid control.

Second Punic War
There were three principal theaters of conflict: Spain, Italy, and North Africa. By 203 BCE, the Carthaginians were confined to Africa.

THE SECOND PUNIC WAR 218–202 BCE

▦ Carthaginian Empire 281 BCE
▦ Carthaginian territory 200 BCE
▦ Roman territory 218 BCE
▦ Roman gains by 200 BCE
▦ Massalian territory 218 BCE
✕ Carthaginian victory
✕ Roman victory
→ Hannibal (219–202)
⇢ Hasdrubal (208–207)
➡ Scipio Africanus (210–206 and 204–202)

ALARMED AT CARTHAGINIAN EXPANSION IN SPAIN, in 226 BCE the Romans sent an embassy to **Hasdrubal**—son of Hamilcar and the new Barcid commander there—and secured an agreement that the Carthaginians would not move north of the Ebro River. In return, the Romans pledged not to move south—although they did forge alliances with cities in the south, such as Saguntum. In 221 BCE, Hasdrubal was assassinated; two years later, **Hannibal**, his brother and successor, attacked Saguntum, rapidly leading to the **Second Punic War** (219–201 BCE).

With the prospect of the Romans sending one army to Spain and another via Sicily to invade North Africa, Hannibal decided to strike first. He marched with 50,000 infantry, 9,000 cavalry, and 37 elephants into northern Spain, across the Pyrenees, through southern Gaul and—to the Romans' astonishment—**crossed the Alps**. Although he now had only around half the force he had started with, his presence encouraged the north Italian Celts to revolt and, at **Trebia** in late 218 BCE, he routed a Roman army. The following year he smashed another large Roman force at **Lake Trasimene**, killing 15,000

Battle of Canae
Some 35,000 Romans survived the battle of Cannae, but half of those were captured by the Carthaginians, and many were sold into slavery.

Romans—including one of the consuls. Faced with many **defections** among the allied cities, the Romans turned to delaying tactics to hold Hannibal at bay. But this was a temporary measure, and the Romans suffered one of their worst ever defeats at **Cannae** in 216 BCE, when

50,000 casualties — 6,000 casualties
FORCES IN THOUSANDS
Roman / Carthaginian
TROOPS

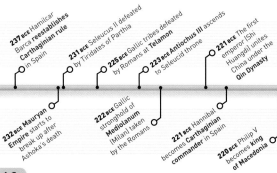

237 BCE Hamilcar Barca **reestablishes Carthaginian rule** in Spain
232 BCE Mauryan **Empire** starts to break up after Ashoka's death
231 BCE Seleucus II defeated by Tiridates of Parthia
225 BCE Gallic tribes defeated by Romans at Telamon
223 BCE Antiochus III ascends to Seleucid throne
222 BCE Gallic stronghold of **Mediolanum** (Milan) taken by the Romans
221 BCE The first emperor (Shi Huangdi) unites China under the **Qin Dynasty**
221 BCE Hannibal becomes **Carthaginian commander** in Spain
220 BCE Philip V becomes king of Macedonia
219 BCE Fourth Syrian War breaks out between Ptolemies and Seleucids over possession of Phoenecia
219 BCE Hannibal besieges Saguntum in Spain, beginning the **Second Punic War**
218 BCE Hannibal **crosses the Alps** to invade Italy
217 BCE Hannibal triumphs over the Romans at Lake Trasimene
217 BCE Egyptians, led by Ptolemy IV Philopator, **crush the Seleucid army** under Antiochus III at Raphia, Palestine
216 BCE Hannibal defeats the Romans at Cannae
215 BCE Romans counterattack against the Carthaginians in Spain
215 BCE Philip V of Macedonia invades Illyria, starting the **First Macedonian War** to 205 BCE
212 BCE Antiochus III campaigns in the east in an unsuccessful attempt to conquer **Bactria and Parthia**
212 BCE In China, the Qin **ban nonscientific books**; standardization and simplification of **Chinese script**

After his death, the First Qin Emperor was buried in a vast mausoleum, in which an army of 8,000 terracotta warriors, each around 6 ft 6 in (2 m) tall, were placed.

HANNIBAL (247–182 BCE)

A brilliant tactician, Hannibal's string of victories against the Romans from 218 BCE was not matched by the strategic judgment to convert them into final victory. Following the surrender of Carthage in 201 BCE, Hannibal served as the city's suffete (chief magistrate) until the Romans had him exiled in 195 BCE. He then offered his service to a succession of Rome's enemies before poisoning himself in Bithynia.

Hannibal's army massacred up to 50,000 of them. But Hannibal did not march immediately on Rome, and his campaign lost momentum. Although Hannibal captured much of southern Italy, including the key city of Capua in 211 BCE, by 212 BCE the Romans had raised 25 fresh legions and stood ready to carry the war back to the Carthaginians.

WHEN THE FIRST QIN EMPEROR DIED IN 210 BCE, resentment against his autocratic rule erupted in a series of peasant revolts. A number of new kingdoms broke away from the center, while the anti-Qin forces found a talented military leader in **Xiang Yu**. In 208 BCE, Li Ssu was executed and a new army, led by **Liu Bang**, a man of peasant origins, emerged to challenge the Qin. By 206 BCE, the **Qin Empire** was fragmented and Xiang Yu and Liu Bang were at war with one another. In 202 BCE, Xiang Yu committed suicide after being defeated at **Gaixia**. With no one left to oppose him, Liu Bang had himself declared emperor as **Gaozu**, the first ruler of the **Han dynasty** (see 200–171 BCE).

With Hannibal making little headway in **southern Italy**, the Romans embarked on a policy of picking off the allies of Carthage. Their first target was **Philip V of Macedonia**, whose attacks on Illyria in 215 BCE had provoked the **First Macedonian War** (215–205 BCE) with Rome. In 211 BCE, the Romans allied with the Aetolians, who fought the Macedonians on land while the Romans launched naval attacks. Philip's invasion of **Aetolia** in 207 BCE forced the Aetolians to sue for peace the next year, and though the Romans sent fresh forces in 205 BCE, the war ended with a recognition of the **status quo** between the two sides.

In Spain, the Romans had retaken **Saguntum** in 212 BCE, but a disastrous defeat the following year in which both consuls died looked set to destroy the Roman position there. The Roman senate sent the young general **Publius Cornelius Scipio** (c. 236–183 BCE) to Spain, where he captured the Carthaginian capital of **Carthage Nova**. In 206 BCE, he crushed a large Carthaginian force at **Illipa**.

In 207 BCE, Hannibal's brother **Hasdrubal** was defeated and **killed** at the **Metaurus River** in northern Italy, denying Hannibal crucial reinforcements. By 204 BCE, many of Hannibal's south-Italian allies had deserted him, and when Scipio landed with a Roman army at **Utica** in North Africa, the Carthaginians recalled Hannibal to head off a threat to **Carthage** itself. The Romans offered relatively lenient peace terms, but the Carthaginians rejected them, and Scipio captured their towns one by one. Aided by the Numidian prince, Massinissa, **Scipio defeated Hannibal's last army** at Zama in 202 BCE. The peace terms the Carthaginians now had to accept were much harsher. All of their territory was forfeit save a band around Carthage itself; their

fleet was reduced to a mere 10 ships; they were not allowed to make war outside Africa at all, and inside it they needed Roman permission to do so. An annual tribute of 10,000 talents payable to the Romans completed the humiliation of what had once been Rome's greatest enemy.

The Continence of Scipio
Scipio was noted for his mercy. In this 19th-century painting, he is seen handing back a captured Carthaginian woman to her fiancé,

owl, the sacred bird of Athena

crescent symbol in post-490 BCE coins

Athenian coin
The Athenian silver tetradrachm has an image of an owl on one side and a helmeted head on the other. It was also stamped with the Greek letters for "ATHE" to identify the city of its origin.

1200 BCE
Shells as money
Beginning from the Maldives, the use of cowrie shells as money spreads throughout the Pacific, and, by the 19th century, into Africa.

Cowrie shells

465–454 BCE
Greek coins
Almost every Greek city-state issues its own coinage, often with the name of the state inscribed on it. Silver replaces electrum as the main metal used.

Prehistory
Cattle as capital
Prehistoric people use cattle as money, with animals such as sheep or chickens sometimes acting as small change.

Cattle

1000–500 BCE
Tool money
In China, common tools are cast in metal, punched with holes (for stringing several together), and used as money.

Knife money

c. 640–630 BCE
First true coins
The state of Lydia produces the first true coins, made of electrum (an alloy of gold and silver) and stamped with an image of a lion or stag.

Lydian coins

27 BCE–14 CE
Augustan aureus
Emperor Augustus reforms the Roman coinage system and issues a new version of the standard gold coin, the aureus, worth 25 silver denarii.

Gold aureus

THE STORY OF MONEY

THE ADOPTION OF MONEY ENABLED EARLY SOCIETIES TO FLOURISH AND GROW INTO COMPLEX CIVILIZATIONS

As societies became more complex, a need arose for a uniform medium of exchange to acquire goods. Money was created to fulfill this role, and it evolved from cattle to precious metals, and finally, to coins and bank notes. Today, money is exchanged more abstractly, through credit cards or electronic transfers.

The earliest forms of money—used in ritual exchanges (for example, as a dowry) and in paying fines—included physical items such as cattle. In the 4th millennium BCE, the growth of trade in Egypt and Mesopotamia led to more compact and portable forms of money. For thousands of years, precious metals were used, often in the forms of bars and ingots. Babylonian king Hammurabi's law code mentions loans paid in silver. In 640 BCE, in the kingdom of Lydia in Asia Minor, the development of money went a stage further with the invention of coinage, which later spread to the Greek world. By the Roman era, a tri-metallic system had been adopted, with coins of gold, silver, and bronze (of least value) circulating across the empire. All had the head of the ruler stamped on them, for propaganda as well as fiscal use.

EXCHANGE NOTES

In 1189, paper money came into use in China during Jin rule. Notes could express larger denominations and, therefore, were more convenient than coins. Gradually, government-backed banks began to issue notes, which were, in theory, exchangeable for an equivalent amount in bullion (a system known as the Gold Standard). However, the economic crisis following World War I forced countries to abandon the Gold Standard. Subsequently, the "real" value of notes and coins became nominal, relying instead on a sense of trust that they could be exchanged for goods. The growth of credit cards from 1950 took this a stage further, as the purchaser passed on nothing save the promise of payment at a later date.

The debasement of Roman coins
Due to inflation, excessive expenditure, and weak control of minting, the purity of the Roman denarius fell from around 90 percent silver under Marcus Aurelius (r. 161–180) to 4 percent during Gallienus's rule (r. 260–268).

TRADE AND PAPER MONEY

The growth in paper money in Europe after the Middle Ages was fueled by the needs of merchants. Traders would deposit funds in a bank in one city and receive a promissory note, which allowed them to withdraw the amount in any other city where the bank had a branch. Great Italian banking houses, such as the Medici, were rich enough to fund the military campaigns of European kings through their loans.

806–821
Paper money
In China, Emperor Xianzong issues the earliest bank notes during a period of copper shortage. The Jin dynasty issues the first true bank notes around 1189.

Song dynasty note

1519
Thalers
Coin minted from silver found in the Joachimsthal mine, Bohemia, becomes standard in the Spanish and Austrian Habsburg empires.

Joachimsthal thaler

1694
First bank note
The Bank of England is founded to fund England's growing national debt. It issues its first bank notes, backed by the bank's own gold reserves.

1949
Credit and debit cards
The first credit cards appear in the US in 1949. By the 1980s, debit cards, which operate as electronic cash (without deferred payment) appear.

Credit cards

1158
Making change
Henry II of England creates high-quality coinage, based on a silver penny, with a cross design that will last over the next 100 years.

Henricus penny

17th century
Modern check
By the 17th century, the use of checks, often backed by goldsmiths, becomes widespread in Europe.

British check from 1659

1862
First dollar bill
The US Treasury issues the first dollar bills for national circulation. These are known as "greenbacks" for their vivid green color.

First one dollar bill

The royal entourage of Gaozu, the first emperor of the Han, depicted in the mountains of China. Gaozu was one of the few Chinese rulers to come from a peasant background.

This wall painting shows Judah Maccabee's revolt in Jerusalem.

THE FIRST HAN EMPEROR OF CHINA, GAOZU, died in 195 BCE, when his successor, Hui Ti, was just 15. Hui Ti fell under the sway of his mother, the empress Lu, who took power for herself on his premature death in 188 BCE. Under her rule **China was invaded** by the Xiongnu from the north and the kingdom of Nanyue to the south, and it was only under Gaozu's son

the beginnings of **political consolidation in central Japan**, especially around the lower Nara basin (near Osaka).

In **India**, the **Sunga dynasty** took power in Magadha in 185 BCE, when its founder Pusyamitra Sunga (r. 185–149 BCE), a former

Mauryan general, assassinated the last Mauryan ruler (see 265 BCE). He is said to have persecuted Buddhists, marking the beginning of the religion's decline in its Indian homeland. He also fought a **long series of wars** with Magadha's neighbors,

including the **Satavahanas**, the **Kalingas**, and the **Indo-Greek** kingdoms of Bactria.

Bactria (in modern Afghanistan) broke away from Seleucid control around 250 BCE, and was ruled by a series of Greek kings, starting with Diodotus. Another **Indo-Greek dynasty** emerged in India, and became powerful under **Menander I** (c. 165–130 BCE), an important patron of Buddhism. Under the Indo-Greek kings, a new **school of art** emerged around Gandhara, which fused Buddhist iconography and Greek naturalism. Gradually, these easternmost Greeks came under pressure from Scythian and Yuezhi nomads and in 125 BCE Bactria collapsed. The last Indo-Greek kingdom of the Punjab survived until 10 CE.

The Roman victory against Philip V of Macedon (see 210 BCE) in the **Second Macedonian War** (200–196 BCE) did not lead to permanent acquisitions in Greece, and the Romans withdrew their army in 194 BCE. After the death of Philip V in 179 BCE, his son Perseus presided over worsening relations with Rome, and in 171 BCE a **Third Macedonian War** broke out. Initial Roman campaigning achieved little except the alienation of their Greek allies, but a more disciplined approach under the consul **Aemilius Paullus** (see 170 BCE) yielded better results.

THE THIRD MACEDONIAN WAR ended In 168 BCE, when Paullus defeated Perseus at the **Battle of Pydna.** A purge of anti-Roman elements swept through the Greek cities, and Macedonia was broken up into four republics to prevent it recovering its strength.

In 149 BCE, Spartan attempts to get the Romans to intervene in a quarrel with the **Achaean League** (a group of Greek city-states) coincided with an **anti-Roman revolt** in Macedonia. By 148 BCE, the Macedonians had been defeated and the Romans turned their attention to the Achaeans. The Roman consul L. Mummius quickly routed the Archaeans and took Corinth, which he razed to the ground. The various leagues of Greek cities were dissolved and **Greece lost its independence**, becoming the Roman province of **Achaea**.

13

THE NUMBER OF **REGIONS** THAT MADE UP **HAN CHINA**

Wendi (r. 180–157 BCE) that **stability was restored**. By 143 BCE, the number of commanderies (regions) under central Han control had risen from 13 to a total of 40.

In Japan, the **Middle Yayoi** period (200 BCE–100 CE) saw an increase in population—possibly to as high as 600,000 people—and

geometrical patterns and shapes

Battle of Pydna
The Macedonian army of Perseus was destroyed at the Battle of Pydna. The Romans killed 20,000 Macedonians and captured 11,000.

Yayoi vase
The Yayoi period in Japanese history (c. 300 BCE to 250 CE) is named for the site near Tokyo where its pottery was first found.

c. 200 BCE Regional cultures appear in **Central Andes**

198 BCE Antiochus III takes Judaea from Ptolemies

200 BCE Second Macedonian War (to 197 BCE)

197 BCE Foundation of library at **Pergamum** in Anatolia

196 BCE Hannibal elected suffete (magistrate) in Carthage and makes reforms to public finances

192 BCE Roman war with **Antiochus III**. He is defeated at Thermopylae and Magnesia (190 BCE)

182 BCE Hannibal commits suicide

180 BCE Wendi becomes Chinese emperor. His 23-year reign provides period of stability

179 BCE Perseus succeeds Philip V as king of Macedon

171 BCE Third Macedonian War (to 167 BCE)

c. 165 BCE First official examination for the selection of Chinese **civil servants**

164 BCE Judah Maccabee enters Jerusalem

c. 200 BCE Small communities in Mexico's **Teotihuacan valley** merge to form larger states

196 BCE Rome declares freedom of the Greeks at **Isthmus of Corinth**

193 BCE The **Aetolian League** revolts against Roman rule and allies with Antiochus

191 BCE The most rigorous **Qin** laws are abolished in China

185 BCE End of Mauryan and start of **Sunga dynasty** in northern India

177 BCE Advance of **Xiongnu nomads** into Henan region of northern China

168 BCE Antiochus IV imposes Greek culture in Judaea, ordering pigs to be sacrificed in Jewish Temple

171 BCE Mithridates I becomes king of **Persia League**

161 BCE Judah Maccabee is **killed in battle**

160 BCE The city of **Pergamum**, ruled by King Eumenes II, becomes a renowned cultural center

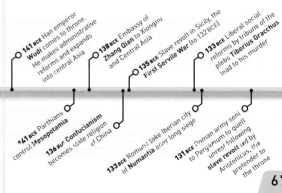

The ruins of Carthage, which was burned and ritually cursed after its capture in 146 BCE. A new Roman town was founded near the city around 48 BCE.

After the end of the Second Punic War, in 202 BCE, the Romans had allowed their ally King Massinissa of Numidia to encroach on Carthaginian territory. The peace conditions that ended the war forbade the Carthaginians to wage

❝ CARTHAGE MUST BE DESTROYED. ❞

Cato the Elder, Roman statesman

war without Roman approval. Unable to act, the Carthaginians were reduced to sending **embassies to Rome** to protest Massinissa's behavior. However, Rome sided with its ally, and one Carthaginian embassy in 162 BCE even resulted in Carthage being

Carthaginean tophet
A memorial stone from the tophet (cemetery) at Carthage, showing Tanit, the goddess of the heavens.

made to pay an annual fine of 500 talents. In 151 BCE, the Carthaginian government sent a military force to relieve a town that had been besieged by Massinissa, and the Romans reacted by **declaring war**. This was the **Third Punic War** (149–146 BCE). Rome's war was encouraged by the anti-Carthaginian senator **Cato**

the Elder, who made a series of speeches to the Senate calling for the destruction of Carthage. The first two years of the Third Punic war saw ineffective Roman attacks on towns around Carthage. In 147 BCE, a new commander was appointed, **Scipio Aemilianus**, who transformed Rome's fortunes in the war within a year.

In 168 BCE, the Seleucid ruler **Antiochus IV** outlawed Jewish religious practices in Judaea, leading to the **revolt of Judah Maccabee** and his brothers. In 164 BCE, Judah Maccabee entered Jerusalem, reconsecrated the temple, and reestablished Judaism. The **Seleucid kingdom** then continued to decline (see also 280 BCE), with the overthrow of its ruler Demetrius I in 150 BCE by Alexander Balas rapidly leading to the **loss of the key satrapies** (provinces) of Media and Susiana.

THE ROMAN REPUBLIC

After the overthrow of the last king in 507 BCE, Rome became a republic, ruled by two annually elected consuls. Over time the consuls came to be supported by other magistrates (praetors and quaestors), and tribunes of the plebs who had a special role in protecting the rights of the lower

orders. Later elections for the consulate became bitterly contested as the office provided great potential for enrichment and personal and family glory. After Augustus became emperor in 27 BCE the office of consul lost any real power, being increasingly awarded to imperial favourites.

> ❝ I SHUDDER TO THINK THAT **ONE DAY** SOMEONE MAY GIVE THE SAME ORDER **FOR ROME.** ❞

Scipio Aemilianus, Roman general and consul, on giving the order to burn Carthage, from Plutarch's *Apophthegmata*

IN CHINA, RAIDS BY NOMADIC XIONGNU TRIBES from 177 BCE gravely threatened the Han dynasty's northern borders. In 139 BCE the imperial envoy, Zhang Qian, set out to Central Asia to seek out **possible allies** against the Xiongnu. His epic journey helped scout the way for Chinese expansion as far as Dunhuang, and the foundation of a number of **new Central Asian commanderies** by 104 BCE. Zhang Qian was held captive by the Xiongnu for some years during his journey before he was able to make an escape. Under emperor Wu (141–87 BCE) the Chinese launched **several offensives** against the Xiongnu, particularly in 121 BCE and 119 BCE, after which the frontier was quiet for almost 20 years.

In the Near East, the shrunken and near-helpless **Seleucid realm** (see 170 BCE) was riven by civil wars and prey to interference from the Parthians, the Hasmonaeans, and, increasingly, the Romans. In 142 BCE, the Maccabees succeeded in wresting Jerusalem from Seleucid control and established a **Hasmonaean kingdom**, with Jerusalem as its

capital, under which a Jewish dynasty ruled until Jerusalem was captured by the Romans in 63 BCE.

On the **Iberian Peninsula**, the Romans had conquered most of southern Spain and parts of Portugal (where the Lusitanians vigorously resisted them) by 174 BCE. A revolt by the Lusitanian leader Viriathus from 147 BCE was joined by several Celtiberian tribes in 144 BCE. This rebellion petered out after Viriathus was murdered in 140 BCE. In 133 BCE, Numantia, the main center of the revolt, finally fell to the Romans after a bitter siege. Its population was sold into slavery and Rome was left in control of all of Iberia, except the far north of Spain.

The **Third Punic War** came to an end when Scipio Aemilianus blocked Carthage's harbor then launched a **successful attack** on the city itself in spring 146 BCE. The last Carthaginian defenders died in an inferno in the city's main temple. The defeat of Carthage brought its 118-year struggle against Rome to an end. The Romans burned the whole city and deported its population to prevent any Carthaginian revival.

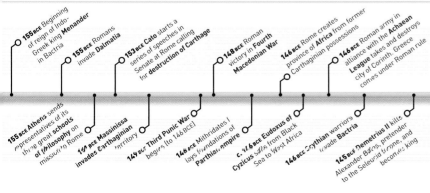

155 BCE Beginning of reign of Indo-Greek king Menander in Bactria

155 BCE Romans invade Dalmatia

153 BCE Cato starts a series of speeches in Senate at Rome calling for **destruction of Carthage**

148 BCE Roman victory in **Fourth Macedonian War**

146 BCE Rome creates province of **Africa** from former Carthaginian possessions

146 BCE Roman army in alliance with the **Achaean League** takes and destroys city of Corinth; Greece comes under Roman rule

141 BCE Han emperor Wudi comes to throne. He makes administrative reforms and expands into central Asia

138 BCE Embassy of Zhang Qian to Xiongnu and Central Asia

135 BCE Slave revolt in Sicily, the **First Servile War** (to 132 BCE)

133 BCE Liberal social reforms by tribune of the plebs **Tiberius Gracchus** lead to his murder

155 BCE Athens sends representatives of its three great **schools of philosophy** on mission to Rome

152 BCE Massinissa invades Carthaginian territory

149 BCE Third Punic War begins (to 146 BCE)

146 BCE Mithridates I lays foundations of **Parthian empire**

c. 146 BCE Eudoxus of Cyzicus sails from Black Sea to West Africa

146 BCE Scythian warriors invade **Bactria**

145 BCE Demetrius II kills Alexander Balas, pretender to the Seleucid throne, and becomes king

141 BCE Parthians control **Mesopotamia**

136 BCE Confucianism becomes state religion of China

133 BCE Romans take Iberian city of Numantia after long siege

131 BCE Roman army sent to Pergamum to quell unrest following **slave revolt** led by Aristonicus, the pretender to the throne

HOWEVER MUCH YOU MAY TRY TO DELAY, YOU ARE FATED TO MEET THE SAME DEATH AS I DID.

Tiberius Gracchus, Roman official, speaking in a dream to his brother Gaius; from an account by Cicero

This 17th-century silk painting from a history of Chinese emperors shows the Emperor Wudi greeting a scholar.

SAKA (SCYTHIAN) TRIBESMEN invaded Punjab, northern India, in **about 125 BCE**. They gradually **occupied more territory**, ending a brief period of Indo-Greek unity (see 200–171 BCE) under the reign of Antialcidas around 110 BCE. Led by **King Maues**, the Sakas took the kingdom of Gandhara and its capital Taxila in about 80 BCE. After Maues died (c. 60 BCE), the Saka kingdom collapsed, but it was revived under his son **Azes I** (r. 58–c. 30 BCE), who conquered much of northwest India. The Sakas held this region until the rise of the Kushan Empire during the 1st century CE.

In southern and central India, the **Satavahanas** began their rise to power after the breakup of the **Mauryan Empire** in the 2nd century BCE (see 200–171 BCE). From his capital in the Deccan, the sixth Satavahana king, **Satakarni II**, extended his sway considerably around 50 BCE, although he and later Satavahana rulers struggled to contain the Saka and Kushan threats from the northwest.

In **Rome**, social turmoil had erupted over the distribution of public land held by the Senate. **Tiberius Gracchus**, who was tribune of the plebs in 133 BCE, sought to ensure that plots of this land would be handed over to poorer families. When the Senate obstructed his plans, he tried to extend his tribunate so that he could pursue his aim. A **mob organized by senators** opposed to the plans beat him to death in the Forum. Tiberius's brother **Gaius became tribune in 123 BCE** and tried to carry on his brother's work. He also reduced the Senate's role in dispensing justice, and pushed through a law to allow the sale of subsidized grain to the poor. In 121 BCE, the Senate declared **Gaius an enemy of the state**, due to his plans to extend Roman citizenship more widely in Italy. He killed himself, and thousands of his political supporters were executed.

Amravati relief carving
This carving depicts the life of the Buddha. It comes from Amravati in Andra Pradesh, southeast India, one of the capitals of the Satavahanas.

IN PALESTINE, THE HASMONEAN KINGDOM (see 146–131 BCE) had continued its expansion until the **fall of Jerusalem** to the Seleucid Antiochus VII in 131 BCE. However, during the reign of John Hyrcanus (r. 134–104 BCE) it recovered much of the ground that had been lost. **Alexander Jannaeus** (r. 103–76 BCE) enlarged the kingdom until it occupied most of modern Israel and the West Bank. After defeats by the Nabataean king Aretas III in 84 BCE and internal strife following Alexander's death, the Hasmoneans were increasingly vulnerable to Roman interference.

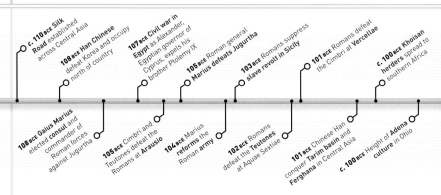

ROMAN MILITARY REFORMS

By the late 2nd century BCE, the Roman army was experiencing difficulty recruiting from the traditional propertied classes. Gaius Marius changed this by opening the army to those who fell below the normal property qualification. The eagle became the universal legionary standard for the first time, and the legions themselves were reformed as a heavy infantry force. From this point onward Roman light infantry and cavalry were organized into "auxiliary" units, which were recruited from noncitizens.

In **North Africa**, the Romans faced a serious challenge when Micipsa, the son of their former ally Massinissa of Numidia (see 170–147 BCE), died in 118 BCE. The Romans ordered the kingdom be divided between Micipsa's nephew **Jugurtha** and his sons. Jugurtha rejected this, killing one cousin and attacking the other, Adherbal, who fled to Rome. After a brief division of Numidia between Jugurtha and Adherbal, Jugurtha renewed his attack on his cousin and the Romans became involved.

YOU DO WELL TO CONSIDER THE OFFICE YOUR OWN, FOR YOU BOUGHT IT.

Julius Caesar's father chastising the future dictator Sulla for having corruptly bought office in 94 BCE; from *Lives* by **Plutarch**

Following several disastrous years of campaigning from 109 BCE, the Romans sent **Quintus Caecilius Metellus**, who captured Jugurtha's strongholds one by one. In **108 BCE, Gaius Marius** replaced Metellus. Finally, trapped in the far west of his territory, Jugurtha was handed to the Romans by his father-in-law **Bocchus of Mauretania**.

In Gaul, two Germanic tribes, the **Cimbri** and **Teutones**, had been defeating the Romans since 107 BCE, notably at Arausio in 105 BCE, where **Roman losses** reached 80,000. Marius took command of the defense against the Germans on his return from North Africa, and in 102 BCE vanquished the Teutones at Aquae Sextiae in Gaul. He next crushed the Cimbri at the **Battle of Vercellae** in 101 BCE. He was rewarded with an unprecedented sixth consulship in 100 BCE.

In China, **Emperor Wudi** (r. 141–87 BCE) strengthened the **Han Empire's** administrative system

---

129 BCE Romans regain control of Pergamum and establish province of Asia

128 BCE Rise of Satavahana dynasty in India

c. 125 BCE Sakas invade Punjab

121 BCE Mithridates II becomes ruler of Parthia

112 BCE Start of war between Romans and Jugurtha of Numidia

126 BCE Anti-Roman revolt in Sardinia

123 BCE In Rome, Gaius Gracchus is elected tribune of the plebs (killed during rioting in 121 BCE)

118 BCE Jugurtha becomes ruler of Numidia

111 BCE Chinese Han dynasty conquers Annam

c. 110 BCE Silk Road established across Central Asia

108 BCE Han Chinese defeat Korea and occupy north of country

107 BCE Civil war in Egypt as Alexander, Egyptian governor of Cyprus, expels his brother Ptolemy IX

105 BCE Roman general Marius defeats Jugurtha

103 BCE Romans suppress slave revolt in Sicily

101 BCE Romans defeat the Cimbri at Vercellae

c. 100 BCE Khoisan herders spread to southern Africa

108 BCE Gaius Marius elected consul and commander of Roman forces against Jugurtha

105 BCE Cimbri and Teutones defeat the Romans at Arausio

104 BCE Marius reforms the Roman army

102 BCE Romans defeat the Teutones at Aquae Sextiae

101 BCE Chinese Han conquer Tarim basin and Ferghana in Central Asia

c. 100 BCE Height of Adena culture in Ohio

Maiden Castle hill-fort in Britain underwent several phases of rebuilding after it was begun around 600 BCE, reaching its final form about 500 years later.

Captured in stone
The Danzante carvings at Monte Alban, Mexico, were once thought to be of dancers, but they are now believed to represent the mutilated bodies of enemies captured in war.

by beginning **civil service examinations**. Official positions for academics had been established in 136 BCE, consolidating the ruling house's stranglehold on the intellectual life of China. In 106 BCE, **Wudi appointed 13 regional inspectors** to monitor the behavior of government officials, raised taxes, and forbade private coin-minting. His armies pushed deep into Central Asia. By 108 BCE, the Han Empire had reached its **largest extent**.

In **Mexico**, the population of **Monte Albán** had reached about 17,000 by around 100 BCE. Monte Albán's control began to reach beyond the immediate vicinity of the **Valley of Oaxaca**, and many large stone platforms and public monuments were built in the city.

AFTER HIS VICTORY AT VERCELLAE, (see 110–91 BCE) Marius became Rome's dominant politician, but the brutal behavior of his ally Saturninus, tribune of the plebs, provoked the Senate. **Political violence** flared, and in 100 BCE Marius had to march an army into Rome. Saturninus was killed in the ensuing riot. As Marius's power waned, discontent rose among Italians without Roman citizenship. In 91 BCE, this erupted into the **Social War**. A protégé of Marius, **Lucius Sulla** (c. 138–78 BCE), took a key role in suppressing the revolt, which was **largely over by 88 BCE**, albeit with some concessions offered by Rome to the rebels.

Sulla was elected consul in 88 BCE. That same year, while waiting to sail with his army to Greece to counter the threat posed by the king of Pontus, **Mithridates VI** (134–63 BCE), Sulla heard that the

Senate had voted to put Marius in charge of the campaign. Enraged, Sulla entered Rome with his troops and seized power. He moved against Mithridates in 87 BCE, and had driven him out of Greece by 84 BCE. Sulla returned to Rome, defeated his remaining opponents (including the aged Marius), and was **appointed dictator** in 82 BCE.

Sulla took savage revenge on the Marians, packed the Senate with his supporters, and curtailed the powers of the tribunes. Anti-Sullan forces regrouped around **Quintus Sertorius**, who had fled to Spain. After Sulla died in 78 BCE, the Senate sent **Pompey** to deal with Sertorius. His military efforts were ineffective; only the assassination of Sertorius allowed Pompey to return victorious to Italy in 71 BCE.

In 73 BCE, a **slave revolt** led by the gladiator **Spartacus** broke out near Naples and grew into the most serious revolt Rome had ever faced. Eventually, the rebel slaves were trapped in southern Italy and defeated by the Roman general **Marcus Licinius Crassus** in 71 BCE.

By the 1st century BCE, the Celtic peoples of southern Britain had started to expand their existing **hill-forts** into *oppida* ("towns") that were defended by extensive fortifications. The greatest *oppida* were formidable obstacles to attackers and some were royal capitals, complete with palaces.

70,000
SPARTACAN REBELS

6,000

spartican rebels crucified

The rebellion by Spartacus
Crassus crucified slaves along the Appian Way, which led to Rome, as a warning to any others who might plan a similar insurrection.

Sacred offering
This 1st-century BCE British Celtic shield was discovered in the Thames River, where it had probably been thrown as an offering to a river god.

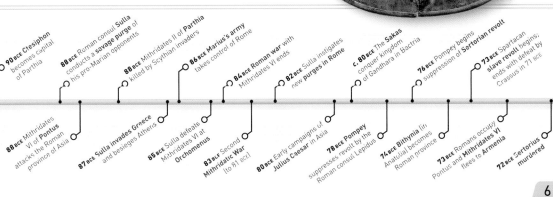

100 BCE Political violence flares in Rome

c. 100 BCE Rise of Aksum (northeast Africa)

99 BCE Serious uprising in eastern China

90 BCE Ctesiphon becomes capital of Parthia

88 BCE Roman consul Sulla conducts a **savage purge** of his pro-Marian opponents

88 BCE Mithridates II of Parthia killed by Scythian invaders

86 BCE Marius's army takes control of Rome

84 BCE Roman war with Mithridates VI ends

82 BCE Sulla instigates new **purges in Rome**

c. 80 BCE The Sakas conquer kingdom of Gandhara in Bactria

76 BCE Pompey begins suppression of **Sartorian revolt**

73 BCE Spartacan slave revolt begins; ends with defeat by Crassus in 71 BCE

c. 100 BCE Celtic hill-forts spread in northwest Europe

91 BCE Social War breaks out in Rome (to 89 BCE)

88 BCE Mithridates VI of Pontus attacks the Roman province of Asia

87 BCE Sulla invades Greece and besieges Athens

85 BCE Sulla defeats Mithridates VI at Orchomenus

83 BCE Second Mithridatic War (to 81 BCE)

80 BCE Early campaigns of Julius Caesar in Asia

78 BCE Pompey suppresses revolt by the Roman consul Lepidus

74 BCE Bithynia (in Anatolia) becomes Roman province

73 BCE Romans occupy Pontus and Mithridates VI flees to Armenia

72 BCE Sertorius murdered

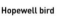

Mound City, Ohio, contains a cluster of more than 20 Hopewell earthwork burial mounds.

A reconstruction of the Roman ramparts at Alesia, where Caesar forced Vercingetorix to surrender.

AFTER POMPEY'S RETURN TO ITALY (see 90–71 BCE), he was elected **consul** for the year, despite still being below the legal minimum age. When war broke out with **Mithridates of Pontus** again, the Romans, under general **Lucullus**, forced Mithridates to retreat to Armenia, which was ruled by his son-in-law Tigranes. However, Lucullus's **troops mutinied in 68 BCE**, and **Pompey** was sent to replace him. Tigranes surrendered and Mithridates retired north of the Black Sea. Having achieved his aim, Pompey entered Syria, where he deposed the last Seleucid king, and then **captured Jerusalem**.

In China, the **Han Dynasty** retreated from modernizing policies under **Zhaodi** (r. 87–74 BCE) and **Xuandi** (r. 74–49 BCE). The **Huo family**, which had dominated the government for decades, was removed from power, and its leading members executed. Government expenditure was cut, and aggressive expeditions

3
THE NUMBER OF **MILITARY TRIUMPHS** AWARDED TO **POMPEY**

in Central Asia were replaced by the establishment of **small, permanent colonies.**

In **Mexico**, the city of **Cuicuilco** in the south of the Valley of Mexico was destroyed by a **volcano** some time in the 1st century BCE. Its disappearance opened the way for **Teotihuacán**, to assert its control over the whole valley and become Mexico's dominant power for more than 500 years.

By the end of the 1st century BCE, the **Adena peoples** of Ohio, in eastern North America, were beginning to develop into the **Hopewell culture.** These people lived by hunting and gathering, but they also built large, elaborate burial mounds for their chieftains.

Hopewell bird
Clay pipes, often in the shape of birds, are one of the most characteristic products of the Hopewell culture.

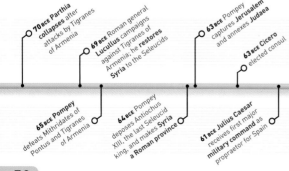

GAIUS JULIUS CAESAR BECAME CONSUL OF ROME for the first time in 59 BCE. Having served a term as governor of Spain, he was popular among the equestrians (wealthy nonsenators), but resistance to him from the Senate (and the obstructiveness of his coconsul Bibulus) led him to join with **Pompey** and **Crassus**, and the three dominated Rome until 53 BCE as the **"First Triumvirate."**

In 58 BCE, Caesar was appointed governor of Narbonensis, the Roman-occupied

area of southern Gaul. He took advantage of the migration of the Germanic **Helvetii** across Gaul toward Italy to cross over the Alps and defeat **Ariovistus**, the Helvetian king. Caesar returned to Rome, but his deputy, Labienus, stayed in Gaul and the following year he pressed on to conquer the **Belgae** of northwestern Gaul. By 55 BCE, Caesar had subdued most of Gaul and had acquired a vast new province for Rome, without ever receiving any approval from the Senate.

In 56 BCE, an **anti-Roman revolt** broke out among the **Veneti** of northern Gaul, apparently supported by the Celtic tribes of Britain. Caesar responded by crossing over to Britain in 55 BCE with two legions. A storm

Caesar at the Louvre
Wearing the laurel wreath of a victorious general, this statue is part of Caesar's cult of personality.

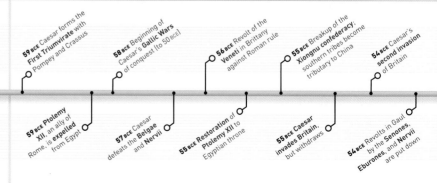

70 BCE Parthia collapses after attacks by Tigranes of Armenia

69 BCE Roman general **Lucullus** campaigns against Tigranes of Armenia; he **restores Syria** to the Seleucids

63 BCE Pompey captures Jerusalem and annexes Judaea

63 BCE Cicero elected consul

65 BCE Pompey defeats Mithridates of Pontus and Tigranes of Armenia

64 BCE Pompey deposes Antiochus XIII, the last Seleucid king, and makes Syria **a Roman province**

61 BCE Julius Caesar receives first major **military command** as propraetor for Spain

59 BCE Caesar forms the **First Triumvirate** with Pompey and Crassus

58 BCE Beginning of Caesar's **Gallic Wars** of conquest (to 50 BCE)

56 BCE Revolt of the **Veneti** in Brittany against Roman rule

55 BCE Breakup of the **Xiongnu confederacy**; southern tribes become tributary to China

54 BCE Caesar's **second invasion** of Britain

59 BCE Ptolemy XII, an ally of Rome, is expelled from Egypt

57 BCE Caesar defeats the **Belgae** and **Nervii**

55 BCE Restoration of **Ptolemy XII** to Egyptian throne

55 BCE Caesar invades Britain, but withdraws

54 BCE Revolts in Gaul, by the **Senones, Eburones,** and **Nervii** are put down

> ## " ...[CAESAR] DREAMED THAT HE WAS FLYING ABOVE THE CLOUDS, AND NOW THAT HE WAS CLASPING THE HAND OF JUPITER. "

Suetonius, recounting Julius Caesar's dream the night before his murder in the Senate House in 44 BCE; from *Lives of the Caesars*

KEY
→ Caesar's movements
✦ Siege
✕ Caesar's victories

prevented the arrival of reinforcements, causing him to retreat, but he returned the next year with five legions (around 30,000 men). The Britons did not resist at first, but later, led by **Cassivelaunus**, chief of the Catuvellauni, they vigorously opposed the Romans all the way to the Thames River. When Cassivelaunus's stronghold at Wheathampstead fell, he sued for peace, and Caesar returned to Rome with hostages and the promise of tribute.

At the end of 54 BCE, shortly after Caesar's second expedition to Britain, another **revolt** in Gaul, this time led by the **Senones**, wiped out much of the Roman force there. After putting down the revolt, Caesar's attentions were diverted to Rome, where **political violence** had resulted in the murder of his former ally Clodius, and where Pompey had been elected sole consul in 52 BCE, rupturing the Triumvirate. Emboldened by the turmoil in Rome, the **Carnutes** revolted in Gaul. They were joined by the Averni, led by **Vercingetorix**, who won several skirmishes against Labienus. Vercingetorix also defeated Caesar himself at Gergovia, but was then trapped at **Alesia** in September 52 BCE. The Romans constructed an encircling rampart around the Gauls' position and managed to beat off a Gaulish relief force. With no hope left, **Vercingetorix surrendered** and was taken back to Rome, where he was strangled in 46 BCE after appearing in Caesar's triumphal parade.

CAESAR ENDED THE GALLIC REVOLT by the end of 50 BCE, but by this point the **Triumvirate** had ended: Pompey's supporters had turned against Caesar, and Crassus had been killed in battle in 53 BCE. The Senate ordered Caesar to disband his army or be declared an enemy of the state. Instead, he **crossed the Rubicon River** into Italy with his troops in 49 BCE. This was illegal, constituting a **declaration of war** against the Senate.

As **Caesar marched toward Rome**, town after town submitted to him. Fearing Caesar, **Pompey** left Rome and **fled to Greece**. Caesar turned first to Spain, where seven legions had declared for Pompey. In August

> ## " THE DIE IS CAST. "

Julius Caesar to his troops on crossing the Rubicon in 49 BCE; from Plutarch's *Parallel Lives*

49 BCE, he forced the Pompeians there to surrender. In December, Caesar set off for Greece in pursuit of Pompey. A military engagement at **Dyrrachium** in July went against Caesar, but he fought back before Pompey's support could grow, and won a resounding victory at **Pharsalus**. Pompey took refuge in Egypt, where he was murdered on the orders of **Ptolemy XIII**, who hoped (in vain) to ingratiate himself with Caesar.

After a short time in Egypt, **Caesar returned to Rome**, where he raised money by confiscating property from the supporters of Pompey. In late 47 BCE, Caesar set sail for Africa, where he defeated a new Pompeian army at **Thapsus** (in modern Tunisia). Pompey's sons Gnaeus and Sextus escaped to Spain to continue the resistance from there, and Caesar annexed the kingdom of King Juba of Mauretania, who had supported them. Caesar then proceeded to Spain, where in

March 45 BCE he defeated Gnaeus Pompey at **Munda**, effectively ending the civil war.

Caesar was now all-powerful. He was made **dictator in 49 BCE**, and in 47 BCE he was given the office for life. Concerns over Caesar's power—in particular, fears that he planned to make himself king—led a group of about 60 conspirators to form around senators **Cassius** and **Marcus Brutus**. They **murdered Caesar** on the **Ides of March** (March 15)

Roman Civil Wars
Caesar won Italy easily, but he had to fight hard to overcome Pompey in his Greek stronghold, and then Pompey's sons and remaining supporters in Africa and Spain.

just before a session of the Senate. If they had hoped to seize power, the conspirators were disappointed: **Mark Antony**, one of Caesar's leading supporters, came to the fore in Rome, while Caesar's great-nephew and adoptive son **Octavian** received widespread support in a bid to take up the mantle of his father.

In India, **Kalinga** (modern Orissa), which had been a client kingdom of the Mauryas (see 200–171 BCE), rose to prominence under **Kharavela** in the mid-1st century BCE. Kharavela expanded Kalinga far to the north and east, conquering the Sunga capital of Pataliputra in Magadha. A strong patron of the Indian religion of Jainism, Kharavela established **trading contacts** as far afield as Southeast Asia.

Murder of Caesar
Conspirators struck Caesar down with daggers. As he fell, Caesar saw Marcus Brutus, a former protégé, and cried out "you too, child?"

53 BCE Expedition of **Crassus** to Parthia ends in disaster, as his army is wiped out at Carrhae in Mesopotamia

52 BCE Vercingetorix leads new Gallic revolt, but is defeated

c. 50 BCE Teotihuacán in Mexico is the largest city in the Americas, with a population of 50,000

50 BCE Construction of a new forum in Rome

c. 50 BCE Kharavela of **Kalinga** carves out an empire in India

49 BCE Caesar crosses the Rubicon into Italy

48 BCE Pompey flees to Egypt and is killed there

48 BCE Herod becomes **ruler of Galilee**, ending the power of the Hasmoneans

47 BCE Caesar defeats Pharnaces of Pontus (son of Mithridates) at **Zela**

47 BCE Caesar appointed **dictator for life**

46 BCE Juba of Numidia commits suicide after defeat at Thapsus; his kingdom is annexed by Rome

46 BCE Julian reform of the calendar; the "Year of Confusion" has 445 days

46 BCE Roman colony of **Carthage founded**; remaining supporters of Pompey defeated at Thapsus

45 BCE Caesar defeats Pompey's sons at **Battle of Munda**

44 BCE Murder of Caesar

44 BCE Cleopatra becomes ruler of Egypt

This 18th-century painting shows Mark Antony fleeing from the battle scene at Actium in 31 BCE. Many of his supporters defected to Octavian's side as a result.

Augustus built a new Forum at Rome, with an imposing new temple to Mars.

IN ROME, THE PERIOD AFTER THE ASSASSINATION of Julius Caesar saw rising tensions between **Mark Antony** and **Octavian**, whom many viewed as Caesar's rightful heir. The two almost came to blows early in 43 BCE, when Octavian marched to raise the **siege of Mutina** (Modena, Italy), where Mark Antony was besieging Decimus Brutus, one of Caesar's assassins. Mark Antony was forced to retreat to Gaul. When the Senate voted to transfer Octavian's legions to Decimus Brutus, Octavian realized he was being sidelined and formed a three-way alliance with Mark Antony and **Marcus Lepidus**, the governor of Transalpine Gaul. This became the **Second Triumvirate**.

The Triumvirate conducted a war against **Cassius and Marcus Brutus**, two more of Caesar's assassins, who had seized much of the territory in the east. In 42 BCE, Mark Antony and Octavian defeated

10
THE NUMBER OF **YEARS** THE **SECOND TRIUMVIRATE** RULED **ROME**

them at **Philippi**, in northern Greece, after which Cassius committed suicide. Three weeks later, they destroyed the remnants of Marcus Brutus's army. Mark Antony stayed in the east until 40 BCE, when he returned to Italy to try to undermine the **growing power of Octavian**. Their two armies refused to fight, and a de facto **division of the Roman world** was

agreed, with Mark Antony ruling the east and Octavian governing the west; Lepidus had to make do with Africa. The **Triumvirate was renewed** in 38 BCE for a further five years, but it was clear that conflict between Octavian and Mark Antony could not long be postponed.

However, Mark Antony was occupied with a **war against the Parthians**, who were allied with remnants of Cassius's army and **attacked Syria** in 39 BCE. In 36 BCE, Mark Antony **invaded Parthia** itself—ostensibly to recover the legionary eagles captured by the Parthians at the **Battle of Carrhae** (see 53 BCE)— and advanced to the capital Phraaspa, but he did not have

Suicide of Cleopatra
This 19th-century painting depicts the death of Cleopatra, who killed herself to avoid being captured by Octavian and taken to Rome.

Battle of Actium
Octavian's fleet outnumbered that of Mark Antony and Cleopatra, with smaller more manoeuvrable ships, and fresher, better trained crews.

sufficient resources to besiege it.
In 33 BCE, the **Triumvirate expired** and Octavian had the Senate declare Mark Antony a **public enemy**. The latter had lost popularity through his relationship with **Cleopatra**, the Egyptian queen, and Octavian quickly rallied public opinion to himself. A fleet was rapidly assembled, and this destroyed Mark Antony's naval force at **Actium**, off western Greece, in September 31 BCE. Mark Antony's land army then **defected** to Octavian, and Antony and Cleopatra **fled to Egypt**, where Octavian caught up with them in the summer of 30 BCE. The Roman warlord and the Egyptian queen both **committed suicide**, and Egypt was annexed to the Roman empire. **Octavian** was now the **unchallenged master** of the whole Roman world.

HAVING DEFEATED HIS ENEMIES, **Octavian** did not take on the title of dictator, as Julius Caesar had. He instead ruled informally as the *princeps*—the **first man of the state**. Having acquired control of Antony's legions, he now had an army of about 500,000 men. He disbanded more than half of these, retaining 28 legions (about 150,000 soldiers), settling the remainder in colonies in Italy and abroad. In 27 BCE, Octavian gave up all his powers, ostensibly **restoring the Republic**. The Senate responded by granting him personal control of Egypt, Gaul, Cilicia, Spain, and Syria. He was also given the title "**Augustus**" and, cementing his position further, was consul each year from 27 to 23 BCE. Over time, the Senate voted Augustus **further powers**, including that of *imperium maius* in 23 BCE, which gave him supreme authority in the provinces he had not previously governed, and the permanent powers of a **tribune of the plebs** in 23 BCE. Although the Senate was, in theory, the supreme authority in Rome, in practice no one could match Augustus's power, and he is seen as the **first Roman emperor**.

North Africa had been a center of strong resistance to both Julius Caesar and Augustus, who settled many army veterans there. In 25 BCE, Augustus gave Mauretania (western North Africa) to **Juba II of Numidia**. Juba, whose wife was the daughter of Mark Antony and Cleopatra, proved a reliable **Roman ally**. Augustus still sent a legion to garrison North Africa, where it stayed for over 300 years.

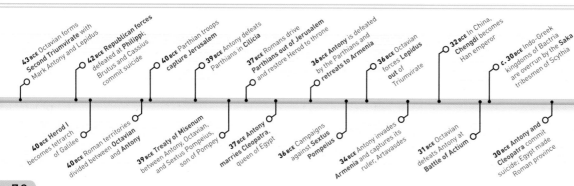

43 BCE Octavian forms Second Triumvirate with Mark Antony and Lepidus

42 BCE Republican forces defeated at Philippi; Brutus and Cassius commit suicide

40 BCE Parthian troops **capture Jerusalem**

39 BCE Antony defeats Parthians in Cilicia

37 BCE Romans drive **Parthians out of Jerusalem** and restore Herod to throne

36 BCE Antony is defeated by the Parthians and **retreats to Armenia**

36 BCE Octavian forces **Lepidus** out of Triumvirate

32 BCE In China, **Chengdi** becomes Han emperor

c. 30 BCE Indo-Greek kingdoms of Bactria are overrun by the **Saka** tribesmen of Scythia

27 BCE Octavian takes the title **Augustus**, becoming in effect the **first Roman emperor**

26–19 BCE Cantabrians of **northern Spain revolt** against Roman rule

40 BCE Herod I becomes tetrarch of Galilee

40 BCE Roman territories divided between **Octavian** and **Antony**

39 BCE Treaty of Misenum between Antony, Octavian, and Sextus Pompeius, son of Pompey

37 BCE Antony **marries Cleopatra**, queen of Egypt

36 BCE Campaigns against **Sextus Pompeius**

34 BCE Antony invades **Armenia** and captures its ruler, Artavasdes

31 BCE Octavian defeats Antony at **Battle of Actium**

30 BCE Antony and Cleopatra commit suicide; Egypt made Roman province

27 BCE Marcus Agrippa completes Roman conquest of northern Spain

25–24 BCE Aelius Gallus fails to conquer Arabia Felix (Yemen) for Rome

> **THOSE WHO SLEW MY FATHER I DROVE INTO EXILE… AND… DEFEATED THEM IN BATTLE.**

Augustus, from the *Res Gestae Divi Augusti*, the testament of Augustus, in Ankara, Turkey

La Maison Carrée, in Nîmes, southern France, is one of the finest surviving Roman temples. It was built around 16 BCE by Marcus Vipsanius Agrippa.

In western Asia, the ruler of Galilee, **Herod I**, was allowed to retain his position by **Octavian**, even though he had supported Mark Antony. He was even **given extra territories**, including parts of Syria and Gaza. Herod had been appointed by Mark Antony in 42 BCE, and by 37 BCE he had conquered the remains of the **Hasmonean kingdom** (see 146–131 BCE). Herod remained a reliable **ally of Rome** until his death in 4 BCE.

Emperor Augustus
Augustus, seen here dressed as a priest, acquired the title of pontifex maximus (chief priest) on the death of Lepidus in 12 BCE.

> **HE COULD JUSTLY BOAST THAT HE HAD FOUND IT BUILT OF BRICK AND LEFT IT IN MARBLE.**

Suetonius, on Augustus's embellishment of the city of Rome; from *Lives of the Caesars*

AUGUSTUS'S MILITARY AND POLITICAL SUCCESSES had relied largely on the abilities of **Marcus Vipsanius Agrippa**, who rose from a minor family to become consul in 37, 28, and 27 BCE. After Agrippa had married Augustus's daughter Julia, he received many promotions, including the power of a tribune of the plebs in 18 BCE. Augustus's own appointed heir had died in 25 BCE, so he **adopted Agrippa's children**, renaming them **Gaius** and **Lucius Caesar**. Agrippa seemed likely to succeed Augustus, but in 12 BCE he died unexpectedly, throwing open the **question of succession**.

By threatening to **invade Parthia** in 20 BCE, Augustus had engineered the return of legionary standards captured by the Parthians at **Carrhae** (see 53 BCE). In 16 BCE, the Roman governor of Macedonia began pushing toward the River Danube, and from 12 BCE **Tiberius**, Augustus's stepson, the son of his second wife Livia, moved north from Illyria to create the Roman province of **Pannonia** (modern Austria and Hungary). Tiberius's brother **Drusus** pushed Roman control across the Rhine toward the Elbe between 12 and 9 BCE, when he died. Around this time, the Romans annexed the provinces of **Raetia** (in modern Switzerland) and **Noricum** (between the Alps and the Danube), **moving the empire's frontiers** almost to a line along the Rhine and the Danube.

Supporters of Tiberius, now the most **high-profile general**, tried to have him displace Lucius and Gaius Caesar as Augustus's heir. Augustus himself did little to resolve the question of succession.

ROMAN LITERATURE AT THE TIME OF AUGUSTUS

The end of the Republic and the reign of Augustus saw a golden age in Latin literature. The orator Cicero and the historian Sallust marked the height of late Republican literature. After Augustus's rise to power, the poets Virgil (right; 70–19 BCE), author of the *Eclogues* and the epic poem *The Aeneid*, and Horace (65–8 BCE), author of the *Odes* and *Carmen Saeculare*, both flourished under the patronage of Maecenas, a close confidant of Augustus.

BY 9 BCE, DRUSUS HAD DEFEATED THE MAIN GERMAN TRIBES and had reached the Elbe River. After his death, Augustus appointed **Tiberius** to replace him. Tiberius won a series of victories in 8 BCE, but then mysteriously **resigned his offices** and went into exile in Rhodes. This left Gaius and Lucius Caesar (both underage) as **heirs apparent** to the Roman Empire.

In China, the **reign of Yuandi** (48–33 BCE) saw the economic retrenchment begun under **Xuandi** (see 70–61 BCE) continue. Some semi-independent kingdoms that the early Han had suppressed began to reappear. Yuandi and his successors **Chengdi** (r. 33–7 BCE) and **Aidi** (r. 7–1 BCE) also created numerous **marquisates**, many of which were granted to the sons of the new kings, weakening the state's central control. Chengdi lacked a **male heir**, resulting in

Khazneh at Petra
The Khazneh is one of Petra's finest monuments. Carved out of a sheer cliff-face, it was probably a royal tomb, perhaps of Aretas IV (c. 9 BCE–40 CE).

the succession of his half-nephew Aidi in 7 BCE. This caused **dissent** among nobles whose candidates for the throne had been overlooked.

The **Nabataean kingdom** of northern Arabia grew rich on its control of the spice trade from southern Arabia, reaching its height in the mid-1st century BCE under **Malichos I** (c. 59–c. 30 BCE). It then faced a growing threat on its northern borders from **Herod I**. A disputed succession in 9/8 BCE between **Aretas IV** and his chief minister **Syllaeus** led the Romans to take an interest in the area. An expedition led by Gaius, grandson of Augustus, may even have briefly annexed Nabataea in 3–1 BCE, but the Romans pulled back, allowing Nabataea another century of independence.

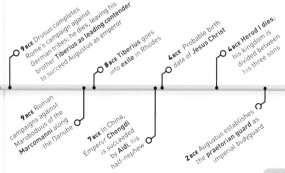

25 BCE Doors to the **Temple of Janus** in Rome are **closed**, signifying peace throughout the Roman world

25 BCE Juba II made king of **Mauretania** by Augustus

c. 25 BCE Buddhist canon written down for the first time in Sri Lanka

23 BCE Romans invade the **Meroitic kingdom** (modern Sudan)

20 BCE Rome and Parthia make peace; the Roman standards captured at the Battle of Carrhae are returned

19 BCE Herod I **rebuilds the temple** at Jerusalem

18 BCE Agrippa, close associate of Augustus, is given the power of a **tribune of the plebs**

15 BCE Roman conquest of **Raetia and Noricum**

14 BCE Major **peasant uprising** in China

12 BCE Death of Agrippa, likely successor to Augustus, opens up question of who will succeed Augustus

12–9 BCE Roman **conquest of Germany** as far as the Elbe

10 BCE Herod I completes building of seaport at **Caesarea**

9 BCE Drusus completes Rome's campaign against German tribes; he dies, leaving his brother **Tiberius as leading contender** to succeed Augustus as emperor

9 BCE Roman campaigns against Maroboduus of the **Marcomanni** along the Danube

8 BCE Tiberius goes into **exile** in Rhodes

7 BCE In China, Emperor **Chengdi** is succeeded by **Aidi**, his half-nephew

4 BCE Probable birth date of **Jesus Christ**

4 BCE Herod I dies; his kingdom is divided between his three sons

2 BCE Augustus establishes the **praetorian guard** as imperial bodyguard

THE RISE OF THE
ROMAN EMPIRE

FROM CITY, TO REPUBLIC, TO DOMINANT EUROPEAN EMPIRE

Soon after its foundation in 753 BCE, the city of Rome began fighting its neighbors to gain new territory. Gradually, the Romans became entangled in campaigns in the Italian Peninsula and beyond. By the 1st century CE, the Roman Empire had become the largest Europe had ever seen.

The early growth of Roman territories was slow, with wars against neighbors often threatening the survival of Rome itself. By 290 BCE the Romans dominated central Italy and began expanding into the Italian Peninsula. Rivalry with Carthage led to the three Punic Wars between 264 and 146 BCE, but victories brought the acquisition of territory in Sicily, Sardinia, Spain, and then North Africa itself.

In the early 2nd century BCE the Romans fought campaigns in the Balkans, leading to the annexation of most of Greece in 146 BCE. The pace of acquisition quickened in the later years of the Republic, as generals competed for political power and used their military successes to bolster their position in Rome. It was in this period that Pompey annexed Syria and Julius Caesar conquered much of Gaul, between 58 and 50 BCE. The collapse of the Roman Republic and the accession of the first emperor, Augustus, in 27 BCE did not end the empire's expansion. The quest for security along the existing frontiers resulted in the frontiers being pushed even farther forward. Rome's final large-scale acquisitions were made in the reigns of Claudius, who oversaw the invasion of Britain in 43 CE, and Trajan, who conquered new provinces in Dacia (modern Romania) and Mesopotamia between 106 and 117 CE.

TARRACO

LUSITANIA

Olisipo
Emerita Augusta
Toletu

BAETIC

Tingis

MAURETANI
TINGITANA

" TO THE **ROMANS** I SET **NO BOUNDARIES** IN TIME OR SPACE. "

Virgil, Roman poet (70–19 BCE), the god Jupiter, prophesying the future greatness of Rome, from the *Aeneid*

7:1 **Roman population**
Around 1 CE, the Roman Empire contained about one-seventh of the world's population— 45 million out of 300 million people.

4.5 MILLION

45 MILLION

An empire of noncitizens
In 1 CE, only a tenth of the Roman population were full citizens. The rest were slaves or had limited civic rights.

1,900,000 mi²
117 CE

1,000,000 mi²
25 BCE

Expanding empire
Between the accession of Augustus and the death of Trajan, the Roman Empire almost doubled in size, acquiring vast new territories in northwestern Europe and western Asia.

KEY
Roman territory

100 CE
By around 100 CE, the Mediterranean had become a Roman "lake," and the acquisition of territories in northwest and Central Europe had brought the northern Roman frontier as far as the Rhine and the Danube.

A GROWING EMPIRE
It took the Romans nearly 500 years to complete the conquest of Italy, but only half that time to enlarge their territories to include Spain, Gaul, parts of Germany, most of the Balkans, much of North Africa, and large parts of western Asia. Over the following 100 years they acquired Morocco, Britain, and Dacia, and made small advances into western Asia, but the empire began to contract after 250 CE.

240 BCE The Romans dominated most of the Italian Peninsula. Victory in the First Punic War (264–241 BCE) brought new territory in Sicily, but the Romans still faced resistance to their rule in northern Italy.

60,000
MILES
THE APPROXIMATE LENGTH OF THE **ROMAN FRONTIERS** AT THEIR **MAXIMUM EXTENT**

Caledonia

North Sea

Baltic Sea

Eboracum

Lindum

Camulodunum

BRITANNIA

Londinium

Colonia Agrippina

Germania

Burgundians

GERMANIA INFERIOR

Augusta Treverorum

Durocortorum

Mogontiacum

LUGDUNENSIS

BELGICA

GERMANIA SUPERIOR

Marcomanni

Quadi

Vindobona

Carnuntum

RAETIA

NORICUM

Brigetio

Virunun

Aquineum

MOSIA INFERIOR

Sarmatians

Lugdunum

AQUITANIA

Aquileia

PANNONIA SUPERIOR

PANNONIA INFERIOR

Apulum

BOSPORAN KINGDOM

ALPS GRAIAE ET POENINAE

Mediolanum

ALPS COTTIAE

Roxolani

DACIA

Durostorum

Black Sea

NARBONESIS

Ravenna

DALMATIA

Sirmium

Viminacium

Trapezus

ALPS MARITIMAE

Massilia

Rome

ITALIA

MODESIA SUPERIOR

Philippopolis

Byzantium

BITHYNIA ET PONTUS

Ancyra

CAPPADOCIA

Samosata

SIS

Corsica

Aleria

Thessalonica

THRACIA

ASIA

GALATIA

Zeugma

Baleares

Sardinia

EPIRUS

MACEDONIA

Delphi

Ephesus

Miletus

LYCIA

CILLCIA

Antioch

alentia

Carales

Messana

Corinth

Athens

Cyprus

SYRIA

arthago Nova

Utica

Mediterranean Sea

Sicilia

ACHAIA

Syracuse

Sparta

Creta

Damascus

MAURETANIA AESARIENSIS

Carthage

Thugga

Tyrus

JUDEA

Jerusalem

Bostra

Sabratha

Leptis Magna

Ptolemais

Alexandria

Petra

ARABIA

Cyrene

Memphis

AFRICA

CYRENE ET CRETA

Sahara

AEGYPTUS

Red Sea

200 BCE The Roman defeat of Carthage in the Second Punic War brought new possessions in Spain and Sardinia. By 200 BCE, a toehold had also been gained in northwestern Greece.

120 BCE Most of Spain had fallen into Roman possession, as well as Carthaginian territory in North Africa. Greece and parts of western Anatolia were also acquired.

60 BCE New North African territories were gained in 96 BCE, and in 63 BCE Syria and parts of Palestine were annexed. The frontiers in Anatolia were also pushed forward.

14 CE The Roman borders had expanded to include Gaul beyond the Alps, as well as new provinces in Raetia and Noricum (Switzerland, south Germany, and Austria), Pannonia (Hungary), and Egypt.

" QUINCTILIUS VARUS, GIVE ME BACK MY LEGIONS. "

Emperor Augustus, on hearing of the Roman defeat in the Teutoberg Forest, 9 CE

WANG MANG WAS IN CHARGE OF BOTH THE CHINESE ARMY and the government under **Emperor Ping Di** (r. 1 BCE–6 CE). He strengthened his influence by marrying his daughter to the young emperor. On Ping Di's death, many of the

28

THE NUMBER OF DIFFERENT **TYPES** OF **COIN** ISSUED BY **WANG MANG**

nobility rejected Wang Mang's choice of successor and rose up in **revolt**. Wang Mang easily put them down, and in 9 he took the title of **first Xin emperor**. He reissued the currency, forbade the selling of private slaves, reorganized the commanderies

(China's administrative regions), and reimposed several state monopolies. Serious floods on the Yellow River in 4–11 led to **famine and revolts** in rural areas. In 23, the peasant rebels called the "**Red Eyebrows**" joined forces with Han loyalists and overwhelmed Wang Mang's armies. When the capital Chang'an fell, **Gengshi** became the first emperor of the **restored Han dynasty**. One of his first acts was to make Luoyang his capital.

In Europe, **Tiberius** (see 20–2 BCE) returned to Germany in 4 to subdue the tribes there. The **Marcomanni resisted**, but a planned attack on them in 6 was postponed because of a revolt in Pannonia, which took three years to quell. A new Roman commander, **Quinctilius Varus**, was sent to Germany, but his **corrupt rule** angered the German tribes. In 9, Varus was ambushed in the **Teutoberg Forest**, and his three legions were annihilated. Augustus then ordered a **withdrawal to the Rhine**, where the Roman frontier remained for the next 400 years.

Consolidating ruler
Rather than extending Roman territory through foreign conquests, Tiberius concentrated on strengthening the existing empire.

When Emperor Augustus (see 20–2 BCE) died in 14, **Tiberius** was his obvious heir (Lucius and Gaius Caesar having died). Tiberius already possessed most of Augustus's powers and had the **loyalty of the Praetorian Guard**—the elite army unit based in Rome, which Augustus had established. Although there were moves in the senate to **restore the Republic**, Tiberius rapidly squashed them. His reign (to 37) was quiet at home. **Germanicus**, Tiberius's nephew, campaigned extensively in Germany up to 16, but his efforts led to no permanent reacquisition of territory beyond the Rhine and he died of poisoning in 19. After Drusus, Tiberius's son, died in 23, the **emperor tired of public life** and retired to the island of Capri, off Naples. **Sejanus**, head of the Praetorian

Guard, took day-to-day power, but his rule was tyrannical and in 31 Tiberius suddenly reasserted himself and had Sejanus executed.

Ponte di Tiberio, Rimini, Italy
Completed in the reign of Tiberius, this bridge carried the Via Aemilia (which ran from Riminia to Piacenza) across the Marecchia River.

GENGSHI'S REIGN AS CHINESE EMPEROR WAS SHORT. He alienated the Red Eyebrows and angered many of China's nobility and bureaucrats by moving the capital from Luoyang back to **Chang'an**. Much of China had already slipped from Gengshi's grasp by 25, when Chang'an was sacked by the Red Eyebrows. The emperor was deposed and replaced by **Guang Wudi** (25–57), who is regarded as the first **Eastern Han** emperor. The new ruler had first to face a **civil war**; by 27, he had defeated the Red Eyebrows, but it took him until 36 to overcome the last of the **warlords** who opposed him. In 37, he abolished all except three of the kingdoms that had sprung up

KEY

- Qin China in 206 BCE
- Territory added by Former Han Dynasty 206 BCE–9 CE
- — Great Wall under the Han

Chinese Han Empire
When Guang Wudi began the Eastern Han Dynasty in 25, Chinese control extended deep into Central Asia. Much of this territory had been won under the Western Han Dynasty.

Ponte di Tiberio, Rimini, Italy

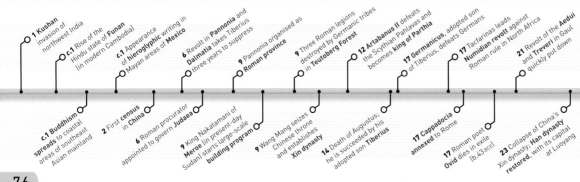

- **1 Kushan** invasion of northwest India
- **c.1** Rise of the Hindu state of **Funan** (in modern Cambodia)
- **c.1** Appearance of **hieroglyphic** writing in Mayan areas of **Mexico**
- **6** Revolt in **Pannonia** and **Dalmatia** takes Tiberius three years to suppress
- **9** Pannonia organised as **Roman province**
- **9** Three Roman legions destroyed by Germanic tribes in **Teutoberg Forest**
- **12 Artabanus II** defeats the Scythian Pahlavas and becomes **king of Parthia**
- **17 Germanicus**, adopted son of Tiberius, defeats Germans
- **17** Tacfarinas leads **Numidian revolt** against Roman rule in North Africa
- **21** Revolt of the **Aedui** and **Treveri** in Gaul quickly put down
- **26** Tiberius retires to Capri, leaving Sejanus, the prefect of the **Praetorian Guard**, in charge in Rome

- **c.1 Buddhism spreads** to coastal areas of southeast Asian mainland
- **2** First **census** in China
- **6** Roman procurator appointed to govern **Judaea**
- **9** King Nakatamani of **Meroe** (in present-day Sudan) starts large-scale **building program**
- **9** Wang Mang seizes Chinese throne and establishes **Xin dynasty**
- **14** Death of Augustus; he is succeeded by his adopted son **Tiberius**
- **17 Cappadocia annexed** to Rome
- **17** Roman poet **Ovid dies in exile** (b.43 BCE)
- **23** Collapse of China's Xin dynasty; **Han dynasty restored**, with its capital at Luoyang
- **26 Pontius Pilate** becomes procurator of Judaea
- **c.33 Crucifixion** of **Jesus Christ**

This ornamental brick from China's Eastern Han period shows a procession that includes horse-drawn carriages.

JESUS CHRIST (c. 4 BCE–33 CE)

Jesus, a carpenter from Nazareth, began his ministry in his early 30s. He taught in the Jewish tradition, calling for the reform of the Temple and for the love of one's neighbour to take precedence over the strict observance of religious law. Jesus gathered a group of twelve disciples around him, but was targeted by Jewish conservatives afraid of his growing influence. In 33, the Roman authorities in Judaea executed Jesus by crucifixion, but the disciples, convinced that Jesus had risen from the dead, continued his teaching.

under his predecessors, and reinstated Luoyang as the capital. He faced renewed tension with the **Xiongnu** on China's northern frontier, but failed to take advantage of their split into two **rival chiefdoms** in 49.

The **Roman Empire** once again faced an **unclear succession** at the death of Tiberius in 37. He had named two heirs, but Gemellus was soon pushed aside because Gaius, nicknamed **Caligula** ("little boots"), was popular with the senate and the army. Caligula's behavior as emperor became increasingly erratic—he had Gemellus executed, and had many of Tiberius's supporters killed. He also had his sister's husband—his heir apparent—condemned to death. After visiting the Rhineland

legions in 39, Caligula marched them to the coast opposite Britain to launch an invasion; when they got there, he merely had them collect seashells along the beach.

Independent **Jewish kingdoms** in Palestine **collapsed** as Roman power grew, creating a powerful ferment of religious change. **John the Baptist** preached in the 20s, followed in around 30 by a new preacher, **Jesus**. After Jesus's death in 33, his disciples began to spread his message more widely. By around 50, communities of Christians, as Jesus's followers were known, would be established throughout Western Asia, with particularly large groups in Antioch and the first appearance of **Christians in Rome**.

IN INDIA, GROUPS OF YUEZHI NOMADS occupying land in Bactria united under Kujula Kadphises (30–80), who founded the **Kushan Empire** and conquered parts of Gandhara. Although few details of Kujula's reign are known, he **minted coins** in imitation of both Greek and Roman models, demonstrating that Bactria and northwestern India remained very much a **cultural crossroads**.

In northwestern Europe, a group of disgruntled officers of Rome's Praetorian Guard **assassinated Caligula** in January 41, tired of his cruel and irrational behavior (see 24–40). In 43, the new emperor, **Claudius** (r. 41–54), sent an invasion force of four legions led by **Aulus Plautius**, governor of Pannonia, to **conquer Britain**. The Romans landed unopposed at Richborough, pushed on to London, and then captured

Christian catacomb, Rome
At first, Roman Christians did not have their own cemeteries. Later, they buried their dead in underground complexes called catacombs.

Colchester, the capital of the principal British resistance leader, **Caractacus**. Claudius himself made a brief appearance at the fall of Colchester, before returning to Rome to bask in the glory of having **acquired a new province**. In 47, the Romans paused briefly in their conquest of Britain, having reached a line roughly between the Humber River in the east and the Severn River in the west. They began **establishing legionary fortresses** in their new province, including at Exeter and Lincoln. Aulus Plautius's replacement, **Ostorius Scapula** invaded Wales, where Caractacus was continuing the resistance. In 50, he defeated an army of Silurian and Ordovician tribesmen, and Caractacus fled to the imagined safety of the Brigantes tribe in northern England. However, the Brigantian queen, **Cartimandua**, handed Caractacus over to the Romans, and Roman Britain remained relatively trouble free during the following decade.

The 40s saw a struggle in the early **Christian community** between those who wanted to remain within the Jewish tradition and those, led by **Paul**, who favored the inclusion of gentiles (non-Jews) in the Christian church. Paul began a series of **missionary journeys** in 46 which led him through Anatolia and Greece to Rome, where he was **martyred** around 20 years later. A charismatic preacher, Paul also wrote a powerful series of **epistles** (letters) to various fledgling Christian groups. In appealing to a wider

EMPEROR CLAUDIUS (10 BCE–54 CE)

Caligula's uncle, Claudius, was an unlikely candidate for Roman emperor. However, he turned out to be intelligent and forceful, putting down two revolts in 42, after which he executed more than 300 senators. He was unfortunate in his choice of wives: he had his wife Messalina executed after she had an affair, and her successor Agrippina (Caligula's sister) is reputed to have poisoned him.

group than the Jews within the Roman empire, Paul ensured that **Christianity spread** sufficiently to help it weather the storms of **persecution** that began under the Emperor Nero in 64. By the late 4th century, Christianity would be the **majority religion** within the Roman Empire.

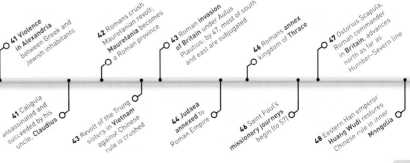

35 Artabanus III of Persia **overthrown** by his cousin, with support of Rome

36 Artabanus III restored as king of **Parthia**

37 Tiberius dies and is succeeded by his great nephew **Caligula**

39 Caligula deposes Herod Antipas as Tetrarch of Galilee and appoints **Herod Agrippa** in his place

40 King Ptolemy of Mauretania assassinated; the **Mauretanians revolt** against Roman rule

c. 40 South American **Arawak** peoples migrate down Orinoco River and settle in Caribbean

41 Violence in Alexandria between Greek and Jewish inhabitants

41 Caligula assassinated and succeeded by his uncle, **Claudius**

42 Romans crush Mauretanian revolt; **Mauretania** becomes a Roman province

43 Revolt of the Trung sisters in **Vietnam** against Chinese rule is crushed

43 Roman **invasion of Britain** under Aulus Plautius; by 47, most of south and east are subjugated

44 Judaea annexed to Roman Empire

46 Romans **annex** kingdom of **Thrace**

46 Saint Paul's **missionary journeys** begin (to 57)

47 Ostorius Scapula, Roman commander in **Britain**, advances north as far as Humber-Severn line

48 Eastern Han emperor **Huang Wudi** restores Chinese rule in inner **Mongolia**

The ruins at Masada, the last outpost of the Jewish revolt against the Romans, which began in 66.

70 THOUSAND

THE NUMBER OF PEOPLE **KILLED** BY **BOUDICCA'S ARMY** DURING THE **ICENI REVOLT**

WHEN CLAUDIUS DIED IN 54, the Roman imperial throne fell to **Nero** (37–68), his adopted son and son-in-law. The young emperor's reign began well when he promised the senate he would avoid making any arbitrary measures. However, the first sign of Nero's tyranny surfaced in 59, when he had his mother **Agrippina** (15–59) murdered. In 62, a new praetorian prefect (commander of the imperial bodyguard), **Tigellinus** (c. 10–69), took office. Tigellinus pandered to the less desirable side of Nero's personality, whose rule became increasingly despotic. Following a **fire** that destroyed much of Rome in 64, Nero is said to have taken terrible retribution on Rome's small Christian population, who proved convenient scapegoats. Later, during the reconstruction of Rome, Nero alienated senators by seizing their land to build himself a new palace. He also ordered additional taxes in Palestine, which sparked a **Jewish revolt** in 66.

In **Britain**, the Romans faced a serious **Iceni** revolt in 60. When the king of the Iceni died, he left his lands to his queen, **Boudicca**. The revolt was triggered when the Roman procurator (chief financial official) ruled that Boudicca could not inherit her lands, and that they would be annexed by Rome. Boudicca raised an army and marched on Camulodunum (Colchester). **Suetonius Paulinus**, the governor of Britain, was away on campaign in Wales, and by the time he returned, Camulodunum had been sacked by the Iceni. The rebels then burned Londinium (London) and Verulamium (St. Albans) before they were finally trapped and defeated by Paulinus. It is said the Iceni lost 80,000 warriors and Boudicca herself was captured, though she died, possibly poisoned, soon after.

Boudicca
This statue of Boudicca stands outside the Houses of Parliament in London, a city that the Iceni queen razed to the ground.

IN THE EAST, Rome faced further troubles with **Parthia** over the border region of **Armenia**, where the Parthian king had installed his own candidate, **Tiridates**, as king in 53. A Roman force invaded Armenia in 58, took its capital cities of Artaxata and Tigranocerta and put in place a pro-Roman king, **Tigranes VI**. His ill-advised invasion of a Parthian ally in 61 led to his removal, and Tiridates was restored. A new Roman army was then roundly beaten by the Parthians in 62, and only a Roman push into Armenia the following year ended the war.

Tiridates was allowed to keep the throne, as long as he travelled to Rome to seek Nero's approval, which he eventually did in 66.

Nero's position as emperor became increasingly precarious when **Calpurnius Piso** led a conspiracy in 65, which prompted Nero to order further executions, including those of many senators. In early 68, a revolt broke out, led by **Gaius Julius Vindex**, governor of Gallia Lugdunensis. Shortly after the revolt of Vindex, the legion based in Spain proclaimed the governor, **Sulpicius Galba**, as emperor. Vindex's revolt was put down by **Verginius Rufus**, the governor of Germany, but **Nero** panicked and **committed suicide**, believing Rufus would be the next to try to claim his throne.

After Nero's suicide, four men became emperor in rapid succession, making 69 the **"Year of the Four Emperors."** First, the praetorian guard recognized **Galba** (3 BCE–69 CE) as emperor, but he made himself unpopular by refusing to give the praetorians the donative, a customary bonus payable on the accession of a new emperor. In January 69, the governor of Upper Germany, **Aulus Vitellius**, revolted, and one of Galba's former supporters, **Salvius Otho** (32–69), angered when Galba recognized another senator as his heir, had the emperor murdered and took the throne. In April 69, the armies of Otho and Vitellius clashed at Bedriacum near Cremona in northern Italy, and the Vitellian army won. Otho committed suicide, but Vitellius soon faced a further conspiracy when T. Flavius Vespasianus

960
COMMITED SUICIDE

7
Survivors

Roman invasion
When the Romans finally breached the walls of Masada, all except seven defenders committed suicide rather than fall into Roman hands.

51 Romans capture **Caractacus**, leader of the British resistance

52 Saint Paul begins spreading Christianity in Greece

57 An ambassador from Japan arrives at the **Han capital** of Luoyang

59 Suetonius Paulinus becomes governor of Britain

c. 60 Mark begins writing the first of the **gospels** recounting the life of Jesus Christ

c. 60 Kushans under Kujula Kadphises advance into northern India, starting the **Kushan Empire**

64 Great **Fire of Rome**; Nero blames the Christians and many are martyred

c. 65 Buddhism reaches China

53 Vologases of Parthia puts his brother **Tiridates** on the throne of Armenia, fueling tensions with Rome

54 Roman emperor **Claudius** is murdered and succeeded by his stepson **Nero**

58 Armenia becomes a Roman protectorate

60 Nero sends an expedition to explore **Meroe** on the east bank of the Nile

60 The **Iceni revolt against the Romans** in Britain

63 Peace of Rhandeia, between Rome and Parthia; **Tiridates** is returned to the Armenian throne

66–70 Jewish revolt against Roman rule

A fresco from Pompei—many of Pompei's elaborate frescoes survived for nearly 2,000 years buried under the ash.

Jewish revolts between 66 and 74

Although the Jewish rebels of 66 initially managed to gain control of a large part of Palestine, by 69 they had lost control of all but the area around Jerusalem.

KEY

- ◼ Area of major revolt 66
- — Area of revolt in 69
- ✿ Siege
- ✕ Jewish victory

(**Vespasian**) (9–79)—the general in charge of suppressing the Jewish revolt—set himself up as yet another rival emperor. The whole of the East and the Balkans defected immediately to Vespasian. At a second **battle near Cremona** in October, Vitellius's forces were crushed. By December Vespasian's army had taken Rome and Vitellius was executed shortly afterward. Rome had an **unchallenged ruler** once again.

Vespasian moved quickly to reestablish the loyalty of the army, dismissing Vitellius's praetorian guard and recruiting another. He also had to face a serious revolt along the Rhine, where **Julius Civilis**, a noble of the Batavian people, joined forces with dissident legionaries and almost established an independent **Gallic empire**.

Judaea had been under direct Roman rule since the death of King Agrippa I in 44. Foreign rule and Roman insensitivity toward

Jewish laws caused great discontent. In 60, the rebuilding of the Temple that Herod had ordered built decades before was finished, and 20,000 unemployed workmen added to the rising tension. The Roman procurator of Judaea aggravated these feelings with his **heavy-handed rule**, and in 66 an uprising broke out. Although the commanders of the uprising were competent, it lacked political leadership and the Jewish strongholds were gradually reduced, first by Vespasian and then by his son Titus (39–81). In 70, **Jerusalem** came under siege, and in late August the city fell and the Temple was destroyed. Perhaps as many as 200,000 people died, many sacred Jewish treasures were taken to Rome, and thousands of Jews were enslaved. Resistance continued at **Masada** until 74, when it fell after a two-year siege.

BY THE MID-70S, CIVILIS'S REVOLT had fizzled out and the rest of Vespasian's reign was largely peaceful. With a reputation for frugality, he restored the empire's finances, imposing levies on a number of provinces, including Egypt. By the time he died in 79, **stability had been restored** to such an extent that the succession of his eldest son, **Titus** (r. 79–81), was unopposed.

Two months after the accession of Titus as Roman emperor, on August 25, 79 the city of **Pompeii**, near modern Naples, was

destroyed by a volcanic eruption. Showers of ash came raining down from **Vesuvius**, and those who did not escape in time were overwhelmed by the pyroclastic flow (a fast-moving mass of hot gases, ash, and debris) from the volcano. Perhaps a tenth of the population of 20,000 died, including the naturalist Pliny the Elder, who was commanding a naval unit nearby and perished in a failed rescue attempt.

In **Britain**, the Roman-controlled area continued to expand, with governor Petillius Cerialis (71–74) occupying the northern English kingdom of **Brigantia**. Julius Frontinus (74–77) completed the subjugation of Wales, defeating the Silures, but it was left to Julius Agricola (77–83/4) to send Roman armies

Figure from Pompeii
The bodies of those who died in the Pompeii eruption were coated in volcanic ash, which then solidified, leaving their outlines behind.

far into Scotland, until a final defeat of the Caledonii at **Mons Graupius** (possibly near Aberdeen) made it likely that all of Scotland would be annexed. But emperor **Domitian** (81–96) was facing trouble on the Danube and a legion was withdrawn from Britain around 86, leaving an insufficient force to garrison northern Scotland, which was evacuated.

Domitian had managed to fend off the threat from the **Sarmatians, Marcomanni, and Quadi** along the **Danube** by 84, but war then erupted with the **Dacians** (of modern Romania) who crossed the Danube and killed the governor of Roman Moesia. By 86, Domitian had defeated the Dacians, under their new king, **Decebalus**. Dacia was not occupied by Rome, leaving Decebalus in place to cause the Romans further trouble.

KEY

- ◼ Atrebates, absorbed 70s
- ▦ Iceni, conquered 60–61
- ◼ Brigantes, conquered 69–74
- → Roman expansion 43–47
- → Roman expansion 47–50
- → Roman expansion 69–74
- → Roman expansion 79–84

Romans in Britain
By 74, Roman legions had reached the north of England. They then pushed north into Scotland until 83.

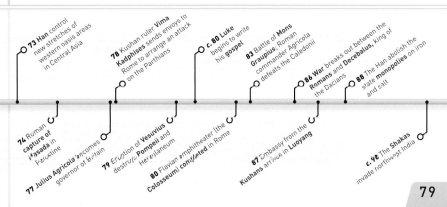

67 Vespasian, commander of the Danubian legions, begins suppression of Jewish revolt, retaking Galilee

68 Emperor **Nero** commits suicide

69 Year of the **Four Emperors**; **Vespasian** becomes emperor

69 Romans defeat the **Garmantians** in North Africa

70 The **Jewish revolt is ended**

73 Han control new stretches of western oasis areas in Central Asia

74 Roman **capture of Masada** in Palestine

77 Julius Agricola becomes governor of Britain

78 Kushan ruler **Vima Kadphises** sends envoys to Rome to arrange an attack on the Parthians

79 Eruption of **Vesuvius** destroys **Pompeii** and Herculaneum

80 Flavian amphitheater (the **Colosseum**) completed in Rome

c. 80 Luke begins to write his **gospel**

83 Battle of **Mons Graupius**; Roman commander Agricola defeats the Caledonii

86 War breaks out between the **Romans** and **Decebalus**, king of the Dacians

87 Embassy from the Kushans arrives in Luoyang

88 The Han abolish the state **monopolies** on iron and salt

c. 90 The **Shakas** invade northwest India

" [AN EMPEROR] UNDER WHOM **EVERYBODY** WAS **PERMITTED** TO DO **EVERYTHING.** "

Fronto, Roman orator, on Emperor Nerva, from Cassius Dio's *History of Rome*

Emperor Domitian
Domitian's reign began well, but his descent into tyranny proved too much for his opponents, who had him assassinated.

DOMITIAN (51–96) BECAME ROMAN EMPEROR after the unexpected death of his brother, Titus (39–81). Domitian had never commanded armies and was unprepared for the exercise of supreme power. He had some success in his early campaigns, but he over-extended himself against the Dacians, and in putting down a legionary revolt led by **Saturninus**, the governor of Germania Superior. This distraction allowed **Decebalus, King of the Dacians** (r. 87–106), to renew his war against Rome, and Domitian was forced to pay off the Dacians with an annual subsidy.

The conspiracy of Saturninus led Domitian to become paranoid and he had many senators executed for treason. In September 96, he was murdered in a palace conspiracy and the Senate chose the aged **M. Cocceius Nerva** (30–98) to replace him. The Senate then voted to destroy all statues of Domitian and to recall those he had exiled. However, in 97 Nerva faced a mutiny of the praetorian guard, who demanded the punishment of Domitian's murderers. Nerva was forced to give in, weakening his authority. His position was further diminished by his lack of an heir. To rectify this he adopted M. Ulpius Traianus (**Trajan**), the governor of Upper Germany, a man with a strong military backing. Nerva died soon afterwards and Trajan became emperor.

In Central Asia, the northern Xiongnu confederation (see 146–131 BCE) collapsed in 89, allowing the Han to make large gains in the region, led by **general Ban Chao** (32–102). Ban Chao became protector-general of the Western Regions in 91, and reestablished control over the key oases along the **Silk Route.** By the time he retired in 102 the Han controlled most of the Tarim Basin. **Chinese state organization** became very complicated under the Han. Three supreme officials supervised large, complex departments. Each of these was subdivided into nine ministries. Governors oversaw each region, with regions divided into over 1,000 counties, each supervised by a magistrate. Eunuchs became increasingly influential at the Han court.

Trajan's Column, in Rome, gives a visual account of Trajan's campaigns against Decebalus in the Dacian Wars.

EMPEROR TRAJAN (98–117) WAS FROM A ROMAN FAMILY who had settled in Spain—he was the first emperor to come from a Roman province rather than Italy. Having returned to Rome from Germany in 100 to claim his throne, he started a new **Dacian War** against Decebalus in 101. From a base at Viminacium (in modern Serbia), he pushed into central Dacia, and fought a major engagement at Tapae, in which both sides suffered serious losses. When Trajan's legions neared the Dacian royal capital at **Sarmizegetusa Regia**, Decebalus sued for peace, agreeing to give up his army's weapons and siege equipment, and to demolish his remaining forts. The Roman army did not withdraw totally, establishing a legionary base near the mountains

Sacred city
This ruined temple is in the Dacian capital, Sarmizegetusa Regia (in modern-day Romania). It contained the kingdom's most sacred shrines.

and building a bridge across the Danube at Drobeta to allow easier access across the river. Three years later, in 105, the Senate declared that Decebalus had violated the treaty, and Trajan embarked on his **Second Dacian War**. This time the legions reached, and took, Sarmizegetusa in 106. Decebalus fled and then committed suicide to avoid capture. The Romans acquired an enormous amount of treasure in Dacia, which allowed Trajan to embark on a building spree, including the construction of a **new Forum** in Rome. Dacia was annexed as Rome's first province across the Danube. It remained in imperial hands for over 160 years.

Some time around 106 the Roman governor of Syria annexed the **Nabataean kingdom**, which became the Roman province of Arabia. It was not Trajan's last acquisition in the east—in 113 he set off on a campaign against **Parthia**. He began by attacking Armenia in 113–114, but it was his

331,000 kg SILVER

165,500 kg GOLD

The Dacian Fortune
The large amount of treasure Trajan acquired in Dacia allowed him to build impressive monuments to commemorate his Dacian victory.

campaign against Parthia itself that gave him greater success in the east than any previous Roman emperor. By late 114 the Armenians had submitted to him, and he pushed into Mesopotamia, capturing the Parthian capital of **Ctesiphon**. By the end of 115, Trajan had reached the Persian

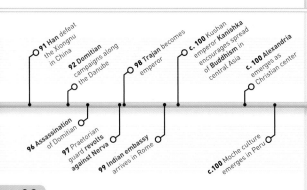

91 Han defeat the Xiongnu in China

92 Domitian campaigns along the Danube

96 Assassination of Domitian

97 Praetorian guard revolts against Nerva

98 Trajan becomes emperor

99 Indian embassy arrives in Rome

c. 100 Kushan emperor **Kanishka** encourages spread of **Buddhism** in central Asia

c. 100 Alexandria emerges as Christian center

c.100 Moche culture emerges in Peru

101 Trajan invades **Dacia** (to 102)

105 Trajan's Second Dacian War

c. 105 Paper invented in China

106 The Nabataean kingdom is annexed by Rome and becomes **province of Arabia**

106 Following defeat of Decebalus, his kingdom is annexed as the Roman province of **Dacia**

109 Pliny the Younger appointed governor of Bithynia

c. 110 Buddhist council in northern India leads to division into two branches, **Mahayana and Hinayana**

113 Trajan completes building of a **new Forum** at Rome

114 Trajan annexes **Armenia** and invades **Parthia**

The remains of Hadrian's Wall in northern England. The central portion of the wall occupies a high position that vastly enhances its defensive value.

Gulf near modern Basra, Iraq, where he is said to have remarked that, had he been younger, he might have pressed on to India. The newly conquered territories were organized as the provinces of **Mesopotamia** and **Assyria**, but they were already in revolt when Trajan returned home in 117. The Parthians rejected Trajan's **puppet king Parthamaspates**, and by the time Trajan died in August 117 almost all of his gains in the east had been lost. On his death-bed Trajan adopted Publius Aelius Hadrianus (**Hadrian**), the governor of Syria, effectively appointing Hadrian as his successor.

In 109, Trajan appointed the historian **Pliny the Younger** (61–c. 112) as his personal representative to govern **Bithynia-Pontus** on the Black Sea coast of Anatolia. This was a controversial move, as Bithynia-Pontus was theoretically a senatorial province. The provinces of the empire had been divided between the emperor and the senate at the accession of Augustus in 27 BCE, with the emperor receiving only the provinces that held legionary garrisons. This division of the provinces persisted into the time of Trajan. Pliny stayed in Bithynia-Pontus for at least two years, trying to sort out the finances of the main cities, which had fallen into confusion. His letters to Trajan are an invaluable insight into the imperial government of the time.

TRAJAN'S SUCCESSOR HADRIAN (r. 117–135) rejected his predecessor's policy of expansion and concentrated on better defense of the **imperial frontiers**. In 122, Hadrian visited Britain, where there had been frontier troubles. He ordered the building of a huge barrier from the Solway Firth in the west to the Tyne River in the east. It took governor **Aulus Platorius Nepos** two years to complete **Hadrian's Wall** (part in stone, and part in turf), which ran 76 Roman miles (113 km), and was equipped with a series of forts and milecastles for its garrison. Hadrian's Wall acted as the northern frontier line of Roman Britain for the next 40 years.

The **Parthian kingdom** was left in some confusion by the campaigns of Trajan. His puppet king, Parthamaspates, was expelled in 117, but the Parthian kingdom then seems to have been divided between **Vologeses**

HADRIAN (76–138)

Hadrian came from a Spanish background and was the adopted son of his predecessor, Trajan. He was mocked by some for his grecophile tendencies, and was the first emperor to sport a beard—a Greek fashion. Hadrian was the first emperor to travel widely throughout the Roman empire, giving him first-hand knowledge of the provinces, from Britain to North Africa.

985

THE NUMBER OF **VILLAGES RAZED** DURING THE **BAR-KOCHBA REVOLT**

III (r. 105–147) who ruled the eastern portion, and **Osroes** (r. 117–129) then **Mithridates IV** (r. 129–140) in the west. There was no further conflict between Parthia and Rome for the time being.

In India, the **Kushan empire** expanded enormously under **Kanishka** (127–140), who conquered Magadha and campaigned against the Chinese in Central Asia; his inscriptions are found from the Oxus river in Afghanistan to as far south as Varanasi and Sanchi. He was a strong patron of Buddhism and presided over the **fourth Buddhist Council**, as well as building a great stupa at his capital Purushapura (Peshawar).

Hadrian's ban on circumcision, his plan to turn Jerusalem into the Roman town of Aelia Capitolina, and his intent to ban Jewish religious practices in Jerusalem caused a furious **revolt in Jerusalem** in 132, as religious Jews rose up against religious reforms. Led by **Shimon Bar Kochba**, the rebels had early successes against Rome. They set up the beginnings of an independent government and minted their own coins. In response, Hadrian summoned **Julius Severus**, the governor of Britain, to conduct a war against the rebels. Severus commanded an army formed of detachments from 12 legions. The rebels had no large towns under their control, and so adopted **guerrilla warfare** while still attempting to defend the smaller forts they held. In 135, the rebel's last main stronghold at **Bethar was captured** amid great slaughter, after which the revolt petered out. Hadrian proceeded with his plan to **outlaw Judaism** in Palestine, and many of the Jews who had survived the rebellion fled abroad.

Treasured goblet
This beautiful vase was found in Kapisa (Bagram) near Kabul, which was the Kushan summer capital in the 1st century.

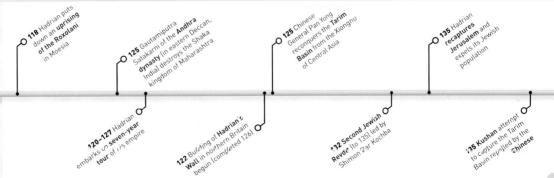

115 Jewish revolt in Cyrenaica against Roman rule

117 Trajan dies

117 Hadrian abandons Mesopotamia and Assyria

118 Hadrian puts down an **uprising of the Roxolani** in Moesia

120–127 Hadrian embarks on seven-year **tour** of his empire

125 Gautamiputra Satakarni of the **Andhra dynasty** (in eastern Deccan, India) destroys the Shaka kingdom of Maharashtra

122 Building of **Hadrian's Wall** in northern Britain begun (completed 126)

125 Chinese General Pan Yong reconquers the **Tarim Basin** from the Xiongnu of Central Asia

132 Second Jewish Revolt (to 135) led by Shimon Bar Kochba

135 Hadrian **recaptures Jerusalem** and expels its Jewish population

135 Kushan attempt to capture the Tarim Basin repelled by the Chinese

200 THOUSAND
THE TOTAL POPULATION OF TEOTIHUACÁN AT ITS PEAK

The Pyramid of the Sun at Teotihuacán in modern Mexico.

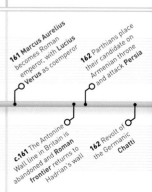

The ruins of Hatra, which was a Parthian-controlled city.

THE CITY OF TEOTIHUACÁN IN THE VALLEY OF MEXICO experienced **massive growth** during the 1st and 2nd centuries, with its population reaching over 80,000 before 200. The city was planned on a grid, with **two huge pyramids**—of the Moon and the Sun—at either end of the main street. The Teotihuacán II phase of the city (0–350) saw the building of the enormous **Temple of Quetzalcoatl** and the acquisition of an empire, with Teotihuacán dominating vast areas of Mexico and overseeing client kingdoms as far south as Guatemala.

Hadrian had adopted **Antoninus Pius** (86–161) as his son and successor, a stop-gap until Antoninus's relative, **Marcus Aurelius** (121–80), was old enough to rule, but Antoninus survived Hadrian by 23 years, and became Roman emperor in 138. He was

turquoise mosaic pieces

Mexican mask
This sumptuous mask from Teotihuacán bears the smooth, flat features that are characteristic of work from the city.

necklace made from coral beads

39 MILES
THE LENGTH OF THE **ANTONINE WALL** IN SCOTLAND

famed for his moderation and rarely left Rome. Disturbances in **Dacia** (in present-day Romania) around 156 and an uprising in North Africa in 145 did not unduly disturb the empire's calm. Antoninus extended the frontier in both Scotland and Upper Germany, ordering the construction of a new turf barrier around 100 miles (160 km) to the north of Hadrian's Wall (see 188–135 BCE) in Britain. This **Antonine Wall** was 39 miles (63 km) in length. The Hadrian's Wall garrison was moved north to a new set of forts, but their stay was short—Marcus Aurelius, Antoninus Pius's successor, ordered a **pull-back to Hadrian's Wall** around 161, where the Roman frontier of Britain remained until the 5th century.

As **Christianity** grew, so did the problem of defining a single doctrine. Among the alternative doctrines that sprang up in the 2nd century was **Marcionism**, which taught that the God of Christians was distinct from the Jewish God of the Old Testament and that Jesus Christ did not have a human nature. **Justin Martyr** (c. 103–165) argued that Christianity was the fulfillment of Jewish prophecy and that Christians were the new chosen people. Justin also wrote to Marcus Aurelius, seeking to explain Christian doctrine.

MARCUS AURELIUS SUCCEEDED TO THE ROMAN THRONE jointly with **Lucius Verus** in 161. Marcus was the more capable of the two, but it was Lucius who was sent, in 162, to rescue the situation in the east after the governor of Cappadocia was defeated and killed by the Persians following a **disastrous invasion of Armenia**. By 163–164 Lucius had brought Armenia back under Roman control, and renamed its capital Kaine Polis ("New City"). A new pro-Roman king was installed there before the legions moved on, pushing deeper into Persian

> **❝ IF IT IS NOT RIGHT, DO NOT DO IT: IF IT IS NOT TRUE, DO NOT SAY IT. ❞**

Emperor Marcus Aurelius, from *Meditations*, 161–180

territory, taking Edessa in Mesopotamia, and reaching the **Parthian capital** of Ctesiphon in 165. The Roman general **Avidius Cassius** (c. 130–175) burned the Parthian palace and then turned back westward. A swathe of Parthian territory down the Euphrates River was annexed as far east as Dura Europos (in southeastern Syria). However, victory celebrations were short-lived, for the troops brought the **plague** back to Rome and by 167 it had spread

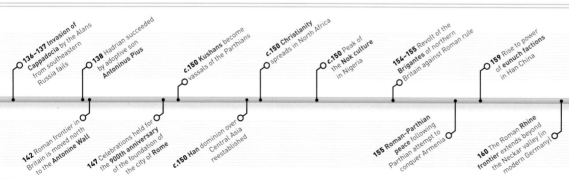

136–137 Invasion of Cappadocia by the Alans from southeastern Russia fails

138 Hadrian succeeded by adoptive son **Antoninus Pius**

c.150 Kushans become vassals of the Parthians

c.150 Christianity spreads in North Africa

c.150 Peak of the Nok culture in Nigeria

154–155 Revolt of the Brigantes of northern Britain against Roman rule

159 Rise to power of eunuch factions in Han China

161 Marcus Aurelius becomes Roman emperor, with **Lucius Verus** as coemperor

162 Parthians place their candidate on Armenian throne and attack Persia

142 Roman frontier in Britain is moved north to **the Antonine Wall**

147 Celebrations held for the **900th anniversary** of the foundation of the city of **Rome**

c.150 Han dominion over Central Asia reestablished

155 Roman–Parthian peace following Parthian attempt to conquer Armenia

160 The Roman **Rhine frontier** extends beyond the Neckar valley (in modern Germany)

c.161 The Antonine Wall line in Britain is abandoned and **Roman frontier** returns to Hadrian's wall

162 Revolt of the Germanic **Chatti**

A painted stucco of the Moche's most important god, Al Apaec, who is often depicted with the fangs of a snake.

widely throughout the **Mediterranean**.

Barely had the Parthian War ended than the **Marcomannic War** began. In early 167, a group of Germanic warriors from the **Langobardi** and **Obii** tribes crossed the Danube to attack the Roman province of Pannonia. They were pushed back fairly easily, but in spring 168 Marcus Aurelius resolved to visit the region to assess the situation. Two more Germanic tribes, the **Marcomanni** and **Quadi** were threatening to force their way across the frontier unless they were admitted to settle in the empire, but Marcus's presence deterred them. However, the expedition was cut short by the death of Lucius Verus from plague in early 169. Marcus returned to Italy, but was back in Pannonia later in the year to launch a **massive offensive** across the Danube. It was a disaster, with the Romans suffering around 20,000 dead and the Marcomanni and Quadi pouring into Italy, where they laid siege to Aquileia. Far from providing an easy victory for Marcus, the war dragged on for another 10 years.

In **China**, the **eunuch faction** at court had become increasingly powerful and had even engineered the murder of the emperor Shaodi in 125. Under **Emperor Huandi** (146–68) a series of natural disasters weakened the authority

Marcus Aurelius
This statue shows Marcus Aurelius adopting a pose of victory, something he claimed but never quite achieved in his Marcomannic Wars.

of the central government, and the emperor relinquished active control of government to the eunuchs. In 168, an attempt by **Dou Miao**, regent for the 12-year-old emperor **Lingdi** (r. 168–89), to have the eunuchs massacred failed—the plot was betrayed and Dou Miao was forced to commit suicide. Several hundred of Dou Miao's supporters were executed and, with its enemies now dead, the eunuch faction was able to exercise power almost unopposed.

THE MOCHE CULTURE EMERGED ON THE COAST OF NORTHERN PERU between 100 and 200. From their bases in the Peruvian valleys of Moche, Chicama, and Virú, these people spread to dominate almost the whole northern coastline. A warlike people, they sacrificed those whom they captured to their deities, including **Al Apaec** ("the decapitator"). They were skilled workers in gold and their pottery has an extraordinarily realistic quality.

The **Roman Empire** was in **crisis** in 170—the Marcomanni and Quadi had occupied parts of northern Italy, and an invasion by the **Iazyges** and **Costobocci** had overun large parts of the Balkans. The Romans trapped the **Marcomanni** as they returned across the Danube and killed many of them. The **Quadi sued for peace later in 171**, but the Marcommani remained recalcitrant, forcing a **new offensive in 172**. The forces of Marcus Aurelius could never quite strike the killer blow, and by 175 the war had reached a **stalemate**.

In May that year, rumors that Marcus Aurelius

Moche stirrup jar
This jar has a typical Moche "stirrup" attached to the back of it. The realism of the paddling figure is characteristic of the culture's ceramics.

THE GERMANIC TRIBES

The Romans had faced Germanic tribes ever since they had reached the Rhine at the time of Julius Caesar. German groups across the Danube, such as the Quadi and Marcomanni, proved troublesome in the 2nd century, but by the late 3rd century new and more dangerous confederations of Germanic tribes arose, such as the Franks, Alamanns, and Goths, who overran much of the Roman Empire by the mid-5th century.

had died while on campaign prompted a revolt by **Avidius Cassius**, the governor of Syria. Avidius was **declared emperor** in Egypt, and received support in Arabia, as well as in his own province of Syria. Critically, however, he failed to secure the support of **Martius Verus**, the

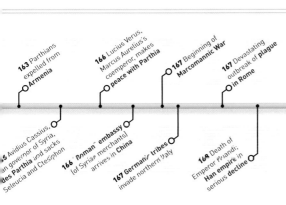

governor of Cappadocia, whom he had fought alongside during the Parthian War.

As Martius's army approached, the loyalty of the usurper's troops wavered, and in July **Avidius Cassius was murdered** by a disaffected centurion, putting an end to his short-lived but dangerous rebellion. There were suggestions that Marcus's wife **Faustina** encouraged Avidius, as she feared for her husband's health and worried her own son Commodus was unfit to rule.

Free from the distraction of Avidius's revolt, Marcus Aurelius returned to the Danube in 177. In the winter of 179–80, the **Roman army** occupied positions deep across the Danube, and it looked as if Marcus might be able to create two new Roman provinces—Marcomannia and Sarmatia. However, Marcus was old and tired—he died in March 180. His son **Commodus** brought the war to a rapid conclusion, allowing him to return to Rome.

Gold dolphin earrings
Earrings adorned with animal-head motifs were especially popular in the eastern Roman empire. This pair bears a symbol of the sea god Neptune.

decorative female head

Plumb line
This bronze weighted plumb line was attached to a groma, an instrument used by the Romans to survey straight lines.

Precious necklace
This necklace, made up of gold and red garnets, seems to form the shape of a spectacular fruit tree.

garnet shaped like a fruit or berry

gold in the form of a leaf

Bone pin
This flat, thin blade or pin is topped by a female head, an ornamental touch for an otherwise humdrum household item.

bronze weight

cart carrying worshipers

ANCIENT ROME
THE ROMANS SPREAD A RICH MATERIAL CULTURE THROUGHOUT THEIR VAST EMPIRE

As Roman political control steadily expanded outside Italy, in its wake came the Roman way of life. Roman surveyors laid out new cities, local elites took up Roman practices, and the masses attended gladiatorial spectacles. On a domestic level, Roman fashions in clothing and accessories also spread.

Although many of the territories that the Romans conquered initially resisted, the populations of these provinces, particularly the former ruling classes, gradually adopted many Roman customs. Influential men became Roman citizens, towns were given new public buildings such as baths and courthouses, Roman legionary garrisons were established in strategic places, and new trade routes brought luxury goods from Rome. As a result, similar Roman artifacts have been found across Europe, the Middle East, and North Africa, dating from around the 1st century BCE to the 5th century CE.

Bronze dividers and foot rule
Dividers allowed engineers to copy scale plans or models at twice or half their size—the gap between the lower points is always twice that between the upper points. The rule, which was one Roman foot long (11¾ in/29.6 cm), folded for easy carrying.

central pivot

metal crest to deflect blows

lower point

head of Oceanus

cursive letter forms

foot rule

Ocean baths
The most important Roman baths were adorned with lavish mosaics, such as this one of Oceanus, the ocean god, from Sabratha in Libya.

Wooden tablet
This type of tablet, made from very thin wood, was used by the Roman military for everyday letters and record-keeping. This one was found at Vindolanda in England.

Procession bowl
This lekane, a type of shallow dish, is decorated with a scene of half-man, half-goat satyrs in a procession in honor of Bacchus, the god of wine.

modern-looking grater

Ancient grater
Cheese played an important part in the Roman diet. Graters such as this one were invented to allow cheese to be used as a topping on other foodstuffs.

Amphora
The Romans transported liquid goods such as oil and wine in amphoras, a type of large, double-handled storage jar.

flask containing oil

strigil for scraping

Bathing tools
At the baths, a Roman's skin was oiled and then scraped to remove sweat and dirt. A ring was used to transport the tools.

Short sword
The Roman military sword, or *gladius*, had a short blade—ideal for attacks at close range. It was used by soldiers and some gladiators.

short blade

ivory grip

satyr carrying cymbals

Military javelin
Each Roman legionary carried two of these *pila* (javelins). The javelin's iron head was designed to bend on impact to prevent an opponent from removing it from shields or wounds.

long iron shank

handle shaped for throwing

Imperial coins
Coins bearing the head of the current emperor (here Augustus and Claudius) acted as powerful propaganda tools across the empire, showing even the masses an image of their ruler.

Latin text

Proof of citizenship
Noncitizens who served 25 years in the Roman army were awarded citizenship and given bronze diplomas such as this one to record the grant.

Sling pellets
Roman legionaries normally relied on their swords, but auxiliary light infantry used other weapons to devastating effect, such as these metal sling pellets.

small size would have offered little protection

gridded visor to protect face

Gladiator helmet
Roman gladiators bore a variety of arms and armor. This sort of helmet was worn by a Thracian, a type of gladiator whose equipment was modeled on that of ancient Thracian warriors.

Bronze gladiator shield
Thracian gladiators—a class of lightly armed gladiator—carried lightweight, round shields such as this one for defense, and a scimitar, with a short, curved blade, to attack their opponents.

In this engraving by Giovanni Stradano, Emperor Commodus shoots an arrow to subdue a leopard. Fighting in the arena as a gladiator was his great passion.

The Severan arch in Leptis Magna (in modern Libya) commemorates a visit by the North African emperor to his home town.

IN CHINA, INCREASING DISSENT caused by the corruption of the eunuchs at the court of Han Emperor Lindi (r. 168–89) and a succession of natural disasters led to the outbreak in 184 of a major insurrection, named the **Yellow Turban revolt** for the color of its supporters' headgear. Up to 400,000 rebels swept westward towards the capital. Another uprising fueled by the **Five Pecks of Rice** sect then succeeded in taking over Sichuan in the southwest. Although the Yellow Turbans had been largely crushed by 185, the rebellion was not finally put down until 204; the **control of the Han emperor was ever weakening**. After Lingdi died in 189, he was replaced by his younger half-brother **Xiandi** (r. 189–220) but he never exercised real power. Instead, control of the empire fell to Han general **Cao Cao**, who contended for 30 years with **a series of rival warlords**, notably **Liu Bei** in the southwest and **Sun Quan** in the south.

18
THE AGE AT WHICH COMMODUS BECAME SOLE EMPEROR

Commodus (r. 180–92), Marcus Aurelius's son, was the first Roman emperor to succeed his father for 90 years, but he proved to be **a disastrous choice**. In 183, after an assassination attempt on him, apparently organized by his sister Lucilla, Commodus became **increasingly despotic**. Many senators who were implicated in the plot were executed and control of the government fell into the hands of **Tigidius Perennis, the praetorian prefect** (the commander of the imperial bodyguard). There were minor wars in Britain and in Dacia (much of modern Romania), but in 185 Perennis was suspected of a plot to make his own son emperor and was executed by his troops. Commodus increasingly **devoted himself to fighting** in the arena as a **gladiator**, while the imperial chamberlain **Cleander** dominated government and sold public offices to the highest bidder. The man in charge of the grain supply, **Papirius Dionysius**, engineered a shortage that led to Cleander's downfall. This did not result in a more stable government, as his replacement only lasted a short time before being murdered. Commodus increasingly identified himself with **Hercules** (the Greek hero) and renamed Rome after himself—*colonia Commodiana*. At the end of 192, the praetorian prefect **Laetus** was convinced that Commodus was planning to have him killed and on **New Year's Day 193** took the initiative and had the emperor **poisoned** and, when that did not work, **strangled**.

> ## BE **HARMONIOUS** WITH **EACH OTHER**, ENRICH THE **SOLDIERS**, IGNORE ALL **OTHERS**...

Septimius Severus, dying words as quoted in Book 77 of Roman historian Dio Cassius's *Roman History*, 211

IN 193, AFTER THE MURDER OF COMMODUS, Helvius Pertinax (126–93), the prefect of the city, was declared emperor, but he was murdered after three months. This was followed by rival claimants to the throne engaging in an auction outside the praetorian camp to decide who would be emperor. **Didius Julianus** (133–93) won, but

Money offered to each soldier by Didius Julianus

25,000
SESTERCES

20,000
SESTERCES

Money offered to each soldier by Flavius Sulpicianus

Buying loyalty
The larger bribes offered to the troops by Didius Julianus meant that he won the auction to be emperor.

his reign was short, as almost immediately the frontier armies rebelled: the army on the Danube proclaimed **Septimius Severus** (c. 145–211) emperor, while the Syrian legions raised their commander **Pescennius Niger** (c. 135–94) to the imperial throne. Severus reached Rome first and, after granting the title of Caesar (junior emperor) to **Clodius Albinus**, governor of Britain, he turned east where, in spring 194, his armies defeated Niger at the **Battle of Issus** in Syria. Severus stayed in the east and in 195 attacked the Parthian Empire. But he was forced to return west to deal with Albinus, who had revolted, and who was killed near Lugdunum (modern Lyon, France) in 197. Severus then returned to Parthia, this time occupying the capital Ctesiphon in 197. He pushed the line of Roman control toward the Tigris and created the **new province of Mesopotamia**.

Trouble in Britain brought the aging emperor to the province in 208. A large-scale Roman advance forced the Caledonians and Maetae north of the provincial frontier to come to terms in 209,

JULIA DOMNA (170–217)

The daughter of a Syrian high priest, Julia Domna married Septimius Severus in 187. A prophecy had predicted that she would wed an emperor, and so it turned out. Forceful and intelligent, she failed to mediate between her sons Caracalla and Geta after their father's death and to prevent Geta's murder. When Caracalla was killed, she deliberately starved herself to death in protest, a move that rallied support for the remaining Severan family.

but they soon broke the peace and a new campaign was launched in 210. Severus was by now very ill, and his son Caracalla took over. In February 211 **Severus died** in Eboracum (modern York, England) and handed succession jointly to sons Caracalla and Geta. After the Scottish war, both rushed back to Rome, but their **joint rule was short-lived**: Caracalla had Geta murdered in December 211.

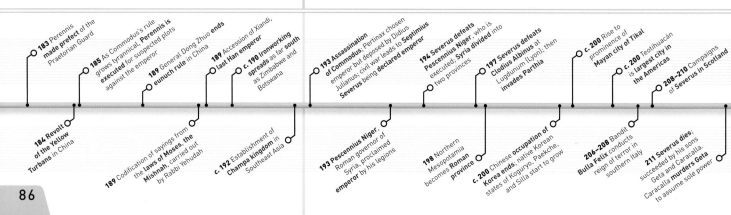

183 Perennis made prefect of the Praetorian Guard

185 As Commodus's rule grows tyrannical, **Perennis is executed** for suspected plots against the emperor

189 General Dong Zhuo ends **eunuch rule** in China

189 Accession of Xiandi, **last Han emperor**

c. 190 Ironworking **spreads** as far **south** as Zimbabwe and Botswana

193 Assassination **of Commodus**; Pertinax chosen emperor but deposed by Didius Julianus; civil war leads to **Septimius Severus** being **declared emperor**

194 Severus defeats **Pescennius Niger**, who is executed; **Syria divided into** two provinces

197 Severus defeats **Clodius Albinus** at Lugdunum (Lyon); then **invades Parthia**

c. 200 Rise to prominence of **Mayan city of Tikal**

c. 200 Teotihuacán **is largest city in the Americas**

208–210 Campaigns **of Severus in Scotland**

184 Revolt **of the Yellow Turbans** in China

189 Codification of sayings from the **laws of Moses, the Mishnah,** carried out by Rabbi Yehudah

c. 192 Establishment of **Champa kingdom** in Southeast Asia

193 Pescennius Niger, Roman governor of Syria, **proclaimed emperor** by his legions

198 Northern Mesopotamia becomes **Roman province**

c. 200 Chinese occupation of **Korea ends**; native Korean states of Koguryo, Paekche, and Silla start to grow

206–208 Bandit **Bulla Felix** conducts reign of terror in southern Italy

211 Severus dies; succeeded by his sons Geta and Caracalla; **Caracalla murders Geta** to assume sole power

A carving of the Buddha from Sarnath in North India, where a school of Buddhist art flourished under the Kushans.

IN INDIA, THE AREA CONTROLLED BY THE KUSHAN DYNASTY began to shrink after the death of King Kanishka in 140, and particularly severe territorial losses were suffered under Huvishka (r. 160–90). Kushan rule finally collapsed under Vasudeva (r. 190–225) when Persian invaders swept through northwestern India. Although Kushan kings continued to rule a much-reduced realm for a further century, their influence was purely local and their **heyday was at an end**.

In Rome, Caracalla's government was unpopular. Among his measures was the **Antonine Constitution of 212**, by which citizenship was granted to almost all free males in the empire. After a successful campaign on the Rhine (in 213), Caracalla ventured further afield, arriving in Egypt in 215. For some unknown reason, he became enraged and ordered the **massacre** of the citizens of **Alexandria**. The next year he launched an invasion of Parthia. His praetorian prefect **Opellius Macrinus** came to suspect that Caracalla wanted him dead, so he persuaded a disaffected soldier to murder the emperor. After Caracalla's murder, **the army declared Macrinus emperor**. There was much residual loyalty

2,000

THE NUMBER OF **BATHERS** THAT COULD USE THE **BATHS** OF **CARACALLA**

to the Severan family, and a revolt broke out in Syria, which aimed to put **Elagabalus** (203–22), grandson of Julia Domna's sister Julia Maesa, on the throne. Macrinus lost support and in June 218 he fled to Cappadocia, where he was killed. In 221, Elagabalus **adopted as his heir** his cousin Alexianus. When the two fell out in 222, the army backed Alexianus and Elagabalus was murdered. Alexianus became **Emperor Alexander Severus** at age 13.

In Persia, Parthian rule had been weakened, both by plague and by the effects of successive Roman invasions. In 207, the kingdom had

Bronze diploma
Diplomas were issued to auxiliary soldiers in the Roman army, granting them citizenship. This practice ceased after the Antonine Constitution.

Arch of Caracalla
Originally the arch was topped by a figure of the emperor riding in a chariot. It stands in Volubilis, the main town of Roman Mauretania Tingitana (in modern Morocco).

been divided into two when Vologeses VI's brother set himself up as a rival king, **Artabanus V**; and a further Roman invasion in 216 ravaged much of the province of Media. Taking advantage of this disorder, the ruler of the southwestern province of Pars, **Ardashir**, expanded his territory and finally defeated Artabanus V c. 224. Ardashir I was then declared king (r. 224–42) as the **first ruler of the Sasanian dynasty**. Although

Persia was temporarily weakened by a civil war, the Sasanians proved to be **much tougher adversaries** to the Romans than the Parthians ever had been.

In China in 220, Cao Cao's son Cao Pi **forced Xiandi to abdicate**. Within two years Cao Pi, Liu Bei, and Sun Quan would each declare himself emperor. The **Han dynasty** and China's unity were at an end.

The Sasanian Empire in Persia
After rapidly acquiring the former Parthian Empire, the Sasanians fought a series of wars with the Romans over control of Mesopotamia.

KEY

Sasanian Empire at greatest extent

East Roman Empire in 3rd century

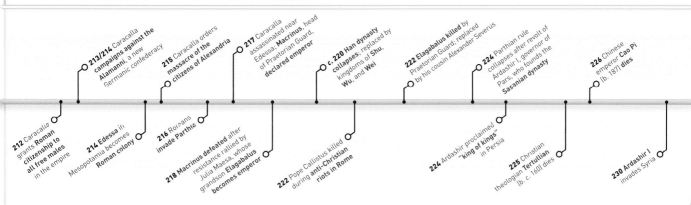

212 Caracalla grants **Roman citizenship to all free males** in the empire

213/214 Caracalla **campaigns against the Alamanni**, a new Germanic confederacy

214 Edessa in Mesopotamia becomes **Roman colony**

215 Caracalla orders **massacre of the citizens of Alexandria**

216 Romans **invade Parthia**

217 Caracalla assassinated near Edessa; **Macrinus**, head of Praetorian Guard, **declared emperor**

218 Macrinus defeated after resistance rallied by Julia Maesa, whose grandson **Elagabalus becomes emperor**

c. 220 Han dynasty collapses; replaced by kingdoms of **Shu, Wu,** and **Wei**

222 Pope Callistus killed during **anti-Christian riots in Rome**

222 Elagabalus killed by Praetorian Guard; replaced by his cousin Alexander Severus

224 Parthian rule collapses after revolt of Ardashir I, governor of Pars, who founds the **Sasanian dynasty**

224 Ardashir proclaimed "**king of kings**" in Persia

225 Christian theologian **Tertullian** (b. c. 160) dies

226 Chinese emperor **Cao Pi** (b. 187) **dies**

230 Ardashir I invades Syria

25 THE NUMBER OF ROMAN EMPERORS THAT RULED BETWEEN 235 AND 284

Roman emperor Gordian III succeeded his father and grandfather.

A mural of St. Cyprian, Bishop of Carthage at the height of the Decian persecution. He was martyred in 257 during a campaign under Valerian.

IN CHINA, THE FINAL COLLAPSE OF THE HAN DYNASTY IN 220 was followed by 350 years of instability. **The Three Kingdoms** period (220–80) saw China divided into the **Wei** kingdom of the north; (initially under Wei Wendi (r. 220–26); the **Shu Han** kingdom in the west whose first ruler was Shu Han Xuande (r. 221–23); and the southern **Wu** kingdom under Wu Wudi (r. 222–52). Wei Wendi was a capable ruler, but his successors struggled to contain attacks by northern tribesmen.

In 235, the Roman emperor Alexander Severus and his mother Julia Mamaea were **murdered** by mutinous troops, putting an **end to the Severan dynasty**. The uprising's ringleader, **Maximinus Thrax** (r. 235–38), an officer from a humble background, was proclaimed emperor, but he spent most of his reign raising funds to reward his troops for their support. This time marks the start of a period of "**military anarchy**" in which Rome had dozens of emperors, most of them short-lived rulers who were raised up by the frontier armies and just as quickly deposed and killed. A rebellion in 238 in North

Art from the Three Kingdoms
High artistic achievements, such as this fine statue, were a feature of the late Han dynasty. Its collapse in 220 did not result in an equivalent decline in China's artistic output.

Africa proclaimed the province's elderly governor as **Emperor Gordian I**, but he was quickly and brutally put down. The Senate declared Maximinus deposed and proposed **Pupienus** and **Balbinus** as candidates. Popular sentiment favored Gordian I's grandson

GOBI DESERT

WEI • Luoyang
Chang'an
Yellow Sea
Chengdu
Jiankang
SHU HAN
WU
Taiwan
South China Sea
Hainan

KEY
▮ Wei, 220–225   ▮ Wu, 222–280
▮ Shu Han, 221–263

China under the Three Kingdoms
Although the Wei kingdom faced the greatest challenges among the three kingdoms, it would eventually conquer the Wu and the Shu Han.

Gordian III (r. 238–44), so all three briefly shared the throne. Balbinus and Pupienus were killed soon after, leaving Gordian III to rule alone. His six-year reign **briefly restored** some semblance of **stability** to the empire, but he was killed while leading an invasion of Persia in 243–44. Compounding the Roman Empire's difficulties was the appearance of **barbarian confederacies** among the Germanic peoples of the Rhine and Danube frontiers. Principal among these were the **Alemanni**. In 213, Caracalla campaigned against them; by 260 they were able to **invade Italy** itself.

PERSIA ATTAINED A POSITION OF RENEWED STRENGTH under Shapur I (r. 241–72). In 244, he won a decisive battle against Gordian III at Misiche near Ctesiphon. Shortly after, Gordian III was killed and replaced by his army commander Philip (or **Philip "the Arab"**). Philip made peace with Shapur but had to pay a large ransom to escape Sasanian territory. His successors broke the terms of the agreement, so in 256 **Shapur I invaded Syria** and captured the towns of Antioch and Europos Dura. **Valerian**, who by then was emperor (r. 253–60), soon retook Antioch. In 260, he fell into a trap and was **imprisoned by Shapur**. The Romans were left

Relief of Shapur I
In this relief, Shapur I triumphs over the Roman emperors Gordian III and Valerian. After Valerian's capture, Shapur is said to have used him as a footstool for mounting his horse.

in disarray and Shapur's armies advanced as far as Iconium (modern Konya, Turkey).

The western part of the Roman Empire also faced increasing pressure. The Romans suffered invasions of Dacia (much of modern Romania) by the **Carpi** people from c. 214. The Carpi, together with a new group, **the Goths**, took part in a raid across the Danube in 239–40. In 248, Emperor Philip **withdrew an annual tribute** he had been paying the Carpi and the Goths, prompting them to pour into Moesia (modern Bulgaria). Philip sent **Quintus Decius** to deal with the invasion; he was so successful that his troops declared him emperor. Early in 249, Decius marched to Rome and defeated and killed Philip. Hearing of the Roman civil war, the **Goths invaded again**, causing Decius to return to the Balkans in 250. Under their warleader **Cniva**, the

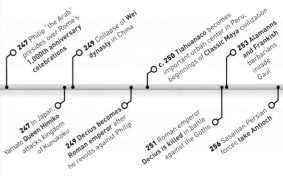

232 Romans **expel Ardashir I** of Persia from Mesopotamia and Cappadocia

235 Serious **Alammanic raids** on the upper Rhine

238 Gordian I declared emperor but lasts only 22 days; **Gordian III** becomes Roman emperor on his grandfather's death

241 Shapur I becomes ruler of Persia

242 Goths **dominate southern Russia**

247 Philip "the Arab" presides over Rome's **1,000th anniversary celebrations**

249 Collapse of **Wei** dynasty in China

c. 250 Tiahuanaco becomes important urban center in Peru; beginnings of **Classic Maya** civilization

253 Alamanns and **Frankish** barbarians invade Gaul

235 Start of "**military anarchy**" in Rome; more than 20 Roman emperors in 50 years

238 Carpi and Goths cross the Danube and ravage Moesia

239 Sasanian Ardashir I captures cities of Carrhae and Nisibis

241 The prophet Mani (founder of Manichaeism) begins preaching in Persia

242 Kushans invade Sasanian province of **Bactria**

244 Gordian III murdered on Persian expedition; **Philip "the Arab"** becomes Roman emperor

247 In Japan, **Queen Himiko** of Yamato attacks kingdom of Kunukoku

249 Decius becomes Roman emperor after he revolts against Philip

251 Roman emperor **Decius is killed** in battle against the Goths

256 Sasanian Persian forces **take Antioch**

The main colonnade at Palmyra, which grew rich on tariffs paid by merchants who plied the desert route that passed through the Syrian city.

SHAPUR I (d.272)

Shapur's early leadership experience came in a role assisting his father, Ardashir, in mopping up support for the Parthian Arsacid dynasty. Shapur's defeats of Gordian III in 244 and of Valerian in 260 established a temporary Persian dominance in Syria and Mesopotamia. He used the many Roman prisoners captured in 256 at Antioch to build the new town of Veh-Antiok-Shapur ("Shapur's town, better than Antioch").

Goths ravaged the province of Moesia, laying siege to the main town of Nicopolis (modern Nikopol, Bulgaria). The campaign went badly for the Romans, ending in defeat and Decius's death at the **Battle of Abrittus** in 251.

In Japan, the **Yamato kingdom** emerged on the plain of Nara (in central Japan) around 250. Its rulers were interred in large burial mounds, and its armies conquered most of central Japan. Much of what is known comes from Chinese sources, who name the Queen of Yamato in 238 as **Himiko**.

VALERIAN'S CAPTURE BY THE PERSIANS

in 260 proved disastrous for the western part of the Roman Empire as well as the east. Valerian's son **Gallienus** (r. 260–68), struggling to contain an invasion of Italy by the Germanic **Iuthungi** had no resources to reinforce the Rhine frontier, which was being breached by **Alemmanic and Frankish raiders**. The Governor of Germania Inferior, **Marcus Postumus**, revolted and killed Gallienus's son Saloninus, who had been left in charge of Gaul and

The Gallic Empire
Postumus began the Gallic Empire in control of Gaul, Germany, Britain, and Spain. By its collapse in 274, the last ruler, Tetricus, had lost Spain.

Germany. Postumus **declared himself emperor**, but unlike previous usurpers did not march on Rome, instead setting up a separate **Gallic Empire**; this initially controlled Britain, Spain, parts of western Germany, and Gaul. He established a form of government that mirrored that of the official empire, complete with its own Senate. In 269, Postumus was murdered by his own troops and later replaced by his praetorian prefect Victorinus. Gallienus—faced with **Gothic invasions** and the revolt of **Zenobia of Palmyra** in the east—was **never strong enough** to put an end to the Gallic Empire. In 268 he was murdered by the army and replaced by Claudius II Gothicus (r. 268–70), who was too busy fighting in the

Balkans to deal with Gaul. Only under **Aurelian** (r. 270–74) was the Roman Empire strong enough, and by then the Gallic Empire was weakened, with its last ruler, Tetricus (r. 270–74), facing splits in the army. In 274, Tetricus was captured near Châlons, and the **Gallic Empire was reabsorbed**.

In the east, a serious **challenge to Roman rule** emerged after 260. The city of **Palmyra** (in Syria) proved Rome's **only reliable ally** against the Sasanian advances of Persia. Its ruler **Septimius Odaenathus** (c. 220–67) received a number of Roman titles, including *Corrector Totius Orientis* ("Marshal of the entire East"), and invaded the Sasanian Empire in 262 and 266. Odaenathus died in 267; and his wife **Zenobia** (r. 267–73) created **an empire of her own**. By 269, her armies had taken Syria and Egypt, and in 271 she declared her son **Vaballathus** emperor. Aurelian marched east and soon rolled back the Palmyrene gains, besieging Palmyra in spring 272. Zenobia was captured while trying to escape, and Palmyra was sacked in 273 when it tried to throw off Roman rule again.

Sepulchral relief from Palmyra
The Palmyrenes buried their dead with exquisite and realistic personal portrayals; the dead were interred in tower tombs outside the city.

In China, **Yuandi** (r. 260–64) restored Wei's fortunes by conquering the Shu Han. But soon after he was overthrown by one of his own generals, **Sima Yuan**, who founded the **Western Jin** dynasty and took the title Wudi (r. 265–89). His armies crushed and annexed the Eastern Wu kingdom in 280, thus **briefly reuniting China**.

> 66 YOU DEMAND **MY SURRENDER** AS THOUGH YOU WERE **NOT AWARE** THAT **CLEOPATRA** PREFERRED TO **DIE A QUEEN** RATHER **THAN REMAIN ALIVE.** 99

Zenobia, Queen of Palmyra, to Aurelian Augustus
from *Historia Augusta* c. 375–400

KEY

- Gallic Empire under Postumus, 260–68
- — Gallic Empire under Tetricus, 270–74
- Roman Empire, 260

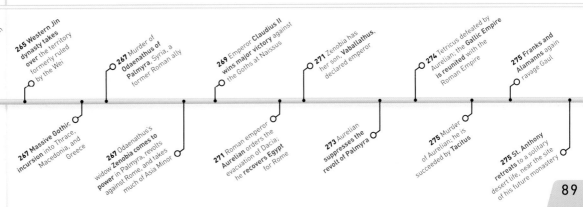

257 Decius issues edict forbidding **Christian worship**

260 Shapur I defeats **Valerian** and takes him prisoner; **Gallienus** declared Roman emperor

265 Western Jin dynasty takes **over** the territory formerly ruled by the Wei

267 Murder of **Odaenathus of Palmyra**, Syria, a former Roman ally

269 Emperor **Claudius II wins major victory** against the Goths at Naissus

271 Zenobia has her son, **Vaballathus**, declared emperor

274 Tetricus defeated by Aurelian; the **Gallic Empire is reunited** with the Roman Empire

275 Franks and Alamanns again ravage Gaul

258 Martyrdom of **Cyprian**, Bishop of Carthage

260 Breakaway **Gallic Empire established** by Postumus

267 Massive Gothic **incursion** into Thrace, Macedonia, and Greece

267 Odaenathus's widow **Zenobia comes to power** in Palmyra, revolts against Rome, and takes much of Asia Minor

271 Roman emperor **Aurelian orders the** evacuation of Dacia; he **recovers Egypt** for Rome

273 Aurelian **suppresses the revolt of Palmyra**

275 Murder of Aurelian; he is succeeded by **Tacitus**

275 St. Anthony **retreats** to a solitary desert life, near the site of his future monastery

> **" PROBUS** WAS ALMOST A **SECOND HANNIBAL** BECAUSE OF HIS **KNOWLEDGE OF WARFARE...** "

Aurelius Victor, Roman historian and official, in *De Caesaribus, c.* 360

The Pyramid of the Moon at Teotihuacán (near modern Mexico City) was built sometime after 200 at one end of the city's Avenue of the Dead; the Pyramid of the Sun sits at the other end.

IN CHINA, THE FIRST EMPEROR OF THE WESTERN JIN DYNASTY, Wudi (r. 265–89), was a strong ruler who secured trade routes to the West and built a bridge over the Yellow River to improve communications. However, the **wars of the Three Kingdoms period** (see 231–244) had impoverished the state and as the tax burden rose, many peasants fled to landowners for protection, resulting in the **rise of private armies**.

In the Roman Empire, Emperor Aurelian—who was murdered in 275—was followed by two short-lived emperors—Tacitus and Florianus—before Probus took power in 276. Within two years, Probus had **defeated the Goths** on the Danube and **pushed back the Franks** from the Rhine. A planned campaign against Persia was frustrated in 281 by the revolt of two usurpers in the West: Bonosus and Proculus. Despite his military successes, in 282 **Probus was murdered by his own troops**, who were resentful at being forced to work on civil engineering projects near Sirmium (in modern Serbia).

Jin sitting bear sculpture
The first half of the Jin dynasty under Wudi gave China a period of comparative peace and stability, which allowed the arts to flourish.

IN 284, THE ROMAN ARMY IN ASIA MINOR PROCLAIMED DIOCLES, the former commander of the imperial bodyguard, **Emperor Diocletian** (r. 284–305). In 285, he defeated **Carinus** (the then emperor of the Western Empire) and started **a radical reorganization of the empire**, reforming the army, and subdividing provinces. The challenges on the frontier were too great to be faced alone; in 285, he appointed **Maximian** (250–310) **to rule alongside him**, first as Caesar (junior emperor) then as Augustus (senior emperor). Other problems with Britain's break from the empire under **Carausius** in 286 convinced Diocletian that more changes were necessary. In 293, he and Maximian appointed two Caesars: **Constantius Chlorus** (r. 293–306) to assist Diocletian in the Western Empire and **Galerius** (r. 293–311) to be Maximian's junior in the East. This **tetrarchy** (four emperor system) enjoyed early successes in Britain (296) and in Egypt (298). In 294, Diocletian **reformed the coinage**, reissuing new bronze and silver coins, and in 301 he issued an **Edict on Maximum Prices** to try to curb rising inflation. Unlike his other measures, this one failed.

Persian frieze
The Paikuli frieze celebrates the victories of Narseh in Armenia and justifies his deposition of predecessor Vahram III.

After the death of Shapur I in 272 Persia faced **a period of political instability**. In 293, **Narseh** (r. 293–302) ascended to the Persian throne. He resolved to recover land in Armenia and Mesopotamia that had been lost

to the Romans. He launched a major invasion in 296, **defeating** the Caesar **Galerius** in 297. The next year, however, Galerius smashed Narseh's army in Armenia and captured the Persian ruler's family. Galerius marched as far as Ctesiphon, which he captured in 298. Narseh was forced to make peace (**Treaty of Nisibis**). Persia remained at peace with the Romans for 40 years.

In the Valley of Mexico, the city of **Teotihuacán reached the peak of its power** around 300. Its main street—the Avenue of the Dead—ran between the Pyramid of the Moon and the Ciudadela (which may have been the palace of the ruler) and was lined with the residences of the lords of the city.

12 SQUARE MILES
THE **AREA** OF **TEOTIHUACAN CITY** AT ITS **PEAK**

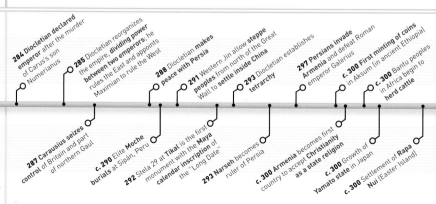

276 Probus becomes **Roman emperor** after brief six-month reign of Tacitus

277 Mani (founder) of Manichaeism) is **crucified by the Persians**

277–79 Probus **expels the Franks** from Gaul, and puts down unrest in Egypt and Illyria

279 Jewish scholars in Tiberias **publish** a collection of Jewish laws and doctrines, **the Talmud**

280 Western Jin conquer the south of China and **unite the country** under their leader, Sima Yuan

282 Probus killed at Sirmium in Illyria after a mutiny

283 Emperor **Carus invades Persia** and takes Seleucia and Ctesiphon; he dies mysteriously near Ctesiphon

284 Diocletian declared **emperor** after the murder of Carus's son Numerianus

285 Diocletian reorganizes the empire, **dividing power between two emperors**; he rules the East and appoints Maximian to rule the West

287 Carausius seizes control of Britain and part of northern Gaul

288 Diocletian makes **peace with Persia**

c. 290 Elite Moche burials at Sipán, Peru

291 Western Jin allow **steppe peoples** from north of the Great Wall to **settle inside China**

292 Stela 29 at **Tikal** is the first monument with the **Maya** calendar inscription of the "Long Date"

293 Diocletian establishes **tetrarchy**

293 Narseh becomes ruler of Persia

297 Persians invade **Armenia** and defeat Roman emperor Galerius

c. 300 Armenia becomes first country to accept **Christianity as a state religion**

c. 300 First minting of coins in Aksum (in ancient Ethiopia)

c. 300 Growth of Yamato state in Japan

c. 300 Bantu peoples in Africa begin to **herd cattle**

c. 300 Settlement of **Rapa Nui** (Easter Island)

This early 16th-century fresco of the Battle of Milvian Bridge is in the Apostolic Palace in the Vatican. Before the battle, the emperor Constantine is said to have seen a Christian monogram in a dream predicting his victory.

SINCE PERSECUTIONS IN THE 250S AND 260S, THE CHRISTIAN COMMUNITY had experienced some 40 years of tranquillity in the Roman Empire. All this changed in 303 when Diocletian issued an **edict** ordering the **destruction of churches** and the handing over and **burning of Christian books**. A sterner edict followed, calling for the arrest of Christian clergy, and one in 304 ordered that all Christians offer a sacrifice to the pagan gods. Devout Christians could not accede to these demands, and many of them were martyred.

In 304, Diocletian fell seriously ill, and in 305 he announced that he and Maximian would abdicate. **Constantius Chlorus** and **Galerius** would take over as Augusti, while the new Caesars were to be **Maximinus** (Galerius's nephew) and **Flavius Severus**

75,000
MAXENTIUS

50,000
CONSTANTINE

Battle numbers at Milvian Bridge
Maxentius's forces outnumbered those of Constantine, but his army became trapped between Constantine's men and the river.

(Galerius's army colleague). The new tetrarchy soon unraveled. **Constantius died** in Eboracum (modern York, England) in July 306 and the troops there proclaimed his son **Constantine** the new Augustus. By October, **Maxentius** (r. 306–12), the son of Maximian, was crowned emperor in Rome. Severus was killed trying to retake Rome from Maxentius, and Maximian restored himself to the position of Augustus. In 308, the **Conference of Carnuntum** was called to settle the disputes, presided over by Diocletian, who came out of retirement. Constantine accepted a demotion to Caesar in the West, with **Licinius** as Augustus (r. 308–24), while **Maximinus Daia** became Galerius's Caesar in the East (r. 310–13). This new arrangement was no more succesful than the old one.

Palace of Diocletian
Diocletian built the great palace at Split, Croatia, for his retirement after his abdication in 305. Here, he tended his cabbages.

In 311, **Galerius died** and **Maximinus became Augustus** in the East. He ordered **renewed measures against Christians**. Constantine, meanwhile, invaded Italy and in October 312 defeated and killed Maxentius at the **Battle of Milvian Bridge**. Before the battle, Constantine is said to have dreamed of the **Chi-Rho symbol** and ordered his troops to mark it on their shields.

Licinius and Constantine met at Mediolanum (modern Milan) in 313, where they agreed to share power and issued the **Edict of Milan**, which granted toleration to all forms of worship, in effect **legalizing Christianity**. Licinius then turned East and defeated Maximinus Daia, securing control

over the Eastern provinces. The alliance between Constantine and Licinius broke down in 316; they patched up a peace in 317, and for six years the Roman Empire relapsed into an uneasy calm.

In China, Wudi's successor **Huidi** (r. 290–306) was mentally disabled and so a succession of regents contended for imperial control. Huidi's brother **Huaidi** (r. 307–11) invited the northern **Xiongnu tribesmen** to help him against the competing Chinese factions, but they took him prisoner. The **last Western Jin emperor Mindi** (r. 313–16) saw the Xiongnu sack the capital of Chang'an (modern Xi'an); the Jin moved south, where **Yuandi** (r. 317–23) became the **first Eastern Jin emperor** in 317.

Chi-Rho symbol
The monogram of Chi-Rho, the first two letters of Christ's name in Greek, became an important early symbol of Christianity.

Early spread of Christianity
Christianity spread in the 2nd and 3rd centuries until there were strong Christian communities in Anatolia, southern Gaul, Italy, Egypt, and the province of Africa (Tunisia).

KEY

░ Areas strongly Christian by 325

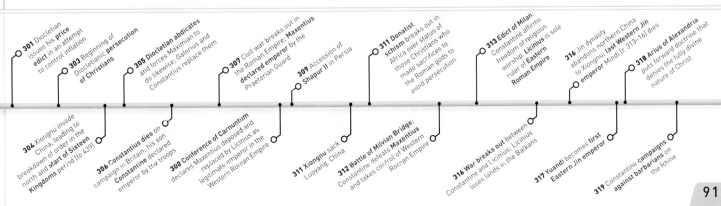

301 Diocletian issues his **price edict** in an attempt to control inflation

303 Beginning of Diocletianic **persecution of Christians**

305 Diocletian abdicates and forces Maximian to do likewise; Galerius and Constantius replace them

307 Civil war breaks out in the Roman Empire; **Maxentius declared emperor** by the Praetorian Guard

309 Accession of **Shapur II** in Persia

311 Donatist **schism** breaks out in Africa over status of those Christians who made sacrifices to the Roman gods to avoid persecution

313 Edict of Milan: Constantine affirms freedom of religious worship; **Licinius** is sole ruler of **Eastern Roman Empire**

316 Jin dynasty abandons northern China to Xiongnu; **last Western Jin emperor** Mindi (r. 313–16) dies

318 Arius of Alexandria puts forward doctrine that denies the fully divine nature of Christ

304 Xiongnu invade China, leading to breakdown of order in the north and **start of Sixteen Kingdoms** period (to 439)

306 Constantius dies on campaign in Britain; his son Constantine declared emperor by the troops

308 Conference of Carnuntum deposed and replaced by Licinius as legitimate emperor in the Western Roman Empire

311 Xiongnu sack Luoyang, China

312 Battle of Milvian Bridge: Constantine defeats Maxentius and takes control of Western Roman Empire

316 War breaks out between Constantine and Licinius; Licinius loses lands in the Balkans

317 Yuandi becomes first Eastern Jin emperor

319 Constantine campaigns against barbarians on the Rhine

It was largely Eastern Church leaders who gathered at the Council of Nicaea (depicted here) in 325; only eight Western bishops made the journey there.

Ammianus Marcellinus (d. c. 330) writing on the character of the Emperor Constantius II in *The Later Roman Empire*

CHANDRAGUPTA I ASCENDED TO THE THRONE of a small kingdom in the western Ganges Plain in 320. Through an **advantageous marriage** to Princess Kumaradevi of the powerful Liccachevi dynasty and by conquest, he **expanded his realm** to include most of the central Ganges, from Magadha (in southern Bihar) to Prayaga (in Uttar Pradesh). His descendants, the Guptas, ruled northern India for almost 150 years.

Having taken up the **cause of Christianity** in 313, the Roman Emperor Constantine (r. 306–337) found that Christians themselves were far from united in **doctrine or organization**. Constantine called a church **council at Nicaea** in western Asia Minor in 325 to establish (and impose) orthodoxy in the face of a division over **Arianism** (the theology of Arius, who held that Jesus Christ was subordinate to God the Father). As well as Constantine, about 300 church leaders attended, and Arius's views were condemned.

The Column of Constantine
The sole surviving monument from the forum that Constantine built for his new city is this column, which sits in central Istanbul today.

14

THE NUMBER OF **DISTRICTS** IN CONSTANTINOPLE

After **defeating Licinius** (r. 308–24) in 324, Constantine **founded a new capital** for the Eastern Roman Empire at the ancient city of **Byzantium**, strategically sited between Europe and Asia. He demolished pagan temples and built new churches, such as Hagia Sophia, providing public buildings to rival those of Rome. The city of **Constantinople** (modern Istanbul) was publicly dedicated on May 11, 330. It was the seat of the Eastern Emperors for over 1,000 years.

8

THE NUMBER OF **TYPES** OF **PURE-GOLD COINS** ISSUED BY **SAMUDRA-GUPTA**

IN 335, SAMUDRAGUPTA (r. 335–75) SUCCEEDED HIS FATHER Chandragupta I as ruler of the Gupta domains in northern India. An inscription he set up in Prayaga survives, recounting a **series of campaigns** he fought in **Uttar Pradesh** and **Mathura**, both of which were annexed to the Gupta kingdom. He also made conquests down the east coast of India, as far as **Madras**, and subdued **West Bengal** as well as parts of **Rajasthan** and the **Punjab**. Various other regions acknowledged his suzerainty, making him the **most powerful Indian ruler** since the Mauryas.

Constantine died in 337, having accepted Christian baptism only on his deathbed. He had made no definite provision for **succession**, leaving his sons to divide the empire between them: **Constantine II** (r. 337–40) held Spain, Gaul, and Britain; **Constans** (r. 337–50) ruled Italy and North Africa, and **Constantine II**

Gold Gupta coin
Many Gupta coins contain images of horses, a possible reference to the ritual horse sacrifice performed by some Gupta rulers.

(r. 337–61) governed the Eastern Empire. Their reigns began with a **massacre at Constantinople** in which almost all of their father's other male relatives were killed in order to remove any possible rivals. Constantine II, who was the eldest, tried to assert his seniority, but **died during an invasion of Italy** in 340. Constans then took control of the entire Western Empire, where he was faced with a series of hard-fought campaigns against **Frankish invaders in Gaul**, and problems in **Britain**, which led him to visit the far-flung province (the last undisputed Roman Emperor to do so) in 343.

Disputes between the two surviving brothers, particularly one over the status of **Athanasius, Bishop of Alexandria** (whom Constantius II had exiled, but Constans wanted restored), soured all relations between them. In 350, a senior military officer, **Magnentius**, revolted at

Augustodunum in southern Gaul (modern Autun, France) and **Constans was killed**. Distracted by a war against Persia, Constantius II tolerated the upstart initially, but in 351 he moved against him. Since Constantius II had no heir, he promoted his cousin **Gallus**—one of the few survivors of the massacre of 337—to the rank of Caesar in 351 and left him **in charge in the East**, while he campaigned against Magnentius in the West. Magnentius's army was **defeated at Mursa** (in present-day Croatia); Italy and North Africa were rapidly recovered, and in 353 **Magnentius committed suicide** in Gaul.

For the next seven years **Constantius II ruled the empire alone**, mainly preoccupied with Frankish incursions into Gaul, the revolt of the usurper Silvanus in 355, and **a series of church councils** that sought to resolve doctrinal disputes (Constantius II favored Arianism over the traditional orthodoxy).

In the end, Gallus proved too ambitious and in 354 he was **deposed and executed**. Constantius II turned instead to Gallus's brother **Julian**, a studious youth with a penchant for pagan philosophy. In 355, after Silvanus's revolt, **Julian was despatched to Gaul** as Caesar, where he proved surprisingly effective at combating Frankish raiders.

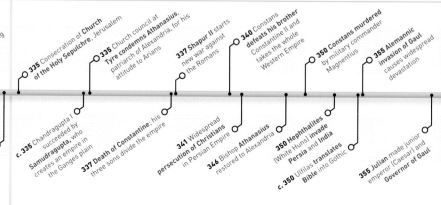

320 Accession of Aksumite king Ezana

320 Chandragupta I, founder of the Gupta Empire of India, ascends throne

321 Constantine campaigns in former Roman province of **Dacia**

c.325 Pachomius founds **monastery of Tabenne** in the Egyptian desert

326 Constantine has his **son Crispus put to death** for plotting

324 Constantine defeats Licinius to become sole Roman emperor; he founds new capital at **Constantinople**

325 Constantine summons **Council of Nicaea** to determine orthodox Christian doctrine

329 Saint Peter's basilica in Rome begun

333 Ezana of Aksum converts **to Christianity**

335 Consecration of **Church of the Holy Sepulchre,** Jerusalem

335 Church council at **Tyre condemns Athanasius,** patriarch of Alexandria, for his attitude to Arians

337 Shapur II starts new war against the Romans

340 Constans **defeats his brother** Constantine II and takes the whole Western Empire

350 Constans murdered by military commander Magnentius

355 Alemannic **invasion of Gaul** causes widespread devastation

c.335 Chandragupta I succeeded by **Samudragupta,** who creates an empire in the Ganges plain

337 Death of Constantine; his three sons divide the empire

341 Widespread **persecution of Christians** in Persian Empire

346 Bishop Athanasius restored to Alexandria

350 Hephthalites (White Huns) **invade Persia and India**

c.350 Ulfilas translates **Bible into Gothic**

355 Julian made junior emperor (Caesar) and Governor of Gaul

The acropolis at Tikal, one of the greatest surviving series of ruins in the Mayan world.

IN ETHIOPIA, THE KINGDOM OF AKSUM became one of the earliest states to **embrace Christianity** outside the Roman Empire. The Syrian Christian missionary Frumentius converted the king, Ezana (r. 320–60) to Monophysitism (a doctrine emphasizing a single nature of Christ, the divine). A letter from Constantius II to Ezana in 357 has survived, **urging Ezana to shift his allegiance to Arianism** and to replace Frumentius with an Arian bishop—evidence that the Roman emperors took seriously the religious loyalties of their neighbors. Ezana conducted military campaigns beyond his borders; an inscription speaks of

6

SQUARE MILES

THE **AREA** OF THE **CITY** OF **TIKAL**, c. 400

expeditions against neighboring "Gaze, then the Agame, and the Siguene," and it seems his armies may have occupied **Meroë city** (in northern Sudan). Enriched by such conquests and the control of trade from sub-Saharan Africa and Arabia, **Aksum** would **dominate the region** until the 7th century.

The **pre-Classic Maya kingdoms** of Guatemala and Mexico underwent a collapse some time in 200–300, with populations declining and building activity ceasing. But the region soon recovered, with the emergence of **a new phase** in Maya civilization, the Classic period (300–900), in which a series of **powerful kingdoms emerged**. Their great urban centers, such as those at Tikal (in Guatemala) and Palenque (in Mexico), are characterized by **huge pyramidal temples and**

Shapur II hunts a stag
Sasanian rulers commissioned lavish silver items depicting themselves hunting wild beasts as a display of their royal power.

palace complexes set in a central "acropolis." The Mayans developed a **hieroglyphic** form of writing that survives on many of the **stelae** (carved stone slabs) they set up to commemorate important events; in Tikal the first such dated monument is from 292. The first named king of Tikal is **Siyaj Chan K'awiil I** (c. 305), and by the reign of Chak Tok Ich'aak I (r. 360–78), Tikal was by far the **largest and most powerful** of the Classic Maya cities.

The **Roman Empire** faced invasions on both its western and its eastern borders in the 340s and 350s. In the West, **the Franks** began to push across the Rhine, and in the early 350s they overran part of the Rhine frontier, occupying some old Roman fortresses. **Caesar Julian** engaged in a series of **campaigns against the Franks** (356–59) and drove them from most of the territory they had taken.

In the East, **conflict** broke out again between the Romans and the Persians, under **Shapur II** (r. 309–79), who took advantage of the political turmoil in the Roman Empire in the 350s. In 359, Shapur II advanced farther west and **took the great Roman fortress of Amida** (modern Diyarbakir, Turkey). Other towns were captured and their populations deported to Persia, threatening the Roman position in the East.

KEY

▮ Northern Maya
▮ Central Maya
▮ Southern Maya
♦ Mayan site
→ Trade route

Maya kingdoms
Classic Maya culture originated in lowland cities, such as Uaxactun and Tikal, but spread to the highlands and the Yucatán peninsula.

Gulf of Mexico
NORTHERN MAYA
Yucatán Peninsula
CENTRAL MAYA
Palenque
Tikal
Peten
Caribbean Sea
SOUTHERN MAYA
PACIFIC OCEAN

356 Bishop Athanasius of Alexandria **exiled once more**

356–57 Constantius II **issues laws** banning divination and sacrifices, and closing pagan temples

358 Huge earthquake devastates western Asia Minor

359 Shapur II **invades Syria** and captures Amida

360 Julian's troops declare him **emperor** in Paris

356 St. Antony, leader of monastic movement in Egypt and "Desert Father," **dies** (born c. 251)

357 Church council at Sirmium issues **pro-Arian creed**

358 Constantius II campaigns across Danube against **Quadi** and **Sarmatians**

359 Church councils at Rimini (of bishops) and at Seleucia in Cilicia agree on the **homoios formula**—a compromise between Arian and orthodox Nicene Christians

360 Council of Constantinople promulgates pro-Arian creed

Here Emperor Julian is seen in religious debate. He attempted to sow discord among Christians by decreeing the return of those who had been exiled for religious reasons.

The church of Hagia Eirene in Istanbul was built by Constantine I.

IN CHINA, THE EASTERN JIN DYNASTY (317–420) brought comparative stability to the south of the country. Although many of the emperors were short-lived, the bureaucracy in the southern capital of Nanjing functioned efficiently and the period saw a **cultural flowering**. Artists such as Gu Kaizhi (c. 345–406) painted masterpieces such as the *Admonitions of the Instructress to the Palace Ladies*, as well as producing works on the theory of painting. **Northern China**, on the other hand, was **highly unstable**, divided between the Sixteen Kingdoms, most of them ruled by **nomadic groups**. The Eastern Jin emperors alternated between a defensive stance towards the Sixteen Kingdoms and aggressive campaigns, notably under Mudi (r. 345–61) who retook Sichuan and Luoyang. All these gains were lost, however, under Emperor Aidi (r. 362–65). In 383, the Eastern Jin

16

THE **NUMBER** OF **KINGDOMS** IN **CHINA** FROM **304** TO **439**

(under Xiaowudi) would be forced to repel a major invasion in the north of the country.

In the Roman Empire, **Julian** was proclaimed **Augustus** by his troops in 360, so he was a direct challenge to Constantius. The threat from the Persians, who were advancing through Asia Minor, was too great for

JULIAN THE APOSTATE (331–63)

The nephew of Constantine I, Julian was educated as a Christian but c. 351 became a pagan under the influence of Maximus of Ephesus. When Julian unexpectedly became emperor in 363, he tried to restore paganism in the empire, including banning Christians from teaching literature. He became known by Christian writers as "the Apostate" for his perceived betrayal of Christianity.

Constantius to meet immediately. **He died** in November 361 as he was finally marching west to deal with the revolt. Now sole emperor, Julian immediately set about **restoring the role of paganism** in the Roman Empire, trying to establish a kind of pagan orthodoxy and an official pagan hierarchy of priests to counter Christianity's strengths. He reopened pagan temples, and **restored the right to sacrifice**.

In 363, Julian set out on **a campaign against Persia**, planning to punish its leader, Shapur II, for his attacks on the empire in 359–60. He reached Ctesiphon, but was then forced to retreat up the Tigris River. Being short of supplies, the Roman army suffered constant harassment from the Persians and, in one such skirmish, **Julian was killed**. The pagan reaction was over.

On Julian's death the army chose **Jovian** (r. 363–64) as emperor,

but he ceded key border provinces to Persia, which lost him popularity, and he died (probably murdered) within months. An officer of the imperial bodyguard, **Valentinian** (r. 364–75), was then raised to the throne, and he selected his brother **Valens** (r. 364–78) to be his **co-ruler**. Valentinian spent much of his reign along the Rhine dealing with Frankish and Alemannic invaders. He died in 375 after suffering some type of seizure, brought on by his anger at barbarian Quadi envoys thought to have insulted him.

The Western Roman Empire was then subdivided between Valentinian's two sons **Gratian** (r. 375–83) and **Valentinian II** (r. 375–92). In the Eastern Empire, Valens was forced to spend most of the early 370s in Syria to contain the Persian threat, but growing trouble with barbarians along the Danube later forced him to turn to the Balkans.

Sarmatian dagger
This dagger belonged to the Sarmatians, a tribe of Iranian origin who specialized in horseback fighting, and were defeated by Valentinian I.

> ... THE **BARBARIANS**, [ARE] LIKE BEASTS ... **BROKEN LOOSE**... OVER THE **VAST EXTENT**... OF **COUNTRY**.

Ammianus Marcellinus, on the Gothic invasion of the Balkans c. 390

IN 376, LARGE GROUPS OF GOTHS ARRIVED AT THE DANUBE FRONTIER, pressing to be admitted to the Roman Empire. **The Huns**, a new nomadic group from Central Asia, were at their rear, and the Goths feared being squeezed between them and the imperial frontier. Emperor Valens did not wait for reinforcements before marching out to meet the Gothic army. On August 9, 378, near Adrianople, **the Romans met the Goths**, under Fritigern. Misled by the temporary absence of the Gothic cavalry, Valens attacked but his army was surrounded by the returning barbarian horsemen. Valens was killed and the **Eastern army destroyed**, leaving the Balkans open to the Goths.

Gratian reacted by turning to **Theodosius**, a Spanish military officer, who he appointed as his imperial colleague. For the next three years Theodosius patiently negotiated, bought off some groups, and struck militarily where he could. In 382, the two

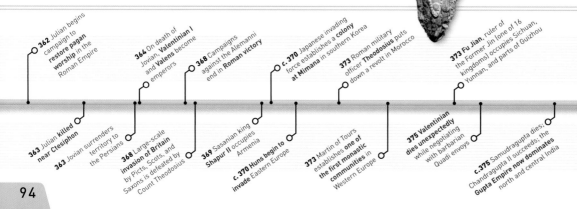

362 Julian begins campaign to **restore pagan worship** in the Roman Empire

364 On death of Jovian, **Valentinian I** and **Valens** become emperors

368 Campaigns against the Alemanni end in **Roman victory**

c. 370 Japanese invading force establishes a **colony at Mimana** in southern Korea

373 Roman military officer **Theodosius** puts down a revolt in Morocco

373 Fu Jian, ruler of the Former Jin (one of 16 kingdoms) occupies Sichuan, Yunnan, and parts of Guizhou

376 Fu Jian, of the Former Jin, **extends control** into Central Asia

376 Goths petition Valens to allow them to settle in the Roman Empire

379 Yax Nuun Ayiin becomes **ruler of Tikal**

363 Julian killed near Ctesiphon

363 Jovian surrenders territory to the Persians

368 Large-scale **invasion of Britain** by Picts, Scots, and Saxons is defeated by Count Theodosius

369 Sasanian king **Shapur II** occupies Armenia

c. 370 Huns begin to invade Eastern Europe

373 Martin of Tours establishes **one of the first monastic communities** in Western Europe

375 Valentinian dies unexpectedly while negotiating with barbarian Quadi envoys

c. 375 Samudragupta dies; Chandragupta II succeeds; the **Gupta Empire now dominates** the north and central India

378 Goths defeat the Romans under Valens at Adrianople

St. Jerome (c. 347–420) completed the *Vulgate*, the first definitive translation of the Bible into Latin, c. 405.

> ## THE **THICKER** THE **HAY**, THE **EASIER** IT IS **MOWED**.
>
> **Alaric the Goth,** speaking of his enemies *c.* 400

sides agreed a truce, whereby the **Goths** were **allowed to settle** in the empire in return for providing troops for the Roman army.

The **Gupta Empire continued to expand** under Chandragupta II (r. 375–415) in northern India. He fought against the Sakas, annexing much of northwestern India. He also made an **astute marriage alliance** that extended his realm to the southwest.

Iron pillar of Delhi
This iron pillar at Qutb complex on the outskirts of Delhi is said to have been erected on the orders of Chandragupta II.

IN CENTRAL AMERICA, THE MAYAN CITY OF TIKAL had reached the peak of its influence in the late 4th century. In 378, a foreign lord called **Siyaj Kak** arrived in the city, possibly from Teotihuacán. His arrival, which may represent a military conquest, led to the **death of Tikal's ruler** Chak Tok Ich'aak and the **destruction of** most of Tikal's **public monuments**. Siyaj Kak installed a new dynasty on the throne of Tikal, possibly drawn from the ruling house of Teotihuacán, with **Yax Nuun Ayiin** ("Curl Snout"; r. 379–404) as the first ruler. Monuments depict him in northern Mexican, rather than Mayan, dress. Under his rule, Tikal's direct influence extended some 30 miles (50 km) away.

In the Western Roman Empire, **Gratian** had spent much of his time since the Battle of Adrianople (378) in northern Italy, where he **continued to act against pagans** in Rome, ordering the removal of the Altar of Victory from the Senate House in 382. In 383, he led an army north to face an invasion of Gaul by the Alemanni, but was then faced with **a revolt in Britain**, where the legions declared their commander **Magnus Maximus emperor**. Many of Gratian's commanders defected and in August 383 he was captured and executed by Maximus, who had crossed over to Gaul. **Theodosius**, fearful of trouble with Persia or a Gothic revolt in the Balkans if he moved west, **recognized Maximus** as his colleague. A peace with Persia in 386, however,

St. Ambrose
A Roman nobleman by birth, Ambrose was Bishop of Milan from 374 to 397. He exercised a powerful influence over Theodosius I.

freed Theodosius to react when Maximus invaded Italy in 387. In August 388, he marched swiftly into northern Italy, **capturing Maximus** near Aquileia and having him executed.

As well as campaigning against the Goths and Maximus, Theodosius was preoccupied with the **imposition of Orthodox Christianity**. He moved against the Arians, deposing the Bishop of Constantinople in 380 and calling a council in 381 in the capital, which reaffirmed the anti-Arian decisions of the Council of Nicaea (see 325). He connived in the **destruction of many pagan temples**, including the great temple of Serapis in Alexandria, and in 391 he **forbade all pagan sacrifices** throughout the empire.

IN 392, VALENTINIAN II, WHO HAD CONTINUED TO RULE OVER ITALY, was found hanged. His military commander Arbogast—suspected by some of Valentinian's murder—promptly made **Flavius Eugenius**, a middle-ranking official, emperor. Theodosius refused to recognize Eugenius, and in 393 he **invaded Italy**. To gain support in the Senate—where paganism was still strong—the Christian Eugenius **revoked** all of Theodosius's **anti-pagan laws**. But, in August 394, he was defeated by the Theodosian army at the **Frigidus River** near Aquileia. Theodosius did not enjoy his rule as sole emperor long, dying in January 395. The empire was then divided between his two sons: the older, Arcadius, taking the eastern part and his younger brother, Honorius, taking the

western one. Although there was no clear intention to do so, this split marked a permanent division; after 395 no one emperor ruled the whole empire again.

The **Goths** had taken part on Theodosius's side at the Battle of the Frigidus River and felt they had not been sufficiently rewarded for their losses. In 395, they rose up, led by **Alaric** (r. 395–410). Despite an attempt by **Stilicho** (c. 365–408), the half-Vandal commander of the Western Roman army, to suppress them, the Goths escaped and marauded throughout Greece in 396. Stilicho moved against Alaric again in 397, but once more failed to defeat him. A **brief halt to the Gothic rampage** came after Alaric's appointment by the Eastern Roman government to *magister militum* (a senior general).

Divided in two
The split of the Roman Empire into Eastern and Western divisions in 395 was permanent. By 476, its Western part would be overrun by barbarians.

KEY
- Eastern Roman Empire
- Western Roman Empire

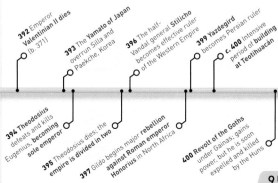

CLASSICAL TRADE

FLOURISHING TRADE BETWEEN CONTINENTS A WORLD APART

The growth of Roman power in the Mediterranean, the unification of China under the Qin and Han, and the establishment of the Parthian Empire in Iran created three large political blocs that provided stable conditions under which very long-distance trade routes could flourish.

The expansion of Han power westward in the 2nd century BCE brought the Chinese into contact with new powers they called An-hsi (Persia) and Li-chien (Rome). A Chinese embassy reached the court of Mithridates II of Parthia around 115 BCE. In the wake of diplomats came merchants, carrying the Chinese silk for which both Parthia and Rome had an insatiable appetite. The main Silk Route ran from China through Central Asia, down into Persia and then across Roman-controlled Syria toward the ports of the Mediterranean.

A thriving trade also spanned the Indian Ocean, transporting spices from the East Indies and southern India to ports in Africa and southern Arabia; from here a land route led up through Petra, in present-day Jordan, to Syria. Control of these trade routes was very lucrative, and towns that lay on them were able to exact heavy tolls from merchants, which they used to build spectacular public monuments.

Farther west, in the Mediterranean, expensive goods such as fine wine were carried by sea; in general land transportation was expensive, and bulky, low-value products tended to be produced and consumed locally.

8,000 MILES
THE LENGTH OF THE TRADE ROUTE FROM **CHANG'AN** TO **ROME**

ROMAN TRADE
The expansion of the Roman Empire to cover much of Europe, western Asia, and North Africa created largely peaceful conditions in which both internal and external trade could flourish.

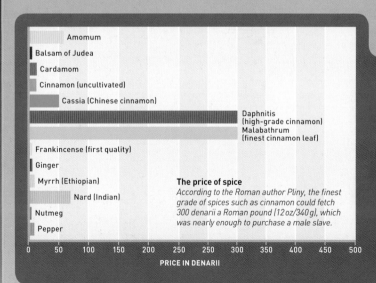

Amomum
Balsam of Judea
Cardamom
Cinnamon (uncultivated)
Cassia (Chinese cinnamon)
Daphnitis (high-grade cinnamon)
Malabathrum (finest cinnamon leaf)
Frankincense (first quality)
Ginger
Myrrh (Ethiopian)
Nard (Indian)
Nutmeg
Pepper

0   50   100 150 200 250 250 300 350 400 450 500
PRICE IN DENARII

The price of spice
According to the Roman author Pliny, the finest grade of spices such as cinnamon could fetch 300 denarii a Roman pound (12 oz/340 g), which was nearly enough to purchase a male slave.

Roman imports
The Romans imported huge quantities of raw materials, including luxury goods such as gold and ivory and cheaper goods such as food.

Roman exports
The Romans paid for their imports with precious metal and coins, and exported products such as wine and glassware.

SLAVES / ANIMALS / SPICES / COTTON / IVORY / INCENSE / SILK / FOOD

WINE / GLASSWARE / OLIVE OIL / SILVER / GOLD

World trade
Trade routes c.1 CE criss-crossed the whole of the classical world. The means of transport used depended on location—Bactrian camels were used in Central Asia, while horses, bullocks, and yaks were used elsewhere. Maritime trade was also extensive—there was an active trading network around the Indian Ocean.

HAN TRADE

The establishment of Chinese control in Central Asia from the late 3rd century BCE opened up a series of routes through Persia to the Mediterranean, which became collectively known as the Silk Route. However, it also involved the Han emperors in continuous and costly defense of their new territories.

Buying safety
To guarantee security on their frontiers and along trade routes, the Han were forced to pay large bribes in silk to barbarian groups such as the Xiongnu.

KEY
● Silk floss (catties) ● Silk fabric (pieces)

Han imports
The Han valued spices as much as the Romans did, but they also sent trade expeditions to Ferghana in Central Asia in search of what they called "heavenly horses."

HORSES · SPICES · PRECIOUS STONES

Han exports
Knowledge of silk in China goes back to at least 2600 BCE, but under the Han it became a staple export item, alongside lacquerware.

SILK · LACQUERWARE

KEY
- Roman Empire and client states
- Han Empire

Trade routes
- Roman
- Trans-Saharan (rudimentary route)
- Indian Ocean
- Silk Route
- China
- East Africa
- Amber
- Incense
- Other (rudimentary route)

Goods traded
- gold
- silver
- tin
- tortoiseshell
- ivory
- animals
- horses
- grain
- spices
- timber
- wine
- olive oil
- amber
- precious stones
- silk
- clothing
- incense
- slaves

Around 200 stone heads decorated Tiwanaku's Semi-Subterranean Temple. They may represent the group that founded the city—their flat headdresses denote high status.

ALTHOUGH THE WESTERN ROMAN EMPIRE SEEMED RELATIVELY SECURE IN 400, within a decade it had suffered a series of disasters. Gothic raids in 401 and again in 405 ravaged northern Italy. Then on the last day of 406, **hordes of Vandals**, joined by two other barbarian groups, the **Alans** and **Sueves**, crossed the frozen Rhine near Mainz, sacked Treveri (modern Trier, Germany) and Remi (modern Reims, France), and forced their way southwest until they reached the Pyrenees.

Meanwhile, the **armies of Britain** had raised up **a series of usurpers** as emperor from 406. The last of these, **Constantine III** (r. 407–11), took most of the remaining Roman troops in Britain and **crossed to Gaul** in spring 407, aiming to seize the throne from the then head of the Western Roman Empire, Honorius. Although he was defeated and captured at Arles in 411, native leaders in Britain had already **expelled the last Roman officials** there in 410—probably in revenge for their abandonment by Constantine's legion. **Britain** was now **independent from Rome**.

In 408, **Alaric** (r. c. 395–410), leader of the **Visigoths, invaded Italy** once more. The Roman

commander Stilicho persuaded the Senate to **agree to pay Alaric a huge bribe** in exchange for leaving the city, but there seems to have been a coup d'état and Stilicho was overthrown and killed. In 409, Alaric had Attalus, the prefect of Rome, declared emperor in an attempt to seize the initiative, but all negotiations failed. So, on August 24, 410, the **Visigoths entered Rome** and subjected it to a **three-day sack**. The event shook the entire Roman world, but Alaric was unable to secure domination over Italy, as he died later the same year.

In South America, **the city of Tiwanaku**, 15 miles (25 km) south

Visigoths ride on Rome
Alaric's sack of Rome in 410 was particularly shocking, as it was the first time the city had fallen since the Gauls took it in 390 BCE.

of Lake Titicaca (on the border between modern Peru and Bolivia), **reached its greatest size** in the 5th century, covering an area some 3 sq miles (8 sq km) in extent. Its central area contained a lavish series of **ceremonial buildings and temples**. These included the Semi-Subterranean Temple, decorated with stone heads of humans and supernatural beings, and structures such as the massive and beautifully decorated **Gateway of the Sun**. These were erected by a major pre-Columbian culture that **dominated the Altiplano** (flat high plateau) of Peru and Bolivia, and whose influence extended into northern Bolivia.

Ransom demands
Alaric initially asked for a huge ransom in return for leaving Rome in 410. Even when he moderated his demands, the Senate refused, and so the city was sacked.

		POUNDS
Pepper		
Gold		
	Silver	

0   10,000   20,000   30,000   40,000

THE BARBARIANS WHO HAD INITIALLY CROSSED THE RHINE IN 406 had gone on to sack a number of cities before moving southwest into Aquitaine and then crossing the Pyrenees into Spain, where they **occupied large swaths of Roman territory**. In 416–18, the Roman army commander Constantius persuaded the **Visigoths under Wallia** (r. 415–18) to invade Spain. There he smashed the Alans and the Siling Vandals, but allowed some of them to settle in southern Spain and left the Asing Vandals and Sueves in possession of northwestern Spain. Wallia was rewarded with official possession of much of southwestern Spain.

On the other side of the Mediterranean in 429, **Boniface**, the Roman Governor of North Africa, revolted against his long-term adversary **Aëtius**, and called on the Siling Vandals for help. The **Vandal king, Gaiseric** (r. 428–77), crossed over the Straits of Gibraltar with—it was said—80,000 of his people and, far from helping Boniface, swiftly occupied most of North Africa. In 435, he made a treaty with the Romans, recognizing his **occupation of Mauretania** (modern Algeria and Morocco). Gaiseric broke this and in 439 his warriors **captured Carthage**, the Roman capital there, and set up an **independent Vandal kingdom**.

The barbarian invasions
Barbarian groups took more and more Roman territory in the first half of the 5th century, leaving the Western emperors virtually powerless.

KEY
- ▪ Roman Empire
- ▫ Sasanian Empire
- → Huns
- → Goths
- → Alans
- → Vandals, Alans, Sueves
- → Burgundians
- → Franks
- → Jutes, Angles, Saxons
- → Irish
- → Picts

401 Visigoths under **Alaric** invade northern Italy

402 Stilicho pushes Visigoths out of Italy

404 St. Jerome completes **The Vulgate** (Latin) translation of the Bible

406 Hordes of **Vandals, Alans, and Sueves** penetrate deep into Roman Empire

407 Usurper **Constantine III,** declared emperor by the army in Britain; crosses into Gaul

408 Constantine III extends his area of rule into **Spain**

409 Vandals, Alans, and Sueves cross into **Spain**; Alaric invades Italy again and besieges Rome

410 Alaric's **Goths** capture and sack Rome

411 Constantine III captured at Arles

c. 411 Sueves establish **kingdom** in northwestern Iberia

415 Kumaragupta becomes ruler of the **Gupta Empire**

c. 420 Moche culture in Peru builds Temple of the Sun, using 50 million bricks

420 Eastern Jin overthrown; **Lui Song dynasty** founded

422 Theodosius II, Eastern emperor, forced to agree to **annual tribute** to the Huns

424 Aëtius invades Italy with Hunnish force intending to support the usurper **John**

425 John defeated; **Valentinian III** becomes emperor in the West

428 Nestorius, Patriarch of Constantinople, **preaches new doctrine** distinguishing Christ's human and divine nature; it is condemned as heretical

429 Vandals cross Strait of Gibraltar into North Africa

429 Bishop Germanus visits Britain on mission to root out Pelagianism

429–31 Struggle between **Boniface** and **Aëtius** for supremacy at Roman court ends in Boniface's death

c. 431 Pope Celestine sends **mission to Ireland** under Palladius

433 Attila becomes **king of the Huns**

A colorful Buddhist mural from the Yungang caves, which were begun under the Northern Wei c. 450.

THE EASTERN JIN DYNASTY IN CHINA HAD ENDED IN 420, with Gongi's abdication. His successor, Song Wudi (r. 420–22), a former fisherman, had risen to become a general and **founded the Liu Song dynasty**. He strengthened the southern kingdom's northern borders against the barbarian tribes, but under his son Wendi (r. 424–53), the northerners captured Luoyang in 424 before, some 25 years later, **besieging** the Liu Song capital of **Nanking**. Although Song Wudi had strengthened the central bureaucracy, the growing power and wealth of the **Buddhist and Daoist monasteries** weakened the economic basis of the state. Wendi's successors were weak and by 479 the Liu Song were overthrown by the short-lived **Southern Qi dynasty** (479–502).

Meanwhile, in northern China, the **Sixteen Kingdoms** had been united under the Toba Wei (a group of Turkic nomads), who founded the **Northern Wei dynasty** (386–534). The Northern Wei ruled over northern China, until its split into two in the early 6th century following a revolt against the imposition of Chinese dress and language on the Wei nomads.

In Europe, the Western Roman Empire continued to lose ground, as barbarians occupied more and more of its territory. In the 420s the **Visigoths under Theodoric**

(r. 418–51) occupied sections of the Mediterranean shore of Gaul, before they were pushed back southwest in 430. Around this time a new group of barbarians, **the Huns**, began to menace the empire. This nomadic group from Central Asia, whose pressure from the rear on the Goths had been indirectly responsible for the crisis of 378 in the Balkans, had since moved farther west. In 424, the Roman general **Aëtius recruited a force of Huns** to help him bolster the cause of John, a usurper raised up at Rome after the death of Honorius in 423. Aëtius continued to use the Huns into the late 420s to secure his power base and his appointment as patrician (the most senior post in the late Roman Empire) in 429.

In 435, he was able to call on them to aid an **attack on the Burgundians** who had raided across the lower Rhine; these were soundly defeated

Northern Wei horse
The art of the Northern Wei often evoked their nomadic origins, as in this beautiful terra-cotta horse.

> **❝ THE WORLD IS PASSING AWAY… LOSING ITS GRIP,** THE WORLD IS **SHORT OF BREATH. ❞**

St. Augustine of Hippo, theologian and philosopher, from *Sermons 81, 8*

and thereafter confined to a region to the northwest of Italy.

These were all just temporary successes, however, as the **area controlled** by the Western Roman emperors **was diminishing steadily**. The loss of almost all of North Africa to the Vandals in 429–39 (and of Sicily in 440), of northern Gaul to the Franks by 450, of southwest Gaul to the Visigoths after 418, and of all save a few isolated outposts in Spain by the 430s meant the remaining strongholds in Italy and southeastern Gaul **could not provide enough tax revenue** to support armies to reconquer the lost provinces. The long reign of **Valentinian III** (r. 425–55) in the Western Roman Empire **did not provide any stability** as he ascended to the throne as a child and never asserted himself until

the very end, when he had **Aëtius**, the Western Empire's last effective general, **murdered**.

The **barbarians** who settled on the former Roman territories began gradually to **establish kingdoms of their own**, notably the Franks in northern Gaul and the Visigoths in southwest Gaul and Spain. In **Britain**, the situation **was rather different**, since the province had rebelled against Rome rather than being subject to barbarian conquest. In a bygone era, the Roman army might have been expected to reassert its control there, but with the empire increasingly dependent on barbarian troops fighting under their own commanders, there was virtually no army left to retake it. The Britons were left to their own devices. It seems that some Roman institutions survived for a while; in 429 Bishop Germanus of Auxerre visited the island and found men bearing Roman titles. But **barbarian raiders**—attracted by the weak British defenses and the lack of a central political authority to counter them—**came in increasing numbers**. Around 446, the leading men of Britain addressed a

FLAVIUS AËTIUS
(c. 395–454)

Born of nobility in Moesia (modern Bulgaria), Aëtius spent time from 408 in the royal court of the Huns. He used these contacts to gain influence and rose to further prominence in the late 420s. The deaths of patricians Felix (in 430) and Boniface (in 433) left him with unrivaled dominance. He shored up the empire's position, and in 451 he scored a notable victory against Attila the Hun. In 454 he was murdered by Valentinian III himself.

desperate letter to Aëtius, appealing for aid. No reply was sent to these "groans of the Britons," and within a few years the **Angle, Saxon, and Jutish raiders** began to occupy parts of the former Roman province.

434 Huns **defeat army of Theodosius II** in Thrace

436 Burgundians defeated by Huns fighting in Roman service

438 Publication of **Theodosian Code**, an attempt to reconcile confusion of conflicting laws in Roman Empire

439 Vandals **capture Carthage**, completing conquest of Roman North Africa

440 Center of Buddhist studies founded on Ganges plain at Nalanda

440 Vandal king, Gaiseric, invades Sicily

442 Gaiseric signs treaty with Valentinian III acknowledging his rule over North Africa

444 Daoism made official religion of Northern Wei

c. 445 Saxons begin to settle in southern England

446 Buddhist rebellion against Northern Wei Daoist reforms

446 Burgundians granted imperial land in Geneva area

447 Huns under Attila **invade Thrace** and extract heavy tribute from the Empire

449 Vortigern, a British ruler, said to have **invited two Saxon leaders**, Hengist and Horsa to settle in Kent

449 Council of Ephesus **accepts Monophysitism**, the doctrine that Christ has a single, divine nature

450 Death of **Cui Hao** (b. 381), train architect of **Northern Wei** administrative reforms

c. 450 Influence of Teotihuacán stretches as far as Guatemala

c. 450 Franks occupy land in Netherlands up to the Somme

c. 450 Nazca people from Peru draw great petroglyph pictures in desert

450 Theodosius II dies; Marcian succeeds him as Eastern Emperor

In this undated painting Attila the Hun is shown with his army—he is said to have been turned aside from sacking Rome only by the pleas of Pope Leo I.

The baptism of Clovis the first: Clovis's baptism made him an easier diplomatic partner for the eastern Roman Empire than his Arian neighbors.

> **[HUNS] TOOK CAPTIVE THE CHURCHES AND SLEW THE MONKS AND MAIDENS.**

Callinicus, disciple of Hypatius, from *Life of Saint Hypatius, c. 450*

IN JAPAN, THE 5TH CENTURY SAW THE RAPID DEVELOPMENT and expansion of the **Yamato state**. Complex irrigation systems began to appear, and rulers built ever larger burial mounds, such as the 1,595ft- (486m-) long Nintoku mound. **Ojin** founded a new line of kings, who exercised firmer control over Japan's main islands from a royal center in the Kawachi-Izumi area. Yamato overseas contacts became more extensive, with ten diplomatic missions visiting China between 421 and 478, and increasing Yamato interference in civil wars between the Korean states of Paekche, Silla, and Koguryo.

The **Sasanian Persian Empire** came under pressure from eastern nomadic groups in the later 5th century. The **Hephthalite Huns** moved into Bactria early in the century, and were a particular threat to the Sasanians, but a famine during the **reign of Peroz (457–84)** caused them to move west again. In 469 Peroz suffered a terrible defeat at the hands of the Hephthalites. He was captured, and only released after leaving his son as a hostage. In 484, Peroz sought revenge in a new campaign against the Hephthalites, but was defeated and killed.

Having demanded, and been refused, the hand in marriage of Honoria, the sister of Roman Emperor Valentinian III in 450, the **Hunnish king Attila** (see 401–450) marched into Gaul. He was defeated near **Châlons** by an army of Romans under Aëtius and Goths under Theodoric.

Pope Leo I
The illustration on this manuscript shows Pope Leo I, an Italian aristocrat, persuading Attila the Hun not to attack Rome.

Clay bear figurine
Clay haniwa figurines have been a feature of rich Japanese burials since the earliest times. The large burial mounds of Yamato rulers contain huge quantities of them.

Undaunted, Attila invaded Italy in 452, but turned back short of Rome. **Attila died** after his wedding feast in 453, and his sons began a civil war that led to the Hunnish empire falling apart.

Following the death of the Roman general Aëtius in 454, real **power in the western Roman Empire** was exercised by a series of barbarian kingmakers, such as **Ricimer**, the leader of the Roman army in Italy. In 457, Ricimer placed **Majorian** on the imperial throne. When Majorian became too independent-minded, Ricimer replaced him with **Libius Severus** (r. 461–65), who he later had poisoned. Deprived of effective leadership, the Roman Empire lost more of its Gallic territories to the **Visigoths** and **Franks**.

IN 456, THE VISIGOTHS, encouraged by the western Roman emperor Avitus, had invaded the Iberian Peninsula. The Visigothic king **Theoderic II** (r. 453–66) defeated the Suevic ruler **Rechiarius**, who was threatening the Roman province of Tarraconensis, and the remaining Sueves retreated. Theoderic took most of Spain for himself, but left the Romans parts of the east coast. This policy was reversed by his successor **Euric** (r. 466–84), who overran the remaining Roman territories in the late 470s. By the time of **Alaric II** (r. 484–507) the Visigothic kingdom encompassed almost all of Spain, as well as Aquitaine and Provence in southern Gaul. The situation in Spain was repeated elsewhere in the Roman Empire, and the area of imperial control shrank to little more than Italy. **Anthemius** (r. 467–472) tried to recover some ground, but an expeditionary force against Vandal-controlled North Africa in 468 ended in disaster. In Gaul, Euric conquered almost all remaining Roman territory in the south by 475. In 472, Anthemius was overthrown by **Gundobad**, a Burgundian. Gundobad placed **Olybrius** (r. 472) and **Glycerius** (r. 473–74) on the throne in quick succession but, despairing of the empire's frailty, he then left for Burgundy. The last embers of the empire were contested in 475–76, between **Julius Nepos** and **Romulus Augustulus**, the son of **Orestes**, commander of the Roman army. Feeling that the

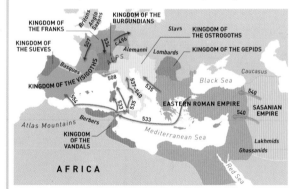
Barbarian kingdoms in Europe c. 500
By 500, most of the former western Roman Empire was divided among several principal barbarian successor states: the Vandals in North Africa, the Visigoths in Spain and southern Gaul, and the Ostrogoths in Italy.

KEY
→ Byzantine reconquests
→ Frankish expansion
→ Ostrogothic expansion
→ Sasanian expansion

interests of the Germanic barbarians in the army were being ignored, Orestes's deputy, **Odoacer**, revolted and deposed Romulus in September 476. He did not appoint a new emperor, claiming that he ruled Italy on behalf of the eastern emperor **Zeno** (r. 474–91). This marked the end of the Roman Empire in the west after 500 years.

However, in the east the Roman Empire survived. The long reign of **Theodosius II** (408–50) had strengthened its position, and after 400 the eastern empire had not had to face such direct threats from Huns, Goths, Vandals, Alamanns, Burgundians, and Franks as the west. **Marcian** (r. 450–57) had consolidated the eastern empire's finances, leaving a surplus of 100,000 pounds of gold at his death. **Leo I** (r. 457–74) fended off residual Gothic threats to the Balkans, and even made an attempt to recover North Africa in 468. **Zeno** faced the challenge of the new Germanic rulers of Italy, led by

Saxon brooch
Anglo-Saxon art in the 5th century valued abstract geometric patterns, as seen on this brooch.

Odoacer. He resolved this by commissioning the king of the Ostrogoths, **Theodoric**, to topple Odoacer in 489. By 500, the eastern Roman Empire under **Anastasius** (r. 492–518) was in little danger of the implosion that had erased its western counterpart just 25 years earlier.

The western Roman Empire was replaced by a series of **Germanic successor states**.

Odoacer ruled as king of Italy, but the legitimacy of his rule was always questionable. In 489, an invasion by Theodoric's Ostrogoths led to a four-year standoff, with Odoacer blockading himself inside the old imperial capital of Ravenna. After the murder of Odoacer in 493, Theodoric established a regime in which the continuation of Roman administrative practices won

the loyalty of the old Roman aristocracy. In 497, the eastern emperor **Anastasius I** recognized Theodoric's right to govern Italy, providing him with a secure base to consolidate his rule and extend it into Gaul.

In northwestern Gaul the Franks had emerged as a threat in the late 4th century, and by the 460s they were carving out a kingdom under **Childeric**. His successor **Clovis** (r. 481–511) transformed that kingdom, defeating **Syagrius**, ruler of a Roman enclave around Soissons, and expanding along the Rhine at the expense of the Alamans in the 490s. In 507, he defeated the Visigoths at the **Battle of Vouillé** and drove them out of most of southwestern Gaul. In the late 490s or early 500s, **Clovis converted** to Catholic Christianity, setting him apart from other barbarian rulers who were mostly Arians (members of an alternative Christian church). In **Britain**, the expulsion of Roman officials had been followed by a period in which petty kingdoms vied for power. These kingdoms were vulnerable to coastal raiders, and, late in the 5th century, groups of Germanic barbarians (**Angles**,

THEODORIC THE GREAT
(454–526)

Son of Theodemir, a king of the Ostrogoths, Theodoric spent 11 years as a Roman hostage, to guarantee the good behavior of his father. He returned home to become king of the Ostrogoths in 471, and for the next 17 years alternately allied with and attacked Roman territories in the Balkans. In 493, Theodoric became the first Ostrogothic king of Italy. His rule was generally pro-Roman, and he was buried in this Roman-style mausoleum.

Saxons, and Jutes) settled in Britain. The arrival of the Saxons has been dated to 449, when they were invited by the British king Vortigern. Seven years later, they revolted and set up a kingdom in Kent. **Aelle** founded a kingdom in **Sussex** around 477 and **Cerdic,** in **Wessex** (around modern Hampshire), by 495. A British victory at Mons Badonicus around 500 stemmed the Saxon tide, but the respite was short-lived.

These 6th-century ivory panels show Emperor Anastasius. He amassed a vast financial surplus, which his successors spent on expanding the Eastern Roman Empire.

This 6th-century mosaic, from the curch of San Vitale, Ravenna, Italy, depicts Emperor Justinian with his retinue of officials, guards, and clergy.

IN THE EASTERN ROMAN EMPIRE (generally called the **Byzantine Empire** from about this date), **Anastasius** (r. 491–518) faced difficulties in the Balkans, as new groups, including the **Bulgars**, pressed southward across the Danube between 493 and 502. More serious were **problems on the eastern frontier**, where the **Persians** insisted on Byzantine financial subsidies to pay for the defense of strategic passes in the Caucasus against barbarian incursions. In 502, the **Persian ruler Kavadh** began a war over the issue; the slow Byzantine reaction allowed him to capture Amida as well as several towns in Armenia. Byzantine forces retook Amida in 505, and Kavadh—preoccupied with a Hepthalite invasion in the east—agreed a truce, which lasted until 527.

Anastasius was almost 60 when he **became emperor** in 491, and his place on the throne was only secured by his marriage in 492 to Ariadne, widow of his predecessor **Zeno**. Almost immediately Zeno's brother **Longinus** revolted, and it took six years for Anastasius to subdue Longinus's home area of **Isauria** (in western Asia Minor). Anastasius gained popularity by abolishing the **chrysargyron tax** for traders and craftsmen. Prosperity continued and over his reign his treasury amassed a surplus of 320,000 pounds of gold. He also implemented monetary reforms in 498 and 512 aimed at stabilizing the currency, which had suffered successive debasements in the 5th century. In religious

red enamel

Frankish fibula brooch
Fibula brooches were practical as well as decorative, being used to fasten clothes. This brooch is decorated with the heads of birds.

terms Anastasius's reign was less tranquil, as he was a follower of **Monophysite Christianity**, which held that Christ had only a single divine nature and did not combine human and divine in his person. At first, Anastasius supported Zeno's **Henotikon**—an "act of union" issued in 482 that tried to broker a compromise between supporters of the orthodox creed (established at the Council of Chalcedon in 452) and the Monophysites. However, later his attitude became more pro-Monophysite, which led to serious rioting in 512, and the revolt of an

army officer, Vitalian, in Thrace in 514. Anastasius left no clear heir, and on his death **Justin** (r. 518–27), head of the palace guard, seized the throne. Justin was of humble origins and relied heavily on his nephew **Justinian**. He restored **Chalcedonian Christianity** and developed good relations with the **Ostrogoths** of Italy and the **Vandals** of North Africa. Abroad, his reign was generally peaceful, apart from a minor campaign against Persia in early 527.

In Gaul, **Clovis, king of the Franks**, had defeated Syagrius, ruler of a Roman enclave near Soissons, in 486, followed by the Alamanns and the Thuringians in 491. The **Visigothic kingdom** in southwestern Gaul was his next target, and it collapsed after a major Frankish victory at Vouillé in 507. Clovis's marriage to Clotilde, daughter of the Burgundian king Chilperic, led him to convert to **Catholic Christianity** in the 490s, and he maintained cordial relations with the Byzantine emperor Anastasius, who gave him the title of consul c. 508. Near the end of his reign, Clovis added several previously independent Frankish domains to his kingdom, notably that of the Ripuarian Franks. On his death in 511, Clovis's kingdom was divided among his four sons—Theuderic, Childebert, Chlodomir, and Chlothar. This tradition of subdivision would weaken the **Merovingian dynasty**, as the descendants of Clovis were known. The Merovingians ruled Francia (France) until the 8th century.

THE REIGN OF THE BYZANTINE EMPEROR JUSTINIAN (r. 527–65) began with important reforms. In 528, he commissioned a new law code to replace the confusion he had inherited. The new code, the **Codex Justinianus**, came into force in 529 (revised in 534). An enthusiastic builder, Justinian ordered the building of the great

THEODORA (c.500–548)

Theodora, who Justinian married in 525, had once been a prostitute and the mistress of Hecebolus, the governor of Libya Pentapolis. After the death of her adoptive mother, Empress Lupicina (who had opposed their relationship), Justinian had the law changed in 524 to allow him to marry Theodora. Theodora became a forceful empress, stiffening Justinian's resolve during the Nika revolt and acting as the protector of Monophysite Christians—she was one herself—during times of persecution.

church of **Hagia Sophia** in 532. The greatest challenge to his rule came in 532, when rioting among the Blue and Green chariot-racing factions got out of hand and turned into the **Nika Revolt**. The uprising almost caused Justinian to flee Constantinople, and its suppression killed 30,000 rebels.

With his throne secure, Justinian looked abroad. In 533 he sent an army under **Belisarius** to Vandal-controlled North Africa, where **Gelimer** had deposed King Hilderic, a Byzantine ally. On September 13, Belisarius defeated Gelimer's army at **Ad Decimum**, just outside Carthage, and Vandal resistance collapsed. Carthage was occupied and Gelimer was sent as a captive to Constantinople.

The rapid conquest of the **Vandal kingdom** encouraged Justinian to intervene in Italy. An excuse was provided by the murder in April 535 of his friend **Amalasuintha**, the Ostrogothic queen. Belisarius launched a strike against Italy in 535, landing on Sicily with 7,000 troops. Sicily was secured by the end of 535, and Belisarius moved into southern Italy early in 536. He took Naples after a three-week siege, causing the Ostrogothic king, **Vitigis**, to retreat northward. On December 9, 536, in a symbolic restoration of the empire's lost provinces, the **Byzantine army occupied Rome**. Rome was soon besieged by Goths. Belisarius finally took the Ostrogothic capital of **Ravenna** in 540. Suspicions that he planned to become emperor led to his recall, encouraging more Ostrogothic resistance.

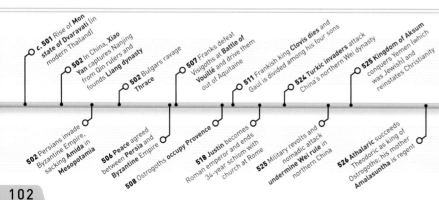

- **c. 501** Rise of **Mon state of Dvaravati** (in modern Thailand)
- **502** In China, **Xiao Yan** captures Nanjing from Qin rulers and founds **Liang dynasty**
- **502** Bulgars ravage **Thrace**
- **507** Franks defeat Visigoths at **Battle of Vouillé** and drive them out of Aquitaine
- **511** Frankish king **Clovis dies** and Gaul is divided among his four sons
- **524** Turkic invaders attack China's northern Wei dynasty
- **525** Kingdom of Aksum conquers Yemen (which was Jewish) and reinstates Christianity

- **502** Persians invade Byzantine Empire, sacking **Amida** in **Mesopotamia**
- **506** Peace agreed between **Persia** and **Byzantine Empire**
- **508** Ostrogoths occupy **Provence**
- **518** Justin becomes Roman emperor and ends 34-year schism with church at Rome
- **525** Military revolts and nomadic attack **undermine Wei rule** in northern China
- **526** Athalaric succeeds Theodoric as king of Ostrogoths; his mother Amalasuntha is regent

- **527** Justinian, nephew of Justin, becomes **Byzantine ruler**
- **529** Platonic Academy at Athens closed down by Justinian
- **529** Korean state of **Silla** expands at the expense of states in the southwest
- **531 Khusrau I** becomes Sasanian ruler of Persia
- **532** In Constantinople, **Nike Revolt** threatens to overthrow Justinian

- **529** Issuing of **Justinian's Code**, reforming Roman law
- **530** Byzantine general **Belisarius** defeats Persians at Dara
- **531** Justinian tries to enlist **Aksum** as an ally in war against Persia
- **532 Peace treaty** between Khusrau I and Justinian

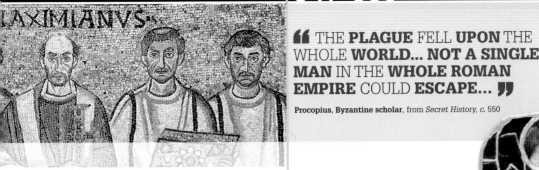

> THE **PLAGUE** FELL **UPON** THE WHOLE **WORLD... NOT A SINGLE MAN** IN THE **WHOLE ROMAN EMPIRE** COULD **ESCAPE...**

Procopius, Byzantine scholar, from *Secret History*, c. 550

Justinian's reconquests
Vandal Italy fell to Justinian's armies in 533, but it was devastated by the 20-year war needed to take it. An attempted Byzantine reconquest of Spain foundered, capturing only a few coastal areas.

KEY
- ▢ Byzantine Empire, 527
- ▢ Justinian's reconquests
- → Byzantine campaigns
- ✕ Battle

Persia entered a new period of greatness under **Khusrau I** (r. 531–79), who came to the throne at a time when the Mazdakites—a populist religious movement—had caused serious social tensions. Khusrau **reformed the tax system** and established **a new army**, encouraging poorer nobles and their followers to serve by paying salaries. Khusrau **captured Antioch** in 540, forcing Justinian to pay 5,000 pounds of gold to regain it. He attacked again, in 544, but a siege of Edessa failed and so he made a truce. A further Byzantine–Persian war (546–61) resulted in a **50-year peace**.

> TO ME, AND TO MANY OTHERS, **THESE TWO SEEMED NOT** TO BE **HUMAN BEINGS, BUT** VERITABLE **DEMONS... VAMPIRES.**

Procopius, Byzantine scholar, on Justinian and Empress Theodora, from *Secret History*, c. 550

THE LATTER PART OF JUSTINIAN'S REIGN lacked the achievements of its first half. A serious outbreak of **plague**, probably bubonic plague, began in Egypt in 540 and caused widespread mortalities, robbing the empire of desperately needed manpower. **Tax revenues fell**, further weakening the administration, and **prices rose**, leading to the passing of laws in 544 to reduce inflation. Further outbreaks of plague occurred in the 6th and 7th centuries, sapping the vitality of the Byzantine Empire.

In Italy, the **Ostrogoths** made rapid advances after the departure of **Belisarius**. Their new king, **Totila**, secured the area north of the Po River, and in 542 took control of much of central Italy. Belisarius was recalled to retrieve the situation in 544, but Justinian starved him of resources and **Rome fell** in 546. Although the Byzantines retook Rome in 547, it fell once more to Totila in 550. Justinian sent two huge armies under **Artabanes** and **Narses** to finish off the Goths. Artabanes entered Ravenna in June 552, and in July Narses defeated Totila at the **Battle of Busta Gallorum** in the Apennines. Totila later died of his wounds. There was still some Ostrogoth resistance, but the war in Italy was effectively over.

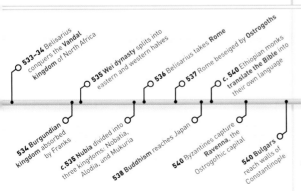

Ostrogothic brooch
This gold and enamel brooch demonstrates the high level of workmanship in the Ostrogothic kingdom of Italy. Its eagle imagery may indicate Roman influence.

533–34 Belisarius conquers the **Vandal kingdom** of North Africa

535 Wei dynasty splits into eastern and western halves

536 Belisarius takes **Rome**

537 Rome besieged by Ostrogoths

c. 540 Ethiopian monks **translate the Bible** into their own language

534 Burgundian kingdom absorbed by Franks

c.535 Nubia divided into three kingdoms; Nobatia, Alodia, and Mukuria

538 Buddhism reaches Japan

540 Byzantines capture **Ravenna**, the Ostrogothic capital

540 Bulgars reach walls of Constantinople

542 Outbreak of **plague** in Constantinople kills many thousands

544 Viet kingdom of Vietnam established

547 Rebellion of **Berber tribes** breaks out in North Africa, but is crushed by Byzantine army

550 Byzantine general Belisarius replaced by **Narses**; Rome falls again

c. 550 Khmer state of **Chenla** throws off suzerainty of Funan

543 Nubian kingdom of **Nobatia** converted to Christianity by Coptic missionaries

546 Ostrogothic king **Totila captures Rome**, which falls again soon after to Belisarius

548 Nanjing sacked as Hou Jing leads rebellion against **Liang dynasty**

c. 550 Turkic **Avar** peoples begin to migrate westward

c. 550 Nubian kingdom of **Alodia** converted to Coptic Christianity

The 13th-century Iona Abbey (pictured) was built on the site of the original monastery founded by St. Columba when he arrived on Iona in 563.

MEROVINGIAN FRANCIA (FRANCE) HAD BEEN DIVIDED into separate kingdoms on the death of Clovis in 511 (see 501–526). Despite this, Frankish power continued to grow. By 558, **Chlothar I** (511–61), who ruled the area of Francia around Soissons, had absorbed the Rheims kingdom and the region around Paris after their rulers died. This left Chlothar as the **sole Merovingian ruler of Francia** for three years, until his death in 561. Francia was once again divided, with Charibert I receiving Paris, Guntram getting Orléans, Sigibert Rheims, and Chilperic Soissons. It was not until 613 that the Frankish kingdom was reunited under **Chlothar II** (r. 613–29).

Ajanta cave art
The Ajanta caves, a Buddhist holy site in Maharashtra, India, experienced a second major phase of use during the 6th century.

Ireland had been converted to Christianity by **Patrick** (d. 461) in the mid-5th century and a strong **monastic tradition** took hold there. From the 6th century, Irish monks began conducting missions abroad. In 563, **Columba** (*c.* 520–97) set up the **abbey of Iona** on an island off Scotland's western coast. Iona became a center of Irish-influenced monasticism, which extended into northern England, Scotland, and Francia with the foundation of the monastic center at Luxeuil in 590.

The **Gupta Empire fell apart** after the reign of Vishnugupta (r. 540–50); and northern India split into a number of **regional kingdoms**. A minor branch of the Guptas ruled Magadha, but they were swept aside by the Maukharis of Kanauj. The region fell to the Vardhana king **Harsha**, who established an empire in the early 7th century.

JAPAN'S SOGA FAMILY CAME TO PROMINENCE IN 536, when Soga no Iname was made chief minister. **Emperor Bidatsu's death** in 585 led to a succession dispute, from which Iname's grandson **Yomei** emerged successful. The next emperor, **Sushun** (r.586–93), had a Soga mother, reinforcing the family's dominance. When Sushun was assassinated in 593, he was succeeded by another Soga, Bidatsu's widow **Suiko** (r. 593–628). Suiko's reign saw the start of the **Asuka Enlightenment**, and was a time of great confidence in foreign affairs, state support for Buddhism, and flourishing arts.

In 572, the Byzantine emperor **Justin II** (r. 565–78) went to **war with Persia** after he refused to pay a tribute due under the terms of Justinian's 50-year peace deal (see 527–540). In 573, Persia struck back, invading Syria and taking the

7 THE NUMBER OF **YEARS** THE **"ENDLESS PEACE"** OF 532 **BETWEEN** THE **BYZANTINE EMPIRE** AND **PERSIA LASTED**

fortress of Dara. On hearing this, Justin went insane. His wife took power, and had to agree a humiliating peace with Persia.

In 567, the **Lombards**, who had settled in the former Roman province of Pannonia (Hungary), destroyed the Gepids and then, under **Alboin** (reign *c.* 560–72), moved southwest into Italy, where the Byzantine authorities were too weak to resist them. In 568–69 they **occupied the plain of the Po River** and set up dukes in major cities. By 572, when Pavia fell to them, they had founded duchies as far south as Benevento. Attempted

Byzantine counterattacks in 575 were a disaster. Under **Agilulf** (r. 590–616) the Lombard kingdom consolidated; the Byzantines were limited to small territories around Rome, Naples, and Ravenna.

Under **Khan Bayan** (r.*c.* 562–82), the **Avars**—nomadic horsemen from the northern Caucasus—exploited the vacuum left by the departure of the Lombards to **carve out a vast territory** around modern Austria. Their conquest of a number of Byzantine towns prompted **Emperor Maurice** (r. 582–602) into a successful campaign to dislodge them.

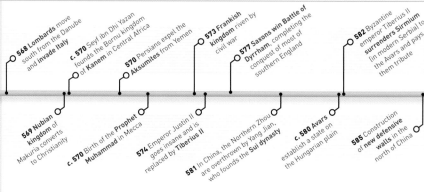

550 Gao Yang deposes China's last Eastern Wei emperor, starting the **Northern Qi dynasty**

555 Byzantines complete their **reconquest of Italy**

557 Yuwen Ju deposes China's Western Wei ruler, founding the **Northern Zhou dynasty**

562 50-year peace signed between Byzantine emperor **Justinian** and **Chosroes I** of Persia

568 Lombards move south from the Danube and **invade Italy**

c. **570** Seyf ibn Dhi Yazan founds the Bornu kingdom of **Kanem** in Central Africa

570 Persians expel the **Aksumites** from Yemen

573 Frankish kingdom riven by civil war

577 Saxons win **Battle of Dyrrham**, completing the conquest of most of southern England

582 Byzantine emperor Tiberius II **surrenders Sirmium** (in modern Serbia) to the Avars and pays them tribute

554 Korean state of Paekche allies with Japan against **Silla**, its Korean rival

558 Chlothar I becomes sole ruler of Francia

563 Irish missionary **Columba begins evangelizing Scotland**

565 Justin II becomes Byzantine emperor

569 Nubian kingdom of Makuria converts to Christianity

c. **570** Birth of the **Prophet Muhammad** in Mecca

574 Emperor Justin II goes insane and is replaced by **Tiberius II**

581 In China, the Northern Zhou are overthrown by Yang Jian, who founds the **Sui dynasty**

c. **580** Avars establish a state on the Hungarian plain

585 Construction of **new defensive walls** in the north of China

Painted c. 581–618, this fresco is from China's Dunhuang caves, in a strategic Silk Road oasis. The caves contain some of the finest examples of Buddhist art.

IN 581, YIANG JIAN, A GENERAL OF THE ZHOU RULERS of northern China, rebelled and took the throne for himself as the emperor **Wendi** (r. 581–604). In 589, he invaded southern China. His forces rapidly overcame those of the last Chen emperor, **Hou Zhu**. Wendi was now the country's sole ruler and the first emperor of the **Sui dynasty**; after three centuries of division, **China** was finally **united**. Wendi disarmed private armies and established agricultural colonies along China's frontiers to strengthen central control in remote areas. He implemented a **major land reform** that increased the number of households liable to the land tax from 4 million in 589, to almost 9 million in 606. Wendi also extended the country's canal system to form a "**Grand Canal**"

" NOT ANGLES, BUT ANGELS. "

Pope Gregory I, on seeing Anglo-Saxon slaves at a market in Rome

that allowed vessels to travel 1,240 miles (2,000 km) from Hangzhou in the southeast to the northeastern provinces around Beijing, via Luoyang in eastern central China. Austere, strict, and occasionally violent, Wendi seemed to have set the Sui dynasty on firm foundations; in the end, it lasted only 14 years after his death, when it was replaced by the Tang.

In 582, **Emperor Maurice** succeeded **Tiberius II** (r. 578–82) as the Byzantine emperor. He had been commander of the palace

POPE GREGORY I (590–604)

From 572 to 574 Gregory I was prefect of Rome, and only became a monk on his father's death. A man of great ability and energy, he was involved in resistance to the Lombards in Italy in the early part of his papacy, but he maintained good relations with the Merovingians in Francia and the Visigothic rulers of Spain. Relations with the Byzantine emperor Maurice broke down over the use of the title "ecumenical patriarch" by the Bishop of Constantinople, which Gregory viewed as a challenge to his authority.

guard and then of the war against the Persians from 578. Tiberius's overspending and ineffective campaigns against the Persians, Lombards, and Avars had **emptied the imperial treasury**, leaving Maurice facing an immediate financial crisis. His subsequent economizing led to **mutinies** by the eastern army in 588 and by that of the Balkans in 593. Maurice made his father Paul head of the Senate and his brother-in-law **Philippicus** head of the palace guard; such nepotism further increased his unpopularity.

In 584, Maurice **renewed the war with Persia**, appointing Philippicus to oversee it. The new commander attacked Arzanene, but his campaign was disrupted by the **defection** of **the Ghassanid Arabs**—former allies alienated by the arrest of their king, al-Mundhir. The mutiny of the eastern troops in 588 caused Byzantine efforts to stall further, and in 589 they lost the city of **Martyropolis** (in present-day Turkey) to the Persians. The Byzantines were saved by the outbreak of a civil war in Persia; the involvement of a Byzantine army in the restoration of one Persian claimant, **Chosroes II**, led to the recovery of Martyropolis and Dara in 592.

In the Balkans, the **Slavs**—a non-Germanic people referred to as "Sclaveni" in contemporary sources—seem to have arrived north of the Danube in the early to mid-6th century. When the Avars moved into the region in c. 559 the Slavs were pushed farther south. By the end of the 6th century, Slavic groups had settled as far south as northern Greece, the Dalmatian coast of the Adriatic, and Macedonia, as well as in those areas of Bulgaria, Bohemia, Moravia, Serbia, and Croatia where the great Slav kingdoms of the Middle Ages would later arise.

In 596, **Pope Gregory I** sent a mission to Britain to revive Christianity, following the invasions by **pagan Anglo-Saxons** in the 5th and early 6th centuries. The missionaries set out under **Augustine**, a former prior of a monastery in Rome, and arrived in Kent the following year. Their reception was reasonably warm as Bertha, the wife of the **Kentish king Aethelberht**, was already Christian. After Aethelberht was baptized a Christian, Augustine was able to establish a church in Canterbury. **King Saebert of Essex** and **King Sigebert of East Anglia**—both

dependent on Kent—also converted, but the infant English Church would suffer a series of setbacks before the last Anglo-Saxon kingdoms became Christian in the late 7th century.

Sui dynasty figurine
This figure depicting a trader on a camel emphasizes China's continuing concern with commerce along the Silk Road through Central Asia.

589 Visigothic king **Recared** announces conversion of the country to **Catholicism** at Council of Toledo

589 The western Turks based in Dzungaria, control **the Silk Road**

589 Yang Jian captures the Yan capital, **reuniting China**

589 Byzantines lose city of **Martyropolis** to the Persians (retaken in 592)

589 Land reform implemented by Sui emperor Wendi in China

590 Slavs begin to move into the **Balkans**

590 Chosroes II deposed as Persian ruler by a military uprising under Bahram; he flees to Constantinople

591 Byzantines **restore Chosroes II** to the Persian throne

590 Gregory I ("the Great") becomes pope

592 Civil war breaks out in China between the pro-Buddhist **Soga** and anti-Buddhist **Mononobe** clans

592 Emperor Maurice launches Byzantine **counterattack** against the Slavs in the Balkans

593 Mutiny of Byzantine army in the Balkans

595 Indian mathematicians use the **decimal system**

597 St. Augustine begins mission to convert England to Christianity

598 Byzantines agree treaty with the Lombards, **conceding northern Italy** to them

TRADE AND INVENTION

600–1449

In the Medieval period, trade and travel unified the Old World in a single network, with new ideas and inventions emerging even as the political landscape was transformed. Meanwhile, in the New World, great civilizations reached their peak.

A coin depicting the Eastern Roman emperor Heraclius.

A Tang dynasty Mendicant friar, with an unusual traveling companion.

This 1721 engraving by Austrian architect Johann Fischer von Erlach shows Al-Haram Mosque and Ka'aba in Mecca.

The ruins of the 7th century Byzantine fortresses at Sbeitla, Tunisia.

UPHEAVAL IN THE EASTERN ROMAN EMPIRE began when the emperor Maurice (r. 582–602) dispatched his armies to the northern Balkans to regain imperial control of the Danube frontier from the Avars (see 568–88). In 602, the army rebelled under officer Phocas and Maurice was killed. **Phocas became emperor** but **Chosroes II** of Sasanian Persia **took advantage** of the eastern empire's weakness, while the Avars invaded from the north. In 610 the son of the military governor of Roman Africa, **Heraclius**, executed Phocas and declared himself emperor.

In 606, in northern India, Harsha (c. 590–647) acceded to the thrones of Thanesar and Kannauj, establishing the **last native Indian empire** of ancient times.

> ❝ THE **EMPEROR HARSHA,** NOBLE IN **BIRTH** AND OF WELL-CHOSEN **NAME,** THE SURPASSER OF **ALL THE VICTORIES WON** BY ALL THE KINGS OF ANCIENT TIMES... ❞
>
> Banabhatta, Indian poet, from *The Deeds of Harsha, c.* 640

Tang dynasty horse sculpture
Horses were symbols of military prowess, especially warhorses from the western fringes of the empire.

SASANIAN CONQUESTS RESTORED THE PERSIAN EMPIRE at the expense of the **Byzantines** with the falls of Jerusalem in 614 and Egypt in 619. By 618, Constantinople was besieged by the Avars, and their Slavic subjects. In 620, Heraclius bought off the Avars in order to focus on repelling the Persians.

In 613 **Clothar II** (584–629) **reunited the Frankish kingdom**, bringing an end to civil war. His Edict of Paris, issued in 614, introduced reforms to the Merovingian church and state.

In 616–17, rebellions against the despotic rule of Yangdi (r. 604–17) caused the collapse of the Sui dynasty in China. A year later military governor **Li Yuan founded the Tang dynasty**, which ruled until 906.

MUHAMMAD FIRST RECEIVED A DIVINE REVELATION IN 610 and began to preach in Mecca from 613; but the start of the Islamic era is traditionally marked by the Hegira or *hijra*, the **flight to Medina.** Hostility from the Meccan authorities forced Muhammad to flee to Medina with his family and followers in 622. In Medina, Muhammad established a political and religious power base. He fought a series of attacks by Meccan forces, with their ultimate surrender in 630 when he took possession of the Ka'aba, the holiest shrine in the Arabian Peninsula. Muhammad's rule was then unchallenged.

Heraclius began to claw back territory ceded to the Persians, starting at the Battle of Issus in 622 and later, in 627, at the Battle of Nineveh. In 628 the **Sasanian and Byzantine Empires** made peace, exhausted by decades of war and unaware of the storm brewing to the south.

In China the emperor's son, **Taizong, consolidated Tang power** by suppressing rebellions across the empire. In 626, Taizong forced his father to step down and inaugurated a golden age of trade, prosperity, and cultural exchange.

MUHAMMAD (570–632)

Born in Mecca, Muhammad ibn Abdallah worked as a merchant and shepherd before growing discontented and retiring to a life of contemplation. In 610, he received the first of a series of divine revelations—these became the Qu'ran. He preached a monotheistic faith based on complete submission to God (Islam). Before his death he unified Arabian tribes within his new religion.

BY THE TIME OF MUHAMMAD'S DEATH IN 632, the young Muslim community—united by Islam, which transcended traditional rivalries—was ready for expansion. Although Muhammad had left no guidance as to his successor (caliph), four men tied to the prophet by marriage emerged as

> ❝ THOSE WHO ARE **PATIENT IN ADVERSITY** AND FORGIVE WRONGS ARE THE DOERS OF EXCELLENCE. ❞
>
> Prophet Muhammad

the Rashidun, or "rightly guided," caliphs. **The first caliph, Abu Bakr** (r. 632–34), suppressed an Arabian rebellion, reestablished Islamic dominion over Arabia, and began the conquest of Syria. His successor **Umar** (r. 634–44) **became caliph** in 634 and oversaw the conquest of **Syria** and the defeat of the Byzantines at Ajnadayn. By 637, Umar controlled Jerusalem and Damascus, and, in the same year, Arab forces conquered **Persia** (modern Iran and Iraq), occupying the Sasanian capital at Ctesiphon. **Umar established several important practices**: the creation of garrison towns in conquered territory to separate the invading Arabic forces from the locals; the recruitment of soldiers through slavery and tribal

602 Eastern Roman emperor **Maurice** killed; **Phocas** succeeds him

606 Harsha begins conquest of northern **India**

613 Muhammad starts preaching in Mecca

618 Sui Emperor Yangdi murdered; **Tang dynasty** established

622 Battle of Issus, first in a string of **victories for Heraclius** over Persians

624 Northern **China subdued** by Tang

628 Sasanian King Chosroes II "the victorious" deposed and slain by his son

630 Heraclius reaches zenith of his power and fame by marching triumphantly into Jerusalem

632 Death of the prophet **Muhammad**; start of caliphate

635 Nestorian Christians reach China

602 Emperor Yangdi orders construction of Grand Canal; completed 610

610 Heraclius becomes Eastern Roman Emperor

613 Clothar II reunites **Frankish** kingdom

619 Persians **conquer Egypt**

626 Tang Emperor overthrown by his son, **Taizong**

629 Dagobert succeeds Clothar II as king of all the franks

630 Xuanxang reaches India on his epic journey to the west

634 Death of caliph **Abu Bakr**; **Umar** becomes second caliph

> ## " THEY **BEQUEATHED THE GLEAMING GOLD,** TREASURE OF MEN, **TO EARTH.** "
>
> From the Old English epic poem, *Beowulf*

One of 20 burial mounds of this type at Sutton Hoo, Suffolk, England, which conceal the graves and funerary treasures of the royal line of East Anglia.

KEY
→ Xuanzang's route

The travels of Xuanzang
The young monk left the Tang capital, Chang'an, in around 630. He crossed Central Asia and reached India in 645.

affiliation—those recruited for fighting were made dependents of tribal members; and a taxation system that favored Muslims and encouraged conversion but allowed Christians and Jews to follow their religions.

Buddhism became increasingly influential in Tang China; the Buddhist monk **Xuanzang** journeyed far and wide in search of wisdom. His travels became legendary and foresaw the increasing mobility of people and ideas along the **Silk Road**, made possible by the power of the Tang and later the caliphate. Also traveling the Silk Road, **Nestorian Christians** reached **China** from Persia in 635.

ISLAMIC EXPANSION CONTINUED as the Arabs defeated the Persian counterattack at the Battle of Nihavand in 642, **dealing the final blow to the Sasanian Empire**; the last emperor, Yazdgird III, died in 651, and with him died Zoroastrianism, the religion of the empire. Conversion of the population to **Islam** proceeded slowly but steadily over the following centuries. The Arabs met with similar success in Egypt where the Byzantines offered only token resistance. The **fall of Alexandria** came in 642, the same year that the Muslims founded the military settlement of Fustat, which later became Cairo. The following year the marauding Islamic armies conquered Tripolitania in North Africa as their advance continued,

89
FEET
THE **LENGTH** OF THE SUTTON HOO **SHIP**

unchecked even by the assassination in 644 of Umar by a Persian slave. His successor, **Uthman**, promulgated the **first written version of the Qu'ran**, which had previously been transmitted orally.

After launching successful expeditions against the Tibetans and Mongolians, but failing to conquer Korea, the **Tang emperor Taizong** (r. 626–49) **died** in 649, and his weak-willed son began to cede increasing influence to the **Empress Wu** (624–705). In Japan, the **Fujiwara** clan enacted the **Taika reforms** in 646, bringing all land into imperial ownership and centralizing power following the Chinese model.

In **England**, Christian converts battled pagan kings for control over territory and the religious and cultural direction of the

region. In 642, for instance, the Christian king **Oswald of Northumbria**, hitherto one of the most powerful kingdoms, was slain by the pagan king **Penda of Mercia**. The great Anglo-Saxon ship burial at **Sutton Hoo**, Suffolk—filled with marvelously worked artifacts, weapons and treasures—is believed to have once contained the body of an **Anglo Saxon king**. One of the last burials of this type in England, the artifacts comprise a fusion of Christian and non-Christian elements, suggesting transition as **Christianity** gained in popularity and strength.

dragon's head crest

Sutton Hoo helmet
This reconstruction is made from iron with highly decorated panels of tinned bronze.

637 Battle of Qadisiyya, Arab forces defeat Persians and conquer Persia as far north as Mosul

639 Death of Dagobert, last of the strong **Merovingian** kings

c. 641 Sutton Hoo burial

641 Death of **Heraclius**

642 End of Sasanian Empire; **Persians crushed** at Battle of Nihavand

642 Death of **Oswald** of **Northumbria**

644 Caliph Umar assassinated; Uthman promulgates Qu'ran to be written down

645 Xuanzang returns to China after pan Asia travels

646 Taika reforms in Japan

647 Death of Indian emperor **Harsha**; his empire breaks up

649 Death of Tang emperor Taizong and rise of **Empress Wu**

The weathered landscape of central Anatolia, a Byzantine territory that suffered repeated raids from Arab forces in the 7th century.

A modern-day depiction of the Battle of Karbala; al-Husayn's death is commemorated in the annual Shiite ritual of the ashura.

THE SPLIT BETWEEN SUNNI AND SHIITE MUSLIMS was the outcome of fierce disagreement over how succession to the caliphate ought to be decided; either by selection (as in the case of the first three caliphs) or by hereditary descent. Caliph Uthman (r. 644–56) had promoted members of his own clan, the **Umayyads**. He was assassinated in 656 by Egyptian soldiers, nursing grievances over their lower status. **Ali Ibn Abi Talib** became the **fourth caliph**. As Muhammad's cousin and son-in-law—next in line by descent—Ali enjoyed unique status in the Islamic world, but he faced many challenges. At the **Battle of the Camel** in 656 Ali overcame a revolt by the prophet's widow A'isha and her allies, opposing his inclusive policies. In 657, the Umayyad emir of Syria, **Mu'awiya**, asserted his claim on the caliphate; Ali was also challenged by the Kharijis, a sect that objected to the application of the hereditary principle. In 661, **Ali was murdered** by a Khariji, opening the way for **Mu'awiya to declare himself caliph**, instituting the Arab Umayyad dynasty. Ali's supporters formed a party of their own, which evolved into a distinctive branch of Islam, **the Shiites**, in opposition to the Sunni.

Emperor Constans II attempted to reestablish

Expansion under the caliphate
The rapid Arab expansion continued throughout the latter half of the 7th century. Islamic armies pushed into Central Asia and North Africa, bringing them within striking distance of Spain.

KEY
- Muslim lands by 656
- Byzantine Empire c.610
- Sasanian Empire c.610
- Frankish Kingdoms c.610

Byzantine claims to Italy by relocating his court to Rome in 663, but raids deep into Anatolia (modern-day Turkey) by Arab forces led to a collapse in his authority; in 668, he was assassinated and **Constantine IV** took the throne. **Arab incursions into** Anatolia continued and by 670 they had reached the Byzantine capital, Constantinople (modern-day Istanbul), launching the **first siege on the city**, which would last until 677.

The **Unified Silla kingdom** in Korea brought to an end the long Three Kingdoms period, with the help of **Tang China**. In 660 the Tang destroyed the kingdom of Paekche, while in 668 Silla and Tang forces combined to overcome Koguryo, thus bringing all of the Korean Peninsula under Silla control.

Stoneware bird
This gray stoneware incense burner dates from the Silla kingdom, which was on the verge of becoming the dominant power during Korea's late Three Kingdoms period.

THE MAYA CITY-STATE OF TIKAL BEGAN ITS RESURGENCE after a century-long period of political and cultural domination by neighboring city-states known as the Tikal hiatus, which had been marked by an absence of inscriptions in the city's petroglyphic record. An inscription dated to 672 records a military campaign against the **rival city-state of Dos Pilas**, and in the following decades Tikal restored its position among the Maya of the Late Classic period (600–900). The city's rulers engaged in a construction programme to match their political ambitions, **building many impressive structures** including massive pyramids, ball courts, causeways, observatories, and palaces.

The Arab forces besieging the city of Constantinople (see 670) were unable to breach its massive walls and were eventually beaten off with the use of a new **Byzantine secret weapon**– "Greek fire" (see 711–20). Its deployment may also have helped destroy the Arab fleet at the Battle of Syllaeum in 677, forcing **the caliphate to agree a 30-year truce**. The truce bought breathing space for the embattled Byzantine Empire, struggling to hold back the Bulgars, who established the **First Bulgarian Empire** in 681 on conquered Byzantine territory north of the Balkan mountains.

ARAB CONQUESTS
Having consolidated their conquests of Persia and Byzantine North Africa, Arab armies pressed on eastward and westward. In Central Asia, Arab forces crossed the Oxus River in 667 and continued to advance to within range of the Silk Road kingdom of Bukhara. In Africa, they crushed the Berber kingdoms, reaching Tangiers in 683.

651 Standardized version of Qu'ran issued by caliph Uthman

654 Penda, King of the **Anglo-Saxon Kingdom** Mercia dies

656 Assassination of Uthman; **Ali becomes caliph** but the succession is disputed

657 Pacal becomes ruler of Maya city-state of **Palenque** and builds astronomical observatory

664 Synod of Whitby—English clergy adopt Roman over Celtic Christianity

668 Silla kingdom unifies Korea

651 Death of Yazdegird III signals **end of Sasanian Empire** and Zoroastrianism

655 Battle of Mast: Arabic navy destroys Byzantine fleet

661 Sunni–Shiite split: Mu'awiya becomes fifth caliph of Islam

664 Arabs conquer much of **Afghanistan**

668 Assassination of Byzantine emperor Constans II; **Constantine IV accedes**

670 First Siege of Constantinople (to 677)

672 Resurgence of Maya city-state of **Tikal**

673 First use of "**Greek fire**" by the Byzantines during siege of Constantinople

c. 680 Indian mathematicians develop base ten and what is later known as the Hindu-Arabic **decimal place-value system**

677 Battle of Syllaeum Byzantine fleet destroys Arabs, securing a 30-year peace

681 Byzantine Empire cedes lands to Bulgars, who establish **First Bulgarian Empire**

Jerusalem's Dome of the Rock—a shrine sacred to all three Abrahamic faiths—has an octagonal floorplan and a massive gold dome.

At the **Battle of Karbala** in 680 the **Shiite leader al-Husayn ibn Ali**, grandson of Muhammad, was surrounded by Umayyad troops, deprived of water for several days, and eventually killed. His death was proclaimed a **martyrdom** by the Shiites, who commemorate it to this day.

In China in 690, the **Empress Wu finally took the throne** in her own name—the only woman in Chinese history to do so—after decades of controlling it through her husband and sons. She even created her own dynasty, **Zhou**, which she headed until 705.

Temple at Tikal
Flanking Tikal's Great Plaza, the 122ft (38m) high Temple II was built during the construction boom of the Late Classic resurgence.

3,000

THE NUMBER OF **MAJOR STONE BUILDINGS** CONSTRUCTED IN TIKAL'S LATE CLASSIC PERIOD

ABD AL-MALIK HAD BECOME CALIPH IN 685, instituting important changes to the way the caliphate was ruled, centralizing government, insisting that all state business was conducted in Arabic, setting up the *barid* (a postal/intelligence gathering service), and issuing, around 697, new coinage: the *dinar* and *dirham*. He also commissioned a great shrine to be built on the

> ❝ I HAVE NOT SEEN THE EQUAL; NEITHER HAVE I HEARD TELL OF ANYTHING… THAT COULD RIVAL IN GRACE THIS DOME OF THE ROCK… ❞
>
> Mukaddasi, Arab geographer, c. 10th century

Temple Mount in Jerusalem, the **Dome of the Rock** (or Qubbat as-Sakhrah), completed in 692.

The harsh 10-year rule of the **Byzantine emperor Justinian II** had aroused widespread opposition and in 695 he was deposed and had his nose cut off by **Leontius**, who became emperor in his stead. However, in 698, the **loss of Carthage**, the last Byzantine stronghold in North Africa, to the Arabs led to another revolt and Leontius suffered the same fate as his predecessor.

The turn of the century was a time of change and unrest in the Americas. In North America, the spear was superceded by widespread **adoption of the bow and arrow**. In the Valley of Mexico around 700, the great **city-state of Teotihuacán**, which once housed over 100,000 people, **collapsed**, bringing six centuries of growth and dominance to an end. Social, economic, and environmental factors were probably to blame.

Ancient Teotihuacán mask
This mask was probably tied to a figurine representing a god. The mask would have been decorated with inlays and ear ornaments.

683 Arabs reach Tangiers

690 Empress Wu takes Chinese throne, establishing **Zhou Dynasty** (to 705)

691 Battle of Sebastopolis: Arabs defeat Byzantine emperor **Justinian II** and take Armenia; Justinian massacres defecting Slavs in revenge

692 Dome of the Rock completed

695 Justinian II deposed by **Leontius** and has nose cut off

695 King Jaguar Paw of Maya city-state of Calakmul **captured and sacrificed by** forces of Tikal

697 Arabs conquer and destroy **Carthage**, found Tunis; loss of Carthage causes Leontius to be deposed

697 Traditional date of semilegendary first doge of Venice, **Paolo Lucio Anafesto**

c. 700 Huare conquer **Moche** in Peru

c. 700 Collapse of city of **Teotihuacán** in the Valley of Mexico

c. 700 North American Indians adopt **bow and arrow**

A detail from the illuminated manuscript of the *Lindisfarne Gospels*.

Greek fire being deployed, as illustrated in the *Madrid Skylitzes* manuscript from the 12th century, which chronicles the history of the Byzantine Empire.

An iconic image of Christ held by Nicephorus, Patriarch of Constantinople

ANGLO-SAXON ART FUSED GERMANIC AND CELTIC ELEMENTS, and, through travelers and Christian pilgrims, it also reflected Roman and Byzantine influences. A product of this unique synthesis was the *Lindisfarne Gospels*, an illuminated manuscript produced c. 701 at the priory of Lindisfarne, on Holy Island, off the northeast coast of England.

In 705, with the help of Bulgar allies, the deposed emperor **Justinian II returned from exile** (see 690–700), regained the Byzantine throne, and exacted brutal revenge on those who had mutilated him.

By 705, **Zoroastrian refugees** fleeing the Islamic conquest of Persia **established communities in India** and became known as the Parsees. Persian Zoroastrian emigration continued during the following centuries.

Ruins of Lindisfarne Priory
The Benedictine Priory, built in the 12th century, replaced an earlier church founded by St. Aidan in 635.

His favorite concubine
This Tang dynasty scroll shows Xuanzong watching his concubine Yang Guifei mount a horse. The emperor's love for her inspired much drama and poetry.

IN 710, THE VISIGOTHIC KINGDOM OF SPAIN had descended into civil war, presenting a tempting prospect to the Islamic armies now established in North Africa, just a short distance away across the Straits of Gibraltar. In 711, a Muslim army under general **Tariq ibn Ziyad**, landed at Gibraltar. Tariq was a Berber (native of northwestern Africa), or, in the parlance of the times, a Moor, and it was a mixed army of Arabs and Moors that achieved the **conquest of Spain**, known to the Islamic world as **al-Andalus**. According to tradition, Tariq defeated the Visigothic king, Roderick, at the Battle of Guadalete, and by the end of the year most of the Iberian peninsula was under Islamic control. Only the northwest, known as **Asturias, managed to**

resist the invaders, with defeat at the Battle of Covadonga in 718 checking the Arab advance. The year 718 is one of the dates traditionally given for the start of the process of Christian reconquest of Spain. Nonetheless, by the end of the decade further expeditions across the Pyrenees, and successful campaigns in Central Asia, had **extended**

caliphate control from Provence to the borders of China.

The Arabs did experience some setbacks, however. In 717, yet another incursion into Byzantine lands triggered a change at the head of the empire, bringing **Leo III**, founder of the Isaurian Dynasty, to the throne. Although unable to prevent the Arabs from reaching the walls of the capital and launching the **second siege of Constantinople** (717–18), Leo's energetic command of the defense, and the deployment of the secret weapon "**Greek fire**," halted Arab advances in the Eastern Mediterranean. Byzantine fleets, wielding Greek fire-spouting siphons, gained control of the seas, and Leo was able to begin restoring the empire.

In 713, the Tang **emperor Xuanzong** came to the throne. His 43-year reign would see **Tang China reach its apogee**, economically and culturally, with the establishment of many schools, patronage of the arts, and a great literary flowering.

GREEK FIRE

The Arab expansion indirectly proved the savior of the Byzantine Empire, when Kallinikos, a Syrian Greek forced into exile by the Arab invasion, brought to Constantinople the recipe for a secret weapon that came to be known as Greek fire. Now believed to have been a concoction of naphtha, sulfur, quicklime, and nitre—a sort of medieval napalm—this highly flammable mixture was sprayed at enemies from a siphon device that could be fitted to the prow of a Byzantine war galley.

CASA GRANDE FLOURISHED AROUND THE 720s. The success of this settlement of the Hohokam, an ancient people of the Sonoran desert in modern-day Arizona, lay in a watering system that allowed a range of crops to be grown, despite the arid environment. The Hohokam lived here for more than a millennium; they were known as "canal builders" because of their sophisticated irrigation technology. Casa Grande was at the **center of a trade network** that stretched from the **Pacific** coast to Tucson and the **Gulf of Mexico**. The earliest structures at Casa Grande were probably pit houses; the "great house" that gives the site its name came much later.

In 725, the **Khazars**, a Turkic people of Central Asian origin, **established their capital at Atil**, on the Volga delta at the northwestern corner of the Caspian Sea. From here they **controlled trade routes to all corners of Asia** and built an empire that would control a huge swathe of Eastern Europe and Western Asia for centuries to come.

In Byzantium in 726, the emperor Leo III (see 711–20) instituted **a policy of iconoclasm** (smashing images deemed sacrilegious) in response to the idea that God was punishing Christian Byzantines by their loss of land to the Arabs and Slavs. The controversy encouraged the Roman papacy to assert their independence from Byzantine imperial authority.

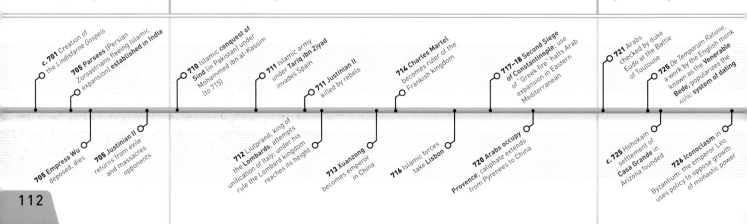

c. 701 Creation of the *Lindisfarne Gospels*

705 Parsees (Persian Zoroastrians fleeing Islamic expansion) **established in India**

710 Islamic **conquest of Sind** (in Pakistan) under Mohammed ibn al-Kassim (to 715)

711 Islamic army under **Tariq ibn Ziyad** invades Spain

711 Justinian II killed by rebels

714 Charles Martel becomes ruler of the Frankish kingdom

717–18 Second Siege of Constantinople: use of "Greek fire" halts Arab expansion in Eastern Mediterranean

721 Arabs checked by duke Eudo at the Battle of Toulouse

725 *De Temporum Ratione*, a work by the English monk known as the **Venerable Bede**, popularizes the AD/BC **system of dating**

705 Empress Wu deposed, dies

705 Justinian II returns from exile and massacres opponents

712 Liutprand, king of the **Lombards**, attempts unification of Italy; under his rule the Lombard kingdom reaches its height

713 Xuanzong becomes emperor in China

716 Islamic forces take **Lisbon**

720 Arabs occupy Provence; caliphate extends from Pyrenees to China

c. 725 Hohokam settlement of **Casa Grande** in Arizona founded

726 Iconoclasm in Byzantium: the emperor Leo uses policy to oppose growth of monastic power

In 1837, artist Steuben depicted the Battle of Tours–Poitiers as a clash over the fate of Christian Europe. In reality Islamic raiders were beaten back in a minor skirmish.

The Great Mosque at Samarra, Iraq, built by the Abbasid Caliphate. Once the largest mosque in the world, the minaret stands at 171 ft (52 m) tall.

1,050

PEOPLE PER SQUARE MILE THE POPULATION DENSITY OF **TIKAL**

SINCE CONQUERING SPAIN, ISLAMIC FORCES had made regular raids across the Pyrenees, striking deep into modern-day France before retreating to al-Andalus. In 721, an incursion into Aquitaine—a dukedom nominally in vassalage to the Frankish kingdom—had been checked by **Duke Eudo at the Battle of Toulouse**. But in 731, Eudo was unable to halt a fresh invasion of Islamic forces under **Abd al-Rahman I**, emir of al-Andalus. After defeat at the Battle of Arles, Eudo was forced to appeal to **Charles Martel**, the Frankish mayor of the palace, for help. Martel raised an army and met the Islamic forces on the banks of the Loire, between Tours and Poitiers, in 732. He was victorious at the **Battle of Tours–Poitiers**, and subsequent Christian historians would depict this as one of the defining clashes of the age—the moment at which Islamic expansion was

checked and Europe preserved for Christianity. Arabic sources record it as a minor skirmish, and in reality its main significance was that it demonstrated the need for 0the Frankish kingdoms to present a unified defense.

The **Maya city-states** of the Late Classic period reached the **peak of their power** and sophistication in the mid-8th century in Central America. The population of **Tikal**, for instance, swelled to at least 60,000, in a city spread out over 47 sq miles (76 sq km). Mayan rulers built stone temples, palaces, ballcourts, and observatories, and controlled a trade network stretching from California to South America. Yet the height of the city-states' glory sowed the **seeds of downfall**, as the populations

overtaxed the surrounding ecology and exceeded their ability to cope with drought. Collapse was just around the corner.

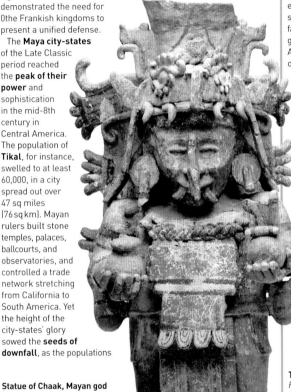

Statue of Chaak, Mayan god
Mayans would have sought help from god of rain and thunder, Chaak, for their crops. Their civilization sat in a region of poor soil and fragile ecology, so rain was vital.

THE FOUNDATION OF THE ABBASID CALIPHATE IN 750 was the culmination of growing tension in the Islamic world. Under the Umayyads (see 651–70) the Arab elite stubbornly maintained their special tax and political status, failing to deal with the growing grievances of the *mawali* (non-Arab Muslims). In 747, revolt broke out in Persian Khorasan, stronghold of the Abbasid clan, who traced their descent back to Muhammad through his uncle, al-Abbas. In 749, **Abu al-Abbas al-Saffah was proclaimed caliph** at Kufa in Iraq, and the following year at the **Battle of the Zab** he defeated Marwan II, the last Umayyad caliph. Marwan fled to Egypt but his head was sent back to Damascus, whereupon al-Saffah instigated a general **massacre of the Umayyad clan** to remove potential opposition.

In 741 **Charles Martel** (see 731–40) **died** and was succeeded by his sons **Pepin the Short** and

Carloman. In 748, Pepin had a son, Charles, who would go on to unite most of Western Europe under one banner (see 761–90).

Tiwanaku, a pre-Columbian city on the altiplano (high plains) of Bolivia, reached its height in around 750. Tiwanaku was the center of a civilization that flourished from the third to tenth centuries (see 951–60). The city itself was probably a **ceremonial and trading center**; its cultural and economic influence spread far through South America, and it would profoundly affect the development of later civilizations in the Andean region. Tiwanaku thrived in the harsh environment of the Bolivian altiplan thanks to its sophisticated **raised-field agriculture system** and extensive use of **terracing and irrigation**, which enabled it to achieve yields in excess of even modern petrochemical farming (see below), and supported the development of a sophisticated culture. The Tiwanaku people built pyramids, temples, and colossal statues.

Tiwanaku yields
Raised fields and irrigation canals enabled Tiwanaku to achieve yields of up to 10 tons/acre (21 tons/ hectare), according to experimental reconstructions.

FARMING YIELDS COMPARED

Bar chart — YIELD (TONS/HECTARE): Traditional ≈ 3, Modern Petrochemical ≈ 14, Tiwanaku Intensive ≈ 21.

The interior of the Mosque of Cordoba, Spain, shows architecture from the earliest phase of construction during the reign of Abd al-Rahman I.

The two-tier crop rotation system introduced in the 760s divided fields between cultivated and fallow land, then alternated, promoting soil fertility.

Roland bids farewell to Charlemagne, in this medieval illustration on vellum.

UNDER THE NEW ABBASID CALIPHS (see 741–50) the Islamic Empire continued to grow. Initial success came in 751 against the Chinese in the Silk Route kingdom of Tashkent. In that year, the Islamic armies were victorious at the **Battle of River Talas** near Samarkand. In 755 a rebellion led by army general An Lushan began, fatally weakening the Tang dynasty's rule in Central Asia. Outlying regions of the caliphate asserted their autonomy. In Spain in 756, one of the last surviving Umayyads, Abd al-Rahman I, declared an independent **Emirate of Cordoba**.

In Europe, the Carolingian Pepin III (c. 714–68) **deposed the last Merovingian king**, Childeric III. With the pope's support **Pepin was crowned** and was soon able to return the papal favor. When the Lombards conquered Ravenna, the **last Byzantine territory in Italy**, the Lombard king, Aistulf then set his eyes on Rome. Pope Stephen II appealed to Pepin for help, and in 755 and 756 Pepin invaded Italy, seizing Ravenna. It was later claimed by the papacy in a document entitled the **Donation of Pepin**, that Pepin had conceded all former conquered territories in northern Italy to the pope, but this was almost certainly not the case.

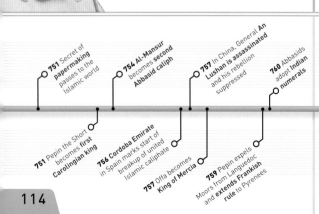

Pepin III
Also known as Pepin the Short, Pepin III was the first Carolingian King of the Franks. This carving from his tomb dates to the 13th century.

THE DEATH OF PEPIN III IN 768, had seen the Frankish kingdom customarily divided between his sons Carloman and Charles (see panel, below).

Meanwhile, the great monastic retreat on the Scottish **isle of Iona** was developing a reputation for piety and scholarship. It is possible that one of the treasures of Celtic Christianity—the **Book of Kells**—was produced by monks in the monastery at Iona. Lavishly decorated and illuminated, this priceless artifact survived the Viking raids (see 791–800), and for safekeeping it was later transferred to a monastery at Kells in Ireland.

The **founding of Baghdad** in 762 signaled the arrival of the first truly Islamic imperial city. Sited near Ctesiphon (the old Sasanian capital), the new city was carefully laid out on a circular plan and was connected to the Tigris and Euphrates rivers by canals. Baghdad became a trading hub that attracted merchants from northern Europe, India, and China.

Map: EUROPE showing Hamburg, Aachen, Paris, Avignon, Barcelona, Bologna, Rome; ATLANTIC OCEAN, Mediterranean Sea

KEY
- Frankish Empire on Charlemagne's accession
- Charlemagne's conquests
- Regions recognizing Charlemagne as overlord

Charlemagne's European Conquests
Charlemagne inherited land from his father then embarked on war after war, continuing the work of his father and grandfather.

THE DEATH OF CARLOMAN IN 771 meant that Charlemagne became sole ruler of the Franks. The following year he launched a series of bloody campaigns with the aim of bringing the peoples east of the Rhine back under Frankish rule—they had been subject to the authority of the preceding Merovingian Dynasty. At this time the various Saxon tribes were still pagans, and Charlemagne was determined to convert them to Christianity and thus bring them under the hegemony of the Frankish state. From 773–74 he conquered the kingdom of the Lombards, **bringing northern Italy into his empire** and establishing his rule over Venetia, Dalmatia, and Corsica, thus extending his reach down both sides of the Adriatic coast and into the Mediterranean. In the late 770s, he attempted to **project his power into Spain** by taking advantage of infighting among the Muslim rulers. Invited to intervene in local politics by disgruntled emirs, Charlemagne

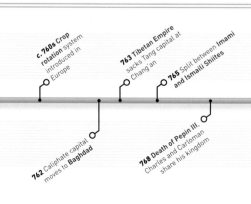

CHARLEMAGNE (748–814)

Athletic and physically impressive, Charlemagne spoke Latin and understood Greek, but never learned to read. His intent was to extend Frankish hegemony, foster a close relationship with the papacy, and reform the Church to ensure divine support for the Frankish Kingdom. This depiction from a 15th century tapestry is testament his enduring legacy.

751 Secret of **papermaking** passes to the Islamic world

754 Al-Mansur becomes **second Abbasid caliph**

757 In China, General **An Lushan is assassinated** and his rebellion suppressed

760 Abbasids adopt Indian numerals

c. 760s Crop **rotation** system introduced in Europe

763 Tibetan Empire sacks Tang capital at Chang'an

765 Split between Imami and Ismaili Shiites

771 Charlemagne **sole king of Franks** after death of Carloman

774 Charlemagne conquers **Lombardy**

751 Pepin the Short becomes **first Carolingian king**

756 Cordoba Emirate in Spain marks start of breakup of united Islamic caliphate

757 Offa becomes **King of Mercia**

759 Pepin expels Moors from Languedoc and **extends Frankish rule** to Pyrenees

762 Caliphate capital moves to **Baghdad**

768 Death of Pepin III, Charles and Carloman share his kingdom

772 Charlemagne begins conquest of East Francia

775 Death of al-Mansur; al-Mahdi becomes caliph

Offa's Dyke, which roughly follows the line of the Welsh–English border, was constructed during the reign of Offa of Mercia; stretches are still visible today.

The giant Buddha at Leshan in China was begun in 713 and finished 90 years later.

sent his armies across the Pyrenees but they **failed to take the city of Saragossa** (modern-day Zaragoza in Spain) and were forced to retreat.

This botched expedition inadvertently launched one of the great romances of medieval times, the **legend of Roland**. In 778, Roland, one of Charlemagne's generals, was killed during an attack on the rearguard of the Carolingian armies as they retreated through the Pyrenean valley of **Roncesvalles**. The attack was actually carried out by Basques, but Roland's Breton followers took up the tale and as it spread through France in the following centuries it morphed into a legend with many fictitious elements: Roland became the nephew of an elderly, white-bearded Charlemagne; his attackers the perfidious Saracens; and Roland was Count of the Marches of Brittany. By the 11th century, the "Song of Roland" appeared as an early *chanson de geste*; a heroic epic of the age of chivalry.

In Constantinople, the **death of Emperor Leo IV** brought to the throne his infant son, **Constantine VI**. During his minority the empire was under the regency of the **Empress Irene**, his mother.

CHARLEMAGNE'S CONQUEST OF WEST SAXONY in 782 comprised a bloody development with the mass execution of 4,500 Saxon prisoners at Werden. This event was appropriated by Nazi historians in the 1930s as a sort of pre-Christian Germanic martyrdom, while others have called into question its details and even occurrence. Meanwhile, concerned about ignorance and illiteracy among the clergy, Charlemagne launched a Carolingian cultural renaissance.

In 786, **Haroun al-Rashid** (r. 786–809) acceded to the caliphate in Baghdad. Under his rule the Barmakid family gained great power as his viziers (high-ranking advisors) and favorites, while the **intellectual and cultural flowering of the Islamic world** gathered pace. Growing enthusiasm among the rich and powerful for books encouraged scholars to begin translating ancient Greek and Roman texts into Arabic.

In 785, Offa of Mercia (r. 757–96), effective overlord of Britain, started constructing the monumental earthwork known as Offa's Dyke, on the border between Wales and Mercia. Originally 89ft (27m) wide and 26ft (8m) high, the purpose of the dyke is unknown, and it probably fell into disuse soon after its completion.

Imperial gift
An exquisite water pitcher sent to Charlemagne by Haroun al-Rashid, probably c. 800.

VIKING RAIDS on the shores of the British Isles started in 789 and gathered pace in the 790s with the looting of the rich monasteries of Lindisfarne and Iona. The "Vikings" (possibly from the Old Norse language) originated in Scandanavia.

In Tang China, the **influence of Buddhism continued to grow**, signaled by monuments such as the **Leshan Buddha**, a giant statue of the seated Buddha carved into a bluff next to the confluence of several major rivers.

In Constantinople (modern-day Istanbul), the emperor invited his **mother Irene to become co-ruler** in 792; four years later she had him blinded and declared herself empress. This move spurred the scholar Alcuin of York to suggest that the imperial seat was effectively vacant, and on December 25, 800, **Charlemagne was crowned Emperor of the Romans** by his ally, Pope Leo III. In the same year he received an embassy from Haroun al-Rashid, emblematic of how the focus of power in Europe had shifted.

In 800, the Abbasid caliphs in Baghdad were forced to recognize

Functional and stylish brooch
Skillfully crafted out of gold, this Viking brooch was not only beautiful but also practical, used to fasten cloaks or other clothing.

more or less **complete loss of authority in Africa west of Egypt**. They conceded to the emir of the province of Ifriqiya (modern-day Tunisia and part of Algeria) the right to make his post hereditary. The emir, Ibrahim ibn Aghlab, thus **founded the Aghlabid Dynasty**. This paid tribute to Baghdad and nominally recognized Abbasid authority, but ruled much of North Africa as an independent state.

> ❝ [CHARLEMAGNE] WAS **LARGE** AND **STRONG** AND OF LOFTY **STATURE**, THOUGH NOT DISPROPORTIONATELY TALL. ❞
>
> Einhard, Charlemagne's friend and Frankish historian, *c.* 830

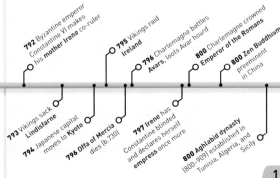

- **778** Failed Carolingian expedition to Spain, **Siege of Saragossa**
- **780** Byzantine **regency of Irene**
- **778** Battle of **Roncesvalles**
- **781** Nestorian Christians in China erect **Nestorian Tablet** in Chang'an
- **781** Carolingian Renaissance begins
- **782** Charlemagne conquers **West Saxony**
- **785** Construction of **Offa's Dyke begins**
- **786** Haroun al-Rashid becomes caliph; **ascendancy of Barmakids**
- **787** Council of Nicaea ends iconoclasm controversy
- **c. 788** Moroccan Shiite revolt under Idris
- **789** First **Viking attack** in Britain
- **790** Army mutinies in Constantinople, depose Irene, and puts **Constantine VI in charge**
- **792** Byzantine emperor Constantine VI makes his **mother Irene** co-ruler
- **793** Vikings sack **Lindisfarne**
- **794** Japanese capital moves to **Kyoto**
- **795** Vikings raid **Ireland**
- **796** Offa of Mercia dies (b.730)
- **796** Charlemagne battles Avars, loots Avar hoard
- **797** Irene has Constantine blinded and declares herself **empress** once more
- **800** Charlemagne crowned **Emperor of the Romans**
- **800** Aghlabid dynasty (800–909) established in Tunisia, Algeria, and Sicily
- **800** Zen Buddhism preeminent in China

504
THE NUMBER OF **STATUES** AT BOROBUDUR TEMPLE

Louis the Pious in a copy of Raban Maur's *Book of the Cross*.

This 14th-century manuscript depicts scholars seated in the House of Wisdom; the Abbasid caliphs recruited scholars of all religions, from Europe to China.

THE TIBETAN EMPIRE EXPANDED in the early part of the 9th century, and extended its control to the Bay of Bengal. Its influence in Central Asia was indicative of **Tang China**'s weakness in the region. Meanwhile, in northern India, the **Gurjara-Prathihara dynasty**, which had united the region and held back the advance of Islam, continued to grow in strength with the conquest of Kanauj in modern-day India by **Nagabhata II**, around 801.

The **Temple of Borobudur**, a **Buddhist monument** in central Java, Southeast Asia, was completed in the early 9th century. The colossal structure, which is the largest Buddhist monument in the world, contains over **2 million stone blocks** and is covered in almost 21,500 sq ft (2,000 sq m) of carvings. The monument is a three-dimensional *mandala*, or cosmic wheel; walking its path, which is a journey of over 2 miles (3km), reenacts the journey toward nirvana (enlightenment). Its construction was an epic achievement, and a testament to the power of the **Srivijayan Empire** (c. 760–1402), which had grown rich from the extensive maritime trade of the region.

For much of this era, **Srivijayan influence** extended over the Southeast Asian mainland, including the **Mekong basin kingdom** formerly known to the Chinese as Funan. But, in 802, **Jayavarman II**, a vassal ruler whose family had been quietly extending their territory since

Jayavarman II
This statue of Jayavarman II, from the 12th-century Bayon temple at Angkor Thom, was constructed by his namesake, Jayavarman VII.

around 770, was powerful enough to establish an independent **Khmer Empire** and have himself proclaimed *chakravartin*, or "universal ruler." In Sanskrit this translates as "god-king"—the authority of Khmer kings rested on their direct link to the gods, which was reflected in the monuments they would construct at the temple city of Angkor in centuries to come (see 880–90).

Around 801, **Bulan**, the Khan of the Khazar Empire (see 861–70), hosted a debate between the three Abrahamic faiths, and chose **Judaism**.

CONFLICT BETWEEN THE BYZANTINES AND BULGARS (see 671–90) continued through the early part of the 9th century. Despite Byzantine emperor **Nicephorus I** (r. 802–11) twice sacking the Bulgar capital Pliskas, in 809 and 811, **the Bulgar khan, Krum**, fought back, meeting his foe in battle later in 811. Nicephorus was killed and Krum had his foe's skull lined with silver for use as a drinking cup. Two years later, Krum attempted to besiege the Byzantine capital **Constantinople**, but was unable to breach the walls and so retreated, **devastating Thrace** instead.

Charlemagne (see 760–800) died in 814 and his last remaining son, **Louis the Pious** (r. 814–40), acceded to the throne. He had been crowned co-emperor by his father the year before.

ISLAMIC SCIENCE

Thanks to the House of Wisdom and other similar centers of scholarship across the Caliphate, Islamic scholars went far beyond the learning of the ancient Greeks and Romans. Islamic scientists made great advances in fields such as alchemy (proto-chemistry), medicine, toxicology, metallurgy, mathematics, and astronomy. This illustration from *The Book of Knowledge of Ingenious Mechanical Devices* shows an innovative handwashing device.

THE HOUSE OF WISDOM, or *Bait al-Hikma*, was an institute devoted to the translation of classical scholarship and the pursuit of learning in **Abbasid Baghdad**. It was the epicenter of the Islamic intellectual renaissance, the heart of the Translation Movement, and the home of great scholars such as **Al-Kharwizmi** (c. 780–850); algebra takes its name from his great treatise on mathematics of c. 830, the *Kitab al-Jabir*, or *The Compendious Book on Calculation by Completion and Balancing*.

The House of Wisdom was consolidated c. 822 by **al-Ma'mun**. After the death of his father **Haroun al-Rashid** (see 791–800), and after a brief struggle, he had succeeded to the Caliphate in 813 and continued the tradition of intellectual patronage, building observatories and gathering the best scholars from around the

400
THOUSAND
THE NUMBER OF **BOOKS** IN THE **HOUSE OF WISDOM**

world. Mimicking the practices of the Abbasid's Persian predecessors, the **Sasanians**, the **Translation Movement** collected manuscripts from other cultures and older traditions, and **translated** them **into Arabic**, thus preserving much ancient scholarship that would otherwise have been lost. Ptolemy's seminal work on cosmology, the *Almagest*, for instance, was translated from Greek into Arabic around 827, and it was only through this translation that European scholars would later be able to access this ancient text.

Civil strife in the **Carolingian Empire** (800–88) resulted from tension between **Louis the Pious and his sons** over their inheritances. After the death in 819 of his first wife—mother of his sons **Lothair, Pepin**, and **Louis the German**—Louis the Pious had married the ambitious Judith of Bavaria, who prevailed on Louis to grant her son, **Charles the Bald** (823–77), lands that had previously been promised to **Lothair**. In retaliation, Lothair,

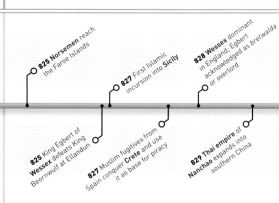

c. 801 Height of Tibetan Empire

c. 801 Khazarian king **Bulan** hosts debate between three Abrahamic faiths, chooses **Judaism**

802 Empress Irene exiled; **Nicephorus** becomes Byzantine emperor

803 Abbasid caliph **Haroun al-Rashid** destroys Barmakids

809 Nicephorus raids Bulgar capital Pliska

811 Krum of Bulgaria kills Nicephorus

811 First paper currency **"flying cash"** in China

825 Norsemen reach the Faroe Islands

827 First Islamic incursion into **Sicily**

828 Wessex dominant in England; Egbert acknowledged as *bretwalda* or overlord

c. 801 In India, Gurjara-Prathihara king **Nagabhata II** conquers Kanauj

c. 801 Construction of **Borobudur temple** in Java

802 Khmer Empire established by Jayavarman II

805 Franks under **Pepin** defeat Avars in Hungary

c. 810 Islamic **algebra** system of Persian mathematician **Musa al-Khwarazmi** established

813 Al-Ma'mun becomes Abbasid caliph

814 Death of **Charlemagne** (born c. 742); Louis the Pious ascends to Frankish throne

c. 820 Founding of the **House of Wisdom** in Baghdad

825 King Egbert of **Wessex** defeats King Beornwulf at Ellandun

827 Muslim fugitives from Spain conquer **Crete** and use it as base for piracy

829 Thai empire of **Nanchao** expands into southern China

The area around Segesta in Sicily, with its Greek ruins, was occupied early in the Aghlabid invasion of the island.

The ancient city of Pagan, in Burma, became the capital of a powerful Buddhist state occupying roughly the same area as the current region.

Louis' co-emperor since 824, rallied his brothers in revolt against their father. In early 830, **Louis was deposed**, and although Lothair's misrule saw his father restored by the autumn, the older man's authority was compromised and the scene set for worse conflict to come.

Wessex, the Anglo-Saxon kingdom in south and west England, became the **dominant English power** as a result of the victory of King Egbert over King Beornwulf of Mercia at the Battle of Ellandun, Wiltshire, in 825. Egbert was subsequently able to conquer the southeastern counties of England, and by around 828 Wessex was the most powerful state in the land, with Egbert recognized as *bretwalda*, or overlord, of England until his death in 839.

The emergence of **Great Moravia** began around 830, with the establishment of the Principality of Moimir, to the west of the White Carpathians, under the rule of **Moimir I**. Moimir was one of two Slavic polities to establish themselves in the power vacuum left by the collapse of the Avars in 805; the other—to the east of the White Carpathians, in what is now Slovakia—was Nitra, under the rule of **Prince Pribina**. In 833, Moimir would conquer Nitra, setting his principality on the path to becoming the **Great Moravian Empire**.

THE ISLAMIC CONQUEST OF SICILY had begun in 827 with the arrival of an invasion force from Aghlabid in North Africa, sent by the **Emir Ziyadat Allah I** (r. 817–38) to take advantage of **internal divisions** among the **Byzantine** rulers of the island. Hindered by outbreaks of plague, the Islamic forces made little headway until 831, when **Palermo** fell after a year-long siege. The city then became the capital of Islamic Sicily, although total conquest of the island did not happen until 902.

The Field of Lies, in Alsace in 833, was a meeting brokered by the Pope to mediate between the **Frankish rulers**, which resulted in the desertion of Louis the Pious and Charles the Bald by their followers, and their subsequent imprisonment. This was one episode in a series of conflicts that saw the collapse of central authority and increasing Frankish vulnerability to raids from the Norsemen to the north and west, **Bulgars** and **Magyars** to the east, and **Saracen** pirates to the south.

Saracen warriors
"Saracens" was a European term for Muslims, especially those occupying Sicily and raiding Europe.

THE TREATY OF VERDUN in 843 marked the definitive division of Charlemagne's empire. After the death of Louis the Pious in 840, his three surviving sons (see 821–30) embroiled themselves in further conflict over land. In 842, Charles the Bald and Louis the German teamed up and swore oaths to impose a settlement on Lothair that saw the **Frankish Empire divided** into regions. These broadly equated to France in the west, Germany in the east, and a middle kingdom that would later become known as *Lotharii regnum*, or Lotharingia (modern Lorraine).

The rise of the **Cholas**, a Tamil dynasty of **southern India**, can be dated to 846, when the Chola king Vijayalaya captured the city of Tanjore from the **Pandya kingdom**.

The **Capitulary of Meersen** was a proclamation by the West Frankish king Charles the Bald in 847, ordering every free man to choose himself a lord. Charles intended the decree to facilitate the levy of armies, but it was also indicative of the increasing inability of the Frankish rulers to protect their subjects. In place of central authority, the peasants relied on local lords; they gave up freedoms and bound themselves to a feudal aristocracy in return

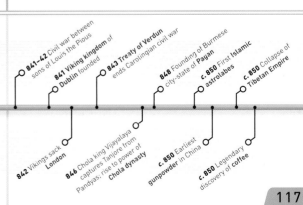

Coffee plant
The coffee bush is native to the mountains of Ethiopia and Yemen, where it was first recorded in use in the mid-15th century.

for protection from **Vikings** and other raiders.

In around 848, the **Burmese city-state of Pagan** was founded in the Irrawaddy Valley. Indian influence is readily perceptible in the architecture of this part of Southeast Asia due to cultural, religious, and mercantile ties.

The legendary **discovery of coffee** is dated to around 850, when it is said that an Ethiopian goatherd named Kaldi noticed that, after eating some red berries, his goats became extremely lively. He brought a sample to a local Islamic holy man, who, disapproving of intoxicants, threw them on the fire, where they roasted and released a delicious aroma.

Monument in the courtyard of the Maya city of Palenque.

The frontispiece of *The Diamond Sutra*, the earliest known printed work, shows Buddha explaining the sutra (sermon) to an elderly disciple.

The landscape of Iceland offered scant welcome, yet Vikings settled here by 874.

THE DECLINE OF THE CLASSIC MAYA civilization continued as the wave of abandonments that began with **Palenque** at the end of the 9th century spread south and east into the Classic Maya heartland. The last recorded inscriptions at Mayan cities Quiriguá and Copán date to 810 and 822; **at Caracol to 859**; and at Tikal to 889. A combination of **drought, famine, disease**, and social upheaval were probably responsible, as overpopulated cities and their overstretched resources reached a tipping point.

The first recorded use of a **crossbow** was in France in 851. Although slower to reload than a longbow, the crossbow, or *arbalest*, required little training or strength to operate.

The **Fujiwara regency**, assumed by Yoshifusa (*c.* 804–72) on the accession of his grandson, the child-emperor Seiwa in 858, marked the Fujiwara clan's domination of Japanese power.

Crossbow versus longbow
Although the longbow could be fired much faster, the crossbow had a greater range and was easy to operate.

KHAZAR EMPIRE

The Caspian Sea is still known in the region as the Khazar Sea for the empire that ruled the area between it and the Black Sea from the 8th to 10th centuries. A contributing cause to the empire's decline may have been a rise of 23ft (7m) in the sea level.

CYRILLIC SCRIPT WAS INVENTED by the Byzantine missionary later known as **St. Cyril** in around 863. Originally named Constantine, Cyril and his brother Methodius were sent to **convert the Slavs** in **Moravia** by Byzantine emperor, Michael III in around 862. Cyril devised a new "Glagolitic" script to **translate the Bible** into Slavic; this later became Cyrillic script.

In 867, Basil, a favorite of Michael III, deposed his master and took the throne as **Basil I**. His reign marked the start of one of the most glorious periods of Byzantine history. Intent on restoring the empire internally and externally, Basil rebuilt the army and navy and revised the legal system.

The **Diamond Sutra** of 868 is the world's oldest surviving printed book. An illustrated Buddhist text, it was found in a cave in Dunhuang, a Silk Road town in northwest China.

Around the mid-9th century, the **Khazars adopted Judaism** (see 801–10). According to tradition, they chose an **Abrahamic faith** to put them on equal footing with Christianity in the Byzantine Empire and Islam in the Caliphate.

Early Cyrillic script
This wax tablet contains psalms of David, written in the early 11th century. It is believed to be the oldest document written in Cyrillic.

ALFRED THE GREAT OF ENGLAND, an educated man who had spent time in Rome with the Pope, acceded to the throne of the Anglo-Saxon kingdom of **Wessex** in 871. During the reign of his elder brother Aethelred I (r. 865–71), **Danish Vikings** had invaded Wessex, but Alfred had helped defeat them at the **Battle of Ashdown** in 870. On assuming the kingship, Alfred averted crisis by defeating the Danes at Wilton in southwest England, but another attack in 875 caught him unawares and he was forced to retreat to the Somerset marshes. According to the popular legend, Alfred was here given shelter by a peasant woman who, unaware of his identity, left him to watch some cakes that were cooking on the fire. Preoccupied with the problems of his kingdom, Alfred let the cakes burn. Nonetheless he was able to summon his armies and defeated the Danish king Guthrum at the Battle of Edington in 878, forcing him to conclude the **Peace of Wedmore**, under the terms of which **Guthrum converted to Christianity** and agreed to a division of the country (see 881–90).

The **settlement of Iceland** demonstrated how the **Vikings** were advancing on other fronts. Irish monks had probably already reached the North Atlantic island, and Viking navigators had other clues to its existence, such as the passage of migrating birds. Vikings had already visited the

King Alfred
A statue of King Alfred was erected at his capital, Winchester, in 1901. His sword doubles as a crucifix, emblematic of his militant faith.

island and even overwintered there, but the first permanent settlement, according to the medieval Icelandic *Landámabók* (Book of Settlement), was by the Norwegian chieftain Ingolfur Arnarson in around 874. According to legend, he selected the spot for his homestead by throwing his

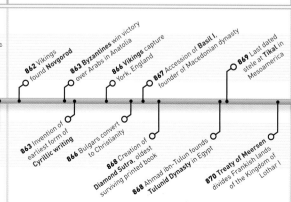

c. 850s Continued decline of Classic Maya civilization

851 Crossbow introduced to France

857 Plague of **ergot poisoning** in Western Europe from infected cereals

857 Founding of **kingdom of Navarre** in Spain

858 Fujiwara regency in Japan; Fujiwara clan cement hold on power

862 Vikings found Novgorod

863 Byzantines win victory over Arabs in Anatolia

866 Vikings capture York, England

867 Accession of **Basil I**, founder of Macedonian dynasty

869 Last dated stele at **Tikal** in Mesoamerica

863 Invention of earliest form of **Cyrillic writing**

866 Bulgars convert to Christianity

868 Creation of **Diamond Sutra**, oldest surviving printed book

868 Ahmad ibn-Tulun founds **Tulunid Dynasty** in Egypt

870 Treaty of Meersen divides Frankish lands of the Kingdom of Lothar I

871 Alfred becomes King of Wessex, England

874 Vikings settle Iceland

874 Persian literary renaissance begins in Bukhara

875 Catalonia in Spain becomes partially autonomous from Carolingian Empire

874 Disappearance of **Al-Mahdi**, the Hidden Imam of Twelver Shi'ites

874 Peasant revolt against Tang after terrible drought in China

878 Battle of Edington, in England, followed by **Peace of Wedmore**

The façade of a building known as the Nunnery annex, at Chichen Itza, the leading Maya city-state of the Late or Terminal Classic Period.

Symeon of Bulgaria, depicted in the center, had been educated as a monk in Constantinople before returning to take control of the Bulgars in 893.

> **WE DISCERN ACROSS THE CENTURIES A COMMANDING AND VERSATILE INTELLIGENCE, WIELDING WITH EQUAL FORCE THE SWORD OF WAR AND OF JUSTICE.**

Winston Churchill, British Politician, on King Alfred, 1956–58

throne pillars overboard and following their drift.

The **Twelfth Imam, al-Mahdi**—believed by some Shi'ites to be the ultimate savior of humankind—miraculously disappeared in 874. According to some Shi'ites, when the Eleventh Imam, Hasan al-Askari, died in 874, his successor, a seven-year-old boy, went into literal and spiritual hiding, and ever since has been said to be "occulted," or hidden until the day of his **messianic return**.

The **Anglo-Saxon Chronicle**, a unique written record of events from wars and politics to the weather, was kept from around 880 until the mid-12th century. It was indicative of the scholarship that King Alfred fostered, inviting scholars to England and translating major classical works himself.

SWEDISH VIKINGS, known as the **Varangians or Rus**, used rivers such as the **Volga** and **Dnieper** to push ever farther inland from the Baltic, establishing dominion over the **eastern Slavs** of the region. Having **founded the settlement of Novgorod** in 862 and launched audacious raids on Constantinople by navigating rivers all the way to the Black Sea, they now colonized ever farther south. In 882, the Rus **prince Oleg** (r. 882–912) defeated his rivals Askold and Dir, **seized** their settlement at **Kiev**, and transferred his capital there from Novgorod. The city would become the capital of **Kievan Rus**, a loose federation of territories, until 1169.

The **Danelaw**—the part of England in which Viking law was upheld—was formalized by the **Treaty of Alfred and Guthrum** in 886, following renewed attacks by Guthrum. Alfred would keep the south, including London, while the area to the north of a line between the Thames and Lea rivers went to the Danish, who would live under their own laws.

In 887, **Charles the Fat** (c. 839–88), the last Carolingian king to rule both the primary Frankish territories, West and East Francia (modern-day France and Germany), was **deposed**. Charles, already king of the East Franks since 879, had been elected king of the West Franks in 884. However, he was a victim of the declining power and authority of the Carolingian monarchs (see 841–50). Unable or unwilling to meet the Vikings in battle—specifically during their **Siege of**

Slavonic–Viking Jewelry
Viking invaders conquered territories along Russia's waterways, establishing a hybrid culture that mixed Slavonic and Viking styles.

Paris in 885–86—he was proven incapable of protecting his people. **Odo**, Count of Paris (c. 860–98), who had led a heroic defense against the Vikings in 885, was elected king of West Francia in 887. From now on, East and West Francia would develop as separate regions.

The catastrophic **decline of the Classic Maya city-states** of the southern lowlands continued throughout the 9th century, and **Tikal was abandoned** by around 889. Maya city-states of the north (the area of Mexico's Yucatán Peninsula) now took precedence in what is known as the Late or Terminal Classic Period. Foremost among these civilizations was **Chichen Itza**, which commanded the advantage of *cenotes*, or water holes; of vital importance in this drought-vulnerable region.

THE GROWING POWER OF THE BULGAR KHANATE (see 811–20) worried the Byzantine emperor **Leo VI**, who in 895 prompted the **Magyars** to attack the Bulgars. However, this merely provoked the new khan, **Symeon** (r. 893–927), to mobilize the Pechenegs—a tribe that had recently arrived on the Dnieper—to invade Magyar lands. The Magyars were forced to migrate west, settling in present-day **Hungary**, from where they launched extensive raids on Frankish territories for years to come. In the summer of 896, Symeon defeated a **Byzantine army** at Bulgarophygon, in

modern-day Turkey, forcing the Byzantine emperor to pay tribute. Symeon would rule for another 30 years, vying for the Byzantine throne, only to be thwarted by the impenetrable walls of its capital, **Constantinople**, on numerous occasions.

The **Toltecs** (c. 800–1000) were probably refugees from the **collapsed Teotihuacan culture** (see 690–700), who settled in the Valley of Mexico, founding a capital at **Tula** c. 900, and forging a militaristic empire that inspired their descendants, the Aztecs.

Toltec coyote
Toltec art, such as this depiction of a coyote-god, influenced other pre-Columbian American civilizations, including the Aztecs.

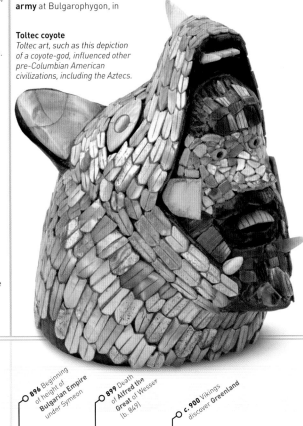

879 Nepal independent from Tibet

880 War in India between **Pandya** and **Cholas**

880 Huang Zhao, peasant rebel turned general, usurps imperial throne from Tang emperor

880 first Anglo-Saxon chronicle written

882 Oleg seizes Kiev, makes it capital of **Kievan Rus**

884 Huang Zhao of Tang China defeated by Turkic armies, but Tang power shaken

887 Odo crowned King of West Francia

887 Carolingian Charles the Fat deposed

889 Tikal abandoned, **Chichen Itza** preeminent

896 Beginning of height of **Bulgarian Empire** under Symeon

c. 900 Development of Toltec kingdom centered on **Tula** in Valley of Mexico

899 Death of **Alfred the Great** of **Wessex** (b. 849)

c. 900 Vikings discover **Greenland**

c. 900 earliest versions of *alf-Layla wa-Layla*, "One Thousand and One Nights"

119

This stone relief is from the Chinese Five Dynasties and Ten Kingdoms period. Breakdown of central authority in the period led to economic contraction.

TANG CHINA HAD BEEN IN MILITARY DECLINE since defeat by the Arabs at the Battle of Talas River in 751–760, and the **Huang Zhao rebellion** of the 880s signaled the end of the dynasty. **Zhuwen** (c. 852–912) was a warlord who had originally been part of the Huang Zhao uprising and then instrumental in the rebel defeat. Richly rewarded for his role, he steadily built up his power base until in 904 he was ready to seize control, **executing the Tang emperor Zhaozong** and most of his sons, and installing the emperor's 13-year-old son on the throne as a puppet ruler. In 907, he took the throne for himself, founding the **Later Liang Dynasty**, but although he controlled the northern heartland of China—the Yellow River Valley region of Huang He—he was unable to prevent the south from

Fatimid era text
Named for Muhammad's daughter, Fatima, the Fatimids proved patrons of learning through their sponsorship of Cairo's al-Azhar school.

fragmenting into ten independent kingdoms. The Later Liang Dynasty was short-lived (907–923), with a succession of groups seizing control of the Huang He region and founding dynasties of their own, but proving unable to hold on to power. This period of anarchy, known as the Five Dynasties and Ten Kingdoms, lasted until the establishment of the **Northern Song Dynasty** (see 951–960), and was a time of great hardship. Authority broke down, the economy collapsed, and barter replaced money in many areas. There was extensive flood and famine as flood defenses and irrigation works fell into disrepair.

To the west and north of the Five Dynasties region, **Shatuo Turks** and **Khitan Mongols** consolidated kingdoms of their own. The Khitans of southern Manchuria established their empire in 905 under the leadership of Yelü Abaoji (872–926). He went on to declare himself emperor in 916, founding the **Liao Dynasty**, which lasted until 1125, including a brief period as one of the Five Dynasties controlling northern China.

In 909, Sa'id ibn-Husayn, an Ismaili Shi'ite, overthrew the **Sunni Aghlabid Dynasty** in Kairouan (modern-day Tunisia), declared himself **al-Mahdi** (the Shi'ite messiah), and **founded the Fatimid Dynasty**, named for the daughter of the prophet Muhammad, from whom he claimed descent.

The **Abbey of Cluny** in Burgundy, founded in 910 by William the

ABBEY OF CLUNY

William the Pious, who donated the land for the abbey in 910, placed no obligations on its Benedictine monks, so that it was free from secular oversight and answerable only to the Pope. Cluny became the center of a monastic empire of great power, governing around 10,000 monks. In 1098, Pope Urban II, a former Abbot of Cluny, declared it "the light of the world."

Pious, Duke of Aquitaine, became the center of a **monastic "empire"** in Europe (see panel, above).

Displaced westward by the Pechenegs (see 891–900), the **Magyars** launched a series of devastating **raids** throughout the decade. In 901, they ravaged

The Five Dynasties
A succession of regimes was unable to consolidate power, leaving warlords to the north and south to set up independent kingdoms. The fractured geopolitical situation is reflected in this map, which shows a tangle of borders and states.

KEY
■ Chinese states
■ States occupied by non-Chinese peoples

Carinthia, in 906 and 907 they wreaked havoc in Moravia, and in 908 they attacked Bavaria, Saxony, and Thuringia. With the Frankish emperor unwilling or unable to help, the East Franks elected regional "dukes" to defend against the incursions.

GANZHOU
SHAZHOU
Uighurs
Khitans
YAN
LATER TANG
Yellow Sea
Tibetans
FORMER SHU
JINGNAN
WU YUE
Man
CHU
WU
MIN
SOUTHERN HAN
ANNAM
South China Sea

ABD AL-RAHMAN III BECAME THE NEW UMAYYAD RULER of the **Córdoba emirate** on the death of his grandfather, Abdallah, in 912. His territories had been reduced by rebellions and he quickly set about regaining much of his lost kingdom. During his reign and that of his successors, **Córdoba** reached the peak of its power (see 921–930).

According to traditional sources, **Prince Igor, ruler of Kievan Rus** from 914–945, was the son of the legendary Rurik, who founded **Novgorod** in 862. Under his protection, **Kievan Rus** (see 881–890) became a

Igor I of Kiev
Igor, who ruled from 914 until his death in 945, gestures to his court in this 19th-century illustration.

c. 900 Era of **castle building** begins in Europe

902 Muslims destroy **Taormina**, last **Byzantine** stronghold in **Sicily**

905 Khitan Empire founded in southern Manchuria

905 Kokinshu, earliest known anthology of **Japanese poetry**, written

907 Oleg of Kievan Rus attacks Constantinople

908 Magyars attack Bavaria, Saxony, and Thuringia

909 Shi'ite Fatimid dynasty founded in Tunis

911 Norse Chieftain **Rollo** granted Normandy

913 Prince Igor becomes ruler of Kievan Rus

901 Magyars ravage **Carinthia**

904 Chinese warlord **Zhuwen** murders Tang emperor, Zhaozong, sets up one of his sons as puppet emperor

905 End of **Tulunid dynasty**; Abbasid caliphate regains control of Syria and Egypt

906–07 Magyars destroy Moravians

907 Collapse of Tang dynasty; start of **Five Dynasties and Ten Kingdoms era** (to 960)

910 Foundation of Benedictine **Abbey of Cluny**

c. 910 Rise of the **Mwene Mutapa Empire** in Zimbabwe

912 Abd al-Rahman III becomes emir, and institutes zenith of **Umayyad emirate** of Cordoba

914 Fatimids take Alexandria

> IN THIS YEAR, **KING AETHELSTAN,** LORD OF WARRIORS, RING-GIVER TO MEN… WON ETERNAL GLORY, IN BATTLE WITH SWORD EDGES, **AROUND BRUNABURH.**

Unknown author, from the Old English poem *The Battle of Brunaburh, 937*

This decorative panel at the Caliph's Palace in Madinat az-Zahra, Spain, was erected by Al-Rahman III in imitation of the Abbasid Caliphs in Baghdad.

Lögberg, or Law Rock, in Iceland is the center of the oldest parliament.

formidable power in the region, earning the respect of the Byzantines by force of arms during the **Rus-Byzantine war** of 941, and winning lucrative trade concessions from them.

In 911, in recognition of helplessness in the face of constant and devastating **Viking raids** (see 881–890), the West Frankish king, **Charles III,** granted a large area of land guarding the mouth of the Seine River, which consisted of a large part of what later became Normandy, to the Norse chieftain **Rollo,** also known as Hrolf, on the condition that he became a Christian. Charles' grip on the crown was tenuous; the authority of the Carolingian monarchs had declined precipitously, with local counts ruling what were

effectively independent fiefs that owed only nominal authority to the king (see 841–850). A powerful faction of West Frankish magnates had elected **Count Odo** of Paris to the kingship in 887, so Charles spent much of his reign engaged in civil war with Odo and his descendants.

One of the tribal dukes who came to power with the impotence of the Carolingians in the face of the Magyar threat, **Henry I,** was elected king of the East Franks in 919, founding the **Saxon Dynasty.** The last Carolingian monarch of the East Frankish kingdom, Louis the Child, died in 911, after which Conrad, duke of Franconia, was elected as king. On his death he nominated his strongest rival, Henry, as successor.

Córdoba's population growth
This estimate shows how Córdoba grew rapidly from a small town to become one of the world's biggest medieval cities.

THE WANING AUTHORITY OF THE ABBASIDS IN BAGHDAD prompted Abd al-Rahman III to declare himself the true caliph in 929, thus amending his kingdom from emirate to **caliphate.** During the 10th century, his capital, Córdoba, became the largest and most developed city in Western Europe.

In 930, **Icelanders** started meeting to decide on justice and legislation at an outdoor assembly on the plains of **Thingvellir.** All free men who had not been outlawed could attend the **Althing,** making it the **oldest representative assembly** in the world.

During what archaeologists call the **Pueblo II phase,** the Pueblo peoples of Chaco Canyon, North America, were thriving. They built immense structures called "great houses," some with up to 700 rooms.

IN 932, THE UMMAYAD CALIPH ABD AL-RAHMAN III (see 911–920) captured Toledo, bringing all of Muslim Spain back under one banner. Al-Rahman also waged a successful war against the Christian kingdoms of **León** and **Navarre** on his northern borders, forcing them to acknowledge his overlordship. In general, Jews and Christians enjoyed tolerance under the caliphate, though they remained second-class citizens, making issues such as tax status a driving force behind conversion.

The **Silla kingdom** (see 651–670) was conquered by the **Koryo kingdom** in 935, completing the reunification of **Korea** under the Koryo leader Wang Kon, who now became **King T'aejo** (r. 918–943). Wang Kon had acceded to power in the Three Kingdoms state of Koguryo in 918, renaming it and leading it in successful military ventures against the Kingdom of Paekche, who were conquered in 934, and the Silla. During his reign, T'aejo consolidated power by incorporating Silla nobility into his new ruling bureaucracy.

In one of the bloodiest battles ever fought on British soil, the Anglo-Saxon king Aethelstan (c. 893–939) crushed an alliance of forces in 937, cementing his control of Britain and his kingship of a now unified **Anglo-Saxon** realm of England. Alarmed by the prospect of Anglo-Saxon expansionism, the king of Alba (in modern-day Scotland) had joined forces with the Vikings and other northern British realms to

counter the threat. The results were immortalized in an Old English poem recorded in the Anglo-Saxon Chronicle (see 871–880), which reported that five kings and seven earls died on the battlefield, alongside "unnumber'd crowds" of soldiers. Victory confined the Welsh and Scottish to their borders, halted Viking expansionism, and helped create **England** as a nation.

In 946, the Persian Shi'ite **Buwayhids** took Baghdad and forced the caliph to recognize Ahmad ibn-Buwayh as supreme commander. Although **Abbasid caliphs** remained in place until 1258, they were mere figureheads; real power now passed to Buwayhid sultans who ruled from their capital in **Shiraz,** Persia.

Henry I (see 911–920) was one of the tribal dukes who came to power in the face of Magyar threat to the Carolingians. Known as Henry the Fowler, he enlarged the kingdom and inflicted the first great defeat that the Magyars (see 901–910) had experienced since beginning their raids into Europe, at the **Battle of Riade** in 933. Henry was powerful enough to ensure that on his death the succession would be hereditary, and the election of 936 was a formality, acknowledging his son, **Otto,** as the new king. Otto's coronation ceremony in 962 consciously emulated that of **Charlemagne** (see 761–770), and he was crowned at Aachen, the old imperial capital.

Statue of Frey
The Vikings worshipped Frey, the Norse god of fertility. This statue from Sweden shows Frey holding his beard—a symbol of growth and virility.

Thor's hammer pendant
Thor's hammer—a symbol of power and virility—was a common theme for jewelry. Thor was the Norse god of thunder.

gold beading and wire work

Gold arm ring
Decorated with patterns made by stamping, beading, and minute engraving, this arm ring from Räbylille, Denmark, has crosses and tree motifs.

sword indicates that rider is a warrior

Silver figure of horseman
This stylized metal figure from Sweden probably represents a warrior on horseback. The Vikings were fine horsemen, but they preferred to travel by ship.

ends of ring are in shape of cat heads

THE VIKINGS

Between the 8th and 11th centuries, the Viking world spanned Europe, from the Pontic Steppes in the south and east to the shores of North America in the west and north. This realm was tied together by a culture of arts and crafts.

The unifying motifs of Viking art and crafts were elaborate ornamentation, interlacing patterns, and stylized animals. The material culture of the Vikings was mostly utilitarian yet finely crafted. Common, ceremonial, and military objects were ornamented heavily. Techniques such as etching, engraving, and inlaying and the use of metal beading helped to create patterns of interweaving tendrils, "gripping beasts," and stylized limbs.

buckle plate for securing baldric

baldric (slinglike shoulder strap)

Wooden shield
Shields were made from spruce, fir, pine, or linden wood with iron handles behind an iron boss. They were painted with bright colors and often had intricate designs.

colors signified intent or allegiance

iron blade

Silver brooch/pin
This gold-coated silver brooch or cloak pin from Sweden is highlighted with niello, a black metallic compound.

double-edged blade

sturdy wooden haft with runic inscription

Ax
Axes were commonly used by poor Vikings, as they were cheaper than swords. This Danish ax has a metal blade and a wooden haft.

Sword
Swords were rare and extremely valuable for the Vikings. This sword could be easily drawn out from its sheath and wielded with one hand.

Buckle plate
This metal plate was fixed to a Viking's leather belt so that it could be buckled. It has two sections, one for each end of the belt.

ornate etching

carved teeth

Hair comb
A typical Viking grooming kit included a comb, tweezers, and scoops for cleaning ears. This wooden comb has a handle secured with iron rivets.

lion figure indicates wind direction

Brooch
This box brooch (top view), from Martens on the Swedish island of Gotland, is decorated with four squatting human figures in gold.

silver and gold inlay work

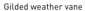

Gilded weather vane
Weather vanes were originally mounted on the prows of ships and later on the tops of churches. This gilded weather vane was found in Sweden.

stylized great beast with sinuous limbs

Early Danish coins
Originally, the Vikings used looted coins, hack silver (chunks), and barter in place of their own money. King Harald Bluetooth started mass minting of coins in 975.

Trading weights
Found in Sweden, these brass-coated iron weights were used to measure quantities of goods and the value of hack silver.

symbol indicates weight

iron crest

carved from an animal horn

Drinking horn
Vikings believed they would use drinking horns like this in Valhalla, the heaven for warriors, if they died in battle. This drinking vessel was used in feasting.

dragon head used to terrify enemies

carved scale patterns

beech panel with tin and iron studs

Helmet
Made from iron plates welded together over a leather cap, this Norwegian helmet has an attached face guard, complete with nose protector.

face guard

Sledge
This oak-and-beech sledge is from a ship burial in Oseberg, Norway. It has finely carved runners and animal heads on each corner post of the box.

Ship's prow ornament
Elements of Viking culture were derived from and prefigured in earlier cultures. For example, this wooden prow ornament is from Saxon times.

This detail from the "Gateway of the Sun," a great stone doorway at Tiwanaku, is carved with a figure known as the Staff God.

This detail from the imperial crown of Otto I shows the biblical figure King Solomon holding a scroll.

THE PRE-INCA, ANDEAN CIVILIZATION OF TIWANAKU declined precipitously in the second half of the 10th century. Sophisticated agricultural and irrigation techniques (see 741–50) had allowed Tiwanaku to support a **population** of up to 60,000 people, with up to **1.4 million** in the wider region, according to some estimates. A **prolonged drought** is believed to have been responsible for its **decline**, and archaeological evidence suggests that the main city was abandoned as citizens

Viking sea routes
By the late 10th century, Viking seafarers had penetrated to every corner of Europe and beyond, reaching as far as Greenland in the north.

KEY
→ Viking expansionist exploration 8–10th centuries

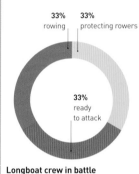

33% rowing   33% protecting rowers

33% ready to attack

Longboat crew in battle
By keeping part of the crew at the oars, Viking raiding parties maintained an aggressive posture without sacrificing mobility.

retreated to smaller, rural settlements, and returned to a pre-urban lifestyle.

The **establishment of the Song dynasty** in China brought an end to the anarchy and warfare of the Five Dynasties and Ten Kingdoms era (see 901–10). Known as the **Northern Song** in its early stages because the capital was at Kaifeng in northern China, the dynasty was founded by **Zhao Kuangyin** (r. 960-76), who was a general under the Late Zhou, the last of the Five Dynasties. He dealt with the threat from external states such as the Khitan Liao (see 901–10), the Tangut kingdom of Xia Xia, a confederation of Tibetan tribes, and conquered several of the Ten Kingdoms to the south. Zhao used the civil service examination system to assert control over the military and centralize power.

Emperor Otto I, "the Great" (912–73), defeated the **Magyars** at the **Battle of Lechfeld** in 955. Since being displaced by **Byzantine–Bulgar conflict** (see 891–900), the Magyars had raided Frankish territories, reaching as far west as Aquitaine in 951. The son of Henry I (see 911–20), Otto vigorously asserted royal authority from his coronation in 936, gaining control of all the East Frankish duchies. His powerful army **ended the Magyar menace** and also defeated the **Wends**—tribes on the eastern border engaged in a long struggle to resist Frankish **colonization and Christianization**.

Bronze Mirror
This intricately decorated mirror from the Song dynasty illustrates the artistic sophistication of China in this period.

THE POPE'S IMPERIAL CORONATION OF OTTO I as emperor in 962 revived the **Carolingian Roman Empire** in the West. In 961, Otto made an expedition to Italy in response to a plea for protection from Pope John XII, and in Pavia he had assumed the Italian crown. The following year he went to **Rome** to receive the imperial crown and assert his authority over the fractious papacy. His son was crowned co-emperor as Otto II in 967.

In 965, the **King of Denmark, Harald Bluetooth**, converted to Christianity, and the **religion** spread rapidly through the Nordic region. Denmark had been forced to accept missionaries as the consequence of defeat by the East Frankish king, Henry I, in 933.

Further afield, Vikings continued to prosper as they penetrated into all parts of Europe.

The **death of** Byzantine emperor **Constantine VII** in 963 brought his infant son **Basil II** (958–1025) to the throne. In practice, authority was assumed by the general **Nicephorus Phocas**. As **Nicephorus II** (r. 963–969), he continued the restoration of the empire that had begun with the reconquest of Crete in 961, regaining Cyprus and Cilicia in 965, subduing the Bulgars in 966–69, and invading northern Syria in 969. That same year he was assassinated by his nephew, **John Tzimisces**.

DURING HIS SHORT REIGN, JOHN TZIMISCES, nephew of Nicephorus II (see 961–70), won a string of victories. Having fought off a revolt by general Bardas Phocas in 971, Tzimisces crushed a campaign by the **Kievan Rus** leader, Sviatoslav, and **conquered Bulgaria** as far as the Danube. In 972, he campaigned in the East, taking Edessa, Damascus, and Beirut, reaching the gates of Jerusalem in 976. He died suddenly that year.

In 980, the **Vikings** started **raiding** England again, though they suffered a reverse in Ireland, where Malachy II forced Viking Dublin to pay tribute.

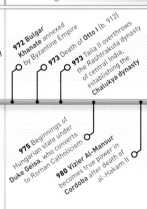

c. 950 Abandonment of **Tiwanaku**

951 Emperor **Otto I** of East Francia invades Italy

954 Construction of **Hindu Lakshmana temple** at Khajuraho in central India

957 Byzantine general **Nicephorus Phocas** takes the city of Hadath, continuing Byzantine advance in Syria

951 Magyars raid as far west as Aquitaine

955 Battle of Lechfeld, Otto I defeats Magyars, who cease raiding and settle in Hungary

958 Byzantine victory at Raban in Syria

960 Founding of **Northern Song dynasty, China**

962 Otto I crowned emperor in Rome

962 Ghaznavid dynasty founded in present-day Afghanistan

965 King Harald Bluetooth of Denmark converts to Christianity

969 Fatimids conquer Egypt

c. 970 Beowulf first written down

963 Death of Byzantine Emperor Constantine VII (b. 905); general Nicephorus Phocas becomes Emperor **Nicephorus II**

965 Khazars destroyed by Kievan Rus

967 Otto II crowned co-emperor to Otto I

969 Byzantine general **John Tzimisces** assassinates his uncle to become emperor

969 First playing cards used in China

972 Bulgar Khanate annexed by Byzantine Empire

973 Death of **Otto I** (b. 912)

973 Taila II overthrows the Rashtrakuta dynasty of central India, establishing the **Chalukya dynasty**

975 Beginnings of Hungarian state under **Duke Geisa**, who converts to Roman Catholicism

980 Vizier Al-Mansur becomes true power in Cordoba after death of al-Hakam II

Venice's modern splendor is the result of control of the lucrative trade routes between Europe, the Byzantine Empire, and the East in the 10th century.

IN 981, THE ISLAMIC FORCES OF CORDOBA defeated the Christian kingdom of **León** in Spain, under the leadership of **Al-Mansur**. "Al-Mansur" was the honorific title taken by Muhammad ibn Abi' Amir, the powerful and energetic vizier who was the true power behind the **Umayyad** throne (see 911–20). He campaigned successfully against León, Navarre, and Catalonia, making their kings subordinate to the caliphate, and extended Umayyad control to Africa via campaigns in **Mauretania** (modern-day Morocco and part of Algeria).

In 986, the Viking explorer **Eric the Red** led a party of Icelandic colonists to the shores of the bleak landmass he misleadingly named

Al-Mansur
This 17th century oil painting depicts Al Mansur, or Almanzor to his Christian subordinates. Al Mansur means "the Victorious."

"Greenland" in the hope of attracting settlers. He succeeded in recruiting 24 boatloads of men, women, and children willing to entrust their lives to Viking longboats and brave the perilous crossing. Only 14 ships arrived, but they quickly established a thriving colony that may have eventually numbered around 5,000 people.

Otto II, the emperor and king of East Francia, died of malaria in

rectangular wool-cloth sail

Viking longboat
Considered by some to be the greatest technical achievement of the early medieval era, the Viking longboat combined river, close-to-shore, and oceangoing capacity.

983 after an expedition to southern Italy. Although his infant son, **Otto III** (r. 983–1001), managed to hold on to the crown thanks to the strong regency of his mother, Theophano, the East Franks were also faced with an uprising among the **Wends**, the forcibly converted Slavic tribes on the eastern border. The Wends restored their pagan religion and resisted Frankish colonization for nearly two centuries.

In 987, **Toltec** forces conquered the Yucatán Maya and made **Chichen Itza** the **capital** of a Toltec–Maya state. According to the early Mayan chronicle *Chilam*

Balam, Chichen Itza was conquered by Toltecs led by Kukulcan, the Mayan name for the Toltec god Quetzlcoatl or "the feathered serpent"—possibly the exiled Toltec king, Topiltzin. Despite the record in the chronicle, however, archaeological findings suggest that the city collapsed around this time.

By the end of the 10th century, the mercantile powers of **Venice** and **Genoa** were beginning to dominate the Adriatic and Tyrrhenian seas, respectively. Venice, in particular, enjoyed lucrative trade links with the Byzantine Empire.

TOLTECS

The Toltecs, who ruled a state centered on Tula in modern-day Mexico, were notable for their aggressive militarism, which changed society in North America, paving the way for militaristic states such as the Aztec. The term "Toltec" came to mean "city-dweller" or "civilized person," but its literal meaning is "reed person"—signifying an inhabitant of Tollan ("Place of the Reeds," the city now known as Tula). Toltec art and architecture, characterized by monumental masonry and giant statues, was greatly influential in the region.

22,000 POUNDS
THE **WEIGHT** IN SILVER OF THE **DANEGELD** IN 991

IN 991, A FORCE OF ANGLO-SAXON WARRIORS made a stand against a much larger army of Vikings at the **Battle of Maldon** in East Anglia, England. They were slaughtered. The English king, **Aethelred II, "the Unready"** (r. 978–1016), was forced to pay a tribute known as the **Danegeld**, to buy off further incursions.

Byzantine emperor **Basil II** launched the first of a long series of **campaigns against** his greatest enemy, the **Bulgarian czar** Samuel, in 996. Basil had won major victories in Syria the year before, but it took him nearly 20 years to finally defeat the Bulgarians.

From around 1000, the inhabitants of **Easter Island** or **Rapa Nui**—an island in the Pacific Ocean—began to carve monumental statues known as *moai*. They practiced sophisticated agricultural techniques and developed a script known as *rongorongo*. At some point their population may have declined dramatically; if and why this happened is one of the many mysteries connected to the island.

These ruins at Pueblo Bonito in Chaco Canyon reveal one of more than a dozen Great Houses constructed by the Anasazi.

One of the greatest but cruelest Byzantine emperors, Basil II became emperor in 976 at age 20, and ruled for nearly 50 years.

The Brihadishvara temple was built by the Cholas in their capital Tanjore.

AROUND 1000, THE ANCIENT PUEBLO CIVILIZATION centered on Chaco Canyon in southwest North America reached its climax. The **Anasazi** used sophisticated dryland agriculture and hydrology to thrive in the arid environment, and controlled trade routes that extended as far as the Pacific coast of present-day California and the Valley of Mexico. They achieved **impressive feats of architecture**, most notably the construction of Great Houses such as Pueblo Bonito, one of 13 such buildings in Chaco Canyon. Pueblo Bonito was six stories high and comprised more than 600 rooms. It probably functioned as a ceremonial center, storage depot, and elite residence. Well-maintained roads—some with stone curbs—connected Chaco Canyon to thousands of smaller Anasazi settlements across the region. The canyon itself may have been home to as many as 10,000 people, and this set the Anasazi on a collision course with the fragile ecology of the region (see 1161–65).

Mahmud of Ghazni (c. 971–1030) was a Muslim intent on **spreading the faith into India**. In 1001, at Peshawar, he defeated Jaipal, raja of Punjab, who then committed suicide.

Probably the **first European to set foot on North America**, Leif Ericson landed in a place he called **Vinland** in around 1002. Shortly after this discovery, Greenlanders under Thorfinn Karlsefni tried to **establish a colony**, spending three winters there. The remains of settlements at L'Anse aux Meadows, in northern Newfoundland, attest to Viking presence in North America.

LEIF ERICSON (970–1020)

Leif was the son of Eric the Red, founder of the Greenland colony (see 981–990). Stories differ on the exact details of his discovery of North America. According to one account, he was returning from a visit to Norway in 1002, where he had been converted to Christianity, and was blown off course, landing at the place he called Vinland because of the grapes growing there. Another account suggests that he aimed for a land sighted to the west by an Icelandic trader.

MURASAKI SHIKIBU (LADY MURASAKI) wrote the novel *Genji Monogatari* (*The Tale of Genji*) in installments between 1011 and 1021. It is regarded as the **first Japanese novel**, and possibly the first psychological novel in world literature.

In 1014, **Brian Boru, High King of Ireland** and self-styled Emperor of the Gael, defeated a coalition of Dublin Vikings and Celtic Leinstermen at Clontarf, Ireland. Although the Norse kingdom was crushed and Viking incursions into Ireland halted, Brian Boru was killed in the battle and his **dream of a united Irish kingdom** fell apart thereafter.

In 1014, at the culmination of an 18-year war (see 991–1000), the **Byzantine emperor Basil II** defeated the armies of the Bulgarian czar at Belasita. Earning the name Bulgaroktonos (Bulgar Slayer), he put out the eyes of 15,000 captured warriors before sending them home. Basil's arch-enemy, Samuel the Bulgarian, was said to have died

Lady Murasaki
A scene from a 16th-century hanging scroll depicts author Lady Murasaki. Of noble birth, she chronicled the affairs of the Heian court.

of shock. By the end of the decade, the Bulgarians finally submitted to **Byzantine annexation**.

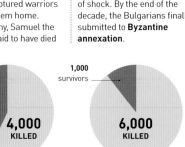

3,000 survivors	1,000 survivors
4,000 KILLED	**6,000 KILLED**
GAELIC	VIKING

The bloody Battle of Clontarf
Fought between the largest armies yet assembled in Ireland, the Battle of Clontarf was a bloody affair. Up to 4,000 Gaels and up to 6,000 Norse and their allies were killed.

IN 1025, THE CHOLA KING RAJENDRA CHOLADEVRA launched an audacious naval expedition against the maritime empire of Srivijaya in Sumatra, also sacking the Pegu kingdom in Burma. Rajendra had inherited a strong kingdom from his father, Rajaraja I, who had conquered Sri Lanka and instituted a program of **Hindu temple building** centered on the Chola capital of Tanjore. Under Rajendra, the Cholas expanded their kingdom to include Bengal, and shattered the power of Srivijaya, securing control of the **lucrative Indian-Chinese trade routes**.

Cnut (also known as Canute) was the son of Sven Forkbeard, king of Denmark and Norway, who had **invaded England** and driven the Anglo-Saxon king, Aethelred II, into exile in Normandy in 1013. After staging his own successful invasion in 1015, Cnut was accepted as overlord of all England in 1016, and went on to expand his empire. By 1030, it included Norway, Denmark, and the Faroe, Shetland, and Orkney islands.

Chola sculpture of Shiva
The Cholas were staunch Hindus and enthusiastic temple builders. Shiva, one of the major Hindu deities, is depicted here as a young and handsome man.

The Seljuks are shown here battling the Byzantines, having already conquered Persia.

Between 1041 and 1048, Bi Sheng invented the first movable type printing system, using clay letters held in wax within an iron frame.

A wise and capable king, Cnut managed conciliation between his Danish and Anglo-Saxon subjects. He collected Danegeld (Danish tax) to pay for a standing navy and army—an important innovation.

IN 1037, THE SELJUKS, UNDER CHAGRI BEG AND HIS BROTHER TUGHRIL BEG, invaded Khurasan in Persia. In 1040, they crushed the Ghaznavids at the Battle of Dandanqan, winning control of eastern Persia, the first step on the road to creating a **new Islamic empire**. The Seljuks were Oghuz Turks, originally nomads from Central Asia who had converted to Islam and moved to Transoxiana, where they served as mercenaries in the region, before turning their attentions to Khurasan.

In 1031, 40 lesser dynasties were founded on the shattered remnants of the **Córdoba caliphate**, in Spain. Known as the Muluk al-Tawa'if ("Party Kings"), these short-lived dynasties took control of different provinces of Córdoba after the strife that brought down the Umayyads following the **execution of Abd al-Rahman Sanchuelo**, son of al-Mansur, in 1009. He was the last leader of the caliphate but his attempt to move out from behind the throne and take the crown led to his downfall. Subsequently, the Berber faction nominated their own candidate for caliph and Cordoba descended into civil war for 22 years. In 1031, the death of Hisham III, the last Umayyad caliph, who had already lost control of several provinces, led

King and Emperor
Ferdinand I was the first ruler of Castile to call himself king. He added the title of emperor after his conquest of León.

to the abolition of the caliphate, with the Abbadids seizing Seville, the Jahwarids taking Cordoba and the Hudids seizing Saragossa. With the Islamic state in disarray the Christian kingdoms to the north were encouraged to expand southwards.

Sancho III of Navarre, who had conquered Castile and was overlord of Christian Spain, died in 1035, and his kingdoms were divided between his two sons. Ferdinand inherited Castile, and in 1037 he killed his brother-in-law, the king of Leon and made himself emperor there in 1039. He went on to conquer Navarre and impose serfdom on parts of Muslim Spain and Portugal.

BANTU IS A FAMILY OF LANGUAGES that originated in the Bantu homeland (now southern Nigeria and northwestern Cameroon). Bantu-speaking people spread from here to the east and south and Bantu became the **dominant language family in sub-Saharan Africa**, although whether this indicates conquest, colonization, or simply cultural influence is less clear. The Bantu expansion started in the Late Stone Age, accelerating as the Bantu-speakers acquired iron technology and cattle-husbandry skills. By the mid-11th century, Bantu tribes had become **sophisticated pastoralists**, able to sustain high population densities and complex social and economic networks. This in turn led to the emergence of chiefdoms, and Bantu speakers dominated Central and southern Africa.

In 1044, Anawrata seized power in the **Pagan kingdom in Burma**. His military prowess and skillful

use of Hinayana Buddhism as a cultural and political driver made Pagan the center of Burmese politics, culture, and religion. He developed Burmese as a written language, instituted a program of building, and forged trade and cultural links to India and China.

In China, sometime between 1041 and 1048, the commoner Bi (or Pi) Sheng invented the **first movable type system**. Block printing had been in use in China for centuries, and since the Later Tang dynasty (923–36) had been used for most book production, but Bi Sheng introduced the innovation of using **tiny clay blocks**—one for each character. The characters were molded on the ends of thin rods of wet clay, which were fired to harden them. Unlike wood, this clay type did not distort when wet and could be used over and over again.

KEY
■ Bantu homeland 2000 BCE
→ Spread of Bantu

Bantu expansion
From their homeland in the border region of southern Nigeria and northwestern Cameroon, Bantu-speaking people spread east and south, through the tropical forest, eventually spreading to all parts of central and southern Africa.

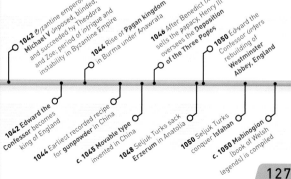

1025 Cholas sack Srivijaya and establish a maritime empire
1028 Sancho III unites Navarre and Castile
1030 Death of Mahmud of Ghazni (b. 971)
1031 Breakup of the Córdoba caliphate
1033 Ferdinand becomes King of Castile
1035 Death of Cnut the Great (born c. 995)
1037 Ferdinand conquers León
1037 Rouen Cathedral constructed
1038 Tibetan revolt against the Northern Song
1039 Henry III elected emperor

1025 Death of Basil II (b. 958)
1029 Cholas are expelled from Sri Lanka
1030 Cnut's empire expands to include Denmark and Norway
1035 Kingdom of Aragon established
1035 William (the Conqueror) becomes Duke of Normandy
1037 Seljuk Turks invade Khourasan (Persia)
1040 King Duncan killed by Macbeth in Scotland
1040 Seljuks conquer Ghaznavid Persia
c. 1040 Bantu expansion climaxes in South Africa

1042 Byzantine emperor Michael V deposed, blinded, and succeeded by Theodora and Zoe; period of intrigue and instability in Byzantine Empire
1044 Rise of Pagan kingdom in Burma under Anawrata
1046 After Benedict IX sells the papacy, Henry III oversees the Deposition of the Three Popes
1050 Edward the Confessor orders rebuilding of Westminster Abbey, England

1042 Edward the Confessor becomes king of England
1044 Earliest recorded recipe for gunpowder in China
c. 1045 Movable type invented in China
1048 Seljuk Turks sack Erzerum in Anatolia
1050 Seljuk Turks conquer Isfahan
c. 1050 Mabinogion (book of Welsh legends) is compiled

Labanga Mosque in Ghana is possibly the oldest mosque in sub-Saharan Africa. Ghana was Islamicized by the Almoravids in the 11th century.

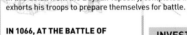

In this detail from the Bayeux Tapestry, completed in 1080, William the Conqueror exhorts his troops to prepare themselves for battle.

IN MOROCCO, IN 1054, A FIREBRAND CLERIC NAMED IBN YASIN inspired the unification of Saharan tribal groups. The confederation—known as the **Almoravids**, from the Arabic "al-Murabitun" ("people of the frontier garrisons")—**built an empire** that would eventually encompass much of northwestern Africa and Muslim Spain (see 1081–90). In 1056, the Almoravids began the **Islamic conquest of**

West Africa, where a number of powerful states had arisen, including that of Ghana.

Yoruba was the name given by outsiders to a group of **city-states in Nigeria** that shared a common language and culture. The oldest and most prestigious Yoruba kingdom was **Ife**, where a **sophisticated urban culture** was well established by the mid-11th century. Ife was the spiritual and mythical center of the Yoruba, but its poor location meant that it never exerted wide-ranging military or political control over the other Yoruba states. Ife is most famous for its artistic achievements, most notably **terracotta and bronze heads**.

In 1059, Pope Nicholas II recognized **Robert Guiscard** the Norman as Duke of **Apulia** and **Calabria**, and Count of **Sicily**—territories under Byzantine and Arab control—legitimizing his attempts to conquer them.

Ife bronze head
This head probably dates from the 14th century, but it represents an artistic tradition stretching back to the 11th century that was at least as sophisticated as any in contemporary Europe.

IN 1066, AT THE BATTLE OF HASTINGS, William Duke of Normandy (*c.* 1028–87) defeated Harold Godwinson (*c.* 1022–66), the last Anglo-Saxon king of England. England had fallen into the Norman orbit earlier, with **Edward the Confessor** spending his youth in exile at the Norman court while Cnut (see 1021–30) ruled England. William claimed that Edward had promised him the English crown, but when Edward died, in 1066, **Harold was elected king**. He marched north to defeat a Norse invasion, before dashing south to Hastings to face William, where **he was killed and his army shattered**. William the Conqueror quickly took southeast England, then the southwest, and suppressed a great uprising in the north in 1069.

Under their leader **Tughril Beg**, the Seljuks had occupied Baghdad and **ended the Buwayhid dynasty** (see 931–50), retaining the Abbasid caliph as a figurehead but giving him the title of sultan. Tughril Beg died in 1063; his successor Alp Arslan **extended Seljuk dominion** into Anatolia, Armenia, and Syria.

2:1

Battle of Hastings
Anglo-Saxon casualties outnumbered Norman losses by two-to-one, thanks in part to their forced march from the north, and the advanced Norman tactics.

INVESTITURE CONTROVERSY

Which was greater: secular or religious authority? This was the question at the heart of the Investiture Controversy. This 12th-century manuscript illumination shows Henry IV requesting mediation from Matilda of Tuscany and Hugh of Cluny. Matilda was one of the most powerful women of the Middle Ages. It was her stronghold of Canossa where Henry made his penitence.

SINCE CHARLEMAGNE'S CORONATION BY THE POPE (see 791–800), the Western emperors had considered it their divine right to appoint—or invest—bishops. Emperors had derived great income and power through their **dispensation of religious offices**, and Emperor Henry III (1017–56) had gone further still, in 1046, insisting that it was the **emperor's right** to appoint the pope. **Pope Gregory VII** represented the opposite view; he held that only popes had the right to invest clerics. In 1075, at the Lent synod, Gregory issued a decree forbidding lay investiture. The emperor, **Henry IV** (1050–1106), who was fighting to reduce the power of German prelates, defied the decree. In 1076, Gregory **excommunicated** him, absolving his subjects of their oaths of loyalty and triggering a **rebellion by Saxon nobles**

against the king. In 1077, Henry IV crossed the Alps in the dead of winter and appeared at Canossa, dressed as a penitent, to submit to the pope (see panel, above). He was absolved but controversy quickly flared up again, with a rival, **Rudolf of Swabia**, being elected to the German (formerly East Frankish) throne. In 1080, Henry had a rival pope elected, while Gregory allied himself with **Roger Guiscard**, Count of Sicily, against the imperial camp.

In 1071, the **Seljuks crushed the Byzantine army** at Manzikert, capturing and ransoming Emperor Romanus IV and going on to conquer Anatolia (present-day Turkey). This began its transformation into a **Muslim Turkish region**. In 1077, the Seljuks established the **Sultanate of Rum** there, while other conquests brought them Syria and Jerusalem.

1054 Founding of Almoravid dynasty; start of Islamic conquest of West Africa

1054 Schism between Eastern (Byzantine) and Western Churches

1055 Gruffydd ap Llywelyn becomes king of all Wales

1057 Death of Macbeth, King of Scotland (b. 1005)

1059 Treaty of Melfi: Pope makes Robert Guiscard the Norman titular ruler of southern Italy and Sicily

1062 Almoravid kingdom establishes capital at Marrakech

1065 Seljuk Turks invade **Transoxiana and Syria**

1068 Dai-co-viet defeats Champa in Vietnam

1071 Normans complete conquest of Byzantine southern Italy

1071 Battle of Manzikert, Seljuks control most of Anatolia and Syria, soon take Jerusalem

1077 Penitence of **Henry IV** at Canossa

1077 Seljuks establish **Sultanate of Rum** in Anatolia

1080 Bayeux Tapestry completed

1055 Death of Jaroslav leads to civil strife in **Kievan Rus**

1055 Seljuk Turks take Baghdad, ending Buwayhid dynasty

1057 Expansion of **Pagan kingdom** in Burma

1066 Battle of Hastings: Norman conquest of England

1069 The Harrying of the North: Normans ravage northern England

1070 Cholas expelled from Sri Lanka

1071 Rebellion of **Hereward the Wake** against Norman rule in England

1075 Start of **Investiture Controversy** between the emperor and pope

1076 Almoravids forcibly convert **Ghana Empire** to Islam

1077 Alfonso proclaims himself **emperor of Spain**

Hassan-i Sabbah leads initiations at Alamut, in an illustration from Marco Polo's 13th-century *Travels*.

> LET SUCH AS ARE GOING TO **FIGHT FOR CHRISTIANITY** PUT THE FORM OF **THE CROSS** UPON THEIR GARMENTS **THAT THEY** MAY **OUTWARDLY DEMONSTRATE** THEIR DEVOTION TO THEIR **INWARD FAITH.**

Pope Urban II, 1095

IN 1090, A GROUP OF ISMAILI SHI'ITES BECAME INVOLVED IN A DISPUTE over the Fatimid succession in Cairo (see 901–10). Under the leadership of the charismatic **Hassan-i Sabbah**, this group recognized the claims of an infant called Nizar, and were therefore known as **Nizari Ismailis**. Forced to flee Cairo, Hassan led the Nizaris to his homeland in Persia where they captured a fortress known as **Alamut** in the mountainous region of Kazvin and made it the base of a de facto **Nizari kingdom**. Thus was born the group later known as the **Assassins**—a name derived from the word "hashashins," a label applied by their enemies who claimed they used intoxicants such as hashish to brainwash devotees into blind obedience.

Alarmed by the advances of **Alfonso VI of Castile**, the **Abbadids** (see 1031) summoned the **Almoravids** from North Africa to defend against the Christian

13 THOUSAND
THE NUMBER OF PLACES LISTED IN THE DOMESDAY BOOK

threat. Defeating Alfonso at Zallaka in 1086, they annexed most of Islamic Spain.

In 1085, **William the Conqueror** (see 1061) commissioned a survey of his new kingdom—known as the **Domesday Book**—probably to regulate military service and assess taxation opportunities.

The Domesday Book
Nicknamed "Domesday" in reflection of the trepidation that the great undertaking inspired in the native English, William's survey actually comprised two manuscripts; the Great and the Little Domesday.

IN 1092, CHINESE POLYMATH SU SUNG DESIGNED AND CONSTRUCTED A COSMIC ENGINE. This mechanical astronomical clock was 30 ft (9 m) high, and was water-driven with an armillary sphere, which showed the position of celestial objects.

In 1094, a Castilian who had served both Christian and Islamic Masters, Rodrigo Diaz de Vivar, known by the Moors as **El Cid** ("the lord"), captured Valencia in eastern Spain and established himself as ruler.

At the **Council of Clermont** in 1095, Pope Urban, a French Cluniac (see 910), preached to an assembly of mainly Frankish clerics and nobles about Muslim "defilement" of the Holy Land, urging his audience to take up arms in a **holy war**. Urban had been entreated by the Byzantines for help against the Seljuks, and saw a way to channel the energies of European nobility away from constant infighting and toward a **Christian expansion** that would benefit the papacy. Fired by religious zeal and spurred by the promise of remission of sins, together with the prospect of winning booty, land, and control of the lucrative trade with the Orient, many nobles of France (formerly West Francia) and Lorraine joined, or "took the cross." Other nations were either in conflict with the papacy or indifferent, so the **First Crusade** was a largely French affair. Taking advantage of disarray in the Muslim world, three groups of Crusaders under Godfrey

Battle of the Crusades
This manuscript illustration shows Crusader knights joining battle with Saracens—the generic term used by Europeans to refer to their Muslim foes. Around 30,000 knights took part in the First Crusade.

and Baldwin of Bouillon, Count Raymond of Toulouse, and the Norman Bohemond of Otranto, took the Seljuk Rum capital of **Nicaea** in 1097, conquered **Edessa** in the same year, captured **Antioch** in 1098, and marched on **Jerusalem** in 1099. Godfrey was elected king of Jerusalem but took the title **Defender of the Holy Sepulchre**; his brother, Baldwin

became king the following year. Under the overlordship of the King of Jerusalem, the Crusaders established **four principal states**: the kingdom of Jerusalem, which thrived on trade mediated by the Italian trading powers; the county of Tripoli, set up by Raymond; the county of Edessa, established by Baldwin; and the principality of Antioch, set up by Bohemund.

75,000 SARACENS

15,000 CRUSADERS

The Siege of Antioch
Islamic forces at the Siege of Antioch outnumbered the Crusaders considerably. In fact Antioch fell only when a traitor opened a gate to a party of knights led by Bohemond of Otranto.

1081 Alexis Commenius accedes to Byzantine throne

1084 Founding of Carthusian monastic order

1085 Alfonso VI takes Toledo and Valencia in Spain

1085 Death of Pope Gregory VII (born c. 1020)

1085 Domesday Book commissioned

c.1085 Thule Eskimos control North American Arctic

1086 Battle of Zallaka in Spain—Alfonso defeated by Almoravids

1089 Fatimids take Palestine

1089 Development of Romanesque style

c. 1090 Assassins take up residence in Alamut

1092 Normans complete conquest of Sicily

1092 Su Sung builds Cosmic Engine mechanical clock in Peking

1092 Death of Seljuk sultan Malik Shah; Seljuk Empire begins to break up

1094 El Cid takes Valencia

1095 Pope Urban proclaims First Crusade

1096 Construction of Basilica San Marco, Venice

1097 Crusaders sack Constantinople

1098 Founding of the Cistercian order

1098 Antioch falls to Crusaders after year-long siege

1098 Council of Bari attempt to reunify Eastern and Western Churches

1099 Crusaders take Jerusalem: end of the First Crusade

1099 Knights Hospitaller established

1099 Death of El Cid (b. 1043)

1100 Baldwin I becomes first king of Jerusalem

1100 William II killed in hunting accident, Henry I becomes king of England

1100 Euclid translated from Arabic into Latin by Adelard of Bath

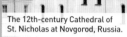

An illustration from Edward Fitzgerald's translation of the *Rubaiyat*; of the 600 verses, only around 120 are thought to have been written by Khayyam himself.

Monumental ruins in the city of Great Zimbabwe, capital of the Mwene Mutapa Empire. After it seized control of the gold trade, the empire grew rich.

The 12th-century Cathedral of St. Nicholas at Novgorod, Russia.

SOMETIME AROUND THE START OF THE 12TH CENTURY, OMAR KHAYYAM (1048–1131), an astronomer and mathematician in the service of the **Seljuk sultans**, composed a series of four-line poems, or "roba'iyat," which became famous thanks to the translation made by **Edward Fitzgerald** in 1859. Khayyam's career reflected the Seljuk era. At **Samarkand**, in the early 1070s, he was able to pursue his **mathematical studies** thanks to patronage from a local jurist, and under the strong Seljuk sultan **Malik Shah** (r. 1072–92), Khayyam was invited to **Isfahan** in 1073 to **set up an observatory** and lead a team of top scholars. In this period he made many **mathematical and astronomical breakthroughs**, including an unprecedented accurate measurement of **the length of the year** to 12 decimal places. Although he is now most famous for the *Rubaiyat*, it is not certain that Khayyam wrote most or any of the verses involved, and he was little regarded as a poet in his own time. Much of the current reputation of the work derives from the very free translation by Edward Fitzgerald.

The success of the **First Crusade** (see 1091–1100) owed much to the disarray of the Islamic regimes it had dispossessed. The **Fatimid Caliphate** in Cairo was rich but decadent; the **Abbasids** in Baghdad were little more than figureheads; the **Seljuk Turks** had failed to forge a unified empire, and instead warlords and tribal groups had set up a patchwork of competing states such as **Rum**, **Danishmend**, and **Damascus**. Throughout the early 12th century, the Crusaders battled constantly against these foes. In 1101, **Raymond IV of Toulouse** (c. 1042–1105) led a new Crusader

Baldwin of Bourcq
This coin features Baldwin of Bourcq, cousin of Baldwin I, who succeeded as count of Edessa, then as king of Jerusalem (see 1118).

army from **Constantinople** against the Sultanate of Rum, taking **Ankara** in June, only to be destroyed by Danishmend Turks in August. **Baldwin I of Jerusalem** (c. 1058–1118) steadily improved his access to the Mediterranean by taking a series of coastal cities from the **Fatimids**, defeating them at **Jaffa** in 1102, **Acre** in 1104, and **Ramleh** in 1105, although Raymond died in an attempt to take **Tripoli** in 1105.

NOTED FOR ITS FINE ARTS AND CRAFTS and construction of **monumental temple mounds**, the post-Moche culture, known as the **Sicán** or **Lambayeque** on the northern coast of Peru, reached its height in the early 11th century. But a prolonged drought, followed by catastrophic flooding, led to **cultural and political collapse**. In the early 12th century, the state recovered from the convulsions of the 11th century and rebuilt around a new capital at **Túcume**. New temples were built and the capital flourished until its conquest by the **Chimú** (see 1375), by which time there were 26 mounds and accompanying enclosures.

In central southern Africa, in what is now Zimbabwe, the **Mwene Mutapa Empire**, also known as **Great Zimbabwe** after its monumental capital, emerged as the most significant regional power. A kingdom of the **Shona** peoples that emerged around 900, Mwene Mutapa was initially based on cattle herding, but from around 1100 it took control of the lucrative **trade routes** linking the gold, iron, and ivory production centers of the interior to the **Arab trading kingdoms** on the east coast, which offered luxury goods from Asia.

Ceremonial knife
This gold knife is from the Middle Sicán culture in Peru. The early 1100s mark the threshold between the Middle and Late Sicán cultures.

inlaid turquoise

THE 12TH CENTURY SAW AN EXPLOSION OF CATHEDRAL BUILDING all over Europe, as population growth, increased wealth, and architectural **advances** combined with religious zeal, **civic pride**, and the personal ambition of potentates. The development of the **Romanesque and Gothic styles** was given expression in the great cathedrals, but each region developed its own, distinctive idiom. In **Novgorod**, for instance, the **Cathedral of St. Nicholas** (started in 1113) was given domed cupolas.

The **Investiture Controversy** between the papacy and the Western emperors rumbled on (see 1071–80). **Henry IV**'s failure to reconcile with the papacy had helped bring about his downfall; concerned that the ongoing dispute was undermining royal authority, his own family had conspired against him, and he was imprisoned. His successor, **Henry V** (1086–1125), launched a powerful expedition to **Italy** to force an **imperial coronation**.

Under duress (he was a prisoner of Henry at the time), **Pope Paschal II** offered major concessions on the investiture issue in the **Treaty of Sutri**, but he repudiated them the following year and the issue remained unsettled (see 1122).

Stained glass window of a Templar Knight in Warwickshire, England.

Guelph and Ghibelline forces join battle in Italy. These factions, based on the German Welf and Hohenstaufen dynasties, would come to dominate Italian politics.

> ❝ IN THIS **RELIGIOUS ORDER** HAS **FLOURISHED** AND IS **REVITALIZED** THE **ORDER** OF KNIGHTHOOD. ❞

From *The Primitive Rule of the Knights Templar*

In **Jerusalem**, in 1119, a group of knights, led by the French Hugues de Payens (c. 1070–1136), formed an order to **protect pilgrims** travelling along the dangerous road from Jaffa, on the coast, to the holy city. The new king of Jerusalem, **Baldwin II** (cousin of Baldwin I and his successor as count of Edessa), assigned them quarters in part of the **Temple Mount** compound, next to the site where the **Temple of Solomon** had once stood. Accordingly, they called themselves the Poor Fellow Soldiers of Christ and of the Temple of Solomon—also known as the **Knights Templar**.

Bologna University was the first in the western world. It was founded in 1119 (or possibly earlier, depending on the source). Institutions such as Bologna University were the incubators for the philosophical school of thought known as **Scholasticism** (see panel, right).

IN 1121, MOHAMMAD IB-TUMART, A BERBER LEADER from the Atlas Mountains, was hailed as the **al-Mahdi** (the Muslim messiah—see 874) and led his forces, known as the **Almohads**, in a **campaign of conquest** against Almoravid territories in Africa.

A synod at the German town of **Worms**, in 1122, presided by a papal legate drew up a concordat (agreement) ending the **Investiture Controversy**—although not the imperial–papal rivalry. A compromise was agreed along the lines already adopted between **Henry I of England** and **Anselm** (see 1107), under which the emperor would be involved in investiture but not control it. Essentially it was a **victory for the papacy**.

In 1123, **Frankish forces** from Jerusalem **defeated a Fatimid army** at Ibelin, while off the coast

Aristotle in translation
A page from a translation of Aristotle's Nicomachean Ethics, written on vellum—a writing material made from calf skin, which is more durable than papyrus or paper.

at Ascalon (Ashkelon), Venetian ships destroyed the Fatimid fleet. This marked the start of the dominance of **Italian maritime power** in the Mediterranean.

Emperor Henry V died in 1125 with no male heir, and an election was held to choose his successor. The closest heir was **Conrad of Swabia** (1122–90), of the house of **Hohenstaufen** (allied to the Salian dynasty and their antipapal policies), but the powerful archbishops of Mainz and Cologne angled for the election of a candidate more friendly to the Church. **Lothair of Saxony** (1075–1137), of the house of Welf, was chosen and became

Emperor Lothair II (III in some sources). Immediately he was plunged into a bitter **civil war** with the Hohenstaufens, and the two opposing sides became entrenched as propapal and proimperial factions known as the **Guelphs** and **Ghibellines** respectively. They would plague relations between and within the **city-states of northern Italy** into the 14th century—long after they had ceased to dominate German power politics—as they became associated with class struggles and **reactionary versus reforming parties**.

The work of **Aristotle** (384–322 BCE) had survived in Byzantium and among the Arabs, but Western Europeans only had access to a translation by the

philosopher **Boethius** of one treatise on logic. This began to change in the early 12th century, as the conquest of Islamic areas such as **Toledo** and **Sicily** gave Christian scholars access to Arabic works. Increasing exposure to the works of Aristotle led medieval scholars to consider him the "**master of those who know**" and the chief authority on matters of reason.

In 1125, the French king **Louis VI** (1081–1137) successfully rallied French nobles to repel an **English–German invasion**. This proved to be a milestone in the French monarchy's attempts to assert its authority, and thus in the emergence of **France as a nation-state**.

SCHOLASTICISM

The school of thought known as Scholasticism—because it was taught by the scholastics, or school masters—developed as the dominant philosophy of learning in medieval Europe, hand in hand with the emergence of the universities. Scholasticism was an approach to learning that used a method of formal discussion and debating. It became the intellectual basis for medieval religious and philosophical dogma.

25 PERCENT
THE APPROXIMATE **PROPORTION** OF **ARISTOTLE'S WORK SURVIVING** TODAY

1118 Baldwin of Bourcq becomes **Baldwin II**, king of Jerusalem

1118 Alexius I Comnenus, Byzantine emperor, institutes a form of feudalism in the empire

1121 Almohads begin **conquest of Almoravid** territories

1123 First Lateran Council; pope outlaws simony (selling of offices)

1123 Fatimids defeated at Ibelin and Ascalon

1123 Founding of **St. Bartholomew's Fair** in London

1124 Baldwin II ransomed, then wins Tyre

1125 Death of Henry V triggers start of what will become known as the **Guelph–Ghibelline conflict**

1125 Jin occupy Beijing; Khitan Liao dynasty collapses

1119 Knights Templar founded in Jerusalem

1119 Foundation of **Bologna University**

1122 Concordat of Worms ends **Investiture Controversy**

1123 Baldwin II captured by Danishmend Turks

1123 Danishmend Turks take Aleppo from Seljuks and found **independent emirate**

1124 Louis IV repels English–German invasion

1124 Hasan i-Sabbah dies (b. 1050s)

1125 Lothair elected king of the Romans; renews expansion into Slavic territory

c. 1125 Death of **David III** of Georgia (b. 1073), who established it as independent state

A mosaic shows Roger II being symbolically crowned by Christ.

St. Alban's Chronicle shows Matilda of England holding a charter.

An illustration from a 15th-century copy of the *History of the Kings of Britain*, by Geoffrey of Monmouth, shows Brutus the Trojan setting sail for Britain.

A scene from the Siege of Damascus, a battle of the Second Crusade.

1126–30

IN 1126, THE JIN—the Jurchen dynasty established by Aguda (see 1115) in Manchuria—turned on their erstwhile Chinese allies, **overrunning northern China** and seizing the Northern Song capital at **Kaifeng**. The Jin took control of northern China and moved the capital to Beijing. This marked the **end of the Northern Song**. However, a Song prince, **Gaozong**, escaped to the south and established the **Southern Song** dynasty in Hangzhou in 1127.

The death of **Pope Honorius**, in 1130, resulted in the election of two rival popes, **Innocent II** and **Anacletus II**. During this papal schism, **Roger II**, count of Sicily, recognized Anacletus as pope—his reward was the throne of Sicily.

Song dynasty porcelain ware
The Qingbai ("blue-white") glaze on this ewer is characteristic of Song dynasty porcelain from southeastern China, where the dynasty survived the Jin invasion.

1131–35

THE DEATH OF HENRY I, IN 1135, PITCHED ENGLAND INTO DYNASTIC STRIFE. His only male heir died in 1120 while crossing the English Channel, and although Henry had made his nobles swear allegiance to his daughter, the **Empress Matilda** (1102–67), she had spent little time in England and her second husband, **Geoffrey of Anjou**, was unpopular with the English nobles. Among those who had sworn fealty to Matilda was Henry's nephew and ward **Stephen of Blois** (r. 1135–54). On his uncle's death he immediately went to London, secured the support of most of the nobles and the Church, and **had himself proclaimed king**. However, Matilda refused to renounce her claim, and their contest would lead to a period of warfare and breakdown of central authority known as the **Anarchy** (see 1136–40).

In 1133, **Lothair II** (1070–1137) went to Italy to intervene in the **papal schism**, installing **Innocent II**. In return, the Pope confirmed the **Matildine inheritance** (the vast estates of Matilda of Tuscany, which she had willed first to the papacy and then to the emperor, sparking a dispute that would become tied up with the Guelph versus Ghibelline contest—(see 1121–25) and **crowned Lothair as emperor**. In 1135, Lothair pacified his rivals, **Conrad of Hohenstaufen** and his brother **Frederick of Swabia**, apparently securing the German crown for his son-in-law **Henry the Proud**, of the House of Welf.

1136–40

IN 1137, LOTHAIR DIED SUDDENLY while returning from a successful campaign in Italy against **Roger of Sicily**. Lothair's plans to concentrate German territories in the hands of the **Welf clan**, and create a stable inheritance for his son-in-law, evaporated when the election of 1138 chose the Waiblinger **Conrad of Hohenstaufen** (1135–95). The Waiblingers were descended from the dukes of Franconia; the name was later corrupted by the Italians into "Ghibelline." Conrad set about reversing the grants of Lothair, taking Saxony away from the Welfs, which promptly sparked renewed civil war.

In 1139, Matilda entered England to reclaim her crown from the usurper Stephen of Blois. Stephen had failed to

Legendary castle
Tintagel, Cornwall, where the ruins of a 13th-century castle still stand, is featured in the Arthurian legends created by Geoffrey of Monmouth.

strengthen his position since taking the crown, alienating many of his nobles on one hand, and powerful clerics on the other. He particularly blundered by arresting his chief minister Roger, Bishop of Salisbury. At a stroke, he lost many of his ablest administrators, and was henceforth unable to rein in the depredations of barons and other landowners, who became laws unto themselves. The country deteriorated into a state of anarchy famously lamented by the author of the Peterborough Chronicle, who wrote that under Stephen's reign the English "suffered nineteen long winters… when Christ and all his saints slept."

Sometime around 1140, the Welsh cleric **Geoffrey of Monmouth** (c. 1100–55) wrote the *History of the Kings of Britain*, an important example of early Anglo-Norman literature that introduced the legend of **King Arthur** to a European audience.

1141–45

IN 1141, JOHN OF SEVILLE TRANSLATED FROM THE ARABIC the *Epitome of the Whole of Astrology*, while in 1142 **Adelard of Bath** translated an Arabic version of Euclid's *Elements of Geometry*, one of the founding texts of mathematics. This **transmission of learning**, ancient and contemporary, via Arabic into Latin, was a key contributor to the emergence of an **intellectual renaissance** in Europe, and beyond that to the scientific achievements of the **Early Modern period** (1500–1800).

In an attempt to end the **civil war** that was convulsing Germany, an 1142 meeting, or diet, at Frankfurt confirmed the Welf **Henry the Lion** (1129–95) as **Duke of Saxony** (which he had already taken by force). Henry engaged in a vigorous renewal of **German expansion** to the east, where his

Pot helm helmet
This type of helmet was typical of those worn by Crusader knights. Made of steel, the pot helm helmet completely covered the head except for two small eye slits.

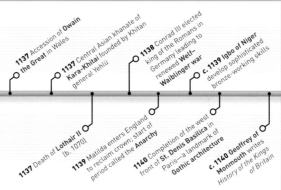

1126 Jurchen Jin defeat Northern Song, and overrun northern China

1127 Conrad elected **king of the Romans** as rival to Lothair

1127 Imad el-Din Zengi founds **Zengid dynasty** in Mosul

1127 Southern Song dynasty established

1127 Stephen II of Hungary takes Belgrade and Sofia from the Byzantines

1130 Roger II becomes **king of Sicily**

1131 Fulk of Anjou becomes king of Jerusalem

1133 Lothair II expels Anacletus, installs **Innocent II** as pope, and is crowned emperor

1134 Gothic tower built at Chartres

1135 Lothair's **year of pacification**—he asserts dominance in Germany

1135 Henry I of England (b. 1068) dies; **Stephen** usurps Matilda

1137 Accession of **Owain the Great** in Wales

1137 Central Asian khanate of **Kara-Khitai** founded by Khitan general Yehlü

1137 Death of **Lothair II** (b. 1070)

1138 Conrad III elected king of the Romans in Germany leading to renewed **Welf-Waiblinger war**

c. 1139 Igbo of Niger develop sophisticated bronze-working skills

1139 Matilda enters England to reclaim crown; start of period called the **Anarchy**

1140 Completion of the west front of **St.-Denis Basilica** in Paris—a landmark of **Gothic architecture**

c. 1140 Geoffrey of Monmouth writes *History of the Kings of Britain*

1141 Battle of Lincoln: Stephen captured; Matilda becomes queen of England

1141 Peace party gains upper hand in **Southern Song** Empire

1141 Kara-Khitai defeat Seljuks at Samarkand

1142 Diet of Frankfurt: an attempt to end Welf-Waiblinger conflict in Germany

Angkor Wat, in Cambodia, was built during the reign of Suryavarman II. It covers nearly 500 acres (200 hectares) and the central tower is 138 ft (42 m) high.

> **THOSE WHO ARE OF GOD... STRIVE TO OPPOSE THE MULTITUDE OF THE INFIDELS, WHO REJOICE IN A VICTORY GAINED OVER US, AND DEFEND THE ORIENTAL CHURCH FREED FROM THEIR TYRANNY BY SO GREAT AN OUTPOURING OF THE BLOOD OF YOUR FATHERS...**

Pope Eugenius III, from Papal bull calling for the Second Crusade, 1145

campaigns against the heathen **Slavs** were given the status of Crusades.

In 1144, the atabeg (governor) of Mosul, **Imad el-Din Zengi** (1085–1146), founder of the **Zengid dynasty**, took advantage of feuding between the Crusader principalities to seize the Crusader county of Edessa. Fulk, king of Jerusalem, had died in 1143 and his successor **Baldwin III** (1130–63) was only a child, under the regency of his mother **Melisende**. She did not have the authority to settle a dispute between Antioch and Edessa, and Imad el-Din besieged Edessa until it fell to him. **The loss of Edessa** caused alarm and outrage in Europe, and provided the trigger for the **Second Crusade** (see 1146–50).

In 1145, Eugenius III issued a call-to-arms in the form of a Papal bull.

IN 1146, THE INFLUENTIAL CISTERCIAN MONK BERNARD OF CLAIRVAUX (1090–1153) egged on by Pope Eugenius III, preached a new Crusade to liberate Edessa from the clutches of the Zengids; **Conrad III of Germany** (1093–1152) and **Louis VII of France** (1120–80) "took the cross." But the expedition was a **disastrous** affair, except for incidental success in Portugal achieved by a contingent of English and Flemish Crusaders who helped Afonso-Henriques, Count of Portugal, take Lisbon from the **Moors** in 1147. Conrad and Louis took different routes to the Holy Land, their armies meeting equally disastrous fates as they struggled through Anatolia. In 1148, forced to hitch a ride on a Byzantine ship, having lost his army at the **Battle of Dorylaeum**, Conrad met up with Louis. Rather than pitch their

French and German Crusaders
The German force outnumbered the French contingent during the Second Crusade. Neither army achieved any success: defeat in Anatolia preceded failure at Damascus.

	CRUSADERS
French	15,000
German	20,000

Koutoubia Mosque in Morocco
The Koutoubia ("booksellers") Mosque, built by the Almohads, reflects the mercantile success of Almohad Marrakech, where book, cloth, and other souqs flourished.

depleted forces against the powerful Zengids, they decided instead to launch an attack on Damascus, the only Muslim state that was friendly to the Crusader kingdoms. Hampered by **lack of supplies** and threatened by the Zengid leader Nur al-Din, successor to Imad el-Din, the **Siege of Damascus** also **failed**. The Second Crusade broke up having failed to achieve anything beyond a damaging fallout. Louis was cuckolded by one of his generals, eventually leading to a divorce from his wife, **Eleanor of Aquitaine** (c. 1122–04), and the loss of her territories (see 1151–55). The **Byzantines** were forced to step in where the Crusade had failed, occupying western Edessa, but **Roger of Sicily** took advantage of Byzantine distraction to invade and plunder Greece in 1147. The disasters of the Second Crusade marked the beginning of the **decline** of the **Frankish Crusader kingdoms**.

In 1147, the **Almohads** under **Abd al-Mu'min** (1094–1163) completed the conquest of Almoravid Morocco, taking **Marrakech**, before invading **Moorish Spain** (although it took them until 1172 to subjugate all the Islamic kingdoms).

Suryavarman II (c. 1113–50) was the most warlike **Khmer king**, although most of his foreign adventures were unsuccessful. He launched attacks against the **Dai Vet** of northern Vietnam and made repeated attempts to subjugate the **Champa**. More significant was his building program, the zenith of which was the **temple of Angkor Wat**. This vast complex includes five towers symbolizing holy mountains, and large numbers of elaborate carvings.

500 ACRES

THE AREA OF ANGKOR WAT

Star-shaped tile
1267 • IRAN
Though distinctively Islamic in its use of luster (a ceramic technology mimicking gilding) and arabesques (stylized foliage), this tile shows Mongol influence with the inclusion of doglike animals.

foliage in gold leaf

Persian ceramic and gold leaf ewer
1200–1399 • IRAN
It was prohibited to make drinking vessels from gold and silver, as these were considered indulgent, so Islamic craftsmen became expert in alternatives such as ceramic, which was then richly decorated.

Bronze vase
18TH CENTURY • CHINA
Although this bronze vase from China displays a text from the Qu'ran in Arabic, it nonetheless shows clear Chinese influence.

THE ISLAMIC WORLD
TECHNOLOGICAL INNOVATION AND RELIGIOUS INSPIRATION COMBINE TO CREATE A UNIQUE HERITAGE OF ARTS AND CRAFTS

Islamic arts and crafts were shaped by religious restrictions, cultural heritage acquired through conquest, and the elaboration of unique features, notably the use of ornamentation and color, and inclusion of Arabic script.

Through its rapid conquest of a huge empire, the Islamic caliphate was exposed to a diverse mix of cultural styles and heritages; Islamic art reflects these while maintaining a high degree of homogeneity due to religious uniformity. Restrictions imposed by Islam, such as prohibitions on representative art and on the use of gold and silver, generated creative responses, especially stylized abstract designs, elaborate ornamentation, strong use of color, and the use of Arabic script and Qu'ranic quotations.

inlaid with ornate foliage

inscription reads "Allah, Muhammad, Fatima, and 'Ali, Hasan, and Husayn"

Jade necklace
1875–1925 • ORIGIN UNKNOWN
This jade necklace is made from five pieces, all different in shape and engraved with verses from the Qu'ran. Such artifacts could serve as amulets with quasi-magical powers.

Surgical scissors and scalpel
10TH CENTURY • ORIGIN UNKNOWN
Islamic physicians made huge advances in medicine and surgery, including devising a range of surgical instruments such as the *mibda* (scalpel) and *miqass* (scissors).

Khanjar
19TH CENTURY • INDIA
Although from India, this curved, double-edged dagger is actually a traditional Omani blade. It is decorated with ornate foliage, a typical Islamic motif.

script border to prevent clipping

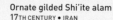

Pendant
18TH CENTURY • INDIA
From the Indian Mughal Empire, this gold pendant shows how Muslim rulers sometimes disregarded prohibitions on representative art and the use of precious metals.

Coins
720–910 • SYRIA/EGYPT
Coins from the Ummayad and Abbadis caliphates, minted in Damascus and Cairo, bear Arabic text in place of pictures of heads of state.

Ornate gilded Shi'ite alam
17TH CENTURY • IRAN
This alam, or standard, made of brass and gold, symbolically recalls the Shi'ite standard planted at the Battle of Kerbala in 680.

Bowl
1000–1199 • IRAN/IRAQ
The bold colors of this simple bowl are typically Islamic, as is the interlacing cord design. The lace of highlighted detail lends a meditative quality to the design.

twisted cord design in ochre, black, and white

head is hinged to body

Feline incense burner
11–12TH CENTURIES • IRAN/AFGHANISTAN
Burners like this, in the shape of a big cat, were used in the courts of Medieval Islamic kings—lions and cheetahs symbolized power. The head tilts to allow insertion of charcoal.

Candlestick
15TH CENTURY • MAMLUK EGYPT
To circumvent the prohibition on precious metals, Islamic metalworkers became adept at combining baser metals like brass with silver and gold inlay.

rim markings indicate city or location

Calligraphy scissors
1700–99 • IRAN
These scissors were used for shaping pens and brushes. The blades are inlaid with gold, a variety of damascening known as *koftgari*.

Qibla compass
DATE AND ORIGIN UNKNOWN
This ornamental compass was used to indicate the direction, *qibla*, of Mecca, so that worshipers could orient themselves properly for prayer.

Pen case
1700–1899 • ORIGIN UNKNOWN
This hexagonal case for carrying pens bares geometric shapes, a typical feature of Islamic design.

Islamic lamp
DATE AND ORIGIN UNKNOWN
This hourglass-shaped lamp bares a design of Arabic script on the side, which is picked out in vibrant blue, a ceramic dye perfected by Islamic craftsmen.

bold colors and gold leaf

no empty space left unfilled

Arabic script inscribed with careful calligraphy

illuminations flout normal prohibitions

Illuminated Divan
1800–99 • INDIA
A Divan, or Diwan, is a collection or anthology of poems, inspired by ancient Persian poetry models. This illuminated Divan of the Persian poet Hafez from 19th-century India has typical Kashmiri painted lacquer covers.

135

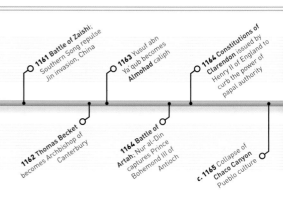

Monks Mound, the largest mound at Cahokia, is over 100ft (30m) high. It has been estimated that it took 15 million baskets of earth to make it.

The University of Bologna was originally a school for jurists.

The Hassan Tower in Rabat, Morocco, is all that was built of what was intended to be an Almohad super-mosque.

THE CITY OF CAHOKIA SPRANG UP AT THE CLIMAX of the Mississippian (or Cahokian) culture of the American Bottom (an area of the Mississippi river valley). Around the mid-12th century they constructed more than **100 mounds**, including one with a base that is larger than that of the Great Pyramid at Giza, along with a huge landscaped plaza that may be the **biggest earthen city square in the world**. The most remarkable feature of Cahokia is the speed with which it came into existence. Until around 1050, **Mississippians** lived in small villages and had never built on anything approaching this scale. By the 1150s the city may have covered **493 hectares (1,200 acres)** and been home to **30,000 people**. Its cultural and economic influence spread across the **Midwest**, from the present Canadian border to the Gulf Coast. Perhaps because urban living was so exceptional for the

Mississippians, Cahokia would **decline rapidly**, within around a century, with a return to low-density farming communities.

In 1152, **Conrad III** (b. 1093), king of the Romans, died and his nephew **Frederick of Swabia**, known as **Barbarossa** (see panel, below) was elected as successor. Of combined Welf and Waiblingen parentage (see 1131–35), he brought relative peace to Germany. His coronation as **emperor** in Rome was delayed because the city was in the grip of a **revolutionary commune** led by radical reformer **Arnold of Brescia** (1090–1155). Frederick allied with the papacy against Arnold and Norman Sicily, making his first expedition to Italy in 1154. The following year, in the face of Roman hostility, he was crowned by the new pope, **Adrian IV** (1100–59), but had to retreat to Germany, abandoning Adrian, who was forced to ally himself with the **Normans**.

FREDERICK BARBAROSSA (1122–90)

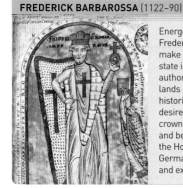

Energetic and ambitious, Frederick I was determined to make Germany the dominant state in Europe, and to reassert authority over all the imperial lands in Italy. Aware of the historic context of his office, he desired to restore the imperial crown to Roman-era glory, and began to style his realm the Holy Roman Empire. In Germany, he pacified rebels and expanded royal lands.

WITH ORIGINS DATING BACK TO PERHAPS 1088, BOLOGNA CLAIMS to be the **oldest university** in the Western world (see 1116–20—in the sense of an institution specifically designated as a *universitas*, as opposed to a *studium generale*, as centers for teaching had previously been known. In 1158, the emperor **Frederick I** (1122–90), on the advice of scholars who may have been **Bologna alumni**, granted the university a charter, firmly establishing the institution as an **independent center of scholarship**. Early universities tended to specialize in one field of study, and Bologna was **dedicated to law**.

In 1159, **Alexander III** (c. 1100–81) was chosen as pope, although his election was opposed by the emperor, **Frederick I**. Frederick had once again invaded Italy, this time intent on assuming his full imperial inheritance. With the aid of the **League of Pavia** (Bresci, Parma, and others), he had subdued Milan and its associated cities, but at the **Diet of Roncaglia**, in 1158, he went too far. Harking back to the Roman era, Frederick insisted that ancient law gave him the right to appoint an **imperial podestà** (local governor) to rule each city. Milan was pushed into revolt, and other cities joined them in forming a **Lombard League** under the auspices of the papacy. Alexander III would earn the title "**the Great**" for leading this anti-imperial rebellion.

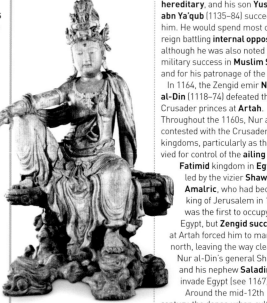

The Bodhisattva Guanyin
This 12th-century Chinese statue depicts the Buddhist deity Guanyin, who protects those in danger—perhaps accounting for his popularity.

IN 1161, THE SOUTHERN SONG REPULSED AN INCURSION by the northern Jin (see 1126–30), securing their kingdom from invasion. A peace treaty of 1165 recognized an uneasy truce between the two powers.

The **Almohad** caliph **Abd al-Mu'min** died in 1163, having destroyed the **Almoravids** and extended Almohad rule from Morocco to Tunisia (the province of Ifriqiya). He made his office

hereditary, and his son **Yusuf abn Ya'qub** (1135–84) succeeded him. He would spend most of his reign battling **internal opposition**, although he was also noted for military success in **Muslim Spain** and for his patronage of the arts.

In 1164, the Zengid emir **Nur al-Din** (1118–74) defeated the Crusader princes at **Artah**. Throughout the 1160s, Nur al-Din contested with the Crusader kingdoms, particularly as they vied for control of the **ailing Fatimid** kingdom in **Egypt**, led by the vizier **Shawar**. **Amalric**, who had become king of Jerusalem in 1162, was the first to occupy Egypt, but **Zengid success** at Artah forced him to march north, leaving the way clear for Nur al-Din's general Shirkuh and his nephew **Saladin** to invade Egypt (see 1167).

Around the mid-12th century, the dense urban culture of the ancient **Pueblo peoples** at **Chaco Canyon** in North America collapsed, probably because their marginal system of agriculture had overtaxed the **fragile dryland ecology**, leaving them vulnerable to drought. Dating of timbers from the Chaco Canyon pueblos shows that the newest timbers date from around the 1160s—in other words, there was no construction after this. Other Pueblo, or **Anasazi**, sites show evidence from this period of fortification, destruction, and even cannibalism, but there is also evidence of orderly abandonment, presumably by people moving to new sites.

c. 1150s Climax of the **Cahokia mound** settlement, North America

1152 Frederick I (Barbarossa) succeeds Conrad as king of the Romans

1153 Jin move their capital from Manchuria to **Beijing**

1151 First use of gunpowder **explosives** in warfare in China

1152 Eleanor of Aquitaine marries Henry of Anjou; their combined lands create the **Angevin Empire**

1154 Henry II becomes king of England

1155 Frederick I crowned emperor

c. 1156 Yoruba city states are flourishing in West Africa

1158 Frederick I grants charter to **Bologna University**, Italy

1159 Election of **Pope Alexander III**, the Great; formation of **Lombard League** to oppose Frederick in Italy

1161 Battle of Zaishi; Southern Song repulse Jin invasion, China

1163 Yusuf abn Ya'qub becomes **Almohad** caliph

1162 Thomas Becket becomes Archbishop of Canterbury

1164 Battle of **Artah**; Nur al-Din captures Prince Bohemond III of Antioch

1164 Constitutions of Clarendon issued by Henry II of England to curb the power of papal authority

c. 1165 Collapse of **Chaco Canyon** Pueblo culture

136

> ❝ WILL NO ONE **RID ME OF THIS TURBULENT PRIEST?** ❞

Attributed to **Henry II**, 1170

The murder of Thomas Becket is depicted in stained glass at Canterbury Cathedral. Canonized in 1173, Becket became one of the most popular English saints.

IN 1170, THOMAS BECKET, ARCHBISHOP OF CANTERBURY, was murdered in Canterbury Cathedral, England, by four knights of the court of **Henry II** (r. 1154–89). Although he swore that he had not ordered the crime, and was absolved of responsibility by **Pope Alexander** in 1172, Henry's famous outburst (see above) had prompted the action of the knights. The context for this outrage was an ongoing dispute over the extent of ecclesiastical versus royal jurisdiction. During the anarchy of **Stephen's reign** (see 1136–40), clerical courts had encroached on areas previously under royal jurisdiction. Following Stephen's death, **Henry Plantagenet** came to the throne. He controlled England alongside the territories of Anjou, Normandy, and Aquitaine—known as the **Angevin Empire**—and set about instituting a badly needed reorganization of his new kingdom. **Taxation reforms**, for instance, replaced the Danegeld with new levies, but it was the **judicial reform** that brought him into conflict with his friend and chancellor **Thomas Becket**. Becket had already been forced into exile after being found guilty of violating the **Constitutions of Clarendon** (see 1164). On his return he vexed Henry by **excommunicating** royally favored bishops.

At its height, in the late 12th century, the commercial **empire of Srivijaya**, based in Sumatra, controlled much of the **Malay Archipelago**. Its authority extended to colonies around the East Indies and as far as **Sri Lanka** and **Taiwan**. Srivijayan power was based almost exclusively on its **maritime prowess**. By securing the seas in the region against piracy, they enabled and directed **trade** between China, India, and the Islamic world, but imposition of heavy duties and taxes stoked resentment and, eventually, revolt.

Frederick I's fourth expedition to Italy, beginning in 1166, prompted the renewal of the **Lombard League** (see 1156–60) and the construction of the mighty fortress town **Alessandria**, named for the pope. With this citadel guarding the mountain passes, **Italy became virtually independent** of imperial authority.

tablet in clay with molded design

Votive tablet
This votive tablet from the trading empire of Srivijaya is engraved with Buddhist figures. The ruling Sailendras were ardent Buddhists.

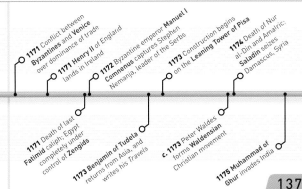

Muhammad of Ghur, traveling by elephant, leads his army in the Islamic conquest of India.

THE GHURIDS WERE A DYNASTY FOUNDED IN 1151 by Ala-ud-Din Husayn, who conquered much of **Ghaznavid Afghanistan** and founded a new state based at **Ghur** in western Afghanistan. In 1173, **Ghiyas-ud-Din** became emir, making his brother Mu'izz-du-Din, better known as **Muhammad of Ghur**, co-emir. Together the brothers brought most of Afghanistan under their control, and in 1175 Muhammad launched the **Islamic invasion** of northern India.

The Spanish rabbi **Benjamin of Tudela** (1130–73) was the **first recorded European** to have approached the borders of **China**, in an epic journey he made from 1159 to 1173. His account, *The Travels of Benjamin of Tudela*, recounts many exotic legends, including **Noah's Ark** resting on Mount Ararat.

In the medieval period, the city of **Pisa**, in Tuscany, became the center of a thriving **city-state**. Its cathedral was constructed in the 11th century, but in 1173 work began on a separate **bell tower**. Even during construction the foundations sank and the tower **began to slant**. Eventually it came to lean 15 ft (4.5 m) from the perpendicular.

During the 1170s, a new **religious movement** emerged in Lyons. Also known as the Poor Men of Lyons and the Vaudois, the **Waldenses** were led by Peter Waldes (c. 1140–1218), a rich merchant who gave away his property and began to preach a radical creed of **gospel simplicity**

Leaning Tower of Pisa
Pisa's famous leaning tower is 179 ft (54.5 m) tall and 57 ft (17.5 m) in diameter at the base.

that rejected many of the teachings of Catholicism. Despite initial blessing by **Pope Alexander III**, the Waldensians' refusal to abide by his injunction against preaching led to their **denunciation as heretics** in 1179 and a long history of persecution (see 1206–10).

In 1174, the Zengid emir **Nur al-Din** died. His nephew **Saladin**, who had already assumed control of **Egypt**, quickly marched north to secure **Syria**, and was duly recognized as **sultan** of Egypt and Syria by the caliph in Baghdad, founding the **Ayyubid dynasty**.

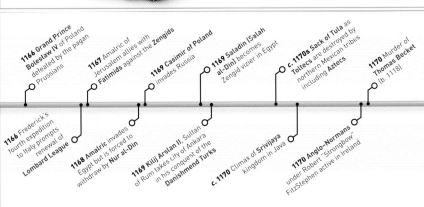

1166 Grand Prince Bolestaw IV of Poland defeated by the pagan Prussians

1167 Amalric of Jerusalem allies with **Fatimids** against the **Zengids**

1169 Casimir of Poland invades Russia

1169 Saladin (Salah al-Din) becomes Zengid vizier in Egypt

c. 1170s Sack of Tula as **Toltecs** are destroyed by northern Mexican tribes including **Aztecs**

1170 Murder of **Thomas Becket** (b. 1118)

1166 Frederick's fourth expedition to Italy prompts renewal of **Lombard League**

1168 Amalric invades Egypt but is forced to withdraw by **Nur al-Din**

1169 Kilij Arslan II, Sultan of Rum takes city of Ankara in his conquest of the **Danishmend Turks**

c. 1170 Climax of Srivijaya kingdom in Java

1170 Anglo-Normans under Robert "Strongbow" FitzStephen active in Ireland

1171 Conflict between Byzantines and Venice over dominance of trade

1171 Henry II of England lands in Ireland

1172 Byzantine emperor **Manuel I Comnenus** captures Stephen Nemanja, leader of the Serbs

1173 Construction begins on the **Leaning Tower of Pisa**

1174 Death of Nur al-Din and Amalric; **Saladin** seizes Damascus, Syria

1171 Death of last Fatimid caliph; Egypt completely under control of **Zengids**

1173 Benjamin of Tudela returns from Asia, and writes his *Travels*

c. 1173 Peter Waldes forms **Waldensian** Christian movement

1175 Muhammad of Ghur invades India

137

This depiction of the Battle of Yashima during the Gempei Wars illustrates a heavily armed Minamoto discovering the terrified mother of Emperor Taira.

EMPEROR FREDERICK BARBAROSSA'S FIFTH EXPEDITION TO ITALY in 1176 (see also 1151–55) ended in disaster for the imperial forces when his army was crushed at the **Battle of Legnano**. The battle marked one of the earliest occasions in the medieval era when cavalry were defeated by infantry. This had class implications as knights on horseback generally belonged to the feudal aristocracy, while footmen with pikes represented freemen of the rising bourgeoisie. In 1177, Frederick was forced to concede the **Peace of Venice** with the pope; a prelude to the more comprehensive Peace of Constance in 1183 (see 1181–85).

Now reconciled with the emperor, **Pope Alexander III** was able to call an ecumenical council at the Lateran Palace in Rome, in 1179. The council decreed that **papal elections** would be solely in the hands of the cardinals, and that a two-thirds majority was needed to elect a pope. It was hoped that this would draw a line under years of contention between papal candidates elected by the antiimperial party and **"anti-popes"**—persons selected by the emperor to oppose the legitimately elected or sitting pope.

In 1176, the army of **Byzantine emperor** Manuel Commenus was destroyed by the Turks of the **Sultanate of Rum** (see 1100–05) at the **Battle of Myriocephalum**. The Byzantines were never again able to send land forces to help the Crusaders.

The **Gempei Wars** (1180–85) in Japan

Pope Alexander III
This 14th-century fresco shows Pope Alexander III presenting a sword to the Venetian Doge for use against the emperor, Frederick Barbarossa.

COAL AND IRON IN MEDIEVAL EUROPE

Growing populations, new agricultural implements, and constant military activity increased the demand for iron in the Middle Ages. Charcoal was still the main source of power for iron forges, but deforestation caused wood shortages. As a consequence, demand for coal increased and scavenging for sea coal was increasingly supplemented by mining. The first record of a coal mine comes from Escomb near Durham, in northern England in 1183.

marked the **end of Taira domination** of Japan (see 641–650), and the start of the **Minamoto shogunate**. Civil wars in 1156 and 1159 had left control of Japan in the hands of Taira no Kiyomori (c.1118–81), who quickly assumed a similar level of power to the **Fujiwara clan** (see 851–860). Not only did he act as prime minister, but he also married his daughters to the imperial family, enabling him to place his infant grandson on the throne as emperor in 1180. But his excessive lust for power and perceived corruption alienated his provincial supporters, and in the same year there was an uprising by the **Minamoto clan** against Taira rule, which grew into the five-year-long Gempei Wars.

> **SALADIN'S** HOPE HAD AN EASY PASSAGE, HIS **PATHS** WERE **FRAGRANT**, HIS **GIFTS POURED OUT**, … HIS **POWER** WAS **MANIFEST**, HIS **AUTHORITY SUPREME.**

Imad al Din, Secretary to Saladin, from *Lightning of Syria*, c.1200

BY THE 1180s, THE CRUSADER KINGDOMS OF OUTREMER ("beyond the sea," as they were known in Europe) were in an increasingly precarious position. Europe was deaf to entreaties for **Crusader reinforcements**, and the Christian Byzantines were preoccupied with other matters, such as war with Norman Sicily. Meanwhile, their Muslim opponents were gathering under the leadership of **Saladin**, or Salah al-Din, (c. 1137–93) the sultan of Egypt and Syria. By 1183, he had suppressed Christian rebels at Edessa and Aleppo, and with both sides reeling from the effects of a drought, had brokered a peace treaty with the leper **king of Jerusalem, Baldwin IV** (c. 1161–85). The uneasy peace was shattered, however, by the actions of Reynald of Châtillon, an adventurer from the Second Crusade, who persistently raided unarmed caravans of Islamic pilgrims, and sponsored a pirate fleet that pillaged the Red Sea.

Saladin mobilized his army, intent on punishing Reynald, but his progress was checked by **Frankish fortresses** and another prolonged **famine**. In 1185, Baldwin died and his sickly infant nephew inherited the crown as **Baldwin V** (1177–86).

In 1183, the peace between Emperor Frederick Barbarossa and his Italian foes was ratified as the Peace of Constance, but although imperial authority over Italy was recognized, the **Lombard** cities were granted effective autonomy.

The **Battle of Dannoura** of 1185 marked the climax of the **Gempei Wars**. Warrior Minamoto Yoshitsune, younger brother of Yoritomo, the founder of the shogunate, destroyed the Taira in the naval battle.

Saladin, sultan of Egypt and Syria
Saladin escapes from battle on a camel in this 18th-century engraving. He was renowned as a generous and principled leader.

1176 Byzantine army defeated by Turks at **Battle of Myriocephalum**

1176 Battle of Legnano between Frederick Barbarossa and the Lombard League

1179 Third Lateran Council held in Rome

1180 Philip II Augustus (r. 1180–1223) becomes **king of France**

1177 Kingdom of Champa sacks Khmer city of Angkor

1177 Peace of Venice between Frederick Barbarossa and the pope

1180 Gempei Wars in Japan (to 1185)

1181 Accession of **Jayavarman VII** of Khmer (reigned until 1215)

1183 Peace of Constance between Frederick Barbarossa and Lombard League

1185 The Taira defeated at **Battle of Dannoura** in Japan

1183 Saladin mobilizes his army against Reynald of Châtillon

1184 Diet of Mainz; leads to Third Crusade

1185 Second Bulgarian Empire is founded (to 1396)

The Horns of Hattin, an extinct volcano crowned with two rocky outcrops, was the site of the Battle of Hattin in 1187.

ON JULY 4, 1187, THE CRUSADER ARMY WAS DEFEATED by the forces of Saladin. The Crusader forces were led by the new king of Jerusalem, **Guy of Lusignan**, who had seized power on the death of the infant Baldwin V in 1186. Baldwin's regents had negotiated another truce with Saladin, but

3:2 Battle of Hattin
Saladin's troops outnumbered the Crusaders by 30,000 to 20,000, yet his success was owed to his tactics and the Christians' desperate thirst.

once again, Reynald of Châtillon had broken it, raiding a caravan of pilgrims and provoking **Saladin** into a final campaign to sweep the Holy Land clear of the Christian principalities. Goaded by Reynald, King Guy led a combined force of Crusader knights, **Templars**, Hospitallers, and English mercenaries (see 1116–20) across a waterless plateau in the blazing heat to take up a position on the **Horns of Hattin**, an extinct volcano. Between them and Lake Tiberias—the main source of fresh water for the thirst-crazed knights—lay the well-rested and provisioned army of Saladin. Using raiding tactics, Saladin drove the Crusaders into desperate confusion, surrounding and capturing them all. More than

200 Templars and Hospitallers were executed, while Saladin personally beheaded Reynald. King Guy was later released, but, with his army annihilated, it was easy for Saladin to cow many of the remaining Crusader strongholds into surrender. He took **Acre** in July and **Jerusalem** in October. Tyre, Antioch, Tripoli, and a few castles were all that remained of the Crusader kingdoms.

The Crusader kingdom of Outremer had been pleading for European assistance for years and the **fall of Jerusalem** in 1187 finally prompted Pope Gregory VIII to preach a **new Crusade**. The dispatch of Anglo-French forces was delayed by disputes between Henry II of England and Philip II of France, and then by the death of Henry and the accession of Richard I in 1189. Richard I and Philip II finally set out in late 1190. Frederick Barbarossa had already set out overland in 1189, but was drowned en route the following year.

horns made of gilded wood

metal plated gloves or *tekko*

skirts split for ease of movement

Samurai armor
This beautifully presented Japanese armor dates from the 19th century, though the first samurai warriors fought with similar armor in the 12th century.

King Richard I of England, also known as Richard the Lionheart, is shown leading Crusaders into battle.

THE THIRD CRUSADE was hampered by infighting among the European factions of the Crusaders of Outremer, and although **Richard the Lionheart** won most of his battles, he was unable to achieve his sworn aim of "liberating" Jerusalem. The Crusade had already gotten off to a bad start (see 1186–90), and there were further delays en route when, in 1191, Richard stopped to conquer Byzantine **Cyprus**. He sold the island to the Templars, who would later pass it on to the diminished Crusader kingdoms, where it became one of the main supports for continuing Christian presence in the **Holy Land**. On arriving in Palestine, Richard joined Philip II of France in the **siege of Acre**, which was actually a double siege—King Guy had laid siege to the city on his release from captivity (see 1186–90), but Saladin had then encircled his forces. Acre was taken by the Crusaders in July and much of the population was massacred. Philip II returned to France, but Richard I had sworn to liberate Jerusalem, and marched along the coast, retaking towns and defeating Saladin at Arsuf in September. Although he would go on to clear Muslim forces from the rest of the coastal strip, and camp within sight of Jerusalem, Richard did not have the forces he needed to take and hold the holy

CRUSADER ARMOR

69 lb THE WEIGHT OF **ARMOR**

3.3 lb THE WEIGHT OF A **SWORD**

0.4 lb THE WEIGHT OF A **MACE**

city. With continued infighting among the Crusader barons, the murder of Conrad of Montferrat by **Assassins** (see 1081–90) soon after being made king, reinforcements arriving for Saladin, and bad news from England—where his brother John was scheming to seize the crown—Richard was forced to conclude a peace treaty with Saladin in 1192. **Outremer** would henceforth be confined to a 90 mile (145km) coastal strip, from Tyre to Jaffa, along with Antioch and Tripoli.

In 1192, **Minamoto Yoritomo** (see 1181–85) awarded himself the title Seii tai-shogun ("barbarian-subduing great general"). Since the end of the Gempei Wars, Yoritomo had dispatched all challengers, including his brother Yoshitsune. As undisputed military dictator, his *bakufu*, or administration, at Kamakura now supplanted the imperial court. Japan would be ruled by **shoguns**—military dictators—for centuries to come.

In 1192, the **Ghurids of Persia** defeated a Hindu rebellion at the Battle of Taraori near Thanesar in India. The following year, Delhi was taken and Muhammad of Ghur founded the **Sultanate of Delhi**.

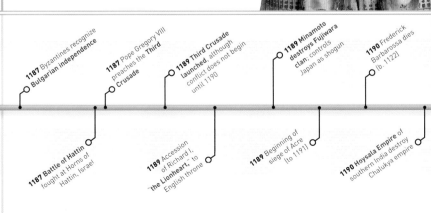

1187 Byzantines recognize **Bulgarian independence**

1187 Pope Gregory VIII preaches the **Third Crusade**

1189 Third Crusade launched, although conflict does not begin until 1190

1189 Minamoto destroys Fujiwara clan; controls Japan as shogun

1190 Frederick Barbarossa dies (b. 1122)

1192 Battle of Tararori; Ghurids crush Hindu confederacy

June 1192 Treaty of Ramla signed between Richard I and Saladin

1187 Battle of Hattin fought at Horns of Hattin, Israel

1189 Accession of Richard I, "the Lionheart," to English throne

1189 Beginning of siege of Acre (to 1191)

1190 Hoysala Empire of southern India destroy Chalukya empire

1198 Innocent III elected pope

A Persian painting shows Temujin, later known as Genghis Khan, battling the Tartars. The Tartar tribes fought constantly with the Mongols.

Peterhouse College, Cambridge, was founded 75 years after the university.

POPE INNOCENT III HAD PROCLAIMED A NEW CRUSADE in 1199, intent on restoring papal supervision to the crusading movement, and hoping to reunite the Greek and Latin churches to fulfill his vision of a **single Christian dominion** under the papacy. In 1201, envoys met Enrico Dandolo, Doge of Venice, to arrange passage to Egypt for the **Fourth Crusade**. Under the **Peace of Venice** (see 1176–80), the Venetians agreed to transport 33,500 men and 4,500 horses for a payment of 85,000 marks. In addition, they would supply 50 war galleys in return for half of the Crusaders' conquests.

When the Crusaders gathered in Venice in 1202, it transpired that there were too few of them, and they could not pay the agreed bill. Instead, they agreed to help Venice by taking Zara, Dalmatia—a rich source of wood for Venetian galleys. Pope Innocent protested, but worse was to come. In 1204, the Crusaders arrived in

Constantinople, where relations with the Byzantines quickly soured; the city was taken for the first time in its history, and was brutally sacked. A new **Latin Empire of the East** was proclaimed under a new emperor, Baldwin of Flanders, while Venice was awarded nearly half the city, numerous Mediterranean islands, and other territories. Although the Byzantine emperors relocated to **Byzantine Nicaea**, the Fourth Crusade marked the end of the Byzantine Empire as a true power, which discredited the Crusading movement and helped the Turks.

In the late 12th century, the Mongolian and Turkic nomads of the steppes were fearsome but disunited. Temujin (c. 1162–1227), who later became known as **Genghis Khan**, was a minor leader who became a *nokhor* (companion) to Toghril, Khan of the Kereits, the dominant tribe in Central **Mongolia**. Through ability and charisma, he rose to become a great general, crushing the

Jayavarman VII
This bronze statue of King Jayavarman VII, in Mahayana Buddhist style, portrays a serene and contemplative king.

neighboring **Tartar** tribes in 1202, but inciting resentment among other Kereits so that in 1203 he clashed with Toghril himself. He emerged from this confrontation as the dominant leader among the Mongol tribes.

Jayavarman VII (c. 1125–1220) had returned from exile to claim the **Khmer** crown in 1181. He

avenged the destruction of the capital by deposing the Champa king in 1191, suppressed a revolt in the west, restored Angkor, and finally gained ascendancy over the Champa kingdom. Jayavarman made **Mahayana Buddhism** the state religion and taxed the resources of the kingdom to build great temples, as well as hospitals, shrines, roads, and bridges. One of his temples, Preah Khan, was served by 98,000 retainers.

In around 1200, the **Chimú** state, centered on their capital at Chan Chan in the **Moche Valley** in Peru, began to expand. Their power rested on their mastery of intensive agriculture techniques and elaborate irrigation. At Chan Chan, Chimú leaders built citadels, or palaces, high-walled buildings with audience chambers and storage depots. It is believed that each new Chimú ruler was obliged to build and fund his own citadel, which drove the expansion of the empire.

In 1202, the **mathematician** Leonardo of Pisa, better known as **Fibonacci** (c. 1177–1250), produced the most influential book in European mathematics to date, the *Liber Abaci*, or *Book of Calculation*. Based on Arabic mathematics, it introduced Europe to Hindu numerals (0–9) and to the word *zephirum*, a Latinized version of an Arabic word that, in the Venetian dialect, became zero in algebra, addition, and the **Fibonacci sequence**.

BY 1206, TEMUJIN HAD UNITED ALL THE TRIBES OF MONGOLIA into the *Khamag Mongol Ulus*, "the All Mongol State," reorganizing tribal society into an army grouped on a decimal system. At the Mongolian capital of Karakorum, he took the title Chinggis Khan or "ruler of the world." His name is now most commonly spelled "Genghis."

In 1208, Pope Innocent III proclaimed a **crusade against heretics** in the south of France—the **Albigensians** (Cathars based around Albi) and **Waldenses** (see 1171–75). Their teachings challenged the worldliness of the established church, while their anticlericalism attracted nobles keen to appropriate church lands; the Cathars, for instance, were under the protection of Raymond of Toulouse, who ruled much of southern France. The pope's declaration gave license to the French king, Philip II (1165–1223), to allow his northern lords to wreak havoc in areas outside of

> **❝ KILL** THEM **ALL, GOD** WILL **KNOW** HIS **OWN. ❞**
>
> **Abbot Arnaud Amaury,** on the Albigensian Crusade

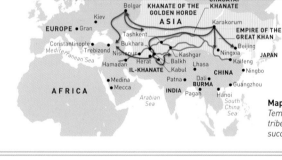

Map of Genghis Khan's empire
Temujin would go on to unite the Mongol tribes and conquer a huge empire. His successors would extend it still further.

KEY
→ Campaigns of Genghis Khan 1206-1227
▥ Empire of Genghis Khan 1227
— Silk road

c. 1200 Emergence of Chimú Empire in Peru, centered on Chan Chan

1201 Establishment of Riga (in present-day Latvia)

1202 King John of England battles Phillip II for his French lands

1202 Crusaders take **Zara** in Dalmatia

1203 Temujin overcomes Toghril to become dominant Mongolian leader

1204 Crusaders sack **Constantinople**

1205 Second Bulgarian Empire defeats Latin Empire and captures Baldwin I

1206 Temujin takes title **Genghis Khan** and begins conquest of Asia

1206 Qutb-ud-din Aibak, Sultan of Delhi, founds dynasty of slave kings, India

c. 1200 Khmer Empire reaches height under **Jayavarman VII**

1202 Fibonacci's book *Liber Abaci* produced

1201 Treaty of Venice makes provision for Fourth Crusade

1204 Establishment of **Latin Empire** under Baldwin I and partition of Byzantine Empire

1204 John of England loses most French territories of the Angevin Empire

1205 Hojo Yoshitoki becomes regent of Kamakura shogunate, inaugurating period of Hojo rule in Japan

1209 Pope Innocent III proclaims **Albigensian Crusade** in Languedoc, France

1209 Massacre of Beziers, Languedoc, by Crusaders

This 19th-century oil painting depicts the Battle of Las Navas de Tolosa, said to have been the decisive battle of the Reconquista.

A detail from the south gate of the great Khmer city of Angkor Thom.

66 I AM THE PUNISHMENT OF GOD... 99

Genghis Khan, Mongolian warlord

PERSECUTION OF THE CATHARS

Although only 200 Cathars lived in the town of Beziers in Languedoc, Crusaders massacred the entire population in 1209. Asked how the attackers should distinguish between Catholics and heretics, crusade leader Abbot Amaury is reputed to have given his famous order to "kill them all." In its pursuit of Cathars, the papacy would eventually create the Inquisition (see 1231–35).

PETER II OF ARAGON (1178–1213) AND ALFONSO VIII OF CASTILE (1155–1214) defeated the Almohads (see 1146–50) at the Battle of Las Navas de Tolosa in 1212. Alfonso had earlier been crushingly defeated by the Almohads in 1195 but had fought off invasions by the other Christian Spanish kingdoms and rebuilt his army. After this decisive victory, the Almohads were soon expelled from Spain, leaving only local Muslim dynasties that could not stand up to the Christian advance. Accordingly, this battle is traditionally said to be a decisive point in the Christian reconquest or Reconquista of Moorish Spain (see 1241–45).

Having lost most of his lands in France, King John of England (1166–1216) joined in alliance with Emperor Otto IV (1178–1215) and others, but they were crushed at the Battle of Bouvines in Flanders in 1214 by Philip II of France and the rival German emperor, Frederick II. This ended Anglo-Norman hopes of regaining French territories. King John's barons were forced to concentrate on England, where they had cause for discontent. Thanks to a dispute with the pope, the king had been briefly excommunicated. More importantly, he was taxing the barons heavily and invalidating the

law when it suited him. The barons revolted and after a brief civil war, John was forced to sign the Articles of the Barons, known in history as the Great Charter or Magna Carta. Although this mainly concerned the rights of barons, its statement that the king was not above the law was an important milestone for human rights. King John immediately disowned the charter, and war

3 clauses still in use

4 surviving copies

63
CLAUSES

40
ORIGINAL COPIES

The Magna Carta
Of the 63 clauses contained in the original Magna Carta, only three survive as laws today. Numerous copies were made, to be distributed around England; four survive.

broke out once more, this time with added French involvement. Retreating from a French invasion force in 1216, the king lost his baggage train—and his royal treasure—while crossing the Wash in Lincolnshire, England, and died soon after. His infant son, Henry III (1207–72) came to the throne.

26 FEET
THE HEIGHT OF THE WALLS OF ANGKOR THOM

JAYAVARMAN VII DIED IN AROUND 1220, having seen his greatest creation take shape. At Angkor, in modern-day Cambodia, he created a new city, Angkor Thom, centered on the great temple of Bayon. The temple comprises towers decorated with huge sculpted faces; the identities of these are disputed, although they may include Jayavarman himself.

Having conquered most of Central Asia and northern China, Genghis Khan's empire (see 1201–05) now bordered the Khwarazm Empire of Persia.

Mongolian dagger
The Mongolians had a deservedly fearsome reputation. After archers had decimated the enemy, fighters with hand weapons would close in.

DOMINGO DE GUZMAN, A CASTILIAN CLERIC, DIED IN 1221. In 1203, he had gone to Rome to ask permission to do missionary work with the Tartars (see 1201–10), but was sent to France to preach to the Cathars of Languedoc instead. By adopting absolute poverty, he was able to challenge the Cathars and make some headway, although ultimately his failure to "correct" the heretics led to the Albigensian Crusade (see 1206–10). However, like Francis of Assisi (see 1226–30), he had created a new kind of monastic order—the Dominicans—adapted to the new urban culture. The Dominicans and Franciscans were mendicant friars, mainly recruited from the middle classes, living off charity rather than farming, and devoted to preaching and charity in towns and cities.

A largely ineffective affair, the Fifth Crusade was the fruit of Pope Innocent's determination to reboot the Crusading movement. Targeting Egypt, the Crusaders took that but then lost Damietta, and failed to account for the Nile floods, which foiled their advance on Cairo. They high-handedly rejected a treaty offered by the sultan that would have given them Jerusalem, and left Egypt in 1221 having accomplished nothing.

his control, preparing the way for an expansion of royal power.

In 1209, Cambridge University was founded by scholars who had relocated from Oxford. By 1226, they had acquired some formal organization.

1209 Founding of Cambridge University, England

1209 Otto IV elected Emperor

1211 Genghis Khan conquers Kara-Khitai, Central Asia and invades Jin China

1211 Civil strife in Germany as Frederick II elected rival emperor to Otto IV

1212 Battle of Las Navas de Tolosa, Spain

1214 Philip II and Frederick II defeat anti-Capetian alliance at Battle of Bouvines, France

1216 Death of King John of England (b. 1166)

1218 Death of Jayavarman VII (b. 1125)

1221 Fifth Crusade ends with loss of Damietta and retreat

1221 Death of St. Dominic (b. 1170), founder of the Dominicans

1221 Genghis Khan sacks Samarkand

1209 Francis of Assisi establishes Catholic Franciscans, religious order

1210 Hindu rebellions against Sultanate of Delhi, India

1215 Magna Carta signed following civil war in England

1215 Fourth Lateran Council calls halt to Albigensian Crusade and calls for a Fifth Crusade to Egypt

1215 Genghis Khan takes Beijing, China

1218 Genghis Khan invades Khwarazmid Empire, Western Asia

1220 Khmer Empire withdraws from Champa, Southeast Asia

1221 Shokyu War in Japan

1221 Toltecs expelled from Chichen Itza, Mexico

1222 Icelandic scholar Snorri Sturlson writes Edda, a book of Nordic mythology

This 13th-century painting by Giotto di Bonodore shows St. Francis of Assisi preaching to the birds.

This 14th-century image shows Pope Gregory IX receiving a list of heretics.

Steppe landscape; little changed since the days of the Mongol Empire.

1,000,000

THE NUMBER OF **PEOPLE KILLED** DURING THE **ALBIGENSIAN CRUSADE**

THE RENEWAL OF THE ALBIGENSIAN CRUSADE (see 1206–10) in 1226 was in spite of the Pope declaring an "official" end to the Crusade at the Fourth Lateran Council of 1215. In reality, the battle for the south of France descended into vicious guerrilla warfare. Renewal of the Crusade was followed eventually by the submission of Raymond VII, Count of Toulouse —the Cathars' protector. Under the **Treaty of Meaux** (also known as the Peace of Paris) of 1229, the town of Toulouse was ceded to the **Capetian dynasty**—the ruling house of France from 987 to 1328.

Crusader coin
A rare Crusader coin from the Kingdom of Jerusalem illustrates the effects of intermingling policy: the inscription is written in Arabic.

Meanwhile, **Emperor Frederick II of Germany** realized that peace with the Muslims was better than military adventures that could not be won. In 1229, he concluded a treaty with the sultan of Egypt that **restored Jerusalem** and some surrounding land to the Christians. The **Sixth Crusade** thus passed without bloodshed, although Frederick was roundly condemned for this achievment.

A former soldier, **Francis of Assisi,** had founded the **Franciscan order** in 1209 (see 1221–25). In 1224, he received the stigmata (the wounds of Christ), and he was canonized just two years after his death in 1226.

Cathar stronghold
The Cathar castle of Peyrepertuse in the Pyrenees was located in a strategic defensive position on the French–Spanish border.

IN 1231, POPE GREGORY IX established the **Papal Inquisition**, a campaign by the church against heresy. Prior to 1231, the investigation of heresy had been the responsibility of bishops but it now became the preserve of specialist **inquisitors**, mostly drawn from the Dominican and Franciscan orders (see 1221–25). In 1233, the Dominicans were charged with bringing the Inquisition to Languedoc in France, where the **Cathar** heresy clung on despite the military defeat of the Count of Toulouse (see 1226–30).

Mongolian expansion continued, although Genghis Khan (see 1201–05) had died in 1227 while suppressing a rebellion in Xia Xia in China. He was succeeded by his second son, **Ogodei** (c. 1186–1241), who was still more ambitious. Ogodei sent armies to the east and west, leading the final assault on the Chinese **Jin Empire** (see 1126–30), which was conquered by 1234. The **Southern Song** had aided the Mongol advance, but when they tried to seize Kaifeng in northern China in 1235, the Mongols turned on them.

In 1235, **Sundiata, king of the Keita,** a Mande people from sub-Saharan Mali, defeated the Susu king Sumnaguru at the **Battle of Kirina**. The Susu had destroyed the old Ghana Empire (c. 830–1235), and Sundiata now built a new Mande empire on the ruins of Ghana.

ON HIS DEATH, GENGHIS KHAN had informally **divided his empire** among four of his sons. Given authority over the west, **Batu Khan** (c. 1207–55) established the Kipchak Khanate, also known as the **Golden Horde Khanate**. In the winter of 1237, when the frozen rivers allowed his cavalry to cross, Batu **invaded Russia**. Over the next four years, his armies conquered the Russian principalities and blazed a trail of destruction deep into Central Europe. Under the overlordship of Ogodei (see 1231–35), the expanding reach of the Mongol Empire had important implications for pan-Eurasian trade. The *Pax Mongolica* or "Mongol Peace" achieved in the lands under Mongolian control made the perilous passage across Central Asia and the silk road increasingly viable, enabling the **first direct contact** between **Europeans and the Chinese** since Roman times in around 1240.

By 1236, the **Teutonic Knights**—a military order formed in 1198 by German merchants serving at the Hospital of St. Mary of the Teutons in Jerusalem—had completed the subjugation of the **Pomeranians**, a pagan tribe in Prussia. Under their grand master, **Hermann von Salza** (c. 1179–1239), the knights established numerous strongholds, and in 1237, they merged with the Livonian Brothers of the Sword and advanced into **Livonia** (present-day Estonia and Latvia).

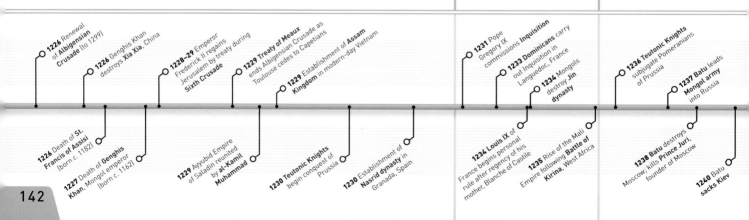

1226 Renewal of **Albigensian Crusade** (to 1299)

1226 Genghis Khan destroys **Xia Xia**, China

1228–29 Emperor Frederick II regains Jerusalem by treaty during **Sixth Crusade**

1229 Treaty of Meaux ends Albigensian Crusade as Toulouse cedes to Capetians

1229 Establishment of **Assam Kingdom** in modern-day Vietnam

1231 Pope Gregory IX commissions **Inquisition**

1233 Dominicans carry out Inquisition in Languedoc, France

1234 Mongols destroy **Jin dynasty**

1236 Teutonic Knights subjugate Pomeranians of Prussia

1237 Batu leads **Mongol army** into Russia

1226 Death of **St. Francis of Assisi** (born c. 1182)

1227 Death of **Genghis Khan**, Mongol emperor (born c. 1162)

1229 Ayyubid Empire of Saladin reunited by **al-Kamil Muhammad**

1230 Teutonic Knights begin conquest of Prussia

1230 Establishment of **Nasrid dynasty** in Granada, Spain

1234 Louis IX of France begins personal rule after regency of his mother, Blanche of Castile

1235 Rise of the Mali Empire following **Battle of Kirina**, West Africa

1238 Batu destroys Moscow; kills **Prince Juri**, founder of Moscow

1240 Batu sacks Kiev

This miniature from the *Annalistic Code* of the 16th century depicts the "Battle of the Ice," fought on the frozen waters of Lake Peipus, Novgorod.

In this 16th-century painting, Ferdinand III, King of Castile and Lon, accepts the surrender of the city of Seville from the Moors in 1248.

IN 1241, THE GERMAN TRADING TOWNS OF LUBECK AND HAMBURG formed an alliance to protect the **Baltic trade routes**. This was the first act in the formation of the **Hanseatic League** (from the medieval Latin *hansa*, meaning a group or association). Lübeck quickly became the center of expanding German trade in the Baltic region, which extended along the Russian rivers as far as **Novgorod**, and linked to the European trading centers of **England and Flanders**.

In 1242, the efforts of the **Teutonic Knights** (see 1236–40)

RECONQUISTA

The notion of the *Reconquista*—the Christian reconquest of Islamic Spain—as a single, continuous project, is a myth, first created by clerical propagandists in the 14th century. In practice, the advance of the Christian kingdoms was by degrees, driven by the need for land, and facilitated by Muslim dissention and advances in military technology.

Medieval trade
A manuscript illumination of the port of Hamburg, a founder member of the Hanseatic League, which had its roots in an alliance of 1241 with Lübeck.

to extend their Livonian territories eastward and launch the conversion of the Russians from the Greek to the Roman church were checked by defeat at the **Battle of Lake Peipus**. Led by **Alexander Nevski**, prince of Novgorod, the Russians checked the knights' progress and Lake Peipus thereafter served as the eastern limit of Livonia.

In a series of stunning victories in Eastern and Central Europe, the **Mongol armies** destroyed all opposition. Early in 1241, an army of horsemen crossed the frozen Vistula River into Poland, sacking Kracow and defeating an alliance of **Poles, Silesians, and Teutonic Knights** at Leignitz in April. Just three days later, another force under **Batu** (see 1236–40) overwhelmed the Hungarian army in their camp at Mohi. By December, Batu was destroying Pest, the largest city in Hungary. The Mongols had reached the gates of Vienna when, in 1242, the news reached them that Ogodei, the Great Khan, had died. As was

traditional, Batu withdrew his forces back to Karakorum, the Mongol capital, for the **election of a new leader.** Elsewhere, Mongol forces had penetrated the Indian subcontinent, sacking Lahore in 1241.

In 1244, **Jerusalem**, which had been under partial Christian control since Frederick II's treaty with the sultan of Egypt (see 1226–30), was **lost to medieval Christians** for the final time. The Egyptian sultan, Ayyub, was engaged in a contest with the Syrian branch of the **Ayyubids** (see 1171–75) at Damascus, which had allied itself with the Christian Crusader kingdoms. In 1244, Ayyub's forces overran Jerusalem and **expelled the Christians**.

IN 1247, FERDINAND III OF CASTILE AND LEON (c. 1199–1252) laid siege to the Moorish city of Seville. It fell to him in 1248, and with it the **last Moorish kingdom in Spain**—with the exception of Granada. Here, Mohammad ibn-Yusuf ibn Nasr had established the **Nasrid dynasty** in 1230. By 1238, the Nasrids had begun to reconstruct an old fortress, the **Alhambra**, which would become one of the wonders of world architecture by the mid-14th century (see 1350–55). In 1246, the emir of Granada agreed to become Ferdinand's vassal, but the last relic of Moorish al-Andalus would resist Christian pressure until 1492 (see 1490–92).

Louis IX of France (1214–70) was much respected throughout Europe and had a reputation for justice. Under his reign, royal control was extended to the Mediterranean, and the previously autonomous realms of Languedoc and Provence would become part of **French Capetian** territories. In 1244, Louis "took the cross," embarking on a crusade in 1248.

Theobald of Navarre had launched a crusade in 1239, but it was so unsuccessful that it is not usually recognized as an ordinate crusade; Louis' crusade of 1248 is accounted the **Seventh**, the last Crusade of this magnitude ever undertaken. Louis landed in Egypt and took Damietta without opposition, but in 1250 his army was **destroyed by the Egyptians** at Fariskur and he was taken captive. His mother, Blanche of Castile, raised a large ransom to buy his freedom.

The **Mamluks** (or Mamelukes) of Egypt were slave soldiers captured from Turkic and Circassian tribes (of the Pontic–Caspian steppes), who formed the main component of the Ayyubid army. Eventually they became strong enough to take power for themselves **murdering Turan Shah**, the last Ayyubid sultan of Egypt, in 1250. At first the Mamluk commander Izz-ad-Din Aybak used the sultan's widow as a puppet ruler, but he soon married her and founded the **Mamluk dynasty**, the first slave dynasty to hold power in its own name.

THE CRUSADES

1096–99	**FIRST**	CRUSADE
1145–49	**SECOND**	CRUSADE
1189–92	**THIRD**	CRUSADE
1202–04	**FOURTH**	CRUSADE
1213–21	**FIFTH**	CRUSADE
1228–29	**SIXTH**	CRUSADE
1248–54	**SEVENTH**	CRUSADE

1241 Mongols ravage Europe and sack Lahore in northern India

1242 Battle of Lake Peipus: Alexander Nevski defeats **Teutonic Knights**

1246 Provence becomes part of Capetian France

1248 Ferdinand III completes conquest of al-Andalus, apart from Granada, with successful **siege of Seville**

1248 Seventh Crusade: Louis IX of France lands in Egypt

1250 Mamluk dynasty founded in Egypt

1241 Formation of **Hanseatic League**

1243 Battle of Köse Dag: Mongols defeat **Seljuk Rum** of Anatolia

1244 Fall of Montsegur, last great stronghold of the **Cathars**

1248 Cologne cathedral burns down; reconstructed in **gothic style**

1247 Franciscan friar **Roger Bacon** records recipe for **gunpowder**

Lip ornament
MIXTEC
This eagle-shaped lip plug, or labret, would have been worn by a member of the Aztec elite. The Mixtec, a conquered tribe, made most Aztec gold jewelry.

eagle head sculpted in gold

Human mask
AZTEC
Found at the Great Temple of the Aztecs in their capital Tenochtitlán (now Mexico City), this greenstone mask was a votive offering.

Warrior effigy pot
MOCHE
This pot from the Moche culture of the north coast of Peru shows a warrior in a headdress grasping a club. Constant warfare was a way of life.

sharp obsidian blade

heavy wooden handle

THE AZTECS, INCAS, AND MAYA

THE EXTRAORDINARY ARTISTIC TRADITIONS OF PRE-COLUMBIAN AMERICA THAT SPANNED MILLENNIA

The Incas, Aztecs, and Maya were advanced civilizations with sophisticated arts and crafts and highly developed graphic systems. The artifacts they created dazzled the medieval European invaders and still fascinate today.

The art and culture of the pre-Columbian civilizations of Mesoamerica and the Andes represent the height of ancient traditions stretching back to the 4th millennium BCE. The conquistadors had a devastating effect on these cultures, but the artifacts that survive are a testament to their rich heritage. Much of Incan culture came from client states, such as the Moche, while the Aztecs and Mayans derived theirs from older cultures, such as the Olmecs.

Obsidian knife
AZTEC
Long-bladed, razor-sharp obsidian knives such as this one were used by warriors and in the gory human sacrifices practiced by the Aztecs.

Maquahuitl
AZTEC
Lacking iron or steel, pre-Columbian Americans used obsidian (volcanic glass) to form cutting edges. The *maquahuitl*—a wooden club fringed with obsidian blades—was a common Aztec weapon.

Sun stone
AZTEC
This sun stone, or calendar stone, is the largest Aztec sculpture ever found. It represents the Aztecs' mythical history of the universe. The Sun, believed to have been formed in the most recent era of creation, is at the center.

decorated with pictoglyphs

band showing days of month

disc is 13 ft (4 m) across

skin of flayed victim

Xipe Totec, god of the springtime
TEOTIHUACAN
The name of this grisly god translates as "our flayed lord"; he is depicted wearing the skin of a sacrificial victim, denoting the spring renewal of the Earth's "skin."

Priceless heart
AZTEC
The heart was considered the most precious organ that could be offered to the gods, and this replica was carved in jade, which the Aztecs regarded as their most valuable substance.

Necklace
INCA

Turquoise was highly valued by the Incas (Aztecs and Mayans preferred jade and other greenstones), and this rare necklace is made from beads of gold, turquoise, and red shell.

ornate headdress

heavy earplugs

hunter disguised as deer

Decorative plate
MAYA

This plate from the Yucatán Maya shows hunting scenes—in the center, a hunter drapes a deer he has caught across his head and shoulders, while round the edges other hunters wear deer masks.

Codex Tro–Cortesianus
MAYA

One of only four surviving Mayan codices, this one records instructions for divination (predicting the future) and priestly rituals. Sheets of bark paper were coated in gesso (chalky paste) to form a writing surface.

Jaina figurine
MAYA

This pottery figure from the island of Jaina shows a powerful man dressed in all his finery, with a heavy bead necklace, massive headdress, and ear plugs.

Tomb figurine
INCA

This cast gold figurine representing an Inca god made up part of the grave goods interred in the tomb of a high-status individual.

size and position of knots records numbers

Panpipes
INCA

Known in Europe as the syrinx, the panpipes were among the most common Inca musical instruments. This unusual set is made of quills from the feathers of a condor.

elaborate carvings

Greenstone yoke
AZTEC

Yokes were worn as protective belts in the sacred ball game *ulama*, played by most Mesoamerican cultures. This ornate yoke was probably a ceremonial replica.

Counting device
INCA

This *quipu*, or counting device, was a versatile accounting tool that helped the Incas keep track of the tribute and population of their empire—data was recorded in lengths of string and knots.

bars and dots represent numbers

codex was read from top to bottom, then left to right

145

Although not as sophisticated as Mayan hieroglyphs, Aztec pictographs such as the one shown could express simple concepts.

This illustration of Mongols battling the Seljuks is from a chronicle by Rashid al-Din, a Muslim minister in the service of the Il-Khanate.

BY THE MID-13TH CENTURY, THE MEXICA TRIBE—better known today as the **Aztecs**—were established in the Valley of Mexico. Aztec legend suggests that they migrated from the ancestral homeland of *Aztlan* in the early 12th century. Settling at Chapultepec, near Lake Texcoco, Mexico, in around 1250, they were soon **expelled by the Tepanecs**, one of the tribal confederations competing for dominance in the wake of the **Toltec collapse** in the early 12th century.

Although the **Mongols** had conquered most of the Russian principalities (see 1236–40), and the **Golden Horde Khanate** had claimed authority over **Russia**, surprisingly little changed for the Russians. In return for tribute and military service, the Russian princes were left in power and the Russian Church was not interfered with. **Alexander Nevski** (c. 1220–63), the prince of Novgorod who had led the Russians to victory against the **Teutonic Knights** in 1242, became the dominant Russian noble, appointed Grand Duke of Vladimir after his brother was driven out by the Mongols.

Under the support of the new **Great Khan**, Mongke (r. 1251–59), his brothers Kublai and Hulagu renewed the **Mongol expansion**.

Prince of Novgorod
This statue depicts Russian leader, Alexander Nevski, whose name derives from the Russian victory at the Battle of the Neva River.

In 1253, Hulagu led a huge army into Western Asia to conquer the **Great Seljuk sultanate** (see 1031–40), while Kublai launched campaigns against the **Southern Song** and the **Kingdom of Nanchao** in China.

HULAGU KHAN (SEE 1251–1255) CONTINUED HIS CAMPAIGN AGAINST THE SELJUKS and other Islamic powers. In 1256, he crushed the **Order of the Assassins** (see 1081–90), taking their stronghold at Alamut in Persia. In 1258, he sacked Baghdad and **executed the Abbasid Caliph**—the figurehead of Islam—in just one of countless atrocities committed by Mongol invaders who massacred hundreds of thousands of Muslims during their campaigns. In 1259, Hulagu penetrated deep into Syria, but as with Batu's campaign in Europe 18 years earlier (see 1241–45), his progress was halted by news of the **death of the Great Khan**, and he withdrew his armies while he returned to the Mongolian capital to help select a new leader.

Taking advantage of Hulagu's withdrawal, the **Mamluk** general **al-Zahir Baybars** marched north and struck at the Mongol garrisons in Syria. At the **Battle of Ayn Jalut** in Palestine, General Baybars **defeated the Mongols** and expelled them from Palestine and Syria. On his return to Egypt he murdered the sultan and took his place. Distracted by dynastic struggles, and later by a protracted inter-khanate war, Hulagu was not able to

KUBLAI KHAN (1215–94)

The grandson of Genghis Khan, Kublai spent eight years campaigning in southern China before succeeding his brother Mongke as Great Khan in 1260. His own kingdom, the Great Khanate, encompassed Mongolia and China, where he founded the Yuan dynasty, moved the capital to Shangdu, and did much to foster trade and international links.

regain his Syrian conquests and the westward expansion of the Mongol Empire was halted. **Hulagu's conquests**, which encompassed Iran, Iraq, most of Anatolia, Armenia, Azerbaijan, and Georgia, became the **Il-Khanate**, or Ilkhanate. Meanwhile, the Mamluks gave refuge to a **fugitive Abbasid prince**, setting him up in Cairo as the **new caliph**. Recognized as guardians of the Islamic faith, the **Mamluks** were

formally made **sultans of Egypt, Syria,** and the **Levant**.

Alfonso X of Castile (r. 1252–1284) won the nickname "the Wise" thanks to his learning, patronage of the arts and Castilian literature, sponsorship of natural philosophy, and judicial reforms. He oversaw the final expulsion of the **Almohads** (see 1121–25) from Spain in 1257.

> ❝ HAD I BEEN PRESENT **AT THE CREATION, I WOULD HAVE GIVEN** SOME USEFUL **HINTS FOR** THE BETTER **ORDERING** OF THE UNIVERSE. ❞

Alfonso X, the Wise, on the Ptolemaic system

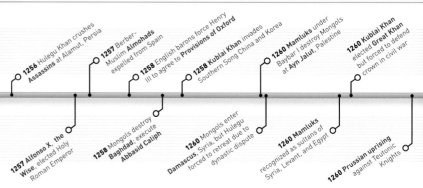

c. 1250s Aztecs settle in Valley of Mexico

1252 Alexander Nevski (1220–1263) becomes leading prince in Russia

1253 Kublai Khan (1215–1294) conquers Nanchao, China, triggering migration of Thai people

1254 Civil war in Crusader states, Western Asia

1254 Teutonic Knights found Konigsberg, Prussia

1252 Formation of pro-Guelph leagues of **and pro-Ghibelline cities,** Italy

1253 Hulagu Khan (c. 1217–1265) begins conquest of Islamic lands

1254 Louis IX of France departs Crusader kingdom of Acre, Western Asia

1254 Death of Conrad IV of Germany (b. 1228)

1254 Manfred of Sicily launches antipapal campaign following Pope Innocent IV's claims on Sicily

1256 Hulagu Khan crushes Assassins at Alamut, Persia

1257 Berber-Muslim Almohads expelled from Spain

1258 English barons force Henry III to agree to Provisions of Oxford

1258 Kublai Khan invades Southern Song China and Korea

1260 Mamluks under Baybar I destroy Mongols at **Ayn Jalut,** Palestine

1260 Kublai Khan elected Great Khan but forced to defend crown in civil war

1257 Alfonso X, the Wise, elected Holy Roman Emperor

1258 Mongols destroy Baghdad; execute **Abbasid Caliph**

1260 Mongols enter Damascus, Syria, but Hulagu forced to retreat due to dynastic dispute

1260 Mamluks recognized as sultans of Syria, Levant, and Egypt

1260 Prussian uprising against Teutonic Knights

This example of Mamluk architecture from the height of the sultanate adorns the entrance to the mausoleum of Qalawun in Cairo, Egypt.

Geneta Mariam church in Ethiopia, built during the Solomonid era.

Former stronghold of the Knights Hospitaller, Krak des Chevaliers or "fortress of the knights" in Syria was taken by the Mamluks and fortified further.

ITALIAN NOBLEMAN AND LATER DOMINICAN MONK, THOMAS AQUINAS (1225–74) became one of the most important philosophers in the history of Western thought. Renowned for his work in **uniting faith and reason**, Aquinas's period of greatest productivity occurred between 1258 and 1273, when he penned his two best-known works, the *Summa contra Gentiles* and the *Summa Theologiae*.

In 1261, Michael VIII Paleologus (r. 1259–61), the Byzantine emperor of Nicaea, concluded the **Treaty of Nymphaeum** with the Genoese, agreeing to cede them all the trading privileges once enjoyed by the Venetians (see 981–990). He had already secured an alliance with the Bulgarians, and was now poised to achieve his dream of re-taking Constantinople from the **Latin Empire** (Constantinople and environs, captured from the Byzantines during the fourth crusade), and reconstituting the Byzantine Greek Empire. In July 1261, a Byzantine army took advantage of the absence of the Venetian fleet to cross the Bosporus strait and take Constantinople. The Latin emperor, Baldwin II fled, and the **Paleologus Empire** was established.

Paleologus would campaign tirelessly to restore lost Byzantine lands.

The **Second Baron's War** in England between 1264 and 1267 was brought about by a combination of newly kindled national consciousness and resentment at foreign interference. **Henry III** of England (r. 1216–72) had introduced many foreign officers into government and taxed the English heavily to fund overseas adventures and papal extortion. Rebels led by **Simon de Montfort**, Earl of Leicester, captured the king and summoned the first European parliament that included elected representatives.

Meanwhile, the **Mamluks** began a push to rid the Holy Land of the Crusader kingdoms once and for all.

Thomas Aquinas
This 15th-century altarpiece depicts Thomas Aquinas, whose philosophy still underpins Catholic dogma.

COST OF PARCHMENT

COST OF PAPER

Cost of paper versus parchment
After paper-making technology was introduced to Italy, the cost of vegetable-based paper fell to 1/6 of the cost of animal-based parchment.

THE SOLOMONID DYNASTY IN ETHIOPIA was founded in 1270 by Yekuno Amlak, displacing the previous Zagwe dynasty, and claiming to have restored the legitimate line of the ancient Christian kings of Aksum. Amlak claimed descent from the biblical Solomon, via the possibly Ethiopian Queen of Sheba.

The town of **Fabriano** in Italy lies close to the Adriatic port of Ancona, which was notable in the 13th century for trade with the Muslim world. This is probably how paper manufacture became established there in the 1270s. Use of animal gelatin in place of more degradable vegetable gel made Fabriano paper more durable, and the town became the principal paper manufacturing site in Europe.

In 1270, Louis IX of France made another attempt at crusading, but on the request of Charles of Anjou, **the Eighth Crusade** was diverted to Tunis, where disease killed Louis and his army.

Travels of Marco Polo
To reach China, Marco Polo traveled through Anatolia, Iran, and Afghanistan. On his return, he sailed to Hormuz in Persia via Sumatra.

KEY
→ Route of Marco Polo 1271–1295
— Silk road

IN 1271, THE VENETIAN MERCHANT AND EXPLORER, MARCO POLO (c. 1254–1324), traveled to China. Arriving at Kublai Khan's court in 1275, the Great Khan employed Marco Polo in various capacities. In 1292, he escorted a Mongol princess to Persia, returning to Italy three years later and writing a **travel memoir** while a prisoner of the Genoese. Polo's memoir, *The Travels*—known by Italians as *Il Milione*, because of the belief that it contains a million lies —is a fascinating portrait of the Mongolian Empire at its height. The *Pax Mongolica* (see 1236–40) allowed freedom of movement through lands under the authority of Il-khanate, and it was said that a virgin with a pot of gold on her head could pass unmolested from Constantinople (modern-day Istanbul) to Beijing.

In 1272, **Edward Plantagenet** (r. 1272–1307), heir apparent to the English throne, returned from the Holy Land, having forced the **Mamluks** to conclude a 10-year truce in his attempts to destroy Acre, one of the last remaining Crusader footholds in Outremer. The Mamluks had already taken the apparently impregnable **Krak des Chevaliers** from the Knights Hospitaller in 1271.

22
PERCENT
THE **WORLD LAND AREA** COVERED BY THE **MONGOL EMPIRE** AT ITS HEIGHT

1261 Genoese–Byzantine **Treaty of Nymphaeum**

1261 Fall of **Latin Empire** and restoration of Byzantine Empire

1264 Thomas Aquinas completes *Summa contra Gentiles*

1264 Second Baron's War in England (to 1267)

1265 Simon de Montfort killed at Battle of Evesham, England (b. 1208)

1262 Civil war in Mongol Empire between **Golden Horde** and **Il-Khanate**

1263 Mamluks begin push to drive Crusaders out of Levant

1265 First representative **English parliament** summoned

1265 Charles of Anjou, brother of the French king, accepts crown of Sicily

1266 Philosopher **Roger Bacon** (c. 1214–94) writes treatise on natural science, *Opus Maius*

1269 Death of **Jatavarman Sundara,** ruler of South India and Ceylon

1270 Solomonid dynasty founded in Ethiopia

1268 Mamluks take Jaffa and Antioch, Crusader States

1270 Death of **Louis IX** of France during Eighth Crusade (b. 1214)

1271 Marco Polo leaves Venice for China

1272 Edward Plantagenet returns to England to become king having signed peace treaty with Mamluks

1274 Rudolf I becomes first Habsburg Holy Roman Emperor

1273 Work starts on **Nasrid Alhambra Palace** in Granada, Spain

1274 Council of Lyons attempts to end schism between Catholic and Byzantine Churches

1274 Kublai Khan's first attempt to invade Japan fails

1275 Marco Polo arrives in China

Statues adorn the Meenakshi Temple in Madurai, India. Originally constructed by Kulasekhara Pandya, the temple was destroyed by Muslim invaders and later rebuilt.

Guglielmo Berardi da Narbona was killed at the Battle of Campaldino.

IN SOUTHERN INDIA, KING KULASEKHARA I (r. 1268–1308) expanded the empire of the **Pandyas** to its greatest extent. The Pandyas were an ancient **Tamil** people of the far south, who contended for supremacy over the centuries with neighboring kingdoms such as the **Cholas** and the island of **Ceylon** (Sri Lanka). Under **Sundara** (r. 1251–68) the Pandya empire had expanded dramatically and reduced some neighboring states to vassalage. His son **Kulasekhara** went on to conquer Kerala, Kongu, and Ceylon, and in 1279 he defeated the last **Chola** king, **Rajendra III**, and annexed his territories. The

Divine wind
An engraving shows the destruction of the Mongol fleet by the kamikaze ("divine wind") in 1281.

greatness of the Pandya court was attested to by Venetian merchant **Marco Polo**, who would pass through in 1293, but the empire was short-lived, breaking up in the early 14th century due to family quarrels and **Muslim invasions**.

By the late 13th century, the **Maori** had settled in **New Zealand** (with the exception of Antarctica, the last land mass to be colonized by humans). Dating the Maori colonization is contentious. According to estimates based on Maori traditions, the first **Polynesians** visited the islands in the early 10th century, and waves of colonization climaxed with the arrival of the **Great Fleet** of ocean-going canoes in 1350. Archaeological findings tell a slightly different story. However, it seems likely that Polynesians, probably from **Tahiti**, arrived in

New Zealand around 1280, dividing the territory between **hapu** (clans). Hapu that traced a common ancestry formed **iwi** (tribes), some of which could trace their lineage back to a single **waka houra** (ocean-going canoe).

Having conquered Korea and most of China, **Kublai Khan** (1215–94) set his sights on **Japan**, sending embassies demanding submission as early as 1268. Under the bold leadership of the **Hojo regency**, the Japanese refused to be cowed. After a failed invasion attempt in 1274, Kublai sent **150,000 men** in two huge fleets in 1281, but the Japanese held off the invading armada until a great typhoon, known in Japan as the **kamikaze** ("divine wind"), devastated the Mongol fleet.

MAORI CARVING

Maori culture is noted for its tradition of arts and crafts; chief among these is *te toi whakairo* (carving). Master craftsmen were believed to channel the voices of the spirits and ancestors, and intricately carved posts and lintels adorning structures around the *marae* (sacred space) and *waka* (canoes) were believed to accumulate and pass on *mana* (spiritual power).

IN THE 1280S, A TRIBE OF TURKOMAN NOMADIC HORSEMEN and raiders based in northwestern Anatolia, known as the **Ottomans**, elected **Osman** (1258–1354) as their chieftain. At this time, the political map of Anatolia was fractured: the Mongol onslaught had broken up Seljuk Rum and replaced it with many small principalities, while also driving waves of Muslim refugees into the region. Meanwhile, the **Byzantine Empire** had been successively **reduced** and broken up by Seljuk and Latin encroachment. Osman was able to lead his tribe in a **territorial expansion**, rapidly conquering Byzantine territory.

Florence, like many other Italian cities, had developed into a largely **autonomous republic** or commune. It was typically easier for the German emperors—the notional feudal overlords—to grant cities powers of self-government than try to control them directly. Since the mid-13th century, Florence had see-sawed violently between **Guelph** and **Ghibelline** regimes (see 1221–25). This **Guelph–Ghibelline** conflict had gripped the Italian city-states, providing a vehicle for the expression of local **class tensions** as well as national and international politics. When one faction gained the upper hand in a city, the other was typically expelled. In the 1280s, the Guelphs had the upper hand, and Guelph partisans exiled from Arezzo encouraged them to take up arms against the rival city. The Florentines defeated Arezzo at the

The Eleanor Cross in Geddington, Northamptonshire, England, features an ogee arch, marking a milestone for the English Gothic style.

William Wallace was outlawed for killing one of Edward's sheriffs in 1296. He was one of the first men to be hanged, drawn, and quartered.

Battle of Campaldino, heralding the start of a period of **Florentine dominance** in Tuscany. Among those battling on the Florentine side was the poet **Dante Alighieri** (see 1311–17).

The line of Slave Kings of Delhi came to an end in 1290 with the seizure of power by **Firuz** of the **Khalji Turks**—a tribe living in Afghanistan—thus founding the **Khalji dynasty**. Firuz is best remembered for releasing into Bengal **1,000 Thugs** or Thuggees, cult followers of the goddess Kali devoted to **murder and robbery** in her name.

Ornate Mughal screen
This screen from the main gateway of the Qutb complex in Delhi was built by the Khalji sultan Ala-ud-din, murderer and successor of Firuz.

IN 1291, AFTER A DESPERATE SIX-WEEK SIEGE, the Mamluks took Acre, the last major Crusader stronghold in **Palestine**, and a few months later they took Beirut, the last remnant of the Crusader kingdom known as **Outremer** (see 1181–85). After nearly 200 years, Christian presence in the Holy Land was extinguished, and the Mamluks **plundered the region** to deter future Crusades.

To limit the risk of disastrous fires, **Venice** moved its **glass-making industry** to the island of Murano in 1291. Venetian glassmakers were the only ones in Europe to master the art of producing **clear glass**. Their expertise in working with glass had earlier borne fruit in the invention of **spectacles** (see 1284).

Edward I of England (r. 1272–1307) had married **Eleanor of Castile** in 1254. Though unpopular with the English, she and Edward enjoyed a happy marriage, and he was devastated when she died in 1290. The following year he ordered the erection of 12 so-called **Eleanor crosses** to mark the passage of her funeral cortege to London.

The contest for **mastery of the Mediterranean** between **Genoa** and **Venice** continued, with a Genoese fleet defeating the Venetians off **Laiazzo** in 1294. The following year, Genoa put together a **huge fleet**, with the aim of landing a killer blow. However, despite a formal challenge being made, it was not engaged. Developments in Venetian shipbuilding, however, were

Murano glass
This Murano glass vessel dates to around 1330. As well as increasing fire safety, concentrating the glass industry on an island helped to regulate it and guard its secrets.

underway. Capable of carrying more cargo and a larger crew, the construction of the first of the great galleys in 1294 heralded a distinct advantage for the Venetians.

165

THE NUMBER OF **GALLEYS** IN THE 1295 FLEET OF **GENOA**

THE EXTINCTION OF THE CANMORE DYNASTY, followed by dissent among the Scottish nobles, had allowed **Edward I** to exercise increasing dominance over the Scots, and in 1292 he awarded the crown to **John Balliol**. However, in 1295, Balliol made an alliance with England's enemy, **France**. The following year Edward launched a campaign to **subdue the Scots**, defeating them at Dunbar, and taking the **Stone of Destiny**—the Scottish coronation stone—back to London. In 1297, the Scottish patriot **William Wallace** (c. 1272–1305) led a revolt against English dominance, overcoming a larger English army at **Stirling Bridge**, but he was defeated at **Falkirk** in 1298 and forced into years of guerrilla warfare and overseas fundraising.

1:4
Battle of Stirling Bridge
Under William Wallace, an estimated 2,500 Scots defeated a much larger force of English soldiers (numbering up to 10,000) at the Battle of Stirling Bridge.

The **Genoese–Venetian naval conflict** continued, with battles in the Black Sea and the Greek islands. At the **Battle of Curzola**, in 1298, the Genoese fleet inflicted a **disastrous defeat** on the Venetians, destroying all but a few of their ships and killing up to 7,000 men.

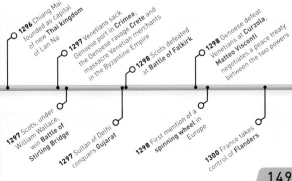

Genoese trade routes
The Genoese opened a lucrative trade route to the North Sea, and competed with Venice to dominate trade with the Byzantines and the East.

KEY
— Trade routes

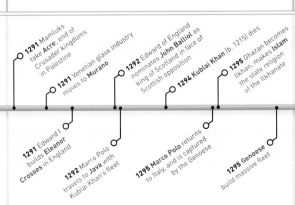

1287 Mongol invasion of Punjab halted at **Lahore**

1289 Mamluks take Tripoli

1289 Battle of Campaldino; Florence is dominant in Tuscany

1290 Firuz founds the Khalji dynasty of the Sultanate of Delhi

1291 Mamluks take **Acre**; end of Crusader kingdoms in Palestine

1291 Venetian glass industry moves to **Murano**

1291 Edward I builds **Eleanor Crosses** in England

1292 Edward of England nominates **John Balliol** as king of Scotland in face of Scottish opposition

1292 Marco Polo travels to **Java** with Kublai Khan's fleet

1294 Kublai Khan (b. 1215) dies

1295 Ghazan becomes Ilkhan, makes **Islam** the state religion of the Ilkhanate

1295 Marco Polo returns to Italy, and is captured by the Genoese

1295 Genoese build massive fleet

1296 Chiang Mai founded as capital of new **Thai kingdom** of Lan Na

1297 Venetians sack Genoese port in **Crimea**; the Genoese ravage **Crete** and massacre Venetian merchants in the Byzantine Empire

1297 Scots, under William Wallace, win **Battle of Stirling Bridge**

1297 Sultan of Delhi conquers **Gujarat**

1298 Scots defeated at **Battle of Falkirk**

1298 First mention of a **spinning wheel** in Europe

1298 Genoese defeat Venetians at **Curzola**; **Matteo Visconti** negotiates a peace treaty between the two powers

1300 France takes control of **Flanders**

> **LET EVIL SWIFTLY BEFALL THOSE WHO HAVE WRONGLY CONDEMNED US—GOD WILL AVENGE US.**
>
> Jacques de Molay, the Grand Master of the Knights Templar, cursing King Philip and Pope Clement V, 1314

The torture of Jacques de Molay, Grand Master of the Knights Templar.

Domenico di Michelino's painting *The Comedy Illuminating Florence*, depicts Dante, the city of Florence, and scenes from the *Divine Comedy*.

ALTHOUGH THE GHIBELLINES HAD BEEN EXPELLED FROM FLORENCE (see 1286–90), factionalism still plagued the city, with a drawn-out **power struggle** between the old aristocratic nobility, the new mercantile nobles, and the powerful guilds. The **Guelph** faction split into Black (extreme) and White (moderate) parties. In 1301, the Whites expelled the Blacks, only for them to return when **Charles, count of Valois**, entered the city. The following year the Black Guelphs sentenced the Whites to death or exile—among them the poet **Dante Alighieri** (see panel, right).

In 1301, **Pope Boniface VIII** (*c.* 1235–1303) supposedly issued a bull asserting **papal supremacy** over France. In fact, the bull was a forgery, put out by the French king **Philip IV the Fair** (r. 1285–1314) to stir up animosity against the pope. Philip "responded" by calling one of the first **Estates General**— including representatives of the towns and clergy—and received their backing. Boniface **excommunicated** Philip and Philip called for the Pope to face **criminal charges**. In 1303, agents acting for Philip forced their way into the papal apartments in Anagni and **arrested the Pope**, who died soon after. Facing tumultuous conditions in Italy, in 1303 the cardinals elected the archbishop of Bordeaux as **Pope Clement V**. Although hoping to establish himself in Italy when the violence subsided, Clement remained in southern France, finally settling in **Avignon** in 1309, then owned by the king of Naples. This temporary arrangement for the papacy would last until 1378.

Palais des Papes
Situated on a rocky outcrop, the papal palace in Avignon is one of the largest and most important medieval Gothic buildings in Europe.

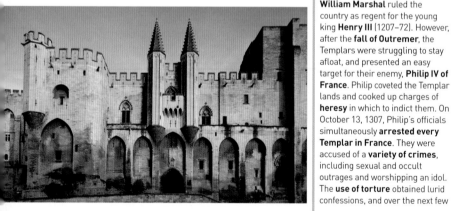

FROM THEIR HUMBLE BEGINNINGS, WHEN THEY HAD BEEN SO POOR that two knights sometimes had to share a horse, the **Knights Templar** had risen to dizzying heights. With the backing of Cistercian abbot **Bernard of Clairvaux** (1090–1153), and subsequently the Pope, they had won exemption from secular jurisdiction and taxation, and thrived as donations of land and money poured in. By the 13th century they had become **de facto bankers** to much of Europe, able to direct a large fleet and maintain the primary **Crusader army** in Outremer. Templar knights rose to prominence all over Europe, especially in England, where the **Master of the Temple** was the first baron of the realm. In the early 13th century, then **Master William Marshal** ruled the country as regent for the young king **Henry III** (1207–72). However, after the **fall of Outremer**, the Templars were struggling to stay afloat, and presented an easy target for their enemy, **Philip IV of France**. Philip coveted the Templar lands and cooked up charges of **heresy** in which to indict them. On October 13, 1307, Philip's officials simultaneously **arrested every Templar in France**. They were accused of a **variety of crimes**, including sexual and occult outrages and worshipping an idol. The **use of torture** obtained lurid confessions, and over the next few

Red Sea

Hereford Mappa Mundi
The world is shown as a disk, with Jerusalem at the center. Trade and pilgrimage routes are illustrated, together with places of interest.

years around **60 Templars were executed**. Elsewhere in Europe, some arrests were made, but there was much less appetite for condemning the order. At the **Council of Vienne** (1311–12), Philip forced Pope Clement to **dissolve the Templars**, and in 1314 the last Grand Master, Jacques de Molay, was burned at the stake.

Hereford, in England, was an important center for the **wool trade**—one of the main sources of wealth in medieval England. Foreign buyers flocked to the country to buy wool for export to the **textile industries** of Flanders and Italy, and the wool trade was described as "**the jewel in the realm.**" The wealth of places such as Hereford was expressed in the magnificence of their cathedrals and the richness of their accessories. At Hereford Cathedral a huge **Mappa Mundi** (map of the world) was created in around 1300 (its creation is variously dated to 1285 and 1314) and used as an altarpiece; it is the largest mappa mundi in existence. Such maps encapsulated the medieval world view on the eve of the **Age of Discovery**.

At the Battle of Bannockburn in 1314, **Robert the Bruce**, king of Scots (r.1306–29), finally expelled the English from Scotland.

DANTE ALIGHIERI
(1265–1321)

Dante is the greatest Italian poet to have lived and one of the most important writers in European literature. He is best known for his epic poem the *Divine Comedy*, and for his tragic love for Beatrice, who married another and died young. Exiled from his native Florence for political reasons, Dante spent much of his life traveling from one city to another. He died in Ravenna in 1321.

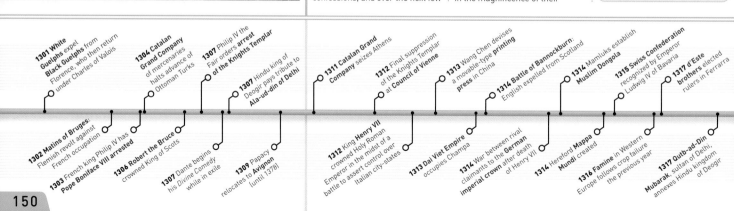

1301 White Guelphs expel Black Guelphs from Florence, who then return under Charles of Valois

1304 Catalan Grand Company of mercenaries halts advance of Ottoman Turks

1307 Philip IV the Fair orders **arrest of the Knights Templar**

1307 Hindu king of Deogir pays tribute to Ala-ud-din of Delhi

1302 Matins of Bruges: Flemish revolt against French occupation

1303 French king Philip IV has Pope Boniface VIII arrested

1306 Robert the Bruce crowned King of Scots

1307 Dante begins his *Divine Comedy* while in exile

1309 Papacy relocates to Avignon (until 1378)

1311 Catalan Grand Company seizes Athens

1312 Final suppression of the Knights Templar at Council of Vienne

1313 Wang Chen devises a movable-type printing press in China

1314 Battle of Bannockburn: English expelled from Scotland

1314 Mamluks establish Muslim Dongola

1315 Swiss Confederation recognized by Emperor Ludwig IV of Bavaria

1317 d'Este brothers elected rulers in Ferrara

1312 King Henry VII crowned Holy Roman Emperor in the midst of battle to assert control over Italian city-states

1313 Dai Viet Empire occupies Champa

1314 War between rival claimants to the German imperial crown after death of Henry VII

1314 Hereford Mappa Mundi created

1316 Famine in Western Europe follows crop failure the previous year

1317 Qutb-ad-Din Mubarak, sultan of Delhi, annexes Hindu kingdom of Deogir

The earliest European illustration of a cannon, from a book by Walter de Milemete, presented to the future Edward III of England in 1326.

The gilded bronze doors on the Baptistry in Florence, sculpted and cast by Andrea Pisano, took six years to make after he won the commission in 1329.

GUNPOWDER WAS SLOWLY BUT STEADILY CHANGING THE FACE OF WARFARE. Arabs and Moors had probably gained knowledge of gunpowder from the **Chinese**, using cannons in Spain as early as 1284. The **Mamluks** are believed to have used **handguns** at Ain Jalut, while the Mongols acquired the technology on conquering China. Europeans probably picked it up from **Spain** and contact with the **Mongols**. The first record of cannons forged from iron comes from Metz in 1324; later that year an English fortress in Gascony was bombarded for a month.

The **Mali Empire** of West Africa reached its height under **Mansa Musa** (r. 1312–37), extending from the Atlantic to Nigeria, and from the Sahara to the rain forest. His great wealth was based on **Mali's gold**, and when he traveled on pilgrimage to Mecca in 1324–25, he dispensed so much gold on his

25

THE **PERCENTAGE** OF **TIMBUKTU'S POPULATION** AT **SANKORE UNIVERSITY**

passage through **Cairo** that he destabilized the economy. On his return, he employed an Andalusian architect to build a new palace at **Timbuktu**, which became a center for **Islamic scholarship**. Mali was later visited by the Moroccan scholar **Ibn Battuta** (c. 1304–69), who first set out on his travels in 1325.

The travels of Ibn Battuta
Ibn Battuta's first journey was the Hajj (pilgrimage) to Mecca. He made seven further journeys, visiting almost every corner of the Muslim world.

KEY
→ Route of Ibn Battuta 1325–1345
— Silk road

FLORENCE IN THE 1320s AND 1330s WAS HOME TO ARTISTS including **Giotto di Bondone** (c. 1267–1337) and **Andrea Pisano** (c. 1290–1349)—both seen as forerunners of the Italian Renaissance (see pp.208–09). Giotto painted naturalistic frescoes on the walls of the **Basilica of Santa Croce** in around 1325, and in 1334 was put in charge of the construction of the **Duomo** (cathedral). Greatly influenced by Giotto, Pisano won a commission to craft a set of **bronze doors for the Baptistry of Florence**, finishing them in 1336.

The **Tughluk dynasty** of the Delhi sultanate had expanded the reach of the **Muslim** state, reducing neighboring **Hindu kingdoms** to vassal status, and repelling a series of **Mongol incursions**. In 1325, **Muhammad Tughluk** (c. 1300–51) murdered his father and took the throne, and established a reputation for cruelty. In 1327, he transferred the capital from Delhi to **Daulatabad** for defensive reasons, forcing the population to relocate. In 1336, **Harihara I** and his brother **Bukka** of the **Sangama dynasty** in the

> ❝ **THE FIRST KING** AFTER THE CONQUEST WHO WAS **NOT A MAN OF BUSINESS.** ❞

William Stubbs, English historian, describing Edward II, 1875

south, led a revolt that resulted in the establishment of the last great Hindu empire in India, centered on the city of **Vijayanagar**.

Edward II of England invested power in favorites, especially **Piers Gaveston** (murdered by resentful barons in 1312) and the **Despenser family**. He also alienated his wife, **Isabella of France**, who was sent to France in 1325 to arrange the marriage of their son. While there, she became the lover of **Roger Mortimer**, and when they returned, in 1326, they led a **revolt against the king**. The Despensers were hanged, Edward was **forced to abdicate** in favor of his teenage son, and **Roger and Isabella ruled as regents**. Eight months later, Edward II was horribly murdered. The regents ceded Gascony to France and acknowledged **Robert the Bruce** as king of an independent Scotland. In 1330, **Edward III** (r.1327–77) had Mortimer hanged and began his own rule. Rising **tension with France** was exacerbated by Edward's embargo on wool exports to

Flanders, which **triggered a revolt** there against French domination. In 1337, Philip VI of France declared Edward's French territories forfeit, while Edward claimed the French crown, triggering the start of the **Hundred Years' War**.

Vijayanagar sculpture
Lord Hanuman, the Hindu monkey god, is shown carved on a rock surface in Vijayanagar, the heart of the last great Hindu empire.

1321 Dante Alighieri dies in Ravenna (b.1265)

1323 Sultan Tughluq of Delhi annexes Telingana and repulses the Mongols

1324 William of Ockham accused of heresy at Avignon for supporting the banned "Spiritual" Franciscans

1325 Aztecs found Tenochtitlán

1324 Cannons used at the Siege of Metz

1324 Musa, emperor of Mali, annexes Timbuktu

1324–25 Musa's pilgrimage to Mecca

1325 The travels of Ibn Battuta begin

1326 Edward II captured by Roger Mortimer then deposed and murdered the following year

1330 Serbs defeat and kill the Bulgarian czar

1332 Negus of Abyssinia repulses an Islamic assault

1333 Black Death starts in China

1336 A Hindu rebellion establishes the Vijayanagar Empire in southern India

1336 Pisano's doors installed on the Florence baptistry

1328 Accession of Phillip VI, first Valois king of France

1328 Ludwig of Bavaria crowned Holy Roman Emperor

1330 Edward III of England begins reign

1331 Ottoman leader Ghazi Orkhan takes Nicaea

1332 Moscow becomes civil and ecclesiastical capital of Russia

1333 In Japan, Emperor Godaigo defeats the Hojo regency

1336 Civil war in Japan; the Ashikaga clan takes power

1337 Flemish rebellion triggered by English wool embargo

1337 Philip seizes Gascony from the English; start of the Hundred Years' War

The Strait of Gibraltar, where Marinid forces destroyed the Castilian fleet.

An illustration from Froissart's *Chronicle*, of 1346, depicts the Battle of Crécy, at which the English used mobile artillery for the first time.

> **WHATEVER THE WORLD FINDS PLEASING, IS BUT A BRIEF DREAM.**
>
> Petrarch, Florentine scholar and poet, from *Canzoniere Number 1 (c. 1352)*

THE BATTLE OF RIO SALADO IS CONSIDERED, BY SOME, to be the defining battle of the **Reconquista**, ending forever the threat of Islamic incursion into the Iberian Peninsula from Africa. The **Marinid dynasty** of Morocco, which had overthrown the **Almohads** in the mid-13th century, gathered a vast force and destroyed the Castilian fleet in the **Strait of Gibraltar**. The Marinids then marched inland to the Salado River, where they were defeated by the Christian kings **Alfonso XI of Castile** (r. 1312–50) and **Afonso IV of Portugal** (r. 1325–57).

800,000
THE AMOUNT IN FLORINS OWED BY EDWARD III

To finance his expensive war in France, **Edward III** of England (r. 1327–77) had taken out **huge loans** from Florentine bankers, especially the **Peruzzi family**. When the money ran out, Edward renounced his loan in 1342. With the king of Naples also defaulting on loans, the Peruzzi were bankrupted, throwing **Florence** into **economic chaos**. Walter de Brienne, the mercenary duke of Athens, was called in to take power in Florence but, eventually, a **mercantile oligarchy** took over.

HAVING GAINED MASTERY OF THE ENGLISH CHANNEL at the naval battle of **Sluys** in 1340, **Edward III** was free to invade France. He landed in **Normandy** in 1346 and took **Caen**, but retreated in the face of a huge French army. At bay, on the borders of the **forest of Crécy**, Edward took up a defensive position and inflicted a **crushing defeat** on the forces of Philip VI. This was largely thanks to the indiscipline and arrogance of the **French knights** and the effectiveness of the **Welsh** and **English longbowmen**. At the cost of a handful of casualties, **the English killed tens of thousands**, including the kings of Bohemia and Majorca, the duke of Lorraine, the count of Flanders, the count of Blois, eight other counts, and three archbishops. The English use of **combined aristocratic and yeoman forces** had produced a powerful new form of army. They would go on to **besiege Calais**,

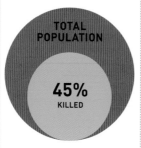

TOTAL POPULATION

45% KILLED

Plague deaths
It is estimated that up to 45 percent of the total population of Europe was killed by the various waves of the Black Death plague.

THE BLACK DEATH

The effects of the Black Death are best recorded in Europe, where it had profound consequences. It depopulated the land, depressed the economy, checked intellectual and artistic progress, changed the social order, contributed to the end of feudalism, and triggered a wave of anti-Semitic pogroms on Jews, who were blamed for the pestilence, forcing many to migrate to Eastern Europe.

which fell in 1347, after a protracted siege.

Also in 1347, the **Black Death** arrived in Europe. It is thought to have been carried initially by Genoese returning from the **Crimea**, where they had been exposed to it by infected Mongols. Transmitted by **fleas that were carried by rats**, the plague was spread by ship to the principal ports, and then to every corner of Europe and Western Asia. A large proportion of the population died.

THE PAPACY WAS REFORMING ITS BUREAUCRACY and improving its finances under the Avignon popes. In 1348, **Clement VI** (1291–1352) bought **Avignon** from Joanne of Naples, and work continued on its papal palace. **Scholars and artists** were attracted to the papal city, briefly among them the Florentine **Francesco Petrarch** (1304–74), who had been crowned **poet laureate** in Rome in 1341. In 1351, Petrarch started to arrange his poems in **sonnet** form. He was also a scholar, whose translation and popularization of **Classical literature** contributed to the emergence of **humanism**, a new school of philosophy that would help to trigger the **Renaissance**.

In 1354, the Nasrid king of Granada, **Yusuf I**, was murdered by his son **Mohammed V** (1338–91) who took the throne. Under Mohammed, the **Alhambra**—the fortress-palace of Granada—was further developed, becoming a **treasure of Islamic architecture**.

The **Ottomans** were invited to **Gallipoli**, on the Dardanelles (the straits separating Asia from Europe), by John Cantacuzenus (c. 1292–1383), claimant to the **Byzantine throne**, to help in his attempt to gain power. Led by Orhan, the **Turkish dynasty** soon seized the peninsula, securing themselves a foothold in Europe.

Architectural jewel
The Court of the Lions is at the heart of the Alhambra palace, built by Mohammed V as the winter residence of the royal family.

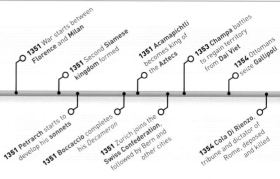

1340 Battle of Rio Salado

1340 Blast furnaces for iron smelting used in Belgium

1344 Aegean Crusade takes Smyrna from the Turks

1342 Edward III renounces debts to Peruzzi bankers

1344 Mongols defeated by Poles and Hungarians

1346 Stephan Dushan IV crowned emperor of the Serbs

1346 Battle of Crécy

1346 Rebellion against the Sultanate of Delhi leads to foundation of Kashmiri kingdom

1348 Teutonic Knights defeat Lithuanian princes at Kovno

1347 Truce between English and French

1347 English take Calais

1347 Black Death strikes Genoa, Constantinople, Marseille, Cyprus, and Naples, and ravages Western Asia

1348 Black Death hits Tuscany, France, Spain, and England

1351 War starts between Florence and Milan

1351 Second Siamese kingdom formed

1351 Acamapichtli becomes king of the Aztecs

1353 Champa battles to regain territory from Dai Viet

1354 Ottomans seize Gallipoli

1351 Petrarch starts to develop his sonnets

1351 Boccaccio completes his Decameron

1351 Zurich joins the Swiss Confederation, followed by Bern and other cities

1354 Cola Di Rienzo, tribune and dictator of Rome, deposed and killed

To many people, Petrarch is known as the "father of humanism."

This mural features Timur Leng, who rose from humble beginnings to found the Timurid dynasty after outmatching the conquests of Genghis Khan.

Constructed of brick and timber, the Bell Tower of Xi'an was built during the early Ming dynasty, in the reign of Zhu Yuanzhang, the first Ming emperor.

BOHEMIA HAD EMERGED AS A POWERFUL STATE under the Premyslid dynasty in the 13th century. Under the **Luxembourg dynasty**, it became the central force in German imperial geopolitics, while its ruler **Charles I** (Charles IV as Holy Roman Emperor) sought to **modernize** the imperial institution and advance the fortunes of Bohemia. In 1348, he had enlarged the kingdom by **granting it territories** such as Moravia and Silesia, and refounded **Prague** to become one of the foremost cities in Europe, with a major university. In 1356, Charles IV issued the **Golden Bull**, which regularized the election of the emperor to a majority vote of seven electoral princes, most of which were hereditary; the papacy would have no role. This, in turn, allowed the electoral principalities to develop **sovereign states**, and set the constitutional basis of the Holy Roman Empire until its final

dissolution in 1806. The Bull established Bohemia as first among the electors and guaranteed its independence.

Timur Leng (1336–1405)—also known as Tamerlane—rose from modest beginnings to become leader of a **Turkic-Mongol Chagatai tribe** in Transoxiana, Central Asia, in around 1362. Despite having a limp, and the fact that he was not of **Chinggid descent** (directly descended from Genghis Khan—only Chinggids could become khans), he was destined to become one of the **greatest conquerors** in history.

Edward of Woodstock, eldest son of Edward III, also known as the **Black Prince** (1330–76), had won his spurs at the **Battle of Crécy** at age 16. He went on to become one of the most effective English commanders. When **hostilities renewed** between England and France in 1355, he invaded France, winning a great victory near **Poitiers** in 1356, in which he captured **King John of France**.

Golden Bull
Edicts issued with golden seals were called Golden Bulls. That of Emperor Charles IV sought to prevent future imperial elections from descending into conflict.

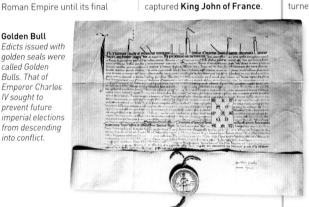

EDWARD, THE BLACK PRINCE, HAD BEEN MADE PRINCE OF GASCONY AND AQUITAINE in 1362, moving to Bordeaux and becoming a major player in continental affairs. In 1367, he intervened in a **dynastic dispute in Castile**, where French ally Henry of Trastamara (1334–79) had deposed English ally Pedro I, thereby **placing control of the Castilian navy in the French camp**. Edward defeated Henry at **Nájera** but was forced to withdraw owing to illness. Subsequently, Henry regained the Castilian throne. In 1372—after **Charles V of France** (r. 1364–80) had fomented a **Gascon rebellion**, restarting the **Hundred Years' War**—the Castilian navy proved instrumental in defeating an English fleet at **La Rochelle**.

China was reunited by conquest from the south, as a native rebellion drove out the **Mongol Yuan dynasty**. In 1368, rebels under **Zhu Yuanzhang** (1328–98)—a former peasant turned Buddhist monk then general—struck north from their base in Nanjing, **displacing the Yuan from Beijing**. Taking the imperial name **Hongwu**, Yuanzhang established the **Ming dynasty**, setting up a strong, centralized government, in which the position of emperor was strengthened, but so was access to the bureaucracy. In 1372, he passed an edict attempting to ban maritime trade and thus **limit contact with foreigners**.

276

THE SPAN, IN YEARS, OF THE **MING DYNASTY**

Under **Murad I** (r. 1362–89), the Ottoman Turks extended their control deep into the **Balkans**. In 1371, Murad defeated an alliance of Serbs, Byzantines, and Bulgars, and held control over much of Thrace, Macedonia, Bulgaria, and Serbia. He also created the **janissaries**, a slave-warrior corps that became the mainstay of Ottoman armies.

Battle of Nájera
Outnumbered by almost three to one, the English–Gascon army defeated the French–Castilian forces with the loss of only around 100 men.

THE STORY OF
PRINTING

A REVOLUTION IN HUMAN COMMUNICATION CHANGES THE WORLD FOREVER

By making it possible to communicate and disseminate information at a speed and scale previously unthinkable, printing wrought changes that are still unfolding today, from triggering religious mania, to scientific and political revolutions—even changing language itself.

Printing is the impression of marks on a medium—most commonly ink on paper. The earliest writing, cuneiform, was a form of printing composed of indentations made by a stylus in clay. Printing in the modern sense of the word first arose in 8th-century China with the development of block printing. Blocks of wood carved into bas-relief were used as stamps to reproduce multiple copies of a single text, complete with images, such as the *Diamond Sutra*, the earliest datable printed book (see 861–70).

MECHANICAL PRINTING
Block printing was laborious and slow, as each block was specific to one page. Movable type was a major advance (see panel, opposite), first achieved in eastern Asia but perfected by German printer Johannes Gutenberg (see 1454–55). His printing press was so advanced that, except for refinements such as new typefaces and mechanization of the presses and paper handling, the basic process remained unchanged until the 19th century.

In the 1880s, the development of linotype allowed a typesetter to compose lines of type using a keyboard, rather than by hand. Stereotyping made it possible to duplicate complete pages for multiple printing. In the 20th century, filmsetting enabled rapid photographic creation of printing plates. By the end of the century, computers allowed every aspect of printing, from typesetting and graphics to inking and drying, to be done on one machine.

bar to lower platen

paper is pressed against form to produce imprint

form, or frame, for setting Gutenberg's special type

wooden coffin, which slides under platen

> ❝ HE WHO FIRST **SHORTENED** THE **LABOUR** OF COPYISTS **BY** DEVICE OF **MOVABLE TYPES** WAS … **CREATING** A WHOLE NEW **DEMOCRATIC WORLD**; HE HAD **INVENTED** THE **ART OF PRINTING.** ❞

Thomas Carlyle, Scottish essayist and historian, 1759–1881

c. 2291–2254 BCE
Sumerian cuneiform
Stamping cuneiform inscriptions, rather than drawing them by hand, is introduced. Stamps are pressed into soft clay bricks, which are then fired.

Sumerian cuneiform

868
Block printed book
The earliest dated book (entire manuscript) is the *Diamond Sutra*, a Buddhist text found in a cave in Dunhuang, China.

The *Diamond Sutra*

1377
Movable metal type
The first metal movable type is cast in bronze in Korea and is used to produce the *Jikji Simche Yojeol*, a Buddhist scripture.

Early Korean book

8th century
Block printing
Printing using carved wooden blocks and ink is known as xylography; the earliest surviving xylographic fragment is a Buddhist *dharani* scroll from Korea.

Japanese *dharani* scroll

c. 1275–1313
Movable type
Invented in China in the 11th century, movable type is refined by Wang Shen, who uses over 60,000 wooden types in his treatise.

c. 1455–56
The printing press
Gutenberg prints the first book in Europe—the Gutenberg or 42-Line Bible (because of the number of lines on each page).

Gutenberg's printing press

1790s–1820s
Metal presses
The all-metal Columbian printing press is the first to replace the screw with levers and weights.

Columbian metal press

screw, or spindle, adapted from wine press

square sleeve, or socket

heavy platen, or printing plate

leather ink balls stuffed with horsehair

sturdy construction for industrial-scale production

MOVABLE TYPE

The key technology in the printing revolution was movable type, in which each character in a script had a corresponding single, small block, or type, allowing lines of type to be assembled, and then reordered for different texts. The first book, printed by movable type cast in bronze, was published in Korea in the late 14th century. Gutenberg improved upon this technology by developing a technique that enabled rapid, precision casting of metal type.

ink impression on paper

raised movable type

Letterpress printing with movable type

Gutenberg's press
Gutenberg created a screw press for pressing inked type, set on a wooden frame, against a sheet of paper. This was a dramatic improvement on the traditional method of taking impressions by means of rubbing.

Late 20th century–present
Desktop printing
The laser printer offers technology that would once have filled an entire workshop.

Laser printer

1886
Linotype
A linotype machine allows a typesetter to make up entire lines of type, using a typewriter-like keyboard, rather than hand-compositing letter-by-letter.

Linotype typesetter

1903
Offset printing
In offset printing, the inked image is transferred (or offset) from the printing plate to the paper via a rubber sheet, achieving smooth, precise transfer and reducing wear on the plate.

Early photocopier

1949
Photocopying
Developed by American Chester Carlson at the Xerox Corporation in the US, the photocopier uses electrostatic distribution of powder ink or toner, rather than wet ink, to create an exact copy.

A 16th-century painting captures the triumphant return of the Doge to Venice after victory over the Genoese.

An illustration from Froissart's Chronicle depicts the Peasants' Revolt, the first great popular rebellion in English history, led by Wat Tyler, who was executed by the mayor of London.

THE WAR OF CHIOGGIA, BETWEEN VENICE AND GENOA, was triggered by the continuing contest for control of the **trade routes through the Dardanelles**, along which flowed the lucrative trade of the **Byzantine Empire** and the **Silk Road** beyond it. In 1376, the Byzantine emperor **John V Palaeologus** (r. 1341–76) granted to Venice the Aegean island of **Tenedos**, key to the Dardanelles. Meanwhile, his son and rival **Andronicus IV** (1348–85) granted it to Genoa. In the ensuing war, the Genoans defeated the Venetians at **Pola** and, in 1379, seized **Chioggia** in Italy and **blockaded Venice**. Under Vittorio Pisano, the Venetians counter-blockaded the Genoese fleet, starving it into submission. **Genoese maritime power was broken** and Venice now controlled the Levantine trade.

Executioner of Cesena
The anti-pope Clement VII was known as the "executioner of Cesena" for his brutal suppression of a rebellion in the Papal States while acting as a papal legate.

> ❝ **NOTHING GREAT** IS EVER ACHIEVED WITHOUT **MUCH ENDURING.** ❞

St. Catherine of Siena, (1347–80)

In 1376, Dominican mystic and miracle worker **Catherine of Siena** travelled to Avignon to convince **Gregory XI** (c. 1336–78) to return the papacy to Rome. A few months later, Gregory went to Rome to attempt to restore order in the Papal States, and died soon after. The **Roman mob** pressured the conclave of cardinals to choose an **Italian pope**, and **Urban VI** (c. 1318–89) was duly elected. French cardinals, meanwhile, elected **Robert of Geneva** (1342–94) as **anti-pope Clement VII**. The French king, Charles V, threw his weight behind Clement, while **Richard II of England** allied with the Holy Roman Emperor Charles IV in supporting the Roman candidate. Thus began the **Western, or Great Schism**, which saw rival popes installed in Rome and Avignon until 1417.

THE BLACK DEATH AND SUBSEQUENT LABOUR SHORTAGES contributed to rising social tension in England. Around 1362, for instance, the poor country priest William Langland had written *Piers Plowman*, a poem in English sympathizing with the plight of the poor peasant. Churchman and scholar **John Wycliffe** (or Wiclif) had caused a stir with writings that prefigured **Protestantism**, and a popular Biblical egalitarian sect, known as the **Lollards**, partially inspired by Wycliffe, was winning widespread support. In 1377, the so-called **Bad Parliament**, dominated by the king's son **John of Gaunt**, Earl of Lancaster and soon-to-be regent to his infant nephew **Richard II** (1367–1400), introduced a **poll tax**; subsequent parliaments extended it, causing **widespread grievance**. In 1381, attempts to reintroduce serfdom triggered the **Peasants' Revolt**, which saw peasants rising against landlords, burning manors, and destroying records. Up to 100,000 men, under **Jack Straw** and **Wat Tyler**, marched on London and siezed the Tower, burning the palace of John of Gaunt and **killing Archbishop Sudbury**, who was blamed for the poll taxes. Richard II cleverly appeased the rebels; Tyler was executed and **the revolt was brutally suppressed**.

Japanese **Noh drama** developed in the 14th century, mainly under the aegis of Kanami Kiyotsugo (1333–84) and his son Zeami Motokiyo (1363–1443), who wrote hundreds of Noh plays and developed the highly stylized and symbolic performances.

Castilian influence in Portugal in the 1380s threatened the independence of the kingdom and sparked **resentment among the Portuguese**. An uprising triggered by a nun resulted in **João** (1358–1453), illegitimate son of Pedro I, seizing control of the country. In 1384, **John I of Castile** (1358–90) invaded Portugal, but João was elected king by the Portuguese parliament and, with English help, defeated Castile at the **Battle of Aljubarrota**, in 1385. In doing so, he freed Portugal from Castilian influence and, after marrying the daughter of John of Gaunt, founded the **Anglo-Portuguese Avis dynasty**.

In 1384, **Philip the Bold of Burgundy** inherited the county of Flanders, adding to his extensive territories. France, ruled by the young and mentally ill **Charles VI**, was now dominated by rivalry between the houses of **Burgundy** and **Orléans**.

Noh mask
In Noh drama, which involves music, singing, speech, and mime, masks are used by the principal character, and by female and elderly characters.

mask usually made of wood or clay

Traveling pilgrims are shown in an illustration from the *Canterbury Tales*. This unfinished poem by Geoffrey Chaucer, 17,000 lines long, vividly illustrates the medieval world view on social, religious, and moral matters.

A miniature from the Topkapi Museum in Istanbul, shows the Battle of Nicopolis, at which the Ottomans destroyed a crusading army.

JAGIELLO OF LITHUANIA (C. 1362–1434), THE LAST PAGAN RULER

in Europe, was crowned king of Poland and converted to Christianity in 1386. Marriage to **Jadwiga of Poland** united the two kingdoms, and brought Lithuania into the Catholic Church, although pagan traditions lingered on.

Timur Leng (see 1356–65) completed his **conquest of Persia** in 1386 and raided deep into the Caucasus, sacking **Tbilisi** in Georgia and capturing the Georgian king. However, when the army of the **Golden Horde** attacked his Central Asian territories, in 1387, he was forced to turn back and meet them. It took another nine years for him to destroy the threat.

Geoffrey Chaucer (c. 1340–1400) was a soldier, scholar, writer, diplomat, government official, and

CHRISTIANIZATION OF EUROPE

In Europe, the medieval period saw the vigorous advance of Christianity until it encompassed the entire region (with just a few exceptions). The spectacular success in converting Europe posed extreme challenges to the Church, as it struggled to reconcile temporal and spiritual power. Internal forces would continue to revolutionize the religion.

Member of Parliament. He was instrumental in the development of **Middle English**—a combination of Old English and French influences. His greatest work, the

Canterbury Tales, partially modeled on Italian author Giovanni Boccaccio's *Decameron*, tells the story of pilgrims on the road to the shrine of **Thomas Becket** (see 1170); it was begun in 1387.

At the **Battle of Kosovo**, in 1389, the Ottomans defeated the Serbs and Bosnians, **smashing the Serbian empire** and absorbing most of its territories. The Ottoman leader, Murad, was killed in the battle but his son **Bayezid the Thunderbolt** (1360–1403) took over. News of Murad's death prompted the **Ottoman vassals** in Europe and Anatolia to **revolt**, but Bayezid swiftly reduced most of them, bringing their territories under **direct Ottoman rule**. The Ottomans now controlled most of Anatolia and the Balkans south of the Danube. Bayezid introduced the **devshirme**—the levy of Christian children who were converted to Islam and used in the administration and **Janissary** corps.

THE START OF THE MING DYNASTY IN CHINA TRIGGERED CHANGE IN KOREA, which was considered a client state by the Ming. The **Koryo empire** had supported the new Chinese dynasty, but this did not prevent the Ming from threatening to invade. In 1388, **Yi Songgye** (1335–1408), a leading general who favored the Chinese, seized power in Korea. In 1392, as **King Taejo**, he founded the **Yi dynasty**, also known as the Choson (or Joseon), a name taken from an ancient Korean kingdom. Taejo restructured his government on the Chinese model, and instituted **wide-ranging land reforms** to redistribute estates from the hands of the oligarchy, replacing them with a new class of technocrats known as the yangban. **Neo-Confucianism** was adopted as the state religion, and a new capital was founded at **Hanseong** (Seoul). The Yi dynasty lasted until 1910.

In **Japan**, the union of the northern and southern imperial courts in 1392 brought to an end the **Yoshino period** (also known as the Period of Northern and Southern

Courts). During this period, the line of the emperor **Godaigo**—driven out of the capital, Kyoto, by the Ashikaga shogun Takauji, in 1336—had maintained a **rival court** in the mountainous Yoshino region south of Nara. Japan was wracked by **civil war** until the shogun **Ashikaga Yoshimitsu** (1358–1408) negotiated a reunification and brought Ashikaga power to its apogee.

The **Nicopolis Crusade** of 1396—intended to roll back the Ottoman advance in the Balkans—saw a Franco-Hungarian expedition led by **Sigismund of Hungary** humiliatingly crushed at the Bulgarian town of Nicopolis on the Danube. A huge army, featuring volunteers from most of the **Christian states**, proved ill-disciplined. The failure of this adventure proved that Christian Europe had to look to its defense.

Gyeongbokgung Palace
This colossal palace, built by King Taejo (Yi Songgye) in 1395, is also known as the "Palace of Shining Happiness" and the "Palace Greatly Blessed by Heaven."

The Timurid Empire
Established by Timur Leng, the Timurid Empire eventually reached a greater extent even than that of Genghis Khan, but it would not long survive Timur's death.

KEY
→ Campaigns of Timur
▨ Extent of Timur's empire

Wladyslaw II Jagiello of Poland prepare for the Battle of Tannenberg.

The wall of skulls at the Templo Mayor archaeological site in Mexico City is made from skulls carved in stone, covered with stucco; the Aztecs practised human sacrifice at the vast temples in the centre of Tenochtitlan.

FOUNDED BY THE AZTECS IN 1325, the city of **Tenochtitlan**—existing on the apparently unpromising site of a marshy island in a partially brackish lake—reached its height at the beginning of the 15th century. Tenochtitlan means "Place of the Fruit of the Cactus"—a reference to the vision that supposedly informed the choice of location. In this vision, the tossed heart of a conquered enemy landed on the island where an eagle wrestled with a snake on a cactus growing out of a rock— as depicted on the present-day Mexican flag. The **Aztecs** drained the island, reclaiming surrounding land, and joined the land together with causeways.

Meanwhile, they expanded their political territory through marriages, alliances, and conquest. After a flood, Tenochtitlan was laid out on a grid pattern, with quarters arranged around a **central sacred district**, regarded as the center of the world. A huge population of up to 200,000 was supported by **intensive agriculture** and extensive **networks of trade** and tribute.

The African **Songhay kingdom** was centered on the trading metropolis of Gao, in the Niger Bend area of **West Africa**. Gao had long been a prosperous city thanks to interregional and trans-Saharan trade with the

Songhay gold coin
This coin from the Songhay Empire is from the Songhay city of Gao; rich and powerful, the city provided the basis for building the empire.

Islamic world, especially in salt, gold, slaves, and ivory. In the mid-13th century, because of the allure of its riches, it became an eastern province of the **Mali Empire** (see 1231–35). However, in the early

15th century, Mali declined and Gao won its independence, beginning the growth of a Songhay Empire that would eclipse the other two largest empires of the late Iron Age in West Africa—Ghana and Mali.

In 1398, **Timur Leng** (see 1356–65) had invaded northern India and destroyed the **Delhi sultanate** with astonishing speed and terrifying cruelty. Marching 160 miles (260 km) in two days, he captured and massacred 100,000 fugitives outside Delhi before sacking the city, supposedly building a huge pyramid from the skulls of his victims. In 1401, Timur massacred the population of Baghdad and launched an invasion of Syria. He then moved against the **Ottomans** (see 1286–90), occupying Anatolia and restoring the old Turkoman principalities.

VALLEY OF MEXICO

Tenayuca

Pantlaco
Atepehuacán
Atzacualco
Coltonco
Tepeyacac
Azcapotzalco
Tacuba
Altepetlac
Popotlan
Tlatelolco
Chapultepec
Lake Texcoco
TENOCHTITLAN
Mixiucan
Tlacateco
Acachinanco
Xola-Xalac
Zacatlalmanco
Tepetlatzinco
Coyoacán
Lake Xochimilco
Mexicatzincgo
Huitzilopochco
Dyke of Netzahualcoyotl

Map of Tenochtitlan
Causeways connected Tenochtitlan to other settlements on the lake and the mainland. The city and its emperor dominated the Valley of Mexico.

KEY
— street
— aqueduct
— causeway
— dyke

HAVING CONQUERED AS FAR AS RUSSIA in the East, **Timur Leng** (see 1386–90) set his sights on the greatest empire—**China**. In 1405, he embarked on a campaign, but died en route to China and was buried at his capital, Samarkand. Despite his possibly exaggerated reputation for cruelty, Timur was a devout Muslim and a **patron of the arts** and architecture. His enormous empire did not long survive him, quickly breaking down into a Timurid state ruled by his son Shah Rukh (1377–1447), which soon fragmented further.

In 1404, John the Fearless (1371–1419) became **duke of Burgundy**, leading opposition to the regency of Louis, duke of Orleans (1372–1407), brother of the mad king, Charles VI of France (1368–1422). In 1407, John ordered the assassination of Louis, triggering **civil war** between the Burgundians and the Armagnacs (named for the count of Armagnac, the father-in-law of Charles, the new duke of Orleans). The **Burgundians**, who favored peace with the English, were popular in Paris and the north, while the **Armagnacs**, who were anti-English and pro-war, had the support of Queen Isabeau of Bavaria, the great nobles, and the south of the country.

In 1404, **Zheng He** (1371–1435) —a Muslim captured from Yunnan in China as a boy, castrated, and pressed into military service—was named grand, or high-ranking, eunuch at the imperial court. The following year he led the first of seven epic voyages of discovery.

THE RELENTLESS ADVANCE OF THE ORDER OF TEUTONIC KNIGHTS (see 1236–40) had brought Prussia and much of the Baltic coast under their control, cutting Poland off from the sea. The union of Poland and Lithuania under King Wladyslaw II Jagiello (c. 1362–1434) posed a new threat to the Order, and the **Great Northern War** ensued. At the **Battle of Tannenberg** in 1410— one of the greatest cavalry confrontations of the age—a huge Polish–Lithuanian army of up to 16,500, including Bohemian mercenaries, Russians, and even Tatars (Turkic Mongols), defeated

Timeline

○ **c. 1400s** Height of Aztec city of **Tenochtitlan**

○ **c. 1400s** Expansion of West African **Songhay Empire**

○ **1401** Timur (1336– 1405) massacres population of Baghdad

○ **1402** Italian architect **Lorenzo Ghiberti** commissioned to design doors of **Florence Baptistry**

○ **1402** Battle of Ankara; **Timur captures Ottoman sultan**

○ **1403** Malay ruler Parmesvara establishes **Sultanate of Malacca**

○ **1405** Breakup of Visconti domains; **Venice seizes Padua,** Verona, and Vincenza

○ **1405** First voyage of explorer **Zheng He**

○ **1405** Death of Timur (b. 1336); **fragmentation of Timurid Empire**

○ **1407** Civil war in France pits Armagnacs against Burgundians

○ **1409** **Donatello** di Niccolo di Betto Bardi completes his masterpiece, *David*

○ **1409** **Council of Pisa** results in three papal claimants

This later depiction of the Battle of Agincourt shows cavalry engaged in conflict; around 10,000 French troops were killed or captured.

This illustration from the Chronicle of Ulrich von Richental shows the papal electors taking their leave from Emperor Sigismund at the Council of Constance.

the forces of the Teutonic Knights who were around 11,000 strong. The Order was crushed, but Jagiello was unable to keep the powerful Polish nobles in order and thus could not press home his advantage. The **Peace of Thorn**, concluded the following year, failed to secure Polish access to the Baltic and enabled the Teutonic Knights to regain some of their advantage.

Andrei Rublev (c. 1370–1430) was a Russian monk and painter, based at the St. Sergius monastery of the Holy Trinity in Moscow. He worked during a period of monastic revival in Russia, when the Eastern Orthodox Church offered comfort in the face of internecine war and the hated **Mongol Yoke**—the tribute and service exacted by the Golden Horde. Though inspired by the great icon painter Theophanes the Greek, Rublev was celebrated for pioneering a new, more serene and symmetrical style.

The Holy Trinity
This detail from Andrei Rublev's greatest icon, painted around 1410, shows the three angels who visited Abraham. Each angel represents a different aspect of the Trinity.

IN 1413, HENRY IV OF ENGLAND DIED and his son, Henry V (1386–1422), came to the throne. In 1415, Henry concluded an alliance with Burgundy and reasserted the **English claim to the French crown** as a pretext for renewing the **Hundred Years' War** (see panel, right). In October, Henry inflicted a terrible defeat on a far superior French force at **Agincourt**, taking the Duke of Orleans prisoner, and going on to conquer Normandy.

> ❝ ...THE LIVING **FELL ON** TOP OF THE **DEAD,** AND OTHERS **FALLING ON** TOP OF **THE LIVING** WERE KILLED AS WELL. ❞

From *Gesta Henrici Quinti*, c. 1416

During **Chinese explorer Zheng He's** fourth and greatest expedition in 1413, he visited Calicut in India, and reached Hormuz on the Persian Gulf, sending ships to explore down the African coast as far as Malindi in Kenya. The fleet included 63 ships of up to 260 ft (80 m) long.

In 1414, anti-pope **John XXIII** one of three men claiming to be pope—was expelled from Rome by King Ladislas of Naples. John sought refuge with the emperor, **Sigismund**, who forced him to convene a general council—the **Council of Constance**—to resolve the split in the Catholic Church known as the **Great Schism** (see 1373–80). In 1415, the Council deposed the existing claimants, and condemned the Bohemian priest, religious reformer, and philosopher **Jan Huss**, who was executed the same year.

THE HUNDRED YEARS' WAR

The series of conflicts from 1337 to 1453, later known as the Hundred Years' War, was triggered by a combination of factors: tensions over the status of the duchy of Guienne, which belonged to the kings of England but owed sovereignty to the French crown; English claims to that crown, based on descent from the Capetians; anxieties of influence on both sides; and the need of English kings to use foreign adventures to shore up support at home. There should have been little contest between France, the most powerful nation in Europe, and smaller, poorer England, but the English used new tactics and weapons, especially the longbow, to devastating effect. The war drained resources on both sides, but also forged a new degree of national identity for both countries.

THE COUNCIL OF CONSTANCE ENDED THE GREAT SCHISM in 1417 by trying and deposing the last antipope, Benedict XIII, and electing Martin V (c. 1348–1431) as the sole true pope.

The burning at the stake of Bohemian religious reformer **Jan Huss** (see 1411–15), and the death of Wenceslaus IV of Bohemia (1361–1419), sparked a **Hussite uprising** in Bohemia. This combined a religious tussle between the papacy and antipapists, with a nationalist struggle between Czechs (Bohemians and Moravians) and Germans. The Hussites, made up of moderate (Utraquist) and extreme (Taborite) factions, united to face a crusading alliance led by Wenceslaus' brother, the emperor Sigismund. The Hussites defeated the alliance outside Prague.

In 1411, **peace** was concluded between **Portugal and Castile** (see 1381–85). Portugal now began to look outward, winning a foothold on the north coast of Africa at Ceuta in 1415. Explorer **Henry the Navigator** (1394–1460) distinguished himself in the expedition; his visit to Africa sparked an interest in exploration, and he may have set up the first school of navigation in Europe at Sagres, in Portugal (see 1434).

45

THE **NUMBER** OF **SESSIONS** HELD AT THE 42-MONTH-LONG **COUNCIL** OF **CONSTANCE**

1421–22

Filippo Maria Visconti of Milan sits in state; having assassinated his brother to become duke of Milan, he restored Visconti hegemony over northern Italy.

SULTAN MEHMED I (1382–1421) had successfully **restored the Ottoman state** after the Timurid invasion (see 1401–03), although his navy had come out worse in a conflict with the **Venetians** at the **Battle of Gallipoli** in 1416, forcing the Ottomans to recognize Venetian claims in Albania. In 1421, Mehmed died and his son, **Murad II (1404–51)**, became sultan. Domestically, he restored the *devshirme* practice of training Christian slaves for key roles in government; externally, he pursued a policy of renewed expansion, beginning with the first **Ottoman siege of Constantinople**. The siege was unsuccessful and Mehmed was distracted by an uprising led by the Sufi theologian and preacher Sheikh Bedreddin—it was suppressed, and the sheikh was executed.

The **Visconti family** had ruled **Milan** since Archbishop Otto Visconti rose to power in 1277; their domain had spread to encompass much of northern Italy, reaching its height under **Gian Galeazzo (1351–1402)**, sole ruler from 1385. He had made marriage alliances with the chief monarchs of Europe; was made hereditary duke in 1395; mastered Verona, Vicenza, Padua, Pisa, Siena, Assisi, and Perugia

Sultan Murad II
Murad defended and extended the Ottoman Empire, and was also a patron of poetry and learning, making his court a cultural center.

between 1386 and 1400; and threatened Florence until his death in 1402. Strife between his sons Gian Maria and Filippo Maria saw this empire disintegrate, but when Filippo had Gian assassinated in 1412, he set about restoring it, **regaining Genoa** in 1421. The Visconti patronized the arts and scholarship, helping to drive the **Renaissance** (see pp. 208–09).

The French had suffered great losses at **Agincourt** (see 1411–15), and in 1420, at the prompting of the pro-English **Burgundians**, Charles VI of France had accepted the **Treaty of Troyes** and acknowledged Henry V of England as his heir and immediate regent. The agreement ceded all the conquered lands up to the Loire to the English and declared the dauphin, Charles, to be illegitimate. The **English** now **controlled northern France**. In 1422, both Henry and Charles died, and under the terms of the Treaty, the infant Henry VI was acclaimed king of both England and France. The dauphin, based at Bourges, refused to accept this, and the **Hundred Years' War** (see 1411–15) continued.

1423–25

The Doge's Palace, seat of the doge of Venice, is a masterpiece of 14th-century Gothic architecture, overlain with 15th, 16th, and 17th century additions.

IN THE 1420S, THE CULTURAL MOVEMENT known later as the Italian or **High Renaissance** gathered pace, particularly in the field of **painting and the visual arts**. In 1424, the sculptor Lorenzo Ghiberti (1378–1455) completed the gilded bronze doors for the **Florence Baptistry** that he had been commissioned to make in 1403; the following year he was commissioned for a further set. Working at the same time as Ghiberti were a host of other artists, including Brunelleschi, Jacopo della Quercia, Masaccio, Donatello, Gentile da Fabriano, Jan van Eyck, and many more.

The Tribute Money
Tommaso di Ser Giovanni di Simone Masaccio died at just 27 years old, but created some of the most influential artworks of the Renaissance.

Although **Florence** was the heart of the Renaissance in the 15th century, the other great Italian power centers of Milan, Rome, and Venice also fostered artistic and architectural achievement. In Venice, the **Doge's Palace**, which had been evolving since its origins in the 9th century, embodied many of the architectural high points of the previous six centuries. The current building began to take shape around 1340; work on the side overlooking the Piazzetta did not begin until 1424, under Doge Francesco Foscari (1373–1457).

In 1424, Timur's descendant, Ulugh Beg (1394–1449)—astronomer and future Mongol leader—built a great **observatory** in Samarkand. It was equipped with a 130-ft (40-m) sextant, and Ulugh and his team of scholars cataloged over a thousand stars.

1426–30

Joan of Arc leads troops into battle, wielding a crossbow.

Bodkin point
This type of arrowhead is an uncomplicated, squared, metal spike, extensively used during the wars of the Middle Ages.

THE DAUGHTER OF A FARMER, JOAN OF ARC (1412–31) was 16 when in 1429 voices in her head commanded her to bear aid to the French dauphin (see 1421–22). The English under John, duke of Bedford (1389–1435), had made further gains against the forces of the dauphin and were **besieging Orleans**, while the dauphin had still not managed to secure his coronation. Joan succeeded in

1421 Murad II becomes Ottoman sultan

1421 Czech estates form autonomous government; repel second anti-Hussite crusade

August 31, 1422 Death of Henry V of England in France; succession of **Henry VI** (b. 1387)

1422 Chinese explorer **Zheng He's** 6th voyage brings giraffes back from Africa

1421 Milan annexes Genoa; defeats Swiss

1421 Chinese imperial court moves to **Forbidden City** at Beijing

October 21, 1422 Death of **Charles VI** of France (b. 1368)

1422 First **Ottoman siege of Constantinople**

August 17, 1424 Duke of Bedford, regent of France, defeats supporters of dauphin Charles at **Battle of Verneuil**

1424 Ulugh Beg (1394–1449), ruler of Samarkand, builds observatory

1424 Ottomans take **Smyrna**, Anatolia

1424 Francesco Sforza succeeds his father as condottierro (leader) of a **mercenary company**, Milan

1424 Italian artist **Lorenzo Ghiberti** completes doors to Florence Baptistry

1424 Renovation begins on Piazzetta facade of **Doge's Palace**, Venice

1426 Hussites under **Procopius the Great** (c. 1380–1434) defeat third anti-Hussite crusade

1427 Venetian forces take **Bergamo** from Milan, northern Italy

1427 Portuguese discover the **Azores**, North Atlantic

1428 Le dynasty in Vietnam wins independence from China

May 1429 Joan of Arc relieves **siege of Orleans**

The Arnolfini Marriage by Jan van Eyck is noted for its detailed interior.

> ❝ WE READ THAT WE OUGHT TO FORGIVE OUR ENEMIES; BUT WE DO NOT READ THAT WE OUGHT TO FORGIVE OUR FRIENDS. ❞
>
> Cosimo de Medici

Painting of the first Medici ruler of Florence, Cosimo.

obtaining an interview with him at Chinon, won him over, and was provided with troops and the title *chef de guerre* ("war leader"). She successfully relieved Orleans, going on to **defeat the English** twice more, and stood next to the dauphin at his coronation as Charles VII at Reims in 1429. Joan failed to take Paris, however, and the following year, she was **captured** by the Burgundians, who ransomed her to their English allies (see 1431–33).

In 1428, Le Loi, leader of Vietnamese resistance to the Chinese occupation, expelled the Chinese and founded the **Le dynasty of Dai Viet**. On admitting Chinese authority, his dynasty was recognized by the Ming.

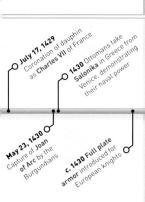

FROM 1431 TO 1433, ZHENG HE (see 1404–07) made a seventh and final expedition, returning to the **Persian Gulf**. Despite this last trip, China's period of exploration had come to an end with the death of **Emperor Yongle** in 1424, after which the **Ming dynasty** returned to its former isolationist policy.

SHIP LENGTHS

72ft COLUMBUS'S SHIP
440ft ZHENG HE'S SHIP

Surrendering the lead in exploration to Portugal and the Europeans would have profound consequences for the Chinese and for world history.

Not all the great Renaissance painters were Italian; **Jan van Eyck** (*c.* 1390–1441) was Flemish. Celebrated for his mastery of realism and his perfection of oil painting, van Eyck produced some of his greatest masterpieces in the 1430s. In 1432, he and his brother Hubert completed their largest surviving work, the altarpiece of St. Bavo's Cathedral in Ghent, Belgium. Later that year, in London, van Eyck painted the *Portrait of an Unknown Man* and the *Man with the Red Turban*; possibly a self-portrait.

In 1431, **Joan of Arc** was turned over by the English to the French ecclesiastical authorities for trial. She was found guilty of heresy, and was **burned at the stake** in Rouen.

SINCE THE 1380S, FLORENCE HAD BEEN DOMINATED by the Albizzi family, who extended the city's control of Tuscany. The attempts of Visconti Milan (see 1421–22) to gain control over all of Tuscany forced Florence into a ruinously expensive war, although alliance with Venice saw **Milan defeated**. A leader of the peace party was wool merchant and banker Giovanni de Medici, possibly the richest man in Europe. After his death in 1429 and a disastrous war with Lucca in Tuscany, the Albizzi succeeded in having Giovanni's son, Cosimo de Medici, banished from Florence in 1433, but new elections saw him returned the following year, marking the start of **Medici domination** of the city. Cosimo combined business acumen with political shrewdness, winning popular support for his policies.

All attempts by **anti-Hussite forces** under the emperor Sigismund to dislodge the Hussites and regain control of the **Czech territories** had failed (see 1416–20). The superior organization and tactics of the Hussites, first under Jan Zizka and, after his death in 1424, under **Andrew Prokops**, made them militarily powerful. In 1430, they invaded Germany and raided as far as Franconia. Negotiations with the ecumenical **Council of Basel** in 1413 led to the Compact of Prague, or *Compactacta*, under which moderate Hussites (the Utraquists) agreed to go back to the Catholic Church. The extreme anti-papist Taborites rejected the Compact, and civil war broke out between the factions, which represented different classes as well as religious ideals. In 1434, at the **Battle of Lipany**, the upper-class Utraquists vanquished the Taborites, killing Prokops.

The rising power of the Sukhothai kingdom of Thailand had increasingly threatened the **Khmer Empire** (see 1201–05) through the 14th century. Repeated **Thai raids**, particularly an incursion in 1431, may have helped

The Windrose
The windrose mosaic at Sagres in Portugal—possibly a sundial—was commissioned by Portuguese navigator Prince Henry.

trigger the 1434 **abandonment of Angkor** (see 1146–50) and the transfer of the Khmer capital to Phnom Penh, farther south, although it is also possible that the new location offered better connections for foreign trade.

Sponsored by Prince **Henry the Navigator** (see 1416–20), Portuguese explorers pushing out into the Atlantic had discovered the islands of **Madeira** and the **Azores**. Henry personally oversaw the colonization of these Atlantic outposts, successfully establishing them as centers of agricultural production and forward bases for **Portuguese exploration**. Henry's next target was to round Cape Bojador on the coast of West Africa, the farthest limit of Portuguese exploration; contemporary European sailors' lore viewed the seas beyond as a dangerous and terrifying otherworld. **Cape Bojador** was finally rounded by Gil Eannes in 1434. The experiences of his sailors on these voyages of discovery convinced Henry that the traditional barca ships in use were unsuitable, and he worked with shipwrights to design a new type of vessel, **the caravel**. This was smaller, lighter, and swifter, with a shallow draft for near-shore operations and more space for stores to allow the ships to stay at sea for longer.

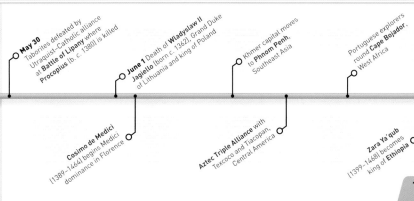

Timeline:

- **July 17, 1429** Coronation of dauphin as **Charles VII** of France
- **1430** Ottomans take **Salonika** in Greece from Venice, demonstrating their naval power
- **May 23, 1430** Capture of **Joan of Arc** by the Burgundians
- **c. 1430 Full plate armor** introduced for European knights
- **May 30, 1431 Joan of Arc** (b. 1412) burned at stake
- **1431** Khmer capital moved from **Angkor** after Thai raid, Southeast Asia
- **1432** Flemish artist **Jan van Eyck** completes the *Adoration of the Mystic Lamb*
- **1433** Tuaregs conquer **Timbuktu**, Mali Empire
- **1433 Compacts of Prague** end Hussite wars
- **1433** Zheng He's last voyage and subsequent **isolation of China**
- **May 30** Taborites defeated by Utraquist-Catholic alliance at **Battle of Lipany** where **Procopius** (b. c. 1380) is killed
- **June 1** Death of **Wladyslaw II Jagiello** (born c. 1362), Grand Duke of Lithuania and king of Poland
- **Cosimo de Medici** (1389–1464) begins Medici dominance in Florence
- **Aztec Triple Alliance** with Texcoco and Tlacopan, Central America
- Khmer capital moves to **Phnom Penh**, Southeast Asia
- Portuguese explorers round **Cape Bojador**, West Africa
- **Zara Ya'qub** (1399–1468) becomes king of **Ethiopia**

This manuscript illustration shows Charles VII entering Paris in triumph.

Founded by King Henry VI of England, construction of Eton college was halted when the king was deposed during the War of the Roses.

Fresco by Domenico di Bartolo (c. 1410–1461), of the Sienese school, from Siena's hospital of Santa Maria della Scala.

> **THE KINGDOM OF FRANCE…** WILL BE THUS **RULED BY** KING **CHARLES VII…** HE WILL ENTER PARIS IN GOOD COMPANY.

Joan of Arc, Christian visionary

THOUGH ALLIED WITH THE ENGLISH OCCUPATION OF FRANCE, the Burgundians (see 1404–07) were increasingly concerned at English gains. With the **Treaty of Arras**, the Burgundians and the French king, Charles VII, made peace but the English, unwilling to accept the terms, withdrew from negotiations. The following year, the French alliance took Paris from English control.

The 1430s saw increasing **tension** between the **papacy** and the **conciliar movement**, which held that the Church ought to be governed by a Church council, rather than an individual pope. Pope Eugene IV summoned a **General Council at Basel** in 1431, but it was dominated by **antipapal sentiment** and, in 1437, he tried to transfer the Council to Ferrara, where it would be more amenable to his influence. Most of the delegates refused to leave Basel, resulting in **two concurrent councils**.

IN 1438, PACHACUTEC (C. 1438–1472) BECAME THE NINTH INCA KING, or *Sapa Inca*. His reign heralded the beginning of a great expansion of the Inca realm, which had been confined to the immediate area around **Cuzco** since its foundation (see 1201–1205). It began with invasion by the rival Chancas, who besieged Cuzco, and were completely defeated. **Inca expansion** was facilitated by the sophisticated nature of most of the kingdoms and tribes they conquered; tight-knit, centralized administration focused on the emperor; a genius for organization and record-keeping (despite having no writing); and an imperial road-building program rivalled only by the Roman Empire.

In 1440, the young king of England founded a new college at Eton. The King's College of Our Lady of Eton near Windsor, now known as **Eton College**, was intended to be part of a large foundation including a massive church, an almshouse, and 70 scholars who were

KEY

▨ Expansion by 1400
▨ Expansion in the reign of Pachacutec

Inca expansion
The Inca Empire had expanded greatly between 1400 and the end of Pachacutec's reign. It would triple in size by the 16th century.

to receive free education before going on to King's College, Cambridge.

With the **Ottomans** (see 1286–90) occupying territories on all sides of the tiny **remnants of the Byzantine Empire**, and threatening Constantinople itself, the embattled Byzantine emperor John VIII Palaeologus (see 1448–49) arrived in Europe to plead for help from the **Council of Ferrara** in 1438.

Gold llama statuette
The Inca were so rich in gold that emperor Atahualpa was able to offer a ransom of 750 tons of it when captured by conquistadors in 1532.

MACHU PICCHU (meaning "Old Peak" in Quechua, the language of the Incas) is a mountaintop citadel about 43 miles (70km) northwest of Cuzco. Construction probably began in the 1440s, under the auspices of **Pachacutec**. The maximum population of Machu Picchu was possibly only around 1,000, and it is thought that it served as a ceremonial center, as well as being an impregnable stronghold for the Inca elite in case of attack.

Resistance to **Ottoman occupation of the Balkans** increased, and in 1443, a crusading army defeated the Ottomans at Nis, in Bulgaria. The Ottoman sultan, Murad II (see 1421–22), was forced out of retirement to take over from his son, Mehmed II, to whom he had

attempted to entrust his crown. At Adrianople, Murad made a 10-year truce with Hungarian military leader Jan Hunyadi and other resistors of Ottoman advance. However, with the pope **preaching crusade**, the resistors were absolved of their oaths of peace and they launched a new attack. Led by Hunyadi and Wladyslaw III of Poland and Hungary (1424–1444), the crusading army—the last major

Machu Picchu
High above the Urubamba Valley in the Peruvian Andes, on an inaccessible ridge, lies Machu Picchu, sacred citadel of the Inca kings.

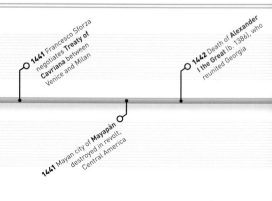

1435 Treaty of Arras; alliance of Burgundians with Charles VII of France against English

1436 Completion of Italian architect **Filippo Brunelleschi's** Duomo, Florence

December 9, 1437 Death of Emperor Sigismund (b. 1368)

1437 Civil war in Scotland

1437 Moors retake Ceuta, North Africa

1438 Byzantine emperor John VIII Palaeologus arrives at Council of Ferrara to seek help against Ottomans

1438 Expansion of Inca Empire begins under Sapa Inca Pachacutec

1438 Francesco Sforza acting for Venice defeats Milanese mercenaries

1439 Council of Basel deposes Pope Eugene IV; elects anti-pope Felix V

1439 Oba Ewuare takes power in Benin Empire, West Africa

1439 Ottoman sultan **Murad II** (1404–51) begins conquest of Serbia

1440 Henry VI founds Eton College, England

c. 1440s Construction of Machu Picchu, Inca Empire, begins

1460 Moctezuma I (c. 1398–1469) becomes Aztec emperor and expands dominion

1441 Francesco Sforza negotiates **Treaty of Cavriana** between Venice and Milan

1441 Mayan city of **Mayapán**, destroyed in revolt, Central America

1442 Death of **Alexander I the Great** (b. 1386), who reunited Georgia

The rocky north coast between Paul and Ribeira Grande in Santa Antao in the Cape Verde islands.

Illustration from a Muromachi period manuscript. The arts flourished in Japan under Ashikaga patronage.

2:1

Battle of Varna
The Hungarian-led crusader army, with a strength of 30,000, suffered heavy losses at the hands of the Ottoman troops, who numbered 60,000.

attempt to expel the Ottomans from the Balkans and relieve Constantinople—was decisively crushed by Murad at the **Battle of Varna**. Wladyslaw disappeared in the battle and was presumed dead, despite rumors of his miraculous survival.

HENRY THE NAVIGATOR'S EXPENSIVE PROJECT to open up the coast of Africa (see 1434) was met with scepticism at home in Portugal, until in 1441, one of his ships returned with **gold dust and slaves**, prompting an acceleration of activity. Between 1444 and 1446, around 35 of Henry's vessels sailed for the **West African coast**. In 1445, sailing in one of Henry's new caravels, explorer **Dinis Dias** sighted the mouth of the Senegal River, which offered a trade route deep into the African interior, and rounded **Cape Verde**, the westernmost point of Africa. Dias returned the following year as part of a fleet of caravels intending to plant the Portuguese flag and explore what Henry believed might be the western branch of the Nile, while another of Henry's captains, Nuño Tristão, sighted the Gambia River.

The marriage of **Margaret of Anjou** (*c.* 1430–82) to Henry VI of England in 1445 was negotiated by William de la Pole, chief advisor to the king and power behind the throne, whose aim was to stop the war in France (see 1435–37). At first, the match and the bride were popular in England, but in 1448, the territory of Maine in northern France was lost to Charles VII and the queen was blamed for her influence over the weak king. Margaret would survive this, however, and become an important player in the **Wars of the Roses** (see 1454–55).

The death of **Filippo Maria Visconti** in 1447 signaled the end of the Visconti ducal line of Milan

(see 1421–22). There were multiple claimants to the ducal throne, and eager to avoid domination by a foreigner, the Milanese powers immediately constituted the *Aurea Repubblica Ambrosiana* of Milan, or the **Ambrosian Republic**, but they faced insurmountable obstacles. Riven by internal dissension and unwilling to lose control of the other cities controlled by Milan, they were soon forced to turn military control over to a *condotierre*, or mercenary soldier-leader—the powerful Muzio Attendolo, nicknamed *Sforza* meaning "exert" or "force."

In the mid-15th century, the Shona kingdom of **Mwene Mutapa**, also known as Great Zimbabwe (see 1106–10), was nearing the end of its glory days. By this time, the riches of the gold fields had funded construction of the Great Enclosure, an elliptical space enclosed by a giant wall 800 ft (244 m) around, and up to 36 ft (11 m) high in places, built from almost a million granite blocks.

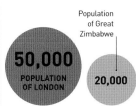

Population of Great Zimbabwe

50,000
POPULATION OF LONDON

20,000

Golden age of Great Zimbabwe
In the mid-15th century, the population of Great Zimbabwe was just under half the size of the population of London.

IN 1449, ASHIKAGA YOSHIMASA (1435–90) BECAME SHOGUN, or military dictator, of Japan. Although his reign marked a cultural highpoint of the Ashikaga, or Muromachi period (1336–1573) it was also a period of increasing civil strife. Repeated famines triggered constant uprisings, while the Ashikaga practice of issuing *tokuseirei* or "acts of grace" to cancel debts, damaged the economy. Despite this, Yoshimasa presided over a cultural flowering at his Higashiyama estate.

The new pope, Nicholas V, elected in 1447, was intent on bringing an end to the schism caused by his predecessor's clash with the **Council of Basel** (see 1435–37), and on restoring peace to Italy and achieving harmonious relations with other rulers. At the **Concordat of Vienna** in 1448, he made concessions to Emperor Frederick III and the other German princes, who in return abandoned the Council of Basel and recognized some papal powers. The following year, the Council of Basel finally disbanded and the anti-pope, Felix V, abdicated in return for a cardinalship. This marked the final **victory of the papacy** over the conciliar movement.

Following the death of Byzantine emperor John VIII, his brother Constantine XI Palaeologus (see panel, right) acceded to the throne in Constantinople—he would be the **last Byzantine emperor**. The Ottomans had defeated another of Jan Hunyadi's crusades to clear

PALAEOLOGUS
(1404–53)

Constantine XI Palaeologus succeeded to the remnants of a once-great empire, left without the resources to defend itself. He was the last emperor of Byzantium, a state that had lasted throughout the medieval period, providing a unique bridge between east and west, ancient and modern. He died on the walls of Constantinople, having done everything in his power to secure its defense.

them from the Balkans at the second Battle of Kosovo in 1448, regaining control of Albania. It was clear that there would be no European rescue for the embattled Byzantines. The Ottomans were closing in on Constantinople.

REFORMATION AND EXPLORATION

1450–1749

The 16th and 17th centuries were determined by new horizons,
as new lands were explored and new ideas formulated.
Religious reform and conflict, global exploration, and a
scientific revolution laid the grounds of a new understanding

A detail from Ghiberti's *Doors of Paradise* for Florence Cathedral's Baptistry. The second pair of doors he completed, they show scenes from the Old Testament.

This 16th-century fresco depicts the siege of Constantinople, which began on April 2, 1453 and ended when the Ottomans took the city on May 29.

THE GREAT ZIMBABWE CIVILIZATION of southeast Africa (see 1106–10) was in decline by the mid-15th century. This coincided with the rise of the **Mutapa Empire** in the fertile, copper-rich uplands between the Zambezi and Limpopo rivers in present-day Zimbabwe and Mozambique. Sustained by lucrative trade in copper, cattle, ivory, slaves, and gold with

into competing regional powers in the aftermath of Timur's invasion of 1398. But in 1451, the new **Afghan Lodi dynasty** reasserted the sultanate's former dominance in the region, which lasted until it was ousted by the Mughal Babur in 1526.

In Europe, Florentine goldsmith **Lorenzo Ghiberti** completed his second set of bronze doors for the Baptistry in Florence in 1452.

> ## ❝ NO ART, HOWEVER MINOR, DEMANDS LESS THAN TOTAL DEDICATION. ❞

Leon Battista Alberti, Italian polymath (1404–72)

Muslim coastal settlements, the Mutapa Empire remained the dominant regional power for more than a century, when repeated Portuguese attempts to infiltrate it finally succeeded (see 1629).

On the Indian subcontinent, the **Delhi sultanate** had fractured

The first door, begun in 1403, took him 21 years; the second, 27 years. In the same year, **Leon Battista Alberti** published *De Re Aedificatoria*, (*Ten Books of Architecture*). Both works were masterpieces in their fields and exemplified the self-confidence and intellectual daring of the Florentine Renaissance.

Mosque pavilion in Mehrauli
The remains of a mosque in Mehrauli, Delhi, built during the reign of the Lodi dynasty (1451–1526), who were the last rulers of the Delhi sultanate.

English defeat at Castillon
The Battle of Castillon decisively ended the hopes of England's French Plantagenet kings to pursue their claim to the French throne.

THE HUNDRED YEARS' WAR, a grimly drawn-out period of Anglo–French conflict (see 1411–15), ended with absolute French triumph in 1453. Any hopes England's French Plantagenet kings had of asserting their rights to the French throne came to a final halt at **Castillon** outside Bordeaux. Two years earlier, Bordeaux, which had been in English hands for 300 years, had fallen to the French. This prompted a last, desperate attempt by the English to reassert themselves against the forces of the French king, Charles VII, which were massing in strength in the southwest of

France. **Bordeaux was recaptured** by the English, but an attempt in July to relieve the English stronghold of Castillon, which was besieged by a large French force, was a calamitous failure. In the first major European conflict to be decided by artillery, the English lost 4,000 men; the French, scarcely 100. Three months later, in October, Bordeaux itself fell again to the French. This brought to an **end the Hundred Years' War** and left **Calais** on the Channel coast as the only remaining English possession in France. For the English, defeat provoked the first of a series of descents into madness by the country's hapless king, Henry VI. For the French, victory brought closer the goal of a properly united kingdom under a single monarch.

In **Western Asia** and on the borders of Christendom, **Constantinople**, capital of the beleaguered **Byzantine Empire**, remained the center of Orthodox Christian civilization. But it faced an imminent threat from the Muslim Ottoman Empire. This threat materialized when the **Ottoman sultan, Mehmed II** ("The Conqueror"), who believed that only relentless conquest would guarantee continued Ottoman supremacy, mustered an army of 80,000 to attack Constantinople; the defenders of the city could call on fewer than 7,000 troops. In addition, Mehmed had the most formidable artillery in the world. The ancient, crumbling walls of the city were

1:12
Siege of Constantinople
Mehmed led 80,000 men against only 7,000 defenders during the siege of Constantinople, a disparity that made the city's fall almost inevitable.

no match for destructive force on this scale, and the city fell to the Ottomans in May 1453.

Conscious of their destiny as world conquerors in need of a suitably imposing capital, the Ottomans were careful to preserve the city after they had taken it: they needed it as a symbol of their own, newly gained grandeur. Its imposing Christian buildings were pressed into service for Muslim worship, and the city itself remained a symbol of **Ottoman military might** for more than 450 years. The Ottoman conquest of Constantinople—now renamed Istanbul—was the clearest possible signal that the Turkish Ottomans were the most dynamic military and political force in the region, and that they were an unmistakable threat, not only to what remained of Christian claims in Western Asia but also to Europe as a whole.

A Turkish miniature painting showing Mehmed II's forces attacking Belgrade, which they tried unsuccessfully to take from Hungary in 1456.

> ## **"IT IS A PRESS,** CERTAINLY, BUT A PRESS **FROM WHICH SHALL FLOW** IN **INEXHAUSTIBLE STREAMS…THROUGH** IT, GOD WILL **SPREAD HIS WORD. "**

Johannes Gutenberg, German inventor and printer (c. 1398–1468)

THE COMPETING AMBITIONS OF ITALY'S CITY-STATES, which had led to almost a century of war, was ended by the **Treaty of Lodi** in 1454. Milan, Venice, Florence, the Papal States, and Naples were the signatories. The treaty had been given additional impetus by the fall of Constantinople to the Ottomans a year earlier, when it became clear there was a need to present a united Christian front.

In 1454 or 1455, **Johannes Gutenberg** produced the first major book to be printed with a movable type **printing press**: the Gutenberg Bible. His method of printing meant that thousands of copies of books could be made relatively easily. The result was an explosion in the **spread of ideas and knowledge**, above all because works appeared in vernacular languages rather than exclusively in Latin and Greek.

In England, on May 22, 1455, armies belonging to the Duke of Somerset and Duke of York clashed in the Battle of St. Albans, the opening conflict of the **Wars of the Roses.** These were a series of civil wars between the **rival Plantagenet houses** of York and Lancaster, both of which had claims to the throne. **Henry VI**, a Lancastrian, was on the throne at the outbreak of the wars, but with the victory and accession of **Edward IV** in 1461, the conflict

King Henry VI
This anonymous portrait is of King Henry VI, reputedly a peaceful, pious man who suffered from prolonged bouts of severe mental illness.

seemed to have been won by the Yorkists. The wars continued until 1485, when Henry Tudor seized the throne (see 1483–85).

By the mid-15th century, **Prussia** (conquered by the Teutonic Knights two centuries earlier) had become resentful of its lowly status within the Baltic territories of the Teutonic Order. In 1454 the Prussian Estates revolted, and asked for Polish military support, beginning what was to become the **Thirteen Years' War** against the Teutonic Knights. The war ended in 1466 with the division of Prussia into two territories: one in the east still controlled by the Order, and so-called Royal Prussia, now a vassal state of the kings of Poland.

Gutenberg Bible
Johannes Gutenberg produced only 180 copies of his Gutenberg Bible, but it marked the start of the age of the printed book.

OTTOMAN EXPANSION CONTINUED IN THE BALKANS AND GREECE as Mehmed II pressed ahead in his determination to conquer the world for Islam. Mehmed attempted to take **Belgrade** in 1456 but was repulsed by Hungary. However, by 1459 the rest of **Serbia** was under Ottoman control. Simultaneously, the Ottomans conquered the Peloponnese in southern Greece, with Athens falling in 1456. Over the next two decades, Ottoman control of the Balkans was consolidated with the conquest of **Bosnia** and **Herzegovina**, and in the Aegean, remaining Christian-held islands—which were chiefly Venetian and Genoan—were clearly under threat.

In 1458, **Matthias Corvinus**, second son of Janos Hunyadi, the man who had led the successful defence of Belgrade against Mehmed II's Ottoman troops in 1456, was elected **king of Hungary.** His reign promised much: not only to draw the Hungarians into the wider European Renaissance, but also to increase the reach and prestige of his country.

Corvinus was permanently distracted by the need to defend Hungary against further Ottoman incursions, but he had **territorial ambitions** to the west. He was successful in substantially expanding Hungarian territory at the expense of **Bohemia**, against whose Hussite ruler, George of Podebrady (r. 1458–71), he obtained papal sanction in 1468 to lead a crusade. During the crusade, Corvinus gained control of **Moravia**, **Silesia**, and **Lusatia**. However, in the longer run his actions destabilized both Hungary and Bohemia, and brought him into conflict with the Holy Roman Emperor, Frederick III. His actions also sparked suspicion among Hungary's nobles, who feared that their own positions would be undermined.

Despite these initial territorial gains engineered by Corvinus, the net result was that most of Hungary fell victim to **Ottoman conquest** in 1526, and Bohemia and the remaining part of Hungary came under direct **Habsburg control**.

April 9, 1454 Treaty of Lodi signed in Lombardy, Italy

February 18, 1455 Italian painter Fra Angelico (b. 1395) **dies**

December 1, 1455 Florentine goldsmith **Lorenzo Ghiberti** (b. 1378) **dies**

July 21–22, 1456 Hungary defeats Ottomans at Battle of Belgrade

January 20, 1458 Matthias Corvinus becomes king of **Hungary** at age of 14

1458 Ottomans take Athens

1454 Thirteen Years' War begins between Poland and Teutonic Order

1454/55 German printer Johannes Gutenberg publishes the **Gutenberg Bible**

April 8, 1455 Calixtus III becomes pope, succeeding Nicholas V

May 22, 1455 Rival claimants to English throne clash in **Battle of St. Albans**, starting the Wars of the Roses

August 20, 1456 Vlad III ("the Impaler") becomes **King of Romania**; his brutality gives rise to the legend of Dracula

1459 Ottomans annex Serbia

167

Czar Ivan III, "Ivan the Great," declared Moscow free of Tartar domination by tearing up the deed (money demand) of Tartar Khan.

Malbork Castle was the headquarters of the Teutonic Knights. It was Europe's largest medieval brick castle and is in what is now Poland.

APTLY NAMED "THE UNIVERSAL SPIDER" Louis XI acceded the French throne in July 1461, marking a critical point in the evolution of the French state. The medieval monarchs of France, whatever their nominal power, were **heavily limited in their influence**. They exercised direct rule over only a limited area, chiefly in the north and center, with the rest of the country controlled by a series of mostly hostile magnates, of whom the **Duke of Burgundy** (Charles the Bold) in 1461 was the most obviously threatening (see 1472–76). By the end of the

Louis XI
Crowned king of France in 1461, Louis XI extended his rule over an increasing number of territories during his 22-year reign.

Hundred Years' War in 1453, France was effectively also bankrupt. Yet by 1481, Louis had not only seen off the last of the dukes of Burgundy, bringing **Artois, Picardy, and Burgundy** itself under his rule, but by a combination of inheritance and clever diplomacy had added **Roussillon, Cerdagne, Maine, Provence, and Anjou**. This extension of centralizing **royal authority** was a crucial step in the subsequent emergence of a unified, much more powerful French state. In reality, relations between the French monarchy and its most powerful subjects would remain fraught well into the 17th century. As elsewhere, it proved necessary both to assert authority and to negotiate with provincial and noble elites. This dual process, central to the making of **early modern France**, led to friction and tension long after the reign of Louis XI.

Expansion on an even more dramatic scale also marked developments in **Muscovy**—the Grand Duchy of Moscow—with the accession of **Ivan III "the Great"** in **March 1462**. The collapse of Mongol rule over the 14th and 15th centuries, and the fall of **Constantinople** (now Istanbul) in 1453, had opened the way for Muscovy not merely to assert leadership of the Orthodox world, but to defy any last Mongol attempts at overlordship. In the process, it sparked a burst of expansion that characterized **Russia** well into the 19th century.

The most notable of these

extensions under Ivan was in the vast **Novgorod Territory**, which, although sparsely populated, economically marginal, and imperfectly known, was rich in natural resources. In 1478, Ivan simply annexed it.

However much it may have increased the stability and prosperity of China, the **Ming dynasty** faced a series of substantial internal threats to its authority as well as continuing conflict with the **Mongols** to the north. If most revolts were the product of famine, a number were also the result of the increasingly autocratic and rigid nature of **Ming rule**. In every case, they were harshly suppressed. In 1464, the same year that the 16-year-old **Emperor Chenghua** came to the throne, such a revolt broke out among the native **Miao and Yao people** in the provinces of Huguang and then Guangxi in south-central China. The revolt took two years to put down. In addition to the **160,000 troops** stationed in the south, a further 30,000 were sent to the two provinces. No accurate estimate of the death toll is possible. The revolt flared up again in 1467 and, on a larger scale, in 1475.

THE THIRTEEN YEARS' WAR between Poland–Lithuania and the **Teutonic Knights**—a military order founded in Palestine—ended with the **Second Treaty of Torun** in 1466. The Teutonic Knights, powerful since the early 13th century (see 1236–40), were

The underlying political fragility of **Japan** and the relative impotence of the **Ashikaga shoguns**, rulers of Japan since 1333, was made starkly clear by the **11-year Onin War**, which broke out in 1467. It left Japan devastated and led to more than

> ## THE CAPITAL THAT WE BELIEVED WOULD FLOURISH FOR TEN THOUSAND YEARS HAS NOW BECOME A LAIR FOR THE WOLVES.

Onin Ki, late 15th–mid 16th century account of the Onin War

obliged to cede much of the western half of their territory to **Prussia**, and, in return for Polish–Lithuanian aid in the war, this territory became the property of the Polish crown.

Samurai sword
This 15th-century katana, with its scabbard, is typical of those used in the Onin war. It could deliver a sweeping cut in a single movement.

a century of turbulence—the *Sengoku jidai* or **Warring States Period**—as a series of regional magnates or *daimyo* attempted to eradicate their rivals. The war began as a succession dispute over who would replace the elderly and retiring **Ashikaga Yoshimasa** as shogun, the Hosokawa clan supporting the claims of Yoshimasa's brother, the Yamana clan those of his

silk binding covers handle

scabbard

> ## THE **LANDLOCKED SEA** IS GREEK OR **ROMAN**, THE **BOUNDLESS SEA** IS **PORTUGUESE.**

Fernando Pessoa, Portuguese poet and writer, 1885–1935

Castile and Aragon
The two kingdoms of Aragon and Castile became a composite monarchy through the marriage of Ferdinand and Isabella in 1469.

infant son. In the process, not only was **Kyoto**, the imperial capital, **entirely destroyed**, but the Hosokawa and Yamana themselves became victims of the conflict, their power and status swept away as the increasingly brutal fighting continued.

The marriage in 1469 of **Isabella**, heir to the **Castilian throne** (which she inherited in 1474), and **Ferdinand**, heir to the throne of **Aragon** (which he inherited in 1479), led directly to the emergence of a **unified, unbendingly Christian Spain**. This resulted in the development of Spain as the most powerful

tempered point

state in early 16th-century Europe. Isabella was 17 years old when she married Ferdinand. In choosing to marry him, she risked the wrath of her older half-brother Henry IV, who perceived her as a threat to his own power. But the marriage, in the Spanish city of Valladolid, was the beginning of an important phase of Spanish history. Within eight years, Ferdinand and Isabella—*Los Reyes Católicos*, the Catholic Monarchs—were jointly ruling Castile and Aragon, although the kingdoms were not formally unified. Administratively, politically, and financially, they remained separate and, as such, were consistently bedeviled by competing priorities and rivalries.

Even at the height of Spanish power in the 16th and early 17th centuries, no Spanish monarch was able to resolve the problem satisfactorily. Nonetheless, Spain's potential to emerge as the dominant force in Renaissance Europe was unmistakable under Ferdinand and Isabella. It was a position that the tirelessly hard-headed Isabella and the politically astute Ferdinand were well placed to exploit.

BY ABOUT 1470, PORTUGUESE exploration of the **west coast of Africa** had reached as far as modern-day Sierra Leone. It had been a hesitant process, limited by ship types, principally galleys and cogs, that were unsuited to long-range exploration. Its goals were uncertain beyond a general hope to trace the **trans-Saharan gold trade** to its source and to exploit the **West African slave trade**. The death in 1460 of **Prince Henry, "the Navigator,"** the early champion of Portuguese exploration (see 1434), had made further progress unlikely. However, in 1469 Portuguese **king Afonso V** agreed—in exchange for an annual fee—to allow a Lisbon merchant, **Fernão Gomes**, to continue to push Portuguese efforts south along the West African coast. The results were spectacular. Within five years Gomes had explored a further

Inca ruler
This 18th-century painting shows Tupac Yupanqui (Topa Inca), the fifth Inca of the Hanan dynasty.

2,500
MILES
THE **EXTENT** OF THE **INCA EMPIRE**

2,000 miles (3,200 km) of coastline. Not only was Portugal able to lay claim to a series of what would prove immensely **lucrative trading stations** (see 1480–82) on the West African coast, Gomes also opened the way to the Portuguese penetration of the South Atlantic.

The **Inca Empire**, more short-lived even than its Aztec neighbor to the north, was formed in a surge of conquest after 1438 from its **Andean heartlands** in central Peru. **Tupac Yupanqui (Topa Inca), who came to the Inca throne in 1471**, had been made **head of the Inca armies** in 1463 and had already substantially enlarged Inca control to the north, well into modern-day Ecuador. The empire extended about 2,500 miles

Portuguese explorers
Fernão Gomes (right) continued the age of exploration begun by Henry the Navigator (left) as depicted in the Monument to the Discoveries, Lisbon.

(4,000 km). Topa Inca's principal contribution to **Inca expansion** came with his conquest from about 1470 of the Peruvian kingdom of **Chimor**.

In southeast Asia, the kingdom of **Champa** (in modern-day Vietnam) had existed since the 7th century. But in **1471 it was effectively destroyed** by Viet troops who laid waste the Champa capital, Vijaya. What remained of the kingdom would henceforth be a vassal state of the Vietnamese.

October 19, 1469 Marriage of Ferdinand and Isabella unites **Castile and Aragon**

1469 Lorenzo de' Medici takes control of **Florence**, beginning a period rich in culture and intellectual thought

October 30, 1470 Henry VI regains throne of England (to 1471)

1470 Inca conquest of **Chimor kingdom**

1471 Portuguese gain **Tangier** and reach **Gulf of Guinea**

1471 Beginning of reign of **Tupac Yupanqui** (to 1493)

1469 Axayacatl assumes control of **Aztec empire** (to 1481)

1470 Ottomans recapture **Negroponte** from Venice

1470 Portuguese begin trading on **Gold Coast**

1470 First **French printing press** established at Sorbonne, Paris

April 11, 1471 Henry VI of England deposed for second time. **Edward IV** regains throne

1471 Collapse of Kingdom of **Champa** (present-day Vietnam)

A carving of the central Aztec deity Quetzalcoatl in Teotihuacán located near present-day Mexico City.

FOLLOWING THE OTTOMAN CONQUEST of Constantinople in 1453, its conqueror, **Mehmed II**, set out not merely to extend Ottoman rule in the Balkans, but also to reassert it in Anatolia, where Ottoman strength had been significantly reduced in the wake of Timur's early 15th-century invasion (see 1401–03). It was now most obviously opposed in the region by a Turcoman people, the **White Sheep Turcomans,** under the rule of **Uzun Hasan**. They had been actively, if not particularly successfully, wooed by various

Expansion of Burgundy
This map shows the territories held by Charles the Bold, who pursued an aggressive expansionist policy. The duchies of Bar and Lorraine gave Charles an almost continuous stretch of land by 1475.

KEY

■ Territories held 1467

▨ Territories added by 1475

— Border of Holy Roman Empire

Christian powers, notably Venice, in an attempt to enlist them in Christian struggles against Ottoman expansion. The result of Uzun Hasan's efforts was a comprehensive defeat in 1473 at the **Battle of Otlukbeli**, the light cavalry of the Turcoman forces swept aside by the Ottomans' overwhelming firepower.

By the mid-1470s, the territories of Burgundy were at their height. Their heartlands were the **Duchy and County of Burgundy**, awarded to the first duke of Burgundy, Philip the Bold, brother of King **Charles V of France**, in 1363. In 1369, with his marriage to Margaret, the countess of Flanders, Philip also acquired **Flanders and Artois**—in effect a significant portion of modern-day **Belgium**. To this constellation of territories, Philip's grandson, **Philip the Good**, then added parts of northeast France and much of modern Holland. These holdings, however imposing, were still far from

Ottoman drums
The Janissaries of the Ottoman army parade with the drums that were used to urge the soldiers into battle.

being a single, continuous territory. Furthermore, as many of them were within the **Holy Roman Empire**, these were at least theoretically subject to the Holy Roman Emperor, just as Burgundy's French lands were nominally subject to the king of France. But their size and, crucially, the fact that they held many of the richest of the burgeoning trading centres of the **Low Countries** made the Burgundians a formidable power. Philip the Good's heir, **Charles the Bold,** inherited this state within states in 1467 and determined not just to make it a continuous territory—which by 1472 he had succeeded in doing through an audacious combination of purchase and

conquest—but to assert its independence as a separate kingdom. The Burgundians were inevitably opposed by the infinitely more calculating French king, Louis XI. In little more than four months in 1476, they suffered two calamitous defeats by **Swiss mercenary armies** in the pay of Louis—at Grandson and at Morat in modern northwest Switzerland.

The rigidly hierarchical **Aztec Empire** (1428–1521) became a formidable military force, imposing itself with brutal finality on its neighbors in **central Mexico** from **Tenochtitlan**, its capital. **Axayacatl**, who came to the Aztec throne in 1469, added substantially to the empire, mainly with the conquest of the state of **Tlatelolco in 1473**.

IN JANUARY 1477, CHARLES THE BOLD'S Burgundian forces confronted the Swiss again, at **Nancy** in Lorraine. They were comprehensively routed and the body of the duke was discovered face down in a frozen pond. While **Louis XI** (see 1461) seized the Burgundians' French territories, those in the Low Countries passed to the Habsburgs with the marriage of Charles's only child, Margaret, to the future Holy Roman Emperor, Maximilian I.

William Caxton (c. 1420–92) was an English merchant whose continental travels introduced him to printing. He established the **first printing press in England in 1476**, printing the first book a year later. He published 87 books, many also translated by him.

Caxton's printing press
The first printing press in England, established by William Caxton in Westminster, London, produced its first book in 1477.

1472 Portuguese discover island of Fernando Po off West African coast

1472 First publication of the Etymologies of Bishop Isidore of Seville, first Christian encyclopedia

August 11, 1473 Ottomans defeat Turkomans at Battle of Otlukbeli

1474 Austrian Habsburgs forced to recognize independence of Swiss League

1474 Treaty of Utrecht grants Hanseatic League major trading advantages in England

March 2, 1476 Swiss defeat Burgundians at Grandson, Switzerland

June 22, 1476 Swiss defeat Burgundians at Morat, Switzerland

January 5, 1477 Burgundians defeated at Battle of Nancy; death of Charles the Bold (b. 1433)

1473 Aztecs defeat and annex **Tlatelolco**

1473 Venetians destroy **Smyrna** and take **Cyprus**

1474 Territories of **Novgorod** incorporated into the Grand Duchy of Muscovy

1475 Burgundian expansion at its height under **Charles the Bold**

1476 Incas conquer south coast of **Peru**

1477 Louis XI of France initiates Royal Postal Service to speed royal communications

The Battle of Nancy was the final and decisive Burgundian War, which left thousands dead, including the Duke of Burgundy, Charles the Bold.

Built in 1482 as São Jorge da Mina, Elmina Castle was one of the first Portuguese trading forts on the west coast of Africa (now Ghana).

> **IT IS NOT NECESSARY TO HOPE IN ORDER TO UNDERTAKE, NOR TO SUCCEED IN ORDER TO PERSEVERE.**

Charles the Bold, Duke of Burgundy (1433–77)

The Ottomans continued their expansion with the **Treaty of Constantinople** of 1479, which ended the intermittent Ottoman–Venetian war that had begun in 1463. It confirmed the **Ottomans as a naval power** of growing importance. It also brought with it Ottoman control of the Greek island **Negroponte (Euobea)** and of Lemnos in the north Aegean. **Venice** remained a major power in much of the region but it was anxious not to jeopardize its lucrative Ottoman trading links.

The accession of **Isabella I** to the throne of Castile in 1474 was challenged by her step-niece,

Joan, wife of King Afonso V of Portugal, in part to disrupt Castilian claims in the exploration of the West African coast. At its heart was a dispute as to which country could lay claim to the Atlantic island groups—the Canaries, the Azores, and Madeira—successively colonized by Spain and Portugal since the early 15th century. The outcome was the 1479 **Treaty of Alcáçovas**, confirming Castile's claims to the Canaries and Portugal's claims to the Azores and Madeira, and Portuguese rights in West Africa.

BY ABOUT 1440, **THREE SEPARATE MOSSI KINGDOMS** had become established in West Africa, roughly in present-day Burkina Faso. These were Tengkodogo, Yatenga, and Wogodogo. Making use of formidable cavalry, from about 1480 they exploited the **gradual decline of Mali** in the face of **Songhay expansion** by raiding deep into Mali territories. They would remain an important presence until colonization by France some 400 years later.

The year 1482 saw two crucial developments in the continuing **Portuguese exploration** and settlement of **West Africa**. The first was the construction of **São Jorge da Mina**, now called Elmina Castle, on what was later known as the **Gold Coast** and is today **Ghana**. It was a strongly fortified trading post, built on royal authority and the first permanent European settlement in sub-Saharan Africa, designed to secure a Portuguese monopoly of the **West African gold trade**. It proved immensely lucrative. By the early 16th century, 1,500 lb (680 kg) of gold a year were passing through Elmina.

The second development was a further series of voyages, led by **Diogo Cão**, southward along the West African coast. The voyages were sponsored by the new king of Portugal, **John II, who came to the throne in 1481** and who committed his country to a deliberately aggressive policy of Portuguese expansion. On **Cão's first voyage**, in 1482, he reached—and claimed for Portugal—the mouth of the Congo. On his second voyage, in 1484–86, he penetrated almost a farther **1,000 miles (1,600 km) south** to Walvis Bay (now in Namibia), once again imperiously claiming the coast in the name of

Cão's cross
Portuguese explorer Diogo Cão marked his discoveries of the west coast of Africa with a series of imposing stone crosses.

the **Portuguese throne**. Both voyages were epics of tenacity, made in the face of consistently unfavorable winds and currents. This was a discouraging discovery. Where sailing conditions around **West Africa to the Gulf of Guinea** were generally benign, aided by northeast trade winds and the Guinea Current, to the south they were much more arduous. Cão's achievement was impressive, but it emphasized that if a practical route existed to the Indian Ocean and the East, it would be left to later Portuguese navigators—notably **Bartolomeu Dias** in 1487—to pioneer the new route, deep into the **South Atlantic**.

87
THE NUMBER OF BOOKS PUBLISHED BY CAXTON'S PRESS

THE SPANISH INQUISITION

Founded by Ferdinand and Isabella in 1478, the goal of the Inquisition was to impose an overarching Christian Catholic identity on all Spanish territories. Tribunals were held in which heretics—which at this time meant Jews and those who had converted to Christianity from Judaism—were punished and expelled. After the fall of Granada in 1492, it was also applied to Muslims. The Inquisition was finally disbanded in 1820.

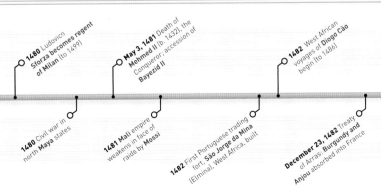

1477 William Caxton publishes first book from London printing press

January 4, 1478 City of Novgorod, surrenders to Ivan III

November 1, 1478 Spanish Inquisition founded

January 25, 1479 Peace of Constantinople: Venice cedes Lemnos and coastal Albania to Ottomans

September 4, 1479 Treaty of Alcáçovas confirms Portuguese and Castile claims in West Africa and the Atlantic island groups

1480 Ludovico Sforza becomes regent of Milan (to 1499)

1480 Civil war in north Maya states

May 3, 1481 Death of Mehmed II (b. 1432), the Conqueror; accession of Bayezid II

1481 Mali empire weakens in face of raids by Mossi

1482 West African voyages of Diogo Cão begin (to 1486)

1482 First Portuguese trading fort, São Jorge da Mina (Elmina), West Africa, built

December 23, 1482 Treaty of Arras; Burgundy and Anjou absorbed into France

VOYAGES OF EXPLORATION

SETTING SAIL AROUND THE GLOBE IN THE AGE OF DICOVERY

Christopher Columbus's voyage across the Atlantic in 1492 sparked an unprecedented opening-up of the world—first by the Portuguese and Spanish, then by the Dutch, English, and French. By 1700, European explorers and colonizers had established themselves globally.

European explorers were motivated by glory, Christian zeal, and—above all—gold, spices, and slaves. The goal was the East, source of legendary riches. With overland routes blocked by Muslim states, maritime routes offered the prospect of outflanking them. By 1488, the Portuguese had rounded southern Africa. Ten years later they reached India and, by 1512, the Spice Islands. There, they were later challenged by the Dutch.

The Spanish went west. Theirs was a more dramatic discovery: an unknown world, America. By the 1550s, they had conquered two empires—the Aztecs and the Incas—and created a huge New World empire. By 1522, they had also completed the first circumnavigation of the globe. English and French efforts were directed initially at finding a way around North America. Though futile, this paved the way for two further European empires there.

> ## " I AND MY COMPANIONS SUFFER FROM A **DISEASE** OF THE **HEART** WHICH CAN BE **CURED** ONLY BY **GOLD.** "

Hernán Cortés, Spanish explorer, on his quest to defeat the Aztecs, 1519

Major European voyages
This map shows the date and routes taken by the first European voyages of discovery and exploration: the earliest Christopher Columbus in 1492, through to Francis Drake in 1577–80. Ships sailed for months at a time to cross the vast oceans, often with crude systems for navigation.

1:13

Survival ratio of Magellan's circumnavigation
Magellan left Spain in September 1519 with 237 men. Just 18 men made it back three years later. Magellan himself was killed in the Philippines, in April 1521.

5
SHIPS IN 1519

1
SHIP IN 1522

Ships commanded by Magellan
Five ships set sail on Magellan's cicumnavigation. Two were wrecked, one abandoned, and one deserted. Only Victoria returned.

ASIA
RICE, BANANAS, YAMS, AND SUGARCANE

AMERICA
CORN, POTATOES, TOMATOES, AND CHILI PEPPERS

EUROPE
HORSES, CATTLE, PIGS AND WHEAT

AFRICA

25 MILLION
CENTRAL AMERICA 1519

population in millions 1565
2.5

ESTIMATED NATIVE POPULATION OF CENTRAL AMERICA

11 MILLION
PERU 1519

population in millions 1565
1.5

ESTIMATED NATIVE POPULATION OF PERU

Effect on populations
The Spanish conquests had a devastating impact on native populations. African slaves were taken over to replace them.

Biological exchange
New foods—and new diseases—passed between Europe and the New World as a direct result of the voyages of discovery. The results were at times beneficial; at others, fatal.

COST AND IMPACT

European maritime exploration was made possible by better ship types and navigation. But journeys were still arduous, and many ships simply disappeared. The fate of Magellan's fleet in 1519–22 reflected these risks.

Relations with native peoples also proved fraught and almost invariably ended violently. Europeans generally saw natives as a resource to be exploited and Christianized. But the startling death tolls in the New World were more the result of the dislocation of settled ways of life and of imported European diseases than of deliberate policy. The sudden intermingling of previously separate worlds had a dramatic impact in both directions, with crops and animal types introduced to new environments.

ASIA

JAPAN
Nagasaki

Macao *Philippine Islands*

Loaisa 1526

PACIFI

Moluccas
New Guinea

Magellan 1519–21

AUSTRALIA

ARCTIC OCEAN

Spitsbergen

Novaya
Zemlya

Barents 1596–97

Willoughby 1553

Greenland

Baffin Island

Iceland

Archangel

Frobisher 1576

ENGLAND

Labrador

Panama

NETHERLANDS

Cabot 1497

EUROPE

ASIA

JAPAN

Corte-Real 1500

Hochelaga
(Montreal)

Cartier 1534–36

SPAIN FRANCE

Nagasaki

NORTH
AMERICA

Azores

PORTUGAL

MING
CHINA

Macao

Philippine
Islands

ATLANTIC
OCEAN

Canary
Islands

Goa

INDIA

Hainan

e 1577–80

Magellan 1519–21

ANNAM

Bahamas

Cuba

Columbus 1492

AFRICA

Calicut

Malacca

Magellan 1519–21

Loaisa 1526

Acapulco

Columbus 1502–04

Cabral
1500

da Gama
1497–98

Pires 1515–16

Drake 1577–80

CEAN

Panama

Cape Tiburón

Cape Sierra Leone

Mogadishu

Sumatra

Borneo

Moluccas

New Guinea

Loaisa 1526

SOUTH
AMERICA

Lima

Magellan 1519–21

Drake 1577–80

Malindi

Kilwa

INDIAN
OCEAN

de Abreu
1511

Java

da Gama 1497–98

Loaisa 1526

Cabral 1500

Sofala

Madagascar

Drake 1577–80

del Cano
(after death of Magellan) 1521–22

AUSTRALIA

Isla de Chiloé

Cape of Good Hope

Puerto San Julián

SOUTHERN OCEAN

Strait of Magellan

Cape Horn

KEY
→ Spanish expeditions
→ Portuguese expeditions
→ English expeditions
→ French expeditions
→ Dutch expeditions

NORTH
AMERICA

EUROPE

ASIA

PACIFIC
OCEAN

ATLANTIC
OCEAN

AFRICA

INDIAN
OCEAN

SOUTH
AMERICA

PACIFIC
OCEAN

AUSTRALIA

SOUTHERN OCEAN

NORTH
AMERICA

EUROPE

ASIA

PACIFIC
OCEAN

ATLANTIC
OCEAN

AFRICA

INDIAN
OCEAN

PACIFIC
OCEAN

SOUTH
AMERICA

AUSTRALIA

SOUTHERN OCEAN

1600 Spain took the lead in exploring and claiming new lands, especially in Central and South America. By 1600, Spain also had claims on the Philippine Islands. Portugal claimed only a handful of coastal trading posts in Africa, India, and the Spice Islands, along with a strip of Brazilian coast.

KEY
◇ Spain and possessions
◇ Portugal and possessions
England and possessions
Denmark and possessions
Dutch (United Provinces) possessions

1800 European expansion continued in the 17th and 18th centuries, with massive areas of the world claimed by Europe by 1800. Britain, in particular, despite losing its American colonies, was gaining ground—in Canada, in southern Africa, and above all, in India.

KEY
◇ Britain and possessions
France and possessions
Denmark and possessions
◇ Spain and possessions
Portugal and possessions
The Netherlands and possessions

Most of what remains of the Great Wall of China was rebuilt during the Ming dynasty.
Dotted with fortifications it extends over 4,000 miles (6,400 km).

IN 1483, THE WARS OF THE ROSES flared up again (see 1454–55). Fought between Lancastrians and Yorkists—rival **Plantagenet** claimants to the English throne—it had appeared to have been settled for good in 1471. In 1470, the **Yorkist Edward IV**, who had seized the throne from the hapless **Lancastrian Henry VI** in 1461, had been forced from it by a group of vengeful magnates. In 1471, with **Burgundian support** from Charles the Bold (see 1472–76), Edward retook the throne. Henry was murdered, probably on Edward's orders.

In 1483, Edward, now grossly corpulent, died. Instantly, the conflict reignited, albeit in a different form. The problem was that the new king, **Edward V**, was only 12 years old and his mother's family, the **Woodvilles**, saw the boy-king as an obvious opportunity to proclaim themselves regents—in effect, to seize the throne themselves, undoing Edward IV's legacy. This at least was the view of the dead king's most consistent champion, his brother the **Duke of Gloucester**, who was competent, intelligent, and loyal. Gloucester characteristically preempted the Woodvilles by seizing the throne himself, as **Richard III**, executing the leading Woodvilles, and **imprisoning Edward V** with his younger brother in the **Tower of London** where both were then murdered. If no definitive proof has ever been offered that Richard III was responsible for the deaths of his nephews, the overwhelming

THE RENAISSANCE

The Renaissance (literally "rebirth") grew out of the Italian Middle Ages and marked a reevaluation of European thought. At its heart was a reinterpretation of Europe's Classical past. It gave rise, first in Florence (left), to an artistic and architectural revolution, and later, to a scientific one. Its early impact was fitful but eventually spread to most of Europe in the following 200 years.

probability is that **he ordered their killings**; his hold on the throne was too shaky to permit any rivals to survive if he could eliminate them. Richard III was vilified in later Tudor propaganda. But given the turbulent treachery of late-medieval England, Richard's actions seem fairly rational. Sooner or later the Woodvilles would have sought an excuse for his death.

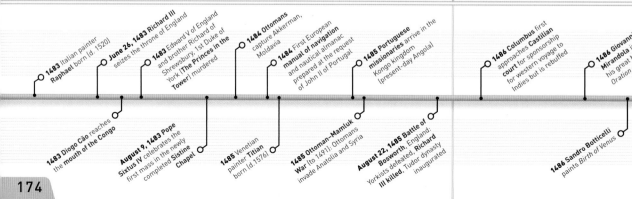

5:8 **Battle of Bosworth**
Henry's Tudor army of 5,000 troops overcame Richard III's much larger force, which was undermined by poor leadership.

But there was a further **Lancastrian claimant, Henry Tudor** (1457–1509). His right to the throne was tenuous at best, but critically he had the support of the French king, **Charles VIII** (r. 1483–98). In August 1485, Henry led an invasion from France. By the end of the month, Richard was dead, killed at the **Battle of Bosworth**, his superiority in numbers undone by the ineptitude of many of his commanders. Henry Tudor, in turn, crowned on the field of the battle, had become **Henry VII**. The Tudor monarch's seizure of the throne might easily have provoked yet another round in this destabilizing infighting. But Henry VII would prove among the most pragmatic, capable, and far-sighted of kings. Under the Tudors, England was significantly strengthened, its magnates tamed, and its government comprehensively overhauled.

FOLLOWING ON FROM EARLIER PORTUGUESE VOYAGES (see 1470–71), two further expeditions were despatched in 1487 to investigate routes to and across the Indian Ocean. **Pêro da Covilhã** was charged with investigating the East African coast as well as the Indian Ocean. From Aden, reached via the Red Sea, he sailed to Calicut in India, as far south as Sofala in **East Africa,** and north to the Strait of Hormuz in the Persian

Gulf, reporting favorably on all these routes in 1492. The second expedition, under **Bartolomeu Dias**, was specifically charged with finding a navigable passage around the presumed southern tip of Africa. In January 1488, rather than simply following the African coast southward as Cão and others before him had done, at around 27°S (several hundred miles short of the tip of south Africa) he headed southwest, away from the coast. By any measure, that was remarkably daring. Miles from land, he picked up the westerlies that blow in the South Atlantic and was carried almost 300 miles (500 km) to the east of the **Cape of Good Hope** on the tip of southern Africa. Dias's voyage provided a better understanding of the wind systems that linked the Atlantic and Indian oceans, and proved vital in calculating the route to the Cape of Good Hope and beyond. Later, **Vasco da Gama** and **Pedro Cabral** exploited this knowledge in their own voyages.

Human sacrifice is a feature common to many early societies.

20,000
THE ESTIMATED NUMBER OF PEOPLE SACRIFICED AT THE INAUGURATION OF THE TENOCHTITLAN PYRAMID

1483 Italian painter Raphael born (d. 1520)

June 26, 1483 Richard III seizes the throne of England

1483 Edward V of England and brother Richard of Shrewsbury, 1st Duke of York (The Princes in the Tower) murdered

1484 Ottomans capture Akkerman, Moldavia

1484 First European manual of navigation and nautical almanac prepared at the request of John II of Portugal

1485 Portuguese missionaries arrive in the Kongo kingdom (present-day Angola)

1486 Columbus first approaches Castilian court for sponsorship for western voyage to Indies but is rebuffed

1486 Giovanni Pico della Mirandola in Florence writes his great humanist tract, Oration of the Dignity of Man

1483 Diogo Cão reaches the mouth of the Congo

August 9, 1483 Pope Sixtus IV celebrates the first mass in the newly completed Sistine Chapel

1485 Venetian painter Titian born (d. 1576)

1485 Ottoman-Mamluk War (to 1491): Ottomans invade Anatolia and Syria

August 22, 1485 Battle of Bosworth, England; Yorkists defeated, Richard III killed, Tudor dynasty inaugurated

1486 Sandro Botticelli paints Birth of Venus

February 1487 Portuguese navigator Bartolomeu Dias rounds the Cape of Good Hope

This 19th-century painting shows the Fall of Granada in 1492, which ended 780 years of Muslim rule in Spain.

None is known to have practiced it with the vigor of the **Aztecs**, however—or on the same gargantuan scale. It is estimated that the Aztecs ritually sacrificed upward of **20,000 victims a year**—slaves, enemies captured in battle, and people simply offered in tribute. The aim was to placate their gods, above all the god of war, **Huitzilopochtil**, whose daily battles with the sun could be sustained only by blood. In 1487, on the opening of the **new great temple** in the Aztec capital, **Tenochtitlán**, up to 20,000 people were ritually executed, their hearts sliced from their bodies, in a single ceremony that may have lasted anything from 4 to 20 days.

In China, the **Ming dynasty** (1368–1644) continued the ambitious rebuilding of the 4,000-mile (6,400-km) long **Great Wall**. First built in 200 BCE, the wall had presented a symbol of superiority as well as a barrier to incursions from barbarians in the north. Under the Ming, its mountainous eastern length was built mostly of brick and stone, its western, desertlike length of clay and earth, often reinforced with wood. It stood on average 25 ft (8 m) high and 18 ft (5.5 m) wide and was studded with 25,000 towers and upward of 15,000 garrisons—a monumental feat of construction.

Tenochtitlán
This mural of the 16th-century Aztec capital imagined by 20th-century Mexican artist Diego Rivera shows the city's massive scale.

Mamluk helmet
This 15th-century iron Mamluk helmet, as worn by Mamluk soldiers, is decorated with inlaid silver calligraphy.

THE OTTOMAN–MAMLUK peace treaty of May 1491 ended a war that had begun in 1485 for control of the Western Asia and Red Sea trade routes. Neither side gained much but the war exhausted the Mamluks financially, making their subsequent conquest by the Ottomans in 1516–17 inevitable.

By 1490, **Vladislas II** (1456–1516) ruled over a vast kingdom, including **Poland–Lithuania, Bohemia, and Hungary**, whose crown he accepted in 1490. Despite the size of these territories, they had little influence on Europe as a whole. Poland–Lithuania—vast, desolate, and impoverished—was on the margins of Europe. Hungary and Bohemia, although more sophisticated, remained not just separate kingdoms but uneasy rivals. The potential of these sprawling lands would never be realized.

On January 2, 1492, Spanish monarchs **Ferdinand and Isabella** (see 1469) presided over the **fall of the Kingdom of Granada**, marking the end of a 10-year campaign to claim the last Moorish territory in Iberia. It was the end of a process begun in the 8th century—the **Christian reconquest** or **reconquista**. It underlined Spain's determination to project itself as an aggressively expansionist Christian power.

In 1492, the Spanish crown finally decided to back **Christopher Columbus's** first Atlantic crossing. Columbus had made a series of extravagant claims about the reward his voyage to the Indies (Asia) would generate. Spain was anxious to match the spoils flowing to Portugal from its West African ventures. It also needed to replace the lost revenues from

"crusading" taxes, previously paid before the fall of Granada. Success depended on Columbus's undoubted navigational ability and on his insistence that Asia lay much farther to the east than conventionally believed. On his arrival in the **New World** on October 12, somewhere in the **Bahamas**, he immediately despatched emissaries to the "Chinese" court. Columbus's self-belief blinded him to the reality of what he had discovered.

> **❝ SAILED** THIS DAY **NINETEEN LEAGUES…** (COUNTED) LESS THAN THE TRUE NUMBER, THAT THE **CREW** MIGHT NOT BE **DISMAYED** IF THE **VOYAGE** SHOULD PROVE LONG. **❞**
>
> Christopher Columbus, 1492

CHRISTOPHER COLUMBUS
(c. 1451–1506)

Born in Genoa, Italy, Christopher Columbus made four transatlantic voyages believing that the riches of the East could be reached by sailing west from Spain. His first journey (1492–93) was followed by others in 1493–96, 1498–1500, and 1502–04. He was the first European to sight South America, in 1498, and charted most of the Caribbean. He died still certain he had reached Asia.

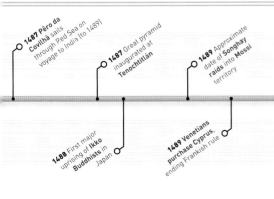

1487 Pêro da Covilhã sails through Red Sea on voyage to India (to 1489)

1487 Great pyramid inaugurated at Tenochtitlán

1489 Approximate date of Songhay raids into Mossi territory

September 18, 1490 Vladislas II, king of Bohemia, becomes king of Hungary

1491 Ottoman–Mamluk accord signed after six years of war

1492 Jews expelled from Spain by royal decree

August 3, 1492 Columbus, in search of Asia, departs Canaries and crosses Atlantic to New World

October 12, 1492 Columbus arrives in Bahamas at what he named "San Salvador"

September 25, 1493 Columbus sets sail on second voyage

1488 First major uprising of Ikko Buddhists in Japan

1489 Venetians purchase Cyprus, ending Frankish rule

1490 Mausoleum of Timur, is erected in Samarkand

1491 Brittany incorporated within France

1492 Last independent Muslim territory in Spain eliminated in conquest of Granada by Ferdinand and Isabella

August 18, 1492 Rodrigo Borgia crowned Pope Alexander VI

January 19, 1493 Charles VIII returns Cerdagne and Roussillon in the Eastern Pyrenees to Spain with the Treaty of Barcelona

1493 Muhammad Ture begins Islamification of African empire of Songhay

This map by Alberto Cantino was the first to show Portugal's discoveries in the West and East and the division between Spanish and Portuguese territories agreed upon at Tordesillas.

This 20th-century painting depicts King Manuel I of Portugal blessing Vasco da Gama and his expedition as they get ready to set sail from Lisbon.

IN 1494, POPE ALEXANDER VI drew up the **Treaty of Tordesillas**, which effectively divided up existing and future New World discoveries between **Spain and Portugal**. It drew a north–south line 370 leagues (about 1,350 miles or 2,000 km) west of the Cape Verde Islands. Land to the west was assigned to Spain; that to the east, to Portugal.

The political crisis provoked in Florence by the **death of Lorenzo ("the Magnificent") de Medici** in 1492 was expoited by a Dominican monk, **Girolamo Savonarola**, who imposed on the city a "Christian and religious republic." In 1494, he denounced tyrants and instituted the **Bonfire of the Vanities**: the destruction of idolatrous goods. He was overthrown, tortured, and executed four years later.

The **Italian Wars**, nominally sparked by the desire of Charles VIII of France (1470–98) to **assert a claim** to the kingdom of Naples, saw an intermittent **65-year struggle** between France and Spain for control of Italy. Its opening salvo, which ended in 1499, was both destructive and inconclusive. The first phase ended with the **Battle of Fornovo**, fought

LEONARDO DA VINCI
(1452–1519)

Born in Italy, Leonardo was a self-taught polymath—a painter, sculptor, inventor, and scientific enquirer—whose restless genius drove him to embrace a limitless range of projects, but to complete almost none. Among his masterpieces are *Mona Lisa* and *The Last Supper*. He died in France in the service of Francois I.

near Parma in July 1495. However, having made his triumphant way to Naples to claim its throne, Charles VIII found his former Italian allies, notably Milan, had joined forces with Venice, the papacy, and the Holy Roman Empire to oppose him in a **Holy League**, ending his dreams of Italian conquest.

By about 1496, an outbreak of what was commonly called the **French pox** (so-named as it was first recorded among French troops there) occurred in Italy. It was syphilis. By the middle of the 16th century, about **one million people** had contracted the disease—probably from a more virulent strain brought by **sailors returning from the New World**.

From about 1490, **Genoese mariner** John Cabot had lobbied Portugal and Spain to sponsor a westward voyage to Asia across the Atlantic, but was rebuffed. He turned his attentions to England, basing himself in Bristol. An early voyage failed, but in May 1497—with royal backing—he set out again. He **reached northern Newfoundland**, then sailed south along 400 miles (650 km) of coast. He returned to England certain he had reached China. The following year, he led a much larger expedition. All but one of its five ships were lost, Cabot with them. But his initial success prompted five more voyages to **Newfoundland** from 1501 to 1505, which confirmed the new discoveries were clearly not Asian. Despite these disappointments, the English ventures were important in proving the existence of a hitherto unsuspected continent—**North America**—and in staking a claim to later English primacy in its exploration and settlement.

1,000,000
THE APPROXIMATE NUMBER OF **EUROPEANS** WHO **CONTRACTED SYPHILIS** IN 50 YEARS **FROM 1496**

THE SOUTHWARD PROBING ALONG the African coast by the Portuguese in the 15th century had reached a climax when **Bartolomeu Dias** rounded the tip of Africa in 1488. In May 1498, **Vasco da Gama** consolidated this achievement when he continued into the Indian Ocean and reached

Battle of Zonchio
This woodcut depicts ships in the first battle of the Ottoman–Venetian War. It was the first time cannons had been used in a naval battle.

Calicut in southwest India. A practical **route to the East had been discovered**. Da Gama's crossing of the Indian Ocean—crisscrossed by Arab and other trade routes since the 9th century—depended on local Muslim knowledge. His route to the Indian Ocean, on the other hand, was new. Where previous Portuguese mariners had hugged the African coast, da Gama made a vast sweep **westward into the South Atlantic**. It was not only the longest ocean crossing yet made,

January 2, 1494 Christopher Columbus establishes first European colony in New World at La Isabella, **Hispaniola**

1494 Florence under religious dictatorship of **Girolamo Savonarola** (executed 1498)

1494 Philip the Fair, son of Maximilian I, becomes ruler of the **Low Countries**

1496 Ottomans invade Montenegro

June 24, 1497 Italian **John Cabot**, sponsored by Henry VII of England, reaches Newfoundland

November 22, 1497 **Vasco da Gama** rounds **Cape of Good Hope** en route to India

1498 Leonardo da Vinci completes The Last Supper

September 22, 1499 Treaty of Basle confirm independence of **Swiss Confederation**

1494 Charles VIII invades Italy, marking start of Franco-Spanish **Italian Wars** (to 1559)

June 7, 1494 Treaty of Tordesillas divides discoveries in New World between **Spain and Portugal**

July 6, 1495 Holy League defeats France at **Battle of Fornovo**, northern Italy

1497 Norway, Sweden, and Denmark **united under King John** (of Denmark)

May 20, 1499 Vasco da Gama reaches **Calicut, India**

August 12–25, 1499 Venetian fleet defeated by Ottoman navy at **Battle of Zonchio**

1499 France seizes Milan

This scene from a fresco in Chehel Stun Palace in Isfahan, Iran, depicts Safavid Emperor Shah Ismail I in battle against Uzbek warriors.

but it also initiated the route used throughout the "Age of Sail" (see pp.172–73).

The ongoing **Ottoman naval threat** to Christendom was underlined by the Venetian–Ottoman War of 1499–1503. Both sides enjoyed profitable trade links. But Venetian sea-power represented an obstacle to Ottoman designs in the **eastern Mediterranean**. The Venetian defeat at the **Battle of Zonchio** in August 1499 made Ottoman naval power strikingly clear.

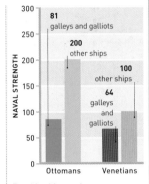

Zonchio ship numbers
The disparity in numbers between the Ottoman and Venetian fleets was compounded by the refusal of some Venetian commanders to fight at all.

A further round in the **Franco-Spanish struggle** for mastery of Italy was launched in 1499, when Louis XII of France (1462–1515) seized Milan. He then allied with Ferdinand of Aragon (1452–1516), agreeing to divide Naples between them. With Naples secured, Louis and Ferdinand fell out. Twice defeated by his former ally, **Louis reluctantly made peace** in 1504.

The burst of **European exploration** sparked by Columbus continued in 1500 when a **Spanish expedition** under Vicente Pinzón and a **Portuguese enterprise** under Pedro Alvares Cabral bound for India made the coast of **Brazil**. Cabral's sighting of this new land would prove important in establishing Portuguese claims to Brazil. Of greater significance was the growing realization that this was indeed a **New World**.

THE YEAR 1501 IS CONSIDERED the date the **Safavid Empire was founded**. With the Ottoman Empire to the west and the Mughal Empire to the east, it formed one of a bloc of sophisticated, centralized, **highly cultured Muslim empires** that dominated West Asia in the 16th and 17th centuries. It began in a burst of conquest launched by **Shah Ismail I**, whose troops surged westward across Persia, putting an end to the political vacuum and infighting that had followed the death of Timur (see 1386–90) in 1405. Proclaiming himself Shah of Persia, Ismail I was a Shi'ite Muslim and vigorously promoted his faith as the official state religion. Checked

Safavid Empire
From modest beginnings on the Caspian Sea, by 1501 the Safavid Empire extended to occupy a swath of Western Asia.

to the west by the military might of the Ottomans, the Safavids increasingly turned their focus to the east. In the process the Safavid capital was moved eastward, finally ending at Isfahan.

The introduction of African slaves by European settlers to the New World began in 1502, hardly 10 years after Columbus's first Atlantic crossing. In part, this was a response to the **alarming death rates** of the native populations, who had been similarly enslaved. The Portuguese rapidly followed suit. This initial phase of the trade, known as the **First Atlantic system**, lasted until around 1580.

The **spread of Islam** in East Africa was reinforced by the

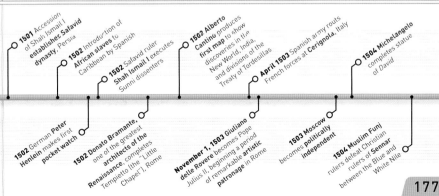

Michelangelo's *David*
Completed by Michelangelo in 1504, this giant marble statue of biblical hero David stands at 17ft (5.2m) tall.

establishment in 1504 of the **Funj Sultanate of Sennar** in the north of Sudan, at the expense of the previous Christian rulers of Sennar. The sultanate rapidly established itself as a major power in the region, threatening both Ethiopia and the Ottomans in Egypt.

In Europe, the **role of Florence** in the early years of the High Renaissance (see pp.204–205) was highlighted by **two remarkable works**: Michelangelo's statue of *David*, which he completed in 1504; and Leonardo's painting *Mona Lisa*, completed sometime around 1505–07.

> **...ANYONE WHO HAS SEEN MICHELANGELO'S *DAVID* HAS NO NEED TO SEE ANYTHING ELSE BY ANY OTHER SCULPTOR...**
>
> **Giorgio Vasari, Italian author,** from *Lives of the Artists*, 1568

> **THE TRUE WORK OF ART IS BUT A SHADOW OF THE DIVINE PERFECTION.**
>
> Michelangelo Buonarroti, Italian artist (1475–1564)

MICHELANGELO BUONARROTI

(1475–1564) was one of the defining figures of the High Renaissance (see pp.204–05). In 1505, he was invited to Rome by Pope Julius II to begin work on a monumental tomb, an association that would last for 40 years. In 1508, he began work painting a fresco on the Sistine Chapel ceiling, which he completed 4 years later.

The pace of **Portuguese expansion** across the Indian Ocean in the early 16th century was remarkable. From 1505, the Portuguese established themselves in a string of ports along the **East African coast**. The goal was simple and ruthlessly pursued—the domination of the lucrative spice trade with India and East Asia. A key player in this campaign was **Afonso de Albuquerque**, who in 1509 became viceroy of the fledgling Portuguese colony in India. By 1510, he had secured **Goa** as the principal Portuguese base in India; by 1511, he had overseen the foundation of the first Portuguese settlement in Southeast Asia, **Malacca**. He also sponsored the first Portuguese voyage to the Spice Islands, the **Moluccas**, which were reached in 1512 by **Francisco Serrão**, who had sailed in company with **Antonio de Abreu** and **Francisco Rodrigues**.

Sistine ceiling

Commissioned by Pope Julius II, the ceiling of the Sistine Chapel in the Vatican is one of the masterworks of Michelangelo. It depicts scenes from the Old Testament.

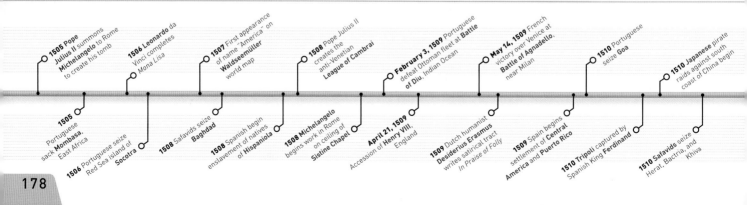

1505 Pope Julius II summons **Michelangelo** to Rome to create his tomb

1506 Leonardo da Vinci completes *Mona Lisa*

1507 First appearance of name "America" on **Waldseemüller** world map

1508 Pope Julius II creates the anti-Venetian **League of Cambrai**

February 3, 1509 Portuguese defeat Ottoman fleet at **Battle of Diu**, Indian Ocean

May 14, 1509 French victory over Venice at **Battle of Agnadello**, near Milan

1510 Portuguese seize **Goa**

1510 Japanese pirate raids against south coast of China begin

1505 Portuguese sack **Mombasa**, East Africa

1506 Portuguese seize Red Sea island of **Socotra**

1508 Safavids seize **Baghdad**

1508 Spanish begin enslavement of natives of **Hispaniola**

1508 Michelangelo begins work in Rome on ceiling of **Sistine Chapel**

April 21, 1509 Accession of **Henry VIII**, England

1509 Dutch humanist **Desiderius Erasmus** writes satirical tract *In Praise of Folly*

1509 Spain begins settlement of **Central America** and **Puerto Rico**

1510 Tripoli captured by Spanish King **Ferdinand**

1510 Safavids seize **Herat, Bactria, and Khiva**

Depiction of the Battle of Agnadello, one of the major battles of the Italian Wars, from the tomb of Louis XII and Anne of Brittany, France.

This detail shows the coronation of Ottoman Sultan Selim I. The empire almost trebled during his nine-year reign.

Where the latter two were forced to turn back in the Banda Sea, Serrão was able to continue to the Moluccas using native craft.

However initially unpromising, it was a measure of the excitement sparked by **Columbus's Atlantic crossings** (see 1492) that within 20 years a variety of **Spanish expeditions** had explored and mapped almost the entire **Caribbean**. This included, in 1508–09, the **Yucatán Peninsula** on the east coast of Mexico, a discovery that led directly to the conquest of Mexico by **Hernan Cortés** (see 1519). The European conquest of the New World was driven largely by greed and effected principally by violence. It nonetheless laid claim to a Christian imperative, given **papal sanction** as early as 1452, by which "saracens, pagans, and any other unbelievers" could be enslaved. It was a view explosively challenged in 1511 in a sermon by a Spanish Dominican friar,

" ARE THEY **NOT MEN?** DO THEY **NOT HAVE** RATIONAL **SOULS?** "

Antonio de Montesinos, Dominican friar, delivering a sermon to Spanish colonists, Hispaniola, December 4, 1511

Antonio de Montesinos, in which, to predictable outrage, he denounced the "cruelty and tyranny" of the settlers.

Similarly aggressive Spanish and Portuguese attempts at colonization in **Morocco**, where both seized coastal strongholds in the 15th and early 16th centuries, partly helped the rise of a new Moroccan dynasty after 1511—the **Sa'dis**—who filled the political vacuum created by the crumbling of Marinid rule in the 1480s.

The **Venetian Republic** was diplomatically isolated and opposed by almost every major Western European power when

Pope Julius II established the **League of Cambrai** in 1508. The Republic was quickly plunged into crisis by its defeat in May 1509 by Louis XII's French army at the **Battle of Agnadello,** one of the major battles of the **Italian Wars** (1494–1559). The following year Julius II allied himself with Venice against France, anxious that Venetian territorial designs in northern Italy had been replaced by identical French ambitions. This shuffling of alliances was typical of the period. It was given a further twist with the formation in 1511 of a new **Holy League**, including England, now directed against France. One outcome of this was a subsequent Franco–Venetian alliance.

Hemmed in on the west by the **Ottomans** and threatened to the south by the Portuguese, the **Safavids** were nonetheless successful in confronting the loose **Uzbek confederation** of peoples of Central Asia to their north. In December 1510, with victory over the Uzbeks outside the city of Merv, substantial territories, including Herat, Bactria, and Kandahar, came under **Safavid** rule.

NO LESS SIGNIFICANT than the Spanish exploration of the Caribbean in the immediate aftermath of Columbus's 1492 crossing was the discovery by **Juan Ponce de León** in April 1513 of the "island" of Florida. It was the first Spanish contact with the mainland of North America and the basis for subsequent Spanish claims to the region. In attempting to circumnavigate his island, Ponce de León made a further discovery almost as important in the age of sail as Columbus's discovery of the wind systems of the central Atlantic— the **Gulf Stream**.

Niccolò Machiavelli was a diplomat in Florence when, in 1513, he wrote the first modern handbook of political science, *The Prince* (published in 1532). Its central theme—that the exercise of political power requires violence and deceit—earned it lasting notoriety. It offers advice about the most effective means of ruling: essentially a pragmatic determination to use all means at hand.

Ottoman territorial expansion was renewed after the civil war of 1509–12 which saw **Selim I** emerge as sultan at the expense of both his father, Bayezid II, who was forced to abdicate, and Selim's older brother, Ahmed, who was killed in battle. Selim initiated this burst of growth—directed south and east against fellow Muslims rather than north against Christian Europe—in 1514 when the Safavids, vastly outnumbered and with no answer to the Ottoman

artillery, were overpowered at the Battle of Caldiran. His Eastern flank secured, Selim swept into **Syria** and **Mamluk Egypt**, which instantly crumbled. Selim I not only dramatically increased Ottoman territories but, in securing almost all the Muslim holy places of the Near East, added substantially to Ottoman prestige (see pp.230–31).

Spice Islands exploration
Portuguese explorer Francisco Serrao successfully reached the Moluccas (Spice Islands) after others had turned back.

KEY
→ Antonio de Abreu / Francisco Rodrigues 1512
→ Francisco Serrão 1512

NICCOLO MACHIAVELLI
(1469–1527)

Philosopher and writer, Niccolò Machiavelli was a functionary in Florence, where he witnessed the power of aggressive rulers first hand, including, in 1502–03, that of the pope's illegitimate son, the ruthless Cesare Borgia. He completed several diplomatic missions, but in 1513 was arrested and tortured. He wrote *The Prince* in the same year. He died aged of 58, impoverished, before his book enjoyed its later notoriety.

1511 England joins anti-French **Holy League** of Pope Julius II

December 4, 1511 Antonio de Montesinos denounces Spanish colonists over enslavement

April 11, 1512 French defeat Holy League at **Ravenna**, Italy

1512 Portuguese reach **Spice Islands**

1512 Accession of **Selim I** in Ottoman Empire

1512 Songhay Empire of West Africa conquers Hausa states of Katsina, Zaria, and Kano

1513 Spanish explorer **Juan Ponce de León** claims **Florida** coast for Spain

1513 Niccolò Machiavelli writes *The Prince*

1514 Ottomans crush **Safavids** at **Caldiran** in northwest Iran and overrun **Syria**

September 13, 1515 Battle of Marignano in northern Italy leaves French in control of Duchy of Milan

1515 Alliance between Habsburg and Polish Jagiellon dynasties in Central Europe

> ❝ WHY DOES NOT THE **POPE**... **BUILD**... **ST. PETER'S** WITH HIS **OWN MONEY**, RATHER **THAN WITH** THE **MONEY**... OF POOR BELIEVERS. ❞

Martin Luther, German priest, from *95 Theses*, 1517

The fall of Tenochtitlán on August 13, 1521 was the result not just of Spanish ferocity but of a 20,000-strong native army recruited by Hernán Cortés.

THE OTTOMAN CONQUESTS IN THE MIDDLE EAST under Selim I—who in 1517 also brought Algeria into the Ottoman orbit—meant that the Ottoman Turkish state was now emphatically an **empire**. It was also rapidly developing as a major naval power. Control of Egypt both consolidated the Ottoman presence in the eastern Mediterranean and, crucially, gave them access to the Red Sea. Already effectively masters of the overland trade routes with the East, the Ottomans were now poised to dominate the lucrative "route of spices." In doing so, they found themselves in direct conflict with the Portuguese, who had been actively probing the Red Sea since 1513. The stage was set for another round of conflict between the Muslim world and the Christian West.

In October 1517, the priest and professor of theology **Martin Luther** (1483–1546) nailed his *95 Theses* to the door of All Saints Church in Wittenberg, Saxony, as part of what was a growing protest movement against religious practices and corruption in the Catholic Church. In 1521, after being excommunicated by the pope, his opposition to the Church hardened. The ready response to Luther's teachings and the influence of the printing press (see pp.154–55) in disseminating his ideas resulted in a major force for religious change known as the **Reformation**.

The arrival of a **Portuguese fleet** under Tomé Pires in **Canton, China**, in August 1517 was the climax of a campaign to open up trading routes across the Indian Ocean, begun when Vasco da Gama rounded the Cape of Good Hope in 1498. However, the early results of these encounters were not promising, as the Chinese regarded the newcomers as **uncouth barbarians**. A Portuguese trade mission to Peking in 1520 was treated with similar scorn.

THE REFORMATION

The Reformation—the religious revolt against the Catholic Church instigated by Martin Luther (right)—tore the Western Church apart. Politics intruded from the start as the revolt spread across Europe. The consequence was a legacy of violent religious division and confrontation between Catholics and Protestants that led to a permanent divide in European Christendom.

THE ELECTION OF CHARLES V AS HOLY ROMAN EMPEROR in 1519 appeared pivotal. Charles (1500–58) was already the ruler of several territories across Europe: in Italy, Austria, the Low Countries, and in Spain. Now, as Holy Roman Emperor, his status appeared unassailable. For the earnest Charles, the imperatives were clear—to preside over a prosperous, pan-European Catholic entity which, properly mobilized, would then **rout the Ottoman menace**. The reality was painfully different. The size of his territories made effective control impossible. Few of his subjects were prepared to surrender traditional "liberties" to a distant, foreign ruler; almost none was prepared to finance him; and religious differences persistently intruded. Simultaneously, the prospect of Habsburg domination alarmed every other major European power, above all France. The result was a **reign of near**

Emperor Charles V
Few rulers were more dutiful than Charles V or as conscious of their divine destiny. However, his best efforts consistently proved in vain.

permanent warfare and dutiful hopes consistently frustrated.

The daring, ruthlessness, and single-mindedness **Spain** brought to overseas adventuring paid dividends with **Hernán Cortés's** march on Tenochtitlán, capital of the Mexican **Aztec Empire**. Beginning in 1519, in less than five years the Spanish force, aided by Tlaxcalan warriors, had subjugated much of Central America. A minor noble and self-financing adventurer, Cortés brought about Spanish domination of Central America.

A further milestone in the cementing of Spain's global role was marked in 1519—the launch

> ❝ HE KNEW **BETTER** THAN ANY OTHER THE **TRUE ART** OF **NAVIGATION.** ❞

Antonio Pigafetta, Italian navigator, on Ferdinand Magellan, 1521

of the **first circumnavigation of the globe**. The expedition leader, **Ferdinand Magellan** (b. 1480) was a Portuguese nobleman who, despite his nationality, succeeded in persuading Charles V to bankroll his scheme to reach the Spice Islands in the Pacific by sailing

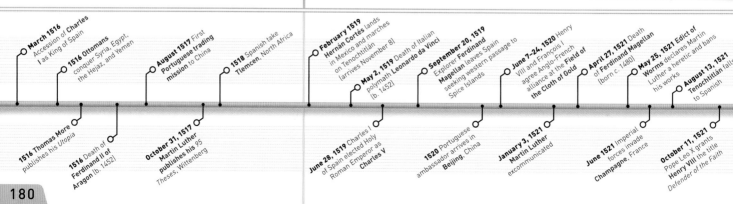

March 1516 Accession of Charles I as King of Spain

1516 Ottomans conquer Syria, Egypt, the Hejaz, and Yemen

August 1517 First Portuguese trading mission to China

1518 Spanish take Tlemcen, North Africa

February 1519 Hernán Cortés lands in Mexico and marches on Tenochtitlán (arrives November 8)

May 2, 1519 Death of Italian polymath Leonardo da Vinci (b. 1452)

September 20, 1519 Explorer Ferdinand Magellan leaves Spain seeking western passage to Spice Islands

June 7–24, 1520 Henry VIII and François I agree Anglo-French alliance at the Field of the Cloth of Gold

April 27, 1521 Death of Ferdinand Magellan (born c. 1480)

May 25, 1521 Edict of Worms declares Martin Luther a heretic and bans his works

August 13, 1521 Tenochtitlán falls to Spanish

1516 Thomas More publishes his *Utopia*

1516 Death of Ferdinand II of Aragon (b. 1452)

October 31, 1517 Martin Luther publishes his 95 Theses, Wittenberg

June 28, 1519 Charles I of Spain elected Holy Roman Emperor as Charles V

1520 Portuguese ambassador arrives in Beijing, China

January 3, 1521 Martin Luther excommunicated

June 1521 Imperial forces invade Champagne, France

October 11, 1521 Pope Leo X grants Henry VIII the title *Defender of the Faith*

At Pavia in 1525, the French army's siege lines were broken by a Spanish relief army, then the soldiers were cut to pieces by pikemen and gunfire.

Babur's Mughal empire could only be created—and sustained—by force.

west. Five ships set out; one returned, three years later, and without Magellan, who had been killed by islanders in 1521. It was, nonetheless, perhaps the most remarkable enterprise of the age of sail, an epic which for the first time revealed the immensity of the Pacific.

1521 saw another round in the **Italian wars** (1494–1559), this time sparked by French fears of a Habsburg-dominated Europe after the election of Charles V as Holy Roman Emperor. France and, at least initially, Venice joined forces to oppose Charles, England, and the papacy. For the French, the war was as unsatisfactory as its predecessors, culminating in a series of defeats.

Portuguese caravel
Magellan's flagship Trinidad *was a caravel like this Portuguese vessel. Typically less than 100 ft (30 m) long, they were sturdily seaworthy ships.*

THE BELIEF THAT THE LANDS IN THE WEST discovered by European explorers from Columbus onward were unknown Asian coasts, rather than a new continent, proved tenacious. It was likewise widely held that a **navigable passage to the East** through these landmasses must exist. It was only the voyages between 1524 and 1528 from Florida to Nova Scotia by **Giovanni da Verrazzano** (1485–1528), a Florentine in the service of François I of France, that revealed the existence of a **continuous coastline**. Yet Verrazzano persisted in the belief that the Pacific was within reach.

The **German Peasants' War** of 1524–25 was a sharp reminder of the way that the language of Protestant reformation could be appropriated by groups who usually lacked a voice in politics. The revolts were attempts by huge numbers of the politically disenfranchised in Germany and in Austria, by no means all of them peasants, to end what they saw as abuses against them—chiefly taxes and labor services—by the Church and the nobility. At the war's height in the spring of 1525, perhaps 300,000 people had

100,000
THE NUMBER OF **REBELS** KILLED IN THE **POPULAR** UPRISING IN **GERMANY**

KEY

Habsburg possessions 1525

— Border of Holy Roman Empire

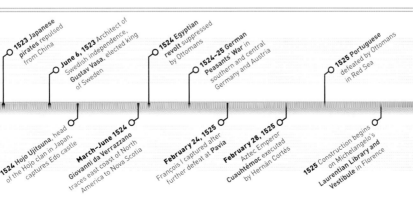

Habsburg Empire under Charles V
The very size of Charles V's empire made it effectively ungovernable. Whatever its potential power, it was riven by religious and political strife.

gathered in a variety of loose groupings and hastily assembled armies. The **uprising was savagely repressed**, with thousands killed. Luther and other leaders of the "official" Reformation vehemently denied any connection with the rebels, and the revolt provoked a brutal clampdown on forms of Protestant religious radicalism, such as **Anabaptism**, which were considered to challenge both social hierarchy and Protestant authority.

The **Battle of Pavia** in 1525 saw **François I captured** and shipped to Madrid, where he was obliged to surrender all claim to Italy. But it was an agreement the French king had no intention of honoring.

8:1 **Battle of Pavia**
The French Army was virtually wiped out at Pavia on February 24, 1525, with 8,000 casualties compared to 1,000 Imperial casualties.

> **IF THERE IS A PARADISE ON EARTH**, IT IS THIS, IT IS THIS, IT IS THIS.

Inscription on Babur's tomb 1530

IN HIS STRUGGLES AGAINST CHARLES V (see 1521), François I had solicited the help of the Ottomans in 1525, in the process initiating a **Franco–Ottoman alliance** that lasted 250 years. The alliance also provided the Ottomans with further justification to renew their conflict with Hungary and, in August 1526, they obliterated a combined Hungarian–Bohemian force at Mohács.

In 1526, the **Mughal Empire** was founded in northern India. It was the creation of **Babur** (1483–1530), a descendant of Genghis Khan (see 1201–05). Babur hailed from Ferghana in central Asia, from where he had been expelled. In 1522, however, he captured Kandahar, an important staging point on the road to India and, in 1526, defeated the Afghan Sultan of Delhi, Ibrahim Lodi, and declared himself emperor. At its height at the beginning of the 18th century, the Mughal empire ("Mughal" is Persian for Mongol) covered almost the entire subcontinent. It was a byword for sophisticated and courtly life, fattened by trade and conquest, and, though Islamic, tolerant of other religions.

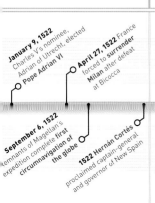

January 9, 1522 Charles V's nominee, Adrian of Utrecht, elected **Pope Adrian VI**

April 27, 1522 France forced to **surrender Milan** after defeat at Bicocca

September 6, 1522 Remnants of Magellan's expedition complete first **circumnavigation of the globe**

1522 Hernán Cortés proclaimed captain-general and governor of New Spain

1523 Japanese pirates repulsed from China

June 6, 1523 Architect of Swedish independence, **Gustav Vasa**, elected king of Sweden

1524 Hojo Ujitsuna, head of the Hojo clan in Japan, captures Edo castle

March–June 1524 Giovanni da Verrazzano traces east coast of North America to Nova Scotia

1524 Egyptian revolt suppressed by Ottomans

1524–25 German **Peasants' War** in southern and central Germany and Austria

February 24, 1525 François I captured after further defeat at Pavia

February 28, 1525 Aztec Emperor **Cuauhtémoc executed** by Hernán Cortés

1525 Construction begins on Michelangelo's **Laurentian Library and Vestibule** in Florence

1525 Portuguese defeated by Ottomans in Red Sea

21 April Battle of Panipat results in Babur establishing the **Mughal Empire**

Babur (1483–1531) conquers Punjab and occupies Delhi, India

Protestant League of Torgau established, Germany

29 August Combined Hungarian and Bohemian armies defeated at Mohács by Ottomans

William Tyndale translates the **New Testament** into English

THE STORY OF
ASTRONOMY

The development of astronomy has been influenced by two key factors: the invention of the telescope, which revealed previously undetectable celestial objects, and advances in mathematics, physics, chemistry, and computing, which have been crucial to explaining astronomical observations.

secondary mirror
primary (main) mirror
supporting strut

Newton's telescope (front view)

Early astronomy was closely linked to mythology, religion, and prognostication. Celestial observations were used to measure time, devise calendars, set the dates of religious festivals, and for astrological prediction. For millennia, it was believed that the Earth was the center of the cosmos. However, this did not fully explain the observed movements of the Moon, Sun, and planets.

MODERN ASTRONOMY
In 1543, Nicolaus Copernicus published his heliocentric model, which put the Sun at the center of the cosmos and is widely considered to mark the birth of modern astronomy. Then, after 1609, the newly invented telescope revealed a host of new astronomical objects. The 17th century also saw the establishment of the laws of planetary motion by Johannes Kepler, and an explanation

of the gravitational force controlling that movement by Isaac Newton. In the 19th century, the distance to the Sun and nearby stars was accurately measured, spectroscopy was introduced, and advances in theoretical physics provided explanations for problems such as how stars generate their energy (by nuclear reactions in their cores). Prior to 1920, many thought the Universe consisted of only our own Milky Way Galaxy. However, Edwin Hubble measured the speed at which distant nebulae were receding, and it was realized that these nebulae were independent galaxies. Not only were the galaxies moving away, but the speed they were moving away increased with distance, implying that the Universe had a beginning, when everything was close together. It was proposed that the expansion had been caused by a massive explosion—the Big Bang. Findings from modern space astronomy have supported the Big Bang theory, but it has also been discovered that much of the Universe consists of dark matter and dark energy, the nature and origin of which are still unknown.

Persian astrolabe
Astrolabes show a representation of the night sky and were used until the 17th century to estimate time and for navigation.

hydrogen beta line   sodium lines

magnesium lines

THE ELECTROMAGNETIC SPECTRUM

Stars and other astronomical objects emit light and other forms of electromagnetic energy, such as X-rays and radio waves. Using spectroscopy, these electromagnetic emissions can be broken up into a spectrum of colors. A star's spectrum is crossed by dark absorption lines, each corresponding to a different chemical element. By investigating the intensity of these lines, a star's chemical composition can be discovered. Further study can also establish its temperature, relative velocity, and the pressure and density of its atmosphere.

2000 BCE
Solar and lunar calendars
The Babylonians produce the first calendar by integrating the 365.25 days of the solar year with the 29.53 days of the lunar month. Similar calendars are used in ancient Egypt.

Babylonian boundary stone

Zodiac of Senenmut

c. **1400 BCE**
Deities and the Zodiac
The ancient Egyptians produce the earliest known representation of the Zodiac, in which stars, planets, and associated deities appear. Zodiacs also appear in Babylonian artifacts.

c. **90–168 CE**
Ptolemy's Universe
Greek polymath Claudius Ptolemy proposes that the Earth is the center of the cosmos, a view that prevailed until the 16th century.

Ptolemy's constellations

1420
Ulugh Beg
The Persian Ulugh Beg builds an observatory in Samarkand. He measures the tilt of Earth's axis to 1/100th of a degree.

Ulugh Beg observatory

1543
The Sun-centered Universe
Nicolaus Copernicus suggests the Earth orbits the Sun and not vice versa. This demotes the Earth to being just one of the six known planets.

The Copernican Solar System

1608/1668
The first telescopes
German-born Dutch lensmaker Hans Lippershey makes the first refracting telescope in 1608. English scientist Isaac Newton makes the first reflecting telescope in 1668.

Newton's telescope

upper tube covered with
decorative vellum

aperture through
which light enters
telescope

lower tube made
of layers of paper
and cardboard

eyepiece lens
magnifies image
35 times

sphere rotates to
point telescope tube
in different directions

30MM THE DIAMETER OF THE **OBJECTIVE MIRROR** IN NEWTON'S TELESCOPE. TELESCOPES USED BY **MODERN ASTRONOMERS** HAVE MIRRORS UP TO **10,400MM IN DIAMETER**.

screw that holds
main mirror in
position

supporting
strut

Newton's telescope
Isaac Newton made his first reflecting telescope in 1668. Shortly afterward, he made a second model (shown here), which stands about 8 in (20 cm) high. Newton's telescope was the first to use a primary mirror rather than a lens to collect light. A secondary mirror then reflects the light through a magnifying eyepiece for viewing.

wooden base

plaque recording that this
telescope was presented to
the Royal Society, London,
in January 1672

1780s
William Herschel
Herschel discovers Uranus (1781) using a homemade telescope. He makes over 400 more, including a 1.26m reflector.

Herschel's 1.26m telescope

1990–present
Space telescopes
Telescopes are put into space near Earth or orbit around it, from where they probe the sky in a range of wavelengths.

Hubble Space Telescope

1920s
Edwin Hubble
Using the US's 2.5m Hooker telescope, Hubble shows that the Universe has more than 100 billion galaxies, and that it is expanding.

The Hooker telescope

1930s
Radio telescopes
A new field of astronomy— radio astronomy—begins when early radio telescopes detect radio waves from the Sun and distant galaxies.

Grote Reber's radio telescope

1960s–present
Exploring other worlds
Spacecraft are used to explore the Solar System. They fly past, orbit, and land on planets, moons, asteroids, and comets.

Mars rover

The Sack of Rome in 1527 shocked Europe and devastated the Church. Although it also deeply embarrassed Charles V, it meant his dominance in Italy was confirmed.

Atahualpa, the last Inca emperor, leads his army at Caxamalca.

THE MOST SHOCKING EVENT OF THE ITALIAN WARS was the **Sack of Rome** in 1527 by Charles V's Imperial troops. It also highlighted the contradictions facing Charles V as he struggled to impose order on his vast territories. As Holy Roman Emperor, Charles V was the natural ally of the Catholic Church just as he was the natural enemy of Lutheranism (see 1517). Yet not only was Charles now at war with the papacy's Holy League—assembled to challenge his dominance in Italy—some of the troops who had laid waste to Rome, when his army ran out of control in protest at their unpaid wages were openly sympathetic to the reformist doctrines of Luther. But, while Pope Clement VII cowered in the Castel San' Angelo as churches and palaces were ransacked and nuns raped and priests murdered, it was clear that Charles's control of Italy was now absolute.

Following their victory at Mohács in 1526 and the conquest of much of Hungary in 1529, the **Ottomans** feared the Habsburgs would try to recapture the lost territories and so laid siege to **Vienna**. It proved too ambitious a task even for the formidable Ottoman army, for the weather proved as arduous a foe as the Austrians. A second attempt on the city in 1532 also failed.

After his victory at Panipat in 1526, **Babur** consolidated his hold over north India the following year, defeating a Rajput army under Rana Sanga at the **Battle of Khanwa**. The final establishment of Mughal power came in 1529 with the destruction of an Afghan army at Ghagra.

In 1531, the **Schmalkadic League** was formed. This was a military alliance, made originally between the Lutheran rulers of

Siege of Vienna
The Ottoman siege of Vienna in 1529 failed because of the bad weather— bitter autumn rains and early snow —and over-extended supply lines.

SULEIMAN I (1494–1566)

The 46-year rule of Suleiman was marked by a succession of victories in the Balkans, the Middle East, and North Africa that left the Ottomans as the most dynamic and dominant presence in the Western Hemisphere. He is known as "Suleiman the Magnificent" in the West and as *Kanuri*, "The Lawgiver," in the Islamic world, and his reign saw a flowering of Ottoman art and culture.

Hesse and Saxony in northern Germany, under which each promised to aid the other if Charles V attempted, by force, to reimpose Catholicism. It rapidly expanded to include other German Protestant states and gained the support of Charles's external enemies, the Ottomans and France. It was also an opportunity for each territory to enrich itself by taking over church property.

SPANISH EXPLORATION AND CONQUEST IN THE NEW WORLD, so decisively reinforced by the subjection of Mexico in 1521, was continued on an even more spectacular scale with the takeover of the Peruvian **Inca Empire** by **Francisco Pizarro** (1476–1541) in 1532. In little more than a year, a force of 188 Spaniards defeated a highly organized state of five million. Like Cortés's invasion of Mexico, its success depended on internal divisions within the Inca Empire, and a combination of religious zeal, greed, and superior military means—steel, guns, and armor against the Incas' weapons of sharpened stones and padded cotton armour—the whole driven by Pizarro, a man of huge ambition.

On the other side of the continent, further European penetration of South America was also taking place, albeit on a far smaller scale. In 1532, Portugal established its first permanent settlement in **Brazil**, at São Vicente. This was the nucleus of what by the end of the century would be a huge colonial enterprise based on slavery and sugar plantations.

In 1532, hostilities between Germany's Schmalkaldic League and Emperor Charles V ceased with the signing of a **treaty at Nuremberg**. The concessions made to the Protestants by Charles, which, most importantly, included freedom of worship, were welcomed by Martin Luther and enabled German Protestants to spread throughout the country in the following decade.

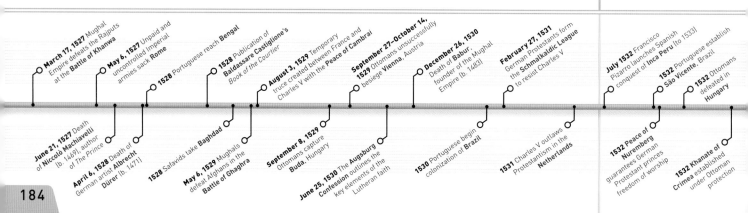

March 17, 1527 Mughal Empire defeats the Rajputs at the **Battle of Khanwa**

May 6, 1527 Unpaid and uncontrolled Imperial armies sack **Rome**

1528 Portuguese reach Bengal

1528 Publication of **Baldassare Castiglione's** *Book of the Courtier*

August 3, 1529 Temporary truce created between France and Charles V with the **Peace of Cambrai**

September 27–October 14, 1529 Ottomans unsuccessfully besiege **Vienna**, Austria

December 26, 1530 Death of Babur, founder of the Mughal Empire (b. 1483)

February 27, 1531 German Protestants form the **Schmalkaldic League** to resist Charles V

July 1532 Francisco Pizarro launches Spanish conquest of **Inca Peru** (to 1533)

1532 Portuguese establish **São Vicente**, Brazil

1532 Ottomans defeated in **Hungary**

June 21, 1527 Death of Niccolò Machiavelli (b. 1469), author of *The Prince*

April 6, 1528 Death of German artist **Albrecht Dürer** (b. 1471)

1528 Safavids take Baghdad

May 6, 1529 Mughals defeat Afghans in the **Battle of Ghaghra**

September 8, 1529 Ottomans capture **Buda**, Hungary

June 25, 1530 The **Augsburg Confession** outlines the key elements of the Lutheran faith

1530 Portuguese begin colonization of **Brazil**

1531 Charles V outlaws Protestantism in the **Netherlands**

1532 Peace of Nuremberg guarantees German Protestant princes freedom of worship

1532 Khanate of Crimea established under Ottoman protection

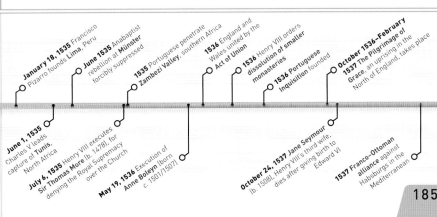

Charles V's seizure of Tunis in June 1935 was almost the only unequivocal success of his reign. Briefly, the prospect of a resurgent Christendom loomed.

" ...THE SCANDAL OF CHRISTENDOM AND A DISGRACE TO YOU. "

Catherine of Aragon to Henry VIII about Anne Boleyn, 1533

HENRY VIII OF ENGLAND had been awarded the title *Fidei Defensor*—Defender of the Faith—by Pope Leo X in 1521 in recognition of his vehement defense of the Catholic Church against Protestant attacks. Henry would remain a devout Catholic to the end of his life, opposed to all attempts to reform Catholic practice. And yet by 1533 he had been excommunicated from the Roman Church. The following year, he completed the rupture, establishing a national church, totally independent from Rome, with himself as its "supreme head." The reasons for this improbable split were simple. Initially, Henry wanted a **divorce** from his aging Spanish wife, **Catherine of Aragon**, who after 24 years of marriage had yet to give birth to a son. Henry had

Anne Boleyn
Henry VIII married Anne Boleyn in secret in January 1533, four months before he divorced Catherine of Aragon. She was crowned in June.

THE JESUIT ORDER

The initial Catholic response to the Reformation was hesitant and uncoordinated, and was led by a series of individuals rather than the Church itself. The Jesuits, the Society of Jesus, were established in 1534 by a Basque nobleman, Ignatius of Loyola. Loyola's goal was to produce a new generation of highly educated priests to spread a new militantly Catholic faith. Given papal sanction in 1540, the Jesuits spearheaded the Catholic revival.

convinced himself this was divine punishment for marrying his brother's widow—in 1501, Catherine had married Henry's elder brother Arthur, who died the following year; Henry and Catherine married in 1509. The pope, under pressure from Catherine's nephew, Charles V, refused to grant a divorce. Henry's response, formulated over several years, was in effect to become his own pope, able to authorize his own divorce. Prompted in addition by the knowledge that, as elsewhere in Europe, any ruler asserting control of the Church in his own country would necessarily increase his own authority, in 1534 the **Church of England** was brought into being under the Act of Supremacy. In pursuit of Henry's personal interests, **Roman Catholicism was abolished**.

HAVING BROKEN WITH ROME, it followed that all the structures of the Catholic Church in England should be taken over by the state. This was not just a question of wanting to eradicate papal authority in England. The Catholic Church in England was immensely wealthy, and this was money that Henry VIII, permanently strapped for cash, was determined to have. In 1535, the king's secretary, **Thomas Cromwell** (c. 1485–1540), took charge of the two-part **dissolution of the country's monasteries**. Starting in 1536 and culminating with all the great monasteries in 1539, the dissolution involved systematic vandalism and saw the greatest transfer of land ownership in England since the Norman Conquest in 1066. Every one of the 560 monasteries in England was

suppressed, yielding the crown an additional income of around £200,000 *per annum*. However, within years the money was gone, squandered by the king.

Henry VIII's divorce from Catherine of Aragon in 1533 had been necessary to allow him to marry **Anne Boleyn**. When she, too, failed to produce a son, Henry had her executed on **charges of adultery** in 1536. In the same year, tensions at the pace and extent of religious change, and the sincere concerns of many that the break with Rome signaled larger changes in the fabric of the traditional Church, had reached the boiling point in the North of England. The **Pilgrimage of Grace** saw the largest uprisings in England since the Peasants Revolt in 1381. Those involved had shown little or no dissatisfaction with the Catholic church and were unprepared to see centuries of settled faith discarded. Faced with protest on this scale, the king

58% of eligible monasteries dissolved

Dissolution of monasteries
Under the Dissolution of Lesser Monasteries Act of 1536, 243 of the 419 eligible monasteries were suppressed or dissolved.

1,175 people burned

29,590 PENANCE IMPOSED

PORTUGUESE INQUISITION

644 effigies burned

Portuguese Inquisition
Between 1540 and 1794, tribunals held in Lisbon, Porto, Coimbra, and Evora led to the death by burning of 1,175 people, most of them Jews.

conceded to the movement's demands. But when the crisis was over, he had the rebellion's leaders executed.

Distracted by events in Europe, Charles V was rarely able to pursue his goal of driving the Ottomans back to their Turkish heartlands. In 1535, however, he achieved a rare success with the **conquest of Tunis** in North Africa. It proved to be a costly victory, provoking an Ottoman raid on Majorca that captured 6,000 Christians and encouraged the French monarch to cooperate more closely with the Ottomans.

While it never achieved the notoriety of its Spanish equivalent (see 1480), the **Portuguese Inquisition**, founded in 1536, was nonetheless vigorous in rooting out heresy in Portugal and, from 1560, in its colonies, such as Goa. Its chief target was Jews, many originally Spanish, who were forcibly converted to Catholicism.

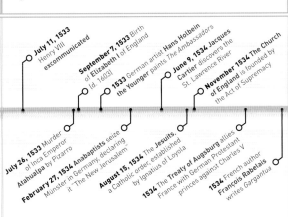

July 11, 1533 Henry VIII excommunicated

September 7, 1533 Birth of Elizabeth I of England (d. 1603)

1533 German artist Hans Holbein the Younger paints *The Ambassadors*

June 9, 1534 Jacques Cartier discovers the St. Lawrence River

November 1534 The Church of England is founded by the Act of Supremacy

July 26, 1533 Murder of Inca Emperor Atahualpa by Pizarro

February 27, 1534 Anabaptists seize Münster in Germany, declaring it "The New Jerusalem"

August 15, 1534 The Jesuits, a Catholic order, established by Ignatius of Loyola

1534 Treaty of Augsburg allies France with German Protestant princes against Charles V

1534 French author **François Rabelais** writes *Gargantua*

January 18, 1535 Francisco Pizarro founds Lima, Peru

June 1535 Anabaptist rebellion at Münster forcibly suppressed

1535 Portuguese penetrate Zambezi Valley, southern Africa

1536 England and Wales united by the Act of Union

1536 Henry VIII orders dissolution of smaller monasteries

1536 Portuguese Inquisition founded

October 1536–February 1537 The Pilgrimage of Grace, an uprising in the North of England, takes place

June 1, 1535 Charles V leads capture of Tunis, North Africa

July 6, 1535 Henry VIII executes Sir Thomas More (b. 1478), for denying the Royal Supremacy over the Church

May 19, 1536 Execution of Anne Boleyn (born c. 1501/1507)

October 24, 1537 Jane Seymour (b. 1508), Henry VIII's third wife, dies after giving birth to Edward VI

1537 Franco-Ottoman alliance against Habsburgs in the Mediterranean

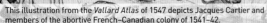

This illustration from the *Vallard Atlas* of 1547 depicts Jacques Cartier and members of the abortive French–Canadian colony of 1541–42.

" I AM INCLINED TO BELIEVE THAT **THIS IS THE LAND GOD GAVE TO CAIN.** "

Jacques Cartier, French explorer, about Canada, 1536

THE BATTLE OF PREVEZA, fought off western Greece in September 1538, further underlined the reach of Ottoman naval power. It pitched the Ottomans against a combined Papal, Venetian, Genoese, and Spanish fleet brought together by Pope Paul III. The **Ottoman victory** highlighted the difficulty the Christians faced in welding together disparate, uneasily allied forces.

In August 1539, **Ghent**, the birthplace of Charles V, **rose in revolt** against him. The issue was tax, demanded by Charles to finance his Italian wars. It revealed the difficulties faced by Charles V in imposing authority over autonomous cities determined to guard their "liberties" by refusing to pay a distant ruler for an equally distant campaign. Charles personally oversaw the suppression of the revolt and the city's notables were forced to parade barefoot. The underlying tension, however, remained.

Despite concerted efforts, the **Spanish exploration of North America** in the 16th century proved discouraging. The myths that drove it—a waterway linking the Atlantic and Pacific, the "Seven Cities of Gold"—proved to be just that. The reality was vast territories that proved hostile and unrewarding. Nonetheless, from 1539, **Hernando de Soto** led a four-year expedition across much of the southern territories of today's US. Similarly, in 1540–42, **Francisco Vázquez de Coronado** headed a still larger force north from Mexico, penetrating as far as Kansas. And in 1542–43, **Juan Rodríguez Cabrillo** led a fleet north along the unknown Pacific coast, discovering San Diego harbor. But none of these ventures would be followed up until the end of the century.

French attempts at settlement in North America, promoted in part by nervousness of being beaten to it by Spain (just as Spain was anxious not to be outflanked by France), proved no more fruitful. Initial efforts had been made in 1534 and then in 1535–36 by **Jacques Cartier** (1491–1557), in the course of which the Gulf of St. Lawrence and then the St. Lawrence River in present-day **Canada** were reached and claimed for France. In 1541, by now thoroughly alarmed by Spanish intentions, France launched a more substantial expedition to Canada with the explicit goal of establishing a permanent settlement. It was led by Jean-Francois de la Rocque de Roberval, with Cartier his deputy, and was a dismal failure. Cartier returned, unauthorized, to France in 1542 with "gold and diamonds" that proved worthless. Roberval abandoned the colony the following year after a winter of near starvation. French efforts in North America would not be renewed for half a century.

A consequence of the Catholic response to the Reformation was the missionary work undertaken between 1541 and 1552 by **Francis Xavier** (1506–52), a cofounder of the **Jesuits** in 1534. Conceived on a heroic scale, its aim was to spread Christianity to East Asia. Xavier traveled via Mozambique to Goa, then to the Spice Islands between 1545 and 1547, and then to Canton and Japan before returning to China, where he died in 1552. His Christian conversions are said to have been exceeded only by St. Paul.

THE FIRST CONTACT BETWEEN EUROPE AND JAPAN WAS IN 1543. According to the Portuguese writer and explorer **Fernão Mendes Pinto**, it occurred on the island of Tanegashima, to the south of the main Japanese archipelago. Not only did the Portuguese introduce firearms to Japan, but they became intermediaries between China and Japan, whose merchants had been forbidden to trade with the Chinese as a result of persistent raids by Japanese pirates.

In 1543, the Polish mathematician **Nicolaus Copernicus** (1473–1543) published *On the Revolution of the Heavenly Bodies*. It was based not on Copernicus's own observations of the heavens so much as on those of Greek and Arab astronomers. Nonetheless, he was able to demonstrate that these much older observations were more readily explained by the **Earth orbiting the Sun** rather

Battle of Préveza
Despite the size of the Christian fleet at the Battle of Préveza in September 1538, it proved no match for the Ottoman fleet led by Khair ed-Din (Barbarossa).

Copernicus's Universe
This painting by Andreas Cellarius from 1660 shows "The system of the entire created Universe according to Copernicus."

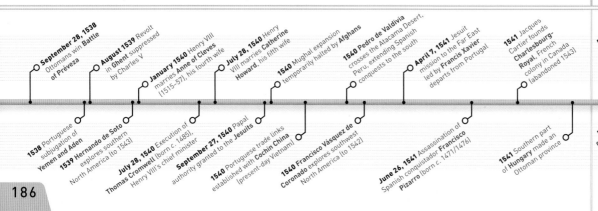

September 28, 1538 Ottomans win Battle of Préveza

August 1539 Revolt in Ghent suppressed by Charles V

January 1540 Henry VIII marries **Anne of Cleves** (1515–57), his fourth wife

July 28, 1540 Henry VIII marries **Catherine Howard**, his fifth wife

1540 Mughal expansion temporarily halted by **Afghans**

1540 Pedro de Valdivia crosses the Atacama Desert, Peru, extending Spanish conquests to the south

April 7, 1541 Jesuit mission to the Far East led by **Francis Xavier** departs from Portugal

1541 Jacques Cartier founds **Charlesbourg-Royal**, French colony in Canada (abandoned 1543)

February 13, 1542 Catherine Howard executed (born c. 1520–25)

August 26, 1542 Spaniard **Francisco de Orellana** completes first navigation of entire Amazon River

1538 Portuguese subjugation of Yemen and Aden

1539 Hernando de Soto explores southern North America (to 1543)

July 28, 1540 Execution of **Thomas Cromwell** (born c. 1485), Henry VIII's chief minister

September 27, 1540 Papal authority granted to the Jesuits

1540 Portuguese trade links established with Cochin China (present-day Vietnam)

1540 Francisco Vásquez de Coronado explores southwest North America (to 1542)

June 26, 1541 Assassination of Spanish conquistador **Francisco Pizarro** (born c. 1471/1476)

1541 Southern part of Hungary made an Ottoman province

May 6, 1542 Francis Xavier arrives in Goa

September 28, 1542 Portuguese explorer **Juan Rodríquez Cabrillo** lands at present-day San Diego while exploring the Californian coast

Natives and llamas were pressed into service to transport silver from Potosí, Bolivia. The sprawling shanty town became the largest in the New World.

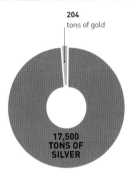

204 tons of gold

17,500 TONS OF SILVER

Gold and silver shipped to Seville
The silver mountain at Potosí meant it dominated the exports of precious metals shipped to Spain from Chile and Mexico from 1503 to 1660.

than the other way around. It took others, notably the Danish astronomer Tycho Brahe in the 1570s, to show by direct observation that Copernicus was right. But a major breach in the geocentric universe theory had been made.

Also published in 1543 was Vesalius's *On the Fabric of the Human Body*. Like Copernicus, **Andreas Vesalius** (1514–64) looked to ancient Greek learning. Unlike Copernicus, he made his own direct observations, based on dissections of human bodies. If any moment can be pinpointed as initiating a **scientific revolution** in the West—the belief the world is best understood by empirical observation—it was perhaps this.

Ever since the formation of the Protestant **Schmalkaldic League** in 1531, Charles V had been forced to skirt its threat to his authority as

Holy Roman Emperor. Persistently distracted by the French and the Ottomans, he had had little option but to appease the league (see 1532) and only in 1546, with France temporarily sidelined after the **Treaty of Crépy** of 1544, did he feel able to confront it directly. The result, decided at the **Battle of Mühlberg** in April 1547, was an overwhelming military success for Charles. The longer-term consequences were mixed.

In 1545, Spanish colonists discovered at **Potosí**, in present-day Bolivia, the biggest single concentration of silver ever found—in effect, an entire mountain of silver. Together with silver found in northern Mexico, it would prove to be the motor of the cash-hungry Spanish Empire, for it was New World silver from Potosí that drove Spanish trade with China just as it financed Spain's attempts at European dominance.

In the same year, at Trent in the Italian Alps, the Catholic Church set out to challenge the Protestant Reformation by reforming and remodeling itself. The **Council of Trent** aimed to eradicate corruption, make the Church's teachings more coherent, and to project itself as a dynamic and competitive religious force. It gave rise to a series of **new Catholic orders** and met twice more, in 1551–52 and 1559–63.

The Portuguese arrive in Japan
Portuguese merchants display some of their wares to the intrigue of the locals on their arrival on Japanese shores in 1543.

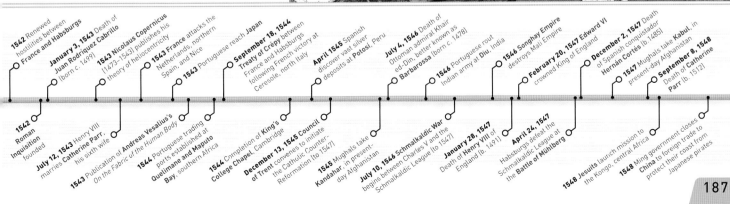

1542 Renewed hostilities between France and Habsburgs

January 3, 1543 Death of Juan Rodríguez Cabrillo (born c. 1499)

1543 Nicolaus Copernicus (1473–1543) publishes his theory of heliocentricity

1543 France attacks the Netherlands, northern Spain, and Nice

1543 Portuguese reach Japan

September 18, 1544 Treaty of Crépy between France and Habsburgs following French victory at Ceresole, north Italy

April 1545 Spanish discover vast silver deposits at Potosí, Peru

July 4, 1546 Death of Ottoman admiral Khair ed-Din, better known as **Barbarossa** (born c. 1478)

1546 Portuguese rout Indian army at Diu, India

1546 Songhay Empire destroys Mali Empire

February 20, 1547 Edward VI crowned King of England

December 2, 1547 Death of Spanish conquistador **Hernán Cortés** (b. 1485)

1547 Mughals take Kabul, in present-day Afghanistan

September 8, 1548 Death of Catherine Parr (b. 1512)

1542 Roman Inquisition founded

July 12, 1543 Henry VIII marries Catherine Parr, his sixth wife

1543 Publication of **Andreas Vesalius's** *On the Fabric of the Human Body*

1544 Portuguese trading ports established at **Quelimane and Maputo Bay**, southern Africa

1544 Completion of **King's College Chapel, Cambridge**

December 13, 1545 Council of Trent convenes to initiate the Catholic Counter-Reformation (to 1547)

1545 Mughals take **Kandahar**, in present-day Afghanistan

July 10, 1546 Schmalkaldic War begins between Charles V and the Schmalkaldic League (to 1547)

January 28, 1547 Death of **Henry VIII** of England (b. 1491)

April 24, 1547 Habsburgs defeat the Schmalkaldic League at the **Battle of Mühlberg**

1548 Jesuits launch mission to the Kongo, central Africa

1548 Ming government closes **China** to foreign trade to protect their coast from Japanese pirates

"ART OWES ITS **ORIGIN TO NATURE...** THIS BEAUTIFUL CREATION... **SUPPLIED** THE **FIRST MODEL,** WHILE THE **ORIGINAL TEACHER WAS** THAT **DIVINE INTELLIGENCE...**"

Giorgio Vasari, from *Lives of the Most Excellent Italian Painters...* 1550

The only surviving child of Henry VIII and Catherine of Aragon, Mary I was the first queen of England to rule in her own right.

This copper engraving depicts the Peace of Augsburg of 1555.

THE ACCESSION OF THE NINE-YEAR-OLD EDWARD VI (1537–53) to the English throne in 1547 marked a violent break with his father's religious settlement. Henry VIII's Church of England (see 1534) was Protestant only in its rejection of papal authority. Edward VI, guided by the actively Protestant **Lord**

Book of Common Prayer
The Book of Common Prayer made English the language of the English Church for the first time. It also provoked bitter protests and uprisings.

Protector, the Duke of Somerset, acting head of the government, and **Thomas Cranmer** (1489–1556), the Archbishop of Canterbury, introduced a new, vehemently Protestant church, given legal force in 1549 by the **Act of Uniformity**. Many of the outward forms of **Catholic worship**, including bell-ringing, were **forbidden**. It was reinforced by the publication

of Cranmer's *Book of Common Prayer*—its use was compulsory.

When the first **Portuguese Governor-General**, Tomé de Sousa, arrived in **Brazil** in 1549 he was accompanied by five Jesuits, sent at the express wish of the Portuguese king, João III, and led by Manuel de Nóbrega (1517–70). The **Jesuits** (see 1533–34), in other words, were central to the Portuguese colonization of Brazil from the beginning. Nóbrega not only celebrated the first mass in Brazil, at Salvador, first capital of the new colony, he established the **first Jesuit College in the New World**. He and his companions proved energetic missionaries, establishing **schools** and **chapels** and, importantly, concentrating their efforts among the natives' children. He was a consistent champion of the Indians in the face of routine brutality by the Portuguese colonizers.

Throughout the 16th century, the **North African coast** was one of the key battlegrounds between the Christian West, chiefly Spain, and the Ottomans for control of the Mediterranean. Spain needed to eradicate the devastating raids by **Barbary pirates**—actively encouraged by the Ottomans—that permanently threatened to disrupt Habsburg communications with its Italian lands. The **fall of Tripoli** to the Ottomans in 1551, with some assistance from French ships, was a striking blow to Habsburg strategic hopes, just as it marked a significant **victory for the Turks**. The city withstood repeated efforts to retake it.

IN 1552, THE LAST CHAPTER of the 60-plus years of the **Italian Wars** (see 1505–12) was opened. It saw France allied with the Ottomans in the Mediterranean, and with a series of German Protestant princes, notably Maurice of Saxony, in Germany. England would make a late and disastrous contribution to the Spanish cause in 1557. This came about because Henry VIII's daughter, **Mary**, became queen in 1553 and **married** Charles V's son, the future **Philip II of Spain**, in 1554. That the ruler of an England that had been Protestant since 1534 should be married to the son of the most militantly Catholic ruler in Europe is easily explained. Where her brother, Edward VI, had been aggressively Protestant (see 1549–51), **Mary I was no less aggressively Catholic**, determined on the full restoration of Catholic—and papal—supremacy. In the

Burned at the stake
Michael Servetus died in Geneva, a copy of his book chained to his leg, uttering the words: "Jesus, Son of the Eternal God, have mercy on me."

4:1 Heretics put to death

During her five-year rule, Mary I had 283 Protestants burned at the stake for heresy—227 of them were men and 56 were women.

space of less than a year, England was wrenched from one religious extreme to another. From 1555, she began the systematic **persecution** of leading **Protestant** figures, 283 of whom she had **burned alive**—hence her later demonization as **Bloody Mary**.

The execution in Geneva in October 1553 of the Spanish theologian and radical **humanist**, **Michael Servetus**, burned at the stake at the express command of the French religious reformer **John Calvin** (1509–64), marked a critical moment in the **Reformation** (see 1516–18). Servetus was a keen exponent, guilty in Calvin's view of "execrable blasphemies" because he rejected Calvin's belief in predestination—that all events are "willed by God," with eternal salvation available only to those who submit to God's will (largely as defined by Calvin). What was significant about the death of Servetus was that for the first time Protestantism was seen to be as intolerant of heresy as Catholicism. The implications were bleakly ominous.

THE FINAL PHASE OF THE ITALIAN WARS made plain that Charles V could never impose himself militarily on those of his nominal subjects within the Holy Roman Empire who had embraced Protestantism. Charles accordingly, and reluctantly, allowed his brother Archduke Ferdinand, Holy Roman Emperor designate, to negotiate a compromise, the **Peace of Augsburg**, agreed in September 1555. At its heart was a formula—*cuius regio eius religio* ("whose realm, his religion")—that allowed each ruler to **impose his own religion** on his territory. Tolerance of this sort suggested a major breakthrough. But the choice was between Catholicism and Lutheranism only—Calvinism (see 1552–54) was not included.

The accession of the 14-year-old **Akbar** to the **Mughal throne** in 1556 marked a decisive moment in the dynasty's fortunes. His father, Humayun, had seen a substantial erosion of Mughal power in the face of Afghan and Hindu advances. Having fought off a determined Hindu attempt on his throne at the **Second Battle of Panipat** in November 1556, Akbar presided over an enormous expansion of Mughal power.

The claims of **Russia's czars** to be the sole legitimate heirs of Rome and, therefore, the only guardians of Christianity led naturally to a belief that the expansion of Russia by conquest was not just desirable but inevitable. Under Ivan IV, known as **"the Terrible"** (1530–84), such ambitious assertions were

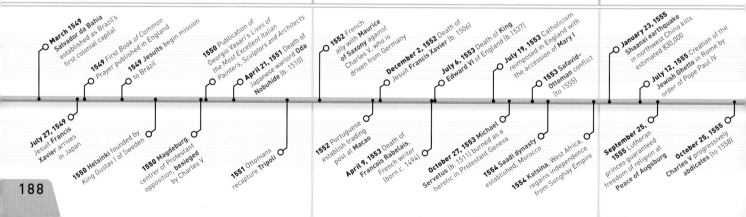

March 1549 Salvador da Bahia established as Brazil's first colonial capital

1549 First Book of Common Prayer published in England

1549 Jesuits begin mission to Brazil

1550 Publication of Georgio Vasari's *Lives of the Most Excellent Italian Painters, Sculptors and Architects*

April 21, 1551 Death of Japanese warlord Oda Nobuhide (b. 1510)

1552 French ally with Maurice of Saxony against Charles V, who is driven from Germany

December 2, 1552 Death of Jesuit Francis Xavier (b. 1506)

July 6, 1553 Death of King Edward VI of England (b. 1537)

July 19, 1553 Catholicism reimposed in England with the accession of Mary I

1553 Safavid-Ottoman conflict (to 1555)

January 23, 1555 Shaanxi earthquake in northwest China kills estimated 830,000

July 12, 1555 Creation of the Jewish Ghetto in Rome by order of Pope Paul IV

July 27, 1549 Jesuit Francis Xavier arrives in Japan

1550 Helsinki founded by King Gustav I of Sweden

1550 Magdeburg, centre of Protestant opposition, besieged by Charles V

1551 Ottomans recapture Tripoli

1552 Portuguese establish trading post at Macao

April 9, 1553 Death of Francois Rabelais, French writer (born c. 1494)

October 27, 1553 Michael Servetus (b. 1511) burned as a heretic in Protestant Geneva

1554 Saadi dynasty established, Morocco

1554 Katsina, West Africa, regains independence from Songhay Empire

September 25, 1555 Lutheran princes guaranteed freedom of religion at Peace of Augsburg

October 25, 1555 Charles V progressively abdicates (to 1558)

This oil painting shows Henri II of France and Philip II of Spain meeting at Cateau-Cambrésis on April 3, 1559 to sign the peace treaty. In reality, it was signed by their ambassadors.

THE TENSE RELATIONS BETWEEN the Portuguese, who had been attempting to establish trading posts in China since 1513, and the **Chinese**, always suspicious of Portuguese intentions, had thawed during the 1540s to the point that by 1552 China agreed to allow **Portugal a trading post in Macau** on the south coast of China. It was the key foothold the Portuguese had been seeking. By 1557, this temporary settlement had become permanent. It would, in turn, prove a crucial link in the Portuguese, later Spanish, global trading system. Macau remained Portuguese until 1999.

In 1557, **Mary I of England** (see 1552–54) was persuaded by her husband Philip II to join Spain in its renewed **war with France**. This proved disastrous, leading directly to the **loss of Calais to the French** in January 1558; Calais had been English since 1360 and was the country's last foothold in continental Europe. Mary had been unable to have children and when she died in November 1558, she was succeeded by her Protestant half-sister Elizabeth I, the daughter of Anne Boleyn.

Capture of Calais
This enamel plaque by French artist Leonard Limosin celebrates the capture of Calais by French forces led by Francis, Duke of Guise on January 7, 1558.

KEY

▪ Territory of Moscow 1300–1505
▫ Expansion of Moscow 1505–1584

Expansion of Moscow
In 1547, Ivan IV transformed the Grand Duchy of Moscow into the Czardom of Russia. In the 1550s, he began the expansion of its boundaries, and its territory and population doubled during his reign.

The **Treaty of Cateau-Cambrésis** of April 1559 marked the definitive **end of the Italian Wars**. It proved a short-lived success. Habsburg Spain was the clear victor, its dominance in Italy absolute (at the expense of the papacy as much as of France). For its part, France kept Calais as well as Metz, Toul, and Verdun. By the terms of the treaty, Philip II was tacitly making plain that the military and financial contributions of the Netherlands to the conflict had been principally to advance Spain's Italian goals. Future conflict in the Spanish Netherlands was more or less guaranteed. A less predictable consequence was the **death of the French king, Henry II** (b. 1519) three months later in a tournament held to celebrate the treaty. The succession of boy-kings that followed led France to 40 years of bitter civil war (see 1572).

In 1558, **Czar Ivan IV** continued his policy of **Russian expansion** with the beginning of the settlement of the Khanate of Sibir (western Siberia). Ivan's conquest of Kazan in 1552 had opened up the way to the Urals and Siberia to the east. Colonization was led by rich merchants, such as the Stroganovs, who had been granted estates and tax privileges by Ivan in the lands they took. Protected by Cossacks, **large-scale migration** into Siberia followed in the 1570s, establishing trade links with local tribes. The Khanate of Sibir was eventually conquered in 1582, greatly increasing the size of Russia.

Akbar the Great in procession
During the 46-year reign of Akbar, Mughal India enjoyed expansion of territory, prosperity, religious tolerance, and cultural richness.

significantly boosted. Although his efforts in the west were thwarted by Lithuanian arms, those to the south were strikingly successful. He had already conquered the Khanate of Kazan in 1552. In 1556, he achieved an even more notable breakthrough, destroying the enfeebled Khanate of Astrakhan.

Russia now found itself not only in control of the **trade routes to Central Asia**, it was also poised to sweep eastward across Siberia.

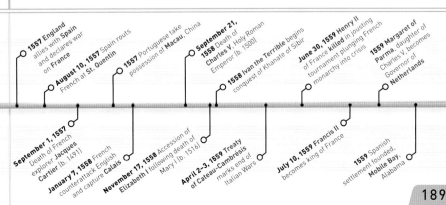

January 27, 1556 Accession of Akbar (1542–1605) to Mughal throne

March 21, 1556 former Thomas Cranmer, Archbishop of Canterbury, executed for heresy

November 5, 1556 Akbar defeats Hindus at Second Battle of Panipat

1557 England allies with Spain and declares war on France

August 10, 1557 Spain routs French at St. Quentin

1557 Portuguese take possession of Macau, China

September 21, 1558 Death of Charles V, Holy Roman Emperor (b. 1500)

1558 Ivan the Terrible begins conquest of Khanate of Sibir

June 30, 1559 Henry II of France killed in jousting tournament plunging French monarchy into crisis

1559 Margaret of Parma, daughter of Charles V, becomes Governor of Netherlands

July 31, 1556 Death of **Ignatius of Loyola**, founder of Jesuits (b. 1491)

1556 Russians seize Khanate of Astrakhan and reach Caspian Sea

1556 John III of Sweden becomes ruler of Finland

September 1, 1557 Death of French explorer **Jacques Cartier** (b. 1491)

January 7, 1558 French counterattack English and capture Calais

November 17, 1558 Accession of Elizabeth I following death of Mary I (b. 1516)

April 2–3, 1559 Treaty of Cateau-Cambrésis marks end of Italian Wars

July 10, 1559 Francis II becomes king of France

1559 Spanish settlement founded, Mobile Bay, Alabama

gold surface

Lacquer inro
1750–1799
Inros were small boxes hung from the belt and secured by a netsuke. This lacquer and gold example is decorated with scenes around Kyoto.

netsuke stops inro from slipping off belt

connecting cord

Wrestler's netsuke
1800–1850
In the Edo period much ingenuity went into the designs of carved toggles called netsuke. This example, depicting a snail on a mushroom, is made of boxwood.

Tea jar
17th century
This formerly lidded jar is Agano stoneware. Its shape, black body, and blue glaze imitate wares imported from China for the tea ceremony.

human figure

Porcelain tea bowl
1700–1750
Used as a delicate cup, this example of blue-and-white Arita ware, decorated with figures, imitates a design of the Chinese Kangxi dynasty period (1662–1722).

typical floral decoration

Imari charger
Edo period
Vast quantities of Imari porcelain, named after its principal port of distribution, have featured this charger's palette, dominated by blue, pink, and orange shades.

bamboo mount gives fan rigidity

EDO PERIOD

JAPANESE ARTS FLOURISHED UNDER THE TOKUGAWA SHOGUNS' RULE

The Edo period (1603–1868) was one of peace. The merchant class grew wealthier and better educated, and began to enjoy arts that were previously the preserve of the landowning elites and the samurai warrior class.

Japanese craftsmen were inspired by the culture of *ukiyo* (Floating World), itself inspired by the Buddhist idea that all is illusion. In Edo Japan *ukiyo* became associated with fleeting pleasures—from dallying with courtesans to attending kabuki dance dramas. Craftsmen strove for an esthetic of otherworldly elegance. Surrounded by beauty, their clients set about their pursuits, from writing to prayer, as though they too were part of the illusory Floating World.

Mount Fuji

top piece emphasizes height

Printed fan
1858
This late Edo artifact is made of split bamboo and paper. On each side is a different silkscreen-printed scene by Hiroshige II (1826–69).

lacquered surface

Lotus throne

Wooden Buddha figure
18th century
Buddhism lay at the heart of Tokugawa ideas of a coherent society. This small figure was kept as a reminder of Buddha.

decorative straw hat

finely carved detail

Ivory figure
18th century
This delicately carved ivory figure of an old woman carrying a bundle of faggots carries the inscription of Gyokusen.

separable component

Brass lantern
18th century
Intended for exterior use, probably at an entrance approach, this monumental brass lantern disassembles into five parts.

Zen ink decoration

Folding screen
Edo period
Sliding panels (*fusuma*) and folding screens served as movable interior walls in Edo Japan.

horns confirm
demonic identity

hair accentuates
wild movement

Brocade picture
18th century
Entitled *Truth-Sincerity*,
this is one of the *nishiki-e*
(brocade pictures) of Suzuki
Harunobu (c. 1725–70), made
by superimposing printings
of woodblocks inked with a
range of colors.

light coloring
denotes an
aristocrat

gaping mouth and
demonic teeth

Theater mask
Edo period
This mask represents Hannya,
a female Noh character turned
into a demon by jealousy and
anger. Noh theater coexisted with
other forms, such as Kabuki.

detail drawn from
nature

water pot   seal block

bamboo
brush

wooden cube
contains
penknife and
a needle

three
volumes
bound
together

Writing tools
1800–1899
Calligraphy was widely practiced by
the well-to-do as a leisure pursuit. The
compartments of this box contain brushes
and other paraphernalia of the art.

grinding
block

ink block

Bound woodblock prints
1779
A monochrome print consists of a single
impression from a carved woodblock.
Some later examples were hand-colored,
in anticipation of color printing.

> ❝ **WITHOUT DESTRUCTION,** THERE IS **NO CREATION…** THERE IS **NO CHANGE.** ❞

Oda Nobunaga (1534–82)

Oda Nobunaga ruthlessly broke the military power of Japan's leading regional warlords in a drive for control that eventually united Japan.

Construction of the austere yet vast royal residence, El Escorial, began in 1563. It was intended to underline the piety as well as the majesty of Spain's rulers.

BY ABOUT 1560, ODA NOBUNAGA, LEADER OF THE ODA CLAN in central Japan, was emerging as the greatest of the country's regional warlords, or *daimyo*. Since the calamitous Onin War, which began in 1466, **Japan had been effectively ungovernable**—the *daimyo* brutally vying for supremacy. The arrival of the Portuguese in the mid-15th century, bringing with them firearms, added to the chaos—the Japanese proved to be ready students of the possibilities of Western-style artillery bombardments (see 1574–77).

From 1561, the substantial **Baltic territories** of the **Livonian Order** (see 1236–40), which had already lost East Prussia in 1525 when the Teutonic Grand Master, Albrecht von Hohenzollern, converted to Protestantism, were **progressively dismembered** by Russia, Sweden, Poland, and Denmark. Originally a Crusading (that is, Christian) frontier entity, Livonia was a victim in part of the Reformation, but more of Polish–Russian rivalries—neither willing to see the other strengthened in the region at its own expense.

Few conflicts were more destabilizing than the **French Wars of Religion**, which began in

Massacre of Huguenots
The killing of 80 Huguenots at Vassy in northeast France in March 1562 was the spark that began the French Wars of Religion.

1562 and dragged on until 1598. There were, technically, eight separate wars; in reality, it was a single, long-drawn-out struggle. On one level, it was a purely religious conflict—was France to be Catholic or Protestant? Inevitably, this meant that the principal **Catholic and Protestant rulers of Europe** were periodically **dragged into the conflict**, neither the pope nor Philip II of Spain wanting a Protestant triumph any more than the Protestant rulers wanted a Catholic one. Yet it was also a matter of determining who exercised authority in France—the

crown or the nobles, whether **Catholic or Huguenot**. The French Protestants were known as Huguenots, from the Swiss-German *Eidgenossen* or "oath companions." The Catholics were in the majority, but the Huguenots were exceptionally well organized. Both parties had powerful aristocratic leaders for whom the struggle was also political. A royal minority always brought political instability in its wake (see 1557–59), but from 1560 it was compounded by three successive kings who had very limited ability to manage the nobles. As none produced an heir and civil war intensified, what was at stake by the end was not just the country's religious destiny but royal authority itself.

44
THE NUMBER OF **KNIGHTS WHO** SERVED AS **GRAND MASTER** OF THE **LIVONIAN ORDER**

IN 1563, SWEDEN AND DENMARK CLASHED FOR SUPREMACY in the Baltic. The **first modern naval war ensued**—that is, with sailing ships, rather than galleys (as was still common in the Mediterranean), heavily armed with cannon. Both countries were competing for control of the maritime invasion routes, the Danes supported by the semi-independent German city of Lübeck. **Seven major naval battles** were fought between 1563 and 1570, by which point both sides were effectively bankrupt. As other countries would discover, custom-built **men-of-war** may have been the most formidably **powerful weapons of the period** but the ships were prodigiously expensive. The war ended with no territorial gain for either side.

Escaping persecution at home, in 1564 a group of **Huguenot settlers** established a **colony in Florida** on the banks of the St. John's River on the site of what today is Jacksonville. Called **Fort Caroline**, it was the **first French colony** in what would become the US. It lasted little more than a year before it was **destroyed by a Spanish force** determined not to allow French settlers, especially Protestant ones, to encroach on a territory where they enjoyed superiority. All the settlers and the relieving force, bar a number of women and children, were killed. In revenge, in 1568, a **French force destroyed a Spanish colony, Fort Matanzas**, built after the destruction of Fort Caroline.

Battle of Oland
The Danes were victorious at the Battle of Oland on May 30–31, 1564, during which the Swedes lost their new royal flagship, Mars.

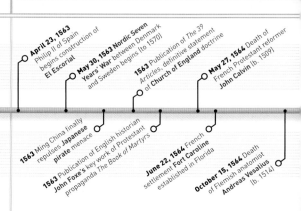

April 19, 1560 Death of German reformer **Philipp Melanchthon** (b. 1497)

December 5, 1560 Death of Francis II (b. 1544): his mother **Catherine de Medici** becomes Regent of France

1560 Portuguese begin **sugarcane cultivation** in Brazil

1560 Diplomat Jean Nicot (1530–1600) introduces **tobacco** from New World to French court

1561 Completion of **St. Basil's Cathedral, Moscow**

1562 Ottomans occupy **Transylvania**

December 6, 1560 **Charles IX** (1550–74) becomes king of France

1560 Foundations laid for the eventual unification of Japan under **Oda Nobunaga** (1534–82)

1561 Collapse of Livonian Order and subsequent partition of Livonia

March 1, 1562 Massacre at Vassy marks start of French **Wars of Religion** (to 1598)

c. 1562 Flemish artist **Peter Breugel the Elder** (c. 1525–69) paints *The Triumph of Death*

April 23, 1563 Philip II of Spain begins construction of **El Escorial**

May 30, 1563 Nordic Seven Years' War between Denmark and Sweden begins (to 1570)

1563 Publication of *The 39 Articles*, definitive statement of **Church of England** doctrine

May 27, 1564 Death of French Protestant reformer **John Calvin** (b. 1509)

1563 Ming China finally repulses **Japanese pirate** menace

1563 Publication of English historian John Foxe's key work of Protestant propaganda *The Book of Martyrs*

June 22, 1564 French settlement **Fort Caroline** established in Florida

October 15, 1564 Death of Flemish anatomist **Andreas Vesalius** (b. 1514)

Although Breugel's *Massacre of the Innocents* has a Biblical subject, in reality it is a commentary on Spanish brutality during the Dutch Revolt.

A priest blesses two soldiers in the Northern Rising of 1569, the last sustained attempt by Catholics in England to protest against the Reformation.

IN ESTABLISHING HIS OWN BRAND of divinely sanctioned Orthodox absolutism, **Ivan IV** (see panel, right) never had to contend with the substantial vested interests—mercantile, aristocratic, or clerical—that frustrated his counterparts in Western Europe. His principal opponents were the Cossacks—free-ranging frontiersmen—and the boyars, the

Spanish settlement
St. Augustine in Florida, founded by Spain in August 1565, is the oldest continuously inhabited European settlement in North America.

hereditary nobility. The **Cossacks were co-opted as allies** by the obvious strategy of bribing them, while, from 1565, the **boyars were dispossessed**, and in most cases slaughtered. Their former estates became Ivan's "private domain," the *oprichina*—a vast area of central Russia—parceled out among a new nobility, the *dvoriane*, loyal to the czar.

The key **maritime challenge confronting Spain** after its conquests in Mexico and Peru

(see 1532) was to link them with the Philippines and the Spice Islands on the western extremity of the Pacific, which, in 1564, Spain determined to colonize. A westward route across the Pacific had been pioneered in 1527, but no return route was known. Between June and October 1565, Spanish navigator **Andrés de Urdaneta** made the critical breakthrough, sailing far to the north to find favorable winds in the **longest nonstop voyage yet made**—11,600 miles (18,700 km). It completed a **vital trade network**.

In much the same way that religious conflict and power politics in the French Wars of Religion produced a savage conflict, so the **Dutch Revolt**—which began in 1566 and lasted until 1648—was the product of a toxic mix of religious intolerance and a drive for political domination. In 1566, **Philip II of Spain, Catholic ruler of the Netherlands**, asserted: "I do not propose nor desire to be the ruler of heretics." Given that there was considerable support for a growing **Protestant** minority in the **Netherlands**, his divine obligation to eradicate these heresies was inescapable. But there was a further complication. The Netherlands, whether Protestant or Catholic, had no desire to submit to Philip's rule given that this would mean surrendering its own "liberties"—

IVAN THE TERRIBLE
(1530–84)

Though capable of bouts of remorse—as when, in 1581, he killed his eldest son and heir by staving in his head with a staff—Ivan IV applied a ruthless brutality to his rule. Hence Ivan "the Terrible". One key consequence was that vast numbers fled Russia during his reign from 1547 to 1584, depopulating the country to the point that serfdom (bonded peasantry) was the only means of retaining an agricultural workforce.

its right to govern itself even while acknowledging Philip as its overall ruler. In particular, it saw no reason why it should pay taxes to finance the Spanish king's campaigns elsewhere. While this was a problem that could never be resolved peacefully, even by the standards of the period, the resulting conflict was shockin in its violence (see 1572–73).

IN 1568, OMURA SUMIDATA, a Japanese *daimyo* who in 1563 had converted to Christianity, gave permission for Portuguese traders and missionaries to establish a port at a fishing village at the southern tip of Japan—**Nagasaki**. Until the suppression of Christianity in Japan in 1614, Nagasaki, a Jesuit colony, was not only almost entirely Catholic—or "kirishitan"—it was Portugal's most important trading center in East Asia.

The most urgent task facing **Akbar** in his consolidation of Mughal power in India (see 1555–56) was the defeat of the **Hindu Rajputs of the northwest**. This was a decade-long campaign, which climaxed in 1569 with the fall of the fortresses of Mewar and Ranthambore. Having secured the submission of the principal Rajput rulers, Akbar married a series of Hindu princesses (he had 36 wives in all), tying his defeated enemies to him in matrimonial alliances.

In 1659, the failure of **Sigismund II**, last of the Jagiellonian rulers of the Grand Duchy of Lithuania and of Poland, to produce an heir led to a formal union between the two states. This new **Polish–Lithuanian Commonwealth** became the **largest territorial state in Europe**. The move was prompted by Sigismund's desire to ensure that his dynasty's territories were preserved, and the need to protect Lithuania from the Ottomans and the Russians. The nobles of both territories quarreled over the new

constitutional arrangement, anxious it should not be to their disadvantage. For the **Poles**, the clinching factor was the **transfer to them of immense territories**, among them the **Ukraine**.

The **Northern Rising** of November 1569 was the **most serious threat to Elizabeth I's pragmatic Protestantism**. Led by the Catholic earls of Westmorland and Northumberland, it swept across northern England before being **savagely repressed**.

In 1569, the Flemish cartographer **Gerardus Mercator** (1512–94) devised a **world map** that for the first time showed the true compass bearing of every landmass. The **Mercator projection** remains the most familiar map of the world.

Gerardus Mercator
Mercator was an engraver and a mathematician as well as a skilled cartographer. He devised his world map of 1569 for marine navigation.

> ❝ **BEAUTY** WILL **RESULT** FROM THE **FORM AND** THE **CORRESPONDENCE OF** THE **WHOLE...** ❞

Andrea Palladio, from *Four Books of Architecture,* 1570

Andrea Palladio, the most influential architect of the later Renaissance.

In the background of this painting of the St. Bartholomew's Day Massacre by the Huguenot François Dubois, Catherine de Medici inspects a pile of corpses.

THE MANILA GALLEON was one of the most distinctive elements of Spain's **New World trading system.** From the 1570s, three galleons (two after 1593) made an annual round-trip between Acapulco in Mexico and Manila in the Philippines. In return for New World silver, Spain imported silks, spices, porcelain, lacquerware, and ivory. It is estimated that by 1600 the value of a single cargo of these ships—the largest in the world—exceeded the entire annual revenue of the English crown.

In 1571, the **Portuguese** attempted to **colonize Angola,** but the Kimbundu people proved impossible to subdue, the soil of the coast was too poor to cultivate, and the salt trade could not be wrested from African control. They did establish trading forts at Luanda and Benguela in 1575 and 1587, boosting their slave trade.

The **Battle of Lepanto,** fought off the coast of western Greece in October 1571, was the last major engagement between galleys— with 208 Christian galleys against 251 Ottoman. The Christian fleet, commanded by **Don Juan of Austria,** illegitimate son of Charles V, triumphed, largely through its artillery. Although the Christians failed in the wider goal to retake Cyprus, the threat of Ottoman expansion in the western Mediterranean was ended.

Battle of Lepanto
An estimated 20,000 Ottomans and 7,500 Christians died at the Battle of Lepanto. The ramming tactics of the Ottoman galleys proved ineffective.

DESPITE THE SPANISH CONQUEST of **Inca Peru** (see 1532), a remnant Inca state was set up in the Upper Amazon in 1539 under a minor Inca noble, Manco Inca Yupanqui, in a small settlement, Vilcabamba. From here, he and his descendants waged an intermittent, generally ineffective campaign against the Spanish. In 1572, Vilcabamba was overrun and **the last Inca leader, Túpac Amaru, was executed.**

In 1566, a delegation of Dutch nobles appeared before **Margaret of Parma** (1522–86), half-sister of Philip II and governor-general of the Netherlands, objecting to Philip's drive against heresy in the Netherlands. They were referred to contemptuously by one of Margaret's counselors as *"gueux"*—"beggars." The name was enthusiastically taken up by the protesting Dutch, particularly the **Sea Beggars,** privateers (or pirates) whose raids on Spanish shipping from 1568 significantly hampered Spain's military efforts. The Sea Beggars depended to a considerable extent on support from England, discreetly doing what it could to disrupt the Spanish. But in the spring of 1572, **Elizabeth I** (see 1586–89), anxious not to offend Spain too obviously, closed English harbors to them. In response, in a more or less desperate gamble, on April 1, 1572 the Sea Beggars seized Brill, Holland. Within three months they had **taken practically every town in Zeeland and Holland,** purging them of royalists and Catholics. **William of Orange** (1533–84), politically and military the most

significant figure in the Revolt, agreed to take command of them. Rebellion had turned to open war.

The **massacre of Huguenots** in Paris on August 24, 1572, St. Bartholomew's Day, was the worst atrocity of the **French Wars of Religion.** It stemmed from an attempt to resolve the wars by a marriage. Henry of Navarre, a leading Huguenot close to the succession of the French throne, was to wed Marguerite of Valois, sister of the young French king, Charles IX. This was largely brokered by the king's mother, **Catherine de Medici** (see panel, right) who, as fearful for her son's throne as she was alarmed by growing Huguenot power, had nonetheless persistently sought to bring the warring factions to terms. In this overheated atmosphere, Catholics and Huguenots descended on Paris for the marriage. However, there was a **plot to assassinate** the Huguenot's dominant figure, **Gaspard de Coligny.** Who was behind it remains uncertain. In

12–15 MILLION	1.5 MILLION
1492	1572

Inca population
The European conquest of the Incas was devastating. Imported European diseases, rather than deliberate genocide, were the chief culprit.

May 20, 1570 Flemish cartographer Abraham Ortelius issues the first modern atlas, *Theatre of the World*

August 8, 1570 Peace of St. Germain ends the Third French War of Religion

1570 First official shipment, via Manila, of **Spanish silver** from South and Central America reaches China

February 13, 1571 Death of Italian artist **Benvenuto Cellini** (b. 1500)

October 7, 1571 Ottomans defeated by combined Christian fleet at **Battle of Lepanto**

1571 Portuguese colony founded in Angola

1570 Cyprus taken by Ottomans

1570 Portuguese trading mission to **Nagasaki,** Japan

1570 Publication in Italy of *Four Books of Architecture* by **Andrea Palladio**

May 1571 Crimean army led by Devlet I Giray starts **Great Fire of Moscow**

1571 Oda Nobunaga destroys rebellious Ikko sect near Nara, Japan

April 1, 1572 Sea Beggars revive opposition to the Spanish in the Netherlands

August 24, 1572 St. Bartholomew's Day Massacre, Paris

1572 Mughals overrun Gujarat, India

February 11, 1573 Duke of Anjou leads Catholic siege of Huguenot **La Rochelle** (to July 6)

1572 Final collapse of Inca resistance to Spanish rule with fall of **Vilcabamba**

1572 Portuguese epic poem *Os Lusíadas* written by **Luís de Camões**

July 13, 1573 Spanish capture **Haarlem,** Netherlands after seven-month siege

July 1573 Edict of Boulogne limits Huguenot worship to La Rochelle, Montauban, and Nîmes

> ❝ **SOVEREIGNTY** IS THE **ABSOLUTE** AND PERPETUAL **POWER OF** A **COMMONWEALTH**... THE **HIGHEST POWER** OF **COMMAND**... ❞
>
> Jean Bodin, French political philosopher, 1576

Hopelessly outnumbered, the Portuguese were in effect exterminated at the Battle of Alcácer Quibir. Portugal lost not only its king but most of its nobles.

CATHERINE DE MEDICI
(1519–89)

The Italian-born Catherine married Henry II of France in 1533. On his death in 1559, she became monarch in all but name as France fell into turmoil, with her first two sons, Francis II and Charles IX, proving too young and inexperienced, and Henry III facing a deteriorating political situation. Her goal to preserve the Valois monarchy was a spectacular failure.

any case, the plot failed—Coligny, though wounded, survived—but the mood in Paris became explosive. Catherine may then have persuaded the king that a Huguenot takeover was in the offing and could be forestalled only by killing all the principal Huguenots in the city. Equally, the subsequent bloodshed may have been spontaneous. At all events, not only was Coligny murdered, but **more than 3,000 Huguenots were killed**. Across France, a further 3,000 may have died in the following weeks.

THE NORTH AFRICAN COAST of the western Mediterranean was a key focus of **Ottoman–Christian rivalry**, with Spain, in particular, seeking to prevent Muslim raids on its shipping. Yet, gradually, the handful of North African cities in Spanish hands were lost—Algiers in 1529, Tripoli in 1551, and Bugia in 1555. By 1574, only Tunis remained. Its final fall in August 1574 to an overwhelming Ottoman fleet marked the **end of Habsburg ambitions in North Africa**, which from now was to remain firmly within the Ottoman orbit.

The **Battle of Nagashino**, fought in June 1575 between the forces of **Takeda Katsuyori** (1546–82) and an alliance led by the warlord **Oda Nobunaga** (see 1560–62), marked a decisive moment in the evolution of warfare in Japan—the first effective use of firearms. The arquebus muskets introduced by

Selimiye Mosque
Built by Mimar Sinan for Selim II in Edirne and completed in 1575, this mosque is the supreme statement of Ottoman Islamic architecture.

Battle of Nagashino
Nobunaga's men outnumbered the Takeda troops by more than 2:1, but it was Nobunaga's skillful use of firearms that won the day for them.

the Portuguese in the 1540s had been eagerly imitated by the Japanese despite being very slow to load. Nobunaga's solution was to have three guns for each man firing them, supported by teams of loaders. The result was a near continuous fire against which the Takeda clan's conventional cavalry and infantry were helpless.

Spain's efforts to suppress the **Dutch Revolt** (see 1572–73) foundered in 1575. Unable to levy taxes in the Netherlands, Philip II could not pay his troops and they mutinied, looting and murdering indiscriminately. Philip's authority in the Netherlands disintegrated. The vacuum was filled by the Dutch themselves—Catholics and royalists as well as the rebellious Protestants. Their agreement was sealed by the **Pacification of Ghent**, signed in November 1576.

JUST AS PHILIP II'S ATTEMPTS TO REASSERT HIS AUTHORITY over the heretical Netherlands were derailed by his simultaneous need to confront the Ottomans in the Mediterranean, so the Sunni Ottomans' attempts to confront the Shi'ite Safavids in Persia were distracted by their conflicts with Spain. The pause in the conflict after the fall of Tunis in 1574, confirmed by a peace treaty in 1580, freed both states to pursue their goals elsewhere. The benefits for the **Ottomans** were immediate—a **string of conquests in Georgia and Azerbaijan** that, by the fall of Tabriz in 1585, saw both incorporated within their empire.

In August 1578, the king of Portugal, Sebastian, was killed at the **Battle of Alcácer Quibir** in northern Morocco. The battle had two consequences. One was to confirm **Ahmad al-Mansur** (1549–1603) as the new sultan of an Ottoman-backed **Morocco**. The other was a **succession crisis in Portugal**. Sebastian's heir was his 66-year-old great-uncle, Henry, a cardinal. He died, childless, 17 months later. Among the claimants to the throne was Philip II (see 1580).

After the Pacification of Ghent (see 1576), Philip II was forced to agree not just to pull out his troops but to restore traditional privileges across the provinces. But on the question of religion, he remained adamant—Catholicism must be restored everywhere. The violence flared again. Philip's envoy, Don Juan,

stormed the city of Namur; in retaliation, Calvinist dissenters established themselves in cities across the south. In January 1579, the Catholic nobility of the south reaffirmed their loyalty to Philip, forming the **Union of Arras**. The northern provinces formed the **Union of Utrecht**. To the miseries of the Netherlands were added the horrors of civil war.

Chichak helmet
The Ottoman rawhide helmet with copper gilt was so effective it was widely imitated in Europe in the 17th century.

Resistance to Philip II's claim on the Portuguese crown in 1580 was weak—while an army advanced on Lisbon, the Spanish fleet assaulted it from the sea.

Toyotomi Hideyoshi's victory at Shizugatake in May 1583 was typical of his ruthless deployment of overwhelming force against his enemies.

THE PUBLICATION IN DRESDEN of the *Book of Concord* in 1580 was a pivotal moment in the development of **Lutheranism** (see 1516–18). While reaffirming the supreme importance of the Holy Scriptures—the Bible—it set out a strict interpretation of them "as the unanimous consensus and exposition of our Christian faith." It remains the basis of Lutheran beliefs today.

Philip II of Spain's claim to the **Portuguese crown** after the throne became vacant (see 1578–79) was made good in August 1580 by a combination of military force and bribery.

> **❝ NOTHING IS SO FIRMLY BELIEVED AS THAT WHICH LEAST IS KNOWN. ❞**
>
> Michel de Montaigne, French Renaissance writer, *Essais Book I*

In July 1581, the northern provinces of the Netherlands—the **United Provinces**—declared their independence by the **Act of Abjuration**, renouncing their oaths of loyalty to Philip II. With the Spanish king now technically deposed, a new throne, that of the Netherlands, was created and accepted by the **Duke of Anjou** (1555–84), brother of Henry III of France. The south remained broadly loyal to Philip, but the Act's

Francis, Duke of Anjou
Foreign support—English or French—was essential to defeat the Spanish, so the Dutch Protestants made the Duke of Anjou their ruler.

assertion that a **legal king could be legally overthrown** would have significant consequences.

The impact of the **Single Whip Reform**, or "simple rule," in 1581 in **Ming China** was immense. The reform meant that not only would all taxes be based on property—itself recorded in a universal census—but they would be **paid in silver**. It was introduced to simplify China's tax system and to avoid problems of inflation created by a paper currency and debased coinage. It was made possible by the inflow of Spanish and Japanese silver. The new tax system created even greater demand for bullion, raised the price of silver still further, and in the long term contributed to destabilizing the entire Ming economy.

THE RITUAL SUICIDE OF ODA NOBUNAGA (see 1560–62) in 1582 brought to power his most able general, **Toyotomi Hideyoshi** (c. 1536/37–98). Within a decade, he had succeeded in **unifying almost the whole of Japan** under his rule. It was a remarkable achievement for one born a peasant. All non-samurai were disarmed to ensure that commoners could not challenge his authority, while his reorganization of the tax system and redistribution of land guaranteed the revenues needed to complete his conquests.

On February 24, 1582, **Pope Gregory XIII** (1502–85) decreed a **revision to the Julian Calendar**, introduced in 46 BCE, which underestimated the length of every year by 11 minutes. By the late 16th century, the Julian date was 10 days adrift from the actual date, meaning that the spring equinox, from which the date of

Songhay Empire
The death of Askia Daud in 1582 followed by the Moroccan invasion (see 1591) were key factors in the Songhay Empire's decline.

[Map labeled: SAHARA, Koumbi Saleh, Timbuktu, Gao, SONGHAY EMPIRE, Jenne, ATLANTIC OCEAN]

KEY
- Songhay territory in 1500
- Songhay territory in 1625

Easter was calculated, fell on March 11 rather than March 21. Thus, for doctrinal reasons, the pope's modest adjustment was made. The change was introduced in October—Thursday the 4th being followed by Friday the 15th—but only in Spain, Portugal, Italy, and Poland-Lithuania. The rest of Europe, especially Protestant Europe, scenting a popish plot, was much slower to follow suit.

Sir Francis Drake (1540–96) became the first English captain to circumnavigate the globe in 1577–80, renewing English interest in the New World. **Sir Humphrey Gilbert** had already voyaged to **Newfoundland** in 1578–79. In 1583, he returned, with Elizabeth I's backing, and claimed it for England. In 1584, again with royal approval, **Sir Walter Raleigh** (c. 1552–1618) sent an expedition to found the **Virginia Colony**, named for the "Virgin Queen." It was established the following year at Roanoke Island, today in North Carolina, but, by 1590, it had disappeared.

The **surrender of Antwerp** on August 17, 1585, to the Duke of Parma was not merely a striking **military triumph for Spain**, but it also brought the city's commercial preeminence to an abrupt end.

Siege of Antwerp
The 13-month siege reduced the city's population from 100,000 to 40,000, but it returned the southern Netherlands to Spanish control.

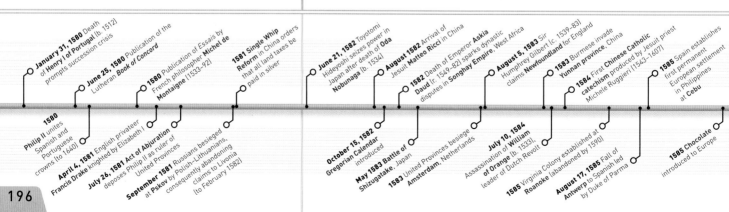

January 31, 1580 Death of Henry I of Portugal (b. 1512) prompts succession crisis

June 25, 1580 Publication of the Lutheran *Book of Concord*

1580 Publication of *Essais* by French philosopher **Michel de Montaigne** (1533–92)

1581 Single Whip Reform in China orders that all land taxes be paid in silver

1580 Philip II unites Spanish and Portuguese crowns (to 1640)

April 4, 1581 English privateer Francis Drake knighted by Elizabeth I

July 26, 1581 Act of Abjuration deposes Philip II as ruler of United Provinces

September 1581 Russians besieged at Pskov by Polish-Lithuanians, consequently abandoning claims to Livonia (to February 1582)

June 21, 1582 Toyotomi Hideyoshi seizes power in Japan after death of **Oda Nobunaga** (b. 1534)

August 1582 Arrival of Jesuit Matteo Ricci in China

1582 Death of Emperor **Askia Daud** (r. 1549–82) sparks dynastic disputes in **Songhay Empire**, West Africa

August 5, 1583 Sir Humphrey Gilbert (c. 1539–83) claims **Newfoundland** for England

1583 Burmese invade **Yunnan province**, China

1584 First Chinese Catholic **catechism** produced by Jesuit priest Michele Ruggieri (1543–1607)

1585 Spain establishes first permanent European settlement in Philippines at Cebu

October 15, 1582 Gregorian Calendar introduced

May 1583 Battle of Shizugatake, Japan

1583 United Provinces besiege Amsterdam, Netherlands

July 10, 1584 Assassination of **William of Orange** (b. 1533), leader of Dutch Revolt

1585 Virginia Colony established at Roanoke (abandoned by 1590)

August 17, 1585 Fall of Antwerp to Spanish led by Duke of Parma

1585 Chocolate introduced to Europe

After keeping her in custody for 19 years, Elizabeth I finally had Mary, Queen of Scots tried and executed for treason in February 1587.

> ❝ I HAVE THE **BODY** BUT **OF** A WEAK AND **FEEBLE WOMAN**, BUT I HAVE THE **HEART AND STOMACH OF** A **KING…** ❞

Elizabeth I, **Queen of England**, addressing the troops at Tilbury, August 19, 1588

ENGLAND'S INTERVENTION IN THE DUTCH REVOLT (see 1572–73) was characterized by the Battle of Zutphen in September 1586—it was a comprehensive defeat of the combined Anglo–Dutch forces by the Spanish. **Elizabeth I** had better luck with her attempts to destabilize Spain. In a series of plundering voyages to the Caribbean, **Drake** had highlighted how Spain's lucrative New World trade could be disrupted. In April 1587, Elizabeth despatched him on a mission to Spain with a goal of further raiding and destruction. Characteristically, she almost immediately changed her mind, but her message recalling Drake never reached him. It was a spectacular success—Spanish and Portuguese vessels and ports were attacked with audacious

abandon. The highlight was a **three-day assault on Cadiz** in southern Spain, in which 23 Spanish ships were sunk (according to Spanish sources; Drake claimed 33) and four were captured. The raid delayed Philip II's Armada by over a year.

Plots and rebellions plagued Elizabeth's reign and she had her Catholic cousin, **Mary, Queen of Scots**, executed in 1587 as a dangerous claimant to her throne.

Christianity in Japan thrived when first introduced by the Portuguese in the mid-16th century. By about 1580, there were an estimated 130,000 Japanese Christians, most in and around Nagasaki. For **Toyotomi Hideyoshi** (see 1582–85) they represented an organized and armed force around which opposition to him could be rallied. A prime motive for the conversion of many warlords had been that it would make it easier for them to obtain gunpowder, since its trade was still largely controlled by the Portuguese. At the same time, Hideyoshi was anxious not to jeopardize the trading links the Portuguese had established. His response was typically hardheaded—trade was still to be encouraged but Christianity would be banned. In July 1587, a **Purge Directive Order to the Jesuits** was issued. In addition, Nagasaki was brought under his direct rule. Though the Order was not fully enforced for a decade or more, Christianity in Japan would in future be forced underground.

Battle of Zutphen
The Anglo–Dutch forces suffered huge losses in the Battle of Zutphen in 1586, which resulted in the city being handed over to the Spanish.

[Bar chart titled ARMY (IN THOUSANDS), y-axis 0–30. Anglo–Dutch army: 6,000 casualties. Spanish army: 4,500 casualties.]

THE SPANISH ARMADA was Philip II's most obvious military gamble—a massive deployment of Spanish naval might meant first to overthrow England, then to crush the Protestant provinces of the Netherlands. It failed entirely. It showed how outright military success was elusive, and that logistical difficulties confronted any long-range military operation. Launched on May 30, 1588, the Armada was the victim of English seamanship, of lengthening lines of supply, and of the weather—the gale-wracked Spanish fleet was forced home in disarray. Spanish hopes of exterminating Protestant heresies were decisively checked.

Spanish Armada
Severe storms and the English fleet caused heavy losses to the Armada, which numbered around 150 ships when it left Lisbon.

ELIZABETH I (1533–1603)

Elizabeth faced many problems on her accession to the English throne in 1558—religious division, economic hardship, and threats from Scotland, France, and Spain. She overcame them with a combination of guile and intelligence and presided over a reinvention of England as a defiantly self-confident Protestant nation.

The death in 1589 of Henry III of France, stabbed by a Dominican monk, brought **Henry of Navarre** (1533–1610) to the throne and plunged France into crisis. Henry IV's claims to the crown were clear, yet he was a Protestant. To the powerful Catholic League

of France, and to Philip II in Spain, **the prospect of a Protestant king of France was unthinkable**. Henry IV's eventual acclamation as king came only in 1593, after a series of debilitating wars, when he—conveniently—converted to Catholicism.

Timeline

September 22, 1586 Anglo–Dutch army beaten by Spanish at **Battle of Zutphen**

1586 Mughals annex **Kashmir**

February 8, 1587 Elizabeth I orders execution of **Mary, Queen of Scots** (b. 1542)

July 1587 Anti-Christian edict issued in Japan

1586 Sir Francis Drake raids Spanish Caribbean settlements

1586 Spanish Renaissance artist **El Greco** (1541–1614) paints *The Burial of the Count of Orgaz*

April 29–May 1, 1587 Sir Francis Drake raids Cadiz, Spain

September 18, 1587 Poles elect a Swedish king, Sigismund III Vasa (1566–1632)

April 4, 1588 Christian IV (1577–1648) becomes King of Denmark

May 30, 1588 Spanish Armada sails from Lisbon

1588 Famine and pestilence sweep China, leading to depopulation and lawlessness

August 2, 1589 Assassination of Henry III (b. 1551) of France and succession of **Henry of Navarre**

May 12, 1588 Day of the Barricades—public uprising in Paris against Henry III

July–August 1588 Spanish Armada defeated by English

September 4, 1588 Death of Robert Dudley (b. 1532), potential suitor of Elizabeth I

January 5, 1589 Death of Catherine de Medici (b. 1519), wife of Henry II of France

1589 Portuguese sack Mombasa, East Africa

Dastana forearm guard
Date unknown
Forearm guards (*dastanas*) were worn by Mughal warriors to shield limbs from glancing blows. The hinged plate also protected the inner arm surface.

elbow protector

Metal turban helmet
Date unknown
The warriors of early Mughal armies wore lightweight but effective turban helmets with nose and neck guards to deflect enemy arrows and blades.

sliding bar for nose protection

Spiked parrying shield
18th century
With its five spikes and central plate, this Mughal device served as an elaborate and dangerously impressive weapon, as well as vital protection for its bearer.

stylized blade with battle spikes

each blade is 7 in (17.7 cm) long

Battle-ax
17th century
Mughal ideals of beauty extended even to weapons, such as this ornate but formidable cavalryman's ax from India's Deccan region.

elaborate tip

Iron mace
18th century
Solid weapons, like this mace, could crush enemy skulls, even through plate armor, and were used by Mughal foot soldiers.

central plate

MUGHAL EMPIRE

OUT OF A POWER STRUGGLE EMERGED AN ADVANCED, WEALTHY, AND INTEGRATED SOCIETY

For over two centuries (1526–1761), Mughal rulers dominated most of India. Through military might and administrative prowess, they integrated Hindus and Muslims into a rich culture of imperial splendor.

With their roots in Mongol and Turkish cultures, seven generations of Mughal kings, beginning with Babur (r. 1526–30), blended Persian and Islamic military and artistic influences into India's indigenous Hindu culture. The result was one of the most impressive medieval empires, which, at its height (1556–1707), commanded vast wealth, assimilated Hindus into its ruling elite, expanded education, and provided patronage in the arts and literature.

antelope features carved in ivory

Ivory priming powder horn
Date unknown
Ivory carving had an ancient history in India, and it became equally revered in Mughal courts. This powder horn, used on hunts, has an antelope shape.

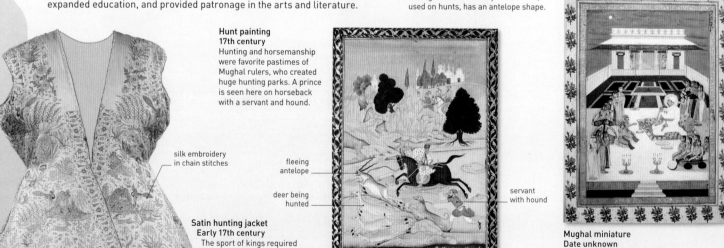

silk embroidery in chain stitches

Hunt painting
17th century
Hunting and horsemanship were favorite pastimes of Mughal rulers, who created huge hunting parks. A prince is seen here on horseback with a servant and hound.

fleeing antelope

deer being hunted

servant with hound

Satin hunting jacket
Early 17th century
The sport of kings required beautifully adorned clothing— this coat is lavishly embroidered with typically Persian floral patterns.

Mughal miniature
Date unknown
Arts and architecture flourished under the patronage of Mughal kings such as Akbar (r. 1542–1605). Miniature painting, introduced as manuscript illustration, was most prized.

Sarpech
Date unknown
The extraordinary wealth of the Mughals was evident in their love of jeweled objects. This *sarpech*, made of gold, emeralds, diamonds, rubies, and a pearl, adorned a royal turban.

large ruby at center

spike can be used as weapon

Hansli necklace
18th century
Cast in gold and heavily encrusted with precious stones, this rigid torque or necklace was known as a *hansli*, because it was designed to rest on the wearer's collarbone—or *hansli* in Urdu.

Talisman
Date unknown
Mughal craftsmen were famed for the intricacy of their work. This talisman, or *tabeez*, is decorated with verses from the Qu'ran.

enameled floral motif

solid jade pestle

floral pattern shows through

Mortar and pestle
17th century
Jade could only be worked using diamond dust, so it was highly prized in Mughal society. This mortar and pestle was carved from one block.

Bowl inlaid with jade
18th century
Parchîn kârî, or inlay, reached its peak during the reign of Jahan (1628–58). This bowl is inlaid with jade and precious stones.

Enameled gold wine goblet
17th century
Records of Mughal courtly life describe kings sipping their wine from enameled gold or silver goblets, and dozens of dishes served on gold and silver plates.

engraving of a dancing girl

bowl for holding tobacco

deer motif

water jar or bowl

golden base

silver incised hookah bowl

Mughal court painting
17th century
The splendor of the Mughal court is clear from this painting of the emperor Jahan (r. 1628–58) among his nobles, grouped in strict hierarchical order around the throne.

Jahan, fifth Mughal emperor

Hookahs
18th century
The Mughals brought the Persian tradition of hookah-smoking to India. Both men and women used hookahs, in which tobacco smoke is cooled with water.

£500,000

THE **GREATEST PRIZE** EVER TAKEN **BY ENGLISH PRIVATEERS,** FROM THE **MADRE DE DEUS**

An estimated 40,000–50,000 people died in Paris in 1590 until the Spanish army led by the Duke of Parma broke the four-month siege in September.

In this Portuguese map of Mombasa, Fort Jesus is depicted bottom right.

BY 1590, TOYOTOMI HIDEYOSHI (see 1582–87) had effectively completed the **unification of Japan**, and the distinctive character of the regime that was to dominate the country for over 250 years was established. Though it was not the capital, from 1590 Hideyoshi based himself at **Edo**, where the feudal nobility, now entirely subservient to him, were required to spend every other year. It proved a highly effective means of preventing rebellion. This elaborate social structure was largely supported by the peasantry, who had to pay heavy taxes.

Attempting to impose himself on France as king, **Henry of Navarre** (see 1588–89) besieged **Paris** in May 1590. The siege was broken in September by Spanish troops under the Duke of Parma.

In 1591, the **Sultan of Morocco, Ahmad al-Mansur,** (see 1578–79), launched an invasion of the troubled **Songhay Empire** (see 1582–85). Al-Mansur's goal was the **trans-Saharan gold trade**. The invasion involved a perilous four-month crossing of the Sahara by a fighting force of 4,000 men sustained by 8,000 camels. In March 1592, a Songhay army over 40,000 strong was routed at the **Battle of Tondibi** by the Moroccans' vastly superior firepower, which included numerous arquebuses and eight English cannons.

Castle complex
Himeji, or "White Egret," Castle is one of 200 massive castles built on the orders of Toyotomi Hideyoshi to ensure his power across Japan.

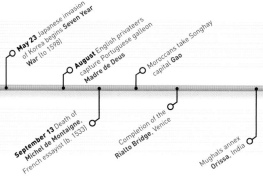

Rialto Bridge
The Rialto Bridge over the Grand Canal in Venice was completed in 1592. It was the fifth bridge built at the site, and the first made of stone.

THE SEVEN YEAR WAR began in the spring of 1592 when **Japanese forces** mounted a sustained **invasion of Korea**. Partly an attempt by Toyotomi Hideyoshi to unite the Japanese in a common cause, it was more particularly the fulfillment of his predecessor Oda Nobunaga's ambitious goal of a **conquest of Ming China** itself. The campaign met with mixed results. Japanese land victories in Korea were matched by Korean naval victories—the heavily armed and protected Korean turtle ships proving decisive against Japan's progressively weakened fleets. **Chinese intervention** late in the year tipped the balance against Japan. By the spring of 1593, the Japanese were forced to sue for peace. By the middle of the year, they had begun to pull out. In 1597, the aging Hideyoshi renewed the campaign, sending larger forces. The result was a **further defeat for Japan** in 1598, but the savage fighting **devastated Korea**. Though the war did not formally end until 1608, by 1599 it was effectively over. Paradoxically, it was Japan that benefited most. The defeat had a significant influence on its subsequent, if never absolute, isolation from the wider world. Korea, by contrast, took years to recover, while the immense cost of the war to Ming China not only provoked riots against the extra taxes levied but weakened its military capacity on its vulnerable northeastern frontier.

From 1592, **Akbar** (see 1555–56) launched a further round of conquests that saw the **Mughal Empire's frontiers** reach their greatest extent during his reign. In the east, Orissa was annexed. In 1594, Baluchistan and the coastal strip of Makran on the Safavid Persian border were conquered. And in 1596, the **key Afghan city of Kandahar**, lost by Akbar's father Humayan, was retaken.

THE OTTOMAN–HABSBURG FRONTIER, generally stable after the renewed Ottoman attempt on Vienna in 1529, was a key focus of Ottoman–Christian conflict. It came center-stage again in 1593 with the **Long War**. A series of inconclusive campaigns followed in Hungary and the Balkans, with the nominal Ottoman vassals of Transylvania, Wallachia, and Moldavia supporting the Habsburgs. The net result of the eventual peace settlement—the **Treaty of Zsitvatorok** of 1606—was to leave the frontier in a state of simmering uncertainty.

On June 10, 1594, in the Spanish settlement of St. Augustine, Florida, Father Diego Escobar de Zambrana baptized Maria, daughter of Juan Jimenez de la Cueva and Maria Melendez. The event was recorded in the oldest public document in what would become the US and is the first authentic record of a **child born to European settlers** there.

Fort Jesus in Mombasa, East Africa was built at the command of Philip II and completed in 1593. It proved to be crucial to Portuguese endeavors in the Indian Ocean throughout the 17th century.

❝ PARIS IS WORTH A MASS. ❞

Henry IV of France, 1593

Timeline

May 21, 1590 Ottoman frontiers extended to the Caucasus and Caspian following **Ottoman-Safavid peace treaty**

September 1590 Duke of Parma ends Henry of Navarre's siege of **Paris**

1590 Toyotomi Hideyoshi (c. 1536/37–98) completes unification of Japan

1591 Moroccans capture **Timbuktu**, Songhay Empire

August 18, 1590 English Virginia Colony at **Roanoke** found abandoned

1590 Publication of *Arcadia* by English poet Philip Sidney (1554–86)

1591 Regent of Russia, **Boris Godunov**, suspected of murdering nine-year-old son of Ivan the Terrible

May 23 Japanese invasion of Korea begins **Seven Year War** (to 1598)

August English privateers capture Portuguese galleon **Madre de Deus**

Moroccans take Songhay capital **Gao**

September 13 Death of Michel de Montaigne, French essayist (b. 1533)

Completion of the **Rialto Bridge**, Venice

Mughals annex **Orissa**, India

July 25, 1593 Henry of Navarre converts to Catholicism

1593 Japanese pull out of Korea after Chinese military intervention

1593 Portuguese complete **Fort Jesus**, Mombasa

1593 Long War between Habsburgs and Ottomans (to 1606)

February 27, 1594 Coronation of Henry IV of France

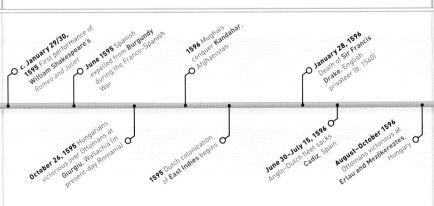
Despite the perils of the venture, all four Dutch ships that set out for the East Indies in 1595 made it back safely to Amsterdam with their cargo in 1599.

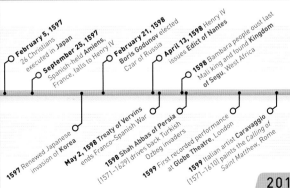
This ceiling fresco at Chehel Sotoun Palace in Isfahan, Iran, shows Shah Abbas I, seated on the right, playing host to Vali Muhammad Khan of Bukara.

THE FINAL CONVULSIONS OF THE FRENCH WARS OF RELIGION

(1562–98) were played out after 1595. **Henry IV** (see 1588–89), by his conversion to Catholicism in 1593, succeeded in winning broad acceptance as king. Yet his conversion aroused the suspicions of the **Huguenots**—fearful he now intended to turn against them—and did nothing to appease the ambitions of the leaders of the **Catholic League**, whose goal was not merely the extermination of Protestantism in France but the seizure of the throne. Henry's response, in January 1595, was to **declare war on Spain**. His aim was both to eradicate the Catholic League, supported by Spain, while demonstrating to the Huguenots that, Catholic or not, he was no puppet of the Spanish monarchy. An early French victory in June

Anglo–Dutch fleet attacks Cadiz
Nominally a joint Anglo–Dutch operation, in reality, of the 150 ships in the fleet that attacked Cadiz in 1596, 130 were English.

1595 against a combined Spanish–Catholic League force in Burgundy was followed the following spring by a renewed Spanish offensive that saw the capture of Calais and Amiens. The inevitable sieges by Henry followed, and the capitulation of Amiens in September 1597 marked his final triumph.

Until the beginning of the Dutch Revolt in 1566, the Netherlands largely dominated the **lucrative maritime trade** between Spain and Portugal and northern Europe—it was Dutch ships that carried spices and other New World goods from Iberia to the north. Thereafter, forbidden to trade with Iberian ports and conscious of the failings of Spain's maritime reach highlighted by the Armada, the **Dutch determined to break into the spice trade**. In 1595, four Dutch ships under Cornelius van Houten sailed for

Anglo–Dutch ships
150

Spanish ships
40

RAID ON CADIZ

10
Anglo–Dutch ships lost

32
Spanish ships lost

Raid on Cadiz
The Spanish lost 80 percent of the fleet anchored at Cadiz. They set many of their ships on fire to deny the Anglo–Dutch raiders their prize.

the East Indies. The crews endured scurvy and repeated clashes with local rulers and the Portuguese, and van Houten was killed in Sumatra. When, in 1599, the beleaguered fleet returned to Amsterdam, it brought with it an apparently meager quantity of spices, yet this was enough to secure a huge profit. The stage for Dutch domination of the East India trade was set (see 1602–03).

One of **England's few successes** in its participation in the Dutch Revolt was a **raid on Cadiz** in southern Spain in July 1596. Much like Drake's raid in 1587, it caused enormous devastation, with most of the city destroyed, and contributed to the bankruptcy of the Spanish crown in 1597.

ALTHOUGH THE BANNING OF CHRISTIANITY IN JAPAN had been

enforced only partially since 1587, in December 1596, certain that Spain and Portugal were using Christian penetration as a prelude to conquest, Toyotomi ordered the **deaths of 26 Christians**—six Franciscan missionaries and 20 Japanese. On February 5, 1597, in Nagasaki, they were strapped to crosses and speared to death. The significance of their deaths was less that Christianity would not be tolerated in Japan, and more that any challenge to the central authority would not be allowed.

The uneasy compromise brokered by Henry IV in France after 1597 was symbolized by the **Edict of Nantes** of April 1598. Under it, Protestants in France were granted the right to organize a quasi-independent state within France. Not only could they practice their religion freely—other than in Paris—but the Crown guaranteed their security, paying them to garrison their towns. Nothing if not pragmatic—and effective enough in the short term in **ending the French Wars of Religion**—inevitably it satisfied no one. The Huguenots still felt themselves unequally treated compared to the Catholics, while the latter were horrified that the Huguenots should be tolerated at all, let alone protected.

The accession in 1587 of the 16-year-old **Abbas I** as the **shah of Safavid Persia** rejuvenated its fortunes. Under his father Shah Mohammed, Persia had been in a state of near civil war created by

WILLIAM SHAKESPEARE
(1564–1616)

William Shakespeare exerted more influence on English literature and European drama than any other writer. The son of a Stratford-upon-Avon wool dealer, he was an actor turned author, and wrote at least 37 plays and 154 sonnets. He is believed to have written the tragedy *Hamlet* around 1599–1602. He also excelled at comedy.

rival factions within the Qizilbash army and had lost substantial territories to the Ottomans and Uzbeks. Abbas set about a **major reform of his rebellious army**, drafting in new troops, principally from the Caucasus, who were directly loyal to him. He rearmed them with muskets supplied by an English diplomat, Sir Anthony Shirley, who was negotiating an Anglo–Persian anti-Ottoman treaty. Between April and August 1598, Abbas launched a **major campaign against the Uzbeks**, driving them from the northwest of Persia.

c. January 29/30, 1595 First performance of William Shakespeare's *Romeo and Juliet*

June 1595 Spanish expelled from **Burgundy** during the Franco-Spanish War

1596 Mughals conquer **Kandahar**, Afghanistan

January 28, 1596 Death of Sir Francis Drake, English privateer (b. 1540)

February 5, 1597 26 Christians executed in Japan

September 25, 1597 Spanish-held Amiens, France, falls to Henry IV

February 21, 1598 Boris Godunov elected Czar of Russia

April 13, 1598 Henry IV issues **Edict of Nantes**

1598 Bambara people oust last Mali king and found **Kingdom of Segu**, West Africa

October 26, 1595 Hungarians victorious over Ottomans at **Giurgiu**, Wallachia (in present-day Romania)

1595 Dutch colonization of **East Indies** begins

June 30–July 15, 1596 Anglo–Dutch fleet sacks **Cadiz**, Spain

August–October 1596 Ottomans victorious at **Erlau** and **Mezőkeresztes**, Hungary

1597 Renewed Japanese invasion of **Korea**

May 2, 1598 Treaty of Vervins ends Franco-Spanish War

1598 Shah Abbas of Persia (1571–1629) drives back Turkish Özbeg invaders

1599 First recorded performance at **Globe Theatre**, London

1599 Italian artist **Caravaggio** (1571–1610) paints the Calling of Saint Matthew, Rome

The English East India Company began trading with Surat, a key center of Indian Ocean trade, in 1608. By 1615, it had ousted the Portuguese.

Tokugawa Ieyasu was 60 years old when he received the title of shogun from Emperor Go-Yōzei. He remained the effective ruler of Japan until his death.

Guy Fawkes (third from the right) and his fellow Catholic conspirators.

BY ABOUT 1600, THE POLYNESIAN PEOPLES OF NEW ZEALAND, the Maori, had become progressively better established in their new lands (see 1276–85). Although theirs was still a Stone Age society—and would remain so until the arrival of Europeans and the introduction of metal—it was remarkably well adapted to the new environment. Known as the **Classic Maori phase**, the culture was distinguished by elaborate wood carving, precisely patterned bone tools and weapons, and substantial earthwork settlements.

The establishment, with royal approval, on December 31, 1600 of the **English East India Company** was a clear statement of English intent that Spain and Portugal could not expect exclusive domination of trade with

Maori weapon
The wahaika, a short wooden club held by a dog-skin thong looped around the thumb and wrist, was used for close combat.

East Asia. That said, from the start the East India Company was a speculative venture at best. It depended not merely on an uncertain ability to reach these distant lands but, once there, to present itself—militarily and diplomatically—as a credible alternative to its European rivals. It called for a combination of seamanship, commercial intuition, and force—the last a permanent necessity. Eventually, it would establish itself almost as an arm of the English, later the British, state. But it was never intended as a means of conquest or colonization—**enrichment for its shareholders was its sole goal**. Ironically, its penetration of these new markets coincided with that of another latecomer, the Dutch. European domination for the riches of the East Indies would be contested not between England and Iberia but between England and the Dutch.

7
CUBIC MILES
THE **VOLUME** OF **MATERIAL EJECTED** FROM **HUAYNAPUTINA VOLCANO,** PERU

FOR AROUND 100 YEARS, THE DUTCH EAST INDIA COMPANY, established in 1602 and exact equivalent of its English rival, was the **most successful commercial venture in the world**. Its navigators not only outflanked the Portuguese in the Indian Ocean—pioneering new routes deep into the Southern Ocean as a means of access to the East Indies—but, having reached their lucrative goals, they exploited them with a single-mindedness that left their predecessors floundering. In 1602, the Dutch had laid claim to Guiana in South America. More importantly, by 1605 they had ousted the Portuguese from the Moluccas (Spice Islands). The foundations of a Dutch East Asian trading empire had been laid.

When **James I** (1566–1625) became **King of England** in 1603 on the death of Elizabeth I, he had already been **King of Scotland**, as James VI, for 36 years. Although they remained two quite clearly separate countries, sharing only a common monarch, James did manage to drive through the repeal of mutually hostile laws. Otherwise, the closest he came to the union he sought was an Anglo-Scots flag, the **Union Jack**, known for his preferred French name, Jacques.

On the very same day as James's accession, **Tokugawa Ieyasu** (1543–1616) became **shogun** of the Tokugawa shogunate of **Japan**. He presided over a rigidly stratified, inward-looking society that endured for 250 years.

French exploration in the New World was resumed by **Samuel de Champlain** in 1603. Over the following 12 years, he made a series of pioneering journeys along the St. Lawrence River toward the Great Lakes. In 1605, he also established a short-lived French colony, Port Royal, in Novia Scotia and, in 1608, a **permanent French base at Québec**. Although partly motivated by a search for a river passage to the Pacific, Champlain recognized that this rugged land was valuable in itself, above all for its **furs**. He subsequently sponsored a series of westward explorations beyond the Great Lakes, championing the potential of *Nouvelle France*.

Ships of Dutch East India Company — **4,800**

Dutch trade goods in million tons — **2.5**

1602–1798

Ships of English East India Company — **2,700**

English trade goods in million tons — **0.5**

Trade in East Asia
The Dutch East India Company was five times as successful as its English equivalent throughout the 17th and 18th centuries.

> ❝ THE **SPANISH ASSAILED** THE UNASSAILABLE; THE **DUTCH DEFENDED** THE INDEFENSIBLE. ❞

Anonymous, Siege of Ostend

WHEN SPANISH FORCES UNDER GENERAL SPINOLA TOOK OSTEND from a combined Anglo–Dutch force on September 16, 1604, it **ended a siege** that had lasted three years, two months, and 17 days. Even by the standards of 17th-century Europe—a century that saw only four years of peace—it was an extraordinarily brutal business. Siege warfare developed in response to artillery, to which the medieval castle, with high, thin walls, was vulnerable. Instead, fortifications became lower, thicker, and very much larger. So much so that many fortified towns were beyond the range of contemporary guns, and a blockade was the only practical means of taking them.

The **death of Czar Boris Godunov** in 1605 brought to a head a **political crisis** rapidly engulfing Russia, one heightened by a terrible **famine** that killed two million people—**a third of the population**—in 1601–03. Hoping to exploit Russia's divisions to its own advantage, and supported by disaffected Russian nobles, an unofficial **Polish–Lithuanian force** had already invaded the

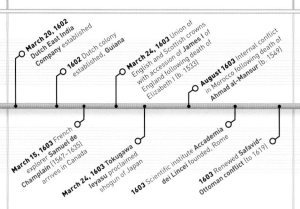

February 19, 1600 Huaynaputina volcano, Peru, erupts, killing around 1,500 people

December 31, 1600 English East India Company established, England

c. 1600 Statue-building culture of Easter Island begins to decline

October 24, 1601 Death of Tycho Brahe, Danish astronomer (b. 1546)

c. 1600 Classic Maori phase in New Zealand

c. 1600 Hausa city-states of West Africa flourish

1601 Russian famine (to 1603) heralds "Time of Troubles"

1601 Deccan kingdoms absorbed by Mughals, India

March 20, 1602 Dutch East India Company established

1602 Dutch colony established, Guiana

March 24, 1603 Union of English and Scottish crowns with accession of James I of England following death of Elizabeth I (b. 1533)

August 1603 Internal conflict in Morocco following death of Ahmad al-Mansur (b. 1549)

March 15, 1603 French explorer Samuel de Champlain (1567–1635) arrives in Canada

March 24, 1603 Tokugawa Ieyasu proclaimed shogun of Japan

1603 Scientific institute Accademia dei Lincei founded, Rome

1603 Renewed Safavid–Ottoman conflict (to 1619)

August 18, 1604 Treaty of London signed, concluding the Anglo–Spanish War

September 16, 1604 Ostend in the United Provinces falls to Spanish

1604 Posthumous publication of Dr. Faustus by English dramatist Christopher Marlowe (1564–93)

A reconstruction of Jamestown, the first permanent English settlement in North America, established in 1607 on the James River in what is now Virginia.

country, its aim in part to claim Orthodox Russia for the Catholic church. With Godunov's death, the interlopers placed on the Russian throne a man claiming to be Ivan the Terrible's youngest son. After less than a year, this False Dimitri was overthrown by **Vasili IV** (1552–1612), who slaughtered the Poles in Moscow, perhaps 2,000. Seeking to strengthen himself against continuing Polish agitation, in 1609 Vasili allied with Sweden, provoking an official Polish declaration of war against Russia. The following year, the **Poles had taken Moscow** and their king, **Sigismund III**, asserted

his own right to the Russian throne. Alarmed at the prospect of Poland–Lithuania taking over Russia, the **Swedes invaded and captured Novgorod**. In 1612, **Russia was saved** when a patriotic rising under Prince Pozharsky forced the Poles out of Moscow and elected the **first Romanov czar, Mikhail** (1596–1645). Though unable to oust the Swedes, Russia came to terms with Sweden in 1617 at the cost of giving up its access to the Baltic. In 1619, the **Polish–Russian conflict was ended** by Russia ceding substantial territories on its western border.

In Strasbourg in 1605, **Johann Carolus** (1575–1634) published what is generally acknowledged as **the world's first newspaper**, *Relation aller Fürnemmen und gedenckwürdigen Historien*— "Collection of all Distinguished and Commemorable News." Carolus already produced a hand-written news-sheet. He realized, however, that a printed version, sold more cheaply and to a wider audience, would be more profitable. By 1617, there were a further four German newspapers.

The hopes of James I of England for religious toleration were dashed with the discovery on November 5, 1605 of a **Catholic plot to blow up the Houses of Parliament**. It is possible that the plotters were encouraged by Robert Cecil, chief minister of James I, in order to stoke anti-Catholic opinion.

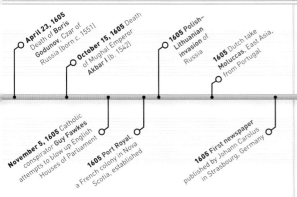

First newspaper on sale
The appearance of the Relation *in Europe in 1605 was early evidence of a growing demand for information in a fast-changing world.*

> ❝ THE **FIFTEENTH** DAY OF **JUNE, WE** HAD **BUILT** AND **FINISHED OUR FORT… THIS COUNTRY** IS A **FRUITFUL SOIL, BEARING** MANY GOODLY AND **FRUITFUL TREES…** ❞

George Percy, English colonist, from *Jamestown Narratives*

IN DECEMBER 1605, PORTUGUESE NAVIGATOR Pedro Fernández de Quiros received royal approval for a second voyage across the Pacific **in search of the presumed southern continent**, *Terra Australis Incognita*. After sailing through the Tuamotu Archipelago in February 1606, he reached the New Hebrides in May, but was swept out to sea by the trade winds and forced to return to New Spain. The expedition had a second ship, under the command of **Luis Váez de Torres**. Continuing to the west, he discovered the strait that bears his name between **New Guinea** and **Australia**, sighting the continent in the process. In the event, his discoveries, meticulously noted but never published, would not be followed up by Spain. It was left to the Dutch to confirm the existence of Australia.

On May 4, 1607, the **first permanent English settlement** was established in **North America**. **Jamestown**, in present-day Virginia, was a highly speculative venture, financed by the London Company (later the Virginia Company). It was intended partly to forestall Spanish, French, and Dutch attempts at settlement, and more particularly to locate a sea passage to East Asia, as well as to prospect for gold and other precious metals. Its early years were unpromising. The site, chosen principally because it was easily defended, was swampy, malarial, and had little arable land. The colonists succumbed to disease and starvation, and relations with the **Powhatan Indians** were tense as well. It was only in 1612, when the **first tobacco crop** was exported, that the colony looked to have any prospects of survival.

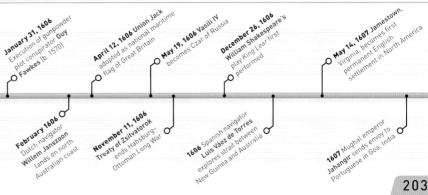

Torres Strait Islanders mask
The sea-faring Torres Strait Islanders had a range of masks for ritual occasions, many of the most elaborate made from turtle shells.

April 23, 1605 Death of Boris Godunov, Czar of Russia (born c. 1551)

October 15, 1605 Death of Mughal Emperor Akbar I (b. 1542)

1605 Polish–Lithuanian invasion of Russia

1605 Dutch take Moluccas, East Asia, from Portugal

January 31, 1606 Execution of gunpowder plot conspirator **Guy Fawkes** (b. 1570)

April 12, 1606 Union Jack adopted as national maritime flag of Great Britain

May 19, 1606 Vasili IV becomes Czar of Russia

December 26, 1606 William Shakespeare's play *King Lear* first performed

May 14, 1607 Jamestown, Virginia, becomes first permanent English settlement in North America

November 5, 1605 Catholic conspirator Guy Fawkes attempts to blow up English Houses of Parliament

1605 Port Royal, a French colony in Nova Scotia, established

1605 First newspaper published by Johann Carolus in Strasbourg, Germany

February 1606 Dutch navigator **Willem Janszoon** lands on north Australian coast

November 11, 1606 Treaty of Zsitvatorok ends Habsburg–Ottoman Long War

1606 Spanish navigator **Luis Váez de Torres** explores strait between New Guinea and Australia

1607 Mughal emperor Jahangir sends envoy to Portuguese in Goa, India

203

facial expression intended to elicit sympathy

sumptuous clothing identifies the artist's patron

Venetian gold ducat
16th century • ITALY
This gold coin depicts the Doge of Venice (right) receiving the city's banner from a dominating St. Mark the Evangelist.

Processional cross
15th century • ITALY
The wealth of the Italian Catholic Church is expressed by this cross, made of gold, silver, and enamel, and paraded on religious holidays.

The Descent from the Cross
c. 1435 • NETHERLANDS
This painting by Rogier van der Weyden (c. 1399–1464) exemplifies Flemish assimilation of the Renaissance move toward idealization of faces and figures.

THE RENAISSANCE

A REBIRTH OF EUROPEAN CULTURE INSPIRED BY ANCIENT GREECE AND ROME

A thousand years after the Roman Empire's collapse, scholars in Florence, Italy, arrived at a renewed understanding of the art, architecture, and literature of the classical period, sparking a cultural revolution.

In the 14th century, trade among European states increased and Florence, as a banking and commercial center—eventually under Medici control—developed a class of wealthy, educated individuals who became patrons of artists and thinkers. If Florence stood initially at the forefront of these artistic and intellectual developments, by the 16th century, the lead had passed to Papal Rome and Venice.

horns represent light rays

beard demonstrates sculptor's skill

larger than life-size figure (8.33 ft/2.54 m high)

Figure of Moses
c. 1515 • ITALY
Sculpted by Michelangelo (1475–1564) for the tomb of Pope Julius II, this statue now stands in the Church of San Pietro in Vincoli, Rome.

floor plan under dome

lantern lets in light and air

Florence Cathedral's dome
15th century • ITALY
The octagonal cathedral dome by Filippo Brunelleschi (1377–1446) consists of three parts, with the innermost visible from inside the building, as shown by this 19th-century engraving.

inner brick dome supports light roof

Mona Lisa
1503–06 • ITALY
Also known as *La Gioconda*, this enigmatic painting by Leonardo da Vinci (1452–1519) is the most famous Renaissance work and the world's best-known painting.

Medici ceramic
15th century • ITALY
This tin-glazed majolica plate, emblazoned with the Medici coat of arms, suggests the wealth and prestige of the Medici dynasty in Florence.

red ball signifies a medicine pill

straight lines represent headings of mariner's compass

Mediterranean sea

Mappa Mundi
1502 • SPAIN
Venice's wealth derived from its dominance of world trade routes. This map shows the Mediterranean and its adjacent seas, which Venetian ships regularly visited to distribute goods that were carried to the west by overland trade routes.

pose of the goddess Venus is based on a Roman statue

The Birth of Venus
c. 1486 • ITALY
This masterly painting of the early Renaissance by Botticelli (c. 1445–1510) refers directly to the Renaissance desire to appropriate and update ancient Roman ideals of beauty.

celestial globe symbolizes navigational skills

torquetum, an astronomical instrument, symbolizes scientific learning

Asian carpet symbolizes exploration

fur-trimmed coat denotes wealth and prestige

distorted skull symbolizes death; when viewed from the side, the skull is undistorted

lute with broken string suggests religious discord

The Ambassadors
1533 • GERMANY
A highly detailed painting with complex symbolism, this portrait of two young French diplomats by Hans Holbein the Younger (c. 1497–1543) includes much evidence of their lives and accomplishments as cultured men of the Renaissance.

kidney

abdominal cavity with intestines removed to reveal underlying organs

Organs in the abdominal cavity
c. 1453 • ITALY
From *De humani corporis fabrica* by Andreas Vesalius (1514–64), this anatomical diagram typifies the Renaissance determination to expand scientific knowledge.

structure based on a bat's wing

Hand-powered wing
c. 1490 • ITALY
Leonardo da Vinci produced several proposals for human-powered flying machines, including this sketch for a hand-cranked wing from his 12-volume *Codex Atlanticus*.

hand-crank mechanism

> **SO LONG AS** THE MOTHER, **IGNORANCE, LIVES,** IT IS **NOT SAFE FOR SCIENCE,** THE OFFSPRING, **TO DIVULGE** THE **HIDDEN CAUSE** OF THINGS.

Johannes Kepler, German astronomer

A copper engraving depicts the assassination of Henry IV, King of France, in Paris. Henry IV had survived 18 previous attempts on his life.

This painting shows the Battle of Kalmar on the Baltic Sea.

ON OCTOBER 2, 1608, HANS LIPPERSHEY (1570–1619), a lens-maker in Zeeland in the Dutch Netherlands, applied for a patent for a device for "seeing things far away as if they were nearby." This was soon known as a **telescope**. Lippershey's device was crude, only magnifying by three times, and was soon exceeded by others. But it was still a milestone in the development of scientific observation in 17th-century Europe.

Since 1606, the Dutch had been trying to broker a truce with Spain to halt the ongoing wars of the **Dutch Revolt**. Forty years of war had left both sides spent, yet each feared the other would use a ceasefire to regroup—as each intended to do. Despite this, in April 1609, a **12-year truce** was agreed.

In 1526, Charles V had decreed that all Muslims in Spain convert to Catholicism. The resulting minority **Morisco** population remained on the margins of Spanish society—valued for their cheap labor, but suspected for their religious affiliation. In 1609, Philip III agreed to **expel** them from Spain entirely. The decision caused whole communities to be summarily expelled and their possessions forfeited. It also created economic dislocation in many parts of the country as a valuable source of labor disappeared. Muslim resentment toward Spain predictably increased.

In 1609, the Dutch East India Company had sent **Henry Hudson** to investigate North America's east coast. He explored the Hudson River to present-day Albany, claiming the region for the Dutch.

Hudson River
New York State's river is named for Englishman Henry Hudson, who explored the river's course.

THE ASSASSINATION OF HENRY IV in Paris on May 14, 1610, stabbed by a one-time monk and teacher, Francois Ravaillac, promised a reawakening of the brutal religious divisions Henry had worked so hard—and killed so many—to avoid. The reality was quite the opposite. Not only was Henry's nine-year-old son immediately accepted as the new monarch, **Louis XIII**, but the threat of renewed conflict between France and Spain was averted. Both had been sparring for control of the duchy of Jülich-Cleves in Germany, threatening a renewed pan-European religious conflict. With Henry's death, both could now legitimately retire with no loss of face. Henry IV, first of the Bourbon kings, was among the most remarkable of France's kings: his **reconstruction** of the pestilential medieval shambles of Paris echoed his far-sighted reconstruction of France itself.

Less than a year after Hans Lippershey claimed to have invented a telescope, **Galileo** (see panel, right), working from no more than descriptions of Lippershey's device, had devised his own. It took him, he claimed, less than one day to put together. It was 10 times more powerful. It was with this basic instrument that, in January 1610, Galileo began to observe the "three fixed stars," invisible to the naked eye, that were next to the planet Jupiter. They were, he realized, **orbiting** the planet. This was a discovery that challenged the accepted notion of how heavenly

GALILEO (1564–1642)

Galileo Galilei, born in Pisa, was an Italian scientist who, despite obstruction from religious orthodoxy, revealed an entirely new, scientific understanding of the world. The Church regarded his revelations as heresy but, reluctant to condemn the scientific pioneer outright, did its best to accommodate him. Heretic or not, Galileo died with his reputation not just growing but assured.

bodies could orbit only one fixed point in the skies: the Earth. This explosive revelation was reinforced later the same year when Galileo began a systematic series of observations of the planet Venus. Its phases—crescent, partial, and full—could be explained only if it, too, was orbiting another body, the **Sun**. Observations made possible by the telescope were poised to revolutionize humanity's understanding of its relationship with a vast, impersonal universe.

IN 1604, KING JAMES I OF ENGLAND authorized a new English translation of the **Bible**. Since the Reformation there had been two previous English translations: the *Great Bible* of 1539 and the *Bishops' Bible* of 1568. However, it was felt that both contained minor **inaccuracies** and neither fully reflected the doctrinal authority and structure of the **Church of England**. The new translation, published in 1611 as *The Holy Bible*, was the work of 47 scholars under the direction of the Archbishop of Canterbury, Richard Bancroft. Though accepted relatively slowly by the Anglicans, by the 18th century it was widely regarded by all English-speaking Protestant churches as the **definitive** English-language Bible. It was only when the revised edition was issued in the late 18th century that it became commonly referred

17 WESTMINSTER ABBEY SCHOLARS
15 OXFORD UNIVERSITY SCHOLARS
15 CAMBRIDGE UNIVERSITY SCHOLARS

King James Bible
Several scholars from each institution translated the Bible from Greek, Hebrew, and Latin into English in 1604–08.

1608 French explorer Samuel de Champlain (c. 1567–1635) founds **Quebec**

1608 First telescope, made by **Hans Lippershey**, Netherlands

April 9, 1609 Twelve Years' Truce agreed between Spain and Netherlands

1609 Polish war with **Russia** (to 1618)

1609 *Astronomia Nova* by **Johannes Kepler** (1571–1630) published; outlines first two laws of planetary motion

January Galileo Galilei reports his discovery, via use of the telescope, of moons of **Jupiter**

August Hudson Bay, North America, discovered by Henry Hudson

Oromo are dominant population in **South Ethiopia** and prominent among Muslims of the **Harar** plateau

Poles occupy **Moscow** after Swedish invasion of Russia

1608 Spain legalizes slavery of **Chilean** Indians

1608 Work restarted on key Roman High Baroque church of **Sant Andrea della Valle**, Rome (completed 1650)

1609 Moriscos expelled from **Spain**

1609 Dutch expedition under **Henry Hudson** explores Hudson River

1609 Samuel de Champlain explores St. Lawrence and eastern Great Lakes, North America

May 14 Assassination of Henry IV of France (b. 1553)

Dahomey kingdom established, West Africa

English trading post established at **Masulipatam**, East India

Tully Castle in County Fermanagh, Northern Ireland, was built in 1619 for Sir John Hume, a Scottish "planter," or settler.

The title page of Don Quixote, part one of which was published in 1605, and part two in 1615. It remains a cornerstone of European literature.

to as the "King James Bible". And it was only in the early 19th century that it came to be known as the Authorized Version.

In June 1611, English explorer **Henry Hudson**, then in the pay of a group of English merchants, was abandoned by his crew after spending an arduous winter on the southern shore of the great bay in **northwest Canada** that bears his name. He was never seen again. Hudson was searching for a northwest passage to Asia. Just as Magellan had discovered a route to the Pacific around the tip of South America, so it was believed that a comparable **northern passage** must exist. The search for it had sparked one of the most heroically futile episodes in global exploration, a series of mostly English endeavors from 1576 that revealed only unnavigable, ice-choked, dead-ends.

Control of **the Sound**—the narrow waterway between **Denmark** and **Sweden** at the mouth of the Baltic—was a central preoccupation in the continuing Scandinavian struggle for supremacy in the Baltic. In 1611, Sweden, determined to end Denmark's stranglehold on this vital waterway, began what became known as the **Kalmar War**. The result, in 1613, was inconclusive, the Dutch and England in particular supporting the Swedes once a Danish victory threatened. Future conflict was, in effect, merely postponed.

OVER THE WINTER OF 1609–10, the fledgling English colony at Jamestown in Virginia endured what was known as the **Starving Time**, a systematic attempt by the Powhatan Indians to starve the colony into submission. All but 60 of the 500 colonists died.

What transformed its prospects was **tobacco**. The Indians themselves cultivated tobacco but the native strain, *Nicotiana rustica*, was so harsh as to be unsmokeable. John Rolfe, who arrived at Jamestown in 1610, had with him seeds of the much sweeter *Nicotiana tabacum*. His first crop, in 1612, found an **instant market** in London. By 1627, the trade was worth £500,000 a year.

Meanwhile, in **Ireland** the deliberate settlement of **Protestants**, many from Scotland, started in 1613. It was intended to reassure James I's Scottish subjects that he had not forgotten their interests and to "pacify" and convert the rebellious **Catholic** population of Ireland. Its results were generally only to inflame religious passions and, by creating a Catholic underclass, to create tensions that still slumber today.

one of 37 pearls

sapphires and emeralds

Old Testament scenes

Czar's orb
This jewel-encrusted orb was used at the coronation of Mikhail Romanov on July 1613.

100,000
THE ESTIMATED NUMBER OF **EUNUCHS** EMPLOYED **BY** THE **MING DYNASTY** IN CHINA

IN STARK CONTRAST TO ENGLAND, where parliamentary authority would progressively increase throughout the 17th century, the influence of **France**'s legislative assembly, the **Estates-General** withered almost entirely. During the crises of the French Wars of Religion and their aftermath, the Estates-General met regularly, if ineffectually: six times between 1560 and 1614. But it would not meet again until 1789, by which point France would be on the verge of revolution.

By 1615, China was grappling with financial crisis and social breakdown. There were **tensions** in the **Chinese government** over conflict between the scholars of the Donglin Academy (literally, "the Eastern Grove Academy") in eastern China, and the court eunuchs—particularly the notoriously capricious and cruel Wei Zhongxian. With the semiretirement of the Wanli emperor, Wei Zhongxian had assumed personal control of the government. The Donglin scholars, adherents of the moral imperatives of Confucianism, objected to the self-glorification and extravagance of the eunuchs. By 1624, Wei Zhongxian had ensured the execution of the leading Donglin academics.

Meanwhile, the **Dutch** started to settle **North America**. In 1615, the Dutch cemented their 1609 claim to the region of present-day Albany by building Fort Nassau at the same site. In 1625, they would build a further settlement at the mouth of the Hudson River, **New Amsterdam**. Dutch colonial settlement would, however, dwindle by the end of the 17th century.

bones in box, shown end on

numbered rod or bone

Napier's Bones
This is an abacus created by John Napier around 1615, which used numbered rods in order to simplify multiplication.

King James Bible published, England

April War of Kalmar: Swedish–Danish conflict for control of the Baltic (to 1613)

1612 First English East India Company **factory** in India, Surat

1612 Portuguese transport approximately 10,000 **slaves** a year from Angola to Brazil

1612 Tobacco cultivation begins, Virginia, North America

January 20, 1613 Peace of Knäred—Sweden pays vast **ransom** for return of fortress of Alvsborg, on the frontiers with Denmark

1612 Poles forced to retreat from Russia

February 21, 1613 Mikhail Romanov elected czar of **Russia** (crowned in July)

1613 Protestant "Plantation" (settlement) of Ireland begins

1614 Scottish mathematician **John Napier** (1550–1617) publishes logarithmic tables

1614 Last meeting of the **French Estates-General** before 1789 Revolution

1614 Romanovs defeat **Cossacks** at Rostokino

1615 England sends first European ambassador to **Mughal** court

1614 Christianity formally prohibited in **Japan**

1615 Internal conflict in **China** between **Donglin** party and corrupt **eunuch** party (to 1627)

1615 Samuel de Champlain reaches Lake Huron, one of the **Great Lakes** in North America

1615 Publication of final part of *Don Quixote de la Mancha*, by Miguel de Cervantes, Spain

> **❝ I HOPE IT WILL BE HARD FOR THE RUSSIANS TO JUMP ACROSS THAT CREEK. ❞**

Gustavus Adolphus, king of Sweden, Treaty of Stolbovo, 1617

An illustration depicts the defenestration of two regents by Protestants in Prague Castle, Bohemia, an event that sparked the Thirty Years' War.

The work of the English philosopher Fr Bacon was to have a lasting impact.

THE SEEDS OF THE LATER FALL of China's Ming dynasty (see 1644) were sown in 1616 when Manchu tribal leader, Nurhaci (1559–1626), **pronounced himself Great Jin**, establishing the Qing dynasty.

20,000
THE NUMBER OF BLUE CEILING TILES THAT GIVE THE BLUE MOSQUE ITS NAME

Since 1599, he had united other Manchu tribes in the **Eight Banners military system**. War with the Ming followed in 1618.

Although the Magellan Strait, linking **the Atlantic and Pacific** in southern South America, had been discovered in 1519, it was difficult to navigate. In 1616, a **Dutch expedition** under Jakob le Maire and Willem Schouten found a new route through open water to the south, naming its southernmost island, **Cape Horn**.

One of **Islam's finest buildings** was completed after seven years in 1616. The Sultan Ahmed Mosque, in Constantinople (now Istanbul), is **known as the Blue Mosque** because of the many ceramic tiles of its interior.

Gorée Island, to the south of Africa's Cape Verde, was purchased by the Dutch from its Portuguese owners in 1617. They turned it into a **major slave trading base**, a role continued by the French, who took it in 1677.

The 1617 **Treaty of Stolbovo** ended the war between Russia and Sweden that had lasted seven years. It drew a new, more **secure boundary for Sweden** that made use of lakes Ladoga and Peipus.

Dutch slave base
This colored engraving shows the fort at Gorée Island when it was controlled by the Dutch. It proved a highly profitable venture for them.

> **❝ THIS IS A SHARP MEDICINE, BUT IT IS A PHYSICIAN FOR ALL DISEASES AND MISERIES. ❞**

Sir Walter Raleigh, last words before execution, October 29, 1618

ON MAY 23, 1618, THE PROTESTANT Count Thurn had the two regents of the Catholic king of Bohemia, and future Holy Roman Emperor, Ferdinand II (1578–1637), thrown from an upper window of Prague Castle, in Bohemia. The **Defenestration of Prague** sparked the brutal **Thirty Years' War**. It was mostly confined to Germany, which by 1648 was a scene of wholesale destruction and slaughter. Initially a religious conflict, **Ferdinand's quest to erase Protestantism** from all his dominions became a Europe-wide fight for supremacy involving, at different points, every major European power.

On October 29, 1618, the English soldier and explorer **Sir Walter Raleigh** (1552–1618) was **executed by beheading** at the Tower of London. He had been one of the early English colonizers of Virginia, North America, but his failure to find the legendary South American **city of El Dorado**, as well as his attacking a Spanish settlement against the expressed wishes of King James I, had sealed his fate.

English privateers (state-sponsored raiders) had bought and sold **African slaves** since the late 16th century, but in 1618 England's involvement in the Atlantic slave trade became deeper when the **first slave shipment to its North American colonies** arrived from West Africa at Jamestown, Virginia.

EARLY SLAVE TRADE

Although it was in the 18th century that the Atlantic slave trade reached its peak, in the early 17th century it was developing rapidly. Slaves were transported from a series of slave forts on the west coast of Africa to the burgeoning European colonial lands of the New World. Male slaves were branded with irons (pictured) on the Atlantic Ocean crossing, in which about 25 percent died.

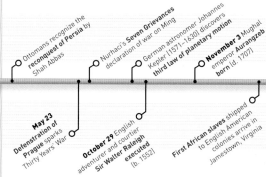

THE DUTCH, IN AGGRESSIVELY SEEKING to supplant the Portuguese in the **East Indies**, had first attempted to establish a **trading post in Java** in 1596. From 1602, they also had to contend with English efforts to infiltrate themselves in the East Indies. In 1619, the **Dutch struck back** decisively, ousting the English and their Javanese allies, and establishing themselves in Jayakarta, which they **renamed Batavia**. It would become not merely the **capital of the Dutch East Indies** but the focal point of the Dutch colonial empire, dismembered only by its conquest by Japan in 1942.

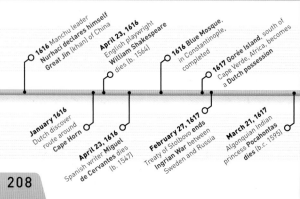

1616 Manchu leader Nurhaci declares himself Great Jin (khan) of China

April 23, 1616 English playwright **William Shakespeare** dies (b. 1564)

1616 Blue Mosque, in Constantinople, completed

1617 Gorée Island, south of Cape Verde, Africa, becomes a **Dutch possession**

January 1616 Dutch discover route around **Cape Horn**

April 23, 1616 Spanish writer Miguel de Cervantes dies (b. 1547)

February 27, 1617 Treaty of Stolbovo ends **Ingrian War** between Sweden and Russia

March 21, 1617 Algonquian Indian princess **Pocahontas** dies (b.c. 1595)

Ottomans recognize the **reconquest of Persia** by Shah Abbas

Nurhaci's **Seven Grievances** declaration of war on Ming

German astronomer Johannes Kepler (1571–1630) discovers **third law of planetary motion**

November 3 Mughal emperor **Aurangzeb** born (d. 1707)

May 23 Defenestration of Prague sparks Thirty Years' War

October 29 English adventurer and courtier **Sir Walter Raleigh** executed (b. 1552)

First African slaves shipped to English American colonies arrive in Jamestown, Virginia

March 1619 Qing defeat Ming at Battle of Sarhu

March 6, 1619 French poet Cyrano de Bergerac born (d. 1655)

1619 Treaty of Deulino ends Polish-Russian War

May 30, 1619 Dutch found **Batavia,** Java

May 8, 1619 Synod of Dort, Netherlands, endorses hardline Calvinist theology

> ❝ **MANY** WILL **TRAVEL** AND **KNOWLEDGE** WILL BE **INCREASED**. ❞

Francis Bacon, English philosopher, from *Novum Organum*, 1620

American Indians of the Powhatan attack a farm in the English colony of Virginia in 1622, massacring all of its inhabitants.

Novum Organum, one of the **great books of philosophy**, was written by English philosopher and scientist Francis Bacon (1561–1626) in 1620. It was a major work in the development of scientific method.

The initial phase of the Thirty Years' War climaxed in the **Battle of White Mountain** in November 1620, when the forces of Holy Roman Emperor Ferdinand II **decisively routed** those of the Calvinist Frederick V (1596–1632), ruler of what was called the Palatinate, in southwest Germany. **Ferdinand's victory** over Frederick had almost exactly the opposite effect from what he

might have expected. It galvanized Protestant opposition to him, importantly including Denmark.

The founding of Jamestown in 1607 as the first permanent **English colony** in the New World was overshadowed by the arrival near modern Boston in November 1620 of the *Mayflower*. The 102 passengers on board were **Puritan pilgrims**, Protestant self-exiles staking all on a new life in a new world.

Battle of White Mountain
This major engagement—a Catholic victory—took place near Prague, and ended the first, or Bohemian, period in the Thirty Years' War.

Population of Plymouth
The population of Plymouth Colony dropped dramatically in the first, difficult year of its founding.

THE PURITAN PILGRIMS of the *Mayflower* had arrived in the New World in 1620 not only late in the year, with the New England winter settling in, but in the wrong place: their original goal was the Hudson River, several hundred miles to the south. Their **early survival** at what they named Plymouth Colony was almost entirely a **matter of luck**, a harsh winter survived largely through American Indian aid. Thereafter, they scraped a **desperate existence**, dependent on uncertain reinforcement from England and their own meagre efforts.

The **expiration in 1621 of the Twelve-Year Truce** between Spain and the Dutch Republic in 1609 was, perhaps predictably, the signal for a further round of **Spanish–Dutch conflict**. Both sides had increased their armies and navies in expectation of a resumption of the war. In addition, Dutch financial if not military help to Frederick V—now in exile in the Dutch Republic after his crushing defeat at White Mountain the year before—provided an obvious motive for **renewed Spanish**

hostility. Yet the subsequent fighting was less an attempt by Spain at the reconquest of the Dutch so much as an **effort to destabilize them politically and economically** by attempts to ban Dutch mercantile activities and to blockade their principal ports. The Spanish were successful in besieging Jülich and Steenbergen in 1622 but an attempted siege of Bergen-op-Zoom had to be abandoned at huge cost.

The **Banda Islands**, in the East Indies, were the only known **sources of nutmeg and mace**, spices that commanded a huge premium in Europe. They were accordingly the focus of bitter, often **violent rivalry**, first between the Portuguese and the Dutch and, by the early 17th century, between the English and the Dutch. In 1621, having ousted the English from the islands, the Dutch, actively encouraged by the Governor-General of the East Indies, Jan Pieterszoon Coen, set about the **extermination of the islanders**. It is estimated that of a population of 15,000, all but 1,000 were killed or expelled.

On March 22, 1622, the **Powhatan American Indians** in what was now the English colony of Virginia, **killed 347 of the settlers**—men, women, and children—approximately 25 percent of the total number of colonists. As early as 1610, **tensions** between the settlers and the American Indians had flared into **open conflict**. By 1622, the Indians, realizing that when the settlers claimed to want peaceful

relations with the Powhatan they meant it exclusively on their own terms, rose against them. The predictable consequence was a **violent English backlash**, which by the middle of the century had all but **eliminated the Powhatan** American Indians.

Determined to end the **power of the Janissaries**—the elite military group that formed the household troops and bodyguard of the Ottoman sultan—Osman II (1604–22) had made a dangerous enemy for himself since becoming sultan in 1618. His attempts to assert himself as an independent ruler provoked a **Janissary uprising** that saw him imprisoned in his own palace. On May 20, 1622, the 17-year-old **sultan was murdered**, probably strangled by one of his captors.

Sultan Osman II
This equestrian portrait of gouache on paper shows the Ottoman sultan Osman II. His short, but brave, reign ended in violent tragedy.

Timeline

June 10, 1619 Protestant defeat in Thirty Years' War at Battle of Sablat

August 28, 1619 Ferdinand II elected Holy Roman Emperor

August 10, 1619 Treaty of Angoulême ends first civil war in France

1620 Imperial, palace of Katsura, Kyoto, completed

August 1620 Louis XIII (1601–43) in civil war victory at Les Ponts-de-Cé

1620 Francis Bacon writes *Novum Organum*

1620 Shogun Tokugawa Hidetada remodels **Osaka castle**

October 1620 Ottomans defeat Poles at Battle of Cecora

November 8, 1620 Battle of White Mountain

November 1620 Pilgrims arrive at Plymouth Colony on Mayflower

1621 Mutapa state of lower Zambezi valley **invaded by Maravi Empire**

1621 Swedes seize Riga

April 1621 Renewed **fighting between Spanish and Dutch** as Twelve-Year Truce expires

1621 Japanese forbidden to travel overseas

1621 Massacre in Banda Islands

1622 Safavid Persians take Kandahar from Mughals, and expel Portuguese from Hormuz

March 22, 1622 Virginia Colony massacre by Powhatan American Indians

October 1622 Dutch end Spanish siege of Bergen-op-Zoom

May 20, 1622 Ottoman Sultan Osman II murdered

October 1622 Louis XIII takes Protestant Montpellier, blockades La Rochelle

1623 Safavid Persians capture Baghdad, Mosul, and Mesopotamia from Ottomans

1623 Territory of New Hampshire established

August 1623 Battle of Stadtlohn in Thirty Years' War sees Protestant army destroyed

March 9, 1623 Massacre of English and Japanese on island of Amboina by Dutch East Indies officials

December 1623 Publication of First Folio of William Shakespeare

> ## " WAR IS ONE OF THE SCOURGES WITH WHICH IT HAS PLEASED GOD TO AFFLICT MEN. "
>
> Cardinal Richelieu, chief minister of France, 1620s

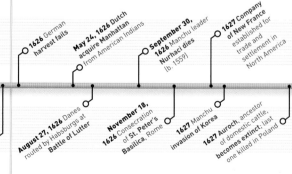

This illustration shows Peter Minuit purchasing the island of Manhattan from the local American Indians, most likely the Lenape people, in 1626.

IN AUGUST 1624, CARDINAL RICHELIEU (1585–1642) became chief minister to the king of France, 23-year-old Louis XIII (1601–43). Richelieu claimed that his goals were "to destroy the military power of the Habsburgs, to humble the great nobles [of France], and to raise the prestige of the **House of Bourbon** in Europe." It was ambitious, and involved alliances with groups that had little commitment to his program. Eventually, the price of confronting enemies abroad and Protestants at home would be popular revolt in France against the financial and military burdens imposed by him. It would also lead to rebellion by the elites that culminated in the civil war of the Fronde (see 1648–49). His political **astuteness and manipulation of factions**, however, prevented political breakdown, and by his death, France was making progress against its Habsburg enemies. Richelieu also knew that Huguenot military power at home (see 1597–98) was a permanent threat to France's stability, but that the persecution of Protestant worship would lead to last-ditch resistance at home and imperil France's alliances with foreign Protestant powers, on which its **anti-Habsburg strategy** rested.

In 1625, the already tangled conflicts of the unfolding **Thirty Years' War** became even more complex. With the Twelve-Year Truce over, Spain squeezed the Dutch, **taking Breda after an 11-month siege**, while France, whose policy was now being directed by the hawkish Richelieu, became covertly involved in supporting an **anti-Habsburg struggle in northern Italy**. This was an attempt by Richelieu to sever the Spanish Road, the tenuous but vital link between Habsburg Italy and the Netherlands. At almost precisely the same moment, Christian IV of Denmark (1577–1648) entered the war, in part seeking to **bolster the Protestant cause**, but more particularly to forestall Swedish ambitions to control northern Germany and the Baltic. In August 1626, his army was **defeated at the Battle of Lutter** (see right) by a Bavarian Catholic army led by Count Tilly and in alliance with the Habsburg emperor. It seemed for the moment that French scheming and Dutch fighting could not prevent a comprehensive victory for the Habsburgs.

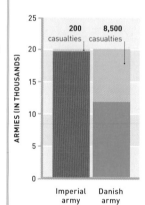

The Surrender of Breda
Justin von Nassau is shown surrendering Breda in 1625 to Ambrosio Spinola, the Spanish commander, after an 11-month-long siege. Breda was retaken in 1637.

ONE OF THE MOST FAMOUS EVER TRANSACTIONS occurred on May 26, 1626 when **Peter Minuit**, director-general of the Dutch West India Company's New Netherlands settlement, **bought Manhattan island**—site of Fort Amsterdam since 1625—from its American Indian inhabitants. The fee was 60 Dutch guilders, estimated since to be around $24. Neither side felt the deal to be overly unreasonable.

The **Thirty Years' War** was a **brutal watershed** in 17th-century Europe, but its cruelty was not merely a grim consequence of battle. Always strapped for money, armies took funding into their own hands and **imposed taxes directly** on the peasants and the towns. Faced by the collection of

BAROQUE ARCHITECTURE

Gathering pace in the early 17th century, the Roman High Baroque was a strong Catholic response to the Protestant Reformation, and reasserted classical Renaissance architecture. Its church building, in particular St. Peter's Basilica in Rome (pictured), sought to advertise and glorify the Catholic Church, and produced numerous new and grandiose buildings.

Battle of Lutter

	Imperial army	Danish army
casualties	200	8,500

Y-axis: ARMIES (IN THOUSANDS), scale 0–25

In 1626, a Danish army, with a huge loss of about 8,500 men, failed to hold ground against a similar-sized Holy Roman Empire force.

overly heavy taxes by soldiers, peasants and poor townspeople became even more **vulnerable to fluctuations in food supply** through bad harvests, military activity, and looting. Across much of Europe, but notably in France, the Austrian Habsburg lands, and Spanish southern Italy, **peasant revolts and urban riots** threatened to take whole areas out of the control of government. With the onset of the Little Ice Age in the mid-17th century (see 1645), the problem intensified.

This 17th-century ink and watercolor miniature of Shah Jahan shows the fifth Mughal emperor with a holy nimbus around his turbaned head.

A hand-colored woodcut depicting the siege of Magdeburg by the Holy Roman Empire. The city was burned and 20,000 killed.

Battle of Breitenfeld
At Breitenfeld in 1631, a strong Swedish–Saxon army inflicted huge numbers of casualties on an army of the Holy Roman Empire.

Queen of France
Portrait of Marie de Medici, the second wife of King Henry IV of France, who attempted to displace Cardinal Richelieu in 1630.

AFTER MORE THAN A YEAR, THE SIEGE OF LA ROCHELLE, the strongest Protestant enclave in France, ended in October 1628 with **defeat for the Huguenots**. The siege was Richelieu's response to lingering hopes of Huguenot opposition to the French Crown, and was designed to both crush Huguenot resistance and dismantle its still formidable military. Although Richelieu acknowledged their right to religious toleration, he made sure they could mount **no further threat to the Crown**.

The publication in 1628 of *On the Motion of the Heart and Blood*, by royal physician **William Harvey** (1578–1657), marked one of the major discoveries of the 17th century. It **explained** both the circulation of the blood and the **functioning of the heart**, by using observation and experimentation.

One of the great leaders of India's Mughal Empire, **Shah Jahan** (1592–1666), was **crowned**

Siege of La Rochelle
Chief minister of France, Cardinal Richelieu, inspects the dyke that he had constructed to blockade the city of La Rochelle from sea-borne relief.

emperor in 1628. His 30-year reign would be a **golden age for Mughal India**, hugely increasing the size of its territory as well as initiating a great flowering of Mughal architecture and culture.

In the 17th century, rulers across Europe embraced the idea of **strong central authority** as the only guarantee of stability. In England, for Charles I (1600–49), absolute monarchy was legitimized by his conviction that he had been divinely sanctioned by God to rule. In 1629, irritated by its checks on his authority, **he dismissed Parliament**, provoking a **growing resentment** among those seeking to share power at what were seen as attempts to impose illegal taxes.

THE ENTRY OF SWEDEN INTO THE THIRTY YEARS' WAR in 1630 added a new dimension to the conflict. It was still essentially a religious war—one that the Catholic Holy Roman Emperor Ferdinand II was clearly winning. Exploiting this, Sweden's Lutheran king, **Gustavus Adolphus** (1594–1632), presented himself as the **savior of the Lutheran princes** of north Germany. Yet he was potentially as much a threat to them as to Ferdinand. Having spent the previous 19 years fighting the Russians, Poles, and Danes for control of the Baltic, he now **hoped to dominate its German coast** too. His intervention might

have led to nothing, however, had the fires that broke out during the storming of the Lutheran stronghold of Magdeburg by the Imperial troops in 1631 not destroyed the city and killed 20,000 inhabitants. This provoked outrage among the Lutheran princes. With their political support, in addition to substantial French funding, Gustavus Adolphus inflicted a **crushing defeat** over an Imperial army at **Breitenfeld**, near Leipzig, in September 1631. At this stage, his army marching triumphantly south, Gustavus Adolphus seems to have conceived a vision of an empire that included both Sweden and Germany. Yet the events of the following year would destroy this hope (see 1632).

On a day in November 1630, forever known as the **Day of Dupes**, the enemies of Cardinal Richelieu attempted to overthrow

him. They commanded Louis XIII to replace Richelieu with **Marie de Medici** (1575–1642), the mother of the king, and when he retired to ponder his decison they believed they had been successful. Yet **powerful friends saved Cardinal Richelieu**, and the king's mother was exiled to Compiègne.

900

THE APPROXIMATE NUMBER OF **PEOPLE BURNT AT THE STAKE** AFTER THE WÜRZBURG **WITCH TRIALS**

copper alloy barrel

Swedish field cannon
This cannon was used by the army of Gustavus Adolphus. The barrel has a caliber (diameter) of 2¾ in (7 cm), and weighs 440 lb (200 kg).

FORCES (IN THOUSANDS)

5,500 casualties — Swedish–Saxon army

20,000 casualties — Imperial army

January 25, 1628 Shah Jahan crowned emperor of Mughal Empire

1628 English physician William Harvey publishes key work on circulation of blood

October 28, 1628 Siege of La Rochelle ends

1629 North Italian Plague breaks out (to 1631)

March 1630 New Holland (Dutch Brazil) established, Brazil

July 1630 Sweden intervenes in Thirty Years' War

November 1630 Richelieu survives Day of Dupes

1631 Renewed conflict between Portugal and Mutapa Kingdom

March 31, 1631 English poet John Donne dies (b. 1572)

September 17, 1631 Swedish army defeats Imperial forces at Battle of Breitenfeld

August 10, 1628 Swedish flagship *Vasa* sinks on maiden voyage, Stockholm

March 10, 1629 Charles I of England dissolves Parliament

September 25, 1629 Treaty of Altmark ends Polish–Sweden War

1629 Mutapa Kingdom, East Africa, defeated by Portugal

September 1630 Boston, Massachusetts Bay Colony, founded

November 15, 1630 German astronomer Johannes Kepler dies (b. 1571)

1631 Magdeburg sacked by Holy Roman forces

July 1631 Würzburg witch trials, Germany, end after five years

December 23, 1631 Swedish army captures Mainz, Germany

An oil painting depicting the trial of Galileo shows the Italian physicist and astronomer sitting before the assembled ranks of the Inquisition, in Rome.

The assassination of Field Marshal Albrecht Wallenstein took place at the Pachelbel House, at Eger, Bohemia. He was awoken and killed by his own men.

2,000,000

THE NUMBER OF **PEOPLE** WHO **DIED IN** THE **DECCAN** FAMINE, 1630–32

ANXIOUS TO RECOVER ITS LOSSES TO POLAND–LITHUANIA under the Treaty of Deulino of 1619, and exploiting the death of the Polish king, Sigismund III Vasa, **Russia besieged Smolensk** in October 1632. Polish forces were unable to attempt a lifting of the siege for almost a year. Their **ultimate defeat of the Russians** in 1634, however, was absolute.

Sweden's success of the previous year in the Thirty Years' War continued with a **defeat of**

	6,000 casualties	6,800 casualties
30		
24		
18		
12		
6		
0	Swedish army	Imperial army

Battle of Lützen
Similar-sized forces suffered similar casualties at the Battle of Lützen. Critically, though, the Swedes lost their leader, Gustavus Adolphus.

the Imperial armies in April 1632 at the Battle of Rain, in Bavaria. A minor triumph in November at the **Battle of Lützen**, near Leipzig, might then have confirmed Swedish territorial ambitions in Germany had **King Gustavus Adolphus** not been **killed in the battle**. At a stroke, the impetus went out of the Protestant campaign. **Habsburg supremacy** seemed to have been assured.

In 1633, Italian astronomer **Galileo Galilei** (1564–1642) was called before the **Roman Inquisition** of the Catholic Church. His crime was to support the heliocentric view of the Solar System that placed the Sun, and not the Earth, at its center. He was **found guilty of heresy**, forced to recant, and spent the rest of his life under house arrest.

Under Japan's **Tokugawa shogunate**, a policy of *kaikin* ("sea restriction") was declared in 1633. **Contact** with the outside world was **strictly controlled**, although trade with Korea and China was allowed, and the Dutch kept a trading post. The idea was to prevent possible territorial incursions into Japan. It remained official policy until 1853.

THE DEFEAT AT LÜTZEN WAS one of the last times that **Albrecht Wallenstein** (1583–1634) led an Imperial army. Although generally successful, he was distrusted by almost everyone and was believed to be negotiating a separate peace. He was charged with treason by Holy Roman Emperor Ferdinand II, but in February 1634 he was **murdered by some of his own officers**, with the tacit approval of Ferdinand. Yet, with the Swedes having failed to follow up their victory at Lützen, the initiative returned to the Imperial

Battle of Nördlingen
Fought in southern Germany, this battle resulted in a crushing victory for the Habsburgs—but it was not a conclusive end to the war.

forces, who crushed the Swedes at the **Battle of Nördlingen** in November 1634. The subsequent Treaty of Prague, in 1635, made clear the extent of the **Habsburg triumph and the Swedish defeat**. Germany's Protestant princes now backed Ferdinand II. It provoked the final and most brutal phase of the Thirty Years' War, and direct **French intervention**.

As in the 16th century, France feared Habsburg encirclement. Up to now, it had sought to secure itself by financing those states most likely to defeat the Habsburg forces, Sweden above all. With the Swedes on the verge of pulling out of Germany, the French now took the field themselves. As Franco–Swedish armies **progressively ravaged Germany**, the Swedes

gradually reversing their previous losses, so Germany was devastated. The **fighting spilled into France** when, in 1636, a Spanish army invaded the northeast, briefly threatening Paris, and again, in 1637, when Spain launched an attack on Languedoc in the south. In 1639, France retaliated by invading Catalonia in the northeast of Spain. In this wave of violence, all the **participants** were by now effectively **bankrupt**. It was Spain that suffered the most, with attempts at raising revenue provoking bitter resentment, even in Spain itself. In 1640, outright revolt against the Spanish Crown broke out in Catalonia and Portugal, both **uprisings openly encouraged by France**. In the

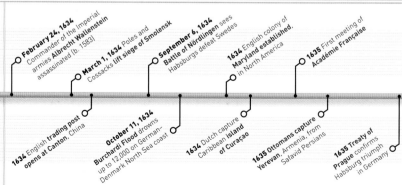
April 1632 Swedish crossing of Rain River destroys Bavarian army, an ally of the Habsburgs

1632 Russians besiege Smolensk

1632 Fasilides becomes emperor of Ethiopia

1632 Deccan Famine, India, ends after two years

February 24, 1634 Commander of the Imperial armies **Albrecht Wallenstein** assassinated (b. 1583)

March 1, 1634 Poles and Cossacks lift siege of Smolensk

September 6, 1634 Battle of Nördlingen sees Habsburgs defeat Swedes

1634 English colony of **Maryland established**, in North America

1635 First meeting of **Académie Française**

1632 Mughal emperor Shah Jahan **destroys Hindu temples**

November 16, 1632 Battle of Lützen; Swedish king, Gustavus Adolphus, killed

June 1633 Galileo condemned by Catholic Inquisition

1633 Shogun Tokugawa Iemitsu (1604–51) **begins isolation of Japan**

1634 English **trading post** opens at Canton, China

October 11, 1634 Burchardi Flood drowns up to 12,000 on German–Denmark North Sea coast

1634 Dutch capture **Caribbean island of Curaçao**

1635 Ottomans capture **Yerevan**, Armenia, from Safavid Persians

1635 Treaty of Prague confirms Habsburg triumph in Germany

> ❝ IT IS **NOT ENOUGH TO HAVE A GOOD MIND;** THE MAIN THING IS TO **USE IT WELL.** ❞

René Descartes, from *Discours de la Méthode*, 1637

This engraving depicts the Ottoman sultan, Murad IV, sitting on a horse. His reign restored internal authority and brought secure borders with Persia.

same year, there was no Spanish New World treasure fleet. By now, the original causes of the Thirty Years' War had been superseded. **Habsburg weakness**, in Spain as much as in Germany, **was increasingly apparent**.

When not conspiring against his enemies, chief minister **Cardinal Richelieu** schemed to promote French prestige, or *gloire*. He championed colonial expansion, and **promoted French arts and learning**. Among his lasting achievements was the **Académie Française**, set up in 1635. Part of a pan-European move toward officially sanctioned institutes of learning, it was also **designed to consolidate** what France saw as one of its chief claims to *gloire*: **its language**. The Académie's 40 members continue to pronounce on language usage today.

In 1635, the system of *sankin kotai* ("alternate attendance"), **introduced to Japan** by Toyotomi Hideyoshi in the 1590s, was made compulsory. The daimyo (feudal lords) were forced to spend every other year at the shogun's court at Edo to participate in lavish rituals. The cost of such submission, plus the time spent at court, **made rebellion less likely**. When they returned to their estates, which they held from the shogun, each daimyo's wife and heir remained behind. **Exacting demands were enforced** regarding dress, types of weapons carried, soldier numbers accompanying each daimyo, and the contributions—military and financial—the daimyo were expected to provide.

Gondar Castle
Part of the Fasil Ghebbi, founded by Fasilides, in Ethiopia, this 17th-century castle shows Arab, Nubian, and Baroque design influences.

ETHIOPIAN EMPEROR since 1632, **Fasilides** (c. 1603–67) founded a permanent imperial **capital at Gondar** in 1636. The buildings he constructed there included the Fasil Ghebbi, a fortress complex that became **home to Ethiopia's emperors** until the 18th century.

An early **speculative bubble burst** in February 1637, when the Dutch price of tulip bulbs peaked

One of the founders of modern philosophy, French writer **René Descartes** (1596–1650), an advocate of rationalism, produced *Discours de la Méthode* in 1637. It was one of the most influential works of Western philosophy.

1,000 PERCENT
THE **RELATIVE PRICE OF TULIP BULBS** COMPARED TO THE **ANNUAL INCOME** OF A SKILLED DUTCH **CRAFTSMAN**

and then suddenly nose-dived, allegedly ruining many investors. A luxury item, they were seen as a safe haven for investment in an uncertain time. Although **Tulip Mania** prices are difficult to be certain about, and have been disputed, anecdotal evidence suggests significant highs.

A major new **encyclopedia**, *The Exploitation of the Works of Nature*, by minor provincial bureaucrat, **Song Yingxing**, was published in China in May 1637. Its wide range of information regarding Chinese technology distinguished it from earlier traditions, and provided an obvious and extensive resource.

THE INTERMITTENT CONFLICT between the Ottoman Empire and the Safavid Persian Empire, which had begun in 1623, climaxed in 1638. **Baghdad fell to the Ottomans** under Sultan Murad IV (1612–40), the last Ottoman ruler to lead his troops in battle. This was followed in 1639 by the **Treaty of Qasr-i-Shirin**, which definitively settled the long-disputed Ottoman–Safavid border, largely to the benefit of the Ottomans. It granted all of **Mesopotamia** (modern Iraq) to the Ottomans, while handing the city of Yerevan (in present-day Armenia) to the Safavid Persians.

The problems that would eventually lead to the execution of **Charles I** of England in 1649 stemmed from the king's high-handed conviction that he could always impose himself on his kingdoms. This was not exclusively a matter of royal versus parliamentary authority. A significant element of **religious controversy** was involved, too. In 1637, Charles, encouraged by William Laud, the archbishop of Canterbury, had made the use of the **Church of England**'s *Book of Common Prayer* compulsory in Scotland. Both Charles and Laud cordially despised the **Calvinist Scottish Kirk** (Church). For their part, Scotland's Kirk elders, much like their Puritan counterparts in England, considered any attempt to **impose Anglican religious uniformity** little better than papism. Their virulent protests in the following year, known as the **Great Covenant**, were followed in

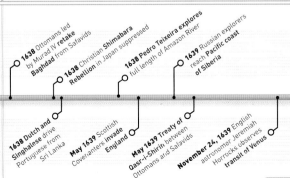

Pedro Teixeira's Amazon expedition
Teixeira's expedition was immense and expensive. Of some political interest, it was financed by the governor of Maranhão, in Brazil.

1639 by the **invasion of England** by a "Covenanter" army **from Scotland**. The king's options were narrowing.

In 1638, **Portuguese explorer Pedro Teixeira** (d. 1641) achieved a remarkable double first in becoming the first person to make the **return journey of the entire length of the Amazon River**, reaching Belém, at the river's mouth, more than two years after he had set out. The previous year Teixeira had been the first person to make the journey upstream, a venture partly inspired by the need to know how far east **Spanish** colonists had advanced beyond the Andes and into the Amazon Basin.

On November 24, 1639, English astronomer **Jeremiah Horrocks** (1618–41) became the first person to both predict and observe a **transit of Venus**. This rare event sees Venus pass directly between the Sun and the Earth. Observing the transit provided information vital to calculating the distance from the Earth to the Sun.

An illustration of Malacca, which was taken from the Portuguese by the Dutch in 1641. An earlier attack by the Dutch in 1605 had failed.

A depiction of the Battle of Rocroi, fought on May 19, 1643. It resulted in the crushing victory of a French army over a Spanish force.

FOLLOWING A SCOTTISH INVASION OF ENGLAND IN 1639, in April 1640 Charles I (1600–49) **recalled the parliament** he had dismissed 11 years earlier. He needed approval to raise taxes for an army. Determined not to submit to its lists of grievances, he dismissed it, but a second invasion in August forced a recall. In December 1641, Parliament presented a **Grand Remonstrance**, an accusation of royal abuses of power. The king responded, in January 1642, with an attempt to arrest his parliamentary opponents. By August, the **country was at war**.

Life dancing to music
Poussin's A Dance to the Music of Time *shows four dancing figures representing poverty, labor, wealth, and pleasure in a perpetual cycle.*

By 1640, French painter **Nicolas Poussin** (1594–1665) completed *A Dance to the Music of Time*, **a key work of the era**. Poussin stressed clarity and order rather than the emotion and color of the Baroque style dominant at that time.

From 1641, a devastating plague struck China, further **weakening a Ming China** threatened by both the Manchu military to the north and increasingly lawless bands of peasants roaming the country, victims of repeated famines. An almost complete **breakdown of central control** in China followed.

Continuing Dutch encroachment on the territory and trade of the Portuguese in Asia saw the **capture of the key trading base of Malacca** in 1641. It would prove a valuable cornerstone of the vast Dutch Empire in the East Indies.

THE COURSE, NOT TO MENTION THE CAUSES, of the **English Civil War** that began in August 1642 was never clear cut. It pitted a **king bent on absolutism** against a Parliament determined not so much to overthrow the monarchy as to reassert its claim to **shared sovereignty in the government** of the kingdom. As the opening battles were fought, Charles I proved himself a surprisingly obstinate and able war leader. However, he was soon to become undone, not just by his compulsive deviousness but by the fact that he found himself confronting increasingly assertive and better organized Parliamentarian forces. These would be largely dominated by the formidably imposing figure of **Oliver Cromwell** (1599–1658), a Puritan, East-Anglian country squire and Member of Parliament. The war's significance, at least in English terms, was to be that Parliament could claim greater legitimacy than that of any king: in short, that **Parliament could restrain a king**, divinely sanctioned or not, held to have broken his trust with his people.

Eleven years after the village of Breitenfeld, in Saxony, had seen King Gustavus Adolphus of Sweden defeat a Holy Roman Empire army (see 1631), the **Second Battle of Breitenfeld** in October 1642 saw another decisive victory for Sweden in the Thirty Years' War. Sweden was subsequently free to occupy Leipzig and the rest of Saxony, further **strengthening Protestantism** in Central Europe,

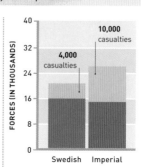

Second Battle of Breitenfeld
The imperial army of the Holy Roman Empire suffered heavy losses at the hands of the Swedish army at Breitenfeld, in Saxony.

and making the Catholics of the Holy Roman Empire more amenable to negotiation.

The overwhelming French defeat of Spain at the **Battle of Rocroi** in northeast France in May 1643 put to an end to hopes of a Spanish triumph against either of the Dutch Republic or France in the Thirty Years' War. **Spain was already on the defensive** against both countries. Rocroi marked the end of its dreams of European imperial dominance. The Spanish army in Flanders was destroyed, **losing almost all its most experienced infantry** in the battle. Combined with its internal struggles against the Catalonians and the Portuguese, and its chronic shortage of money, Spain risked permanent eclipse. In the short term, defeat reduced the threat from the Dutch, who were anxious that they had potentially swapped the prospect of Spanish

domination for that of control by the French. In the longer term, **Spanish decline seemed inevitable**.

In 1643, Italian physicist and mathematician **Evangelista Torricelli** (1608–47) made a major contribution to scientific method in Europe with his **invention of the mercury barometer**. He had not intended to make this invention, but while working on a water pump for the Duke of Tuscany, and substituting the much heavier mercury for water, he realized that the rising and falling of a column of mercury in a tube sealed at one end was due to **changes in atmospheric pressure**.

Torricelli's barometer
In this engraving, Torricelli demonstrates the existence of atmospheric pressure through the use of mercury-filled tubes.

April 1640 Short Parliament, in England, called by Charles I

May 1640 Catalan revolt against Castilian military impositions breaks out

November 1640 Long Parliament called, ending Charles I's personal rule

1641 Dutch take Portuguese possession of Malacca

1640 Nicolas Poussin completes *A Dance to the Music of Time*

December 1640 End of Iberian Union; John IV proclaimed king of Portugal

1641 Revolts begin against Ming rule in China; plague sweeps through China

November 22, 1641 Grand Remonstrance of English Parliament

January 4, 1642 Charles I attempts arrest of parliamentary opponents

January 8, 1642 Italian astronomer and physicist Galileo Galilei dies (b. 1564)

October 23, 1642 Battle of Edgehill is drawn in First English Civil War

1642 Kaifeng Flood kills 300,000 in China

1642 Dutch painter Rembrandt van Rijn (1606–69) paints *The Night Watch*

May 14, 1643 Accession of infant Louis XIV, France

1642 Montreal founded by French

October 23, 1642 Second Battle of Breitenfeld sees Swedes defeat Imperial army

1642 Dutch sailor Abel Tasman (1603–59) discovers Tasmania and New Zealand

January 4, 1643 English astronomer, mathematician, and physicist Isaac Newton born (d. 1727)

May 19, 1643 Battle of Rocroi sees French crush Spanish

1643 Evangelista Torricelli invents mercury barometer, Tuscany

> " WE STUDY THE GLORY OF GOD, AND THE **HONOUR** AND **LIBERTY** OF **PARLIAMENT, FOR WHICH WE… FIGHT,** WITHOUT SEEKING OUR OWN INTERESTS… "

Oliver Cromwell, English Parliamentarian general, Battle of Marston Moor, 1644

Carisbrooke Castle, on the Isle of Wight, England, was where Charles I was imprisoned for 14 months, from 1647, after his defeat in the English Civil War.

ON APRIL 24, 1644, AS A REBEL MING ARMY under Li Zicheng prepared to take Beijing, the **Chongzhen Emperor,** the last Ming ruler, **committed suicide.** In February, Li had proclaimed the Shun dynasty, but it was not to last long. In May, the Manchus, allying with a remnant Ming force, crushed Li's army at the Battle of Shanhai Pass. By the autumn, the **first Manchu Qing emperor** of China, the six-year-old Shunzhi Emperor (1638–61), had been installed in Beijing. Ming resistance in the south continued until 1681. The Qing themselves ruled until their collapse in 1911.

In the **English Civil War,** the Battle of Marston Moor in July 1644 saw a **decisive victory for Parliament.** The following summer, at Naseby in June 1645, ultimate victory was virtually guaranteed when the main army of Charles I was annihilated by Parliament's newly formed **New Model Army.** Led by Oliver Cromwell and Sir Thomas Fairfax, the New Model Army brought a greater professionalism and mobility into the conflict, and

Potala Palace in Tibet
The Potala Palace, seen atop the Marpo Ri hill in this view from the south, rises more than 1,000 ft (300 m) above the valley floor.

emphasized the ultimately superior resources of the Parliamentary cause.

From about 1645, the Northern Hemisphere saw **crop failures** brought about by abnormally cold winters. The result was **famine** on a massive scale, leading to both war and the collapse of state structures across the globe. These **climatic changes,** known since 1976 as the Maunder Minimum, were the result of reduced sunspot activity, the direct consequence of which was the **Little Ice Age,** in which global temperatures fell by several degrees.

In 1645, the 5th Dalai Lama, Lozang Gyatso (1617–82), began the construction of the **modern Potala Palace,** in Lhasa, Tibet. Construction finally ended in 1694, and it remained the seat of the Dalai Lama up to 1959.

POWER IN THE EARLY YEARS OF THE QING DYNASTY was exercised by the child-emperor's uncle, **Prince Dorgon** (1612–50). A distinctive feature of the Qing was their hair, shaved at the front, braided into a pigtail at the back, and known as a "queue." Dorgon

attachment for holding strap

now made this **compulsory for all male Han Chinese** (the Queue Order). Clashing with Confucian contention that hair, as a gift from your parents, should never be cut, to wear a Manchu pigtail was seen as a mark of servility, as Dorgon intended. **Thousands** who refused to adopt it **were put to death.**

On May 26, 1647, the **Massachusetts Bay Colony banned Jesuit priests** from the colony. Founded as a staunchly Puritan enclave, the colonists loathed the Jesuits as a sinister manifestation of popery. Also, increasingly alarmed by the French Jesuit missionaries in Canada, who had converted many Huron and Algonquin American Indians, they were determined that a movement **"subversive to society"** should have no place in the new colony.

After escaping Parliament's siege of Oxford in April 1646, King **Charles I surrendered** to a Scottish army. The next year they delivered him to Parliament. He was **imprisoned at Carisbrooke Castle,** on the Isle of White. From there, he continued to try to bargain with the various parties, but his secret negotiations with the Scottish Presbyterians to invade England led to a **renewal of the English Civil War.**

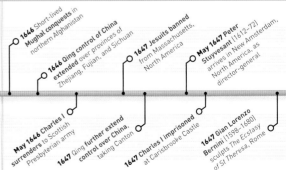

English Civil War armor
Metal breastplates with appended tassets (to protect the legs and lower body) were used by foot soldiers on both sides during the civil war.

KEY
- Under Manchu control by 1644
- Under Qing control by 1660
- Under Qing control by 1770

RUSSIAN EMPIRE
AMUR
OUTER MONGOLIA
MANCHURIA
Mukden
XINJIANG
Beijing
Sea of Japan
TIBET
Lhasa
Nanjing • Suzhou
Chongqing • Changsha
Fuzhou
PACIFIC OCEAN
Guangzhou
INDIA
Macao
Bay of Bengal

GROWTH OF QING EMPIRE

Having secured control of China proper in 1644, the Qing Empire continued to expand throughout the 17th and 18th centuries, provoked in part by the threat of Russian, British, and French moves into Asia. Only some areas of the vast empire were governed directly by the Manchu or settled by the Chinese. Much was secured, at huge expense, through military garrisons.

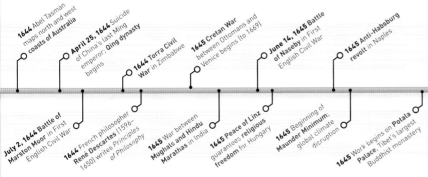

1644 Abel Tasman maps north and west coasts of Australia

April 25, 1644 Suicide of China's last Ming emperor; **Qing dynasty** begins

1644 Torra Civil War in Zimbabwe

1645 Cretan War between Ottomans and Venice begins (to 1669)

June 14, 1645 Battle of Naseby in First English Civil War

1645 Anti-Habsburg revolt in Naples

July 2, 1644 Battle of Marston Moor in First English Civil War

1644 French philosopher René Descartes (1596–1650) writes *Principles of Philosophy*

1645 War between Mughals and Hindu Marathas in India

1645 Peace of Linz guarantees religious freedom for Hungary

1645 Beginning of **Maunder Minimum;** global climate disruption

1645 Work begins on Potala Palace, Tibet's largest Buddhist monastery

1646 Short-lived Mughal conquests in northern Afghanistan

1646 Qing control of China extended over provinces of Zhejiang, Fujian, and Sichuan

1647 Jesuits banned from Massachusetts, North America

May 1647 Peter Stuyvesant (1612–72) arrives in New Amsterdam, North America, as director-general

May 1646 Charles I surrenders to Scottish Presbyterian army

1647 Qing further extend control over China, taking Canton

1647 Charles I imprisoned at Carisbrooke Castle

1647 Gian Lorenzo Bernini (1598–1680) sculpts *The Ecstasy of St Theresa,* Rome

THE STORY OF
ARMS AND ARMOR

FROM STICKS AND STONES TO A DEADLY ART FORM

cherub's head decoration

hole to attach crest

rope comb

two sections of skull plate join at comb

French 16th-century embossed helmet
Armor reached its greatest decorative heights during the Renaissance. Suits and helmets were embossed and etched, gilded or silvered, particularly for tournaments— and to show the owner's wealth and status.

Whether for hunting or sport, conflict or contests of skill, handheld arms have played a crucial role in human existence and advancement. The first weapons developed out of survival tools: found objects, such as stones, were used to bludgeon prey, or to fend off predatory animals or rival humans.

As prehistoric humans' skills advanced, clubs and stone hand-axes gave way to carefully crafted wooden spears used to hunt animals or impale fish. Even more effective weapons married wooden shafts with razor-sharp flint blades to form axes, daggers, spears, and arrowheads. Soft, easily worked metals such as copper replaced flint, followed by stronger, sharper, and longer Bronze Age and Iron Age swords, daggers, javelins, and battle-axes. Until the advent of firearms, the history of handheld weapons is one of variations on a theme, culminating in the sophisticated forging processes of Japan's samurai swords, which at their height in the 14th–16th centuries wrapped super-sharp steel around a flexible iron core.

THE DEVELOPMENT OF ARMOR

Early "armor" consisted of padding: thick layers of cloth with a stiff leather "helmet" to protect the head. Plated helmets, breastplates, and wooden shields were used by classical Greek and Roman armies, but elsewhere, ordinary soldiers relied on padding, leather, and luck—a situation that changed little in Europe until chain mail was perfected in 11th-century France. Full suits of armor were costly, so they were also used as status symbols.

SHIELDS

Like arms and body armor, shields—a type of "accessory armor"—could be functional, decorative, or both. During the medieval period in Europe, when knights held high status in society, shields were often embellished with elaborate scenes of courtly devotion or prowess in battle. Decoration like this was thought to bring added protection to the bearer.

15th-century Flemish shield

750,000–50,000 BCE
Flint cutting edges
Razor-sharp flint daggers, spears, and axes are used for both hunting and warfare.

Flint dagger

5500–3300 BCE
Flint arrowheads
The wooden bow combined with arrowheads made from sharpened flint proves a deadly combination, allowing users to strike their victims from a safe distance.

2500 BCE
Helmets
The first part of the body to be protected is the head. Early armies use plated helmets, but most soldiers rely on leather caps.

Attic helmet

6th–mid-5th centuries BCE
The crossbow
Crossbows can be cocked well in advance of firing—providing one of the earliest "loaded" weapons.

Early Chinese crossbow

450,000–400,000 BCE
Wooden weapons
Easily worked and readily available, wood is shaped into spears for hunting or defense.

Wooden spear

3700–2300 BCE
Metal weapons
Metalworking gives rise to sophisticated and effective blades in the Bronze and Iron Ages.

Bronze ax

c. 1400 BCE
Suit armor develops
Plated body armor is an early invention, but it is expensive and not always practical for movement in battle.

Mycenaean armor

3rd–4th centuries
Steel blades
Adding carbon to iron produces steel, which allows bladed weapons to be mass-produced. Blades also become stronger and longer.

Roman gladius

surface is made from bright steel

closed visor protects face, but limits field of view

single pivot for visor and face guard

breastplate is combined with a neck guard

separate plates offer protection, but allow movement

peg for lifting visor

The return of armor
During World War I, body armor was revived. German machine gunners wore suits like this one when firing from exposed places.

upper bevor decorated with figures in Roman armor

neck guard

77 lb THE APPROXIMATE WEIGHT OF A FULL SUIT OF EUROPEAN 16TH-CENTURY TOURNAMENT ARMOR

Wheel-lock pistol

15th–17th centuries
Firearms developed
With the invention of guns, body armor shrinks back to the cuirass (breastplate), to allow for drawing of pistols.

1939–1945
Flak jackets
Based on the same design as the cuirass, World War II flak jackets stop shrapnel, but not bullets.

Reinforced flak jacket

11th century
Mail perfected
Lighter and less bulky than armor plate, chain mail worn over a gambeson (padded jacket) saves lives.

Chain mail

1100 onward
Swords improve
The cross-guard is added to protect the hand, and marks the first big change to sword design since Roman times. Refined edges mean swords can now cut and stab.

15th century
First suits of full plate armor develop
Suits of armor provide the best protection. Gloves now have jointed fingers, while shoulder plates bring freer movement and less exposure.

19th century
Automatic-loading firearms
The advent of the revolver, with its rotating cylinder, meant that multiple shots could be fired before reloading.

Colt 1849 pocket pistol

20th–21st centuries
Kevlar and "liquid" body armor
Kevlar threads are five times stronger than steel. Soaked in shear thickening fluid (STF), it can withstand bullet penetration.

Cannon and gunners are seen in this 17th-century painting commemorating the actions of the royalist forces in defeating the Fronde uprising in France.

This depiction of the execution of King Charles I of England outside the Banqueting House, in London, was painted by English artist John Weesop.

THE DEATH OF LOUIS XIII in May 1643 had brought to the French throne the **four-year old Louis XIV**, under the regency of his mother, Anne of Austria (in direct defiance of Louis XIII's will). Whatever France's successes in the Thirty Years' War (see 1635) and its emerging supremacy over Spain, the country was not only **strapped for cash**, it had to confront continuing **peasant uprisings** brought about by harvest failures and punitive **demands for tax**. In addition, those nobles that Cardinal Richelieu (see 1624) had excluded from government were invited back to counter those supporters of Richelieu who were hostile to Anne and her new chief minister, Cardinal Mazarin (1602–61). Bungled attempts to

> ❝ DO YOU NOT KNOW, MY SON, **WITH** WHAT **LITTLE WISDOM THE WORLD IS GOVERNED?** ❞

Axel Oxenstierna, Swedish chancellor, Westphalia, 1648

manage factional rivalries while maintaining a costly war were to lead to government breakdown in 1648 with the **Fronde**—initially a parliamentary protest, but later an **aristocratic uprising**. Four years of turmoil followed: Paris was taken, the royal family fled, and Mazarin was

Dahomey panther mask
This bronze pendant in the shape of a stylized head of a panther, dating from 17th-century Dahomey, shows the country's cultural sophistication.

ON JANUARY 30, 1649, Charles I of England was beheaded. He remains the only **king of England** to have been **legally executed**. His conviction by the High Court of Justice as "tyrant, traitor, and murderer" was carried by a vote of 68 to 67. Throughout his trial, Charles consistently rejected any idea that any court could legally try a king. "I would know by what power I am called hither... Remember I am your King, your lawful King." In reality, there is little doubt that since the triumph of the parliamentary New Model Army, **dominated by Oliver Cromwell**, his death became a possible outcome to the crisis. The awkward question was whether one form of tyranny was being swapped for another. Nonetheless, what counted was the assertion that a body of law

Oliver Cromwell
This portrait of Oliver Cromwell, the chief instigator of the trial and execution of the king, was painted by English artist Robert Walker.

twice forced into exile. When it fizzled out in 1652, the way lay open to a better management of aristocratic loyalties that was to come with the personal rule of Louis XIV from 1661.

In October 1648, after four years of negotiations, the **Thirty Years' War** in Germany was brought to a close with a series of treaties collectively known as the **Treaty of Westphalia**. France was still at war with Spain (as it would be until 1659), but Germany's horrors at least had been ended. France secured rather vaguely defined gains on its eastern border; Sweden was confirmed in its possession of Pomerania on the Baltic coast, as well as receiving a huge cash payment from the **Holy Roman Emperor**, Ferdinand III, to withdraw its troops. Among the German states, **Brandenburg–Prussia** gained the most.

Crucially, Spain also recognized the independence of the Dutch Republic, and Germany's local rulers were given the right to make **alliances with foreign powers**, in effect confirming them as sovereign states. The authority of the Holy Roman Emperor appeared **fatally undermined**.

separate from the person of the king existed that no one, legal ruler or not, could disregard: **Parliament, not the king, was the law's rightful custodian**.

At the end of the 1640s, the **Kingdom of Dahomey** began to emerge as a **powerful force** under King Wegbeja (d. 1685). After uniting the lands of the Aja and the Fon, he introduced new laws, **reformed government** and bureaucracy, and initiated a religion and culture that would characterize this **West African state** for more than two centuries.

Treaty of Westphalia
This document was agreed over several months and signed by the Holy Roman Emperor and the king of France, ending 30 years of war.

— seal of one of 109 parties

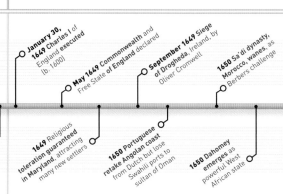

Timeline (1648):

- **January** Khmelnytsky Uprising (to 1651): Ukrainian Cossacks seek independence from Poland–Lithuania
- **January 17** Long Parliament breaks off negotiations with Charles I, leading to **Second English Civil War**
- **October 24 Treaty of Westphalia** ends Thirty Years' War in Germany
- **April Portuguese defeat Dutch army** in Brazil
- **Russian serfs lose rights**; anti-tax risings in Moscow
- **September 12** Battle of Stirling fought during **Scottish Civil War**
- **January 30 Eighty Years' War** between Dutch and Spanish ends
- **The Fronde**, a French aristocratic rebellion against Cardinal Mazarin, begins (to 1652)
- **Mughals transfer imperial court** to Shahjahanabad (Delhi)
- **Ottomans besiege** Venetian-held Crete
- Russian explorer Semyon Dezhnev (1605–72) **discovers Bering Strait**
- **December 11 Pride's Purge** expels majority from England's Long Parliament, **creating Rump Parliament**

Timeline (1649–50):

- **January 30, 1649 Charles I** of England executed (b. 1600)
- **May 1649 Commonwealth** and Free State of England declared
- **September 1649 Siege of Drogheda**, Ireland, by Oliver Cromwell
- **1650 Sa'di dynasty, Morocco, wanes**, as Berbers challenge
- **1649 Religious toleration guaranteed in Maryland**, attracting many new settlers
- **1650 Portuguese retake Angolan coast** from Dutch but lose Swahili ports to sultan of Oman
- **1650 Dahomey emerges** as powerful West African state

> **IT IS NOT WISDOM BUT AUTHORITY THAT MAKES A LAW.**

Thomas Hobbes, English philosopher, from *Leviathan*, 1651

The Coronation of Louis XIV, a tapestry from a painting by Charles Le Brun, court artist to Louis XIV, shows the young Louis about to receive his crown.

CHARLES I'S EXECUTION did not mark the final collapse of the royalist cause in England. A rump army, much of it Scottish, was still active. The royalists had an obvious **figure to rally round**, Charles's elder son, also called Charles. Yet his **defeat at Worcester** in September 1651 marked the final battle of the English Civil War, and saw Charles forced into a nine-year exile.

One of the foundations of **Western political philosophy** appeared in 1651 when Thomas Hobbes (1588–1679) published *Leviathan*. It argued for the **absolutism of a sovereign authority**. Though recognizing the liberty of the individual, Hobbes believed that anarchy could only be averted through a strong central government. It was an early example of **social contract theory** (individuals in society are united by mutual consent) and was profoundly influential.

In 1648, the **Khmelnytsky Uprising** saw a Cossack revolt against the rule of the Polish–Lithuanian Commonwealth in the Ukraine, which had been awarded to Poland under the Treaty of Lublin of 1589. The uprising climaxed in 1651 with the **Battle of Berestechko**, the largest single battle of the 17th century. The result was a victory of sorts for the Polish–Lithuanians. However, the ultimate effect of the struggle was a **weakening of the Commonwealth**, which was already wracked by numerous internal disputes among its querulous nobles.

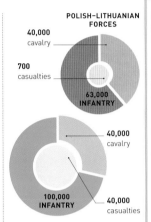

POLISH–LITHUANIAN FORCES

40,000 cavalry

700 casualties

63,000 INFANTRY

40,000 cavalry

100,000 INFANTRY

40,000 casualties

COSSACK–CRIMEAN TARTAR FORCES

Battle of Berestechko, 1651
The Cossack–Crimean Tartar forces suffered 40,000 casualties at Berestechko, far more than their Polish–Lithuanian adversaries.

The first of three **wars between England and the Netherlands** began in 1652 (two followed in 1665–67 and 1672–74). All were naval wars fought for command of the sea and **shipborne commerce**. For the Dutch, a small nation with few natural resources, but still the leading mercantile power of Europe, they assumed vast importance. For the English, they marked the **emergence of a new bullish confidence**. England's eventual victory signaled the decline of Dutch commercial preeminence, and launched a new **Anglo–French rivalry** for commercial and colonial supremacy.

ONE OF THE WORLD'S ICONIC structures, the **Taj Mahal**, in Agra, India, was completed in 1653 after 19 years. A mausoleum built by Mughal emperor Shah Jahan (1592–1666) **in memory of his third wife, Mumtaz Mahal**, it combined Indian, Persian, and Islamic styles of architecture.

In December 1653, **Oliver Cromwell** was made **Lord Protector of England**. Various types of government for the new republic had previously been tried, including military rule, while **parliaments were formed and dissolved**, generally by the irascible Cromwell, with great rapidity. Cromwell resisted the idea that he be made king. In the end, after his death in September 1658, it appeared desirable and inevitable that the vacuum could be filled only by the restoration of the actual king-in-waiting, the future Charles II.

Weakened by its struggle with the Cossacks during the Khmelnytsky Uprising, the partial **dismemberment of the Polish–Lithuanian Commonwealth** by neighbors eager for territorial gains became inevitable. The **resulting devastation**—its population almost halved, its economy all but destroyed—is known as The Deluge. Not only did Poland endure a Russian invasion in June 1654, in what became known as the **Thirteen Years' War**, the following year Sweden, too, invaded the country. The most enduring consequence of this calamitous period was not merely **Poland's loss of the Ukraine** to Russia under the Treaty of Andrusovo in 1667; rather, that Orthodox Russia was immensely boosted, and its czars' claims to rule "all the Russias" made tangible.

On June 7, 1654, the 15-year-old **Louis XIV was crowned king of France**. Since acceding to the throne when aged four, first his mother and then Cardinal Mazarin acted as regent. His subsequent reign, of 72 years and 110 days, remains one of history's longest.

Taj Mahal
This view of the white-domed marble of the Taj Mahal, in India, has made it one of the most recognizable and admired buildings in the world.

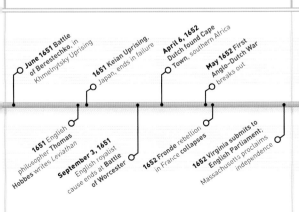

June 1651 Battle of Berestechko, in Khmelnytsky Uprising

1651 Keian Uprising, Japan, ends in failure

April 6, 1652 Dutch found Cape Town, southern Africa

May 1652 First Anglo–Dutch War breaks out

1651 English philosopher Thomas Hobbes writes *Leviathan*

September 3, 1651 English royalist cause ends at Battle of Worcester

1652 Fronde rebellion in France collapses

1652 Virginia submits to English Parliament; Massachusetts proclaims independence

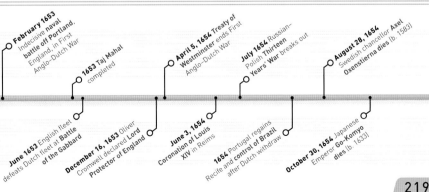

February 1653 Indecisive naval battle off Portland, England, in First Anglo–Dutch War

1653 Taj Mahal completed

April 5, 1654 Treaty of Westminster ends First Anglo–Dutch War

July 1654 Russian–Polish Thirteen Years' War breaks out

August 28, 1654 Swedish chancellor Axel Oxenstierna dies (b. 1583)

June 1653 English fleet defeats Dutch fleet at Battle of the Gabbard

December 16, 1653 Oliver Cromwell declared Lord Protector of England

June 3, 1654 Coronation of Louis XIV in Reims

1654 Portugal regains Recife and control of Brazil after Dutch withdraw

October 30, 1654 Japanese Emperor Go-Komyo dies (b. 1633)

219

This engraving on wood depicts Brandenburg forces storming Polish positions at the Battle of Warsaw in 1656 during the First Northern War.

A manuscript showing Ottoman troops on the island of Lemnos.

4,600,000
SQUARE MILES

THE APPROXIMATE **SIZE OF** THE **EMPIRE** CLAIMED BY **PORTUGAL**

FEARFUL OF RUSSIAN DOMINATION OF THE BALTIC, Sweden entered the Thirteen Years' War between Russia and Poland–Lithuania in 1655, thus creating the **First Northern War**. Other countries were sucked in and alliances changed. In 1656,

the Polish capital Warsaw was taken by a Swedish–Brandenburg force, further **undermining the Polish–Lithuanian state**.

One of the **greatest paintings in Western culture** was created in 1656 when Spanish artist Diego Velázquez (1599–1660) painted

Las Meninas, an enigmatic work that has been hugely influential.

A renewed phase of **Ottoman** confidence began when Köprülü Mehmed (1575–1661) became **grand vizier** in 1656, Sultan Mehmed IV handing him control of the empire. He ruthlessly stamped out opposition and embarked on a series of military campaigns—completed after his death in 1661—that saw the **empire at its greatest extent**.

Las Meninas
Diego Velázquez's painting of Margarita, the daughter of Philip IV of Spain, and her entourage, is known for its complex composition.

ON MARCH 2, 1657, the Great Fire of Meireki began in Edo (Tokyo). In two days, fed by relentless winds, it destroyed almost 70 percent of the city, consuming the paper and wooden buildings and **killing around 100,000** people.

Although an offshoot of the First Northern War, the **Swedish–Danish Wars** of 1657–58 and 1658–60 developed into a largely separate conflict over control of the Baltic when, in June 1657, Denmark joined the coalition confronting Sweden in Poland. Sweden had made consistent **gains at Denmark's expense** since the mid-16th century; the prize, control of The Sound—the strategically and economically vital entrance to the Baltic—still under Danish control in 1657. In the winter of 1657–58, Charles X of Sweden (1622–60) outflanked the Danes, marching his troops into Denmark and then, in February, across the frozen Baltic to Copenhagen itself. The **Treaty of Roskilde** in 1658 confirmed Sweden's territorial dominance. The second war, if less favorable to Sweden, still underlined **Sweden's Baltic superiority**.

With the Ottoman Empire now reinvigorated by Grand Vizier Köprülü Mehmed, in late 1657 its fleet **captured the Aegean islands of Lemnos and Tenedos** from the Venetians. The islands, which dominated the approaches to the Dardanelles, had been used by the Venetians to **blockade Constantinople**, the Ottoman capital. The Venetians would not pose such a threat again.

IN JUNE 1658, AURANGZEB (1618–1707), or Alamgir ("Conqueror of the World") as he called himself, was **crowned Mughal emperor**. It ended two years of infighting between him and his brothers for their father, Shah Jahan's, throne—this despite Shah Jahan still being alive. All three **brothers were subsequently executed** (two by Aurangzeb). His reign would prove paradoxical. Mughal India was still immensely rich and powerful. Under Aurangzeb, a devout Muslim, it reached it **greatest territorial extent** (see p.234). Yet the near continuous warfare of his 49-year reign, in which immense

Conqueror of the World
This portrait of the Mughal emperor, Aurangzeb I, seen here with his courtiers, is attributed to the Indian artist Bhawani Das.

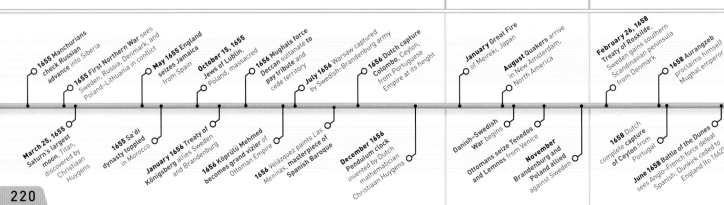

1655 Manchurians check Russian advance into Siberia

1655 First Northern War sees Sweden, Russia, Denmark, and Poland–Lithuania in conflict

May 1655 England seizes Jamaica from Spain

October 15, 1655 Jews of Lublin, Poland, massacred

1656 Mughals force Deccan sultanate to pay tribute and cede territory

July 1656 Warsaw captured by Swedish–Brandenburg army

1656 Dutch capture Colombo, Ceylon, from Portuguese Empire at its height

March 25, 1655 Saturn's largest moon, Titan, discovered by Christian Huygens

1655 Sa'di dynasty toppled in Morocco

January 1656 Treaty of Königsberg allies Sweden and Brandenburg

1656 Köprülü Mehmed becomes grand vizier of Ottoman Empire

1656 Velázquez paints *Las Meninas*, masterpiece of Spanish Baroque

December 1656 Pendulum clock invented by Dutch mathematician Christiaan Huygens

January Great Fire of Meireki, Japan

August Quakers arrive in New Amsterdam, North America

Danish–Swedish War begins

Ottomans seize Tenedos and Lemnos from Venice

November Brandenburg and Poland allied against Sweden

February 26, 1658 Treaty of Roskilde, Sweden gains southern Scandinavian peninsula from Denmark

1658 Aurangzeb proclaims himself Mughal emperor

1658 Dutch complete capture of Ceylon from Portugal

June 1658 Battle of the Dunes sees Anglo–French force defeat Spanish; Dunkirk ceded to England (to 1662)

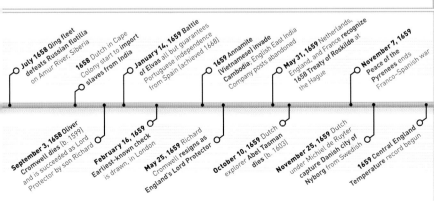

The Peace of the Pyrenees in 1659 saw Louis XIV of France (center left) meet Philip IV of Spain to ratify the treaty that ended Franco–Spanish conflict.

> **THE TRUTH IS, I DO INDULGE MYSELF A LITTLE THE MORE IN PLEASURE,** KNOWING THAT **THIS IS THE PROPER AGE** OF MY LIFE TO DO IT.

Samuel Pepys, English diarist, diary entry, 1660

Swedish Empire

The Swedish Empire reached its peak in 1658 in the reign of Charles X, following the Treaty of Roskilde. However, the need to defend its new territories forced it into a series of unsustainably expensive wars.

[Map of the Swedish Empire showing North Sea, Baltic Sea, with locations: Trondheim, Christiania, Stockholm, Copenhagen, Malmö, Stralsund, Helsingfors, Narva, Riga; regions: NORWAY, SWEDEN, FINLAND, DENMARK, BREMEN, RUSSIA, POLAND–LITHUANIA]

LOUIS XIV (1638–1715)

Louis XIV, known as *Le Roi Soleil* (Sun King), had a greater impact on France than any other monarch. Determined to be the absolute ruler of his nobles and his country, he centralized the state, fought numerous wars, and also encouraged culture. By his later reign, France had expanded its territory and was the leading nation in Europe, much admired and imitated.

campaigns were launched against the Sikhs and the Marathas, **exhausted the country's treasuries** and highlighted the internal flaws of his vast empire. By his death in 1707, it was visibly in decline.

Near Dunkirk, in northeastern France, on June 14, 1658 a combined Anglo–French force defeated the Spanish. This was the last decisive conflict of the **Franco–Spanish War** that had begun in 1635, and as such the last battle of the Thirty Years' War. It was also the last confrontation of the **Anglo–Spanish War,** which had begun in 1654. For the French, the imperative, as ever, was dominance in Europe; for the English, to steal whatever advantage, commercial or territorial, they could over Spain, hence the **pragmatic alliance** between Oliver Cromwell's Puritan England with Louis XIV's Catholic France.

The year 1659 marked the start of one of the most remarkable developments of the **scientific revolution** in Europe with the beginning of what is now known as the **Central England Temperature,** or CET, record. It was a scientific experiment on an unprecedented scale, an attempt to measure temperatures almost nationally, but in reality within a triangle bounded in the north by Manchester, the east by London, and in the west by Bristol. Today, it constitutes the oldest continuous **measurement of temperatures** in the world. It had a precedent of sorts in 1657 in Italy, the Accademia del Cimento (Academy of Experiment) in Florence instituting what has been called the "world's first weather observation network." If Europe's scientific revolution depended on **accurate observation** and measurement, the CET was a crucial forerunner.

The **Peace of the Pyrenees** in November 1659 ended the enduring Franco–Spanish conflict in Europe. France was now **Europe's major power,** and Spain, its New World revenues diminishing, its internal tensions multiplying, and its support from

£400
THE VALUE OF THE EARLIEST-KNOWN CHECK

Austria curtailed, was slowly subsiding. The change roused those states able to confront an assertive France to do just that, putting France on a collision course with the other **emerging powers in Europe**: England, the Dutch, and Habsburg Austria.

"I... BLESSED GOD... IT WAS THE LORD'S DOING." With these words diarist John Evelyn recorded the overwhelming reception accorded Charles II (1630–85) in London in May 1660 on his **restoration as king of England.** By any measure, Charles's restoration was a triumphant vindication of the principles of kingship, as well as of the contradictory limitations of Oliver Cromwell's republican experiment. Charles II swept back to his throne on a wave of popular sentiment. Worldly, knowing, and, at heart, lazy, Charles was always **ready to compromise** with his parliamentary opponents. His charm was legendary. That said, his weakness for pleasure-seeking combined with his instinctive sympathy for Catholicism, especially when funded by Louis XIV in France, highlighted a **still unresolved political crisis.** Charles, by turns vengeful and forgiving, never

resolved this dilemma. It was left to his successor, the rather less shrewd James II, to provoke the crisis that would later definitively propel England into a **unique parliamentary revolution** (see 1688).

The famous **English diarist Samuel Pepys** (1633–1703) began putting his daily thoughts on paper in 1660. Pepys was a high-ranking naval official, and his diary, which he kept until 1669 but which was not published until the 19th century, provided one of the most valuable sources of information on **life during the English Restoration.**

The death of Cardinal Mazarin (see 1648) in 1661 began the **personal rule of the 22-year-old Louis XIV.** He would remain on the French throne for a further 53 years. A childhood in which France was divided made him aware of the need to develop a style of personal assertiveness and grandeur. This was to impress on the French elites that they were part of his great project for French glory and **preeminence in Europe.** United under a ruler who recognized their privileges and status, French nobles and officials supported a series of wars to assert this position. However, these wars would bring France to the brink of disaster and pauperize most of its population. Yet the **cultural impact** of Louis' rule remained; no other European country would approach France in the second half of the 17th century for such a projection of national preeminence.

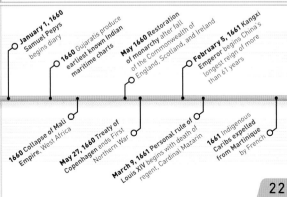

July 1658 Qing fleet defeats Russian flotilla on Amur River, Siberia

1658 Dutch in Cape Colony start to import slaves from India

January 14, 1659 Battle of Elvas all but guarantees Portuguese independence from Spain (achieved 1668)

1659 Annamite (Vietnamese) invade Cambodia; English East India Company posts abandoned

May 31, 1659 Netherlands, England, and France recognize 1658 Treaty of Roskilde at the Hague

November 7, 1659 Peace of the Pyrenees ends Franco–Spanish war

January 1, 1660 Samuel Pepys begins diary

1660 Gujaratis produce earliest known Indian maritime charts

May 1660 Restoration of monarchy after fall of the Commonwealth of England, Scotland, and Ireland

February 5, 1661 Kangxi Emperor begins China's longest reign of more than 61 years

September 3, 1658 Oliver Cromwell dies (b. 1599) and is succeeded as Lord Protector by son Richard

February 16, 1659 Earliest-known check is drawn, in London

May 25, 1659 Richard Cromwell resigns as England's Lord Protector

October 10, 1659 Dutch explorer Abel Tasman dies (b. 1603)

November 25, 1659 Dutch under Michiel de Ruyter capture Danish city of Nyborg from Swedish

1659 Central England Temperature record begun

1660 Collapse of Mali Empire, West Africa

May 27, 1660 Treaty of Copenhagen ends First Northern War

March 9, 1661 Personal rule of Louis XIV begins with death of regent, Cardinal Mazarin

1661 Indigenous Caribs expelled from Martinique by French

A 1635 view of Fort Zeelandia, in Tainan, present-day Taiwan.

The people of New Amsterdam plead with its director-general, Peter Stuyvesant, not to resist the English warships gathering in the harbor.

This representation of London's Great Plague shows, in the center foreground, the Angel of Death holding an hourglass and a spear.

FOR ALMOST FOUR DECADES the **Dutch East India Company** had controlled western **Formosa** (Taiwan), with its trading base Fort Zeelandia at its heart. Hostile to this alien presence, the Chinese Ming dynasty besieged the fort, which was inadequately supplied by water, and captured it in February 1662. The **Dutch** were forced to **abandon Formosa**.

The **pace of scientific investigation** in the 17th century led Europe's scientists to share ideas, and then to form bodies devoted to a better understanding of science. In 1662, the **Royal Society**, the world's oldest such scientific body, was founded in London. That it had royal approval showed how both the practical application of **science** and the pursuit of **pure knowledge** had become of interest to the state.

5 MILLION
THE **PRICE** IN LIVRES FOR WHICH **FRANCE BOUGHT DUNKIRK**

NUMEROUS ENGLISH RAIDS on Dutch shipping and trading posts in this year were the result of an **English desire to win** as much Dutch trade as possible. The most successful of these took place on August 27, when a small English fleet arrived at **New Amsterdam**, the capital of the Dutch North American colony of New Netherland, and demanded its surrender. Director-general Peter Stuyvesant eventually complied. By March 1665, the Second Anglo–Dutch War broke out.

The **Austro–Turkish War** that broke out in 1663 reached a climax in August 1664, when an

Battle of St. Gotthard
This woodcut, based on a drawing by Adolf Ehrhardt, shows an attack by the Habsburg cavalry in the defeat of the Ottomans at St. Gotthard.

> ❝ ONE IS EASILY **FOOLED BY** THAT **WHICH ONE LOVES.** ❞

Molière, from *Tartuffe*, 1664

Ottoman army, intent on capturing Vienna, was defeated by a Habsburg force at **St. Gotthard, Hungary**. Although the Ottomans gained favorable peace terms, their **invasion was curtailed**.

Alarmed at English and Dutch domination of trade with Asia, in 1664 the **French East India Company** was established, with royal patronage. It was lavishly funded, but it resulted only in the settlement of the island of Réunion in the Indian Ocean and a **handful of trading posts** in India.

THE PUBLICATION IN THIS YEAR OF *Micrographia*, by English natural philosopher and polymath Robert Hooke (1635–1703), was the first work **under the patronage of the Royal Society**. It was not merely the first time that those other than a closed circle of specialists had been made aware of the remarkable world revealed by **microscopes**. His drawings of an ant, louse, and flea, lovingly detailed and precisely executed, sparked particular astonishment at the complexity of this hitherto **unsuspected microworld**. It was, according to diarist Samuel Pepys, "the most ingenious book that I ever read in my life." Of greater significance was that Hooke was the **first to use the term "cell"** for the smallest unit

Hooke's findings
This page from Robert Hooke's 1665 publication, Micrographia, shows a detailed illustration of an ant. Hooke had drawn the ant after viewing it under his microscope, which is shown here.

of a living organism, the term derived from the fact the cells Hooke observed reminded him of a monk's cell.

The year 1665 also saw the last outbreak of **bubonic plague in England**. The disease was concentrated mostly in London, where, at its height in September, 7,000 a week were dying. In the 18 months the **plague ravaged the city**, 100,000 people died.

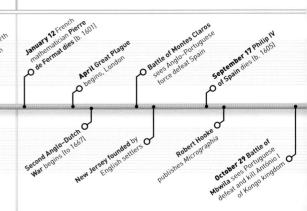

1662 Charles II sells Dunkirk, English since 1658, to Louis XIV

February 1662 Chinese force Dutch to **abandon Formosa**

July 1662 Royal Society, London, founded

1663 Austro–Turkish War begins (to 1664)

England attacks **Dutch West African** trading posts

Dutch **partially take Guiana** from England

French East India Company established

September 24 Peter Stuyvesant surrenders **New Amsterdam**, in North America, to an English naval force

August 1 Battle of **St. Gotthard** sees Austrians defeat Ottomans

French playwright **Molière** (1622–73) writes *Tartuffe*

Marathas capture Surat, India

Treaty of Vasvar ends Austro–Turkish War

January 12 French mathematician Pierre de Fermat dies (b. 1601)

April Great Plague begins, London

Second Anglo–Dutch War begins (to 1667)

New Jersey founded by English settlers

Battle of Montes Claros sees Anglo-Portuguese force defeat Spain

Robert Hooke publishes *Micrographia*

September 17 Philip IV of Spain dies (b. 1605)

October 29 Battle of **Mbwila** sees Portuguese defeat and kill Antonio I of Kongo kingdom

In 1666, a major fire swept through the central parts of London, consuming thousands of houses and wiping away centuries of history.

> **THE MIND** IS ITS OWN PLACE AND IN ITSELF, **CAN MAKE** A **HEAVEN OF HELL,** A **HELL OF HEAVEN.**

John Milton, English poet, from *Paradise Lost*, 1667

A woodcut portrait of the admiral and privateer Henry Morgan.

1666

79 SHIPS

10 ships lost

ENGLISH FLEET

84 SHIPS

4 ships lost

DUTCH FLEET

Four Days' Battle
In one of the longest naval engagements ever, the Four Days' Battle, fought in June 1666 during the Second Anglo–Dutch War, saw the Dutch inflict a defeat on the English.

THE BIGGEST ENGAGEMENT OF THE SECOND ANGLO–DUTCH WAR, which had begun in 1665, the **Four Days' Battle** was an English attempt to destroy the Dutch fleet before it could grow to challenge them. However, the **English** suffered such **losses** that it handed the initiative to the Dutch. Disaster then followed for England in June 1667 after a daring **Dutch raid** on the Medway River, in the Thames estuary. With discontent at home, England brought the war to a halt.

As the Great Plague ended, a new **disaster overtook London**, the **Great Fire**, which burned from September 2 to 5. London was still a medieval city, filthy and unplanned, with no great spaces and few public buildings of note. The City, which was the commercial heart, was especially overcrowded and unsanitary. It was here the fire began. Although the risk of fire was well known, no effective precautions were taken. Though **drought and a heat wave** had made the city especially vulnerable, a crucial added factor was a strong easterly wind. The result was that the **whole of the City was destroyed**, including the medieval St. Paul's Cathedral, 87 other churches, and upward of 13,000 houses. The official death toll of six has long been disputed.

Not to be outdone by the founding of the Royal Society of London (see 1662), in December 1666 Louis XIV gave his blessing to the creation of the **French Academy of Sciences**, which in 1699 became the Royal Academy of Sciences and was installed in the Louvre Palace, in Paris. Today, it is part of the *Institut de France*. It was at the heart of a **drive for verifiable scientific knowledge**. As an arm of the state it was also interested in discoveries that could enrich its country, such as in agriculture and armaments.

1667

THE TREATY OF ANDRUSOVO in January 1667 ended the Polish-Lithuanian Commonwealth's calamitous war with Russia that had begun in 1654. It also climaxed The Deluge—its **dramatic decline** above all **in the face of Russian expansion**. Russia, granted Smolensk and present-day Belarus, could for the first time claim to have **unified the Slavic peoples of the region**.

The completion in 1667 of the **Piazza San Pietro**, by Gian Lorenzo Bernini (1598–1680), saw the high point of urban planning in Baroque Rome. Many of Rome's public spaces were ambitiously rebuilt by a series of architects to make them deliberately imposing, and worthy to be at the center of the Catholic Church.

The **War of Devolution** began in May 1667 as a result of Louis XIV's continuing **claims to the Spanish Netherlands**. It saw France take some Habsburg cities in Flanders, as well as Franche-Comté to its east. However, a Triple Aliance of

80,000
THE NUMBER OF **PEOPLE KILLED IN** THE **SAMAKHI EARTHQUAKE** IN AZERBAIJAN

England, Sweden, and the Dutch Republic forced the isolated Louis to return most of his gains by the 1668 **Treaty of Aix-la-Chapelle**.

In 1667, the **epic poem** *Paradise Lost*, by English poet John Milton (1608–74), gave the English language one of its **greatest literary achievements**. It told the Christian story of man's fall from grace in the Garden of Eden.

Siege of Lille
Louis XIV directs French forces at Lille during the War of Devolution. Its capture provided one of France's few gains from a frustrating conflict.

1668

THE PORTUGUESE TRADING POST AT BOMBAY (Mumbai) had **passed to the English Crown** in 1662 as part of the dowry of Catherine of Braganza, Charles II's Portuguese wife. In 1668, the king leased it to the **East India Company** for an annual rent of £10, making it the Company's third trading post in India after those at Surat and Madras. With Bombay Castle completed in 1675, from 1687 it became the focus of all the Company's trading in India, resisting attempts to storm it by the Mughals and the Dutch.

In 1668, the **Welsh privateer** (state-sponsored raider) **Henry Morgan**, famous for his attacks on Spanish settlements in the Caribbean, succeeded in one of the **most daring assaults ever** when his ships captured the well-protected **Spanish trading city of Porto Bello**, in Panama. It won him both great wealth and further English support for his buccaneering endeavors.

Just as Philip II's seizure of the Portuguese crown in 1580 was a sign of Spanish power, so its **recognition of Portuguese independence in 1668** under the Treaty of Lisbon, which confirmed the House of Braganza as rulers of Portugal, was evidence of its decline. From 1640, Portugal had been in open revolt against Spain, and in June 1665 at the **Battle of Montes Claros** a combined Anglo–Portuguese force inflicted a crushing defeat on them. Close to bankruptcy, and sure of further French hostility, the Spanish had little option but to concede.

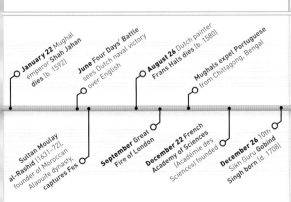

January 22 Mughal emperor **Shah Jahan** dies (b. 1592)

June Four Days' Battle sees Dutch naval victory over English

August 26 Dutch painter **Frans Hals** dies (b. 1580)

Mughals expel Portuguese from Chittagong, Bengal

Sultan Moulay al-Rashid (1631–72), founder of Moroccan Alaouite dynasty, **captures Fes**

September Great Fire of London

December 22 French Academy of Sciences (Académie des Sciences) founded

December 26 10th Sikh Guru Gobind Singh born (d. 1708)

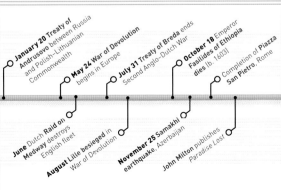

January 20 Treaty of Andrusovo between Russia and Polish–Lithuanian Commonwealth

May 24 War of Devolution begins in Europe

July 31 Treaty of Breda ends Second Anglo–Dutch War

October 18 Emperor **Fasilides of Ethiopia** dies (b. 1603)

Completion of **Piazza San Pietro**, Rome

June Dutch Raid on Medway destroys English fleet

August Lille besieged in War of Devolution

November 25 Samakhi earthquake, Azerbaijan

John Milton publishes *Paradise Lost*

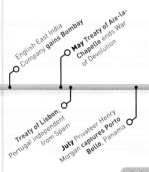

English East India Company **gains Bombay**

May Treaty of Aix-la-Chapelle ends War of Devolution

Treaty of Lisbon; Portugal independent from Spain

July Privateer Henry Morgan captures Porto Bello, Panama

The Badshahi Mosque, Lahore, was commissioned by Aurangzeb.

ONE OF THE REASONS GIVEN FOR THE DISINTEGRATION of the Mughal Empire after the death of **Aurangzeb** in 1707 has been his supposed religious **persecution of Hindus** and other minorities. Where his predessor Akbar I had pursued an active policy of religious toleration as the most effective means of controlling his Hindu vassals, Aurangzeb—himself a Sunni Muslim—was said to have **systematically destroyed Hindu temples**. In addition, he banned the use of music, central to Hindu practice, issuing a decree, perhaps in 1669, to this effect. He also had drawn up an **exhaustive digest of Muslim law**, the *Fatawa-e-Alamgri*, said to have been rigorously imposed. All these claims are disputed, however. In fact, the number of Hindu temples said to have been destroyed varies improbably from 80 to 60,000. That Aurangzeb was **strongly anti-Christian**, though, seems certain to have been true.

£100 MILLION
THE ANNUAL REVENUE RAISED BY AURANGZEB'S EXCHEQUER

" COME QUICKLY, I AM DRINKING THE STARS. "

Attributed to Dom Pérignon, while tasting champagne, 1670

IN MAY 1670, THE HUDSON'S BAY COMPANY WAS FORMED under British royal charter on the initiative of two French fur trackers, Pierre-Esprit Radisson and Médard de Groseilliers. They had learned that **the best furs** came from the **Cree territory** to the north of Lake Superior. Easier to reach via Hudson Bay rather than via the rivers and lakes to the south, they proposed a base there. Rebuffed in France, they **solicited support in England**. The Hudson's Bay Company would become one of the great commercial enterprises of England, the **basis of its claim to Canada**, and source of regional rivalry with France.

The claim that in 1670 **Dom Pérignon** (1638–1715), a monk at the Benedictine Abbey of Hautvillers, in Champagne in northeast France, **invented the sparkling wine** of that name, is largely discounted today. In fact,

Cossack leader
Stepan Razin, the Cossack leader who rose up against the nobility and the czar's bureaucracy, is seen here on the Volga River, South Russia.

he was devoted to **eliminating the bubbles** such wines produced, as the pressure they built up in the bottles tended to explode them. But as cellar master of the Abbey, he did make a major contribution to the **production of white wines**, by using grapes otherwise used in red wine. It was not until the early 18th century that the **taste for sparkling wines**, in England and France, grew rapidly.

A **Cossack uprising** in South Russia in 1670 was **brutally suppressed** by the czar, and its leader Stepan Razin was executed the following year. An attempt to protect Cossack independence against the **centralized Russian state** had become a revolt by a disaffected peasantry that saw several cities sacked and looted.

Portuguese glazed tiles decorate the São Miguel Fortress in Luanda, a key military strongpoint in the colonization of Angola in the later 17th century.

IN 1671, PORTUGAL ENDED THE INDEPENDENCE of the kingdom of Ndongo, in what is today Angola. A Portuguese colony had largely **dominated the Ndongo** since the 16th century, but a rebellion by their king, Philip, in 1671, saw **Portuguese troops capture the capital** and take control of its entire territory.

Just as fears of Spanish dominance in Europe had allied France, England, and the Dutch Republic, so French dominance after 1659 saw **anti-French alliances** throw Spain and the Dutch Republic together. Spain opposed Louis XIV's claim to the Spanish Netherlands by marriage, while the Dutch preferred a weak Spain as a neighbor to a strong France. The War of Devolution of 1667–68 had seen French gains, and then losses, yet in the Spanish Netherlands, but in 1672 Louis, allied with England and Sweden, tried again in the **Franco–Dutch War**. The war ended with the Dutch granting New Amsterdam to England, while the French—although their conquest of the Dutch Republic failed—gained the former Burgundian territory of the Franche-Comté and a string of border territories in the Spanish Netherlands. Yet the peace proved a brief pause in Louis' attempts to expand and safeguard France.

FUR TRADE

A valuable natural asset of North America was fur. It drove the French westward into Canada and saw the English establish the Hudson's Bay Company (see 1670). It also led to Anglo–French conflict there. While the French would accompany the American Indians on fur-trapping expeditions, the English, and the Dutch (pictured) before them, usually took delivery of furs from the Indians at their trading posts. All depended on Indian aid, while the Indians became dependent on European weapons and tools.

March 11 Mount Etna, Sicily, erupts, killing 20,000

Aurangzeb issues **codification of Muslim law**, *Fatawa-e-Alamgri*

September 6 Ottomans take Candia, Crete, from Venice

Coffee drinking introduced to Paris by Ottoman ambassador

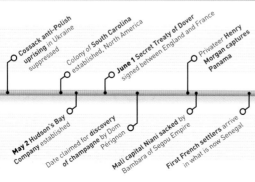

Cossack anti-Polish uprising in Ukraine suppressed

Colony of **South Carolina** established, North America

June 1 Secret Treaty of Dover signed between England and France

Privateer **Henry Morgan captures Panama**

May 2 Hudson's Bay Company established

Date claimed for **discovery of champagne** by Dom Pérignon

Mali capital Niani sacked by Bambara of Segou Empire

First French settlers arrive in what is now Senegal

1671 Ndongo defeated by Portugal and cede territory to Portuguese colony in Angola

1671 Spain allies with Dutch Republic against France

June 16, 1671 Execution of Cossack leader Stepan Razin (b. 1630)

December 30, 1671 French Royal Academy of Architecture founded

April 1671 Battle of Saraighat sees Mughal defeated by Ahom kingdom

1671 German mathematician Gottfried Leibniz builds **first calculator**

1672 English Royal African Company established

March 12, 1672 Third Anglo–Dutch War begins (to 1674)

Marquette and Jolliet descend the Mississippi River with their guides.

The Qing emperor Kangxi oversaw the complete suppression of the Three Feudatories revolt.

Frederick William I leads his troops at the Battle of Fehrbellin.

Leibniz mechanical calculator
One of the first calculating machines, developed by Gottfried Leibniz, this device multiplies by making repeated additions.

In 1671, German mathematician **Gottfried Leibniz** (1646–1716) demonstrated one of the **world's first mechanical calculators**. It was the first such machine that could perform all four of the basic arithmetic functions. Leibniz went on to further refine his calculating machines, thus providing the basis of the modern calculator.

Repeated **Cossack and Crimean Tartar revolts** against the weakened Polish–Lithuanian Commonwealth in 1672 drew their Ottoman allies into a four-year **Polish–Ottoman War**. Polish resistance under Jan III Sobieski (1629–96) was greatly undermined by grudging support from the Polish parliament, the Sejm, and was hardly equal to the progressively larger armies of the Ottomans. The result was the **loss of what little prestige Poland could still claim** as well as most of its Ukrainian territories.

THE EXTENSIVE WATERWAYS OF North America provided a ready-made means of exploring its interior. In 1673, **French–Canadian explorer** Louis Jolliet and French Jesuit Jacques Marquette **traveled down the Mississippi River** to within 370 miles (600 km) of the Gulf of Mexico. They turned back for fear of arousing Spanish hostility but discovered the Missouri and Ohio rivers, as well as confirming that the river led to the Gulf and not the Pacific. **English exploration** inland from their scattered coastal settlements was much more hesitant, rarely coordinated, and additionally blocked by the **Appalachian mountain chain**. It almost always depended on native assistance. For example, it was after spending a year with a group of Tomahitan Indians in present-day Georgia that Gabriel Arthur traveled with them **across the Cumberland Gap**, unwittingly discovering what in the 18th century would be the principal route to Kentucky and the west.

2,000
MILES, THE
LENGTH
OF THE
APPALACHIAN
MOUNTAINS

FOLLOWING THEIR TAKEOVER OF CHINA WITH THE COLLAPSE of the Ming dynasty in 1644, the Qing coopted some of the more **powerful Ming generals**, making them regional governors and allowing them considerable latitude in their rule over what became almost independent territories. It was felt that if they **enriched themselves**—as they did on a prodigious scale—the less likely it was that they would revolt. The risk was that their progressively greater revenues would be matched by greater **pretensions to rule China**. In 1674, the **Revolt of the Three Feudatories** broke out across southern China in those provinces controlled by the three most prominent rebels, Wu Sangui, Shang Kexi Gungdong, and Geng Jingzhong, joined by lesser Ming governors. Led by the Kangxi Emperor (1654–1722), the Qing response, with its **superior military**, was successful,

Statue of Shivaji
This bronze statue of Shivaji on horseback in Maharashtra, India, commemorates his leadership of the Maratha campaign for self-rule.

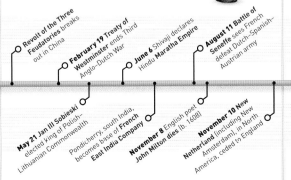

albeit not until 1681. With the rebels as wary of each other as they were of the Qing, they rarely cooperated, **allowing the Qing to pick them off** one by one. Those rebels who did not commit suicide were executed.

After freeing the Hindu Maratha from the Sultan of Bijapur, **Shivaji** (1630–80) was crowned Maratha king in 1674, establishing the **Maratha Empire** (see p.242) that would later defeat the Mughals to dominate India until the early 19th century.

IN 1675, MUGHAL EMPEROR AURANGZEB ORDERED THE EXECUTION of Tegh Bahadur, ninth guru of the Sikhs, after he had refused to convert to Islam. It brought to the Sikh throne his nine-year-old son, **Gobind Singh** (1666–1708). It would be several years later that, under Singh's leadership, the Sikhs would pose a growing **military threat to Mughal rule**, and contribute significantly to its collapse. However, the pattern of **religious opposition to the Mughals** was already well established in many parts of India, most obviously in the Western Ghats, where Shivaji had declared the Maratha Empire.

On June 18, 1675, a combined Prussian and Brandenburg army, led by Frederick William I, Elector of Brandenburg (1620–88), met and **defeated a Swedish army**, led by Count von Wrangel, near **Fehrbellin**, in Brandenburg. This relatively insignificant battle in the **Scanian War**, itself a by-product of the Franco–Dutch War, nonetheless marked a crucial moment in Sweden's long struggle to impose itself as the dominant Baltic power. Defeat at the hands of an otherwise relatively minor German state **dealt the Swedes a lasting blow**. Swedish pretensions to great power status were revealed as precarious at best.

April 1672 Franco–Dutch War begins with invasion of Dutch Republic (to 1678)

June 7, 1672 Battle of Solebay in Third Anglo–Dutch War is inconclusive

July 4, 1672 William III of Orange appointed **Stadtholder of Holland**

October 18, 1672 Treaty of Buczacz between Ottoman Empire and Polish–Lithuania Commonwealth

February 17 French writer and actor **Molière** dies (b. 1622)

May Jolliet and Marquette begin **exploration of Mississippi River**

English explorer Gabriel Arthur **crosses Appalachians**

Battles of Schooneveld between English and Dutch fleets

Revolt of the Three Feudatories breaks out in China

February 19 Treaty of Westminster ends Third Anglo–Dutch War

June 6 Shivaji declares Hindu **Maratha Empire**

May 21 Jan III Sobieski elected king of Polish–Lithuanian Commonwealth

Pondicherry, south India, becomes base of **French East India Company**

November 8 English poet John Milton dies (b. 1608)

August 11 Battle of Seneffe sees French defeat Dutch–Spanish–Austrian army

November 10 New Netherland (including New Amsterdam), in North America, ceded to England

Sikh leader, **Tegh Bahadur**, executed by Mughals

June 18 Battle of Fehrbellin sees Brandenburg and Prussia defeat Sweden

Development of haiku poetry, Japan

War between English colonists and Algonquian American Indian tribes

225

Horseshoe Falls, on the Canadian side of Niagara Falls, is about 2,600 ft (800 m) wide. Europeans first discovered this natural wonder in 1677.

A 19th-century image of the Asante, wh[o] dominated West Africa from the 1680s.

IN FRANCE, LOUIS XIV'S principal architectural endeavors concentrated on his **immense palace at Versailles**, just outside Paris. Louis was also determined to continue the transformation of the French capital, begun by his grandfather Henry IV at the start of the 17th century. Henry's intent had been to lift the city from medieval slum to a **capital worthy of the first power of Europe**—a city to rival Rome for its imposing public buildings and commanding spaces. The Louvre Palace, predictably, was significantly enlarged and remodeled, notably the east wing, whose stately façade encapsulated the **French taste for Classicism** at its most austere and precise. But the building that most memorably reflects Louis's contribution to Paris is **Les Invalides**, or more properly *L'Hôtel National des Invalides*. Part hospital, part retirement home for French soldiers, it was completed in 1676. Designed by Libéral Bruant (1635–97), Les Invalides was conceived on an grand scale, with vast formal gardens

sweeping up to its immense façade and 15 courtyards clustered behind. Its most memorable feature, the **lavish royal chapel** *L'Église du Dôme*, was added slightly later. Placed at the southern end of the complex, it was designed with a vast dome and spire, with details picked out in gold.

Louis XIV's reign marked one of the most **fertile periods of French literature**. The year 1677 saw the first performance of *Phèdre*, the greatest tragedy of French dramatist **Jean Racine** (1639–99). Dramatists such as Racine, Pierre Corneille (1606–84), and **Molière** (1622–73) thrived under royal patronage, captivating court audiences in different ways. Corneille and Racine reflected courtly concerns through their use of formal verse, classical themes, and emphasis on honor, virtue, and renunciation, while Molière's racy dramas mocked the social pretensions of the bourgeoisie. As a result of this rich and growing theatrical tradition, the **Comédie-Française** was established in Paris under

royal patronage. This official state theater aimed to showcase the glories of the French stage and French culture as widely as possible.

European explorers began to realize the **immensity of North America** as the 17th century progressed. The extraordinary variety and natural beauty of its landscape also continued to amaze. The **discovery of Niagara Falls** in 1677, a waterfall hugely larger than any in Europe, with over 6,000,000 cu ft (170,000 cu m) of water thundering over it every minute, provoked wonder in the Old World. There is doubt as to which European can claim to have seen the falls first. However, the French Franciscan missionary Louis Hennepin (1626–1701), exploring at the request of King Louis XIV, is generally credited with their discovery, in 1677.

engraving of author

Religious work
This is the frontispiece from the third edition of John Bunyan's The Pilgrim's Progress, a hugely influential work in the 17th century.

One of **literature's most significant religious works** was published in February 1678. *The Pilgrim's Progress* was written by English writer and Christian preacher **John Bunyan** (1628–88), who completed much of the work while imprisoned in Bedford Gaol (jail). It was published in two parts (the second part appeared in 1684) and is an **allegorical tale** of an everyman's journey from this world to heaven. *The Pilgrim's Progress* has become one of the most translated books in history.

Les Invalides, Paris
These sumptuous buildings now contain museums and monuments relating to France's military history, and a hospital for war veterans.

IN 1679, THE ENGLISH PARLIAMENT passed the **Habeas Corpus Act**. Like Magna Carta (see 1215), it represented a cornerstone of English liberty. It is the legal assertion that **no one may be unlawfully detained**. The law was passed for pragmatic reasons rather than as a liberal **principle of justice**. Its aim was to prevent James, Duke of York, the Catholic brother and heir of Charles II, from arresting his Protestant opponents without legal justification, as Charles's

> ❝ YOU MAY **HOLD THE BODY,** SUBJECT TO EXAMINATION. ❞

English writ of Habeas Corpus, 1679

chief minister, the Earl of Clarendon, had begun to do. The underlying principle of the Act, which is incorporated into the **American Constitution**, remains fundamental to most Anglo-Saxon legal systems as an **ultimate guarantee of individual liberty**. However, in reality the law is hardly ever invoked.

In August 1680, the **Pueblo people** of the colony of New Mexico **rose against the Spanish occupiers** and drove them from the area for 12 years. Spanish claims to New Mexico, though dating back to Francisco Coronado's expeditions of the

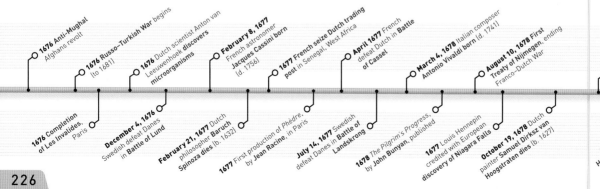

1676 Anti-Mughal Afghans revolt

1676 Russo–Turkish War begins (to 1681)

1676 Dutch scientist Anton van Leeuwenhoek **discovers microorganisms**

February 8, 1677 French astronomer **Jacques Cassini born** (d. 1756)

1677 French seize Dutch trading post in Senegal, West Africa

April 1677 French defeat Dutch in **Battle of Cassel**

March 4, 1678 Italian composer Antonio Vivaldi born (d. 1741)

August 10, 1678 First Treaty of Nijmegen, ending Franco–Dutch War

1679 Renewed Mughal–Rajput conflict (to 1709)

May 27, 1679 Habeas Corpus, cornerstone of English liberty becomes law

1676 Completion of Les Invalides, Paris

December 4, 1676 Swedish defeat Danes in Battle of Lund

February 21, 1677 Dutch philosopher Baruch Spinoza dies (b. 1632)

1677 First production of *Phèdre*, by Jean Racine, in Paris

July 14, 1677 Swedish defeat Danes in Battle of Landskrong

1678 *The Pilgrim's Progress*, by John Bunyan, published

1677 Louis Hennepin credited with European discovery of Niagara Falls

October 19, 1678 Dutch painter Samuel Dirksz van Hoogstraten dies (b. 1627)

1679 Colony of New Hampshire established

December 1679 Second Treaty of Nijmegen ending Franco–Dutch War

> **HE THAT DOES GOOD** FOR GOOD'S SAKE **SEEKS NEITHER PARADISE NOR REWARD, BUT** HE **IS SURE OF BOTH** IN THE END. 〞

William Penn, English Quaker, establishing Philadelphia, 1682

mid-16th century, had never amounted to much more than statements of priority and Christian preeminence over the region. New Mexico was seen as a land of marginal value as it was **remote and arid**. The Pueblo revolt was provoked partly by drought and by the suffering such natural events inevitably brought in their wake, but more particularly by Spain's determination to **crush local religious practices**—Pueblo shamen were consistently accused of witchcraft and executed. When the Spanish returned in 1692, they did so in overwhelming numbers.

The **Asante kingdom**, founded in about 1680, was formed from the Akan, who dominated West Africa. The most prominent group of the Akan was the Oyoko. Using diplomacy and warfare, the **Oyoko consolidated the Akan** tribes in the 1670s, uniting them against the threat of the neighboring Denkyira, who they eventually

conquered in 1701 at the Battle of Feyiase (in modern Ghana).

Few projects revealed the determination of Louis XIV's France to extend itself than the construction of the **Canal du Midi**, a navigable inland waterway that stretched between the Mediterranean Sea and the Atlantic Ocean. Its construction was necessary because it would replace a perilous and indirect sea passage with a simple canal route. The technical problems, no less than the cost, were daunting. The main problem was how to ensure a sufficient supply of water to the highest parts of the canal. It was easily the most complex engineering problem undertaken by any 17th-century European state, calling for labor on a massive scale, and used entirely untried engineering solutions. When **completed in 1681**, the Canal du Midi stretched a distance of 149 miles (240 km).

PUEBLO POTTERY

The Pueblo of southwest North America, so called by the Spanish for their *pueblos*, or villages, were famed for their sophisticated and elaborate pottery. It is characterized by a light background on which are painted stylized animals and repeated abstract patterns in ocher, black, and gray coloring.

Penn in America
This detail from a painting shows English Quaker William Penn's meeting with American Indians in what is now the state of Delaware.

THE 1682 CORONATION OF nine-year-old **Peter the Great** (1672–1725) as czar of Russia brought to a close this vast nation's vague, imperial influence as a semipower on the margins of Europe. Peter's childhood was scarred by revolt, and it left him determined to punish his internal enemies and reshape **Russia as a western European power**. In a life of compulsive energy, he built a new capital, **St. Petersburg**, and ruthlessly imposed himself on his boyars (nobles). His version of Versailles, recreated on the edge of the Baltic, did not amount to much more than a statement of intent, but by the end of his reign **Russia** was a massive power-in-waiting, **looming over Europe**.

In 1682, nine years after Jolliet and Marquette had ventured down the **Mississippi**, confirming that these territories contained neither easily exploited wealthy natives nor obvious sources of gold, **Robert de La Salle** (1643–87), a veteran of North American exploration, determined to follow the river to its mouth. With his party of 19 American Indians, he reached it on April 9, 1682, and **proclaimed the river** and its hinterlands a **French possession**, **Louisiana**, named after the French king. This formed the basis of a French claim to a vast swathe of North America. Yet a

follow-up expedition by sea in 1684 failed to find the river and saw three of its four ships wrecked. La Salle was murdered by the remainder of his party.

In 1682, **William Penn** (1644–1718), an English Quaker and philosopher who had been granted land in North America belonging to James, Duke of York, founded the settlement that would grow into the city of **Philadelphia**, **Pennsylvania**. Penn promised religious freedom and material wealth to all those Europeans who settled there.

French claims to North America
This map depicts the vast areas of North America claimed by France, as well as the areas under Spanish and British control in the late 17th century.

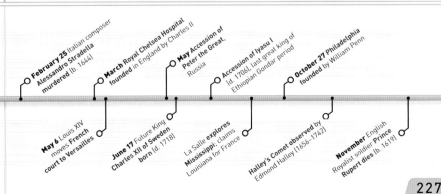

KEY
- British control and settlement
- Spanish control and settlement
- French control and settlement
- French influence
- approximate western limit of French claim

Timeline

1680 Asante kingdom founded, West Africa

March 4, 1680 Shivaji, founder of the Maratha Empire, dies (b. 1630)

August 1680 Pueblo revolt

August 1680 Comédie-Française established, Paris

1681 Canal du Midi completed, France

1681 War of Twenty-Seven Years between Marathas and Mughals begins (to 1707)

1681 Rozwi defeat Torwa of Zimbabwe; new capital at Danangombe

December 1681 Revolt of the Three Feudatories, China, ends with victory for Qing dynasty

February 25 Italian composer Alessandro Stradella murdered (b. 1644)

May 6 Louis XIV moves French court to Versailles

March Royal Chelsea Hospital founded in England by Charles II

May Accession of Peter the Great, Russia

June 17 Future King Charles XII of Sweden born (d. 1718)

La Salle explores Mississippi, claims Louisiana for France

Accession of Iyasu I (d. 1706), last great king of Ethiopian Gondar period

Halley's Comet observed by Edmond Halley (1656–1742)

October 27 Philadelphia founded by William Penn

November English Royalist soldier Prince Rupert dies (b. 1619)

The Battle of Kahlenberg saw a Polish–Imperial army lift the Ottoman Empire's two-month siege of Vienna.

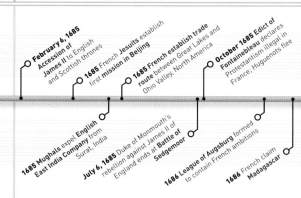

This 19th-century illustration shows Friedrich Wilhelm I, elector of Brandenburg, welcoming French Protestant Huguenots to Berlin in 1685.

ON JULY 14, 1683, AN OTTOMAN army **besieged Vienna.** As with the previous Ottoman attempt on the city in 1529, this was a direct assault on the Christian West. In the event, the siege failed just as it had in 1529. But whereas 1529 had been the climax of a series of conquests that had seen the Ottomans sweep across Hungary, the 1683 Ottoman assault was a **frantic final attempt to regain former glories** in the face of internal weakness. Confronted with renewed resistance, the **siege was broken** in September **at Kahlenberg** by a combined Imperial–Polish force led by the Polish king, Jan III Sobieski. The **collapse of Ottoman rule in Hungary** followed, with a Holy

Thames Frost Fair, 1683–84
Frost fairs were a regular feature on the Thames River, in London, during the winters of the Little Ice Age, with tents and coaches on the ice.

League of the Holy Roman Empire, Poland, and Venice, formed in 1684 under papal authority, driving them south across the Balkans.

Taiwan's Tunging kingdom, a supporter of China's ousted Ming, had supported military **assaults against the Qing** since 1661. By 1683, negotiations toward a settlement had led nowhere and so the Kangxi Emperor (1654–1722) launched the Qing's military might, securing a huge **naval and land victory** over the Tunging at the **Battle of Penghu,** resulting in their kingdom becoming part of the Qing empire.

The climatic changes of the Maunder Minimum, which had begun in 1645 as a result of reduced sunspot activity, had by the 1680s initiated a particularly cold period of the **Little Ice Age** across the world, and global temperatures had fallen by several degrees. Amid its many

Battle of Penghu
So seriously did the Qing take the Tunging threat that it sent a huge land and naval force, including more than 200 ships, to guarantee victory.

bitter winters, that of 1683–84 was considered by many to be the worst. The Little Ice Age did not end until the 19th century.

Dissatisfied with the Treaty of Nijmegen in 1679, Louis XIV strove to **extend France's frontiers** at the expense of the German states and the Spanish Netherlands with bids to **occupy territory** in Flanders and the Rhineland—the latter crucial in controlling trade on the Rhine. Using bluster, threat, and bogus legal claims, he gained Alsace, Luxembourg, and key forts in Flanders, consolidated by the **Treaty of Ratisbon** in 1684 at the end of the brief War of the Reunions of 1683–84. Now at the peak of his power, Louis was **determined to impose himself** on Europe, but succeeded only in uniting Protestant and Catholic Europe alike against him.

THE EDICT OF NANTES, AGREED by Henry IV in 1598, was essential to ending the French Wars of Religion. Of necessity, it was a compromise, and it saw France's substantial **Protestant Huguenot minority granted religious toleration** in return for accepting Henry as king. In October 1685, with the **Edict of Fontainebleau,** Louis XIV **revoked it.** His decision was entirely logical. There was practically no European state that permitted religious toleration. Louis's absolutism clearly demanded nothing less than an **officially sanctioned state**

brutality—that it aroused not just the **indignation of Protestant Europe** but reinforced its alarmed perception that Louis XIV's France had to be opposed at all costs.

The consequence of Louis XIV's obvious designs on Europe was the establishment in 1686 of the anti-French **League of Augsburg,** subsequently known as the **Grand Alliance.** The League was created initially by the newly confident Holy Roman Emperor, Leopold I (1640–1705)—vanquisher of the Ottomans—and urged on by William III of Orange (1650–1792), ruler of the Dutch Republic. In

900,000
THE NUMBER OF **HUGUENOTS** IT WAS **CLAIMED FLED FRANCE AFTER** LOUIS XIV ISSUED **THE EDICT OF FONTAINEBLEAU**

religion, and that religion was Roman Catholicism. In every other respect, however, it was a disaster for France. The **huge numbers of Huguenots who fled the country** were among the most industrious in France, and they were eagerly embraced by those countries to which they emigrated, chiefly England, the Dutch Republic, and Prussia. Simultaneously, so naked an act of aggression was this against France's Protestants—the policy was imposed with consistent

time, every western European state bar Switzerland was **ranged against France.**

In 1685, the aging **James II** (1633–1701), younger son of Charles I and younger brother of Charles II, **brought a curious incompetence** to a brief occupation of the English and Scottish thrones. **Determined to reimpose Catholicism** on a now Protestant, parliamentary nation, in less than three years he would overturn the delicately cynical political settlement of Charles II.

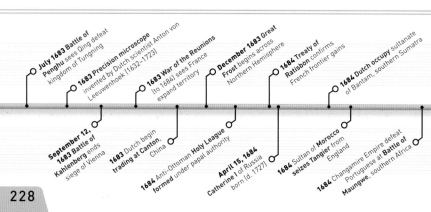

July 1683 Battle of Penghu sees Qing defeat kingdom of Tungning

1683 Precision microscope invented by Dutch scientist Anton von Leeuwenhoek (1632–1723)

1683 War of the Reunions (to 1684) sees France expand territory

December 1683 Great Frost begins across Northern Hemisphere

1684 Treaty of Ratisbon confirms French frontier gains

1684 Dutch occupy sultanate of Bantam, southern Sumatra

September 12, 1683 Battle of Kahlenberg ends siege of Vienna

1683 Dutch begin trading at Canton, China

1684 Anti-Ottoman Holy League formed under papal authority

April 15, 1684 Catherine I of Russia born (d. 1727)

1684 Sultan of Morocco seizes Tangier from England

1684 Changamire Empire defeat Portuguese at **Battle of Maungwe,** southern Africa

February 6, 1685 Accession of James II to English and Scottish thrones

1685 French Jesuits establish first mission in Beijing

1685 French establish trade route between Great Lakes and Ohio Valley, North America

October 1685 Edict of Fontainebleau declares Protestantism illegal in France; Huguenots flee

1685 Mughals expel English East India Company from Surat, India

July 6, 1685 Duke of Monmouth's rebellion against James II of England ends at **Battle of Sedgemoor**

1686 League of Augsburg formed to contain French ambitions

1686 French claim Madagascar

This Dutch painting shows William III's fleet departing the Netherlands for England at the start of the Glorious Revolution of 1688.

> **I HAVE CONQUERED AN EMPIRE BUT I HAVE NOT BEEN ABLE TO CONQUER MYSELF.**
>
> Peter I (the Great), czar of Russia, reflecting on his rule, 1672–1725

IN OCTOBER 1688, DESPITE FINANCIAL WEAKNESS, Louis XIV's forces devastated the Rhineland Palatinate, in Germany, provoking the **Nine Years' War**. His goal was to force Leopold I to recognize French rule over the frontier territories previously annexed, as well as create a devastated strip of land that would be difficult for armies to cross to attack France. The next month, **William III of Orange landed in England** with an army of 15,000. These two events provoked a kind of volcanic eruption in European political history. Whereas Louis's invasion, almost immediately bogged down in winter mud, eventually led to **an eclipse of French power** in the face of a Europe united in opposition to him (see 1685–86), within three months William III had become not just the joint monarch of England (with his wife, Mary) but the leader of the **pan-European, anti-French Protestant alliance**. At stake was a fundamental clash over the nature of legitimate rule.

ISAAC NEWTON (1642–1727)

In 1687, the English physicist Isaac Newton published the universal law of gravitation, one of the most remarkable of all scientific discoveries. It explained what holds the universe together: that all heavenly bodies exert a force called gravitas, or weight. Newton's work would dominate science's views on the physical universe for almost 300 years.

If Louis XIV's apparently absolute monarchy seemed the pattern by which modern princes could most effectively exercise power, the **accession of William III** to the English and Scottish thrones made plain a radical alternative: that Parliament was the ultimate arbiter of who should rule. No one had disputed the right of William's ousted predecessor, James II, to the English throne. His clumsily active promotion of Catholicism, however, was wholly at odds with the **strongly Protestant sympathies of the ruling elite**, whose power was exercised through Parliament. It was a consortium of English magnates of all parties who invited William to take over the

Nine Years' War coin
This German commemorative coin—a form of propaganda—shows the destruction of the Rhineland Palatinate by French troops during the Nine Years' War.

throne of England in what was, legal inventions aside, a direct deposition of a reigning monarch. The consequence, known as the **Glorious Revolution of 1688**, was a triumph of Parliamentary authority, and England would be immeasurably strengthened.

However, for Louis XIV the **result of the Nine Years' War**, which would be mainly fought around France's borders, but also in Ireland, North America, and India, would not be the one he had intended. Although **France** had fought well, it was **crippled by economic woes**, and eventually welcomed a settlement with the Grand Alliance, which too was **financially exhausted**. By 1697, although Louis would retain Alsace, he would have to return the Duchy of Lorraine and all his gains on the east bank of the Rhine, as well as accept William as king of England and a string of Dutch fortresses along his border with the Spanish Netherlands.

WHEN CONFRONTED WITH THE INVASION OF WILLIAM III IN 1688, James II of England abandoned an army he sent to confront William and **fled to Louis XIV's France**. Charles II had been happy to be financed by Louis XIV, but he had disguised the fact. James II now actively reveled in French backing. In March 1689, he **landed with a French-financed army in Ireland**, and attracting substantial Catholic support briefly threatened the new Dutch Protestant settlement. However, William's victory in 1690 at the Battle of the Boyne saw James back in France three days later. Henceforward, the Stuart Jacobite claim to its thrones in Britain (see 1715 and 1745) would complicate French diplomacy, and seem unlikely to change political reality.

In **New York**, the Glorious Revolution produced a short-lived echo when German Calvinist **Jacob Leisler overthrew the royal governor** in May 1689 in the name of William III. An English force arrived to compel Leisler to surrender in January 1691, and he was executed for treason.

Since 1682, a young **Peter I** (1672–1725) had ruled Russia jointly with his disabled half-brother Ivan V, but the real power had been his **sister and regent, Sophia**. The power struggle came to a climax in 1689 when, gaining the support of the Streltsy royal guardsmen, he overthrew Sophia, forcing her into a convent and leaving him and Ivan as co-czars.

Leisler's Rebellion

Jacob Leisler is shown swearing in volunteers to support his overthrow of the governor of New York. He captured Fort James, Manhattan, briefly renaming it Fort William.

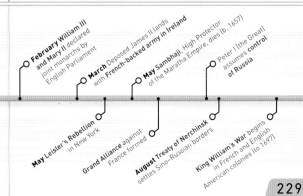

March 19, 1687 French explorer Robert Cavelier de La Salle murdered on Mississippi expedition

April 4, 1687 Declaration of Indulgence briefly brings religious toleration to England

August 12, 1687 Battle of Mohács sees Holy League defeat Ottomans in Hungary

December 1687 French Huguenots settle in Dutch Cape Colony, Africa

November 1688 Nine Years' War begins (to 1697)

December 1688 In England, Glorious Revolution sees James II deposed

July 1687 Isaac Newton's *Principia* explains gravity

September 1687 Venetians attack Ottomans in Dalmatia and Greece

1688 Genroku Era, Japan, flowering of kabuki theater

November 1688 William III of Orange arrives in England

1688 Lloyds coffee house (venue of Lloyds insurance) opens, London

1688 Holy League captures Belgrade from Ottomans

February William III and Mary II declared joint monarchs by English Parliament

March Deposed James II lands with French-backed army in Ireland

May Sambhaji, High Protector of the Maratha Empire, dies (b. 1657)

Peter I (the Great) assumes control of Russia

May Leisler's Rebellion in New York

Grand Alliance against France formed

August Treaty of Nerchinsk settles Sino-Russian borders

King William's War begins in French and English American colonies (to 1697)

229

THE RISE AND FALL OF THE
OTTOMAN EMPIRE

AN ENDURING POWER THAT DOMINATED IN EUROPE AND THE MIDDLE EAST FOR NEARLY 500 YEARS

The long decline of the Ottoman Empire in the 19th century disguised the fact that for 450 years after its emergence in about 1300, it was not just one of the most dynamic and sophisticated polities in the world, but also one of the largest. It dwarfed its European and Middle Eastern rivals.

At its height, toward the end of the 17th century, the Ottoman Empire stretched from the gates of Vienna to the Indian Ocean, and from the Crimea to Algiers. Though the Mongol leader Timur had checked Ottoman ambitions in the early 15th century, once Murad I took the throne in 1413, the expansion program was vigorously renewed. His son, Mehmed II (r. 1451–81), extended Ottoman rule across the Balkans and seized Constantinople (Istanbul) in a blaze of conquest. Under Selim I (r. 1512–20), the Safavids were contained at

Caldiran and much of the Middle East and North Africa was conquered. Suleimân the Magnificent (r. 1520–66) expanded Ottoman territories deep into Hungary and almost as far as the Atlantic. Faced with such potency, the Christian West could do little. Enormously rich, technologically advanced, and buoyed by its leadership of the Muslim world, Ottoman power seemed irresistible. The empire's decline after the failure of the siege of Vienna in 1683 was the result less of internal weakness than of the growing strength of its European opponents.

ATLANTIC
OCEAN

PORTUGAL

SPAIN

● Madri

Lisbon ●

Oran

● Fez

MOROCCO

FORMIDABLE OPPONENTS

The Ottoman state began as a small frontier principality preying on Christian Byzantium. Under a succession of 14th-century warrior-sultans, a series of rapid conquests were launched, notably at Kosovo in 1389, when a combined Christian–Balkan force was defeated. Bayezid I (r. 1389–1402) exploited this victory by annexing Bulgaria and invading Hungary. Ottoman success was based on a highly trained army. The most feared troops, the janissaries, were recruited from the conquered peoples of the Balkans, converted to Islam. In addition, Ottoman artillery in the 15th and 16th centuries was among the most destructive in the world.

Size of the Ottoman Empire
By the turn of the 20th century, the Ottoman Empire had shrunk to a third of the size it been three centuries earlier. Modern Turkey is a fraction of that.

2 MILLION SQ MILES

0.7 MILLION SQ MILES

301,384 sq miles

KEY
● 1683   1914   ● Modern Turkey

16th-century Empire
At its peak, the Ottoman Empire was not just a land power—its navy dominated the eastern Mediterranean and the maritime routes with the Indian Ocean. It challenged not merely European but its Middle Eastern rivals, too: Mamluk Egypt, conquered in 1517, and Safavid Persia, an equally dynamic and sophisticated state.

HOLY ROMAN EMPIRE   HUNGARY   Black Sea   Caspian Sea

Mediterranean Sea

AFRICA   Red Sea   Arabian Peninsula

1481 From a small nucleus c. 1300, the Ottomans went on to conquer a vast area, covering much of Anatolia and the area around the Black Sea by 1481.

KEY
Empire at 1300
Empire at 1481

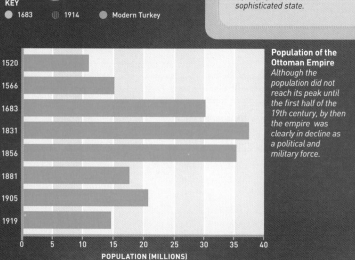

Population of the Ottoman Empire
Although the population did not reach its peak until the first half of the 19th century, by then the empire was clearly in decline as a political and military force.

Year	
1520	
1566	
1683	
1831	
1856	
1881	
1905	
1919	

0   5   10   15   20   25   30   35   40
POPULATION (MILLIONS)

POLAND-
LITHUANIA

HOLY ROMAN EMPIRE

RUSSIAN EMPIRE

KHANATE OF THE CRIMEA

JEDISAN

MOLDAVIA

TRANSYLVANIA

HUNGARY

WALLACHIA

Esztergom (Gran)

Vienna

Koszeg (Güns)

Buda

Mohács

Szigetvár

Belgrade

Khotin

Bender

Jassy

Sofia

Kiev

Astrakhan

Azov

Sea of Azov

Kaffa (Kefe)

Black Sea

GEORGIAN STATES

Trebizond

Caucasus

Derbent

Caspian Sea

Baku

Tiflis

Ganja

Kars

Nakhichevan

Tabriz

Tehran

Adrianople (Edirne)

Amasya

Erzurum

Çaldiran

Hamadan

Isfahan

FRANCE

VENETIAN REPUBLIC

Venice

Corsica

Sardinia

NAPLES

Reggio

Sicily

Algiers

Tunis

Malta

ALGIERS

TUNIS

Tripoli

REPUBLIC OF RAGUSA

Constantinople

ANATOLIA

Taurus Mountains

Preveza

Monemvasia

Crete

Rhodes

Cyprus

Tripoli

Mediterranean Sea

Marj Dabiq

Aleppo

SYRIA

Damascus

Jerusalem

Alexandria

Cairo

Al Raydaniyya

Suez

MESOPOTAMIA

Baghdad

Basra

Persian Gulf

Bahrain

TRIPOLI

EGYPT

HEJAZ

Medina

Mecca

Jedda

Suakin

Massawa

Arabian Peninsula

Red Sea

Aden

KEY

- Ottoman Empire and vassals 1512
- Conquests of Selim I 1512–20
- Conquests of Suleiman I 1520–66
- Ottoman conquests 1566–1639
- → Major Ottoman campaigns

" THE PRESENT TERROR OF THE WORLD. "

Attributed to a European ambassador *c.* 1600

1913 Ottoman power had dwindled. Greece, Serbia, Romania, and Montenegro were now independent, and other European powers had taken over North Africa and the Black Sea.

EUROPE

AUSTRO-HUNGARIAN EMPIRE

Black Sea

Caspian Sea

PERSIA

GREECE

Mediterranean Sea

NEJD

TUNISIA

LIBYA

EGYPT

Arabian Peninsula

Red Sea

AFRICA

1923 The Ottomans' remaining Arab territories were divided between Britain and France. Turkey was reduced to its Anatolian heartlands, sparking nationalist conflict with Greece and Armenia.

EUROPE

Black Sea

Caspian Sea

TURKEY

PERSIA

GREECE

SYRIA

IRAQ

NEJD

PALESTINE

TRANSJORDAN

EGYPT

Mediterranean Sea

Arabian Peninsula

Red Sea

KEY

- Turkey 1923
- French mandate
- British mandate

Fort William, shown here in the 1700s, was built after the English East India Company moved its main Bengal trading station to Calcutta in 1690.

This woodcut, taken from the title page of a pamphlet, shows the devastation of Port Royal, Jamaica, by both an earthquake and a tsunami in June 1692.

THE ENGLISH EAST INDIA COMPANY had been a presence in Bengal since the early 17th century. **Seeking greater security for their trade**, a new base, **Fort William**, named after William III, was established in 1690 in what is now Calcutta. The fort, continually enlarged and improved, would be critical to the later British dominance in India.

In 1690, **English philosopher John Locke** (1632–1704) wrote *An Essay Concerning Human Understanding*. It marked Locke as a **key thinker** in the Western philosophical tradition, above all for his assertion that knowledge of the world came through experience of it, and that the basis of this understanding was reasoned, empirical (based on observation) thought. Reinforcing many of his established ideas about property rights, religious

Philosopher John Locke
John Locke contended that there is a contract between monarch and people under which the monarch can be overthrown if he abuses it.

toleration, and monarchy, it also ensured his influence in debates about **liberty and reason** in 18th-century France and America.

The **turnip**, a basic root crop of the agricultural revolution of the 17th century, was **first cultivated in England in about 1690**. The Dutch, to make best use of their limited lands, had already discovered that **crop rotation** (arable crops alternated with root crops rather than leaving fields fallow) not only improved fertility but provided food for sheep whose manure furthered productivity.

On July 12, 1690, William III's victory over the deposed Catholic James II at the **Battle of the Boyne**, in Ireland, was decisive in maintaining the **Protestant supremacy** that had been established there by the Glorious Revolution of 1688. In Ireland, brutal **sectarian violence** would continue for centuries.

Orange forces of William III	Jacobite forces of James I
35,000 TROOPS	**21,000 TROOPS**

BATTLE OF THE BOYNE

Orange casualties	Jacobite casualties
500	**1,500**

Battle of the Boyne, Ireland
The Orange army of William III inflicted a decisive defeat on the Jacobites of James II, giving the lie to William's "bloodless revolution."

❝ THE EUROPEANS ARE VERY QUIET; THEY DO NOT EXCITE ANY DISTURBANCES… THEY DO NO HARM TO ANYONE, THEY COMMIT NO CRIMES… ❞

Kangxi, Chinese Qing emperor, announces the Edict of Toleration, 1692

ALTHOUGH THE NINE YEARS' WAR had quickly settled in 1688 into a stalemate on land that would last to 1697, at sea the Grand Alliance enjoyed a clear superiority over France. The six-day **Battle of La Hogue** from May to June 1692 saw much of the French fleet either beached or destroyed by fireships. It **ended hopes of a French invasion of England**.

At 11:43am on June 7, 1692, a catastrophic **earthquake struck Port Royal**, capital of the English colony of Jamaica, and one of the most important ports in the Caribbean, as well as a legendary base for pirates. **Most of the city sank beneath the sea**. With the subsequent tsunami and outbreaks of disease, the death toll was about 5,000.

In **Salem**, Massachusetts, in late 1691, young girls started having fits and hallucinations, citing demonic possession. This led to claims of witchcraft, which by 1692 had reached the point of

hysteria. On June 10, an elderly widow, Bridget Bishop, was **hanged as a witch**, and by September a further 18 people had been executed on the same charge, and one man crushed to death. Trials for witchcraft were no longer common in England by this time, and the **mass hysteria** of Salem remains hard to explain.

Jesuit missionaries had been in East Asia since the 16th century. In contrast to Japan (see 1597–99), in China they were **valued by a succession of emperors**, not least for their knowledge of western science. They made many converts, and in 1692 the Kangxi Emperor issued an **edict of toleration of Christianity**.

Salem Witch Trial
The trial of George Jacobs was one of many in a Puritan community riven by petty jealousies, where none disputed the existence of Satan.

The summit vent of Mount Etna, an active volcano on the east coast of Sicily, in Italy, has witnessed many destructive eruptions, not least in 1693.

The forces of the Grand Alliance, led by William III of England, gather outside Namur, where a French garrison is besieged. The siege lasted two months.

IF SOUTHERN EUROPE had been spared the worst of the Little Ice Age (see 1683–84), the eruption on January 11, 1693 of **Mount Etna**, in Sicily, proved a cruel reminder of the power of nature. The eruption **set off an earthquake** that **devastated Sicily** and large areas of southern Italy and Malta. About 60,000 were killed in Sicily alone, and thousands of square miles became uninhabitable due to lava flows and tsunamis.

For several years after the summer of 1693, a series of **famines swept western Europe**. In France alone, about two million died. These were among the most calamitous **consequences of the Little Ice Age**, with bitter winters giving way to dismal, rain-soaked summers, and stunted crops rotting in sodden fields. Even in years of relative plenty, the vast **majority of Europe's peasants**, themselves the overwhelming majority of the continent's population, had a subsistence existence at best, with root vegetables, bread, and oatmeal as their staple diet. When the crops failed, they starved. In the face of these near Biblical visitations of mass misery, there seemed to be no answer. Almost entirely dependent on the food surpluses generated by its heavily taxed peasant population, even as obviously powerful a state as late-17th-century France could do

Dodo
The dodo stood about 3ft 3in (1m) in height and weighed about 44lb (20kg). It had a long, hooked bill, grayish or brownish plumage on a fat body, and very small wings.

little more than suffer and accept its unavoidable fate.

In 1598, on the **isolated island of Mauritius**, in the Indian Ocean, the Dutch admiral Wybrand van Warwijck described a bird he called a "walghvogel." Later Dutch settlers there called it a "dodaars," which was a reference to what they saw as the knot of tails at its rear. Portuguese sailors that visited the island called it a "doudo," meaning "fool" or "crazy." By perhaps 1693, the **dodo, a flightless bird** that was related to the pigeon, had **become extinct**. The dodo is the first animal whose extinction can be specifically ascribed to man; it was a victim of its trusting nature, the destruction of its woodland habitats, and the introduction of cats, rats, pigs, and dogs that hunted it to its extinction.

IN JULY 1694, ENGLAND FOUND A NOVEL SOLUTION to the problem of a lack of funds that had plagued the combatants of the Nine Years' War. The **Bank of England** served both Crown and government, and was closely modeled on the Bank of Amsterdam, founded in 1609. A private venture (until 1931), it **immediately loaned the government** £1.2 million—raised by its investors in 12 days—at an annual interest rate of 8 percent and for an annual service charge of £4,000, in return for the right to print bank notes. It also **created a National Debt**, but at the same time allowed England not merely to finance its own part in the war but to finance its allies. The bank was possibly the most significant factor in Britain's subsequent emergence on the world stage.

European colonialism in the 17th and 18th centuries had the simple goal of money. In the New World, the Spanish had conquered two rich civilizations and found a vast silver mine. The **Portuguese in Brazil** had found only native peoples and tropical jungles; sugarcane plantations worked by slave labor were the source of its marginal profits. Then, in **Minas Gerais**, in the southeast, **gold was found** in 1695. It transformed colonial Brazil, as did the later discovery of diamonds in the same region. Vast, lawless towns appeared, chiefly Ouro Preto

("Black Gold") and Diamantia, and the region's **population exploded**, from scattered handfuls to 320,000 (half of them slaves). A result was the near collapse of the sugarcane industry, stripped of most of its workforce.

One of the few moments of significance in the Nine Years' War took place in September 1695, when the **Grand Alliance retook the city of Namur** after three years in French hands. The loss of the most important fortress in the Netherlands further weakened an already defensive French position.

In 1696, **China** began an **eastward expansion** that by the end of the 18th century would see it **almost double in size**. It was provoked by the invasion of Khalkha (Outer Mongolia) by the nomadic Zunghar people of Central Asia in 1690, who were anxious to forestall a possible Chinese takeover of the region. The **invasion failed**, sparking only a confused series of campaigns under the Zunghar ruler, Galdan, as well as a civil war. In 1696, the Kangxi Emperor led a Khalkha–Chinese army across the Gobi Desert into Mongolia and crushed the Zunghar. **Outer Mongolia** was **incorporated within the Chinese empire** the following year.

Russia fought two campaigns in 1695–96 to capture the **Ottoman-held fortress port of Azov**. The port was key to Russia because it

Battle of Azov
In this painting by Robert Kerr Porter, Peter the Great is seen personally leading his galley fleet during the capture of Azov in 1696.

blocked access to the Black Sea, a factor that had contributed to the failure of its Crimean campaigns against the Ottomans in 1687–89. Finally, Peter I (the Great), the sole czar of Russia since the death of his disabled half-brother, Ivan, attacked Azov with a combined land and naval force, capturing the city in July 1696. A lesson learned was that Russia needed a navy, and it embarked on a massive shipbuilding program.

Caucasian pistol
This ornately fashioned pistol with a long barrel and a short, gently curved handle was typical of the weaponry employed in the Azov campaigns.

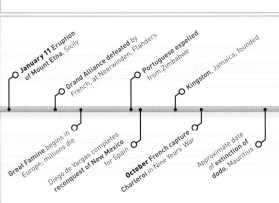

> ❝ THE **GREATEST COMFORTS** AND **LASTING PEACE** ARE **OBTAINED**, WHEN ONE **ERADICATES SELFISHNESS FROM WITHIN.** ❞
>
> Guru Gobind Singh, 10th Sikh Master, 1697

An engraving depicting 16-year-old Philip, duke of Anjou, being recognized as Philip V, king of Spain, on October 2, 1700.

THE NINE YEARS' WAR THAT HAD SEEN FRANCE TAKE ON the Grand Alliance of England, the Holy Roman Empire, Spain, and the Dutch Republic was **ended by the Treaty of Ryswick** in 1697. It established that all territory taken since 1679 was to be returned.

The Ottoman defeat at the Siege of Vienna in 1683 marked not just the beginning of a protracted Ottoman decline, but the **emergence of Habsburg Austria** as a European power to challenge France, England, and the Dutch Republic. After 1683, Austrian Imperial armies pursued the retreating Ottomans south across the Balkans, a process that climaxed at the **Battle of Zenta**, in Serbia in September 1697. Under the Italo-French general Eugene of Savoy (1663–1736), who

Treaty of Ryswick
The treaty was signed at the palace of Huis ter Nieuwburg, the country house of William of Orange, in Ryswick, in the Dutch Republic.

was rapidly emerging as one of the foremost commanders in Europe, an Imperial army surprised the Ottomans as they attempted to cross the Tisa River. The Ottomans were massacred: about 10,000 killed or drowned. The **Treaty of Karlowitz** in 1699 confirmed the Austrian gains, including the gradual

absorption of Hungary by the Austrian crown.

In July 1698, English military engineer **Thomas Savery** (1650–1715) **registered a patent** for "a new invention for raiseing of water... of great use and advantage for drayning mines." Basic forms of steam power had existed since the 1st century CE, but none of these had ever been translated into working machines. Savery's **steam engine was basic**, prone to violent explosions, and unable to pump water more than 33 ft (10 m) below it, meaning that in mines it had to be installed, dangerously, underground. It was only in 1721 when an English ironmonger, Thomas Newcomen (1664–1729), working with Savery, produced his **atmospheric engine**, that a viable commercial use was found. Yet, the real potential of steam as **an engine of industrialization** would not be realized until the invention by the Scot, James Watt (1736–1819), in 1769, of a separate condenser, and then only with the backing of English businessman Matthew Boulton (see pp.274–75).

MUGHAL EMPIRE

The crushing of a Sikh revolt in the Punjab in 1699 saw the Mughal Empire at its zenith. From its Afghan heartlands, it had grown under Akbar, taking all but the tip of India's subcontinent by the end of the 17th century. The harsh rule of Aurangzeb saw many revolts, and the later rise of the Marathas (see 1720) left the Mughals as puppets.

KEY
- ■ Akbar's domains, 1556
- ■ Additional areas held by Mughals at Akbar's death, 1605
- ■ Additional areas acquired up to the death of Aurangzeb, 1707

THE DEATH IN 1700 OF CHARLES II, the childless king of Spain, caused a major crisis when he nominated Philip of Anjou (1683–1746), the grandson of Louis XIV of France, as his successor. Charles hoped that French power would preserve the **Spanish Empire** if **ruled by a Bourbon**. Louis accepted the vast increase in family prestige and French influence, but **opposition** to the succession and its increase in French power **grew hugely**.

The accession in 1697 of the 15-year-old Charles XII (1682–1718) to the throne of Sweden was the signal for **Sweden's Baltic rivals**, Denmark, Saxony, Poland, and, increasingly, Russia, to attempt to end Swedish pre-eminence. In fact, in the conflict that followed, the **Great Northern War** of 1700–21, Charles, "the Swedish Meteor," would prove himself a general of genius. In the four months from August 1700, he successively defeated the Danes and then, over on the other side of the Baltic, at Narva,

Stradivarius violin
The Stradivarius violin, made by Italian Antonio Stradivari, entered a golden age in 1700. These violins were larger than earlier models.

annihilated a Russian army four times the size of his own. The following July, he inflicted a similarly crushing defeat on a combined Polish–Saxon force at Klissow in Poland. With **Sweden never more dominant**, Charles's bold campaigning, whatever the odds against him, had apparently been wholly vindicated.

From about 1700, a **major development in European culture** began to take shape: a musical tradition, part courtly, part church-based, known as the **High Baroque**. It evolved from later Renaissance music, above all in Italy, but developed to reach a new level of polyphonic tonal and **instrumental complexity**. It was made possible by both new and more elaborated musical forms: the concerto, fugue, oratorio, prelude, cantata, and opera. It was made possible by **new forms of existing instruments**: the organ, harpsichord, and, above all, violin. It depended also on **composers of genius**, such as Johann Sebastian Bach (1685–1750) and George Handel (1685–1759), and on a more extensive world of courtly and private patronage of them.

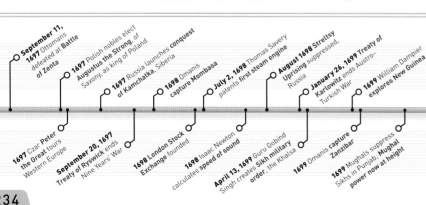

September 11, 1697 Ottomans defeated at Battle of Zenta

1697 Polish nobles elect **Augustus the Strong** of Saxony, as king of Poland

1697 Russia launches **conquest** of Kamchatka, Siberia

1698 Omanis **capture Mombasa**

July 2, 1698 Thomas Savery patents first steam engine

August 1698 Streltsy Uprising suppressed, Russia

January 26, 1699 Treaty of Karlowitz ends Austro–Turkish War

1699 William Dampier explores New Guinea

1697 Czar Peter **the Great tours** Western Europe

September 20, 1697 Treaty of Ryswick ends Nine Years' War

1698 London Stock Exchange founded

1698 Isaac Newton calculates speed of sound

April 13, 1699 Guru Gobind Singh creates Sikh military order, the Khalsa

1699 Omanis **capture Zanzibar**

1699 Mughals suppress Sikhs in Punjab; **Mughal power now at height**

January 26 Cascadia Earthquake, North America

February 12 Great Northern War begins

May 12 English poet John Dryden dies (b. 1631)

November 1 Death of Charles II of Spain (b. 1661); accession of Philip V

Vietnamese gain control of entire Indochina Peninsula

Rise of Bantu kingdom of Buganda, East Africa

Russo-Turkish War ends after two years

November 20 Sweden defeats Russia at Battle of Narva, in Estonia

Jethro Tull's seed drill is shown here being operated manually. It sowed seeds in rows, performing work that previously required several laborers.

A REVOLUTION IN AGRICULTURE BEGAN IN 1701 when English agriculturalist **Jethro Tull** (1674–1741) created the horse-drawn **seed drill** (see pp.250–51). A major time- and labor-saving device, it sowed great numbers of seeds in neat rows. Although not taken up at once, it later proved popular with large landowners and would lay the basis of modern **productive agriculture**.

No sooner had the Nine Years' War ended than Europe's powers found themselves in another lengthy and costly war. The surprise choice of Philip, duke of Anjou, as King Philip V of Spain (see 1700), greatly **disturbed the European balance of power**, and Louis XIV did nothing to discourage fears of a Franco-Spanish military alliance. He took over military duties in Philip's lands, moving troops into the Spanish Netherlands to defend them from the English and the Dutch. With renewed confidence in France's European status, Louis then **recognized James III**, son of the exiled James II (1633–1701), as king of England. With England and the Dutch Republic **backing Austria's claims** to the Spanish throne—in the form of their candidate, Archduke Charles of Austria   armed opposition to France was now guaranteed. The **War of the Spanish Succession** that began in 1701 saw a Grand Alliance oppose the unification of the French and Spanish thrones. It would last until 1713–14 and redraw the map of the continent and the world.

25 SHIPS **18 SHIPS**

ANGLO-DUTCH FORCES | FRANCO–SPANISH FORCES

Battle of Vigo Bay, October 1702
In an early encounter in the War of the Spanish Succession, 25 ships of an Anglo–Dutch fleet defeated a Franco–Spanish fleet at Vigo Bay.

Freelance **Samurai warriors known as ronin** emerged from the Japanese civil wars of the 14th and 15th centuries. In 1651, they engaged in rebellion and continued to **instigate dissent** into the 18th century. In 1701, a respected lord, Asano Nugatory, was forced to commit suicide after assaulting an official who had insulted him. In revenge, 47 of his samurai became ronin and murdered the official, an act normally punished by execution. But because Confucianism taught that it is honorable to avenge a lord's death, they were allowed to commit suicide in turn.

The **kingdom of Prussia**—later the forerunner of the German state—**was proclaimed in 1701** when Frederick I, duke of Prussia and elector of Brandenburg, was crowned the first "king in Prussia," in Konigsberg Castle.

Revenge of the 47 ronin
This color woodcut is one of a series on the 47 ronin uprising, the most famous incident of the samurai code of honor, bushido.

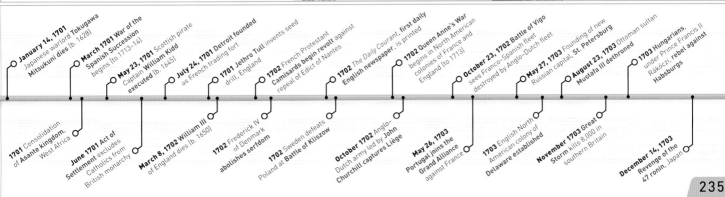

January 14, 1701 Japanese warlord Tokugawa Mitsukuni dies (b. 1628)

March 1701 War of the Spanish Succession begins (to 1713–14)

May 23, 1701 Scottish pirate Captain William Kidd executed (b. 1645)

July 24, 1701 Detroit founded as French trading fort

1701 Jethro Tull invents seed drill, England

1702 French Protestant Camisards begin revolt against repeal of Edict of Nantes

1702 *The Daily Courant*, **first daily English newspaper**, is printed

1702 Queen Anne's War begins in North American colonies of France and England (to 1713)

October 23, 1702 Battle of Vigo sees Franco–Spanish fleet destroyed by Anglo–Dutch fleet

May 27, 1703 Founding of new Russian capital, St. Petersburg

August 23, 1703 Ottoman sultan Mustafa III dethroned

1703 Hungarians, under Prince Francis II Rákóczi, rebel against Habsburgs

1701 Consolidation of Asante kingdom, West Africa

June 1701 Act of Settlement excludes Catholics from British monarchy

March 8, 1702 William III of England dies (b. 1650)

1702 Frederick IV of Denmark abolishes serfdom

1702 Sweden defeats Poland at Battle of Kliszow

October 1702 Anglo-Dutch army led by John Churchill captures Liège

May 26, 1703 Portugal joins the Grand Alliance against France

1703 English North American colony of Delaware established

November 1703 Great Storm kills 8,000 in southern Britain

December 14, 1703 Revenge of the 47 ronin, Japan

This modern photograph shows Halley's Comet, named after the British astronomer Edmond Halley, who was the first to determine that the comet returned periodically, every 76 years.

This picture depicts the Mughal emperor Aurangzeb hunting nilgai.

THE BATTLE OF BLENHEIM, fought in 1704 near the village of Blindheim on the Danube in Bavaria, Germany, ended in victory for the Duke of Marlborough and the Grand Alliance (see 1701), and turned the **War of the Spanish Succession** in favor of the Grand Alliance. The battle halted a Franco–Bavarian march on Vienna, and Bavaria played no further part in the war.

Meanwhile, the **Gibraltar peninsula** on the Spanish mainland was seized by a combined Dutch–English force in 1704; Gibraltar was ceded perpetually to Britain in 1713.

Victor of Blenheim
The Duke of Marlborough (in red) sits astride his horse in this tapestry, now hanging in his eventual home, Blenheim Palace, England.

300

THE NUMBER OF **POCUMTUCKS** AMONG THE **RAIDERS** AT **DEERFIELD**

In Tunisia to the southeast, the **Husaynid dynasty** was established in 1705 when Al-Husayn ibn 'Ali (1669–1740) was recognized by the Ottoman sultan as governor of the province. The Husaynid dynasty lasted until Tunisia gained independence in 1957.

In North America, **Deerfield, Massachusetts**, was the scene in 1704 of a massacre of English colonists by a combined force

News from home
Published weekly, The Boston News-Letter provided English colonists in America with news of England's political events and wars.

of French-Canadians and American Indians. Also in 1704, *The Boston News-Letter*, North America's first continuously published newspaper, appeared, largely funded by the British government.

In 1706, the most decisive event in the War of the Spanish Succession occurred in North Italy, where the Duke of Savoy, allied with Austria and Britain, was defending his territory against French invasion and siege of the capital, Turin. The French were crushed when the Duke of Savoy and Prince Eugene broke through French lines and routed the army, driving them out of North Italy.

Also in 1706, Spanish conquistador **Juan de Uribarri** claimed southeastern Colorado, an area populated by warring American Indian tribes, and joined it to **Spanish New Mexico**.

In England, the **first steam engine** using moving parts was built in 1704 by **Thomas Newcomen** (1663–1729) and Thomas Savery (see 1698). The first working Newcomen engine was installed to pump water from a mine in Staffordshire in 1712.

Edmond Halley (1656–1742), English mathematician and astronomer, published *A Synopsis of the Astronomy of Comets* in 1705, in which he described the parabolic orbits of 24 comets. He proved that three sightings, many decades apart, were of a single comet—the comet that is now known as Halley's Comet—and determined that this comet returns to the solar system every 76 years.

Battle of Blenheim losses
About 112,000 troops took part in the Battle of Blenheim, with 20,000 French casualties but almost half as many from Britain and its allies.

THE DEATH IN 1707 OF AURANGZEB, sixth Mughal emperor of India (b. 1618), marked the start of the decline of the Mughal Empire. Aurangzeb's successors squandered the dynasty's fortunes while losing control of regional governors, who went on to built their own empires. Aurangzeb, disturbed by the growing power of the **Sikh Guru Gobind Singh**, had

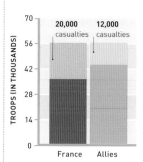

GURU GOBIND SINGH
(1666–1708)

The tenth and last guru of Sikhism, Gobind Singh was a powerful figure in Indian history. In 1699 he transformed Sikhism by creating the Khalsa (Pure), a community of the faith that trained as warriors; now the Khalsa embraces all Sikhs. Aurangzeb considered coming to terms with Gobind Singh, but the rajas of the Sivalik Hills remained hostile, and Gobind Singh was assassinated in 1708.

February 29, 1704 English colonists in Massachusetts massacred and **Deerfield sacked**

1704 British inventors Thomas Newcomen and Thomas Savery build **first steam engine** with moving parts

November 1705 Capitol building completed in **Williamsburg**, capital of English colony of **Virginia**

September 7, 1706 French defeated by Austrian and Savoyard forces in **Battle of Turin**

March 17, 1707 Mughal Emperor **Aurangzeb** (b. 1618) dies

April 25, 1707 Defeat of Grand Alliance at **Almanza**, Spain

August 13, 1704 Grand Alliance and Franco-Bavarian troops fight **Battle of Blenheim**

1705 British astronomer Edmond Halley publishes *A Synopsis of the Astronomy of Comets*

January 17, 1706 A future Founder of the US, **Benjamin Franklin**, is born (d. 1790)

1706 Southeastern Colorado claimed by Spanish New Mexico

May 1, 1707 Acts of Union come into effect, uniting **Scotland** and **England**

In a detail of a painting by Ignace Jacques Parrocel, Prince Eugene of Savoy's troops are shown confronting the French at the Battle of Malplaquet.

48 YEARS REIGN

27 YEARS OF WAR

Aurangzeb's reign

Emperor Aurangzeb reigned for 48 years, from 1658 until his death in 1707, but for 27 of those years he was at war with the Marathas.

summoned him, but died before they could meet. Gobind Singh became friends with the new emperor, Bahadur Shah (r. 1707–12), but was assassinated in 1708 on the orders of a rival leader, Nawab Wazir Khan.

Far from India, the kingdom of **England** and the kingdom of **Scotland** were formally unified as Great Britain by the **Acts of Union** of 1707. Henceforth, both were ruled by a single monarch and by a parliament based in London.

Britain, still embroiled in the War of the Spanish Succession, joined Dutch forces to seize **Minorca** and **Sicily** from France in 1708; both were used as military bases. Also in 1708, British settlers lost control of the Canadian east coast after a defeat by the French at **St. John's, Newfoundland**.

THE BATTLE OF MALPLAQUET in 1709 was the bloodiest of the **War of the Spanish Succession** (see 1701) and, indeed, the entire 18th century. Grand Alliance forces under the Duke of Marlborough attacked the French at Malplaquet, France, southwest of the French-held fortress of **Mons**, which lay over the present-day Belgian border. In gaining possession of the battlefield, the Allies suffered more than 21,000 casualties, twice as many as the French, but the French retreated in good order and remained a future threat.

Meanwhile, in the **Great Northern War** (1700–21) between Russia and its western neighbors (see 1700), Charles XII of Sweden had been leading forces in a march on Russia. The Swedish army of 17,000 men attacked the fort of **Poltava** in the Ukraine in

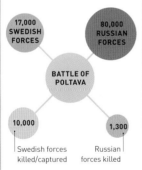

17,000 SWEDISH FORCES

80,000 RUSSIAN FORCES

BATTLE OF POLTAVA

10,000 Swedish forces killed/captured

1,300 Russian forces killed

Forces in the Battle of Poltava

In the Battle of Poltava, 60 percent of the Swedish troops were killed or captured, while less than 2 percent of the Russian troops were killed.

July 1709. The Swedes were faced by Peter the Great's army of 80,000, which eventually ran them from the battlefield. Charles, exiled in Moldavia, persuaded the **Ottoman Empire** to go to war with Russia in 1710, but Peter the Great (1672–1725) accepted terms in 1711.

In 1709, the Persian Safavid rulers of southwestern **Afghanistan** were overwhelmed by an **uprising** organized by **Mirwais Khan Hotak** (1673–1715), a tribal chief of the Ghilzai Pashtuns and founder of the Hotaki dynasty (which lasted from 1709 to 1738). Furious at Safavid cruelty and attempts to force them to convert from Sunni to Shia Islam, the Afghans assassinated their Safavid governor, Gurgin Khan, and massacred many Persians.

In Britain, revolution of an industrial kind was in the making. In 1709, **Abraham Darby** (1678–1717), a Quaker ironmaster who was **smelting iron** using charcoal, was the first to produce high-quality pig iron using **coke**. His new process freed iron smelting from its dependence on wood supplies, and coke processed from coal—was much more plentiful. In 1710, it was Germany's turn to transform an industry. In that year, the **Meissen** factory, near Dresden, produced the first successful **European porcelain**.

North of Germany, **Denmark** was taking an interest in the Great Northern War between Sweden and Russia. Denmark had lost the

provinces of **Scania**, **Halland**, and **Blekinge** to Sweden in 1700 but still had hopes of seizing them back. Assuming Sweden to be weakened by the Battle of Poltava, Denmark found pretexts to declare war on October 18, 1709. In November, a large Danish invasion force landed in Sweden virtually unopposed. However, by February 1710, Sweden had managed to amass 16,000 men, and this force defeated the Danes in the **Battle of Helsingborg**. Denmark lost 7,500 men in the battle and thereafter abandoned hope of regaining its former possessions.

In 1710, French settlers of the Canadian east coast region of **Arcadia** (now Nova Scotia) endured a third, and this time successful, British attempt to seize **Port Royal**. The victory secured Britain their first French colonial possession and helped to obstruct French colonization of Canada for years to come.

German chinoiserie
This 18th-century Meissen porcelain vase has moldings picked out in gold leaf. Its form and decorative motifs were inspired by imported Chinese porcelain.

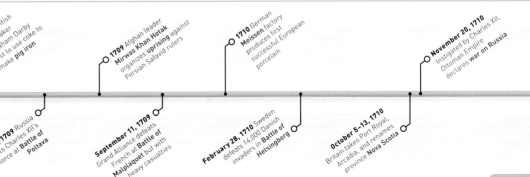

July 29–August 31, 1707 Grand Alliance defeats French fleet at **Battle of Toulon**

October 7, 1708 Sikh Guru Gobind Singh **assassinated**

1708 British and Dutch capture **Minorca** and **Sicily** from France

1709 British ironmaker Abraham Darby first to use coke to make **pig iron**

July 8, 1709 Russia defeats Charles XII's force at **Battle of Poltava**

1709 Afghan leader **Mirwais Khan Hotak** organizes **uprising** against Persian Safavid rulers

September 11, 1709 Grand Alliance defeats French at **Battle of Malplaquet** but with heavy casualties

1710 German **Meissen** factory produces first successful European porcelain

February 28, 1710 Sweden defeats 14,000 Danish invaders in **Battle of Helsingborg**

October 5–13, 1710 Britain takes Port Royal, Arcadia, and renames province **Nova Scotia**

November 20, 1710 Instigated by Charles XII, Ottoman Empire declares **war on Russia**

THE STORY OF
NAVIGATION

THE QUEST TO EXPLORE AND MAP THE WORLD'S OCEANS AND CONTINENTS

H1 chronometer

Perhaps the most surprising fact in the history of navigation is that, until the 18th century, it was impossible for explorers and mariners to determine their position accurately. Today, thanks to developments in navigational technology, it is possible to pinpoint locations to within a few meters.

The earliest sailors had no means of accurate navigation other than by sight, relying on landmarks along coastlines, judging distances and directions from the positions of the Sun, Moon, and stars, and using simple sounding devices, such as weighted lines, to keep ships from running aground. The invention of instruments such as the magnetic compass, astrolabe, and sextant

John Harrison
English clockmaker John Harrison was the first to make accurate timepieces that enabled longitude to be calculated with precision.

enabled direction and latitude to be gauged reasonably accurately (by measuring the angle of the Sun or a star above the horizon) but the problem remained of how to determine longitude.

ACCURATE NAVIGATION
Calculating longitude depends on comparing local time with "universal" time (the time at an agreed location, which is now Greenwich, England). Each hour's difference equates to 15 degrees' difference in longitude. Calculating longitude therefore relies on accurate timepieces, which did not exist until John Harrison developed his chronometer in the 18th century. The next major advances in navigation did not come until the 20th century, with the advent of the gyroscopic compass, radar, and, from the 1990s, of the global positioning system (GPS).

LATITUDE AND LONGITUDE

LATITUDE
Latitude lines (parallels) run horizontally on a map and are measured in degrees north or south of the equator. Each degree is about 69 miles (111 km) apart.

latitude line

LONGITUDE
Longitude lines (meridians) run vertically on a map and are measured in degrees east or west of Greenwich, England. They meet at the poles and are farthest apart at the equator.

longitude line

" ONE OF THE MOST **EXQUISITE MOVEMENTS** EVER MADE. "

William Hogarth, English artist, on Harrison's H1 chronometer, from *Analysis of Beauty*, 1753

winding handle

3000–1500 BCE
Early sounding
Ancient Egyptians use sounding reeds to measure water depth and gauge their position from coastal landmarks.

12th-dynasty sailing boat

11th century
Dead reckoning
Sand clocks are used for dead reckoning: measuring the time traveled and speed to estimate a vessel's position.

Sand clock

1300–1500
Navigational charts
Portolan charts of the Mediterranean and European coastlines allow sailors to navigate from port to port using compass bearings.

Portolan chart

c. 150
Ptolemy's maps
A Roman based in Egypt, Ptolemy creates maps using a grid system that influenced navigational maps until the 17th century.

Ptolemy's map

c. 1100
The compass
Chinese sailors are the first to use a magnetic compass (which uses a magnetized needle to show the direction of north and south) for navigation.

Mariner's compass

c. 1480
The astrolabe
Sailors start to use astrolabes to estimate latitude by measuring the angle of the Sun or a particular star above the horizon.

Mariner's astrolabe

seconds hand

Harrison's H1 chronometer
John Harrison's first "sea clock" was the
H1, which he made to solve the longitude
problem—how to measure time accurately
enough at sea to calculate longitude.
However, the H1 was impractically
large, a problem Harrison solved in
1759 with his H4 chronometer.

minute hand

1735–59
The chronometer
John Harrison makes the first marine
chronometer (the H1) in 1735. He
then makes improved versions,
culminating in the H4 in 1759.

calendar hand,
indicating date
of the month

hour hand

1907
Gyroscopic compass
American Elmer Sperry
invents the gyroscopic
compass, a major advance
for accurate navigation
because it always points
to true north and is not
subject to deviation.

Ship's compass

1930s–40s
Radar
The invention of radar
makes it possible to
determine an object's
position even when it
cannot be seen.

Radarscope

Late 20th century
**Global positioning
systems**
The introduction of
satellite-based GPS
makes it possible
to pinpoint locations
and navigate to within
a few yards.

GPS chart plotter

> **RIGHT IS RIGHT,** EVEN IF **EVERYONE** IS **AGAINST IT;** AND **WRONG IS WRONG,** EVEN IF **EVERYONE** IS **FOR IT.**

William Penn, founder of Pennsylvania, 1681

On completion, St. Paul's Cathedral dominated the north bank of the Thames River. It remained the tallest building in London until 1962.

IN AN EXTENSION OF THE WAR OF THE SPANISH SUCCESSION

(see 1701–03) in South America, a squadron of French ships attacked Portuguese-held **Rio de Janeiro**, incapacitated Portuguese ships in the harbor, and only spared the city's defenses from destruction on payment of a ransom. French morale, which had been at a low since their withdrawal from the Battle of Malplaquet (see 1709), was raised by this proof that French long-range naval power had not been extinguished.

In North America, the **Tuscarora War** began in **North Carolina** between Tuscarora American Indians and settlers from Britain, Germany, and the Netherlands. The settlers and northern Tuscarora American Indians began to kidnap the Tuscarora in the south, sell them into slavery, and appropriate their lands. The southern Tuscarora retaliated in September with widespread attacks on settlements in which hundreds of settlers were killed.

In Asia, the Persian Safavid rulers of western **Afghanistan**

Losses at Rio de Janeiro
Caught unawares by a French naval attack in Rio de Janeiro harbor, Portuguese ships tried to escape. Three drifted aground, and one was destroyed by its crew.

moved to counter the uprising organized by Mirwais Khan Hotak (see 1709–10), but the Safavid army and its leader, Khosru Khan, were annihilated, and **Afghan independence** was secured.

In December 1711, **St. Paul's Cathedral**, London's most iconic building, was completed. Designed by Christopher Wren, it was the fourth church to occupy its site; its predecessor was badly damaged in the Great Fire of London in 1666. The building had the **first triple dome** in the world: a light, timber-framed outer dome, supported by a hidden brick cone, and inside it, the inner dome that is visible from the interior.

Attack on Rio de Janeiro
French corsair René Duguay-Trouin's ships enter Rio de Janeiro harbor to salvage French honor—and profit at the same time.

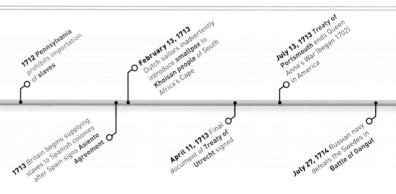

Smallpox epidemic
1:9 *In the South African Cape, smallpox ravaged the native Khoisan population, killing nine people for every one survivor.*

ON 7 JUNE 1712, PENNSYLVANIA,

under moral pressure from its Quaker population, freed all the slaves in the state, an early step in the abolition of slavery. However, Queen Anne reversed the decision in the following year. Quaker state-founder and slaver trader William Penn (1644–1718) was not himself an opponent of slavery.

In **South Africa's Cape** region, Dutch sailors infected with **smallpox** inadvertently caused a catastrophic decimation of the native **Khoisan people** in 1713. The disease rapidly spread from laundrywomen infected by the sailors' dirty linen to the wider population because no one had immunity or medicine. The epidemic killed 90 percent

An end to war
This painting from the French royal almanac for 1714 shows signatories of the Treaty of Utrecht, which ended the War of the Spanish Succession.

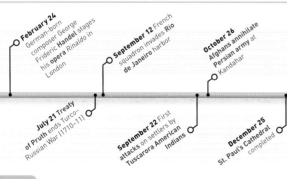

February 24 German-born composer George Frideric **Handel** stages his opera *Rinaldo* in London

July 21 Treaty of Pruth ends Turco-Russian War (1710–11)

September 12 French squadron invades **Rio de Janeiro** harbor

September 22 First attacks on settlers by Tuscarora American Indians

October 26 Afghans annihilate Persian army at Kandahar

December 25 St. Paul's Cathedral completed

1712 Pennsylvania prohibits importation of slaves

1713 Britain begins supplying slaves to Spanish colonies after Spain signs **Asiento Agreement**

February 13, 1713 Dutch sailors inadvertently introduce **smallpox** to **Khoisan people** of South Africa's Cape

April 11, 1713 Final document of **Treaty of Utrecht** signed

July 13, 1713 Treaty of Portsmouth ends Queen Anne's War (began 1702) in America

July 27, 1714 Russian navy defeats the Swedes in **Battle of Gangut**

William Penn, English Quaker leader and colonialist.

The flag of English pirate Edward Teach, known as Blackbeard, became notorious in the Caribbean between 1717 and his death in 1718.

> **...SUCH A FIGURE, THAT IMAGINATION CANNOT FORM AN IDEA OF A FURY FROM HELL, TO LOOK MORE FRIGHTFUL.**

Captain Charles Johnson describing Edward Teach, from *A General History of the Robberies and Murders of the most notorious Pyrates*, 1724

of the southwest Cape's Khoisan. Survivors fleeing inland were killed by neighboring tribes to limit the disease's spread.

In 1713, the **Treaty of Utrecht** was signed; together with the **Treaty of Rastatt** in 1714, it was to **end the War of the Spanish Succession**. Underlying the Utrecht Treaty (actually a series of treaties) was the principle of maintaining the balance of power between France, Spain, and their neighbors, so that no state could dominate Europe. The lines of succession of the two countries were separated, so no Spaniard could claim the French throne, and vice versa. Savoy gained Sicily, Austria received the Spanish Netherlands, and Britain was ceded Newfoundland, Nova Scotia, and Gibraltar. In addition, the **Asiento Agreement** gave Britain a 30-year contract to supply slaves and goods to Spanish colonies.

In Britain, after the death of Queen Anne in 1714, **George I** (1660–1727) became the **first monarch** of the German **House of Hanover** to rule Great Britain and Ireland. The Hanoverian succession in 1714 ended the reign of the House of Stuart, which had ruled Scotland from 1371, and Great Britain and Ireland since 1603.

In 1714, the **Ottomans declared war on the Venetian Republic**. The final conflict between the two powers, the war ended in 1718 with an **Ottoman victory** and Venice's loss of the Peloponnese, its major possession in Greece.

THE STATE OF WAR BETWEEN THE MAJOR EUROPEAN POWERS in the late 17th and early 18th centuries created a profound sense of **lawlessness**. This was most marked in regions where desperate efforts were being made to seize colonial power. With the standing navies at war, some of the work of policing the new colonies fell to **privateers**. For many it was only a short step to becoming outright **pirates**. One of the most notorious, Edward Teach, known as **Blackbeard** (c. 1680–1718), became a target for the authorities after he took charge of his own ship in November 1717. He was finally murdered in November 1718.

In **North America**, the signing of the Treaty of Utrecht (see 1713) had failed to bring an end to the hostilities between the European colonizing powers, and, in turn, these were struggling to dominate competing American Indian tribes. In 1716, in an attempt to block French expansion westward from Louisiana, the **Spanish entered east Texas**, they established

Qing cloisonné
This ornamental elephant with two miniature vases exemplifies the sophistication that cloisonné enamel-work reached during the Qing dynasty period.

> **NO CHINESE CATHOLICS ARE ALLOWED TO WORSHIP ANCESTORS IN THEIR FAMILIAL TEMPLES.**

Pope Clement XI, Papal bull, 1715

several missions and, in 1718, the town of San Antonio. While the latter became the target of raids by Apache American Indians, the Spanish successfully encouraged the Yamasee and other tribes in their attacks on hundreds of British settlers in South Carolina, a conflict known as the **Yamasee War** (1715–17).

In Asia, **Zunghar Mongols** invaded Outer Mongolia and Tibet in 1717, and **sacked** the Tibetan capital of **Lhasa**, looting the tomb of the fifth Dalai Lama. Tibet appealed to the Qing Kangxi emperor (1654–1722) for assistance. The Zunghars defeated an invading Qing army in 1718, and the Qing Empire was not to liberate Lhasa for three years (see 1720). Meanwhile, in the Chinese homeland, **Jesuit missionaries** found themselves under threat. Impressed by their services, the Kangxi emperor

had ensured their protection with an Edict of Toleration (see 1692). However, in 1715 Pope Clement XI issued a Papal bull condemning Chinese ancestor worship. In retaliation, the Kangxi emperor would repeal his edict in 1721, officially forbidding Christian missions in China.

In Europe, King **Louis XIV** of France **died in 1715**, leaving the infant Louis XV as his heir. Ignoring the terms of the Treaty of Utrecht, King Philip V of Spain claimed the throne of France if the infant were to die. In 1717, a **Triple Alliance** was signed by the Dutch Republic, France, and Great Britain in an effort to compel Philip to abandon his expansionist ambitions. Austria's joining of the alliance in the following year turned this into a Quadruple Alliance against Spain (see 1718–19).

In Britain, the Hanoverian succession (see 1714) had provoked anger among Jacobites—supporters of the deposed Stuart king James VII of Scotland and II of England—and in 1715 this erupted into the **First Jacobite Rebellion**. Over-estimating the support they could count on in England, about 4,000

men (mainly Scottish) marched toward London but were defeated in November by Hanoverian forces at the **Battle of Preston**. While his lieutenants countered the threat to his reign in the north, life for Hanoverian king George I in London was seemingly unaffected: there were several performances for the king and members of the court of *Water Music* by the German Baroque composer **George Frideric Handel** (1685–1759), who had made his home in London in 1712.

BAROQUE MUSIC

A style of European music that began around 1600 and lasted until about 1750, baroque developed from the masses and madrigals of the Renaissance. It had a stronger emphasis on counterpoint and rhythm, greater expression of emotion, and gave greater importance to the solo voice and instrumental solos. It also established opera, with Monteverdi and Cavalli being early practitioners. Notable baroque composers include Peri and Allegri (early baroque); Lully, Pachelbel, and Purcell (middle); and Bach, Handel, Telemann, and Vivaldi (late baroque).

BAROQUE LUTE

August 1, 1714 George of Hanover becomes King **George I of Britain**

March 19, 1715 Pope Clement XI issues **Papal bull** against Chinese ancestor worship

September 9, 1714 Ottomans declare **war on Venice**; ends in 1718 with an Ottoman victory

April 15, 1715 Murder of a government delegation triggers **Yamasee War, South Carolina**

September 1, 1715 French king **Louis XIV** (known as the "Sun King," b. 1638) **dies**

August 27, 1715 Scottish Jacobite leaders rally to **march on London**

January 27, 1716 Massacre in Tugaloo, Georgia, sets Creek American Indians against the Cherokees in Yamasee War

November 9–14, 1715 Hanoverians defeat Jacobites at **Battle of Preston**

February 10, 1716 James Stuart escapes **to France** after failure of First Jacobite Rebellion

August 5, 1716 Prince Eugen of Savoy, Imperial commander, defeats Ottomans at **Battle of Petrovaradin**

Summer 1716 Spanish **reoccupy east Texas** after absence of 23 years

January 1, 1717 Britain, France, and Dutch Republic sign **Triple Alliance** against Spain

1717 Zunghar Mongols invade Tibet during ongoing conflict with China

July 17, 1717 First performance of Handel's **Water Music** for King George I of England

November 1717 English pirate **Blackbeard** (Edward Teach) begins to operate in the Caribbean

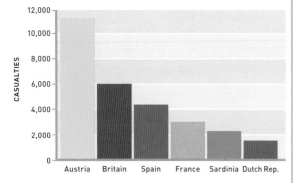

Admiral Sir George Byng's British fleet sail into the Straits of Messina prior to the Battle of Cape Passaro, in a painting by Richard Vale.

This detail of a map by Willem Blau (c. 1650) shows the position of British-controlled Honduras, lying on the east coast of the Yucatán peninsula

THE TREATY OF UTRECHT (see 1713) had ceded Sardinia and Sicily to Savoy, but the treaty was ignored by King Philip V of Spain (1683–1746), who sailed to capture the islands in 1717. Set against Philip was the **Triple Alliance** (see 1717) of Britain, France, and the Dutch Republic, which Austria joined on August 2, 1718, expanding it into the **Quadruple Alliance**. On July 21, Austria—under Holy Roman Emperor Charles VI (1685–1740)—had signed the **Treaty of Passarowitz**, ending the Austro–Turkish War (1716–18). This freed Charles's forces to turn their attention to Spain, and the **War of the Quadruple Alliance** was declared on December 17, 1718.

Previously, the Triple Alliance had set an ultimatum for the

withdrawal of Philip's invasion force. The British fleet, led by Sir George Byng, clashed with the Spanish invasion fleet—which had not been informed of the ultimatum—in the **Battle of Cape Passaro** on August 11, 1718. The larger Spanish warships were captured, while the smaller ships escaped. Later that year, an Austrian army landed at Messina, Sicily, to oust the Spanish garrison, but was defeated on October 15 in the first **Battle of Milazzo**.

In 1719 there were further attempts by the **Quadruple Alliance**, now joined by **Savoy**, to curb Spain. France invaded the Spanish **Basque Country** and then **Catalonia**, but disease forced both forces to withdraw. The Austrians attacked in **Sicily** and eventually the Spanish occupiers capitulated, their supplies having been blocked by the British navy. In another example of Spain's vulnerability from the sea, the British captured the port of **Vigo** in October.

War casualties
In the War of the Quadruple Alliance, 28,350 men were killed or wounded, including more than 2,000 from Sardinia, which was invaded by Spain.

THE BRITISH COLONY IN HONDURAS (now Belize), the only British possession in Central America before it gained full independence in 1981, was established on the eastern coast of the Yucatán peninsula by **British buccaneers**. By the turn of the 18th century the colony had begun to exploit the region's logwood (*Haematoxylum campechianum*), which yielded an important dye used for textiles and paper. In 1720, **slaves**—many from Jamaica and others directly from Africa—were first imported to this area of the so-called Mosquito Coast to expand logging operations on the Belize River.

The year 1720 saw the end of the War of the Quadruple Alliance (see 1718) with the signing of the **Treaty of the Hague**. Philip agreed to abandon his claims to Sicily and Sardinia, which came under the control of Austria and the Duchy of Savoy respectively, with the duke being titled king of Sardinia. In North America, the French returned **Pensacola** in Florida to King Philip V, along with places they had occupied in the north of Spain, receiving trade advantages in exchange. The treaty also confirmed **Texas** was a Spanish possession.

Meanwhile, the **Maratha**, a sub-ethnic group inhabiting the Maharashtra region of western India, began a major expansion of the empire that it had

Maratha expansion
The Maratha expanded their empire to the north, south, and east. Such was their reputation that they were able to raise taxes even beyond areas of their direct administration.

KEY
☐ Maratha Empire
→ Maratha campaigns

reestablished in 1674. The catalyst for the expansion, which began in 1720, was the death in 1719 of Balaji Vishwanath (b.1680) and the succession of his son **Bajirao** (1700–40), who was only 20 years old at the time but already a charismatic and dynamic leader. Recognizing the weakness of the grip that the **Mughal Empire**, based in Delhi, had on the states around him, Bajirao's army struck out into Hindustan. The campaign was successful and gained Bajirao great credit at home. This helped him negotiate peace treaties with Mughal authorities in the Deccan. With the security of the Maratha homeland assured, Bajirao began further

Maratha mace
The head of 118 spikes and a quadrangular top spike on this Maratha mace testify to its fearsome effectiveness as a weapon.

expansions in 1728, when he also moved his capital from Satara to **Pune**.

Far to the northeast, the **Zunghar Mongols** had taken possession of **Tibet** (see 1717). In 1720, a force of Qing and Tibetan warriors drove the Zunghars from Tibet. The Zunghars had killed the sixth Dalai Lama, claiming he was an impostor. The Qing force brought with it a replacement, Kelzang Gyatso, who was made the **seventh Dalai Lama**. Tibet became a tribute-paying protectorate of Qing China, and the Tibetan region of Kham was annexed to China's Sichuan province. However, disputes over who should govern under the Qing emperor resulted in **harsh suppressions** by the Chinese in the years that followed.

(map labels: HONDURAS, NICARAGUA, MAR DEL ZUR)

(India map labels: Plateau of Tibet, Himalayas, THAR DESERT, SINDHIA, GAIKWAR, HOLKAR, Ujjain, Baroda, Maheshwar, Nagpur, BHONSLE, PESHWA, Arabian Sea, Pune, Satara, Deccan, Kolhapur, SAVANUR, GOOTY, Eastern Ghats, Western Ghats, Malabar Coast, Coromandel Coast, Bay of Bengal, INDIAN OCEAN, TANJORE, Ceylon, Decan)

CASUALTIES

12,000	
10,000	
8,000	
6,000	
4,000	
2,000	
0	Austria Britain Spain France Sardinia Dutch Rep.

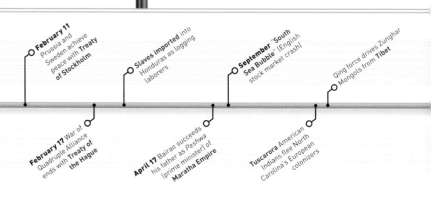

Timeline:

May 17, 1718 French found **New Orleans**, Louisiana

July 21, 1718 **Treaty of Passarowitz** signed

August 2, 1718 Austria joins Triple Alliance, forming **Quadruple Alliance**

August 11, 1718 British beat Spain in **Battle of Cape Passaro**

November 30, 1718 King Charles XII of Sweden (b. 1682) dies

December 17, 1718 Quadruple Alliance declares war on Spain

April 1719 France invades **Basque Country**

April 25, 1719 Danel Defoe (c. 1659–1731), British novelist, publishes *Robinson Crusoe*

May 1719 French capture **Pensacola**, Florida

October 1719 British capture Spanish port of **Vigo**

February 11 Prussia and Sweden achieve peace with **Treaty of Stockholm**

February 17 War of Quadruple Alliance ends with **Treaty of the Hague**

Slaves imported into Honduras as logging laborers

April 17 Bajirao succeeds his father as Peshwa (prime minister) of **Maratha Empire**

September "**South Sea Bubble**" (English stock market crash)

Tuscarora American Indians flee North Carolina's European colonizers

Qing force drives Zunghar Mongols from **Tibet**

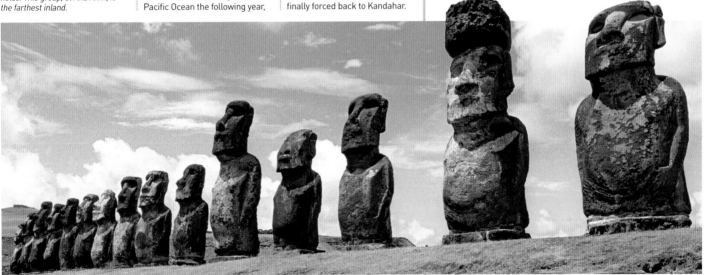

Brilliant polychromatic decoration characterizes this detail of a rectangular Persian dish made in the 18th century during the Safavid dynasty.

THE GREAT NORTHERN WAR

(1700–21) between Sweden and Russia was brought to an end by the conclusion of the **Treaty of Nystad**. In 1719, Russia had successfully challenged Sweden's supremacy in the Baltic by attacking cities on the Swedish east coast. An alliance of the British and Swedes in 1719 then gave Sweden British navy protection that discouraged further raids. The Nystad Treaty restored Finland to Sweden, but former Swedish **Baltic territories** in Estonia and elsewhere went to

Deified ancestors

Moai were erected by clans on Easter Island to watch over their fields. This group, at Ahu Akivi, is the farthest inland.

Russia. Sweden was irrevocably diminished by the terms of the treaty, while Russia, with its new Baltic ports, now dominated Eastern Europe.

In one of the landmark moments of Dutch exploration, Jakob Roggeveen (1659–1729) set out in 1721 to find **Terra Australis**, the mysterious southern continent earlier mapped in part by Spaniard Juan Fernández and Dutchman Abel Tasman, among others. A former employee of the Dutch East Indies Company but now sponsored by its West Indies counterpart, Roggeveen and his three ships sailed to the Falkland Islands, Chile, and the Juan Fernández Islands. While crossing the South Pacific Ocean the following year,

the three ships chanced upon **Easter Island** (now Rapa Nui), so-named because it was discovered on Easter Sunday. Roggeveen also discovered the **Society Islands** and **Samoa** before returning home.

In 1722, the declining **Safavid dynasty** of Persia was deposed by **independent Afghans** to the east. Mahmud Hotaki (c. 1697–1725), son of Mirwais Khan Hotak (see 1709), brought an army to the Safavid capital of Isfahan, sacked the city, and proclaimed himself **shah of Persia**. It was not until 1729, and the defeat of the Hotaki dynasty by Afsharid Persians who were descended from the Mongols at the **Battle of Damghan,** that the Afghans were finally forced back to Kandahar.

EUROPEAN SUCCESS in procuring slaves in West Africa for transporting to the new colonies depended on the enthusiastic cooperation of certain tribes. In **Dahomey**, in what is now the Republic of Benin, King Agadja (r. 1708–40) presided over a culture of enslavement and human sacrifice. His conquest of neighboring Allada in 1723 provided a ready source of **captives for sale**, and by 1724 Dahomey had become the Europeans' principal source of slave labor.

In 1724, the *Code Noir*, King Louis XIV of France's extensive definition of the conditions of slavery, was introduced in the

French territory of Louisiana, North America. The code was partly intended to give slaves basic protection from their masters—all were to be given food and clothes, for example— but it also legitimized **cruel punishments**: runaway slaves were to be branded, their ears cut off, and, after a second offence, crippled by having their hamstrings cut.

Also in 1724, the disintegrating Mughal Empire saw the **Indian state of Oudh** gain independence under Saadat Ali Khan (c. 1680– 1739). He founded the Moghul **Awadh dynasty**, which ruled until its power was seized by the British in the early 19th century.

> ## " YOU ARE NOW **TRAVELING INTO** THE **PARADISE OF THE SCHOLARS.** "

Caspar Wolff, **German scientist**, praising the Academy of Sciences in a letter to mathematician Leonhard Euler. *c.* 1779

Peter the Great's Academy of Sciences in St. Petersburg, founded in 1725, was rehoused in this building of 1783–85 on the Neva River.

The Shinto gate (*torii*) at the entrance to the Itsukushima Shrine, Japan.

THE TREATY OF THE HAGUE

(see 1720) did not end rivalries between the major European powers. In 1725, Austria signed the **Treaty of Vienna** with Spain, gaining trading advantages in the colonies for its Imperial Ostend Company; in exchange, Austria abandoned all claims to the Spanish throne and also promised to help Spain recapture Gibraltar. In 1726, Britain embarked on an attempt to blockade Spanish treasure ships at Porto Bello, Panama, but withdrew without success in 1727 after severe losses from disease.

Emboldened by its promise of Austrian support, which was negated by a secret pact made between Britain and Austria, **Spain besieged Gibraltar** in 1727, an act that precipitated the **Anglo–Spanish War.** The four-month siege failed, costing Spain 1,400 men to British casualties of 300. The war ended with the Treaty of Seville in 1729.

In Russia, the **St. Petersburg Academy of Sciences** was founded in 1725 by Peter the Great (1672–1725). The most eminent scholars of all disciplines were invited to work there—for example, German embryologist Caspar Wolff (1733–94) offered Swiss mathematician Leonhard Euler a 200-rouble salary as an enticement, which he accepted.

CATHERINE I (1684–1727)

The orphaned daughter of Lithuanian peasants, the future wife of Peter the Great was born Marta Skowrońska. She was secretly married to Peter in 1707, and she reigned as Russia's first female monarch from his death until her own. In her reign, she was supported by the Supreme Privy Council, which wanted to deny power to the aristocracy.

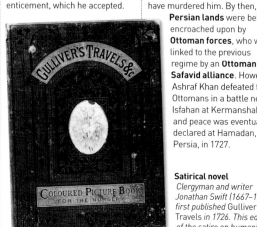

To the southeast, the Afghan shah of Persia, Mahmud Hotaki (see 1721–22), died in 1725. He was succeeded by his cousin, Ashraf Khan (d. 1730), who may have murdered him. By then, **Persian lands** were being encroached upon by **Ottoman forces,** who were linked to the previous regime by an **Ottoman–Safavid alliance.** However, Ashraf Khan defeated the Ottomans in a battle near Isfahan at Kermanshah, and peace was eventually declared at Hamadan, Persia, in 1727.

Satirical novel
Clergyman and writer Jonathan Swift (1667–1745) first published Gulliver's Travels in 1726. This edition of the satire on humanity was published in the 1860s.

Coffee in Brazil
This 19th-century woodcut shows a Brazilian coffee plantation. From small beginnings in 1727, Brazil grew into the world's largest coffee producer.

Also in 1727, the **Treaty of Kyakhta** was signed by **Imperial Russia** and the **Chinese Qing Empire**; it remained the basis of relations between the two until the mid-19th century. Mongolia's northern border was mapped and agreed on, and routes established for trade in furs and tea.

The late 1720s saw the start of **coffee-growing** in the Caribbean and South America. Seedlings were first brought to Martinique around 1720, and in 1727 the king of Portugal sent to French Guinea for seeds. His envoy, Francisco de Mello Palheta, persuaded the French governor's wife to provide seeds and seedlings, and these enabled the Portuguese to start a coffee industry in Brazil.

THE RUSSIAN EMPEROR PETER THE GREAT was determined to discover the full **extent of his lands to the east.** A Danish seaman, Vitus Bering (1681–1741), was commissioned to follow the Siberian coast northward from the Kamchatka Peninsula, and in 1728 **Bering** sailed into the narrow **strait,** now named after him, that **separates Siberia and Alaska.** By sailing farther north, Bering established that Siberia reaches its eastward limit at the strait. Bering suspected that there must be land farther east, but it was only during a second voyage, in 1741, that he first saw the coast of Alaska across the strait.

On the Indian subcontinent, the **Maratha** people, after nearly a decade of consolidating their power under Bajirao (see 1720), struck out into the Deccan region surrounding their homeland. In 1728, in the **Battle of Palkhed,** they confronted rival prince Asaf Jah I of Hyderabad (also known as Nizam-ul-Mulk) who had been laying claim to Maratha leadership and who was refusing to pay them *chauth* (a tribute tax). In a strategic masterstroke, the Marathas cornered the nizam's army in a waterless zone, where it refused to fight. In consequence, the nizam abandoned his leadership claim and payment of *chauth* was resumed.

The year 1729 was a pivotal point in **trading** relations **between China and the West** because the Qing Yongzheng emperor banned almost all

January 28, 1725 Peter the Great (b. 1672) dies. Catherine I continues work of founding his Academy of Sciences

April 22, 1725 Afghan-born Shah Mahmud Hotaki of Persia (born c. 1697) dies or is murdered

April 30, 1725 Austria and Spain sign **Treaty of Vienna**

1726 Vast Chinese encyclopedia *Gujin Tushu Jicheng* printed using movable type

February 11, 1727 Spain begins siege of Gibraltar (to 12 June)

1727 Portuguese introduce coffee to Brazil

August 23, 1727 Russia and China sign **Treaty of Kyakhta** in Mongolian border town

November 18, 1727 Foundation stone laid of new city of Jaipur, India

February 28, 1728 Maratha defeat Asaf Jah I, ruler of Hyderabad, in **Battle of Palkhed**

May 18, 1728 Peter II crowned czar of Russia, succeeding Catherine I importation of **opium**. Chinese goods were in high demand in Europe, but the Chinese were unimpressed by European goods and accepted payment only in silver—which Britain, in particular, had to obtain at exorbitant cost. In the early 18th century, British traders had begun to trade Indian opium for Chinese goods, and there was soon a growing number of **addicted Chinese** that greatly reduced Europe's silver requirement. European opium smugglers remained a major problem for China into the 19th century.

Also in 1729, after more than a decade of mistreatment, **Natchez American Indians killed** more than 200 French **settlers at Fort Rosalie**, Mississippi. However, by 1731 the French, assisted by the Choctaw people, were to retaliate by enslaving a large

Bering Strait
This satellite image shows the Bering Strait, a 56-mile (96-km) stretch of water that separates Asia and North America.

number of Natchez for work on Caribbean plantations.

The short-lived **Ottoman Tulip Period** (1718–30) was ended by a rebellion against unpopular measures led by a janissary (soldier), **Patrona Halil**, that caused Sultan Ahmed III to be supplanted by Mahmud I. The Tulip Period was one of stability in the Ottoman Empire and was marked by increased interest in Western ways. Just as Western Europe had been fascinated by tulips in the 17th century, the Ottoman court became equally

obsessed. Ottoman **architecture and art were invigorated**, but high prices for tulips and tulip bulbs distorted the economy. The instatement of Mahmud I in 1730 brought an end to the Tulip Period, but **Halil was strangled** in front of the sultan in 1731 for overreaching himself.

In **Japan**, whose population had been ruled by the Tokugawa shogunate since 1603, there was a resurgence of the **Shinto religion.** Beginning around 1730, it was fueled by the writings of scholars such as Kada no Azunamaro (1669–1736) and Kamo no Mabuchi (1697–1769). The Shinto scholars rejected Chinese and Buddhist influences and sought to identify a purely **Japanese spiritual identity**. Shintoism was reinstated as the national religion of Japan more than a century later in 1868.

Meanwhile, the Arabian state of **Oman** was expanding its dominions in Africa. The Portuguese-held Kenyan city

Massacre at Fort Rosalie
On November 28, 1729, Natchez American Indians killed 242 settlers at Fort Rosalie, Mississippi, in retaliation for years of mistreatment.

of **Mombasa** and the island of Pemba had been captured by the Omanis in 1698, and by 1730 they had driven the Portuguese from the Kenyan and Tanzanian coasts and gained control of the island of **Zanzibar** (now part of Tanzania).

In **West Africa**, Islamic Fulbe, or Fulani, people began to unify into larger communities in what is now known as

the **Fulbe Revolution**. The first such state was Bondu, in Guinea, formed in the late 17th century. Then came Futa Jallon (centered in Guinea but sprawling over neighboring territories), where the Islamic Fulbe took power from the existing leaders and non-Islamic Fulbe people.

A **confederation of provinces** was formally created in 1735 with its capital at Timbo, Guinea. Other areas that were profoundly affected by the Fulbe Jihad—as the seizure of power was termed—included the formerly declining **Bornu Empire** (in present-day Nigeria), the fortunes of which underwent a significant revival.

In 1731, formerly independent **Dahomey** in West Africa finally accepted the suzerainty of the **Yoruba Oyo Empire** (present-day Nigeria). The Yoruba had invaded and defeated them after a protracted and bitterly fought campaign in 1728, but resistance in Dahomey did not end until 1748.

Opium pipe and poppy
This traditional Chinese opium pipe has a knob-shaped bowl in which the drug (dried latex from the opium poppy) is vaporized when the bowl is heated.

> **" ...IN LESS THAN TWO HOURS** THEY **MASSACRED** MORE THAN **200** OF THE **FRENCH. "**
>
> **Father le Petit, missionary,** in a letter to Father D'Avaugour, Procurator of the Missions in North America, 1730

CASUALTIES bar chart: Men (~150), Women (~35), Children (~55), y-axis 0–180

Timeline:

August 14, 1728 Danish explorer Vitus Bering discovers **Bering Strait** is eastward limit of Siberia

October 20–23, 1728 More than a quarter of **Copenhagen**, Denmark, **destroyed by fire**

1728 Nigerian **Oyo Empire** invades **Dahomey**

1729 Persians under Nader Shah defeat occupying Afghans in **Battle of Damghan**

April 21, 1729 Catherine II (the Great) of Russia born (d. 1796)

July 30, 1729 City of **Baltimore**, Maryland, **founded**

November 9, 1729 Britain, France, Spain, and Dutch Republic sign **Treaty of Seville**

November 28, 1729 Natchez American Indians kill settlers **at Fort Rosalie**, Mississippi

1729 Qing emperor bans sale and smoking of **opium in China**

January 29, 1730 Anna of Russia becomes czarina on death of Peter II (b. 1715) from smallpox

September 1730 Patrona Halil leads rebellion that topples Ottoman emperor Ahmed III

September 20, 1730 Mahmud I succeeds Ahmed III as Ottoman emperor

March 16, 1731 Austria, Britain, Dutch Republic, and Spain sign **Treaty of Vienna**

1731 Dahomey accepts suzerainty of Nigerian Oyo Empire

"Tavern Scene" is one of the eight paintings of British artist William Hogarth's *A Rake's Progress* (1732–33), which depicts the downfall of a rich merchant's feckless heir.

OBSESSED WITH CREATING a strong, independent state, Frederick William I (r. 1713–40), the "Soldier King" of **Prussia**, instituted **compulsory military service**: every young man had to serve in the military for three months of each year. In this way, the Prussian army became the fourth-largest in Europe, with 60,000 soldiers, despite having the twelfth-largest population.

In **America**, the state of **Georgia** was founded in 1732, becoming the last of the Thirteen Colonies established by Britain on the Atlantic coast. Named after Britain's King George II, the new state was intended to strengthen the British presence in the south. The first settlers began to arrive in 1733 and included many released from debtors' prisons.

> **WHERE SOME STATES HAVE AN ARMY, THE PRUSSIAN ARMY HAS A STATE.**

Voltaire, French thinker (1694–1778)

Also in 1733, Danish seaman Vitus Bering (1681–1741), after whom the Bering Strait is named (see 1728), began the **Great Northern Exploration**. Empress Anna of Russia (1693–1740) had authorized a large expedition involving 3,000 people in three separate groups: one group was to map northern Siberia; the second, to explore north of Japan, and Bering's group, to determine what lay east of the strait. It was not until June 1741, just months before his death in December, that Bering first caught sight of Mount St. Elias

Prussian blue
The conscripted army of Prussian king Frederick William I wore dark blue coats with red linings and red-and-white facings.

on the **Alaskan mainland**. In the same month, his second ship sent men ashore on Alaska's Prince of Wales Island.

Meanwhile, during the **Kyoho era** (July 1716 to April 1736) in Japan, **famine** had struck. In 1732, swarms of locusts attacked the crops, especially rice, of agricultural communities around the inland sea. Heavy rains then destroyed winter crops of wheat and barley, and insects decimated the following year's rice crop. The worst-affected area was the north of Kyushu Island, where around 15,000 people died. In cities such as Edo (present-day Tokyo) and Osaka, the cost of rice rose seven-fold, and in 1733 rice shops were attacked during **food riots**.

In 1733 Poland's King Augustus II died. Stanislaw Leszczyński was made king when 12,000 Polish nobles voted for him in the Sejm election. However, 3,000 nobles who voted for Augustus III used

1:4 **Polish election, 1733**
Stanislaw Leszczyński gained 12,000 votes and temporarily became king of Poland. Augustus III gained only 3,000 votes but succeeded him in 1734.

20% DEAD

TOTAL POPULATION

Kyoho famine in Japan
In the Fukuoka Domain, northern Kyushu, about 20 percent of the population died during the 1733 famine of the Kyoho era.

the backing of Russia and Austria to install Augustus as king in 1734. What began as a civil war developed into the **War of the Polish Succession** (1733–38) as the Bourbons (France and Spain), the Habsburgs (Austria), Prussia, Saxony, and Russia campaigned outside Poland to seize territories lost after the War of the Spanish Succession (see 1701). Only with the **Treaty of Vienna** in 1738 did Stanislaw give up his legal claim.

British culture in this period came to be dominated by **radical humanism**, a conviction that human identity, ethics, and knowledge need not be based on a belief in God. Alexander Pope (1688–1744) wrote in his poem *An Essay on Man* (1734), "Know then thyself, presume not God to scan / The proper study of Mankind is Man." Secular humanism spread to the arts, with artists such as William Hogarth (1697–1764) bringing sharp **social criticism and satire** to their depictions of humanity.

Another British development was the patenting in 1733 of a **flying-shuttle loom** by John Kay

(1704–80). The loom had a wheeled, thread-carrying shuttle, which greatly increased the rate at which fabrics could be made. Kay's new loom **threatened the livelihood of weavers**, who attempted to get the loom banned. However, they were unsuccessful, and Kay's invention was adopted widely.

VOLTAIRE (1694–1778)

Born François-Marie Arouet in Paris, Voltaire was a prolific writer, historian, and philosopher of the French Enlightenment (see 1763) who disseminated his radical humanist ideas in works that ranged from essays and historical works to poems, plays, and novels. His ideas—on social reform and civil liberties, for example—often met with hostility, forcing him to flee several times, but they had a major influence on thinkers of the French and American revolutions.

February 22, 1732
George Washington, first president of the US, born (d. 1799)

1732 Locusts destroy food crops and begin **Kyoho famine** in Japan

December 27, 1732 Russian empress Anna issues a last edict concerning **Great Northern Exploration**

February 1, 1733
King Augustus II of Poland (b. 1670) dies

May 29, 1733
Canadians given the right to have Indians as **slaves** and sell them

September 12, 1733
Stanislaw Leszczyński (1677–1766) elected as (disputed) **king of Poland**

1733 Famine leads to **food riots** in Edo and Osaka, Japan

1732 King Frederick William I of Prussia institutes **conscript training system**

June 9, 1732 King George II of Britain grants charter for establishment of state of **Georgia**

1732–33 British artist **William Hogarth** completes eight-painting series *A Rake's Progress*

February 12, 1733 first British settlers land at **Savannah**, Georgia

July 1733 British inventor John Kay begins manufacturing **flying-shuttle loom**

October 10, 1733 France declares war on Austria in **War of the Polish Succession**

June 30, 1734 Stanislaw is deposed and **Augustus III** becomes king of Poland

An illustration depicting sugar processing in the Caribbean from *Histoire des Antilles* by French clergyman and plantation owner Jean-Baptiste Labat.

CHARLES MARIE DE LA CONDAMINE (1701–74), French explorer, scientist, and mathematician, joined an expedition to Peru in 1735. After falling out with his colleagues, he continued alone to Quito, Ecuador, from where he traveled down the **Amazon** to Cayenne, thereby making the first scientific exploration of the river. Returning to Paris in 1744, he published the journal of his travels and discoveries in 1751. When in **Ecuador**, La Condamine was the first European to encounter **rubber**—the Mayans had been making flexible rubber for centuries—and in 1736 he introduced the product to Europe when he sent sheets of processed rubber to Paris.

By the early 18th century, the Portuguese, Spanish, British, French, and Dutch had **slave-worked sugar plantations** in Brazil and throughout the Caribbean. In 1735, the French East India Company began to develop plantations on the islands of **Ile-de-France** and **Bourbon** (now Mauritius and Réunion). Soon to follow was the first **sugar refinery** on Mauritius, built at Ville Bague in the north.

ax head inlaid with silver calligraphy

Weapon of conquest
This finely decorated battle-ax belonged to Nader, who was crowned shah of Persia in 1736. He led the Persians to war with Afghanistan in the following year.

In North America, pressure from expanding British colonies forced the French to strengthen their claim to **Indiana** by establishing a **permanent settlement**. In 1732, a trading fort had been erected at the site of present-day Vincennes, but in 1735 the traders were joined by a wave of agricultural workers. **Vincennes** quickly grew, becoming not only the foremost French trading post in Indiana but also the dominant **center of French culture** in the region.

Meanwhile, the year 1736 marked the **end of Safavid rule** in Persia. Persian military leader **Nader Shah** (1698–1747) had become more powerful than the Safavids he served (Tahmasp II until 1732, and Tahmasp's young son, Abbas III). When Nader proposed himself as **shah**, few stood against him. He was crowned in 1736. In 1737, Nader moved against Persia's former Afghan overlords by occupying southern **Afghanistan**. When Tahmasp and Abbas were murdered in 1740, the Safavid dynasty was extinguished.

The **Russo–Austrian–Turkish War** (1735–39)

signaled that no treaty could easily end the War of the Polish Succession (see 1733). In addition, Russia, joined by Austria in 1737, intended to seize the **Crimea** and gain access to the Black Sea, at the same time ending raids by Crimean **Tartars**. One Russian army captured part of the Crimea in 1736, but was forced by disease to retreat. Another army recovered **Azov** from the Ottomans in Romania and advanced to **Jassy** (Iaşi), Moldavia. In 1737, renewed Russian gains in the Crimea were reversed due to a lack of supplies.

By 1737, the **Maratha Empire** in India (see 1728) was enjoying its greatest **expansion** to the north, at the expense of the Mughal Empire. Peshwa (prime minister) **Bajirao I** (r. 1721–40) masterminded this expansion, but almost as powerful as the Peshwa were Maratha chieftains called Sardars—among them Gaekwads of Baroda, Shindes of Gwalior, and Holkars of Indore—who established their own kingdoms in the captured lands.

In 1737, Swedish taxonomist and botanist **Carolus Linnaeus** (1707–78) published *Genera Plantarum*, later joined by *Species Plantarum* (1753). Along with his earlier *Systema Naturae* (1735), these works laid the foundation for the system of biological classification still used today.

Plant anatomy
Carolus Linnaeus's Genera Plantarum classified plants by their sex organs—the numbers of stamens and pistils in their flowers.

Tab. I

Timeline:

1735 Carolus Linnaeus publishes first edition of *Systema Naturae*

April 1735 French explorer La Condamine embarks on expedition to **Peru**

1735 Vincennes, Indiana, is established on Wabash River

October 3, 1735 Signing of Preliminary **Peace** ends fighting in War of the Polish Succession

October 8, 1735 Qianlong succeeds Yongzheng as Qing **emperor of China**

March 8, 1736 Nader Shah, founder of Afsharid dynasty, crowned **shah of Persia**

June 19, 1736 Russian army seizes **Azov**, Romania, from Ottomans

1736 La Condamine sends first samples of **processed rubber** to Europe

June 30, 1737 Russian army storms Ottoman fortress of **Ochakov**, Romania

July 1737 Austria joins Russia in its war with **the Ottomans** but suffers several defeats

July 1737 Russian army defeats army of **Crimean khan** but withdraws due to lack of supplies

1737 Carolus Linnaeus publishes first edition of *Genera Plantarum*

The ruins of the old Kandahar citadel, Afghanistan, lie on the hilltop behind the 12th-century arch. In the Persian siege, Hussein Hotaki took refuge in the citadel but surrendered after it was bombarded by Nader Shah.

Frederick II (left) converses with the Marquis d'Argens near Sanssouci.

THE AFGHAN HOTAKI DYNASTY had been expelled from Persia in 1729 by Nader Shah (1698–1747), and he was also determined to eliminate the remaining threat posed by the Afghan **Ghilzai** people. Having occupied southern Afghanistan in 1737, he besieged the Hotaki stronghold of **Kandahar** in 1738. Nader Shah exiled Hussein, last of the Hotakis, destroyed the towns of Kandahar and Qalat-i-Ghilzai, and finally **crushed the hopes of the Ghilzais** by backing the rise of the rival Afghan **Durrani** people. Afghanistan was then part of the Mughal Empire, centered in Delhi, but the Mughal governor had been powerless to stop Nader Shah's **Persian force**, which swept through Kabul and **crossed the Indus** in December 1738. After defeating the forces of Mughal Muhammad Shah in the **Battle of Karnal** in February

8:1

Battle of Karnal
Trying to prevent Nader Shah's Persian invading army from reaching Delhi, the Mughals lost 20,000 men while the Persians lost only 2,500.

1739, around 68 miles (110km) from Delhi, Nader Shah entered the city victorious on March 9, 1739. The Mughal treasury was empty but the shah **seized the emperor's personal jewels**, including the famous Koh-i-Noor and Darya-e-Noor diamonds.

Also in 1739, the **Austro-Turkish War** (1737–39) was ended by the Treaty of Belgrade. In the same year, the Treaty of Niš brought the **Russo–Turkish War** (1735–39) to a conclusion. Both these treaties confirmed Austria's loss of northern Serbia and Belgrade to the Ottomans, obliging Russia to abandon hopes of capturing the Crimea, although the Russians were allowed to build an unfortified port at Azov and trade on the Black Sea.

Hostilities broke out once again between **Britain** and **Spain** in 1739. Britain had been awarded limited rights to trade slaves and goods in the Spanish colonies (see 1713), but increasingly, the Spanish were seizing British cargoes. In 1731, Spanish coastguards had severed the ear of a British captain, Robert Jenkins, and in 1739 the case led to a war, which was later dubbed the **War of Jenkins' Ear** by the Scottish historian Thomas Carlyle. Britain began to attack Spanish possessions in the New World, such as the Spanish naval base of Porto Bello in Panama. Following the **Battle of Porto Bello**, the British took possession of the settlement in November 1739. The Viceroyalty of New Spain, first established in the early

Administration of empire
The Viceroyalty of New Spain, centered on the Caribbean and Gulf of Mexico was the first of four created to govern Spanish New World territories.

16th century, responded by increasing its defenses around the Caribbean coast.

In **North America**, French colonists were maintaining their drive to **push westward** into Spanish territories. A priority was to identify a route to **link the**

Battle of Porto Bello
Fought in 1739, in the early stages of the War of Jenkins' Ear, the Battle of Porto Bello resulted in the British seizing the settlement from Spain.

Mississippi Basin with Spanish **Colorado** and **Santa Fe**. In 1739, two French brothers, **Pierre and Paul Mallet, opened up a route** by negotiating the Missouri and Platte rivers, traveling southward to the Arkansas River, from where a local man guided them to Santa Fe. Despite the continuing existence of a buffer state of warring American Indian tribes, a link between the French and Spanish settlements was established.

WITH THE DEATH OF KING FREDERICK WILLIAM I OF PRUSSIA in 1740, his son, Frederick II (1712–86), ascended to the throne. In his youth, Frederick II had been fond of music, poetry, and philosophy. He studied the works of Niccolò Machiavelli (see 1513) in preparation for kingship, and in 1739 wrote a refutation of the Renaissance Florentine's ideas, *Anti-Machiavel*, which he published anonymously in 1740. His rule was characterized by modernization, tolerance, and patronage of the arts. Yet he became known as **Frederick the Great** for the political and military feats by which he first expanded the borders of Prussia (until 1701 known as Brandenburg–Prussia) far beyond their historical limits, then defended these acquisitions against massive coalitions of powerful enemies. Frederick II's first opportunity to expand Prussia's frontiers arrived quickly after his accession. The Habsburg emperor, Charles VI, died in 1740 and was succeeded by his daughter, Maria Theresa (1717–80), who was to rule Austria's hereditary domains with her husband, Francis Stephen, as Holy Roman Emperor. Immediately, Prussia and France challenged the arrangement. Most of Europe took sides in what became the **War of the Austrian Succession** (1740–48), with Britain, the Dutch Republic, Sardinia, and Saxony supporting the queen. Frederick, claiming inheritance of **Silesia**—parts of present-day Poland, Germany,

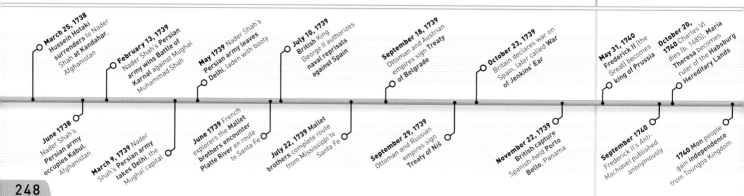

March 25, 1738 Hussein Hotaki surrenders to Nader Shah at Kandahar, Afghanistan

June 1738 Nader Shah's Persian army occupies Kabul, Afghanistan

February 13, 1739 Nader Shah's Persian army wins Battle of Karnal against Mughal Muhammad Shah

March 9, 1739 Nader Shah's Persian army takes Delhi, the Mughal capital

May 1739 Nader Shah's Persian army leaves Delhi, laden with booty

June 1739 French explorers the Mallet brothers encounter Platte River en route to Santa Fe

July 10, 1739 British King George II authorizes naval reprisals against Spain

July 22, 1739 Mallet brothers complete route from Mississippi to Santa Fe

September 18, 1739 Ottoman and Austrian empires sign Treaty of Belgrade

September 29, 1739 Ottoman and Russian empires sign Treaty of Niš

October 23, 1739 Britain declares war on Spain, later called War of Jenkins' Ear

November 22, 1739 British capture Spanish-held Porto Bello, Panama

May 31, 1740 Frederick II (the Great) becomes king of Prussia

September 1740 Frederick II's Anti-Machiavel published anonymously

October 20, 1740 Charles VI dies (b. 1685). Maria Theresa becomes ruler of the Habsburg Hereditary Lands

1740 Mon people gain independence from Toungoo Kingdom

> **"...TOWARD THE NORTH,** FROM THERE SHONE **FREDERICK, THE NORTH STAR, AROUND WHOM** GERMANY, EUROPE, EVEN THE WORLD SEEMED TO TURN. "**

Johann Wolfgang von Goethe, German writer (1749–1832), on Frederick the Great

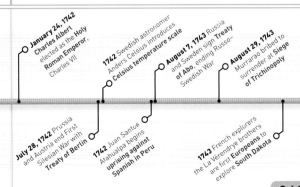

Poppelsdorf Castle, Germany, exemplifies Rococo style, which became popular during the 18th century, particularly in France, Germany, Bohemia, and Austria.

and the Czech Republic—seized the territory from Habsburg, Austria, and made it a Prussian province. It was later incorporated into the German Empire, in 1871.

In Asia, the Mon kingdom centered in **Pegu**, Burma (Myanmar), rebelled in 1740 against the northern Burmese **Toungoo kingdom** that had first subjugated it in 1539. After the rebellion, a Burmese monk with Toungoo royal heritage was made king of Pegu. The independent kingdom lasted until 1757.

Also in 1740, a major expansion of the **Lunda kingdom** of Central Africa began when a party exploring to the west established the kingdom of **Kazembe**. For the next hundred years, an aggressive policy of annexation increased Kazembe's size to cover most

of Katanga in the present-day Democratic Republic of the Congo.

Meanwhile, the War of the Austrian Succession was having repercussions in the north. Sweden, still bridling at losing its **Baltic territories** after the Great Northern War (see 1721–22), deployed troops on the Russian border and declared the **Russo–Swedish War** (1741–43). The threat to St. Petersburg pushed forward a planned coup d'état in Russia, but the new tsarina, Elizabeth Petrovna (1709–62), continued with the war rather than cede the Baltic territories to Sweden, as had been promised.

In Ulster (Northern Ireland), **emigration to North America** increased dramatically. Those leaving included many members of the **Scottish Presbyterian**

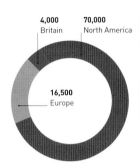

4,000 Britain	70,000 North America
	16,500 Europe

The Ulster diaspora
Between 1680 and 1750, 70,000 Scottish–Irish emigrants left Ulster for North America, 4,000 moved to Britain, and 16,500 left for Europe.

Church, most of whom were descendents of families who had colonized the Irish north in the 17th century. Ireland's English overlords distrusted the Scottish–Irish colony, which supported Scottish interests. Presbyterian ministers were **fined or incarcerated**, and economic activities of the Scottish Presbyterians were curtailed, causing poverty and famine. In the early 18th century, this discrimination worsened; they were forced to pay tithes in support of the Church of England and excluded from important office. A severe **famine** in 1741–42 resulted in about 12,000 annually leaving for the New World. These **Scottish–Irish emigrants**, resentful of their treatment by the English, later gave fierce support to the cause of American independence from Britain in the 1770s and 1780s.

THE OPPORTUNISTIC SEIZING OF SILESIA by Frederick II of Prussia (see 1740–41) proved a successful gambit. The Austrian army had challenged the Prussians but had been defeated in the Battle of Mollwitz in 1741. In 1742, Maria Theresa of Austria and the victorious Prussians signed the **Treaty of Berlin**, by which a large part of Silesia was ceded to Prussia. The treaty brought an **end to the First Silesian War** (1740–42), though the wider European conflict known as the War of the Austrian Succession continued until 1748.

In 1742, Swedish astronomer **Anders Celsius** (1701–44) developed the Celsius, or centigrade, **thermometer**. Celsius actually set the melting point of ice at 100 degrees and the boiling point of water at zero degrees, an arrangement that was reversed in 1744 by Swedish botanist Carl Linnaeus (1707–78).

In **Spanish Peru**, a new leader of the native people, **Juan Santos Atahualpa**, a Jesuit-educated man claiming to be a direct descendant of the murdered Inca king Atahualpa (1497–1533), began a **rebellion in Quisopango** in 1742. The Spanish mounted a military campaign against him in 1742, and again in 1743, 1746, and 1750, but never defeated him in his home territory in the Andes.

Celsius thermometer
This 18th-century French instrument, intended for measuring outdoor temperatures, features Celsius's scale, with a range of –15 to +45 degrees.

In India, the **struggle** for power continued between the **Maratha** people (see 1720) and the **nizam of Hyderabad**, the semi-independent representative of the Mughal Empire. The Marathas seized **Trichinopoly**, leaving Murrarao Ghorpade as governor of the town, and refused to pay tribute to the nizam. In 1743, the nizam, determined to regain control of the area, had 80,000 men besiege the town. Defeated, Murrarao accepted payment to change allegiance.

The Russo–Swedish War (1741–43) was ended by the **Treaty of Abo** in 1743. Intent on reducing the Swedish threat to St. Petersburg, Russia had occupied **Finland**, and the treaty moved the Swedish border north. Most of Finland was returned to the Swedes, who in exchange accepted **Adolf-Frederick of Holstein-Gotthorp** (1710–1771), a client of Empress Elizabeth of Russia, as heir to the Swedish throne.

In North America, **South Dakota** was first **explored by Europeans** in 1743, when the French de La Vérendrye brothers returned west after being the first Europeans to see the **Rockies** during their attempt to reach the Pacific.

Growth of Brandenburg-Prussia
In the late 17th and 18th centuries, successive leaders enhanced the power and territory of Brandenburg–Prussia through military and political means.

KEY
- Brandenburg 1648
- Acquisitions 1648–1786

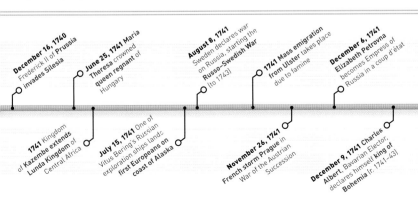

THE STORY OF
AGRICULTURE

FROM HUNTER-GATHERERS AND DOMESTICATION TO CULTIVATION AND GENETIC MANIPULATION

No other activity has made a greater impact on both human society and the environment than agriculture. Its discovery and use first allowed small, previously nomadic, hunter-gathering societies to settle in one place, transform the landscape, form communities, and establish civilizations.

Most archaeologists agree that the earliest plants were domesticated in the Fertile Crescent region of the Middle East around 10,000 BCE. While the fig is thought to be the first truly cultivated food, emmer wheat, barley, lentils, chickpeas, and flax were also common early crops. The first animals to be domesticated were sheep and goats, followed by small breeds of cattle.

On the other side of the world, in what is now South and Central America, squash and corn were being planted, joined by beans; these three plants became known as the "Three Sisters" crops and represented an early knowledge of nutrition: planting them together not only retained soil nutrients but provided essential vitamin and minerals needed for human health.

TOOLS OF THE TRADE

Neolithic farmers used digging sticks—long, flat blades with rounded points—to scrape shallow depressions in the earth, into which they dropped seeds. They also cleared areas of woodland using axes as well as fire to make space for crops and animal enclosures. However, sophisticated farming techniques such as irrigation and large-scale monocropping were practiced in Sumeria as early as 5000 BCE, while in Egypt, farmers made use of plows and sickles, and boasted a range of crops and livestock.

The light scratch plow used by Mediterranean countries dominated farming in Europe until the Middle Ages, when the heavy horse-drawn plow and a three-field system of crop rotation revolutionized agriculture and greatly increased food supplies. Voyages to Asia and the discovery of the New World in the 15th century had a profound impact on agriculture worldwide, as crops and animals were exchanged between Europe, Asia, and the Americas. This changed agriculture on a scale not seen again until engine-driven farm machinery and mass-production techniques, including the use of chemical fertilizers and pesticides, became the norm in the 20th century.

attachment point

coulter cuts thin vertical strips of turf

share cuts deep horizontal slices of earth

c.10,700–9000 BCE
Domestication of plants
In the Middle East, figs are among the first crops to be cultivated actively by man.

c. 5000 BCE
Sumerians develop core agriculture
Large-scale cultivation, monocropping, irrigation, and the use of a specialized agricultural labor force allows the Sumerian culture to flourish and expand.

Sumerian plow

1st century
Roman trade
Foods such as olives, olive oil, and wine are traded across the Roman Empire, where agriculture is an important business.

c.8000–2000 BCE
The Three Sisters
The planting together of squash, teosinte (a primitive form of corn), and beans in the Americas shows a knowledge of companion planting techniques.

2500–1500 BCE
Egypt cultivates the Nile
The Egyptians use a sophisticated system of planting and harvesting crops that is dependent on the annual flooding of the Nile Delta.

Green figs

Teosinte corn cob

Egyptian harvest

Roman millstone

Small's wooden plow
Scottish inventor James Small was a major contributor to the development of the plow. In the mid-1700s, he significantly redesigned the single-furrow horse plow and remodelled the mouldboard, which was now made of iron, making it stronger and more efficient at turning soil.

handle

1950
3,400,000

1907
600

US 20th-century tractor usage
Tractors became more widespread as their design improved. They became smaller and mass production made them more affordable.

moldboard turned
soil to one side

THE AGRICULTURAL REVOLUTION

From the end of the 16th century in Europe, landowners began to take a more scientific approach to farming. This entailed following such practices as crop rotation to ensure that soil fertility was not depleted, using more efficient machinery such as improved plows, and cross-breeding livestock to avoid genetic weaknesses. While the success of these practices resulted in more food, it came at a cost: the need for farm laborers was greatly reduced, and land enclosures dispossessed many peasants who had nowhere to go.

1050–1300
The Middle Ages
The heavy plow, pulled first by teams of oxen then draft horses, changes the shape of fields, gives bigger yields, and greatly improves the way medieval Europe feeds itself.

Wooden
plow

Late 18th century
The cast-iron plow
The invention of first a cast-iron moldboard, then a cast-iron plowshare greatly improves plowing efficiency in both Old and New World agriculture.

1890s–early 1900s
Gasoline-powered vehicles
The internal-combustion engine-powered agricultural tractor signals the end of horse-drawn farming. By World War I, tractors become common parts of farm machinery in the US.

The Ivel tractor

1492
Columbian exchange
Columbus's discovery of the New World results in an unprecedented cultural exchange of animals and plants, including tobacco and corn.

Tobacco
leaves

1800–40
The mechanical reaper
Although still horse-drawn, the mechanical reaper is the first step in the mechanization of farming, harvesting crops in much less time than could be achieved by hand.

McCormick's reaping machine

1970s
Move to sustainability
In a countermovement to the high-impact and environmentally damaging chemical practices of the mid-20th century, green and sustainable practices begin to be developed.

2000–present
Urban farming
As world populations rise, the search for new ways to feed more people increases. Vertical hydroponic farms in urban spaces have proved successful.

This 18th-century, hand-colored copperplate engraving shows disciplined ranks of red-coated Hanoverian troops falling upon Jacobite Highlanders at the Battle of Culloden, the last battle of the Jacobite uprising.

THE EAST AFRICAN PORT OF MOMBASA was used in the 18th century for trade in gold, ivory, and slaves. Mombasa was held for 200 years by the Portuguese, until a native rebellion drove them out in 1729. The **Arabs of Oman** took over, and in 1744, with a new dynasty installed in Oman, the new governor of Mombasa seized power there from the Omanis. He was killed by Omani assassins in 1745, but his brother, 'Ali ibn Athman (r. 1746–55) stirred up a rebellion and the assassins were executed. 'Ali ibn Athman proclaimed himself **Sultan of Mombasa**, thereby securing the port's independence from Oman.

Meanwhile, Prussia's war with Austria (see 1740) continued. In the **Second Silesian War** (1744–45), the Austrians tried to regain Silesia, but the Prussians eventually defeated the forces of Empress Maria Theresa in 1745 in the battles of **Hohenfriedberg**, Soor, and Kesselsdorf. Maria Theresa finally recognized

9,000
AUSTRIANS AND SAXONS

5,000
PRUSSIANS

Losses at Hohenfriedberg
In this battle the victorious Prussians had significantly fewer casualties than the Austrians and their allies from Saxony.

Deadly Coehorn mortar
The Hanoverian army at Culloden had six short-barreled Coehorn mortars; easily portable, they were deadly weapons on the battlefield.

Frederick II's sovereignty in Silesia by signing the **Treaty of Dresden** at the end of the year; in return, Prussia recognized her husband, Francis, as Holy Roman Emperor. This left only France prosecuting the War of the Austrian Succession (1740–48).

In 1744, France attempted a major **invasion of Britain** in support of Prince Charles Edward Stuart (1720–88)—grandson of the deposed Stuart King James II and the "**Young Pretender**" to the Hanoverian throne of Britain. But the invasion foundered due to terrible weather. In 1745, "**Bonnie Prince Charlie**," as Charles became known, crossed to Scotland and rallied the **Jacobite chiefs** of several Scottish Highland clans to march on England. The Scots defeated a Hanoverian force in the **Battle of Prestonpans** and eventually reached Derby but then retreated, having gained little support from the English or the French. Military successes followed on their return to Scotland, but in 1746

the Scottish force was overcome by a Hanoverian force at the **Battle of Culloden**. The hounding and killing of fleeing and wounded Highlanders earned the Hanoverian commander, William Augustus, Duke of Cumberland, notoriety as the "**Butcher of Culloden**." The battle ended the Second Jacobite Rebellion and wiped out Jacobite hopes of regaining power in Britain.

In 1745, an English farmer began experiments in selective animal breeding that were to revolutionize **animal husbandry**. The principle of mating animals with desired traits was already known, but the methods developed by farmer **Robert Bakewell** were better than earlier ones. His work resulted in the New Leicester breed of sheep and New Longhorn cattle breed, both of which are still widely influential in animal breeding today.

In Japan, the hold of the **Tokugawa dynasty** on power was weakening. In 1745, Tokugawa Ieshige (1712–61) was elected as

shogun. The retiring shogun's eldest son was poor in health, defective in speech, and had little interest in government affairs, but his father demanded his succession as primogeniture dictated. Natural **disasters and famine** characterized his reign, and as the power of the mercantile class grew, his own authority declined, the result of poor decisions and **delegation of power** to subordinates.

Meanwhile, France was still at war with Austria and its allies. In 1746 a French force, authorized by Governor-General Joseph Francois Dupleix (1697–1763), took the British-held Indian port of **Madras**. In 1747, Dupleix followed this with an **attack on Fort St. David**, the strongly

fortified British headquarters in southern India, 100 miles (160 km) south of Madras, but this time he was unsuccessful. However, the French remained in occupation of Madras until the **Treaty of Aix-la-Chapelle** (see 1748) returned the port to the British in exchange for Louisbourg in Nova Scotia.

In China, during the reign of the Qianlong Emperor (r. 1736–99), **Christians** were subjected to renewed **persecution** from 1746 to 1748 as a matter of **imperial policy**. In 1715, Pope Clement XII had criticized idolatrous elements in Chinese religious practices, and the Qianlong Emperor realized that Chinese Christians felt greater **loyalty to foreign powers** than to him. As a result,

Selectively bred sheep
This 1842 engraving depicts a New Leicester ram, a breed developed by Robert Bakewell's new breeding methods at his Leicestershire farm.

February 24, 1744 Tempest scatters French **invasion fleet** approaching Britain

June 4, 1745 Prussia defeats Austria in **Battle of Hohenfriedberg**

September 29, 1745 Prussia defeats Austria in **Battle of Soor**

1745 Tokugawa Ieshige elected **shogun** of Japan

December 15, 1745 Prussia defeats Austria in **Battle of Kesselsdorf**

April 16, 1746 Jacobite Scottish Highlanders massacred at **Battle of Culloden**

1746 'Ali ibn Athman proclaims himself **Sultan of Mombasa**

1745 British farmer Robert Bakewell begins **animal breeding** program

September 21, 1745 Jacobite Scottish Highlanders defeat Hanoverians in **Battle of Prestonpans**

December 1745 Marching Jacobite **Scottish Highlanders** reach Derby, England

December 25, 1745 Prussia and Austria sign **Treaty of Dresden**

September 7–9, 1746 France captures **Madras**, India, from British

May 20, 1747 British naval surgeon James Lind begins experiments to discover cause of **scurvy**

> ## " THE MOST SUDDEN AND VISIBLE GOOD EFFECTS WERE...FROM ORANGES AND LEMONS. "

James Lind, British surgeon, from *Treatise of the Scurvy*, 1753

A fireworks display on the Thames River on May 15, 1749, organized by the Duke of Richmond to celebrate the signing of the Treaty of Aix-la-Chapelle.

Map of Madras
This 1750 engraving depicts the Indian port of Madras, together with its British Fort of St. George, both captured by a French naval expedition in 1746.

evangelization was banned, and Chinese Christians were forced to go into hiding. Wherever missionaries were discovered flouting the law by preaching, the persecution of Christians was intensified.

Another scientific breakthrough in 1745 was the **Leyden jar**, probably the most important 18th-century development in the understanding of **electricity**.

Early capacitor
The Leyden jar could store electric charge, which was created by an electrostatic generator and conducted into the jar through its metal rod.

Invented by the Dutch scientist Pieter van Musschenbroek of the University of Leiden, this device, an early type of **capacitor**, demonstrated that electricity could be stored. From this developed the idea of a battery, originally a group of Leyden jars combined to generate a more powerful electric charge.

In 1747, the powerful Persian overlord **Nader Shah** (b. 1688), who had become paranoid and mercilessly cruel, was **murdered** by his bodyguards. A grand assembly in Kandahar, Afghanistan, recognizing the

resulting weakness of the Persian Empire, elected Nader's Afghan lieutenant, **Ahmad Khan Abdali**, (also known as Ahmad Shah Durrani, 1722–73) as head and founder of the **modern state of Afghanistan**. Abdali was to unify the country under his rule and develop a large empire, including parts of present-day Iran, Pakistan, and India.

In West Africa, the **Yoruba** people, occupying territory from eastern present-day Benin to southern Nigeria, invaded the **Kingdom of Dahomey** in 1747. The kingdom was rich from trade in slaves and commodities such as palm oil, and was forced to pay tribute to the **Yoruba Empire of Oyo**, an arrangement that lasted until 1818.

1747 also saw a development that was to improve the lives of **sailors**. In a pioneering study, James Lind, a surgeon of the Royal Navy, proved that **scurvy**, a sometimes fatal disease common during long voyages, could be treated by eating **citrus fruit**. However, only in 1795 did the Royal Navy begin to use lemon juice to prevent and treat scurvy.

THE WAR OF THE AUSTRIAN SUCCESSION (see 1740) was concluded by the signing of the **Treaty of Aix-la-Chapelle** (present-day Aachen) in 1748. Prussia's conquest of Silesia was recognized, France regained some of its colonies in exchange for withdrawing from the Netherlands, and Britain's **Asiento** contract with Spain (see 1713) was renewed.

Nader Shah's lucrative **sacking of Delhi** (see 1739) became the incentive for a second attack, this time on the **Punjab** by Ahmad Khan Abdali (see 1747). His army of 12,000 horsemen was met in the **Battle of Manupur** by a defensive Mughal force of 60,000. Abdali's Afghans held their own until 1,000 of them were killed by an exploding gunpowder store; devastated, they fled. Meanwhile, a rising power in the south was the **Kingdom of Mysore** under the control of Hyder Ali (1720–82), father of the famous Tipu Sultan (1750–99). Under Hyder Ali, the Mysore Empire **seized territory** from the Marathas, Hyderabad, and neighboring kingdoms.

In **North America**, the British presence in Nova Scotia was consolidated with the establishment of **Halifax** in 1749; the area capital was transferred there from Annapolis Royal. In violation of a previous treaty, Lieutenant General **Edward Cornwallis** (1713–76) arrived with transport ships containing **2,500 settlers**, sparking a war in which the French and native Mi'kmaq

Unrefined platinum ore
Platinum was discovered in South America by Spanish conquerors. The name is derived from the Spanish term platina, *meaning "little silver."*

kept the British settlement constantly under attack.

In Pennsylvania, the **first Lutheran Synod** was founded in 1748 by Henry Melchior Mühlenburg (1711–87). German Lutherans had first arrived in Pennsylvania in 1683, but it was the creation of the Synod that **unified the Lutheran community**.

South America's gold and silver had long been valued in Europe, but it was not until 1748, with a report from Spanish explorer Antonio de Ulloa (1716–95), that the value of **South America's platinum** was realized. A dense, corrosion-resistant metal, it was mined in the Cordillera Occidental of **Colombia** and in central **Peru**.

Another Spaniard, Giacobbo Rodríguez Pereire (1715–80), made history in 1749 when he took a pupil to the Paris Academy of Sciences to demonstrate his new **sign language** for deafmutes in which the sign alphabet required the use of only one hand.

1747 French attack on **Fort St. David**, India, falls

October 1747 Ahmad Khan Abdali formally becomes head of **Afghanistan**

1747 British scientist William Watson demonstrates **electric circuit** using Leyden jar

March 11, 1748 Ahmad Khan Abdali defeated by Mughals at **Battle of Manupur**

October 18, 1748 European powers sign Treaty of **Aix-la-Chapelle**

April 27, 1749 First performance of German-British composer George Frederick Handel's *Music for the Royal Fireworks*

1747 Dutch scientist Pieter van Musschenbroek invents **Leyden jar**

June 10, 1747 Nader Shah of **Persia** (b. 1688) murdered by bodyguards

1747 Yoruba invade Kingdom of **Dahomey** in West Africa

August 16, 1748 First **Lutheran Synod** of Pennsylvania formed

June 21, 1749 Edward Cornwallis establishes **Halifax**, Nova Scotia

THE AGE OF
REVOLUTION

José I of Portugal's coat of arms on the ceiling of Coimbra University.

A detail from engraver William Hogarth's 1751 work *Gin Lane* depicts the public drunkenness and social problems caused by cheap gin.

This Buddha statue is in the Sulamani Pahto temple in Bagan, Burma, which was built in 1181 but contains images and frescos from the Konbaung period.

THE COLONIAL BOUNDARY BETWEEN SPAIN AND PORTUGAL in the New World was settled by the **Treaty of Madrid**, signed on 13 January, which significantly amended the **Treaty of Tordesillas** (1494). The previous agreement stipulated that the Portuguese empire extend no further than 370 leagues west of the Azores (around 46 degrees west), but the new treaty took into account the extent of Portuguese settlement in Brazil. Spain hoped that by allowing Portugal some concessions it would discourage any further Portuguese territorial expansion in the region.

MARQUIS OF POMBAL
(1699–1782)

The Marquis of Pombal was a controversial political figure, appointed prime minister of Portugal in 1750, the year José I (1714–77) took the throne. His 27 years in power saw economic and social reform, and the expulsion of the Jesuits.

17

THE NUMBER OF **VOLUMES** OF THE ENCYCLOPÉDIE PUBLISHED BETWEEN 1751 AND 1765

ENGLAND WAS EXPERIENCING AN ALCOHOL CRISIS, fuelled by the popularity of cheap gin, as illustrated by the darkly satirical engraving *Gin Lane* by **William Hogarth** (1697–1764), issued in 1751. Gin production had been refined over the previous 50 years, and the spirit proved hugely popular – by the year Hogarth's print was completed, the British were drinking more than two gallons of gin per capita a year. Public outcry over the social effects of gin led to the Gin Act of 1751, which attempted to limit the amount that could be bought.

In France, intellectuals led by the writer and philosopher **Denis Diderot** (1713–84) began the publication of the *Encyclopédie, ou dictionnaire raisonné des sciences, des arts et des métiers*. Known as the **Encyclopédie**, it became one of the defining works of the

Enlightenment (see 1763). Many influential French thinkers – such as **Montesquieu** (1689–1755), **Jean-Jacques Rousseau** (1712–78), and **Voltaire** (1694–1778) – contributed to tens of thousands of articles in the work, which attempted to catalogue the depths of human knowledge in science, philosophy, politics, and religion. With its emphasis on reason, the volumes were banned in some countries, such as Spain, where the **Catholic Inquisition** objected to its content.

Halfway across the world, China was extending its power in the **Dzungaria and Tarim basin** by fighting the Mongolian tribes for control to this key part of the steppes. The basin's importance lay in its proximity to the **Silk Road** (see pages 100–01), the vital trade route between China and the West.

ROCOCO

This 18th-century painting on the ceiling of a Bavarian church exemplifies the work of the Rococo movement that dominated European decorative arts, architecture, painting, and sculpture. Rococo evolved out of Baroque (see 1626), but its details and flourishes were even more ornate and often playful. The period is often associated with French design during the reigns of Louis XV (r. 1715–54) and Louis XVI (r. 1774–92).

BURMA (MYANMAR) HAD LONG BEEN DIVIDED among warring factions until a chief, **Alaungpaya** (1714–60), began to unite the country through a series of military victories, and established the **Konbaung dynasty**. Not only did he have to bring disparate groups together, he also faced the challenge of troops from Britain and France, who were eager to gain territory in Burma and who were willing to arm Alaungpaya's enemies. But for the next seven years, Alaungpaya resisted both threats, and British and French troops were driven out. Under successive kings, the unified kingdom continued to become stronger, and over the following decades it went so far as to make incursions into Siam (Thailand).

In Britain, the public went to bed on 2 September and woke up on 14 September. The government

> ❝ ENERGY AND PERSISTENCE **CONQUER ALL THINGS.** ❞

Attributed to Benjamin Franklin, American inventor, politician, and diplomat

had made the decision to change from the **Julian calendar** to the **Gregorian** one, joining the other western European countries that had made the change hundreds of years before. This calendar was introduced in 1582 by Pope Gregory XIII, who chose to make the change when it became clear that the old Julian calendar put around 11 extra days between vernal equinoxes, making the celebration of Easter arrive earlier each year.

In British North America, scientific discoveries were making their own leap forward. Inventor, politician, and diplomat **Benjamin Franklin** (1706–90) invented the **lightning conductor**. Before the advent of Franklin's lightning rod, buildings were often destroyed by fires started by lightning. Franklin thought there was a relationship between lightning and **electricity** and was said to have flown a kite in a lightning storm to prove his theory. The rod, developed after this experiment, attracts lightning, which is conducted into the ground, bypassing the building and keeping it safe from a lightning strike.

January 13 Treaty of Madrid signed

The Sino-Tibetan War follows Tibetan anger and subsequent murder of Chinese people in Tibet

José I ascends to Portuguese throne, and the **Marquis de Pombal** becomes his prime minister

September 12 Britain captures **Arcot**, a turning point against the French in India in **Second Carnatic War**

Denis Diderot begins publication of *l'Encyclopédie*

William Hogarth's *Gin Lane* is completed

Benjamin Franklin invents the lightning rod

February 11 First **hospital** in the present-day US opened, in Pennsylvania

August The **Liberty Bell**, symbol of American independence, arrives in Philadelphia from foundry in London

September Britain adopts Gregorian calendar

1753

Based on the work of the botanist Carl Linnaeus, this botanical drawing of blackberries is by J. Miller.

BY THE TIME SIR HANS SLOANE (1660–1753), an Irish-born physician and collector, died, he had amassed 71,000 different objects, ranging from samples of flora and fauna from all over the world, to books and manuscripts about a wide range of subjects. Like other intellectuals and scientists across Europe, he was part of wider Enlightenment intellectual currents, and he had realized the scholarly value of his collection, which he bequeathed to Britain. In

exchange, he wanted a payment of £20,000 to his estate – well below the value of the collection. The English Parliament approved the deal and passed an act establishing the **British Museum**. Parts of the collection were put on public display a few years later.

Sloane's contemporaries across Europe were engaged in collecting and other scientific pursuits. In the same year, Swedish botanist **Carl Linnaeus** (1707–78) published his *Species Plantarum*, which classified more than 7,000 species of plants by putting each genus into a class and order, a system that is still used today.

Golden collection
Used for determining positions of stars, this gold astrolabe, was part of Hans Sloane's collection.

1754

This scene shows troops mounted on elephants during the Carnatic War.

THE SECOND CARNATIC WAR (1749–54) and the **French and Indian War** (1754–63) were both precursors to the larger **Seven Years' War** (1756–63). However, the theatre of these Anglo-French disputes was not Europe. The

```
INDIA
                        Hughli
              Chandernagar   Chinsura
       Surat  Diu · Daman      Calcutta
  Bassein    · Bombay
       Goa              · Vizagapatam
                         · Yanam
Cannanore ·            · Masulipatam
  Mahe ·              · Pulicat
Calicut ·            · Madras
        Cochin ·    · Pondicherry
                   · Karikal
                   · Nagapatam
                   · Jaffna
         Colombo · · Trincomale
           Galle · Matara
```

KEY
- ● Portuguese settlements
- ○ French settlements
- ● British settlements
- ○ Dutch settlements

Europe in India
By the mid-18th century, European powers held territories and established settlements in India.

French and Indian War
ranged from Virginia in the south to Nova Scotia in the north of North America. Battles of the **Second Carnatic War** took place in South India. The **Treaty of Pondicherry** temporarily halted tensions between France and Britain, whose troops were technically employed by corporations – the **East India companies**. The treaty recognized the British-backed Mohammad Ali as the new **Nawab of Carnatic**, which had been a key factor behind the dispute.

1755

A painting depicts the desperate search for survivors in Lisbon after the city was heavily damaged by an earthquake in November.

> I AM NOT SO **LOST IN LEXICOGRAPHY** AS TO FORGET THAT **WORDS** ARE THE DAUGHTERS OF EARTH. 🙶

Samuel Johnson, English writer, from the preface of his *Dictionary of the English Language*, 1755

AN EARTHQUAKE KILLED TENS OF THOUSANDS OF PEOPLE in Lisbon, Portugal, when it shook the city on the morning of 1 November. It was later estimated by scientists to be around an 8.7 magnitude event. Estimates of the number of deaths range from 10,000 to 100,000 in a population of 200,000. The earthquake also triggered a tsunami that destroyed settlements further south in the Algarve region. The disaster had a profound effect across Europe – **Voltaire** (1694–1778) was inspired to write his *Poème sur le désastre de Lisbonne* about the event, and German philosopher Immanuel Kant (1724–1804) wrote a series of essays about it. The **Marquis of Pombal** (see panel, left) immediately took action, making sure fires were put out and the dead were quickly buried. He then began the rebuilding of the city, including the construction of buildings meant to withstand another earthquake.

Earlier in the year, in England, the writer **Samuel Johnson** (1709–84) had completed the commission he had received for a *Dictionary of the English Language* from a syndicate of London printers. It took him eight years and six assistants to finish it. Although it was not the first English dictionary, it quickly became the most celebrated and authoritative. Some of its more notorious definitions include "patron: commonly a wretch who supports with insolence, and is paid with flattery" and "oats: a grain, which in England is generally given to horses, but in Scotland supports the people".

English by definition
This is the front cover of the first edition of Samuel Johnson's Dictionary of the English Language.

This detail taken from an engraving by Paul Revere depicts the British capture of the French fort in Louisbourg, Nova Scotia. The fort was built to protect France's interests in the region and became a target for the British when war was declared in 1756. The town was attacked by land and sea, falling to the British in 1758.

THE SEVEN YEARS' WAR (1756–63) was fought in theaters from India to North America to Europe, making it a truly global conflict. Its roots, however, were European. The earlier **War of Austrian Succession** (see 1740) left many territorial issues unresolved. **The Treaty of Aix-la-Chapelle** (1748) did not settle the dispute between **Prussia** and **Austria** over the province of **Silesia**, located in southeast Prussia and bordering Austria. At the same time, **British** and **French** tensions continued to simmer. Because of complicated

FREDERICK II (1712–86)

Known as "Frederick the Great," the Prussian King Frederick II ruled for 46 years. With his interest in culture and philosophy, Frederick's reign was marked by a liberal spirit. But it was his military prowess that earned Frederick II his reputation, as he transformed the small kingdom of Prussia into a European power.

alliances, these situations escalated into what became known as the Seven Years' War.

By 1756, some key incidents had made the battle lines clear. In April, **France invaded Minorca** in the Mediterranean, which Britain had taken from Spain in 1708. The French sent 15,000 troops to the island, where the British had only around 2,500. Britain formally declared war on France. The conflict brought in the **Electorate of Hanover**, in northwest Germany, which was willing to send the British extra troops.

Prussia's **Frederick II** (1712–86), meanwhile, was increasingly suspicious of the alliance between **France and Russia**. In May, his troops entered the **Electorate of**

Saxony, between Prussia and Russia. They outnumbered those in Saxony by more than 3:1, but Austria's leader, **Maria Theresa** (1717–80), was quick to send more troops. The war had begun.

Britain and Prussia formed an alliance against France, Russia, Austria, Sweden, Saxony, and eventually Spain. But each country was also pursuing its own interests: Britain wanted France

out of **India** and **North America**; Austria and Prussia both wanted Silesia. Russia wanted to curb Frederick II's growing powers and assist Austria and France.

The European conflict had been preceded by skirmishes in colonial territories: the British and French had been fighting in North America, as well as in India. **Anglo–French tensions** had spilled over into disputes with

local rulers in India, leading to an infamous incident—the **Black Hole of Calcutta**. The Nawab of Bengal, **Siraj-ud-Dawlah** (1733–57), who France supported, attacked the British in Calcutta and imprisoned many of them in a small cell in Fort William. Estimates of the captives range from 60 to 150. Overnight, between 40 and 123 of them died due to overcrowding and heat.

Men at arms
The sizes of the armies involved in the Seven Years' War are shown here. Although some of the important battles were at sea, most of the fighting was done by army soldiers.

RUSSIA	AUSTRIA	FRANCE	PRUSSIA	BRITAIN
333,000	201,000	200,000	145,000	90,000

The Seven Years' War
The battlefields of this conflict spanned the globe, stretching from Canada to India to Europe, making it the first global war. The colored crosses show the victors in the key battles.

Zorndorf 1758
Minden 1759
Krefeld 1758
Kolin 1757
Rossbach 1757
Quiberon Bay 1759
SWEDEN
BRITAIN
PRUSSIA
RUSSIAN EMPIRE
EUROPE
Bohemia
HOLY ROMAN EMPIRE
FRANCE
PORTUGAL
SPAIN
Minorca 1756
ASIA
AFRICA
INDIA
Wandiwash 1760
Pondicherry 1761
INDIAN OCEAN

Quebec 1759
NORTH AMERICA
NEW FRANCE
ATLANTIC OCEAN
Havana 1762
Cuba
Guadeloupe 1759
Martinique 1762
PACIFIC OCEAN
SOUTH AMERICA

KEY

- ✕ Britain
- ✕ Prussia
- ✕ Anglo–German alliance
- ✕ Austria
- ✕ France

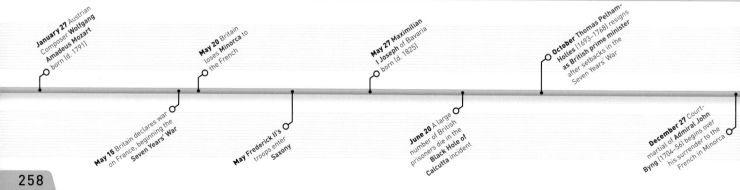

January 27 Austrian Composer **Wolfgang Amadeus Mozart** born (d. 1791)

May 15 Britain declares war on France, beginning the **Seven Years' War**

May 20 Britain loses Minorca to the French

May Frederick II's troops enter **Saxony**

May 27 Maximilian I Joseph of Bavaria born (d. 1825)

June 20 A large number of British prisoners die in the **Black Hole of Calcutta** incident

October Thomas Pelham-Holles (1693–1768) resigns as British prime minister after setbacks in the Seven Years' War

December 27 Court-martial of **Admiral John Byng** (1704–56) begins over his surrender to the French in Minorca

1757

Barbary pirates in an engagement with the Venetian navy.

1758

Frederick II leads his soldiers to victory at the Battle of Zorndorf.

1759

Spain's new king, Charles III, would rule for nearly 30 years. Luis Paret y Alcázar (1746–99) depicts palace life in his painting *Charles III Eating Before his Court*.

THE BRITISH-PRUSSIAN ALLIANCE (see 1756) received a number of boosts during 1757. **Robert Clive** (1725–74) recovered Calcutta for the East India Company (see 1600) in India and Britain by defeating the Nawab of Bengal at the **Battle of Plassey**. The Holy Roman Emperor **Francis I**—who was married to Austria's Maria Theresa—officially declared war on Prussia. **King Frederick II** then attacked Bohemia, though he was defeated by Austrian troops. Although Prussia defeated Austro-French forces in Rossbach in November, they lost to Austrian troops in Leuthan in December.

In Morocco, **Muhammad III** (c. 1710–90) brought stability to the country as sultan after 30 years of unrest. Muhammad was known for curbing the power of the **Barbary pirates**, who raided towns across the Mediterranean.

Robert Clive
Calcutta was recaptured for the British by Major General Robert Clive at the Battle of Plassey. The victory secured Clive's control over Bengal.

AS THE SEVEN YEARS' WAR CONTINUED, the British won key victories over France by taking **Fort Duquesne** and **Louisbourg** in North America and **Pondicherry** in India (see map, opposite), and by claiming **Senegal** in West Africa. In Europe, Britain and Prussia defeated the French near the banks of the Rhine at **Krefeld** in June and Russia at the battle of **Zorndorf**, on Prussian soil, in August.

Meanwhile, in India, warfare was breaking out on a different front—between Afghans and Marathas. Territorial disputes were behind the **Afghan–Maratha War** (which continued until 1861). After the death of **Nader Shah** (1688–1747), his Persian empire began to disintegrate and Afghanistan emerged independent under the rule of **Ahmad Shah Durrani** (c. 1722–73) who wanted to gain control of the nearby territories of the **Punjab** and the **Upper Ganges**. Durrani had sacked the Mughal city of **Delhi** the previous year. The neighboring Marathas, who felt they should rule over the territory, then went to war against the Afghans.

In the **Arabian Peninsula**, significant—though not violent— political change was taking place as the chieftains of the **Utub** confederation elected **Sabah bin Jaber (Sabah I)** (c. 1652–1762) emir of an emerging territory that would soon become known as **Kuwait**. His family, the al-Sabah dynasty, continues to rule Kuwait to the present day.

> ## ALL IS FOR THE BEST IN THE **BEST OF ALL** POSSIBLE WORLDS.

Voltaire, French writer, from *Candide*, 1759

FOR THE BRITISH, THE SEVEN YEARS' WAR reached a turning point. They took the French West Indian island of **Guadeloupe** in May, Canadian territory in July, and Quebec in September. They also defeated French naval forces off Portugal at **Lagos Bay** in August and at **Quiberon Bay**, in the west of France, in November. Anglo-Prussian troops defeated the French at the **Battle of Minden** in Germany in early August, although less than two weeks later Prussia faced a humiliating surrender at **Kunersdorf**, in

Germany, followed in November by further defeat by the Austrians in the **Battle of Maxen** in Saxony.

In Spain, the throne was taken by the Bourbon **Charles III** (1716–88), who would become known for his reforming zeal.

Portugal, meanwhile, had grown suspicious of the activities of the Catholic **Jesuit** order (see 1533), expelling it from its territories.

Cultural developments included the publication by the Frenchman **François Marie Arouet de Voltaire** of *Candide*, a satire about mindless optimism.

ABOLITIONISM

The image of a kneeling slave and the inscription "Am I not a man and a brother?" became a famous symbol of the British abolitionist movement and was later adopted by the American Anti-Slavery Society, founded in 1833. The seal was made by Josiah Wedgwood for the Society for Effecting the Abolition of the Slave Trade. After decades of pressure, the British slave trade ended in 1807. Abolitionist groups were also established in other countries involved in slavery, such as the French *Société des Amis des Noirs*.

Wedgwood pottery
Born into a family of English potters, Josiah Wedgwood transformed his craft with his style and technique. He set up his own business in 1759 and became potter to Queen Charlotte. His "creamware" dishes were hugely popular.

A caricature of George III and his wife Queen Charlotte. King George III was born in Britain, which he ruled for nearly 60 years.

Hyder Ali, the ruler of the Indian kingdom of Mysore, who became an enemy of British East India Company troops.

WHEN GEORGE III (1738–1820) TOOK THE THRONE OF ENGLAND in 1760, he was the first king from the German royal dynasty, the Hanoverians, to be born in Britain. Unlike his German-speaking grandfather, **George II** (1683–1760), English was his first language. The crown skipped a generation owing to the death of George's father, Frederick Lewis (1707–51). Before his death, he left instructions for the 12-year-old George to separate the Electorate of Hanover from England and reduce the national debt, when he took the throne.

After the death of his father, George fell under the influence of **John Stuart, Third Earl of Bute** (1713–92), who was his tutor and adviser. During the early years of George III's reign, Bute held much sway. This was especially evident in the souring of relations with **William Pitt the Elder** (1708–78) and the Newcastle–Pitt coalition, which governed Britain during the height of the **Seven Years' War**

Fleet size in the Seven Years' War
Many important battles were at sea, and British naval strength became even more superior to that of France.

KEY

	British Royal Navy	French Navy
●	battleships	battleships
○	cruisers	cruisers

Price of a male slave
As British Caribbean colonies began to increase sugar production, they had to bring in more African slaves as labor, as did the French.

(see 1756). Most significant in this period is George III's desire to have the war come to an end, as well as have Britain distance itself from Prussia. These wishes were made manifest when Bute became prime minster in 1762.

While George III was embroiled in British and European politics, his dominions in the **Caribbean** had undergone a transformation. They were no longer imperial outposts, but wealthy sugar colonies. However, these riches depended on the use of thousands of **African slaves** to work on the plantations. The population of British America had reached two million by 1760, and of this, more than 300,000 were slaves. Similarly, the slave population in France's Caribbean colonies would reach 379,000 by the end of the decade. In the Spanish sugar islands, however, Cuba had fewer than 40,000 slaves, but its sugar boom would come later.

The British island of **Jamaica** had become a large sugar producer and seen a rapid rise in the importation of slaves, many of whom ran away or rebelled. A rebellion took place on Easter Sunday in 1760, when a **revolt led by a slave** named Tacky began in St. Mary's parish. It spread from there, and some 30,000 slaves participated before it was suppressed the following year.

Meanwhile, in **Qing China**, the **ongoing revolts** in the northwest frontier by **Mongol tribes**, which started around 1755, had finally been suppressed. The conflict had begun after the Mongols refused to pay the annual tribute the Chinese government had demanded—indeed, the Mongols went so far as to kill the Chinese revenue collectors. However, China was eventually able to overpower the Mongols and bring their territory under their dominion by 1760.

AS THE SEVEN YEARS' WAR INTENSIFIED within Europe, it also reached a climax in the colonial possessions. The British effectively destroyed French power in India when they seized **Pondicherry** (see map, below). The port had been settled by the French East India Company in 1674 and had become one of France's main bases of operations for trade as well as ongoing fights against the British East India Company. This victory followed another one against the French the previous year in **Wandiwash**, in southeast India.

At the same time in India, the fighting between **Afghans and Marathas** (see 1758) came to a head in the battle of **Panipat**, in the north of the territory, on January 14. The battle was bloody, with high casualty rates—some 75,000 Marathas were killed and 30,000 captured. However, Ahmad Shah Durrani, who led the Afghans, was forced by his troops to return to the throne in Afghanistan. This outcome meant that the Marathas and British began to divide the former Mughal territory among themselves. The war contributed to the weakening of the Maratha Confederacy and the further decentralization of its power, leading to the breakup of its kingdoms and subsequent battles over territory with Britain.

Farther south, in **Mysore**, another future enemy of Britain, **Hyder Ali** (1720–82), was building up his army and consolidating his power base in order to take control of the territory.

Halfway across the world, British and French troops were fighting in the **Caribbean**. The British used the island of Guadeloupe, which they had captured two years earlier (see map, 1756), as a base from which to take Dominica from the French. The following year they stormed Martinique.

To complicate matters further, **Spain** had entered the conflict, and Britain's naval fleet was making preparations to attack Spanish ships. However, the attack plans would go beyond naval skirmishes, as British troops managed to not only invade and occupy the Cuban port of **Havana** the following year, they also used ships stationed in India to mount a similar attack on **Manila**, the capital of the Spanish colony of the Philippines.

Conflicts in India
India was the site of important battles in 1761, not only for Britain and France, but also in the fight between Marathas and Afghans.

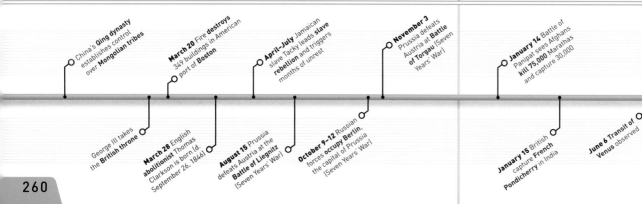

China's **Qing dynasty** establishes control over **Mongolian tribes**

March 20 Fire **destroys** 349 buildings in American port of **Boston**

April–July Jamaican slave Tacky leads **slave rebellion** and triggers months of unrest

November 3 Prussia defeats Austria at **Battle of Torgau** (Seven Years' War)

George III takes the **British throne**

March 28 English abolitionist Thomas Clarkson is born (d. September 26, 1846)

August 15 Prussia defeats Austria at the **Battle of Liegnitz** (Seven Years' War)

October 9–12 Russian forces **occupy Berlin**, the capital of Prussia (Seven Years' War)

January 14 Battle of Panipat sees Afghans **kill 75,000 Marathas** and capture 30,000

September 8 George III **marries** Charlotte of Mecklenburg-Strelitz

January 15 British capture French **Pondicherry** in India

June 6 Transit of Venus observed

Slavery abolished in mainland Portugal

1762

> **I SHALL BE AN AUTOCRAT, THAT'S MY TRADE; AND THE GOOD LORD WILL FORGIVE ME, THAT'S HIS.** "

Attributed to **Catherine the Great, Empress of Russia**

RUSSIA SAW THE ARRIVAL OF TWO RULERS over the course of 1762, first with the ascension of **Peter III** (1728–62) and later **Catherine II** (1729–96), who became known as Catherine the Great. When Peter III became emperor, he made clear his support of Prussia in the Seven Years' War and then pulled Russia out of the conflict. His views were deeply unpopular with ministers and the public. A conspiracy against him was quickly organized, leading to his arrest. His wife, Catherine, was installed as empress of Russia. Peter III was imprisoned, where he died in dubious circumstances. Catherine the Great's reign was marked by **Russian aggression and territorial expansion.** She introduced wide-ranging reforms in agriculture, industry, and education. She also relaxed Russia's censorship laws and was known for her love of literature and particular fondness for French philosophers and writers—including Voltaire, with whom she corresponded for 15 years.

As the Seven Years' War continued, **Spain** became further drawn into events as the British occupied its key Caribbean port of Havana. In addition to this, Britain was able to use troops in India to occupy Manila, in the Philippines, which was also a Spanish colony. At the same time, **Spain and France** entered a secret agreement known as the **Treaty of Fontainebleau.** Under the terms of the treaty, Spain received France's Louisiana territory in

Catherine the Great
The German-born empress of Russia, who reigned from 1762 until 1796, oversaw the territorial expansion of her adopted country.

North America, which stretched west of the Mississippi River. The treaty was partly to thank Spanish Bourbons for their support of French forces, and also to get rid of a potential drain on resources. Spain also benefited from the deal because it would block British expansion toward Spanish territory, especially nearby Mexico.

In France, the philosopher and writer **Jean-Jacques Rousseau** (1712–78) published his influential treatise, *The Social Contract* (*Du Contrat Social*) in which he examined the relationship between governments and the governed, and the question of freedom in the face of political authority. It was immediately banned by French authorities.

1763

A print of a fireworks display in London celebrating the Peace of Paris, which ended the Seven Years' War.

OUT OF MONEY AND EXHAUSTED, THE EUROPEAN POWERS fighting the Seven Years' War **brought the conflict to a close** with the Treaty of Paris (also known as the Peace of Paris) and the Treaty of Hubertusburg. The cost had been enormous—the lives of hundreds of thousands of soldiers, and mountains of money. Britain's national debt rose from £75 million to £133 million; Prussia raised taxes and debased the taler three times. For Austria it cost 392 million gulden (the original estimate was 28 million) and French national debt rose from 1,360 million livres in 1753 to 2,350 million livres in 1764.

The **Treaty of Paris** involved Britain, France, and Spain. The French faced the largest losses: they ceded to Britain their territories in present-day Canada, with the exception of the islands of St. Pierre and Miquelon; their territories in present-day US east of the Mississippi River; the Caribbean islands of Grenada, Dominica, St. Vincent and the Grenadines, and Tobago; Minorca in the Mediterranean; and Senegal in West Africa. They also formalized their cessation of the **Louisiana territory** to Spain. In exchange, Britain returned to France the valuable Caribbean sugar islands of Martinique and Guadeloupe; Belle Island, off the coast of Brittany; and the slave-trading island of Gorée in West Africa. France also regained its Indian factories, but they were not allowed to fortify them. The Spanish were forced to give their Florida territory to Britain, but in

exchange British troops left Havana and Manila. In Europe, France agreed to evacuate German territories.

Under the **Treaty of Hubertusburg,** the borders of 1756 were reinstated, so Austria retreated from Silesia and Prussia left Saxony, and Europe reverted to its former boundaries.

In the Ohio River valley territory, Pontiac (1720–69), a chief of the **Ottawa people,** was angered by the deal, which would put the land under British rule. In what became known as **Pontiac's Rebellion,** he led attacks against settlements, a situation that lasted until a deal between the Ottawa and British was reached in 1766.

1764

Wolfgang Amadeus Mozart, age 8, around the time he visited Britain.

IN AN ATTEMPT TO FILL THE COFFERS DEPLETED BY WAR, the British government brought in the **Sugar Act,** which clamped down on tax avoidance on imported molasses in North America, a move that angered traders and colonists.

At this time, the musical prodigy **Wolfgang Amadeus Mozart** (1756–91) was on a three-year tour of Europe with his family. He visited Munich, Brussels, Paris, and London, where his father Leopold presented him to play at the royal courts. While in London he met the German composer **Johann Christian Bach** (1735–82), who became an important musical mentor.

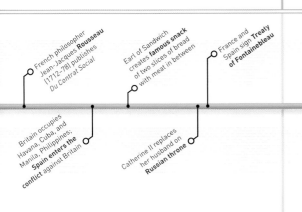

ENLIGHTENMENT IN EUROPE

The Enlightenment was a time of questioning many established beliefs in Europe—a change in ideas reflected in the writings and other cultural output from around the mid-18th century. It is also marked by scientific curiosity and advancement. This painting by Luke Howard (1772–1864) shows a fascination with weather that led him to classify and name many cloud types.

French philosopher Jean-Jacques **Rousseau** (1712–78) publishes *Du Contrat Social*

Earl of Sandwich creates **famous snack** of two slices of bread with meat in between

France and Spain sign **Treaty of Fontainebleau**

February 10 Treaty of Paris signed, ending **Seven Years' War**

February 15 Treaty of Hubertusburg signed, allowing **Prussia to keep Silesia**

Austrian musical prodigy **Wolfgang Amadeus Mozart** composes his first symphony

Britain occupies Havana, Cuba, and Manila, Philippines; **Spain enters the conflict against Britain**

Catherine II replaces her husband on **Russian throne**

Native American tribes led by Pontiac **rise up against British** soldiers and settlers

September 29 Sugar Act for British American colonies **taxes molasses** from non-British colonies

Jesuits **expelled** from French territories

EUROPEAN
NATION STATES

PLANNING PEACE FOR A CONTINENT AT WAR

Europe at the dawn of the 19th century bore little resemblance to the peaceful political unit of cooperative countries that it has become in the 21st century. Indeed, prior to 1815, the power balances and political alliances were constantly shifting, leading to near-continual confrontation.

The Napoleonic Wars had seen Europe in a cycle of almost constant conflict for more than a decade and left Europe in a state of imbalance. To address the questions of how to reorganize the war-ravaged continent, a congress was called at Vienna in 1814. Decisions were made on what to do with the new states that Napoleon had created, such as the Grand Duchy of Warsaw (see map below), and the regions of Germany, Italy, and the Low Countries that had been annexed to France. The peacemakers aimed to avoid a repetition of the conflicts that had

torn Europe apart and a spirit of conservatism and restoration prevailed—though not all deposed rulers were restored, and not all possessions lost in the Napoleonic Wars were regained.

The national boundaries resulting from the Treaty of Vienna in 1815 stayed in place for more than four decades. Fear of revolution led to a desire among Europe's statesmen to maintain the status quo. Although there were threats from liberal and nationalist elements, the Vienna system survived and disputes were largely settled by diplomacy.

NAPOLEONIC EMPIRE

When Napoleon became First Consul of France in 1799, he soon made clear his imperial ambitions by crowning himself emperor of France in 1804 and mounting military campaigns throughout Europe.

1815 The Congress of Vienna's reorganization of Europe led to the creation of the German Confederation. The growth of liberalism and nationalism in Europe saw uprisings across the continent but the Vienna system held firm until the revolutions of 1848.

KEY

🗡 Threat to Vienna system

--- Internal frontiers 1815

— German confederation

1812 Since coming to power in 1799, Napoleon had managed to extend France's power in Europe dramatically, controlling the Low Countries, parts of Germany and Italy, Spain, and Poland, although his attempts to encroach on Russia were met with a humiliating defeat in 1812.

KEY

French territory ruled directly from Paris 1812

Dependent state 1812

Population chart

Prussia	
England	
Habsburg Empire	
France	

| 0 | 10 | 20 | 30 | 40 |

POPULATION IN 1800 (MILLIONS)

At the beginning of Napoleon's rule, France had a far larger population than the surrounding states. This chart shows population figures c. 1800.

2,000,000 NATIVE FRENCH SOLDIERS 1804–15

1,000,000 CASUALTIES 1804–15

French forces

Over the course of the Napoleonic Wars, soldiers from all over the French Empire fought, and died, in Napoleon's army. At its height, it comprised nearly 600,000 men.

200

THE NUMBER OF **STATES** REPRESENTED AT THE **VIENNA CONGRESS**

Map labels (Napoleonic Empire map): ATLANTIC OCEAN, Edinburgh, North Sea, Stockholm, DENMARK, Copenhagen, SWEDEN, Baltic Sea, Riga, Dublin, BRITAIN, London, Hamburg, Tilsit, RUSSIAN EMPIRE, PRUSSIA, Berlin, Brussels, Hanover, GRAND DUCHY OF WARSAW, Paris, CONFEDERATION OF THE RHINE, Prague, FRENCH EMPIRE, Zurich, Munich, AUSTRIAN EMPIRE, Corunna, Bordeaux, Lyon, HELVETIA, KINGDOM OF ITALY, Vienna, SPAIN, Madrid, Toulouse, Marseille, CATALONIA, Rome, Belgrade, Sofia, ILLYRIAN PROVINCES, Lisbon, PORTUGAL, Gibraltar, Tangier, KINGDOM OF SARDINIA, Naples, KINGDOM OF NAPLES, Corfu, OTTOMAN EMPIRE, Mediterranean Sea, Palermo, Tunis, Athens, MALTA, KINGDOM OF SICILY, Crete

Map labels (right map): BRITAIN, SCOTLAND, Edinburgh, IRELAND, 1822–29: Catholic Emancipation campaign, Dublin, ENGLAND, 1830–32: First Reform Act crisis, WALES, 1840s: Chartist agitation, London, ATLANTIC OCEAN, revolution, Bay of Biscay, 1831: Vendean uprising, FRANCE, Bordeaux, 1820: revolution in Portugal against British control of country, Oporto, 1833–39: First Carlist War, ANDORRA, PORTUGAL, Lisbon, 1820: revolution Madrid, SPAIN, Barcelona, Balearic Islands, 1846–48: Second Carlist War, GIBRALTAR to Britain

NORWAY
1814: Denmark forced to cede Norway to Sweden

FINLAND
1808–09: Russia invades, then annexes Finland

SWEDEN

Helsingfors

Stockholm

St Petersburg

North Sea

Copenhagen

Baltic Sea

Riga

DENMARK

SCHLESWIG-HOLSTEIN

Bornholm

Amsterdam

Hamburg

Danzig

EAST PRUSSIA

RUSSIAN EMPIRE

UNITED NETHERLANDS

HANOVER
in personal union with Britain

1817–31: German student protests

Hanover

Posen

Berlin

PRUSSIA

Brussels

PRUSSIA

Cologne

SAXONY

Prague

Warsaw

POLAND

1830–31: national revolt

Brest-Litovsk

1831: Belgium gains independence from United Netherlands

BAVARIA

PRINCIPALITY

Stuttgart

WURTTEMBERG

Cracow

REP. OF CRACOW
1847: to Austria

1847: peasant uprising

GALICIA

NEUCHATEL

BADEN

BAVARIA

Munich

AUSTRIAN EMPIRE

Geneva

SWITZERLAND

Vienna

SARDINIA

Lyon

1821: Piedmontese revolution

Milan

Venice

LOMBARDY-VENETIA

Buda Pest

HUNGARY

MODLAVIA

MONACO

PARMA

ILLYRIAN KINGDOM

TRANSYLVANIA

Marseille

MODENA

MASSA AND CARRARA

SAN MARINO

1807–33: Serbian revolts

Belgrade

WALLACHIA

Bucharest

1821: revolts in Wallachia and Moldavia

LUCCA

TUSCANY

PAPAL STATES

BOSNIA

SERBIA

Corsica

MONTENEGRO

BULGARIA

RUMELIA

Rome

DALMATIA

OTTOMAN EMPIRE

1820: revolution

SARDINIA

Naples

ALBANIA

THRACE

Salonica

KINGDOM OF THE TWO SICILIES

1821: revolution

Palermo

Corfu
1815: to Britain

GREECE

Smyrna

Ionian Islands
1815: to Britain

Athens

1821–33: War of Independence

Malta
1800: to Britain

Mediterranean Sea

Crete

A RETURN TO WAR

Many of the ongoing tensions between countries that arose in the 19th century gained momentum in the 20th. The assassination of the Austrian archduke Franz Ferdinand by Serbian nationalists in 1914 sparked World War I, a global conflict that would reshape Europe.

ATLANTIC OCEAN

North Sea

Baltic Sea

Mediterranean Sea

1914 The Vienna system was swept away by the wave of nationalism that crossed Europe from the mid-19th century. Countries such as Italy and Germany were unified by the time Europe sat on the brink of war in 1914. However, at Versailles in 1919, the map would be redrawn yet again.

KEY

- German Empire
- Austro–Hungarian Empire
- Russian Empire
- Netherlands
- France
- United Kingdom
- Norway
- Spain
- Switzerland
- Sweden
- Belgium

- Montenegro
- Portugal
- Romania
- Italy
- Greece
- Ottoman Empire
- Albania
- Luxembourg
- Denmark
- Serbia
- Bulgaria

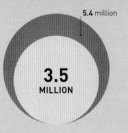

5.4 million

3.5 MILLION

13:6 **Rival populations**
The population of the Allied countries at the outset of World War I was more than double the population of the Central Powers.

KEY

Allied Powers: Russia, France, Britain, Belgium, and Serbia

Germany and Austria–Hungary

Troop numbers
The Allied Powers had far greater forces to mobilize in 1914 than the armies of the Central Powers.

> ❝ ANY **PLAN** CONCEIVED IN MODERATION **MUST FAIL** WHEN THE CIRCUMSTANCES ARE SET IN THE EXTREMES. ❞

Prince Klemens von Metternich (1773–1859), Austrian foreign minister

A cartoon about the Stamp Act shows the Treasury Secretary, George Grenville, with a child's coffin bearing the words "Miss Ame-Stamp, born in 1765, died 1766."

Jacobites toast Charles Stuart—"Bonnie Prince Charlie"—in Edinburgh. Many of his supporters were Scottish.

THIS YEAR WOULD BE ONE OF GROWING DISCONTENT with colonial rule within British and Spanish colonies in the Americas. In May, the residents of the Andean city of **Quito** (in today's Ecuador) protested against the imposition of a new system of tax administration aimed at increasing revenues for Spain's depleted treasury. The rioters drove out the royal officials, installing in their place a government that controlled the city until troops arrived a year later to reestablish royal control.

Farther to the north, Britain's American colonists were growing angry at similar revenue-raising exercises. Following the unpopular Sugar Act (see 1764) was the **Stamp Act**. This piece of legislation stipulated that all American colonists would have to pay a **tax on every piece of printed paper** they used. This meant that products from legal documents to newspapers and

playing cards would carry the duty. The colonists feared the tax represented a form of press censorship. They also resented the tax's introduction, not so much because of the cost, but because the Crown was beginning to look at internal American commerce and not just external trade for additional revenue, something not done before. In addition, Britain was imposing taxes without the consent of the colonists, who responded with **protests**, and the act was repealed the following year.

Meanwhile, in Lancashire, England, a weaver and carpenter named James Hargreaves (1720–78) had completed work on an invention known as the **spinning jenny**. The device was an improvement on the spinning wheel because it could power multiple spindles. Hargreaves supposedly came up with the idea for the device after observing a spinning wheel lying overturned

on the ground. He realised that by creating a machine that was horizontal, more spindles could be added. The spinning jenny enabled cloth production to increase by eightfold, and other inventors continued to modify Hargreave's design to make the machine even more efficient.

In Germany, **Joseph II** (1741–90) became Holy Roman Emperor and also co-ruler of the Habsburg family lands with his mother Maria Theresa until her death in 1780. Joseph later began a program of reform that included the emancipation of serfs and improvement of the education system, a reflection of the Enlightenment works he read. He was considered to be an "enlightened despot."

Dawn of the machine age
A woman working at a spinning jenny in an early 19th-century mill. James Hargreaves' invention revolutionized cloth production.

> **IF OUR TRADE** BE **TAXED,** WHY NOT OUR **LANDS,** OR **PRODUCE,** IN SHORT, EVERYTHING **WE POSSESS?…**

Samuel Adams, American politician, on the Sugar Act, 1764

JAMES FRANCIS EDWARD STUART DIED IN 1766 at the Palazzo Muti in Rome, having failed in his mission to be **restored to the British throne** as James III. His birth in 1688 had initiated the Glorious Revolution, forcing his father James II (1633–1701) to take his family to France to live in exile. At the heart of the matter was the Stuart faith: **Catholicism.** After the royal family had fled, the English Parliament passed the Act of Settlement of 1689, barring any Roman Catholics from succession to the throne. The Stuarts, however, had many supporters in England, Scotland, and Ireland. They were known as Jacobites after "Jacobus," the Latin for James.

Several attempts were made to return James III, or the "Old Pretender" as he became known, to the throne, the most notable being the risings of 1715 and 1745. All proved unsuccessful. Over the course of the Old Pretender's exile his son, **Charles Edward Stuart** (1720–88)— known as "Bonnie Prince Charlie" or the "Young Pretender"—also took up his father's fight, but to little avail. Charles never recovered from his defeat at the Battle of Culloden (the last clash of the 1745 rising—see 1744–47), although he made later efforts to secure support from France and the Holy Roman Empire for further uprisings. By the time the **Old Pretender died** and Charles became the official claimant to

Bonnie Prince Charlie's star and garter
The star and garter worn by Charles Stuart indicated he was the son of a legitimate sovereign. It was awarded while the family was in exile.

the Stuart throne, the battle that had consumed both their lives had been lost, though admiration for the cause continued.

In Denmark, **Christian VII** (1749–1808) **became king** shortly before his seventeenth birthday. Later that year, he married Caroline Matilda, one of the sisters of Britain's George III. His reign was marked by his **mental instability** and **debauchery.** During his early days of rule, the German doctor **Johann Freidrich Struensee** (1737–72) infiltrated the court and exercised much influence over the weak king, eventually enacting policy and having an affair with the queen. Struensee was finally arrested and executed. The later years of Christian's reign were in name only, and from 1784 his son, Frederick VI (1768–1839), acted as regent.

May 18 A serious **fire in Quebec** destroys one-quarter of the city

Mughal emperor grants *diwani* (right to collect revenue) to **Bengal,** establishing British control of the territory

December Burmese–China **War** (to 1769) begins when **China invades Burma** after Burmese troops enter Chinese territory

Stamp Act for British American colonies meets with protests

May 22 Riots in Quito start over imposition of a new tax system

August 18 Josef II (1741–90) becomes Holy Roman Emperor

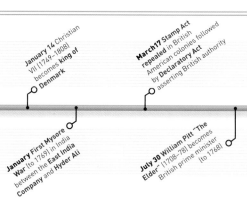

January 14 Christian VII (1749–1808) becomes **king of Denmark**

March 17 Stamp Act **repealed** in British American colonies followed by **Declaratory Act** asserting British authority

January First Mysore **War** (to 1769) in India between the **East India Company** and **Hyder Ali**

July 30 William Pitt "The Elder" (1708–78) becomes British prime minister (to 1768)

A depiction of the Jesuits being expelled from the kingdom of Spain.

Captain James Cook and his crew at the watering place in the Bay of Good Success, Tierra del Fuego.

Detail of the bell tower at the Mission of San Diego de Alcalá in California.

102 NEW SPAIN

78 PERU

42 NEW GRANADA

Jesuit settlements in the New World
The Society of Jesus was instrumental in the settlement of territory in the Americas and by 1767 had extensive missions.

LIKE THE PORTUGUESE NEARLY A DECADE EARLIER, the Spanish Crown grew concerned about the **Jesuits** and the order's activities in the American colonies. One of the underlying causes for concern had been Jesuit resistance to paying **tithes** to the Crown, and this reluctance was symptomatic of longer-running struggles between the order and the king. At issue was the Jesuits' **growing influence and wealth** in Spanish America through their schools, extensive landholding, and agricultural success. Claiming he was "moved by weighty reasons," Charles III decided to expel the Jesuits from his realm. This enabled the Crown to confiscate valuable Jesuit land and property. Thousands of the order's members fled to the Papal States and Corsica.

CAPTAIN JAMES COOK (1728–79) made his name in the Royal Navy with his excellent navigational skills and cartography of Canadian waters during the Seven Years' War (1756–63). These accomplishments paved the way for his next assignment—an expedition to the South Pacific. The mission was organized by the Royal Society, with the Admiralty providing the ship. The *Endeavour* set off from Plymouth on August 25 and arrived in Tahiti—via Madeira, Rio de Janeiro, and Cape Horn—on April 13, 1769. Cook then headed further south encountering the island later known as **New Zealand**. He eventually sailed from there to the unknown eastern coast of Australia where he landed in what became known as **Botany Bay**. The *Endeavour* returned to England in 1771 and Captain Cook's expedition was hailed a success.

The Endeavour
A model of the ship that took Captain James Cook to the Southern Hemisphere.

As Cook was sailing the Pacific, other changes were afoot in Britain. Reflecting the growing desire for knowledge (the Enlightenment), the first volume of the *Encyclopaedia Britannica*, was published in Edinburgh. It was "compiled upon a new plan in which the different Sciences and Arts are digested into distinct Treatises or Systems." It soon sold out and by 1771 a three-volume set was completed.

Meanwhile, in London, former soldier **Philip Astley** (1742–1814) opened a riding school in 1768 called **Halfpenny Hatch** based in Lambeth, where he performed tricks on horseback in a ring. He added musicians, acrobats, and clowns to provide entertainment during the interludes, and the **modern circus was born**.

In Russia, events had taken a serious turn. Tensions with the Ottoman Empire had pushed the two into the **Russo–Turkish War** of 1768–74. The root cause was Catherine the Great's refusal to comply with the treaty ending the previous war with the Ottomans (1736–39), as well as her interventions in Poland. The Ottomans declared war after Russia sacked a Turkish town.

Further east, **Prithvi Narayan Shah** (1723–75) brought together kingdoms in the Kathmandu Valley to create the kingdom of **Nepal**.

96
THE NUMBER OF **CREW** AND **CIVILIANS** WHO SET OFF **WITH CAPTAIN COOK**

THE SETTLEMENT OF NORTH AMERICA showed no sign of abating, though its inhabitants still knew very little about the vast western territory. In 1769, an American named **Daniel Boone** (1734–1820) set off for a hunting expedition in present-day Kentucky, an area virtually unknown to white settlers. Along the way he worked out a better route along the Cumberland Gap, a plateau in the Appalachian mountains. This became part of the Wilderness Road, a trail blazed by Boone and the Transylvania Company, and later used by settlers to cross the mountains and reach the Kentucky territory. Boone and his family moved to Kentucky in 1775 and established one of the first towns, Boonesborough. He spent the rest of his life working as a hunter and explorer.

The **Spanish**, too, were looking to expand their territory in North America. They had claimed a region in present-day southern California that **Charles III** was eager to populate with Spanish settlers after rumors that Russia was planning to move into the area. To this end he sent Franciscan friars to establish missions in the region. Spanish Franciscan **Junípero Serra** (1713–84) began work on a series of missions throughout Spain's California territory. The first one, established in 1769, was **San Diego de Alcalá**, and over the course of the next 54 years a chain of 20 further missions was built along the California coast.

Charles III **expels the Jesuits** from all Spanish territories

English geographer **James Rennell** (1742–1830) appointed Surveyor-General and begins survey of India

January 9 Soldier and equestrian Philip Astley stages **first modern circus** in Lambeth, London

Encyclopaedia Britannica begins publication in Edinburgh, with three-volume set on sale by 1771

Ali Bey al-Kabir (1728–73) deposes Ottoman governor in Egypt

August 25 English explorer James Cook (1728–79) begins his first Pacific voyage (to 1771)

September 25 Russian-Ottoman War (to 1774) begins over Russian advances into Poland and plans for Crimea

Kingdom of Nepal unified under Prithvi Narayan (1723–75)

Former English wigmaker **Richard Arkwright** (1732–92) invents **water-powered spinning frame**

Scottish inventor **James Watt** (1736–1819) patents **steam engine**

French East India Company dissolves

265

An engraving depicting the violence of the Boston Massacre.

The Cromford Mill set up by Richard Arkwright in Derbyshire.

An engraving showing the assassination of Gustavus III of Sweden (bottom), whose constitution and reforms angered the nobility and led to his death.

AFTER THE FAILURE OF THE STAMP ACT

AFTER THE FAILURE OF THE STAMP ACT (see 1765) the British government was still left with the question of how to raise money in the colonies. The answer came in a series of acts formulated by the Chancellor of the Exchequer, **Charles Townshend** (1725–67). The legislation included duties on paint, paper, glass, lead, and tea imported to the American colonies, as well as a reorganization of customs to cut down on smuggling. In addition, another act suspended the New York legislature because it refused to comply with the **Quartering Act**, which demanded that colonial assemblies provide basic necessities for British soldiers in the territories. On March 5, a group of dock workers began to

Marie Antoinette miniature
A cameo of Marie Antoinette, who would become one of the most infamous queens of France.

harass some British soldiers on patrol near a customs house in Boston, and a crowd formed. More soldiers arrived and opened fire on the colonists—the majority of whom were unarmed—killing five and wounding a further six. This episode became known as the **Boston Massacre** and fuelled resentment between Britain and its American colonies.

In Europe, the Dauphin of France, the future **Louis XVI** (1754–93), married the daughter of Maria Theresa of Austria, **Marie Antoinette**. They were 15 and 14 years old, respectively, at the time.

14

THE AGE AT WHICH MARIE ANTOINETTE MARRIED LOUIS XVI

THE BIRTH OF THE INDUSTRIAL REVOLUTION

THE BIRTH OF THE INDUSTRIAL REVOLUTION came a step closer when Englishman **Richard Arkwright** (1732–92) worked with clockmaker John Kay to develop a **spinning frame**. By 1771 they had decided to use a waterwheel to power it—hence the name "**water frame**"—and built a factory—Cromford Mill—in northern England, making this the first **water-powered textile mill**. The venture was a success and the textile factories became profitable, leading Arkwright to open a series of factories in Engand and Scotland.

Arkwright's inventions are considered an important part of the **Industrial Revolution**, which transformed Britain from an agricultural economy to a manufacturing one. The mills saw the development of the **mass-production** factory system which would be adopted all over the world.

INDUSTRIAL REVOLUTION

The Industrial Revolution was an economic transformation that took place in Europe during the late 18th and early 19th centuries, changing rural, agrarian economies to ones based on manufactured goods, which were often made in cities. This transformation began in England, and was facilitated by the arrival of inventions such as the spinning jenny (see 1765) and the use of steam power (see 1775), which led to the growth of industries such as textiles in cities like Manchester. New technologies soon spread throughout Europe, and other countries such as France, Germany, and Belgium were seeing similar economic shifts as agricultural workers left the countryside for jobs in growing urban centers, or to work in the coal mines that powered the urban factories.

Partition of Poland
Russia, Austria, and Prussia recieved parts of Poland in the first partition.

POLAND FACED

POLAND FACED the first of three **partitions** of its territory. This resulted from **Russia's defeats of the Ottoman Turks** in the Russo–Turkish War (see 1768), which had alarmed **Austria** and **Prussia.** Frederick II aimed to shift Russian expansion from Turkish territory to the Polish–Lithuanian Union, which was weakened by civil war. On August 5, Russia, Prussia, and Austria signed a **treaty**—ratified by the Polish legislature (Sejm)—depriving Poland of a third of its land, of which all three powers took a share.

In Sweden, **Gustavus III** (1746–92) took the throne, though the monarchy had been weakened by a government faction wishing to limit the Crown's power. In response, Gustavus staged a coup and issued a new constitution. He introduced judicial reforms and strengthened Sweden's navy. However, he was unpopular with the nobility, of whom he was critical, and was denounced for his expenditure of public funds. He was assassinated in 1792.

In England, a legal case was mounted over a slave, **James Somersett**, who had been brought from Jamaica to England in 1771 and was due to be sent back. The Lord Chief Justice, Lord Mansfield, ruled Somersett must be freed. This set a precedent that people could not be taken out of England against their will.

March 5 Five colonists killed in **Boston Massacre** anti-British riots

April 29 Captain Cook arrives at Botany Bay, Australia

Belgian inventor **John-Joseph Merlin** (1735–1803) develops forerunner of modern **wheelchair**

Richard Arkwright sets up the first **water-powered mill** in Derbyshire, England

February 12 Gustavus III (1746–92) of Sweden reestablishes absolute monarchy

June 22 The decision delivered in the trial known as **Somerset's case** leads to abolition of slavery within Britain

Captain Cook leaves on his second voyage, after a brief return to Britain

April 19 Marriage of France's **Louis XVI** (1754–93) to **Marie Antoinette** (1755–93)

July 5–7 Russians beat Turks at naval **Battle of Chesma**

July 12 English carpenter and weaver **James Hargreaves** (1720–78) patents the **spinning jenny**, which he invented in 1765

October 17 Mozart premieres his opera, *Ascanio in Alba*, aged 15

August 5 First **partition** of **Poland** by Austria, Prussia, and Russia

1773

A painting by Vasily Perov shows Cossack leader Emelyan Pugachev holding court and passing judgment on his enemies.

BRITAIN'S AMERICAN COLONISTS were becoming increasingly agitated by the number of restrictions being placed on them—even if some had unexpected benefits, such as a reduction in the price of tea. Indeed, because of the **Tea Act of 1773**, which allowed direct exportation from India to North America, as well as having it taxed at source rather than upon arrival, American colonists would pay less than anyone in Britain for their tea. However, there were many colonial merchants who dealt in smuggled tea and so faced ruin if legal tea became cheaper than

Boston Tea Party
Merchants dump chests of tea worth £10,000 from an East India Company ship into Boston harbor.

their contraband goods. They put pressure on East India ships to not dock in American ports. The *Dartmouth*, however, proceeded to anchor in Boston. On December 16, angry traders took 342 chests of tea worth £10,000 from the *Dartmouth* and tipped it into the city's harbor. This was heralded as a key moment of resistance to British governance.

Russia also was experiencing unrest, led by a Cossack called **Emelyan Pugachev** (1742–75). Pugachev served in the Seven Years' War, though he deserted in 1762. He traveled around Russia, claiming to be the deposed emperor Peter III, and promising to abolish serfdom. Through his travels he managed to rally about 25,000 willing troops. Despite early victories against Catherine

the Great's army, his troops were eventually overpowered. He was executed on January 10, 1775.

The Ottoman Empire was facing upheaval in Egypt. **Ali Bey al-Kabir** (1728–73) had been Egypt's de facto ruler, but in 1769 he deposed the Ottoman governor of Egypt and tried to make the country independent. He also sent troops into the territories of Palestine and Syria, but by 1773 he was defeated by Ottoman forces and died from his wounds while in prison in Cairo.

On his ship in the South Atlantic, Captain James Cook crossed the **Antarctic Circle**. He had set out on another mission the year before, in a ship called the *Resolution*, determined to explore the vast and unknown areas of the southern hemisphere.

1774

The funeral procession of Louis XV (1710–74), whose nickname had been "the well-beloved." Louis XV ruled France for almost 60 years.

IN THE AMERICAN COLONIES, representatives from each of the 13 colonies except Georgia met in Philadelphia to discuss what to do about a slew of legislation that became known as the **Intolerable Acts**. These acts were issued in retaliation for the dumping of tea in Boston harbor (see 1773) and growing American rebellion. They stipulated that Boston harbor must be closed to all but British ships; that the colonists must house British troops if necessary; that British officials would not be tried for crimes in the colonies but in Britain instead, allowing them to act with impunity; and self-government in Boston was to be stopped. Also included was the **Quebec Act**, which enlarged the boundaries of the Canadian province, permitted a degree of self-rule through a governor and appointed councillors, guaranteed religious freedom for the many Catholic settlers, and allowed the continuation of French civil law in conjunction with British criminal law. This act added insult to injury for many American settlers. They objected to the expansion of Quebec into territory they believed was theirs, and many were suspicious of the type of government that had been installed there. The **Continental Congress**—a group of delegates drawn from each of the thirteen colonies—decided to take action, and agreed to boycott British goods and trade, sending a strong message to the English king, George III.

Louis XVI
The king of France, Louis XVI, wearing his coronation robes. He came to power at just 17 years old.

In France, **Louis XVI** became the king at the age of 17 after the death of his grandfather, Louis XV.

Meanwhile, fighting between **Russia** and the **Ottoman Empire** came to an end. They signed the **Treaty of Kuchuk Kainarji** in July, which granted Russia the right of free navigation in the Black Sea and recognized the Crimean Peninsula as independent, meaning **Crimea** was free from Ottoman rule. The region soon aligned itself with Russia.

The Ottomans faced further disruption with the death in October of Sultan **Mustafa III** (1717–74), succeeded by his brother, **Abdul Hamid I** (r. 1774–89). When Mustafa became ruler, the empire was in decline, as earlier economic growth had faltered. The situation was exacerbated by the costly and disastrous war with Russia.

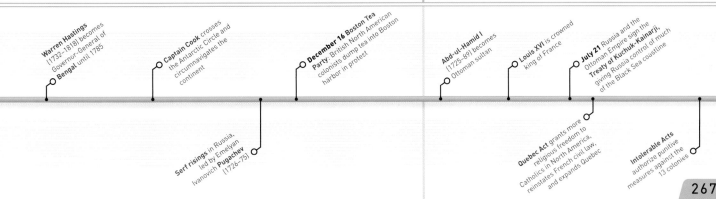

Warren Hastings (1732–1818) becomes Governor-General of Bengal until 1785

Captain Cook crosses the Antarctic Circle and circumnavigates the continent

December 16 Boston Tea Party: British North American colonists dump tea into Boston harbor in protest

Serf risings in Russia, led by Emelyan Ivanovich **Pugachev** (1726–75)

Abd-ul-Hamid I (1725–89) becomes Ottoman sultan

Louis XVI is crowned king of France

July 21 Russia and the Ottoman Empire sign the **Treaty of Kuchuk-Kainarji**, giving Russia control of much of the Black Sea coastline

Quebec Act grants more religious freedom to Catholics in North America, reinstates French civil law, and expands Quebec

Intolerable Acts authorize punitive measures against the 13 colonies

The opening shots of war between the British troops (in red) and the American colonial militia (in the foreground) on Lexington Common in Massachusetts, by English artist William Barnes Wollen (1857–1936).

THE ANGRY RECEPTION GIVEN TO LEGISLATION and discontent over the issue of **"taxation without representation"** in the 13 American colonies had begun to worry British officials and they feared an armed rebellion. On April 18, General Thomas Gage (1721–87), who was also Governor of Massachusetts, sent British soldiers (known as "redcoats") to seize the guns and ammunition being stored by the colonists in the town of Concord, just outside of Boston. Aware that the British might execute such a plan, the colonists had set up a system of alerts should any event come to pass. Once news was received of the planned raid on Concord, Boston silversmith and engraver **Paul Revere** (1735–1818) set off from the city that night to warn fellow organizers that British troops were on the march. Minutemen (militia who were ready to fight "at a minute's notice") grabbed their guns and waited for the arrival of the redcoats.

On the morning of April 19 the "shot heard around the world" was fired and battle ensued between colonists and British troops in **Lexington** and nearby **Concord**. The **American Revolutionary War** had begun.

Fighting continued through the summer. Colonial forces, under the command of **General George Washington** (1732–99) captured key points near **Lake Champlain**, but the British defeated them at the **Battle of Bunker Hill** on June 17, despite losing half their troops in the process.

Within the colonies the war was divisive. Not all colonists were willing to fight against Britain and soon people were divided into **patriots** and **loyalists**. Some 20 percent of the population of the 13 colonies were estimated to have supported the Crown. Within this number were **American Indians** and **slaves**. In the case of the former, some tribes sided with the British because they were valued trading partners. Many also thought their interests, such

spent steam escapes via smokestack

four-way valve controls admission and release of steam

Steam power
James Watt's work on steam engines allowed for the development of steam-powered trains.

Continental soldier's hat
This style of tricorne was worn by American colonists fighting for the Continental army.

as territorial boundaries, stood a better chance of being protected by Britain. For slaves, the incentive to side with the British Crown was the possibility of **emancipation**—they had been told they would be freed if they fought for the king. Some residents, such as the **Quakers**, opposed warfare. Many others simply wanted to avoid participation in either side of the conflict.

Halfway around the world, British East India Company troops were embroiled in the domestic troubles of the Marathas (see 1758). The **First Anglo-Maratha War** (1775–82) was the result of the East India Company's intervention into the Maratha Confederacy, a union of five clans that came to power after the collapse of the kingdom of Maharashtra. This war left many issues unresolved and tensions would rise again between the British and Marathas, leading to two further wars (see 1803).

In Britain, Scottish inventor and engineer **James Watt** (1736–1819) had struck up a business partnership with Matthew Boulton (1728–1809), who owned an engineering works. Watt had improved the **Newcomen steam engine**, which had been around since the turn of the century. He developed a separate condensing chamber for the engine, which made it lose less steam and be more efficient. In partnership with Boulton, Watt began to manufacture these engines in 1775. At this point steam engines were used mostly to pump water from mines, but Watt saw more potential uses for steam and continued working on engines for the rest of his life. His inventions allowed later engineers to revolutionize transportation and he thereby effectively laid the foundations of modern industry.

THOMAS PAINE

Thomas Paine (1737–1809) was born in Norfolk, England. He emigrated to America and advocated independence. He returned to England and wrote *Rights of Man*, defending the French Revolution, which cemented his reputation as a radical propagandist.

February 15 Pope Pius VI succeeds Pope Clement XVI

July 30 Captain Cook lands at Portsmouth, ending his second voyage

April 19 American Revolutionary War begins with battles in Lexington and Concord

First Maratha War (to 1782) between the Maratha Confederacy and British East India Company

November 7 Freedom is promised to male slaves who fight for the British in the American Revolutionary War

James Watt patents his steam engine

Ecstatic colonists tear down a statue of King George III in New York in celebration of the signing of the Declaration of Independence.

A colonial map of the city Colonia del Sacramento in Uruguay.

A view of the opulent interior of La Scala opera house in Milan.

A Xhosa family, from a painting by French naturalist Pierre Sonnerat.

> **WE HOLD THESE TRUTHS TO BE SELF-EVIDENT, THAT ALL MEN ARE CREATED EQUAL, THAT THEY ARE ENDOWED BY THEIR CREATOR WITH CERTAIN UNALIENABLE RIGHTS, THAT AMONG THESE ARE LIFE, LIBERTY AND THE PURSUIT OF HAPPINESS.**

US Declaration of Independence, July 4, 1776

AS THE AMERICAN REVOLUTIONARY WAR WAS GAINING MOMENTUM, on July 4 the **First** Continental Congress issued a **Declaration of Independence**, formally announcing the separation of the North American colonies from British rule and calling this collective the **United States**. The document outlined reasons for the decision to separate from Britain while asserting certain natural rights. The ideas put forth in this declaration—that all men were created equal and had the right to "life, liberty and the pursuit of happiness"—would not, however, apply to everyone. Enslaved Africans—some of whom had been fighting on the Americans' side—were excluded.

The year 1776 also witnessed the publication of many influential works. In January, the writer and radical thinker **Thomas Paine** (see panel, opposite), who had been living only a short time in Philadelphia, issued a pamphlet entitled *Common Sense*, calling for American independence and the establishment of a republican government. The pamphlet, initially published anonymously, was hugely influential both nationally and internationally and had a significant role in furthering the cause. In Britain, Scottish philosopher **Adam Smith** (1723–90) published *An Enquiry into the Nature and Causes of the Wealth of Nations*, which outlined the advantages of a system of free trade, changing the way politicians and the public thought about economic expansion.

Also in this year, the first volume of *The History of the Decline and Fall of the Roman Empire* by English historian **Edward Gibbon** (1737–94) was published. The work struck a chord and was a success. It was also noteworthy for Gibbon's methodology, which was objective and meticulous in its use of reference material, making it the yardstick for future historians. A further five volumes were published over the following decade.

IN BAVARIA, there was unrest over the succession to the throne. Elector **Maximilian III Joseph** (1727–77), last of the Wittelsbach line, died, and **Charles Theodore** (1724–99), Elector Palatine was crowned. Charles had no legitimate heir but several bastards for whom he sought land. He signed a treaty with Joseph II of Austria to cede Lower Bavaria to Austria in exchange for part of the Austrian Netherlands. This angered Frederick II of Prussia and in 1778, the **War of the Bavarian Succession** broke out, ending in 1779.

Spain and Portugal finally settled ongoing disputes in the **Río de la Plata** region with the **First Treaty of San Ildefonso**. Spain ceded territory in the Amazon basin in return for control over the Banda Oriental (in present-day Uruguay).

Charles Theodor
The Elector Palatine, Charles Theodore, had no legitimate heirs but he had several illegitimate ones. He proved an unpopular king.

Clubs used against Cook
Traditional Hawaiian clubs like these may have been used in the attack that caused James Cook's death.

WITH TWO SUCCESSFUL VOYAGES TO HIS NAME, Captain James Cook (see 1773) set out for a third in 1776, this time to search for the **Northwest Passage**, a fabled Arctic shortcut that was supposed to connect the Atlantic and Pacific Oceans. By 1778 he had made the first European contact with the **Hawaiian islands**. He continued on to the Arctic circle, but failed to find the passage. He later sailed back to Hawaii, where a dispute over a missing boat led to his being killed by Hawaiians in 1779.

In **Milan**, a grand opera house was opened **La Scala**. It was founded under the patronage of Maria Theresa of Austria (the city was under Austrian rule) to replace a theater that had been destroyed in a fire. The new theater was built on the site of the church of Santa Maria alla Scala and financed by wealthy patrons. It opened on August 3 with a performance of *L'Europa riconosciuta*, an **opera** by Antonio Salieri (1750–1825).

THE RELOCATION OF THE BOERS (Dutch-speaking settlers) to remote regions hundred of miles north of Cape Town was causing problems for the **Xhosa** people. These tribes had settled in the territory long before the Boers' arrival. Both groups were cattle farmers and competed for rich pasture land for their herds.

Attempts were made to establish a border between the **Fish and Sundays Rivers**, although both groups violated any agreement. Tension turned to violence, with the Xhosa raiding Boer cattle and murdering some herdsmen, possibly in retaliation for the death

Boer house
Dutch settlers in South Africa moved away from Cape Town, deep into rural areas where they raised livestock.

of a tribesman. The Boers then attacked and captured more than 5,000 head of cattle.

These skirmishes, amounting to the first **Xhosa War**, did not resolve the root cause of the dispute— access to grazing lands and water. Intermittent battle continued for almost a century.

A mural from Daria Daulat Bagh, the summer palace belonging to Tipu Sultan, ruler of the southwestern Indian kingdom of Mysore from 1782–99.

Lord Cornwallis, left, surrenders his sword to George Washington, right, after the British defeat at the Battle of Yorktown.

AS BRITAIN'S EAST INDIA COMPANY attempted to extend its reach outside of Bengal, it often met resistance from Indian princely states. This was especially true of the southwestern kingdom of Mysore, which was under the rule of the powerful **Haidar Ali Khan** (1722–82). Disputes over territory had led to the First Mysore War (1767–69), which was soon followed by the **Second Mysore War** (1780–84). The fighting did not completely settle the conflict between them, which continued until 1799.

Unrest in India was not the only military preoccupation for Britain, which was now fighting on many fronts. In addition to the ongoing war in North America, dispute broke out with the Dutch. The **Fourth Anglo–Dutch War** (1780–84), which saw no actual fighting, was a direct consequence of the conflict in America. The Dutch were supplying arms to the rebelling colonists, and a dispute erupted over Britain's seizure of Dutch ships. The

Dutch maintained Britain should respect their neutrality, but the British did not agree.

The North American colonists were not alone in their struggle, as their southern neighbors in Peru took up arms in the **Túpac Amaru revolt** (1780–82), which was prompted by dissatisfaction with the Spanish colonial regime. Some 75,000 Indians and Creoles (those born in Peru but of Spanish descent) rose up in protest at their treatment. The leader Túpac Amaru II (see box, below) was captured and killed in 1781, but it took another year and 60,000 Spanish troops to quell the unrest.

In Africa, the kingdom of **Buganda**, located on the northern shore of Lake Ukerewe (Lake Victoria), emerged as a regional power as it expanded its territory. Around the same time, the **Masai**, who occupied the southeastern side of the lake, were also becoming a significant presence in the region and were moving farther south and east—helped by their large, organized warrior class.

TUPAC AMARU II (c. 1742–81)

Born José Gabriel Condorcanqui in Cuzco, Peru, around 1742, Túpac Amaru II renamed himself after the last Inca leader, who ruled the Incan Empire from 1545–72. Of *mestizo* (Indian and Spanish) heritage, he fought against the colonial regime to gain better conditions for the indigenous population of Peru.

THE ONGOING WAR between Britain and North American colonists took a decisive turn at the battle of **Yorktown**, Virginia, on October 19. The **Continental Army** had received a boost from French support the previous year, and the **Comte de Rochambeau** (1725–1807) led troops alongside the American **General George Washington** (1732–99). Their combined force of ground soldiers meant that when rebel forces took

20 American
600 British
52 French

Deaths at the Battle of Yorktown
Yorktown took a high toll on British troops and proved decisive in the quest to end British rule in America.

their positions on September 28 **General Charles Cornwallis** (1738–1805) was outnumbered by more than two to one, and his reinforcements failed to arrive in time. That, along with a French naval blockade, gave Cornwallis no option but to surrender. Although this was the last major battle of the **Revolutionary War**, official recognition of American independence would not come until later.

The politics of the American colonies was changing. The **Articles of Confederation** had been ratified earlier in the year, on March 1. The process of ratification had started in 1777 under the **Second Continental Congress**. The agreement set up a "firm league of friendship" for what were to be known as the **United States of America**, while outlining what the responsibilities of the central government would be. The document would eventually be replaced with the US Constitution (see 1787).

In Europe, tensions between the Dutch and British led to a convoy of British ships setting off from India on August 9 with orders to destroy Dutch settlements in **Sumatra**. When the British arrived, the small Dutch population in the outposts surrendered immediately and all the Dutch factories and warehouses in **Padang** were turned over to the British crown.

Meanwhile, colonial subjects in the **Viceroyalty of New Granada**—which comprised present-day Colombia, Venezuela, Panama, and Ecuador—were discontent with the Spanish regime. They revolted over mounting taxes on tobacco and

American riflemen
This cartoon depicts an American rifleman as worn out and badly equipped. However, these soldiers defeated British regular troops.

alcohol in what became known as the **Comunero Rebellion**. Plans to march on Bogotá were abandoned after a deal was reached over taxes but the Spanish viceroy then attacked the *comuneros* and killed two of their leaders.

Revolution of an intellectual kind was taking place in Prussia with the publication of the *Critique of Pure Reason* by the philosopher **Immanuel Kant** (1724–1804). His work challenged existing notions about the nature of knowledge.

> **SCIENCE IS** ORGANIZED **KNOWLEDGE. WISDOM IS** ORGANIZED **LIFE.**

Immanuel Kant, German philosopher, from *Critique of Pure Reason*, 1781

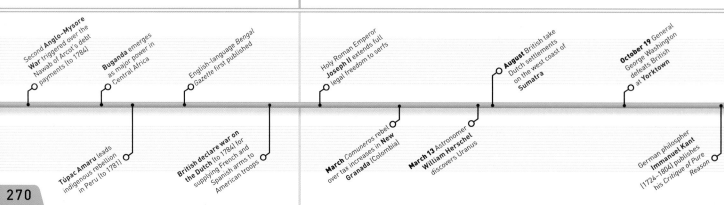

Second **Anglo–Mysore War** triggered over the Nawab of Arcot's debt payments (to 1784)

Buganda emerges as major power in Central Africa

English-language Bengal *Gazette* first published

Holy Roman Emperor **Joseph II** extends full legal freedom to serfs

August British take Dutch settlements on the west coast of **Sumatra**

October 19 General George Washington defeats British at **Yorktown**

Túpac Amaru leads indigenous rebellion in Peru (to 1781)

British declare war on the Dutch (to 1784) for supplying French and Spanish arms to American troops

March *Comuneros* rebel over tax increases in **New Granada** (Colombia)

March 13 Astronomer **William Herschel** discovers Uranus

German philospher **Immanuel Kant** (1724–1804) publishes his *Critique of Pure Reason*

Chakri Mahaprasad Hall in Bangkok was built under Rama I.

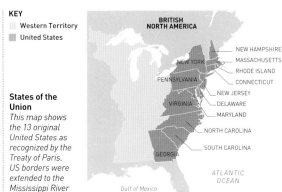

A bronze frieze depicts the signing of the Treaty of Paris in 1783, in which Britain recognized the independence of its former American colonies.

A cartoon depicts the political implications of the India Act.

WHILE THE VICTORIOUS FORMER COLONIES OF NORTH AMERICA entered into complicated and protracted negotiations with Britain over their official recognition and their future, **Ireland** found that it was also in a position to receive a **new political settlement** from the British government. The Declaratory Act of 1720 and Poynings' Law of 1494 were repealed. These laws had been designed to place Ireland under the rule of the English Parliament. With many of the restrictions in these Acts lifted, Ireland was able to establish some degree of **legislative independence**. Despite the new freedoms, however, political participation was only open to **Protestants**, and the unrest this arrangement eventually prompted in the largely Catholic territory meant that self-rule had a short life span.

In **Siam (Thailand)**, a new ruling dynasty was established—the **Chakri**—after a power struggle following the demise of the previous ruler, **King Taksin**, who had left no heir. The Chakri remains Thailand's ruling house. It was established by **Rama I** (1737–1809), who had been the chief commander in the army and had won loyal support fighting against the Burmese. Rama I spent much of his reign on the **reconstruction of Siam** after years of warfare, building extensively, including a royal palace and Buddhist temples, though he remained a strong military leader, and repelled five further invasions from Burma.

NEARLY TWO YEARS AFTER THE SURRENDER at Yorktown, the **Treaty of Paris**, which formally ended the **Revolutionary War**, was finally signed on September 3 between Britain and its former American colony, calling for them to "forget all past misunderstanding and differences." The document gave formal recognition to the United States and established the boundaries of the 13 states that it comprised. Although the settlement saw the establishment of the United States, there was still a significant European presence, with Spain holding large territories to the west.

Another treaty was signed between Britain, France, and Spain, in which Britain surrendered **Tobago** and **Senegal** to France and agreed to Spain

KEY

▢ Western Territory
▢ United States

States of the Union
This map shows the 13 original United States as recognized by the Treaty of Paris. US borders were extended to the Mississippi River under the treaty.

BRITISH NORTH AMERICA

- NEW HAMPSHIRE
- MASSACHUSETTS
- RHODE ISLAND
- CONNECTICUT
- NEW YORK
- PENNSYLVANIA
- NEW JERSEY
- DELAWARE
- VIRGINIA
- MARYLAND
- NORTH CAROLINA
- SOUTH CAROLINA
- GEORGIA

ATLANTIC OCEAN

Gulf of Mexico

retaining **Minorca**—which it had regained the year before—and its territories in **Florida**.

In a small village called Annonay, in the southeast of France, two brothers were about to make

aviation history. On June 4, **Joseph** (1740–1810) and **Etienne Montgolfier** (1745–99) had the first public trial of a **hot air balloon** officially recorded. Only a couple of months later, and after some design modifications, they gave a demonstration of their balloon in front of Louis XVI and Marie Antoinette at Versailles. In the September 19 flight—one of several flights made in 1783—they put a sheep, a duck, and a rooster in the balloon's basket to see how the animals would fare at a high altitude. The first manned free flight, when the balloon was not tethered to the ground, took place on November 21 of the same year.

Balloon ride
This engraving shows a later Montgolfier balloon, named Le Flesselles, ascending over Lyon with seven passengers, on January 19, 1784. One of those on board was Joseph Montgolfier.

BECAUSE THE BRITISH PRESENCE IN INDIA had evolved through the East India Company (EIC), the 18th century saw a growing tension between the EIC and the British government. The **India Act 1773** had already brought the company under tighter control, but its demands for government money to cover the cost of its many battles had prompted further action. The **India Act 1784**, which was ushered in under the government of British prime minister **William Pitt the Younger** (1759–1806), placed the EIC under even more scrutiny by establishing a Board of Control to look after civil, military, and

> ❝ EVERY **RUPEE** OF **PROFIT MADE** BY AN **ENGLISHMAN** IS **LOST** FOR EVER TO **INDIA.** ❞
>
> **Edmund Burke, British politician, on the East India Company, 1783**

financial affairs, which would include members of the British government. The Act also stipulated that trade and territorial rule were to be two separate activities. Legislation that followed in the 19th century went even further, abolishing the EIC's monopoly and opening up trade, as well as allowing the settlement of Christian missionaries in the region.

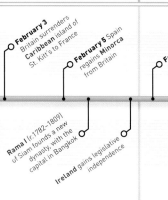

February 3 Britain surrenders **Caribbean island of St. Kitt's** to France

February 5 Spain regains **Minorca** from Britain

Rama I (r.1782–1809) of Siam founds a new dynasty, with the capital in Bangkok

Ireland gains legislative independence

February 5–March 28 Calabrian **earthquakes** in southern Italy wreak destruction and kill thousands

June 8 Laki volcano erupts in Iceland, causing widespread famine across Europe

September 3 Treaty of Paris signed, Britain recognizes **independent United States**

December William Pitt the Younger (1759–1806) becomes British prime minister (to 1801)

April 8 Russian Empire annexes **Crimea**

November 21 First manned **hot-air balloon flight** by Montgolfier brothers in Paris

Spanish crown authorizes a **botanical expedition** to South America

Pitt's **India Act** puts more government control on East India Company

British **Loyalist settlement** founded at New Brunswick, Canada

December 13 Samuel Johnson, English poet and essayist, dies (b. 1709)

The power loom transformed the textile industry.

Frederick II of Prussia was feared and admired throughout Europe for his military prowess.

This 19th-century engraving depicts the coastal settlement of Sierra Leone, West Africa.

IN 1784, EDMUND CARTWRIGHT (1743–1823), an English clergyman, paid a visit to a cotton-spinning mill established by Richard Arkwright (see 1771). What he saw inspired him to invent similar machines to weave textiles. By 1785 he had patented his first **power loom.** Cartwright's loom became an integral part of the textile industry in Britain. The design was later improved by the American businessman **Francis Cabot Lowell,** who had seen the looms in operation on a visit to Britain, and its use was widespread on both sides of the Atlantic after 1820.

In Burma, the Konbaung dynasty's **King Bodawpaya** (1745–1819) had captured the coastal kingdom of Arakan the previous year. Bolstered by this victory, he decided to move to the east and invade the kingdom of Siam (Thailand), but was defeated.

Round-the-world expedition
Jean-François de Galaup, the comte de Lapérouse, was sent by Louis XVI on an expedition to map out the uncharted waters of the Pacific.

THE US WAS EXPERIENCING AN ERA OF TECHNOLOGICAL innovation. In Philadelphia, Pennsylvania, inventor **John Fitch** (1743–1798) had set up the Steamboat Company with the aim of designing a steam-powered boat. Fitch found success ahead of his rivals in August 1787 when the **Perseverance** successfully sailed on the Delaware River. By 1790, a fledgling steamer service was running between Philadelphia and Trenton, New Jersey, but Fitch struggled as he had trouble attracting investors. It would take the more advanced boat designs and superior business acumen of **Robert Fulton** (1765–1815) before steamboat travel became a viable commercial enterprise.

First steamboat
John Fitch managed to take steam-engine technology and apply it to boats. However, commercial success was some way off.

Shipping still had its perils and **pirate** raids were common. US merchants wishing to trade in the Mediterranean markets risked attack and the **Barbary corsairs** were particularly feared. On July 23, the US signed a treaty with Morocco which assured safe passage for US ships in exchange for trading on equal terms.

In Europe, Prussia mourned the death of **Frederick II.** He had turned **Prussia** into a formidable power, and reshaped Europe's political balance.

> ❝ AN **EDUCATED PEOPLE** CAN BE **EASILY GOVERNED.** ❞

Attributed to Frederick II, king of Prussia

AFTER THE RULING IN THE SOMERSETT CASE (see 1772), which established that slaves who arrived in Britain were free, many slaves were abandoned by their masters and the "**black poor**" of London were left with no means of support. Abolitionist Granville Sharp (1735–1813) arranged for a free settlement to be established in **Sierra Leone,** West Africa. The ship *Nautilus* returned some 400 former slaves to Africa. These initial settlers were later joined by slaves from **Nova Scotia,** Canada, who had fought for the British in the American Revolutionary War. At the same time, West Africa was still rife with other European slavers.

In the US, there was a growing call for a stronger central government and, from May to September, the **Constitutional Convention** met, ostensibly in order to amend the Articles of Confederation (see 1781). But

Slave settlement
Sierra Leone is located on the west coast of Africa. Previously a trading post for slavery it became a place of settlement for freed slaves.

instead, the delegates drew up a new system of government. They created a **bicameral legislature** in which all states would be equally represented in the Senate and proportionally based on population in the House of Representatives.

In Russia, designs on Ottoman territory led to the **Russo–Turkish War,** lasting until 1792.

US CONSTITUTION

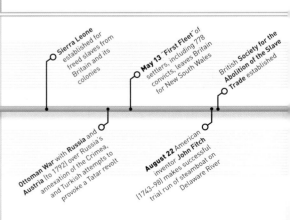

The US Constitution is the oldest written constitution in the world still in use. It was adopted on September 17, 1787 and has been amended 27 times to deal with issues such as freedom of speech. George Washington (left) led the Constitutional Convention and became the first US president in 1789. During his presidency, the first ten amendments, known as the Bill of Rights, were ratified.

Edmund Cartwright revolutionizes weaving with invention of the power loom

Lapérouse sets off on his voyage to **map the Pacific**

Burma's King Bodawpaya (1745–1819) invades Siam, triggering **Siamese–Burmese War** (to 1792)

Ottoman authority reasserted over Egypt

Marquess Cornwallis (1738–1793) becomes Governor-General of Bengal (to 1793)

August 11 Captain Francis Light takes control of **Penang** on Malay coast for British East India Company

August 17 **Frederick II,** king of Prussia, dies

Sierra Leone established for freed slaves from Britain and its colonies

Ottoman War with Russia and Austria (to 1792) over Russia's annexation of the Crimea, and Turkish attempts to provoke a Tatar revolt

May 13 "First Fleet" of settlers, including 778 convicts, leaves Britain for New South Wales

August 22 American inventor **John Fitch** (1743–98) makes successful trial run of steamboat on Delaware River

British **Society for the Abolition of the Slave Trade** established

35 MILLION PESOS
THE AMOUNT OF **MONEY SPAIN** RECEIVED ANNUALLY FROM ITS **COLONIES** AT THE TIME OF **CHARLES III'S DEATH**

A portrait of Charles IV (center right) and his family by Spanish painter Francisco Goya (1746–1828).

AFTER ALMOST 30 YEARS ON THE SPANISH THRONE, the "enlightened despot" Charles III died, and his son, **Charles IV** (1748–1819), inherited the crown. Unlike his father, Charles IV was not a strong leader. His wife, **Maria Luisa** of Parma (1751–1819), and her political protégé **Manuel de Godoy** (1767–1851), who eventually became prime minister, ran the country and the empire, leading it into disaster. This period was marked by **constant warfare with France**, culminating in an occupation in 1808, when Charles was forced to abdicate (see 1808).

In France, as in Britain, there was growing public support for the **abolition** of slavery. The Committee for the Abolition of the Slave Trade had been established in Britain in May 1787 with the aim of ending the slave trade. Shortly afterward, in February 1788, a group of Parisian men met to set

Arrival in Port Jackson
Colonists arrive in the bay that would later become Sydney, Australia. Native women are shown watching them on the shore.

up the **Société des Amis des Noirs** (Society of the Friends of the Blacks), which called not only for the abolition of the slave trade and slavery, but also urged equality for people of mixed race, the treatment of whom was a growing issue in the French Caribbean sugar colonies.

Meanwhile, in Sweden, **Gustav III** was trying to realize his imperial ambitions by declaring war against Russia without the approval of parliament. He hoped to capture **Finnish** territory while the **Russians** were occupied with their **war against Turkey.** Gustav's efforts failed initially due to a conspiracy by aristocrats and officers angry at the expansion of the Crown's power at the expense of the **Riksdag** (parliament) and the nobility. Officers attempted to negotiate with Catherine the Great of Russia without Gustav's prior knowledge. **Denmark** later joined the **Russo–Swedish War** (to1790) as an ally of Russia, and laid siege to the key port of Gothenburg, in the southwest of Sweden.

In the neighboring Habsburg Empire, the **Magyar** (Hungarian) nobles were unhappy about Joseph II's reforms (see 1765), in particular the introduction of German as the official language of government and secondary education. Joseph was also planning to restructure the land

First Fleet
Despite its reputation, only about half of those on the First Fleet were convicts. The remainder included marines, crew, and their families.

1,487
PEOPLE ON FIRST FLEET

778
CONVICTS

tax system, and had already abolished serfdom. By the time of his death in 1790, the Magyars were on the brink of a rebellion, and even appealed to Prussia to support them. However, their discontent did not escalate to armed conflict due to the intervention of Leopold II (1747–92), who succeeded his brother and promised to rescind the previous reforms. He swore to treat Hungary as an independent kingdom and allow for it to be administered under its own laws.

In Britain, Royal Navy Captain Arthur Phillip (1738–1814) had set sail on May 13, 1787 with 11 ships full of convicts destined for settlement at **Botany Bay** in Australia. Captain James Cook (see 1768) had first come across the bay in1770, and the British government was eager to settle the territory. At the same time, the shipping of convicts to Australia presented a way of relieving Britain's overcrowded prisons. Known as the **First Fleet**, these ships carried more than 1,400 people, with convicts making up 778 passengers. The fleet arrived in Botany Bay in 1788, but Phillip soon decided the site was not suitable for permanent settlement and the colony moved farther inland to Port Jackson, which would later become known as **Sydney**. Although the early days of settlement were difficult, a stream of ships continued to bring felons, and less than 50 years later there were nearly 60,000 settlers in Australia.

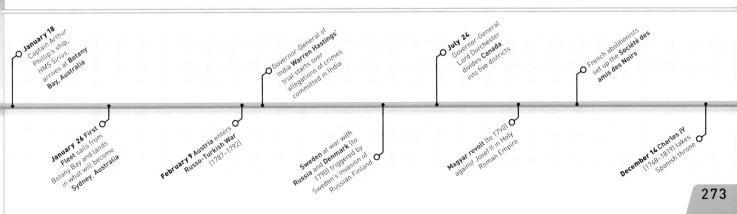

January 18 Captain Arthur Phillip's ship, *HMS Sirius,* arrives at **Botany Bay, Australia**

January 26 First Fleet sails from Botany Bay and lands in what will become **Sydney, Australia**

February 9 Austria enters **Russo-Turkish War** (1787–1792)

Governor-General of India **Warren Hastings'** trial starts over allegations of crimes committed in India

Sweden at war with **Russia** and **Denmark** (to 1790) triggered by Sweden's invasion of Russian Finland

July 24 Governor-General Lord Dorchester divides **Canada** into five districts

Magyar revolt (to 1790) against Josef II in Holy Roman Empire

French abolitionists set up the **Société des amis des Noirs**

December 14 Charles IV (1748–1819) takes Spanish throne

Beam engine

The engine developed by Thomas Newcomen and improved by James Watt works by the beam at the top rocking back and forth, which transfers power from a piston that moves up and down in a cylinder.

beam goes back and forth

connecting rod

large flywheel rotates

piston rod moves up and down

steam condensed in cylinder

crankshaft connects to piston

1679
The first boiler
French inventor Denis Papin designs a device that can convert liquid to vapor, making it the first pressure cooker.

Papin's steam digester

1698
The high-pressure steam engine
In England, Thomas Savery uses steam power to create "The Miner's Friend" to pump water out of coal mines, although it was not a success.

1765
James Watt's engine
Scottish inventor James Watt makes improvements to the Newcomen engine by adding a condenser, and develops an engine that rotates a shaft instead of pumping.

1801–04
Trevithick's engine
English mine engineer Richard Trevithick develops a smaller, lighter steam engine and puts it on wheels, creating a "road locomotive."

1st century CE
Hero's engine
The Greek scientist Hero describes an aeolipile, which has a rotating ball that is spun by jets of steam.

The Hero engine

1712
Newcomen's engine
Thomas Savery joins forces with Thomas Newcomen and they create the much-improved atmospheric steam pumping engine.

Newcomen's atmospheric engine

1769–70
The steam car
In France, Nicholas Cugot invents a road vehicle that can run on steam by converting it into piston action and rotary motion.

1802–07
The steamboat
In the US, Robert Fulton applies steam power to a passenger boat, and it proves a success in sailing against currents.

THE STORY OF
STEAM POWER
HOW WATER VAPOR WAS UTILIZED TO DRIVE THE INDUSTRIAL REVOLUTION

Although the power of steam was not harnessed until the 17th century, scientists had understood its potential for hundreds of years. As far back as the 1st century CE, the Greek scientist Hero of Alexandria had discussed a device—the aeolipile—that illustrated the possibilities of water vapor.

The aeolipile worked by heating water in a mounted sphere that had two bent nozzles. When steam was released through the nozzles, the sphere would rotate. Although it had no practical use at the time, this was the first indication of experiments with steam power. More dramatic developments took place in the 17th century, when the first boiler was invented. Although it was little more than a pressure cooker, from this point onward, a steady stream of innovations followed.

POWERING INDUSTRY

By the 18th century, engineers had realized how steam-powered devices could be used to pump water out of mines—an important issue in light of the growing demand for coal in Europe during the Industrial Revolution. Scientists soon realized that steam could also be used to power engines. Thomas Newcomen had invented a steam engine in 1712, but it was the improvements made by James Watt that made the device more efficient. Watt's key innovation consisted of condensing steam, so that the engine did not need to heat and cool the cylinder, making it far more efficient. Soon, steam power was being used to fuel ships and locomotives, enabling them to travel farther and faster. By the 19th century, it was being used to produce electricity, something that continues to the present day, using much of the technology developed over the preceding centuries.

Richard Trevithick
In addition to developing the world's first steam railroad locomotive, the English engineer Richard Trevithick also adapted his high-pressure engine for use in iron mills and steam-powered barges.

> ❝ IN THE WHOLE HISTORY OF **TECHNOLOGY** IT WOULD BE DIFFICULT TO FIND **A GREATER SINGLE ADVANCE** THAN THIS. ❞

L. T. C. Rolt, English writer and engineer, *Thomas Newcomen: The Prehistory of Steam*, 1963

Savannah steamship

1819
Crossing the Atlantic
The US vessel *Savannah* becomes the first ship to cross the Atlantic using steam power as well as sails. The era of sails ends soon after.

1867
The water-tube boiler
In the US, George Babcock and Stephen Wilcox invent the water-tube boiler, in which water circulates in tubes. It is used to make electricity in 1882.

Babcock and Wilcox steam boiler

Early 20th century
Geothermal power
Scientists in Lardarello, Italy, discover "geothermal," or "dry steam," energy and build the first power station of its kind in 1911.

Geothermal power station

Stephenson's "Rocket"

1829
Stephenson's "Rocket"
English engineer Robert Stephenson applies steam power to locomotives, and his "Rocket" becomes a commercial success.

1884–97
The steam turbine
Sir Charles Algernon Parsons develops a steam turbine generator, which produces huge amounts of electricity. It is used to power large ships, such as the *Titanic*.

The *Titanic* powered by Parson's steam turbine

20th century
Steam turbines and nuclear power
Controlled nuclear chain reactions create heat in reactors, which boils water to produce steam and drive a steam turbine in order to produce electricity.

" LIBERTÉ, EGALITÉ, FRATERNITÉ! "

Liberty, Equality, Fraternity!
Rallying cry of the French Revolution, 1789

Representatives of France's "Third Estate"—the people—swore the "Tennis Court Oath" not to separate until they had established a constitution in France.

BY 1789, FRANCE'S LOUIS XVI was facing multiple crises: he was bankrupt from endless warfare, there was popular unrest, and the failure of the 1788 grain crop meant riots over bread. The decision was made to summon the **Estates-General**, France's representative assembly. It had not met since 1614, so between January and April elections were held to select deputies. The Estates-General was composed of three "estates" or orders: the

The three estates
These figures (from left to right) symbolize each of the estates representing France: the nobility, the people, and the clergy.

First Estate (the clergy); the Second Estate (the nobility); and the **Third Estate—the people**. The assembly met at Versailles on May 5. The immediate issue was how much voting power to give the Third Estate; the First and Second Estates wanted voting to be by estate rather than a vote per head, so that they would not be outnumbered by the public's representatives. By June 17 the

frustrated Third Estate declared itself a **National Assembly** and decided to proceed without the nobles and clergy. This prompted officials to lock them out of their usual meeting place, so they occupied Louis XVI's indoor tennis court and swore an oath on June 20 to remain united until they produced a constitution for France, a pledge that became known as the **Tennis Court Oath**. All but one of the 577 deputies signed; Joseph Martin Dauch from Castelnaudary refused to endorse it because it was not sanctioned by the king.

Louis XVI felt he had no option but to give in to the demands of the Third Estate and urged the nobility and clergy to join when by, July 9, was named the **National Constituent Assembly** (though it continued to be called the National Assembly).

A few days later, Paris was awash with rumors, including that troops were on their way into the city to disperse the National Assembly. In response, on the afternoon of July 14, some 600 people armed with weapons seized from the Hôtel des Invalides attacked the **Bastille**, a medieval fortress used as a prison. The Bastille held only seven prisoners at the time of the attack, but it symbolized the despotism of the monarchy and contained ammunition the people wanted to seize. The uprising, in which a whole garrison and 98 attackers died, became a defining moment of the **French Revolution**, which was now underway.

600

THE NUMBER OF **PEOPLE** WHO **STORMED** THE **BASTILLE**

Storming of the Bastille
The crowd of around 600 people that gathered outside the prison calling for its surrender was peaceful at first, but violence soon broke out.

During late July and early August, rumors spread throughout the French countryside, which was already in a state of unrest due to grain shortages. There were fears of bandits sweeping the land and stories of crops being burned. During this period, known as the **Great Fear**, panic set in among many peasants, who armed themselves and attacked nobles and their châteaux.

By August 4, the National Constituent Assembly sought to control the situation and so decreed the **abolition of feudalism** and the tithe. This was followed on August 26 by the publication of the *Declaration of the Rights of Man and of the Citizen*, which proclaimed that "men are **born free** and **remain free** and equal in rights" and that "the source of all sovereignty lies essentially in the Nation."

Throughout this period of upheaval, uncensored newspapers reported events and **political clubs** formed where people could voice their opinions. Despite the onslaught of new freedoms and monumental social reform, the Revolution was in its infancy— France's future was far from clear.

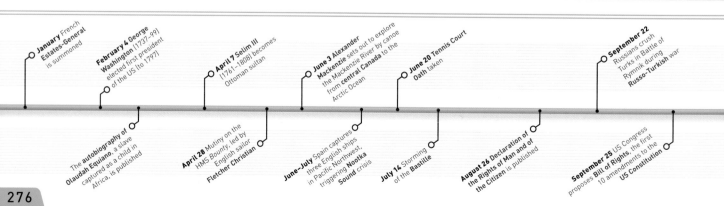

January French Estates-General is summoned

February 4 George Washington (1737–99) elected first president of the US (to 1797)

The **autobiography of Olaudah Equiano**, a slave captured as a child in Africa, is published

April 7 Selim III (1761–1808) becomes Ottoman sultan

April 28 Mutiny on the HMS *Bounty*, led by English sailor **Fletcher Christian**

June 3 Alexander Mackenzie sets out to explore the Mackenzie River by canoe from **central Canada** to the Arctic Ocean

June–July Spain captures three English ships in Pacific Northwest, triggering **Nootka Sound** crisis

June 20 Tennis Court Oath taken

July 14 Storming of the Bastille

August 26 Declaration of the Rights of Man and of the Citizen is published

September 22 Russians crush Turks in Battle of Rymnik during **Russo-Turkish war**

September 25 US Congress proposes **Bill of Rights**, the first 10 amendments to the US Constitution

General Josiah Harmar met with defeat when he mounted a campaign against a coalition of American Indians in the Northwest Territory.

Plantations go up in flames in Le Cap in the north of Saint-Domingue (Haiti) during the slave rebellion.

NEWS OF THE EVENTS IN PARIS spread to French colonies. As the National Assembly knew, **slavery** did not sit well with the ideas espoused in the *Declaration of the Rights of Man*. Neither did the inequity that **free people of color** faced in France and its empire.

Part of the French Empire was Saint-Domingue (Haiti), half of the island of Hispaniola—the other half of the island, Santo Domingo (Dominican Republic), belonged to Spain. In 1790, two wealthy mixed-race planters from Saint-Domingue, **Vincent Ogé** (1750–91) and **Julien Raimond** (1744–1801), were in Paris, where they argued that because they were property owners, they ought to be given full rights. Ogé was frustrated by the Assembly's failure to confront white planters on this issue and continued his protest back in Saint-Domingue. He led a **revolt** of some 200 supporters in the town of Grande-Rivière. It was quickly suppressed, and Ogé fled to Santo Domingo.

Throughout 1790, the National Assembly continued working on a **constitution**, pushing through the official ban on the nobility and suppressing the **religious orders**.

Revolutionary cartoon
This illustration shows a version of the French Revolutionary emblem issuing the famous call for liberty, equality, and fraternity or death.

In the US, General Josiah Harmar (1753–1813) had been ambushed by a coalition of American Indians. The attack near the Maumee River (Ohio) in the **Northwest Territory** was led by **Chief Little Turtle** (1752–1812). Harmar was ordered to lead an expedition against the Indians, but his force of 1,100 militiamen and 320 troops was forced to **retreat**.

> ❝ MEN ARE BORN AND REMAIN **FREE** AND **IN EQUAL RIGHTS. SOCIAL DISTINCTIONS** MAY BE FOUNDED ONLY UPON THE **GENERAL GOOD.** ❞

Article 1, *Declaration of the Rights of Man and of the Citizen*, 1789

IN JANUARY, VINCENT OGÉ and **Jean-Baptiste Chavannes** (*c.* 1748–1791), who had helped Ogé organize the 1790 revolt, were in hiding in the Spanish colony, Santo Domingo. They were, however, returned by the Spanish to Saint-Domingue, where their bones were broken on a wheel and their **heads placed on stakes**. This was met with outrage in France, and by May political rights were granted to free people of color, if born of two free parents.

Slaves in Saint-Domingue had also been hearing a mixture of news and rumors about events in Paris and begun to hope they would see abolition. In the end, they decided not to wait for France to grant it to them.

One hot August evening, a slave leader named **Dutty Boukman** (?–1791) gathered slaves at a religious voodoo ceremony in Bois-Caïman and told them to "listen to the voice of liberty that

500,000
SLAVES

30,000
Settlers

Slaves vs. settlers
The high number of slaves imported to Saint-Domingue to work in the sugar industry became a liability when they launched a rebellion.

speaks in all of us." A week later, Boukman and his followers launched a **massive revolt** in the north of the island. They attacked estates, killed slave owners, destroyed tools, and torched cane fields. They had numbers on their side: the slave population in Saint-Domingue was more than

15 times the population of whites. Unlike previous revolts, this one would prove **unstoppable**.

In France, Louis XVI and his family had tried to **flee** to the royalist stronghold of Montmédy on the eastern border. They reached **Varennes**, in the northeast of the country, before being stopped and forcibly returned to Paris. After this failed attempt at escape, Louis lost all credibility as a monarch.

Haitian revolution
The slave revolt in French Saint-Domingue later become an international conflict when Britain and Spain went to war with France.

KEY
■ 1791: original center of the slave revolt
— 1790: border between Saint Domingue (French) and Santo Domingo (Spanish)
— 1820: border between the Republic of Haiti and Santo Domingo (Spanish)

Map labels: Tortuga, Port-de-Paix, Le Cap, Fort Liberté (Fort Dauphin), ATLANTIC OCEAN, Santiago, San Francisco de Macorís, SAINT DOMINGUE, SANTO DOMINGO, Gonâve, Hispaniola, Jérémie, Port-au-Prince, Santo Domingo, Cayes, Caribbean Sea

VOODOO AND SAINT-DOMINGUE

Haitian Voodoo (or Voudou) is a religion that was born out of slavery. It draws on a range of African traditions, especially those of Benin, the former home of many slaves. It also incorporates Catholicism, the religion forced on the slaves by their captors, and may also have links to the practices of the indigenous Arawak people. The Catholic practices slaves adopted enabled them to disguise their true religion from their masters, with Catholic saints standing in for *Loa* (spirits) worshiped in Voodoo. This new system of belief allowed slaves to form their own identity and also provided a way of organizing resistance, as in Saint-Domingue.

Leopold II (1746–92) becomes emperor of the Holy Roman Empire

August 14 Russo-Swedish War ends with Treaty of Värälä

March 2 Semaphore telegraph demonstrated in France

June 21 Louis XVI and the royal family attempt to flee Paris

The Constitutional Act **splits Canada** into Upper and Lower Canada

September 30 Premiere of Mozart's opera *The Magic Flute* in Vienna

Third Anglo-Mysore War (to 1792) leads to the defeat of Tipu Sultan (1750–99)

October Vincent Ogé and Jean-Baptiste Chavannes lead first **revolt** in France's **Saint-Domingue**

The monumental **Brandenburg Gate** in Berlin is finished

August 20 Danish navigator **Vitus Jonas Bering** discovers Alaska

August 21 Large-scale slave uprising begins in **Saint-Domingue**

December 5 Austrian composer **Wolfgang Amadeus Mozart** (b. 1756) dies

A detail from the painting *Battle of Valmy*, by French artist Emile-Jean-Horace Vernet, shows Prussia's defeat by France.

This image shows the execution of Louis XVI by guillotine in the Place de la Révolution, Paris. His wife Marie Antionette was executed a few months later.

EVENTS IN FRANCE TOOK A DRAMATIC TURN on April 20, 1792 when the National Assembly declared war on the Holy Roman Empire, perceiving it as a threat. Emperor Leopold II had signed the **Declaration of Pilnitz** with Frederick William II of Prussia, swearing to defend Louis XVI and destroy Paris should anything befall him. Provoked by the French call to war, Austrian and Prussian troops set off for France.

News of this enraged the French people, who thought they had been betrayed by their king and the aristocracy, and on August 10 a group of revolutionaries found **Louis XVI** when they stormed the **Tuileries Palace**. The king and the rest of the royal family were **jailed in the Temple** prison.

By early September, fears that royalist prisoners were organizing a counter-revolutionary plot were growing, and on September 2 an armed group of Parisians attacked and killed some prisoners who were being transferred to a different jail. This set off a wave of action, known as the **September Massacres**, in which angry mobs in Paris and elsewhere took suspects from prison and executed them. Around **1,200** people were killed in five days.

The war began with setbacks for France, but by September 20, the French successfully held off the Prussians at the **Battle of Valmy**, in northeastern France, then attacked the Austrian Netherlands winning a victory at **Jemappes** in what is now Belgium. In Paris, a new ruling body, the **National Convention**, met and the following day abolished the constitutional monarchy in favor of establishing a **republic**.

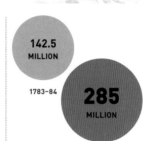

142.5 MILLION

1783–84

285 MILLION

1792–93

Tea export
The British public's taste for tea became evident, as the pounds of tea the East India Company exported from China doubled.

By this point the rest of Europe was concerned about events within France and its boldness beyond its borders, so Holland, Spain, Austria, Prussia, and Russia established the **First Coalition**, with Britain joining in 1793. They fought against France throughout the following six years during the **War of the First Coalition**.

Meanwhile, halfway across the world, the East India Company had found that supplying the British with **Chinese tea**—for which they were paying China in opium produced in Bengal—was proving a profitable trade. Exports doubled in a decade as the hot drink became popular in Britain and North America. Conducting business with China, however, was complicated for the Company. It was only allowed commercial access through one port, **Canton** (Guangzhou), as the Chinese kept strict controls on the entry of foreigners to the rest of the country.

ON JANUARY 18, THE NATIONAL CONVENTION OF FRANCE condemned Louis XVI to death. On January 21 he was taken to the Place de la Révolution, Paris, where he was guillotined. His wife, **Marie Antoinette**, remained in prison until October, when she appeared before a Revolutionary tribunal. She met the same fate as her husband on October 16.

Marie Antoinette's death occurred during the **Reign of Terror**, which was the result of a decree on September 5 that made "terror" the means of governance. A couple of weeks later the **Law** of Suspects was passed, which established **Revolutionary Tribunals**. Anyone suspected of being an enemy of the Revolution was tried and if deemed guilty received a death sentence. The activities of hundreds of thousands of people were monitored, and many were arrested. The **Committee of Public Safety**, led by **Maximilien**

Eli Whitney's cotton gin
This machine separated cotton seeds from the plant's fiber more quickly than if done by hand, which increased cotton production greatly.

MARY WOLLSTONECRAFT (1759–97)

Mary Wollstonecraft was an English writer and early advocate for women's rights. Deeply influenced by events in France and subsequent debates in Britain, she published, *A Vindication on the Rights of Woman*, in 1792. The work, calling for the education system to allow girls the same advantages as boys, was controversial. It would be many years before any changes were enacted, but the book has endured as a work of early feminist philosophy.

March 16 Attempted assassination of **Gustavus III** of Sweden, who dies from his wounds on March (b. 1746)

April 20 War of the First Coalition (to 1797): France declares war on Holy Roman Empire, Prussia, and Piedmont

April 25 French national anthem, **La Marseillaise**, composed by Claude-Joseph Rouget de Lisle

September 21 France abolishes monarchy and declares itself a republic

English writer **Mary Wollstonecraft** (1759–1797) publishes *A Vindication of the Rights of Woman*

September Léger-Félicité Sonthonax arrives to Saint-Domingue to quell slave rebellion

Denmark abolishes the slave trade

January 21 Louis XVI is executed

January 23 Second partition of **Poland**

February Second Nootka Convention signed by **Britain and Spain**

France declares war on Britain, the Dutch Republic, and Spain; Britain enters fighting in **Saint-Domingue**

"MY PEOPLE, I DIE INNOCENT!"

Louis XVI of France, before his execution

This detail from a fresco depicts the battle of Raclawice on April 4, 1794, when Polish troops led by General Tadeusz Kosciuszko defeated the Russians.

Robespierre (1758–94), was, in effect, in control of the government. Members of the same political club as Robespierre—the **Jacobins**—also become involved in the surveillance of potential suspects.

In **Saint-Domingue (Haiti)**, fighting on the island was complicated by the arrival of **British troops**. Prompted by the French declaration of war in 1792, Britain hoped to seize control of the island and add it to their other Caribbean sugar islands, such as Jamaica. The struggle lasted for five years.

In the US, **Eli Whitney** (1765–1825) perfected a machine called the **cotton gin**, which he patented the following year. Many planters wanted to diversify into the cotton trade, but the long-staple variety of cotton grown—which yields long, silky fibers—could only be cultivated near the coast. Heavily seeded **short-staple** cotton—producing shorter fibers—was the only other option, but removing the seeds was a laborious and time-consuming task. Whitney's machine, however, combed cotton very quickly, and it led to the development of the cotton industry in the American South.

Back in Europe, **Poland** faced a **second partition**, this time with Prussia and Russia taking some 115,000 square miles (300,000 sq km), leaving Poland a fraction of its former size. Poland ceded eastern provinces from Livonia to Moldavia to Russia, while Prussia was given Great Poland, Torun, and the port city of Gdansk.

17,000

THE NUMBER OF **PEOPLE EXECUTED** DURING **"THE TERROR"**

Britain and Spain averted a war over the **Nootka Sound** in the Pacific, northwest of the American territory, by signing the Second Nootka Sound Convention. Another agreement was signed the following year in which Spain capitulated to British demands. The diplomatic standoff—which eventually involved the European allies of both sides—had started in 1789 when Spain seized three British ships sailing nearby. This escalated into a battle of words over who had **the right to settle** in that territory.

In China, East India Company officer George Macartney (1737–1806) had arrived in Beijing (Peking) in 1792 with a party of 94 people and a range of British goods. He was finally presented to the emperor Quinlong (1735–99) in September 1793. The British government and the East India Company were eager to expand trade between Britain and China, but Qing officials were not interested and they refused to negotiate a treaty.

THE REIGN OF TERROR in France eliminated the enemies of the Committee of Public Safety on the left and right by 1794. However, the committee felt the need to go further and suspended a suspect's right to public trial and legal assistance, with juries instructed to issue either acquittal or death. This measure was passed in June, but little more than a month later a revolt in the National Convention ended the reign of Robespierre. Known as the **Thermidorian Reaction**, it refers to 9 Thermidor Year II (July 27, 1794), the date in the French Revolutionary Calendar. This change to the calendar system began in 1792 and lasted until 1806. The calendar began on the year of the anniversary of the

Maximilien Robespierre
The head of the Committee of Public Safety tried to eliminate his enemies, but he ended up dying on the guillotine.

Revolutionary coin
The French king Louis XVI was replaced on the country's coinage by the figure of Hercules, flanked by Liberty and Equality.

proclamation of the Republic (September 21, also the autumn equinox). Each month was 30 days long, and was divided into "decades" of 10 days.

On July 27, Robespierre was arrested and he and another 100 supporters faced the same **guillotine** used on their enemies.

This was a turning point in the French Revolution, as the National Convention asserted its strength, but the Terror had exacted a high price—some 17,000 people were officially executed and hundreds of thousands arrested.

In Saint-Domingue, the former slave turned military leader, General **Toussaint Louverture**, was persuaded to leave the Spanish and join French Commissioner **Léger-Félicité Sonthonax** (1763–1813) to lead French Republican troops—though he later broke with the French (see 1803). Sonthonax was posted to Saint-Domingue in 1792 to keep the island under control after the slave rebellion, and to enforce the National Convention's ruling that free people of color were to have equality. However, France's declaration of war against Britain had complicated the situation, and Spain and Britain fought alongside the former slaves. This prompted Sonthonax to look to existing slaves as possible troops. In 1793 he promised slaves in the north of the island **freedom** if they fought for the French cause, and by that August he decreed the **abolition of slavery**, ratified by the National Convention on February 4, 1794.

Meanwhile, in **Poland**, anger had mounted over the devastating partition the previous year, and patriots organized the **Polish Rebellion of 1794**. Despite an initial victory in Russian-held Warsaw, the Poles were crushed by Russia's forces.

"I WAS **BORN** A **SLAVE,** BUT **NATURE GAVE** ME A **SOUL** OF A **FREE MAN...**"

Toussaint Louverture, former slave and military leader

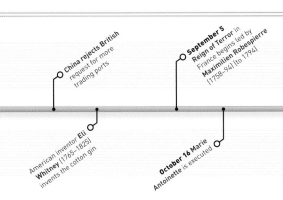

China rejects British request for more trading ports

American inventor **Eli Whitney** (1765–1825) invents the cotton gin

September 5 Reign of Terror in France begins led by **Maximilien Robespierre** (1758–94) (to 1794)

October 16 Marie Antoinette is executed

January 11 Third Nootka Convention between Britain and Spain ends dispute over Pacific Northwest

February 4 France abolishes slavery

March 24 Polish uprising begins against Russia and Prussia over partitions

June 26 First use of aircraft in battle when French use **observation balloon** in battle of Fleurus against Austrians

July 28 Maximilien Robespierre executed

Start of Qajar **dynasty** in Persia

A view of the island of Penang, north of the Dutch settlement of Malacca. The Strait of Malacca remains a key trade route linking Europe and Africa to China.

One of a series of portraits depicting the Persian Shah's family and harem. It was commissioned by Fat'h Ali Shah, the second Qajar ruler.

A painting of Marquis Wellesley viewing an elephant fight.

THE SECOND PARTITION OF POLAND had sparked an uprising in 1794 led by Polish officer Tadeusz Kościuszko (1746–1817). After eight months of fighting, a Prussian–Russian alliance defeated the Poles, and the **Third Partition** of 1795 occurred. This saw the remaining Polish territory divided among Russia, Prussia, and Austria. After this final partition, Poland ceased to exist.

Elsewhere in Europe, the War of the First Coalition was drawing to a close, negotiated partially with three treaties under the **Peace of Basel**. These agreements gave German lands west of the Rhine River to France, and ended Franco–Spanish fighting around the Pyrenees mountains through Spain's cessation of Santo Domingo to France. This meant the French now had control of

Maroon colony, Jamaica
This engraving shows a maroon settlement in Jamaica. Maroons were former runaway slaves who had established their own autonomy.

300,000

THE NUMBER OF **NEWSPAPERS SOLD EACH DAY** IN **REVOLUTIONARY FRANCE** AROUND **1795**

the whole island of Hispaniola, although the fighting that had begun in Saint-Domingue showed few signs of abating.

In **Jamaica**, the peace that had been established in 1739 between the British and former runaway slaves, known as **maroons** (from the Spanish word for runaways, *cimarrón*) ended. Maroons had initially invaded and raided colonists but, on signing a treaty that granted them land and autonomy, had largely desisted. However, in 1795, an incident in which the British severely whipped two maroons for stealing pigs triggered a revolt. Fearful that the island could follow the example of Saint-Domingue, the governor brought in troops to suppress it. Upon surrender, some maroons were shipped to **Nova Scotia**.

Farther afield, the Dutch-controlled **Cape of Good Hope** in South Africa and the port of **Malacca** in the Strait of Malacca, which connects the Indian and Pacific Oceans, were seized by the British.

OVER A YEAR AFTER SETTING OUT to find the Niger River, **Mungo Park** (1771–1806), a Scottish surgeon and explorer, finally located it. He had been sent on the expedition by the Association for Promoting the Discovery of the Interior Parts of Africa, in order to "ascertain the course" of this large African river. He embarked from the River Gambia in 1795, and on July 20, after prolonged illness and four months spent captive, he reached Ségou (in present-day Mali), which lies on the river.

The first documented inoculation was completed by British physician **Edward Jenner** (1749–1823) on May 14. In an attempt to prevent the deadly **smallpox** virus, which had killed thousands across Europe, Jenner experimented by using **cowpox**, a similar but less lethal virus often contracted by milking infected animals. His experiment entailed inoculating eight-year-old James Phipps with cowpox taken from Sarah Nelmes, a dairymaid. The early success of this experiment led to the development of the **modern vaccine**.

In Europe, French army commander **Napoleon Bonaparte** (see panel, right) took charge of the French army in northern Italy in March. He was given orders to seize Lombardy, and went on to win many victories over the Austrian army, subsequently forcing Austria into peace negotiations. The result was the **Treaty of Campo Formio**, signed the following year, in which

Austria recognized the French puppet state, the Cisalpine Republic, and ceded the Austrian Netherlands (Belgium) to France.

In **Persia**, a new dynasty—the **Qajar**—was established. The leader, **Agha Mohammad Khan** (1742–97), had spent the past decade attempting to unite disparate factions in the region, eventually asserting his authority over territory as far as Georgia in the Caucasus mountains. He declared himself shah (king) in 1796, but died the next year. His family continued to rule until 1925.

Farther east, China was in the throes of a rebellion. The **White Lotus**, a secret Buddhist sect, sought to overthrow their **Manchu** rulers and restore the previous ruling dynasty, the **Ming**. The White Lotus attracted much support, but ultimately failed after eight years of fighting.

A PERIOD OF AGGRESSIVE EXPANSION of Britain's territorial claims in Bengal began when Irish nobleman Richard Wellesley (1760–1842) was appointed **Governor-General of Bengal** in 1797. He left for Calcutta in November and set about increasing British territory through both military and diplomatic channels.

During his term as governor (1797–1805), some of the most powerful rulers in India were defeated—including Tipu Sultan, who was known as the Tiger of Mysore (see 1761 and 1799). This period also saw efforts to professionalize the East India Company. These included setting up a **college** in order to teach junior clerks subjects such as Indian languages, though some of these measures were considered controversial at the time.

NAPOLEON BONAPARTE (1769–1821)

Napoleon Bonaparte was born in Corsica and educated in France, where he became an army officer in 1785. His successful campaign in Italy (1796–97) was followed by further military and political victories. In 1804, he was declared emperor and led France on to more battles, though with diminishing success, draining the nation's resources and ultimately leading to his downfall. He died in exile on the remote island of St. Helena, in the South Atlantic.

January 19 French conquer the Dutch and establish the **Batavian Republic** (until 1806)

August Second Maroon War in Jamaica between runaway slave community and the British

May 14 English scientist **Edward Jenner** (1749–1823) tests smallpox vaccine

July 20 Mungo Park is first European to reach the Niger River

White Lotus rebellion in China (to 1804) attempts to restore Ming dynasty

January 31 German composer **Franz Schubert** born (d. 1828)

Third partition of **Poland**

War of the First Coalition ends with **Peace of Basel** treaties

September 16 Dutch territory in the **Cape of Good Hope** seized by the British

France's **Napoleon Bonaparte** (1749–1821) begins Italian Campaign (to 1797) in the French Revolutionary Wars

August 19 Treaty of San Ildefonso joins Spain and France against Britain (French Revolutionary Wars)

November 17 Catherine the Great (b. 1729) dies and is succeeded by Paul I

East India Company takes Sri Lanka (**Ceylon**) from the Dutch

March 4 John Adams becomes second US president

November 16 Frederick William III (1770–1840) becomes king of Prussia (to 1840)

This painting shows the destruction of the French flagship *L'Orient* during the Battle of the Nile, Egypt, where Britain's Royal Navy destroyed France's fleet.

> **" THE REVOLUTION IS OVER. I AM THE REVOLUTION. "**
>
> Napoleon Bonaparte, 1799

DESPITE THE TERMINATION OF the War of the First Coalition in 1795, France still considered Britain an enemy. The French mooted the idea of a possible **invasion**, but it was ultimately rejected due to Britain's superior **sea power** and naval defenses. Seeking a way to get around the Royal Navy—as well as disrupt valuable trade—Napoleon proposed to attack the British on the colonial front in India, via **Egypt**, which he also hoped to conquer. Setting off from France, he took **35,000 troops**, capturing the Mediterranean island of Malta along the way. Upon reaching Alexandria in July, Napoleon quickly defeated **Mameluke** troops at the **Battle of the Pyramids**. However, on August 1,

Irish Revolt
Protestant prisoners, suspected of being loyal to British rule, were executed by Irish nationalists in Wexford during the revolt.

10–25
THOUSAND
ESTIMATED NUMBER OF **IRISH DEAD AFTER THE REBELLION**

French forces were completely destroyed by the British navy, under the command of **Horatio Nelson** (1758–1805), at the **Battle of the Nile**. Napoleon and his troops were left stranded in Egypt, but the defeat and humiliation did little to hamper the French commander's imperial ambitions.

In 1796, the British had taken advantage of warfare in Europe to wrest the island of **Sri Lanka** from Dutch control, meeting with very little resistance. The British

named the island off India's coast **Ceylon**, and ran its administration from Madras. By 1798, the British had begun to realize the strategic importance of the island, and **Frederick North** (1766–1827) was sent there as the colony's first governor. Not all of Ceylon was under British control, however. The kingdom of **Kandy**, whose subjects occupied the interior of the island, remained independent. Their autonomy would become a cause for concern for British governors in Ceylon.

At the same time, in **Ireland**, resentment at British rule had turned to rebellion, led by nationalists called the **Society of United Irishmen**. Headed by Theobald Wolfe Tone (1763–98) and James Napier Tandy (1740–1803), the group had made numerous attempts to enlist the support of Revolutionary France, but the British, learning of these plots, had forced the rebels to change their plans. They decided to rise up, although lacking French reinforcements, and managed to seize control of **County Wexford**. A French expeditionary force sent to assist them was intercepted by British troops and the revolt soon collapsed. Tone committed suicide while awaiting his execution.

ONCE NAPOLEON BONAPARTE had returned to France from Egypt, he began to focus on his political future, and was soon plotting a **coup d'état** that involved dissolving the Directory, the body that had been governing the country since 1795. The outcome of the **18 Brumaire Coup** of November 9 was that the Directory was replaced with the Consulate, and Napoleon took charge of France as **First Consul**.

The Rosetta Stone
The translations between three different scripts on this large piece of granite unlocked the world of hieroglyphics and ancient Egypt.

While in Egypt, French soldiers had unearthed an object that transformed the understanding of the ancient world. A block of black **granite** inscribed with strange writing, it was named the **Rosetta Stone** after the town where it was found. It fell into British possession by 1801, although it took years of study before anyone was able to **translate** it. Eventually scholars established a relationship between the three scripts on the stone: **hieroglyphics**, demotic script (Egyptian handwriting used in everyday life), and Greek. It became clear that this discovery would permit the transcription of hieroglyphics, a type of communication not used since the 4th century CE. Deciphering the stone provided a window into Egyptian antiquity.

In India, soldiers for the East India Company emerged victorious from a violent battle with the fearsome **Tipu Sultan** (1750–99), the ruler of **Mysore**. Tipu had made alliances with French troops in India, and on this pretext the British Governor-General Richard Wellesley (see 1797) authorized the **Fourth Mysore War**, intent on driving out the French and annexing the territory. Tipu was killed in battle, and the East India Company took half of his territory.

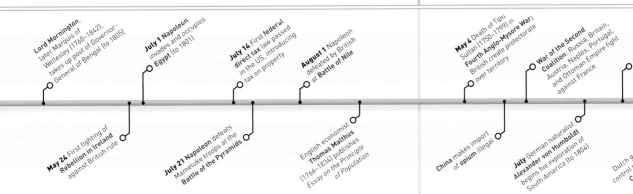

Lord Mornington, later Marquis of Wellesley (1760–1842), takes up post of Governor-General of Bengal (to 1805)

May 24 First fighting of **Rebellion in Ireland** against British rule

July 1 Napoleon invades and occupies **Egypt** (to 1801)

July 21 Napoleon defeats Mameluke troops at the **Battle of the Pyramids**

July 14 First federal **direct tax** law passed in the US, introducing tax on property

August 1 Napoleon defeated by British at **Battle of Nile**

English economist **Thomas Malthus** (1766–1834) publishes the *Essay on the Principle of Population*

May 4 Death of Tipu Sultan (1750–1799) in **Fourth Anglo-Mysore War**; British create protectorate over territory

China makes import of **opium** illegal

War of the Second Coalition: Russia, Britain, Austria, Naples, Portugal, and Ottoman Empire fight against France

July German naturalist **Alexander von Humboldt** begins his exploration of South America (to 1804)

Discovery of **Rosetta Stone** in Egypt

Dutch government takes control of **Dutch East India Company**'s territories

THE STORY OF
MEDICINE

ANCIENT BELIEFS GIVE WAY TO SCIENTIFIC ADVANCES, TRANSFORMING HUMAN HEALTH

Understanding of the human body and disease made important advances during the 18th and 19th centuries, laying the foundation for modern medical care. Ancient practices, such as bloodletting to cure illness, were replaced with ones that were born of a more rigorous scientific approach.

People have attempted to treat disease since prehistoric times, but until the 18th century medicine was based largely on superstition, natural remedies, and unscientific practices and theories, such as the theory that the body had four fluids (humors) that needed to be in balance for health. There had been progress in anatomy and surgery, but overall, medicine remained primitive.

THE DEVELOPMENT OF MODERN MEDICINE

In the 18th century, medicine started to become more scientifically rigorous, and significant advances were made, such as the development of a vaccine for smallpox in 1796. The 19th century saw the establishment of the germ theory of disease,

the introduction of antiseptic techniques and anesthetics, and the use of X-rays to image the body. Around 1900, pharmacology began to make great progress, with the invention of aspirin in 1897 and the first synthetic antibacterial drug in 1908. During the 20th century, more vaccines and drugs were developed, such as antibiotics and anticancer drugs. Surgical techniques also became more sophisticated; successful organ transplants were performed, and keyhole surgery became routine. In diagnosis, scanning techniques were invented, and screening became widely used. From the late 20th century, genetics also began to have a significant impact on medicine as genetic causes of diseases were discovered and genetic testing was developed.

- paper tube
- wooden tube
- unit housing sound sensor

Monaural stethoscope | Electronic stethoscope

THE STETHOSCOPE

The stethoscope was invented in 1816 by French physician René Laennec, who used a simple tube (a monaural stethoscope) to listen to a woman's chest. In 1851, British physician Arthur Leared invented the binaural stethoscope, with an earpiece for each ear, and, in the 1940s, Americans Maurice Rappaport and Howard Sprague developed the modern acoustic stethoscope, which has two "bells," one for listening to the heart, the other for listening to the lungs. The latest development is the electronic stethoscope, which uses an electronic sound sensor and amplifier.

> ❝ THE **DEVIATION OF MAN** FROM THE STATE IN WHICH HE WAS ORIGINALLY PLACED BY **NATURE** SEEMS TO HAVE PROVED TO HIM **A PROLIFIC SOURCE OF DISEASES.** ❞

Edward Jenner, English surgeon, *An Inquiry into the Causes and Effects of the Variolae Vaccinae, or Cow-Pox*, 1798

c. 5100–4900 BCE
Neolithic trepanation
Trepanation, which involves drilling holes in the skull, is used as far back as the Neolithic period to treat a variety of health problems.

Trepanned skull

c. 420 BCE
Hippocrates develops diagnostics
Hippocrates, the Greek physician considered to be the father of modern medicine, moves health away from religion and into the realm of science.

1543
Andreas Vesalius
The Brussels-born surgeon writes his influential anatomical work, with accurate diagrams of human anatomy based on many dissections and operations.

De Humani Corporis Fabrica

1818
First blood transfusion
British obstetrician James Blundell performs the first successful human-to-human blood transfusion, using a syringe to transfer blood between the patients.

c. 1550–700 BCE
Ancient Egyptian surgery
Medical and especially surgical knowledge advances due to the practice of mummification, which gives doctors greater insight into anatomy.

Egyptian knives and curettes

c. 1000–1300
Arab medical advances
The Arab world adds to medical progress with the development of pharmacists, who work with plants and use them to find new cures.

Arabic medical manuscript

1796
Vaccination
British scientist Edward Jenner develops a vaccine for smallpox. It is the first vaccine created for any disease, and Jenner's work saves countless lives.

Jenner's inoculation point

switch
for fan

gears for
powering fan

clockwork motor

roller

crank for winding
clockwork motor

outlet for
antiseptic
spray

hammer to tap
antiseptic powder
container

container for
antiseptic powder

housing of fan

Antiseptic machine
Patented by British surgeon Anthony Bell in 1879,
this device was used to make the air in operating
rooms free of disease-causing microorganisms.
Using a clockwork-powered fan, the machine blows
antiseptic powder and carbolic acid into the air.

1865–67
Antisepsis
British surgeon Joseph
Lister pioneers
antiseptic surgery by
using a solution of
carbolic acid to kill
infectious organisms
during operations.

1881
**Blood pressure
measurement**
Samuel von Basch
invents a noninvasive
way of measuring blood
pressure using a bulb
connected to an
anaeroid manometer.

Blood pressure
apparatus

1954
Organ transplant
The first successful organ
transplant between living
patients (a kidney transplant
between identical twins) is
carried out in Boston by a team
led by Joseph Murray, J. Hartwell
Harrison, and John P. Merrill.

Late 20th century
Keyhole surgery
Laparoscopic (keyhole)
surgery becomes widely
used after the first
laparoscopic appendix
removal using a
microchip camera is
performed in 1981.

21st century
Robotic surgery
Developments in
robotics allow for
more precise, less
invasive surgery,
with faster healing
and less pain for
the patient.

Robotic suturing

1846–47
Practical anesthesia
In 1846, US dentist Henry Morgan
publicly uses ether for
anesthesia. In 1847, Scottish
doctor James Simpson
uses chloroform.

Chloroform inhaler

1901
Blood types identified
US scientist Karl
Landsteiner publishes his
discovery of the four main
human blood groups (A, B,
AB, O), which allows for
more successful
transfusions.

Blood
bag

1971 and 1977
CT and MRI scans
British scientist
Godfrey Hounsfield
invents the first
commercial CT scanner
in 1971. The first MRI
scan of a human is
carried out in 1977.

MRI scan

1800

The Battle of Marengo was a victory for France over Austria.

AS A NEW CENTURY BEGAN, unrest in Europe continued. Despite previous treaties, French military action increased in aggression. Mistrust of France prompted the formation of the **Second Coalition** in 1798; by 1799, it comprised Austria, Britain, Russia, Portugal, Naples, and the Ottoman Empire. On June 14, Napoleon scored a significant victory against Austria in the **Battle of Marengo**, the result of which was French control of northern Italy.

Spain, meanwhile, had done little to develop its Louisiana territory in North America, lacking the resources to settle it. So when Napoleon put pressure on Charles IV to return Louisiana, the Spanish monarch obliged. Under the terms of the secret **Treaty of San Ildefonso**, Napoleon agreed not to give the land to a third power.

Napoleon's saber used at Marengo
Sabers were much in use during Napoleon's wars and were carried by both cavalry and infantry.

1801

An engraving depicting peace celebrations in Milan, Italy, after the Treaty of Lunéville, in which Austria was forced to recognize France's growing borders.

IN THE AFTERMATH OF THE IRISH REBELLION (see 1798), British prime minister William Pitt the Younger concluded that the solution to the "Irish question" was a political union. In 1800 a bill outlining these plans was presented to the Irish parliament. After much controversy, the bill was passed. The **Act of Union**, also approved by the British Government, came into effect on January 1, 1801. It saw the Irish parliament closed down and representation moved to London, where 32 Irish peers were put in the House of Lords and 100 MPs in the House of Commons. Pitt had hoped the move would allow the granting of concessions to Catholics, but the bill maintained a ban on their holding public office.

In Europe, Austria's defeat at Marengo in 1800 forced them to accept the **Treaty of Lunéville**, which recognized France's frontiers to the Rhine, Alps, and Pyrenees.

Russia, meanwhile, was expanding to the south, encroaching on the kingdoms of **Kartalinia-Kakhetia** (present-day eastern Georgia). In a 1783 treaty, the ruling Bagratid dynasty agreed to Russian protection, in return for assurances that its territorial integrity would be preserved. However, Russian emperor **Paul I** (1754–1801), who had succeeded Catherine the Great upon her death in 1796, decided to formally annex the territory.

1802

The mausoleum of emperor and Nguyen dynasty founder, Gia Long.

AFTER 30 YEARS OF CIVIL WAR, Vietnam was united under the leadership of **Nguyen Phuc Anh** (1762–1820), a powerful general who, with the help of French mercenaries, was able to defeat the rival Trinh family. Nguyen Anh declared himself emperor, taking the name **Gia Long**, and reestablished the Nguyen family as the ruling dynasty.

Ongoing warfare in Europe and further afield came to an end with the **Treaty of Amiens.** Signatories included Britain, France, Spain, and the Netherlands (which was known as the Batavian Republic from 1795 until 1806).

Under the terms of the treaty, Britain kept the colonies of **Trinidad**, which had been taken from Spain, and **Ceylon**, which had been captured from the Dutch. **Egypt** was restored to the Ottoman Empire, and France agreed to relinquish **Malta**. This state of affairs was short-lived.

France and Britain at the table
A political cartoon of Britain's William Pitt and France's Napoleon Bonaparte carving up the globe around the Peace of Amiens.

1803

Jean-Jacques Dessalines who fought for Haitian independence.

IN SAINT-DOMINGUE (HAITI), THE ONGOING WAR TOOK A DECISIVE turn with the capture and exile of **General Toussaint Louverture** in 1803. He had joined the French Republican cause ten years earlier (see 1793) and drove out the remaining British forces on the island, before taking up the title of **governor** in 1801. Napoleon was, however, displeased with Louverture's successes and was infuriated when he defied orders, riding into Santo Domingo—then under French control—and freeing the slaves. In 1802, Napoleon **reinstated slavery** and sent 25,000 troops to reclaim the island. After months of fighting, Louverture was invited to negotiate a settlement. He was then seized and exiled. The battle for abolition then fell to his deputy **Jean-Jacques Dessalines**.

With most of Napoleon's troops in Saint-Domingue killed on the battlefield or ravaged by **yellow fever**, Dessalines' men drove out the remaining soldiers. French reinforcements were held up by a British **blockade** of French ports as part of the ongoing war, and France abandoned the island.

The cost of fighting in Haiti had put further strain on France's troubled finances and it occurred to Napoleon that he could raise revenue by selling the large and mostly undeveloped land controlled by France in North America. The US had become interested in the Louisiana Territory, especially the port of **New Orleans** as more people

---

THOMAS JEFFERSON
(1743–1826)

Virginia-born planter and slave owner Thomas Jefferson was a leading republican and one of the primary authors of the United States' Declaration of Independence. He remained politically powerful all through his life, serving as vice president (1797–1801) and president (1801–09). Yet for all the influence of his writings on issues like liberty, he did not free his own slaves during his lifetime.

In Vienna, composer **Ludwig van Beethoven** (1770–1827) finished composing his Piano Sonata 14 in C-sharp Minor Op. 27 No 2, known as the "*Moonlight Sonata*," which became one of his most famous works and is thought to be dedicated to his pupil, the Countess Giulietta Gucciardi, who did not return his affections.

The United States saw the election of **Thomas Jefferson** (see panel, above) as the country's third president.

" FREEDOM OR DEATH! "

Inscription from Haiti's Act of Independence and on Haitian flag

A sketch of an evergreen shrub leaf from William Clark's diary. He and Meriwether Lewis spent years exploring the vast Louisiana territory.

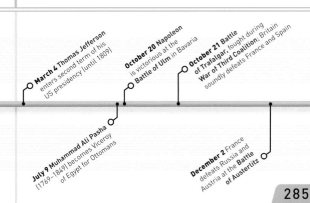

This painting shows the aftermath of the Battle of Trafalgar, in which France and Spain suffered heavy losses at the hands of Britain's Royal Navy.

KEY

▢ Territory gained by US from France in 1803

→ Onward route of Lewis and Clark

Territory gained by the US
The massive Louisiana Territory almost doubled the size of the US. The following year it was extended south to include New Orleans.

settling farther west came to depend on trade along the Mississippi River. On May 2 a deal, the **Louisiana Purchase**, was signed in which the US bought the territory stretching from the Gulf of Mexico to the Rocky Mountains—an area of 829,000 square miles (2,147,000 square kilometers). The price agreed was $15,000,000, but, including interest, the total paid was closer to $27,000,000.

Napoleon faced further challenges in Europe as Britain declared war on France, beginning the **Napoleonic Wars**. Meanwhile, British East India Company troops were waging another war involving the internal politics of the Maratha Confederacy, the **Second Maratha War** (to 1805). The Company's attempt to gain control of the territory in India only set the stage for further conflict.

AFTER FINALLY DRIVING THE FRENCH OUT of Saint-Domingue, Jean-Jacques Dessalines declared the independence of the **new republic of Haiti** on January 1, 1804. The name was based partly on the original indigenous name for the island. It was the first—and only—former slave colony to throw off colonial rule and slavery. Despite this, its birth was met with a wary reception—some in the slave-owning US did not want Haiti setting an example for the southern states, a concern shared by Britain, whose slave colony of Jamaica was also in close proximity.

The defeat in the Caribbean did little to weaken Napoleon's stranglehold on power in Europe. In 1804, he made France a **hereditary empire**, ostensibly to ward off any assassination attempts, but also to showcase his own might. The coronation ceremony on December 2 was remarkable as Napoleon was not crowned by Pope Pius VII (1742–1823) who officiated, but placed the crown on his own head, crowning himself **Napoleon I**. In this year he also made sweeping reforms to the legal system in France and French territories, known as the Napoleonic Code (see panel, right).

In the US, two explorers—**Meriwether Lewis** (1774–1809)

and **William Clark** (1770–1838)—set off on an expedition through the newly acquired Louisiana Territory (see map, left). They were under instructions from President Thomas Jefferson to find the Missouri River, establish relations with the indigenous people of the region, and find the fabled **Northwest Passage**. They made detailed maps and recorded the flora and fauna of the region. The two explorers finally returned to St. Louis in 1806.

In West Africa, **Usman dan Fodio** (1754–1817), a Muslim scholar and teacher, began a four-year **jihad** (holy war) that resulted in the creation of the **Sokoto Caliphate** in 1808 and the **Fulani empire** in Hausaland (in present-day northern Nigeria).

NAPOLEONIC CODE

One of Napoleon Bonaparte's most far-reaching reforms was to codify French law. Enacted in 1804, the Napoleonic Code (*Code Napoléon*) was a civil code created with the intention of breaking from the institutions of the past. Based on reason, it was also heavily

influenced by Roman law, and declared all men equal, ending any hereditary nobility. Women fared less well, as they were put under male control. The laws also dealt with issues such as property rights, marriage, and civil rights. The Napoleonic Code was disseminated throughout French-controlled territory in Europe and beyond, making it highly influential—an adapted version is still in force in the Dominican Republic today. It was also later adopted by some of the new Latin American republics, including Bolivia and Chile.

FRANCE'S DEFEAT IN THE CARIBBEAN at Saint-Domingue was soon overshadowed by victory against Russia and Austria, which had been pulled back into war. Napoleon had also declared himself the king of Italy, then comprising Venice and northern Italian kingdoms. This act provoked the formation of a **Third Coalition** against France, with Britain, Austria, Russia, and Sweden as members. Deciding against an invasion of Britain, Bonaparte sent forces to **Ulm**, Bavaria (September 25–October 20), where he was victorious. However, the day after the Battle of Ulm ended, France suffered a humiliating naval defeat at the hands of the British in the **Battle of Trafalgar**, under the command

Casualties of Trafalgar
This sea battle saw heavy losses for France and Spain, though British Admiral Horatio Nelson was among the dead.

of Napoleon's old enemy, Horatio Nelson (see 1798). The battle, fought near Cape Trafalgar, between Cadiz, Spain, and the Strait of Gibraltar, saw the meeting of 18 French and 15 Spanish ships against 27 British vessels. Britain was victorious, capturing or destroying 18 ships, but Nelson, fatally wounded in action, died before the end of the battle. Napoleon decided to change tactics and turned to Europe, occupying Vienna and defeating Russia and Austria at the **Battle of Austerlitz** on December 2.

In Egypt, the Macedonian-born soldier **Muhammad Ali** (1769–1849) was named viceroy, or pasha, to the Ottoman sultan. Ali had arrived in Egypt in 1801 as part of a regiment sent to drive out the French.

Casualties of Trafalgar (bar chart)

	CASUALTIES
UK Dead	
UK Wounded	
France Dead	
France Wounded	
Spain Dead	
Spain Wounded	

0   1,000   2,000

Timeline

Mecca falls to Wahhibis, challenging Ottoman control

New elements Rhodium, Palladium, Osmium, Iridium, and Cerium **discovered**

November 18 Saint-Domingue: Former slaves led by Jean-Jacques Dessalines defeat French army at Battle of Vertières

January 1 Republic of **Haiti established** after French defeat in Saint-Domingue

May 18 Napoleon declared emperor of the French; introduces **legal code**

February 14 First Serbian uprising against Ottoman Empire (to 1813) over demands for autonomy

Russian war with **Persia** (to 1813) over Russia's annexation of Georgia and Karabakh

Pitt the Younger returns as British prime minister until 1806

March 4 Thomas Jefferson enters second term of his US presidency (until 1809)

July 9 Muhammad Ali Pasha (1769–1849) becomes Viceroy of Egypt for Ottomans

October 20 Napoleon is victorious at the **Battle of Ulm** in Bavaria

October 21 Battle of Trafalgar, fought during War of Third Coalition; Britain soundly defeats France and Spain

December 2 France defeats Russia and Austria at the **Battle of Austerlitz**

Napoleon after his victory at the Battle of Jena in Saxony.

> **" YOU MAY CHOOSE TO LOOK THE OTHER WAY** BUT YOU CAN NEVER SAY AGAIN THAT **YOU DID NOT KNOW. "**
>
> **William Wilberforce,** to the English parliament prior to the vote on the Abolition Bill, 1789

Francisco Goya's painting *The Third of May* depicts the French troops executing Spanish insurgents involved in the Madrid uprising.

PRUSSIA SUFFERED A DEVASTATING defeat against France at the **Battle of Jena** on October 14. Fought in Jena and Auerstädt in Saxony (southeast Germany), 122,000 French troops and 114,000 Prussians met in combat. As a result, Frederick William III (1770–1840) decided that internal reform in Prussia was necessary in order to bolster the country's flagging fortunes. Among the numerous measures taken, **serfdom** was abolished. Although the transition later proved profitable for agriculture, it took years to implement the changes.

In addition to his other conquests, Napoleon wanted control of the **Holy Roman Empire**, which would expand his territory in Germany. Emperor Francis II (1768–1835) was in no position to challenge France and **abdicated**, officially ending the empire, of which France took possession.

In the Middle East, the Islamic holy pilgrimage site of **Mecca** was invaded by members of the Arabian **Saudi** dynasty who practiced a strict version of the religion known as **Wahhabi**. In 1805, they had captured **Medina**, which, like Mecca, was under the control of the Ottoman Empire. They also made incursions into the Arabian Peninsula, sacking the city of **Karbala**, in Iraq (also under Ottoman rule), and extending their influence south to **Yemen**, a cause for concern among Ottoman officials.

THE LONG BATTLE LED BY English abolitionist and politician **William Wilberforce** (1759–1833)—and the thousands of members of the British public who supported his campaign—finally came to fruition in 1807 as the bill to **abolish the slave trade** was passed with an overwhelming majority. The legislation, however, only ended the trade in Britain. It did not end the practice of slavery.

Russia, alongside Prussia, had reentered the hostilities against France with the **Battle of Eylau** (February 7–8) in eastern Prussia. The battle was inconclusive and resulted in a stalemate, with both sides losing more than 20,000 troops. After a decisive Russian defeat at the later **Battle of Friedland**, Russia signed one of

Elite force
A Janissary, left, in Cairo. Initially the bodyguards of the sultan, the Janissaries became the elite troops of the Ottoman Empire army.

the **Treaties of Tilsit** on July 7, while Prussia signed the other on July 9. Under the terms of the treaties, France and Russia formed an alliance, while the territories of Austria and Prussia were significantly reduced.

In the Ottoman Empire, auxiliary troops called **Yamaks** erupted into a revolt over attempts to introduce European-style reforms to the military. They were soon joined by the elite **Janissary** soldiers. The unrest culminated in the assassination of Selim III (1761–1808).

ALREADY IN CONTROL OF MOST of western and central Europe, Napoleon now turned toward the Iberian Peninsula. Enraged by the Portuguese refusal to back a French boycott against Britain, he sent troops into Portugal via northern Spain. The presence of French troops, as well as previous unpopular concessions to France, provoked the Spanish people to rise up, calling for the abdication of their monarch, **Charles IV**, in favor of his son, **Ferdinand VII** (1784–1833). Ferdinand took the throne, but it was to be very short-lived.

Lured to Bayonne, France, by Napoleon's offer to mediate, Ferdinand VII was forced to abdicate. As Charles VII had already abdicated, Napoleon was now able to declare his brother, Joseph Bonaparte (1768–1844), the new king of Spain, triggering the **Peninsular War**. When news of these events reached Spain's colonies, there were furious outbursts. In Santo Domingo, loyalists mounted the **War of Reconquest** (to 1809), driving out the occupying French troops and declaring the island once more under Spanish control.

LONG-STANDING ENEMIES, Spain and Britain now fought alongside each other as they united against France. British troops met early defeat at the **Battle of La Coruña,** northwest Spain, fighting French troops under Napoleon's direct command. Britain was subsequently victorious at the **Battle of Talavera** (July 27–28), southwest of Madrid, under the leadership of Arthur Wellesley (1769–1852), later known as the **Duke of Wellington**.

The Spaniards, while fighting the French, had also been establishing provincial bodies, called **juntas**, in order to organize their resistance. The central junta in Spain had also issued a decree declaring the American territories to be more than just colonies, but still a part of the monarchy. Across the Atlantic it was obvious that there was a crisis of **legitimacy** in Spanish rule—without a king, to whom did allegiance lie? While debates about this were underway, similar American juntas were set up, and it soon it became clear that not all the colonies would stay on the path of loyalty to the Crown.

Pistol from Peninsular War
Flintlock pistols were widely used in this period. The term "guerrilla" also arose, named for Spanish tactics.

hammer

ramrod

French urge **Ottomans** to declare war on Russia; fighting lasts until 1812

August 6 Formal abolition of **Holy Roman Empire**

British take **Cape Colony** from the Dutch again to prevent French control

October 14 Napoleon defeats Prussians at twin of **Jena** and **Auerstädt** battles

February 7–8 Napoleon defeats Russia at **Battle of Eylau**

March 25 Britain **abolishes the slave trade** in all its territories

Janissary revolt leads to deposition of Ottoman leader Selim III, replaced by **Mustapha IV** (1779–1808)

June 14 Russians defeated by France at **Battle of Friedland**

British fail to take **Buenos Aires** during attempt to seize colonies of Spain, the ally of France

November Portuguese royal family flees to **Brazil** after France invades **Portugal**

Peninsular War (to 1814): Spain, Portugal, and Britain against France

Sierra Leone comes under British control

June 6 Joseph (1768–1844), Napoleon's brother, is placed on the Spanish throne

January 16 Peninsular War: British defeated at La Coruña, Spain

February 8 Austria declares war on France

September 17 Sweden cedes Finland to Russia under the **Treaty of Hamina**

A mural by José Clemente Orozco (1883–1949) depicting Miguel Hidalgo, whose anticolonial document sparked the Mexican War of Independence.

A caricature compares the Luddites to mobs of the French Revolution.

When Napoleon Bonaparte's troops arrived in Moscow, they found the city ablaze, as portrayed by this painting by Jean-Charles Langlois (1789–1870).

KEY

▪ Spanish territory
▪ Portuguese territory

Latin America on the eve of independence
Spain and Portugal still controlled the majority of Central and South America during the early days of the Peninsular War.

USING THE EXISTING POLITICAL CHAOS as an opportunity for reform, Spanish politicians called a congress, known as a **Cortes**, on September 24 in the port of Cadiz. Deputies numbered 104, with 30 representing the colonial territories, although more arrived later. The Cortes declared itself the source of national sovereignty and began to draw up a constitution, although Spaniards were divided as to the extent they wished the government to be restructured. There was also the question of how much political **representation** to allow overseas territories. The colonies represented a population far greater than Spain's, meaning they could, in theory, dominate the Cortes. The peninsular politicians wished to avoid this, yet needed the colonies' continued support.

Some members of the public in the colonies began taking matters into their own hands. In Dolores, Mexico, a parish priest named **Miguel Hidalgo y Costilla** (1753–1811) distributed a document calling for the end of Spanish rule, while advocating racial equality and land redistribution, an act known as the *Grito de Dolores* (Cry of Dolores). Thousands responded to his call and set off for Mexico City, where they were put down by loyalist troops the following year. But Hidalgo's actions had sparked the Mexican struggle for freedom.

In other Spanish colonies, similar upheavals took place. The viceroyalty of **New Granada** also declared its independence on July 20, and there had been uprisings in Quito and Buenos Aires.

Meanwhile, on the **Hawaiian islands** in the Pacific Ocean, **King Kamehameha I** (1758–1819) became the first ruler of a united Hawaii, helping the islands withstand European incursions.

ON JULY 5, THE SOUTH AMERICAN TERRITORY of Venezuela joined New Granada (see map, left) and Mexico in declaring independence from Spain. One of the rebels involved in the deliberations for independence, **Simón Bolívar** (see panel, below), had recently returned from England, where he had tried to elicit British support for their cause, but was unsuccessful.

Bolívar's trip was confined to London, but had he traveled farther north, he would have seen rebels of another kind: the group known as the **Luddites,** who were attacking textile mills in the industrial north of England. The Luddites aimed to destroy the new machinery in the mills. They feared the machines would eventually **replace** them, thereby forcing them into unemployment and poverty.

SIMON BOLIVAR (1783–1830)

Simón Bolívar was born in Caracas to a wealthy family. He was sent to Europe at 16, where he was inspired by the writings of Enlightenment thinkers on the issue of liberty. Soon after returning to South America in 1807, he became involved in independence conspiracies. Later known as *El Libertador*, he led much of northern South America to independence from Spain. He also ruled Gran Colombia, but the political union ultimately failed.

RUSSIA, LIKE PORTUGAL, DECIDED to resist Napoleon's **Continental System**, measures intended to damage the economy of Britain. Russia had withdrawn from it in 1810, and Napoleon resolved to mount an invasion in retaliation. He sent more than **500,000 troops** to Russia in June and won early victories at the battles of **Smolensk** on August 17 and **Borodino** on September 7, arriving with his forces in Moscow on September 14. There they found the city gutted, and its inhabitants all gone. Russian troops held off any further advance, and as the brutal Russian winter set in, Napoleon's troops began to falter. The **Grand Armée** was running short on food and many soldiers, unaccustomed to such extreme cold, died. Napoleon had no other option but to make a humiliating **retreat** in December. Only around 30,000 French soldiers survived.

In North America, merchants prospered in their trade with France, claiming to be a neutral party in the dispute between the British and the French. Britain refused to recognize this **neutrality** and began to seize American ships, often capturing the American sailors and pressing them into service with the British Royal Navy. This triggered the **War of 1812** (to 1814), which also included battles on the mainland where Britain persuaded American Indians loyal to the Crown to attack settlements in the Northwest Territory.

In Spain, the Cortes had finally produced a **constitution**. It limited the power of the monarchy—although Ferdinand VII was still in exile—and did not provide any special representation in the Cortes for the nobility or the clergy. Its liberal ideas provoked an angry reaction among some supporters of the Crown and Church, and triggered a long-running fight between liberals and conservatives, which would continue for decades.

In Egypt, Muhammad Ali was ordered on a campaign to reestablish Ottoman rule in the holy city of **Mecca**, and drive out the Wahhabis, who had seized much of Arabia. His troops took Medina in 1812, and Jeddah and Mecca the following year.

An engraving of a palanquin (litter) being carried in Mauritius.

A painting depicts the 17th-century Temple of Tooth, located in the kingdom of Kandy, where one of Buddha's teeth is preserved.

A native inhabitant in Alaska, territory which Russia had claimed.

NAPOLEON BONAPARTE, AFTER HIS HUMILIATING RETREAT IN Russia (see 1812), began to experience the rapid decline of his military might. This was driven home by the decisive defeat at the **Battle of Leipzig** (also known as the Battle of the Nations) fought October 16–19. France had nearly 185,000 troops, but the allies outnumbered them with more than 300,000 soldiers from Austria, Russia, Prussia, and Sweden. Even after this loss, Napoleon still refused to sign a peace deal that would put France's boundary back to the Rhine River and the Alps.

While Russia was caught up in the Napoleonic conflict, it was also entangled with territorial deals further east; Russia and Persia signed the **Treaty of Gulistan**, in which Russia was given a large area of Persian Caucasus territory. The deal brought to an end the **Russo–Persian War** (1804–13), which had been triggered by Russia's annexation of Georgia and the **Karabakh** (a region in present-day Azerbaijan). The territories, which had been a dominion of Persia, had appealed to Persia's shah for help in resisting Russia.

In **Venezuela**, Simón Bolívar (see 1811) had won an important victory against the Spanish and captured **Caracas**, though Spain's forces would later defeat him, forcing him into exile for two years. During this period he went to Jamaica and Haiti to regroup and enlist further support before returning to Venezuela in 1816.

ALLIED TROOPS PURSUED Napoleon to Paris, where he was captured. He abdicated on April 6 and was exiled to the island of Elba, off the Tuscan coast of Italy. To replace him, **Louis XVIII** (1755–1824)—brother of the beheaded Louis XVI—was placed on the French throne. Afterward, the European powers convened the **Congress of Vienna** (September 1814 to June 1815). Part of the resulting settlement gave Prussia two-fifths of Saxony; set up a German Confederation; and allowed Britain to retain France's Indian Ocean islands of **Mauritius** and the **Seychelles**, which it had captured.

ALTHOUGH HE WAS EXILED FROM FRANCE, Napoleon rallied enough supporters to help him mount his return, and he entered Paris on March 20—just 11 months after his forced departure. Louis XVIII fled, and what became known as the "**Hundred Days**" began. Once he had an army assembled, Napoleon mounted attacks against his enemies, defeating Prussia at **Ligny** (in present-day Belgium) on June 16. He fared much worse two days later at the **Battle of Waterloo**, against British troops led by the Duke of Wellington, who had brought the Peninsular War (see 1808) to an end the previous year. Napoleon had been on the verge of victory, but the arrival of Prussian reinforcements secured his defeat. Napoleon was forced to abdicate once again, but this time he was to be exiled much further away—the island of **St. Helena**, a British outpost in the South Atlantic, where he died in 1821.

At the same time, Britain's troops in **Ceylon** (Sri Lanka) had taken control of the kingdom of **Kandy**, which meant the entire island was under British rule.

Battle of Waterloo
This clash was the definitive defeat of Napoleon Bonaparte, after which he was forced to abdicate and go into exile.

A RUSSIAN ORTHODOX PRIEST, Father Sokoloff, was sent to **Sitka**, in the Alaska territory, to build a church in the town as part of Russia's bid to colonize the region. Alaska had lingered as an outpost but settlements began to grow as trade in sea otter furs flourished.

In southern Africa, **Shaka** (c. 1787–1828), a fierce warrior, took over the rule of the **Zulus**. He reorganized the army, leading his tribe to military victory, and incorporated conquered tribes into the Zulu nation.

Charter Act ends East India Company monopoly and allows missionaries to enter India

October 19 Napoleon defeated by Allies at **Leipzig** (Battle of the Nations)

Egyptian forces recapture **Jeddah** and **Mecca** from Wahhabis

Simón Bolívar leads invasion of **Venezuela** and is proclaimed "El Libertador" (The Liberator)

January 14 Treaty of Kiel: Denmark gives Sweden Norway in exchange for Pomerania

April 6 Napoleon abdicates; exiled to island of Elba, returning less than a year later

May 30 Treaty of Paris signed

April 11 Louis XVIII (1755–1824) regains French throne (to 1824)

War in Nepal between East India Company troops and Gurkhas over annexation of villages (to 1816)

December 11 Ferdinand VII (1784–1833) is returned to Spanish throne; scraps liberal reforms

British annex Ceylonese **kingdom of Kandy**

April 23 Second Serbian Uprising (to 1817) gives Serbs more autonomy

June 18 Battle of Waterloo ends in Napoleon's surrender

Napoleon exiled to island of St. Helena, where he later dies in 1821

United Provinces of the Río de la Plata set up as independent states in South America

July 9 Argentina gains independence from Spain

Shaka (c. 1787–1828) becomes Zulu king

August 27 Bombardment of **Algiers** by Anglo-Dutch allies seeking release of Christian slaves

Java returns to **Dutch** rule after a period of British control

1817

Argentine general José de San Martín with his horse and officers.

| | 121 dead or injured | 1,100 dead or injured |

Battle of Chacabuco
A bold risk by rebel leader José de San Martín resulted in a highly successful ambush against the Spanish, who sustained heavy losses.

THE FIGHT AGAINST SPANISH rule took a decisive turn when Argentine-born General **José de San Martín** (1778–1850) led around 3,000 troops from Argentina into Chile through treacherous passages in the **Andes** mountains, and launched a surprise attack on royalist forces on February 12—the **Battle of Chacabuco**. He then moved on to take Santiago. He refused the offer of governorship of Chile, passing it instead to fellow soldier **Bernardo O'Higgins** (c. 1776–1842), who became the territory's "supreme director."

Serbia had also been fighting once more for independence, after being invaded by the Turks in 1813. The **Second Serbian Uprising** was successful, and most of their former rights were regained by 1817.

1818

> ❝ **LET US BE FREE.** THE REST MATTERS NOT! ❞

José de San Martín, revolutionary leader

THE BATTLE IN ARABIA, ongoing since 1811 between Egypt and the Wahhabi sect of Islam, drew to a close in 1818. Egyptian forces led by Muhammad Ali recaptured the holy cities of Mecca and Medina. **Wahhabi** power had spread quickly, and from their Arabian base they had secured control of Mecca, Medina, and Jedda. Syria was under threat when Muhammad Ali received his orders to defeat the Wahhabi and return the cities to Ottoman rule. A final siege of the capital **Diriyah** (in present-day Saudi Arabia) put a temporary end to Wahhabi ambitions.

In South America, the effort led by José de San Martín at the Battle of Maipú on April 5 secured **independence for Chile** when loyalist troops suffered a crushing defeat. With a small naval fleet of seven ships under the command of British mercenary Lord Thomas Cochrane, the rebels also managed to break the Spanish hold on the coastline.

In Paris, German inventor Baron Karl von Drais de Sauerbrun was impressing crowds with a display of his **draisienne,** a two-wheeled machine that was the precursor to the modern **bicycle.** Made of wood and propelled by pushing the feet along the ground, rather than by pedals, it was known in German as the **Laufmaschine,** or "running machine." While testing the design the previous year, he had managed to ride it 9 miles (14 km). The idea was soon picked up and modified by other inventors,

Mary Shelley
The English novelist Mary Shelley published her first novel, Frankenstein, *in 1818, and it remains a literary classic today.*

including Briton **Denis Johnson** (c. 1759–1833), a coachmaker by training, who designed a "pedestrian curricle," later known as a **dandy horse.**

In England, **Mary Shelley** (1797–1851), the daughter of writer Mary Wollstonecraft (see 1792) and wife of poet Percy Bysshe Shelley (1792–1822), published the novel *Frankenstein; or, The Modern Prometheus.* The novel concerns a scientist who artificially creates another human being, and the consequences they both suffer. The work was an instant success, and is considered a classic work of **Gothic** literature as well as one of the earliest examples of science fiction.

1819

A depiction of the Peterloo Massacre in which a peaceful political protest in Manchester, England, was attacked by armed cavalrymen.

ON AUGUST 16, A POLITICAL RALLY of around 60,000 people on St. Peter's Field in Manchester, England, turned from a protest about high food prices and lack of popular suffrage into the **Peterloo Massacre.** Magistrates, concerned about the size of the crowd, ordered the Yeomanry (voluntary cavalry officers) to arrest the speakers, but they **attacked** the crowd when they refused to make way. A regiment, the 15th Hussars, was then sent in, and an estimated 15 people were killed and more than 500 injured.

Upon his return from exile, Venezuelan general **Simón Bolívar** had begun to make considerable headway against royalist forces. In 1819, he led his troops from Venezuela over the Andes to launch an attack. The Spanish were defeated at the **Battle of Boyacá** on August 7 and Bolívar marched south to Santa Fé de Bogotá, which secured the independence of **New Granada.** Bolívar was named the president of the new Republic of Colombia.

In a bid to challenge Dutch dominance of trade routes between China and India (see 1795) the British East India Company sought a new base in the Malay peninsula. **Stamford Raffles** arrived in **Singapore,** which was then part of the Riau-Johor empire. He negotiated a deal with the local ruler and founded a port.

THE EAST INDIA COMPANIES

The East India Companies monopolized trade between Europe and Southeast Asia, India, and the Far East from the early 17th century. However, the French Compagnie Française des Indes Orientales ceased trading at the time of the French Revolution (see 1789). The charter for the Dutch Vereenigde Oost-Indische Compagnie was revoked in 1799 when the government took control of it. Sweden's Svenska Ostindiska Companiet folded in 1813, while Britain's East India Company (above) traded until 1874.

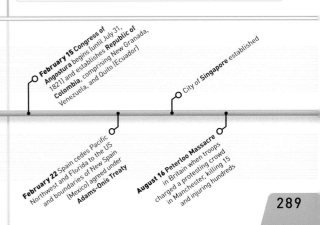

March 8 New York Stock Exchange founded

November Third Maratha War (to 1818)

Argentine general **José de San Martín** (1778–1850) wins decisive victory against Spanish in Chile

Wahhabis defeated by Egyptian forces

April 5 Battle of Maipú secures Chilean independence

Dutch take Malacca back from Britain

Haitian president **Jean Pierre Boyer** (1776–1850) unites divided island

English writer **Mary Shelley** (1797–1851) publishes *Frankenstein*

February 15 Congress of Angostura begins (until July 31, 1821) and establishes **Republic of Colombia,** comprising New Granada, Venezuela, and Quito (Ecuador)

February 22 Spain cedes Pacific Northwest and Florida to the US and boundaries of New Spain (Mexico) agreed under **Adams-Onís Treaty**

City of **Singapore** established

August 16 Peterloo Massacre in Britain when troops charged a protesting crowd in Manchester, killing 15 and injuring hundreds

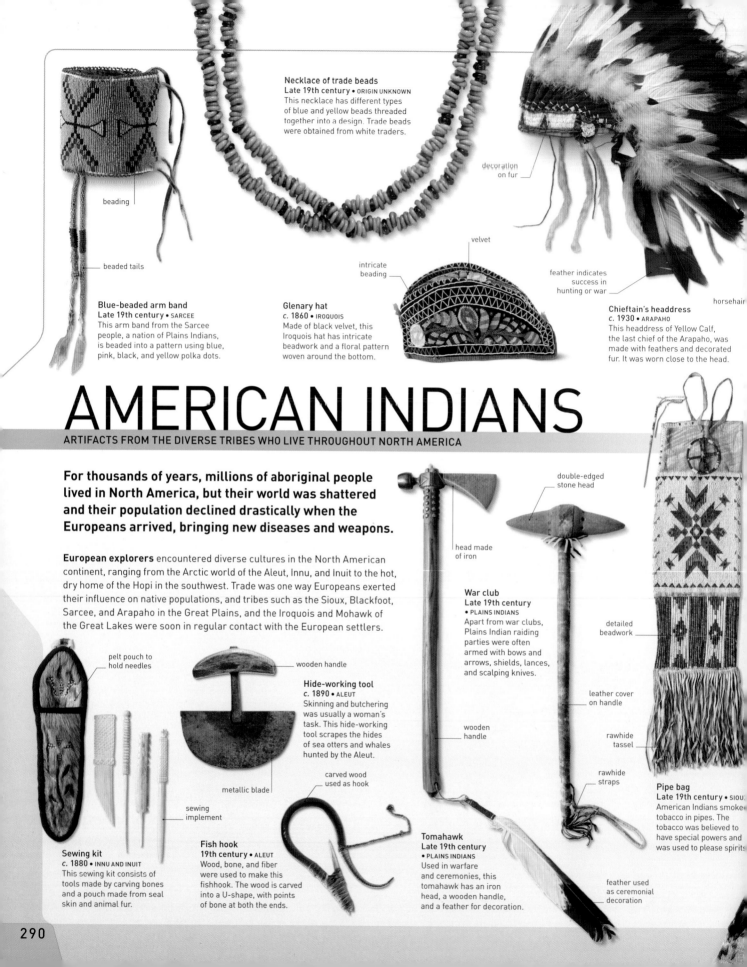

Necklace of trade beads
Late 19th century • ORIGIN UNKNOWN
This necklace has different types of blue and yellow beads threaded together into a design. Trade beads were obtained from white traders.

decoration on fur

velvet

intricate beading

feather indicates success in hunting or war

horsehair

beading

beaded tails

Blue-beaded arm band
Late 19th century • SARCEE
This arm band from the Sarcee people, a nation of Plains Indians, is beaded into a pattern using blue, pink, black, and yellow polka dots.

Glenary hat
c. 1860 • IROQUOIS
Made of black velvet, this Iroquois hat has intricate beadwork and a floral pattern woven around the bottom.

Chieftain's headdress
c. 1930 • ARAPAHO
This headdress of Yellow Calf, the last chief of the Arapaho, was made with feathers and decorated fur. It was worn close to the head.

AMERICAN INDIANS
ARTIFACTS FROM THE DIVERSE TRIBES WHO LIVE THROUGHOUT NORTH AMERICA

For thousands of years, millions of aboriginal people lived in North America, but their world was shattered and their population declined drastically when the Europeans arrived, bringing new diseases and weapons.

European explorers encountered diverse cultures in the North American continent, ranging from the Arctic world of the Aleut, Innu, and Inuit to the hot, dry home of the Hopi in the southwest. Trade was one way Europeans exerted their influence on native populations, and tribes such as the Sioux, Blackfoot, Sarcee, and Arapaho in the Great Plains, and the Iroquois and Mohawk of the Great Lakes were soon in regular contact with the European settlers.

double-edged stone head

head made of iron

War club
Late 19th century
• PLAINS INDIANS
Apart from war clubs, Plains Indian raiding parties were often armed with bows and arrows, shields, lances, and scalping knives.

detailed beadwork

leather cover on handle

wooden handle

rawhide tassel

rawhide straps

Pipe bag
Late 19th century • SIOU
American Indians smoke
tobacco in pipes. The tobacco was believed to have special powers and was used to please spirits

pelt pouch to hold needles

wooden handle

Hide-working tool
c. 1890 • ALEUT
Skinning and butchering was usually a woman's task. This hide-working tool scrapes the hides of sea otters and whales hunted by the Aleut.

carved wood used as hook

metallic blade

sewing implement

Sewing kit
c. 1880 • INNU AND INUIT
This sewing kit consists of tools made by carving bones and a pouch made from seal skin and animal fur.

Fish hook
19th century • ALEUT
Wood, bone, and fiber were used to make this fishhook. The wood is carved into a U-shape, with points of bone at both the ends.

Tomahawk
Late 19th century
• PLAINS INDIANS
Used in warfare and ceremonies, this tomahawk has an iron head, a wooden handle, and a feather for decoration.

feather used as ceremonial decoration

Sashes
Mid-19th century
• MOHAWK
These sashes display intricate beadwork. The one on the left has a floral motif, which was often copied from white settlers in the area.

tribal symbol

intricate beadwork

Jacket
c. 1890 • SIOUX
This jacket is made of buckskin and decorated with beads, which were brought in by white traders.

buckskin exterior

Beaded moccasins
Late 19th century • SIOUX
Leather moccasins with decorative beading were worn by Sioux hunters and traders. The sole extends over the toes.

beading on leather

Wooden bears
Early 20th century • INUIT
These wooden polar bears were made by the Inuit people, who live in the Arctic and subarctic regions of North America.

inner fur lining

carved from wood

painted with bright colors

Kachina figure
20th century • HOPI
Hopi kachina figures of this type were used to teach children about the world of spirits.

seal or reindeer skin on the exterior

fur-lined hood for warmth

Mukluks
Early 20th century • INUIT
These boots for children have seal or reindeer skin on the outside and fur on the inner lining.

carved tooth

Carved and pierced teeth
19th century • INUIT
Used by shamans—or medicine men—in their practices, these teeth, some shaped into birds, are strung together along a ring.

skin is waterproof

horn

Winter coat
Late 19th century • INNU
Anoraks were winter coats, typically loose at the bottom to allow the wearer to draw in cold air if ventilation was needed.

seal skin insulates body from cold

cavities stuffed with sage and grass were an offering to the buffalo

Buffalo skull
19th century • BLACKFOOT
Used in the Sun Dance ritual of the Plains Indians, this Blackfoot buffalo skull has horns and is decorated with polka dots.

Egyptian Mameluke soldiers were former slaves. By invading Sudan, Egypt hoped to add Sudanese captives to their ranks.

A woodcut illustrates the battle for independence in Mexico.

A depiction of the coronation of Pedro I as emperor of Brazil. Pedro, the son of the king of Portugal, had declared the colony's independence.

AS THE UNITED STATES began the settlement of western territories, the issue of **slavery** could not be ignored. Most of the northern states had abolished the practice, but the southern states had become increasingly dependent on slave labor. When the Missouri territory petitioned for statehood in 1817, it caused a political crisis over whether the federal government had the right to restrict slavery in this territory. The solution was the **Missouri Compromise**, which allowed slavery in Missouri, but not in any new state north of 36°30' latitude.

Much of Europe, meanwhile, was convulsed by political unrest, with **revolts** in the Italian states, Portugal, France, and the Low Countries. In **Spain**, Ferdinand VII had returned to the throne in 1814, rejecting the new constitution (see 1812) and arresting liberal leaders. Following public unrest, Ferdinand was forced to accept the 1812 Constitution, marking the start of the **Trienio Liberal**—three years of a liberal regime (1820–23). In 1823, France's Louis XVIII—who

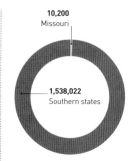

10,200
Missouri

1,538,022
Southern states

Slave population
Although the slave population was small in Missouri, the question of permitting slavery in the state caused a political crisis in the US.

had been restored to the throne (see 1815)—sent in troops to "free" Ferdinand. These soldiers toppled the liberal regime, and returned Ferdinand to power.

Egypt invaded its southern neighbor, **Sudan**. Pasha Muhammad Ali wanted Sudanese gold and slaves for his army. By 1821, Sudan had fallen and the Egyptian Empire extended down the Nile to what is now Uganda.

IN GREECE, A FIGHT FOR INDEPENDENCE FROM THE TURKS began. Resentful at years of living under oppression, people from across Greek society—including the **Orthodox Church**—began to plot their liberation. Some rebel groups had been organizing through secret patriotic societies such as the **Philikí Etaireía** (Society of Friends). These organizations involved people living on the islands, but also had significant support from the large **Greek diaspora**.

At the same time, rebels in the **Americas** were able to take advantage of Spain's internal crisis and weakness to make the final **push for independence**. **Mexico** managed to secure its liberation after Mexican royalists, upon hearing the news of events in Spain (see 1820), decided that self-rule was the only way to **avoid a liberal regime** as had happened in Spain. On August 24, a treaty was signed recognizing Mexican independence, and on May 19 the former royalist Agustín de Iturbide (1783–1824) crowned himself emperor **Agustín I**.

Farther south, the **Congress of Cúcuta** was formed and formally established **Gran Colombia**, consisting of present-day Colombia, Panama, Venezuela, and Ecuador. **Simón Bolívar** was named president and Bogotá was made the capital.

In Peru, **José de San Martín** led his troops into Lima and declared **Peru independent**, though fighting to secure its freedom continued.

THE RELATIONSHIP BETWEEN PORTUGAL AND BRAZIL had been fundamentally affected when the Portuguese court, fleeing Napoleon, arrived in Brazil in 1808. After **John VI** (1769–1826) returned to Portugal in 1821, he left his son, **Dom Pedro** (1798–1834), in charge of the kingdom of Brazil, as Prince Regent. Dom Pedro, frustrated by the attempt of the Portuguese Cortes to reduce Brazil to its pre-1808 colonial status, issued his **Grito de Ipiranga** (Cry of Ipiranga) declaring Brazil's independence and crowning himself Emperor Pedro I.

Even the loyalist **Santo Domingo**, on the island of Hispaniola, was swept up in the revolutionary spirit of the time, declaring **independence** in 1821, though it failed to realize a plan to join Gran Colombia. Santo Domingo's neighbor, **Haiti** (previously Saint-Domingue), grew concerned that France or Britain might sneak through the

AFRICA

LIBERIA

ATLANTIC OCEAN

Liberia
Located on the West Coast of Africa, alongside slaving ports, a colony for freed slaves was established by the American Colonization Society.

12 THOUSAND

THE NUMBER OF **FREED SLAVES RELOCATED** TO LIBERIA FROM 1822 TO 1862

now poorly guarded ports in Santo Domingo and launch an attack to recolonize and **re-enslave** the island. With this pretext—and the fact that slavery still persisted in Santo Domingo—Haiti's president, **Jean-Pierre Boyer** (in office 1818–50), arrived in Santo Domingo with his forces. The provisional government turned control over to Boyer, who united both sides of the island under Haitian rule.

The issue of slavery remained contentious in the US, and there arose the additional question of how to treat **freed slaves**. The American Colonization Society, founded in 1816, advocated they be returned to Africa. The society secured agreements with local rulers in West Africa, near **Cape Mesurado**, establishing a settlement that would become known as **Liberia**.

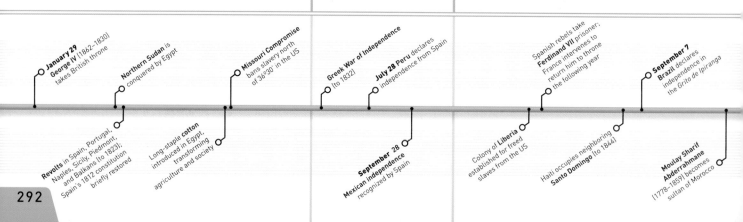

January 29
George IV (1762–1830) takes British throne

Northern Sudan is conquered by Egypt

Missouri Compromise bans slavery north of 36°30' in the US

Greek War of Independence (to 1832)

July 28 **Peru** declares independence from Spain

Spanish rebels take **Ferdinand VII** prisoner; France intervenes to return him to throne the following year

September 7 **Brazil** declares independence in the *Grito de Ipiranga*

Revolts in Spain, Portugal, Naples, Sicily, Piedmont, and Balkans (to 1823); Spain's 1812 constitution briefly restored

Long-staple **cotton** introduced in Egypt, transforming agriculture and society

September 28 **Mexican independence** recognized by Spain

Colony of **Liberia** established for freed slaves from the US

Haiti occupies neighboring **Santo Domingo** (to 1844)

Moulay Sharif Abderrahmane (1778–1859) becomes sultan of Morocco

292

The Alaungpaya dynasty's invasion of northern India led to Britain declaring war and eventually capturing the coastal city of Rangoon, pictured.

This print depicts the Ottoman siege of Missolonghi, where the Greeks had established a provisional government during their war for independence.

IN HIS ANNUAL MESSAGE TO THE US Congress on December 2, President James Monroe (see panel, below) outlined a new diplomatic policy: the **Monroe Doctrine**. Concerned about the possibility of European incursion into the new republics of Latin America, Monroe attempted to **set boundaries** between Europe and the Americas. The doctrine stated that the US would not interfere in the internal affairs or wars of European powers, nor in any colonies in the Americas, but likewise declared the western hemisphere now closed to any further European attempts at **colonization**. Interference with territories in the Americas would now be viewed as hostile acts against the US.

Earlier in the year, another republic had joined the Americas: the **United Provinces of Central America**, which was composed of Guatemala, El Salvador, Nicaragua, Honduras, and Costa Rica. They had achieved independence from Spain in 1821, but were joined to the empire of Mexico. The local leaders decided to break away and establish a federal republic, with the capital in **Guatemala City**.

The **Alaungpaya Dynasty** of Burma (present-day Myanmar, see 1752), had been making incursions into the northern Indian state of **Assam**, bringing them into contact with the British, who were occupying the region. In an effort to protect their interests in India, Britain launched the **First Anglo–Burmese War** the following year (1824–26). This resulted in the British capture of much of the territory of Burma, including **Rangoon**, which was taken in 1825.

US ISOLATIONISM

James Monroe (1758–1831, see right) was the fifth president of the United States, serving from 1817–25. His time in office was a period during which the US began to emerge as a serious global power. This period was known as the "era of good feelings," and was marked by significant economic growth and general public optimism. With its aversion to interference in other nations' affairs set out in the Monroe Doctrine, the US began to pursue a policy of isolationism.

Lord Byron
The Romantic poet Lord Byron was inspired by the Greek struggle for independence from the Ottoman Empire, and went to Greece to fight.

AS THE FIGHT FOR GREEK INDEPENDENCE INTENSIFIED, it attracted the public's attention across Europe, especially among writers and artists. One such person was the English **Romantic** poet **Lord Byron** (1788–1824), famed for his poem *Don Juan*. Byron had arrived in Greece the previous year to help fight in the struggle. However, while he was abroad, he contracted a serious illness and died on April 19 in **Missolonghi**.

In Peru, a decisive victory at the **Battle of Ayacucho**, on December 9, meant the end of Spanish rule, though to the north, in the territory known as **Upper Peru**, loyalist forces were still holding out against rebel troops, in one of the last bastions of fighting.

THE TERRITORY OF UPPER PERU received a much-needed boost with the arrival of Simón Bolívar (see 1811) and **Antonio José de Sucre** (1785–1830), whose troops helped to defeat the Spanish. Bolívar wanted this territory to **unite** with the rest of Peru, but Sucre had already agreed with the rebel leaders that it would become a separate **republic**. In honor of Bolívar's help, the rebels named the new nation **Bolivia**, and they invited Sucre to be its first president, which he accepted. With the creation of Bolivia, all the former Spanish colonies—with the exception of Cuba, Puerto Rico, and the Philippines—had become independent nations.

In England, there was great excitement over the opening, on September 27, of the **Stockton to Darlington** railroad line, in the industrial north of the country.

Technological innovations in the use of steam (see 1775 and 1786) to power engines had led to the development of railroad **locomotives**, such as the one designed by English inventor **John Blenkinsop** in 1812. **George Stephenson** (1781–1848), a colliery mechanic, improved on that design and caught the attention of a group of investors wishing to link the towns of Stockton and Darlington. Darlington was in the middle of a **coal mining** region and the Pennine mountains made transportation difficult. The 25-mile (40-km) line opened the way for further rail development.

Crowd puller
The opening of the Stockton to Darlington rail line marked the first time that a locomotive was used to pull a passenger train.

January 10 Edward Jenner, smallpox vaccine pioneer (b. 1749), dies

September 10 Simón Bolívar named president of **Peru**

April 19 Poet Lord Byron (b. 1788) dies in Missolonghi, Greece

Dutch cede Malacca to British

March 4 John Quincy Adams becomes sixth US president

June 20 Bourbon Charles X crowned King of France

September 27 Opening of the Stockton–Darlington Railway in Britain marks start of passenger rail travel using locomotives

United Provinces of Central America declare their independence (Guatemala, Honduras, Nicaragua, Costa Rica)

December 2 New diplomatic policy by US, the Monroe doctrine, posits nonintervention by US and Europe in the Americas

First Anglo–Burmese War (to 1826) over Burma's occupation of territory in northeast India

December 9 Battle of Ayacucho in Peru is a decisive victory over Spain

Javanese revolts against Dutch rule (to 1830)

August 6 Bolivia gains independence from Spain

October 26 Erie Canal opens in New York State, linking Lake Erie and the Hudson River

The signing ceremony at the Treaty of Turkmanchai, in which Persia returned contested land in the Caucasus region to Russia.

18 MILES PER HOUR
THE TOP SPEED OF THE **FIRST US STEAM LOCOMOTIVE**

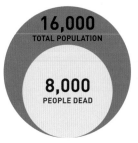

A depiction of the uprising that led to the Belgian independence.

TENSIONS BETWEEN RUSSIA AND Persia restarted (see 1813) over the Caucasus region, with the Persians attempting to take back the territory of **Georgia** in 1825. However, a crushing defeat at the **Battle of Ganja** on September 26, 1826 halted the Persian advance. Russian troops then marched into Persia, eventually taking Tehran, leaving the Persians no option but to accept **defeat**. They negotiated the **Treaty of Turkmanchai**, which put the Russian border at the Aras River, returning the Caucasus territory to Russia.

In **Hawaii**, US missionaries had started to settle on the islands and America had become one of the kingdom's largest trading partners. The US was looking to protect its growing interests there by formalizing trade arrangements in the face of possible European competition, so it convinced the regency government of **King Kamehameha III** (1813–54) to sign the **Hawaii–United States Treaty** of 1826. The treaty stipulated that there would be peaceful and friendly political and trading relations between the two.

In France, inventor **Joseph-Nicéphore Niépce** (1765–1833) took the world's first **photograph**, known as *View from the Window at Le Gras*, which was of a barnyard in France. His technique involved making an eight-hour exposure onto a pewter plate using a **camera obscura**, which was a dark box with a tiny hole—a forerunner of the modern camera.

AS GREECE'S BATTLE AGAINST the Ottoman Empire continued, neighboring powers began to call for an end to the conflict. Britain, France, and Russia joined together to sign the **Treaty of London** on July 6, which demanded the establishment of an independent Greek state. The Ottomans refused, confident they had the land and sea power to defeat the Greeks.

By autumn, the Ottoman resources were put to the test as a Turkish–Egyptian fleet went up against a naval force comprising British, French, and Russian ships at the **Battle of Navarino** on October 20. The Russo–European ships sunk three-quarters of the Ottoman fleet, and this humiliating defeat led to the eventual withdrawal of Turkish troops from Greece, which won independence in 1832.

A one-sided battle
A Turkish warship burns fiercely at the Battle of Navarino, in which the Ottoman fleet was devastated but not a single allied ship was lost.

José Gervasio Artigas
Artigas was the father of the Uruguayan independence movement, but had been in exile for several years when it was finally liberated.

THE TREATY OF MONTEVIDEO RECOGNIZED the independence of Uruguay in August 1828. The area, then known as the **Banda Oriental**, was disputed between Brazil and Argentina. It had been under Spanish control but during the wars of independence in South America, under the leadership of **José Gervasio Artigas** (1764–1850), the territory established its independence from Spain and Argentina in 1815. However, the following year, **Brazil invaded** and occupied it. This led to a further war, led by **Juan Antonio Lavalleja** (1784–1853) and his group known as the "thirty-three immortals." Lavalleja, with Argentinian support, defeated Brazilian troops and founded an independent Uruguay.

Territorial disputes were also behind another conflict between the **Ottoman Empire** and **Russia**, with the Russians capturing **Vidin** and **Varna** (in present-day Bulgaria).

DEBATE OVER IRELAND HAD intensified after the Act of Union (see 1801). **Daniel O'Connell**, a Catholic lawyer, called for England to repeal its **anti-Catholic laws**, arguing that it could not claim to be representing the people of Ireland. In addition, he staged mass meetings about the issue of **Catholic emancipation**. In 1828, O'Connell stood for parliament and won, though he was not allowed to sit in government because of his Catholicism. His victory, however, attracted the attention of the British prime minister, Arthur Wellesley, the **Duke of Wellington** (see 1815), who was Irish though not Catholic. He oversaw the **Catholic Relief Act 1829**, which allowed Catholics in Ireland and England to take seats in Parliament and hold public office.

Elsewhere in England, inventor George Stephenson (see 1825) unveiled a new locomotive engine, known as the *Rocket*, which reached speeds of about 36 miles (58km) per hour. He had entered the **Liverpool and Manchester Railway** competition for best new engine. The *Rocket* was the victor.

This year also saw progress of the railroad in the US, with the first American-built steam locomotive, **Tom Thumb**. In 1830, a race was staged against a horse-drawn cart to prove the **superiority of steam power**. Although the horse won on this occasion due to a techinal fault with the train, the point was made and the owners of the **Baltimore and Ohio Railroad** agreed to switch to steam trains.

EUROPE HAD SCARCELY RECOVERED from the unrest of the previous decade (see 1820) when France was convulsed by the **July Revolution**, an insurrection that forced the abdication of Charles X (r. 1824–30), who was replaced by **Louis-Philippe**, duke of Orléans (r. 1830–48). The rebellion had been triggered by Charles's attempt to enforce repressive ordinances, such as suspending the freedom of the press and modifying electoral law so many people lost their right to vote.

Louis-Philippe's succession to the throne signaled the arrival of power for the **bourgeoisie**, who were his chief support, rather than the aristocracy, and he remained in power until 1848.

Around the same time, **revolts** were taking place in the Italian and German kingdoms; in the Netherlands; and in Russia, as the **Polish** living under Russian rule rose up against the czar.

16,000
TOTAL POPULATION

8,000
PEOPLE DEAD

Cherokee deaths on Trail of Tears
Thousands of American Indians were forcibly relocated from the Southeast US, traveling a route later called the Trail of Tears.

British occupy **Fernando Pó** (off West Africa) to use as base for antislaving raids

British Straights settlement established, comprising Penang, Malacca, and Singapore

July 6 Treaty of London signed between France, Britain, and Russia; calls for Ottoman Empire to agree armistice in Greece

August 27 Uruguay's independence recognized by treaty

Russia acquires **Armenia** and declares war on Ottomans (to 1829)

March 4 Andrew Jackson (1767–1845) becomes seventh US president (to 1837)

Catholic Relief Act passed enabling Catholics to sit as MPs

Venezuela and **Ecuador** withdraw from Gran Colombia

July 16 Second Russo–Persian War (until 1828) begins over Persian attempt to retake Georgian territory

October 20 Russo–European fleet defeats Ottomans at **Battle of Navarino**

Romanian **Petrache Poenaru** (1799–1875) invents the fountain pen

September 22 Shaka Zulu, leader of the Zulu Kingdom, South Africa, assassinated

Louis Braille (1809–52) publishes first book using his first reading system for blind people in France

French invade **Algeria** and take control

> **NO MINISTER** EVER STOOD, OR **COULD STAND,** AGAINST **PUBLIC OPINION.**
>
> Robert Peel, British politician, on the Reform Act, 1834

Also during this period, French troops arrived in **Algiers**, with the intention of taking control. A few years earlier, in 1827, the provincial Ottoman ruler, or dey, Husayn (r. 1818–38), had struck a French consul with a fly whisk, giving the French a pretext for war. The source of the tension was an unpaid debt between France and the dey. During a French

Liberty leading the people
This famous painting by French artist Eugène Delacroix (1798–1863) was inspired by the July Revolution, and depicts "Liberty" as a woman.

blockade of Algiers, matters escalated. By July 5, the French had raised their flag over the kasbah in Algiers and this marked the start of French control over this North African territory.

In **South America**, political alliances were also fragile. Before his death in 1830, Simón Bolívar (see 1811) had witnessed the secession of **Venezuela and Ecuador** from Gran Colombia, which ended his dream of **political unity** among the new republics.

Farther north, more settlers in the US were making their way west, and this was known as

the **era of the wagon train**. Settlers, traveling in groups of horse-drawn wagons carrying all of their possessions, headed out to unknown territory to set up farms and settle the land.

Meanwhile, to facilitate settlement in the east, the US government passed the **Indian Removal Act** in 1830. This stripped American Indians of legal rights, and forced them to leave their desirable territory in the southeast of the country and relocate to sparsely populated land west of the Mississippi. The moves resulted in many deaths.

THE KINGDOM OF THE NETHERLANDS was caught up in the turmoil across Europe. The Congress of Vienna (see 1815) had forced the Belgian territories, which had been under French control, to unite with the Dutch, thereby creating a buffer between Russia and France. This move proved unpopular and tensions grew over the intervening years.

By August 1830, inspired by events in France, the **Belgian Revolution** had begun. The result was a clear break from the kingdom of the Netherlands. Later that year a **constitution** was issued, which created a constitutional monarchy and a parliamentary system. On January 20, 1831, the new state of **Belgium** was officially recognized by Britain and France, though not the Netherlands. The Belgians were forced to choose a monarch with no direct connection to other major European powers. They finally elected Leopold of Saxe-Coburg-Saalfeld—the uncle of Britain's Queen Victoria—and he ruled as **Leopold I** until 1865.

The same year, Syria was annexed by Egypt until 1840, when the latter was finally forced to return the region to the Ottomans.

The English Reform Act
A cartoon shows the reformers' attack on the "Old Rotten Tree," which symbolizes the corrupt "rotten" boroughs. They wanted a fairer distribution of parliamentary seats.

BRITAIN ALSO SAW UPHEAVAL AND SOCIAL CHANGE in the 1830s. There had been growing public discontent over the outdated voting system (see 1819). A bill was drafted, aimed at transferring votes and redistributing seats from small "rotten" boroughs controlled by the nobility to the more populous industrial towns. The first **Reform Bill** failed to be passed in parliament. This caused serious riots in many cities, as well as a political crisis with the prime minister, **Charles Grey** (1764–1845), who threatened to step down over the matter. The bill finally became law on June 4, 1832. This legislation allowed more middle-class men the vote, but the working class and women were still excluded.

February 7 Belgian constitution recognized; **Belgium** declares independence

First wave of **rebellion** and social unrest in Europe calling for liberal political reforms

August 25 Start of the Belgian Revolution (to 1831)

November 29 Polish **uprising** against Russia

Egypt occupies **Syria** (to 1840)

First official Ottoman newspaper *Takvim-i Vekayi* begins publication

June 4 British parliament passes the **Reform Act**, which makes significant changes to the electoral system

Russia annexes Duchy of Warsaw

May 26 US Congress passes **Indian Removal Act**

June 26 William IV (1765–1837) ascends to the British throne

August 9 Louis Philippe (1773–1850) declared king of France after revolution in Paris

August 21 Nat Turner slave **rebellion** in US, leaving more than 50 white people in Virginia dead

August 30 Treaty of London creates an independent kingdom of Greece and installs a monarchy.

1833–34

This engraving shows children working in an English mill. The size of the first cotton spinning machines meant they were best operated by children.

48

THE MAXIMUM HOURS PER WEEK CHILDREN AGED 9–12 COULD WORK IN ENGLISH MILLS

IN BRITAIN, INDUSTRIAL development and urban growth progressed rapidly. Laws were introduced to address exploitation of labour and the growing cost of providing for the poor. The **1833 Factory Act** appointed inspectors to monitor factories and limited the hours that children could work.

In England, local parishes provided some relief for the elderly, ill, and impoverished. Out of this grew a system of **workhouses**, aiming to give employment to the able-bodied. The **Poor Law Amendment Act of 1834** stipulated that the poor could only receive assistance if they went to workhouses, which were to be built in every parish. Conditions in the workhouses were deliberately harsh and the legislation immediately proved unpopular.

In China, British merchants were granted permission to **engage in trade** after legislation ended the East India Company's monopoly. Although there had been private traders in Canton before the act, now more were allowed to sell their wares and export Chinese goods, such as **tea**, the imports of which rose 40 per cent after the beginning of free trade.

In 1832, **Egypt invaded Syria**. Muhammad Ali, the pasha, was angered by a failed promise from the Ottoman sultan to give him the territory. Ali took Gaza and Jerusalem in the **First Turko–Egyptian War**, and by 1833 the Ottoman government begged Russia for help, and 18,000 troops were sent to Constantinople. Britain and France got involved, demanding a settlement, in which Egypt was given Syria, and Russia withdrew.

Commemorative coin
The Slave Emancipation Act outlawed the buying or selling of people, set free young children, and compensated planters in most of the British Empire.

1835

A Galápagos cactus finch, one of the species noted by Charles Darwin.

IN THE PACIFIC OCEAN, almost 600 miles (1,000km) from the coastline of South America, English naturalist **Charles Darwin** (1809–82) took extensive notes on the nature of the **Galápagos Islands**. Darwin had accepted a post on a scientific voyage aboard the *Beagle*, which left England on December 27, 1831, arriving in the Galápagos in September 1835 (see also 1839). It was in the Galápagos where Darwin first noticed the difference in the species of wildlife on the island compared with mainland South America. This discovery laid the foundation for his later scientific work on the **evolution** of different species (see 1859).

In Britain, the **National Colonisation Society** had been set up to facilitate the settlement in Australia of people who were not convicts. Founder **Edward Gibbon Wakefield** (1796–1862)—who had served time in prison—came up with a scheme for populating colonies based on the sale of land and a tax on the price, which would pay for the transportation to the colony. A fleet set off for **South Australia**, where the city of Melbourne was established in 1835, and Adelaide a year later.

> **IT SEEMS TO BE A LITTLE WORLD WITHIN ITSELF.**

Charles Darwin, from *Journal of Researches*, September 1835

1836

The Alamo, the site of a key battle for Texan independence.

AS SETTLERS IN THE US MOVED WEST, many decided to live in the Texas territory, which was part of **Mexico**. However, Mexican authorities wanted tighter control over this large territory and the settlers rebelled in October 1835, launching the **Texas War of Independence**. The following March, after months of unrest, General Antonio López de Santa Anna (1794–1876) marched into Texas with 5,000 Mexican troops. Although massively outnumbered, the rebels managed to hold them off during a battle at a San Antonio fortress, called the Alamo. The rebels were eventually defeated but the Alamo proved a rallying point for Texans bent on revenge. Soon after, General **Samuel Houston** (1793–1863) led a Texan army into the battle cry **"Remember the Alamo!"** and beat Santa Anna at the Battle of Jacinto on April 21, forcing Mexico to recognize the new republic of Texas.

5,000 MEXICANS

182 Texans

Battle of the Alamo
Texans were vastly outnumbered by Mexican forces in the battle fought between 23 February and 6 March and there were very few survivors.

1837

A painting of Queen Victoria's coronation in Westminster Abbey.

Long-distance communicator
This is a single-needle electric telegraph machine, which later developed into double-needle and four-needle instruments.

EXPERIMENTS had been taking place for decades over the question of how to transmit electric current through wires. In 1837, two British inventors, William Fothergill Cooke and Charles Wheatstone, made a breakthrough and secured a patent for an **electric** telegraph device that allowed for communication through wires and had **needles that could point to specific letters and numbers**. At the same time in the US, **Samuel Morse** received a patent on an electromagnetic transmitter that could transfer information

---

1833 Slave Emancipation Act abolishes slavery in British Empire; not in force until 1838

1833 Isabella II (1830–1904) takes Spanish throne, with Maria Christina (1806–78) as regent

1833 Factory Act in Britain prohibits employment of children under age of nine

1833 First Turko–Egyptian War ends; Egypt retains Syria, which it had invaded in 1832

1834 Poor Law Amendment Act passed in Britain calling for the poor to support themselves

1834 British East India Company's monopoly on trade to China abolished

1834 First Carlist War in Spain over succession to the throne (to 1839)

May 5 First railway in continental Europe opens in Belgium

August 30 Founding of the town of Melbourne in Australia

December 1 Danish author Hans Christian Andersen publishes first book of fairy tales

March 2 Texans rebel against Mexican rule and declare their territory a republic

Spain recognizes **independence of Mexico**

March 6 Defeat of Texans at Battle of the Alamo

October 24 A. Phillips patents the **match**

December 28 Colony of South Australia officially proclaimed

Death of **Muhammad Bello**, whose kingdom of Sokoto (northern Nigeria) reached a population of around 10 million

Charles Wheatstone and **William Cooke** patent the telegraph in Britain; **Samuel Morse** in US

March 4 Martin van Buren becomes third US president

> ## " HE'LL HAVE US GOING TO THE MOON YET. "

Great Western Railway director, on Isambard Kingdom Brunel

The East India Company's steamer, *Nemesis*, attacks Chinese war junks in Anson's Bay, at the mouth of the Pearl River, China, during the First Opium War.

using dots and dashes. Morse's telegraph was far simpler than the Cooke Wheatstone design, and soon became the standard instrument worldwide, revolutionizing the global movement of information.

When Britain's King William IV died on 20 June, he had no surviving legitimate heir, so the crown passed to **Victoria**, his niece (see panel, below). She was the daughter of Edward, Duke of Kent, and granddaughter of George III. Her reign was viewed as a time of growing prosperity, technological innovation, and colonial expansion.

In **Japan**, **Tokugawa Ieyoshi** (1793–1853) became shogun. At the time of his rule Japan was experiencing social and economic decline. He introduced measures known as the **Tempo Reforms**, restricting migration to urban areas and instigating price controls—but they failed.

TRANSPORTATION TECHNOLOGY was rapidly changing. Along with the expansion in rail transport, travel by sea was also being revolutionized by many innovations. The power of steam was finally harnessed in an efficient way that allowed for much quicker sea crossings (see 1786). On 8 April 1838, the *Great Western* left Bristol for its maiden transatlantic voyage, and arrived

Brunel's *Great Western*
The Great Western steamship shown off the west coast of England. The sails helped to propel the ship and keep it on an even keel.

in New York 15 days later; the paddle-wheeled steamship had cut the voyage time in half and arrived with fuel to spare. The ship had been designed by leading British civil engineer **Isambard Kingdom Brunel** (1806–59), who had also been involved in other engineering projects, including the Great Western Railway. The idea for the steamship started as a suggestion by Brunel to Great Western Railway directors that the train line could be extended to New York by way of a regular transatlantic service. Soon after, the **Great Western Steamship Company** was set up to facilitate the construction of the ship.

In the Americas, **Guatemala**, **Honduras**, and **Nicaragua** became independent nations.

QUEEN VICTORIA (1819–1901)

Ruling for 63 years and 216 days, Queen Victoria was one of the longest-reigning monarchs of Britain. In 1840, she married her cousin, Albert of Saxe-Coburg and Gotha (1819–61). She adored him and they had nine children together. The Victorian era contrasted sharply with the excesses of previous Hanoverian rulers, and Victoria's domestic life was held up as the model for families in this period.

WHILE BRITISH TRADE IN CHINA CONTINUED TO EXPAND, so too did the Chinese opium problem. Decades earlier, the East India Company had started exporting the drug, produced from **poppies** grown in Bengal, to China in order to trade it for tea, which it then sent to Britain. Despite numerous attempts to ban the importation of the substance, British ships continued to import it. On March 30, 1839, one frustrated Chinese commissioner ordered British warehouses and ships in Canton to be destroyed. Britain sent warships in retaliation, attacking China's coastline in the **First Opium War**.

Meanwhile, tensions between Egypt and the Ottoman sultan erupted again in the **Second Turko–Egyptian War**. This time it was triggered by an Ottoman attempt to invade Syria, which it had previously ceded to Egypt (see 1833).

At the same time, British political meddling in Afghanistan triggered the **First Afghan War** (to 1842). Worried about Russia's

growing influence over the Afghan emir, **Dost Muhammad Khan** (1793-1863), Britain attempted to replace him with an emir more sympathetic to British interests in northern India, including the protection of overland trade routes through the region.

In England, naturalist Charles Darwin (see 1835) published an account of the diary he kept while on the ***Beagle***. The journey had taken Darwin around the world. He had set off from Plymouth in 1831 for the Cape Verde Islands, then Brazil, Argentina, Uruguay, and Tierra del Fuego. He then sailed north along the Pacific Coast of South America, stopping at the Galápagos Islands, before going onward to Tahiti, New Zealand, Australia, Mauritius, and finally back to England, arriving in October 1836. Darwin's account helped make his name in science.

DARWIN'S JOURNEY

Feb 1832 ➝➝➝➝ Sep 1835

Darwin's *Beagle* voyages
Charles Darwin's five-year voyage (1831–36) on the Beagle, a warship carrying ten cannons, led him to consider scientific evidence in new ways.

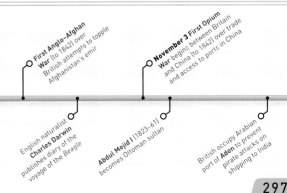

Timeline:

June 20 **Victoria** (1819–1901) becomes British monarch

Upper Canada and Lower Canada rebellions against British rule are put down

Chartist movement begins to form, calling for social reform in Britain

Guatemala, Honduras, and Nicaragua become independent

May 26 **Cherokee** tribe forcibly relocated in US in the **Trail of Tears**

Proteins discovered by Swedish chemist, **Jöns Jakob Berzelius** (1779–1848)

First Anglo–Afghan War (to 1842) over Britain attempts to topple Afghanistan's emir

November 3 **First Opium War** begins between Britain and China (to 1842) over trade and access to ports in China

Louis Daguerre develops the **daguerreotype**, a photographic process

September 28 **Akbar Shah II**, last Mughal emperor of India, dies (b. 1760)

April 8–23 Isambard Kingdom Brunel's (1806–59) Great Western steamship **crosses Atlantic in record time**

June 10 **Myall Creek Massacre**, Australia, in which 28 Aborigines killed by settlers

December 16 Battle of Blood River, South Africa, in which **Boers win victory** over Zulus

English naturalist **Charles Darwin** publishes diary of the voyage of the Beagle

Abdul Mejid I (1823–61) becomes Ottoman sultan

British occupy Arabian port of **Aden** to prevent pirate attacks on shipping to India

THE STORY OF
ELECTRICITY
HARNESSING THE FORCE THAT BUILT THE MODERN WORLD

When Thales, a mathematician and philosopher in ancient Greece, experimented with a piece of amber—known as "elektron" in Greek—little could he have known that his initial observations would still hold a significant place in science more than 2,000 years later.

What Thales noticed was that if he rubbed a piece of amber against fur it would attract bits of dust and feathers lying nearby—although he did not know it, he had stumbled on what we know today as static electricity. Over the following centuries, scientists all over the world experimented with this form of electricity, as well as magnets and magnetism. By the 17th and 18th centuries, technological leaps had been made, although the connection between electricity and magnets would not be clear until the 19th century (see panel, right).

POWER TO THE PEOPLE
As the 1800s progressed, understanding about electricity rapidly increased, and new innovations were rolled out in quick succession. By the dawn of the 20th century, many of the technologies were in place that are still with us today—such as batteries and light bulbs—though they have since been further adapted and refined. Today, the scientific challenge is to find ways of generating electricity that do not cause pollution.

metal brushes move charges

metal foil sectors produce a charge

static electricity is stored in Leyden jars

Wimshurst machine
The English inventor James Wimshurst developed a device that could generate static electricity and store it in a vessel called a Leyden jar. For many years, scientists studying electricity used Wimshurst machines to produce electric charge.

Edison's screw-in light bulb
Although US inventor Thomas Edison is often credited with inventing the light bulb, what he really did was improve an existing idea (see below). He spent years working out a way—using incandescent bulbs—to make electric lighting practical and safe for public use.

600 BCE
Amber
Thales of Miletus rubs a piece of amber against fur and notes that it attracts bits of nearby feathers.

Amber

1700–10
Electrostatic generator
English inventor Francis Hauksbee develops a device that can generate static electricity by using a glass globe and wool threads.

Voltaic pile

1799–1800
The first voltaic pile
The Italian inventor Alessandro Volta creates the first battery, known as the voltaic pile—the unit "volt" is later named after him.

1820s–30s
Faraday experiments
English scientist Michael Faraday further illustrates the relationship between electricity and magnetism with his induction ring.

Faraday's induction ring

1600
Gilbert's *De Magnete*
English physician William Gilbert publishes his famous work on magnetism.

Leyden Jar

1745–46
The Leyden jar
Pieter van Musschenbroe and Ewald Georg von Kleist independently invent a device that allows static electricity to be stored.

1752
Lightning conductor
US scientist Benjamin Franklin flies a kite during a storm, with a key tied to the string, and proves that lightning is a form of electricity.

1820
Electromagnetism discovered
Danish physicist Hans Christian Ørsted notices that a magnet is affected by a nearby wire connected to a battery, and discovers the relationship between magnets and electricity.

" GENIUS IS ONLY ONE PERCENT INSPIRATION, AND NINETY-NINE PERCENT PERSPIRATION. "

Thomas Edison, US inventor, *c.* 1903

inert gas must be placed in bulb

a partial vacuum in bulb means filament can reach high temperatures without catching fire

wires carry electricity to and from filament

metal end screws into lamp

contact transmits electricity

carbonized bamboo filament moves electrons

filament becomes incandescent when current passes through it

MICHAEL FARADAY (1791–1867)

This English inventor played an important role in furthering knowledge about the relationship between magnets and electricity. His discovery of what he called "electromagnetic rotation" was a vital step in the development of what would become the electric motor. Faraday worked out that the interaction between electricity and a magnet would lead to the constant rotation of current, something he tested using a wire carrying electricity, a magnet, and a bowl of mercury.

1878–79
The electric light bulb
British inventor Joseph Swan creates an incandescent "electric lamp." The idea is improved by US scientist Thomas Edison, and the light bulb is born.

Hoover Dam

1882
Hydroelectric power
Scientists begin to realize that the force of water can generate electricity, and build dams and hydroelectric power plants to harness this energy.

Steam turbine

1884
Electricity from steam
Like liquid water, steam is also harnessed for electricity by devices like the turbine, created by Charles Patton.

Early 21st century
Sustainable electricity
Growing worries about pollution caused by the older ways of generating energy lead to the development of "green" technology, such as wind turbines.

Wind turbines

1825
The electromagnet
This device, built by Joseph Henry, uses two metal plates, which are put in acid in order to form a voltaic cell.

Henry's electromagnet

1881
The world's first public electric lighting
The English town of Godalming, Surrey, brings to a close the era of the gas lamp when it wires its streets with electric lighting.

1883–84
The Tesla coil
Serbian-American inventor Nikola Tesla develops a coil that can transmit electricity over long distances—it is a crucial discovery that aids the spread of electricity.

Tesla coil

1950s
Nuclear power
Scientists discover that atoms can be used—in controlled nuclear reactions—as a source of energy to heat water, which then generates electricity. By 1951, the first nuclear power plant is built in Arco, Idaho, in the US.

Horse and coach at a London station leaving to deliver mail. The development of stagecoaches meant mail could be delivered all over Britain.

The port of Hong Kong was key to Britain's trade in the East.

An illustration depicting a caravan of African slaves. The slave trade remained prevalent in many parts of the world despite a growing effort to eradicate it.

EUROPEAN SETTLEMENT OF New Zealand had gradually increased over the previous decade, and included the introduction of many missions. Settlers traded with the **Maori**, who were already living on the island—exchanging European muskets for Maori crops and livestock. This had led to an arms race between rival tribes in the Maori **Musket Wars** (1820–35).

The British wanted to establish a colony and the **New Zealand Company** was set up, selling land for settlement (see 1835). A ship of settlers left for New Zealand in 1839. All involved were aware of potential hostility from the Maori. In 1840, William Hobson (1792–1842), lieutenant-governor of New Zealand, approached Maori chiefs with the **Treaty of Waitangi**. This offered protection by the British in exchange for ceding sovereignty.

Tamati Waka Nene
Nene was a warrior and chieftain of the Maori Ngatihoa tribe in the early 19th century. He spoke out in favor of the Treaty of Waitangi.

The Maori would keep their land on the basis that if they sold it only the British Crown could buy it. There was much opposition to the treaty but some Maori chiefs believed the British presence would bring stability to the country. On May 21 sovereignty was proclaimed over the territory.

In Britain, the **postal system** was reformed. Improved transportation made it possible to deliver mail all over the country, but costs rose as postage was paid for on receipt, based on distance traveled. A "**penny post**" system was proposed, whereby any letter could be sent anywhere in the country for a penny, and postage would be prepaid using stamps. These measures came into force in 1840 and was the first system of its kind in the world.

2,050
non-Maori
population

80,000 MAORI POPULATION

New Zealand's population in 1840
The European population was still very small at the end of 1840, though the Treaty of Waitangi opened the way for further settlement.

AS CHINESE AND BRITISH TROOPS continued to fight in the **Opium War**, Britain's ships sailed up the Pearl River, capturing forts around Canton, followed by the ports of Amoy and Ningpo. The British also occupied the key port of Hong Kong. A preliminary agreement to end the war, drafted in January and known as the **Convention of Chuenpee**, ceded Hong Kong to the British, but the document was written amid continued hostilities and was never ratified.

Egypt and the Turks, meanwhile, ended their second **war over Syria** (see 1839), with Egyptian troops withdrawing from Syria.

THE OPIUM WAR between Britain and China finally came to an end after British troops took further territory, reaching Nanking in August. Chinese officials sued for peace, resulting in the **Treaty of Nanking** on August 29. China was forced to pay an indemnity of $20 million to the British and officially cede Hong Kong. It was also made to open the ports of Canton, Amoy, Foochow, Ningpo, and Shanghai to British trade. These cities became known as "**treaty ports**."

Industrialization and the **mining** industry resulted in many children being forced to work under dirty and dangerous conditions. In Britain, social reformer Anthony Ashley Cooper, seventh earl of Shaftesbury (1801–85), became a driving force for the **Mines Act of 1842**, prohibiting children under ten and women from working in mines. In the US, the state of Massachusetts passed legislation to **limit a child's work day** to ten hours. Belgium's King Leopold I also tried to regulate child and female labor conditions, but his plans were rejected.

The **slave trade** and the practice of slavery still persisted in many countries. France had brought slavery back to its colonies (see 1803), and while Spain had signed a treaty over abolition in 1817 with the British, who had abolished the slave trade in 1807, it was not enforced for decades. Likewise, **Portugal's** 1818 treaty with Britain and subsequent treaties were not honored, nor was slavery abolished in its colonies. However, in 1842, a further treaty allowed British ships to attack Portuguese slave ships off East Africa. The Portuguese colony of **Mozambique** was a huge slave port, with 15,000 slaves a year taken from 1820 to 1830.

Treaty of Nanking
This treaty ended the three-year Opium War, gave Britain control of Hong Kong, and opened up five "treaty ports" to traders.

February 6
Britain takes over New Zealand under Treaty of Waitangi between Maori chiefs and British Crown

June 4 Frederick William IV (1795–1861) takes Prussian throne

April 4 US President William Henry Harrison dies in office (b.1773)

February 7 Battle of Debre Tabor. Ethiopia; Ras Ali Alula, Regent of Emperor of Ethiopia, defeats warlord Wube Haile Maryam of Semien

August 29 Treaty of Nanking cedes Hong Kong to British, opening five ports to foreign trade

May 1 World's first postage stamp issued in Britain —the Penny Black

July 15 Convention of London: European powers and Ottoman Empire try to check power of Egypt's Muhammad Ali, who threatens Ottoman Empire

July 26 Britain occupies Hong Kong

March 30 Anesthesia used for first time in an operation

August 9 US–Canada border agreed by Webster–Ashburton Treaty

Mines Act prohibits the underground work of women and young children in Britain

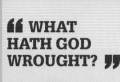

" WHAT HATH GOD WROUGHT? "

Samuel Morse, American artist and inventor, in his telegraph message

A portrait of Abdul Rahman. His father, Faisal, revived Saudi fortunes.

With the backing of the US Congress, Samuel Morse managed to have wires built that could transmit messages.

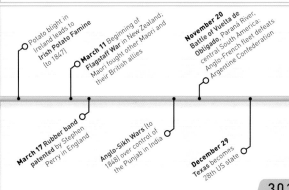

A painting depicts sufferers of the Irish famine. One million died when the potato crop failed over successive years, while millions more left the island forever.

THE OTTOMAN DESTRUCTION OF the first Saudi state (see 1818), established by the Wahhabi movement and **Saud** family, did not prevent the founding of a second Saudi state in 1824. After initial upheavals, **Faisal al-Saud**, second leader of the second state, resumed his rule in 1843, and led the state successfully until 1865.

In South Africa, after a series of victories against the Zulu people, Boer settlers (see 1880) established the **Republic of Natal** in the southeast of the country. The territory was annexed by the

12,000
THE NUMBER OF **BOERS** WHO **MIGRATED** FROM THE **CAPE COLONY**

British in 1843. Many Boers decided to move farther north to what later became the Transvaal and the Orange Free State, joining the emigration of Boers from the Cape Colony, in a move known as the **Great Trek**.

Despite the treaty between the Maori and the British in New Zealand (see 1840), the issue of illegal land sales caused increased tensions, culminating in the **Wairau Massacre** on June 17, in which a chief's wife and 22 Europeans were killed.

Friedrich Engels
The Prussian philosopher wrote about the condition of the working classes in England. His work with Karl Marx made him famous.

FRIEDERICH ENGELS (1820–95) was the son of a prosperous businessman who owned textile mills in Prussia and a cotton mill in England. He went to work at the family firm in Manchester in 1841, but he lived a double life. In his spare time he met workers and studied the economic conditions of people in England, and the result of his work was a book, *The Condition of the Working Class in England in 1844*, in which Engels

described working-class life. Around this time he also began a lifelong friendship with fellow writer and philosopher, **Karl Marx** (1818–83), and the two went on to publish hugely influential works about capitalism and communism.

In the Caribbean, a group of conspirators known as **La Trinitaria**, led by Juan Pablo Duarte (1813–76), launched their fight for the independence of the Spanish-speaking side of the island of Hispaniola (see 1822). With neighboring Haiti distracted by its own civil war, Duarte and his fellow rebels were able to eject the Haitians and declared the new **Dominican Republic** independent from Haiti on February 27.

Meanwhile, Samuel Morse (see 1837) had managed to get funding from the US government to build the first **telegraph line** in the US from Baltimore to Washington. The line was completed in 1844. In his first public demonstration of the telegraph that year he sent a message that famously read "What hath God wrought?"

Glass and iron
The Palm House at the Royal Botanical Gardens, Kew, UK, was built in 1844, constructed with plate glass and iron. It was the first large-scale structure to be made using wrought iron.

Population decline in Ireland
Partly due to famine deaths, but mostly due to massive emigration to escape deprivation, Ireland's population had halved by the 1900s.

SUCCESSIVE FAILURES OF THE potato crop in Ireland triggered a famine that lasted five years and left more than one million people dead. The crop failure, due to **late blight** (see panel, right), was particularly devastating because for millions of the rural poor, the **potato** was their staple food. The British government's response was limited. Rather than intervene directly, it directed landlords to shoulder the burden. However, as many small tenant farmers had no crops to sell, rents went unpaid and landlords ran their tenants off the land. Landowners soon were unable or unwilling to provide local poor relief. To compound matters, many larger farms continued to export grain, meat, and other foods to Britain as there was no market for them in Ireland, given that there was little extra money available for the purchase of such goods. The fact that these foods were not given to the millions who were starving in Ireland, further strained relations

between the Irish people and the British government. Many Irish decided to **emigrate** and more than two million people left for Britain, Canada, and the US, contributing to the decline in population from 8 million to 6.5 million between 1841 to 1851.

On the other side of the Atlantic, the Republic of **Texas** had been trying unsuccessfully to join the US since 1836. When it became clear that Britain had a stake in keeping Texas independent, to halt US westward expansion, the suit was finally approved in December.

POTATO BLIGHT

The blight responsible for the failure of Ireland's potato crop was *Phytophthora infestans*, a mold that caused rot within two weeks. Blight spreads quickly when humidity stays above 75 percent and temperatures above 50°F (10°C) for two full days; both factors were present during the summer of 1845. By autumn the crop was lost and people abandoned the land.

June 17 First New Zealand War (land Wars) (to 1847) begins with **Wairau Massacre**

Fortunes of Saud family restored by **Faisal bin Turki** al-Saud (1785–1865)

February 27 Santo Domingo wins independence from Haiti and becomes **Dominican Republic**

German political theorist and author **Friedrich Engels** (1820–95) publishes *The Condition of the Working Class in England*

May 1 Hong Kong Police Force, first Asian police force, formed

May 24 American inventor **Samuel Morse** (1791–1872) sends first telegraph message

June 24 Charles Goodyear patents **vulcanized rubber** in the US

Potato blight in Ireland leads to **Irish Potato Famine** (to 1847)

March 11 Beginning of **Flagstaff War** in New Zealand; Maori fought other Maori and their British allies

November 20 Battle of Vuelta de Obligado, Parana River, central South America; Anglo-French fleet defeats Argentine Confederation

March 17 Rubber band patented by Stephen Perry in England

Anglo-Sikh Wars (to 1848) over control of the Punjab in India

December 29 Texas becomes 28th US state

The Battle of Palo Alto, the first battle of the Mexican War, fought near Brownsville, Texas. The war was triggered by a boundary dispute.

A poster from 1848, showing the Parisian public facing the municipal guards during the February revolution against the government.

DIPLOMATIC RELATIONS BETWEEN MEXICO AND THE US became strained after Texas became the 28th state (see 1845). The **Mexican** government did not want to accept this annexation and refuted the US claim that the new state's southern border was at the Rio Grande, stating it lay farther north, at the Nueces River. A diplomatic mission was sent to Mexico City in 1845 to settle the matter, as well as to attempt the purchase of the New Mexico and California territories, but these efforts were met with a snub. The following year, on April 25, Mexican troops crossed the Rio Grande and attacked soldiers stationed there. The US President, **James K. Polk** (1795–1849) declared war, and fighting lasted until Mexico surrendered in 1847.

The US also faced **boundary** disputes with the British, over the Oregon Territory, which lay between 42º N and 54º40´ N. The US claim for land as far north as 54º40´ N gave rise to Polk's campaign slogan of "Fifty-four Forty or Fight!" However, under the 1846 **Treaty of Oregon** the boundary was set at 49ºN.

In Britain, the control of the import and export of grains—known as the **Corn Laws**—had been the source of controversy for decades. Poor harvests, blockades, and disruption to supplies during wartime had led to fluctuating wheat prices. Legislation to protect domestic agriculture by limiting the **import** of cheap grain and fix prices had proved unpopular and led to the establishment of the **Anti-Corn Law League** in 1839. The League argued that the laws impeded prosperity as restrictions on grain imports caused a price increase and a consequent rise in the cost of wages. The control of exports also limited the external market for British goods. A combination of pressure from the League and the failure of the potato crop in Ireland (see 1845) led to the repeal of the laws.

In **Japan**, there was international pressure for the **isolationist nation** to open up its ports to foreign trade. The Dutch, who were the only Europeans allowed limited access to trade in Japan, sent a mission in 1844 urging the country's rulers to open up trade. This was followed by the French and British requesting trading rights. In 1846, a US delegation arrived and was also sent away empty-handed, but the US would soon try again in its quest for access to Japanese ports (see 1853).

100,000
FRENCH TROOPS

10,000
Algerian troops

Rebellion of Abd al-Qadir
Although the Algerian troops were hugely outnumbered by the French, Abd al-Qadir made effective use of guerilla tactics.

IN THE YEARS FOLLOWING FRANCE'S ATTACK and colonization of **Algiers** (see 1830), the French faced much resistance from Algerians, including emir **Abd al-Qadir al-Jaza'iri** (1807–1883). He gained the support of Algerian tribes who aided him in his fight against the French. After a series of defeats, he was forced to **surrender** in 1847. He was taken prisoner, but was later freed.

In Germany, a **telegraph** line connecting Frankfurt to Berlin was installed by a firm owned by **Werner Siemens** (1816–92), who had developed a technique for seamless insulation of copper wire.

Meanwhile, English author **Emily Brontë** (1818–48) published *Wuthering Heights*. Although not met with much critical acclaim, it later became one of the most influential literary examples of the **Romanticism** movement.

FRIEDRICH ENGELS AND KARL MARX (see 1844) joined a revolutionary group of Germans known as the League of the Just who soon changed their name to the **Communist League**. Engels and Marx were charged with developing a program of action for the group, and the result was a pamphlet that became known as the *Communist Manifesto*. This called for the overthrow of the bourgeoisie, with the cry of "working men of all countries, unite." Marx believed the gulf between rich and poor in Europe meant conditions were ripe for a socialist revolution.

Europe in revolt
Republican uprisings in 1848 saw an end to the monarchy in France, although revolutionaries in other countries were less successful in their aims.

In February, only a couple of weeks after the manifesto's publication, the streets of **Paris** erupted into revolution. Although it was dramatic and violent, it was not a socialist insurrection. **France** had been suffering an economic depression and a minister named **François Guizot** had come to symbolize the government's inability to alleviate the situation. The monarchy fared little better as the king, Louis-Philippe (see 1830), was also very unpopular with the public. Fighting broke out on February 22 and quickly became violent, with soldiers opening fire on the

KEY
- Small German states
- Areas in revolt against Louis–Napoleon in 1851
- German Confederation
- Revolution in 1848–49

FIFTY-FOUR FORTY OR FIGHT!

William Allen, Governor of Ohio, during his election campaign

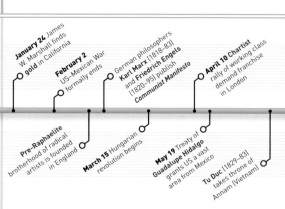

Protectionist **Corn Laws** abolished in Britain after years of protest

Second Carlist War fought in Spain between Carlist forces and Isabella II's forces

Rotary printing press invented by Richard March Hoe in the US

Ottoman Empire cedes Abadan Island in Iran to **Persian Empire**

Resistance to French in **Algeria**

January 24 James W. Marshall finds **gold** in California

February 2 US–Mexican War formally ends

German philosophers **Karl Marx** (1818–83) and **Friedrich Engels** (1820–95) publish *Communist Manifesto*

April 10 Chartist rally of working class demand franchise in London

US goes to war with **Mexico** (to 1848) over Texas territory

Sewing machine patented by Elias Howe in the US

September 23 Planet **Neptune** observed for first time by German astronomers Johann **Gottfried Galle** and **Heinrich Louis d'Arrest**

July 26 Liberia gains independence

Pre-Raphaelite brotherhood of radical artists is founded in England

March 15 Hungarian revolution begins

May 19 Treaty of Guadalupe Hidalgo grants US a vast area from Mexico

Tu Duc (1829–83) takes throne of Annam (Vietnam)

Merchant ships crowd the bay at San Francisco during the gold rush years, when tens of thousands of fortune seekers arrived in California.

COMMUNISM

With the publication of the *Communist Manifesto* Marx and Engels laid the foundation of a political movement that sought to share the means of production, such as land or factories, equally among the public. Communists aimed to create a classless and stateless society, as well as abolish the capitalist trappings of private property and wage labor.

crowds. The following day, Guizot was forced out of office and Louis-Philippe abdicated from the throne. A provisional government was set up and the **Second Republic** established, eventually producing a constitution and extending the vote. However, internal power struggles led to a workers' rebellion in June. By the end of the year, another Bonaparte was in power—this time Napoleon's nephew, **Prince Louis-Napoleon Bonaparte** (1808–73), had been elected president.

This unrest was not limited to France. The rebellions had started in Sicily in January, and spread from there. There were a number of factors involved: high food prices, economic depression, **nationalist movements**, desire for **constitutional reforms**, and frustration with monarchies. The revolutions varied in intensity and

success. In some places, they amounted to large-scale protests, such as the **Chartists'** demonstrations for changes to the voting system in Britain, or the call for institutional reforms in Belgium and the Netherlands.

It was in France, the Austrian Empire, Germany, and the Italian states where the real agitation lay. In the **Kingdom of the Two Sicilies** (see map, left), the king was forced to grant a constitution. **Germany** saw street fighting in Berlin in March, with the king of Prussia promising to grant Germany a constitution. **Austria**, too, saw fighting break out in Vienna, and a new government was appointed, while many of its territories, such as **Hungary**, called for more autonomy. In broad terms, however, the events of 1848 ended in failure and further social repression.

> ## "...DISGRACED BY THE STINK OF REVOLUTION, BAKED OF DIRT AND MUD. "

Frederick William IV of Prussia, on the Crown after the 1848 Revolution

WITH THE END OF THE WAR BETWEEN THE US AND MEXICO in 1847, the US gained—through the Treaty of Guadalupe Hidalgo (1848) —a vast area of land that included **California**. The following year, a carpenter named James Wilson Marshall noticed shiny metal nuggets in a river near present-day Sacramento, which he soon realized were **gold**. News of this discovery spread throughout the country—aided by President James K. Polk's announcement— and by 1849 the **rush** had begun. That year some 40,000 people arrived in San Francisco by boat and another 40,000 by wagon train from around the US and other countries. Most of the prospectors ended up empty-handed but many stayed in California, making the West Coast a booming region in the mid-19th century.

In **southern Africa**, a British explorer and missionary named **David Livingstone** (1813–73) had finally reached a lake in the interior that he had heard about—known today as **Lake Ngami**. He had been living in South Africa since 1841 and had been traveling extensively in the region. In order to find this body of water, Livingstone had to cross the **Kalahari Desert**, where he also encountered the Botletle River, which he thought could be "the key to the Interior."

In **India**, the previous four years had seen two wars between the British East India Company troops and the Sikhs in the northwest. The **First Sikh War** (1845–46) had

been triggered by the death of their ruler Ranjit Singh (1781–1839). Previously, the Company considered Singh's force of 100,000 Khalsa warriors far too powerful to confront. But after his death, British troops moved in and took areas near the border, seizing the city of **Lahore** by 1845. A treaty between the two forced the Sikhs to give up even more territory. A revolt against the British in 1848 triggered the **Second Sikh War**, and by 1849 the Punjab region had been annexed by the British.

Yemen, at the foot of the Arabian Peninsula, was fighting against imperial advances from the **Ottoman Empire**, which was trying to reassert its authority in the Tihama region, on the **Red Sea**. In the south of the country,

Livingstone's compass
The magnetic compass used by David Livingstone, who spent much of his time as a missionary exploring Africa's interior.

the British East India Company had already taken control of the **port of Aden** a decade earlier in order to set up a coaling station for British ships en route to India.

PRE-RAPHAELITES

Three young artists frustrated with the state of British painting at the Royal Academy, where they were students, decided to create a movement to bring a moral seriousness into art—in contrast to the pomposity and frivolity they perceived in Victorian art. Known as the Pre-Raphaelite Brotherhood, Dante Gabriel Rossetti, William Holman Hunt, and John Everett Millais painted religious and romantic subjects with realist clarity, although their work was also symbolic.

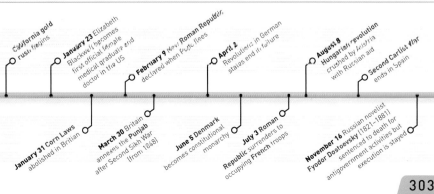

October 24 First Schleswig War is fought between Prussia and Denmark (to 1851)

November 1 First medical school for women opens in Boston, Massachusetts

December 2 Emperor Ferdinand I of Austria abdicates for nephew, Emperor Franz Josef I

October 28 First railroad in Spain is opened

November 4 Second Republic established in France with Louis-Napoleon Bonaparte (1808–73) as president

California gold rush begins

January 23 Elizabeth Blackwell becomes first official female medical graduate and doctor in the US

February 9 New Roman Republic declared when Pope flees

April 2 Revolutions in German states end in failure

August 8 Hungarian revolution crushed by Austria with Russian aid

Second Carlist War ends in Spain

January 31 Corn Laws abolished in Britain

March 30 Britain annexes the Punjab after Second Sikh War (from 1848)

June 5 Denmark becomes constitutional monarchy

July 3 Roman Republic surrenders to occupying French troops

November 16 Russian novelist Fyodor Dostoevsky (1821–1881) sentenced to death for antigovernment activities but execution is stayed

A depiction of one of the many bloody battles during the Taiping Rebellion.

A hand-colored lithograph shows the Crystal Palace at the Great Exhibition of 1851 in London's Hyde Park. Some six million people visited it in six months.

The Royal Navy played a significant role in the Anglo–Burmese War.

Commodore Matthew Perry brought Japan a railroad car as a gift.

IN THE SAME WAY CHINA HAD TRIED TO KEEP European ships from its ports, it had also tried to drive out Christian missionaries, thereby limiting the influence of **Christianity**. Despite this, by the mid-19th century some 200,000 Chinese had been **converted**, and thousands more were familiar with the religion.

In 1850, officials sent troops to disband a religious society whose beliefs were loosely based on **Protestant** ideas. This sect was led by **Hong Xiuquan** (1814–64) who, believing himself to be the younger brother of Jesus Christ, launched a revolt that became the **Taiping Rebellion**. Drawn by his call to share property, many starving peasants joined the ranks and fighting went on for 14 years, claiming millions of lives.

20 MILLION
THE NUMBER OF **PEOPLE KILLED** OVER THE COURSE OF THE **TAIPING REBELLION**

> ## " IT IS A WONDERFUL PLACE—**VAST, STRANGE, NEW,** AND **IMPOSSIBLE TO DESCRIBE.** "

Charlotte Brontë, English novelist, on visiting the Great Exhibition

IN LONDON, THE WORLD WAS ON DISPLAY. An exhibition had been organized, billed as the "Great Exhibition of the Works of Industry of all Nations." The **Great Exhibition**, as it became known, was housed in the Crystal Palace, an exhibition hall made of glass and iron built for the occasion. Some six million people pored over the 100,000 exhibitions between May 1 and October 31. Of the 14,000 participating exhibitioners, almost half were from overseas. An enormous variety of agricultural and manufactured items were on display, ranging from the **Koh-i-Noor diamond** from India to tapestries from Persia, and British engineering equipment.

In the same year as this global event, a **telegraph cable** was laid across the English Channel, facilitating rapid international communication.

Britain by this point had seen a large **population** boom and become more **urbanized** as agricultural workers moved to the cities to work in the growing number of factories (see 1771). Detailed censuses showed that the population of London had surged from about one million in 1801 to over two million by 1851.

In **Australia**, the discovery of gold in Victoria and New South Wales the same year prompted a **gold rush** that tripled the country's population over the next ten years.

In Siam (Thailand), **King Mongkut** (1804–68) began his rule. His reign saw increased relations with the West. During this period, he employed an English governess, **Anna Leonowens** (1831–1915), whose memoirs inspired the 20th-century musical *The King and I*.

Rise in Britain's population
The population of England, Scotland, and Wales nearly doubled in fifty years, from 10.6 million in 1801 to almost 21 million by 1851.

HOSTILITIES HAD ONCE AGAIN flared up between British troops and the Burmese. After making extensive territorial gains in the last war against **Burma** (see 1823), Britain was eager to control more of the area. Wider control would create an overland coastal connection from Calcutta in Britain's Indian territory to the British port in Singapore. The East India Company also wanted access to the **teak forests** in Burma. In 1852, the British seized a ship belonging to Burma's king, and this was enough to start the **Second Anglo–Burmese War.** Lasting only a few months, British troops were able to take southern territory, ousting the reigning king, Pagan Min (1811–80), and installing his brother, Mindon Min (1814–78), who was willing to accept British control of the southern portion of the kingdom.

In **West Africa**, in present-day Senegal, Muslim Tukulor chief **Umar Tall** (1797–1864) capitalized on unrest between the Dinguiraye and Bambara people to wage a jihad (holy war) on part of upper **Senegal**, taking control of the territory. His empire would eventually stretch to **Timbuktu** in present-day Mali. His rule was a time of further entrenchment of Islam in West Africa.

In South Africa, the British acknowledged the independence of the **Transvaal** after refusing to accept the previous Boer Republic of Natal (see 1843). This was followed two years later with a similar acceptance of the settlers' new **Orange Free State**.

US COMMODORE MATTHEW PERRY (1794–1858) had been charged with opening up trade between the US and the secluded **Japan**. Japan had been under international pressure to open up its ports to foreign merchants for years. The Dutch, who were the only Europeans allowed very limited **access to trade** in Japan, sent a mission in 1844 urging the country's rulers to allow in more ships. This was followed by French and British requests for trading rights. A delegation from the US was sent away empty-handed (see 1846). However, the US government was eager to secure trading rights in East Asia and so sent Perry to further negotiate. He arrived on July 8 and refused to leave until he had delivered his letters. The Japanese relented after a few days and took his papers, which requested a trade treaty. They eventually consented to the terms, and the **Treaty of Kanagawa** was concluded the following year.

As **China** was contending with the Taiping Rebellion (see 1850), another uprising broke out in the central and eastern provinces. The rebels were composed of many outlaws, as well as peasants from famine-stricken areas. With the government otherwise engaged, the rebels were able to form armies and begin the **Nien Rebellion**. Over the course of the next 15 years they gained control of much of northern China, although they were eventually defeated.

Taiping Rebellion leads to civil war in China (to 1864)

December 16 First **settlers** for Christchurch arrive in **New Zealand**

April 1 Rama IV (1804–68) takes the **Thai** throne

May–October Great Exhibition of Industry takes place in **Crystal Palace** in Hyde Park, London

Gold deposits found in southeast Australia; Australian population triples over next ten years

September 30 *Eugenie*s begins voyage from Sweden; becomes first Swedish Royal Navy vessel to **circumnavigate world**

October A **telegraph cable** is successfully installed across the **English Channel**

Second Anglo–Burmese War (to 1853) begins

Independent Boer republic of **Transvaal** in South Africa recognized by Britain

Louis-Napoléon becomes Emperor **Napoleon III**

American writer **Harriet Beecher Stowe** (1811–96) publishes abolitionist novel *Uncle Tom's Cabin*

March 20 Taiping Rebellion: Rebel army takes Nanjing, killing 30,000 Imperial troops

March 30 Dutch painter **Vincent Van Gogh** born (d. 1890)

October 4 Crimean War (to 1856) begins over disputed territory within Ottoman Empire

October 12 New **Zealand** becomes independent

> **❝ MEN, REMEMBER** THERE IS **NO RETREAT** FROM HERE. YOU MUST DIE WHERE YOU STAND. **❞**
>
> Colin Campbell, Commander of the Highland Brigade, at the Battle of Balaclava, October 25, 1854

A painting of King Mongkut of Siam, who was also known as Rama IV.

US filibusterer William Walker surrenders to Costa Rican troops.

THE TENSIONS THAT HAD BEEN mounting between **Russia** and the **Ottoman Empire** in the previous year spilled over into a war. Britain and France joined the fight from October. The conflict was fueled by the decision of Czar Nicholas I (1796–1855) to declare the right to protect **Orthodox Christians** living under Ottoman rule. When this claim was rejected by the Ottomans, Nicholas sent troops into Moldavia and

The Crimean War
Brigadier Scarlett leads the British Heavy Brigade uphill at Balaclava, on October 25, 1854 against the Russians during the Crimean War.

Wallachia, and the Ottoman Empire declared war. By March 1854, Britain and France had also declared war on Russia, and in September they landed troops in Russia's **Crimea** territory and began a siege of **Sevastopol**. In October, a brigade of British troops at the **Battle of Balaclava** misinterpreted orders, charging down a valley instead of up it, allowing Russians to bombard the 673 soldiers on all sides. Had it not been for French intervention, the casualty rate would have been higher than 40 percent. This incident was memorialized in the poem by Lord Alfred Tennyson, *The Charge of the Light Brigade*.

Austria threatened to enter the war against Russia in 1856 and a preliminary peace was arranged on February 1, followed by the March 30 **Treaty of Paris**.

The Crimean War was the first conflict to be covered by newspapers, which were taking advantage of the new telegraphic and photographic technology. The war also established the reputation of the "**Lady with the Lamp**," British nurse Florence Nightingale (1820–1910), whose reforms to field hospitals caused a dramatic reduction in deaths from disease during wartime. She helped promote nursing as a respectable career for women.

MISSIONARY DAVID LIVINGSTONE was exploring the interior of Africa (see 1849) on his second expedition. He was convinced a trade route to the sea existed, and sailed up the **Zambezi River** in November 1853 to find it. Two years later, he and his party came across a gigantic waterfall, known as **Mosi-oa-Tunya**, "the Smoke that Thunders." He was the first European to see the falls and renamed them **Victoria Falls**.

To the East, in Siam (Thailand), King Mongkut (see 1851), known for his interest in the West, signed commercial agreements with Britain and the US in an effort to open up **Siamese** trade.

IN NICARAGUA, US-BORN WILLIAM WALKER (1824–60), who had arrived in the country in 1855 with 58 men, declared himself **president**. He was initially invited by Francisco Castellón (1815–55), who had been trying to organize a liberal revolt. This was a period of **filibustering**: attempts by privately funded mercenaries to take over small countries and annex them to the US. Walker intended to establish Nicaragua as a **slave state**; southern US states wanted to enlarge slave-holding territory as abolitionism grew. Walker was eventually captured by invading Costa Rican forces and later shot.

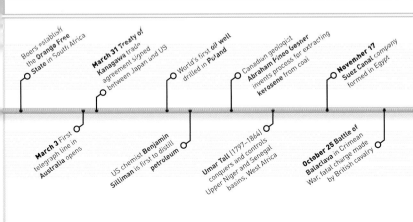

Boers establish the **Orange Free State** in South Africa

March 3 First telegraph line in **Australia** opens

March 31 Treaty of Kanagawa trade agreement signed between Japan and US

US chemist **Benjamin Silliman** is first to distill **petroleum**

World's first **oil well** drilled in **Poland**

Umar Tall (1797–1864) conquers and controls Upper Niger and Senegal basins, West Africa

Canadian geologist **Abraham Pineo Gesner** invents process for extracting **kerosene** from coal

October 25 Battle of Balaclava in Crimean War, fatal charge made by British cavalry

November 17 Suez Canal company formed in Egypt

February 1 **Kassa Hailu** crowned Tewodros II, emperor of Ethiopia

Start of British **trade with Siam**

March 17 Taiping army of 350,000 invades **Anhui**, eastern China, during **Taiping Rebellion**

David Livingstone is first European to see **Victoria Falls**, as he renames them

March 30 Treaty of Paris settles Crimean War

English engineer **Henry Bessemer** (1813–98) invents process for mass **production of steel**

Second Opium War (to 1860) over trade between China and Britain

William Walker (1827–60) proclaims himself president of Nicaragua; tries to establish slave plantations

English painter Thomas Jones Barker's *The Relief of Lucknow*, completed in 1859, depicts British forces defending this colonial city after the end of a prolonged siege during the Sepoy Rebellion.

IN 1857, A RUMOR SPREAD THROUGH THE INDIAN TROOPS— known as **sepoys**—in the Bengal Army stationed at Meerut, Northern India. Their new rifle cartridges were reputed to be greased with pork and beef fat. The cartridges were for a new type of rifle, the **Enfield**, and to load them the ends of the paper cartridges needed to be bitten off. For Hindu and Muslim soldiers, allowing beef or pork fat in their mouths went against their respective religions beliefs. Added to this rumor were various other grievances, together with a

British — 45,000 | Indian

311,000

British–Indian army in 1857
A much larger proportion of Indians than British served in the army, making an uprising involving the Indian troops a serious threat.

growing suspicion that the British were also trying to undermine Indian culture and traditions. The soldiers refused to use the cartridges, and the subsequent dispute that broke out between Indian troops and British commanders sparked the revolt known as the **Sepoy Rebellion** (also known as the **Indian Mutiny**).

The unrest lasted for more than a year, as the mutineers were joined by peasants angry at their exploitative landlords, as well as those who resented the recent British annexation of the north Indian region of Oudh. The rebels managed to capture Delhi and "restore" an aging Mughal emperor, **Bahadur Shah II** (1775–1862), to power, while killing the British in Delhi and the nearby cities of Kanpur and Lucknow. The retaliation by the British army was similarly brutal, and they recaptured Delhi in September and Lucknow the following March. The revolt was suppressed by June 1858.

This conflict was the culmination of frustration with the East India Company's rule as well as creeping **westernization** as Britain annexed more territories and sent out more officials. The uprising provoked deep concern

in Britain, and the East India Company was stripped of its power to control India. The Company by this point was hated throughout India, and the British government thought it could no longer be relied on to keep stability (see panel, 1858). The Mutiny had shown the level of Indian discontent and anger, which would continue to grow under British rule, while at the same time helping to fuel the independence movement.

In additon to the conflict in India, British troops had returned to battle in **China**. Britain demanded greater freedom of trade in China in the wake of the Treaty of Nanjing (see 1842), but the Chinese resisted. In 1856, the British sent an expedition with the French to attack China's ports, culminating in the **Second Opium War**.

Anglo–French forces attacked Canton in 1857. By the following year, the **Treaties of Tianjin** were negotiated between China, Britain, and France, as well as with Russia and the US. These agreements called for China to open more ports and to legalize opium importation. In addition, foreign diplomats were given the right to live in **Peking**. The Chinese refused to ratify these agreements until 1860.

In the US, the **abolitionist** cause suffered a serious setback when a Supreme Court ruling in the case Dred Scott v. John F. A. Sandford declared slavery to be **legal** in all US territories. The case was brought by **Dred Scott**. He was taken by his owner, John Emerson, from the slave state of Missouri (see 1820) to the "free" Wisconsin territory, later returning to

> ❝ **A FREE NEGRO** OF THE AFRICAN RACE…**IS NOT A 'CITIZEN' WITHIN** THE MEANING OF THE **CONSTITUTION OF THE UNITED STATES.** ❞
>
> **Chief Justice Roger Taney** in the Dred Scott v. Sandford case, April 1854

Dred Scott
A slave in the US, Dred Scott sued his owner for his freedom. The case went to the US Supreme Court, where his emancipation was denied.

Missouri. Scott, with the aid of abolitionists, filed a lawsuit claiming the move from slave to free state had broken his chain of servitude. The case reached the Supreme Court in 1857, where the justices voted against freeing Scott on the grounds that he was not entitled to rights as a **US citizen**, including the right to sue in a court of law. The judges also declared the Missouri Compromise (see 1820) unconstitutional because Congress could not deprive citizens of their property. It was up to the states to decide to ban slavery, and there was nothing to stop new territories becoming slave states.

muzzle-loading barrel

paper cartridges containing powder and bullet

Enfield rifle and cartridges
The paper cartridges contained powder and a bullet. After removing the cartridge's end, the powder was poured out into the barrel. The cartridge and bullet were then rammed in.

Kuala Lumpur, Malaysia, is founded as tin-mining settlement

March 6 In US, slave **Dred Scott** sues unsuccessfully for freedom in landmark case heightening tensions over abolition

March 21 Earthquake in Tokyo, **Japan**, kills over 100,000

March 23 First safety **passenger elevator** installed in New York by inventor **Elisha Otis**

May 10 Sepoy troops rebel in northern India, unleashing uprisings against the British

May 11 Indian rebels capture Delhi during **Sepoy Rebellion**

July 15 Second **massacre at Kanpur** by Indian rebels

October 13 Financial panic in New York; banks close until December 12

November 1 Area of present-day **Pakistan** becomes part of Indian Empire

November 30 Félix María Zuloaga succeeds Ignacio Comonfort as president of Mexico

A contemporary oil painting illustrates the 1860 Battle of Guadalajara during the Mexican Reform War between liberals and conservatives.

US Marines under the command of Colonel Robert E. Lee smash the armory door at Harpers Ferry, behind which John Brown and his men were besieged.

> **...THE CRIMES OF THIS GUILTY LAND WILL NEVER BE PURGED BUT WITH BLOOD!**
>
> **John Brown, American abolitionist,** before his execution, December 2, 1859

AFTER MEXICO'S DEFEAT BY THE US (see 1846), many Mexicans were in favor of reform, including the middle-class liberal **Benito Juárez** (1806–72). Installed in the government as justice minister, Juárez and other liberals, including president **Ignacio Comonfort** (1812–63), drafted a new constitution curbing military and ecclesiastical privileges, such as the allocation of special courts for civil trials, and some landholding rights. The constitution, which also prohibited slavery and called for a democracy in Mexico, went into effect in 1857.

RISE OF THE RAJ

With the end of the East India Company's administration in 1857, India was governed directly from London by the Viceroy. This was brought about on November 1, 1858 by governor-general Charles John Canning (1856–62) who became the first Viceroy of India. The period, known as the Raj, lasted until Indian independence in 1947.

However, the Catholic Church and the military refused to accept these reforms, and the antagonism turned into the **War of the Reform** (1857–60). With the conservatives in charge of the military, the liberals found themselves pushed out of Mexico City, and were eventually forced to make a new capital at the port of **Veracruz** in 1858. The US decided to intervene in the conflict, recognizing the liberal government at Veracruz in 1859 and sending it much-needed arms. This aided the rebels in their retaliation, and they managed to defeat conservative forces. Juárez returned to Mexico City on January 1, 1861 as president, taking control of the whole country, and he once again put the constitution into effect.

France, meanwhile, was embroiled in battles not only in China, but in other kingdoms in East and Southeast Asia where the French sought a foothold in trade. France was concerned about the rise of Siamese power, as well as the continuing attacks on French missionaries in Vietnam. By the end of 1858, a Franco–Spanish expedition had seized the city of Da Nang in Vietnam, starting the **Cochinchina Campaign**. In 1859, the coalition captured the key port of **Saigon**, where a garrison of 1,000 troops later faced a year-long siege from 1860 to 1861. The war finally ended in a settlement with Vietnam's king, **Tu Duc** (1829–83), in 1863, in which three provinces were ceded to France.

KEY

- ■ Great Britain
- ■ France
- ■ Russia
- ■ Netherlands
- ■ Spain
- ■ Japan

EUROPE IN SOUTHEAST ASIA

Throughout the 19th century European powers vied for control of the profitable trade routes from China through Southeast Asia. Goods such as spices were imported to Europe from colonies in Asia, while textiles were exported. The opening of the Suez Canal in 1869 made trade between Europe and Asia quicker and cheaper.

CONSTRUCTION WORK HAD FINALLY BEGUN ON A CANAL that would link the Mediterranean Sea and the Red Sea. It would cut voyages between Europe and Asia by thousands of miles by allowing ships to avoid sailing around the Cape of Good Hope. In 1854, French official **Ferdinand de Lesseps** (1805–94) managed to obtain permission from the khedive (viceroy) of Egypt, Said Pasha (1822–63), to construct a canal at Suez. In 1856, the Suez

Canal Company (*Compagnie universelle du canal maritime de Suez*) was set up and given the right to run the canal for 99 years after its completion.

In the US, abolitionist **John Brown** (1800–59) attacked a federal armory in **Harpers Ferry, Virginia** on the night of October 16. He also took more than 60 slave owners hostage, hoping that the slaves of these people would join his cause. They were attacked by the local militia

and the rebellion was finally ended by federal troops, led by Colonel Robert E. Lee. Of the 22 men who participated in the raid, 10 were killed, including Brown's two sons. Brown himself was later hanged.

Meanwhile, in England, naturalist **Charles Darwin** (see 1835, 1839) cemented his reputation with the publication of *On the Origin of Species by Means of Natural Selection*. The work explained the process of **evolution** and he set out his ideas about species adaptation and the survival of the fittest.

In the US, Abraham Lincoln (1809–65) won the race for presidency as the candidate for the newly formed **Republican** party, which had been established to curtail the power of existing slave states and stop the creation of new ones. The Democrats had split and fielded two candidates.

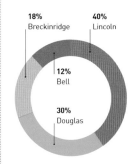

18% Breckinridge	40% Lincoln
12% Bell	
30% Douglas	

A clear majority
The Democratic candidates, Douglas and Breckinridge, combined had more of the popular vote, but Lincoln won the necessary electoral votes.

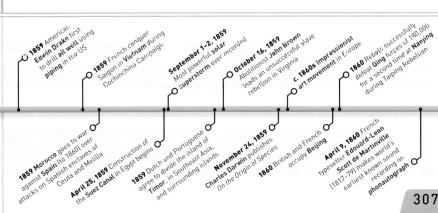

January 14 Assassination attempt on Napoleon III in Paris led by Felice Orsini fails

May–July Mahtra War: Peasants in Governorate of Estonia, Russian Empire, revolt against serfdom (already officially abolished)

Early attempts to lay **transatlantic telegraph cable**

Wars of Italian Unification (to 1870)

June 20 Last rebels of the **Sepoy Rebellion** surrender in Gwalior

Government of India Act passes control of India from British East India Company to British Crown

1859 American Edwin Drake first to drill oil well using piping in the US

1859 French conquer Saigon in Vietnam during Cochinchina Campaign

September 1–2, 1859 Most powerful solar superstorm ever recorded

October 16, 1859 Abolitionist John Brown leads an unsuccessful slave rebellion in Virginia

c. 1860s Impressionist art movement in Europe

1860 Rebels successfully defeat Qing forces of 190,000 for a second time at **Nanjing** during Taiping Rebellion

1859 Morocco goes to war against **Spain** (to 1860) over attacks on Spanish enclaves of Ceuta and Melilla

April 25, 1859 Construction of the Suez Canal in Egypt begins

1859 Dutch and Portuguese agree to divide the island of **Timor**, in Southeast Asia, and surrounding islands

November 24, 1859 Charles Darwin publishes *On the Origin of Species*

1860 British and French occupy Beijing

April 9, 1860 French typesetter Edouard-Leon **Scott de Martinville** (1817–79) makes world's earliest known sound recording on **phonautograph**

The Confederate battery at Fort Moultrie firing on Fort Sumter in Charleston harbor on April 12, 1861. The attack triggered the Civil War, which devastated the US.

THE SPLIT IN THE US DEMOCRATIC PARTY ahead of the 1860 election precipitated a much larger, more dangerous fracture that came in 1861—the **secession** of Southern states to a confederacy. Many northerners, President Lincoln included, initially thought that slavery might just die out if it were not allowed in any new territories. But a gradual approach was not possible, since abolitionism kept growing, with more of the public supporting it over the 1850s.

The US was economically divided, which intensified the debate over slavery. The South was mostly rural, and slave labor was used to grow cotton, tobacco, and rice. The more urban Northern states, in contrast, had a high population of immigrant workers.

Lincoln's presidential victory was the last straw for Southern slave owners, and by December 1860 South Carolina had seceded from the Union. Over the next few

Union cap
Forage cap, with insignia badge for a volunteer regiment, as worn by northern Union soldiers during the Civil War.

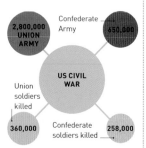

Costly civil war
The conflict between the North's federal government and 11 Southern states was brutal and bloody with a high rate of casualties and deaths.

months, it was followed by Georgia, Alabama, Louisiana, Mississippi, Texas, and Florida. These states formed the **Confederacy** and elected Jefferson Davis (1808–89) as their president. They were soon joined by Virginia, Arkansas, Tennessee, and North Carolina in the spring, although the slave-holding states of Kentucky, Missouri, Maryland, and Delaware did not secede. One of the underlying causes of secession, besides slavery, was the issue of the **states' rights** versus that of **federal** government. South Carolina and the other Confederate states argued that states held the right to own slaves and to leave the Union.

The situation grew increasingly tense. The continued presence of Union forces at **Fort Sumter**, in the harbor of Charleston, South Carolina, made many people there feel that their new sovereignty

was being compromised. So, at 4:30 a.m. on April 12, Brigadier-General P. G. T. Beauregard gave the order to fire on the soldiers stationed there. These would be the **opening shots** of the **American Civil War**.

Meanwhile, the second Italian War of Independence, which began in 1859 and was part of the wider struggle for unification of the **Italian states**, was coming to a close. France and Piedmont–Sardinia had formed an alliance to drive out Austrian rule in Italy, which they achieved through a series of victories in 1859. But during negotiations of the **Peace of Zurich**, Napoleon III of France allowed Austria to retain Venetia (mostly Venice), causing uproar among supporters of Italian independence. In the south, **Giuseppe Garibaldi** (1807–82), an Italian military commander, attacked the Kingdom of Two

Alexander II
Alexander was the emperor of Russia from 1855–81. He freed the serfs and reformed the judicial and education systems.

Sicilies, seizing Palermo in 1860. With most of the Italian kingdoms in a degree of upheaval, **Victor Emmanuel II** (1820–78) of Piedmont–Sardinia was declared "king of Italy." The struggle was not yet over, however, as France occupied Rome while Venice was under Austrian rule. Garibaldi's attempt to liberate the Papal States (Rome) in 1862 at the Battle of Aspromonte on August 29 ended in defeat, leaving the project of unification still incomplete.

In Russia, **serfdom** was abolished in wide-reaching changes by Russian emperor **Alexander II** (1818–81) who, after defeat in the Crimean War (see 1854), wanted to reform the country, starting with labor. He set out the **Edict of Emancipation** in 1861, despite opposition from landowners. Earlier attempts to abolish serfdom had been made around 1818, but with little success. Some 10 million people were freed on February 19 and were promised their own land.

> **IT IS BETTER TO ABOLISH SERFDOM FROM ABOVE THAN TO WAIT FOR IT TO ABOLISH ITSELF FROM BELOW.**
>
> **Czar Alexander II of Russia**

January 1 Benito Juárez captures **Mexico City**, ending War of Reform against conservatives

January 2 Friedrich Wilhelm IV of Prussia dies; succeeded by **Wilhelm I**

February 9 Southern Confederacy elects **Jefferson Davis** president

February 19 Abolition of serfdom in Russia

March 4 Abraham Lincoln (1809–65) becomes first Republican US president

March 19 End of **First Taranaki War** (from 1860) part of **New Zealand Land Wars**

March 17 Italian unification wars: **Victor Emmanuel II** of Piedmont–Sardinia declared **king of Italy**

April 12 Attack on Fort Sumter starts the **American Civil War** (to 1865)

March 30 Physicist and chemist, Sir **William Crookes** (1832–1919), declares discovery of element **thallium**

June 15 Benito Juárez becomes president of **Mexico**

June 25 Abd al-Aziz (1861–76) succeeds **Abd al-Mejid I** as sultan of the Ottoman Empire

July 1 Rebel Taiping forces defeated by French and Imperial Chinese troops at **Battle of Shanghai**

President Pedro Santana (1801–64) tries to return **Dominican Republic** to Spanish rule

1862

" POLITICS IS THE ART OF THE POSSIBLE. "

Otto von Bismarck in a remark to Meyer von Waldeck, August 11, 1867

IN MEXICO, AN EXPEDITION OF British, French, and Spanish forces arrived to collect payment on the money they were owed. After the War of the Reform (see 1858) President Benito Juárez had declared in 1861 that he was placing a **moratorium** on the payment of interest **on foreign debt** for two years. The lending countries disputed his decision, and soon resorted to **armed conflict**. France sent in troops, which faced a defeat

OTTO VON BISMARCK
(1815–98)

One of Prussia's most influential leaders, Otto von Bismarck came into power as prime minister in 1862 and he masterminded the unification of Germany (see 1871). Bismarck built up the army and also tried to develop a German national identity; he fought against the Catholic Church and tried to stem the growth of socialism.

early on, but reinforcements eventually reached Mexico City. Napoleon III saw an opportunity to establish an empire in Mexico.

Farther north, in the **American Civil War**, Union troops attempted, but failed, to capture the Confederate capital, Richmond, by advancing up the peninsula east of **Yorktown**. This was followed by the **Second Battle of Bull Run** (August 28–30, see p.310), which saw 70,000 Union troops defeated by 55,000 Confederates. A few weeks later, on September 17, one of the bloodiest battles of the war took place at **Antietam**, in Maryland, where Union troops suffered around 12,000 casualties and the Confederates around 11,000. Farther west, Union troops under General **Ulysses S. Grant** (1822–85) won a crucial victory at the **Battle of Shiloh**, Tennessee.

In Japan, the **Tokugawa** regime had become increasingly suspicious of foreigners (see 1853), taking measures that included the passing of **anti-foreigner acts** and efforts to expel people. This precipitated attacks on ships from the US, Britain, France, and the Netherlands. In retaliation, in 1863 the US fired on two Japanese ships and French warships fired on—and subsequently burned down—a small village. The following year, France, Britain, the Netherlands, and the US sailed into the **Straits of Shimonosekei** and destroyed Japanese batteries along its coast. They eventually secured a treaty giving them free passage and the right to trade.

1863

Workers hurry to catch their morning train at the Gower Street station on the Metropolitan (underground) railroad in London.

30 THOUSAND
THE NUMBER OF PASSENGERS ON THE FIRST DAY OF THE METROPOLITAN LINE

THE SITUATION IN MEXICO became more complex as conservative Mexicans, still angry about their defeat in the War of the Reform (see 1858), capitalized on the fighting between French and Mexican troops (see 1862) and conspired with **Napoleon III** to overthrow the government. As a result, Austrian archduke Ferdinand Maximilian Joseph (1832–67) was invited to become **emperor** of Mexico. He accepted, thinking that he had been voted in by the people, and became **Maximilian I** the following year.

In the US, Abraham Lincoln tried to persuade Confederate states to return to the Union by giving them

Emancipation proclamation
Abraham Lincoln reads the Emancipation Proclamation before his cabinet members. The decree abolished slavery in the US.

the option of abolishing slavery gradually, rather than immediately. Not one state took up his offer, so on January 1, he followed through with his plan and issued the **Emancipation Proclamation**, abolishing slavery in the South.

On the battlefields, Union troops were making serious gains in the south, as General Grant captured the Mississippi port of Vicksburg in July, giving Union forces control over key parts of the Mississippi River. The Union Navy, meanwhile, had captured the port of **New Orleans**, and occupation of the city followed. Farther north, Confederate defeat at the **Battle of Gettysburg**, Pennsylvania, from July 1–3, had marked a turning point in the war.

In Britain, Londoners were thrilled by the opening of the **Metropolitan Railway**, which ran underground, from Farringdon Street to Paddington. This was the first part of what would eventually become the **London Underground**, also known as the Tube. Other train companies soon followed suit.

1864

Prussia and Denmark went to war over Schleswig and Holstein.

IN THE ONGOING AMERICAN CIVIL WAR, President Lincoln made General Grant commander-in-chief of the Union forces. A few months later, Union general **William T. Sherman** (1820–91), began his "march to the sea." Sherman pursued a "scorched earth" policy, destroying rail lines and setting towns on fire from Atlanta to Savannah, Georgia.

Relations between **Denmark** and **Prussia**, part of the German Confederation, had soured. A brief war was the result of a revolt by the Germans in the duchies of **Schleswig** and **Holstein**, which were living under Danish rule. Prussian troops occupied the territory and by August 1, Denmark gave up rights to the duchies, which were to be placed under joint Austrian and Prussian rule—a situation that would become a future source of conflict (see 1866).

38,000 Danish troops

61,000 German Confederation

The Prussian–Danish War
The war began when Prussian forces crossed the border into Schleswig, and Denmark was forced to relinquish control of the duchy.

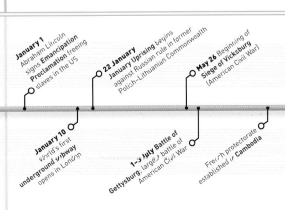

March 9 First battle between two ironclad warships, the USS Monitor and USS Virginia

Umar Tall conquers Massina in present-day Mali, West Africa

British annex **Lagos**

April 6–7 Confederate defeat at Battle of Shiloh

France, Britain, and Spain launch expeditions to Mexico, starting French intervention

August 29–30 Second Battle of Bull Run (American Civil War)

September 17, Battle of Antietam, costly battle ending in strategic victory for Union

September 23 Otto von Bismarck takes office as prime minister of Prussia

January 1 Abraham Lincoln signs **Emancipation Proclamation** freeing slaves in the US

January 10 World's first underground subway opens in London

22 January January Uprising begins against Russian rule in former Polish–Lithuanian Commonwealth

1–3 July Battle of Gettysburg, largest battle of American Civil War

May 26 Beginning of Siege of Vicksburg (American Civil War)

French protectorate established in **Cambodia**

February 1 Danish–Prussian War begins (to October 30); part of Wars of German Unification (to 1870)

April 10 Maximilian I of Austria (1832–67) crowned Mexican emperor

Umar Tall killed attempting to suppress Fulani rebellion, West Africa

November–December General Sherman's "march to the sea" in American Civil War

ORIGINS OF THE CIVIL WAR

As the US expanded, the issue of which states would be allowed to have slaves became the central political focus between North and South. By 1860, the 18 free states of the North and the 15 slave states were on the brink of war.

1820: THE MISSOURI COMPROMISE

Slavery became a more pressing political issue as the US began to settle its western territories. When the Missouri territory petitioned to become a state in 1817, its slavery status prompted a political crisis. The outcome was the Missouri Compromise, which allowed slavery in Missouri but not in any new state north of 36°30' latitude.

1850: A NEW COMPROMISE

Thirty years after the Missouri Compromise, the debate over slavery intensified as the US extended farther west. Senator Henry Clay organized a series of bills that were considered a compromise. California was to be admitted as a free state but the controversial Fugitive Slave Act, which penalized officials who did not arrest alleged runaway slaves, was also passed, angering abolitionists.

1861: CIVIL WAR

The bombardment of Fort Sumter in South Carolina triggered a ferocious conflict that would consume the whole country for four brutal, bloody years, until the Confederacy had no choice but to surrender.

KEY
- Free states
- Free territories
- Slave states
- Territories where slavery legal

KEY
- Union States 1861
- Confederate states 1861
- States that voted to join Confederacy
- Union front line to December 1861
- Union front line to December 1862
- Union front line to December 1864
- Union movements
- Confederate movements
- Union forts
- Confederate forts
- Union naval blockade
- Union victory
- Confederate victory
- Inconclusive battle
- City destroyed by Union forces

1854: THE KANSAS–NEBRASKA ACT

One of the compromise acts in 1850 was to allow the Utah and New Mexico territories to reach a decision on slavery when they became states. The Kansas–Nebraska Act applied this principle for people in those states, allowing them to vote on the issue. This act also controversially repealed the Missouri Compromise, causing further anger in the North.

KEY

■ Free states	■ Territories where slavery legal
■ Free territories	■ Territories newly opened to slavery 1854
■ Slave states	■ Area not subject to standard territorial laws

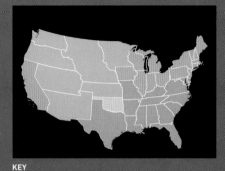

1857: THE DRED SCOTT DECISION

The growing abolitionist cause received a setback when the Supreme Court ruled in the case of Dred Scott v. John F. A. Sandford (see 1857) that slavery was legal in all the territories. The judges also declared that the Missouri Compromise was unconstitutional. They argued that it was up to states to decide to ban slavery, but that territories were not states.

KEY

■ Free states	■ Territories opened to slavery
■ Slave states	■ Area not subject to standard territorial laws

AMERICAN
CIVIL WAR
THE CONFLICT THAT TORE THE UNITED STATES APART

The shells fired at Fort Sumter, South Carolina, in 1861 not only ripped the country in two, but also began a deadly conflict that would pit families against each other, with brother fighting brother on the battlefield, as the Confederacy of Southern states took up arms in defense of slavery.

The issue was not only ideological, but also economic. Southerners felt that their rural, agrarian livelihood was under direct threat from the policies of the federal government. And for the industrial and urban North and President Abraham Lincoln, the question was about more than freedom for slaves. Without the 15 slave states, what would the future hold for the Union? The war cost billions and destroyed the Southern economy. The Union navy blockaded ports causing prices in the South to skyrocket; the price of a cup coffee in

a restaurant in Richmond, Virginia, reached around $5 by 1864. By the time the South conceded defeat and surrendered in 1865, both sides had been heavily battered—but the country emerged united.

The war was also significant because it was the harbinger of modern warfare. Infrastructure developments, such as railroads, and technological innovations in armaments like breech-loading rifles had changed the nature of battle, and led to a much higher number of casualties.

OVER THE COURSE OF THE CIVIL WAR, THE UNION PROVIDED SOLDIERS WITH

1 BILLION ROUNDS OF **AMMUNITION**

100 MILLION POUNDS OF **COFFEE**

10 MILLION PAIRS OF **PANTS**

1 MILLION HORSES AND **MULES**

KEY
● Union army expenditure ● Union navy expenditure

Cost of the war
Billions were spent fighting the Civil War, with the army and navy costing the Union millions during this period. The estimated cost to the Confederacy, including the emancipation of the slaves, was around $2.1 billion, inflicting serious damage to the Southern economy.

Populations
The industrial North had a much larger population than the mostly agrarian Southern states.

23 MILLION UNION POPULATION

9 MILLION CONFEDERATE POPULATION

$1,200
THE COST OF **A BARREL OF FLOUR** IN VIRGINIA BY 1865

1:3

Outnumbered
Despite the South being significantly outnumbered, the fighting continued for four years, leaving some 600,000 dead.

French painter Edouard Manet's *The execution of Maximilian I.*

The War of the Triple Alliance devastated Paraguay. This painting by Cándido López depicts the arrival of the Allied Army at Itapiru, Paraguay.

THE AMERICAN CIVIL WAR DREW TO A CLOSE. By the spring, Union troops had captured the Confederate capital of Richmond, and after several other defeats, Confederate general **Robert E. Lee** (1807–70) saw no other option but to **surrender** on April 9, signaling the end to the bloodiest conflict the US had seen. The war had left the US intact, but more than 600,000 men had been killed and half a million wounded. The new peace was soon marred: only a few days after the Union's victory, President Lincoln attended Ford's Theater in Washington, DC. There, Confederate **John Wilkes Booth** crept into the state box and shot him. Lincoln died the following morning on April 15.

The American Civil War was over, but the situation in **Mexico** remained complicated. US troops were deployed there because the US government under Andrew Johnson (1808–75) objected to French intervention in Mexican affairs (see 1863).

Farther south, a war had erupted between **Paraguay** and its neighbors Uruguay, Brazil, and Argentina. Brazil invaded Uruguay in 1864 to assist in the overthrow of the ruling party. In response, the president of Paraguay, Francisco Solano López (1827–70), declared war on Brazil, and shortly after, on Argentina. Uruguay aligned itself with Brazil and the **War of the Triple Alliance** (also Paraguayan War) began. López was killed in battle on March 1, 1870, and a peace treaty was negotiated. The war devastated Paraguay, reducing the population of 525,000 to 221,000.

In **Jamaica**, a group of peasants who had been denied government land for planting stormed the

50,000
PARAGUAY

26,000
Alliance of Argentina, Brazil, and Uruguay

Forces in War of Triple Alliance
Although Paraguay had the far larger force at first, it was untrained and without a chain of command López, as leader made all decisions.

courthouse in **Morant Bay** during a meeting of the parish council, and 19 white people died in the altercation. In retaliation, governor **Edward Eyre** led a ruthless attack on the black community, declaring martial law, and killing hundreds of people while imprisoning hundreds more. When news of this reached Britain there was a public outcry and Eyre was recalled to England.

Lincoln's death
This painting by Alonzo Chappel depicts the death of Abraham Lincoln, 16th President of the United States.

IN 1866, PERU DECLARED WAR ON SPAIN, JOINED BY CHILE. The cause of the war dated back to the Talambo Affair in 1862, when Spanish immigrants were attacked by Peruvian workers on the Talambo estate in northern **Peru**. Spain's demand for compensation was ignored, so it seized the **Chincha Islands** off the coast of Peru in 1864. These were valuable as a source of **guano**, used as fertilizer. Spain demanded 3 million pesos in exchange for the islands in 1865.

Peru's General Mariano Ignacio Prado declared war on Spain in January 1866. Chile, fearful of a renewed Spanish presence in South America, joined Peru. They tried to close their ports, but Spain managed to bombard **Valparaiso** in Chile on March 31 and **Callao** in Peru on May 2 before a ceasefire the following week. This was the last attempt by Spain to recapture South American territory.

Battle of Callao
A detail of a painting shows Peruvian troops defending the fortified port of Callao, Peru, while being bombarded by the Spanish navy.

> ## A SPECTRE IS HAUNTING EUROPE; THE SPECTRE OF COMMUNISM.

Karl Marx, from the *Communist Manifesto*, 1848

FRANCE'S ATTEMPT TO GAIN CONTROL OF MEXICO (see 1863) seemed doomed with the arrival of US reinforcements. France abandoned Mexico's emperor, Maximilian I, who had been installed at their behest as well as that of Mexican monarchists. He was captured by liberal forces, court-martialed, and executed on June 19. Benito Juárez then returned to his post as president.

Farther north, the size of the US received a huge boost with the **purchase of** the vast **Alaska** territory from Russia. For the price of $7.2 million, the US received 663,268 sq miles (1,717,856 sq km) of territory.

In Europe, Karl Marx (see panel, right) had published the first of three volumes in what would become one of his most influential works, *Das Kapital*. The book, through an examination of the capitalist system, tried to address larger economic and historical questions about the nature of class and social relations.

In **Prussia**, tensions with Austria had led to the **Seven Weeks' War** the previous year. Under the resulting Treaty of

War of the Triple Alliance (to 1870) between Paraguay and an alliance of Argentina, Brazil, and Uruguay

April 14 Assassination of Abraham Lincoln (b. 1809)

July 31 First narrow gauge mainline railroad in the world opens at Grandchester, Queensland, **Australia**

October 11 Paul Bogle leads the **Morant Bay Rebellion** in Jamaica

Spain fails to retain Chincha Islands off coast of **Peru**

June 14–August 23 Austro-Prussian war starts over the Prussian occupation of the duchy of Holstein

January 11 Benito Juárez (1807–72) becomes president of **Mexico**

Dual monarchy of **Austria–Hungary** established

April 9 Confederate General Robert E. Lee **surrenders** to General Ulysses S. Grant, effectively **ending American Civil War**

June 23 Last significant rebel army in American Civil War surrenders in Oklahoma Territory

August 16 Dominican Republic regains independence from Spain

December 10 Léopold II becomes king of **Belgium**

Russian novelist **Fyodor Dostoyevsky** (1821–81) publishes *Crime and Punishment*

October 14 French troops land at Ganghwa Island, **Korea**, in retaliation for execution of French Jesuit priests

January 30 Emperor Kōmei dies; Crown Prince **Mutsuhito** becomes emperor of **Japan**

Karl Marx publishes first part of *Das Kapital*

This painting shows battleships in the Ten Years' War (1868–78), which was part of the long-running struggle for Cuba's independence from Spain.

" …REJOICE THAT I HAVE **LIVED TO SEE THIS DAY,** WHEN THE **COLORED PEOPLE… HAVE EQUAL PRIVILEGES** WITH THE MOST FAVORED. "

Thomas Garrett, American abolitionist, on the passing of the 15th Amendment

KARL MARX (1818–83)

Karl Marx was a German philosopher, political economist, historian, political theorist, sociologist, and communist revolutionary, whose ideas played a significant role in the development of modern communism and socialism—theories collectively known as Marxism. His critique of capitalism, *Das Kapital*, remains influential today.

Prague, Prussia received Schleswig-Holstein, Hanover, Hesse-Kassel, Nassau, and Frankfurt, allowing it to organize the **North German Confederation**. The king of Prussia, **William I** (1797–1888) was at its helm, backed by Prime Minister **Otto von Bismarck** (see 1862). Austria also gave up control of the Venetia (Venice), allowing the region to be unified with Italy.

WITH THE FALL IN 1868 OF THE TOKUGAWA SHOGUNATE in Japan and the rise of the emperor Meiji Tenno (1852–1912), the island reversed its policy of isolationism and began a program of Westernization, with the aim of being able to stand up to the Western powers that were demanding access to Japan (see 1853). This period, known as the **Meiji Restoration**, was a time of long-lasting fundamental social reforms, such as the ending of feudalism, formation of a national army, and implementation of tax systems, with a constitutional government being convened by 1890. There was a boom in infrastructure modernization throughout this period, with the arrival of railroads and the telegraph.

In **Cuba**, discontent with the Spanish regime had been growing. When Queen Isabella II (1830–1904) was deposed by a military rebellion in Spain, Cubans seeking independence took the opportunity to launch a war against the Spanish rulers on their island. Led by Carlos Manuel de Céspedes, this uprising, known as *El Grito de Yara* (The Cry of Yara), resulted in The Ten Years' War (1868–78), a campaign of guerilla warfare that ended in failure for the Cuban rebels.

Meiji vase
A Japanese Satsuma cabinet vase from the Meiji period. Art was well supported by the Japanese government during this period.

In the same year, there was also an uprising against Spanish rule in Puerto Rico. The Lares uprising, or *El Grito de Lares*, was shortlived and, like the Cuban uprising, also ended in failure.

In **South Africa**, British control was spreading. Boer settlers had moved away from the Cape Colony, taking land from local tribes, including the neighboring Basutoland. Sotho leader **Moshoeshoe I** (c. 1786–1870) asked Britain for help against further incursions into **Sotho territory**, and the result was that the kingdom was annexed to the British Crown in 1868, becoming a protectorate. On Moshoeshoe's death in 1870, it was made part of the Cape Colony region without consulting the Sotho people.

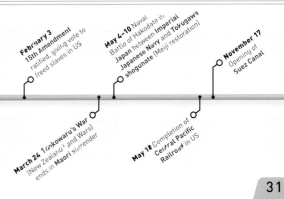

AS RECONSTRUCTION CONTINUED in the war-torn southern US, Congress enacted an amendment to the Constitution—ratified by the states in February 1869—that extended the right to vote to all black men, whether they had been enslaved or not. The **Fifteenth Amendment** declared that "the rights of the citizens of the United States to vote shall not be denied or abridged by any State on account of race, color, or previous condition of servitude".

Meanwhile, westward expansion in the US continued to grow, aided by the arrival of railroads. By 1869, the **first transcontinental railroad** had been completed by the Central Pacific Railroad. The project was supported by government bonds. Part of the track was started from Sacramento, California, heading east and joining with existing lines in Promontory, Utah, on May 10, 1869. Much of the work on this stretch of railroad was done by more than 10,000 Chinese

Grand opening
The opening of the Suez Canal, Port Said, Egypt. The project took a decade to complete but its impact on global trade was immediate.

immigrant laborers. The construction of this line allowed rapid coast-to-coast travel in the US, further facilitating western settlement.

Another feat of engineering also opened around the same time—the **Suez Canal** (see 1859). After a decade of construction, this canal linked the Mediterranean and Red seas, and provided a much quicker passage to the Indian Ocean.

In South Africa, **diamonds** had been discovered in the **Northern Cape province** in 1866, and soon a rush was on between the Boers, British, and native people to mine them. The British swiftly stepped in to annex the territory while **thousands of prospectors** arrived to try their luck.

October 18 Transfer ceremony held after US buys **Alaska territory** from Russia

August 18 Helium discovered by French astronomer **Pierre Janssen** (1824–1907)

September Spain's Isabella II **forced to flee** during liberal uprising

October 1 Rama V (1853–1910) takes Thai throne and ushers in **era of reform**

February 3 15th Amendment ratified, giving vote to freed slaves in US

May 4–10 Naval Battle of Hakodate in Japan between **Imperial Japanese Navy** and **Tokugawa shogunate** (Meiji restoration)

November 17 Opening of Suez Canal

June 19 Emperor of Mexico, **Maximilian I** executed

Diamond fields discovered in **South Africa**

Japan's **Meiji period** of social and political reform (–1912)

September 23 Puerto Rico's *El Grito de Lares*, a bid for independence from Spanish rule, ends in failure

October 10 Cuba starts Ten Years' War of independence against Spain

March 24 Tohkowaru's War (New Zealand) and Wars) ends in Maori surrender

May 10 Completion of **Central Pacific Railroad** in US

This 19th-century painting depicts Prussian hussars firing up at a French observation balloon during the Franco–Prussian War in 1870.

Men at their battery during the war between the Third Republic and the Paris Commune that erupted at the end of the Franco-Prussian war.

> ❝ THE **ARMY** IS THE **TRUE NOBILITY** OF OUR **COUNTRY.** ❞

Napoleon III, Emperor of the French

PRUSSIA'S VICTORY IN THE SEVEN WEEKS' WAR (see 1867) gave the impetus to further pursue plans for German unification, this time by bringing the southern German states into the union. Attempts had also been made to place Prince **Leopold of Hohenzollern-Sigmaringen** (1835–1905) on the Spanish throne, left vacant after Queen Isabella II's deposition in 1868 (see panel, 1872). Intense French diplomatic pressure from Napoleon III prevented this. Otto von Bismarck, the Prussian prime

minister, however, wished to provoke France into war. To these ends he published the **Ems telegram** (as it was later known), editing it to appear as though insults had been exchanged between King Wilhelm I of Prussia and the French Ambassador. France declared war on Prussia on July 19. Prussia was victorious at the battles of **Gravelotte** on August 18, and **Sedan** on September 1, where an ill Napoleon **surrendered** to German forces and was taken prisoner. While Napoleon was held captive, a provisional government for national defense was set up in Bordeaux where it was decided to depose him and establish the **Third Republic**. By mid-September, the Prussians had besieged Paris. The city was forced to surrender in early 1871 after severe food shortages. By March, an armistice had been

Immigration in Argentina
This graphic shows the steady rise in the percentage of Spanish and Italian immigrants who arrived in Argentina between 1869 and 1929.

agreed and Germany was given the regions of **Alsace** and **Lorraine**.

Meanwhile, a steady stream of **immigrants** escaping poverty and war in Europe flowed to the Americas. In the US, the **population** hit 40 million and by the end of the century it would nearly double to 76 million. Likewise, in **Argentina** the 1870 population of 1.8 million would reach 8 million by 1914, with many immigrants from Italy and Spain—both places that had been seriously affected by years of warfare.

Siege of Paris
The siege resulted in the capture of the city by Prussian forces, leading to a humiliating French defeat in the Franco–Prussian War.

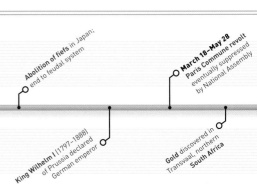

German unification
This map shows the newly unified German Empire, which was organized after Prussia's victory in the Franco–Prussian War.

KEY

- Prussian gains by 1866
- other states in North German Confederation 1867
- other German states 1866
- Austro-Hungarian empire 1867
- → Prussian invasion of France in Franco-Prussian War of 1870-71
- — boundary of German Empire 1871

ITALIAN TROOPS HAD ENTERED ROME the previous September and in October a **plebiscite**, or referendum, made Rome the capital of the united Italy—which became official by 1871. The pope, however, was not pleased with his settlement offer and **excommunicated** Italian king Victor Emmanuel II, entrenching himself in the Vatican while Rome developed as the new capital. The tension between the Vatican and the Italian government would not be resolved until the 20th century.

While France and Prussia were negotiating the end of the Franco–Prussian war in 1871, angry Parisians had risen up over the surrender and established the

radical **Paris Commune**. A council of citizens—including republicans, Jacobins, socialists, and anarchists—governed Paris for over two months. The retaliation of the National Assembly, which had relocated to Versailles, was swift. Troops were sent to Paris and 20,000 people were killed.

Following victory against France, Wilhelm I of Prussia declared himself **Emperor of Germany** and named Bismarck (see 1862) as **Chancellor**.

In South Africa, a diamond rush (see 1869) in the Northern Cape was followed by the discovery of **gold** in the **Transvaal** region. This sparked the arrival of thousands of prospectors to the region.

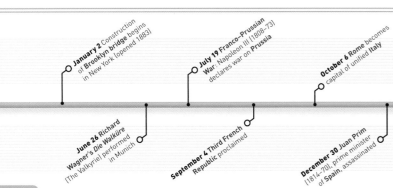

January 2 Construction of **Brooklyn bridge** begins in New York (opened 1883)

June 26 Richard Wagner's *Die Walküre* (The Valkyrie) performed in Munich

July 19 Franco–Prussian War: Napoleon III (1808–73) declares war on **Prussia**

September 4 Third French Republic proclaimed

October 6 Rome becomes capital of unified **Italy**

December 30 Juan Prim (1814–70), prime minister of **Spain**, assassinated

Abolition of fiefs in Japan; end to feudal system

King Wilhelm I (1797–1888) of Prussia declared German emperor

March 18–May 28 Paris Commune revolt eventually suppressed by National Assembly

Gold discovered in Transvaal, northern **South Africa**

1872

A portrait of the US women's suffragist leader Susan B. Anthony, who brought her campaign to public attention by illegally voting in 1872.

100 DOLLARS

THE FINE IMPOSED ON SUSAN B. ANTHONY FOR VOTING

IN THE AFRICAN KINGDOM OF ETHIOPIA, Yohannes IV (1831–89) was crowned emperor. He was considered a strong ruler, staving off the increasing incursions from Europeans as well as from African neighbors. By the end of the following decade, Ethiopia had defeated **invasions** by Egyptian forces, as well as Italian forces.

In the US, pressure was growing for women to be given the **right to vote**. One of the leading advocates was **Susan B. Anthony** (1820–1906), who, during the 1872 presidential election, marched up to the polling station in Rochester, New York and cast her vote in defiance of the law. She was arrested and fined. Although she refused to pay the fine, the court case did not continue and Anthony carried on with her crusade.

Meanwhile, in New York, Captain Benjamin Briggs set out to cross the Atlantic on the ship *Mary Celeste* on November 7. By December 4, the crew of the *Dei Gratia* spotted the *Mary Celeste* drifting around the coast of Portugal completely **deserted**. The life boat was missing and the ship had drifted some 700 miles (1,100 km) from the last point entered in the log. Its crew was never seen again, and the **maritime mystery** was never solved.

In France, physicist Louis Ducos du Hauron had been working on creating a **color photograph** using a three-color principle. He patented his process in 1868 and went on to produce some of the earliest color photographs.

CARLIST WARS IN SPAIN

The 19th century in Spain was dominated by the Carlist Wars. These civil wars began in 1834, triggered by the death of Ferdinand VII. The conservative Carlists did not want the king's daughter, Isabella (1830–1904), to take the throne, but rather Ferdinand's brother, Don Carlos (1788–1855). After three wars, the dispute was resolved in 1876 with the accession of Isabella's son Alfonso XII (1857–85) to the throne, who drove some 10,000 Carlists out of Spain.

1873

> ❝ THE **MAIN THING IS** TO **MAKE HISTORY, NOT** TO **WRITE IT.** ❞
>
> Otto von Bismarck, 19th-century German statesman

Royal Canadian Mounted Police
"Mounties," as they became known, wearing their distinctive uniforms at an annual sports event at Regina, Saskatchewan, Canada.

EAGER TO PROTECT GERMANY'S GROWING POWER, Bismarck proposed the **Three Emperors' League**, an alliance between Germany, the Austro-Hungarian Empire, and Russia, with the purposeful exclusion of France. Formed in 1873, the league lasted for three years, was later reestablished in secret in 1881 and renewed in 1884, and finally collapsed in 1887. At issue were the continued conflicts of interest between Austria–Hungary and Russia in the Balkan territory.

In the Caribbean, the island of **Puerto Rico** finally abolished slavery. Although the slave trade had been suppressed earlier, the practice had continued on the island and in neighboring Cuba. Both were still under Spanish control. The end of slavery was announced in May 1873, although an **apprenticeship** system was put in place, extending slave conditions for some until 1876.

In **Canada**, the North West Mounted Rifles was formed to enforce the law on a national and local level. The force was charged with policing the largely rural provinces of the huge Canadian territory. The initial few hundred officers had some 300,000 sq miles (800,000 sq km) under their jurisdiction. But the US was uncomfortable with the idea of armed troops patrolling the border, so the force's name was changed to the North West Mounted Police—though later the name would be altered again to the **Royal Canadian Mounted Police**, which is still in use, along with the famous abbreviation of "Mounties."

1874

A depiction of Garnet Wolseley's reception among the Asante people.

IN MARCH, BRITISH ARMY OFFICER CHARLES GEORGE GORDON (1833–85) arrived in the province of **Equatoria**, in the south of Egyptian-occupied Sudan. He was to take control of the territory but under the auspices of the khedive (viceroy) of **Egypt**. Gordon was tasked with establishing way stations up the White Nile and to attempt to suppress the ongoing **slave trade**. He mapped parts of the Nile and set up outposts along the river as far as Uganda. He became governor-general of Sudan in 1877.

Meanwhile, in West Africa, a British expedition led by **Sir Garnet Wolseley** (1833–1913) defeated the **Asante Empire** (present-day Ghana) and asserted control over the southern part of their territory, known as the **Gold Coast**.

Charles George Gordon
A British general and colonial administrator, Gordon was invited by Egypt's khedive to govern part of Egypt's Sudan territory.

scene of birds

decorative panel

painted doors

flowers   fruit

Elm chair
c. 1850
This Ming-style elmwood chair has a shaped crest rail and curved backsplat with openwork cartouches above a beaded apron.

Jade brush holder
c. 18th century
The detail of this jade brush holder contains the figure of Taoist philosopher Laozi. The ancient Taoist practices were popular in the Ming period but fell out of favor with Qing rulers.

Elm cabinet
c. 1860
The doors of this black lacquered elm cabinet of rectangular outline are painted with a colorful decoration that includes birds and flowering trees.

Soapstone Lohan
1600–1799
This statue shows a Lohan, a human who achieved enlightenment through meditation on the teaching of Buddha. Buddhism flourished during the Qing period.

THE QING DYNASTY

OBJECTS FROM THE EMPIRE THAT RULED CHINA FOR MORE THAN TWO CENTURIES

The Qing dynasty was established after the last Ming emperor was overthrown in 1644. Rule was instituted by Manchu chieftains, and the Qing period of rule lasted until 1911. It was a time in which China witnessed a tripling of its population to around 450 million.

Although the Manchus were seen as outsiders by the Chinese, they maintained their rule for so long by continuing to use the existing form of government from the Ming dynasty (1368–1644). This continuity spilled over into the arts and crafts as well, and much of the work produced in the Qing years was heavily influenced by Ming designs, especially porcelain.

Flask
1736–95
Supported on a spreading circular foot, this flask has a short, contracted neck and right-angle handles. The sides have bands of exotic blooms.

copper-red underglazing

cinnabar lacquer

head is made of chalcedony

dragon

hook is carved from jade

Covered box
1736–95
The top of this peach-shaped covered box (the fruit is a symbol of long life) shows a *chun* (spring) character enclosing, in the center, Shou Lao, the god of longevity, with a dragon on either side.

intricate carving

Ax head
19th century
Made from chalcedony, this translucent green and red ax head has a flat, curved cutting edge. Carved in relief is a Taotie mask and sleeping silkworms.

Belt hook
19th century
This jade belt hook has a Taoist design, shaped as two dragons and a bat laid on the outside, a phoenix on one side, and a silkworm pattern on the reverse.

Blue tea set
1850–99
Part of a set of two, this porcelain bowl with lid and saucer is decorated with famille rose enamel colors on a blue background.

interior is lined with silver

Pewter tea caddy
18th century
This tea caddy is constructed from pewter. Its simple design is embellished with floral and calligraphic engravings.

Brass wedding bowl
18th century
This brass wedding bowl is part of a set of two. This one is lined with silver—the other has a gilt silver interior—and the base has an engraved design.

panels depict the seasons

lacquered wooden case and brass caps

Portable set of eating implements
1736–95
The contents of this traveling set of eating implements include two pairs of chopsticks, a knife, a pair of forks, and an ivory pick.

Sancai teapot
1662–1772
This teapot is sancai porcelain and has a rectangular shape, with raised panels on each side illustrating the four seasons.

large bead called Buddha head separates smaller beads

subsidiary string of beads

Ivory necklace for civil servant
1900s
These beads are made of painted ceramic and gold leaf. The larger beads, called Buddha heads, divide up the smaller beads into groups of 27. There are also subsidiary strands of 10 blue beads.

incised inscription

Golden nail guards
c. **19th century**
These elaborate nail guards have gold openwork with a "cracked ice" pattern. The device was designed to protect the nail of the little finger.

Xian seal
19th century
This oval Xian seal has an incised inscription on each of the long sides. The base reads "Living by the Golden Tower."

peaches symbolize longevity

fine silk

rounded designs popular in 19th century

Pair of bowed shoes
1800–1900
These bowed shoes with pointed toes and high heels were worn for outdoor activities by a woman with bound feet. The sides have an intricate embroidered decoration of birds and flowers.

Silk robe
c. **19th century**
This woman's black silk robe has a pattern of flowers woven into the fabric. The design also includes a springtime scene involving flowers and butterflies.

317

A painting entitled *The Victor* by Russian war artist Vasily Vereshchagin (1842–1904) depicts Turks celebrating a victory during the Russo–Turkish War. Hostilities between Russia and the Ottoman Empire were long-running and the two had gone to battle many times over the previous two centuries.

THE RIFT BETWEEN THE OTTOMAN EMPIRE AND ITS SUBJECTS IN Bosnia and Herzegovina grew wider as **Christian** inhabitants of the two territories **rebelled** against Ottoman rule, requesting aid from neighboring **Serbia**, which had a much higher degree of autonomy. Buoyed by Russian promises of support and inspired by the nationalism sweeping through the region, Serbia too declared war on the Ottoman Empire on June 30, 1876; **Montenegro** followed suit the next day, leading the weakening empire into another destabilizing conflict. Montenegro was initially successful, with a victory in Herzegovina, but Russian support in Serbia did not materialize and the Turks won the battle of Aleksinac on August 9, 1876. This forced the Serbs to appeal to other nations for help.

In other parts of the Ottoman world, **Egypt** continued to make incursions into **Ethiopia**, leading its king, Yohannes IV (see 1872), to declare war on the Egyptians. The conflict arose because Ismail Pasha (1830–95), the khedive (viceroy) of Egypt, wanted to put settlements on strategic points along the **Red Sea** coastline in Ethiopian territory (present-day Eritrea). By 1875 Egypt had succeeding in occupying many coastal towns, as well as the inland city of Harar. The fighting lasted until 1877, by which time Ethiopia had managed to defeat two Egyptian campaigns.

ANGER AND UNREST HAD BEEN growing among American Indians in the US, many of whom had been forced off their land. This issue often resulted in armed conflict with US troops. One of the most infamous confrontations was the **Battle of Little Bighorn** where, on June 25, Lieutenant Colonel George A. Custer (1839–76)

> ❝ THE NATION THAT **SECURES CONTROL OF** THE **AIR WILL** ULTIMATELY **CONTROL** THE **WORLD.** ❞
>
> Alexander Graham Bell, Scottish inventor

and his men were killed by a coalition of Eastern **Sioux** and Northern **Cheyenne** Indians. Around the same time, US forces were fighting the **Apache** people,

who lived near the border with Mexico. They too were angered by attempts to move them onto a reservation, and attacked white settlements. This conflict continued for another decade until their leader, **Geronimo** (1829–1909), surrendered in 1886.

Elsewhere in the US, a Scottish-born inventor named **Alexander Graham Bell** (1847–1922) patented his device for "transmitting vocal or other sounds telegraphically"—**the first telephone**. This development would change forever the way the world communicated.

In Mexico, former soldier **Porfirio Díaz** (see panel, right) tried to launch a revolt against president Sebastián Lerdo de Tejada. His attempt in early 1876 failed and he fled to the US. He returned in November and defeated the government's troops. In May 1877 he was elected president and controlled Mexico for decades.

Explorer **Henry Morton Stanley** (1841–1904), meanwhile, was trying to follow the uncharted Lualaba River in the **Congo** to

PORFIRIO DIAZ
(1830–1915)

Mexican general, politician, and president, Porfirio Díaz was of mixed European and indigenous descent. From a humble background, he made a name for himself in the military. After he was elected president, he shored up his support and created a political machine that kept him in power and the opposition divided and suppressed, leaving him to control politics in Mexico for more than 30 years.

establish which river it joined. Stanley's African exploits were already famous; he had been previously sent by a US newspaper to find fellow explorer David Livingstone (see 1855) and in 1871, on the shores of Lake Tanganyika, he had supposedly uttered the celebrated words, "Doctor Livingstone, I presume?"

IN CHINA, FAMINE SPREAD through the northern provinces. A drought the previous year affecting the **Yellow River** —a vital source of water—was compounded by a lack of rain in 1877 and the arrival of locusts. When the rains returned toward the end of the following year, some 9 to 13 million people had died in a region of 108 million.

In South Africa, the discovery of **gold** (see 1871) had exacerbated tensions between the Boer settlers and the British, who by this point governed much of the country. By 1877 the British managed to **annex the Transvaal**. However, the Afrikaners rebelled against this move and regained their independence a few years later (see 1881).

Famine in China
An illustration in a French magazine shows the state of poverty during the famine years in China, when millions died in the northern region.

Early telephone
This early example of a telephone—known as a box telephone—had a trumpetlike mouthpiece and it transmitted sound through the use of an electromagnet.

mouthpiece

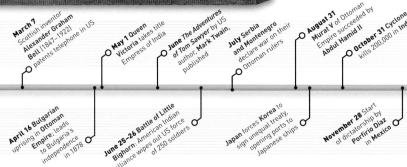

Revolts in **Balkans** over Ottoman rule

Asia's first **stock exchange** opens in present-day **Mumbai**

March 7 Scottish inventor **Alexander Graham Bell** (1847–1922) patents telephone in US

May 1 Queen **Victoria** takes title Empress of India

June *The Adventures of Tom Sawyer* by US author, **Mark Twain**, published

July Serbia and Montenegro declare war on their Ottoman rulers

August 31 Murat V of Ottoman Empire succeeded by **Abdul Hamid II**

October 31 Cyclone kills 200,000 in India

Russia declares war on **Ottoman Empire** (to 1878) over Ottoman control of Serbia

Great North China Famine (until 1879)

March 3 French composer Georges **Bizet's** (1838–75) opera *Carmen* debuts in Paris

September 7 Egyptian invasion of Ethiopia defeated

April 16 Bulgarian uprising in Ottoman **Empire**; leads to Bulgaria's independence in 1878

June 25–26 Battle of Little Bighorn: American Indian alliance wipes out US force of 250 soldiers

Japan forces **Korea** to sign unequal treaty, opening ports to Japanese ships

November 28 Start of dictatorship by **Porfirio Diaz** in **Mexico**

May 6 Chief Crazy Horse (c.1840–1877) of Oglala Sioux surrenders to US army; later killed in custody

Romania declares independence from Ottoman Europe

Vasily Vereshchagin's *Mass for the Dead (The Defeated)* shows the aftermath of a Russian defeat during the Russo–Turkish War of 1877–78.

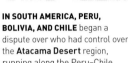

This oil painting shows the defense of Rorke's Drift on January 22, where a handful of British soldiers faced an attack by of 4,000 Zulu soldiers.

RUSSIA DECIDED TO ONCE AGAIN DECLARE WAR on the Ottoman Empire on April 24, 1877, in an attempt to aid the Serbians in their fight against the Ottomans (see 1875). Russia was aided by Romania (the united Moldavia and Wallachia). The **Russo–Turkish War of 1877–78** included a five-month siege of the Ottoman Bulgarian town of Plevna, which eventually fell to Russian forces. Russia also managed to take some key fortresses and a truce was called. A settlement was reached on March 3, 1878, known as the **Treaty of San Stefano**, which gave Serbia, Romania, and Montenegro their independence, while Bulgaria was granted some autonomy and put under Russian authority.

However, European powers were not satisfied with this settlement as there were many competing interests. **Prussia** backed Great

Siege of Plevna
Although the Russians eventually overcame the Turks, the small Turkish force heroically held up the Russian advance into Bulgaria.

Afghan fighters
A photograph of Afghan soldiers holding hand-crafted rifles, at Jalalabad, Afghanistan, during the second Anglo–Afghan conflict.

Britain's desire to curb Russian expansion into Bulgaria—which at this point reached the Aegean Sea—by refusing to let Russia extend naval power in the Mediterranean. **Austria-Hungary** wanted to continue occupation of Bosnia and Herzegovina to keep its regional influence intact and stem growing Slav nationalism.

Meanwhile, Britain had signed the **Cyprus Convention** with Turkey. This deal would allow British administration of the island while it remained under Ottoman sovereignty. This allowed Britain to establish a presence and a naval base in the eastern part of the Mediterranean, with the aim of blocking further Russian incursions into the region.

Away from the European diplomatic bargaining table, the British were once again caught up in warfare with Afghans. The **Second Afghan War** (to 1880)

was ignited when British agents learned of negotiations between Afghan leader Sher Ali Khan (1825–79) and Russia. This was compounded by Sher Ali's refusal to receive a British delegation. In November 1878, British forces invaded the region. Sher Ali turned to Russia for support, but was told to make peace with Britain. Sher Ali died the next year and his son, Mohammad Yaqub Khan (1849–1923), signed a **treaty** ceding the **Khyber Pass** to the British. Soon after, a British envoy was murdered and British troops returned to take Kabul. Yaqub was forced to flee. He was succeeded by Abdur Rahman Khan (c. 1844–1901), who ended the conflict and supported British interests.

IN SOUTH AMERICA, PERU, BOLIVIA, AND CHILE began a dispute over who had control over the **Atacama Desert** region, running along the Peru–Chile border. In the previous decade the valuable mineral **sodium nitrate** had been discovered there. Initially Chilean companies went into the desert to extract the mineral and issues over territorial control soon arose. Chile and Bolivia at first agreed that the 24th parallel was their boundary. But Bolivia, dissatisfied with the deal, entered into a secret agreement with Peru to defend its interests in the desert. Bolivia later seized the property of Chilean companies, prompting Chile's president to send in troops. Chile formally declared **war on Bolivia and Peru** on April 5. The war of the Pacific took place on land and sea, and was not resolved until 1883, with Chile keeping control of the mineral-rich Antofagasta region.

In South Africa, British forces came up against the Zulu nation in the **Anglo–Zulu War**. The British wanted to expand into Zulu territory, but this was met with resistance by King Cetshwayo

139 British forces	**4,000 ZULU FORCES**
	BATTLE OF RORKE'S DRIFT
32 British casualties	**550** Zulu casualties

Battle of Rorke's Drift
Although the Zulus had some rifles, these were put to little effective use, and superior British firepower won out despite overwhelming numbers.

(1826–84), who organized some 60,000 warriors. The British established a depot at **Rorke's Drift**, which was later attacked by Zulus after their victory in Isandlwana. The Zulus were successfully repelled after 550 warriors were shot by the handful of British troops stationed at the depot. After seven months of conflict, the British managed a final victory over the Zulus in the Battle of Ulundi on July 4, and took control of their territory.

Sunken ship in War of the Pacific
This scene from the Battle of Iquique, during the War of the Pacific, shows Chilean and Peruvian ships. The dispute also included Bolivia.

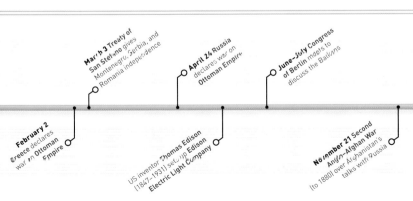

March 3 Treaty of San Stefano gives Montenegro, Serbia, and Romania independence

April 24 Russia declares war on Ottoman Empire

June–July Congress of Berlin meets to discuss the Balkans

January 11 Anglo–Zulu War begins

January 14 War of the Pacific (to 1883) begins: Chile declares war on Bolivia and Peru

February 3 First electric streetlight in Britain

February 2 Greece declares war on Ottoman Empire

US inventor Thomas Edison (1847–1931) sets up Edison Electric Light Company

November 21 Second Anglo–Afghan War (to 1880) over Afghanistan's talks with Russia

January 22 Battle of Isandlwana: Zulu troops massacre British troops

July 4 Anglo–Zulu War ends with British victory at Battle of Ulundi

December 31 Thomas Edison gives first public demonstration of incandescent light bulb in Menlo Park, New Jersey, US

West Indian laborers cutting a channel during the first—and failed—attempt to construct a canal in Panama connecting the Atlantic and Pacific oceans.

> **THE DOOR THAT NOBODY ELSE WILL GO IN AT, SEEMS ALWAYS TO SWING OPEN WIDELY FOR ME.**
>
> Clara Barton, American humanitarian

Clara Barton was the founder of the American Red Cross organization.

BUOYED BY THE SUCCESS OF THE SUEZ CANAL (see 1869), Ferdinand de Lesseps (see 1859) began to draw up plans for a waterway connecting the Atlantic and Pacific oceans through the isthmus of **Panama**. However, the project got off to a difficult start the following year in 1881. There were disagreements over the canal's plans, the machinery did not function well in the terrain, and many workers died of disease in the tropical heat.

Meanwhile, the development of commercial **refrigeration** began to alter the relationship between consumers and producers. Cheese and meats could now be exported long distances. On February 2, the first shipment of frozen meat to survive the journey intact arrived in London from Australia. The following years saw

THE BOERS

The Boers ("farmers" in Dutch) in South Africa were settlers of Dutch, French Huguenot, and German descent that left the Cape Province in search of autonomy farther north. They spoke Afrikaans, a language that evolved from Dutch. The earliest settlers arrived in the Cape of Good Hope after the Dutch East India Company established a port in 1652. The Boers had a strong ethnic identity and clashed often with the Zulus and the British.

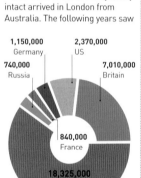

1,150,000 Germany
2,370,000 US
740,000 Russia
7,010,000 Britain
840,000 France
18,325,000 REST OF THE WORLD

Shipping tonnage 1881
This chart shows total goods shipped by country in vessels over 100 tons. Refrigeration sparked a rise in food transport and the use of vast ships.

a boom in **shipments** of meats and other agricultural goods from Australia, New Zealand, and Argentina to Europe.

Around the same time, the problem of creating a safe means of artificial light was solved by the US inventor **Thomas Edison** (1847–1931). He had perfected existing designs on **lightbulbs** of the day (see pp.298–99) by preventing them from overheating and making them much safer to use. Almost as soon as he had patented the design, lighting systems began to spring up on the streets, in businesses and hotels, and in homes.

IN SOUTH AFRICA, TENSIONS BETWEEN BOER SETTLERS (see panel, above) and the British over the annexation of the Transvaal (see 1877) had tipped into violence. Boers had established the **South African Republic** in the Transvaal area and begun to use arms to support their claim, starting the First Anglo–Boer War in 1880. British troops suffered a defeat at the hands of the Boer settlers in the battle at Majuba Hill on February 27, 1881, bringing the dispute to an end by March. The **Convention of Pretoria** treaty granted the South African Republic independence over its affairs, although Britain was allowed to maintain an unclear

"suzerainty" over it. This did little to rectify the situation, and the simmering resentment between the British and Boers would erupt again before the end of the century (see 1899).

France, meanwhile, was attempting to extend its influence in North Africa. With Algeria under its control, it looked to the neighboring Ottoman territory of **Tunisia**. The past 50 years had seen Tunisian rulers caught in between Ottoman demands and European creditors, especially after the government went bankrupt in 1869, after which a British, French, and Italian financial commission was imposed on the territory. France decided to send in 36,000 troops in 1881, under the pretext that Tunisians had been moving into Algerian territory. Under the **Treaty of Bardo** that same year, Tunisia became a **French protectorate**. French military occupied the territory and a French minister was installed to liaise with the Tunisian bey (ruler), who now only had limited control.

In **Russia**, there was an outbreak of anti-Jewish violence culminating in **pogroms** in the south of the country, including Kiev, that continued until 1884. This was triggered by the **assassination** of the reformist **Alexander II** (1818–81) who was killed by a group known as People's Will. False rumors circulated that Jewish people were responsible and that the government was

going to instruct the public to take their revenge on Jews. The violent attacks caused many Jewish people to emigrate to Western Europe, the US, and Palestine.

In the US, teacher and nurse **Clara Barton** (1821–1912) organized the American Red Cross, a part of the growing International Red Cross relief organization that had been founded in 1863.

Meanwhile, in New Mexico, sheriff **Pat Garrett** (1850–1908) captured one of the United States' most notorious outlaws, **Billy the Kid** (c. 1859–81) on April 30. Born William H. Bonney Jr., Billy the Kid became an infamous gunfighter, and was rumored to have killed at least 27 men by the age of 21. After his arrest he was jailed and sentenced to death, but he escaped until Garrett tracked him down and shot him dead on July 14.

Garrett's gun
A replica of the holster that held Pat Garrett's gun around the time he captured Billy the Kid.

Census puts **US population** at 50 million

May 2 First shipment of **frozen meat** from Melbourne, Australia to **Britain**

July 22 Abdur Rahman Khan becomes emir of **Afghanistan**

March 13 Alexander II of Russia **assassinated** by bomb, triggering **anti-Semitic** violence

French protectorate established in **Tunisia**

July 23 Boundary treaty between Chile and **Argentina** establishes exact border between them

June 29 Tahiti cedes to France

December 20 First Anglo–Boer War (to 1881) over annexation of the **South African Republic** (Transvaal region)

January 16 Russia attacks Turkmen Fort in **Turkmenistan** which later becomes part of **Russia**

May 21 US nurse Clara Barton sets up the **American Red Cross**

July 20 Indian Wars: **Chief Sitting Bull** surrenders **Sioux** people to US troops

August 3 Official end to **First Anglo–Boer War** with Pretoria Convention treaty; **South African Republic** in Transvaal reestablished

1882

This illustration shows the bombardment of Alexandria—a sea battle won by the British, who succeeded in destroying the port's fortified batteries.

OVER THE COURSE OF THE PREVIOUS FEW YEARS, the power of French and British interests had grown substantially in Egypt. This led to increasing European interference in Egyptian affairs—considered legitimate because of the financial debt Egypt owed to Britain and France. By 1882, Egypt was bankrupt and the khedive (viceroy) was scarcely able to hold on to his own authority. Ismail Pasha (1830–95) had been deposed by the Ottoman sultan in 1879—under pressure from Britain and France—in favor of his son, Muhammad Tawfiq Pasha (1852–92). This **Dual Control** by the French and British persisted while there was growing internal nationalist unrest.

Britain was fearful of what a nationalist uprising might mean for the Suez Canal, in which it had a substantial interest. So British forces decided to mount an attack to stifle any further action; the Royal Navy bombarded the forts of **Alexandria** on July 11, 1882. Egypt was then placed under military occupation, becoming a British protectorate.

Farther south, in **Sudan**, British troops were continuing to fight the **Sudanese War** (1881–99) against the followers of the powerful **Muhammad Ahmad bin Abd Allah** (1844–85), who had declared a holy war after taking the title Mahdi. His mission was to restore justice to the world, believing it was soon going to end.

In Europe, an **anti-French union** was being formed, known as the **Triple Alliance**. It consisted of Germany, Austria–Hungary, and Italy. The first two had signed previous unions (see 1873), which included Russia. Italy joined after disputing France's territorial claims in North Africa.

Meanwhile, in France, scientist **Louis Pasteur** (1822–95)—known for his development in 1863 of the **pasteurization** process that reduced harmful germs in food and drink—had turned his attention to vaccines (see 1796). He investigated anthrax, a bacterial disease that had killed many sheep in Europe and also affected humans. By 1881, he had conducted successful large-scale experiments with animals, and vaccines were produced.

1883–84

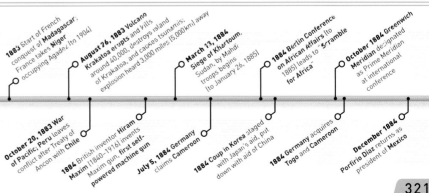

A hand-colored woodcut showing the island of Krakatoa, Indonesia, before its destruction, when its volcano erupted in 1883.

BRITISH TROOPS SUFFERED EARLY DEFEATS IN THE WAR IN SUDAN at the hands of the **Mahdi** revolutionary army (see 1882). At the beginning of the year on January 26, Ahmad and the Mahdi troops captured the city of El Obeid, situated in the center of the territory. Mahdi troops continued their march toward **Khartoum**, which had earlier been placed under British administration by the Egyptian khedive (see 1874), capturing the city after a siege of nine months.

Brooklyn Bridge
The Great East River Suspension Bridge in New York City was built between 1870 and 1883. It stretches 5,988 ft (1825 m) across its span.

Meanwhile, France had seized more of the territory around the **Niger River** (Niger) and became involved in conflict on the island of Madagascar off the coast of East Africa in a bid to protect French territory. In 1883, France invaded the island in the **Franco–Hova War** against the Hova people—the largest Malagasy group on the island—and bombarded the coastal towns of Majunga and Tamatave from the sea. In 1885, they reached a settlement allowing the French occupation at Diégo-Suarez in the north. However, tensions continued and the French sent in 15,000 troops in 1885, landing at Majunga and capturing the capital.

Triggered by the ongoing **Berlin Conference on Africa** (see 1885) Germany claimed territory in southwest Africa (Namibia), Togoland (Togo), Cameroon, and part of the island of Zanzibar off the coast of Tanzania, East Africa. **Italy** took control of Eritrean coastal towns along the Red Sea, though made no farther inroads into **Ethiopian** territory.

In the **Pacific**, Britain and Germany divided up more territories. By the 1870s, Britain had established settlements along the coast of the eastern half of **New Guinea** (present-day Papua New Guinea), annexing it by 1884. Germany took control of the northeast part of the island.

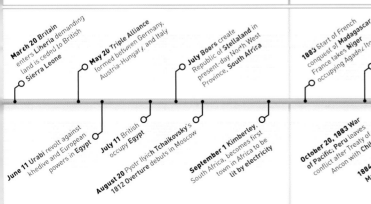

March 20 Britain enters Liberia demanding land is ceded to British Sierra Leone

May 20 Triple Alliance formed between Germany, Austria-Hungary, and Italy

July Boers create Republic of **Stellaland** in present-day North West Province, **South Africa**

June 11 Urabi revolt against khedive and European powers in **Egypt**

July 11 British occupy **Egypt**

August 20 Pyotr Ilyich Tchaikovsky's 1812 Overture debuts in Moscow

September 1 Kimberley, South Africa, becomes first town in Africa to be lit by electricity

1883 Start of French conquest of **Madagascar**; France takes **Niger** occupying Agadez (to 1904)

August 26, 1883 Volcano Krakatoa erupts and kills around 40,000, destroys island of Krakatoa, and causes tsunamis; explosion heard 3,000 miles (5,000 km) away

October 20, 1883 War of Pacific; Peru leaves conflict after Treaty of Ancon with **Chile**

1884 British inventor **Hiram Maxim** (1840–1916) invents Maxim gun, first self-powered machine gun

March 13, 1884, Siege of Khartoum, Sudan, by Mahdi troops begins (to January 26, 1885)

July 5, 1884 Germany claims Cameroon

1884 Coup in Korea staged with Japan's aid, put down with aid of China

1884 Berlin Conference on African Affairs (to 1885) leads to "Scramble for Africa"

1884 Germany acquires Togo and Cameroon

October 1884 Greenwich Meridian designated as Prime Meridian at international conference

December 1884 Porfirio Díaz returns as president of **Mexico**

A village in the valley of the Congo River in Africa in the 1800s. Congolese territory was put under the control of the Belgian king, Leopold II, in 1885.

British troops of the Somersetshire Light Infantry cross a river in Burma, during the Anglo–Burmese War.

AS SOME OF THE NATIONS IN EUROPE became more powerful—especially the new nations of Germany and Italy—they were eager to participate in the growing European colonization of overseas territories, notably in Africa. To this end, the **Berlin Conference on Africa** was held from November 15, 1884 until February 26, 1885. Later known as the meeting that triggered the "**Scramble for Africa**," competing powers jostled for territory—although no African leaders were even consulted, much less invited. The meeting was initiated by Portugal in the interests of protecting its claim to part of the **Congo** estuary. This claim would, however, be rejected and the river basin was declared neutral in order to protect trade in the region. A group of European investors were given part of the Congo region, which was put under the control of Belgium's King Leopold II (1835–1909), and named the **Congo Free State**.

> ❝ **BESIDE LEOPOLD,** NERO, CALIGULA, ATTILA, TORQUEMADA, GENGHIS KHAN AND SUCH **KILLERS OF MEN ARE** MERE **AMATEURS.** ❞

Mark Twain, American author, on Leopold II's regime in the Congo

Meanwhile, in Germany, engineer **Gottlieb Daimler** (1834–1900) patented a high-speed internal-combustion engine. Daimler and partner Wilhelm Maybach (1846–1929) conducted further research with the engine, placing it on bicycles and carriages. Around the same time fellow German **Karl Benz** (1844–1929) had also been experimenting with engines. He came up with the idea for the Benz car, and in 1885 assembled the **first automobile** in the world. He set up Benz & Co, which would later merge with Daimler to make **Mercedes–Benz** cars.

In **India**, a growing political awareness and the burgeoning nationalist movement led to the establishment of the **Indian National Congress**, which held its first meeting in December.

Early Benz
A side view of a gasoline-driven, three-wheeled Benz Motorwagen. German engineer, Karl Benz, patented his design in 1886 and the motorcar was born.

EMANCIPATION FINALLY ARRIVED FOR SLAVES IN CUBA in October 1886, after a long struggle. Although Britain had decided to end the slave trade in 1807 and abolish the practice of slavery in 1833, Spain and other European colonial powers did not follow suit. In 1817, the Spanish agreed a treaty with Britain to stop the slave trade—and then ignored it. With the loss of most of its Central and South American colonies, Spain turned to its remaining sugar islands of **Cuba** and **Puerto Rico** to refill its coffers. To this end, slavery not only continued, but increased over the course of the 19th century, although British antislavery patrols tried to stop ships between the west coast of Africa and Havana. Despite their efforts, the numbers continued to rise. In 1840, around 14,500 slaves were brought to Cuba; by 1859 this number reached nearly 30,500. By 1866, slave imports had fallen to just over 1,000 and the following year, the slave trade was finally outlawed by the Spanish legislature. However, this act did not free the considerable number of slaves on the island. Years of gradual abolition culminated in a royal **decree** that **emancipated the slaves** in 1886. Meanwhile on January 1, Britain annexed **Burma**, heralding a long period of insurgency.

Third Burmese War
Although the war lasted a few weeks, the Burmese insurgency that followed lasted until 1899, claiming many more lives—as shown in this chart.

The annexation was the culmination of the **Third Anglo–Burmese War** in 1885, which had only lasted a few weeks. The war was triggered by Burmese king **Thibaw's** negotiations with France over a political alliance and the construction of a railway line to the Indian border. Britain was unable to air its concerns as Thibaw refused a visit from the British envoy. Britain had already annexed Lower Burma after the previous war (see 1852) and the British decided to react by now seizing **Mandalay** and northern Burma. Thibaw was deposed and the territory was annexed to India, giving Britain control of the former kingdom. Although this marked the end of the official war, there was a sporadic guerrilla campaign by the Burmese that would continue to cause unrest in the region for another four years.

Chart: FORCES (IN THOUSANDS) vs COUNTRIES
- British: **4,000 casualties**
- Burmese: **2,500 casualties**

Timeline 1885:

January 4 First successful **appendectomy** performed

March 31 Bechuanaland (present-day Botswana) becomes British protectorate

Belgium's **Leopold II** (1835–1909) establishes **Congo Free State**

One of the world's first **skyscrapers** built in Chicago

September 18 Eastern Rumelia unites with Bulgaria

Tanganyika becomes German protectorate

Indian political party, **Indian National Congress**, meets for first time

Germany annexes **Marshall Islands**, Pacific Ocean

Serbia defeated in war with Bulgaria

Development of first automobiles by German engineers **Gottlieb Daimler** (1834–1900) and **Karl Benz** (1844–1929)

September 30 British abolish Boer republic of Stellaland, adding it to Bechuanaland

November Third **Anglo-Burmese War** (to 1886) leads to British annexation of Burmese territory

Timeline 1886:

January 1 Britain annexes **Burma**

March 3 Treaty of Bucharest officially ends **Serbo-Bulgarian War**

September 4 Indian Wars: Geronimo chief of Apache surrenders warriors to US Army

January 29 Karl Benz patents first modern gasoline-driven **automobile**

May 8 Soft drink **Coca-Cola** first sold

October 7 Spain abolishes slavery in **Cuba**

1887

A crest belonging to Czar Ferdinand I, who was elected ruler of Bulgaria.

BULGARIA HAD BEEN CAUGHT UP in the wave of nationalism that swept through Europe in the earlier part of the 19th century (see 1848). Bulgaria's independence struggle—during which 15,000 Bulgarians were massacred by Turkish troops in 1876—had attracted Europe's attention. A couple of years later a small Bulgarian principality was established and Britain and Austria-Hungary ensured Russia would not have influence there. By 1885, Bulgaria had merged with **Eastern Rumelia**, and after a coup d'état, the two states were unified. This altered the Balkan balance of power and Serbia declared war. The conflict was brief and peace was restored by 1886. On July 1887, **Prince Ferdinand** of Saxe-Coburg-Gotha (1861–1948) was elected ruler of Bulgaria.

Czar Ferdinand I
Postage stamp, with Czar Ferdinand. He was elected to the position after political infighting led Bulgarians to look further afield for a leader.

1888

An engraving depicts slaves washing diamonds at a Brazilian mine.

720,000 BRAZILIAN

200,000 CUBAN

Slave population
At the time of their respective abolitions, Brazil and Cuba had large slave populations. Freedom was initially slow in coming to slaves.

BRAZIL, LIKE CUBA, CONTINUED TO MAKE USE OF SLAVES much later than other former colonies. In South America, the republics that emerged from the Spanish Empire had abolished slavery by the middle of the century. And like Spain, **Brazil** had been put under pressure by the British to end the trade, which eventually occurred in 1850. Over the next thirty years, growing **abolitionist sentiment** reached the highest level, as the emperor **Dom Pedro II** (1825–91) became sympathetic to these ideas. He was interested in the gradual abolition of slavery but was aware of the dangers of a slaveholder backlash. He had observed not only what had happened in Cuba, but also in the US Civil War (see 1861). In 1871, a gradualist measure known as the **Rio Branco Law**, which freed children born to slave mothers, was enacted. Later measures in 1885 freed slaves who were older than 65. Eventually, a **proclamation in May 1888** completely abolished slavery.

1889

> IF THERE BE A **GOD**, I THINK THAT WHAT HE **WOULD LIKE ME TO** DO IS **PAINT** AS MUCH OF **THE MAP OF AFRICA BRITISH RED** AS POSSIBLE...

Cecil Rhodes, British politician, on colonization

IN PARIS, ENGINEER GUSTAVE EIFFEL (1832–1923) DAZZLED the city and all of Europe with his **tower**, which was opened to the public on March 31. Eiffel won a design contest to build the tower as part of the **International Exposition** of 1889 in honor of the centenary of the French Revolution. With its 984-ft (300-m) tower—twice the height of the Great Pyramid in Giza—nothing like it had ever been seen. The tower attracted almost two million visitors in the first six months after it opened.

Brazil, meanwhile, faced political upheaval as a military coup overthrew leader **Dom Pedro II**. The military, clergy, and aristocracy had been angered by

Eiffel Tower
Initially criticized by the Parisian public who thought it unsightly, the tower has come to be an iconic Parisian landmark.

some of Pedro's reforms and, although still popular with the public, he abdicated and a republic was declared.

Farther north, in Panama, the canal project (see 1880) had collapsed, and work on it came to a halt. The **Compagnie Universelle du Canal Interocéanique** and the French public had lost faith in the enterprise as the death toll mounted and construction was plagued by endless problems.

In Africa, British rule was expanding apace as **Cecil John Rhodes** (1853–1902)—who had already established his reputation in the gold and diamond mines in South Africa—received a charter for his **British South Africa Company** in 1889. The company was expected to respect local law and beliefs. However, Rhodes's

IMPERIALISM

The late 19th century was a time of extensive colonial rule by European powers. "The Rhodes Colossus" (right) from an 1892 *Punch* magazine depicts British colonizer, Cecil Rhodes, straddling the continent after the announcemount of his proposed telegraph line from Cape Town to Cairo. But this was also a period infamous for European exploitation of natural resources, as well as the indifferent or cruel treatment of native peoples.

aim was to acquire territory in Southern Africa and continue the extraction of valuable minerals. Rhodes came to symbolize the excesses of **colonial greed**.

22,000 THE NUMBER OF WORKERS WHO **DIED DURING A FAILED ATTEMPT TO BUILD** THE **PANAMA CANAL**

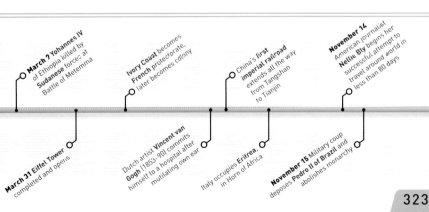

January 24 Battle of Dogali: Italians defeated by **Ethiopia**

First automatic rifle, the **Mondragón**, patented by General Manuel Mondragón (1600)–1914)

Bulgaria, independent of Ottoman Empire, becomes leading Balkan state

March 4 Gottlieb Daimler (1834–1900) reveals his first **automobile**

November 8 Emile Berliner (1851–1929) patents gramophone

November 13 Bloody Sunday—violent clash between Irish protesters and police in London

"Jack the Ripper" murders occur in London

Slavery abolished in **Brazil**

June 15 Wilhelm II becomes German emperor

Kodak snapshot camera becomes available to the public

Earliest known **recording** of classical music made on a **wax cylinder**

March 9 Yohannes IV of Ethiopia killed by Sudanese forces at Battle of Metemma

March 31 Eiffel Tower completed and opens

Ivory Coast becomes French protectorate, later becomes colony

Dutch artist **Vincent van Gogh** (1853–90) commits himself to a hospital after mutilating own ear

China's **first imperial railroad** extends all the way from Tangshan to Tianjin

Italy occupies **Eritrea**, in Horn of Africa

November 14 American journalist **Nellie Bly** begins her successful attempt to travel around world in less than 80 days

November 15 Military coup deposes Pedro II of Brazil and abolishes monarchy

THE IMPERIAL
WORLD

THE ERA OF EUROPEAN COLONIAL EXPANSION ACROSS THE GLOBE

Throughout the 18th and 19th centuries the world witnessed a relentless European drive to control territories all over the globe. Colonies provided not only direct supplies of valuable natural resources, but also a theater of conflict in which Europe's antagonisms were played out.

The Imperial Age saw Spain, Britain, France, Germany, Holland, Portugal, Italy, and to a lesser extent, Denmark and Sweden, scramble for territories. A country could lose colonies in one war, only to reclaim them later through trade in a wider political game. Colonies often started out as trading posts, in places such as India, but through political maneuvering and exercising military might European countries began to take control. People living in the Americas, Africa, India, and Southeast Asia were often on the receiving end of racial prejudice and political oppression. Economic exploitation of colonial territories and their people also frequently occurred, as raw materials were exported out of the country, and slave labor was used. This situation persisted until after World War II, when many colonies around the world began to demand their independence (see pp.422–23).

EMPIRE BUILDING

In the 18th century, most colonial outposts were located along the world's coastlines, as settlements sprung up where ships stopped off. Trading posts grew into cities, often with European-style architecture to reflect the political changes. Over time, improvements in military power, transportation, and health—tropical diseases killed thousands of Europeans—saw the spread of colonial rule throughout the 19th century. This was especially true for Britain and France. However, Spain, which had begun empire-building earlier and controlled large parts of Latin America at the beginning of the period, had lost almost all of its territories by the 1820s.

" THE SUN NEVER SETS ON THE BRITISH EMPIRE. "

Popular saying coined during the early 1800s

BELGIAN CONGO

1,037,451

5,764,731

Belgium

Expansion
Following the example of Britain and the Netherlands, the small state of Belgium exploited the vast territory of the Congo, which was 76 times larger than Belgium.

Colonial minority
Native Spaniards were in the minority in the Spanish colony of New Spain (Mexico and Central America). In 1810, they made up just under a fifth of the total population.

LENGTH OF RAILROAD LINE (MILES)

North and South Rhodesaia · Sudan · British East Africa & Uganda · Sierra Leone · Gold Coast · Nyasaland

2500 · 2000 · 1500 · 1000 · 500 · 0

BRITISH AFRICAN TERRITORIES

Making tracks
By 1914, the vast expanse of colonial British Africa was spanned by thousands of miles of railroad track, opening the region up to trade and aiding communication between territories.

Imperial land
By 1910, Britain was well ahead in the imperial race, with an empire covering more than twice as much of the globe as its closest rival, France.

US · PORTUGAL · BELGIUM · GERMANY · FRANCE · BRITAIN

Imperial population
Millions of people across the world lived under colonial rule by 1910. Britain governed subjects in Africa, the Americas, Asia, and Australasia.

24 · 21 · 18 · 15 · 12 · 9 · 6 · 3 · 0
SIZE OF EMPIRE (MILLION SQ MILES)

0 · 50 · 100 · 150 · 200 · 250 · 300 · 350 · 400
COLONIAL POPULATION (IN MILLIONS)

ALASKA

CANADA

NEWFOUNDLAND

Rocky Mountains

Great Lakes

Chicago

St. Pierre and Miquelon

UNITED STATES OF AMERICA

New York
Washington DC

Appalachian Mountains

Los Angeles

Bermuda

ATLANTIC

MEXICO

CUBA
US occupation
Havana

Bahamas

DOMINICAN REPUBLIC
Puerto Rico
Virgin Islands
St. Martin
Leeward Islands
Guadeloupe
Martinique
Barbados
Windward Islands
Trinidad and To

Mexico

Jamaica · HAITI

BRITISH HONDURAS *West*
HONDURAS *Indies*
Curaçao

GUATEMALA
SALVADOR
NICARAGUA
COSTA RICA

VENEZUELA

BRITISH GUIAN

COLOMBIA

Guiana Highlands

DUTC
GUIA
FREN
GUIA

Galapagos Islands

ECUADOR

Amazon Basin

Andes

PACIFIC OCEAN

ACRE

BRAZIL

Lima

PERU

BOLIVIA

Rio de Jan
São Paulo

PARAGUAY

CHILE

Andes

ARGENTINA

URUGUAY

Santiago

Buen
Aires

Patagonia

FALKLAND
ISLANDS

1700 In the 18th century, European expansion, with the exception of Spanish Central and South America, was mostly confined to port cities. Huge swaths of the world were under the control of the older Ottoman and Qing empires in the East.

1800 A century later, Spain, France, and Britain had taken control of almost all of the Americas. The British had also made a series of incursions into India, as the Mughal Empire broke down, while also undertaking exploration into Africa.

1850 By the middle of the 19th century, the world map had been reconfigured with the independence of Latin America. British and French attention had turned to the resource-rich lands of Africa, while the Dutch continued to expand into Southeast Asia.

1900 At the turn of the 20th century, European colonialism had reached across the globe. The "Scramble for Africa" in the 1880s saw the major powers jostling for territory and taking land from Africans. The US gained territories in the Caribbean and Southeast Asia.

Greenland

ICELAND
NORWAY
SWEDEN
FINLAND
DENMARK
BRITAIN
NETH.
London
BELGIUM
Paris
PORTUGAL
Lisbon
SPAIN
Madrid
GIBRALTAR
Ceuta
Melilla
Canary Islands
Madeira
IFNI
RIO DE ORO
Verde Islands
GAMBIA
PORTUGUESE GUINEA
SIERRA LEONE
LIBERIA
GOLD COAST
SAO TOME AND PRINCIPE
RIO MUNI
Ascension
BAROTSELAND-NORTHWESTERN RHODESIA
St. Helena
GERMAN SOUTHWEST AFRICA
WALVIS BAY to Cape Colony
Cape Town
CAPE COLONY

OCEAN

GERMAN EMPIRE
Berlin
POLAND
SWITZ.
Vienna
AUSTRO-HUNGARIAN EMPIRE
ROMANIA
Budapest
SERBIA
BULGARIA
FRANCE
ITALY
Rome
Malta
TUNIS
GREECE
Athens
Istanbul
CYPRUS
British occupied
MOROCCO
ALGERIA
OTTOMAN EMPIRE
Sahara
Sahel
FRENCH WEST AFRICA
French in terms of 1899 Franco-British agreement. French control in part notional
NIGERIA
TOGO
KAMERUN
FRENCH CONGO
ANGOLA
SOUTHERN RHODESIA
BECHUANA-LAND
SOUTH AFRICAN REPUBLIC
NATAL
BASUTOLAND
ORANGE FREE STATE

RUSSIAN EMPIRE
Siberia
Gobi
St Petersburg
Moscow
Black Sea
Caspian Sea
KHIVA
BUKHARA
Tehran
PERSIA
AFGHANISTAN
Red Sea
EGYPT
Ottoman dominions under British control
Cairo
BEDUINS
Arabian Peninsula
OMAN
Aden
Socotra
ERITREA
ANGLO-EGYPTIAN SUDAN
HADHRAMAUT
FRENCH SOMALILAND
Addis Ababa
ABYSSINIA
BRITISH SOMALILAND
ITALIAN SOMALILAND
LADO
CONGO FREE STATE
nominally independent under Belgian control
GERMAN EAST AFRICA
Zanzibar
BRITISH EAST AFRICA
Seychelles
BRITISH CENTRAL AFRICA
Amirante Islands
Comoro Islands
NORTHEASTERN RHODESIA
MADAGASCAR
Mauritius
Réunion
PORTUGUESE EAST AFRICA

QING EMPIRE
NEPAL
BHUTAN
Himalayas
Delhi
INDIA
Chandernagore
Gwadar to Oman
BAHRAIN
TRUCIAL OMAN
Diu
Damāo
Bombay
Goa
Mahé
Madras
Pondicherry
Karikal
CEYLON
Maldive Islands
Yanaon
BURMA
SIAM
Bangkok
FRENCH INDOCHINA
Saigon
Singapore
SUMATRA
Batavia
JAVA
Chagos Islands
Cocos Islands
Christmas Island

Port Arthur
Beijing
Weihaiwei
Jiaozhou
Nanjing
Shanghai
KOREA
JAPAN
Tokyo
Taiwan
Macao
Hong Kong
Guangzhouwan
Manila
PHILIPPINE ISLANDS
BRITISH NORTH BORNEO
SARAWAK
MALAYA
BRUNEI
BORNEO
DUTCH EAST INDIES
PORTUGUESE TIMOR

PACIFIC OCEAN

INDIAN OCEAN

AUSTRALIAN COLONIES
Sydney
Lord Howe Island
NEW ZEALAND

KEY

- Ottoman Empire
- Britain and possessions
- France and possessions
- Denmark and possessions
- Spain and possessions
- Portugal and possessions
- Swedish Empire
- Netherlands and possessions
- German Empire in 1900; Hohenzollerns in 1700; Prussia in 1800 and 1850
- Austrian Empire in 1850; Austrian-Habsburg Empire in 1700 and 1800
- Italy and possessions in 1900; Venetian Republic in 1700
- Russian Empire and possessions
- Japan and possessions
- Qing Empire
- US and possessions

A colored engraving depicts the massacre of Sioux Indians at Wounded Knee Creek, South Dakota, by US soldiers of the 7th Cavalry Regiment.

The Trans-Siberian Railway during its construction in Russia.

The Great Mosque of Djenne, Mali, was built after the French took control.

IN THE US, TENSIONS AND SPORADIC FIGHTING in the west between US troops and American Indians had continued since the **Battle at Little Bighorn** (see 1876). In addition to this, American Indians faced increasingly harsh living conditions: poverty, disease, and crop failures were rife. By the 1880s, a new mysticism called the **Ghost Dance** had emerged among the **Sioux** people, based on the belief that an Indian messiah would come in 1891 and unite all the displaced native peoples. This newfound belief manifested in trances, dances, and a mass frenzy, which worried the US agents who oversaw the reservations. They attempted to stop the dances, and the Sioux people rebelled, with US army troops being called in by the end of the year.

The reservation of Wounded Knee Creek in South Dakota was the scene of a massacre on December 29, when around 150 American Indians—men, women, and children—were killed and 50 were wounded by US troops. During disarmament of the Sioux tribe a scuffle had broken out, and in the ensuing carnage around 25

US soldiers were also left dead, many due to friendly fire from US machine guns. This was the last major conflict between American Indians and the US Army, although poor relations persisted between the two groups.

In Europe, a small island off the North Sea coast of Germany, near the territory of Schleswig-Holstein, **Heligoland**, had formally come into British possession in 1814, having been seized by the Royal Navy seven years earlier. However, as Germany's European and African expansion continued, a deal was struck for Britain to hand over the island to Germany in exchange for the islands of **Zanzibar** and **Pemba**, near Tanzania's port of Tanga off the East African coast. Germany developed Heligoland into a large naval base. Zanzibar was added to Britain's substantial territory in Africa, building on earlier deals struck with Germany, as well as claims made following the Berlin Conference (see 1885). In the following year, Britain formally established the **Nyasaland Districts**

Protectorate. This became known as the "British Central Africa Protectorate" in 1893 and was then officially designated as "Nyasaland" in 1907. Part of this territory lay along Lake Nyasa and the Shire valley in present-day Malawi).

Sioux weapon
A 19th-century style knife and beaded rawhide sheath, as carried by American Indian Sioux warriors.

6:1
Wounded Knee dead
The massacre left 150 Sioux dead, while 25 troops from the US army were killed. A further 50 Sioux were wounded during the conflict.

5,785
MILES
THE **DISTANCE BETWEEN MOSCOW** AND **VLADIVOSTOK** ON THE **TRANS-SIBERIAN RAILWAY**

IN RUSSIA, CONSTRUCTION HAD BEGUN ON AN EXTENSIVE RAILROAD SYSTEM across its vast territory. The project was the idea of Alexander III (1845–94), and it was known as the **Trans-Siberian Railway**. It stretched from Moscow to the port of **Vladivostok**, 5,715 miles (9,198 km) to the east. Russia received permission from China to run tracks through parts of Manchuria, allowing the completion of a trans-Manchurian line by 1901. The work began from west and east ends and eventually met in the center. By 1904, the sections linking Moscow and Vladivostok were connected and running. The railroad facilitated the quicker movement of people through Russia and allowed for the further settlement of sparsely populated **Siberia**.

French in Africa
A postage stamp from French West Africa shows an illustration of a native mask. France managed to gain control of much of the region.

BRITAIN AND FRANCE WERE CONTINUING THEIR PUSH into West Africa. The British had secured ports along the coast, annexing Lagos in 1861. Lagos provided a key point from which to seize control of surrounding **Yorubaland**, situated around the lower parts of the Niger River, corresponding with much of modern southwest Nigeria. The British took advantage of existing internal divisions among Yoruba rulers, and in 1892, they overthrew the **Ijebu** government, part of the Yoruba political system.

Likewise, the French exploited divisions in the Muslim **Tukulor Empire** by signing treaties with its neighbors and building forts within Tukulor territory. By 1892, the French controlled much of the region around the Senegal River.

January 15
Pyotr Ilyich Tchaikovsky's *Sleeping Beauty* performed at St. Petersburg, Russia

July 1 Heligoland-Zanzibar treaty between Britain and Germany

November 23 William III of Netherlands dies; Luxembourg breaks away over succession to throne

March Construction of the **Trans-Siberian Railway** begins (finishes 1917)

Malawi becomes a British protectorate

January 7 Abbas II becomes khedive of Egypt (to 1914)

May 19 British defeat Ijebu (present-day Nigeria) with machine gun at River Ye...

June 28 Cecil Rhodes' British South Africa Company begins **colonization of** Southern African territory

July 29 Dutch post-Impressionist artist **Vincent van Gogh** dies two days after shooting himself (b. 1853)

December 29 Massacre at Wounded Knee in which the US Army kills 150 Sioux, including women and children

March 29 George Seurat (1859–91) leading figure in **neo-Impressionist movement** dies

October Paleoanthropologist **Eugene Dubois** (1858–1940) finds first remains of *Homo erectus*

Dimitri Ivanovsky (1864–1920) discovers **viruses**

1893

ALTHOUGH FRANCE HAD MADE GAINS IN THE WEST AFRICAN INTERIOR, the coastal territories around the kingdom of **Dahomey** (present-day Benin) had proven difficult to subdue. In 1889, Britain had handed over to France the coastal city of **Cotonou** in Dahomey without consulting the Dahomeans. The result was the First Franco–Dahomean War (1889–90), which concluded with a treaty that ceded Cotonou and Porto Novo to France in exchange for payments to the king of Dahomey. However, tensions remained, and by 1892 another war had begun, this time over the issue of **slavery**. The king, Behanzin (1844–1906), was still allowing slave raids, despite the abolition of slavery. In addition, he attacked a French gunboat. France retaliated, this time with an army of French and Senegalese troops, and they overpowered the kingdom, bringing it under French control in 1893.

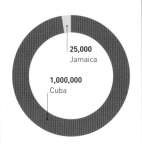

25,000
Jamaica

1,000,000
Cuba

Sugar production in tons
In 1893, Cuba, then the dominant world sugar grower, produced 1 million tons of sugar, four times as much as Jamaica.

Halfway around the world, in the British colony of **New Zealand**, women won the right to vote. The push for women's **suffrage** was gaining momentum in many places, but these islands were the first to grant the right, after formidable efforts by suffragists and tireless campaigners, such as **Kate Sheppard** (1847–1934). Shortly after this act was passed, there was a general election in which 65 percent of women cast their votes.

Meanwhile, **Cuba** was experiencing a sugar boom, with profits of $64 million in 1893. However, a US **tariff** the following year would cause profits to drop to $13 million by 1896.

Ruler of Dahomey
A painting of Behanzin, king of Dahomey (modern Benin), shows him holding symbols of kingship while surrounded by attendants.

1894

An engraving showing the coronation ceremony of Emperor Nicholas II and the Empress Alexandra, who would be Russia's last ruling monarchs.

IN RUSSIA, AFTER THE DEATH OF ALEXANDER III, Nicholas II (1868–1918) became the next, and last, emperor of Russia. He presided over an increasingly troubled country, and would not be able to withstand the social **revolution** that engulfed Russia in the early 20th century.

Russia's neighbor, **China**, had become entangled in a local conflict in **Korea** that escalated into the **Sino–Japanese War**. The confrontation had started over an internal revolt in Korea. The monarch asked both nations for help, and both sent troops. Yet they also refused to leave once the rebellion was suppressed. Japan was allied with the modernizing government in Korea, while China backed the royal family. Tensions between China and Japan mounted and

conflict broke out, with Japan declaring war on China on August 1.

In the Ottoman Empire, the **Christian Armenian** people were also caught up in the nationalist spirit of the time, and they tried to assert their independence. However, their efforts met with a particularly brutal **suppression**, ordered by Sultan Abdul Hamid II (1842–1918). This saw systematic massacres of Armenian people throughout the empire, resulting in the collapse of the independence movement a few years later.

The death toll has been estimated to be around 250,000 Armenians killed out of a population of 2 million, between 1894 and 1897.

Sino–Japanese War
A painting of the Sino–Japanese War shows the Japanese forces conquering Jiuliancheng after defeating the Chinese at Pyongyang.

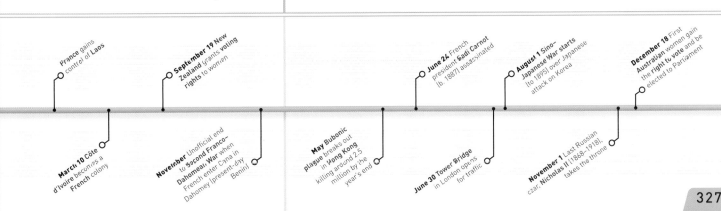

France gains control of **Laos**

March 10 Côte d'Ivoire becomes a French colony

September 19 New Zealand grants voting rights to women

November Unofficial end to **Second Franco– Dahomean War** when French enter Cana in Dahomey (present-day Benin)

May Bubonic plague breaks out in **Hong Kong** killing around 2.5 million by the year's end

June 24 French president **Sadi Carnot** (b. 1837) assassinated

June 30 Tower Bridge in London opens for traffic

August 1 Sino– Japanese War starts (to 1895) over Japanese attack on Korea

November 1 Last Russian czar, **Nicholas II** (1868–1918), takes the throne

December 18 First Australian women gain the right to vote and be elected to Parliament

> **EVERY DAY SEES HUMANITY MORE VICTORIOUS IN THE STRUGGLE WITH SPACE AND TIME.**

Guglielmo Marconi, Italian inventor

This scene from the Italian invasion of Abyssinia in 1896 shows the Abyssinian forces routing the Italian troops.

TECHNOLOGICAL DEVELOPMENTS WERE PROLIFERATING RAPIDLY all over the world. In Italy, physicist and inventor **Guglielmo Marconi** (1874–1937) invented a **wireless telegraph**. In his initial experiments, using a telegraph key to operate a **transmitter**, he was able to send electromagnetic waves in bursts that corresponded to **Morse code**. He then used a transmitter to ring a bell that had been placed 30 ft (9 m) away. He worked on the **receiving antennae** and by the end of the year he could transmit a signal 1.5 miles (2.5 km). However, he found little enthusiasm for his work, so he went to Britain, where he patented

Marconi's wireless
The wireless telegraph (replica shown) developed by Guglielmo Marconi paved the way for the development of radio technology.

the device the following year, and laid the foundation for **radio technology**. Meanwhile, German physicist **Wilhelm Conrad Röntgen** (1845–1923) had been experimenting with electric currents and cathode-ray tubes. The outcome was a type of radiation that allowed objects to **appear transparent** on photographic plates. Röntgen called this **X-radiation**, an early version of the modern X-ray.

In **Korea**, the clash between Japanese and Chinese forces (see 1894) came to an end after the **Chinese defeat** in Pyongyang, and subsequent naval victories by the **Japanese fleet**. China sued for peace on February 12 and the resulting **Treaty of Shimonoseki**, which had involved Russian, French, and German intervention, forced China to give up the island of **Formosa** (modern Taiwan) to Japan, as well as the nearby Pescadores (Penghu) Islands. China also had to recognize **Korean independence**, open more ports to Japanese trade, and pay a large indemnity.

Early X-ray
One of the first X-ray photographs made by German professor Wilhelm Conrad Röntgen (1845–1923) captured a woman's hand with rings.

GREECE SAW THE MODERN REBIRTH OF THE ANCIENT OLYMPIC GAMES, which was organized by an enthusiastic Frenchman, Baron **Pierre de Coubertin**. In 1890, he met **William Penny Brookes**, who had orchestrated a British Olympic Games in 1866. Coubertin and Brookes wanted to create an **international festival of modern sport**. After years of campaigning, Coubertin was finally able to organize the event in **Athens** from April 6–15. It was an enormous success—almost **300 contestants** competed in track and field, gymnastics, tennis, swimming, cycling, fencing, shooting, weightlifting, and wrestling, while **40,000 spectators** cheered them on. However, Brookes did not live to be present at the games, having died the previous year.

Meanwhile, **Italy** was trying to extend its reach in Africa with an invasion of the **Abyssinian Empire** (modern Ethiopia). Its previous attempt to annex the kingdom had ended in failure by 1889 (see 1872). Under the terms of the **Treaty of Uccialli**, Italy thought it had the right to establish a protectorate over **Abyssinia**, but this was contested. By 1895, the

1896 OLYMPIC GAMES

43 THE NUMBER OF **EVENTS**

14 THE NUMBER OF **COUNTRIES**

241 THE NUMBER OF **ATHLETES**

SCRIBNER'S

The Olympic Games and their Revival

Stories

Lord Leighton

Cathode Photography

Quarrel of the English Speaking Peoples

APRIL

Olympic revival
The cover illustration for the April edition of Scribner's Magazine *celebrated the revival of the Olympic Games, being held in Athens, Greece. There were 43 events, in nine different sports.*

disagreement between Italy and Abyssinian emperor **Menelik II** (1844–1913) had turned into an armed conflict. The turning point was the **Battle of Adwa** on March 1, 1896, at which 80,000 Abyssinians defeated 20,000 Italian soldiers.

7,000 THE NUMBER OF **ITALIANS KILLED** AT **ADWA**

March 4 Formosa (Taiwan) ceded from China to Japan

April 17 Treaty of Shimonoseki marks end of China–Japan war

November 8 Wilhelm Conrad Röntgen discovers the **X-ray**

March 1 Abyssinian army defeats Italians at **Battle of Adwa**

May 18 US Supreme Court establishes a "**separate but equal**" doctrine between blacks and whites

June 15 Earthquake and tsunami in Sankiru, Japan, kills 27,000 people

August 16 Discovery of gold along the **Klondike River**, northwest Canada, sparks a **gold rush**

March 30 German **Rudolf Diesel** (1838–1913) patents the Diesel engine

July 31 Basque Nationalist Party founded

December 28 World's **first moving picture film** shown in Paris

April Revival of the Olympic Games in Athens, Greece

June 4 Henry Ford's first automobile, the **Quadricycle**, completed

September 22 Queen **Victoria** becomes longest reigning monarch in British history

A cartoon entitled "The concert of nations," in an 1897 edition of *Le Petit Journal*, satirizes the Thirty Days' War, also known as the Greco–Turkish War.

Four soldiers raise their rifles over the brush of San Juan Hill, Cuba, as they fight from trenches during the Spanish–American war.

Cyclists of the Lancashire Fusiliers took part in the South African War.

ALTHOUGH THE TEN YEARS' WAR HAD BEEN UNSUCCESSFUL (see 1868), many Cubans were unwilling to accept continued control by Spain. Leading the renewed cries for independence was the **Cuban Revolutionary Party**. It declared a republic in eastern Cuba and began a guerilla war, known as the **Cuban War of Independence**. Soldiers managed to reach **Havana** by the following year, although they were driven back. The US would end up getting involved when the **battleship** *Maine* **was blown up** in the Havana harbor (see 1898).

Trouble was brewing between **Greece** and the **Ottoman Empire** over the situation in **Crete**. There had been a brutal suppression of a Christian uprising on the island the year before, and Greece was determined to annex the territory. However, the **Thirty Days' War** did not have the outcome Greece desired. When an armistice was agreed in August, it was forced to pay an **indemnity** and it lost part of the territory of **Thessaly**. The Turks withdrew their troops from Crete and the island was made an international protectorate.

JOSE MARTI (1853–95)

A writer, philosopher, journalist, and political theorist, José Martí became a key figure in the Cuban revolutionary struggle. He is considered a national hero for his planning and leadership during the Cuban War of Independence. He died on the battlefield at Dos Ríos, in the east of the island.

Meanwhile, Britain was undergoing a remarkable **boom in coal mining**. The level of coal production had doubled since the 1860s. The mining industry was also a major employer—in 1897 the number of **miners** in Britain was around 695,200, rising from about 216,200 in 1851.

Coal mining in Britain
By 1897, Britain was the world leader in coal production. Its output of 200 million tons put it ahead of the US and Germany, who were also large coal producers.

WITH THE DESTRUCTION OF THE *USS Maine*—blown up while docked in Havana's harbor—the **US** made the decision to go to **war against Spain**. Cuba's struggle for independence had already attracted much support in the US. The government blamed the *Maine* incident—in which **260 crew members were killed**—on Spain. Although Cuba and Spain had agreed an armistice on April 9, the US began the **Spanish–American War** only a few weeks later, on April 25. Battles were fought in two theaters: the Atlantic and the Pacific. US Navy ships sailed into Manila Bay, in the **Spanish Philippines**, while another fleet made incursions into the southern harbor of Cuba, **Santiago**, where troops then disembarked. By July 25, **Spain had capitulated**. It would pay a steep price for what the US Secretary of State John Hay (1838–1905) called "a splendid little war" in a letter to his friend and future US president **Theodore Roosevelt** (1858–1919), who had led the First Volunteer Cavalry (known as the "Rough Riders"). Under the terms of the **Treaty of Paris** of December 10, Spain had to give up its remaining colonies, **allowing Cuba its independence** and ceding Puerto Rico, Guam, and the Philippines to the US. However, the US continued to occupy Cuba, and the following year tried to exclude Cubans from governing, and disbanded the army. Around the same time the US also managed to annex the islands of **Hawaii**.

Hawaii annexed
In a contemporary illustration, Hawaiians in Honolulu receive news of their annexation by the US. The US would also take control of Guam and the Philippines.

Meanwhile, in **Egypt**, Britain and France became embroiled in the **Fashoda Incident**, which involved territorial disputes over their respective attempts at expansion in Africa. The British wanted to build a **railroad linking Egypt and Uganda** while France wanted to continue its eastward drive into the **Sudan**. Although their troops met in Fashoda on September 18, the situation did not escalate into war, as all sides wanted to **avoid battle**. Instead they decided that British, French, and Egyptian flags should fly over the fort that the French had occupied. Eventually, they agreed that their **boundaries** would be marked by where the **Nile and Congo rivers** divided.

HOSTILITIES BETWEEN THE BOERS AND BRITISH were once again heading toward conflict. They had already clashed in the **First Boer War** (see 1880). This time Boers were demanding that British troops protecting mining interests should withdraw from the **Transvaal**, but this request was ignored. So the South African Republic and the Orange Free State **declared war** on Britain in October. The **South African War** would last less than three years but, for the British, it would become the largest since the Napoleonic Wars, as its forces reached some 500,000 men. The war was fought across a **hostile terrain**, which the Boers—whose troops numbered less than 90,000—could use to their advantage. The war became infamous because of the **treatment of Boer civilians**, who saw their farms burned and women and children put into **camps** where up to 25,000 died.

War medal
The Queen's South Africa Medal, awarded to military personnel who served in the war, is engraved with a Jubilee bust of Queen Victoria.

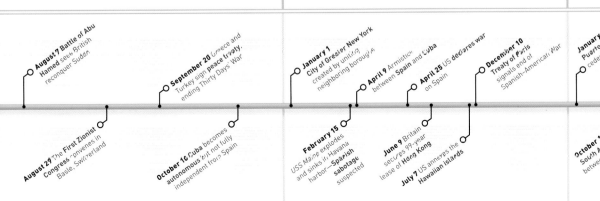

August 7 Battle of Abu Hamed sees British reconquer Sudan.

August 29 The First Zionist Congress convenes in Basle, Switzerland

September 20 Greece and Turkey sign peace treaty, ending Thirty Days' War

October 16 Cuba becomes autonomous but not fully independent from Spain

January 1 Greater New York City of Greater New York created by uniting neighboring boroughs

February 15 USS *Maine* explodes and sinks in Havana harbor—**Spanish sabotage** suspected

April 9 Armistice between Spain and Cuba

April 25 US declares war on Spain

June 9 Britain secures 99-year lease of Hong Kong

July 7 US annexes the **Hawaiian Islands**

December 10 Treaty of Paris signals end of Spanish–American War

January 1 Puerto Rico ceded to US

October 11 Start of **South African War**, between British and Boers (to 1902)

July 29 Peace Conference at the Hague establishes an international court of arbitration

November Sigmund Freud (1856–1939) publishes *The Interpretation of Dreams*

COAL (MILLIONS OF TONS) chart: 250, 200, 150, 100, 50, 0 — 1865 (~100), 1897 (~190)

This illustration shows the storming of Beijing by the international force that arrived to fight the anti-Western attacks during the Boxer uprising.

Queen Victoria's funeral procession makes its way through London.

Prince Saud Ibn Abdul-Aziz, the first monarch of the modern Saudi state.

THE GROWING PRESENCE OF WESTERNERS—especially Christian missionaries—in China was starting to cause public anger. This eventually erupted into the **Boxer Rebellion**, which was a peasant uprising that aimed to eject all foreigners from China. The group behind the attacks had earlier founded a secret society known as the "Righteous and Harmonious Fists," hence the sobriquet "Boxer." Members of the group were also found among the Qing court, and so the movement's violent attacks on foreigners and Chinese converts to Christianity were officially sanctioned. An international **relief force** of 2,100 troops from Britain, France, Italy, Germany, Russia, Japan, and the US was eventually sent to the port of Tianjin in June 1900, but the Boxers

continued to burn down churches and kill Christians. After the international troops seized several forts, the empress dowager **Tz'u Hsi** (1835–1908) ordered all foreigners to be killed, and many foreign ministers were murdered. After the arrival of reinforcements, the international force made its way to Beijing, which it captured. The empress dowager fled, and a truce was negotiated with the imperial princes in September 1901. This put an end to the violence and provided for reparations to be made. While these events were taking place, the **Russians** took the opportunity to occupy southern **Manchuria**, which bordered southern Russia.

In Africa, mining began in **Katanga**, a southern region of the present-day Democratic Republic of the Congo. The discovery of rich **copper** deposits—as well as other minerals, including zinc, cobalt, and tin—led to the rapid establishment by Europeans of mining infrastructure, such as railroad lines, and towns began to spring up in this region. As mining companies proliferated, Katanga was soon one of the most highly industrialized areas

Going underground
A Metro sign built into a lamp-post in Paris, France. The first underground train line was opened in Paris in 1900.

[Graph]

MILLIONS: 0, 10, 20, 30, 40, 50, 60, 70, 80
X-axis: 1800, 1850, 1900

Growing nation
Thanks to decades of immigration, the population of the US had soared, reaching more than 75 million by 1900.

of the Congo, but the many Africans employed performed the dirty and dangerous work in the mines for very little pay.

Meanwhile, in West Africa, British troops faced a rebellion by the **Asante**, which took eight months to subdue. Unrest in the **Gold Coast** region continued throughout the following decade as Africans continued to resist British rule.

Across the Atlantic, in the US, decades of **immigration** had caused the country's population to nearly double. There were around 35.5 million people living in the US in 1870, and by 1900 that number had reached more than 75 million. Much of this growth had been in **urban areas**—some 40 percent of the population were living in cities rather than settling in rural communities.

THE MANY COLONIES THAT HAD BEEN FOUNDED IN AUSTRALIA—Victoria, New South Wales, Queensland, South Australia, Western Australia, and Tasmania—ushered in a new era on January 1, after the drafting and approval of the **constitution** and official establishment of the Commonwealth of Australia.

A few weeks later, Great Britain and its colonies mourned the loss of **Queen Victoria**, who died on January 22. She had ruled the nation and empire for 63 years, making her reign the longest by a British monarch. Her son, **Edward VII** (1841–1910), took the throne, and the largely peaceful—though very socially stratified—period under his rule was known as the **Edwardian era**.

[Stamp image: VICTORIA / STAMP DUTY]

Commonwealth stamp
This stamp showing Queen Victoria is from Australia, which brought its colonies into a federation the same year the monarch died.

THE SOUTH AFRICAN, OR ANGLO-BOER, WAR between Boer settlers and the British ended on May 31. The end of the war was hastened when the British adopted a "scorched earth" policy, which involved destroying crops and livestock to limit Boer supplies. The dispossessed Boer women and children were rounded up into concentration camps. Under the **Treaty of Vereeniging**, the Boers were forced to recognize British sovereignty in South Africa, ending the independence of the Orange Free State and the South African Republic. The whole territory was now under British control.

Meanwhile, **Ibn Saud** (c. 1880–1953) recaptured the Saud dynasty's formal capital of Riyadh, after decades of civil war (see 1843). In 1901, Saud, who was living in Kuwait, set out to take back the territory he had been forced to leave by the rival Rashids. He and his men reached Riyadh in January 1902 and crept into town, waiting to ambush the Rashidi governor the following morning. Soon Saud had taken the city and the territory, with the help of a growing number of supporters. This became the kingdom of **Saudi Arabia** in 1932, and it remains under the Saud family's rule to the present day.

On the Caribbean island of Martinique, the violent eruption of **Mount Pelée** killed around 30,000 people and destroyed the port of Saint-Pierre on May 8. The volcano had previously erupted in 1792 and 1851, but on nowhere near the scale of the 1902 eruption.

January 24 Second Anglo-Boer War: British attempt to relieve Ladysmith at the Battle of Spion Kop ends in defeat

April 30 Hawaii becomes an official US territory

May 18 Tonga becomes a British protectorate

July 2 First zeppelin flight takes place in Germany

August 14 Boxer Rebellion in China: international forces invade Beijing to free European hostages

Nigeria becomes British protectorate

April 22 Battle of Kousséri: the French take control of Chad after defeating and killing warlord **Rabi az-Zubayr**

June 5 British soldiers take Pretoria in Second Anglo-Boer War

July 19 First subway line opens in Paris

October Russian occupation of Manchuria

January 222 Queen Victoria dies; **Edward VII** (1841–1910) ascends British throne

June 11 New Zealand annexes the Cook Islands

September 14 Theodore "Teddy" Roosevelt (1858–1919) elected US president

September 25 Britain annexes Asante kingdom (part of Ghana)

February 15 Berlin U-Bahn underground opens

May 20 Cuba becomes independent of US

May 31 End of Second Anglo-Boer War with Treaty of Vereeniging

December 10 Egypt opens first Aswan Dam

The original 1903 airplane designed by Wilbur and Orville Wright makes its first flight on December 17, 1903 in Kitty Hawk, North Carolina.

The French newspaper *Petit Journal* shows how the Russian sick and wounded were transported on skis during the Russo–Japanese war.

TWO BROTHERS IN THE US, WILBUR (1867–1912) AND ORVILLE (1871–1948) WRIGHT, became obsessed with the growing science of aviation and were determined to fly. They pumped the profits from their bicycle shop into their experiments and built a biplane. In the town of Kitty Hawk, on the coast of North Carolina, they began to conduct experiments. On the morning of December 17, their work paid off when Orville made what is considered to be the **first successful flight** in an airplane that the pilot had complete control over (as opposed to earlier attempts with gliders). He traveled 197 ft (60 m) in 12 seconds. Later that day Wilbur flew 850 ft (259 m) in 59 seconds.

Farther south, in **Panama**, the US had resurrected the idea of building a canal between the Atlantic and Pacific, the first attempt at which had failed more

Lion in the path
The United States publication Judge *depicts the Panama Canal as the "lion in the path" in this political cartoon.*

than a decade before (see 1889). The US wanted to purchase the assets of the former French holding company and begin construction, but talks with the **Colombian** government (which still controlled the isthmus) broke down. Soon after, in 1903, Panama, with the backing of the US, declared its **independence**. By 1904, Panama and the US had agreed on the terms of the Panama Canal Zone, in which the US would be permitted to exercise its jurisdiction until 1979, and work on the canal began.

In **France**, cyclist Henri Desgrange (1865–1940) organized a race that would become one of the most prestigious in the world: the **Tour de France**. Its roots,

however, were intertwined with the infamous **Dreyfus Affair**. This was a scandal involving Alfred Dreyfus (1859–1935), a French officer who was accused of treason. Evidence came to light that cleared Dreyfus, but it was suppressed. Dreyfus was Jewish, and France became divided over the issue of **anti-Semitism**. During the scandal, the sports newspaper *Le Vélo* supported Dreyfus. Angry advertisers decided to set up a rival periodical, *L'Auto-Vélo*, later called *L'Auto*. Cycling promoter Desgrange was hired as editor. However, *L'Auto's* sales were initially poor, and so a race was organized to promote it. Desgrange devised a month-long cycling contest (though it was later shortened) which followed the route of Paris–Lyon–Marseille–Toulouse–Bordeaux–Nantes–Paris. On July 1, 60 competitors set off. The event's first winner was Maurice Garin.

JAPAN AND RUSSIA HAD BEEN COMPETING to expand their influence in Manchuria and Korea. Russia had built its Trans-Siberian railroad (see 1891), which now had a line running into **Manchuria**, annexed during the Boxer crisis in China (see 1900). During this time, **Japan** had begun to build up its army and navy, and approached Russia in 1903 to suggest they recognize each other's mutual interests in these regions. The talks broke down on February 6, 1904, and three days later Japan attacked Russian warships, sinking two of them and triggering the **Russo–Japanese War.** Japan then sent troops into Manchuria and Korea, forcing the Russians farther north over the course of

Russo–Japanese War
This map shows the course of the conflict in which a victorious Japan drove Russia out of Manchuria, forcing Russia to give up its expansionist policy in East Asia.

the year. A peace deal was brokered by US President Theodore Roosevelt (1858–1919), and on September 5 a treaty was signed that forced Russia to leave Manchuria, cede part of the island of **Sakhalin** to Japan, and recognize Japan's interests in **Korea**, as well as grant fishing rights off the coast of Siberia. Japan's victory against Russia marked its emergence as a major world power.

In Africa, German troops were facing rebellions in their colonies. Revolts broke out in **German South West Africa** (Namibia), where the **Khoikhoi** people had risen up in 1903, followed by the **Herero** in 1904. Many Africans were rounded up and put into concentration camps, where the work conditions were so dire that more than half of the prisoners died. By the time Germany had suppressed the rebellion, in 1908, about 80 percent of the Herero and 50 percent of the Khoikhoi peoples had been killed, either in the course of the conflict or while interned in the camps.

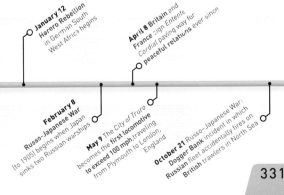

KEY

- Japan
- Qing China
- □ to Russia 1897, to Japan 1905
- area leased to Japan 1895
- → Japanese advances 1904–05
- route of Russian Baltic fleet
- ✕ Japanese victory, with date

12 SECONDS
THE DURATION OF THE WRIGHT BROTHERS' FIRST FLIGHT

June 11 Serbia's King Alexander Obrenović (b. 1876) and Queen Draga (b. 1864) are **assassinated**

September 29 **Prussia** is first to require **drivers' licenses** for automobiles

November 18 Deal signed between US and Colombia to start on **Panama Canal** (canal opens in 1914)

November 4 Panama declares **independence** from Colombia with US backing

December 17 Inventor brothers Orville and Wilbur **Wright** make first flight at Kitty Hawk, North Carolina

January 12 **Herero Rebellion** in German South West Africa begins

April 8 **Britain** and France sign Entente Cordiale paving way for **peaceful relations** ever since

February 8 **Russo–Japanese War** (to 1905) begins when Japan sinks two Russian warships

May 9 The *City of Truro* becomes the **first locomotive to exceed 100 mph**, traveling from Plymouth to London, England

October 21 Russo–Japanese War: **Dogger Bank** incident in which Russian fleet accidentally fires on British trawlers in North Sea

THE STORY OF
THE CAR

FROM THE MODEL T TO HYBRIDS, CARS HAVE BEEN A DRIVING FORCE FOR CHANGE

Ford Model T

After thousands of years of slow transportation using ships, horses, or even traveling on foot, the development of the automobile revolutionized the way the world thought about distance and speed. Instead of spending days on a trip, people and goods could move hundreds of miles in a matter of hours.

Although the late 19th century witnessed many significant technological innovations in the realm of transportation, such as the development of steamships, none would come close to having the widespread and immediate impact of the development and mass production of the car. Although automobile ownership was at first only the preserve of the wealthy, the US inventor Henry Ford was able to increase output and push down prices, so that by the 1920s many eager consumers could buy a car. This had a profound effect on the landscape as highways sprang up, and by the 1950s, suburbs in the US were planned around the idea that residents would be driving.

THE AGE OF THE AUTOMOBILE

Despite the subsequent problems—especially pollution and traffic jams—the love affair with the car has never ceased. Indeed, as people in developing countries become richer, they too want to be car owners. Now the challenge is to find more fuel-efficient and environmentally friendly ways to power cars, and more manufacturers are experimenting with other forms, such as hybrids (see panel, right). However, in spite of these issues, the automobile continues to be an integral part of transportation networks all over the world.

HYBRID CARS

Automobile engineers have long been trying to find ways to run cars on other fuels than gasoline, including solar power and battery power. Hybrid cars combine a fuel engine with a battery engine, giving the driver better fuel consumption and producing less pollution.

Rolling off the assembly line
Workers on the assembly line at the Ford Motor Company assemble a Model T. Ford's innovative factories allowed the company to assemble millions of cars very quickly.

> ❝ ANY CUSTOMER CAN HAVE A CAR PAINTED **ANY COLOR** THAT HE WANTS **SO LONG AS IT'S BLACK.** ❞

Henry Ford, US industrialist, *My Life and Work*, 1922

Trevithick's road locomotive

15th century
Leonardo da Vinci's car
The Renaissance Italian designs the world's first self-propelled wagon.

Reconstructed da Vinci car

1801
The steam-powered car
Richard Trevithick, a British inventor, creates a smaller, lighter version of the steam engine and calls it the "road locomotive."

1867–77
The four-stroke Otto engine
The German inventor Nikolaus August Otto patents his four-stroke internal-combustion engine.

Otto engine

1769–70
The first true automobile
The French engineer Nicolas Cugnot builds a steam-powered vehicle that can reach speeds of up to 2 mph (3 kph).

Cugnot's Faradier

1860
The coal–gas engine
Belgian Jean-Joseph Étienne Lenoir invents a two-stroke internal-combustion engine fired by coal gas.

Lenoir gas engine

Benz three-wheeler

1885
Internal combustion improves
The Germans Karl Benz and Gottlieb Daimler separately develop practical cars with internal-combustion engines.

1913 Ford Model T
Henry Ford's design classic has many of the features found in today's cars. As well as being relatively cheap, it was sufficiently robust and reliable to withstand the rough roads of the US at the time.

brass-framed windscreen with two panels

brass wing mirror

brass struts support windshield

open-bodied model had no doors

brass horn with rubber squeeze bulb

acetylene-powered headlight

kerosene-powered sidelight

solid rubber tire

wooden wheel

starting handle

shock absorber

N 1098

1885–86
The four-wheeled car
Gottlieb Daimler makes improvements to the engine and adds a fourth wheel to the body, producing the first modern car.

1903–30
The Ford Model T
The US car manufacturer Henry Ford begins production of the mass-market Model T. By 1927, some 15 million cars have been produced, thanks to Ford's moving assembly lines.

1930s
Volkswagen's "compact car"
Developed in Germany, the "people's car" marks the rise of the affordable, fuel-efficient car.

Volkswagen Beetle

1889–90
Front-mounted engines
René Panhard and Émile Levassor of France are the first to build entire cars for sale and to put the engine at the front.

Panhard et Levassor Dos-a-Dos

1890s–early 1900s
Early electric cars
Not all cars are developed with gasoline engines. Some 28 percent were using electricity by 1900.

1940s–50s
The rise of the luxury car
Brands such as Rolls Royce and Cadillac become bywords for the most luxurious cars for sale.

Rolls Royce Silver Dawn

1997–present
Hybrid cars
Car makers look for cleaner, cheaper ways to fuel cars.

Toyota Prius

> ❝ THE **ETERNAL MYSTERY** OF THE WORLD IS ITS COMPREHENSIBILITY. ❞

Albert Einstein, in the *Franklin Institute Journal*, March 1936

German-born Albert Einstein became one of the world's most famous scientists after the development of his Special Theory of Relativity.

The ruins of the San Francisco City Hall after the 1906 earthquake.

Life for Romanian peasants was harsh and many wanted land reform.

IN RUSSIA, DISCONTENT WITH THE CZAR, NICHOLAS II, had been growing, and there were calls for a constitutional monarchy. This was compounded by the humiliating defeat in the Russo–Japanese War (see 1904). **Protests** spread around the country. In February, Nicholas promised to set up an **elected assembly**, but this did nothing to stop the unrest. Finally, the military joined in, and June saw a mutiny by the crew of the **battleship *Potemkin***. By October, Nicholas promised a constitution and an elected legislature, but this was insufficient for the protesters, who organized themselves into **soviets** (revolutionary councils). One of the leaders, **Leon Trotsky** (1879–1940), was jailed. Although the protests continued, anti-revolutionary forces finally suppressed what became known as the **Russian Revolution of 1905**. The following year, Nicholas implemented reforms, the **Fundamental Laws**, which included the creation of an elected legislature, or **Duma**.

In **Switzerland**, the German physicist **Albert Einstein** (1879–1955) had received his doctorate and international acclaim for his publications. The most influential was known as the **Special Theory of Relativity**, which explained the relationship between mass and energy in the equation $E=mc^2$. In 1921 he would receive a Nobel Prize for his scientific contributions.

In **India**, the British viceroy Lord Curzon (1859–1925) was facing increased nationalist opposition. He decided to **partition** the province of **Bengal**, joining East Bengal and Assam, with a capital in Dhaka. This move was attacked as an attempt to stifle the **nationalist movement**, which had strong support throughout Bengal.

Film poster
The film Battleship Potemkin (1925), made by the Russian director Sergei Eisenstein, dramatized the 1905 mutiny of the ship's crew.

SAN FRANSISCO EARTHQUAKE

25,000 BUILDINGS **DESTROYED**

450–700 PEOPLE **DIED**

$350 MILLION OF **DAMAGE**

SITUATED ON ONE OF THE WORLD'S MOST ACTIVE FAULT LINES—the San Andreas, which runs for 810 miles (1,300 km)—the city of **San Francisco** is susceptible to **earthquakes**. By 1906, people in the growing city were used to the earth moving—there had been recorded quakes in 1836, 1865, 1868, and 1892—but nothing had been done to make the city of 400,000 people better prepared. On April 18, San Francisco bore the brunt of what was later estimated to be a **7.8 magnitude earthquake**, while people as far afield as Los Angeles and Nevada also felt shaking. The quake lasted less than a minute, but it **wreaked damage** that would take years to repair, as buildings collapsed and many caught fire throughout the city.

In India, the **All India Muslim League** was established—initially with the support of the British government—with the aim of protecting the rights of Muslims. Some 3,000 delegates attended its first meeting on December 30. By 1913 it had joined the growing call for **self-rule in India**.

PEASANT UNREST THAT HAD BEEN SPREADING throughout the countryside in **Romania** culminated in a **revolt** in 1907. This was fueled by land issues, as the peasants were forced into **exploitative contracts**, meaning many farmers had to live in poverty. As the rioting spread through villages, up to **10,000 people were killed** before it was suppressed by the military.

In Southeast Asia, **Cambodia** had clawed back some of its western provinces from Thailand due to **French pressure**. By 1863, France had established a strong presence in Cambodia, eventually restricting the Cambodian king's powers and installing a governor. This paved the way for **colonization** by the French, but angered Cambodian nationalists. The resistance was quelled by 1907.

The French in Thailand
A 19th-century French gunboat, armed with a Hotchkiss Cannon, patrols the waters of the Chao Phraya River in Bangkok, Thailand.

January 22 Bloody Sunday massacre of 500 Russian demonstrators at the Winter Palace, St Petersburg

April 4 Earthquake in Kangara, India, kills 20,000

May 27 The Japanese fleet destroys the Russian fleet at the **Battle of Tsushima** in the Russo–Japanese War

June 7 Norway gains independence

October 16 Partition of Bengal and nationalist agitation in India

March 31 Start of the **First Moroccan Crisis** in which Germany challenges France's dominance in Morocco

May 15 Las Vegas founded in the US

June 30 Special Theory of Relativity published by German physicist **Albert Einstein** (1879–1955)

April 18 Great San Francisco earthquake almost destroys the city

August 23 US troops appear in Cuba at request of ousted president

December 30 Foundation of All India Muslim League

March Peasant revolt in Romania against feudal laws

July 25 Korea becomes a protectorate of **Japan**

March 15 Nineteen women elected to Finnish parliament

August 31 Creation of **Triple Entente**, an alliance between Britain, France, and Russia

An engraving in the Italian newspaper *La Domenica del Corriere*, from February 1908, depicts the assassination of Charles I, king of Portugal. He was murdered during a period of increased calls for a republican government.

PORTUGAL WAS CONVULSED BY REVOLUTION following the assassination of its king, **Charles I** (1863–1908), in February. Already a highly unpopular monarch, he made matters worse by deciding to appoint his own prime minister —**bypassing parliament** in the process. Events took a violent turn on February 1 when Charles and his eldest son, Lúis Filipe, were shot while they were traveling in a carriage in Lisbon. Charles was succeeded by his son, **Manuel II** (1889–1932), who managed to survive on the throne for just a couple of years before being overthrown (see 1910).

In Africa, the **Congo Free State** (see 1884) was abolished and Belgium's government established the **Belgian Congo**. The Free State had been run by a private company with Belgian **King Leopold II** (1835–1909) ruling over it personally. Africans working in the Free State provided the company with valuable **rubber and ivory**. However, reports of the appalling labor conditions led to an **international**

outcry and calls for reforms. Belgium's answer to these demands was to make the territory an **official colony** and rule it from Brussels, ensuring the continued supply of Congolese products. But the brutal conditions persisted, and the **population dropped** from an estimated 20–30 million in 1884 to around 8.5 million by 1911.

Meanwhile, **Austria–Hungary** also reconfigured its colonial relationships—in its case with **Bosnia–Herzegovina**, which it had already occupied (see 1878). It had become worried about the implications of the **Young Turk Revolution** underway in the neighboring Ottoman Empire (see 1909). Austria–Hungary was concerned that its power in the Balkans might be undermined because, technically, Bosnia–Herzegovina was still under

Ottoman suzerainty and one of the Young Turks' aims was to reclaim the territory. After securing **Russia's** support, Austria–Hungary **annexed Bosnia–Herzegovina**. This move immediately angered nearby **Serbia**, which called for a section of Bosnia–Herzegovina that would give it access to the Adriatic Sea. Russia was soon caught in the middle of what would later be known as the **Bosnian Crisis**. At first it sought to secure some concessions for Serbia, but it later bowed to the demands of Austria–Hungary and its allies. During this period, **Bulgaria's Prince Ferdinand** (see 1887)— whose role as leader was not yet recognized by Russia and many other European countries—took advantage of the crisis to proclaim **Bulgarian independence** from the faltering Ottoman empire.

KEY

- ■ The Kingdom of Hungary
- ■ The Austrian Empire
- ▥ Bosnia–Herzegovina
- — Border of Austria–Hungary

The Austro–Hungarian Empire
In 1908, Austria–Hungary was eager to assert its control over the Balkan states of Bosnia and Herzegovina in order to prevent the Ottoman Empire from taking the territory.

Sultan Mehmed V
The 35th Ottoman sultan, Mehmed V (1844–1918), was effectively a puppet for the Young Turks' Committee of Union and Progress.

FOLLOWING THE SUCCESSFUL REBELLION BY THE YOUNG TURKS the previous year, in 1909 the **Committee of Union and Progress**—the group's political wing—had taken control of the levers of power within the **Ottoman Empire**—something they would maintain for the next couple of years, despite internal disputes. The Young Turks had wanted to force the sultan to **restore the constitution**, and once this was accomplished Abdul Hamid II (r. 1876–1909) ruled as a constitutional monarch, although only briefly—he was deposed on April 27. They then proceeded to make his brother, **Mehmed V** (r. 1909–1918), the new sultan.

Many of the Young Turks had been students and members of the Ottoman intelligentsia and they organized themselves while living in Europe and British-

controlled Egypt. Although they were initially seen as "liberal," many of their policies were considered repressive, especially elsewhere in the empire. Much of the anger lay in the Young Turks' **nationalism**, which meant they wanted to push a **Turkish identity** at the expense of the many large ethnic groups throughout the Ottoman world, such as the Arabs and Slavs. However, they did implement some **progressive reforms**, such as secularizing the legal system and improving education, including allowing women better access to schooling. They also wanted to limit the amount of **foreign influence** throughout the empire in areas such as Bosnia–Herzegovina (see 1908).

MUSTAFA KEMAL ATATURK (1881–1938)

Having been involved with the Young Turk Revolution of 1908, Mustafa Ataturk led the Turkish national movement in the Turkish War of Independence. When the Republic of Turkey was established in 1923 he became its first president.

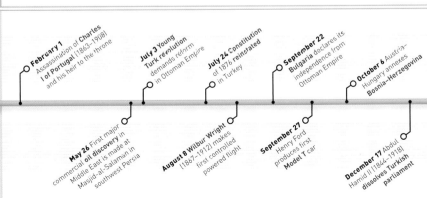

February 1 Assassination of Charles I of Portugal (1863–1908) and his heir to the throne

July 3 Young Turk revolution demands reform in Ottoman Empire

July 24 Constitution of 1876 reinstated in Turkey

September 22 Bulgaria declares its independence from Ottoman Empire

October 6 Austria-Hungary annexes **Bosnia-Herzegovina**

May 26 First major commercial oil discovery in Middle East is made at Masjid-al-Salaman in southwest Persia

August 8 Wilbur Wright (1867–1912) makes first controlled powered flight

September 27 Henry Ford produces first **Model T car**

December 17 Abdul Hamid II (1844–1918) **dissolves Turkish parliament**

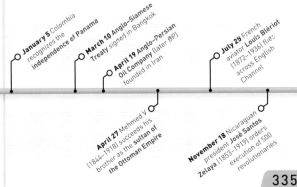

January 5 Colombia recognizes the **independence of Panama**

March 10 Anglo-Siamese Treaty signed in Bangkok

April 19 Anglo-Persian Oil Company (later BP) founded in Iran

July 25 French aviator **Louis Blériot** (1872–1936) flies across English Channel

April 27 Mehmed V (1844–1918) succeeds his brother as the **sultan of the Ottoman Empire**

November 18 Nicaraguan president Jose Santos Zelaya (1853–1919) orders execution of 500 revolutionaries

> ## IT'S BETTER TO **DIE UPON YOUR FEET** THAN TO **LIVE UPON YOUR KNEES!**

Emiliano Zapata, leader during the Mexican Revolution

Emiliano Zapata was one of the leaders involved in the fight to oust Porfirio Díaz from office and put in place a revolutionary government led by Franscisco Madero. Zapata was instrumental in organizing guerrilla troops.

Imperial officials flee from Tientsin during the Chinese Revolution, which precipitated the end of the Qing dynasty, rulers of China since the 1600s.

A CENTURY AFTER ITS FIRST REVOLUTION (see 1810), Mexico was once again caught up in the throes of political change. Liberal reformers had begun to resent **Porfirio Díaz**'s political machine (see 1876) and the **Regeneration movement** was formed. Members of the group were often jailed, and the publication of their newspaper was suppressed. In 1906, they published a manifesto calling for a **one-term presidency** and reforms to land—the return of land confiscated by the Díaz regime to its rightful owners—and education. Díaz eventually allowed the development of an opposition, and other groups emerged. However, Díaz jailed one popular presidential candidate, **Francisco Madero** (1873–1913), on the eve of

the 1910 election, reneging on his promise for fair elections. Madero escaped to Texas and began to **organize an uprising** for November 20, the anniversary of the previous Mexican revolution. It was not a large rebellion, but involved small towns being attacked by pockets of **guerrilla groups**, which the army was able to suppress. However, by the following year, the revolutionary militias—many of them peasant farmers—led by **Francisco "Pancho" Villa** (1877–1932) and **Emiliano Zapata** (1879–1919), stepped up their attacks against the army. Díaz surrendered his office under the **Treaty of Ciudad Juarez**, and by November 1911 Madero was installed as president. However, he now came

in for attacks from the right and the left as groups splintered from the revolutionary movement. This **political fighting spilled over into violence**, with warfare continuing for decades.

In East Asia, **China invaded Tibet** once again, trying to assert its claim to rule the territory. This invasion came after British attempts to occupy Lhasa in 1904, which were fueled by fears that Tibet could fall under the influence of Russia. This was followed by a 1907 **treaty between China and Britain** that recognized China's sovereignty over Tibet. Tibet did not consider it valid, and the Tibetans were able to use the **revolution** that began in China the following year (see 1911) as an opportunity to drive out the Chinese.

For nearby **Korea**, the consequences of the Russo–Japanese war (see 1904) had severe ramifications. It had allowed Japan to use the peninsula for military operations and in the resulting **Treaty of Portsmouth**, in 1905, Korea was made a **Japanese protectorate**, and by 1910 had been officially annexed.

Casa Mila
Designed by the Catalan architect Antoni Gaudi (1852–1956), Barcelona's iconic Casa Mila was constructed between 1905 and 1910.

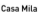

6000
THE NUMBER OF **DIAMONDS** IN GEORGE V'S **CROWN**

EVENTS IN CHINA TOOK A DRAMATIC TURN AS THE QING DYNASTY—which had been in power for more than 260 years—faced a rebellion. Despite its longevity, many Chinese always considered the ruling **Manchus** as foreigners. They were also resentful at the **growing number of Westerners**, who had been permitted to move inland from the port cities. The 20th century had been full of unrest for China (see 1900) and this continued to grow as **revolutionary groups** began to form around the country. In October, a revolutionary plot was uncovered and the members arrested and executed. Soldiers in **Wuchang** who knew of the plot decided to push forward with a revolt; they led a **mutiny** on October 10, which soon spread throughout the country, and the rebels **declared China a republic**. They were met with little resistance because many officials accepted that the

Manchus' days were numbered. In the US, exiled revolutionary leader **Sun Yat-sen** (1866–1925) had heard about the events in China and returned home. He was elected **provisional president** of the country, although prime minister **Yuan Shikai** (1859–1916) had been given full power by the imperial court. The two struck a deal, although Yuan would try to make himself **emperor** in 1915; his efforts ended in failure three months before he died in 1916.

Meanwhile, in **India**, the British were trying to display their colonial might with an enormous **durbar**, or assembly, in Delhi. This was to mark the visit of **King George V and Queen Mary**. During the visit, the king announced that the **colonial capital would be moved from Calcutta to Delhi**. Around the same time, the unpopular policy of **partition in Bengal** was ended (see 1905), and the territory was reunited. Over the following years,

Sun Yat-sen
The cover of the magazine Je sais tout *shows a picture of Sun Yat-sen, president of the Chinese Republic.*

Je sais tout

February 20 Egyptian prime minister **Boutros Ghali** assassinated (b. 1846)

March Albanian uprising against Ottoman rule

May 31 Union of South Africa created

August 28 Montenegro becomes an **independent kingdom** under Nicholas I

November Mexican Revolution begins

May 6 George V (1865–1936) takes the British throne

October 5 Monarchy overthrown in Portugal: a **republic proclaimed**

October 23 Vajiravudh (1881–1925) crowned **Rama VI**, King of Siam

December Plague in northeastern China kills more than **40,000 people**

May 25 Porfirio Díaz resigns as president of Mexico

September 29 Italy declares war on the Ottoman Empire through the **conquest of Libya**

October 10 Wuchang Uprising, leads to collapse of Qing dynasty in China

November Francisco Madero (1873–1913) becomes president of Mexico

An illustration of General Lyautey, the French governor of Morocco.

A photograph captures the moment when suffragist campaigner Emily Davison is trampled by George V's horse at Epsom on Derby Day.

Rubber boom
Technological innovations, especially the tires used on the increasingly popular motorcar, fueled a rise in the use—and price—of rubber.

a new part of Delhi was built, with a monumental **Viceroy's house** and government buildings designed by the leading British architect **Edwin Lutyens** (1869–1944). However, such displays did little to quell the growing nationalist sentiment.

In Europe, **Marie Curie** (1867–1934), a Polish-born French scientist, won her second **Nobel Prize**, this time in chemistry for her work on **radioactivity**. She and her husband, Pierre (1859–1906), had been the recipients of the 1903 Nobel Prize for Physics.

In 1911, the world **price of rubber** was beginning to soar, fueled by its use in **new technologies**, especially in the production of automobile tires. Rubber came from the sap of trees that grew in the forests of Brazil, Southeast Asia, and West Africa.

THE OTTOMAN EMPIRE FACED FURTHER UPHEAVAL with the **First Balkan War**. The conflict ended with the Turks losing Albania, which became independent, and Macedonia, which was to be shared among the Balkan allies (see 1913).

In March 1912, **Morocco** was established as a French **protectorate** under the **Treaty of Fez**. The year before the new sultan **Abd al-Hafiz** (c.1875–1937), besieged in his palace, had asked the French to help him suppress internal dissent.

WOMEN'S RIGHT TO VOTE

By the early 20th century, the fight for women to be given the vote had gained momentum all over the world. Australia had followed New Zealand (see 1893) by giving women suffrage in 1902. In northern Europe, Finland had given women the right to vote in 1906, while Norway followed in 1913. While, women suffragists in Britain would have to wait until after World War I, countries such as Russia and the US (see above—states with full suffrage are gold) also began to peel back voting restrictions around this time.

THE TREATY OF LONDON OF 1913 OFFICIALLY SIGNALED THE END of the First Balkan War. However, the Balkan League—Serbia, Bulgaria, Montenegro, and Greece—that had challenged the Ottoman Empire soon began to disintegrate. Bulgaria attacked Serbia in June because of a disagreement over the **division of Macedonia**, although the fighting ended a couple of months later with a **Serbian– Greek alliance**. Greece and Serbia would receive most of Macedonia with Bulgaria only receiving a small part. This internal division opened a vacuum for the Turks. The **Young Turk government** in charge of the Ottoman Empire was not satisfied with the outcome of the **Treaty of London** and it mounted another invasion, this time recapturing Adrianople (modern Edirne) on July 20. However, by this point it had lost almost all of its Balkan territory.

In Britain, the **suffragist battle** to give women the right to vote (see panel, left) took a violent turn as campaigner **Emily Davison** (1872–1913) threw herself in front of King George V's horse during the Epsom Derby in June. The horse, Anmer, struck Davison's chest and she was knocked down and remained unconscious for four days, until she died of her injuries on June 8. It remains unclear if her intention was to commit suicide. A public funeral was held for her in London on 14 June.

By 1913, **Henry Ford** (1863– 1947), the head of the US Ford Motor Company, which he set up in 1903, had sold nearly **250,000 Model T cars**. Although other companies were making cars, they were far too expensive for average consumers. Ford wanted to make them more affordable so he began production of the basic **Model T**. He also developed new and more efficient production techniques through the use of

Coup d'etat
An illustration from Le Petit Journal *depicts the murder of Nazim Pasha, Ottoman minister of war, during the First Balkan War.*

moving **assembly lines** that he had installed in his Michigan factory. This improvement meant that a completed chassis (car body) could be made in just over an hour and a half, while his competitors took hours longer.

> **❝ HISTORY IS MORE OR LESS BUNK.** IT'S TRADITION. ❞

Henry Ford, US industrialist,
in an interview in the *Chicago Tribune*, May 25, 1916

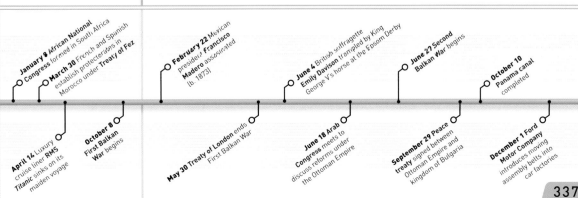

December 14 Roald Amundsen's expedition reaches the South Pole

December 29 Sun Yat-sen becomes first president of the Chinese Republic

December Delhi Durbar marks the coronation of King George V

December Outer Mongolia declares its independence

January 8 African National Congress formed in South Africa

March 30 French and Spanish establish protectorates in Morocco under Treaty of Fez

April 14 Luxury cruise liner RMS Titanic sinks on its maiden voyage

October 8 First Balkan War begins

February 22 Mexican president Francisco Madero assassinated (b. 1873)

May 30 Treaty of London ends First Balkan War

June 4 British suffragette Emily Davison trampled by King George V's horse at the Epsom Derby

June 18 Arab Congress meets to discuss reforms under the Ottoman Empire

June 29 Second Balkan War begins

September 29 Peace treaty signed between Ottoman Empire and kingdom of Bulgaria

October 10 Panama canal completed

December 1 Ford Motor Company introduces moving assembly belts into car factories

337

TECHNOLOGY AND SUPERPOWERS

1914–2017

Technological progress brought the wonders of space flight and
the internet, but radical projects to transform society failed.
Despite two World Wars, the human population quadrupled,
creating new economic and environmental challenges.

Young German men cheer as they march down Pariser Platz in Berlin. Many Germans reacted enthusiastically to being called up for war.

EARLY IN THE YEAR, ATTENTION WAS FOCUSED ON CENTRAL AMERICA. In January, the first ship completed its passage through **the Panama Canal**. This amazing feat of American engineering cost around $300 million to construct and claimed the lives of around 4,000 workers.

In April, the US intervened in **Mexico's civil war** by sending a force of Marines to **occupy the port of Veracruz**, which prevented President Victoriano Huerta from receiving arms shipments from Germany. The US held the port for six months, contributing to Huerta's fall from power in July.

Meanwhile, Europe began its descent into war. **World War I was sparked** by the assassination of Archduke Franz Ferdinand (1863–1914), heir to the Austro–Hungarian throne, and his wife Sophie. They were shot on June 28 during an official visit to Sarajevo in Austrian-ruled Bosnia. The fatal shots were fired by 19-year-old Bosnian Serb, Gavrilo Princip. **The Austrian government blamed Serbia for the assassinations.** Assured of Germany's full support by Kaiser Wilhelm II (1859–1941), on July 23 the Austrians sent an ultimatum to Serbia. Its demands were intended to be so humiliating that Serbia would reject them, giving the Austrians a pretext for military action. Although the

Raising the Stars and Stripes
American soldiers raise the flag over the Mexican port of Veracruz. The occupation cost 17 American lives and lasted for six months.

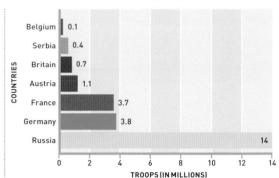

Serbians were prepared to make concessions, Austria–Hungary declared war on July 28. In response, Russia began mobilizing its army in support of Serbia.

Within a week, **all the major European powers were at war.** Brushing aside last-minute peace initiatives by Germany's Kaiser Wilhelm and Russia's Czar Nicholas II (1868–1918), German military chiefs insisted that **Germany declare war on Russia.** Since their military plans demanded a swift victory in the west as a prelude to defeating Russia in the east, Germany also **declared war on France.** Germany did not want to fight the British, but in order to invade France they needed to send an army through Belgium, whose neutrality was guaranteed by Britain. On August 4, after German troops had crossed the Belgian frontier, **Britain declared war on Germany.** Although many people privately regarded the onset of war with

Army sizes at the outbreak of war
Russia's army was huge, but it was poorly equipped and badly organized. Britain had a relatively small army, and depended on its navy for defense.

dismay, it was greeted by cheering crowds. The traditionally antimilitarist and internationalist **German Social Democrat Party** rallied to the war effort, convinced Germany had to defend itself against Russian conquest. In France, most previously antimilitarist radicals and socialists adhered to the *union sacrée* (sacred union), which called for a political truce with prowar parties and vetoed any strike action. In the UK, **Ulster Protestant paramilitaries**, who had been on the verge of an armed rebellion against the British government's plans for Irish Home Rule, and their Catholic opponents, the **Irish Volunteers**, volunteered en masse for the British Army.

In continental Europe, millions of men were called up and

COUNTRIES / **TROOPS (IN MILLIONS)**

Country	Troops (in millions)
Belgium	0.1
Serbia	0.4
Britain	0.7
Austria	1.1
France	3.7
Germany	3.8
Russia	14

January 1 First daily passenger air service in the US

January 7 First ship completes transit of the Panama Canal

March 20 Curragh Mutiny in Ireland; British officers refuse to act against **Protestant paramilitaries**

April 21 US forces occupy Mexican port of **Veracruz**

May 10 Antimilitarist radicals and socialists triumph in **French elections**

May 25 British parliament passes the Irish **Home Rule bill**

June 13 Pancho Villa defeats President Huerta's troops at Zacatecas during Mexican civil war

15 July Mexican president Victoriano **Huerta** forced to resign

August 1 Germany declares war on Russia

August 4 German troops enter Belgium; **Britain declares war** on Germany

March 16 Wife of French government minister Joseph Caillaux **shoots newspaper editor** Gaton Calmette dead

April 20 Sopwith Tabloid biplane wins **Schneider Trophy race**, flying at 92 mph (148 kph)

April 28 More than 180 miners killed in **explosion in coal mine** in Eccles, West Virginia

May 29 Canadian steamship *Empress of Ireland* sinks in St. Lawrence River, **killing 1,073 people**

June 28 Austrian **Archduke Franz Ferdinand** and his wife assassinated

July 28 Austria declares **war on Serbia**

July 31 French antiwar socialist leader **Jean Jaurès assassinated**

August 3 Germany declares war on France

August 14–24 French army suffers major losses in **Battle of the Frontiers**

August 15 Panama Canal officially inaugurated

> **THE PLUNGE** OF CIVILIZATION **INTO** THIS **ABYSS OF BLOOD** AND **DARKNESS... IS** TOO **TRAGIC FOR** ANY **WORDS.**
>
> Henry James, American author, August 4, 1914

dispatched by train to the frontiers, while a much smaller force of British regular soldiers was sent to France as the **British Expeditionary Force (BEF)**. Lord Kitchener (1850–1916), the British secretary for war, launched a drive to recruit volunteers. The response was overwhelming, with three-quarters of a million British men enlisted by the end of September. Most people expected a short war with high casualties, and at first this expectation seemed justified.

German troops surged into Belgium, adopting an official policy of "Schrecklichkeit" (frightfulness). They committed atrocities against the Belgian population—in the worst incident 674 civilians were massacred at Dinant—and laid waste the historic city of Louvain, burning its famous university library.

The **BEF experienced its first action at Mons**. Unable to resist the German onslaught, the British and French were driven back **toward Paris**. Meanwhile, the French launched their own offensive along the eastern

KEY
→ German advance (Aug 2–Sept 5)
The Allies (and allied states)
Germany
Neutral states

GERMAN INVASION OF FRANCE

The German war plan, devised in 1906 by then chief of staff Count Alfred von Schlieffen, assumed that, if attacked on two fronts, France would concentrate its forces along its eastern border. The bulk of the German army was to advance through Belgium and Luxembourg, encircling the French armies. The aim was to defeat the French in six weeks, before the Russians could enter the fray.

French–German border, but they suffered heavy losses for no gain. By the beginning of September the situation was desperate for the British and French armies. The Germans

were also forced to change their operation, abandoning their plan to advance to the west of Paris, and instead marching to the east of the city. French army commander General Joseph Joffre (1852–1931) launched a **counteroffensive at the Marne**, while troops from Paris—some of whom were carried to the front in buses and taxis—attacked the German flank. The German army was forced to retreat, their

Refugees flee Belgium
Roads in Belgium were lined with refugees like these, carrying whatever possessions they could, and fleeing from the advancing German army.

250,000

THE **TOTAL NUMBER** OF **BRITISH, FRENCH,** AND **GERMAN CASUALTIES** AT THE **FIRST BATTLE OF YPRES**

hopes of a swift victory in ruins.

On the Eastern Front the Russians mobilized more quickly than Germany had anticipated, but as they advanced into East Prussia the Russian First and Second Armies were crushed at the **Battles of Tannenberg and the Masurian Lakes**. The victorious German General Paul von Hindenburg (1837–1934) and his chief of staff General Erich Ludendorff (1883–1918) became national heroes.

On the Western Front, from September through to November, a series of battles were fought northward into Flanders (see pp.467–47). They culminated in the encounters known collectively as the **First Battle of Ypres**. With neither side able to inflict a decisive blow, the armies dug trenches along a line that was to remain broadly unchanged for three years.

Meanwhile, **the war was widening into a global conflict**. Ottoman Turkey joined in on the side of Germany, declaring a jihad (Muslim holy war) against the

Recruitment poster
British War Secretary Lord Kitchener's face adorned recruitment posters that called for volunteers to join up and fight.

British Empire. British troops from India landed in Turkish-ruled Iraq and seized Basra, while Japan joined the Allies and swiftly seized German possessions in China and the Pacific. In Africa, British troops invaded German East Africa and South African forces attacked German Southwest Africa—they also put down a revolt by the Boers, who had sided with the Germans.

At **Christmas, occasional fraternization** between opposing troops along the Western Front appalled generals, who feared their men would lose the will to fight, but the war continued. By the end of the year around half a million French and German troops were dead, and a third of the British men who had arrived in France in August had been killed.

1915

A submarine embarks on a mission in the Atlantic. German U-boats terrorized the seas, attacking Allied naval and merchant shipping at will.

A German airship taking off from its base for a bombing raid on London.

AT THE START OF 1915, THE GREAT POWERS OF EUROPE remained locked in a war for which they had been unprepared. The fighting had exhausted munition supplies, so to continue the war the

Chemical warfare
Before the advent of the gas mask, troops, such as these French soldiers, protected themselves from a gas attack in any way they could.

combatants had to **vastly expand their armaments industries.** Governments became aware that the war would be won, or lost, as much in the factories as on the front line. Britain set up a new Ministry of Munitions, and in Russia the czarist government set up a special War Industries Committee. The French, meanwhile, had to recall conscripts from the trenches to work in factories, their production problems accentuated by the German occupation of industrial areas of northeast France.

On the **Western Front**, the **stalemate continued** along a double line of trenches that stretched from the Channel to the Swiss border. Generals assumed that sufficient numbers of men and shells hurled against these defenses would achieve a breakthrough, but they were wrong.

The British attempted their first offensive of the trench war at **Neuve Chapelle** in March, with Indian troops leading the assault and the Canadian Expeditionary Force fighting for the first time. They gained a mere 1.2 miles (2km) of ground for 11,000 casualties. The Germans had a similar experience attacking at **Ypres** in April, and

the French suffered in repeated offensives throughout the year. Mass offensives led only to mass casualties—**over 300,000 British and French losses** in the autumn Champagne-Loos offensive. On the Eastern Front, the fighting was far more mobile, and the **Russians were forced to retreat** from Poland and Lithuania.

In an attempt to break the deadlock on the Western Front, the Germans **used poison gas for the first time** at Ypres in April, releasing lethal chlorine to drift across to the Allied trenches. The first victims were French colonial troops on April 22, followed two days later by soldiers of the First Canadian Division. But German troops failed to take advantage of the initial impact of the gas; Allied soldiers quickly discovered means of protection, and the Allies also adopted gas as a weapon against the Germans.

WOMEN AT WAR

A shortage of manpower meant that women were recruited into a range of jobs traditionally reserved for men. By 1918, around a third of the 1.7 million workers in French munitions factories were women, and they constituted over half of the total German industrial workforce. Women also replaced men as agricultural laborers, for example in the British Women's Land Army.

BRITISH NAIL CLUB

BRITISH SPIKED CLUB

GERMAN METAL ROD

Savage attacks
Soldiers raiding enemy trenches often carried primitive weapons for close-quarters combat. As well as clubs like these, they used trench knives, knuckle dusters, and even spades in savage melees.

On April 26, **Italy signed the Treaty of London**, committing it to enter the war on the side of Britain and France. Before the war, Italy had been an ally of Germany and Austria–Hungary, so this was a diplomatic coup for the Western Allies. Italy duly declared war on Austria on May 23, and the fighting on the **Italo–Austrian Front** quickly descended into the same static stalemate as on the Western Front.

While stalemate persisted on the ground, **war in the air developed on a substantial scale.** Slow-moving aircraft flew over enemy trenches taking reconnaissance photographs and engaged in small-scale bombing missions, while nimbler fighter aircraft intercepted them.

Away from the battlefield, Germany's Zeppelin and Schütte-Lanze airships embarked on the **world's first long-range bombing campaign**, with Britain as their main target. German Navy airship commander Captain Peter Strasser believed that Britain could be "overcome by means of

airships...through increasingly extensive destruction of cities, factory complexes, dockyards...." This was, in reality, far beyond the airships' capacity, but from May 31 onward **night raids** on London and other major cities still managed to cause many civilian casualties and forced Britain to divert resources from the Western Front to **home defense**.

At sea, Germany responded to an ongoing blockade of its ports by the British Royal Navy by attempting to impose its own blockade on Britain through the use of submarines. From February **German U-boats** were authorized to attack merchant shipping in British home waters without warning. On May 7, the Cunard liner *Lusitania*, bound from New York to Liverpool with almost 2,000 passengers and crew on board, was torpedoed off southern Ireland by the submarine *U-20*. More than 1,200 people were drowned, including 128 Americans citizens. The attack provoked anti-German riots in British cities and a hostile response in the US. After the

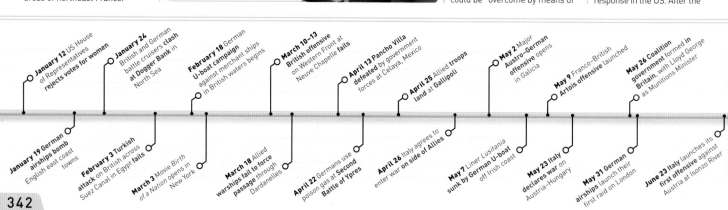

January 12 US House of Representatives rejects votes for women

January 24 British and German battle cruisers **clash at Dogger Bank** in North Sea

February 18 German U-boat campaign against merchant ships in British waters begins

March 10-13 British offensive on Western Front at Neuve Chapelle **fails**

April 13 Pancho Villa **defeated** by government forces at Celaya, Mexico

April 25 Allied troops land at Gallipoli

May 2 Major Austro–German offensive opens in Galicia

May 9 Franco–British Artois offensive launched

May 26 Coalition government formed in Britain, with Lloyd George as Munitions Minister

January 19 German airships bomb English east coast towns

February 3 Turkish attack on British across Suez Canal in Egypt **fails**

March 3 Movie Birth of a Nation opens in New York

March 18 Allied warships fail to force passage through Dardanelles

April 22 Germans use poison gas at Second **Battle of Ypres**

April 26 Italy agrees to enter war **on side of Allies**

May 7 Liner Lusitania **sunk by German U-boat** off Irish coast

May 23 Italy **declares war** on Austria–Hungary

May 31 German airships launch their first raid on London

June 23 Italy launches its first offensive against Austria at Isonzo River

British troops on the Western Front are silhouetted against the sky, wearing the steel Brodie helmets that were first introduced in October 1915.

sinking of another passenger liner, *Arabic*, off Iceland on August 19, the **Germans felt obliged to curtail U-boat attacks in the Atlantic to avoid provoking the US** into entering the war.

TAKE UP THE SWORD OF JUSTICE

Fighting a just war
This British recruitment poster uses the sinking of the Lusitania as propaganda to prove the justice of the Allied cause.

> " ... ACROSS THE RIDGES OF THE **GALLIPOLI PENINSULA** LIE SOME OF THE **SHORTEST PATHS** TO A **TRIUMPHANT PEACE.** "

Winston Churchill, First Lord of the Admiralty, urging the case for a renewed offensive at Gallipoli, June 5, 1915

Seeking an alternative to the costly stalemate on the Western Front, Britain and France devised a plan to **crush Germany's ally Turkey**. British and French warships were to sail through the Dardanelles Straits into the Sea of Marmara, bringing the Turkish capital, Constantinople, under their guns. When the naval attack was made on March 18, however, three battleships were sunk and consequently it was decided that the Dardanelles Straits should be seized before the navy could pass through.

Allied forces landed at Gallipoli on April 25, including a large contingent of the Australian and New Zealand Army Corps (**ANZAC**). Faced with tough Turkish resistance on difficult terrain, they failed to break out of their landing zones. Renewed landings at **Suvla Bay** in August achieved no greater success. Trench warfare, similar to that in France but with conditions exacerbated by heat

and disease, quickly developed. By the time the operation was abandoned in January 1916, the Allied forces had suffered almost a quarter of a million casualties.

Success at Gallipoli was a boost to Turkish morale, which was much needed after the Turkish Third Army had been virtually destroyed fighting the Russians in the Caucasus earlier in the year. Claiming that the Armenian population of eastern Turkey was collaborating with the Russians, the Turks embarked on a **mass deportation of Armenians** from the war zone. The deportation, which was accompanied by widespread massacres, has since been interpreted as an **act of genocide**. Between 800,000 and 1.5 million Armenians are thought to have died as a result of Turkish action.

The second half of 1915 was also marked by the terrible **sufferings of Serbian troops and civilians**. Serbia stoutly resisted Austrian offensives throughout the first year of the war, but in October 1915 its army collapsed in the face of a combined attack by the Germans, Austrians, and Bulgarians. Britain and France landed troops at **Salonika in Greece**, intending to aid the Serbs, but they were too late. Serbia was overrun, and as many as 200,000 Serbians died in a winter retreat through Kosovo into Albania.

While the war was being fought in Europe, **Hollywood** was establishing itself as the center of movie production. Director D.W. Griffith's civil war epic *Birth*

of a Nation was a runaway box office success. With the racist Ku Klux Klan as its heroes, Griffith's masterpiece provoked protests from African Americans and triggered race riots, but with a running time of three hours

and ten minutes its ambition surpassed that of any previous film. Less controversially, British actor **Charlie Chaplin** blended slapstick comedy with pathos to achieve stardom in *The Tramp*.

The ANZACS at Gallipoli
An Australian soldier carries a wounded colleague at Gallipoli. More than 26,000 Australians were killed or wounded in the campaign.

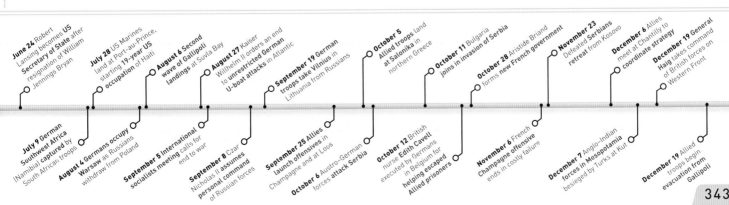

June 24 Robert Lansing becomes US Secretary of State after resignation of William Jennings Bryan

July 9 German Southwest Africa (Namibia) captured by South African troops

July 28 US Marines land at Port-au-Prince, starting 19-year US occupation of Haiti

August 4 Germans occupy Warsaw as Russians withdraw from Poland

August 6 Second wave of Gallipoli landings at Suvla Bay

August 27 Kaiser Wilhelm II orders an end to unrestricted German U-boat attacks in Atlantic

September 5 International socialists meeting calls for end to war

September 8 Czar Nicholas II assumes personal command of Russian forces

September 19 German troops take Vilnius in Lithuania from Russians

September 25 Allies launch offensives in Champagne and at Loos

October 5 Allied troops land at Salonika in northern Greece

October 6 Austro-German forces attack Serbia

October 11 Bulgaria joins in invasion of Serbia

October 12 British nurse Edith Cavell executed by Germans in Belgium for helping escaped Allied prisoners

October 28 Aristide Briand forms new French government

November 6 French Champagne offensive ends in costly failure

November 23 Defeated Serbians retreat from Kosovo

December 6 Allies meet at Chantilly to coordinate strategy

December 7 Anglo-Indian forces in Mesopotamia besieged by Turks at Kut

December 19 General Haig takes command of British forces on Western Front

December 19 Allied troops begin evacuation from Gallipoli

THE GREAT
WAR

THE CONFLICT THAT CHANGED THE NATURE OF WAR FOREVER

World War I (Aug 1914–Nov 1918) was initially known as the Great War. Although it was a global conflict, the focus was Europe, where the Central Powers— Germany, Austria-Hungary, and Turkey—fought an alliance led by France, Britain, and Russia. The US entered the war on the Anglo-French side in 1917.

From the outset, the decisive arena of conflict was Germany's Western Front. The Germans invaded neutral Belgium and Luxembourg, overcoming Belgian resistance at Liege and Antwerp. French and British forces were driven into retreat southward after clashes at Mons and Charleroi. At the Marne, however, French commander General Joseph Joffre rallied his forces for a counter-offensive and the Germans were pushed back.

After a desperate struggle at Ypres in the fall of 1914, the rival armies dug into trenches that stretched from the North Sea to Switzerland. Massive resources were committed to offensives— by the Germans at Verdun and by the Western Allies at the Somme—without breaking the stalemate. Up to 1918, only a voluntary withdrawal by the Germans to the fortified Hindenburg Line significantly changed the position of the armies.

From March 1918 a series of large-scale German offensives broke through Allied defenses and advanced the front line toward Paris. But, aided by the arrival of US troops, the Allies halted the Germans at the Marne. A successful British offensive at Amiens in August initiated the "Hundred Days," a series of advances that pushed the fighting back close to the German border.

BRITAIN

London

The Western Front
Millions of troops were compressed into a restricted area of northeastern France and western Belgium. It was here that most of the largest and bloodiest battles of the war were fought.

English Channel

KEY
- - - Front line 1914–1916
━━━ Hindenburg Line
- - - Front line Mar 1918
━━━ Furthest extent of German advance 1918
- - - Armistice Nov 1918
✕ Major battle

A WAR ON ALL FRONTS

On the Eastern Front, Germany and Austria-Hungary faced the forces of the Russian Empire. From the battle of Tannenberg in August 1914, the German Army established an ascendancy over the Russians, but the Austro-Hungarians enjoyed no such superiority, suffering defeat in the Russian Brusilov offensive in 1916. Revolution in Russia in 1917 led to the country's exit from the war, and a humiliating peace treaty with Germany signed at Brest-Litovsk in March 1918.

The entry of the Turkish Ottoman Empire into the war as an ally of Germany in the fall of 1914 spread the conflict to the Middle East. An Anglo-French bid to attack the Turkish capital, Constantinople, failed dismally at Gallipoli.

Bulgaria also joined the Central Powers, helping to crush Serbia in 1915 and Romania the following year. Allied troops based at Salonica in northern Greece from 1915 remained largely passive until the final months of the war, when their advance northward in September 1918 helped deliver a decisive blow to the collapsing Central Powers.

THE EASTERN FRONT
Fought mostly in East Prussia, Poland, and Galicia, the war between Russia and the Central Powers brought Russia to political and military collapse. Peace terms enabled Germany to occupy Russian territory.

KEY
━━━ Front line 1914–15 (limit of Russian advance)
━━━ Limit of Austro-German advance 1915–16
━━▶ Brusilov offensive 1916
━━▶ Armistice line Dec 1917
━━━ German penetration into Russia by 1918
✕ Major battle

THE BALKANS Serbia resisted attacks by Austria-Hungary, but was overrun once Germany and Bulgaria joined in. The Allies landed troops at Salonica and Gallipoli, and many retreating Serbs joined the Allies at Salonica.

KEY
━━━ Salonican front Sep 1918
━━▶ Austrian, German, and Bulgarian advance 1915
━━▶ Retreating Serbs 1915
━━▷ Allied offensive Sep 1918
━━▶ Romanian offensive Aug–Sep 1916

North Sea

NETHERLANDS

Strait of Dover

Calais

Ostend

GERMANY

Passchendaele
Jul 31–Nov 6, 1917

Antwerp
Sept 28–Oct 10, 1914

Ypres
Oct 19–Nov 22
1914

Lys
Apr 9–29, 1918

Messines
Jun 7–14, 1917

Loos
Jun 7–14, 1915

● Brussels

BELGIUM

Arras
Apr 9–May 16, 1917

Mons
Aug 23, 1914

● Namur

Liège
Aug 4–16, 1914

Somme
Jul 1–Nov 18, 1916

Charleroi
Aug 21, 1914

Cambrai
Nov 20–Dec 7, 1917

Albert

Amiens
Aug 8–11, 1918

LUXEMBOURG

● Sedan

Chemin des Dames
Apr 16–May 9, 1917

Rheims

Verdun
Feb 21–Dec 18, 1916

Chateau-Thierry
Jul 18, 1918

First Marne
Sep 5–12, 1914
Second Marne
Jul 15–Aug 6, 1918

Argonne
Sep 26–
Nov 11, 1918

St Mihiel
Sep 12–19, 1918

Paris ●

FRANCE

Nancy

SWITZERLAND

War in the skies

Military aviation expanded massively through the war. In August 1914, around 500 aircraft were deployed by all combatants combined. By the end of the war some 12,000 military aircraft were in action at the front.

FRONTLINE COMBAT AIRCRAFT

5,000
4,000
3,000
2,000
1,000

France Britain Germany Italy US

COUNTRIES

KEY
■ 1914
■ 1918

War casualties

The total military death toll in World War I was around 9.7 million. Germany suffered the heaviest loss at over 2 million, followed by Russia (1.8 million), and France (1.4 million).

6%
Other combat-related deaths

4%
Poison gas

10%
Rifle fire

60%
Artillery

20%
Machine gun fire

SWITZERLAND

AUSTRIA-HUNGARY

Caporetto
Oct 24 –Nov 19 1917

● Bolzano

Trento

Vittorio Veneto
Oct 24 –Nov 3, 1918

11 battles
of the Isonzo
Jun 1915–Sep 1917

River Piave
Jun 15–23, 1918

Piave River

Isonzo

● Verona

Venice

Trieste

ITALY

Adriatic
Sea

THE ITALIAN FRONT An ally of Germany and Austria-Hungary before the war, Italy remained neutral in 1914, and the following year entered the conflict on the side of Britain and France. A series of ineffective Italian offensives on the mountainous border with Austria at the Isonzo River were followed by headlong retreat after a crushing defeat at the battle of Caporetto. With British and French reinforcements, the Italians held firm at the River Piave in summer 1918.

KEY
↝ Italian advance
↝ Austro-German advance
— Allied offensive
— Front line Sep 1917
— Front line Dec 1917–Oct 1918
✕ Major battle

RUSSIAN EMPIRE

Black Sea

antinople

OTTOMAN EMPIRE

↝ Central Powers advance Sep 1916 –Jan 1917
✕ Major battle

The cost of war

The huge financial cost of the war became a major issue in the postwar period, when Britain and France sought reparations payments from Germany to pay debts owed by them to the US.

COST IN US DOLLARS (BILLIONS)

40
30
20
10
0

Austria-Hungary Britain France Germany Italy Russia US

MAJOR COUNTRIES INVOLVED IN THE WAR

This Irish Republican barricade was set up across Townsend Street in Dublin during the Easter Rising to delay the advance of British troops fighting to retake the city.

A YEAR OF BATTLES OF UNPRECEDENTED SCALE opened with a German offensive against the French city of **Verdun** in February (see pp.344–45). German commander-in-chief Erich von Falkenhayn (1861–1922) aimed to "bleed the French army white" by drawing it into costly combat. The French reacted as he had hoped by sending reinforcements, decimated by the German heavy guns. German losses also mounted up, as French resistance stiffened under the inspirational leadership of General Philippe Pétain (1856–1951). Repeated **German offensives** continued until mid-July, after which **French counteroffensives** succeeded into December. Little territory changed hands and both sides suffered around 400,000 casualties.

Meanwhile, the US was fighting a war on a quite different scale.

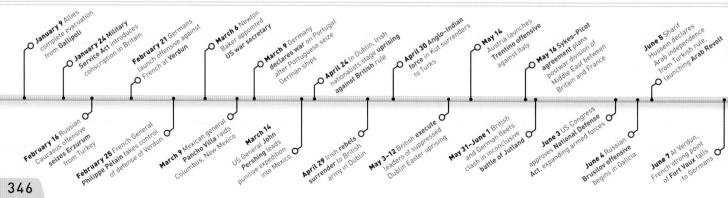

In March, Mexican general **Pancho Villa** (1878–1923), the flamboyant leader of one of the revolutionary armies engaged in Mexico's ongoing civil war, made a **cross-border raid into the US**. His attack on Columbus, New Mexico, was rebuffed by the US Cavalry. The provocation was too great for the US to ignore, and President Woodrow Wilson (1856–1924) ordered General John Pershing (1860–1948) to lead an expedition into Mexico. Around 5,000 US troops fought engagements with both Villa supporters and Mexican government forces before withdrawing in January 1917.

Britain suffered a **military disaster** in the spring in Mesopotamia (Iraq), then part of the Turkish Ottoman Empire. The area had been occupied by British forces from India. From December 1915, Anglo–Indian troops had been **under siege by Turkish forces at Kut-al-Amara**, between Basra and Baghdad. Relief forces failed to fight their way through to Kut, so, facing starvation, they were forced to surrender. Taken prisoner, the British and Indian soldiers endured terrible hardship, less than half surviving captivity.

Bandit leader
Originally a bandit chief, Pancho Villa became a key figure in the Mexican Revolution and Mexico's clash with the US in 1916.

Prussian wappen, or helmet plate

German helmet
The German spiked Pickelhaube helmet was replaced in the course of 1916 by the metal Stahlhelm, which provided better protection.

This disaster was offset by the **Arab revolt against Turkish rule**. Encouraged by Britain, Hussein bin Ali, Sharif of Mecca (1854–1931), launched an uprising in June. Arab forces defeated the Turkish garrisons of Mecca, Medina, and other towns in the Hejaz, and Hussein proclaimed himself Sultan of the Arabs. The British sent **T.E. Lawrence** (1888–1935), a junior officer in Cairo, to act as adviser to Hussein's son Feisal, the most active leader of the revolt. Between them, Lawrence and Feisal organized an effective military force. They used guerrilla tactics to push for the liberation of Arabs throughout the Turkish-ruled Middle East.

In April, **Britain faced a revolt against its rule in Ireland**. The Irish Republican Brotherhood sought German support for a nationalist uprising, but Germany's attempt to supply rifles to the rebels was intercepted by the British. **Republicans** still went ahead with the **uprising on Easter Monday**, occupying key buildings in Dublin, and proclaiming a Provisional Government of the Irish Republic. The British sent troops to Dublin, and after five days of fighting the rebels surrendered. Fifteen republican leaders were executed after a secret trial by a British military court. Although few Irish had supported the rebellion, the executions stimulated a wave of pro-Republican sentiment.

At the end of May, the German High Seas Fleet and the Royal Navy's Grand Fleet met in the **Battle of Jutland** in the North Sea. The British spotted a sortie by the German fleet and sent a far superior naval force to attack it. German Admiral Reinhard Scheer (1863–1928) was caught by surprise, but British Admiral John Jellicoe (1859–1935) failed to profit from the advantage. The German warships were able to make a fighting withdrawal to port, while inflicting heavier losses than they suffered. Despite a disappointing performance, the Royal Navy had confirmed its superiority—it was the German fleet that had retreated.

In June, General Aleksei Brusilov (1853–1926) mounted

Russia's most successful **offensive** of World War I, almost destroying the Austrian army in Galicia. The Austrians were only rescued by the arrival of German troops to support them. Brusilov's initial success was based on subtle tactics—surprise and the rapid movement of shock troops to exploit breakthroughs. Unfortunately, the British did not learn from their Russian allies. On July 1, General Douglas Haig

GENERAL DOUGLAS HAIG (1861–1928)

Cavalry officer Douglas Haig performed well as a corps commander in the first year of World War I. As British army commander-in-chief, his assaults on German defenses at the Somme in 1916 and Passchendaele in 1917 resulted in huge losses. In 1918, Haig held firm in the face of the formidable German spring offensives, then presided over a string of British victories.

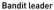

January 9 Allies complete evacuation from Gallipoli

January 24 Military Service Act introduces conscription in Britain

February 21 Germans launch offensive against French at Verdun

March 6 Newton Baker appointed **US war secretary**

March 9 Germany declares war on Portugal after Portuguese seize German ships

April 24 In Dublin, Irish nationalists stage **uprising against British rule**

April 30 Anglo–Indian force in Kut surrenders to Turks

May 14 Austria launches **Trentino offensive** against Italy

May 16 Sykes–Picot agreement plans postwar division of Middle East between Britain and France

June 5 Sharif Hussein declares Arab independence from Turkish rule, launching **Arab Revolt**

February 16 Russian Caucasus offensive **seizes Erzurum** from Turkey

February 25 French General Philippe Pétain takes control of defense of Verdun

March 9 Mexican general **Pancho Villa** raids Columbus, New Mexico

March 14 US General John **Pershing** leads punitive expedition into Mexico

April 29 Irish **rebels surrender** to British army in Dublin

May 3–12 British **execute** leaders of suppressed Dublin Easter uprising

May 31–June 1 British and German fleets clash in inconclusive **battle of Jutland**

June 3 US Congress approves **National Defense Act**, expanding armed forces

June 4 Russian **Brusilov offensive** begins in Galicia

June 7 At Verdun, French strong point of **Fort Vaux** falls to Germans

" SUCCESS WILL COME TO THE SIDE THAT HAS THE LAST MAN STANDING. "

General Philippe Pétain, 1916

French soldiers arriving at Verdun in eastern France. The standard tour of duty at the front was eight days—all a man could be expected to stand.

launched a massive offensive at **the Somme** (see pp.344–45). Rather than destroy enemy defenses, the eight-day artillery bombardment had alerted the Germans to an imminent attack. British troops marched forward in lines, because the generals believed their conscripted troops were incapable of executing more intelligent tactics, and were mown down by German machine guns. Almost 20,000 men were killed, **the heaviest losses ever experienced by the British army** in a single day's fighting. Haig kept the men fighting for five

months, introducing tanks as soon as this new weapon was available, and allowing his subordinates to experiment with varied tactics including night attacks. But there was no breakthrough, and the only result was attrition—a gradual wearing down of the armies.

By the second half of 1916, the strain of two years of warfare had left countries with the option of either ratcheting up their war effort or seeking a path to peace. In August, Germany changed its leadership. General Paul von Hindenburg (1847–1934) and his

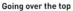

Casualties of the Somme offensive
The Somme was one of the bloodiest battles of the war. Between July 1 and November 18 over a million men were killed or wounded.

Quartermaster-General Erich Ludendorff (1865–1937) were given supreme command of the German army and control of the entire German war effort. In order to wring every drop of productivity out of German industry, they created a state-directed economy that has been dubbed "**war socialism.**" By contrast, their Austrian allies were losing their will to fight. The death of Emperor Franz Josef I (1830–1916) in November marked the beginning of the **end of the Austrian Empire**. His successor, Charles I (1887–1922), was desperate for a way out of the war.

The collective madness of the battlefield provoked an **influential art movement** that gave itself the nonsense name **Dada**. Dadaists such as Hugo Ball and Hans Arp gathered at the Cabaret Voltaire in Zurich, in neutral Switzerland, and advocated a crazy antiart that satirized a world afflicted by mass slaughter. Their anarchic works rejected the social order that legitimized war.

A more rational spokesman for peace was **President Woodrow Wilson, elected for a second term** of office in November. As the man who had kept the US out of the European war, Wilson put himself forward as a peacemaker. He issued a "**peace note**" that called on combatant countries to

Performing artists
Leading Dada artist Hugo Ball performing at Cabaret Voltaire, which he founded in 1916. Dadaists protested against the war.

state their war aims as a prelude to ceasefire negotiations. Germany's civilian government came up with its own "peace offer," but the country's military leaders would not permit any of the concessions that might have made peace a practical possibility.

The **Russian Empire** was desperate for an end to the fighting, and its czarist regime was leaking popular support. In December, court conspirators assassinated Grigori **Rasputin** (1869–1916), an hirsute "holy man" whose hold over the czar's wife had become a public scandal. The assassination was widely welcomed, but it could not halt the czarist **government's slide toward collapse**.

Going over the top
British soldiers prepare to attack during the Battle of the Somme, leaving the relative shelter of the trench for exposed ground.

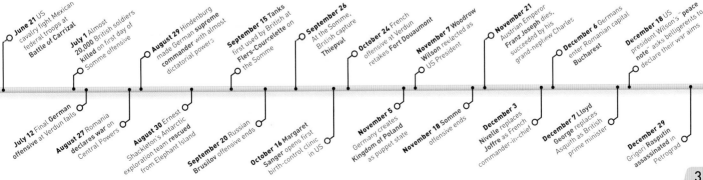

June 21 US cavalry fight Mexican federal troops at **Battle of Carrizal**

July 1 Almost 20,000 British soldiers **killed** on first day of Somme offensive

July 12 Final German **offensive** at Verdun fails

August 27 Romania **declares war** on Central Powers

August 29 Hindenburg made German **supreme commander** with almost dictatorial powers

August 30 Ernest Shackleton's Antarctic exploration team **rescued** from Elephant Island

September 15 Tanks first used by British at **Flers-Courcelette** on the Somme

September 20 Russian **Brusilov offensive ends**

September 26 At the Somme, British capture **Thiepval**

October 16 Margaret Sanger opens first birth-control clinic in US

October 24 French offensive at Verdun retakes **Fort Douaumont**

November 5 Germany creates **Kingdom of Poland** as puppet state

November 7 Woodrow **Wilson** reelected as US President

November 18 Somme offensive ends

November 21 Austrian Emperor **Franz Joseph** dies, succeeded by his grand-nephew Charles

December 3 Nivelle replaces **Joffre** as French commander-in-chief

December 6 Germans enter Romanian capital **Bucharest**

December 7 Lloyd **George** replaces Asquith as British prime minister

December 18 US president Wilson's "**peace note**" asks belligerents to declare their war aims

December 29 Grigori Rasputin assassinated in Petrograd

Armed workers and soldiers taking part in the overthrow of Russia's Provisional Government by the Bolsheviks in Petrograd. They established a communist revolutionary regime.

ON JANUARY 9, GERMAN KAISER WILHELM II (1859–1941) approved the decision of his military commanders to engage in **unlimited submarine warfare**. The Germans knew that this would mean sinking American merchant vessels and would probably bring the neutral US into the war, but they believed they could sink enough ships to force Britain to sue for peace and make US intervention ineffectual. When an American cargo ship, the *Housatonic*, was sunk by a U-boat on February 3 off the Scilly Isles, the US broke off diplomatic relations with Germany.

Anticipating US entry into the war, German foreign minister Arthur Zimmermann decided to offer Mexico an alliance, encouraging it to fight to regain Texas, New Mexico, and Arizona from the US. A **telegram from Zimmermann** detailing

WAKE UP, AMERICA !

CIVILIZATION CALLS EVERY MAN WOMAN AND CHILD !

MAYOR'S COMMITTEE 50 EAST 42" ST.

this plan was intercepted, decoded by British intelligence, and passed to the US government. When it was published in the US press it caused a sensation, stoking anti-German feeling already ignited by the U-boat campaign.

VLADIMIR ILYICH LENIN (1870–1924)

Born into Russian minor gentry, Vladimir Ilyich Ulyanov became a Marxist activist, adopting the name "Lenin." Living in exile in Western Europe, he led the Bolsheviks from 1903. Returning to Russia in 1917, he was determined to radicalize the revolution through a Bolshevik seizure of power. Once in control, he ruthlessly stamped out all opposition, and founded the world's first communist state.

Propaganda poster
New York's Mayor's Committee on National Defense declared April 19 "Wake Up America Day," and publicized it with this poster.

On April 2, US president Woodrow Wilson (1856–1924) asked Congress to vote for a war "to make the world safe for democracy." Four days later, the **US declared war on Germany**, keeping independence of action by not formally allying itself with Britain and France. The slow process of building and equipping a mass conscript army began.

While the US was entering the war, Russia was caught up in revolutionary turmoil. A momentous sequence of events was triggered by food riots, strikes, and a mutiny of soldiers in Petrograd (St. Petersburg). On March 15, **Czar Nicholas II (1868–1918) abdicated** and a Provisional Government was established by politicians from the Duma (Russian parliament). Committees set up by workers and soldiers, known as "soviets," created a competing focus of political power. On April 16, **Vladimir Ilyich Lenin** (see panel, left), leader of the Marxist Bolshevik Party, returned to Petrograd from exile in Switzerland. Lenin sought to radicalize the revolution by proposing an end to the war and "all power to the soviets."

The dominant personality in the Provisional Government, moderate socialist **Alexander Kerensky** (1881–1970), was

committed to continuing the war. The failure of the campaign he launched on July 1, known as the **Kerensky Offensive**, was followed by widespread mutinies in the army at the front and desertion. Attempts to suppress the Bolsheviks failed. The Provisional Government survived a coup attempt, but on November 7 it succumbed to an armed takeover organized by Lenin's associate, **Leon Trotsky** (1879–1940). Lenin set up a **revolutionary government** of People's Commissars and proclaimed a unilateral armistice.

Meanwhile, on the Western front stalemate and slaughter

continued. At the start of the year newly appointed French commander-in-chief Robert Nivelle (1856–1924) promised a crushing onslaught that would win the war in days. When the **Nivelle Offensive** was launched in mid-April, however, it proved no more successful than previous offensives. The disappointment was bitter. There were widespread mutinies and the French army threatened to disintegrate. Hastily appointed to replace Nivelle, General Philippe Pétain (1856–1951) restored order with a mixture of concessions and punishments, and ruled out any further French offensives.

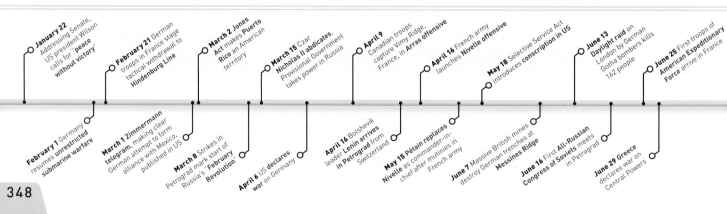

January 22 Addressing Senate, US president Wilson calls for **"peace without victory"**

February 1 Germany resumes unrestricted submarine warfare

February 21 German troops in France stage tactical withdrawal to **Hindenburg Line**

March 1 Zimmermann telegram, making clear German attempt to form alliance with Mexico, published in US

March 2 Jones Act makes **Puerto Rico** an American territory

March 8 Strikes in Petrograd mark start of Russia's **"February Revolution"**

March 15 Czar Nicholas II abdicates, Provisional Government takes power in Russia

April 6 US declares war on Germany

April 9 Canadian troops capture Vimy Ridge, France, in **Arras offensive**

April 16 Bolshevik leader Lenin arrives in Petrograd from Switzerland

April 16 French army launches **Nivelle offensive**

May 15 Pétain replaces Nivelle as commander-in-chief after mutinies in French army

May 18 Selective Service Act introduces **conscription in US**

June 7 Massive British mines destroy German trenches at **Messines Ridge**

June 13 **Daylight raid** on London by German Gotha bombers kills 162 people

June 16 First **All-Russian Congress of Soviets** meets in Petrograd

June 25 First troops of **American Expeditionary Force** arrive in France

June 29 Greece declares war on Central Powers

> ❝ THE **WORKERS'** AND **PEASANTS'** GOVERNMENT… **PROPOSES** TO ALL **WARRING PEOPLES**… **NEGOTIATIONS** LEADING TO A JUST, **DEMOCRATIC PEACE.** ❞
>
> **Lenin,** *November 8, 1917*

These British Mark IV tanks are transported to the Cambrai offensive. They carry bundles of wood to fill the trenches, so that they can drive across them.

The British army remained committed to an offensive strategy. In the second half of the year, General Douglas Haig (1861–1928) began **a new push at Ypres** (see pp.344–345), hoping to break through to the ports where German U-boats were based. Haig's offensive ran into persistent bad weather that reduced the battlefield to a sea of mud. The offensive persisted into November, until British and Canadian troops reached **Passchendaele**, the village that finally gave its name to the battle.

The mud in Flanders rendered tanks, an increasingly important element of British weaponry,

Dawn breaks at Passchendaele
Dead and wounded soldiers lie in the muddy desolation of the battlefield in the Ypres salient, where the battle of Passchendale was fought.

3 THE NUMBER OF **CREW** THAT FLEW AND OPERATED A **GERMAN GOTHA BOMBER**

inoperative. On harder ground at **Cambrai** in November, massed tanks helped British forces advance 4 miles (6 km) in one day—three times the distance achieved at Passchendaele in three months. Any celebrations were premature, however, as a German counterattack soon retook most of the lost ground.

The long stalemate between Italy and Austria–Hungary ended when German troops were transferred to the Italian front in October. At the **Battle of Caporetto**, an Austro-German offensive drove Italian forces into retreat. A line was stabilized in November behind the Piave River, just 19 miles (30 km) from Venice (see p.345).

From June, civilians living in Paris and London were subjected to sporadic **air attacks by German**

Gotha bombers and even larger R-VI "Giants." These fixed-wing aircraft were faster and more difficult to shoot down than the German airships (see 1915), although defense by antiaircraft guns and fighter aircraft soon forced them to attack exclusively by night. Physical damage and casualties were not great, but the psychological impact of these raids was considerable, as citizens were driven to hide underground in cellars and subway stations.

In all combatant countries war weariness and worsening conditions made it hard for governments to maintain solidarity. Food shortages and socialist sentiments, excited by the revolutionary uprising in Russia, led to widespread **strike action in German factories**. The German Reichstag (parliament) passed a resolution calling for peace negotiations in July, but it had no control over the military-dominated German government.

In France, scandals and strikes rocked the political system through the summer and fall, but the appointment of the fiercely pro-war Georges Clemenceau (1841–1929) as prime minister in November stiffened resolve.

The British royal family, meanwhile, found it prudent to change its name from the Germanic Saxe-Coburg and Gotha to Windsor.

The British public was cheered in December by the **capture of Jerusalem from Turkey**. This military success gave practical importance to the previous month's **Balfour Declaration**, which expressed British government support for Zionist aspirations to "a national home for the Jewish people in Palestine." Britain's Arab allies, fighting alongside the British army against the Turks, had not been consulted.

Howitzer Mark I
Used to great effect by the British Army during World War I, this gun could fire two rounds of 290 lb (132 kg) shells every minute.

— hydraulic recoil buffer

— carriage

British merchant shipping losses to U-boats
German unrestricted submarine warfare increased attacks on merchant ships from February to April. The adoption of a convoy system in May reduced sinkings to a sustainable level.

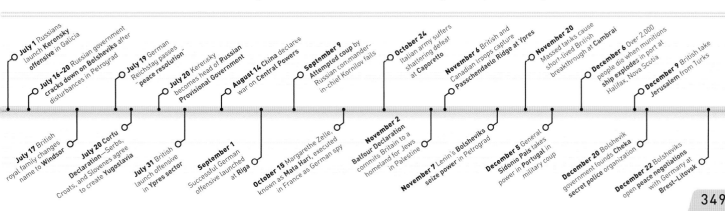

July 1 Russians launch **Kerensky** offensive in Galicia

July 16–20 Russian government cracks down on **Bolsheviks** after disturbances in Petrograd

July 17 British royal family changes name to **Windsor**

July 19 German Reichstag passes "**peace resolution**"

July 20 Kerensky becomes head of **Russian Provisional Government**

July 20 Corfu Declaration—Serbs, Croats, and Slovenes agree to create **Yugoslavia**

July 31 British launch offensive in **Ypres sector**

August 14 China declares war on **Central Powers**

September 1 Successful German offensive launched at **Riga**

September 9 Attempted coup by Russian commander-in-chief Kornilov fails

October 15 Margarethe Zelle, known as **Mata Hari**, executed in France as German spy

October 24 Italian army suffers shattering defeat at **Caporetto**

November 2 Balfour Declaration commits Britain to a homeland for Jews in Palestine

November 6 British and Canadian troops capture **Passchendaele Ridge at Ypres**

November 7 Lenin's Bolsheviks **seize power in Petrograd**

November 20 Massed tanks cause short-lived British breakthrough at **Cambrai**

December 5 General Sidonio Pais takes power in **Portugal** in military coup

December 6 Over 2,000 people die when munitions **ship explodes** in port at Halifax, Nova Scotia

December 9 British take **Jerusalem** from Turks

December 20 Bolshevik government founds **Cheka** secret police organization

December 22 Bolsheviks open peace negotiations with Germany at **Brest-Litovsk**

Revolutionary hero
DATE UNKNOWN
In this painting for a poster from the 1917 Revolution period, Lenin appears in front of the battleship *Aurora*, which was used in the Bolshevik seizure of power.

battleship *Aurora*

Red horsemen
c. 1920
The 1917 revolution was followed by the Russian Civil War, between the Bolsheviks and the "White" armies led by czarist officers. This poster is dedicated "to the peoples of the Caucasus Red Army."

cavalry played an important part in Communist victory

SOVIET PROPAGANDA
ART FOR THE FURTHERANCE OF COMMUNIST POLITICAL IDEOLOGY AND REVOLUTIONARY IDEALS

For the Communists who seized power in Russia in November 1917, art had to serve the socialist revolution and disseminate its ideology. Propaganda mobilized the populace in support of the regime and pilloried its enemies.

During the early phase of Communist rule, many avant-garde artists believed their revolutionary ways of making art would accord with the political revolution. However, under the dictatorship of Joseph Stalin, from the late 1920s Soviet artists were required to depict workers and peasants in a heroic-realist style, their images reflecting the supposed happiness and progress of Communist life.

Modernist poster
1919
Avant-garde artist El Lissitzky produced this Civil War poster. His red wedge represents the Communist Red Army beating the anti-Communist White armies.

The Revolution needs you
1928
The labor force underwent radical reorganization under the Communists. This poster urges Soviet citizens to become members of workers' cooperatives.

Rapid industrialization
1928
The Communist leadership launched an industrialization drive in the late 1920s. Workers are compelled to increase production by this poster.

Collectivization
1930
A tractor driver and peasant woman call on their comrades to join a collective farm during Stalin's brutal drive to abolish private farms.

grand schemes to rebuild Moscow were derailed by World War II

Life under Stalin
1930s
Celebrating the unity and strength of the Soviet people under the banner of Stalin, this poster proclaims: "Onward to the heights of joy and happiness of mankind."

Military strength
1940s
A poster of the World War II era depicts bomber aircraft and a Soviet airman displaying the obligatory optimism of any Communist citizen portrayed in Stalinist art.

piglike capitalist being held up

Commemorating victory
1940s
The slogan on this poster commemorating the Soviet victory in World War II says: "Having won the war, the soldier has brought spring."

Cold War propaganda
1950s
This anti-American poster from the Cold War caricatures the Statue of Liberty, portraying the US as bloatedly capitalist and militaristic.

Peace and progress
1970s
A Salyut space station is superimposed on a dove of peace in this poster from the era of "peaceful coexistence" with the capitalist world.

German prisoners of war in France—in the last three months of the war 363,000 German soldiers were captured by the advancing Allies.

ALTHOUGH THE US ENTERED WORLD WAR I IN APRIL 1917, at the start of 1918 its Expeditionary Force in Europe was still not ready for combat. Despite this, in anticipation of victory, US President Woodrow Wilson announced a **14-point program** for a just and durable peace. His proposals included freedom of the seas and free trade, general disarmament, self-determination for European peoples who did not have their own nation-states, and an international organization to guarantee new borders against aggressors. Germany would have to hand back the territory it had occupied during the war as well as Alsace–Lorraine, which was taken from France in 1871.

The Germans had quite different ideas, however. In March, they used their military dominance over the newly installed Bolshevik government (see 1917) to impose punitive peace terms on Russia through the **Treaty of Brest-Litovsk**, which marked Russia's exit from World War I. With Poland, Ukraine, Belarus, Finland, and the Baltic States nominally independent as client states of Germany, the treaty deprived Russia of about a third of its prewar population. The German military authorities then set about ruthlessly exploiting resources in the eastern regions they now controlled.

The humiliating treaty did not bring peace to Russia, which was already slipping into civil war. Determined to concentrate all the power in Bolshevik hands, **Lenin forcibly dispersed a democratically elected Constituent Assembly** in January—the Bolsheviks had won only 25 percent of votes cast. His regime faced opposition from groups as diverse as rival socialist revolutionaries, czarist generals, Ukrainian anarchists, and Don Cossacks. Lenin survived an assassination attempt in August, but throughout the year ever larger areas of Russia fell out of his followers' control.

Meanwhile, relieved of the need to fight a war on two fronts, Germany attempted to win a decisive victory in the west before American manpower could irreversibly tip the balance. On March 21, the **Spring Offensive or "Kaiserschlacht"** struck the British line on the Somme front. An initial bombardment by 9,000 guns and mortars, with munitions including 2 million gas shells, prepared the way for an infantry attack spearheaded by German Stormtroopers, many armed with flamethrowers. More than 20,000 British troops surrendered on the first day of the offensive, and by March 25 the leading German units had advanced 40 miles (65 km). **The stalemate that had lasted on the Western front since 1914 was at an end.**

In early April, the Germans opened a fresh offensive at Lys in Flanders. In an emotional appeal to his troops, British commander General Douglas Haig (1861–1928) declared: "With our backs to the wall and believing in the justice of our cause, each one of us must fight on to the end." More practically, the French general **Ferdinand Foch (1851–1929) was appointed Supreme Commander** to coordinate the operations of the

Poster of a German aircraft
A German poster advertising an exhibition of items captured in the air war. Most World War I aircraft were made of canvas and wood.

MURDER OF THE RUSSIAN ROYAL FAMILY

After abdicating in 1917, Czar Nicholas II, his wife, four daughters, and only son were sent to Siberia, where they lived in reasonable comfort. But in April 1918 the family was moved to Ekaterinburg in the Urals and placed under close guard by local Bolsheviks. On the night of July 16–17, Bolshevik secret police had the entire family shot in a cellar, along with their doctor and servants. Their bodies were buried and not discovered until 1991.

Allied armies, including US troops. Although the Allies made further retreats and remained on the defensive until July, the Germans failed to achieve the decisive success they needed.

One victim of the fighting in April was Germany's most renowned air ace, Manfred von Richthofen (1892–1918). **The "Red Baron" was shot dead** by ground fire while engaged in a dogfight with Canadian pilot Roy Brown over the Allied lines. His death symbolized the exhaustion of Germany's war effort. Richthofen's fighter wing, known to the British as the "Flying Circus," had an impressive reputation in combat and the Baron himself was credited with 80 "kills." But the German pilots were overwhelmed by the sheer number of allied aircraft— British and French factories built 55,000 aircraft in 1918 alone.

By June, over a **million American soldiers were in France**, under the command of General John Pershing (1860–1948). Their contribution was vital to stabilizing the Allied line in the face of German offensives. The fighting qualities of the US Marines particularly impressed

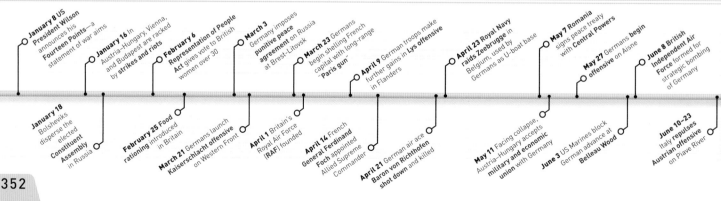
January 8 US President Wilson announces his **Fourteen Points**—a statement of war aims

January 16 In Austria–Hungary, Vienna, and Budapest are racked by **strikes and riots**

February 6 Representation of People Act gives vote to British women over 30

March 3 Germany imposes **punitive peace agreement** on Russia at Brest-Litovsk

March 23 Germans begin shelling French capital with long-range "**Paris gun**"

April 9 German troops make further gains in **Lys offensive** in Flanders

April 23 Royal Navy raids Zeebrugge in Belgium, used by Germans as U-boat base

May 7 Romania signs peace treaty with **Central Powers**

May 27 Germans **begin offensive** on Aisne

June 8 British **Independent Air Force** formed for strategic bombing of Germany

January 18 Bolsheviks disperse the elected **Constituent Assembly** in Russia

February 25 Food rationing introduced in Britain

March 21 Germans launch **Kaiserschlacht offensive** on Western Front

April 1 Britain's Royal Air Force (**RAF**) founded

April 14 French General **Ferdinand Foch** appointed Allied Supreme Commander

April 21 German air ace **Baron von Richthofen** shot down and killed

May 11 Facing collapse, Austria–Hungary accepts **military and economic union** with Germany

June 3 US Marines block German advance at **Belleau Wood**

June 10–23 Italy repulses **Austrian offensive** on Piave River

> ## " I HOPE WE MAY ALL SAY THAT **THUS,** THIS FATEFUL MORNING, **CAME TO AN END ALL WARS.** "

David Lloyd George, British Prime Minister, November 11, 1918

British soldiers, an American sailor, and a Red Cross nurse celebrate the signing of the armistice on November 11, ending four years of mass slaughter.

their German enemies—a German reference to the Marines as "Devil Dogs" stuck as a nickname for the Corps.

The **turning point** was an **attack at Amiens** on August 8, spearheaded by Australian and Canadian infantry, and supported by massed British and French tanks. Described by the German general Erich Ludendorff (1865–1937) as "the black day of the German army," it initiated the "Hundred Days" of relentless Allied offensives, with large-scale use of tanks and aircraft.

In September, Pershing achieved his ambition of commanding an independent US operation—the capture of the **St. Mihiel salient.** This was followed by a combined American and French offensive in the **Argonne forest,** the costliest single battle in American history, with 117,000 US casualties.

On September 29, with their Hindenburg Line defenses breached and their ally Bulgaria on the point of surrender, the **German High Command**

sought an armistice. They approached President Wilson (1856–1924), hoping to make a deal with the US, but Wilson aligned himself with the British and French, who insisted that Germany should surrender. Although German troops were still putting up a stubborn defense, and there were not yet any Allied troops on German soil, the country was disintegrating from within. A mutiny in the German navy at the end of October was followed by strikes and socialist uprisings in major cities, where food shortages had fueled political discontent.

Germany's main allies, Turkey and Austria–Hungary, stopped fighting. On November 9, the Social Democrat Philipp Scheidemann declared Germany a republic, and Kaiser Wilhelm II (1859–1941) fled to the Netherlands. Two days later, a German delegation **signed an armistice** in a railroad car in the Compiègne forest. The guns fell silent at 11 a.m. on November 11.

50 MILLION PEOPLE DIED IN THE FLU PANDEMIC OF 1918–19

Peace celebrations erupted in London, Paris, and other Allied cities, but even in the victor nations the reaction was muted by the memory of the millions who had died. There were no celebrations in the collapsed empires destroyed by the conflict— Germany, Austria, Russia, and Turkey—which faced an uncertain future amid political turmoil.

Meanwhile, a global pandemic of "**Spanish Flu**" was at its peak. One of the worst natural disasters in human history, the spread of the disease was probably aided by large-scale movements of troops and by the weakened immune systems of populations suffering from malnutrition. The disease killed more than 50 million people.

Signing the armistice
The Allied delegation, led by Marshal Foch, photographed outside the railroad carriage at Compiègne where the armistice was signed.

Troop numbers and deaths
Around 65 million men fought in World War I, of whom 8.5 million died. Germany suffered the highest number of casualties.

KEY
● Military strength
● Casualties

Chart axis — TROOPS (IN MILLIONS): 0, 3, 6, 9, 12, 15

Allied powers: Russia, France, British Empire, Italy, US
Central powers: Germany, Austria–Hungary, Turkey, Bulgaria

butt

drum-pan magazine stores ammunition

steel water jacket cools gun barrel

Rifle with bayonet
ITALY

Bolt-action M91 Carcano rifles and carbines armed the Italian infantry in World War I. This carbine has its bayonet fixed, for use in trench fighting in close quarters.

retractable bayonet

Lewis gun
BRITAIN

Originally an American design, the Lewis gun was adopted by the British Army as its standard light machine gun in 1915. It armed aircraft and tanks, as well as infantry.

antiseptics and painkillers

list of contents of pouch

Maxim machine gun
GERMANY

The German Army's heavy machine gun, the Maschinengewehr '08, was derived from the gun invented by American Hiram Maxim in 1884. It could fire 400 rounds a minute.

First-aid pouch
GERMANY

German medical orderlies carried a pouch containing basic painkillers and antiseptics, such as iodine, to treat wounded men before they were sent to dressing stations.

leather pouch

WORLD WAR I
MASS-PRODUCED WEAPONRY ALLOWS THE SLAUGHTER OF MILLIONS

World War I has been described as "industrial warfare" as manpower and economic resources of industrialized states were mobilized for fighting. Modern firearms provided armies with firepower on an unprecedented scale.

Formidable defensive systems of trenches, barbed wire, and machine-gun posts made offensive operations costly and tended to lead to stalemate. Weapons used in trench warfare ranged from grenades and flamethrowers to homemade clubs and knives. From 1916, the first slow and unreliable tanks made their appearance. Aircraft added a new dimension to warfare, carrying out reconnaissance and bombing, and strafing ground targets.

barrel

brake

wheeled gun carriage

Artillery shells
FRANCE

Artillery ammunition in World War I ranged from shrapnel to high-explosive and gas shells. These shells were fired by the French 75-mm field gun.

Howitzer
BRITAIN

Howitzers such as this 6-inch British gun were effective in trench warfare because they launched a shell on a high trajectory, dropping onto the concealed enemy.

Officer's compass
BRITAIN
A compass was vital on a night patrol or raid. Without it, soldiers could lose their way in the no man's land between the trenches, rendered featureless by shelling.

mother-of-pearl face catches the light

handset

wooden box

Gas mask
GERMANY
Effective masks were developed that protected the eyes and face from contact with poison gas and, through a filter respirator, neutralized the gas for breathing.

screw-on metal filter canister

Folding shovel
ITALY
For an infantryman, a shovel was essential equipment, needed to dig trenches or temporary shelters. This folding shovel was used by Italian alpine troops.

Nail club
BRITAIN
Primitive wooden clubs, with nails or other metal objects at the striking end, were used by soldiers on both sides as a silent, deadly weapon in trench raids.

adjustable eye pieces

Stereoscopic periscope
GERMANY
Soldiers in trenches used periscopes to keep watch on the enemy line. Snipers quickly picked off men who exposed their heads above the parapet.

Field telephone
GERMANY
Although radios were also used, field telephones were the main communications link in trench warfare. Where telephone cables had been ripped up by shelling, runners carried messages to the front line by hand.

leather balaclava

leather face mask

Aviator's headgear
BRITAIN
Flying in open-cockpit aircraft, many aviators in World War I wore leather balaclavas and face masks to protect themselves against the cold and wind.

Turkish bayonet and grenade
TURKEY
The Turkish Army in World War I had some obsolete equipment, such as swords and bayonets, but also state-of-the-art German-supplied weaponry such as fragmentation grenades.

steel canister

leather skull cap

barrel could fire 1-pound shell

Anti-aircraft gun
BRITAIN
Armies adapted existing guns, firing time-fused explosive shells for air defense. This British "pom-pom" gun, mounted on a pedestal, was used in defense of London against air attack.

Desert shoes
BRITAIN
British troops fighting against the Turks in the Palestine campaign sometimes wore wire sand shoes over their army boots to facilitate marching on desert sands.

Tank helmet
BRITAIN
British tank crews found that when bullets struck their armored vehicle, metal shards flew inside the hull. Helmets protecting the head and face were swiftly adopted to limit injuries.

pivot changes direction and angle of gun

The "Big Four"—David Lloyd George, Vittorio Orlando, Georges Clemenceau, and Woodrow Wilson—meet amiably at the Paris Peace Conference.

IN JANUARY 1919, LEADERS OF THE VICTOR COUNTRIES FROM WORLD WAR I met for a peace conference in Paris. US President Woodrow Wilson's liberal idealism was the focus for popular hopes that a new and better world would be built on the ruins of the old. Wilson was one of the **"Big Four"** who dominated the proceedings in Paris, the others being French prime minister Georges Clemenceau (1841–1929), British prime minister David Lloyd George (1863–1945), and Italian prime minister Vittorio Orlando (1860–1952). Each European leader had his own agenda, inevitably dominated by issues of national self-interest. Wilson's idealism expressed itself in an agreement to create a **League of Nations**, which was to provide "collective security" against

area lost to Poland
area lost to Denmark
area lost to France

3,984
14,500

57,000 sq km

German loss of territory
After World War I, Germany lost 13 percent of its territory. Most went to the new state of Poland, while France regained Alsace-Lorraine.

aggression and replace war with negotiated settlement of disputes, but Clemenceau believed the best guarantee for the future peace of France was in a permanent weakening of Germany.

Defeat in war had reduced Germany to a state of economic and social collapse. In January, communist revolutionaries, known as **the Spartacists**, tried to imitate the success of the Bolsheviks in Russia (see 1917) by staging an uprising in Berlin. The **attempted revolution** was crushed by the army and right-wing paramilitary Freikorps; the two most prominent Spartacist leaders, Karl Liebknecht and Rosa Luxembourg, were captured and killed. In February, an elected assembly, sitting in the city of Weimar, set about drawing up a constitution for an impeccably

Russian Red Army cap badge
The hammer-and-plow insignia from the Civil War period symbolizes the union of industrial workers and peasants in the revolutionary cause.

democratic republic, but on the streets of Germany **extremism of right and left continued to flourish**. In the southern German state of Bavaria, communists proclaimed a Soviet regime in April, only to be crushed by the army and Freikorps in May.

With Germany in no position to resume hostilities, the victorious Allies were able to impose peace terms in the **Versailles Treaty** without negotiation. Germany lost all its colonies and substantial territory in Europe. The European territorial loss consisted largely of areas needed to form the **new state of Poland**, and Alsace-Lorraine, which Germany had taken from France during the Franco–Prussian War (see 1870). Tight restrictions were placed on German armed forces and the Rhineland was demilitarized.

The Germans were also required to make reparations payments, which were justified by the assertion that Germany had been guilty of starting the war. The **"war guilt" clause**

Revolutionary leader
Trotsky's organizational and leadership skills were essential to Bolshevik success in Russia. He is seen here addressing troops of the Red Army.

outraged Germans more than any other part of the treaty. The crew of the German High Seas Fleet—interned since the armistice at **Scapa Flow** in the Orkney Islands north of Scotland—scuttled their vessels as an act of defiance. But left with no choice, German delegates signed the treaty in the Hall of Mirrors at the Palace of Versailles on June 28.

While peace was being formalized in Western Europe, **civil war raged in Russia**, as Lenin's Bolshevik government fought for survival against various "White"

counter-revolutionary armies. The Whites had the backing of foreign powers, who landed intervention forces at ports around Russia—US and Japanese at Vladivostok, French at Odessa, and British at Murmansk and Arkhangelsk—but these foreign interventions were half-hearted and mostly short-lived. The Bolshevik People's Commissar for War, **Leon Trotsky** (1879–1940), created a mass Red Army by conscripting peasants at gunpoint and subjecting them to harsh discipline. Fighting between the

January 12 Paris Peace Conference opens

January 15 Uprising of German communists in Berlin is suppressed

January 23–30 Poland and Czechoslovakia fight border war in Silesia

February 5 Charlie Chaplin, Douglas Fairbanks, Mary Pickford, and D. W. Griffith found **United Artists**

February 14 President Wilson presents **Covenant of League of Nations** to peace conference

March 9 Arrest and exile of Egyptian nationalists sparks **uprising in Egypt** against British

March 23 In Italy, Benito Mussolini **founds Fascist movement**

April 11 Britain and US reject **racial equality** clause in League of Nations Covenant

April 30 China **withdraws** from peace conference after Shandong is handed to Japan

May 3 Communist revolutionaries lose **control of Bavaria**

May 6 Afghan forces attack British India, beginning **Third Anglo–Afghan War**

January 21 Sinn Fein MPs elected to Westminster meet in Dublin to **form Irish parliament**

January 31 British government uses troops to quell **workers' protests in Glasgow**

February 6 German national assembly meets at Weimar

March 6 Third International (Comintern) founded to **promote communism worldwide**

March 21 Hungary proclaimed a Soviet republic under leadership of Bela Kun

April 6 Bavaria formally declared a **Soviet republic**

April 10 Revolutionary leader Emiliano **Zapata assassinated** in Mexico

April 13 Indian **protestors massacred** by British authorities at Amritsar

May 4 Student demonstrations in Beijing spark nationwide protests against foreign domination of China

May 27 US Navy Curtiss seaplane **completes crossing of Atlantic** in three stages

May 29 Observation of a solar eclipse confirms Einstein's **General Theory of Relativity**

> ❝ WE'VE HAD A **TERRIBLE VOYAGE**... THE **WONDER** IS WE ARE HERE AT ALL. ❞

John Alcock, officer in the British RAF, after flying nonstop across the Atlantic, June 15, 1919

John Alcock and Arthur Whitten Brown in the plane they flew on the first nonstop transatlantic flight from Newfoundland in Canada to Ireland.

Red and White armies was vicious, and accompanied by massacres and atrocities on a vast scale.

In the midst of this mayhem, Russia hosted a congress in Moscow to found the **Third International**, known as Comintern. Its aim was to promote the spread of communist revolution worldwide; its effect was to split the international socialist movement, forcing people on the political left to choose between social democracy and revolutionary communism.

The vision of an imminent world revolution had some credibility at a time when radical workers' and anti-colonial movements were challenging the established authority in many countries.

Outside Russia, it was only **in Hungary** that **communists** established a national government in 1919. The collapse of the Austro–Hungarian Empire was a disaster for Hungary, which faced the loss of two-thirds of its prewar territory to Czechoslovakia, Romania, and Yugoslavia. The communist **Bela Kun** (1886–1938) took power in March, launching military offensives against Czechoslovakia and Romania. He followed the Bolshevik example by forming a Red Army and exercising a reign of terror against his opponents, but after 133 days in power he was defeated by the Romanians. Admiral Miklós Horthy's counter-revolutionary National Army marched into Budapest to suppress the communists with another reign of terror. In 1920, Horthy took power in Hungary as "Regent."

In **Italy**, people of all political persuasions were disgusted with their country's limited share in the spoils of victory. Orlando was forced to resign as prime minister on his return from the Paris Peace

Conference, after failing to secure either Dalmatia or the port of Fiume (Rijeka) for Italy. In September, Gabriele D'Annunzio (1863–1938), a flamboyant right-wing nationalist poet and aviator, seized Fiume with a band of armed followers. He held the port-city, ruling as dictator of the Regency of Carnaro, until he was driven out by the Italian Navy after a peace deal between Italy and Yugoslavia in November 1920, which made Fiume a Free State.

Meanwhile, **Britain was facing opposition to its rule in India**. The British were committed to a promise made during World War I to grant the Indians a measure of self-government, but they suspended civil liberties in a crackdown on what were described as "anarchical and revolutionary crimes." On April 13, British officer General Reginald Dyer (1864–1927) ordered troops to fire on an unarmed crowd of protestors at the Jallianwalla Bagh, a public

Italians enter Fiume
Gabriele D'Annunzio's nationalist legionnaires salute the flag of the short-lived Regency of Carnaro in Fiume, now the Croatian city of Rijeka.

garden in Amritsar, Punjab. At least 379 people were killed. Although the British government condemned the killings and dismissed General Dyer, the **Amritsar massacre** caused widespread outrage in India and increased pressure for independence.

Despite the world's troubles, technological and scientific progress continued. On June 14, British pilot Captain John Alcock (1892–1919) and his navigator Lieutenant Arthur Whitten Brown (1886–1948) took off from St. John's, Newfoundland, to attempt the **first nonstop flight across the Atlantic**. After a perilous 16 hours 27 minutes, their Vickers Vimy bomber aircraft landed nose-down in a bog in Galway, Ireland. Their feat won them a hero's welcome in London, but Alcock's triumph was short-lived, as he was killed in an air crash just six months later.

At the time when Alcock and Brown made their famous flight, British scientists were analyzing the results of an expedition sent to the African island of Principe to observe a solar eclipse. The

expedition was intended to test the validity of the **General Theory of Relativity**, a revolutionary concept in physics formulated during World War I by Albert Einstein (1879–1955). In September it was announced that the observations did indeed confirm Einstein's theory, fundamentally changing the notions of time and space that had underpinned Isaac Newton's view of the universe.

ALBERT EINSTEIN
(1879–1955)

Einstein was born to Jewish parents in southern Germany. In 1905, he published his Special Theory of Relativity, which was followed by the General Theory of Relativity in 1915. His theories revolutionized understanding of the relationship between time, space, matter, and energy. From the 1920s Einstein was fêted worldwide, but chose exile in the US, away from Hitler's Germany.

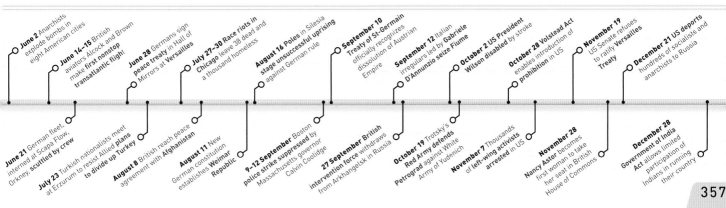

June 2 Anarchists explode bombs in eight American cities

June 14–15 British aviators Alcock and Brown make **first nonstop transatlantic flight**

June 28 Germans sign peace treaty in Hall of Mirrors at Versailles

July 27–30 Race riots in Chicago leave 38 dead and a thousand homeless

August 16 Poles in Silesia stage **unsuccessful uprising** against German rule

September 10 Treaty of St-Germain officially recognizes dissolution of Austrian Empire

September 12 Italian irregulars led by Gabriele D'Annunzio **seize Fiume**

October 2 US President Wilson disabled by stroke

October 28 Volstead Act enables introduction of prohibition in US

November 19 US Senate refuses to ratify Versailles Treaty

December 21 US deports hundreds of socialists and anarchists to Russia

June 21 German fleet, interned at Scapa Flow, Orkney, **scuttled by crew**

July 23 Turkish nationalists meet at Erzurum to resist Allied **plans to divide up Turkey**

August 8 British reach peace agreement with Afghanistan

August 11 New German constitution establishes **Weimar Republic**

9–12 September Boston police strike suppressed by Massachusetts governor Calvin Coolidge

27 September British intervention force withdraws from Arkhangelsk in Russia

October 19 Trotsky's Red Army defends **Petrograd** against White Army of Yudenich

November 7 Thousands of left-wing activists **arrested** in US

November 28 Nancy Astor becomes first woman to take her seat in British House of Commons

December 28 Government of India Act allows limited participation of Indians in running their country

> **WHAT** HAVE I GOT **FOR IRELAND? SOMETHING SHE** HAS **WANTED THESE LAST 700 YEARS.**

Michael Collins, Irish revolutionary leader, 1921

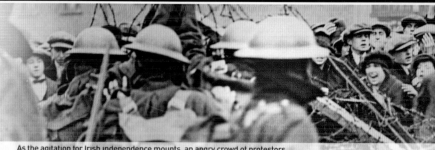

As the agitation for Irish independence mounts, an angry crowd of protestors in Dublin try to force a street barricade manned by British soldiers.

GERMANY REMAINED IMMERSED IN THE TURMOIL that had followed defeat in World War I (see 1919). In March, units of the nationalist paramilitary Freikorps occupied Berlin and declared the Weimar Republic overthrown. As conservative politician Wolfgang Kapp attempted to form a government, Weimar ministers called for a **nationwide general strike** to resist the Freikorps "putsch." Workers walked out, factories and transport shut down, and within days the Kapp regime had collapsed.

The Weimar government reluctantly engaged in talks with the victorious Allies over **implementation of the Versailles peace treaty** (see 1919). Germany began disbanding much of its armed forces and paying war reparations in kind, through deliveries of coal to France and large numbers of cattle, sheep, and horses to France and Belgium.

Farther east, war continued to rage. The Bolsheviks triumphed over the White generals in the Russian Civil War. Asserting Bolshevik authority over Ukraine and Belarus brought the Red Army into conflict with the Poles. After some early success against Polish forces, the **Red Army** invaded Poland. Led by General Józef Piłsudski (1867–1935), the Poles mounted a counter-offensive outside Warsaw that crushed the Red Army. Lenin (see 1917) was forced to end the war on Polish terms.

The terms imposed on the Ottoman sultan by the victorious Allies in the Treaty of Sevres meant **breaking up the Turkish empire**. In April, General Mustafa Kemal (1881–1938), the Turkish hero of Gallipoli (see 1915), headed a nationalist parliament in opposition to the sultan and began a war to win control of what he regarded as Turkish national territory—much of which had been given to Greece by the Allies.

The year saw the beginning of prohibition in the US. The **18th Amendment** to the Constitution banned the manufacture and sale of "intoxicating liquors," a move that had little influence on alcohol consumption, but provided a massive boost to organized crime. The more momentous **19th**

Dividing up reparations

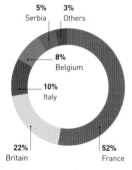

- **5%** Serbia
- **3%** Others
- **8%** Belgium
- **10%** Italy
- **22%** Britain
- **52%** France

The Allies agreed to divide up German reparations payments after a complex calculation of the losses they had suffered during World War I.

More Easy Money—A Clever Crook Story—In this Issue

September 11, 1920

Price–15 Cents
Subscription Price $7.00 a year

Leslie's

Illustrated ...paper

Vol. CXXXI. No. 3385

VOTING BOOTH NO 1

Victory for suffrage

This magazine cover celebrates the passing of the 19th amendment to the US Constitution, which gave women voting rights.

Polish Cross of Valor

This military decoration was introduced by Poland during the war with Bolshevik Russia in 1920 to recognize Polish deeds of heroism.

Amendment, ratified in August, guaranteed American women the vote on equal terms with men.

The US did not take part in the initiation of the **League of Nations**. This international body—dedicated to the peaceful resolution of disputes and the collective deterrence of aggression—was the brainchild of American president Woodrow Wilson, but the US Congress

January 16 Prohibition comes into effect in US

February 2 Russia recognizes Estonia's independence by **Treaty of Tartu**

February 7 White Russian leader Admiral Kolchak executed by Bolsheviks

March 1 Admiral Horthy becomes Regent of Hungary

March 8 Arabs proclaim Syria an independent state

March 13–17 The **Kapp Putsch fails** in Berlin; left-wing uprising in the Ruhr

March 26 Britain deploys Black and Tans against IRA in **Irish Independence War**

April 7 French troops **occupy German cities** in response to dispatch of German troops to the Ruhr

April 25 Supreme Allied Council assigns Britain a mandate to rule Palestine and Mesopotamia, and France to rule Lebanon and Syria

May 7 Polish troops fighting Russian Bolsheviks **occupy Kiev** in Ukraine

May 20 President Carranza of Mexico assassinated

July 24 French troops **occupy Damascus** to enforce French rule over Syria and Lebanon

August 10 Turkish Ottoman Sultan signs **peace treaty of Sevres** with the Allies

August 13–25 Bolshevik Red Army defeated by Poles in **Battle of Warsaw**

August 26 The **19th Amendment** to US Constitution guarantees **votes for women**

September 16 Bomb **explodes on Wall Street**, New York, killing 38 people

November 2 Warren Harding wins US presidential election

November 14 Wrangel's White Russian forces defeated by Red Army and **evacuated from Crimea**

November 15 First meeting of General Assembly of **League of Nations**

November 21 Bloody Sunday in Ireland: British forces open fire on football crowd after IRA kills British agents

December 1 Alvaro Obregón becomes president of Mexico, bringing stability after decade of civil conflict

5 MILLION
THE ESTIMATED **NUMBER OF PEOPLE** WHO **DIED** IN THE **RUSSIAN FAMINE** OF **1921**

Russian famine victims receive food from a relief train. The US played a leading role in the international effort to feed the starving.

refused to ratify it. Representatives of 41 countries attended the League's first General Assembly in Geneva in November, but neither Germany nor Russia was among them.

Meanwhile, **war had broken out in Ireland**, where Britain was resisting the declaration of an Irish Republic. British World War I veterans were recruited into two new units, the Black and Tans and the Auxiliaries, to fight the Irish Republican Army (IRA). On November 21, in an operation planned by IRA intelligence chief **Michael Collins** (1890–1922), the IRA killed 13 people in Dublin. The Auxiliaries responded the same afternoon by firing into a Gaelic soccer crowd, killing 14 people.

In the same month, on the second anniversary of the armistice ending World War I, Britain and France each **buried an Unknown Soldier**. The French soldier was entombed at the Arc de Triomphe in Paris, and the British soldier in Westminster Abbey in London. It was intended to commemorate all those who had given their lives, irrespective of rank or social class.

The last major event of the year was the accession of **General Alvaro Obregón** (1880–1928) as president of **Mexico**. Obregón had been one of the chief players in the civil conflicts that had torn the country apart since the Mexican Revolution (see 1910). His armed overthrow of President Venustiano Carranza (1859–1920) gave Obregón the chance to establish a relatively stable government.

IN 1921, RUSSIA experienced one of the most **destructive famines** of the 20th century. Years of warfare and revolution had laid waste to the Russian countryside, which was further devastated by drought in the Volga region. As hundreds of thousands died of starvation and disease, Lenin's Bolshevik government reluctantly appealed for foreign relief. The most prominent participant in the **international humanitarian effort** was the American Relief Administration, led by future US president Herbert Hoover (1874–1964). Despite the distribution of food aid to around 10 million people, millions died by the time the famine abated the following year.

The **Bolsheviks** continued to impose the will of their party upon their devastated country. In March, workers, soldiers, and sailors rebelled at the naval

Division of Ireland
Northern Ireland, with a mainly Protestant population, was separated from southern Ireland, which became the Irish Free State.

fortress of Kronstadt, demanding free elections, freedom of speech, and the right of peasants to own land and cattle. The **rebellion** was crushed by Bolshevik forces, but faced with popular discontent and economic devastation, the Bolsheviks had to retreat from some of the communist measures they had adopted. **Lenin's New Economic Policy** (NEP) allowed a limited capitalist market economy. Once peasants were permitted to sell their produce at a profit, the rural economy quickly recovered and food supplies were assured.

Despite the tribulations of the Russian Bolshevik government, its example continued to stimulate the foundation of Communist parties across the world. This included the **Communist Party of China**, which held its founding congress in Shanghai in July.

In Ireland, Britain attempted to fulfill its pre-World War I commitment to **Irish Home Rule** (see 1914). To appease the Irish Protestants the country was divided. Home Rule parliaments were established in Dublin and Belfast, and both parts remained within the United Kingdom. This was accepted by the Protestants, but rejected by Irish Republicans. **Negotiations** opened in London, and on December 6 the Irish delegation agreed to accept the **division of Ireland** in return for Dominion status within the British Commonwealth. Southern Ireland became the **Irish Free State**, but many Irish Republicans were outraged by the compromises

MAO ZEDONG (1893–1976)

The son of a farmer, Mao helped to found the Chinese Communist Party in 1921. He developed the idea of basing a revolution on support from peasants, rather than industrial workers. From 1949 he ruled Communist China as party chairman. His radical policies, including the Great Leap Forward in 1958 and the Cultural Revolution of the 1960s, caused vast disruption and loss of life.

in the Anglo–Irish Treaty, which led to civil war (see 1922).

Britain also had **troubles at home**. A brief post-war economic boom was followed by the collapse in demand for products from many of the country's traditional industries, such as coal mining and shipbuilding. By June, more than **2 million people were unemployed**. For the men who had fought in World War I, it was a bitter irony to find themselves lining up for unemployment benefits.

In the US, racism and anxieties about political subversion were rife. In **Tulsa**, Oklahoma, the most destructive **race riot** in American history saw most of the African-American section of the town destroyed in white attacks. Support for the white supremacist Ku Klux Klan rose rapidly, and concerns about the racial makeup of the US population

were reflected in tight limits on foreign immigration. **The Emergency Quota Act** linked the right of entry to country of origin, blocking mass immigration from southern and eastern Europe. Asians were entirely excluded.

The assumption of white racial superiority suffered a severe blow in **Morocco**, which the **French and Spanish** had casually divided into "spheres of influence." Spanish troops attempting to control the mountainous Rif region were surrounded and massacred by local **Berbers** at the Battle of Annual in July. The Berber leader Abd el-Krim declared the region an **independent Rif republic**, but it succumbed to a combined French and Spanish counter-attack four years later.

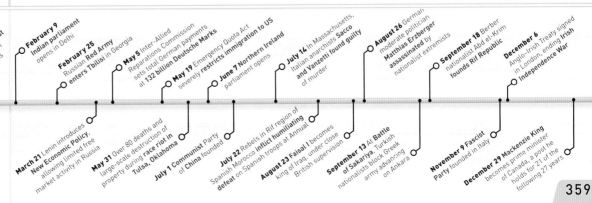

December 22 Congress of Soviets adopts ambitious **plan for electrification** in Russia

December 30 **French Communist Party** founded at Tours congress

December 23 Government of Ireland Act **creates separate parliaments** for northern and southern Ireland

February 9 Indian parliament opens in Delhi

February 25 Russian Red Army enters Tbilisi in Georgia

March 21 Lenin introduces **New Economic Policy**, allowing limited free market activity in Russia

May 5 Inter-Allied Reparations Commission sets total German payments at **132 billion Deutsche Marks**

May 19 Emergency Quota Act **severely restricts immigration to US**

May 31 Over 80 deaths and large-scale destruction of property during **race riot in Tulsa, Oklahoma**

June 7 Northern Ireland parliament opens

July 1 Communist Party of China founded

July 14 In Massachusetts, Italian anarchists **Sacco and Vanzetti found guilty** of murder

July 22 Rebels in Rif region of Spanish Morocco **inflict humiliating defeat** on Spanish troops at Annual

August 23 Faisal I becomes king of Iraq, under close British supervision

August 26 German moderate politician **Matthias Erzberger assassinated** by nationalist extremists

September 13 At Battle of Sakariya, Turkish nationalists block Greek army advancing on Ankara

September 18 Berber nationalist Abd el-Krim **founds Rif Republic**

November 9 Fascist Party founded in Italy

December 6 Anglo-Irish Treaty signed in London, ending **Irish Independence War**

December 29 Mackenzie King becomes prime minister of Canada, a post he holds for 21 of the following 27 years

359

Demonstrators gather on the streets of Delhi to protest against the arrest of Indian nationalist leader, Mohandas Gandhi.

> **❝** ...ONE SHOULD BE **FREE TO GIVE** THE FULLEST **EXPRESSION TO HIS DISAFFECTION** SO LONG AS HE **DOES NOT CONTEMPLATE,** PROMOTE, OR **INCITE VIOLENCE. ❞**
>
> **Mohandas Gandhi**, in a statement during his trial, March 18, 1922

FOUR YEARS AFTER THE CONCLUSION OF THE "WAR TO END WAR," serious progress was made toward a more peaceful future. Meeting in the US in February, the world's five major naval powers—Britain, France, Italy, Japan, and the US—signed **the Washington Treaty**, limiting the size of their navies. The same conference also called for an end to the military use of poison gas and banned submarine attacks on merchant shipping. It was the first effective arms limitation agreement between major powers. Britain sacrificed most, accepting naval parity with the US after long domination of the world's oceans, but the treaty was most controversial in Japan, where nationalists objected to naval inferiority to Britain and America.

Another hopeful sign of the flowering of peace was the **development of international air travel in Europe**. Small, noisy, uncomfortable aircraft had begun scheduled flights between European cities, exploiting the surplus of trained pilots and aircraft manufacturing capacity left over from the war. Navigation was primitive, and most pilots simply followed roads or railroads. This resulted in the **first commercial air disaster** in April, when a passenger aircraft flying from London to Paris met an aircraft following the same route in the opposite direction.

In the **Middle East**, Britain faced intractable problems reorganizing its League of Nations mandates from former Ottoman territory.

THE BRITISH MANDATE FOR PALESTINE

Former territories of the Ottoman Empire were divided between Britain and France, an arrangement legalized by League of Nations mandates. In accordance with the Balfour Declaration (see 1917), Britain had agreed to allow Jewish settlement in Palestine, but had also given wartime promises to the Arabs. In 1922, it divided its Palestinian mandate territory along the line of the Jordan River. Jewish settlement was allowed to the west, and to the east Transjordan would remain purely Arab land.

The immigration of Jews to Palestine (see panel, above), which Britain was committed to allowing, led to **clashes between Jews and Arabs** that the British could not control.

In another former Ottoman territory, **Egypt**, Britain faced determined nationalist opposition to the protectorate it had established in 1914. Unable to agree on a settlement, in February Britain unilaterally **declared Egypt independent**, while retaining the right to station troops there.

A more positive side effect of the British presence in Egypt was the discovery by British archaeologists of **the tomb of Tutankhamun**. The Earl of Carnavon (1866–1923) and Egyptologist Howard Carter (1874–1939) entered the tomb to find unparalleled treasure, including a gold face mask and jewel-studded chariots. Carnarvon's death the following year inspired a myth, "the curse of the tomb," that magnified the impact of the discovery.

In India, nationalist opposition to British rule had found a leader in **Mohandas Gandhi** (1869–1948). Winning the support of the peasant masses for the Indian National Congress independence movement, he organized a nationwide campaign of civil disobedience, including a boycott of British goods. Although Gandhi advocated strict nonviolence, his campaign generated widespread disturbances, including the massacre of 23 police officers at Chauri Chaura in February. **Gandhi was arrested** by the British authorities in March and sentenced to six years prison, of which he served only two.

Implementation of the **Anglo–Irish Treaty** (see 1921) led to a vicious **civil war**. Michael Collins (1890–1922), head of a provisional Irish Free State government in Dublin, was opposed by anti-Treaty republicans. In April, the Irish Republican Army (**IRA**) occupied Dublin's Four Courts building. After a lengthy standoff, in June Collins used artillery loaned by Britain to bombard the Four Courts, and retake the building. On August 22, Collins was killed in an ambush on a country road in County Cork. More numerous and better armed, the Free State troops had crushed most opposition by the time the treaty came into effect on December 6. The Protestant northern province of Ulster remained part of the United Kingdom.

In **Turkey**, nationalists led by **Mustafa Kemal** (1881–1938) were at **war with Greece**, which aspired to create a "Greater Greece" including Constantinople and much of western Anatolia. In August, a Turkish offensive at Dumlupinar drove the Greeks into retreat. The predominantly Greek city of Smyrna (Izmir) was occupied by pursuing Turkish

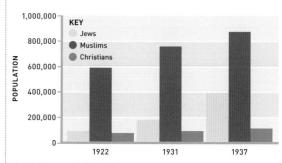

Population growth in Palestine
Through immigration, the proportion of Jews in Palestine increased rapidly. This provoked a violent reaction from the Muslim majority.

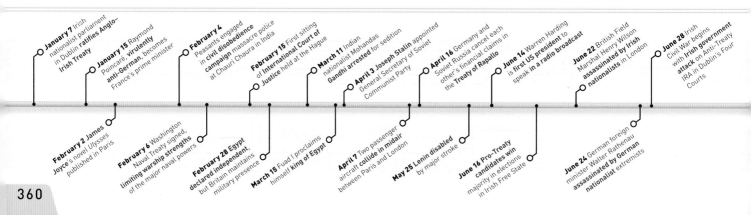

January 7 Irish nationalist parliament in Dublin **ratifies Anglo–Irish Treaty**

January 15 Raymond Poincaré **virulently anti-German**, becomes France's prime minister

February 2 James Joyce's novel *Ulysses* published in Paris

February 4 Peasants engaged in **civil disobedience campaign massacre police** at Chauri Chaura in India

February 6 Washington Naval Treaty signed, **limiting warship strengths** of the major naval powers

February 15 First sitting of **International Court of Justice** held at the Hague

February 28 Egypt declared independent, but Britain maintains military presence

March 11 Indian nationalist Mohandas **Gandhi arrested** for sedition

March 15 Fuad I proclaims himself **king of Egypt**

April 3 Joseph Stalin appointed General Secretary of Soviet Communist Party

April 7 Two passenger aircraft **collide in midair** between Paris and London

April 16 Germany and Soviet Russia cancel each other's financial claims in the **Treaty of Rapallo**

May 25 Lenin disabled by major stroke

June 14 Warren Harding **is first US president to speak in a radio broadcast**

June 16 Pro-Treaty **candidates win** majority in elections in Irish Free State

June 22 British Field Marshal Henry Wilson **assassinated by Irish nationalists** in London

June 24 German foreign minister Walter Rathenau **assassinated by German nationalist extremists**

June 28 Irish **Civil War begins** with Irish government **attack on Anti-Treaty IRA** in Dublin's Four Courts

Benito Mussolini mingles with his Fascist Blackshirt paramilitaries in Rome after being appointed prime minister by the Italian king in October.

forces and devastated by fire. Britain contemplated intervening against the Turks, but in an **armistice** agreed to at **Mudanya** in October both the European powers and Greece accepted the Turkish military victory. Under the agreed to peace terms there was a large-scale exchange of people, with over a million Greeks expelled from Turkey and half a million Turks forced to leave Greece. Abandoned Greek villages in western Turkey still bear witness to this human tragedy. **The Republic of Turkey was founded** the following year, with Mustafa Kemal as its first president.

1922 was the year when **Benito Mussolini** (1883–1945) achieved power in Italy. Since the end of World War I, Italy's ruling class had been intimidated by waves of militant action, with socialist workers occupying factories and peasants taking over large estates. In this troubled situation, Mussolini founded the *fasci di combattimento*, a **nationalist militia** that attacked socialists and seized power by force in some Italian towns. In October, Mussolini threatened to lead his **Fascist** followers in a "March on Rome" unless he was made head of government. Italy's king, Victor Emmanuel III (1869–1947), eventually gave in and Mussolini assumed office as prime minister. Once in control, Mussolini began

dismantling Italy's system of parliamentary democracy.

As Mussolini was muscling his way to power, the **first national radio broadcasting company** was being established in Britain. Like the early radio stations that were starting up in the US, the British Broadcasting Company (later Corporation) was financed by manufacturers of radio sets, eager to create a market for their products. And it worked; by March 1923, daily broadcasts of concerts, news, and talks had attracted 125,000 people to buy licenses from the Post Office for their "wirelesses." The US would not have a major broadcasting network until the formation of the

National Broadcasting Company (NBC) in 1926.

New **modernist trends in literature** were prominent in 1922. Irish writer James Joyce's novel *Ulysses*, published in Paris in February, broke all literary conventions, but its language and subject matter ensured that it was banned as obscene in countries with tighter censorship rules than France. The more decorous American expatriate poet T. S. Eliot caused a sensation with his long and obscure poem *The Waste Land*, which came with notes to help the reader follow its numerous literary allusions. Experimentation was also rife in **the movies**, from German director F. W. Murnau's expressionist horror movie *Nosferatu* to American filmmaker Robert Flaherty's groundbreaking documentary *Nanook of the North*.

Russia was entering a period of relative tranquillity, after the upheavals of revolution and civil war. At the year's end the former Russian Empire was reconstituted as the **Union of Soviet Socialist Republics** (USSR), but by then

Early airwaves
Early radio sets were often impressive-looking pieces of equipment. This one, from 1925, has an unusual, star-shaped antenna.

the founder of the world's first communist state, **Vladimir Lenin** (see 1917) had been disabled by a stroke. Despite this, he dictated a document, later known as **"Lenin's Testament,"** that was critical of several of his colleagues. In particular, it warned against the rudeness and intolerance of **Joseph Stalin** (1978–1953), newly installed as the Soviet Communist Party's General Secretary, and proposed that he be removed from his post. After Lenin's death, knowledge of the document was restricted to a communist inner circle, and action against Stalin was never taken.

"Father of the Turks"
Mustafa Kemal, the founder of the Turkish Republic, talks with camel drivers during the Turko-Greek War. He later took the name Ataturk.

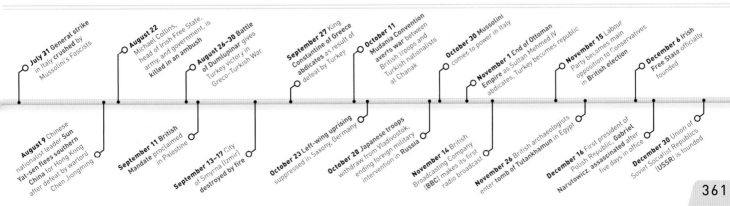

July 31 General strike in Italy crushed by Mussolini's Fascists

August 9 Chinese nationalist leader **Sun Yat-sen flees southern China** for Hong Kong after defeat by warlord Chen Jiongming

August 22 Michael Collins, head of Irish Free State, army, and government, is **killed in an ambush**

September 11 British Mandate proclaimed in Palestine

August 26–30 Battle of Dumlupinar gives Turkey victory in Greco-Turkish War

September 13–17 City of Smyrna (Izmir) **destroyed by fire**

September 27 King Constantine of Greece **abdicates** as result of defeat by Turkey

October 23 Left-wing uprising suppressed in Saxony, Germany

October 11 Mudania Convention averts war between British troops and Turkish nationalists at Chanak

October 28 Japanese troops withdraw from Vladivostok, ending foreign military intervention in Russia

October 30 Mussolini comes to power in Italy

November 14 British Broadcasting Company **(BBC) makes its first** radio broadcast

November 1 End of Ottoman Empire as Sultan Mehmed IV abdicates, Turkey becomes republic

November 26 British archaeologists enter tomb of Tutankhamun in Egypt

November 15 Labour Party becomes main opposition to Conservatives in **British election**

December 16 First president of Polish Republic, Gabriel **Narutowicz, assassinated** after five days in office

December 6 Irish Free State officially founded

December 30 Union of Soviet Socialist Republics **(USSR) is founded**

Officers of Spain's Guardia Civil stand by debris from a bomb explosion in Barcelona during the disturbances preceding the seizure of power by de Rivera.

IN 1922, THE GERMAN GOVERNMENT had declared itself unable to pay war reparations, which were due to the victorious Allies in gold Marks. The French, led by fiercely anti-German prime minister Raymond Poincaré (1860–1934), were determined to take action. In January 1923, **French and Belgian troops occupied the Ruhr,** Germany's industrial heartland. The German government responded by encouraging passive resistance—strikes stopped production in mines and factories.

The occupation triggered **hyperinflation,** and a collapse in the value of the German Mark. Inflation was already difficult to control before the Franco–Belgian

occupation, but the German government's decision to print banknotes to pay striking Ruhr workers was fatal. By the summer, the Mark was almost worthless. The exchange rate against the US dollar rose hourly, and eventually reached 5.72 trillion Marks to the dollar. By the time inflation peaked, savings of 68,000 Marks would buy no more than a postage stamp. In contrast, those who owed money had their debts eradicated. In August, **Gustav Stresemann** (1878–1929), a respected German politician, formed a **coalition government,** and the following month called off passive resistance in the Ruhr. In November, the Mark was replaced by the **Rentenmark,** knocking 12 zeros off the old currency and restoring public confidence.

The chaotic state of Germany tempted a minor political extremist, **Adolf Hitler** (see panel, right), to make a bid for power in the **Munich Putsch**

Worthless paper money
The collapse of the German currency resulted in the printing of 500 million Mark notes. Smaller notes were so worthless they were use to light stoves.

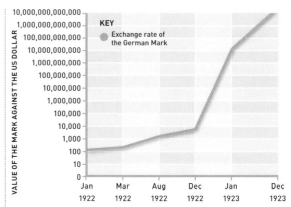

KEY
● Exchange rate of the German Mark

VALUE OF THE MARK AGAINST THE US DOLLAR

10,000,000,000,000
1,000,000,000,000
100,000,000,000
10,000,000,000
1,000,000,000
100,000,000
10,000,000
1,000,000
100,000
10,000
1,000
100
10
0

Jan 1922 | Mar 1922 | Aug 1922 | Dec 1922 | Jan 1923 | Dec 1923

German hyperinflation
The value of the Mark against the US dollar reflects the acceleration of German inflation. Ten years earlier a dollar had been worth 2.3 Marks.

on November 8–9. Hitler had made himself leader of the Nationalist Socialist Party (Nazis). He had also won powerful allies, including war hero General Erich Ludendorff (1865–1937). Hitler planned to use the Bavarian capital, Munich, as the base for a "March on Berlin" in imitation of Mussolini's "March on Rome" (see 1922). But, at the last moment, Bavarian leaders opposed the putsch. Hitler and Ludendorff were confronted by the army and police on the streets of Munich. After a brief gunfight, the attempted revolt disintegrated. Hitler was arrested two days later and charged with high treason (see 1924).

While Hitler's attempted coup failed, **in Spain General Primo de Rivera** (1870–1930) succeeded in seizing power. In the aftermath of the Spanish defeat by Abd el-Krim's Berbers at Annual (see 1921), the Spanish parliament had launched an investigation into the army and Spain's King Alfonso XIII (1886–1941) to apportion blame. Primo de Rivera dismissed parliament and established a **military dictatorship** under the king. Sadly, his desire to end Spain's economic problems and bitter political divisions proved far beyond his power or ability.

A more successful military man was Turkey's Mustafa Kemal (1881–1938), later known as Ataturk. Victorious in the war against Greece (see 1922), **Kemal formally founded the Turkish Republic** in October. He embarked upon a series of radical reforms designed to turn Turkey

ADOLF HITLER
(1889–1945)

Born in Austria, Hitler fought in the German army in World War I. An inspired orator, he won mass support for his National Socialist (Nazi) Party from the late 1920s. From 1933, he established a ruthless dictatorship that resulted in the Holocaust (see 1942). His expansionist policies caused a war in 1939 that finally led to the destruction of his Reich.

into a modern secular state. He banned traditional dress, abolished the Muslim caliphate system of government, and replaced Arabic script with the Roman alphabet.

In **Japan,** one of the worst natural disasters of the century struck on September 1. Known as the **Great Kanto earthquake,** a tremor measuring 7.9 on the Richter scale **devastated Tokyo** and the surrounding area. The quake started fires that were whipped up by high winds into

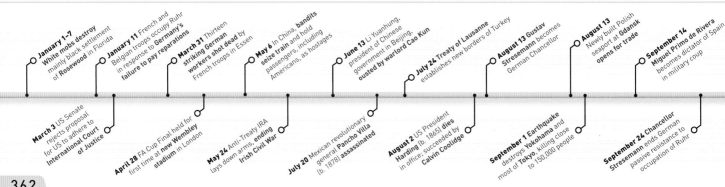

January 1–7 White mobs destroy mainly black settlement of **Rosewood** in Florida

January 11 French and Belgian troops occupy Ruhr in response to Germany's **failure to pay reparations**

March 31 Thirteen **striking German workers shot dead** by French troops in Essen

May 6 In China, **bandits seize train and hold** passengers, including Americans, as hostages

June 13 Li Yuanhung, president of Chinese government in Beijing, **ousted by warlord Cao Kun**

July 24 Treaty of Lausanne establishes new borders of Turkey

August 13 Gustav Stresemann becomes German Chancellor

August 13 Newly built Polish seaport at Gdansk **opens for trade**

September 14 Miguel Primo de Rivera becomes dictator of Spain in military coup

March 3 US Senate rejects proposal for US to adhere to **International Court of Justice**

April 28 FA Cup Final held for first time at **new Wembley stadium** in London

May 24 Anti-Treaty IRA lays down arms, **ending Irish Civil War**

July 20 Mexican revolutionary general **Pancho Villa** (b. 1878) **assassinated**

August 2 US President Harding (b. 1865) **dies** in office; succeeded by **Calvin Coolidge**

September 1 Earthquake destroys Yokohama and most of **Tokyo,** killing close to 150,000 people

September 24 Chancellor Stresemann ends German passive resistance to occupation of Ruhr

Tokyo in ruins after the earthquake of 1923. More than 140,000 people were killed in the disaster, which destroyed half a million buildings.

Queen Mary, wife of King George V, visits the Empire Exhibition at Wembley, mounted to inspire enthusiasm for Britain's imperial glory.

a firestorm. A tsunami up to 30 ft (10 m) high struck coastal districts, including the port of Yokohama. The death toll was estimated to be close to 150,000.

At this time, the US appeared as a beacon of prosperity in a dark world. President Warren Harding (1865–1923) died in office and was succeeded by his vice president, **Calvin Coolidge** (1872–1933). Coolidge became notorious for his placid complacency, describing the US as enjoying "a state of contentment seldom before seen." Indeed, the US was becoming the **world's first modern consumer society**, producing nine out of 10 of the world's automobiles.

African–American jazz musicians provided the soundtrack of this era of prosperity. Concentrated in the northern cities, such as Chicago and New York, jazz was popularized by the new medium of radio. New York's Harlem district became the center of an African–American cultural explosion, in literature as well as music, and the **Cotton Club opened** there in 1923. It became one of the most famous venues for live jazz, but black people were only admitted as performers.

Despite its problems, Germany was still culturally vibrant. The **Bauhaus** crafts and design school was founded by architect Walter

The Bauhaus exhibition
Joost Schmidt, a teacher at the Bauhaus, designed the poster for the 1923 exhibition, which linked modern art to industrial technology.

Gropius (1883–1969) in 1919, rejecting the traditional artist's hostility to modern technology and mass production. By the time of its first major exhibition in 1923, its mission was to bring functional modernist aesthetics to the everyday world, from the design of apartment buildings and electrical appliances to tubular-steel chairs and typography.

VLADIMIR ILYICH LENIN (1870–1924), founder of the Soviet Union, died of a massive stroke on January 22. Hundreds of thousands filed past his body in Moscow's Hall of Columns. Largely at Stalin's insistence, Lenin's body was embalmed and placed on permanent display; his brain was removed for study by Soviet scientists, who were tasked with discovering "the substance of his genius." Lenin statues were erected across the Soviet Union, and the city of Petrograd was renamed Leningrad in his honour.

In **Britain**, the **Labour Party**, led by Ramsay Macdonald (1866–1937), enjoyed its first **brief spell in government**. Despite Macdonald's moderation, the presence of socialists in government was a shock to the British establishment. When an election was called in October, a letter, purportedly sent by Soviet Comintern chief Grigory Zinoviev, was leaked to the press. It was used to accuse Labour of being soft on communism, and contributed to their election defeat.

The **British Empire Exhibition**, held at Wembley in London from April, was a conscious attempt to promote the imperial idea as a source of strength and security in a troubled world. Its opening was the first occasion that a British monarch, George V (1865–1936), made a speech on the radio.

Political and economic conditions in Germany began to recover from postwar chaos, with the help of the US. **The Dawes Plan**, named for American banker and politician Charles G. Dawes, arranged for the withdrawal of French and Belgian troops from the Ruhr (see 1923), and for German payment of reparations with the help of US loans.

Meanwhile, Nazi leader Adolf **Hitler was put on trial** for his attempted Munich Putsch (see 1923). Seizing the opportunity to make political speeches in court, he became a national celebrity. He was found guilty of high treason, but given a lenient five-year prison sentence, of which he served less than a year. During his time in Landsberg prison, he wrote the first volume of *Mein Kampf* (*My Struggle*), a statement of his political beliefs.

Meanwhile, in Italy the murder of socialist parliamentary deputy Giacomo Matteotti (1885–1924) drew attention to the lawless violence underpinning **Benito Mussolini's** Fascist government (see 1922). Matteotti was presumed to have been killed by **Fascist Blackshirts**. Opposition deputies withdrew from parliament in protest, opening the way for Mussolini to move more swiftly toward a single-party dictatorship.

900,000

THE NUMBER OF **PEOPLE** WHO **FILED PAST LENIN'S BODY** AS IT LAY **IN STATE** FOR **FOUR DAYS**

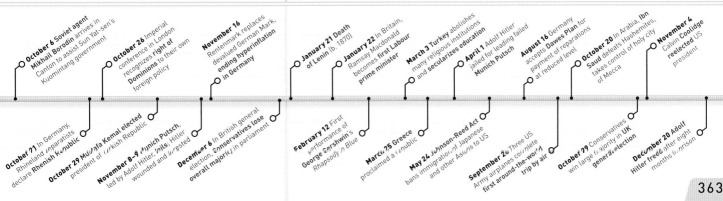

October 6 Soviet agent Mikhail Borodin arrives in Canton to assist Sun Yat-sen's Kuomintang government

October 26 Imperial conference in London recognizes **right of Dominions** to their own foreign policy

November 16 Rentenmark replaces devalued German Mark, **ending hyperinflation in Germany**

January 21 Death of Lenin (b. 1870)

January 22 In Britain, Ramsay Macdonald becomes **first Labour prime minister**

March 3 Turkey abolishes many religious institutions and **secularizes education**

April 1 Adolf Hitler jailed for leading failed **Munich Putsch**

August 16 Germany accepts **Dawes Plan** for payment of reparations at reduced level

October 20 In Arabia, Ibn Saud defeats Hashemites, takes control of holy city of Mecca

November 4 Calvin Coolidge reelected US president

October 21 In Germany, Rhineland separatists declare Rhenish Republic

October 29 Mustafa Kemal elected president of Turkish Republic

November 8–9 Munich Putsch, led by Adolf Hitler, fails; Hitler wounded and arrested

December 6 In British general election, Conservatives lose overall majority in parliament

February 12 First performance of George Gershwin's *Rhapsody in Blue*

March 25 Greece proclaimed a republic

May 26 Johnson-Reed Act bans immigration of Japanese and other Asians to US

September 26 Three US Army airplanes complete first around-the-world trip by air

October 29 Conservatives win large majority in UK general election

December 20 Adolf Hitler freed after eight months in prison

THE STORY OF
FLIGHT

FROM HOT-AIR BALLOONS TO SUPERSONIC JETS, FLIGHT HAS COME A LONG WAY

Side view

Until the 20th century, human flight was an area of experiment for enthusiasts. Ascents in balloons sparked the first flying craze but had little practical effect. In the 19th century, engineers calculated the forces involved in winged flight and experimented with gliders, but it was the arrival of gasoline engines that made powered flight practicable.

wing with anhedral angle (pointing downward at back)

wingstrut

wooden ribs covered in muslin

chain propeller mechanism

1783
Hot-air balloon
French brothers Joseph and Etienne Montgolfier complete the first manned flight in a hot-air balloon.

Montgolfier balloon

1900
First Zeppelin flight
On July 2, German pioneer Ferdinand von Zeppelin's LZ-1 successfully takes to the skies.

Zeppelin airship

1903
The Wright Flyer
On December 17, the Wright brothers complete the first sustained, controlled flight in a powered, heavier-than-air machine at Kill Devil Hills, North Carolina, US.

1919
Airlines progress
The first scheduled international passenger air service is inaugurated between London and Paris; the first airlines are set up.

c. **1485–1510**
Leonardo's flying machine
Early concepts of human flight, like those sketched by Leonardo da Vinci, are based on bird flight but are technically impractical.

Da Vinci's ornithopter

1852
First powered flight
Frenchman Henri Giffard attaches a steam engine to a balloon filled with coal gas; powered flight begins.

Giffard's airship

1909
Long-distance flight
On July 25, Frenchman Louis Blériot flies across the English Channel from France to England.

Louis Blériot

1914
Aircraft in warfare
Use of aircraft for combat transforms aviation; tens of thousands of aircraft are mass-produced for the first time.

" WE COULD NOT UNDERSTAND THAT THERE WAS ANYTHING ABOUT A **BIRD THAT COULD NOT BE BUILT** ON A LARGER SCALE. "

Orville Wright (1873–1948), American aviation pioneer

American brothers Orville and Wilbur Wright made the first viable powered winged aircraft by attaching an engine to a glider in 1903. They solved the problem of controlling an aircraft in flight and by 1905 had a machine that would stay airborne until its fuel ran out. In the beginning, airships outperformed winged aircraft, but they were slow and fatally accident-prone. Successors to the

Wright brothers showed that winged aircraft had astounding potential for increase in size, range, and speed. By the 1930s, high-performance aircraft could exceed 400 mph (640 kph), while the development of flying instruments improved safety. Long-distance flying feats made pilots heroes in the 1920s and 1930s. But, by the 1940s, the same flights were available to paying

passengers in the comfort of pressurized cabins. Jet engines carried aircraft performance to supersonic speed and altitudes at the edge of space. Rocket technology then propelled humans into space itself. From the 1970s, falling prices turned flight into a worldwide mass transportation system and made it accessible to the majority. Air travel had bridged distances and shrunk the world.

narrow wing made from ash ribs

uniquely designed propeller blades

forward elevators

landing skids

Wright Flyer
The Wright brothers' home-built aircraft, which they used for trial flights in December 1903, had a complex control system with rudders and elevators.

Sikorsky VS-300

1930s
Helicopters evolve
The first helicopters are developed by Louis Breguet in France, the Focke-Wulf company in Germany, and Igor Sikorski in the US.

1939
Jet aircraft
Englishman Frank Whittle invents the first jet engine. The first jet-propelled aircraft, the Heinkel He 178, makes successful test flight.

de Havilland Comet

1952
First commercial jet
The prototype de Havilland Comet, the first commercial jet, takes off. Passenger air travel zooms into the jet age.

Concorde in flight

1976
Concorde enters service
Concorde, the world's first supersonic passenger aircraft, enters commercial service.

1927
First non-stop transatlantic flight
On May 20–21, American Charles Lindbergh flies solo, non-stop from New York to Paris in a single-engine monoplane.

Spirit of St. Louis

1935
Air travel becomes cheaper
The Douglas DC-3 passenger aircraft makes flight cheaper and more viable.

1947
Supersonic flight
American aviator Chuck Yeager becomes the first to pilot the rocket-powered Bell X-1, the first aircraft to break the sound barrier.

1961
Manned spaceflight
Soviet cosmonaut Yuri Gagarin becomes the first man in space, orbiting the Earth in his Vostok spacecraft.

Space shuttle *Columbia*

1981
Reusable space craft
The space shuttle *Columbia* becomes the first shuttle to be launched into Earth's orbit, on April 12.

1925

American dancer and singer Josephine Baker was described by writer Ernest Hemingway as "the most sensational woman anyone ever saw."

PARIS REASSERTED ITS CLAIM as the world leader in taste and style with the **International Exhibition of Modern Industrial and Decorative Arts**. The exhibition gave a name—**Art Deco**—to the design trend toward angular shapes, abstract patterns, exuberant African, Aztec, and Egyptian motifs, and materials such as chromium and ivory. Art Deco soon set the style for everything from scent bottles and skyscrapers to ocean liners and movie theaters.

Less noticed at the time was a small exhibition of works in a Parisian gallery by artists calling themselves "**Surrealists.**" The group, which included the Catalan artist **Joan Miró** (1893–1983) and

Surrealist style
Harlequin's Carnival *exemplifies the playful, anarchic style developed in the 1920s by Joan Miró, a Spanish Catalan artist living in Paris.*

the American **Man Ray** (1890–1976), were dedicated to the exploration of dreams and unconscious impulses to subvert everyday reality. Over the following decade Surrealism was to become a major international art movement.

Man Ray was one of **a host of American expatriates** who **flocked to Paris** in the mid-1920s, lured by the vibrant cultural scene and the favorable exchange rate. American writers based in the city included Gertrude Stein (1874–1976), Ernest Hemingway (1899–1961), and F. Scott Fitzgerald (1896–1940), whose classic work *The Great Gatsby* was published in 1925. African-American erotic dancer **Josephine Baker** (1906–1975) became a star of Parisian nightlife, performing at the Theatre des Champs-Elysées. For their part, the French took an adoring interest in American jazz.

Back in the US, in Dayton, Tennessee, biology teacher **John Scopes was put on trial** for teaching Darwin's theory of evolution. Scopes was backed by the American Civil Liberties Union to test Tennessee's newly passed Butler Act, which had outlawed the teaching of evolution. Christian fundamentalists brought in former US Secretary of State William Jennings Bryan to act for the prosecution, and after a trial that enthralled America, Scopes was **found guilty**, although the verdict was later quashed.

The general world **political and economic outlook** was better than at any time since World War I. In April, Britain's Chancellor of the Exchequer, Winston Churchill, returned his country's currency to the prewar **Gold Standard**. This set the value of sterling artificially high, creating problems for British exporters, but it was an important gesture toward the restoration of international financial stability.

In December, **the Locarno Pact was signed**. This was a series of treaties designed to restore normal peacetime relations between Germany and the European victors of World War I. The agreement depended on the relationship established between the German and French foreign ministers, Gustav Stresemann and Aristide Briand, and opened the way for Germany's admission to the League of Nations in 1926.

1926

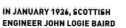

Reza Khan Pahlavi on his throne after being appointed shah of Iran. His aim was to modernize his country along secular Western lines.

revolving disc containing lenses
puppet head is filmed

The first television camera
Logie Baird gave the first demonstration of television using a mechanical system with a spinning disk as the scanner.

IN JANUARY 1926, SCOTTISH ENGINEER JOHN LOGIE BAIRD (1888–1946) made the **first** demonstration of a **television transmission** in a loft in London's Soho district. Fifty members of the Royal Institution saw the indistinct, but recognizable moving image of a face.

In May, Britain experienced its only **General Strike**. This nationwide industrial stoppage, in support of coal miners, paralyzed transportation networks and docks, and closed down factories and newspapers. The government responded by mobilizing troops and recruiting volunteers to maintain essential services. After nine days the unions backed down and ordered a return to work.

In **Poland**, the nation's military hero **Marshal Jozef Pilsudski** (1867–1935) **led a coup d'état** in May, in reaction against the unstable parliamentary government. Pilsudski declined the presidency, but effectively took dictatorial powers.

In Iran, another military strongman, **Reza Khan Pahlavi** (1878–1944), **established a new dynasty** by crowning himself as shah on April 25; his intention was to modernize his country. The Pahlavi dynasty he founded ruled in Iran until the 1970s.

160 MILLION
THE NUMBER OF **WORKING DAYS LOST TO STRIKES** IN THE **UK** IN **1926**

"I OWNED THE WORLD THAT HOUR AS I RODE OVER IT..."

Charles Lindbergh, American aviator

Aviator Charles Lindbergh poses alongside the *Spirit of St Louis*, the aircraft in which he achieved the first nonstop solo flight from New York to Paris.

IN MAY 1927, 25-YEAR-OLD CHARLES LINDBERGH (1902–1974) **flew solo across the Atlantic,** a feat that made him the most famous American alive. The offer of a cash prize for the first nonstop flight between New York and Paris had stimulated feverish competition. On May 8, famous French war aces Charles Nungesser and François Coli attempted the flight from Paris; they set off westward over the Atlantic and were never seen again. Such dramas had wrought excitement to a high pitch when the unknown Lindbergh, an airmail pilot, took off from Roosevelt Field on May 20 aboard a custom-built monoplane. Not only did he succeed in reaching **Paris in 33 hours and 30 minutes,** but he did it alone. Lindbergh was mobbed on landing in France and the mixed blessing of celebrity accompanied him for the rest of

The Great Mississippi Flood
Following months of heavy rain, the Mississippi broke its levees in spring 1927, submerging a vast area of land (in purple) and killing 246 people.

his life. His achievement stimulated the rapid growth of commercial aviation in the US.

America's upbeat mood was ripe for the world's **first modern consumer boom,** which was built around the purchase of cars and electrical goods. By 1927, there was one car for every six Americans—enough to ensure that even quite modest families might aspire to a Model T Ford. Levels of saving were high, and many chose to invest their spare cash in the rising stock market.

Not everything was as positive, however. Falling prices for agricultural goods were hitting rural areas worldwide, and the US, with almost half its population working the land, was not immune. Farm owners were heavily in debt and farm workers were badly paid.

The terrible conditions experienced by many rural workers was highlighted in April 1927 by the **Great Mississippi**

Car ownership in the US
In the eight years from 1919 to 1927 the number of cars on America's roads tripled. Five-sixths of the world's automobiles were in the US.

Flood, which was the worst flood disaster in American history. Many of its victims were black and very poor; ill-treated and neglected in refugee camps after the disaster, many thousands of them swelled the movement of African-Americans from the south to new lives in northern cities.

Two of the greatest works in cinema history were released in 1927: Fritz Lang's futuristic *Metropolis* and Abel Gance's historical epic *Napoleon*. But these hugely ambitious silent movies were upstaged by the success of Al Jolson (1886–1950) in a sound film, *The Jazz Singer*. A new era of "**talkies**" had arrived.

Second only to the Lindbergh flight in media coverage in 1927 was the controversy surrounding the **execution of the anarchists** Ferdinando **Sacco** and Bartolomeo **Vanzetti**. Italian immigrants dubiously convicted of a murder in Massachusetts in 1920, their case became a focus of protests by liberals and socialists, and their execution by electric chair on August 23 provoked riots in a number of cities across the world.

Meanwhile, in the Soviet Union, **Leon Trotsky**

First feature-length "talkie"
The first successful full-length sound feature film, The Jazz Singer, took $2.6 million at American box offices and made Jolson a household name.

(1879–1940) was expelled from the central committee of the ruling Communist Party in November, along with his allies Grigori Zinoviev and Lev Kamenev. Once the favorite to succeed Lenin (1870–1924) as Soviet leader, Trotsky had been ruthlessly outmaneuvered by the party's General Secretary Joseph

Stalin (1878–1953). Accused of "factionalism," Trotsky was sent into internal exile in Kazakhstan the following January and finally **expelled from the Soviet Union** in February 1929. Zinoviev and Kamenev submitted to Stalin, but he had them executed in 1936.

Warner Bros. Supreme Triumph
AL JOLSON
THE JAZZ SINGER

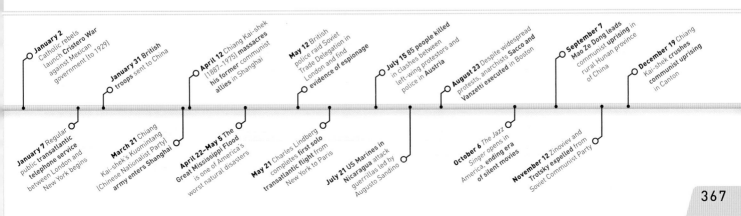

January 2 Catholic rebels launch Cristero War against Mexican government (to 1929)

January 7 Regular public transatlantic telephone service between London and New York begins

January 31 British troops sent to China

March 21 Chiang Kai-shek's Kuomintang (Chinese Nationalist Party) army enters Shanghai

April 12 Chiang Kai-shek (1887–1975) massacres his former communist allies in Shanghai

April 22–May 5 The Great Mississippi Flood is one of America's worst natural disasters

May 12 British police raid Soviet Trade Delegation in London and find evidence of espionage

May 21 Charles Lindberg completes first solo transatlantic flight from New York to Paris

July 15 85 people killed in clashes between left-wing protestors and police in Austria

July 21 US Marines in Nicaragua attack guerrillas led by Augusto Sandino

August 23 Despite widespread protests, anarchists Sacco and Vanzetti executed in Boston

September 7 Mao Ze Dong leads communist uprising in rural Hunan province of China

October 6 The Jazz Singer opens in America, ending era of silent movies

November 12 Zinoviev and Trotsky expelled from Soviet Communist Party

December 19 Chiang Kai-shek crushes communist uprising in Canton

Bacteriologist Sir Alexander Fleming surrounded by test tubes in his laboratory. Fleming discovered the antibiotic properties of penicillin in 1928.

IN THE SOVIET UNION, JOSEPH STALIN (1878–1953) began radical **economic and social reform**. Abandoning the compromise of Vladimir Lenin's New Economic Policy (see 1921), Stalin launched a **Five-Year Plan** to transform the Soviet Union into a major industrial country. He cracked down on businessmen and successful peasants who had made money out of the revolution. Hundreds of "bourgeois experts" —people, such as engineers, who had been valued for their skills rather than their involvement in the revolution—were arrested and **convicted of sabotage**.

In China, Chiang Kai-shek (1887–1975), leader of the nationalist **Kuomintang** (National People's Party), was close to establishing his rule over the entire country. The warlords who ruled different areas of China either became his allies or were defeated by his army. In June, Kuomintang forces took Beijing, and in October Chiang Kai-shek formally established a national

Chinese suffering
Prisoners taken during fighting between Chinese nationalist forces and those of the northern warlord Zhang Zuolin.

government, but he still faced resistance. Former allies of the Kuomintang, the **communists** suffered heavy losses when Chiang Kai-shek turned against them in 1927. Forced out of the cities they continued their struggle in remote rural areas—a large area of mountainous Jiangxi and Fujian provinces came under the control of the communist leader Mao Zedong (see 1921).

Political violence was also widespread elsewhere. In Yugoslavia, hostility between Croats and Serbs led to the **killing of Croatian Peasant Party leader Stjepan Radić (1871–1928)**. He was shot by a Montenegrin Serb political opponent in the Yugoslav parliament on June 20, and died later of his wounds. With his realm torn apart by nationalist passions, the following year Yugoslavia's King Alexander I (1888–1934) banned political parties and assumed dictatorial powers.

In Mexico, General **Alvaro Obregón (1880–1928)**, the dominant figure in his country's

politics since 1920, was **assassinated** after being elected president for a second term. His killer, José de León Toral, was a member of the **Catholic Cristero** movement that had launched an armed rebellion in response to the Mexican government's anticlerical policies. The desire for stability after the shock of Obregón's assassination led to the formation of the **National Revolutionary Party**, which, under a variety of names, dominated Mexican politics for more than 70 years.

In Germany, stability seemed to have been achieved after the chaotic post-World War I period. In elections to the Reichstag in May, Adolf Hitler's extremist **Nazi Party won less than three percent of the popular vote**, compared with almost 30 percent for the moderate Social Democrats. Under the German Republic's rigorous proportional representation system, the Nazis' minimal support gained them 12 seats in parliament.

In August, Germany was one of the original signatories of an agreement for "the renunciation of war as an instrument of national policy." This supremely optimistic document, commonly known as the **Kellogg–Briand Pact** after US Secretary of State Frank B. Kellogg (1856–1937) and French Foreign Minister Aristide Briand (1862–1932), obliged states to only resort to war in self-defense. Within a year it had been signed by all the world's major powers.

Of more practical consequence was the **discovery of penicillin**. Scottish scientist Alexander Fleming (1881–1955) accidentally discovered the antibiotic mold in contaminated specimen dishes, but the development of penicillin for medical use was the work of other scientists in the 1940s.

Prohibition era weapon
A sawn-off, double-barrelled shotgun hidden in a violin case was a typical weapon for an American gangster of the 1920s.

JOSEPH STALIN (1878–1953)

Born Josif Dzhugashvili, in Georgia, Stalin joined Lenin's Bolsheviks in 1903. After Lenin's death he cleverly outmaneuvered other leading Bolsheviks to achieve dictatorial power by 1929. He ran a ruthless police state that murdered millions of its citizens, yet he presided over the country's transformation into a major industrial power and led it to victory over Nazi Germany in 1945.

ON FEBRUARY 14, SEVEN PEOPLE WERE SHOT DEAD in a garage on Chicago's North Side. The perpetrators of the **St. Valentine's Day Massacre** were probably members of the gang headed by Al Capone (1899–1947), a prominent figure in organized crime. The victims belonged to the rival gang of Bugs Moran. Both Capone and Moran drew their main income from bootlegging—the illegal trade in alcoholic drinks that flourished under prohibition (see 1920). The massacre focused public outrage on the crime and violence that was rife in American cities. The authorities were forced to take action, which led to the arrest and imprisonment of Capone on charges of tax evasion in 1931.

On March 4, Republican **Herbert Hoover** (1874–1964) was inaugurated as US president. His arrival in office coincided with a high point of complacency about US economic progress. Through the 1920s the US had become the world's first automobile-owning society, with 26 million cars on the road by 1929. Optimism and easy credit drove share prices on Wall

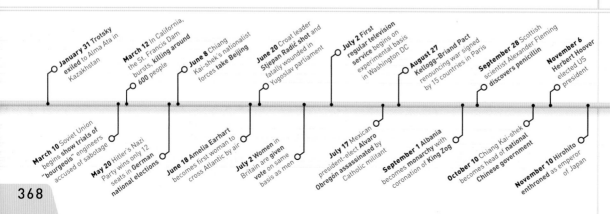

January 31 Trotsky exiled to Alma Ata in Kazakhstan

March 12 In California, the St. Francis Dam bursts, **killing around 600 people**

June 8 Chiang Kai-shek's nationalist forces **take Beijing**

June 20 Croat leader **Stjepan Radić shot** and fatally wounded in Yugoslav parliament

July 2 First regular television service begins on experimental basis in Washington DC

August 27 Kellogg–Briand Pact renouncing war signed by 15 countries in Paris

September 28 Scottish scientist Alexander Fleming **discovers penicillin**

November 6 Herbert Hoover elected US president

January 5 King Alexander takes control of Yugoslavia, **abolishing parliamentary constitution**

March 10 Soviet Union begins show trials of "bourgeois' engineers accused of sabotage

May 20 Hitler's Nazi Party wins only 12 seats in German **national elections**

June 18 Amelia Earhart becomes first woman to cross Atlantic by air

July 2 Women in Britain are given **vote** on same basis as men

July 17 Mexican president-elect Alvaro **Obregón assassinated** by Catholic militant

September 1 Albania becomes monarchy with coronation of King Zog

October 10 Chiang Kai-shek becomes head of national Chinese government

November 10 Hirohito enthroned as emperor of Japan

February 11 Lateran Treaty agreed between Mussolini's Italian government and Vatican

> ## ANY **LACK OF CONFIDENCE IN** THE **ECONOMIC FUTURE OF** THE **UNITED STATES** IS **FOOLISH.**
>
> **President Herbert Hoover,** in a speech after the stock market crash, November 15 1929

Herbert Hoover being sworn in as US president. His inauguration speech foresaw "the day when poverty will be banished from this nation."

Street in an apparently endless upward curve—about 30 million Americans had some form of stock market investment. In the prevailing mood, it was easy for the president to view problems in the economic scene—the ruin of small farmers through falling crop prices and poverty-line wages of many urban workers— as temporary problems that could be overcome.

Moviegoing was one boom area of the US economy. **Hollywood** had become the center of film production, and its "Big Five" studios churned out hundreds of movies a year. The **film industry**

Winning movie
The first movie to win the Academy Award for Best Picture was Wings, *a silent film about World War I fighter pilots, staring actress Clara Bow.*

was going through a technological revolution, with the transition from silent to sound movies. It was also becoming intensely conscious of its status and image. The Academy of Motion Picture Arts and Sciences made its **first annual "Oscar"** awards in 1929, awarding Best Picture to the war film *Wings*—the only silent movie to win the accolade.

In Italy, **Benito Mussolini's** (1883–1945) Fascist regime achieved a diplomatic triumph in signing the **Lateran Treaty** with Pope Pius XI. Since the unification of Italy in 1871 there had been an unresolved dispute between the Italian state and the papacy, with successive popes regarding themselves as "prisoners" in the Vatican. The Lateran Treaty recognized the **Vatican City** as an **independent state** and acknowledged Catholicism as Italy's official religion. Unofficially it assured the Fascist regime the support of the Catholic Church.

Another attempt was made to draw a line under World War I when the wartime Allies set up a committee, headed by American industrialist Owen Young, to reconsider **German reparations payments**. Accepting that the Dawes Plan (see 1924) had fixed payments too high, the **Young Plan** made proposals for Germany to pay a reduced annual sum until 1988. Although the deal was accepted by the German government, it was denounced by conservative nationalists and by the Nazis. They forced a referendum on reparations, which

they described as "the enslavement of the German people." Although only 14 percent of voters backed it, the referendum campaign significantly raised Hitler's political profile in Germany.

The long shadow cast by World War I was also evident in a **wave of antiwar books**. They included American writer Ernest Hemingway's novel *A Farewell to Arms*, British poet Robert Graves's (1895–1985) war memoir *Goodbye to All That*, and *All Quiet on the Western Front*, written by German novelist Erich Maria Remarque (1898–1970). Presenting war as a futile waste of human lives, they captured the popular mood of the time.

By far the most important event of the year, however, was the **Wall Street Crash**. In September, the

share rise faltered. By October 23, shares prices were falling, and the following day, "Black Thursday," the **market dropped** in a stampede of selling. In vain, President Hoover assured the American public that "the fundamental business of the country" was "on a sound and prosperous basis," but the selling of shares went on, and there were further sharp falls. Speculators who had bought shares on credit were ruined, as were thousands of modest individuals who had entrusted their life savings to the market. Experts spoke of a temporary "market correction," and Hoover took action to stimulate the economy and create jobs, but the crash was the start of a long-lasting collapse in share prices, and the signal for the start of a **worldwide depression**.

Wall Street index
Share prices on the New York stock exchange experienced a speculative boom in the 1920s, which was followed by an unstoppable collapse.

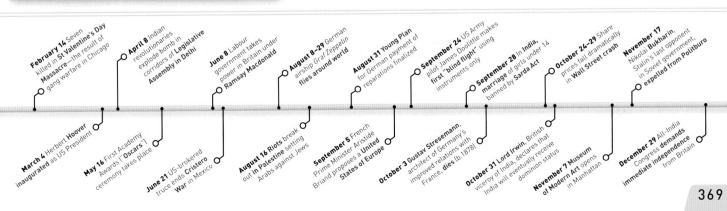

February 14 Seven killed in **St Valentine's Day Massacre**—the result of gang warfare in Chicago

March 4 Herbert **Hoover** inaugurated as US President

April 8 Indian revolutionaries explode bomb in corridors of **Legislative Assembly in Delhi**

May 16 First Academy Awards ("**Oscars**") ceremony takes place

June 8 Labour government takes power in Britain under **Ramsay Macdonald**

June 21 US-brokered truce ends **Cristero War** in Mexico

August 8–29 German airship *Graf Zeppelin* **flies around world**

August 16 Riots break out in Palestine setting Arabs against Jews

August 31 Young Plan for German payment of reparations finalized

September 5 French Prime Minister Aristide Briand proposes a **United States of Europe**

September 24 US Army pilot James Doolittle makes first "**blind flight**" using instruments only

September 28 In India, marriage of girls under 14 banned by **Sarda Act**

October 3 Gustav Stresemann, architect of Germany's improved relations with France, **dies** (b.1878)

October 24–29 Share prices fall dramatically in **Wall Street crash**

October 31 Lord Irwin, British viceroy of India, declares that India will eventually receive dominion status

November 7 Museum of Modern Art opens in Manhattan

November 17 Nikolai **Bukharin**, Stalin's last opponent in Soviet government, **expelled from Politburo**

December 29 All-India Congress demands **immediate independence** from Britain

369

> ❝ WE ARE **50 OR 100 YEARS BEHIND** THE **ADVANCED COUNTRIES.** WE MUST **MAKE GOOD** THIS **DISTANCE** IN **TEN YEARS.** ❞

Josef Stalin, in a speech to the first All-Union Conference of leading personnel of Socialist Industry, February 4, 1931

Unemployed men waiting for food handouts in New York during the Depression. There was no federal unemployment benefit or welfare in the US.

IN THE EARLY MONTHS OF 1930, THE SOVIET UNION was thrown into turmoil by the mass **collectivization of agriculture**—the replacement of privately owned peasant farms with large, state-owned farms operated by a peasant collective. In the eyes of dictator Joseph Stalin (see 1928), who wanted to transform the Soviet Union into a modern industrial state, small-scale peasant agriculture was an obstacle to be ruthlessly swept aside—both inefficient and tainted with antisocialist self-interest. The peasants, however, were ferociously attached to their land and farm animals, and when communist officials were sent to villages to organize collective farms, they met **widespread resistance**. Peasants slaughtered their animals rather than hand them over to the state, and attacked the communists with stones and clubs. The authorities responded with **mass arrests of "kulaks"**—better-off peasants—and troublemakers. By March it was announced that 14 million Soviet farms had been collectivized, but the chaos it created was so disruptive to food production that Stalin had to order a pause in the campaign.

It was no coincidence that the following month an agency known as the **Gulag was set up** to run a system of forced labor camps across the Soviet Union. Of about one million peasants arrested in the early 1930s, hundreds of thousands ended up in Gulag camps, providing slave labor to drive the developing Soviet economy. **Collectivization failed** to produce an increase in agricultural output, and the vision of vast Soviet prairies farmed by tractors and mechanical harvesters remained largely a fantasy; instead there was famine (see 1933). But it did stimulate a mass movement of peasants to the cities, where they found work on construction sites and in factories. **Soviet industrial projects**, many using Gulag prison labor, developed on a vast scale, while the rest of the world plunged into an economic recession.

In **India** the charismatic nationalist Mohandas Gandhi (see panel, right) was mounting a campaign of **civil disobedience** against British rule. Gandhi dramatized his opposition to the government salt monopoly by staging a march from Ahmedabad to the Indian Ocean. Setting out on March 12, he reached the sea on April 6, and scooped up a handful of salt water in public defiance of the government's ban on unlicensed salt gathering. Although Gandhi advocated strict nonviolence, the **Salt March triggered riots** that redoubled after his arrest on May 5. Despite this, the British were willing to make some concessions to Indian participation in local government, but opposed all ideas of independence.

The exploits of adventurous **aviators** continued to fascinate the public, as they had done through the 1920s. Pilots became national heroes through pioneering **long-distance flights**. In May, Jean Mermoz (1901–36), who was employed by the French Aéropostale airmail company, made the first **postal flight across the South Atlantic**, flying a float plane nonstop from Dakar in West Africa to Natal in Brazil. This completed an unbroken airmail link that stretched from France to Chile. Meanwhile, the British cheered as **amateur pilot Amy**

MOHANDAS GANDHI
(1869–1948)

Known as Mahatma ("Great Soul"), Gandhi was born into a privileged Indian family and studied law in London. His first campaigns of non-violent civil disobedience were in South Africa. Returning to India in 1915 he led the opposition to British rule, although many nationalists rejected his non-violence. In 1948 he was assassinated by Hindu extremists, outraged by his conciliatory attitude toward Muslims.

Johnson (1903–41) flew solo from Croydon in England to Darwin, Australia in a second-hand De Havilland Gypsy Moth biplane. The journey, which took 19 days, was especially remarkable since she had never even flown across the English Channel.

This amateur triumph of British aviation stood in stark contrast with the fate of an expensive government project, the **R101**

powerful light for working at night

wheel studs to prevent tractor from skidding

Soviet tractor
By the 1930s the Soviet Union was manufacturing its own tractors. There were about 200,000 tractors in the Soviet Union by 1934.

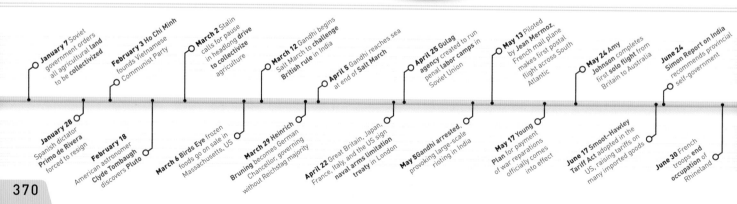

January 7 Soviet government orders all agricultural land to be **collectivized**

January 28 Spanish dictator **Primo de Rivera** forced to resign

February 3 Ho Chi Minh founds Vietnamese Communist Party

February 18 American astronomer **Clyde Tombaugh** discovers **Pluto**

March 2 Stalin calls for pause in headlong drive **to collectivize** agriculture

March 6 Birds Eye frozen foods go on sale in Massachusetts, US

March 12 Gandhi begins Salt March to challenge **British rule** in India

March 29 Heinrich Bruning becomes German Chancellor, governing without Reichstag majority

April 5 Gandhi reaches sea at end of **Salt March**

April 22 Great Britain, Japan, France, Italy, and the US sign **naval arms limitation treaty** in London

April 25 Gulag agency created to run penal labor camps in Soviet Union

May 5 Gandhi arrested, provoking large-scale rioting in India

May 13 Piloted by **Jean Mermoz**, French mail plane makes first postal flight across South Atlantic

May 17 Young Plan for payment of war reparations officially comes into effect

May 24 Amy Johnson completes first **solo flight** from Britain to Australia

June 17 Smoot-Hawley Tariff Act adopted in the US, raising tariffs on many imported goods

June 24 Simon Report on India recommends provincial self-government

June 30 French troops **end occupation** of Rhineland

The burned-out wreckage of British airship *R101* lies in a field outside Beauvais in northern France. Britain's Air Secretary was killed in the crash.

Famous flight
British aviatrix Amy Johnson after her solo flight from England to Australia. Pilots were among the leading celebrities of the time.

airship. On its maiden voyage in October, *R101* was intended to carry the British Secretary of State for Air and other dignitaries from England to India. The badly designed craft only reached northern France, where it crashed in bad weather, killing 48 of the 54 people on board.

By far the worst disaster of 1930, however, was the **collapse of the world economy**. In the US, at the start of the year, most commentators believed that, in the wake of the stock market crash (see 1929), the country was facing a temporary and modest economic downturn. In May, **President Herbert Hoover** (1874–1964) reassured Americans that they had "now passed the worst." Instead, unemployment continued to rise, bread lines became a common sight, farmers began to go

bankrupt in large numbers, and over 1,300 US **banks failed** during the year. The US unwisely sought relief for its farmers and unemployed workers through blocking imports. The **Smoot–Hawley Tariff Act**, which became law in June, placed heavy duties on thousands of imported goods. When the US's trading partners retaliated, the world was set on

course for a disastrous reduction in overall levels of trade.

In **Germany**, economic crisis triggered political extremism and the **collapse of democratic government**. In March, the governing coalition fell apart because the Social Democrats would not agree to cuts in unemployment benefit. Heinrich Brüning (1855–1970), leader of the Center Party, formed a government without majority support in the Reichstag. He dissolved parliament in July, calling a general election against a background of massive unemployment. Adolf Hitler's Nazi Party mounted a spectacular and violent election campaign, blaming all of Germany's problems on the Versailles Treaty (see 1919). The **Nazis increased their seats** in the Reichstag from 12 to 107, becoming the second largest party in the country. Brüning responded

to a polarized Reichstag by ignoring it and clinging to power, ruling by Emergency Decree.

Many observers outside Germany were disturbed by the growing support for Hitler's aggressive nationalist extremism. France showed its lack of trust in a peaceful future by beginning construction of formidable defensive fortifications along its border with Germany. In the pursuit of absolute security, **the Maginot Line** consumed much of France's defense budget during the 1930s.

South American countries were especially vulnerable to the Depression because of their role as suppliers of food and raw materials to the industrialized US and Europe. Many experienced **political upheavals** as economic conditions worsened. In **Argentina**, a military coup ushered in a decade of political conflict and government corruption. In **Brazil**, an army revolt brought Getúlio Vargas (1882–1954) to power in

November. Vargas installed a populist dictatorship that pushed for the industrialization of Brazil and suppressed political dissent, while introducing social welfare measures for the poor.

In Japan, radical nationalists, including many army and navy officers, believed the answer to **Japan's economic problems** lay in military conquest. The civilian government of prime minister **Osachi Hamaguchi** (1870–1931) outraged them further by seeking cuts in military spending to help offset a budgetary deficit. On November 14, Hamaguchi was shot at Tokyo station by a member of a nationalist secret society. He never recovered, and died nine months later. It was an ominous sign of the Japanese militarists' determination to pursue their own aggressive expansionist policies.

Japanese assassination
Japanese Prime Minister Hamaguchi after being shot by a nationalist extremist at Tokyo station. He died the following year.

Nazi vote in federal elections 1928–1932
A minority extremist party in 1928, the Nazi party grew to be the largest single party by summer 1932. They peaked at 37.4 percent of votes cast.

Bar chart — NUMBER OF VOTES (IN MILLIONS):
- May 1928: 2.6%
- Sept 1930: 18.3%
- July 1932: 37.4%
- Nov 1932: 33.1%

> THE **CAPITALIST CHAIN** IS AGAIN **THREATENING TO BREAK** AT THE WEAKEST LINK. **SPAIN** IS **NEXT IN ORDER.**

Leon Trotsky, Russian revolutionary,
speaking on the revolution in Spain, January 1931

Demonstrators in Madrid celebrate the revolution of April 1931 that overthrew the Spanish monarchy. Among the new reforms was women's right to vote.

Scaling new heights
Photographer Lewis Hine documented the casual risks taken by workers during construction of the Empire State Building.

ON APRIL 14, 1931, KING ALFONSO XIII OF SPAIN (1886–1941) abdicated and fled into exile, after his supporters were defeated in municipal elections. The victors in this bloodless revolution, a coalition of moderate republicans and socialists, set up a provisional government headed by Niceto Alcalá-Zamora (1877–1949). The departure of the king and **founding of Spain's Second Republic** gave the urban and rural poor, as well as nationalists in the Basque country and Catalonia, hope, but army officers, landowners, industrialists, and the Catholic hierarchy were adamantly opposed to change. Spain was on the path to civil war.

In New York on May 1 the **Empire State Building was officially opened**. Standing 1,454 ft (443 m) tall to the top of its spire, it surpassed the Art Deco Chrysler Building, which had been the **world's tallest building** for just 11 months. Begun in 1929, at the height of the US stock market boom, the Empire State Building expressed the boundless optimism of the time. But its completion also came against a background of farm bankruptcies and rising unemployment.

Meanwhile, the world economic recession took a sharp turn for the worse through a major **European banking crisis**. In May,

Austria's largest bank, the Creditanstalt, failed, and by July many major German banks also faced collapse. German Chancellor Heinrich Brüning proposed a customs union between Germany and Austria, and suggested Germany might renege on payment of war reparations. France's hostile response was to refuse to help prop up the German financial system. Germany and Austria were forced to take emergency measures to block foreigners from withdrawing funds.

Britain had made substantial loans to German banks—money that was now frozen. As a **crisis loomed**, financial experts advised **Ramsay Macdonald's** (1886–1937) **Labour government** to cut expenditure to balance the budget. In August, proposals to cut unemployment benefit and government employee pay provoked a mass resignation by Labour ministers. Macdonald stayed as prime minister, forming a coalition National Government with the other two main parties,

the Conservatives and the Liberals. A Royal Navy strike over pay at Invergordon panicked foreign investors and triggered a run on the pound, reducing the value of sterling by a quarter.

The most ominous event of the year was **Japanese aggression against China**. On September 18, Japanese army officers guarding the South Manchurian Railway carried out an attack on the tracks, which they blamed on the Chinese. This "Mukden incident" provided the pretext for the Japanese **military occupation of Manchuria**. The occupation was condemned by the League of Nations as an act of aggression, but the Japanese refused to withdraw. The following year Japan set up a puppet government in Manchuria under **Pu Yi** (1906–67), China's last emperor, who had been deposed in 1912.

From September to December a Round Table **Conference on the future of India** was held in London. The Indian National Congress, the principal Indian nationalist movement, was

Occupation of Manchuria
Korea became a Japanese colony in 1910. In 1931, the Japanese extended into Manchuria, which became the puppet state of Manchukuo.

KEY
⬜ Japanese Empire 1930
⬜ Japanese sphere of influence 1930
⬛ Japanese conquests 1931–3

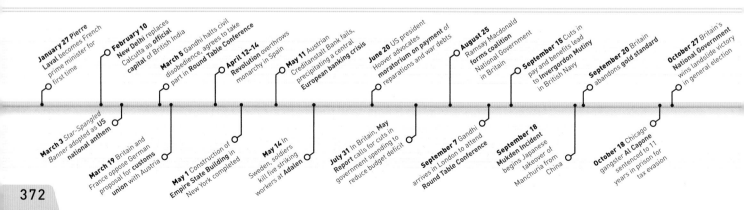

January 27 Pierre Laval becomes French prime minister for first time

February 10 New Delhi replaces Calcutta as official capital of British India

March 5 Gandhi halts civil disobedience, agrees to take part in Round Table Conference

April 12–14 Revolution overthrows monarchy in Spain

May 11 Austrian Creditanstalt Bank fails, precipitating a central European banking crisis

June 20 US president Hoover advocates **moratorium on payment of** reparations and war debts

August 25 Ramsay Macdonald forms coalition National Government in Britain

September 15 Cuts in pay and benefits lead to Invergordon Mutiny in British Navy

September 20 Britain abandons gold standard

October 27 Britain's National Government wins landslide victory in general election

March 3 *Star-Spangled Banner* adopted as US national anthem

March 19 Britain and France oppose German proposal for **customs union** with Austria

May 1 Construction of **Empire State Building** in New York completed

May 14 In Sweden, soldiers kill five striking workers at **Adalen**

July 31 In Britain, **May Report** calls for cuts in government spending to reduce budget deficit

September 7 Gandhi arrives in London to attend **Round Table Conference**

September 18 Mukden Incident begins Japanese takeover of Manchuria from China

October 18 Chicago gangster Al Capone sentenced to 11 years in prison for tax evasion

American pilot Amelia Earhart arrives in England after her historic solo transatlantic flight in a Lockheed Vega monoplane.

Japanese troops in Manchuria
The Japanese occupation of the northern Chinese province of Manchuria can be seen as their first step toward World War II.

represented by **Mohandas Gandhi** (1869–1948). He had negotiated a pact with the British Viceroy of India, Lord Irwin, to suspend the civil disobedience campaign (see 1930). The conference was not a success, however, and on his return to India Gandhi resumed his nonviolent campaign against the British.

In contrast with the British treatment of India was the passage of the **Statute of Westminster** by the British parliament in December. This law **recognized full equality** between Britain and the dominions—Australia, New Zealand, Canada, South Africa, the Irish Free State, and Newfoundland. For them, the British Empire had truly become a Commonwealth of Nations.

42 THE NUMBER OF STATES WON BY ROOSEVELT IN THE **1932 US** ELECTIONS

THE PEAK YEAR OF THE GREAT DEPRESSION saw declining output and sharply reduced levels of trade bring **mass unemployment** to the world's leading industrial nations. At least 13 million Americans, around 3 million Britons, and more than 5 million Germans were unemployed. In Europe, national unemployment benefit programs helped the jobless to survive, but in the US, where only piecemeal local welfare programs existed, unemployment led to abject poverty. Thousands became homeless, living in shanty towns ironically called "**Hoovervilles**" after the US president.

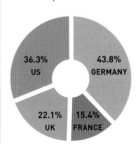

Industrial unemployment
German industrial workers had the worst unemployment rate at the peak of the depression, closely followed by the US.

In Ireland, **Éamon de Valera (1882–1975)** became president after an election victory for his Fianna Fàil party in March. As a republican who had taken part in the Easter Rising (see 1916) and had led the Irish Republican Army (IRA) in the Irish Civil War (see 1922), De Valera was renowned for his anti-British sentiments. He revoked the Oath of Allegiance to the British crown and entered into a **trade war with Britain** that damaged both countries.

In Germany, Nazi leader Adolf Hitler (1889–1945) suffered frustration in his campaign to win power through the democratic process. He stood for president in the spring elections, but was eventually beaten by the incumbent Paul von Hindenburg (1845–1934). Although in elections to the Reichstag the **Nazis were the largest single party**, they continued to be excluded from government. Ignoring the Reichstag, Hindenburg installed a conservative clique in power.

There was relief from the grim news of the Depression when American pilot Amelia Earhart (1897–1937) became the **first woman to fly solo across the Atlantic**. Taking off from Newfoundland in Canada on

the morning of May 20—the fifth anniversary of Charles Lindbergh's famous flight (see 1927)—she landed in a field in Northern Ireland 14 hours and 56 minutes later.

The US presidential election was held in November, against a background of bank failures, farm bankruptcies, and rising unemployment. Herbert Hoover's inability to halt his country's

slide into the Depression gave him little hope against the Democratic challenger, and former governor of New York, **Franklin D. Roosevelt** (see 1933). During his campaign, Roosevelt promised "a new deal for the American people." He won with 57.4 percent of the popular vote, but what Roosevelt actually intended to do about the Depression remained unclear.

THE BONUS ARMY

In summer 1932, more than 20,000 unemployed World War I veterans gathered in Washington, D.C., to demand payment of a "bonus" promised by the government in recognition of their military service. They established a shanty town within sight of the Capitol and vowed to stay until the money was paid. Their protest attracted widespread sympathy from Americans distressed at mass unemployment, but President Hoover refused to pay out. On July 28, infantry, cavalry, and tanks were deployed to attack the protesters' camp and disband the Bonus Army.

Pie chart data:
- 43.8% GERMANY
- 36.3% US
- 22.1% UK
- 15.4% FRANCE

Timeline

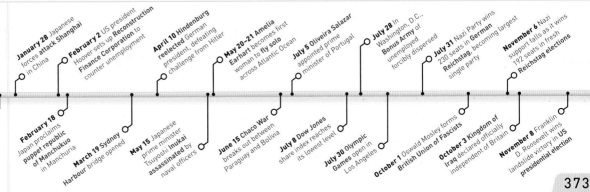

November 7 Japanese Chinese Soviet Republic proclaimed by First All-China Soviet Congress

December 10 Alcalá-Zamora becomes president of Spanish Republic

December 31 Statute of Westminster creates British Commonwealth of Nations

January 28 Japanese forces attack Shanghai in China

February 2 US president Hoover sets up Reconstruction Finance Corporation to counter unemployment

February 18 Japan proclaims **puppet republic of Manchukuo** in Manchuria

March 19 Sydney Harbour bridge opened

April 10 Hindenburg reelected German president, defeating challenge from Hitler

May 15 Japanese prime minister Tsuyoshi Inukai **assassinated** by naval officers

May 20–21 Amelia Earhart becomes first woman to fly solo across Atlantic Ocean

June 15 Chaco War breaks out between Paraguay and Bolivia

July 5 Oliveira Salazar appointed prime minister of Portugal

July 8 Dow Jones share index reaches its lowest level

July 28 In Washington, D.C., **Bonus Army** of unemployed forcibly dispersed

July 30 Olympic Games open in Los Angeles

July 31 Nazi Party wins 230 seats in German Reichstag, becoming largest single party

October 1 Oswald Mosley forms **British Union of Fascists**

October 3 Kingdom of Iraq declared officially independent of Britain

November 6 Nazi support falls as it wins 192 seats in fresh Reichstag elections

November 8 Franklin D. Roosevelt wins landslide victory in US presidential election

THE STORY OF
COMMUNICATION

ELECTRICITY TRIGGERS A REVOLUTION IN BROADCASTING AND PERSONAL COMMUNICATION

Instant worldwide communication has become a defining characteristic of the modern world. Until 200 years ago, most long-distance messages could travel no faster than the horse or ship carrying them. It was the advent of electricity in the 19th century that transformed communications.

In the 18th century, the French navy developed a system for transmitting orders between ships using semaphore flags. From the 1790s, semaphore was used on land, with lines of stations relaying coded messages using large signalling devices, each visible to the next station in the chain. From the 1830s, the development of electric telegraph replaced this medium. American Samuel Morse produced a robust and practical system, a simple on-off key generating a code that was transmitted along a wire. By the 1860s, telegraph wires spanned continents, and underwater cables enabled almost instant communication across oceans.

In the late 19th and early 20th centuries, the invention of the telephone enabled electronic transmission of speech. The discovery that radio waves could transmit sound opened the new possibility of broadcasting. From the 1920s, "wireless sets," providing entertainment and news, became a common feature of households. Television, however, did not become a mass medium until the 1950s.

THE INFORMATION AGE

Several lines of development revolutionized communications after World War II, creating the "Information Age." The advent of transistors made electronic goods smaller and cheaper, and advances in rocket technology allowed satellites to be placed in space, enabling global access to communication networks. The triumph of digital technology and microprocessors from the 1980s made computers almost universal. The potential flow of information worldwide was effectively limitless.

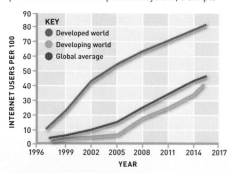

The rise of the Internet and social media
With half the world population on the internet and more than 30 percent engaging in some form of social media, both are now integral parts of our everyday lives.

KEY
- Developed world
- Developing world
- Global average

INTERNET USERS PER 100

YEAR
1996 1999 2002 2005 2008 2011 2014 2017

Long-distance call
Alexander Graham Bell initiates the first telephone link between New York and Chicago in 1892. By then, New York was already linked to Boston and Philadelphia.

receiver

Prehistory
Smoke signals
Fire allows smoke signals to be sent over considerable distances. However, this method is limited to a simple set of prearranged messages.

1st–2nd centuries
Letters by courier
Letters are written on papyrus or on wood in the Roman Empire. The Vindolanda tablets from Roman Britain include a birthday invitation.

Vindolanda tablet

1784
Mail coaches
Britain introduces four-horse coaches that are faster than passenger-carrying stagecoaches to carry post between major cities.

Morse receiver

1837
Electric telegraphy
American inventor Samuel Morse develops the electric telegraph in the US. British Railways uses an electric telegraph.

Sumerian tablet

3100–2500 BCE
Cuneiform writing
Writing is a giant step forward in communication. Mesopotamian cuneiform script is inscribed on clay tablets.

2900–2350 BCE
Carrier pigeons
Pigeons are used to carry messages in ancient Egypt and Persia. They will continue to be used by armies in World War I and World War II.

17th century
Newspapers
Newspapers, which disseminate information to a large public, develop in 17th-century Europe. The development of the printing press contributes to their growth.

The London Post

1791–95
Visual telegraphy
French inventor Claude Chappe pioneers a semaphore system that allows coded messages to be transmitted by chains of relay stations.

Chappe telegraph

ebonite earpiece

mouthpiece

> ❝ THAT'S **AN AMAZING INVENTION,** BUT WHO WOULD EVER WANT TO USE ONE OF THEM? ❞
>
> **Rutherford B. Hayes, US President,** to Alexander Graham Bell after a demonstration of the telephone, 1876

crank, which drives a dynamo to send a signal to the exchange

bell, which rings when an incoming signal is sent from the exchange

Early table telephone
Made of metal, the Ericsson table telephone dates from 1890. It combined the transmitter and receiver into a single handset. The handle cranked a generator that rang a bell at the telephone exchange to contact the operator.

1870s
The telephone
Inventors, including American Alexander Graham Bell, demonstrate early telephones in the US. The first telephone exchanges in North America and Europe date from 1878.

1920s
Airmail
The carrying of mail by aircraft, initiated on a small scale before World War I, becomes important, transforming delivery times on long-distance routes.

Apple iPhone

Early 21st century
Mobile communication
Mobile phone usage becomes a mass phenomenon in the first decade of the 21st century.

Penny Black

1837–40
Postage stamp
Britain introduces a low, uniform rate for postage, paid by buying an adhesive stamp.

1850s–60s
Transatlantic cable
Telegraph cables laid across the Atlantic seabed allow messages to be exchanged between Europe and North America in minutes.

Early 1900s
Radio
Wireless telegraphy and sound transmission developed, leading to radio broadcasting.

Wireless

1920s–30s
Television
Transmission of moving images leads to public television broadcasting, though few people own televisions until the 1950s.

1960s
Communication satellites
Telstar enables the first live transatlantic television broadcast in 1962.

Telstar

Late 20th century
The Internet
Global computer networks create instant communication through email.

375

> ## " ... THROUGH GOD'S POWERFUL AID, WE HAVE BECOME ONCE MORE TRUE GERMANS. "
>
> Adolf Hitler, German chancellor, 1933

Adolf Hitler being greeted by his followers at the annual Nazi Party rally at Nuremberg in September 1933—it was a celebration of his rise to power.

IN GERMANY, AT THE END OF JANUARY, after backroom negotiations with the conservative clique of politicians and army officers surrounding the president Paul von Hindenburg (1847–1934), Nazi leader **Adolf Hitler (1889–1945)** was invited to become **Chancellor** (head of government). The conservatives believed they would have Hitler under their control, since only three members of the coalition government were Nazis. Hitler, however, celebrated his appointment as if it was a revolutionary **seizure of power**.

On February 28, the **Reichstag building in Berlin burned down**. The fire was blamed on a Dutch communist named Marinus van der Lubbe. It provided a pretext for an **Emergency Decree** that gave the government and its police almost limitless powers. The Nazis fell short of a majority in elections five days later, but on March 23, with the support of the Nationalist and Catholic parties, Hitler won a parliamentary vote for an **Enabling Act** that **transferred all authority** from the Reichstag to his government. The German parliament had voted for its own destruction; Hitler soon banned all other political parties, and created a **single-party state**.

The consequence of Nazi rule soon became evident. The first improvised **concentration**

Reichstag fire
A Dutch communist was executed for causing the fire at the Reichstag building, but the view persists that the Nazis were responsible.

Jewish boycott
A Nazi Stormtrooper, accompanied by an elite Schutzstaffeln (SS) soldier, posts a notice on a Jewish shop window—"Don't buy from Jews!."

camps opened in March; in April a one-day nationwide **boycott of Jewish businesses** was enforced; and in May the German Student Association organized the **burning of books** described as "un-German." These highly publicized acts were just the beginning. As the protection of the law was withdrawn from communists, socialists, and Jews, hundreds of **opponents** of the regime were **murdered** and thousands tortured and beaten.

Nazi violence troubled many Germans, but support for the regime was guaranteed by a sharp turnaround in the economy and the rapid disappearance of mass unemployment. This was

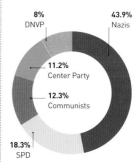

- **43.9%** Nazis
- **8%** DNVP
- **11.2%** Center Party
- **12.3%** Communists
- **18.3%** SPD

German election results
The Reichstag election of March 1933 showed stubborn support for the communists and the socialist SPD despite intimidation.

partly achieved through ambitious public works programs, most prominently the building of a network of autobahns (highways), that provided employment. There was also a **restoration of confidence**, through the Nazis' projected image of Germany as united, powerful, and dynamic.

The US also found a strong, new leader in the person of President **Franklin D. Roosevelt** (see panel right). In his inauguration speech on March 4, Roosevelt told Americans that "the only thing we have to fear is fear itself." He immediately applied this principle to the tottering US banking system. **On March 6 every bank in the US was closed.** The president announced that banks would not reopen until the federal authorities had established they

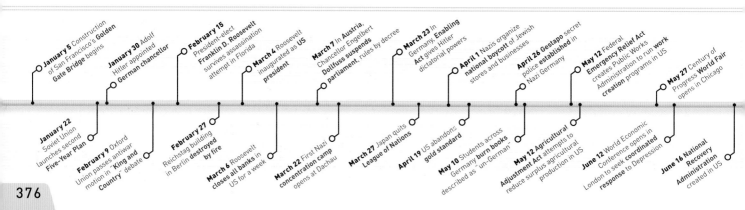

January 5 Construction of San Francisco's **Golden Gate Bridge** begins

January 30 Adolf Hitler appointed **German chancellor**

February 15 President-elect **Franklin D. Roosevelt** survives assassination attempt in Florida

March 4 Roosevelt inaugurated as **US president**

March 7 In Austria, Chancellor Engelbert **Dollfuss suspends** parliament, rules by decree

March 23 In Germany, **Enabling Act** gives Hitler dictatorial powers

April 1 Nazis organize **national boycott** of Jewish stores and businesses

April 26 Gestapo secret police **established** in Nazi Germany

May 12 Federal **Emergency Relief Act** creates Public Works Administration to run **work creation** programs in US

May 27 Century of Progress **World Fair** opens in Chicago

January 22 Soviet Union launches second **Five-Year Plan**

February 9 Oxford Union passes antiwar motion in "**King and Country**" debate

February 27 Reichstag building in Berlin **destroyed by fire**

March 6 Roosevelt **closes all banks** in US for a week

March 22 First Nazi **concentration camp** opens at Dachau

March 27 Japan quits **League of Nations**

April 19 US abandons **gold standard**

May 10 Students across Germany **burn books** described as "un-German"

May 12 Agricultural Adjustment Act attempts to reduce surplus agricultural production in US

June 12 World Economic Conference opens in London to seek **coordinated response** to Depression

June 16 National Recovery Administration created in US

" I PLEDGE MYSELF TO A NEW DEAL FOR THE AMERICAN PEOPLE. "

Franklin D. Roosevelt, at his nomination acceptance speech, 1932

Young women in Florida having their backs decorated with the Blue Eagle of the National Recovery Administration, a major plank of Roosevelt's New Deal.

were solvent. Americans accepted Roosevelt's assurance that the banks were now safe and came forward to deposit their savings —a confidence trick that worked.

Through the frenetic first 100 days of his administration, Roosevelt pushed through a raft of legislation to fulfil his promise of a **"New Deal."** The measures were neither entirely coherent nor uniformly successful. The wages of federal employees were cut. Farmers were paid to leave land fallow and slaughter animals, to raise farm prices. The **National Recovery Administration** pressured businesses to raise wages and prices, to increase profitability and consumer demand. The Tennessee Valley Authority brought electricity and modernization to one of the most economically backward regions in the US. Most popular were

direct work creation programs such as those organized by the **Civil Works Administration**. These ranged from important construction projects to "boondoggles"—futile jobs to keep men employed.

Above all, Roosevelt's personal leadership had a dramatic effect on American morale. His warm-hearted radio broadcasts, known as **"fireside chats,"** convinced many Americans that they truly had a friend in the White House.

The British, meanwhile, were desperate to restore international free trade, and to end the slide toward protectionism and devalued currencies. When a **World Economic Conference** assembled in London, however, Roosevelt insisted on the right of the US to manipulate its own exchange rate and to deploy tariffs in its national interest.

4.4 YEARS
THE AVERAGE LIFE EXPECTANCY OF A MALE CHILD BORN IN UKRAINE IN 1933

The conference failed and, in the absence of international cooperation, all the countries that attended continued to pursue aggressive nationalist policies, blocking the overall recovery of the world economy.

While capitalist countries struggled with the Depression, the communist **Soviet Union** seemed immune to such problems. Hidden from the outside world, its people suffered a different catastrophe. While Soviet propaganda celebrated rising output, in 1932–33 **famine gripped the Ukraine** and other grain-producing areas, killing millions of the rural population. It mainly came about as the result of the collectivization of agriculture (see 1930). But the scale of the disaster was vastly increased by Stalin's insistence

on forcibly extracting grain from starving rural areas to feed cities.

At a time of widespread distress and upheaval, it was perhaps ironic that the **Chicago World's Fair**, opening in May, celebrated a "Century of Progress." The American public loved the fair's celebration of the onward march of technology, but not everything was devoted to "progress." The burlesque dancer Sally Rand was a major hit with her "fan dance," so too was the arrival of 24 Italian flying boats commanded by marshal of the Italian Air Force Italo Balbo, and a visit from the German airship *Graf Zeppelin*.

The Chicago Fair's emphasis on achievements in the air was timely, for this was the year in which the technology of **air travel** reached a critical turning point. The introduction of the all-metal, streamlined, monoplane **Boeing 247** airliner, which was capable of cruising at over 150 mph (241 kph), transformed journey times. The 247 could carry 10 passengers coast-to-coast across the US in just 20 hours. The Douglas Aircraft Company responded with the **DC-1** and **DC-2**, which shaved a further two hours off a transcontinental scheduled flight. Air travel was still expensive though and remained a form of transport used only by the well off.

World's Fair program
The 1933 Chicago World's Fair, staged on the shore of Lake Michigan, took the theme of science, technology, and industry.

A **strange incident** occurred in January 1933. The game of **cricket**, the playing of which was one of the ritual bonds holding together the British Commonwealth, **led to a diplomatic crisis**. The English team touring **Australia** adopted intimidating "bodyline" tactics, its fast bowler Harold Larwood aiming deliveries at the Australian batsmen's chests and heads. After two Australian players were injured at Adelaide, Australian protests went to government level. Intervention by the **British foreign office**, eager to maintain good relations with an assertive Commonwealth state, ensured that the unapologetic Larwood never played Australia again.

FRANKLIN D. ROOSEVELT (1882–1945)

Franklin Delano Roosevelt entered politics as a Democrat before World War I. As governor of New York from 1928 he led efforts to provide relief for the unemployed. Elected president four times, from his first presidential campaign in 1932 he transformed American politics by attracting the votes of labor unions, ethnic minorities, and African-Americans. His New Deal policies won him enduring popularity, reinforced by his leadership during World War II.

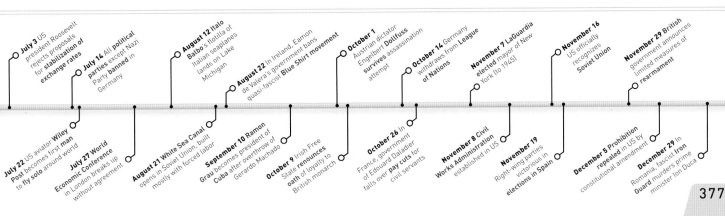

July 3 US president Roosevelt rejects proposals for **stabilization of exchange rates**

July 14 All **political parties banned** in Germany except Nazi Party

July 22 US aviator Wiley Post becomes first man to fly solo around world

July 27 World Economic Conference in London breaks up without agreement

August 12 Italo Balbo's flotilla of Italian seaplanes lands on Lake Michigan

August 21 White Sea Canal opens in Soviet Union, built mostly with forced labor

August 22 In Ireland, Eamon de Valera's government bans quasi-fascist **Blue Shirt movement**

September 10 Ramon Grau becomes president of **Cuba** after overthrow of Gerardo Machado

October 1 Austrian dictator Engelbert Dollfuss **survives assassination** attempt

October 9 Irish Free State **renounces oath of loyalty to** British monarch

October 14 Germany withdraws from **League of Nations**

October 26 In France, government of Edouard Daladier falls over **pay cuts** for civil servants

November 7 LaGuardia **elected mayor of New** York (to 1945)

November 8 Civil **Works Administration** established in US

November 16 US officially recognizes **Soviet Union**

November 19 Right-wing parties victorious in **elections in Spain**

November 29 British government announces limited measures of **rearmament**

December 5 Prohibition **repealed in US** by constitutional amendment

December 29 In Romania, fascist Iron Guard murders prime minister Ion Duca

> **VERY FEW** OF THESE **PANIC-MONGERS HAVE** ANY PERSONAL KNOWLEDGE OF THE **COUNTRIES** THAT ARE ALREADY **UNDER BLACKSHIRT GOVERNMENT.**

Lord Rothermere, *Daily Mirror*, January 22, 1934

Black-shirted paramilitaries of Oswald Mosley's British Union of Fascists give the Nazi salute. Mosley was inspired by the example of Mussolini and Hitler.

Ethiopian tribal warriors gather to fight for their emperor, Haile Selassie.

IN A YEAR DOMINATED BY POLITICAL VIOLENCE and assassinations, the **French Third Republic** was rocked by the **Stavisky affair**. A crooked financier, Alexandre Stavisky committed suicide on January 8, after the collapse of a dishonest investment scheme. The right-wing press accused leading French politicians of profiting from Stavisky's fraudulent deals. On February 6, various nationalist and anti-Semitic groups assembled in Paris, intending to march on the Chamber of Deputies and overthrow the allegedly corrupt Republic. In a night of **street fighting** between thousands of demonstrators and police, 15 people were killed and many more injured. The attempt to force the government to resign failed, and the **Republic survived**.

In the US, the public was distracted from the woes of the **Depression** by the exploits and violent deaths of outlaws and gangsters. **Bonnie Parker** and **Clyde Barrow** led a gang that robbed banks, stores, and gas stations, roving from Texas to Minnesota. Their shoot-outs with police and narrow escapes were reported with feverish excitement in the press. Parker and Barrow were finally **ambushed and shot dead** by police at Bienville Parish, Louisiana, on May 23, 1934, sealing the legend of "Bonnie and Clyde." Another "most wanted" criminal was the

Bonnie and Clyde
American outlaw Bonnie Parker playfully targets her partner-in-crime Clyde Barrow. This photo was on a reel of film found by police in 1933.

gangster **John Dillinger**. Arrested in January, he escaped from custody, but was tracked down by federal investigation chief J. Edgar Hoover. On July 22, Dillinger was gunned down by federal agents as he left the Biograph Theater, a movie house in Chicago.

Another man to die by the bullet in 1934 was **Sergei Kirov**, the Communist Party boss in Leningrad and a close associate of Soviet dictator **Joseph Stalin**. On December 1, a man walked up behind Kirov in a corridor outside his office and shot him in the back of the neck. The **assassination** was blamed on Leonid Nikolaev, an expelled party member with a grudge, but suspicions persist that Stalin may have arranged the assassination himself. Whatever the truth, the Soviet dictator used Kirov's death to pass a **new antiterrorist law**, which was later used to justify the **arrest and execution** of thousands of people.

In Germany, on June 30–July 1, Adolf Hitler confirmed his hold on power by a massacre, known as the **Night of the Long Knives**. The main target of the killings was the leadership of the SA (Sturmabteilung or Stormtroopers). These paramilitaries had provided the muscle for Hitler's rise to power, but now the disorderly street-fighters had become an embarrassment. SA chief **Ernst Röhm** was one of the hundreds that were killed. He was **arrested** early on the morning of July 1 by Hitler, who was accompanied by SS guards. Röhm was asked to

kill himself, but refused and was **shot in his cell** by two SS officers. As well as the SA leadership, scores of individuals who had criticized the Nazi regime were also murdered, including former chancellor Kurt von Schleicher.

In **Austria**, a Nazi attempt to seize power failed. The Austrian chancellor **Engelbert Dollfuss** had established an authoritarian single-party state. In February, Dollfuss suppressed a left-wing uprising in Vienna, using artillery against the socialists' stronghold in the Karl Marx Hof housing estate. He also banned the Austrian Nazi Party. In July, the Nazis attempted an armed coup, probably intending to achieve the unification of Austria with Nazi Germany. Although Dollfuss was killed, the coup failed. **Kurt Schuschnigg**, a member of Dollfuss's party, succeeded him as chancellor.

Fascism was on the rise even in Britain. Former Labour minister Oswald Mosley had founded the **British Union of Fascists** (BUF) in 1932, hoping to turn Britain into an authoritarian state under his rule. In June 1934, Mosley staged a rally at Olympia in London that degenerated into a brawl as BUF paramilitaries fought with anti-fascist protestors. Such political violence had little appeal for the British, who were also alienated by the fascists' links with the Nazis—Hitler was a guest at Mosley's wedding. Although it enjoyed the backing of some national newspapers, the BUF remained a minority party without significant electoral support.

THROUGH THE FIRST HALF OF THE 1930S, parts of the US and Canada were swept by giant dust storms as topsoil blew off land ruined by a combination of persistent drought and intensive farming. The worst of these "black blizzards" occurred in April 1935, affecting a vast area of the plains of Kansas, Oklahoma, Texas, New Mexico, and Colorado. The **Dust Bowl** created by this

850 MILLION TONS

THE ESTIMATED **AMOUNT OF TOPSOIL BLOWN OFF** THE **SOUTHERN PLAINS** OF THE **US BY DECEMBER 1935**

ecological disaster could no longer support small farmers, who were forced to migrate in their thousands. Many of them found their way to migrant camps in California, where they were exploited as seasonal labor.

Meanwhile, President Roosevelt's administration was pressing ahead with a raft of reforms often referred to as the **Second New Deal**. These policies were more radical than

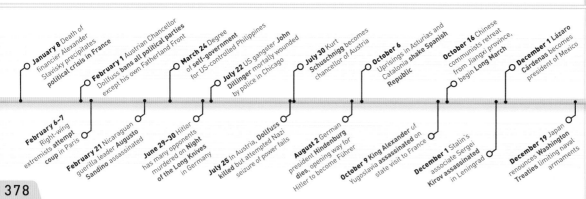

January 8 Death of financier Alexander Stavisky precipitates **political crisis in France**

February 1 Austrian Chancellor Dollfuss **bans all political parties** except his own Fatherland Front

March 24 Degree of self-government for US-controlled Philippines

July 22 US gangster **John Dillinger** mortally wounded by police in Chicago

July 30 Kurt **Schuschnigg** becomes chancellor of Austria

October 6 Uprisings in Asturias and Catalonia shake **Spanish Republic**

October 16 Chinese communists retreat from Jiangxi province, begin **Long March**

December 1 Lázaro Cárdenas becomes president of Mexico

January 17 Leading Soviet communists, including Kamenev and Zinoviev, **convicted** of complicity in Kirov's murder

February 6-7 Right-wing extremists attempt **coup** in Paris

February 21 Nicaraguan guerilla leader Augusto **Sandino assassinated**

June 29-30 Hitler has many opponents murdered on **Night of the Long Knives** in Germany

July 25 In Austria, Dollfuss **killed** but attempted Nazi seizure of power fails

August 2 German president Hindenburg **dies**, opening way for Hitler to become Führer

October 9 King Alexander of Yugoslavia **assassinated** on state visit to France

December 1 Stalin's associate Sergei **Kirov assassinated** in Leningrad

December 19 Japan renounces Washington Treaties limiting naval armaments

January 13 Saarland chooses to become part of Germany

March 16 Hitler introduces conscription in Germany in open defiance of **Versailles Treaty**

BENITO MUSSOLINI (1883–1945)

Benito Mussolini imposed his authoritarian, militaristic rule on Italy from 1922 to 1943. His Fascist state was widely admired, but dreams of conquest led to military adventures and an alliance with Nazi Germany. Unwisely leading his country into World War II, he was deposed as the Allies invaded Italy in 1943 and eventually killed by partisans.

Roosevelt's original New Deal (see 1933), favoring labor unions over big business and the poor over the rich. The **Wagner Labor Relations Act** placed the government on the side of workers who went on strike to gain union rights. The **Social Security Act** provided federal pensions for the elderly and subsidies for state-run unemployment and sickness benefit schemes. Such measures, financed by higher taxes on the rich, were denounced as socialist by most US newspapers and their millionaire owners, but **confirmed Roosevelt's popularity** with the bulk of the American people.

In the **civil war** raging in **China**, communist guerrillas escaped destruction by the forces of Chiang Kai-shek's Nationalist government through a series of **strategic withdrawals** to remote areas of the north and west. During the **Long March** from Jiangxi to Shaanxi, a journey of around 6,200 miles (10,000 km),

Mao Zedong asserted himself as the foremost communist leader. In December 1935, Mao declared that the Long March had been "a manifesto, a propaganda force... proclaiming to the world that the

Long March survivors
Chinese communists of the First Front Army arrive at Yan'an in Shaanxi province at the end of the strategic retreat known as the Long March.

Red Army is an army of heroes." But for the time being these "heroes" remained hunted rebels.

In Germany, Hitler's Nazi regime formalized its anti-Semitism through the **Nuremberg Laws** in September. Jews were deprived of German citizenship and, by the **Law for the Protection of German Blood and German Honor**, marriage and extramarital sexual relations between Jews and non-Jews were banned. A problem in the application of **anti-Semitic legislation** was identifying to whom it applied, since Jewish Germans had been intermarrying with non-Jewish Germans for generations. The Nuremberg Laws formally defined a Jew as a person with three or four Jewish grandparents.

Worried by Hitler's plans to expand German forces, Britain and France sought to enrol Italian Fascist dictator **Benito Mussolini** as an ally against Germany. This policy was wrecked by Mussolini's imperialist ambitions in Africa. In October, troops from Italy's east African colonies, Eritrea and Italian Somaliland, **invaded** the independent African state of **Ethiopia**. Ethiopian Emperor **Haile Selassie** was able to raise a large army, and although his forces were poorly equipped, they put up stout resistance. Ethiopia was a member-state of the League of Nations (see 1919). The League denounced Italy as an aggressor and called for economic sanctions. The British and French governments concocted a peace plan that would have given

Luxury liner
The Normandie was the largest, fastest, and most luxurious of the liners plying the Atlantic. Its interior was a riot of Art Deco features.

Mussolini a large chunk of Ethiopian territory. When news of the deal leaked out, public opinion in the democracies was outraged. British foreign secretary Samuel **Hoare** and French prime minister Pierre **Laval** were forced to resign, economic sanctions against Italy went ahead, and **Mussolini** was **pushed into the arms of Hitler**.

Despite the continuing effects of the economic Depression and the world's grave political problems, there were many **signs of technological progress**. The Hoover Dam was the most spectacular of a series of dam projects that would provide electric power and irrigation for large areas of the US. For those who could afford it, **luxury travel**—stylish ocean liners and intercontinental air travel—**flourished**. For the masses who could not afford this kind of luxury, there was always the cinema. The movie *Top Hat* marked the peak of the Hollywood musical, Fred Astaire and Ginger Rogers transporting viewers into a magical world of wealth and glamour.

slanted bow and slim hull increased ship's speed

April 14 France, Britain, and Italy agree **common policy** against Germany at **Stresa Conference**

May 27 **Setback for New Deal** as US Supreme Court rules National Recovery Administration unconstitutional

June 18 In Anglo-German naval agreement, Britain implicitly accepts German **rearmament**

September 3 British driver Malcolm Campbell sets new **land speed record** of 301 mph (484 kph)

September 15 Nazis introduce anti-Semitic **Nuremberg Laws**

October 2 Italian troops **invade Ethiopia**

October 23 **Mackenzie King** returns to power as Canadian prime minister

December 9 In Hoare–Laval **Pact**, Britain and France agree to offer deal to Italy on Ethiopia

May 6 **Works Progress Administration** founded in US to provide employment

May 29 Luxury ocean liner *Normandie* embarks on its **maiden voyage**

July 5 In US, **Wagner Act** becomes law, protecting rights of **trade unions**

August 14 **Social Security Act** gives Americans old age pensions and other benefits

September 8 Huey Long, controversial governor of Louisiana, is **shot**; dies two days later

September 30 **Hoover Dam** dedicated

October 20 Long **March** of Chinese communists from Jiangxi to Shaanxi **completed**

November 30 Greece becomes monarchy again, George II returning from exile

December 18 Hoare **forced to resign** as British Foreign Secretary; replaced by Anthony Eden

22 THOUSAND THE NUMBER OF GERMAN TROOPS THAT MARCHED INTO RHINELAND

German troops march across a bridge into the demilitarized Rhineland. Hitler feared a military response by the Western democracies that never came.

EUROPE HAD BEGUN TO SLIDE inexorably down the slope toward a **major war**. On March 7, Hitler sent troops into the Rhineland, a part of Germany that had been demilitarized under the terms of the Locarno Pact (see 1925). The operation was perfectly stage-managed, the marching soldiers greeted by cheering crowds and women throwing flowers. However, behind the scenes Hitler and his generals were racked by nervous tension. **German rearmament** was still in its early stages and the German army could not have resisted if France had opted for a military response, but strong public opinion and domestic issues inhibited a stronger stand. By doing nothing, the Western allies showed they would not act to uphold international agreements.

The **British and French** nonetheless embarked on **expansion of their armed forces** in response to developments in Germany. In Britain, Conservative leader Stanley Baldwin had won a general election in 1935 partly due to his promise to limit rearmament. Despite having a mandate for military expansion, Baldwin continued to proceed cautiously.

The main focus was on achieving an effective defense of Britain against attack by the **German Luftwaffe** (air force). Two days before Hitler's occupation of the Rhineland, a new fighter aircraft, the **Supermarine Spitfire**, made its maiden flight. RAF Fighter Command was created on May 1, responsible for air defense. It was

to be equipped with the Spitfire and the Hawker Hurricane, also then under development.

The importance of air power was demonstrated in the **conquest of Ethiopia** by Fascist Italy (see 1935). Italian aircraft were used to deliver poison gas onto Ethiopian troops, contributing to the defeat of Emperor Haile Selassie and the

EL PARTIDO UNICO DEL PROLETARIADO
APLASTARA *al* FASCISMO

occupation of Addis Ababa in May. **Selassie fled to exile** in Britain. The following month he made a memorable speech at the League of Nations, ending with the ominous prophecy: "It is us today; it will be you tomorrow."

Confronted with the successes of Fascism and Naziism, the Soviet-controlled **Comintern**

Workers unite
Armed workers trample on Nazi and Fascist symbols in this Spanish Civil War poster. Communists were initially a minority in the Republican camp.

(Communist International) had decided that communist parties should seek to form "**Popular Front**" alliances with social democrat and center parties. This policy bore fruit in France in May, when the Popular Front, led by socialist **Léon Blum**, won a large majority in parliamentary elections. At the same time, a workers' strike had led to the occupation of factories and department stores across France. Blum's first act as prime minister was to settle the strike by negotiating the **Matignon agreements**, which gave workers improved conditions including a 40-hour week and paid vacations. Struggling to maintain the support of communists on one side and centrist radicals on the other, however, the Blum government was soon bogged down in economic problems and the diplomatic dilemma posed by the outbreak of civil war in Spain.

A Popular Front of communists, socialists, republicans, and

The Spanish Civil War
Crossing from Spanish Morocco, Nationalist troops advanced north. The Republicans held on to Madrid in desperate fighting.

KEY
- Republican zone
- Nationalist gains
- Initial Nationalist zone

anarchists won **Spanish elections** in February. The Popular Front government promised sweeping land reforms and autonomy for **Catalonia**, but events soon ran out of their control, with peasants seizing large estates and anti-clerical attacks on convents and churches. On July 13, José Calvo Sotelo, a leading anti-Popular Front politician, was murdered by socialist militants. Four days later, **Nationalist army** officers based in Spanish Morocco launched a **military uprising**. Resisted by hastily armed socialist and anarchist militias, and a significant proportion of the Spanish armed forces, the revolt failed across much of Spain—Madrid, the Basque country, and Catalonia remained in Republican hands. When German and Italian aircraft began to ferry General Francisco Franco's **Army of Africa** from Morocco into southern Spain, the military revolt turned into civil war.

At first, a rapid Nationalist victory appeared probable. While Germany and Italy provided men, tanks, and aircraft to support the

Map of Spain showing: Bay of Biscay, FRANCE, Oviedo, Bilbao, Barcelona, Salamanca, Madrid, PORTUGAL, SPAIN, Valencia, Badajoz, ATLANTIC OCEAN, Seville, Granada, Mediterranean Sea, SPANISH MOROCCO, ALGERIA

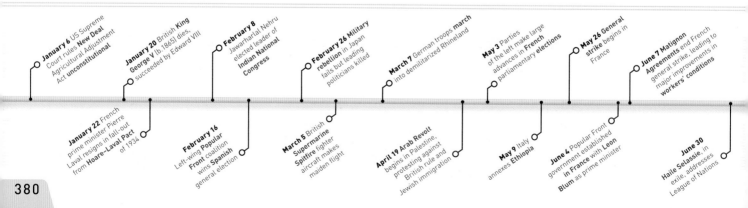

Timeline:

January 6 US Supreme Court rules **New Deal** Agricultural Adjustment Act **unconstitutional**

January 22 French prime minister Pierre Laval resigns in fall-out from **Hoare–Laval Pact** of 1934

January 20 British **King George V** (b.1865) dies; succeeded by Edward VIII

February 16 Left-wing **Popular Front** coalition wins **Spanish** general election

February 8 Jawaharlal Nehru elected leader of **Indian National Congress**

February 26 Military rebellion in Japan fails but leading politicians killed

March 5 British **Supermarine Spitfire** fighter aircraft makes maiden flight

March 7 German troops **march** into demilitarized Rhineland

April 19 Arab Revolt begins in Palestine, protesting against British rule and Jewish immigration

May 3 Parties of the left make large advances in **French parliamentary elections**

May 9 Italy annexes **Ethiopia**

May 26 General strike begins in France

June 4 Popular Front government established **in France** with **Leon Blum** as prime minister

June 7 Matignon Agreements end French general strike, leading to major improvements in **workers' conditions**

June 30 Haile Selassie, in exile, addresses League of Nations

> ## "IF YOU DON'T TRY TO WIN YOU MIGHT AS WELL HOLD THE OLYMPICS IN SOMEBODY'S BACKYARD. "

Jesse Owens, US athlete, at the Olympic Games, 1936

US athlete Jesse Owens stands on the podium after winning the long jump at the Berlin Olympics. German silver medal winner Luz Long gives the Nazi salute.

rebels, France and Britain adopted a neutral stance, leaving only the Soviet Union to back the Republic. Franco's Army of Africa advanced inexorably on Madrid, carrying out massacres along the way.

Meanwhile, Comintern was recruiting volunteers from many European countries and North America to fight in Spain. The first of these **International Brigades**

GENERAL FRANCISCO FRANCO (1892–1975)

Franco was a career officer who commanded the Spanish Foreign Legion in Morocco in the 1920s. A Catholic monarchist, he joined the military uprising against the Republic in July 1936 and was recognized as sole leader of the Nationalist rebels in September. After victory in the Civil War in 1939 he imposed a harsh dictatorship. He kept Spain neutral in World War II and remained in power until his death in 1975.

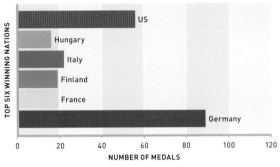

1936 Olympic Games medal tally
The most successful countries in the 1936 Berlin summer Olympics were Germany and the US. The Soviet Union and Spain were among countries that did not take part.

played a vital role in the defense of Madrid in November. The Nationalist advance was halted and Madrid remained Republican.

In the highly charged political atmosphere of 1936, the holding of the summer **Olympic Games** in **Berlin**—agreed to before the Nazis came to power—was inevitably a propaganda coup for Hitler. He seized the opportunity to present the Third Reich in a favorable light. The Olympics were staged on an unprecedentedly lavish scale with impeccable efficiency. Germany topped the medal table, but black American athlete **Jesse Owens** attracted the most attention by winning four gold medals in sprint events and the long jump. Hitler was accused of snubbing Owens because his success ran counter to Nazi theories of Aryan racial superiority. Owens himself felt more insulted by the lack of

congratulations from Roosevelt.

The Berlin Olympics were the occasion for the **first live TV broadcasts.** Seventy hours of fuzzy black-and-white coverage were shown in special viewing rooms around the city, as well as picked up by a handful of private TV sets. Later in the year, the BBC began the first regular high-definition television service, broadcast from Alexandra Palace in London.

In the fall, two events took place that would enter Britain's political mythology. The **Jarrow Crusade** was a march by 200 cloth-capped jobless workers from a Depression-blighted shipbuilding town on the Tyne River. Jarrow had 70 percent unemployment. The workers sought to publicize its plight by presenting a petition to parliament in Westminster. Their 280-mile (450-km) journey took almost a month, attracting

sympathetic coverage in the press. Its effect was zero, but it became for the British a symbol of the era of mass unemployment.

On October 4, the black-shirted **British Union of Fascists** (BUF) staged a march through a predominantly Jewish area of London's East End. There they clashed with antifascists in what became known as the **Battle of Cable Street**. The march was abandoned. This humiliation for the BUF was followed by a government ban on political uniforms. British fascism never regained its momentum.

In the US, **Roosevelt** (see 1933)

Marconiphone television receiver
Early televisions like this one made by Marconi were luxury products—the Marconiphone sold in Britain for 60 guineas, equivalent to about $4,500 (£3,000) today.

325
THE NUMBER OF **DAYS EDWARD VIII REIGNED** AS KING BEFORE HE ABDICATED

won a landslide victory in the presidential elections in November, securing a second term and confirming the popularity of his New Deal policies.

Three weeks after Roosevelt's reelection, a further critical step toward a new world war was taken when Germany and Japan signed the **Anti-Comintern Pact**. Explicitly an agreement to resist communist subversion, the pact was aimed against the Soviet Union. It created an ideological link between the Nazis and an increasingly militaristic Japan.

On November 16, Britain's king **Edward VIII** (1894–1972) informed Prime Minister Stanley Baldwin that he intended to marry American divorcee **Mrs. Wallis Simpson**. Political opinion was solidly behind Baldwin, who told the king that he must choose between Simpson and the throne. **Edward abdicated** and his brother, Albert, inherited the throne as George VI (1895–1952).

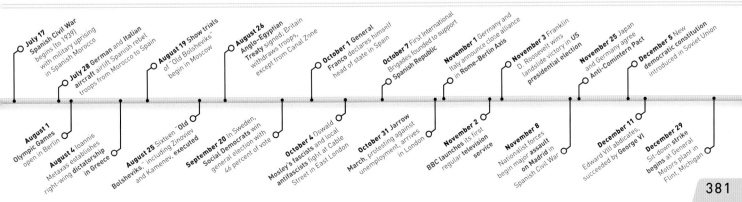

July 17 Spanish Civil War begins (to 1939) with military uprising in Spanish Morocco

July 28 German and Italian aircraft airlift Spanish rebel troops from Morocco to Spain

August 19 Show trials of "Old Bolsheviks" begin in Moscow

August 26 Anglo-Egyptian Treaty signed; Britain withdraws troops, except from Canal Zone

October 1 General Franco declares himself head of state in Spain

October 7 First International Brigades founded to support Spanish Republic

November 1 Germany and Italy announce close alliance in Rome–Berlin Axis

November 3 Franklin D. Roosevelt wins landslide victory in US presidential election

November 25 Japan and Germany agree Anti-Comintern Pact

December 5 New **constitution** democratic constitution introduced in Soviet Union

August 1 Olympic Games open in Berlin

August 4 Ioannis Metaxas establishes right-wing **dictatorship** in Greece

August 25 Sixteen "Old Bolsheviks," including Zinoviev and Kamenev, **executed**

September 20 In Sweden, Social Democrats win general election with 46 percent of vote

October 4 Oswald Mosley's fascists and local antifascists fight at Cable Street in East London

October 31 Jarrow **March**, protesting against unemployment, arrives in London

November 2 BBC launches its first regular television service

November 8 Nationalist forces begin major assault **on Madrid** in Spanish Civil War

December 11 Edward VIII abdicates, succeeded by George VI

December 29 Sit-down strike **begins** at General Motors plant in Flint, Michigan

George VI at his coronation in Westminster Abbey on May 12. He ascended the throne following the abdication of his brother, Edward VIII.

" I SEE ONE-THIRD OF A NATION ILL-HOUSED, ILL-CLAD, ILL-NOURISHED. "

Franklin D. Roosevelt, American president, in his inauguration speech, January 20, 1937

THE YEAR BEGAN WITH FRANKLIN D. ROOSEVELT starting his second term in office as US president. In his inauguration speech on January 20, Roosevelt drew attention to **persistent poverty** in America. He pledged to end this injustice, denouncing "heedless self-interest" as bad morals and bad economics. The president's **radical policies** brought him into conflict with the Supreme Court, while across the country a wave of **sit-down strikes** pitted workers against their employers. As the number of jobless more than doubled between 1936 and 1938, it was not obvious that Roosevelt's approach was working. This period was ironically dubbed "Roosevelt's Depression."

For Britain and its empire, this was a year of change. In May, the country saw a **new king crowned**, George VI (1895–1952), and a new

prime minister in Downing Street, Neville Chamberlain (1869–1940). In Ireland, a referendum in July approved a proposal for a new constitution. The **Irish Free State became Ireland** (Eire in Gaelic), and in effect a fully independent country, although officially still a dominion of the British Commonwealth. British India took another step toward self-government with implementation of the **India Act**, but the limited powers of its elected assembly fell far short of satisfying Indian nationalists. The British also failed to find a solution to the

Picasso's vision of war
In response to the German bombing of the Basque town of Guernica, Pablo Picasso painted this large mural in support of the Spanish Republicans. It was displayed at the 1937 Paris Exhibition.

problem in **Palestine**, and their proposal to split it between the Jews and Arabs was rejected by both sides.

In Spain, the ongoing civil war (see 1936) was progressing badly for the Republican Loyalists. Political divisions, with Communists determined to suppress anarchists and Trotskyists, nullified the courage and determination of their military efforts. The Nationalist rebels continued to enjoy the support of German and Italian forces, especially in the air. On April 26, the Basque town of **Guernica** became famous worldwide when, on a busy market day, it was

devastated by aircraft of the German Condor Legion. Estimates of the death toll varied from 300 to 1,700. Graphically described by journalists who visited the town in the wake of the attack, the event focused **fears about aerial bombardment**, specifically the impact of the German Luftwaffe in any future war between the major powers.

In an increasingly divided world, art and literature were becoming politicized. **Prominent writers went to Spain**, either to fight in the Civil War (mostly on the Republican side) or as war tourists and journalists. Among these were George Orwell and

W. H. Auden from Britain, Ernest Hemingway from the US, and André Malraux from France. The most famous response to the bombing of Guernica was Pablo Picasso's painting, which was first exhibited in the Spanish Republic's pavilion at the Paris International Exhibition in summer 1937.

The **Paris Exhibition** also featured grandiose Nazi German and Soviet Russian pavilions, both using monumental sculpture to trumpet the glories of their rival political systems. The Nazis also took the extraordinary decision to mount a show of the art they despised, displaying confiscated

" AT 2 A.M. TODAY WHEN I VISITED THE TOWN, THE WHOLE OF IT WAS A HORRIBLE SIGHT, FLAMING FROM END TO END. "

George Steer, British journalist, reporting the bombing of Guernica for *The Times*, April 27, 1937

January 1 Anastasio Somoza García takes power in Nicaragua

January 20 Roosevelt inaugurated for second term as US president

February 8 In Spanish Civil War, Nationalist and Italian troops take Malaga

February 8–27 International Brigades resist Spanish Nationalists in **Battle of Jarama**

February 16 DuPont Corporation patents **nylon**

February 19 Rodolfo Graziani, viceroy of Italian East Africa, survives assassination attempt in Eritrea

March 8–16 Defensive victory for Republicans at **Battle of Guadalajara** in Spanish Civil War

March 30 In US, General Motors recognizes **United Automobile Workers** union after sit-in strikes

April 26 Guernica **bombed** by German aircraft supporting Nationalists in Spain

May 3–10 Uprising against Communist-dominated Republican government **crushed** in Barcelona

May 6 Hindenburg airship **explodes** in flames on arrival in New Jersey

May 12 Coronation of **George VI** in Britain

May 25 World Exhibition begins in Paris

May 27 Golden Gate Bridge opens in San Francisco

May 28 Neville Chamberlain becomes British prime minister

May 30 Memorial Day Massacre battle between police and strikers in Chicago

June 12 Purge of Soviet armed forces begins with **shooting of eight generals**

June 19 Spanish Nationalists capture **Bilbao**

June 21 Léon Blum resigns as French prime minister

The German Zeppelin airship *Hindenburg* exploding into a fireball while docking at Lakehurst in New Jersey. The cause of the disaster remains uncertain.

paintings by modernists and Jews at a "**Degenerate Art**" exhibition in Munich, to be laughed at by the German public.

Meanwhile, under the dictatorship of Joseph Stalin (1878–1953), the Soviet Union had begun the **Great Terror**. The Soviet regime had always been ruthless toward those it defined as enemies—for example, peasants who resisted collective agriculture (see 1930)—but now the unbridled power of the secret police was turned against the leadership of the Soviet armed forces, and of the ruling party itself. The process began in 1936, with the arrest, trial, and execution

of "**Old Bolsheviks**"—men who had participated in the 1917 Revolution. While arrests of Old Bolsheviks continued through 1937, other people also came under suspicion. Between 1937 and 1939 almost half the senior army commanders were executed, imprisoned, or fired. Although the fate of the Soviet elite attracted most attention, Stalin's reign of terror spread through the entire population. At least 680,000 people were killed during the purges, and some historians believe the real figure could even be closer to 2 million.

In summer 1937, gradual **Japanese encroachment on Chinese territory** erupted into full-scale war. Japanese and Chinese forces clashed at the Marco Polo Bridge outside Beijing in July, and the following month large-scale fighting developed in Shanghai. **Chiang Kai-shek**'s Chinese Nationalist forces put up much stiffer resistance than the Japanese expected, inflicting around 50,000 casualties on the invaders, but they were forced to abandon the city. The Japanese then advanced on the Chinese Nationalist capital, **Nanking**, which they took in December. Nanking's civilian population was subjected to a brutal attack by Japanese troops, while thousands of surrendered Chinese soldiers were also killed. This massacre, witnessed by Christian missionaries and other Western

observers, shocked the public in the US and solidified the sympathy of the US government for the Chinese. US hostility to Japan's actions in China was the **first step on the path to the Pacific War** (see 1941).

Elsewhere, the year was marked by **air disasters**. German airships had begun scheduled transatlantic passenger flights. On May 6, the airship *Hindenburg*, with 97 passengers and crew on board, burst into flames as it docked at Lakehurst, New Jersey. Within seconds the fire had spread through its hydrogen-filled gasbag. Remarkably, only 35 people were killed, but the disaster brought an abrupt end to the brief era of luxury airship travel. Two months later, America's most famous woman pilot, **Amelia Earhart** (1887–1937), took off from New

sickle is the symbol of agriculture

hammer is the symbol of industry

sculpture made from stainless-steel panels

Worker and peasant
This giant sculpture, by Vera Mukhina, dominated the Soviet pavilion at the World's Fair in 1937. It is an example of Socialist Realist style.

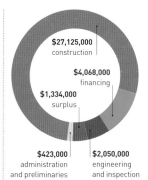

$27,125,000 construction

$4,068,000 financing

$1,334,000 surplus

$423,000 administration and preliminaries

$2,050,000 engineering and inspection

Golden Gate Bridge building costs
The original budget for building San Francisco's Golden Gate Bridge was $27 million, but the actual building costs totaled $35 million.

Guinea with co-pilot Fred Noonan for the Pacific leg of an attempted **around-the-world flight**. Their aircraft was never seen again.

Technology continued to progress throughout the year, culminating in the race for the first successful **trials of turbojet engines**, between Frank Whittle in Britain and Hans von Ohain in Germany. Whittle won, but the Germans forged ahead with development of a jet aircraft Ohain's engine powering the first jet flight in August 1939.

Another marker for progress was the opening of the **Golden Gate Bridge** in San Francisco. At 4,200 ft (1,280 m), its central span was the longest of any suspension bridge in the world, a record that stood until it was surpassed by the Verrazano-Narrows Bridge in New York in 1964.

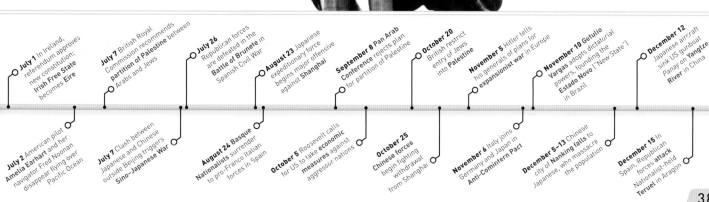

British prime minister Neville Chamberlain (right) visited Nazi Germany for the Munich Conference on September 28.

WALT DISNEY'S REWORKING OF THE FAIRY TALE OF SNOW WHITE and the Seven Dwarfs marked the transition of animated movies from cartoon shorts aimed primarily at children to a major strand in film culture. Dismissed in advance as "Disney's Folly," *Snow White* was an immediate hit, briefly holding the record for the **highest grossing movie** of all time before being overtaken by *Gone with the Wind* (see 1939). The ability of Hollywood to manufacture universally appealing, mass-market films, along with the influence of American **big-band** "swing" dance music, was laying the foundations for a US-dominated, **international popular culture**.

All was not well with the **US economy**, however. A sharp **rise**

Animated feature
Walt Disney's Snow White and the Seven Dwarfs *was the first feature-length animated movie to be released worldwide, in 1938.*

in **unemployment** in 1938 drew attention to the fact that President Roosevelt's New Deal (see 1933) had failed to solve the economic problems of the US Depression.

By comparison, although pockets of high unemployment persisted in Britain, the **British economy** was performing well in the late 1930s, with high levels of house building, burgeoning production of consumer goods—from cars to vacuum cleaners—nationwide electrification, and growth in high-tech industries such as aircraft manufacturing. A symbol of **Britain's technological success** was the performance of the streamlined A4 Pacific-class locomotive *Mallard*. On July 3 it reached 126 mph (203 kph), setting a **world speed record** for a steam engine that has never been surpassed.

The year's first major international crisis came in March, with the German **annexation of Austria**—the **Anschluss** ("unification"). Hitler had been applying mounting pressure on the government of Austrian Chancellor

Economic growth
The Soviet Union achieved high economic growth in the 1930s. Japan and Germany also recovered well from the Depression.

Kurt Schuschnigg (1897–1977) to back the Nazi movement inside Austria. When Schuschnigg attempted to hold a **referendum on Austrian independence**, Hitler forced his resignation and launched an **invasion**. German troops crossed the border unopposed; Hitler was greeted in Vienna by cheering crowds. The annexation was accompanied by widespread attacks by Nazis on Austria's large Jewish population.

Although the unification of Germany and Austria was a major **breech of the Versailles Treaty** (see 1919), Britain and France made no attempt to intervene. Instead, British prime minister **Neville Chamberlain** embarked upon an active policy of "**appeasement**," based on the

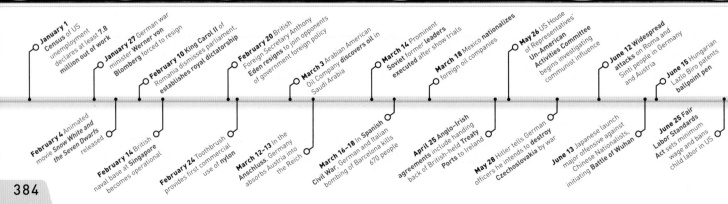

January 1 Animated movie *Snow White and the Seven Dwarfs* released

January 1 Census of US unemployment declares at least **7.8 million out of work**

January 27 German war minister Werner von Blomberg forced to resign

February 4 British naval base at Singapore becomes operational

February 10 King Carol II of Romania dismisses parliament, **establishes royal dictatorship**

February 14 British naval base at Singapore becomes operational

February 20 British Foreign Secretary Anthony Eden resigns to join opponents of government foreign policy

February 24 Toothbrush provides first commercial use of **nylon**

March 3 Arabian American Oil Company **discovers oil** in Saudi Arabia

March 12–13 In the **Anschluss**, Germany absorbs Austria into the Reich

March 14 Prominent Soviet former **leaders executed** after show trials

March 16–18 In Spanish Civil War, German and Italian bombing of Barcelona kills 670 people

March 18 Mexico **nationalizes** foreign oil companies

April 25 Anglo-Irish agreements include handing back of British-held **Treaty Ports** to Ireland

May 26 US House of Representatives **Un-American Activities Committee** begins investigating communist influence

May 28 Hitler tells German officers he intends to **destroy Czechoslovakia** by war

June 12 Widespread **attacks on Roma and Sinti people** in Germany and Austria

June 13 Japanese launch major offensive against Chinese Nationalists, initiating **Battle of Wuhan**

June 15 Hungarian Lazlo Biro patents **ballpoint pen**

June 25 Fair Labor Standards Act sets minimum wage and bans child labor in US

Arab prisoners are guarded by a British soldier in the Old City of Jerusalem, during the suppression of the revolt against Britain's rule in Palestine.

belief that a durable peace could be secured by settling Germany's "legitimate claims." Attention focused on the German minority in Czechoslovakia, concentrated in the **Sudetenland** area. Hitler stirred up unrest among the Sudeten Germans, while ordering his generals to prepare for an invasion of Czechoslovakia. The British and French governments were desperate to avoid war, but France was formally committed to defending the Czechs. In September, Chamberlain embarked on an unprecedented diplomatic initiative, flying twice to Germany for **face-to-face talks with Hitler.** Although Britain pressured the Czech government into making major concessions, this only made Hitler raise his demands.

10,000,000

THE APPROXIMATE **ADDITION TO** THE **GERMAN POPULATION** BY THE **ANNEXATIONS** OF **AUSTRIA** AND **SUDETENLAND**

War seemed inevitable, and military preparations were under way in Britain and France when, on September 28, Italian dictator **Benito Mussolini** proposed a **four-nation conference.** Hitler accepted and met the French premier Édouard Daladier (1884–1970), Chamberlain, and Mussolini at Munich. A deal was struck that preserved peace at the expense of Czechoslovakia, which had to **hand over the Sudetenland** to Germany. Chamberlain and Daladier were greeted as heroes when they returned home, the British and French people profoundly relieved to have avoided war. Conservative MP Winston Churchill (1874–1965) was among the minority who **denounced the Munich agreement**, calling it "a defeat without a war."

Post-Munich optimism only lasted until November, when **Kristallnacht** ("the Night of Broken Glass") provided graphic evidence of the extremist nature of the Nazi regime.

Night of broken glass
A shopkeeper clears up shattered glass from a looted Jewish shop in the wake of attacks on German and Austrian Jews in November.

The assassination of a German diplomat by a Jew in Paris served as a pretext for Nazi-orchestrated attacks on Jewish homes and businesses across Germany and Austria. Synagogues were burned down and sacred objects desecrated; 30,000 Jewish men were rounded up and taken to concentration camps, where beatings and torture were routine.

Those countries still committed to democracy and freedom expressed **outrage at Nazi anti-Semitism**, but they were not keen to provide a home for Jews now desperate to escape Nazi persecution. At an **international conference** on the issue held at Evian in July, the Australian representative T. W. White stated bluntly: "As we have no racial problem, we are not desirous of importing one." Britain agreed to accept a limited number of Jewish children, without their parents, and the US maintained its existing barriers to immigration. **Jews were trapped** because, although the Nazis were ready to let them leave, they had nowhere to go.

One potential destination for Jews from Europe was **Palestine**, which was recognized by the British as a site for a **Jewish homeland** (see 1917). But the British were struggling with an armed uprising by **Palestinian Arabs** who were **bitterly opposed** to the expansion of Jewish settlement. In an attempt to defuse the situation, Britain imposed tight limits on Jewish immigration.

The high pitch of anxiety in the world at the time became evident when a radio broadcast induced **mass panic** in the US. Orson Welles's radio version of the alien-invasion classic *The War of the Worlds* was broadcast by CBS at Halloween. The news bulletin format convinced millions of Americans that a genuine invasion by Martians was underway. When genuinely frightened listeners finally understood their mistake, there was widespread anger.

MALLARD

Steam record holder
Designed by Nigel Gresley, the steam locomotive Mallard *was a masterly fusion of form and function. It achieved an enduring world speed record.*

Spanish women in Madrid, celebrating the victory of Franco's Nationalists in the country's civil war. Defeated opponents of Franco faced harsh oppression.

BY 1939 MILITARY DICTATORSHIPS WERE SPREADING ACROSS EUROPE. Only a handful of countries, chiefly Britain and France, maintained a liberal democratic system. In the spring, General Francisco Franco's **Nationalists triumphed in the Spanish Civil War**, occupying the surviving Republican strongholds of Barcelona and Madrid. Tens of thousands of Franco's enemies were executed. Others fled into exile, and many were interned in camps in France. Meanwhile, Italy's dictator Benito **Mussolini** (1883–1945) had **annexed Albania**, and driven out its monarch, King Zog (1895–1961).

More threatening for the peace of Europe was German Führer Adolf Hitler's **occupation of Prague**. The Munich agreement (see 1938) had left Czechoslovakia

> ## " WHEN STARTING AND WAGING **WAR** IT IS **NOT RIGHT THAT MATTERS, BUT VICTORY.** "

Adolf Hitler, military and political leader of Germany, January 30, 1939

a defenseless state, and the Germans encouraged Slovakian nationalists, who were resentful of Czech domination, to declare independence. In March, **Hitler's troops marched unopposed into Prague**, turning the Czech lands of Bohemia and Moravia into a German "protectorate." Poland and Hungary also annexed small portions of territory, and Czechoslovakia ceased to exist as a country.

The German occupation of Prague forced the leaders of the Western democracies to acknowledge the ruthlessness of Nazi expansionism. It was obvious **Poland was to be the next target**. Believing a threat of force would deter Hitler, the British and French gave the Poles a guarantee of military support, but Hitler was not deterred. In April he began military planning for an invasion of Poland.

Desperate Jews tried to flee the expanding area coming under Nazi control, but many countries refused to let them in. Among the more fortunate were those rescued by the **Kindertransport** scheme that arranged for almost

Invasion of Poland
German forces invaded Poland from East Prussia, Germany, and Slovakia on September 1. With Nazi agreement, the Soviets occupied eastern Poland.

KEY

→ German advance/operation

→ Soviet advance

— German/Soviet demarcation line in Poland

EVACUATION OF THE CITIES

At the start of September, Britain and France began to evacuate civilians from danger areas. Expecting air attacks, the British evacuated 1.5 million children from large cities, along with mothers with babies and young children. The French carried out mass evacuations from the border provinces of Alsace and Lorraine in eastern France. Germany did not carry out mass evacuations until heavy bombing began in 1942.

10,000 unaccompanied **Jewish children** to find **refuge** in Britain. Adults were not allowed to accompany them, however, and many of the children never saw their parents again.

While all eyes were focused on Europe, the **Soviet Union was fighting an undeclared war with Japan** in Asia. Throughout the summer, clashes occurred along the border between Mongolia, a Soviet client state, and Japanese-occupied Manchuria. Soviet General Georgy Zhukov's hard-fought victory at the battle of Khalkhin Gol decided the outcome. This defeat influenced the Japanese to pursue naval-led expansion in the Pacific and Southeast Asia, rather than further land conquests in East Asia.

Anticipating a war with Germany, Britain and France unenthusiastically pursued

World War II British gas mask
All British civilians were issued gas masks for protection against poison gas air attacks. This brightly colored mask is for a child.

During the period known as the "phony war," preparations for conflict in suburban Britain often seemed bizarre, with no real enemy to fire at.

a military alliance with the Soviet Union—a country they disliked and distrusted. No one anticipated a deal between Hitler and the Soviet leader Joseph Stalin, but on August 23 the Soviet and German foreign ministers, Vyacheslav Molotov (1890–1986) and Joachim von Ribbentrop (1893–1946), signed a nonaggression treaty, known as the **Molotov–Ribbentrop Pact**, which included a secret agreement to divide Poland between them.

German forces invaded Poland on September 1. Two days later, unable to escape their commitment to the Poles, the **British and French governments declared war on Germany**. Australia, New Zealand, Canada, and South Africa followed. Britain brought India into the war without consulting its elected representatives, while **Ireland** and the **US** declared their

36
THE NUMBER OF **DAYS GERMANY** TOOK TO **OVERRUN POLAND**

Finnish Rifle
The Finnish Lahti anti-tank rifle was used against the Soviets during the Winter War, which began with the Russian invasion of Finland.

10-round magazine

cheek rest

neutrality. Much to Hitler's annoyance, Italy also declared itself neutral. The war was greeted by all countries with fear and resignation. There were no cheering crowds in Berlin, London, or Paris.

The **destruction of Poland** was achieved with breathtaking speed. German troops reached the outskirts of Warsaw within a week. The Poles fought with courage and tenacity—Germany sustained more than 40,000 casualties—but once Soviet troops moved in from the east all was lost. **Warsaw surrendered** on September 28, and the fighting stopped a week later. Dividing the country between them, the Soviets and Nazis set about imprisoning and massacring Poles in large numbers.

Throughout the autumn the Germans began confining Poland's Jews to **ghettos**, a major step toward the Holocaust (see 1942). Hitler had already signed an order in Germany at the start of the war for the killing of people with incurable mental disabilities. Over **70,000 German mental patients were murdered** by lethal injections or gassing,

before the operation was suspended in August 1941.

With Poland crushed, the Western democracies entered the period known as the "**phony war**." After the fall of Poland the British and French rejected a peace offer from Hitler, but the troops they assembled in France remained passive. The lack of military action was a relief to the British and French governments. German air attacks and massive civilian casualties had been expected, but did not occur.

The only dramatic action in Britain's war against Germany was at sea. In October, the German Navy's U-boat *U-47* penetrated the defenses of Britain's main naval base at Scapa Flow, in the Orkney Islands off

Scotland, and **sank the battleship** *Royal Oak*. British morale was raised two months later when the German battleship *Graf Spee* was driven by British cruisers to take refuge in the neutral port of Montevideo in Uruguay, where the Germans scuttled it.

At the end of November, the **Soviet Union** launched an **attack on Finland**. **The Winter War** revealed severe deficiencies in the organization, equipment, and leadership of the Soviet Red Army. By the end of the year, the Finns still held their Mannerheim Line

Movie attendance
Movies of the late 1930s achieved extraordinary ticket sales. Around 80 million movie tickets were sold in the US every week.

defenses, and the Soviets had suffered heavy losses.

Remaining neutral, the US seemed a world away from the blacked-out cities of Europe. The **New York World's Fair**, opened in April, taking "The World of Tomorrow" as its theme. Around 44 million visitors came to see such novelties as nylon stockings and color photography.

Hollywood was enjoying a **golden era**, with classic releases including *Gone With the Wind*, *The Wizard of Oz*, and *Stagecoach*. Grand picture palaces, some of which could accommodate more than 4,000 customers, were filled. The American economy was poised for a decisive upturn as an **amendment to the Neutrality Act** allowed US factories to equip the British and French war effort.

MOVIES

Star Wars 1977
The Sound of Music 1965
Bambi 1942
Gone With the Wind 1939
Snow White and the Seven Dwarfs 1937

0 100 200 300 400 500 600 700 800 900 1000
MOVIE ATTENDANCE (IN MILLIONS)

Off to see the Wizard
Judy Garland played Dorothy in the 1939 movie The Wizard of Oz—perfect fantasy entertainment for hard and dangerous times.

August 15 Premier of movie *The Wizard of Oz*

August 20 Soviets defeat Japanese at Kalkhin Gol in Mongolia

25 August IRA bomb explodes in Coventry, killing five people

September 1 Germans invade Poland, **starting World War II** in Europe (to 1945)

September 3 Britain and France declare **war on Germany**

September 17 Soviet Union invades eastern Poland

October 8 Poland partitioned between Germany and Soviet Union

October 11 Albert Einstein informs US president Roosevelt of possibility of **atom bomb**

November 4 US Neutrality Act authorizes sale of arms to combatants on cash-and-carry basis

December 15 Premier of movie *Gone With the Wind*

August 23 Molotov–Ribbentrop Pact allies Soviet Union with Nazi Germany

August 27 The Heinkel He 178 makes **first jet-powered flight**

September 16 War in Mongolia ends in victory for Soviet Red Army over Japanese

October 6 Poles **defeated** by Soviet Union and Germany

October 10 Britain rejects peace proposal from Hitler

October 14 British battleship *Royal Oak* sunk in Scapa Flow by German U-boat

November 30 Soviet Union attacks Finland, beginning **Winter War**

December 17 German pocket battleship *Graf Spee* scuttled after **Battle of River Plate** four days earlier

German expansion
Between September 1939 and August 1942 Nazi German forces conquered most of mainland Europe, seizing control of an area from Norway to Crete, and from France to the Black Sea. Britain remained free of German domination, but was subjected to air attacks. Nazi U-boats also preyed on Britain's shipping lanes.

KEY
➡ German advance
✕ Major battle
✕ Major German air attack
✕ Major Allied air attack

THE WAR IN
EUROPE
THE ALLIED BATTLE TO TURN BACK THE TIDE OF NAZI CONTROL

The German invasion of Poland in September 1939 provoked Britain and France to declare war on Germany. At first the Germans won an astonishing series of victories, but from 1942 onward they were overwhelmed by the combined strength of the US, the Soviet Union, and Britain.

After the rapid defeat of Poland in April 1940, the Germans invaded Denmark and Norway. Their devastating campaign swiftly overran the Netherlands, Belgium, and France. British Forces escaped from Europe through an evacuation from Dunkirk in France. The Luftwaffe failed to overcome the RAF in the Battle of Britain in summer 1940, but British cities were subjected to night bombing raids during the Blitz.

The entry of Italy into the war in June 1940 spread the fighting to the Mediterranean and North Africa. Needing to rescue Italian forces from defeat, the German army swept south to Crete and intervened in North Africa. Hitler's invasion of the Soviet Union in June 1941 brought German forces to the gates of Moscow and Leningrad. But the German drive eastward came to a catastrophic end at Stalingrad in late 1942.

Defeated in North Africa, the Germans then faced an Allied invasion of Italy. In summer 1944, the Allies landed in Normandy and broke out to liberate France and Belgium. A final German counterattack in the Ardennes was repulsed, and Germany was finally invaded from east and west.

US lend-lease
The US provided its Allies with vast quantities of war equipment and supplies, under the lend-lease program. Britain and the Soviet Union were the major beneficiaries.

EUROPE IN 1942 By 1942 Nazi Germany dominated mainland Europe. Its allies and satellites included Italy, Hungary, Bulgaria, Slovakia, Croatia, and Vichy France. Greater Germany expanded before and during the war to include Austria, French Alsace-Lorraine, and much of Poland (which ceased to exist as a state in October 1939). Although the Nazis found some willing collaborators, their ambition to found a "New Order" in Europe eventually came to nothing.

ATLANTIC OCEAN

NORWAY · SWEDEN · FINLAND

USSR

North Sea · DENMARK · ESTONIA

IRELAND · Baltic Sea · LATVIA · Moscow ●

UNITED KINGDOM · NETHERLANDS · EAST PRUSSIA · LITHUANIA

London · Hamburg · ✕ Minsk Jun 29–Jul 4, 1944

D-day landings Jun 6, 1944 · ✕ Arnhem Sep 17–26, 1944 · ✕ Battle of Berlin Apr 16–May 2, 1945 · ✕ Kursk Jul 5–13, 1943

BELGIUM · ✕ Dresden · ✕ Stalingrad Aug 23, 1942– Feb 2, 1943

✕ Ardennes Dec 16–Jan 25, 1945 · GERMANY · POLAND · UKRAINE · Caspian Sea

Paris · ✕ Pforzheim · SLOVAKIA

Bay of Biscay · SWITZERLAND · AUSTRIA · HUNGARY · ROMANIA

FRANCE · Budapest Dec 29–Feb 13, 1945 · Black Sea

CROATIA · SERBIA

PORTUGAL · SPAIN · Anzio Jan 22–Jun 5, 1944 · ITALY · MONTE-NEGRO · BULGARIA

Cassino Jan 17–May 18, 1944 · Rome · Salerno Sep 9, 1943 · TURKEY

MOROCCO · Messina · ALBANIA

ALGERIA · Sicily · GREECE

Mediterranean Sea

TUNISIA

LIBYA · El Alamein Oct 23–Nov 5, 1942 · EGYPT ✕

KEY
➤ Allied advance
✕ Major battle
✕ Major Allied firebomb attack

Allied offensives
The tide of war turned with the British victory at El Alamein in North Africa and the Soviet triumph at Stalingrad. Italy surrendered in 1943 after the Allies landed, and after the Normandy invasion on D-day in 1944, Germany was crushed between Soviet forces advancing from the east and the Western Allies attacking from the west.

KEY
— Frontiers 1937
···· Frontiers Nov 1942
▨ Greater German Reich
▨ German occupation
▨ Axis satellite
▨ Italy and Italian occupied territory
▨ Finnish territory
▨ Neutral
▨ Allied territory

KEY
▨ RAF
▬ USAAF

BOMBS DROPPED ON EUROPE (IN 100,000 TONS)

YEAR: 1939 1940 1941 1942 1943 1944 1945

Stategic Allied bombing in Europe
RAF Bomber Command and the US Army Air Force carried out a sustained, large-scale bombing campaign on mainland Europe. The Allies dropped 3 million tons of bombs, killing around 500,000 people. The US bombed industrial objectives by day, while the RAF attacked cities by night.

THE IRON CURTAIN
After World War II, Eastern European countries that were occupied by the Soviets were placed under communist governments. In Yugoslavia, an independent communist regime refused Soviet tutelage. The divide between communist east and capitalist west, which ran down the middle of Germany, was dubbed the Iron Curtain.

KEY
▨ Soviet territory
▨ Soviet-dominated communist states by 1949
▨ Members of NATO 1949
▨ Independent communist state
— Iron Curtain in 1949
● Cities divided into zones of occupation

Allied soldiers form lines on the beach at Dunkirk, France, awaiting boats to carry them to England. German air attacks harassed the evacuation.

United Commonwealth
A British propaganda poster shows men from the dominions and colonies united in the war effort. Even in 1940 Britain did not "stand alone," prime minister by **Paul Reynaud** (1878–1966).

ALTHOUGH BRITAIN AND FRANCE WERE AT WAR WITH GERMANY, the only fighting in Europe in early 1940 was between the **Soviet Union** and **Finland** (see 1939). The British and French governments, both strongly anticommunist, planned to send an expeditionary force to aid the Finns. Troops were assembled, but Soviet military successes led Finland to seek peace in March. In France, the failure to help the Finns led to the fall of the government of **Edouard Daladier**, who was replaced as

Also in March, Soviet dictator **Joseph Stalin** (see 1928) **approved the killing** of all Polish officers who had fallen into Soviet hands through the occupation of eastern Poland (see 1939). Most of the region's educated elite— doctors, lawyers, and teachers— were also murdered. Some 22,000 victims were buried in **mass graves** in Katyn Forest and elsewhere. In June, when the Soviet Union occupied the Baltic states—Lithuania, Latvia, and Estonia—tens of thousands more

people were executed or deported to labor camps. Stalin's reach extended as far as Mexico, where his exiled rival **Leon Trotsky** had found refuge. In August, Trotsky was killed by Ramon Mercader, an agent of Stalin's secret police.

On April 4, British prime minister **Neville Chamberlain** announced that Hitler had "missed the bus" by failing to launch a major offensive as **British rearmament accelerated**. Five days after this complacent speech, German forces **occupied Denmark** and **invaded Norway**. Britain and France sent troops and warships to aid the Norwegians but could not prevent a German victory. Norway's King Haakon VII was evacuated to Britain with his government to continue the fight from exile.

In Britain, the disastrous campaign in Norway destroyed confidence in the Chamberlain government. On May 10, **Winston Churchill** became prime minister at the head of a broad coalition.

On the same day, **German forces** invaded the **Netherlands**, **Belgium**, and **Luxembourg**. After Rotterdam was heavily bombed, the Dutch forces surrendered to avoid further destruction. Dutch Queen Wilhelmina defiantly set up a government-in-exile in London.

Allied troops in northern France advanced into Belgium to meet the German offensive. The Germans unexpectedly delivered a powerful thrust **through the Ardennes region into France** and broke through the French defenses at Sedan. Fast-moving German formations of tanks and motorized

WINSTON CHURCHILL (1874–1965)

Churchill led an adventurous life as a soldier and war correspondent before entering politics. As First Lord of the Admiralty in World War I he was blamed for the Gallipoli disaster. A backbench MP during the 1930s, he opposed the appeasement of Hitler. In 1939, he returned to the Admiralty before becoming prime minister in May 1940. He led Britain through the war but lost the 1945 general election.

Battle of France
After the Dunkirk evacuation of the Allied forces, German troops advanced into central and western France.

KEY
- → German advance
- — Allied front line May 16
- — Allied front line May 21
- — Allied defensive line May 28
- — Allied front line Jun 4
- — Allied front line Jun 12

infantry supported by Stuka dive-bombers drove northward to reach the Channel coast and cut off the Allied forces in Belgium and northeast France. The Allies established a defensive perimeter around the **port of Dunkirk** and a remarkable escape operation was mounted. Between May 26 and June 4, 338,000 Allied troops were evacuated by sea before Dunkirk fell to the Germans.

Belgian **King Leopold III** (1901–83) **surrendered** on May 28, overruling his government's wish to continue fighting.

The French army was driven into retreat, allowing the Germans to **occupy Paris** on June 14. France was also attacked by Italy, Mussolini belatedly entering the war to pick up some of the spoils of German victory. The French government, along with much of the population, fled to the southwest. In Bordeaux, a new government was formed under the defeatist Marshal Pétain (1856–1951). **General Charles de Gaulle**, a junior minister under Reynaud and a serving army officer, escaped to Britain and

January 8 Food rationing introduced in Britain

February 11 In Winter War, Soviet forces breach Finnish Mannerheim defensive line

March 5 Stalin orders massacre of Polish officers and educated Poles at Katyn

March 12 Moscow Peace Treaty ends war between Soviet Union and Finland

March 21 Paul Reynaud replaces Edouard Daladier as French prime minister

March 23 Muslim League calls for autonomy for predominantly Muslim areas of India

April 9 German forces invade Norway and Denmark

April 13 Royal Navy sinks eight German destroyers at Narvik in Norway

April 16 Allied troops land in Norway

April 28 Allied troops begin withdrawal from central Norway

May 10 German forces invade Belgium and Netherlands

May 10 Winston Churchill becomes British prime minister

May 22 Emergency Powers Act gives British government almost unlimited powers over citizens

May 26–June 4 Allied troops evacuated from Dunkirk

May 28 Belgian forces ordered to surrender by King Leopold III

June 10 Italy declares war on Britain and France

June 14 Germans occupy Paris after French government flees to Bordeaux

June 15–17 Soviet Union annexes Estonia, Latvia, and Lithuania

June 18 General de Gaulle broadcasts from London, calling for French to fight on

June 22 French government of Marshal Pétain signs armistice with Germany

> **FRANCE HAS LOST THE BATTLE, BUT FRANCE HAS NOT LOST THE WAR.**
>
> Charles de Gaulle, French General, June 18, 1940

German troops march down the Champs-Élysées after the occupation of Paris in June 1940. The French capital was an open city and taken without fighting.

launched an emotional plea for continued resistance, but few heeded the call. Pétain sought an **armistice**, which was **agreed on June 22**. At Hitler's insistence, the armistice was signed in the same railroad car in which the 1918 armistice had been signed.

German troops occupied the north and west of France. Pétain established a regime in the town of **Vichy** that held responsibility for all of France, although policy in the occupied part had to be agreed with the Germans. Taking almost dictatorial powers as head of state, he affirmed conservative principles of religion, patriotism, and the family. The **Vichy French collaborated** on some points with the Nazis, introducing their own anti-Semitic laws.

In **Britain**, Churchill quashed defeatism. He encouraged a popular **mood of defiance** with his broadcast speeches and pushed through radical measures to stiffen resistance. These ranged from the internment of aliens to the creation of the **Home Guard** militia to resist German invasion.

Since the British refused to negotiate a peace deal, Hitler began preparing a cross-Channel

Supermarine Spitfire
The Spitfire, the RAF's most famous fighter aircraft of World War II, could match the performance of the German Messerschmitt 109.

— laminated wood propeller blade

449
THE NUMBER OF **GERMAN BOMBERS INVOLVED IN** THE **10-HOUR RAID ON** THE BRITISH CITY OF **COVENTRY**

invasion. In August, the Luftwaffe began a sustained air campaign over southern England, initiating the **Battle of Britain**. British air defenses were well prepared, with radar early warning stations linked to command centers that coordinated a response by Spitfire and Hurricane fighters. Despite this, RAF

Fighter Command was hard pressed as waves of bombers with fighter escort attacked airfields, radar stations, and aircraft factories. It was a relief for the RAF when the Luftwaffe switched to **bombing London** from early September. On September 15, attacked by over 1,000 German aircraft, the British shot down 60 for the loss of 28 of their own. Such figures meant that Germany could not win the command of the air needed to cover an invasion.

German invasion plans were abandoned in October, but from autumn 1940 until May 1941, British cities were **subjected to the Blitz**, a series of night raids by Luftwaffe bombers that caused heavy casualties—more than 40,000 civilians were killed—and widespread destruction. Contrary to prewar predictions, however, the raids brought neither social breakdown nor the collapse of morale. British stoicism under fire won many admirers in the neutral US.

In 1940, **Franklin D. Roosevelt** stood for and won a third term in office. Before the election, Roosevelt had made his hostility to Nazi Germany and Japan clear. He had begun rearmament and introduced a measure of conscription, but he was aware of the antiwar feeling among people in

Going underground
During the Blitz, thousands of Londoners spent the night in Underground stations to shelter from the bombing.

the US. In a "fireside chat" on radio, Roosevelt told Americans their country was to become the "**arsenal of democracy**," its factories providing the arms for Britain to fight the Axis.

— all-metal monocoque fuselage structure

CITY OF WINNIPEG

AE ⊙ A EP20

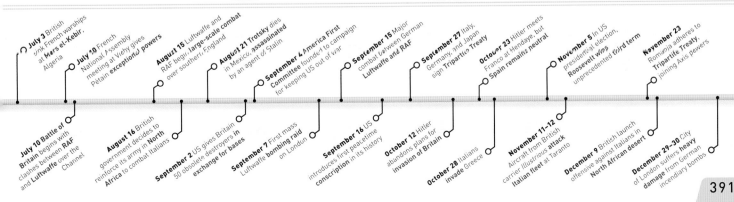

July 3 British sink French warships at Mers el-Kebir, Algeria

July 10 French National Assembly meeting at Vichy gives Pétain **exceptional powers**

July 10 Battle of Britain begins with clashes between **RAF** and **Luftwaffe** over the Channel

August 15 Luftwaffe and RAF begin **large-scale combat** over southern England

August 16 British government decides to reinforce its army in North **Africa to combat Italians**

August 21 Trotsky dies in Mexico, assassinated by an agent of Stalin

September 2 US gives Britain 50 obsolete destroyers **in exchange for bases**

September 4 America First Committee founded to campaign for keeping US out of war

September 7 First mass Luftwaffe **bombing raid** on London

September 15 Major combat between German **Luftwaffe and RAF**

September 16 US introduces first peacetime **conscription** in its history

September 27 Italy, Germany, and Japan sign **Tripartite Treaty**

October 12 Hitler abandons plans for **invasion of Britain**

October 23 Hitler meets Franco at Hendaye, but **Spain remains neutral**

October 28 Italians **invade Greece**

November 5 In US presidential election, **Roosevelt wins** unprecedented **third term**

November 11–12 Aircraft from British carrier *Illustrious* **attack Italian fleet** at Taranto

November 23 Romania adheres to **Tripartite Treaty**, joining Axis powers

December 9 British launch offensive against Italians in **North African desert**

December 29–30 City of London suffers heavy damage from German incendiary bombs

> ❝ **DON'T FIGHT** A **BATTLE IF** YOU **DON'T GAIN ANYTHING** BY WINNING. ❞
>
> **Erwin Rommel, German Field Marshal and commander of the Afrika Korps,** in his war diaries *Infanterie Greift An*, 1937

German tanks and infantry, belonging to Erwin Rommel's Afrika Korps, advance across Libya during the hard-fought campaign in North Africa.

THE ENTRY OF FASCIST ITALY INTO WORLD WAR II IN JUNE 1940 extended the war into the Mediterranean and North Africa, where Italy had colonies, including Libya. Early in 1941, British Commonwealth forces, advancing from Egypt, captured the Libyan port of Tobruk and took 130,000 Italian prisoners. In response, Hitler sent General (later Field Marshal) Erwin Rommel (1891–1944) to North Africa with an armored force—the Afrika Korps—to rescue his fascist ally. Rommel soon pushed the British back and placed Tobruk under siege, while German aircraft based in Sicily attacked British shipping and bombed the island of Malta, a vital British naval base.

The Italian army also attempted an **invasion of Greece** in 1940, but once again the Germans had to step in. Axis forces invaded **Yugoslavia** in April, which was rapidly defeated and dismembered, creating an **independent Croatia** under the rule of the fascist **Ustaše movement**.

German troops pressed south into Greece, which was swiftly overrun. British Commonwealth forces attempted to defend the **Greek island of Crete**, but it fell to the Germans after an initial assault by paratroopers.

For Hitler, the Mediterranean was merely a sideshow. He had already set in motion preparations for an **invasion of the Soviet Union**, codenamed **Operation Barbarossa**. Nazi intentions were genocidal. Hitler told his generals to plan "a war of annihilation," Special SS death squads, known as **Einsatzgruppen**, were detailed to follow the armies and kill communists and Jews in occupied territory. Nazi administrators anticipated the extermination of 30 million Soviet citizens to free up food supplies for Germany.

Launched on June 22, Operation Barbarossa was warfare on a vast scale. Hitler had assembled more than **4 million troops**, including a million from his Axis allies. At first the invasion was an overwhelming success. In a series of encirclements, around 3 million Soviet soldiers were taken prisoner. The invaders reached the gates of Leningrad and thrust toward Moscow, but the **Axis advance** slowed with the autumn rains and eventually **ground to a halt in the snow.** The Soviets launched furious, often suicidal, counterattacks to drive the enemy back from the outskirts of Moscow. For the first time

German parachute badge
German paratroopers, like airborne forces all over the world, were considered to be an elite, a status reflected in their stylish badge.

Airborne operation
The Germans used paratroopers to great success in their invasion of Greece at Corinth, and in the subsequent attack on Crete.

Axis war casualties
The casualties suffered by Germany and its Axis allies rose dramatically between 1939 and 1941, as the war widened its grip on Europe.

DEATHS (IN THOUSANDS): 800, 650, 400, 200, 0 — 1939, 1940, 1941

Operation Barbarossa
The Axis invasion of the Soviet Union made great progress in the second half of 1941. It inflicted heavy losses on Soviet forces, but failed to achieve the quick victory that Hitler needed.

KEY
→ German/Axis advances
— Front line June 21, 1941
— Front line Sept 1, 1941
— Front line Nov 15, 1941
— Front line Dec 5, 1941

Germany had failed to achieve a lightning victory.

In the Baltic republics (Estonia, Latvia, and Lithuania), Belarus, and Ukraine, much of the population **initially welcomed the Germans** as liberators from Stalinist rule. However, few maintained their enthusiasm once they experienced the brutality of Nazi rule. In Leningrad, placed under siege by German and Finnish forces, thousands died every day, mostly from starvation. Almost all the **prisoners of war** captured by the Axis were **executed or perished** from starvation and neglect.

The Jews suffered the worst. At **Babi Yar**, outside the Ukrainian capital Kiev, more than 30,000 Jewish people were murdered in two days. The Nazis also began systematic killing of Jews in Poland, using gas vans at an extermination center at Chelmno.

Throughout 1941, Britain fought on against the Nazis, ignoring a bizarre **peace initiative by Hitler's Deputy Führer Rudolf**

January 20 Inauguration of Roosevelt for third term as US president

January 22 British troops capture Libyan port of Tobruk from Italians

February 7 Italians defeated by British at Beda Fomm, Libya

February 12 Rommel arrives in North Africa to take command of Afrika Korps

March 1 Bulgaria joins Axis forces

March 11 President Roosevelt signs Lend-Lease Act to supply arms to Britain

April 6 German, Italian, and Bulgarian troops **invade Yugoslavia and Greece**

April 10 Rommel besieges British Commonwealth troops in Tobruk

April 17 Yugoslavia surrenders to Axis forces

April 27 Greece surrenders to Axis forces

1 May Orson Welles' movie *Citizen Kane* premieres in New York

2 May British invade Iraq to overthrow pro-Axis government

May 5 Emperor Haile Selassie liberated from Italians, returns to Ethiopia

May 10 Hitler's deputy Rudolf Hess flies to Scotland

May 20 German airborne **invasion of Crete**

May 27 German battleship *Bismarck* sunk in Atlantic

June 8 Allied forces **invade Syria and Lebanon**, held by Vichy French

June 22 Germany and its allies invade Soviet Union in **Operation Barbarossa**

June 29 Soviet forces defeated at Minsk, losing more than 400,000 men

> **THAT THE PEARL HARBOR ATTACK** SHOULD HAVE SUCCEEDED IN ACHIEVING **SURPRISE SEEMS** A **BLESSING FROM HEAVEN.**

Hideki Tojo, Japanese Prime Minister

Battleships USS *West Virginia* and USS *Tennessee* are engulfed in smoke and flames during the surprise Japanese raid on Pearl Harbor.

Hess (1894–1987). On May 10, Hess parachuted into rural Scotland, convinced that he could persuade the British government to ally itself with Germany. Instead, he was arrested and remained a prisoner for the rest of his life.

The chief threat to Britain at this stage in the war lay in the **Battle of the Atlantic**—German attempts to cut off the country's seaborne supplies of food and war material. In May, the German battleship *Bismarck* sortied into the Atlantic. After sinking the Royal Navy battle cruiser HMS *Hood*, *Bismarck* was tracked down, halted by torpedoes dropped from Swordfish biplane aircraft, and then sunk by British battleships. The British and

1,000,000

THE NUMBER OF LENINGRAD'S RESIDENTS THOUGHT TO HAVE DIED DURING THE SIEGE

Canadian navies were less successful at protecting merchant convoys against **German submarines**, however, and losses were soon mounting. The British people felt the effect of this in reduced food rations.

Britain did not hesitate to ally itself with the **Soviet Union**, despite Prime Minister Winston

Fighting in the snow
A German soldier experiencing the Russian winter during the invasion of the Soviet Union. Axis forces were ill-equipped to cope with the conditions

Churchill's (see 1940) strong dislike of Soviet communism. But the British really needed the US to enter the war.

President Roosevelt (see 1933) made no pretense of neutrality. In March, he introduced **Lend-Lease** to supply Britain with military equipment paid for by the US government. American shipyards and factories benefited greatly from this, as did American workers with plentiful and well-paid jobs. Later in the year, free military aid from the US was extended to the Soviet Union.

In August, Roosevelt and Churchill met at Placentia Bay in Newfoundland, Canada, where they signed the **Atlantic Charter**, a statement of joint war aims embodying liberal democratic principles. American warships were already escorting convoys in the eastern Atlantic, and in October a US destroyer was sunk by a German torpedo, but

Roosevelt felt he lacked the popular support needed for a declaration of war.

Roosevelt's dilemma was resolved by the Japanese. The US opposed Japan's expansion into Asia, and after Japanese troops entered French Indochina in July **Roosevelt imposed an oil embargo**. Since Japan was entirely dependent on imported oil, its government had the choice of abandoning its military ambitions or fighting a war with the US.

Following a plan advocated by Admiral Isoroku Yamamoto, on

ISOROKU YAMAMOTO
(1884–1943)

In the 1930s, Japanese Admiral Isoroku Yamamoto became a leading advocate of naval air power. As naval commander-in-chief he was the architect of the raid on Pearl Harbor in 1941. He was killed in April 1943 when his aircraft, identified by American intelligence, was shot down over Bougainville Island in the Pacific.

Pearl Harbor badge
The slogan "Remember Pearl Harbor" was widely used in the US to inspire patriotic support for the war against the Japanese.

December 7, Japanese carrier aircraft delivered **a surprise attack** on the American naval base at Pearl Harbor in Hawaii. The raid sank or damaged 18 warships and destroyed around 300 aircraft, but failed to destroy America's vital aircraft carrier force. Other Japanese forces invaded the Philippines and the British colony of Malaya.

The shock of the raid on Pearl Harbor ensured popular American support for war against Japan, but not against Germany. To the relief of both Churchill and Roosevelt, Hitler chose to declare war on the US in support of his Japanese allies. At the **Arcadia Conference** in Washington at the end of the year, **Britain** and the **US** agreed a **military strategy** that gave priority to defeating the Germans. The two countries also agreed to unify their military command under the Combined Chiefs of Staff.

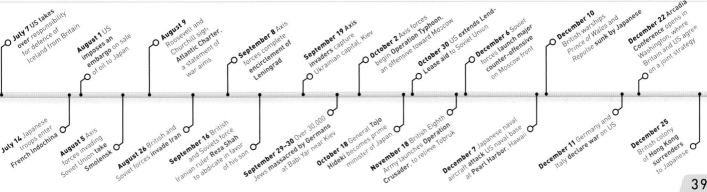

July 7 US takes over responsibility for defence of Iceland from Britain

August 1 US imposes an embargo on sale of oil to Japan

August 9 Roosevelt and Churchill sign **Atlantic Charter**, a statement of war aims

September 8 Axis forces complete encirclement of Leningrad

September 19 Axis invaders capture Ukrainian capital, Kiev

October 2 Axis forces begin Operation Typhoon, an offensive toward Moscow

October 30 US extends Lend-Lease aid to Soviet Union

December 6 Soviet forces launch major counter-offensive on Moscow front

December 10 British warships *Prince of Wales* and *Repulse* sunk by Japanese

December 22 Arcadia Conference opens in Washington, where Britain and US agree on a joint strategy

July 14 Japanese troops enter French Indochina

August 5 Axis forces invading Soviet Union take Smolensk

August 26 British and Soviet forces invade Iran

September 16 British and Soviets force Iranian ruler Reza Shah to abdicate in favor of his son

September 29–30 Over 30,000 Jews massacred by Germans at Babi Yar near Kiev

October 18 General Tojo Hideki becomes prime minister of Japan

November 18 British Eighth Army launches Operation Crusader, to relieve Tobruk

December 7 Japanese naval aircraft attack US naval base at Pearl Harbor, Hawaii

December 11 Germany and Italy declare war on US

December 25 British colony of Hong Kong surrenders to Japanese

WAR IN THE
PACIFIC

THE ALLIES DEFEAT IMPERIAL JAPAN IN THE PACIFIC

At war with China since 1937, the Japanese decided in 1941 to take a gamble that, if successful, would secure them an empire in Asia and the Pacific. On December 7, they attacked the US base at Pearl Harbor in Hawaii and launched an invasion of the Philippines and European colonies in Southeast Asia.

The British and Dutch colonies in Southeast Asia proved easy prey for Japan—the British base at Singapore fell with virtually no resistance. Within five months, the Japanese had reached the border of British India in Burma. Australia seemed threatened, but Japan's southward push was checked by a clash with US aircraft carriers at the

Battle of the Coral Sea. A new phase of the war began with an ambitious thrust by the Japanese navy against Midway Island, which led to heavy losses. From August 1942, the most intense fighting focused around Guadalcanal, which the US eventually held. It was not until 1944 that the US had built up sufficient strength for a sustained advance.

The Japanese navy was routed at the battles of the Philippine Sea and Leyte Gulf, while the seizure of the Mariana Islands brought the Japanese within range of US bomber aircraft. In August 1945, defeated in Burma and Okinawa, facing a Soviet invasion of Manchuria, and the destruction of cities by atom bombs, the Japanese surrendered.

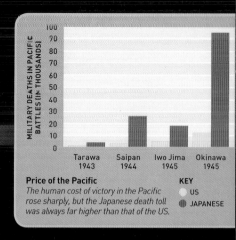

Price of the Pacific
The human cost of victory in the Pacific rose sharply, but the Japanese death toll was always far higher than that of the US.

KEY
○ US
● JAPANESE

Japan on the offensive
The Japanese onslaught, begun in December 1941, gave their armies control of the Philippines, Indonesia, Malaya, and Burma, while their navy established a defensive perimeter in the mid-Pacific. A naval defeat at Midway in June 1942 ended the period of Japanese expansion.

KEY
✕ Major land battle
✕ Major Japanese air attack
✕ Major sea battle
→ Japanese advance
--- Japanese sphere of influence

The Big Six

City	Number of raids	Percentage of city destroyed
Tokyo	5	50%
Nagoya	4	31%
Kobe	2	56%
Osaka	4	26%
Yokohama	2	44%
Kawasaki	1	33%

Between March 10 and June 15, 1945, six major Japanese cities, including Tokyo and Kobe, were decimated by heavy US bombing raids.

3:2

Burma campaign
Sixty percent (three in five) of the Japanese troops who fought in the Burma campaign in 1942–45 lost their lives. Total Japanese casualties numbered around 200,000, compared with the 71,000 British and British Indian men who were killed and wounded.

KEY
✕ "Big Six" fire bomb target
✕ Atomic bomb target

Attacks on Japan
Taking off from bases in the Mariana Islands, US B-29 Superfortress bombers devastated Japanese cities with incendiary devices from March 1945. The dropping of atom bombs on Hiroshima and Nagasaki (August 6 and 9, 1945) was followed by Japanese surrender.

> " I REALIZE THE **TRAGIC SIGNIFICANCE** OF THE **ATOM BOMB**… WE THANK GOD IT HAS COME TO US INSTEAD OF OUR **ENEMIES**… "

US president Harry S. Truman, August 9, 1945

Allied counterattack
The US army led a fightback against the Japanese in the southwest Pacific, from New Guinea to the Philippines. In the Central Pacific, the US navy and marines spearheaded a thrust from the Gilbert Islands to the Marianas. The loss of Okinawa in June 1945 placed Japan under imminent threat of an Allied invasion.

KEY
✕ Major land battle
✕ Major sea battle
→ Allied advance

Wounded Allied soldiers are carried through the jungle by New Guineans. The harsh environment was as deadly an enemy as the Japanese.

ON JANUARY 20, 1942, SS GENERAL REINHARD HEYDRICH (1904–1942) chaired a conference at Wannsee, a suburb of Berlin. The purpose of the meeting was to brief German civil servants and foreign ministry officials on plans to systematically **deport Jews** en masse from every country in Europe. The Jews were to be transported to camps—chiefly in Poland—from which, it was made clear, none would return.

Meanwhile, a Japanese tide of conquest flowed across Southeast Asia. **The fall of Singapore**, a major British base that was surrendered to the Japanese

THE HOLOCAUST

The Nazis murdered people from many groups, including Slavs, homosexuals, and gypsies, but their treatment of the Jews was without parallel. By 1942 they had embarked upon the total extermination of European Jews. To achieve this "final solution," the Nazis transported Jews to specially built camps equipped with gas chambers. Most were killed within hours of arrival, but some were kept alive and used as slave labor. About 6 million Jews were murdered, two-thirds of Europe's Jewish population.

in February after token resistance, was a blow to the prestige of the British Empire. About 120,000 British, Australian, and Indian troops were taken prisoner.

Determined resistance by American and Filipino soldiers on the Bataan peninsula in the **Philippines** ended in April. Large numbers of the troops died as prisoners of the Japanese on the brutal **Bataan Death March**—a 62-mile (100-km) trek that was forced upon the malnourished and disease-ridden men.

As the Japanese advance swept over Dutch-ruled Indonesia and British-ruled Burma, Australians worried that their country might be next. An **attack** by Japanese naval aircraft on the **port of Darwin** in Northern Australia in February caused over 500 casualties, and Japanese midget submarines penetrated Sydney Harbor at the start of June. In a sharp change of attitude, Australia began to look on the US, rather than Britain, as its chief military ally.

Amid intense anti-Japanese feeling, in February President Roosevelt signed **Executive Order 9066**, which allowed Japanese Americans living in the western United States to be deported to **internment camps**. About 120,000 ethnic Japanese were interned during the war.

As the United States geared up for total war, the **fight back against Japan** began. The naval battles in the Coral Sea in May and at Midway in June were duels between aircraft carriers, fought without the Japanese and American fleets coming within sight of each other. The **Coral Sea** encounter brought neither side decisive advantage, but **Midway** was a disaster for the Japanese Navy, which lost four aircraft carriers to American dive-bombers and torpedo aircraft.

The American victory at Midway was a turning point, but far from decisive in itself. When **American forces landed on Guadalcanal** in the Solomon Islands in August, the Japanese responded with ferocious determination, landing their own troops to counterattack and initiating a series of naval

I CAME OUT OF BATAAN AND I SHALL RETURN.

General Douglas MacArthur, US commanding officer, after his escape to Australia following defeat in Bataan, March 20, 1942

battles in which both sides suffered heavy losses. In **New Guinea, Australian troops** played a leading role in fighting in hostile jungle terrain.

In **India**, the British faced a political as well as a military challenge. With Japanese troops threatening an invasion from Burma, in August Mohandas Gandhi (1869–1948) and other National Congress leaders launched the **Quit India**

Movement, demanding full independence. Their campaign of civil disobedience was ruthlessly repressed by the British authorities, and more than 100,000 Indians were arrested, including Gandhi. Some Indian nationalists joined **Subhas Chandra Bose's Indian National Army**, which fought alongside the Japanese, but far more fought for Britain: around 2.5 million Indians volunteered for the Indian Army.

Nazi death camps
The Germans built death camps, mostly in occupied Poland, expressly for the killing of Jews. There were many other concentration camps in which tens of thousands died.

KEY
● Nazi extermination camp

January 2 Japanese forces **capture Manila**, in the Philippines

January 20 At **Wannsee Conference**, German officials plan extermination of Jews

February 15 British surrender **Singapore** to Japanese

February 19 US President Roosevelt signs executive order **authorizing internment** of Japanese Americans

February 19 Japanese aircraft attack town of Darwin, in Australia's Northern Territory

February 27 Japanese navy defeats Allied fleet at **Battle of Java Sea**

March 8 Japanese troops capture Rangoon in Burma

March 27–28 British Commandos raid Normandie dock at St. Nazaire in Occupied France

April 9 American and Filipino troops **surrender to Japanese**, in the Philippines

April 15–29 Many American and Filipino prisoners of war die on **Bataan death march**

April 18 Carrier-launched American bombers attack Japan in **Doolittle Raid**

May 8 Japanese and American aircraft carriers clash in **Battle of the Coral Sea**

May 12–28 Soviet forces **suffer massive losses** in failed counter-offensive at Kharkov

May 26–June 11 Free French troops resist Axis tanks in North African desert at **Bir Hakeim**

May 27 Nazi **Reinhard Heydrich fatally wounded** by British-trained Czech agents in Prague

May 30–31 Cologne is target of first "thousand bomber raid" by **RAF Bomber Command**

June 4–7 US carriers inflict heavy losses on Japanese at naval **Battle of Midway**

June 17 Roosevelt approves initial $90 million budget for **Manhattan Project** to develop atomic bomb

June 26 Axis forces **retake Tobruk** in Libya after Rommel's victory at Gazala

Soviet infantry fight amid the ruined buildings of Stalingrad. German defeat in the city was a decisive turning point in World War II.

Naval power
US Navy dive-bombers fly over Midway Island in the Pacific. This was the location of a decisive duel between American and Japanese aircraft carriers in June 1942.

In the **desert war in North Africa**, after suffering repeated defeats at the hands of Field Marshal Erwin Rommel (1891–1944), the British Eighth Army, commanded by General Bernard Montgomery (1887–1976), won a great offensive victory at **Alamein** in October–November.

As Rommel's Axis army retreated westward across Libya, Allied forces, including a large contingent of American troops commanded by General Dwight D. Eisenhower (1890–1969), landed in French North Africa during

Operation Torch. Opposition from French colonial forces loyal to the Vichy government (see 1940) was easily overcome, leaving Rommel trapped between armies to his east and west. The Germans responded by extending their military occupation of France to the Vichy-ruled area.

The war being fought in the **Soviet Union** (see 1941) came to its climactic turning point at the **Battle of Stalingrad**. The eastward advance of Axis forces had continued through most of the year, reaching the Caucasus by July and threatening the vital oilfields of Azerbaijan. Hitler insisted his troops capture

Yank tank
American-built Grant tanks were supplied to the British in North Africa. This one was used by General Montgomery as an observation post.

the city of Stalingrad—of symbolic importance because of its name. German soldiers entered the city in September, but the Soviets defended it street-by-street amid the ruined buildings. In November, Soviet General Giorgi Zhukov (1896–1974) masterminded a counterattack. Striking from north and south, his armies encircled the Axis forces, trapping a quarter of a million men inside Stalingrad. Ordered by Hitler to stay and fight, by the end of the year they were starving, freezing, and short of ammunition. The German commander, Field Marshal Friedrich Paulus, was among the 90,000 men who lived to surrender the following February—and one of only a handful who then survived Soviet imprisonment.

American industrial miracle
The output of US factories and shipyards soared during World War II. The number of workers employed in shipbuilding alone rose from around 100,000 in 1940 to 1.7 million late in the war.

Chart 1 — WARSHIPS (NUMBER IN THOUSANDS OF TONS): 1941; 1942; 1943; 1944; 1945

Chart 2 — PLANES (NUMBER IN THOUSANDS): 1941; 1942; 1943; 1944; 1945

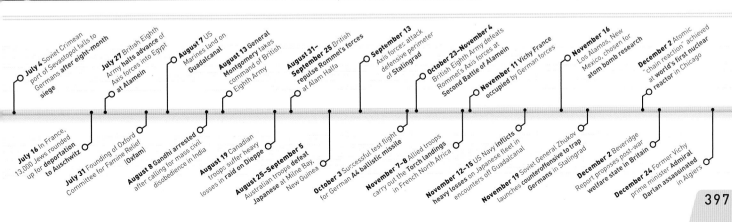

July 4 Soviet Crimean port of Sevastopol falls to Germans **after eight-month siege**

July 16 In France, 13,000 Jews rounded up for **deportation to Auschwitz**

July 27 British Eighth Army **halts advance of** Axis forces into Egypt **at Alamein**

July 31 Founding of Oxford Committee for Famine Relief (**Oxfam**)

August 7 US Marines land on Guadalcanal

August 8 Gandhi arrested after calling for mass civil disobedience in India

August 13 General Montgomery takes command of British Eighth Army

August 19 Canadian troops suffer heavy losses in **raid on Dieppe**

August 25–September 5 Australian troops defeat Japanese at Milne Bay, New Guinea

August 31– September 25 British repulse Rommel's forces at Alam Halfa

September 13 Axis forces attack defensive perimeter of Stalingrad

October 3 Successful test flight for German **A4 ballistic missile**

October 23–November 4 British Eighth Army defeats Rommel's Axis forces at **Second Battle of Alamein**

November 7–8 Allied troops carry out the **Torch landings** in French North Africa

November 11 Vichy France occupied by German forces

November 12–15 US Navy inflicts heavy losses on Japanese fleet in encounters off Guadalcanal

November 16 Los Alamos, New Mexico, chosen for **atom bomb research**

November 19 Soviet General Zhukov **launches counteroffensive to trap** Germans in Stalingrad

December 2 Atomic "chain reaction" achieved at **world's first nuclear reactor** in Chicago

December 2 Beveridge Report proposes post-war **welfare state in Britain**

December 24 Former Vichy prime minister **Admiral Darlan assassinated** in Algiers

US President Roosevelt and British Prime Minister Churchill meet at Casablanca in January to discuss the conduct of the war.

French Resistance fighters pose for a group portrait. The Resistance carried out acts of sabotage, gathered intelligence, and mounted guerrilla warfare operations.

IN JANUARY 1943, Franklin D. Roosevelt met British prime minister **Winston Churchill** for a conference in **Casablanca**, Morocco, which set the future course of World War II in Europe. Britain persuaded the US to **plan for an invasion of Sicily**, knowing this meant an invasion of northern France would have to be postponed until 1944. The Allied leaders also agreed that their air forces would mount a combined bomber offensive against Germany. At the end of the conference, Roosevelt announced that the Allies would **accept nothing less than the "unconditional surrender"** of their enemies.

The surrender of Axis forces at Stalingrad (see 1942) in February was a massive setback for Germany, but the Germans remained in occupation of most of Europe. In many places, **armed resistance movements** contested the occupation. A turning point for the **resistance in France** was the decision in 1943

JOSIP BROZ TITO (1892–1980)

Born in Croatia, Josip Broz adopted the name Tito as a communist activist in the 1930s. After the German occupation of Yugoslavia in 1941, Tito led a guerrilla movement that took control of the country by 1945. He made Yugoslavia a communist state, but resisted the dominance of the Soviet Union. He remained Yugoslav president until his death.

Casablanca
The general release of the film Casablanca *was timed to take advantage of the widely reported Casablanca Conference.*

fought hard against the Germans, but were also actively hostile to the Chetnik guerrillas, led by Serb nationalist and monarchist **Draza Mihailovic**. In France, Resistance leader **Jean Moulin** strove to unite rival factions, but in May he was arrested, tortured by Gestapo chief Klaus Barbie, and died in captivity.

Spring 1943 brought the climax of the struggle against German U-boats known as the **Battle of the Atlantic**. In March, the Allies lost 285,000 tons (260,000 metric tons) of merchant shipping to German submarine attacks and there seemed a risk that Britain's lifeline of seaborne supplies would be severed. German U-boats operated in groups known as "wolf packs," coordinated by radio. But then, a combination of factors, including increased use of aircraft on ocean patrols, intelligence from decrypted German naval messages, and the equipping of convoy escorts with improved radar and radio direction-finding equipment, tilted the balance against the submarines. By May, **U-boat losses** were so high that submarine commander Admiral Karl Dönitz had to withdraw his forces from the Atlantic. The U-boat offensive never regained its momentum.

By far the heaviest land fighting of 1943 was on **Germany's eastern front**. Despite the

> ## GERMANY IS A FORTRESS, BUT IT IS A FORTRESS WITHOUT A ROOF.

Franklin D. Roosevelt, US President, 1944

disaster at Stalingrad, Axis forces were able to mount a successful counteroffensive at **Kharkov** in the spring. This left the Soviets holding an exposed bulge of territory, or salient, at **Kursk**. German generals planned to attack from north and south to trap the Soviet forces inside the salient and destroy them. But deputy supreme commander **Georgi Zhukov** anticipated the German offensive and prepared a formidable defensive system. The forces assembled at Kursk were huge—the two sides together

Soviet badge
This badge was awarded to Soviet tank crewmen during World War II. The Soviets lost around 5,000 tanks at Kursk in summer 1943.

totaled over 2 million men, with more than 6,000 tanks and 5,000 aircraft. The Axis onslaught began on July 5, initiating the **largest tank battle in history**. Soviet losses were heavy, but after four days the Axis offensive had stalled and the Red Army launched a counterattack. The Germans organized a fighting withdrawal but the tide of the war in the east had turned for good.

While the battle of Kursk was at its height, the Western Allies mounted a **large-scale invasion of Sicily**. US and British armies were put ashore and advanced around opposite sides of the island, receiving little opposition from Italian forces, who quickly surrendered. The campaign turned into a race between US general **George S. Patton** and British general **Bernard Montgomery**. Patton was first to reach Messina, but between them the two armies allowed most of the Axis forces to escape to mainland Italy.

The loss of Sicily was a fatal blow to the Italian dictator Benito Mussolini. After **a vote of no confidence** from the **Fascist Grand Council**, Mussolini was dismissed by King Victor Emmanuel III (1869–1947) and arrested. His replacement,

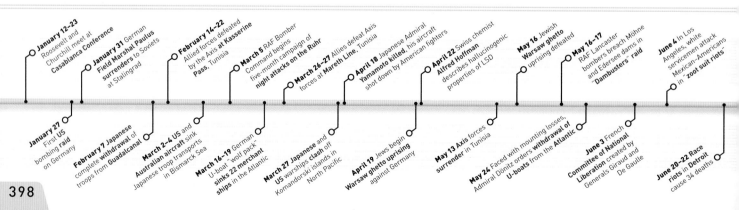

January 12–23 Roosevelt meet at Churchill meet at Casablanca Conference

January 31 German Field Marshal Paulus **surrenders** to Soviets at Stalingrad

February 14–22 Allied forces defeated by the Axis **at Kasserine Pass**, Tunisia

March 5 RAF Bomber Command begins five-month campaign of **night attacks on the Ruhr**

March 26–27 Allies defeat Axis forces at Mareth Line, Tunisia

April 18 Japanese Admiral **Yamamoto killed**, his aircraft shot down by American fighters

April 22 Swiss chemist **Alfred Hoffman** describes hallucinogenic properties of LSD

May 16 Jewish **Warsaw ghetto** uprising defeated

May 16–17 RAF Lancaster bombers breach Möhne and Eder see dams in "**Dambusters**' raid"

June 4 In Los Angeles, white servicemen attack Mexican-Americans in "**zoot suit riots**"

January 27 First US bombing raid on Germany

February 7 Japanese complete **withdrawal** of troops from Guadalcanal

March 2–4 US and Australian aircraft sink Japanese troop transports in Bismarck Sea

March 16–19 German U-boat 'wolf pack' **sinks 22 merchant ships** in the Atlantic

March 27 Japanese and US warships **clash** off Komandorski Islands in North Pacific

April 19 Jews begin **Warsaw ghetto uprising** against Germany

May 13 Axis forces surrender in Tunisia

May 24 Faced with mounting losses, Admiral Dönitz orders **withdrawal of U-boats** from the Atlantic

June 3 French **Committee of National Liberation** created by Generals Giraud and De Gaulle

June 20–22 Race riots in Detroit cause 34 deaths

Men of the US Coast Guard cutter *Spencer* watch the explosion of a depth charge that sank a German U-boat in the Atlantic on April 17.

Women at war
A US poster suggests that working in munitions factories can be as glamorous as joining the various uniformed women's services.

Germany came under **heavy air attack** through 1943. RAF Bomber Command, equipped with the new Lancaster bomber, achieved a spectacular success in the "Dambusters" raid in May. Using "bouncing bombs," Lancasters made a low-level night attack on four Ruhr dams, breaching two of them. In July, bombers saturated the port city of **Hamburg** with incendiary devices. In hot, dry weather conditions, separate fires blended into a single immense firestorm. More than 37,000 people were killed, most of them civilians.

While the RAF bombed Germany by night, the **US Army Air Force** began a **daylight bombing campaign**. The US bombers, bristling with guns, were expected to fight off attacks by German aircraft and drop bombs on targets using technologically advanced bombsights. In practice, the B-17s and B-24s suffered alarmingly heavy losses and precision bombing proved hard to achieve under combat conditions.

The **impact of bombing** on the German civilian population was huge. Aside from the casualties, hundreds of thousands were made homeless and there were severe food shortages. Over **two million children** were **evacuated** from the cities. Many factories were relocated underground to avoid the bombing.

Flying fortress
The crew of an American Eighth Air Force B-17 Flying Fortress at a base in England prepares for a bombing mission over Germany. The Eighth Air Force lost 26,000 men between 1942 and 1945.

The shortages experienced by German civilians were replicated, in greater or lesser degree, in all European countries, including neutral Spain. In Britain, labor shortages led to the **conscription of women for work** in civil defense, military auxiliary services, factories, and in agriculture. In the US, women workers were employed in heavy industrial jobs traditionally reserved for men.

Black workers also took jobs that in peacetime were reserved for whites. This led to **racial tensions** that erupted into **rioting** in Detroit in June. White and black mobs clashed, and 34 people were killed before federal troops restored order.

One of the worst tragedies of 1943 was the **Bengal famine** that killed more than a million people in British India. Responsibility for this catastrophe is disputed, but Prime Minister Churchill refused to allow shipping space, which

prevented food from reaching the starving.

In Asia, 60,000 Allied prisoners of war (POWs) and almost 200,000 Asian laborers were **forced to build a railroad** from **Thailand** to supply Japanese troops in **Burma**. Around 16,000 POWs and 90,000 Asian workers died while they were building it.

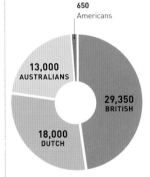

650 Americans
13,000 AUSTRALIANS
29,350 BRITISH
18,000 DUTCH

Building the Burma Railroad
Alongside Asian forced laborers, chiefly British, Australian, and Dutch prisoners of war were used by the Japanese to build the railroad.

Marshal Pietro Badoglio (1871–1956), signed an armistice with the Allies in early September. But the Germans had time to take over key positions in Italy and defend the peninsula against Allied invasion forces. German paratroopers rescued Mussolini from captivity. They set him up as ruler of a puppet **Italian Social Republic**, which was founded in the town of Salo. As Allied forces fought their way northward from Naples toward Rome, the **Badoglio government joined the Allies**, declaring war on Germany.

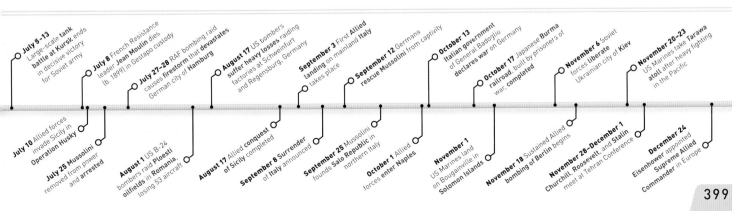

July 5–13 Large-scale tank **battle at Kursk** ends in decisive victory for Soviet army

July 10 Allied forces invade Sicily in **Operation Husky**

July 8 French Resistance leader Jean Moulin dies (b. 1899) in Gestapo custody

July 25 Mussolini removed from power and arrested

July 27–28 RAF bombing raid causes firestorm that devastates German city of **Hamburg**

August 1 US B-24 bombers raid Ploesti oilfields in Romania, losing 53 aircraft

August 17 US bombers **suffer heavy losses** raiding factories at Schweinfurt and Regensburg, Germany

August 17 Allied **conquest of Sicily** completed

September 3 First Allied landing on mainland **Italy** takes place

September 8 Surrender of Italy announced

September 12 Germans **rescue Mussolini** from captivity

September 25 Mussolini founds Salo Republic in northern Italy

October 1 Allied forces enter Naples

October 13 Italian government of General Badoglio declares war on Germany

October 17 Japanese **Burma railroad**, built by prisoners of war, completed

November 1 US Marines land on Bougainville in Solomon Islands

November 6 Soviet forces liberate Ukrainian city of Kiev

November 18 Sustained Allied bombing of Berlin begins

November 28–December 1 Churchill, Roosevelt, and Stalin meet at Tehran Conference

November 20–23 US Marines take Tarawa atoll after heavy fighting in the Pacific

December 24 Eisenhower appointed Supreme Allied Commander in Europe

150,000
THE NUMBER OF ALLIED TROOPS THAT LANDED ON THE NORMANDY BEACHES

9,000
THE NUMBER OF ALLIED CASUALTIES DURING THE LANDINGS

American soldiers wade ashore from a landing craft during the invasion of Normandy on June 6. The landings began the liberation of Occupied France.

IN EARLY 1944 THERE WAS HEAVY FIGHTING IN ITALY as German troops blocked the Allied advance on Rome. In January, Allied seaborne landings at **Anzio**, behind the Germans' defensive Gustav Line, failed to break the deadlock. In February, Allied commanders decided to bomb the medieval abbey at Monte Cassino, a key point in the Gustav Line, but this much-criticized act of desecration was also ineffectual. **Monte Cassino eventually fell to the Polish infantry** in May, allowing Rome to be liberated the following month.

In the spring, British Indian troops withstood a Japanese attempt to invade northeast India from Burma. The **Japanese offensive** was so successfully repulsed that Allied forces were able to mount their own offensive to retake much of Burma later in the year. With the Quit India movement (see 1942) also suppressed, the British had reasserted their authority over the subcontinent.

Meanwhile, Allied preparations for an **invasion of Occupied France** turned southern England into an armed camp. Operation **Overlord**, was commanded by General Dwight D. Eisenhower (1890–1969). The Allies chose Normandy as the target for their invasion. Postponed because of bad weather, the **Normandy landings** took place on June 6, referred to as **D-Day**.

During the night, 18,000 airborne troops landed by parachute or glider behind the German coastal defenses. At dawn, a fleet of 5,000 ships carrying around 130,000

Burma Star
This military medal was awarded to British and Commonwealth soldiers for service in the Burma campaign between 1941 and 1945.

soldiers arrived offshore. It was the **largest amphibious operation in history**. Three of the five landing beaches, codenamed **Sword**, **Juno**, and **Utah**, were taken with relative ease by British, Canadian, and US troops, but the British at **Gold** beach and especially the Americans at **Omaha** beach suffered substantial losses before securing ground.

Two ingenious innovations, the **Mulberry floating harbor** and the Pluto undersea oil pipeline, allowed supplies to reach Allied forces once ashore. A grueling struggle ensued to break out of Normandy, and German resistance was not overcome until August.

Meanwhile, **Adolf Hitler** (1889–1945) survived an **assassination attempt**. A plot was mounted by patriotic German officers and officials to overthrow the Führer and seek peace with the Western allies. On July 20, Colonel Claus Schenk von Stauffenberg (1907–1944) carried a bomb in his briefcase to a meeting at Hitler's headquarters at Rastenburg, East Prussia. He placed the bomb under a table at which Hitler was sitting. It

exploded, devastating the room and killing four people, but the **dictator survived unscathed**. Stauffenberg and some of the other leading conspirators were shot by firing squad; thousands more were arrested and tortured, many suffering lingering deaths. Field Marshal Erwin Rommel (1891–1944) was also implicated in the plot, but he was permitted to commit suicide.

The breakout of Allied forces from Normandy in August (see p.389) led rapidly to the **liberation of Paris**. After French Resistance fighters began an uprising in the city on August 19, General Charles de Gaulle's Free French forces, fighting as part of Eisenhower's Allied armies, raced for Paris. A column of French tanks reached central Paris on August 25.

D-Day Landings
The Allies landed on five Normandy beaches—Sword, Juno, Gold, Utah, and Omaha. Allied troops also parachuted in behind enemy lines.

KEY
→ Allied landing/advance
▽ Allied parachute landing
— Allied front line June 7, 1944

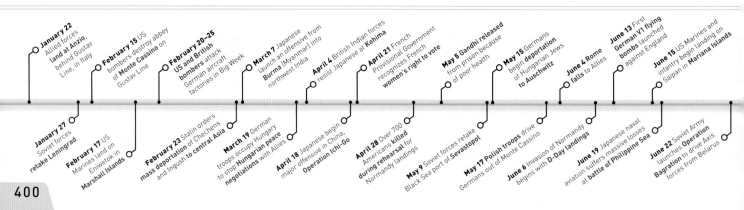

January 22 Allied forces land at Anzio, behind Gustav Line, in Italy

January 27 Soviet forces retake Leningrad

February 15 US bombers destroy abbey of Monte Cassino on Gustav Line

February 17 US Marines land on Enwetok in Marshall Islands

February 20–25 US and British bombers attack German aircraft factories in Big Week

February 23 Stalin orders mass deportation of Chechens and Ingush to central Asia

March 7 Japanese launch an offensive from Burma (Myanmar) into northwest India

March 19 German troops occupy Hungary to stop Hungarian peace negotiations with Allies

April 4 British Indian forces resist Japanese at Kohima

April 18 Japanese begin offensive in China, major offensive Operation Ichi-Go

April 21 French Provisional Government recognizes French **women's right to vote**

April 28 Over 700 Americans killed during rehearsal for Normandy landings

May 5 Gandhi released from prison because of poor health

May 9 Soviet forces retake Black Sea port of Sevastopol

May 15 Germans begin **deportation of Hungarian Jews to Auschwitz**

May 17 Polish troops drive Germans out of Monte Cassino

June 4 Rome falls to Allies

June 6 Invasion of Normandy begins with D-Day landings

June 13 First **German V1 flying bombs launched** against England

June 19 Japanese naval aviation suffers massive losses at battle of Philippine Sea

June 15 US Marines and infantry begin landing on Saipan in Mariana Islands

June 22 Soviet Army launches **Operation Bagration** to drive Axis forces from Belarus

Soldiers of US 7th Armored Division patrol the snowy Belgian town of St. Vith, a site of fierce fighting during the German Ardennes offensive in December.

Flying bomb
The German unmanned V-1 flying bomb was propelled by a primitive jet engine and packed with explosives. In summer 1944 more than 100 a day were fired at London.

As the Germans withdrew, the celebrations in Paris began, and so too did **reprisals against alleged collaborators**. Around 9,000 French people were summarily executed and tens

Liberation of Paris
Parisians celebrate the liberation of their city, and welcome the return of General de Gaulle to France as leader of the Free French.

of thousands subjected to public humiliation—for example, women were paraded with shaved heads—before **De Gaulle formed a provisional government** and restored order.

At the beginning of August the **Polish resistance movement** staged an uprising against the Germans in Warsaw. The Soviet Red Army had almost reached the city, after pushing westward through the summer, but Stalin had no desire to help the Poles, who were mostly anti-Russian and anticommunist. The Red Army stopped short of Warsaw, and did little for two months while the Polish uprising was crushed by Nazi troops. Several hundred thousand Poles were killed. After the survivors surrendered in early October, the Germans destroyed Warsaw.

In the west in September, with the Allies in control of most of Belgium, British general Bernard Montgomery (1887–1976) devised a plan to end the war quickly by an **airborne invasion of the occupied Netherlands**. British, US, and Polish paratroopers attempted to seize and hold a series of bridges that would allow Allied tanks to advance into northern Germany. The last bridge at **Arnhem** was not taken, however, and the operation failed leaving the Netherlands to suffer a harsh winter under the Nazis.

The US **offensive in the Pacific** gathered momentum through the year (see pp.394–95). Outnumbered and militarily outclassed, the Japanese fought with suicidal

determination. In the battle for the **island of Saipan** between June 15 and July 9, almost the entire garrison of 30,000 Japanese soldiers were killed. The Japanese Imperial Navy was almost wiped out in two great battles—the **Philippine Sea** in June, and **Leyte Gulf** in October.

Facing near certain death in unequal combat with superior US forces, some Japanese naval pilots mounted "**kamikaze**" suicide attacks, deliberately crashing their aircraft into US warships. These tactics proved

Prayer for safety
For good luck, some Japanese servicemen carried their national flag with a special prayer written on it, asking for a safe return.

so effective that they were adopted as a form of mass attack, using hundreds of virtually untrained rookie pilots.

Facing defeat in Europe, Hitler put his faith in secret weapons. The first jet aircraft, the German **Messerschmitt 262**, entered the conflict, but failed to reverse the

mounting dominance of Allied air forces. The **V1 flying bombs** launched against London caused heavy casualties, but had no decisive effect, nor did the **V2 rockets**, the world's first ballistic missiles. Around 3,000 V2s were launched, mostly at London and Antwerp. They arrived without warning and there was no defense against them, but they were inaccurate, and failed to have the impact Hitler desired.

In December, the German Führer made his last gamble with a surprise offensive in the

Ardennes, which became known as the **Battle of the Bulge**. German tanks broke through the US front line and headed for Antwerp. Stiffening resistance, especially by US airborne troops at Bastogne, was followed by a well-organized Allied counter-attack. The German tanks ran out of fuel, and improved weather allowed Allied aircraft to strike in support of ground forces. Hitler's last throw of the dice had failed.

US and Japanese naval strengths
A combination of vastly productive US shipyards and heavy Japanese losses enabled the US to win naval dominance in the Pacific.

	1941	1942	1943	1944	1945
NUMBER OF SHIPS	A B S	A B S	A B S	A B S	A B S

NAVAL UNITS

KEY
- US
- Japan

- A Aircraft carriers
- B Battleships
- S Submarines

Party member
GERMANY
This membership book, dated July 15, 1937, certified that the holder was a member of the Nazi party, the ruling party in Germany during World War II.

Yellow star
GERMANY
From September 1941, all Jews in the German Reich were forced to wear a yellow star with *Jude* (German for "Jew") written on it.

Anti-submarine weapon
BRITAIN
Depth-charge launchers were carried by British Navy ships to counter attacks by German U-boats. The charge exploded at a preset depth.

depth-charge launching tube

symbol of British monarch (King George VI)

SS dagger
GERMANY
Ceremonial daggers were issued to all members of the Nazi elite SS. The blade bears the SS motto *Meine Ehre heißt Treue* ("My Honor is Loyalty").

SS motto

symbol of the Third Reich

FAITES VITE... FAITES BIEN

LEUR *Victoire* SERA LA VÔTRE

French Canadian poster
CANADA
This poster, addressed to Canada's French-speaking population, appeals for naval volunteers to join the fight against German U-boats.

WORLD WAR II

A GLOBAL CONFLICT THAT INVOLVED NOT ONLY MILITARY PERSONNEL BUT ALSO CIVILIANS

World War II cost more lives than any other conflict in human history. Battle was joined on land, at sea, and in the air, with weapons ranging from the bolt-action rifle to the atomic bomb.

World War II involved more than 100 million military personnel and most nations of the world. As well as being the most widespread war in history, it was also marked by mass casualties among civilians, who were subjected to large-scale aerial bombardment, massacre by German and Japanese soldiers and security forces, and the dropping of atomic bombs on Japan.

paper tape on which encrypted message was printed

setting knob

Cipher machine
US
The M-209 was a mechanical cipher machine that provided swift and basic encryption, providing sufficient security for use on the battlefield.

rifle bolt

Lee Enfield bolt-action rifle
BRITAIN
This rifle, which fired .303 cartridges from a 10-round magazine, was the standard British and Commonwealth infantry rifle in both world wars.

foresight

scale marked in degrees

movable arm

eyepiece

Field telephone
US
Portable telephones, such as the American EE8 shown here, were used for battlefield communication over relatively short distances.

Identification card
JAPAN
This wooden card belonged to a Japanese serviceman. It lists his military unit and gives permission to go out, perhaps after curfew.

Naval sextant
JAPAN
Used to calculate a ship's position, the naval sextant dates from the age of sail but was still in use during World War II.

rotatable mirror

Suicide pill
BRITAIN
The British sent agents into Nazi-occupied Europe to liaise with local resistance fighters. Each agent carried a suicide pill to swallow if captured.

Sniper rifle
USSR
The Soviet Red Army made extensive use of snipers, especially in the Battle of Stalingrad. They used a standard-issue Mosin-Nagant infantry rifle with a telescopic sight.

telescopic sight

Improvised boots
GERMANY
German troops invading the USSR in 1941 were not equipped to face the Russian winter. Some made straw boots to protect against frostbite.

viewing window shows code letters

Civilian ration card
GERMANY
Shortages of food, fuel, and other essentials led most combatant countries to introduce rationing. This German ration card is for meat.

Der Feind sieht Dein Licht!

Verdunkeln!

Blackout poster
GERMANY
A dramatic poster calls on German citizens to observe blackout regulations during air raids. The slogan says "The enemy sees your light! Make it dark!"

scorpion badge of Long Range Desert Group

Desert headgear
NEW ZEALAND
The Long Range Desert Group, set up by the British, was initially formed of New Zealanders. They found Arab-style headgear a good defense against desert conditions.

Red Cross parcel
BRITAIN
Prisoners of war received Red Cross food parcels. As a result, by the end of the war, Allied POWs were better fed than their captors.

plugboard; its setting can be altered to change the cipher

Anti-tank mine
GERMANY
This Teller mine had a fuse activated by the pressure of tank tracks. Over three million of these mines were made in World War II.

pressure activation plate

Enigma cipher machine
GERMANY
The Germans believed messages encrypted by Enigma were secure, but with the help of an early electromechanical computer, Allied codebreakers cracked the code.

Klappe schließen

Nuclear relic
JAPAN
This melted glass bottle shows the extreme heat generated by the US atom bomb that destroyed Hiroshima on August 6, 1945.

> ## THIS IS **YOUR VICTORY!** IT IS THE **VICTORY OF** THE CAUSE OF **FREEDOM IN EVERY LAND.** "

Winston Churchill in an address to the crowds in London, May 8, 1945

Exuberant Londoners celebrate on Victory in Europe (VE) Day, May 8, after the announcement of the final unconditional surrender of German forces.

IN FEBRUARY 1945, JOSEPH STALIN, FRANKLIN ROOSEVELT, AND WINSTON CHURCHILL met for the last time at a conference at **Yalta** in the Crimea. Stalin agreed to hold democratic elections in Poland—a promise he did not intend to keep. To aid the Soviet troops invading Germany from the east, the Western leaders agreed to step up bombing of German rail centers, including **Dresden**. On the night of February 13–14, Britain's RAF dropped explosive and incendiary bombs on Dresden, causing a firestorm that destroyed the city's historic center and killed some 25,000 people.

There was little pity for the Germans, as the **liberation of the death camps** exposed Nazi crimes. The major extermination centers, including **Auschwitz**, were liberated by the Soviet Red Army. The Western Allies met

Landing on Iwo Jima
American Marines are pinned down by Japanese fire on a beach of the volcanic island of Iwo Jima during the landings on February 19.

their most graphic experience of Nazi barbarity at **Belsen**, a concentration camp in Saxony. Liberating the camp in mid-April, British troops found thousands of prisoners dying of starvation, mistreatment, and disease, and bodies dumped in mass graves or left unburied. Cinema newsreel footage of Belsen convinced most people that the war against Germany had been justified.

The **human cost** of the war with Japan **continued to mount**. In February–March, US Marines

Dresden in ruins
Inhabitants of the German city of Dresden attempt to cope with the aftermath of Allied bombing that created a firestorm in the city.

suffered 26,000 casualties capturing the island of **Iwo Jima**, a volcanic rock in the Pacific defended to the death by an 18,000-strong Japanese garrison.

The **American invasion** of the much larger **Okinawa Island**, launched in April, resulted in a bloodbath. Japanese soldiers as usual fought to the death and tens of thousands of the island's civilian population also died, many by suicide. The Allied fleet offshore was battered by **mass kamikaze attacks** (see 1944).

Meanwhile, American B-29 bombers began the **systematic destruction of Japanese cities**. An incendiary raid on Tokyo

on March 9–10 killed at least 80,000 people.

President Roosevelt did not live to see the defeat of Germany and Japan. The news of his **death** on April 12 came as a shock to the American people. The inexperienced **Harry S Truman**, vice-president for less than three months, took over at the White House, facing formidable responsibilities.

The Allies had agreed that the Soviet Union should have the honor of **capturing Berlin**, and the heavy casualties that went with it. Hitler was determined to fight to the end, although much of the defense of Germany had devolved upon adolescents and the elderly. While American and Soviet troops advancing across Germany from west and east met amicably at the Elbe River, the Red Army fought street by street to take Berlin. As the Soviets drew near his bunker, on April 30 **Hitler shot himself**. By then, former Italian dictator **Benito Mussolini** was also dead, **executed** by communist partisans.

11.5 MILLION THE ESTIMATED NUMBER OF "DISPLACED PERSONS" IN EUROPE IN 1945

January 12 Soviet troops resume offensive in Poland and eastern Germany

January 22 F. D. Roosevelt inaugurated for fourth term as US president

February 3 US troops begin battle to retake Philippine capital Manila

February 13–14 Dresden destroyed by Allied bombing

February 19 US Marines land on island of Iwo Jima

March 9–10 American air raid on Tokyo causes firestorm that kills around 80,000 people

April 12 US President Roosevelt dies; he is succeeded by **Harry S Truman**

April 25 Soviet and American troops meet at the Elbe River

April 30 Hitler commits suicide in Berlin

May 2 Soviet forces complete victory in battle for Berlin

May 7–8 Final German surrender ends war in Europe

January 27 Soviet Red Army liberates Auschwitz–Birkenau death camp

January 30 *Wilhelm Gustloff* sunk in the Baltic by a Soviet submarine, drowning 9,400 German refugees

February 4–11 Roosevelt, Churchill, and Stalin meet at Yalta

March 7 US troops seize bridge over Rhine at Remagen

March 8 Josip Broz Tito establishes provisional government in Yugoslavia

April 1 US troops land on Okinawa

April 15 Allied troops liberate Belsen and Buchenwald concentration camps

April 28 Benito Mussolini and his mistress killed by Italian partisans

June 5 Allied Control Council formally takes power in Germany

June 26 United Nations Charter signed by representatives of 50 countries

A formally dressed Japanese delegation prepares to sign the surrender papers on board the American battleship USS *Missouri* in Tokyo Bay on September 2.

World War II casualties
More civilians than servicemen died in World War II. The Soviet Union and Germany had the heaviest military death tolls. Poland lost one in five of its population, including most Polish Jews.

KEY
● Military toll
● Civilian toll

CASUALTIES (IN MILLIONS)

China — Soviet Union — Poland — Germany — Britain and Commonwealth — Japan — France — Italy — US

His body and that of his mistress Clara Petacci were hung upside down from meat hooks in a Milan gasoline station.

The **surrender of German forces** was complete by **May 8**, sparking heartfelt victory celebrations in Allied countries. Although war continued with Japan, the British Labour Party withdrew from the wartime coalition to fight a general election against the Conservatives led by Churchill. To general astonishment, **Labour** won a **landslide victory**, their promise of a welfare state and democratic socialism outweighing the popular appeal of Churchill's war record.

On July 16, the New Mexican desert was lit up by the **world's first atomic explosion**. This was the culmination of the top-secret **Manhattan Project**, a feat of science and engineering that had cost America $2 billion, spent on presidential authority without Congressional approval. The explosion produced temperatures higher than those at the core of the sun.

The successful atomic test coincided with the gathering of Allied leaders for a conference at Potsdam, near Berlin. Although differences between the Western Allies and the Soviet Union were growing, Stalin agreed to join in the war on Japan. At the end of the conference the Allies issued the **Potsdam Declaration**, calling on Japan to surrender immediately or face "prompt and utter destruction." The **Japanese government rejected the call to surrender** as "of no important value."

Preparations for dropping atom bombs on Japanese cities were well advanced even before the first atomic test. The first bomb was dropped on **Hiroshima** as soon as it was ready and weather conditions permitted (see panel, right). Three days later, on August 9, a second bomb devastated the city of **Nagasaki**, killing at least 35,000 people. The **Soviet invasion of Manchuria** was a further shock to Japan.

Since June, the Japanese government had been split between those who wanted a negotiated peace and militarists insisting on a fight to the death. On August 10 **Emperor Hirohito intervened** decisively **in favor of the peace faction**. The Japanese agreed to

Raising the red flag
Taken by a Red Army photographer, this photo reconstructs the moment when soldiers raised the Soviet flag on the Reichstag building in Berlin.

HIROSHIMA

The American B-29 bomber, *Enola Gay*, piloted by Colonel Paul Tibbets, took off from Tinian Island in the Marianas at 2:45 on the morning of August 6 carrying an atom bomb. It dropped the bomb on the Japanese port city of Hiroshima at 8:15. Heat, light, and the explosion killed some 70,000 people instantly. The lingering effects of radiation raised total deaths to an estimated 140,000.

surrender if the status of the emperor was guaranteed. Although Truman refused to offer any such assurance, on August 15 Hirohito told his people the war had developed "not necessarily to Japan's advantage," and that he was making peace.

The **war had ended** with unexpected suddenness. Dealing with the **aftermath** of devastated cities, broken economies, occupied enemy countries, refugees ("displaced persons"), and war criminals posed almost as great a challenge as the war itself.

Time of death
A pocket watch retrieved from the body of a citizen of Hiroshima records the exact moment when the atom bomb exploded above the city.

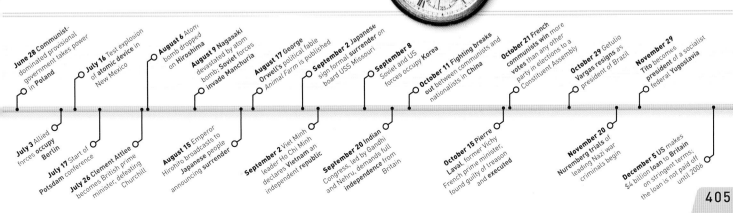

June 28 Communist-dominated provisional government takes power in Poland

July 3 Allied forces occupy Berlin

July 16 Test explosion of atomic device in New Mexico

July 17 Start of Potsdam conference

July 26 Clement Attlee becomes British prime minister, defeating Churchill

August 6 Atom bomb dropped on Hiroshima

August 9 Nagasaki devastated by atom bomb; Soviet forces **invade Manchuria**

August 15 Emperor Hirohito broadcasts to Japanese people announcing **surrender**

August 17 George Orwell's political fable *Animal Farm* is published

September 2 Viet Minh leader Ho Chi Minh declares **Vietnam** an independent **republic**

September 2 Japanese sign formal **surrender** on board USS Missouri

September 20 Indian Congress, led by Gandhi and Nehru, demands full **independence** from Britain

September 8 Soviet and US forces occupy **Korea**

October 11 Fighting breaks out between communists and nationalists in China

October 15 Pierre **Laval**, former Vichy French prime minister, found guilty of treason, and executed

October 21 French communists win more **votes** than any other party in elections to a Constituent Assembly

October 29 Getulio **Vargas resigns** as president of Brazil

November 20 Nuremberg trials of leading Nazi war criminals begin

November 29 Tito becomes **president** of a socialist federal Yugoslavia

December 5 US makes $4 billion **loan to Britain** on stringent terms; the loan is not paid off until 2006

Jewish refugees make their way to Palestine. Thousands attempted this journey before Britain stopped allowing illegal entry into Palestine.

REPRESENTATIVES OF 51 NATIONS BEGAN THE YEAR BY FORMING the **United Nations (UN) General Assembly**, the successor to the League of Nations (see 1919). Its aims were to provide a forum for the nations of the world and to **uphold peace and security**.

The peace after World War II was short-lived, as relations between **Western allies** and the **Soviet Union** continued to cool. In March, **Winston Churchill** summed up the threat of communism in a speech that described an "**iron curtain**" falling across Europe.

The Soviet Union tightened its grip on Europe by creating "**satellite states.**" **Communist governments** were set up in Czechoslovakia, Bulgaria, Albania, Poland, Romania, and Hungary. In France and Italy, communist parties narrowly missed coming to power.

Tensions increased in **India** following Britain's declaration that India would gain **independence** after the war. The leader of the Muslim League, **Muhammad Ali Jinnah** (1876–1948), demanded a **separate Muslim state**, while Hindus opposed this idea. On

> ## " AN IRON CURTAIN HAS DESCENDED ACROSS THE CONTINENT. "

Winston Churchill, British politician, March 5 1946

August 16, Jinnah declared a **Direct Action Day**, a mass protest against British proposals for an all-India government. Violent fighting erupted and thousands died. In response, **Mohandas Karamchad Gandhi** (1869–1948) began a campaign for reconciliation between Hindus and Muslims.

The US granted **independence** to the **Philippines** in July, though the gift had strings attached: the **US kept sovereignty** over several military bases, the Philippine economy was dependent on US markets, and a "parity" clause gave US citizens equal economic rights with Filipinos.

The drive for liberation in **Africa** continued with the establishment of the **Pan-African Federation** by **Kwame Nkrumah**, from Ghana, and **Jomo Kenyatta**, from Kenya. They aimed to promote African unity and end racial discrimination.

In **Palestine**, conferences were held to resolve the growing crisis of admitting **Jewish refugees into Palestine**, but no agreement was reached. The problem was compounded in August, when boats carrying refugees were blocked by **British warships**. Britain told the US it would no

longer allow illegal entry into Palestine, igniting a diplomatic war.

Civil war resumed in China, having been suspended during the world war. The communist leader **Mao Zedong** (1893–1976) declared war on the ruling Kuomintang nationalist party and its leader **Chiang Kai-shek** (1887–1975).

France remained determined to hold on to its colonies in Indochina, beginning one of the longest **guerrilla wars** in history. In November, clashes intensified between the Viet Minh, led by **Ho Chi Minh** (1890–1969), and the

Juan Perón
Fiercely nationalistic, anti-US, and anti-communist, Perón pledged a "Third Way" between capitalism and communism.

Dead Sea Scrolls
The discovery of the Dead Sea Scrolls was one of the most important archaeological finds of the century. The scrolls are fragments of manuscripts of the Old Testament.

Far East Expeditionary Corps, led by France. **The First Indochina War**, involving the rebellion of Vietnam, Cambodia, and Laos against France, was declared on December 19 (see 1954).

The Argentine former secretary of labor, **General Juan Domingo Perón** (1895–1974), was installed as president of Argentina on June 4. With strong working-class support and military backing, he promised **social security** and **higher wages**.

Technicians at the University of Pennsylvania began operating the **first practical electronic digital computer**. The machine was first used for military purposes. It occupied 1,800 sq ft (167 sq m), had 18,000 vacuum tubes, and weighed almost 50 tons.

The division of post-war Europe
After the war, Britain, France, and the US occupied West Germany, while the Soviet Union controlled East Germany. Lithuania, Latvia, Moldavia, and Estonia were absorbed into the USSR.

The UN General Assembly in session in Central Hall, London. The General Assembly is the only part of the UN where all members have equal representation.

LORD LOUIS MOUNTBATTEN WAS APPOINTED THE LAST VICEROY of India to oversee the **end of British imperial rule**. He believed that the only way forward for the country was to **partition** it, dividing it in two parts based on the religion of those areas. In July, the British passed the **Indian Independence Act**, dividing the Raj into **India** (Hindu and Sikh) and **Pakistan** (Muslim), leaving Kashmir to determine its own fate. Pakistan was split into **East** and **West Pakistan**, with India separating the two areas. On August 14, Pakistan gained independence, and **Muhammad Ali Jinnah** became its first governor-general. The next day an **independent India** was born. Partition set off waves of violence and displaced millions of Hindus and Sikhs who had lived in what was now Pakistani territory, as well as Muslims who lived in newly Indian territory.

The partition of India
Partition split the former British Raj into two separate new states: India and Pakistan. Pakistan was formed of two territories, 1,050 miles (1,700 km) apart.

The rulers of **Kashmir** were left with a momentous decision: to become independent, or to join India or Pakistan. In October, **war broke out between India and Pakistan** after Pakistan supported a Muslim insurgency in Kashmir. India agreed to a request for armed assistance from Kashmir's **maharaja**, in return for the accession of Kashmir to India once the hostilities between India and Pakistan ceased (see 1949).

After six years of war, **Britain**'s status had diminished, and the **US** emerged as the only power capable of matching the **Soviet Union**. The "Truman Doctrine" was established on March 12, when Winston Churchill requested US aid in **Greece**, where a **civil** war had broken out between communists and the royalist government. In response, 400 million dollars were sent to Greece to help end the **communist threat**. President Truman's doctrine pledged support to all states struggling to uphold democracy against the threat of communism.

With fears that all of Europe could fall to communist regimes, the US secretary of state **George Marshall** (1880–1959) introduced a plan to help Europe's shattered economies recover from the war, helping victors and vanquished alike. The European Recovery Program, or **"Marshall Plan,"** provided fuel, raw materials, loans, food, and machinery, aiming to help jump-start economic growth.

Anne Frank's diary
The publication of Het Achterhuis (The Secret Annex) on June 5 introduced Anne Frank, a young Jewish girl whose diary chronicled her years hiding from the Nazis in Amsterdam during World War II.

The **crisis in Palestine** (see 1946) continued to worsen as Britain referred the situation to the UN. A plan was devised to partition the area into **separate Jewish and Arab states**. The UN General Assembly agreed to this resolution on November 29, but it was unpopular with Arabs.

While the British organized their withdrawal from the region, Arab and Jewish communities clashed and **terrorist attacks** intensified (see 1948).

Uprooted by partition
Partition caused the largest mass migration in history—around 10 million people were displaced. These Sikh refugees are leaving the Muslim section of the Punjab.

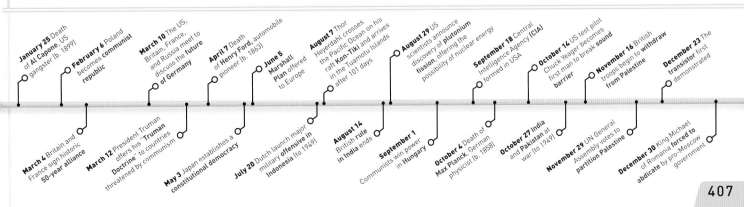

January 25 Death of Al Capone, US gangster (b. 1899)

February 6 Poland becomes communist republic

March 4 Britain and France sign historic 50-year alliance

March 10 The US, Britain, France, and Russia meet to discuss the future of Germany

March 12 President Truman offers his "Truman Doctrine" to countries threatened by communism

April 7 Death of Henry Ford, automobile pioneer (b. 1863)

May 3 Japan establishes a constitutional democracy

June 5 Marshall Plan offered to Europe

July 20 Dutch launch major military offensive in Indonesia (to 1949)

August 7 Thor Heyerdahl crosses the Pacific Ocean on his raft Kon-Tiki and arrives in the Tuamotu Islands after 101 days

August 14 British rule in India ends

August 29 US scientists announce discovery of plutonium fission, offering the possibility of nuclear energy

September 1 Communists win power in Hungary

September 18 Central Intelligence Agency (CIA) formed in USA

October 4 Death of Max Planck, German physicist (b. 1858)

October 14 US test pilot Chuck Yeager becomes first man to break sound barrier

October 27 India and Pakistan at war (to 1949)

November 16 British troops begin to withdraw from Palestine

November 29 UN General Assembly votes to partition Palestine

December 23 The transistor first demonstrated

December 30 King Michael of Romania forced to abdicate by pro-Moscow government

Mohandas Gandhi lies in state after his assassination by a Hindu fanatic who blamed him for the partition of India.

THE CROWNING ACHIEVEMENT OF MOHANDAS GANDHI (b. 1868) was realized when **India won independence** in 1947. However, the concessions he made to Muslims led to his assassination by a **Hindu fanatic** who blamed him for the partition of India, even though Gandhi had bitterly opposed the splitting up of the subcontinent. The news of **Gandhi's assassination** had a profound effect throughout the world, and a state of mourning was declared in India.

South Africa held May elections that saw the **National Party** take power from Jan Smuts' United Party. **Dr D. F. Malan** (1874–1959) became prime minister and formed the first government dominated by **Afrikaners**. Immediately after the election, the government began institutionalizing **segregation.** Malan believed that Africans threatened the prosperity and purity of the Afrikaner culture.

Segregation sign
Under apartheid, separate residency areas were created, and social contact between different races was strictly prohibited.

He based his policy on a system that became known as **apartheid** and enforced a racial hierarchy privileging white South Africans (see 1994).

Anticolonial sentiment grew in the **Malay Peninsula** after World War II. Groups of guerrillas took to the jungle, led by communist insurgent leader **Chin Peng** (b. 1924). In February, there were terrorist attacks on European settlers, and later an "emergency" was declared.

All-Korean elections had been called for in 1948, but **Kim Il Sung** (1912–94), the leader of North Korea, persuaded the **Soviets** not to allow the UN north of the **38th parallel** (the boundary between the northern zone of the Korean Peninsula, occupied by the USSR, and the southern zone, controlled by US forces), believing he could not possibly win a free election. As a result, a month after the South was granted independence as the **Republic of Korea**, on August 15, the **Democratic People's Republic of Korea** (DPRK) was proclaimed, with Kim as premier. On October 12, the Soviet Union declared Kim's regime the only lawful government on the peninsula. By 1949, **North Korea** was a full-fledged **communist dictatorship**.

The UN had devized a plan to split **Palestine** into Jewish and Arab nations, but it was not adhered to when the **state of Israel** was proclaimed by its first prime minister, **David Ben-Gurion**, on May 14. The last British troops withdrew on

UN PARTITION PLAN 1947

☐ proposed Arab State
☐ proposed Jewish State
☐ proposed International zone

Plan for Palestine
The UN General Assembly proposed to split Palestine into Jewish and Arab states, with Jerusalem under international administration.

May 15. Five **Arab armies** from Jordan, Egypt, Syria, Lebanon, and Iraq immediately invaded the new Jewish state but were repulsed. The Israeli army crushed pockets of resistance and extended its borders in what became known as the **first Arab–Israeli War** (see 1949). The realization that the Israeli nation might survive increased anti-Israeli and anti-Jewish sentiment throughout the Arab world.

The **Organization of American States** (OAS) came into being on April 30. Its members were

the independent states of North and South America. They pledged to **fight communism**, increase security, and aid economic growth.

Harry Truman (1884–1972) had steered the US through the end of World War II and the beginning of the Cold War. However, he was not expected to win the **1948 presidential election** against the Republican Thomas E. Dewey, due to his pro-Civil Rights policies, which had alienated many southern Democrats. As the campaign continued, he won the following of the people and was reelected in one of the biggest **election upsets** in history.

In **Britain**, the debate over free healthcare had been ongoing since the 19th century. After Labour's election victory in 1945, **Aneurin Bevan** (1897–1960) presented a plan to provide free healthcare to all for the first time. Bevan formally launched

the **National Health Service** (NHS) on July 5.

With World War II over, the Olympic committee (IOC) could once again select a nation to host the **Olympic Games**. London was chosen, but six years of war had left Britain with shortages of food and clothing, and the 1948 celebrations became known as the "Austerity Games." These Olympics saw the **first defection** from the communist East to the West when the head of the Czechoslovakian gymnastics team, **Marie Provaznikova**, refused to return home.

Czechoslovakia had been moving toward democracy after World War II, but the Soviets did not intend to allow any state within their sphere of influence to become a democracy. **Communists**, supported by the Soviets, carried out a **coup in Prague**, in February. The Czech president, **Edvard Beneš** (1884–1948), was removed from

DAVID BEN-GURION (1886–1973)

The founder of the state of Israel, Ben-Gurion was born in Poland and immigrated to Palestine in 1906. He became an active supporter of the struggle for an independent Jewish state and was expelled from Palestine in 1915 due to his nationalist activities. During World War II, he helped Jews fleeing from the Nazi Holocaust. Ben-Gurion retired from politics in 1970.

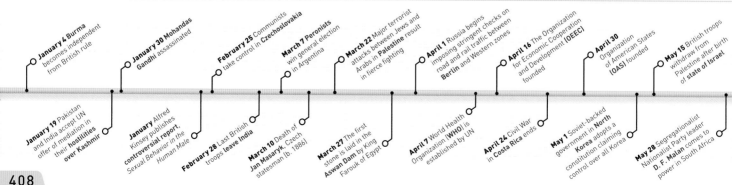

January 4 Burma becomes independent from British rule

January 19 Pakistan and India accept UN offer of mediation in their **hostilities over Kashmir**

January Alfred Kinsey publishes **controversial report,** *Sexual Behavior in the Human Male*

January 30 Mohandas Gandhi assassinated

February 25 Communists take control in **Czechoslovakia**

February 28 Last British troops leave India

March 7 Peronists win general election in Argentina

March 10 Death of Jan Masaryk, Czech statesman (b. 1886)

March 22 Major terrorist attacks between Jews and Arabs in **Palestine** result in fierce fighting

March 27 The first stone is laid in the **Aswan Dam** by King Farouk of Egypt

April 1 Russia begins imposing stringent checks on road and rail traffic between **Berlin** and Western zones

April 7 World Health Organization (**WHO**) is established by UN

April 16 The Organization for Economic Cooperation and Development (**OEEC**) founded

April 24 Civil War in Costa Rica ends

April 30 Organization of American States (**OAS**) founded

May 1 Soviet-backed government in **North Korea** adopts a constitution claiming control over all Korea

May 15 British troops withdraw from Palestine after birth of **state of Israel**

May 28 Segregationalist Nationalist Party leader D. F. Malan comes to power in South Africa

> **I KNOW OF NO OTHER MAN IN OUR TIME, OR INDEED IN RECENT HISTORY, WHO SO CONVINCINGLY DEMONSTRATED THE POWER OF THE SPIRIT OVER MATERIAL THINGS.**

Sir Stafford Cripps, British statesman, on Gandhi, 1948

Harry Truman holds up a newspaper that prematurely announced Thomas Dewey had won the election.

power and replaced by the leader of the Czech communist party, **Klement Gottwald** (1896–1953; see 1989). This was a tense period in Czechoslovakia. **Jan Masaryk**, the Czech foreign minister, had tried to assure the Soviets that a democratic Czechoslovakia posed no security threat. However, he had been in favor of accepting aid from the **Marshall Plan** (see 1947), which Stalin refused to endorse. On March 10, the Czech government reported that Masaryk had committed suicide. Despite suspicions that the communists had murdered Masaryk, nothing was proven.

Berlin was divided into **four zones** after World War II, under an agreement between Britain, France, the US, and Russia (see 1961). Berlin as a whole was an enclave within Soviet-occupied East Germany. The Soviets were determined to force Western powers out of Berlin and, in the **first crisis of the Cold War**, cut

The Berlin Airlift
A crowd of Berliners watch a Douglas C-54 Skymaster plane carrying vital supplies to the Allied sectors of the city.

road and rail links between the city and the West in June. The Allies responded to the "**Berlin Blockade**" by organizing a massive **airlift** to supply the people of Berlin, and the blockade was lifted in May 1949.

The end of World War II brought **mass movements of refugees** as millions of displaced people fled or were expelled from Eastern Europe. Many were treated brutally and found it hard to assimilate. In response, the UN adopted the **Universal Declaration of Human Rights**, which guaranteed a "right to seek and to enjoy in other countries asylum from persecution," as well as the Convention on the Prevention and Punishment of the Crime of Genocide.

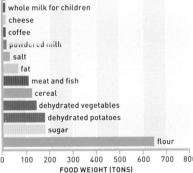

- fresh yeast for baking
- whole milk for children
- cheese
- coffee
- powdered milk
- salt
- fat
- meat and fish
- cereal
- dehydrated vegetables
- dehydrated potatoes
- sugar
- flour

0 100 200 300 400 500 600 700 800
FOOD WEIGHT (TONS)

Feeding Berlin
At the height of the Berlin blockade, one plane reached Berlin every 30 seconds. This graph shows the quantity of food that was flown in daily to sustain Berlin's 2 million citizens.

May 31 President Syngman Rhee of **South Korea** asserts jurisdiction over all of Korea

June 1 Israel and Arab League agree to **month-long truce**

June 20 Lord Mountbatten leaves India; new governor-general is **Chakravarti Rajagopalachari**

August 15 South Korea formally becomes **Republic of Korea**

August 20 Greek government defeats communist rebels

September 9 President Kim Il Sung declares **North Korea a republic**

October 30 Chinese leader Chiang Kai-shek concedes defeat to the communists in **battle for Manchuria**

December 9 Convention on the Prevention and Punishment of the Crime of Genocide adopted by UN

December 19 Dutch launch second military offensive in **Indonesia**, capturing Republican capital at Yogyakarta

June 18 Malayan "emergency" declared (until 1960) due to **communist insurgency**

June 24 Beginning of **Berlin** blockade (to May 1949)

August 16 Death of Herman "Babe" Ruth, legendary US baseball player (b. 1895)

September 3 Death of Edvard Beneš, former Czech president (b. 1884)

September 11 Death of first Pakistani leader, governor-general **Mohammed Ali Jinnah** (b. 1876)

November 2 US president Harry S. Truman reelected

December 10 Universal Declaration of **Human Rights** established by UN

December 16 Cambodia gains independence from France

December 23 Death of General Tojo Hideki, Japanese prime minister during WWII (b. 1884)

"...A ROOF STRETCHING OVER THE ATLANTIC OCEAN."

Ernest Bevin, British foreign secretary, describing the North Atlantic Treaty

At the signing of the North Atlantic Treaty in Washington, D.C., on April 4, US president Harry S. Truman gave an address on its significance.

KEY
- Original signatories
- Joined after 1949

NATO alliance
This map illustrates the 12 nations that originally signed up to NATO in 1949. The alliance enabled the US to keep military bases in Europe.

A TRUCE WAS REACHED IN THE ARAB–ISRAELI WAR (see 1948), bringing an end to eight months of hostilities. The Israelis referred to it as their "**War of Independence**," while the Arabs called it "*Al Naqba*," or "**The Catastrophe**." The Arab states negotiated separate armistice agreements. Egypt was the first to sign on February 24, followed by Lebanon, Jordan, and Syria. The agreement established a line between Israel and the Jordanian-held West Bank, which became known as the **Green Line**.

Representatives of Belgium, Britain, Canada, Denmark, France, Iceland, Italy, Luxembourg, the Netherlands, Norway, Portugal, and the US met in Washington, D.C., in April, to sign an historic treaty that established the **North Atlantic Treaty Organization**, or **NATO**. The alliance was intended for **mutual defense**; countries promised to develop their capacity to resist armed attack, and to consult one another when any of the countries was

threatened. The treaty also provided that member countries would try to **settle disputes by peaceful means**.

The **Soviet Union** stunned the West by exploding its **first atomic bomb**, on August 29, at a remote test site in Kazakhstan. Named "**First Lightning**," its development was facilitated by US spies, such as Julius and Ethel Rosenberg, and British spy Donald Maclean, who had passed technological secrets to the Soviets (see 1951). The loss of nuclear supremacy led US president Harry Truman to order the development of the much more powerful **hydrogen bomb**.

The **Berlin Airlift** (see 1948) by the Western Allies had aided solidarity with the West German leaders. On May 23, the western occupied zones were united to form the **Federal Republic of**

Germany. West Germany held the first free elections since 1932, and the Christian Democrats under **Dr. Konrad Adenauer** (1876–1967) won a small majority.

In July, the Vatican issued the *Acta Apostolicae Sedis* under Pope Pius XII, which effectively **excommunicated Catholics** who collaborated with or supported the Communist Party. The decree represented a significant counteroffensive by the Holy See in a **religious Cold War** against the communist regime, following the persecution of Catholics in communist states.

On Easter Monday, April 18, Eire became the **Republic of Ireland**, following the bill of 1938. It meant Ireland had officially broken free of allegiance to the British crown. In May, the British Parliament approved a bill continuing the status of Northern Ireland as a part of Great Britain; six northern Irish counties had shown a majority in favour of remaining British in the **Northern Ireland General Election** held on February 19.

The **Fourth Geneva Convention** was adopted in August. It brought together the elements of the previous three Geneva Conventions of 1864, 1906, and 1929, and added rules to protect civilians during war. It came in response to **Nazi atrocities** during World War II and the practice of "total war." The international treaty governed the **treatment of civilians during wartime**, including hostages, diplomats, spies, bystanders, and civilians in territory under military occupation.

Civil war in China (see 1946) drew to an end in 1949. Beiping was taken by the communists and its name changed back to **Beijing**, and between April and November, most major cities passed to communist control with minimal resistance. **Mao Zedong** (see 1921) proclaimed the founding of the **People's Republic of China** on October 1, and in December, Chiang Kai-shek and his Nationalist troops fled from the mainland to the island of Formosa (Taiwan), naming **Taipei** the **temporary capital of China**.

The Dutch finally gave up their struggle over **Indonesia** in

People's Republic
Following the proclamation of the People's Republic of China, propaganda posters showed a smiling Chairman Mao Zedong encouraging his people to build a new, prosperous country.

December and conceded independence after four years of war. **President Ahmed Sukarno** (1901–70), who had cooperated with the Japanese in the war, emerged as the strongest national leader; he was faced with the task of welding all the separate regions into a **united nation** under a new constitution, with **Jakarta** as the capital of the Republic. On September 26, 1950, Indonesia was **admitted to the UN** (see 1965).

New **7-inch vinyl records** (also called 45s) were introduced in the US by record company RCA on January 10. With its format of one song per side, the "**single**" was perfect for rock 'n' roll, and it went on to revolutionize the **pop music business**. In the first year of production, RCA pressed more than **25 million** 45s.

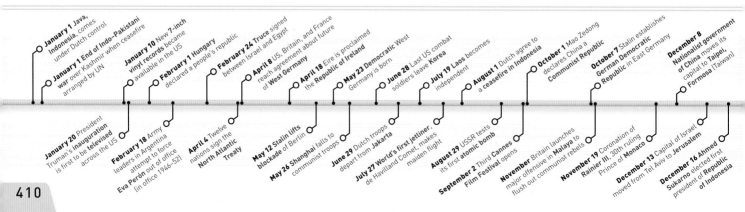

January 1 Java, Indonesia, comes under Dutch control

January 1 End of Indo-Pakistani war over Kashmir when ceasefire arranged by UN

January 10 New 7-inch vinyl records became available in the US

February 1 Hungary declared a people's republic

February 24 Truce signed between Israel and Egypt

April 8 US, Britain, and France reach agreement about future of West Germany

April 18 Eire is proclaimed the Republic of Ireland

May 23 Democratic West Germany is born

June 28 Last US combat soldiers leave Korea

July 19 Laos becomes independent

August 1 Dutch agree to a ceasefire in Indonesia

October 1 Mao Zedong declares China a Communist Republic

October 7 Stalin establishes German Democratic Republic in East Germany

December 8 Nationalist government of China moves its capital to Taipei, Formosa (Taiwan)

January 20 President Truman's inauguration is first to be televised across the US

February 18 Army leaders in Argentina attempt to force Eva Perón out of office (in office 1946–52)

April 4 Twelve nations sign the North Atlantic Treaty

May 12 Stalin lifts blockade of Berlin

May 26 Shanghai falls to communist troops

June 29 Dutch troops depart from Jakarta

July 27 World's first jetliner, de Havilland Comet, makes maiden flight

August 29 USSR tests its first atomic bomb

September 2 Third Cannes Film Festival opens

November Britain launches major offensive in Malaya to flush out communist rebels

November 19 Coronation of Rainier III, 30th ruling Prince of Monaco

December 13 Capital of Israel moved from Tel Aviv to Jerusalem

December 16 Ahmed Sukarno elected first president of Republic of Indonesia

> ❝ WE SHALL LAND AT **INCHON**, AND I SHALL **CRUSH THEM.** ❞
>
> Douglas MacArthur, US General, 1950

The civil war in Korea quickly escalated and drew in troops from across the world under UN command, including these British machine gunners.

AFTER NEARLY 100 YEARS OF BRITISH RULE, India became a **republic** on January 26. India had been managing its own affairs since the partition in 1947, but this day marked the official cutting of all ties. In a formal ceremony, **president Rajendra Prasad** (1884–1963) took the oath of office and a new constitution came into force.

Since it was first created as **Transjordan** after World War I, the **Hashemite Kingdom of Jordan** faced problems arising from its disputed status, weak economy, and artificial frontiers. On April 24, King Abdullah of Jordan (1882–1951) **annexed Arab Palestine** to create an expanded kingdom, to the fury of his Arab neighbors. The annexed territory included East Jerusalem and **doubled Jordan's population**.

South Africa, with its oppressive apartheid laws (see 1948), began

> ❝ **COMMUNISM** IS **A HAMMER** THAT WE USE TO **CRUSH THE ENEMY.** ❞
>
> Mao Zedong, 1950

Emblem of India
India adopted this emblem, taken from a sculpture called Lion Capital of Ashoka, *after it became a republic. The words "truth alone triumphs" are inscribed in Devanagari script.*

to witness **increasing racial tension**. Whites and blacks were segregated on a large scale, and **identity cards** specifying a person's race were introduced. On May 1, a **general strike** was held protesting against all discriminatory laws. **Police opened fire** in the Alexandra Township, killing 18 people and wounding 30.

A year after communists had assumed power in **China** they invaded neighbouring **Tibet**. The military assault took place in October, and by April 1951, Tibet's leaders claimed to have been strong-armed into signing a treaty, known as the **"Seventeen Point Agreement,"** which gave China control over Tibet's external affairs and allowed **Chinese military occupation**.

Anti-communist witch-hunter **Senator Joseph McCarthy** launched a "red scare" crusade in America on February 9, claiming that the US State Department was harbouring 205 communists. His claims were never substantiated,

but many lost their jobs and their reputations (see 1954).

In June, a **new crisis** divided former wartime allies in **Korea**. Split into a Soviet-occupied northern zone and an American-occupied southern zone, once these two powers had withdrawn, the **north**—still backed by the USSR—**invaded the south**. The US, determined not to appease the Russians, provided the main contingent for a **United Nations army** that went to the support of the South Koreans. Within four months, the UN force had driven deep into North Korea; only the intervention of **China** saved North Korea from collapse (see 1953).

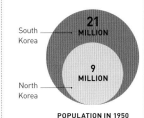

South Korea — **21 MILLION**
North Korea — **9 MILLION**

POPULATION IN 1950

135,000 North Korea
95,000 South Korea

ARMY SIZE IN 1950

Korean population and army
Despite having less than half the population of South Korea in 1950, North Korea's army was superior in size and much better equipped.

AN AMERICAN'S LOYALTY...
STRONGER THAN
COMMUNIST TREASON!

McCARTHYISM

Named for senator Joseph McCarthy (1908–57), McCarthyism became synonymous with the hunt for communists in US public life during the 1950s. The triumph of communism in Eastern Europe and China provoked a severe crisis in the US. Fears of a worldwide communist conspiracy resulted in a campaign against people suspected of communist leanings. McCarthy held senate hearings to "out" communists, and so-called "anti-American" books were removed from public libraries.

The **first human organ transplant** took place on June 17 at the Little Company of Mary Hospital in Illinois. A kidney from a dead body was used to replace a damaged kidney. Although it was later rejected, the transplant gave the patient's remaining kidney time to recover.

German-born physicist **Albert Einstein** (see 1919), who had become actively involved in advocating nuclear disarmament and civil rights, published *"On the Generalized Theory of Gravitation"* in April's *Scientific American*. In this paper, he attempted to unify **gravity** and

electro-magnetism in a way that led to a new understanding of **quantum mechanics**.

The first **modern credit card**, which could be used at a variety of stores, was introduced in the US by Diners Club on February 8. It was established mostly for businessmen to use for travel and entertainment expenses. Cardholders had up to 60 days to pay in full. Merchants were quick to accept the card because they found that **customers** who used a credit card **usually spent more** if they were able to "charge it."

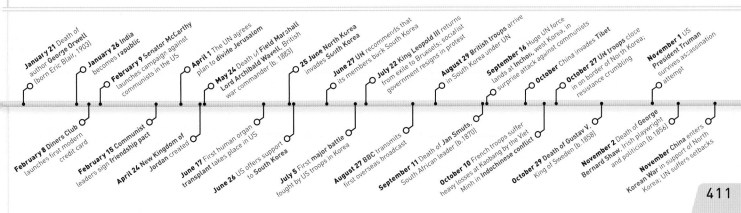

January 21 Death of author George Orwell (born Eric Blair, 1903)

January 26 India becomes **republic**

February 9 Senator McCarthy launches campaign against communists in the US

April 1 The UN agrees plan to **divide Jerusalem**

May 24 Death of Field Marshall Lord Archibald Wavell, British war commander (b. 1883)

25 June North Korea invades South Korea

June 27 UN recommends that its members back South Korea

July 22 King Leopold III returns from exile to Brussels; socialist government resigns in protest

August 29 British troops arrive in South Korea under UN

September 16 Huge UN force lands at Inchon, west Korea, in surprise attack against communists

October China invades **Tibet**

October 27 UN troops close in on border of North Korea; resistance crumbling

November 1 US President Truman survives assassination attempt

February 8 Diners Club launches first modern credit card

February 15 Communist leaders sign friendship pact

April 24 New Kingdom of Jordan created

June 17 First human organ transplant takes place in US

June 26 US offers support to **South Korea**

July 5 First major battle fought by US troops in Korea

August 27 BBC transmits first overseas broadcast

September 11 Death of Jan Smuts, South African leader (b.1870)

October 10 French troops suffer heavy losses at Kaobang by the Viet Minh in **Indochinese conflict**

October 29 Death of Gustav V, King of Sweden (b.1858)

November 2 Death of George Bernard Shaw, Irish playwright and politician (b.1856)

November China enters Korean War in support of North Korea; UN suffers setbacks

radio antennae 8–10 ft (2.4–2.9 m) long

steel sphere weighing 185 lb (84 kg)

Sputnik 1
1957 • USSR
The first artificial satellite, launched ahead of the US version, contained a radio transmitter. Orbiting hundreds of miles above the Earth, it helped scientists understand more about Earth's atmosphere.

ДЕНЬ КОСМОНАВТИКИ
СССР

12
1961

Marine award
1962 • US
John Glenn, the first American to orbit the Earth, was awarded a special medal by the US Marine Corps to commemorate the event. Alan Shepard had become the first American in space in the previous year.

Gagarin poster
1961 • USSR
This Soviet poster shows a beaming Yuri Gagarin, who made history as the first man in space aboard Vostok I.

Cosmonaut's suit
1965 • USSR
Soviet Aleksei Leonov was the first man to walk in space, in March 1965. His suit, the Berkut, came with a backpack life-support system.

seal connects helmet to suit

suit includes an airtight insulation layer

pressure gauge

insulated gloves with rubber fingertips to assist grip

THE SPACE RACE

TWO SUPERPOWERS COMPETE TO PROVE THEIR TECHNOLOGICAL MIGHT

Two nations dominated the race to explore space in the 1960s—the US and the USSR. What had begun as a search for long-range missiles became a battle for international prestige, which neither wanted to lose.

In 1957, the Soviet Union stunned the US when it launched Sputnik 1 into orbit. Then, in 1961, Soviet cosmonaut Yuri Gagarin became the first human to orbit the Earth. It looked like the US was lagging behind. But after the creation of the Apollo program, the US eventually won the ultimate prize: Neil Armstrong and Buzz Aldrin stepped onto the lunar surface on July 21, 1969, marking the beginning of a new era in space exploration.

Moon rock
1969
Collected by Apollo 11 astronauts, Moon rock resembled volcanic lava found on Earth, suggesting that the Moon was once molten.

Scoop

Brush

Sample testing kit
1969 • US
The crew of Apollo 11 took special tools and containers with them to collect rocks, soil, and dust from the lunar surface to return to Earth.

LIFE
SPECIAL SECTION
THE VIEW FROM THE MOON
IN COLOR: PICTURES FROM APOLLO VIII

2/6
JANUARY 20 · 1969

Life **magazine**
January 20, 1969 • US
Images from the Apollo 8 mission appeared on the front cover of *Life* magazine, such was the interest in space exploration. The Apollo 8 crew were the first to orbit the Moon.

tunnel hatch

rendezvous window

access hatch

Lunokhod 1 space probe
1970 • USSR
Lunokhod, meaning "moonwalker" in Russian, was the first of two roving remote-controlled robots to land on the Moon on November 17.

directional helical antenna

solar cell recharges batteries

Apollo 10 command module
1969 • US
This module, carrying three crew, went into orbit around the Moon in a rehearsal for the Apollo 11 mission that landed on the Moon two months later.

independently powered wheels

sachet of freeze-dried food

Space food tray
DATE AND PROGRAM UNKNOWN
This food tray is magnetic to combat low gravity, with metal cutlery and Velcro fastenings to secure shrink-wrapped food packages and liquid.

magnetized surface

Apollo patch
1969 • US
An eagle carrying an olive branch perches on the lunar surface in the Apollo 11 patch, which was designed by the crew.

Mir patch
DATE UNKNOWN • USSR
This is the official mission patch for the Russian Space Station Mir program. The word "Mir" appears in Cyrillic.

Space tools
DATE AND PROGRAM UNKNOWN
Special tools were designed to help astronauts collect specimens. Because bulky space suit gloves made grasping difficult and tiring, tool handles were thicker than normal.

sheet cutters

¡UN CUBANO EN EL COSMOS!
TRIPULACION CONJUNTA SOVIETICO-CUBANA
YURI ROMANENKO Y ARNALDO TAMAYO CIRCUNDAN LA TIERRA EN LA SOYUZ-38
¡VIVA LA AMISTAD SOVIETICO-CUBANA!

soft lunar boots ideal for spacewalking

APOLLO SOYUZ
20 FILTER CIGARETTES

СОЮЗ АПОЛЛОН
20 СИГАРЕТ С ФИЛЬТРОМ

Commemorative cigarettes
1975 • US AND USSR
These cigarettes were made to celebrate the Apollo–Soyuz mission in 1975, when craft from the US and USSR docked together in space. The packets were printed in both English and Russian.

Cuban newspaper
1980 • CUBA
During the space race, astronauts from many communist countries, such as Cuba, went into space as crew members on Soviet spacecraft.

" IT HAD TO BE. "

Julius Rosenberg, convicted **spy,** on his death sentence, 1951

Thousands of suspected Mau Mau activists in Kenya were arrested following open revolt against British rule.

EGYPT RENOUNCED ITS 1936 TREATY THAT GRANTED BRITAIN a lease on the Suez base, in October. Britain refused to withdraw and a guerilla war began in the **Suez Canal Zone**.

In March, the Iranian government nationalized its oil industry, which had been dominated by the **Anglo–Iranian Oil Company**. Britain responded with a **worldwide embargo** on Iranian oil.

A new era dawned in **nuclear power** when the first nuclear power plant, in Idaho, produced around 100 kW of power—enough for four 100 watt light bulbs.

Fears about the **spread of communism** deepened as **Julius and Ethel Rosenberg** were accused of stealing information from the US for the Soviets. British Foreign Office officials **Guy Burgess** and **Donald Maclean** disappeared on 28 May—it was later found out that they had **defected** to the Soviet Union.

The Rosenbergs awaiting trial
Americans Julius and Ethel Rosenberg were found guilty of smuggling atomic secrets to the Soviet Union.

INDOCHINA PROVED VOLATILE THROUGHOUT THE YEAR. In April, the French launched a big push to smash the **Viet Minh resistance** northwest of Saigon. In October, another French operation targeted Viet Minh supply bases.

A **peace treaty** that **Japan** had signed in San Fransisco, US, in 1951 went into effect on April 28, making the country an **independent state** again.

On May 27, **East Germany** closed its border with **West Germany**. A 30-ft (10-m) wide "**control strip**" was dug along the border.

King George VI of Britain died on February 6. His daughter, **Elizabeth**, was officially proclaimed queen two days later.

Opposition to British rule led to the **Mau Mau Rebellion** in **Kenya**. The Mau Mau were an anticolonial insurgent army. They began raiding white-settler farms, and by the end of the year the British had declared a state of emergency.

The **European Coal and Steel Community** came into being in July. Comprised of six nations, it created a "**common market**" for coal and steel, and laid down the

50
THOUSAND
THE NUMBER OF **AFRICANS** WHO DIED IN THE **MAU MAU UPRISING**

EVA PERON (1919–52)

Maria Eva Duarte de Perón, or "Evita," played a crucial role in helping her husband, Juan Perón, become Argentinian president. She was idolized by the poor, and began many programs of social welfare and reform. She died of cancer at age 32.

foundations for the future European Union.

A **military coup in Egypt** headed by Colonel Gamal Abdal Nasser's **Committee of Free Officers** seized control of the government in July. Egypt became a republic in 1953.

The first atomic bombs had been dropped on Hiroshima and Nagasaki in 1945. The much more powerful **hydrogen bomb**, or H-bomb, was tested by the US on November 1.

The world's first successful use of a **mechanical heart** was announced in the US, on July 3. The **Dodrill–GMR** machine kept blood circulating for 50 minutes during open-heart surgery.

STALIN'S POLICIES WERE BECOMING INCREASINGLY ANTI-SEMITIC. At the end of 1952, he told his Politburo that all Jews were sympathetic to America. On January 13, nine doctors were arrested for conspiring to murder prominent figures in the Soviet armed forces. Six of them were Jews. These accusations were

Hillary and Norgay
Edmund Hillary and Sherpa Tenzing Norgay become the first to successfully reach the summit of Mount Everest, the highest point on Earth, during the British Everest Expedition of 1953.

met by reactions of foreboding in Western Europe. The doctors were freed after **Stalin died** of a stroke in March.

Stalin's death led to a major **power struggle** in the Kremlin where a moderate coalition, headed by **Georgi Malenkov** (1902–88), took over. His moderate policies became unpopular and **Lavrenty Beria** (1899–1953), who had been the head of Stalin's secret police, tried to gain power.

Beria was **charged with treason** and was then shot in the back of a truck, in what seems to have been a summary **assassination**.

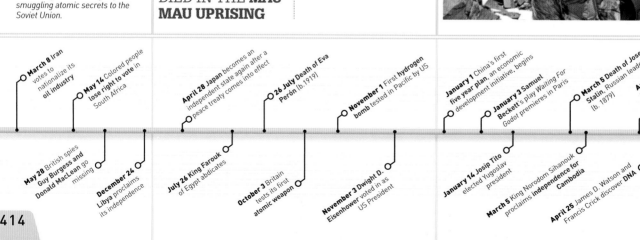

March 8 Iran votes to nationalize its oil industry

May 14 Colored people **lose right to vote** in South Africa

May 28 British spies **Guy Burgess and Donald Maclean** go missing

December 24 Libya proclaims its independence

April 28 Japan becomes an independent state again after a peace treaty comes into effect

July 26 King Farouk of Egypt abdicates

26 July Death of Eva Perón (b.1919)

November 1 First **hydrogen bomb** tested in Pacific by US

November 3 Dwight D. Eisenhower voted in as US President

January 1 China's first **five year plan**, an economic development initiative, begins

January 14 Josip Tito elected Yugoslav president

January 3 Samuel Beckett's play *Waiting For Godot* premieres in Paris

March 5 King Norodom Sihanouk proclaims **independence for Cambodia**

March 5 Death of Joseph Stalin, Russian leader (b. 1879)

April 25 James D. Watson and Francis Crick discover **DNA**

April 8 Jomo Kenyatta, Mau Mau leader, arrested and jailed

May 29 Everest conquered by Edmund Hillary and Tenzing Norgay

The Indochinese conflict lasted eight years, ending in 1954. This photograph shows French forces evacuating Hanoi.

DNA

A scientific breakthrough was made in 1953, when the blueprint of life, DNA (deoxyribonucleic acid), was mapped out by James Watson and Frances Crick. DNA is the hereditary material that contains the coded information needed to build and maintain all living organisms. Watson and Crick proposed a model for DNA called a double helix. It explained heredity and led to the development of an entire biotechnology industry.

chromosome

coiled structure

base pair

War in Korea (see 1950) ended when an **armistice** was signed on July 27, but a state of suspended hostility remained. The **Republic of Korea** (South) and the **Democratic People's Republic of Korea** (North) chose not to sign the peace treaty.

Mount Everest, the world's highest mountain, was first climbed on May 29, by New Zealander **Edmund Hillary** (1919–2008) and the Nepalese Sherpa **Tenzing Norgay** (1914–86). They stayed only 15 minutes at the summit as they were low on oxygen.

A new "absurdist" play, *Waiting for Godot* by **Samuel Beckett** premiered at the Theatre de Babylone in Paris on January 5. Critics were at once divided over its merits.

FRENCH RULE IN INDOCHINA CAME TO AN END ON 21 JULY. **Laos** and **Cambodia** became independent, while Vietnam was divided into **North Vietnam**, with a communist government, and **South Vietnam**. In all three noncommunist states, communist guerrilla movements sprang up.

Senator **Joseph McCarthy** intensified his campaign to root out communists (see 1950). He set his sights on the US army and made unsubstantiated allegations against them. This led to his being censored by the Senate on December 2. Public support dwindled, and McCarthy's reign of fear ended.

A **vaccine for polio** was tested in a huge field trial in the US, in April. The trials were successful, and a **nationwide vaccination** scheme was started the following year.

ISRAELI FORCES CONDUCTED A SURPRISE RAID on the Egyptian-held **Gaza Strip** in February. The raid was the largest of its kind against Arab forces since the end of the First Arab–Israeli War in 1949 (see 1956).

Under its **apartheid** legislation, the South African government forcibly evicted 60,000 black people from **Sophiatown**, in February, to make it a white-only suburb. The **African National Congress** (ANC), an antiapartheid organization, responded with a day of prayer.

The Friendship, Cooperation and Mutual Assistance Treaty, known as the **Warsaw Pact**, was signed on May 14. The treaty set up a military alliance of communist states to **counter NATO** in the West.

The **Soviet Union** ended its occupation of **Austria**, which had been ongoing since the end of World War II, on condition that

Eastern alliance
The Warsaw Pact united the Eastern Bloc in a similar alliance to NATO. The signatories were Albania, Bulgaria, Czechoslovakia, East Germany, Hungary, Poland, and the USSR.

ROSA PARKS (1913–2005)

Rosa Parks made history when she refused to give up her seat on a bus for a white man. Her arrest mobilized a boycott of the bus system, which ended segregation on Montgomery's buses. The boycott also brought international attention to the civil rights cause. Parks remained committed to her cause, and was a symbol of the struggle for civil rights until her death in 2005, aged 92.

Austria remained neutral. The **Austrian State Treaty** was signed on May 15, reestablishing Austria as an independent sovereign state. It joined the UN the same year.

Juan Perón's position as president of Argentina was weakened by his wife's death and a quarrel with the Roman Catholic Church. He was **overthrown** in a coup on September 19, and exiled to Paraguay.

There was a turning point in the US **Civil Rights movement** on

December 1, when **Rosa Parks** broke Alabama race laws by refusing to move to the back of a bus. Thousands boycotted the bus company in protest.

In the West, by the mid-1950s, **teenagers** stood out as a distinct group with interests, musical tastes, and their own fashions. This led to disapproval from adults who feared **juvenile delinquency**. New slang was condemned, dances were closed, and some institutions banned the wearing of jeans.

POLAND
EAST GERMANY
SOVIET UNION
ROMANIA
CZECHOSLOVAKIA
HUNGARY
ALBANIA BULGARIA

KEY
■ Signatories of the Warsaw Pact

June 18 After coup in Egypt the previous year, its army proclaims a **new republic**

June 19 Julius and Ethel Rosenberg executed for espionage

July 27 End of the Korean War (began 1950)

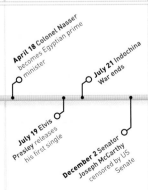

April 18 Colonel Nasser becomes Egyptian prime minister

July 21 Indochina War ends

July 19 Elvis Presley releases his first single

December 2 Senator Joseph McCarthy censored by US Senate

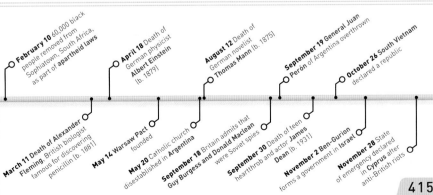

February 10 60,000 black people removed from Sophiatown, South Africa, as part of **apartheid laws**

April 18 Death of German physicist **Albert Einstein** (b. 1879)

August 12 Death of German novelist **Thomas Mann** (b. 1875)

September 19 General Juan Perón of Argentina overthrown

October 26 South Vietnam declared a republic

March 11 Death of Alexander Fleming, British biologist famous for discovering penicillin (b. 1881)

May 14 Warsaw Pact founded

May 20 Catholic church disestablished in Argentina

September 18 Britain admits that Guy Burgess and Donald Maclean were Soviet spies

September 30 Death of teen heartthrob and actor **James Dean** (b. 1931)

November 2 Ben-Gurion forms a government in Israel

November 28 State of emergency declared in Cyprus after anti-British riots

" WHAT COULD WE DO? THERE WAS A REIGN OF TERROR. "

Nikita Krushchev, on Stalin, February 25, 1956

Nikita Krushchev, photographed during an eight-day visit to London. Khrushchev's "de-Stalinization" of the USSR prompted a thaw in the Cold War.

The Soviets began the "Race for Space" with the launch of the world's first satellites, Sputnik I and II—an achievement celebrated by this poster.

Chevrolet Bel Air Convertible
The 1956 Chevy was just what the American public wanted—it was fast, big, and affordable. It soon became a classic symbol of the American Dream.

THE US CIVIL RIGHTS MOVEMENT experienced a turbulent time this year when a black student began attending the University of Alabama. White community members attacked African-Americans, and the activities of the **Ku Klux Klan**, an organization of white supremacists, increased.

Morocco declared its **independence** from France on

KEY
▨ Areas affected by the Suez Crisis

The Suez Crisis
The Suez Canal was a vital trading route from the Mediterranean to the Red Sea. It was especially important for the shipment of oil.

March 2, although Spain retained control of Ceuta and Melilla on the coast. Border disputes with Algeria led to fighting in 1963.

Riots erupted in **Cyprus** in March, after British authorities deported **Archbishop Makarios**, leader of the **campaign to unify Cyprus with Greece**. He was accused of fostering terrorism.

Egypt's **President Nasser** nationalized the **Suez Canal** on July 26. Britain and France had shares in the Suez Canal Company, and concluded a secret pact with Israel in October agreeing that Israel should attack Egypt. This provided a pretext for an Anglo–French invasion of the Suez Canal Zone. On October 29, **Israel invaded the Sinai Peninsula**. The US pressured Israel to withdraw, and UN forces were stationed along the Egypt–Israel border. The Anglo–French assault was launched on November 5. However, a threat from the US to withhold financial loans and a possible USSR intervention led to a ceasefire and withdrawal. Tensions

remained high between Egypt and Israel following the crisis, which became known as the **Second Arab–Israeli War**.

Nikita Khrushchev, Communist Party First Secretary of the Soviet Union, **denounced Stalin** as a "brutal despot" in a speech on February 25. It outraged Stalinists, but led to the prospect of a **thaw in relations** with the US. In Eastern Europe it had a dramatic effect on raising expectations for change.

The **Hungarian Revolution**, in October, led to the formation of a liberal government. **Imre Nagy**, a moderate, became prime minister. On November 3, Nagy announced a plan to withdraw from the Warsaw Pact. After an initial willingness to withdraw forces, Warsaw Pact troops invaded Budapest and crushed the rebellion the next day.

KASHMIR WAS FORMALLY INCORPORATED INTO INDIA on January 26, defying a UN ruling. It was granted **special status** under India's constitution, which ensured, among other things, that non-Kashmiri Indians could not buy property there. Pakistan strongly objected (see 1917, 1965).

Ghana became the first black African country to gain its **independence** from colonial rule on March 6. The first prime minister, Dr. **Kwame Nkrumah** (1909–72), initiated ambitious development programs and spearheaded the political advancement of Africa.

The **Treaty of Rome** was signed on March 25. It set up the **EEC** (European Economic Community) and provided for the countries' social and economic programs. It also gave former colonies free trade with the EEC, and made them eligible for aid.

The suppression of communist guerillas in **Malaya** had been a constant source of concern to

Britain (see 1948). Eventually, Britain realized that this situation could not be resolved by military means, and made constitutional advances that culminated in the **independence of the Malayan Federation** on August 31.

President Sukarno of Indonesia had struggled to maintain a parliamentary democracy since independence in 1945. On March 14, he decided to dispense with parliament and imposed **martial law**. On December 3, Sukarno nationalized Dutch businesses; two days later he expelled all Dutch nationals.

The **Space Age** began on October 4, when Russia launched its **Sputnik I** satellite into orbit. It was followed a month later by **Sputnik 2**, which carried a dog called **Laika**.

European Economic Community
This map shows the composition of the EEC at its inception in 1957, when six countries signed the Treaty of Rome.

February 25 Nikita Khrushchev gives anti-Stalin speech to Communist Party

March 2 Morocco gains independence

April 18 Nikita Khrushchev and Premier Bulganin of the Soviet Union visit Britain

July 26 President Nasser of Egypt nationalizes Suez Canal

August 14 Death of Bertolt Brecht, German playwright (b. 1898)

October 29 Israel attacks Sinai Peninsula; Second Arab–Israeli War

March 10 Renewed anti-British riots in Cyprus

June 29 Riots break out in Poland against communism

October 26–November 5 Hungarian revolution against Soviet domination

November 5 Joint Anglo-French attack on Suez Canal zone

November 8 UN imposes ceasefire on allies in Suez Canal zone

January 14 Death of Humphrey Bogart, US actor (b. 1899)

January 26 Kashmir joins India

March 25 Treaty of Rome paves way for the European Economic Community (EEC)

May 2 Death of US Senator Joseph McCarthy, renowned for McCarthyism (b. 1908)

September 25 Desegregation takes place in Little Rock, Arkansas, US; African American children attend school

March 6 Ghana becomes independent

August 7 Nikita Khrushchev visits East Germany

August 31 Malaya becomes independent

October 4 Soviets are first in space with launch of Sputnik I

Elvis Presley, seen here singing to an adoring young crowd, joined the US Army and set sail for Germany, putting a temporary halt to his extraordinary career.

MAO ZEDONG, FOUNDER OF THE PEOPLE'S REPUBLIC OF CHINA, initiated a program of reform in 1958 that would ultimately kill millions. The "**Great Leap Forward**" was intended to rapidly industrialize China's rural economy. However, Mao's scheme plunged the country into one of the worst famines in history. At least 35 million people were worked, starved, or beaten to death in the following four years.

Great Leap Forward
This propaganda poster urges workers to make more steel as part of Mao Zedong's "Great Leap Forward," an attempt to modernize China.

35 MILLION

THE NUMBER OF DEATHS IN THE GREAT LEAP FORWARD

The **Middle East** felt the repercussions of the **Suez Canal crisis** this year (see 1956). In February, Egypt and Syria merged to form the **United Arab Republic**. Pro-Western regimes in the Middle East saw the union as a threat to their security, and Iraq and Jordan formed a loose union. In July, a **civil war** broke out in Lebanon between the predominantly Christian and strongly pro-Western regime of **President Camille Chamoun** and the **Muslim Socialist National Front**. On July 14, a group of Iraqi Free Officers led by Brigadier Abdul Karim Qasim captured power in Baghdad in a savage **military coup**. King Faisal II, the regent Abdul Illah, and Prime Minister Nuri al-Said were murdered.

CHARLES DE GAULLE (1890–1970)

A soldier, politician, and statesman, Charles de Gaulle became head of the provisional government of France in 1944. Elected president in 1945, he resigned in 1946, returning to power in 1958 to solve the crisis brought about by the Algerian War. He resigned again in 1969 after being defeated in a referendum on constitutional reform.

The Iraqi coup threatened to **destabilize Western control** over the Middle East and its oil resources. To counter this, within 48 hours of the Baghdad coup the US sent a battalion of marines into Lebanon in **Operation Blue Bat**, to help prop up the tottering regime of President Chamoun. Tensions eased, and the US withdrew its forces on October 25 without a shot being fired.

French wars in Indochina, civil war in Algeria, and a series of unstable governments led to the recall of **General Charles De Gaulle** (see panel, above) to French politics. He demanded special powers for six months to restore order, and to draft a new constitution for a **Fifth Republic**, which was submitted to the French public in a referendum on September 28. De Gaulle won an **easy victory to become president** on December 21, 12 years after he had relinquished power.

Russia's success in launching a satellite in 1957 spurred the Americans into forming **NASA**, the North American Space Agency. On July 29, President Eisenhower signed the **National Aeronautics and Space Act**, and NASA opened formally three months later.

Elvis Presley had become a huge star with a series of chart-topping records, and this year would prove to be pivotal. On January 20, he began work on his fourth motion picture, *King Creole*. Then, at the height of what seemed a promising career, Presley was **conscripted into the army**, and in September he set sail for Germany. Billboard noted a drop in sales of his records and Elvis's army years would mark a clear line between the old Elvis and the new.

以 鋼 为 綱 . 全 面 跃 进
YI GANG WEI GANG QUAN MIAN YUE JIN

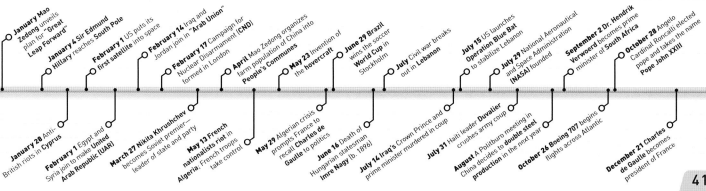

January Mao Zedong unveils plan for "Great Leap Forward"

January 4 Sir Edmund Hillary reaches **South Pole**

February 1 US puts its first satellite into space

February 14 Iraq and Jordan join in "Arab Union"

February 17 Campaign for Nuclear Disarmament (CND) formed in London

April Mao Zedong organizes farm population of China into **People's Communes**

May 23 Invention of the **hovercraft**

June 29 Brazil wins the soccer **World Cup** in Stockholm

July Civil war breaks out in Lebanon

July 15 US launches **Operation Blue Bat** to stabilize Lebanon

July 29 National Aeronautical and Space Administration (**NASA**) founded

September 2 Dr. Hendrik Verwoerd becomes prime minister of South Africa

October 28 Angelo Cardinal Roncalli elected pope and takes the name **Pope John XXIII**

January 28 Anti-British riots in Cyprus

February 1 Egypt and Syria join to make **United Arab Republic (UAR)**

March 27 Nikita Khrushchev becomes Soviet premier—leader of state and party

May 13 French nationalists riot in Algeria; French troops take control

May 29 Algerian crisis prompts France to recall **Charles de Gaulle** to politics

June 16 Death of Hungarian statesman **Imre Nagy** (b. 1896)

July 14 Iraq's Crown Prince and prime minister murdered in coup

July 31 Haiti leader **Duvalier** crushes army coup

August A Politburo meeting in China decides to **double steel production** in the next year

October 26 Boeing 707 begins flights across Atlantic

December 21 Charles de Gaulle becomes president of France

> **"** A **REVOLUTION** IS **NOT** A BED OF ROSES. **"**

Fidel Castro, prime minister of Cuba from 1959–76

John F. Kennedy and his wife, Jacqueline, smile from the back of an open-top car during Kennedy's inauguration celebrations.

THE RACE BETWEEN THE US AND USSR TO SEND A MAN INTO SPACE accelerated in 1959. On January 2, the Soviets launched the first spacecraft to escape Earth's orbit and reach the Moon, **Luna 1**. The US also had its first successful mission this year, when the **Juno 2** rocket sent the **Pioneer 4** probe toward the Moon. **Luna 2** was launched on September 12, and on October 7, pictures taken by **Luna 3** gave mankind its first look at the **far side of the Moon**.

Cuba had been ruled by a **series of dictators**, culminating in the corrupt regime of **Fulgencio Batista** (r. 1940–44 and 1952–59). A group of revolutionaries led by law student **Fidel Castro** took up arms and set up a base in the Sierra Maestra mountains, provoking Batista to indiscriminate repression. Batista's regime collapsed, and **Castro took over**—he was sworn in as prime minister on February 16. A "honeymoon" period with the US soon ended as Cuba became a **totally socialist state**.

In **Vietnam**, northern guerrillas under **Ho Chi Minh** (1890–1969) attacked the southern army in March. Ho Chi Minh aimed to unite

FIDEL CASTRO (1926–2016)

Fidel Castro was jailed for his revolutionary activities in Cuba in 1953. After his release he went into exile, but returned in 1956. He was Cuban prime minister from 1959–76 and the first communist head of state in the Americas. His relations with the US were originally good, but speedily deteriorated. Although still a prominent figure, he retired as president in 2006.

Vietnam under communist rule. The US, seeking to stop the spread of communism, trained the **Army of the Republic of Vietnam** (ARVN) and provided advisors to South Vietnam. On July 8, two Americans were killed by Viet Minh troops. These were the first American deaths in the **Vietnam War**.

The **Dalai Lama**, the spiritual leader of Tibet, fled his country on March 31 and **escaped to India** with his ministers. This came after widespread **open rebellion against Chinese rule** within Tibet, which had culminated in a full uprising. Thousands

were reported killed as **China suppressed the revolt**. Over the next few months, an estimated 80,000 Tibetans fled to India.

Antiapartheid riots continued in South Africa. Those in the township of **Sharpeville** resulted in the deaths of 70 demonstrators, and the **African National Congress** (ANC, see 1994) was banned. These events prompted **worldwide condemnation** of South Africa's apartheid policies. When the British prime minister **Harold Macmillan** visited the South African parliament in February 1960, he made a speech highlighting the "**wind of change**" which he believed would bring independence for black Africans.

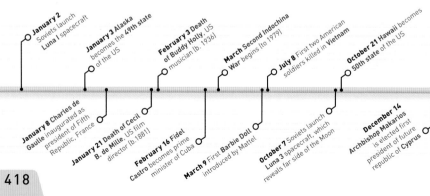

VW Beetle
Produced by the German company Volkswagen, the Beetle survived the war and decorated Beetles became a symbol of peace around the world.

THE STRAIN ON DIPLOMATIC TIES BETWEEN CHINA AND THE USSR became public in June, at the congress of the Romanian Communist Party, when **Nikita Khrushchev** and China's **Peng Zhen** clashed openly. The Soviets were alarmed with China's "**Great Leap Forward**" (see 1958), while the Soviets reneged on their earlier commitment to help China develop nuclear weapons, and were seen as too conciliatory to the West. At a meeting in November, the Chinese delegation clashed with the Soviets again, but eventually a compromise was reached, preventing a formal split.

The **Belgian Congo** became independent on June 30, ushering in a period of turmoil. It was renamed the **Federal Republic of Congo**, with Joseph Kasavubu as president, and Patrice Lumumba —a socialist—as prime minister. In July, the province of Katanga declared independence and asked for Belgian help—Belgium sent an invasion force in response, causing Kasavubu to **appeal to the UN**. In September, Kasavubu dismissed Lumumba as prime minister, and in December he was arrested. **Lumumba was murdered** the following year.

In September, the major oil-exporting countries outside the communist bloc set up the Organization of the Petroleum Exporting Countries (**OPEC**). They combined to fix oil prices by controlling supply (see 1973).

The **laser** was first operated on May 16. A device that emits an intense beam of light, it was

invented by the US physicist **Theodore Maiman** (1927–2007). It drew the attention of scientists around the world and led to **advances** in engineering, medicine, and technology.

The influential civil rights activist **Martin Luther King** (1929–1968) rose to international prominence in the early 1960s. King was arrested in Atlanta, Georgia, during a "sit-in" on October 19. He was sentenced to a four-month term in prison. Presidential candidate **John F. Kennedy** (1917–1963) intervened to secure King's release after eight days in jail.

John Fitzgerald Kennedy was elected as 35th President of the US in November. He narrowly defeated the Republican candidate Richard Nixon after some fiercely contested television debates.

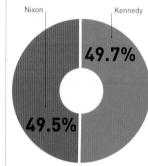

Nixon | Kennedy

49.7%

49.5%

Race for the White House
The presidential race between Nixon and Kennedy was incredibly tight. Kennedy beat Nixon by less than 1 percent—just 118,574 votes.

January 2 Soviets launch Luna I spacecraft

January 3 Alaska becomes the 49th state of the US

February 3 Death of Buddy Holly, US musician (b. 1936)

March Second Indochina War begins (to 1979)

July 8 First two American soldiers killed in Vietnam

October 21 Hawaii becomes 50th state of the US

January 8 Charles de Gaulle inaugurated as president of Fifth Republic, France

January 21 Death of Cecil B. de Mille, US film director (b. 1881)

February 16 Fidel Castro becomes prime minister of Cuba

March 9 First Barbie Doll introduced by Mattel

October 7 Soviets launch Luna 3 spacecraft, which reveals far side of the Moon

December 14 Archbishop Makarios is elected first president of future republic of Cyprus

March 21 Sharpeville Massacre in South Africa

April 25 Violent race riots in Mississippi, US

June 22 Chinese-Soviet split becomes apparent

August 11 Chad gains independence from France

August 20 Senegal gains independence from France

October 1 Nigeria gains independence from Britain

May 16 Laser beam first operated, in US

June 30 Congo gains independence from Belgium

August 16 Cyprus becomes republic

September 14 Organization of the Gasolineeum Exporting Countries (OPEC) founded

November 8 John F. Kennedy elected as US president

November 16 Death of Clark Gable, US actor (b. 1901)

Paratroopers hold back a crowd of French nationals angry at news of self-determination for Algeria.

First man in space
Yuri Gagarin is pictured here in the cockpit of his spacecraft, Vostok 1. His groundbreaking first flight into space lasted 1 hour 45 minutes.

THE PORTUGUESE LUXURY PASSENGER LINER SANTA MARIA was hijacked in January while sailing in West Indian waters. The hijackers were **Iberian leftists** who opposed the Portuguese government and the fascist regime in Spain. The 900 people on board were released after 11 days.

The Soviet Union scored a victory in the **space race** when **Yuri Gagarin** (1934–68) became the first man to be launched into space. He **orbited the Earth** just once on April 12, traveling at more than 17,000 miles per hour (27,000 km per hour) in his **Vostok 1** spacecraft.

In 1960, the Russians had scored a triumph by winning the allegiance of **Fidel Castro**, the newly installed dictator of Cuba (see panel, opposite). Washington responded in April by financing 1,500 anti-communist exiles in the ill-fated "**Bay of Pigs**" expedition. This badly conceived attempt at invasion on the southern coast was immediately repulsed (see 1962).

One of **John F. Kennedy's** first proposals as US president was the establishment of a **Peace Corps** to help in developing nations. The aim was for young people to take one or two years **working abroad** as teachers, healthcare workers, or advisors in Africa, Asia, and South America.

Worldwide action to conserve the **natural world** was put in place on April 29, in Switzerland. The "**Morges Manifesto**" became the blueprint for the first global green organization, the World Wildlife Fund (**WWF**). The organization's headquarters were established in Switzerland, and national offices were gradually set up across the world, starting with Britain, in November. South America's first ever **National Park** was also established this year, in Brazil. The government created the 5.6 million acre (2.3 million hectare) **Xingu National Park** to resettle the indigenous people of Brazil, as their lands were taken over and developed. Seventeen tribes were settled in the new park.

South Africa focused on its anti-British policies and won the vote for **independence** on May 31.

It became a republic and left the Commonwealth. In the same year, **Nelson Mandela** (1918–2013) led the ANC's new military wing, and launched a sabotage campaign.

President Charles de Gaulle called for **self-determination in Algeria** (see 1954), but the atmosphere between France and Algeria remained murderous. French settlers living in Algeria reacted with outrage, and France braced itself for civil war. On October 17, thousands of **Arab Algerians converged on Paris** to protest against repressive measures taken against them. About 10,000 people were arrested and **hundreds were killed**.

Berliners found themselves living in a physically divided city on August 13, as troops in East Germany closed the border between **East and West Berlin**. Barbed wire fences up to 6 ft (2 m) high were erected. Within days, these were replaced by concrete blocks, and the **wall became permanent** (see 1989).

Dividing wall
The Berlin Wall enclosed the three sectors of West Berlin, separating it from East Berlin and East Germany.

KEY
— Berlin Wall
- - Berlin city limits

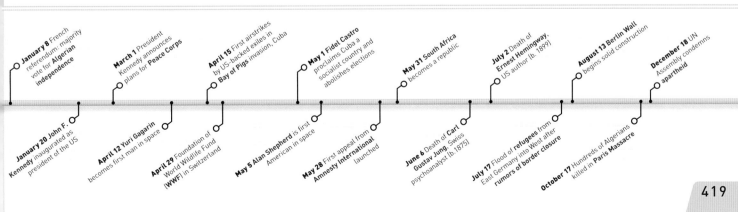

January 8 French referendum: majority vote for Algerian independence

January 20 John F. Kennedy inaugurated as president of the US

March 1 President Kennedy announces plans for Peace Corps

April 12 Yuri Gagarin becomes first man in space

April 15 First airstrikes by US-backed exiles in Bay of Pigs invasion, Cuba

April 29 Foundation of World Wildlife Fund (WWF) in Switzerland

May 1 Fidel Castro proclaims Cuba a socialist country and abolishes elections

May 5 Alan Shepherd is first American in space

May 28 First appeal from Amnesty International launched

May 31 South Africa becomes a republic

June 6 Death of Carl Gustav Jung, Swiss psychoanalyst (b. 1875)

July 2 Death of Ernest Hemingway, US author (b. 1899)

July 17 Flood of refugees from East Germany into West after rumors of border closure

August 13 Berlin Wall begins solid construction

October 17 Hundreds of Algerians killed in Paris Massacre

December 18 UN Assembly condemns apartheid

Soviet missiles are displayed at a parade in Havana. The US came close to confrontation with the Soviet Union over the establishment of Soviet nuclear installations on Cuba.

Martin Luther King salutes the crowd from the steps of the Lincoln Memorial.

" WE'RE **EYEBALL TO EYEBALL** AND THE **OTHER FELLOW** JUST **BLINKED.** "

Dean Rusk, US Secretary of State, on the Cuban Missile Crisis in 1962

PRESIDENT CHARLES DE GAULLE OF FRANCE reached an agreement with Algerian nationalists in March to proceed with Algerian independence. **The Organization Armée Secrète** (OAS), a secret organization of army officers who wanted Algeria to remain a French colony, launched a wave of bomb attacks across Paris and made repeated attempts on De Gaulle's life. **Algeria** gained **independence** from France on July 3, after a referendum held in January backed the move. It brought an end to eight years of civil unrest and guerrilla warfare. French officials estimated it had cost 350,000 lives; Algerian sources put the figure at 1.5 million.

Telstar, the world's **first communication satellite**, was launched on July 10 from Cape Canaveral. In the early hours of July 11, live transatlantic television pictures were sent from Maine in the US to Goonhilly in Cornwall, England.

The US was back in the news when screen idol **Marilyn Monroe**, was found dead in her Los Angeles apartment on August 5. She was 36 years old. There was much speculation about the cause of her death; the coroner reported a "probable suicide," but many believed she had accidentally overdosed on sleeping tablets.

Meanwhile, **Nelson Mandela**— leader of Umkhonto we Sizwe, the armed wing of the African National Congress (ANC)—was arrested on August 5 after 17 months on the run. Convicted of sabotage, he was **jailed for five years** on November 7.

Jamaica became **independent** within the British Commonwealth on August 6, with **Alexander Bustamante** (1884–1977) of the Jamaica Labor Party as prime minister. He would oversee several years of economic growth under his moderate centre-left government.

The people of Berlin were not celebrating any such freedom after the construction of the **Berlin Wall** (see 1961). **Peter Fechter**, an 18-year-old German bricklayer, became one of the first victims of the Berlin Wall's border guards after he was shot trying to cross from East to West Berlin.

In Britain, Liverpool-based rock band **The Beatles** finally signed with the record company EMI on June 4. They had previously auditioned for several record companies, but despite the enthusiasm of their manager, Brian Epstein, they had been turned down. "**Love Me Do**," their first single, was released on October 5, and spent 18 weeks in the charts.

In the US, concerns were growing over the alliance of **Cuba** and the **USSR**. The installation of Soviet missiles on Cuba had reduced the warning time of a nuclear attack on the US from 15 minutes to two. In October, **President Kennedy** ordered a blockade of the island to prevent the arrival of more missiles, and delivered an ultimatum to the Russian leader, **Nikita Khrushchev**, to remove existing missiles. The world was on the brink of nuclear war, but Khrushchev finally backed down. This incident became known as the **Cuban Missile Crisis**.

India and **China** were fighting their own battle in a short but bloody **border war** over their claims to the Aksai Chin Plateau, on India's northeast frontier. Chinese troops advanced into India on October 20, but declared a ceasefire on November 21.

5,000 attempted to cross the wall

around **150** were killed trying to cross over

Crossing the Berlin Wall
Many people made desperate attempts to escape over the Berlin Wall from East to West Germany between 1961 and 1989.

THE 1960S SAW THE REKINDLING of the women's liberation movement. **Betty Friedan** (1921–2006) identified some of the frustrations felt by American housewives in her book *The Feminine Mystique*, which was published in February, and helped start a "**second wave**" of **feminism** in the US.

In another display of unity, the heads of states of 32 African countries signed a charter on May 25, setting up the **Organization of African Unity** (OAU). Their aims were to promote African solidarity, end colonialism, and to coordinate the economic, political, health, scientific, defence, and cultural policies of the members. The conference, hosted by **Haile Selassie** of Ethiopia, also planned to support African freedom fighters by supplying arms, training, and military bases.

Kenya, an early member of the OAU, became the 34th African nation to achieve independence. **Jomo Kenyatta** (1894–1978) was elected leader of the Kenya African National Union after nine years in prison, and won the national election in May. Kenyatta became prime minister and led Kenya from self-government to **full independence** on December 12.

In Europe, US **president John F. Kennedy** made a morale-boosting **speech in Berlin** on June 26. In it he offered solidarity to the citizens of West Germany, who were alarmed at the construction of the Berlin Wall. Thousands gathered in

Gable Monroe Clift in The John Huston Production **the Misfits** **Thelma Ritter Eli Wallach** Arthur Miller Frank E.Taylor John Huston

Marilyn Monroe
At the time of her death Marilyn Monroe was a huge star who had appeared in 29 movies. The Misfits was her last film.

January 8 French vote for **Algerian independence**

May 10 President Kennedy sends US marines into **Laos**

July 10 Launch of *Telstar*, communication satellite

August 6 Jamaica gains independence

October 14–28 Cuban Missile Crisis brings world to brink of nuclear war

October 10–November 21 Indo-China war

January 13 Military coup in **Togo**

January 29 Death of US poet Robert Frost (b. 1874)

May 31 Adolf Eichmann hanged for Nazi war crimes

July 3 Algeria gains independence from France

August 5 US film star, Marilyn Monroe, found dead (b. 1926)

August 17 Peter Fechter gunned down on Berlin Wall

November 7 Nelson Mandela jailed for five years in South Africa

February 19 Publication of Betty Friedan's *The Feminine Mystique*

April 23 Death of Israeli president Yitzhak Ben-Zvi (b. 1884)

SECOND WAVE OF FEMINISM

The "first wave" of feminism addressed legal obstacles, such as votes for women, while the second focused on sexuality and family. Simone de Beauvoir's *Le Deuxième Sexe* defined the woman's movement and exploded the myth that women were second-class citizens.

SIMONE DE BEAUVOIR

LE DEUXIÈME SEXE

I

LES FAITS ET LES MYTHES

nrf

GALLIMARD

front of the Rathaus Schöneberg (City Hall) to hear him speak. In a strongly defiant message to the Soviets, Kennedy described West Berlin as a symbol of freedom.

His speech dashed any hopes held by Moscow that the allies would abandon West Berlin.

Relations between East and West were still strained following the **Cuban Missile Crisis** (see 1962). The incident had raised worldwide concerns about nuclear contamination, which led to talks about a treaty to ban **nuclear testing** in the atmosphere, space, and under water. The **Test Ban Treaty** was signed in Moscow by the foreign ministers of the Soviet Union, the US, and Britain on August 5. It was ratified by the US Senate on September 24 and came into force on October 11.

Meanwhile, the **campaign for racial equality** in the US moved a step closer to victory on August 28. A crowd of over 250,000 civil rights protestors gathered at the Lincoln Memorial for a mass "March on Washington" for jobs and freedom. Many leading figures spoke, including **Martin Luther King Jr.,** who famously stated "**I have a dream,**" while predicting a day when the promise of freedom and equality for all would become a reality in the US.

Another consequential day for the US was November 22, when president John F. **Kennedy was assassinated** as he traveled through Dealey Plaza, Dallas, in a open-top car. Texas governor John Connally was also injured. Both of their wives, who were with them, were unharmed. Secret Service agents immediately stormed the School Book Depository building, where shots had been heard, and found a rifle with a telescopic lens. Just under an hour later, a policeman approached **Lee Harvey Oswald** and was shot dead. Oswald was arrested and charged with the murder of the policeman and Kennedy's assassination.

Traveling back to Washington, DC, on board the presidential plane, *Air Force I*, Vice President **Lyndon B. Johnson** was sworn in as the 36th US president. Kennedy's **funeral** took place on November 25. The world's reaction to the news was one of overwhelming shock.

Two days after Kennedy's assassination, Lee Harvey Oswald, the man charged with the murder, was shot and killed. Oswald, a former marine, was being transferred from police headquarters to jail. He was surrounded by police and journalists. In the melee, **Jack Ruby**, a Dallas nightclub owner, stepped forward and shot Oswald. He later stated that he had done it "for Jackie Kennedy." The murder was filmed and seen live on televisions across the US. Oswald had denied he was responsible for Kennedy's death, which fueled conspiracy theories. In an attempt to investigate the truth, the **Warren Commission** was set up on November 29 to examine the facts.

Kennedy funeral
Over one million people lined the route of Kennedy's funeral procession, which ended at Arlington National Cemetery. Millions more watched it on TV.

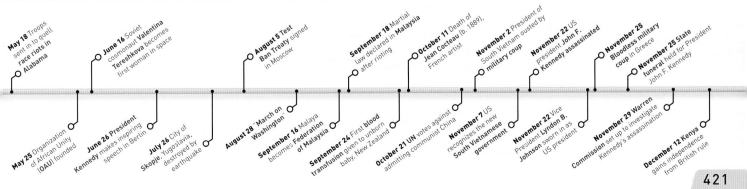

May 18 Troops sent in to quell race riots in Alabama

May 25 Organization of African Unity (OAU) founded

June 16 Soviet cosmonaut **Valentina Tereshkova** becomes first woman in space

June 26 President **Kennedy** makes inspiring speech in Berlin

July 26 City of Skopje, Yugoslavia, destroyed by earthquake

August 5 Test Ban Treaty signed in Moscow

August 28 "March on Washington"

September 16 Malaya becomes Federation of Malaysia

September 18 Martial law declared in Malaysia after rioting

September 24 First blood transfusion given to unborn baby, New Zealand

October 11 Death of **Jean Cocteau** (b. 1889), French artist

October 21 UN votes against admitting communist China

November 2 President of South Vietnam ousted by military coup

November 7 US recognizes the new South Vietnamese government

November 22 US president John F. **Kennedy assassinated**

November 22 Vice President **Lyndon B. Johnson** sworn in as US president

November 25 Bloodless military coup in Greece

November 25 State funeral held for President John F. Kennedy

November 29 Warren Commission set up to investigate Kennedy's assassination

December 12 Kenya gains independence from British rule

END OF
EMPIRE

COLONIAL DOMINATION CRUMBLES AS INDEPENDENCE MOVEMENTS GROW

Empire in 1938
Imperialism was still widespread before World War II. The largest foreign-held territories were in Africa, a product of the "Scramble for Africa" in the 19th century. France and Britain were the leading colonial powers.

KEY
◆ ▪ United Kingdom and possessions
▪ France and possessions
▪ Denmark and possessions

Up until World War II, empires belonging to Britain, France, Belgium, Portugal, and the Netherlands stretched back centuries. At the end of the war, the political landscape had changed significantly, and there was mounting opposition and challenge to imperial rule. In the modern world, all that is left of the European empires is a sprinkling of islands.

By 1945 the empires of Italy, Germany, and Japan had collapsed. The British Empire emerged from the war relatively unscathed, but it was the British who made the first move to end colonialism when they granted India independence in 1947. However, change was slow. In the mid-1950s, the globe was still circled by British possessions.

Despite a widespread belief that imperialist nations had a responsibility to protect their people from Communism, many were crippled by postwar austerity and, increasingly, discontent arose among their populations. Nationalist movements flourished, supported by Soviet Russia, and encouraged by the US. This clash of ideologies complicated the transition to independence; civil war often filled the vacuum.

The last throw of the imperial dice for France and Britain came with the Suez crisis in 1956. The French were being defeated in Indo-China and were engaged in a brutal civil war in Algeria, while Britain was trying to put down rebellions in Cyprus, Kenya, and Malaya. When Egyptian president Nasser nationalized the Suez Canal, it was a further blow to British imperial powers. British and French troops invaded, but were forced into a humiliating climbdown (see 1956). The dismantling of colonies in Africa followed: France had to give up Algeria, and Belgium the Congo. But the wealth of their past rulers was never inherited by the new nations, and many former colonies struggled with foreign intervention, corruption, and poverty.

MODERN OVERSEAS TERRITORIES

Overseas territories are countries that often have a degree of autonomy, but do not possess full political independence or sovereignty as a state. Many colonies fought for self-rule after World War II, but several of them rejected independence. Some overseas territories, for example, are too small and lack the resources to survive as viable independent countries. Others, such as French Guiana in the Caribbean, which is ruled by France, and the Falkland Islands in the South Atlantic, which are ruled by Britain, are of special strategic or economic importance to the states that control them, so not easily let go.

AUSTRALIA	Ashmore and Cartier Islands
	Heard Island and the McDonald Islands
	Christmas Island
	Coral Sea Islands
	Cocos (Keeling) Islands
	Norfolk Island

Modern imperialism
The world today looks very different: colonies in the West Indies, Africa, and Asia have gained independence. The remaining colonial areas consist chiefly of small islands.

- Spain and possessions
- Portugal and possessions
- Netherlands and possessions
- Norway and possessions
- Belgium and possessions
- Italy and possessions
- Australia and possessions
- US and possessions
- Japan and possessions
- 1960 Date of independence

UNITED KINGDOM
Anguilla
Bermuda
British Indian Ocean Territory
British Virgin Islands
Cayman Islands
Falkland Islands
Gibraltar
Guernsey
Jersey
Isle of Man
Montserrat
Pitcairn Islands
Saint Helena
South Georgia and the South Sandwich Islands
Turks and Caicos Islands

DENMARK
Faroe Islands
Greenland

NEW ZEALAND
Cook Islands
Niue
Tokelau

FRANCE
Bassas da India
Clipperton Island
Europa Island
French Guiana
French Polynesia
French Southern and Antarctic Islands
Glorioso Islands
Guadelope
Juan de Nova Island
Martinique
Mayotte
New Caledonia
Réunion
Saint Pierre and Miquelon
Tromelin Island
Wallis and Futuna

THE NETHERLANDS
Aruba
Netherlands Antilles

NORWAY
Bouvet Island
Jan Mayen
Svalbard

THE US
American Samoa
Baker Island
Guam
Howland Island
Jarvis Island
Johnston Atoll
Kingman Reef
Midway Islands
Navassa Island
Northern Mariana Islands
Palmyra Atoll
Puerto Rico
US Virgin Islands
Wake Island

DISPUTED TERRITORIES
Antarctica
Gaza Strip
Parcel Islands
Spratly Islands
West Bank
Western Sahara

Nelson Mandela was among eight men sentenced to life imprisonment during the Rivonia Trial—they left the court with their fists raised in defiance.

THE YEAR BEGAN WITH INCREASING TENSION between Greek and Turkish Cypriots. In March, the UN sent 7,000 troops into **Cyprus** to try to keep the peace. Strong diplomatic pressure finally brought an end to the violence on August 10.

On May 27, **Jawaharlal Nehru**—the first prime minister of an independent India, and regarded by many as the founder of modern India—died, aged 74. Gathering in mile-long lines, 250,000 men, women, and children filed past his body to pay their respects.

In South Africa, **Nelson Mandela** (1918–2013) a prominent figure of the **antiapartheid** struggle, was jailed for life on June 12. During the trial, Mandela and other members of the **African National Congress** (ANC, see 1994) admitted trying to bring down the government.

Beatlemania begins
The Beatles took the US by storm in 1964. Their faces were splashed across newspapers and magazines as their tour of 23 cities sold out.

Meanwhile, race equality in the US took a positive turn when the **Civil Rights Bill** became law on July 2. The bill created equal rights for all, regardless of race, religion, or color. The signing was witnessed by civil rights activist **Martin Luther King, Jr.**, who had emerged as the symbolic leader of the worldwide struggle for civil rights. At 35, he became the youngest man to receive the **Nobel Peace Prize** for his work.

In Vietnam, the US was adamant that **South Vietnam** should not fall to the communists. On August 7, US president Johnson received approval from Congress to "**take all necessary action**" against the communist regime in North Vietnam. As a result the war escalated, but it was largely kept from the American public, and in November Johnson won a landslide victory (see 1965).

Capturing the American public's attention, the **Warren Report**, investigating the assassination of Kennedy (see 1963) was released on September 28. It asserted that there had been no conspiracy, and concluded that gunman Lee Harvey Oswald had acted alone.

In the East, Nikita **Khrushchev**, leader of the Soviet Union, was "retired" in October, having been in power since 1958. His policies had become increasingly unpopular and he was removed from office.

The Beatles made it big this year, sparking a hysteria known as "Beatlemania." Appearing on US TV in February, by April their singles occupied all five top spots on the *Billboard* Hot 100 chart.

" NOTHING IS MORE IMPORTANT THAN INDEPENDENCE AND FREEDOM. "

Ho Chi Minh, president of North Vietnam, on a propaganda poster during Vietnamese war

Hostile terrain
The US army was technologically superior in Vietnam, but struggled with unfamiliar territory such as the swamp that these marines are wading through.

ON FEBRUARY 18, THE GAMBIA ACHIEVED INDEPENDENCE from British rule. Dawda Kairaba Jawara became the first prime minister, and was knighted the following year. By contrast, **Southern Rhodesia**, led by prime minister Ian Smith, announced a **Unilateral Declaration of Independence** on November 11. Britain declared this action illegal, and through the UN most countries applied **economic sanctions** against Southern Rhodesia.

In **Vietnam**, the conflict was escalating. President Johnson ordered Operation Rolling Thunder, a massive **bombing campaign against North Vietnam**, and in March the first American ground troops landed in South Vietnam. By June they were fighting alongside South Vietnamese forces against the **Viet Cong**.

Back in the US, racial tension was at boiling point. Following the arrest of a black man for drunk driving, Watts, a suburb of Los Angeles, erupted into violent **race riots**. Some blamed the heat wave, while others pointed the finger at police brutality.

In September **India** launched an **invasion of West Pakistan**, following covert operations by Pakistan across the ceasefire line. Since the ceasefire line had been established in 1949, both countries had laid claim to **Kashmir**. After three weeks of fighting, they agreed to a **UN ceasefire**.

President **Sukarno** of **Indonesia** barely survived an attempted coup in November. **General Suharto**, commander of the army's strategic reserve, emerged the victor in the power struggle.

Meanwhile, the lights went out in the US on November 9 during the biggest **blackout** in US history. More than 30 million people in the northwest were left without electricity, which was caused by human error.

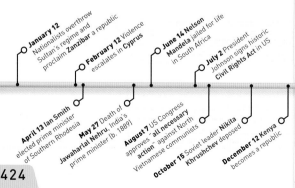

January 12 Nationalists overthrow Sultan's regime and proclaim **Zanzibar** a republic

February 12 Violence escalates in **Cyprus**

April 13 Ian Smith elected prime minister of Southern Rhodesia

May 27 Death of **Jawaharlal Nehru**, India's prime minister (b. 1889)

June 14 Nelson **Mandela** jailed for life in South Africa

July 2 President Johnson signs historic **Civil Rights Act** in US

August 7 US Congress approves "**all necessary action**" against North Vietnamese communists

October 15 Soviet leader Nikita **Khrushchev** deposed

December 12 Kenya becomes a republic

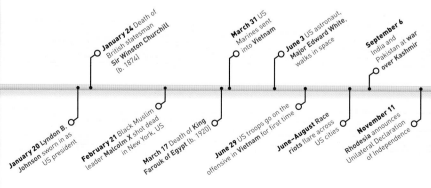

January 20 Lyndon B. Johnson sworn in as US president

January 24 Death of British statesman **Sir Winston Churchill** (b. 1874)

February 21 Black Muslim leader Malcolm X shot dead in New York, US

March 17 Death of King **Farouk of Egypt** (b. 1920)

March 31 US Marines sent into Vietnam

June 3 US astronaut, Major Edward White, walks in space

June 29 US troops go on the offensive in Vietnam for first time

June–August Race riots flare across US cities

September 6 India and Pakistan at war over Kashmir

November 11 Rhodesia announces Unilateral Declaration of Independence

1966

The Black Panthers, a black nationalist group based in Oakland, California, argued for working-class unity. Here supporters hold up copies of Mao Zedong's *Little Red Book*.

WITH INCREASED FIGHTING IN VIETNAM, 1966 SAW THE US launch its **largest offensive** against the Viet Cong in Operation Crimp, to capture the Viet Cong's Saigon area headquarters. By the end of 1966, the number of US troops in Vietnam had reached 385,000, amid **increased public protests** about the war.

Pakistani and **Indian** leaders met more peacefully in January at Tashkent in Uzbekistan to sign a declaration agreeing to resolve their dispute (see 1965) by **peaceful means**. Shortly afterward, Lal Bahadur Ahastri, prime minister of India, died of a heart attack. He was succeeded by Indira Gandhi, daughter of Nehru.

In **Northern Ireland**, violence erupted following the 50th anniversaries of the Battle of the Somme and the Easter Rising—symbolic dates for Protestants and Catholics respectively. The murder of two Catholics by a "loyalist" terror group called the **Ulster Volunteer Force** (UVF) sparked more riots in May and June. The UVF was banned, but the cycle of sectarian killings, known as **the Troubles**, had begun.

The shock assassination of **Hendrik Verwoerd**, prime minister of South Africa and the architect of apartheid, raised queries about the future of South Africa. He was stabbed to death on September 6 by Dimitri Tsafendas, who claimed not enough was being done for whites.

Race continued to be a dominant issue in the US, with **race riots** occurring in many cities throughout

The Little Red Book
Full of Mao's quotations, this book added to his cult and had a profound impact on the masses during the Chinese Cultural Revolution.

In August, Chinese communist leader Mao Zedong launched the **Cultural Revolution**, aiming to purge the country of "impure" elements and restore his authority over party rivals. One-and-a-half million people died and much of the country's cultural heritage was destroyed. In September 1967, with many Chinese cities on the verge of anarchy, Mao sent in the army to restore order.

By the end of 1966, the decade known as the "**Swinging Sixties**"—so called because of the collapse of social taboos relating to race, sex, and gender—was in full swing. It was epitomized by rock music, photography, and fashion, with London and youth culture at its heart.

State of play in Vietnam
This map shows North and South Vietnam in 1964, divided by a demilitarized zone. In 1966 the North Vietnamese crossed the zone and one of the largest battles to date broke out near Dong Ha.

the mid-1960s. Student radicals were becoming impatient with Martin Luther King's strategy of nonviolence, and in June, activist Stokely Carmichael popularized the term "**Black Power**." In October he formed the **Black Panther Party**, combining traditional civil rights slogans with Marxist rhetoric, and the language of black separatism.

KEY
- ▪ North Vietnam
- ▪ South Vietnam
- — Demilitarized zone

1967

Donald Campbell was attempting to break the world speed record when his speedboat *Bluebird* crashed, killing him instantly.

THE YEAR BEGAN WITH THE TRAGIC DEATH OF DONALD CAMPBELL, who was killed on January 4 at Coniston Water in the Lake District, England, while attempting to break his own **water speed record**. He was traveling at more than 300 mph (480 kph) when his boat flipped.

Tensions were running high in the Middle East after Egypt asked for UN forces in the Sinai to be removed. The Israelis responded with a **pre-emptive attack**, which ended after six days with Israel in control of Sinai, Gaza, the West Bank, the Golan Heights, and Jerusalem.

Meanwhile, in Bolivia, **Ernesto "Che" Guevara** (see panel, right) was captured and shot dead, on the Bolivian president's orders, on 9 June. Guevara was in Latin America helping guerrilla groups.

More interested in saving lives, South African surgeon Christiaan

CHE GUEVARA (1928–67)

Ernesto "Che" Guevara was born in Argentina in 1928, and became involved in the opposition to Juan Peron. He traveled extensively through Latin America, where he saw poverty and social injustice that helped forge his radical political views. Che became an associate of Fidel Castro, and played a role in the fight for Cuba. He left Cuba to help revolutionaries abroad, and was executed in Bolivia.

11,500 EGYPT
1,000
6,094 JORDAN
Syria

Casualties in the Six-Day War
Israel won a decisive victory in the Six-Day War between Israel, Egypt, Jordan, and Syria, with 759 casualties. Arab losses, in contrast, were high.

Barnard conducted the **first heart transplant** on December 3. Although the patient died later of pneumonia, the procedure was a great step forward for medicine.

In Europe, Nicolae **Ceausescu** became premier of **Romania** on December 9, defying the Soviets by establishing diplomatic relations with West Germany.

In **Greece**, after army officers seized power on April 21, a counter coup by King Constantine II failed, and he fled to Rome.

During the first manned mission to the Moon, the three astronauts on board Apollo 8 beamed back images of Earth as a planet in space.

THE MY LAI MASSACRE IN VIETNAM SENT SHOCK WAVES through the US political establishment. My Lai lies in the South Vietnamese district of Son My, an area where the **Viet Cong** were deeply entrenched. On March 16, **US troops**, who had been on a "search and destroy" mission to root out communist fighters, **killed more than 500 Vietnamese civilians** in cold blood, many of them women and children. The massacre helped to **turn public opinion** against the Vietnam War, although the story was not made public until the following year.

By 1968, the Vietnam War was costing the US $66 million a day. **Protests against the war escalated** as people questioned the US's role in the conflict. Vivid news reports showed horrific civilian casualties. On August 28, during the Democratic national convention in Chicago, **10,000 antiwar protesters gathered** and were confronted by 26,000 police and national guardsmen. The event was covered live on network TV.

War paraphernalia
A Chinese compass, a map case, and a map with enemy bases marked on, formed the basic kit for Vietcong militia during the Vietnam War.

On 4 April, the African-American civil rights leader **Martin Luther King, Jr.** (see panel, right) was assassinated in the southern US city of Memphis, Tennessee. King was shot on the balcony of his hotel as he was preparing to lead a march of sanitation workers **protesting against low wages**. The day before his assassination,

he delivered his famous speech, "I have seen the mountaintop ..." in Memphis, which seemed to predict his end, "... **I've seen the promised land**. I may not get there with you".

King's death sparked **widespread race riots** across the US that cost dozens of lives and led to damage worth millions of dollars. It hastened the process of "**white flight**" from the inner cities that left many American downtowns virtually abandoned. **James Earl Ray**, a petty criminal, was convicted of King's murder and sentenced to 99 years in prison.

Senator Robert Kennedy (1925–68), increasingly opposed to the Vietnam War, struggled over his decision to challenge the Democratic party's incumbent president, **Lyndon Johnson**. His younger brother, Edward (Teddy), was against it; his wife, Ethel, urged him on. Many feared he would suffer the same fate as his brother John, who had been assassinated in 1963. He **announced his candidacy** on March 16, and two weeks later Johnson dropped out of the race. America was a wounded nation, reeling from the war and inner-city riots. Kennedy based his presidential election campaign on **inequality and social justice**.

On 5 June, **Robert Kennedy was shot** in a Los Angeles hotel after giving a victory speech to celebrate his win in the California Primary. A **Palestinian immigrant**, **Sirhan Sirhan**, fired at Kennedy as he was being escorted through the kitchen pantry of the Ambassador Hotel. Robert Kennedy's **support for Israel** was believed to have prompted the attack. He died the following day. His death, coming 63 days after that of Martin Luther King, Jr., made 1968 one of the most **volatile and traumatic**, years in US history.

On November 6, Republican **Richard Nixon** (1913–94) emerged victorious in the US **presidential election**. He had based his campaign on rising crime and claimed he would restore law and order. It was a

dramatic comeback; Nixon was Dwight D. Eisenhower's vice-president and lost the presidential race to John F. Kennedy in 1960.

Enoch Powell (1912–98), a British right-wing politician, made a hugely **controversial speech** on April 20, in which he warned the government against opening the "floodgates" to **black immigrants**. He called for an immediate reduction in immigration, and viewed the future with foreboding. Quoting the Roman poet Virgil, he said, "... like the Roman, I seem to see the river Tiber foaming with much blood." His speech caused a **storm of protest**, and ended Powell's political ambitions.

Elsewhere in Europe, **France** experienced student **riots**, mass **protests**, and **strikes** throughout May, which brought the country

MARTIN LUTHER KING, JR. (1929–68)

A leading African-American civil rights campaigner in the US, Martin Luther King, Jr. rose to prominence in 1955, when he led a boycott of buses in Montgomery, Alabama, in protest against the state's transport segregation laws. In this, and his subsequent campaigns, he insisted on non-violence. King was awarded the Nobel Peace Prize in 1964. Four years later, he was assassinated by a white gunman in Memphis, Tennessee.

200,000
THE **NUMBER OF WARSAW PACT TROOPS** THAT **INVADED CZECHOSLOVAKIA**

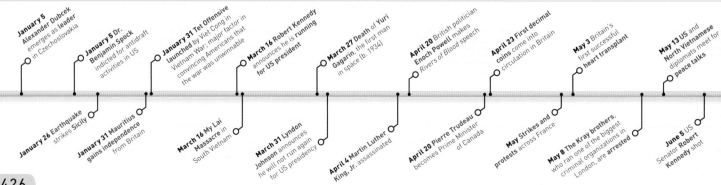

January 5 Alexander Dubcek emerges as leader in Czechoslovakia

January 5 Dr. Benjamin Spock indicted for antidraft activities in US

January 31 Tet Offensive launched by Viet Cong in Vietnam War; major factor in convincing Americans that the war was unwinnable

March 16 Robert Kennedy announces he is running for US president

March 27 Death of Yuri Gagarin, the first man in space (b. 1934)

April 20 British politician Enoch Powell makes *Rivers of Blood* speech

April 23 First decimal coins come into circulation in Britain

May 3 Britain's first successful heart transplant

May 13 US and North Vietnamese diplomats meet for peace talks

January 26 Earthquake strikes Sicily

January 31 Mauritius gains independence from Britain

March 16 My Lai Massacre in South Vietnam

March 31 Lyndon Johnson announces he will not run again for US presidency

April 4 Martin Luther King, Jr. assassinated

April 20 Pierre Trudeau becomes Prime Minister of Canada

May Strikes and protests across France

May 8 The Kray brothers, who ran one of the biggest criminal organizations in London, are arrested

June 5 US Senator Robert Kennedy shot

to its knees. It began as a series of student protests that broke out at universities in Paris, following confrontations with administrators and police. Further police action inflamed the situation, leading to a **general strike** by over 10 million workers across France—roughly two-thirds of the workforce. The government came close to collapse; President Charles de Gaulle (1890–1970)

Protest in Paris
When French strikers took to the streets in May, the country was on the verge of revolution. The largest rallies were held in Paris.

called for new parliamentary elections on June 23. Although De Gaulle won the election, the Paris riots were regarded as a **cultural and social revolution**.

Troops from five **Warsaw Pact countries** (see 1955) stormed into **Czechoslovakia** on August 20 to seize control and restore communism to the country. During an eight-month period that became known as the **Prague Spring**, the incumbent prime minister Alexander Dubcek had made **substantial reforms**, including freedom of speech. He was arrested, and his government replaced with

a **repressive regime** (see 1989). The invasion drew condemnation from around the world. Jan Palach, a Czech student, **burned himself to death** in protest over the Soviet occupation. An estimated 500,000 gathered to watch his funeral procession.

On September 7, a prominent gathering of women disrupted the staging of **Miss America**, a long-standing **beauty pageant** held at Atlantic City's convention hall. The protest was organized by the **New York Radical Women** (NYRW), a group active in the civil rights and antiwar movements. They attacked the pageant's

beauty standards as racist—no black woman had ever made it to the final. The demonstrators brandished signs that read "**Women's Liberation**," and threw bras into bins as a sign of protest, which began the myth that feminists "burn their bras."

Americans, finally, had cause to rejoice at the end of the year when **Apollo 8**, the first manned craft to **orbit the moon**, was launched into space on December 21. Live pictures of the lunar surface were beamed back to Earth. The crew, Frank Borman, James Lovell, and William Anders, returned on December 27 as **national heroes**.

150
WOMEN PROTESTERS

52
BEAUTY CONTESTANTS

Beauty and backlash
The glamorous contestants appearing in the Miss America Pageant, in Atlanta, were outnumbered three to one by the protestors.

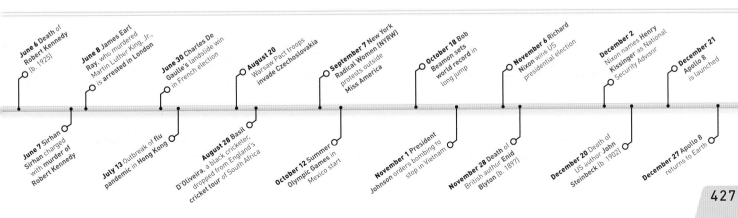

THE STORY OF
GENETICS

THE SEARCH FOR THE BLUEPRINT OF LIFE AND THE MECHANISM OF HEREDITY

Watson and Crick's DNA model

For thousands of years, humans have wondered how characteristics are inherited, but it was not until the 19th century that scientists began to understand the fundamental mechanisms. Now, the knowledge that DNA carries genetic information has provided insight into the basis of life itself.

One of the earliest theories of heredity was that of the ancient Greek Hippocrates, who proposed that elements from all of the body became concentrated in semen, which then made a human in the womb containing the characteristics of both parents. Charles Darwin later called this mechanism of inheritance "pangenesis."

It was not until the 19th century that the basic rules of heredity were discovered, by the Austrian monk Gregor Mendel. At about the same time, the Swiss scientist Friedrich Miescher extracted from the cell nucleus a substance he called "nuclein" (now known as DNA). In the early 20th century, American biologist Thomas Hunt Morgan's experiments with fruit flies confirmed that genes reside on chromosomes. However, it was still thought that protein, not DNA, was the substance that transmits inherited traits.

THE SIGNIFICANCE OF DNA

In the 1940s, Oswald Avery, Colin MacLeod, and Maclyn McCarty discovered that DNA is the hereditary molecule in most organisms and is the chemical basis of genetic information. In the early 1950s, Maurice Wilkins and Rosalind Franklin discovered that DNA has a helix shape, and in 1953, these findings were put together by Francis Crick and James Watson in their double-helix model of DNA. The Human Genome Project went further, mapping all the human genes.

GENETIC CODE

A gene is a portion of DNA containing information for making a specific protein (comprising a specific sequence of amino acids). This is encoded as an "alphabet" of bases: A (standing for adenine), C (cytosine), G (guanine), and T (thymine). These are arranged into "words" (codons) of three letters; each codon corresponds to a particular amino acid. In a cell, a gene's codon sequence is translated into a sequence of specific amino acids, making the specific protein coded for by that gene.

> ❝ **YOU,** YOUR JOYS AND YOUR SORROWS, YOUR MEMORIES AND AMBITIONS, YOUR SENSE OF PERSONAL IDENTITY AND FREE WILL, **ARE ... NO MORE THAN THE BEHAVIOUR OF... NERVE CELLS AND ... MOLECULES.** ❞

Francis Crick, *The Astonishing Hypothesis: The Scientific Search for the Soul*, 1994

---

c. 460–375 BCE
Hippocrates' pangenesis hypothesis
Hippocrates devises the theory that hereditary material collects from throughout the body and reassembles inside the womb to form human life.

Hypocrates

1859
Theory of natural selection
Charles Darwin publishes *The Origin of Species*, in which he puts forward his theory that the fittest organisms survive and pass on their traits.

The Origin of Species

c. 1868–69
Nuclein discovered
Swiss scientist Friedrich Miescher discovers a substance he calls "nuclein" in the nuclei of white blood cells. Later called nucleic acid, nuclein is now known as DNA.

White blood cell

1663–65
Cells first described
English scientist Robert Hooke coins the term "cell" to describe the microscopic units he observed while examining a section of cork with an early compound microscope.

Robert Hooke's microscope

1863
Gregor Mendel
Experimenting with peas, Austrian monk Gregor Mendel finds that traits, such as whether peas are round or wrinkled, are passed on by independent units, later called genes.

Round and wrinkled peas

1880s
Meiosis discovered
Meiosis, the process of cell division that produces gametes (sex cells), is described in the early 1880s. Its significance for inheritance is elucidated in the 1890s by German biologist August Weismann.

1888
Chromosomes discovered
German anatomist Heinrich Waldeyer notices that the central part of the cell (the nucleus) sometimes contains threadlike bodies, for which he coins the term "chromosomes."

aluminum plates represent four chemical bases in DNA model

plate representing the base cytosine

plate representing the base guanine

plate representing the base thymine

Watson and Crick's DNA model
James Watson and Francis Crick made a model of the DNA molecule using metal plates and rods in their laboratory in Cambridge, England. They proposed that DNA was a double-helix polymer, shaped like a twisted ladder, and noted that this structure allows for replication of genetic material. This reconstruction uses some of the plates from the original model.

plate representing the base adenine

bonds between bases represented by rods

Early 20th century
Role of chromosomes in heredity
Working with fruit flies, American geneticist Thomas Hunt Morgan establishes that genes controlling heredity are positioned along chromosomes, and links the inheritance of a specific trait with a particular chromosome.

1953
Structure of DNA discovered
American biologist James Watson and British biologist Francis Crick discover that the DNA molecule consists of two helical chains of nucleotides wound loosely around each other.

1972
Recombinant DNA
American biochemists Paul Berg and Herb Boyer produce the first recombinant DNA molecules (recombinant DNA is DNA that has been created artificially), an achievement that is considered the birth of modern biotechnology.

1905
Sex chromosomes identified
American geneticists Nettie Stevens and E. B. Wilson independently identify the XY chromosome sex-determination system: males have XY and females have XX sex chromosomes.

X chromosome

1940–44
DNA identified as genetic messenger
Using *Streptococcus pneumoniae* bacteria, American scientists Oswald Avery, Colin MacLeod, and Maclyn McCarty discover that DNA is the hereditary material in most living organisms.

Streptococcus pneumoniae

1989–present
Human Genome Project
The Human Genome Organization maps the human DNA sequence and discovers it contains only about 20,000 to 25,000 genes. Full analysis of the results continues.

January 2 Violence flares on the streets of **Londonderry**, Northern Ireland

February 3 Yasser Arafat (1929–2004) becomes leader of the **Palestine Liberation Organization (PLO)**

February 13 Human egg fertilized in test tube for the first time by Robert Edwards

March 2 Anglo–French **Concorde makes maiden flight**

March 10 James Earl Ray pleads guilty to the murder of **Martin Luther King** and is jailed for life

March 17 Golda Meir (1898–1978) becomes premier of Israel

March 19 British troops invade island of **Anguilla** in the Caribbean

March 28 Death of Supreme Allied Commander and former president **Dwight D. Eisenhower** (b. 1890)

April 28 Charles De Gaulle (1890–1970) resigns as President of France

May 1 Major **James Dawson Chichester–Clark** becomes new prime minister of Northern Ireland

June 8 Spain closes its land border with **Gibraltar** (to 1985)

June 30 Nigeria bans relief aid to Biafra during civil war

July 1 Prince Charles invested as **Prince of Wales**

> ## THAT'S ONE SMALL STEP FOR [A] MAN, ONE GIANT LEAP FOR MANKIND.

Neil Armstrong, on first setting foot on the Moon, on July 21, 1969

This photograph shows hijacked planes that were set on fire by Palestinian militants belonging to Popular Front for the Liberation of Palestine (PFLP).

YASSER ARAFAT (1929–2004), A PALESTINIAN FREEDOM FIGHTER, became the leader of the **Palestine Liberation Organization (PLO)** in February. He had formed the radical group **Al-Fatah** in the late 1950s, which was merged with the Popular Front for the Liberation of Palestine (PFLP) to form the PLO.

In Libya, **Mu'ammar al-Gaddafi** (1942–2011) led a group of army officers to depose King Idris (1890–1983) on September 1, in a bloodless coup, and established the **Libyan Arab Republic**.

Nigeria banned food aid from the Red Cross to the breakaway state of **Biafra**, bringing millions of people to the brink of **starvation**. Biafra accused Nigeria of using starvation and genocide to win the civil war (1967–70), and pleaded for help from the world.

On August 14, **Britain sent troops into Northern Ireland** following three days of violence in the predominantly Catholic bogside area of **Londonderry**. Although intended to be a brief intervention, the troops remained after the **violence intensified**.

Willy Brandt (1913–92) was sworn in as the **Chancellor of West Germany** on October 21, becoming the first Socialist politician to lead a German government since 1930.

Eagle returns
Apollo 11's *lunar module* Eagle, holding astronauts Neil Armstrong and Buzz Aldrin, makes its way back to the command module.

Biafra starves
A child suffers the effects of hunger and malnutrition during the Biafran blockade. Pictures of the famine garnered worldwide sympathy.

Concorde, the supersonic airliner, made its **maiden flight** in March. Piloted by André Turcot, the Anglo-French plane took off from **Toulouse** in France; it reached 10,000 ft (3,050 m), and was in the air for 27 minutes.

Elsewhere in Europe, Beatle **John Lennon** (1940–80) and his wife **Yoko Ono** spent **two weeks in bed**, drawing the world's attention to peace. They spent the first week at the Hilton Amsterdam, in March, and the second at the Queen Elizabeth Hotel in Montreal, where the song *Give Peace a Chance* was recorded, in May.

Large-scale **music festivals** were held in Europe and the US during a summer that epitomized the **hippie movement**. The British band The Rolling Stones played a free concert at Hyde Park, London; the American musician Bob Dylan (b. 1941) performed the headline act at the **Isle of Wight Festival**, England; and up to 400,000 turned up at **Woodstock**, New York.

Millions marched across the US on October 15 to protest against the **Vietnam War**. In Washington, DC, 250,000 people gathered to participate in **antiwar rallies** and hear activists speak.

On July 21, **Neil Armstrong** (b. 1930) and **Edwin Aldrin** (b. 1930) took man's **first steps on the moon** from their spacecraft *Apollo 11*. Millions watched this televised event that represented a **symbolic victory** for the US over the USSR during the Cold War space race.

Time spent on the moon:
21 hours, 31 minutes, and 20 seconds

Mission duration
8 days, 3 hours, 18 minutes, and 35 seconds

The lunar mission
The prime mission objective of Apollo 11 was stated simply as: "perform a manned lunar landing and return."

IN CAMBODIA, THE HEAD OF STATE, PRINCE NORODOM SIHANOUK (b. 1922) was overthrown by **General Lon Nol** in a **coup**, on March 18. Lon Nol claimed to have support from the US. In April, **President Richard Nixon** (1913–94) ordered US troops and B-52 bombers into **Cambodia** to destroy North Vietnamese and Vietcong sanctuaries and supplies.

In early September, **Palestinian militants** forced two planes to fly to the Jordanian desert, where the hijackers **blew up the aircraft** after releasing most of the hostages. A third plane was flown to **Cairo** and was also blown up. After 24 days of talks, the remaining **hostages were freed** in exchange for seven Palestinian prisoners. On September 16, fighting broke out between Jordanian troops and PLO guerrillas. Egyptian President **Gamal Abdel Nasser** (b. 1918) **brokered a settlement** on September 27. **Nasser died** of a heart attack the next day. He had become the most powerful figure in the Middle East while **attempting to unify Arab nations**.

A **catastrophic cyclone** hit East Pakistan (modern Bangladesh) on November 12. The **Bhola Cyclone** was the **deadliest ever recorded**, with up to 500,000 casualties. Alleging neglect and lack of help from West Pakistan, the Bengalis went on to vote for Sheikh Mujibur Rahman's **Awami League**, which demanded autonomy from West Pakistan in the following elections (see 1971).

Elections were held in Chile on September 4, and **Salvador Allende's Marxist coalition** was elected. Allende instituted a program of sweeping **nationalization and reforms**.

In April, the German pharmaceutical company **Grünenthal** pledged to pay DM 100 million to **thalidomide victims**. Thalidomide, a drug given to pregnant women for nausea, was withdrawn in 1961 after nearly 10,000 babies were born with **major disabilities**.

Charles De Gaulle (b. 1890), who led the French resistance to the Nazi occupation during World War II and became the President of liberated France, **died** on November 9. His funeral was held on Armistice Day, November 11.

The Beatles, the most famous music band in the world, split when Paul McCartney (b. 1942) announced his decision to leave in April. The **group officially disbanded** on December 31.

500 THOUSAND
THE NUMBER **KILLED** IN THE **CYCLONE** IN **BANGLADESH**

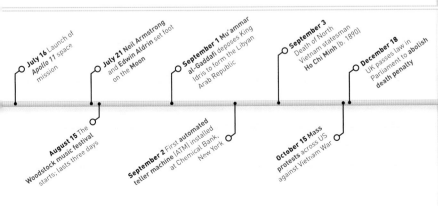

- **July 16** Launch of *Apollo 11* space mission
- **July 21** Neil Armstrong and Edwin Aldrin set foot on the Moon
- **August 15** The Woodstock music festival starts; lasts three days
- **September 1** Mu'ammar al-Gaddafi deposes King Idris to form the Libyan Arab Republic
- **September 2** First automated teller machine (ATM) installed at Chemical Bank, New York
- **September 3** Death of North Vietnam statesman Ho Chi Minh (b. 1890)
- **October 15** Mass protests across US against Vietnam War
- **December 18** UK passes law in Parliament to abolish death penalty
- **January 12** Civil war between Nigeria and Biafra ends
- **January 23** First Boeing 747 arrives at Heathrow airport, London
- **March 2** Rhodesia (modern Zimbabwe) becomes a republic
- **April 30** US sends troops to Cambodia
- **June 19** Edward Heath becomes prime minister of Britain
- **July 27** Death of former Portuguese leader **Antonio Salazar** (b. 1889)
- **September 28** Death of Egyptian president Nasser (b. 1889)
- **October 19** Major oil find in the North Sea
- **November 9** Death of General Charles De Gaulle (b. 1890)
- **December** Antigovernment riots rock Poland

1971

> ## " I AM **NOT** A POLITICIAN, BUT A **SOLDIER.** "

Idi Amin, in his first speech to the Ugandan nation, January 1971

IN UGANDA, GENERAL IDI AMIN SEIZED POWER from President Milton Obote in a **military coup** on January 25, while the president was out of the country attending the Commonwealth conference in Singapore (see 1979).

Sierra Leone, in West Africa, and **Qatar**, in the Middle East, formally achieved independence from Britain in this year.

In March, a **civil war** broke out between **Pakistan** and its dominion, **East Pakistan** (modern Bangladesh). Nearly nine million **refugees** fled to India. In December, Indian troops entered East Pakistan, following a **surprise attack on Indian airfields**. There was also heavy fighting in **Kashmir**. In a campaign lasting only 13 days, Indian troops crushed Pakistani forces in the east. On December 20, the independent state of **Bangladesh** was born (see 1972).

In **Northern Ireland**, the **Provisional IRA** stepped up its campaign against British security forces (see 1969). In August, the Northern Ireland government introduced **internment without trial** to stop the growing violence.

On September 15, a small team of activists set sail from Vancouver, Canada, on the ship *Phyllis Cormack* to protest against US nuclear tests in **Alaska**. They later adopted the name **Greenpeace**.

The **Walt Disney World** resort officially opened near Orlando in Florida on October 1. It featured Adventureland, Fantasyland, Frontierland, Liberty Square, and Tomorrowland.

IDI AMIN (1925–2003)

Idi Amin became known as the "Butcher of Uganda." After seizing power in 1971, he ruled by terror—an estimated 300,000 people died during his reign. His behavior was both barbaric and eccentric: famously, he declared himself the "King of Scotland." Idi Amin's rule ended in 1979 after he was ousted by troops from neighboring Tanzania then forced to flee the country.

On October 25, **China's admission to the UN** boosted the country's international status. The US president, Richard Nixon (1913–94), sent his national security adviser, **Henry Kissinger** (b. 1923), to China for secret talks. Kissinger also began talks with the **USSR**, which led to a number of formal agreements, including one regarding **access to Berlin**.

1972

British troops remove civil rights protestors from Londonderry, Northern Ireland, after the army opened fire on demonstrators during "Bloody Sunday." Among the 13 civilians killed were seven teenagers.

BRITISH MINERS WALKED OUT ON NATIONAL STRIKE on January 9 after refusing a government pay offer. All 289 pits across the country were closed. On February 19, they agreed to a **new pay deal** and returned to work on February 25.

On January 30, British troops opened fire on demonstrators in **Londonderry**, Northern Ireland, **killing 13 people** and injuring 14. The marchers were protesting against the policy of internment without trial. This day came to be known as "**Bloody Sunday.**"

In the largest attack on mainland Britain since "**The Troubles**" (see 1966), the **IRA** bombed the 16th Parachute Brigade headquarters at Aldershot, Hampshire, on February 22, killing seven civilians.

President Nixon flew to China in February and met **Mao Zedong** (1893–1976), marking a new **cordiality in US–China relations**. In May, Nixon paid a state visit to **Moscow** to sign 10 agreements, the most important of which were the nuclear arms limitation treaties known as SALT I.

On June 8, South Vietnamese planes dropped a **napalm bomb** on **Trang Bang**, which was under North Vietnamese occupation. Napalm was an incendiary liquid that burned everything it touched. Images of **burned civilians** were shown around the world and increased pressure on the US to withdraw from Vietnam.

The prime ministers of India and Pakistan, **Indira Gandhi** (1917–84) and **Zulfikar Ali Bhutto** (1954–79), signed the **Simla Agreement** in July, in the wake of the 1971 war.

The agreement reiterated the promises for peaceful negotiations made in **Tashkent** (see 1966).

The terrorist group **Black September**, a faction of the Palestine Liberation Organization (PLO), took members of the **Israeli team** hostage during the **Summer Olympics** at Munich, West Germany. They later **killed 11 athletes**, launching a new era of international terrorism.

New horizons

For the Munich Olympics, leading artists made 35 posters, including the one shown below. Their aim was to erase the memory of the 1936 games, held during Hitler's reign.

January 2 Crowd barriers collapse at **Ibrox stadium**, Glasgow, Scotland, killing 66 people

January 25 Idi Amin siezes power in Uganda

April 19 Sierra Leone becomes a republic

September 3 Qatar becomes a republic

September 11 Death of **Nikita Khrushchev**, former Soviet leader (b. 1894)

December 3 Pakistan attacks India

January 10 Death of "**Coco**" of Gabrielle Chanel (b. 1883)

March 26 Civil War between East and West Pakistan

August 9 Northern Ireland government introduces policy of **internment without trial**

December India defeats Pakistan in 13-day war

December 20 Bangladesh born out of East Pakistan

January 13 Ghana becomes a dictatorship after military coup

January 25 First combined **pancreas and kidney transplant** performed at Guy's Hospital, London

February 21 President Nixon visits China

May 29 Nixon and **Brezhnev** sign treaties reducing risks of nuclear war

July 2 Pakistan and India sign **Simla Peace Agreement**

August 26 Olympics open in Munich

December 25 Earthquake in Nicaraguan capital, Managua

January 25 National Organ Matching and Distribution Service (NOMDS) founded in London

January 30 Paratroopers fire on protesters in **Londonderry**, Northern Ireland

March 25 British prime minister Edward Heath imposes **direct rule over Northern Ireland**

August 6 Idi Amin expels 50,000 Asians with British passports

September 5 Israeli Olympic quarters stormed by **Arab militants**

November 7 Richard Nixon reelected as US president

December 26 Death of US statesman **Harry Truman** (b. 1884)

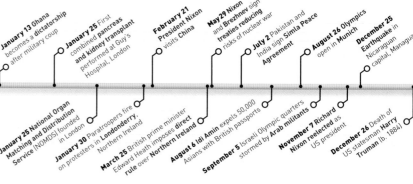

> ❝ THERE WILL BE **NO WHITEWASH** AT THE **WHITE HOUSE.** ❞

Richard Nixon, US president, in a TV speech on Watergate, April 30, 1973

The White House, the official residence of the US President, was rocked by the Watergate scandal and the subsequent resignation of President Nixon.

Emperor of Ethiopia, Haile Selassie, had been crowned "King of Kings."

ON JANUARY 30, SEVEN MEN WERE CONVICTED of breaking into the Democratic Party's **Watergate** headquarters in Washington, DC and **bugging** it. **President Nixon**, who had just been reelected, continually denied any connection between Watergate and the **White House**. However, *Washington Post* reporters **Bob Woodward** and **Carl Bernstein** brought to light the president's involvement in the bugging, which would eventually lead to his **impeachment** and **resignation** from office (see 1974). Their work on the "**Watergate scandal**," helped by crucial information from the mysterious informant, "Deep Throat," led to the *Washington Post* being awarded the **Pulitzer Prize**.

Allende's reforms
The Chilean president's sweeping nationalization and reforms resulted in costly welfare schemes and economic chaos in the country.

In a landmark judgement referred to as the **Roe v. Wade** case, the Supreme Court **legalized abortions** in the US. The ruling came after Norma McCorvey, under the pseudonym "Jane Roe," challenged the criminal abortion laws in Texas.

The **Vietnam war** was officially over for the US, when it signed a **ceasefire agreement** in January after months of talks in Paris.

Britain, **Ireland**, and **Denmark** became full-fledged members of the **European Economic Community** (EEC) in January, bringing the number of member states to nine. It was the first enlargement of the organization since its inception in 1957.

The **IRA** extended its **bombing campaign** in mainland Britain. On September 8, there were bombs in Manchester city center and at Victoria station, London. Two days later, explosions ripped through King's Cross and Euston stations. On November 14, an IRA gang was **convicted of the bombings**.

In September, Chilean president **Salvador Allende** (1908–73) was killed in a coup led by his trusted ally **General Augusto Pinochet** (1915–2006), and backed by the **US**. Pinochet killed 3,000 supporters of the Allende regime, **shut the Chilean Parliament**, and banned all political activity. In 1974, he made himself president (see 1998).

In December, the Basque separatist movement, **ETA**, killed Spanish prime minister Admiral **Luis Carrero Blanco** in Madrid, in retaliation for the execution of Basque militants (see 1959).

Costing dear
When OPEC shut off oil supplies to the western nations that had supported Israel, it sent prices shooting up from less than $3 a barrel to $11 in a matter of weeks.

Heavy fighting broke out between **Arab and Israeli forces** in what came to be known as the **Yom Kippur War**, in October. Egyptian forces broke the Israeli line on the eastern bank of the Suez Canal, and in the north, Syrian troops battled with Israeli defenses along the **Golan Heights**, seized by Israel from Syria in 1967. A peace deal, signed on November 11 between Egypt and Israel, ended the strife. Following the war, the Arab oil-producing countries imposed an **oil embargo** on all the countries that had supported Israel. In October, **oil prices soared** around the world, from under $3 a barrel before the war to over $11 by early 1974.

THE POLITICS OF OIL

The Arab oil embargo caused global chaos. The Organization of Petroleum Exporting Countries (OPEC) switched off supply at a time when the market was already starting to suffer shortages. The crisis revealed oil as a powerful political weapon. Countries in the Middle East were seen to have acquired control of a vital commodity, and Western nations were vulnerable because they relied on oil imports.

THE OIL EMBARGO OF 1973 HAD A DRASTIC EFFECT on the developed world, leading to a long-term recession. Unemployment and inflation soared, and **stock markets crashed** globally.

In Portugal, **General Antonio de Spinola** (1910–96) led a bloodless military coup, ending 50 years of dictatorship. Known as the **Carnation Revolution**, this event ushered in a new era of democracy in the country.

In Britain, the **IRA** attacked the Houses of Parliament on June 17, the Tower of London in July, and a Guildford pub in October.

In July, **Turkish troops** invaded northern **Cyprus** following a coup in which **President Archbishop Makarios**, a Greek Cypriot, was deposed. The island was split in two parts, with Greek-Cypriots fleeing to the south and the Turkish community, to the north.

After years of war and famine in Ethiopia, **Emperor Haile Selassie** (1892–1975) was overthrown in a coup, on September 12. General **Tafari Benti** (1921–77) became head of state.

In the US, the **Watergate** breakin (see 1973) was traced to a Nixon support group. In July, the Supreme Court ordered Nixon to turn over the **tape recordings** relating to the scandal. He was impeached, and **resigned from office** in August.

Disco, a genre of dance music that had started in the clubs of New York in the late 1960s, peaked at this time with new music, polyester suits, and films such as *Saturday Night Fever*.

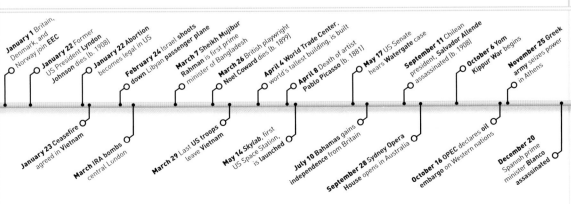

> ❝ **VIETNAM WAS LOST** IN THE **LIVING ROOMS OF AMERICA,** NOT ON THE **BATTLEFIELDS OF VIETNAM.** ❞

Marshall McLuhan, media commentator, writing at the end of the Vietnam War

Two punks kiss on the Kings Road in London. Punk rock emerged during the mid-70s as an angry expression of contempt for politics and society.

MARGARET THATCHER BECAME THE FIRST WOMAN to lead a political party in Britain on February 11, when she won the Conservative Party vote.

In the Middle East, Saudi Arabia's **King Faisal** (1906–75) was **assassinated** by his nephew, Prince Faisal Ibu Musaed.

Prince Juan Carlos was sworn in as King of Spain, two days after dictator General Francisco Franco died on November 20.

In April, the Cambodian capital, **Phnom Penh,** fell to the radical communist movement, the **Khmer Rouge,** led by **Pol Pot.** They transformed Cambodia into a communist, rural society. All inhabitants of cities were expelled to work in agricultural communes.

After almost two decades of fighting, the **Vietnam War** finally

Fall of Saigon
The North Vietnam troops (pictured) met little resistance in Saigon, but the final hours of America's presence were marked by chaos.

Vietnamese war casualties
More than one million North Vietnamese troops died, compared to around 220,000 from South Vietnam, and 58,000 from the US.

ended on April 30 as the government in Saigon surrendered to the **North Vietnam** forces. Saigon was renamed **Ho Chi Minh City** and the following year, North and South Vietnam were reunified.

Mozambique became **independent** on June 25, after a coup in Portugal ended colonial rule (see 1974). Four months later, **Angola** also gained its independence (see 1976).

Iraq stepped up its military pressure against **Kurdish rebels** in northern Iraq. The **Kurds** were **crushed** with the razing of Zakho and Qala Diza.

In **Lebanon,** Christian militia attacked a bus full of Palestinians in

Beirut. This started a **civil war** that lasted for 15 years (see 1990).

This was a year of global terrorism, as **Arab terrorists** held **hostages** at Orly airport in Paris; a German left-wing group seized the **German Embassy** in Stockholm, Sweden; and South Moluccan terrorists took over the **Indonesian Embassy** in Amsterdam, the Netherlands.

In November, **oil** began to flow from the **North Sea** from sources that British Petroleum (BP) discovered six years earlier.

Microsoft was officially founded on April 4 by **Bill Gates** (b. 1955) and **Paul Allen** (b. 1953), starting the world of personal computing.

US Purple Heart
A US military decoration awarded to the wounded or killed, 351,794 Purple Hearts were awarded during the Vietnam War.

THE MARXIST PEOPLE'S MOVEMENT FOR THE LIBERATION OF ANGOLA (MPLA) took nominal control of the whole country by February, and the new **Angola People's Republic** was recognized. This was preceded by intense fighting that also involved the National Front for the Liberation of Angola (FNLA) and the Union for the Total Independence of Angola (UNITA).

Antiapartheid protests in Soweto, **South Africa** turned violent on June 16. Demonstrators clashed with police and more than 300 people were killed.

40–70
MILLION
THE NUMBER OF **DEATHS** CAUSED BY **MAO'S REGIME**

Mao Zedong (b. 1893), the founder of the People's Republic of China, died of a heart attack on September 9.

Syrian peacekeeping troops entered **Lebanon** on 9 June. In December, after more than 50 ceasefires had been violated, uneasy peace prevailed.

The **Seychelles gained independence** from Britain on June 29, with James Mancham as president and France Rene as prime minister of the coalition.

THE ARCHBISHOP OF UGANDA, DR. JANANI LUWUM (b. 1922), was murdered on February 16 for being an Anglican, and for protesting against the excesses of **Idi Amin's regime** (see 1971).

Steven Biko (see panel, right), a prominent black rights leader in South Africa, **died in prison** on September 12. He had been detained under the terrorism act. His death caused **international outrage** but an inquest cleared the police of any wrongdoing.

In Pakistan, Zulfiqar Ali Bhutto's **Pakistan People's Party** (PPP) was accused of **vote rigging.** This prompted Army Chief General Mohammed Zia ul-Haq to depose Bhutto in a **military coup** on July 4.

The right-wing **Menachem Begin** (1913–92) had a surprise win at the Israeli elections in May, ending 29 years of Labor rule. As premier, he initiated a **peace process** with Egypt (see 1979).

Fruit of knowledge
Apple Inc. computers went on sale this year. The distinctive logo—a rainbow-colored apple with a bite taken out—symbolized knowledge.

March 25 Death of King Faisal of Saudi Arabia (b. 1906)

April 4 Microsoft officially founded by Bill Gates and Paul Allen

April 13 Civil War in Lebanon

April 17 Phnom Penh falls to Khmer Rouge

April 30 Vietnam War ends with the fall of Saigon

July 11 Terracotta army discovered near Xian, China

July 21–24 Short border war between Libya and Egypt

August 15 Death of Sheikh Mujibur Rahman of Bangladesh (b. 1920)

August 27 Death of Emperor Haile Selassie of Ethiopia (b. 1892)

November Britain and Iceland confront each other over the amount of cod caught in the North Atlantic

November 3 North Sea oil begins to flow from North Sea

November 11 Angola gains independence from Portugal

November 20 Death of General Francisco Franco of Spain (b. 1892)

November 27 IRA murders Ross McWhirter

January 21 First commercial flight of Concorde

June 16 Soweto riots in South Africa

July 17 Olympic Games open in Montreal

September 9 Death of Mao Zedong (b. 1893)

November 2 Jimmy Carter elected US president

February 18 Maiden flight of the Space Shuttle atop Boeing 747

April Apple II computer launched

August 16 Death of Elvis Presley (b. 1935)

May 17 Menachem Begin wins Israeli elections

July 5 Military coup in Pakistan

" ALL EXAMINATIONS SHOWED THAT THE **BABY** IS **QUITE NORMAL. "**

Obstetrician Patrick Steptoe, after the birth of Louise Brown

Dr. Robert Edwards holds the world's first test tube baby, Louise Brown. It was a medical breakthrough fraught with controversy.

STEVE BIKO (1946–77)

In 1968, Steve Biko was the first president and cofounder of the all-black South African Students' Organization (SASO), which aimed to raise black consciousness. The government banned him in 1973, but he continued to spread his word. On August 18, 1977, the police seized Biko, held him for 24 days, and tortured him to death. The *Rand Daily Mail* exposed their brutality.

Amnesty International, the human rights organization, won the **Nobel Peace Prize** for having "contributed to securing the ground for freedom, for justice, and thereby also for peace in the world." The movement proclaimed 1977 "**Prisoners of Conscience Year.**" The following year, Amnesty also received the United Nations Human Rights Award.

ISRAELI SOLDIERS CROSSED THE LEBANESE BORDER on March 14, in Operation Litani. Thousands of **Palestinians fled** the area and hundreds died. Israel claimed Palestinian fighters were using southern Lebanon to mount attacks against civilian and military targets in Israel.

Demonstrators on the streets of **Tehran**, capital of Iran, had been shouting dissent all year, but in September, **protests grew** against the policies of Iran's supreme ruler, **Shah Mohammed Reza Pahlavi** (1919–80). The challenge stunned the Shah and his generals, and rioters were attacked. Many people were killed, and **martial law** was imposed in major cities.

Egyptian President **Anwar Sadat** (1918–81) arrived in Washington, DC for talks with **President Jimmy Carter** (b. 1924), in February. His visit represented a change in **Egyptian foreign policy** which had previously sought favor from the **Soviet Union**. Shortly after, Israeli Prime Minister **Menachem Begin** met President Carter. These initial talks paved the way for historic joint meetings at Camp David, Maryland, in September 5–17. Here, both sides signed the **Camp David Peace Accord** for peace in the Middle East. Sadat and Begin later received the Nobel Peace Prize.

Cambodia was **invaded by Vietnam** on December 25 in a lightning assault. The Vietnamese forced out **Pol Pot's Khmer Rouge** regime, but the war that followed continued to be a major source of international tension. Pol Pot's army was not completely defeated; thousands of his troops fled to the **Thai–Cambodia border**, where they were able to build up their strength, and skirmishes forced the Vietnamese to stay in Cambodia for the next decade (see 1991).

Former Italian prime minister **Aldo Moro** was **kidnapped** in Rome on March 16. The extreme left-wing **Red Brigade**, which wanted revolutionary transformation of Italian society, claimed responsibility and demanded that the trial of their leader, Renato Curcio, be stopped. The government refused, and eight weeks later, **Moro's body** was found in the trunk of a car in Rome.

The oil tanker *Amoco Cadiz* ran aground on Portsall Rocks, three miles off the Brittany coast, when its steering mechanism failed. The entire cargo of 1.6 million barrels spilled into the sea, causing an **oil slick** 18 miles (30km) wide and 80 miles (130km) long. Dozens of Breton **beaches were polluted**. Devastating scenes of marine animals covered in oil and dying were broadcast around the world.

The world's **first test tube baby, Louise Brown**, was born in Oldham, Lancashire, England, with the help of gynecologist **Patrick Steptoe**, who had pioneered the technique along with **Dr. Robert Edwards** (see 1969).

Khmer Rouge fighter
Under Pol Pot, Khmer Rouge soldiers, often teenagers, controlled Cambodia. They were responsible for killing over 1 million people.

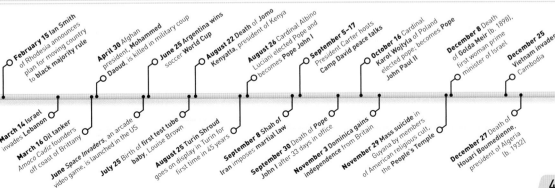

September 12 Death of anti-apartheid activist Steven Biko (b.1946)

December 25 Death of Charlie Chaplin, actor and director (b. 1889)

November 18 President Sadat of Egypt is first Arab leader to **visit Israel**

February 15 Ian Smith of Rhodesia announces plan for moving country to **black majority rule**

March 14 Israel invades Lebanon

March 16 Oil tanker Amoco Cadiz founders off coast of Brittany

April 30 Afghan president, Mohammed Daoud, is killed in military coup

June 25 Argentina wins soccer World Cup

June Space Invaders, an arcade video game, is launched in the US

July 25 Birth of **first test tube baby**, Louise Brown

August 22 Death of Jomo Kenyatta, president of Kenya

August 26 Cardinal Albino Luciani elected Pope and becomes Pope John I

August 25 Turin Shroud goes on display in Turin for first time in 45 years

September 5–17 President Carter hosts **Camp David peace talks**

September 8 Shah of Iran imposes martial law

September 30 Death of Pope John I after 33 days in office

October 16 Cardinal Karol Wojtyla of Poland elected pope; becomes Pope John Paul II

November 3 Dominica gains independence from Britain

November 29 Mass suicide in Guyana by members of American religious cult, the People's Temple

December 8 Death of Golda Meir (b. 1898), first woman prime minister of Israel

December 25 Vietnam invades Cambodia

December 27 Death of Houari Boumedienne, president of Algeria (b. 1932)

> **" IN ISLAM, THE LEGISLATIVE POWER AND COMPETENCE TO ESTABLISH LAWS BELONG EXCLUSIVELY TO GOD. "**
>
> Ayatollah Khomeini, from his lectures on Islamic Government

Iranian women holding posters of Ayatollah Khomeini show support for the Islamic Revolution. Mass demonstrations brought the country to a halt.

20:1

War casualties
Afghans paid a heavy price for the Soviet invasion—for every Soviet who was killed or wounded, 20 Afghan soldiers lost their lives.

VIETNAMESE FORCES ENTERED CAMBODIA in 1978, in response to repeated border attacks by the **Khmer Rouge** (see 1978). On January 7, 1979, they seized the Cambodian capital of **Phnom Penh** and the Khmer Rouge were driven from power. **Pol Pot**, leader of the Khmer Rouge, fled to the jungle in Thailand and began a **guerrilla war** against a succession of Cambodian governments. On April 2, Vietnamese forces discovered a **mass grave** in the northeast—this was the first of many mass graves from the Pol Pot era to be discovered. It became apparent that between 1975 and 1979 Pol Pot was responsible for the slaughter of more than 1 million people.

Rings of Jupiter
An image taken by NASA's Voyager 2 spacecraft shows Jupiter's ring system, never seen before, being bombarded by tiny meteorites.

China viewed the Vietnamese attack on Cambodia as a serious provocation, and, on February 17, Chinese forces **invaded Vietnam**. Casualties on both sides were high, and each side claimed to have won the upper hand.

When **Afghan communists** took power through a coup in 1978, they found themselves pulled three ways: between the **Soviets**, the **Americans**, and the Islamic regime in **Iran**. In March, a resistance group declared a **holy war** against the "godless" Marxist regime and killed Soviet citizens in Herat, western Afghanistan. In the countryside, revolt grew against repressive government initiatives, and the Afghan army faced total collapse. In light of this, the Soviet Union feared an Iranian-style **Islamist revolution**. Citing the 1978 Treaty of Friendship, the **Soviets invaded**

Afghanistan on December 24. In doing so, they were confident of military superiority. However, the US had been covertly training anti-government forces, the **Mujahideen** (warriors), and the Soviets were met with fierce resistance when they stormed into Kabul.

As the political situation in **Iran** deteriorated (see 1978), the **Shah** was forced into exile. **Ayatollah Ruhollah Khomeini** (1902–89), a Shi'ite Muslim cleric, returned from 15 years of exile to jubilant crowds, and the **Islamic Republic of Iran** was proclaimed on April 1. Western influences were suppressed, and many who had been educated in the West fled the country. Young supporters of Ayatollah Khomeini, angered by America's long support of the Shah, took control of the US embassy in **Tehran**. They seized 63 hostages, and vowed not to release them until the US returned the Shah for trial. In response, **President Carter embargoed Iranian oil**. Female and non-US citizen hostages were released, and then a male hostage who became seriously ill, in 1980, but 52 Americans remained hostage until 1981.

The left-wing **Sandinista National Liberation Front** succeeded in overthrowing the US-backed regime in the republic of **Nicaragua** and took the capital, Managua. This ended seven years of civil war against the **Somoza** government. The Sandinistas established a revolutionary government on July 20, led by **Daniel and Humberto Ortega**.

Both the Irish Republican Army (**IRA**) and the Irish National Liberation Army (**INLA**) were active

rear sight

detachable magazine

barrel

AK–47 Kalashnikov assault rifle
The AK-47 became an iconic weapon during the Soviet war in Afghanistan. Used by both sides, Kalashnikovs were cheap and readily available.

this year. On March 30, shadow Northern Ireland secretary **Airey Neave** was killed by an INLA car bomb. On August 27, **Lord Louis Mountbatten** (a member of the British royal family) was killed by an IRA bomb blast. Hours later, 18 soldiers were killed in booby-trap bomb explosions close to the border with the Irish Republic. The deaths triggered a wave of sectarian murders.

Ugandan leader **Idi Amin** (1925–2003) was forced to flee the capital city of Kampala on April 11 as Tanzanian troops, along with exiles and the **Uganda National Liberation Front**, closed in. Two days later, Kampala fell and a coalition government took power. **Yusufu Lule** (1912–85), who had been driven into exile by Amin, became president. Amin escaped to Libya, leaving behind a country with its economy in tatters.

The **Sony Walkman** was launched in **Japan** on June 22. The first Walkman featured a cassette player and the world's first lightweight headphones. It cost US$200, and sold out within a month.

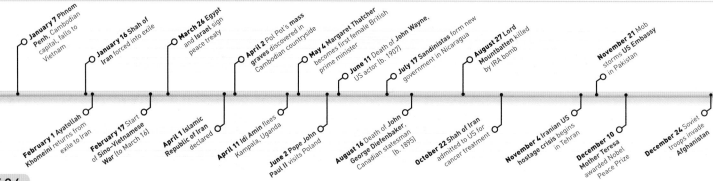

January 7 Phnom Penh, Cambodian capital, falls to Vietnam

January 16 Shah of Iran forced into exile

February 1 Ayatollah Khomeini returns from exile to Iran

February 17 Start of Sino-Vietnamese War (to March 16)

March 26 Egypt and Israel sign peace treaty

April 1 Islamic Republic of Iran declared

April 2 Pol Pot's mass graves discovered in Cambodian countryside

April 11 Idi Amin flees Kampala, Uganda

May 4 Margaret Thatcher becomes first female British prime minister

June 2 Pope John Paul II visits Poland

June 11 Death of John Wayne, US actor (b. 1907)

July 17 Sandinistas form new government in Nicaragua

August 16 Death of John George Diefenbaker, Canadian statesman (b. 1895)

August 27 Lord Mountbatten killed by IRA bomb

October 22 Shah of Iran admitted to US for cancer treatment

November 4 Iranian US hostage crisis begins in Tehran

November 21 Mob storms US Embassy in Pakistan

December 10 Mother Teresa awarded Nobel Peace Prize

December 24 Soviet troops invade Afghanistan

15 MILES
THE HEIGHT OF THE **ERUPTION COLUMN** IN **THE MOUNT ST. HELENS** EXPLOSION

Mount St. Helens in Washington State erupted, with a massive avalanche in May, and a cloud of ash that screened out all sunlight as far as 250 miles (400 km) away.

ROBERT MUGABE WON A SWEEPING VICTORY on March 4, becoming prime minister of **Rhodesia**. A Marxist guerrilla fighter, he was hated by Ian Smith's white-minority regime. On April 18, Rhodesia became **Zimbabwe**.

Parts of **Africa** suffered extreme deprivation due to **famine** in 1980. Drought, cattle raiding, and a breakdown in civil order caused a food shortage. The **famine in Uganda** is regarded as one of the worst in history—21 percent of the population died.

Smallpox was declared **extinct** on May 8 by the World Health Organization, 21 years after the global eradication program had begun. The last natural case of smallpox was in Somalia in October 1977. Around **300 million** people died from smallpox in the 20th century alone.

The **Iranian Embassy** in **London** became involved in a dramatic siege on April 30, when

Smallpox eradication
A global vaccination campaign led to WHO declaring smallpox eradicated in 1980. Smallpox was a devastating illness, with a mortality rate of 30%.

30% DIED

70% SURVIVED

six gunmen from a group opposed to **Ayatollah Khomeini** took over the building. They demanded the release of 91 Iranian political prisoners. The siege ended after a raid by the **Special Air Service** (SAS). Nineteen hostages were set free, but one died and two were injured in the cross-fire.

On September 22, **Iraq** invaded **Iran** sparking a bitter eight-year war, which destabilized the whole region. By the end of October, **Khorramshahr**, the largest port in Iran, fell to Iraqi forces.

Under President Tito's grip (see 1943), **Yugoslavia** had achieved internal peace. **Tito's death**, on May 4, combined with the decline of communist ideology, led to the weakening of Yugoslavia's unifying factors. Ethnic and

nationalist differences flared, and individual republics began pushing for **independence**.

A huge bomb ripped through a railway station in **Bologna**, Italy, on August 2, killing 85 people and injuring hundreds in one of the worst terrorist attacks in Italian history. **Right-wing extremists** were thought to be responsible.

Poland experienced a turning point with the **Gdansk shipyard strike**: the first political mass movement to emerge in the Soviet bloc. On August 30, the Polish government reached an agreement with striking shipyard workers, led by **Lech Walesa**. It authorized the establishment of **Solidarity**, a new trade union free of communist control. Membership rapidly swelled to over 10 million.

Mount St. Helens, a volcano in Washington State, northwest US, **violently erupted** on May 18, spewing a huge cloud of ash. It triggered an earthquake measuring 5.2 on the Richter scale; the north face of the mountain collapsed, and 57 people died.

Ronald Reagan, a former Hollywood actor and Republican governor of California, won the **US presidential election** on November 4, beating Jimmy Carter in a landslide victory. He would go on to serve two terms.

Iran–Iraq War
An Iraqi soldier watches an oil refinery burn during the Iran–Iraq war. Oil fields and refineries were heavily targeted by both sides.

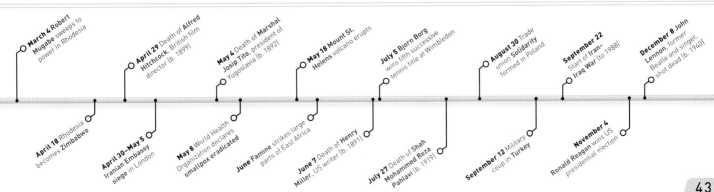

March 4 Robert Mugabe sweeps to power in Rhodesia

April 18 Rhodesia becomes Zimbabwe

April 29 Death of Alfred Hitchcock, British film director (b. 1899)

April 30–May 5 Iranian Embassy siege in London

May 4 Death of Marshal Josip Tito, president of Yugoslavia (b. 1892)

May 8 World Health Organization declares smallpox eradicated

May 18 Mount St. Helens volcano erupts

June Famine strikes large parts of East Africa

June 7 Death of Henry Miller, US writer (b. 1891)

July 5 Bjorn Borg wins fifth successive tennis title at Wimbledon

July 27 Death of Shah Mohammed Reza Pahlawi (b. 1919)

August 30 Trade union Solidarity formed in Poland

September 12 Military coup in Turkey

September 22 Start of Iran–Iraq War (to 1988)

November 4 Ronald Reagan wins US presidential election

December 8 John Lennon, former Beatle and singer, shot dead (b. 1940)

437

Demonstrators carry a banner reading *Solidarność*, or "Solidarity," the name of the first noncommunist Polish trade union.

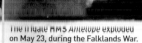

The frigate HMS *Antelope* exploded on May 23, during the Falklands War.

FORMER ACTOR RONALD REAGAN BECAME THE 40TH PRESIDENT of the US on January 20. Two months later he survived an assassination attempt by **John Hinckley**, who was obsessed with actress Jodie Foster, and believed an assassination of the president would impress her.

Pope John Paul II survived being **shot four times** on May 13 as he travlled through crowds in his "popemobile" in St. Peter's Square, Rome. Police arrested Mehmet Ali Hagca, a Turkish citizen, who was sentenced to life imprisonment in July.

A **state of emergency** was declared in **Egypt** after **President Anwar Sadat** was assassinated at a military parade. A group calling itself the **Independent Organization for the Liberation of Egypt** said it carried out the attack. Vice-President Hosni Mubarak succeeded President Sadat as head of state.

> IF WE RESIGN TODAY WE WILL BURY **OUR HOPES FOR FREEDOM** FOR MANY YEARS TO COME. SEVERAL THOUSAND PEOPLE **CANNOT OVERCOME TEN MILLION.**

Solidarity, trade union, message to the people of Poland, December 1981

On January 20, **Iran** finally agreed to **release 52 American hostages**, who had been held for 444 days. This followed a guarantee from the US that it would release Iranian assets that had been frozen in American banks since the US embassy was seized in Tehran.

Iran also saw renewed political terrorism this year. The **Mujahidin**, a group of muslim fighters, mounted waves of **bombings and assassinations**. In August, both the new president **Ali Rajai** and the prime minister **Javad Bahonar** were killed. In October, **Ali Khamenei** was elected president in a landslide victory.

Spain was in turmoil after an attempted **right wing coup**, led by Lieutenant Colonel Antonio Tejero Molina (b. 1932), who stormed

Spanish coup
Colonel Antonio Tejero stormed the Spanish parliament, firing shots into the air as he announced a military coup. The coup collapsed within hours.

the Spanish parliament along with 200 soldiers. Armed forces put down the coup on February 23.

Israel shocked the world by blowing up a **nuclear plant** near Baghdad, **Iraq**, on June 7. They claimed it had the capability of making nuclear weapons to destroy Israel—Iraq denied this.

In the face of union protests, the **Polish government** declared a **state of emergency** on December 13, and placed leaders of the **Solidarity** trade union under arrest. In response, members of Solidarity called for a **national strike** (see 1982).

Brixton, south London, erupted into **riots** on April 11 after a black man was arrested by police. The violence spread to other cities where there had been unrest due to poor relations between black communities and the police.

Columbia became the first **shuttle** to fly into space on April 12. The maiden flight was piloted by veteran US astronauts **John Young** (b. 1930) and **Robert Crippen** (b. 1937), and heralded a new era in space exploration.

Bob Marley (b. 1945), the international face of reggae music, died of cancer on May 11.

He was 36 years old. Bob Marley and the Wailers was the world's most recognized **reggae band**.

AIDS (see panel, below) came to the fore in June after the deaths of five men in Los Angeles. Previously, no cases had been reported outside the gay community; it became clear that the disease affected other groups. The unknown condition came to be named **Acquired Immune Deficiency Syndrome** (AIDS).

HIV VIRUS

HIV is a virus that causes Acquired Immune Deficiency Syndrome (AIDS), a disease of the immune system. The HIV virus was discovered in May 1983 by doctors at the Pasteur Institute in France. The isolation of the HIV virus made it possible to develop drugs that could dramatically extend the life expectancy of those with AIDS, although no vaccine has yet been found. At least 28 million people worldwide have died from the disease; Africa has been the worst-affected area.

ARGENTINA INVADED THE BRITISH TERRITORY of the **Falkland Islands** in the South Atlantic on April 2. The sovereignty of the islands had long been disputed. British prime minister **Margaret Thatcher** (1925–2013) sent a naval task force to liberate the islands. The subsequent conflict cost the lives of hundreds of Argentine and British servicemen, many of them through **missile attacks on navy warships**. The conflict ended on June 14, when the commander of the Argentine garrison at **Port Stanley** surrendered to the British.

Iran launched **Operation Undeniable Victory** in March, as part of its war against Iraq (see 1980). This marked a major turning point, and Iran forced the Iraqis to retreat. Within a week, Iran

January 20 Ronald Reagan (1911–2004) inaugurated as US president

January 20 Iran releases American Embassy hostages after 444 days

February 23 King Juan Carlos of Spain survives military coup

April 12 US space shuttle Columbia launched

May 5 IRA prisoner Bobby Sands dies while on hunger strike

May 30 President Ziaur Rahman of Bangladesh assassinated (b. 1936)

July 29 Wedding of Prince Charles to Lady Diana Spencer at St. Paul's Cathedral, London

August 5 President and prime minister of Iran both assassinated

November 1 Antigua and Barbuda gains independence

January 8 Spain calls off its siege of Gibraltar

March 25 Nicaragua declares state of emergency

February 4 Prime minister Thatcher announces further plans to privatize nationalized British industries

March 30 President Reagan survives assassination attempt

May 10 Francois Mitterrand (1916–96) becomes president of France

June Scientists identify the AIDS virus

August 1 MTV (Music Television) launched in US

October 6 President Anwar Sadat of Egypt assassinated (b. 1918)

November 10 Hosni Mubarak (b. 1928) becomes new president of Egypt

April 2 Falkland War begins between Britain and Argentina

> ## "A FLAGRANT VIOLATION OF INTERNATIONAL LAW. "
>
> **UN Security Council**, on the US invasion of Grenada in 1983

King of pop
The dominant pop star of the '80s, Michael Jackson released the album Thriller in 1982. It became, and remains, the best-selling album of all time.

2:5 Falklands casualties
During the Falklands War, which lasted 74 days, 255 British and 649 Argentine soldiers were killed. More than 11,000 Argentine soldiers were taken prisoner.

succeeded in destroying a large part of three Iraqi divisions. Iranian president **Ali Khamenei** (b. 1939) rejected an Iraqi offer of a ceasefire and sent thousands of young Iranians to their death in "**human-wave**" **attacks** that cleared the way for Iranian tanks. However, by the year's end, Iraq had been resupplied with new **Soviet arms**, and the ground war

entered a new phase (see 1983).
Israel invaded **Lebanon** on June 6, in an attempt to wipe out **guerrilla positions** on Israel's northern border. By September 15, the Israeli army occupied West Beirut. On September 16–18, the pro-Israel **Phalangist Party** killed hundreds of Palestinians in refugee camps. Defense minister **Ariel Sharon resigned** after an Israeli inquiry stated he had failed to act to prevent the massacre.

The **IRA** continued their campaign against British rule in Northern Ireland by exploding **two bombs** in London parks. The first, at **Hyde Park**, killed four soldiers from the Household Cavalry. Horses were also slain. The second, placed underneath the bandstand in **Regents Park**,

Israel attacks Lebanon
Many cities were bombarded by heavy artillery during the Israeli invasion of Lebanon—an attempt to drive out the PLO.

killed seven soldiers.
Solidarity (see 1981), the Polish Trade Union Movement, was **banned by the Polish government** on October 8. This was greeted by **international condemnation** and street protests. US President Ronald Reagan put pressure on Poland by imposing economic sanctions. **Lech Walesa** (b. 1943), the Solidarity leader, was released on November 12, after 11 months of internment.

Leonid Brezhnev (b. 1906), leader of the Soviet Union, died on November 10. He had served as general secretary for 18 years. He was succeeded by **Yuri Andropov** (1914–84). During his leadership, Brezhnev had pushed for better relations with the West, and increased Soviet military and industrial strength, but living standards remained poor.

The world's **first test tube twins** were born in Manchester, England, on April 28. The twins were conceived outside the womb after their mother underwent in-vitro fertilization (**IVF**).

ON JANUARY 17, NIGERIA ANNOUNCED that it would **expel all resident aliens**. Over a million foreigners were forced out. The move was condemned abroad, but appeared popular in Nigeria.

Drought struck Ethiopia this year. Harvests failed and there were massive food shortages. The crisis was exacerbated by the communist government's military spending and censorship of the emerging crisis.

The **US embassy in Beirut** was hit by a suicide bomber on April 19. The US government believed the attack was carried out by **Hezbollah**, a militant Islamic group. Later in the year, terrorists bombed the French and American peacekeeping headquarters in Beirut, with extensive loss of life.

In the **Iraq–Iran War**, Iraq had begun using **chemical weapons** —the blister agent mustard gas was deployed as Iraq fought back against attacks from the "human waves" of Iranian troops.

Vicious attacks were carried out against members of the **Tamil** ethnic group in **Sri Lanka** on

Secret hunger
A mother holds her child during the Ethiopian famine. The Ethiopian government initially hid the famine from the rest of the world.

July 23. These followed a deadly ambush by **Tamil Tigers**, which killed 13 Sri Lankan soldiers. The year marked the start of **civil war**.

The **Soviets** were accused of **shooting down a South Korean airliner**. They claimed the airliner flew into their airspace and did not respond to communication.

President Reagan had spearheaded a strategy to support **anticommunist insurgencies** bent on overthrowing Marxist regimes. In May, Reagan openly expressed support for the **Contras**, the Nicaraguan opposition to **Communist Sandinista** rule. In October, the US overthrew the Marxist government of **Grenada**.

On March 23, President Reagan launched his **Strategic Defence Initiative** (SDI), an ambitious scheme to combat nuclear weapons in space. Reagan's SDI became known as "**Star Wars**."

$20 BILLION
THE PROPOSED COST OF "STAR WARS"

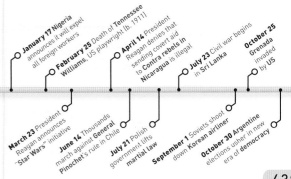

April 25 British marines recapture **South Georgia** from Argentina

May 2 Argentine cruiser **Belgrano** sunk by British forces

June 6 Israel invades **Lebanon**

June 14 Argentine forces **surrender** to British, ending Falklands War

August 31 PLO driven out of Beirut as Yassir Arafat leaves

November 10 Death of **Leonid Brezhnev**, Soviet leader (b. 1906)

January 17 Nigeria announces it will expel all foreign workers

February 25 Death of Tennessee **Williams**, US playwright (b. 1911)

April 14 President Reagan denies that sending covert aid to **Contra rebels in Nicaragua** is illegal

July 23 Civil war begins in Sri Lanka

October 25 **Grenada** invaded by US

May 25 HMS Coventry bombed during Falklands conflict

July 20 IRA bombs two London parks

October 8 Solidarity, the Polish trade union movement, is **banned**

November 12 Lech Walesa, leader of Solidarity, **released** from internment

March 23 President **Reagan** announces "Star Wars" initiative

June 14 Thousands march against General **Pinochet's rule in Chile**

July 21 Polish government lifts **martial law**

September 1 Soviets shoot down Korean airliner

October 30 Argentine elections usher in new era of democracy

Arthur Scargill, leader of the National Union of Miners (NUM), confronts a battalion of police during the British miners' strike, which lasted a year.

Two billion viewers in 60 countries watched the Live Aid concerts.

BRITISH COAL MINERS WENT ON STRIKE from March 12 over pay and mine closures. The dispute lasted an entire year.

Police constable Yvonne Fletcher was killed outside the **Libyan Embassy** in London during a demonstration on April 17. Her death led to a **police siege** of the building. Subsequently, the UK expelled Libyan diplomats from the country.

On December 19, **China** and **Britain** signed a treaty to transfer **Hong Kong**, a British colony, to Chinese rule in 1997.

An **IRA bomb** went off at the Grand Hotel, **Brighton**, on

Red ribbon
A symbol of solidarity for those suffering from HIV/AIDS, the Red Ribbon Foundation was formed in 1993 to promote awareness about the disease.

October 12, targeting the British cabinet who had gathered for the **Conservative Party conference**. Prime Minister Margaret Thatcher (1925–2013) had a narrow escape.

Major General Mohammed Buhari (b. 1942) seized power in Nigeria in a bloodless **military coup** on January 1, citing the government's corruption record.

Indira Gandhi (b. 1917), the prime minister of India, was **assassinated** on October 31. The killing was carried out by **Sikh extremists** in response to an attack on the Sikh shrine, the **Golden Temple of Amritsar**. Ghandi ordered the attack, known as **Operation Blue Star**, to remove Sikh separatists, who were thought to be amassing weapons at the temple. The operation resulted in up to **1,000 deaths**.

On December 3, a **poison-gas leak** at the US-owned Union Carbide pesticide plant near **Bhopal**, India, became one of the worst industrial accidents in history.

The US president **Ronald Reagan** (1911–2004) declared the withdrawal of peacekeeping troops from the Lebanese capital of **Beirut**, on February 7, following increased terrorist attacks.

55,000

15,000

3,000

have died since

died within weeks

Bhopal gas victims
The Bhopal tragedy injured many thousands and killed 3,000 people within weeks. At least 15,000 are thought to have died subsequently.

Free in space
US astronaut Bruce McCandless floats free in space. He used a jet pack to fly nearly 300 feet (91 m) away from the shuttle Challenger.

TANCREDO NEVES (1910–85) WAS ELECTED PRESIDENT OF BRAZIL on 15 January, after 21 years of military rule. Democracy also returned to **Uruguay**, in March, and to **Bolivia**, in August.

On 25 May, hundreds died in attacks on Palestinian strongholds in **Beirut** by Syrian-backed **Shi'ite troops**. Prime minister **Shimon Peres** (b.1923) withdrew Israeli troops from Lebanon, but Israel held a 12 mile- (19 km-) wide **security zone** in the south. Later in the year, on October 7, Palestinian Liberation Organization (**PLO**) militants hijacked an Italian cruise liner, the *Achille Lauro*, demanding the release of **50 Palestinian prisoners** held in Israel. The crisis ended after they

Hole in the ozone layer
This graph shows the average size of the hole in the ozone layer in each year from 1985–95. As a comparison, the area of Europe is about 4 million sq miles (10 million sq km).

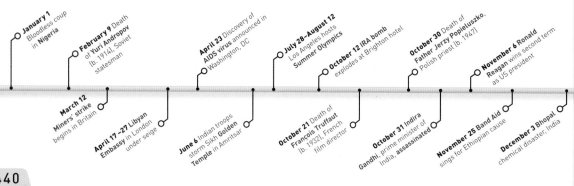

January 1 Bloodless coup in **Nigeria**

February 9 Death of Yuri Andropov (b. 1914), Soviet statesman

March 12 Miners' strike begins in Britain

April 17–27 Libyan Embassy in London under seige

April 23 Discovery of AIDS virus announced in Washington, DC

June 6 Indian troops storm Sikh **Golden Temple** in Amritsar

July 28–August 12 Los Angeles hosts **Summer Olympics**

October 12 IRA bomb explodes at Brighton hotel

October 21 Death of Francois Truffaut (b. 1932), French film director

October 30 Death of Father Jerzy Popieluszko, Polish priest (b. 1947)

October 31 Indira Gandhi, prime minister of India, **assassinated**

November 6 Ronald Reagan wins second term as US president

November 25 Band Aid sings for Ethiopian cause

December 3 Bhopal chemical disaster, India

15 January Brazil elects first civilian president in 21 years

4 February Siege of Gibraltar ends

5 February Terry Waite negotiates release of UK hostages held in Libya

11 March Mikhail Gorbachev (b. 1931) becomes Soviet leader

May Scientists reveal depletion in **ozone layer**

The Russian space station *Mir* (peace) provides a home for visiting astronauts. The first crew arrived on March 15.

killed a passenger, on October 10, when the hijackers abandoned the liner in exchange for safe conduct.

The **Siege of Gibraltar** ended after 16 years, when the Spanish government opened the border, on February 4. The dispute over the island's sovereignty continues.

British scientists discovered a **hole in the ozone layer** over Antarctica. Their findings, published in the May issue of *Nature*, rallied environmentalists.

Live Aid rocked the world in July with two huge concerts held simultaneously in London and Philadelphia to raise money for **famine relief in Ethiopia**.

MIKHAIL GORBACHEV
(1931–)

Mikhail Gorbachev became leader of the Soviet Union on March 11, 1985. He was the architect of *glasnost* (openness) and *perestroika* (restructuring). He built bridges with the West and renounced Stalinist ideas. He won the Nobel Peace Prize in 1990, but his policies led to the implosion of the Soviet Union.

KEY

▪ Highly contaminated area
— Broad range of radiation

Nuclear fallout
Following the nuclear power plant accident at Chernobyl, radiation spread across Europe as far as Paris.

WITH THE IRAN–IRAQ WAR IN ITS SIXTH YEAR, Iran launched a surprise assault and **captured** the abandoned **Iraqi oil port of Faw** in February. Iraq was accused of using mustard gas in its efforts to hold off the attack.

"Irangate," a scandal involving US president **Ronald Reagan**, came to light in October in the US. The Reagan administration had been selling **arms to Iran** to secure the release of US hostages in Lebanon. The profits of the deal were used to fund **Contra rebels** fighting the Marxist regime in **Nicaragua**. Reagan survived, but his chief of staff, **Donald Regan**, and national security adviser, **John Poindexter**, resigned.

US planes **bombed** military targets in **Tripoli**, Libya, on April 15. President Reagan cited self-defense to justify the move. Days earlier, US soldiers had died in a **bomb attack** at the La Belle disco in West Berlin, believed to have been ordered by Libya.

John McCarthy (b. 1956), a British journalist, was **kidnapped** by Islamic terrorists in Beirut, on April 17. On the same day, three British hostages were killed in retaliation for Britain's support of the US bombing of Libya (see 1991).

Yemen experienced turmoil in January as power struggles within the **Yemen Socialist Party** (YSP) led to a **brutal war** between the north and south. Britain's Royal yacht, *Britannia*, helped evacuate British citizens.

Challenger badge
On January 28, the American space shuttle Challenger broke apart 72 seconds after takeoff, causing the death of all seven crew members.

The **Soviet Union** admitted to an accident at a nuclear power station in **Chernobyl**, Ukraine, on April 26. The accident was the worst disaster in the history of nuclear power. It released a high level of **radioactive contamination**, which spread to Europe.

Mir, the Soviet space station, was launched on February 20, as part of a **space city** to house cosmonauts. The first crew arrived on board the space station on March 15.

On June 12, **South Africa** imposed a **state of emergency** before the 10th anniversary of the black student uprising in **Soweto**. The government enforced curfews and banned television cameras from filming "unrest."

Ferdinand Marcos (1917–89) was forced to quit as **dictator of the Philippines** on February 25, after the military and a tide of world opinion turned against him. **Corazon Aquino** (1933–2009), the first female leader of the country, was sworn in as his successor.

Nearly **50,000 students** gathered in Shanghai's **People's Square** on December 21, urging for more social freedom.

50,000
THE **NUMBER OF STUDENTS** WHO **MARCHED** IN SHANGHAI FOR **DEMOCRACY**

SWEDISH DEMOCRATS

Olof Palme led the Swedish Social Democratic Party from 1969. As prime minister he initiated major reforms and was an avid supporter of women's rights, healthcare, and welfare standards. His party was also a forerunner of green politics. He was accused of being pro-Soviet, which some thought led to his assassination in 1986.

Students all across China held demonstrations in major cities, demanding **democratic reforms**.

Spain and **Portugal** joined the **European Union** (EU) on January 1, taking its membership to 12. A new flag was also adopted as the official symbol of Europe.

The **Australia Act**, signed on March 3, made Australian law **independent** of the British legal system. It also transferred control of Australian constitutional documents into Australian hands.

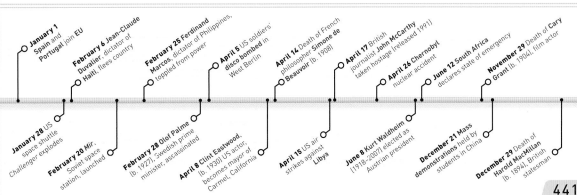

June 23 Air India jumbo jet crashes into Irish Sea

July 13 Live Aid concerts for Ethiopia in London and Philadelphia

November 13 Volcano erupts in Colombia

September 3 Titanic wreck found

November 15 Anglo-Irish Treaty signed

December 11 Unabomber claims first victim in 17-year mail-bomb campaign in US

January 1 Spain and Portugal join EU

February 6 Jean-Claude Duvalier, dictator of Haiti, flees country

February 25 Ferdinand Marcos, dictator of Philippines, toppled from power

April 5 US soldiers' disco bombed in West Berlin

April 14 Death of French philosopher Simone de Beauvoir (b. 1908)

April 17 British journalist John McCarthy taken hostage (released 1991)

April 26 Chernobyl nuclear accident

June 12 South Africa declares state of emergency

November 29 Death of Cary Grant (b. 1904), film actor

January 28 US space shuttle Challenger explodes

February 20 Mir, Soviet space station, launched

February 28 Olof Palme (b. 1927), Swedish prime minister, assassinated

April 8 Clint Eastwood, (b. 1930) US actor, becomes mayor of Carmel, California

April 15 US air strikes against Libya

June 8 Kurt Waldheim (1918–2007) elected as Austrian president

December 21 Mass demonstrations held by students in China

December 29 Death of Harold MacMillan (b. 1894), British statesman

NORWAY

SWEDEN

FINLAND

Barents Sea

Kara Sea

Laptev Sea

Tallinn

St. Petersburg
(Leningrad)

Arkhangel'sk

Plesetsk

Siberia

Riga

Kaliningrad

ESTONIA

LITHUANIA • Vilnius

LATVIA

• Minsk

BELARUS

R U S S I A N   F E D E R A

Ural Mountains

Chernobyl •

• Kiev

MOLDOVA

UKRAINE

Odessa

• Dnipropetrovs'k

• Donets'k

• Rostov

• Moscow

Tula •

Ryazan' •

• Nizhny Novgorod

• Yashkar Ola

• Kazan

• Voronezh

Samara •

• Perm'

• Ufa

• Yekaterinburg

• Tyumen'

• Chelyabinsk

West Siberian Plain

• Tomsk

• Krasnoyarsk

Lake Baikal

• Novosibirsk

Volgograd
(Stalingrad)

Black Sea

Groznyy •

Caspian Sea

GEORGIA

T'bilisi •

Yerevan •

ARMENIA

Baku •

AZERBAIJAN

• Omsk

• Irkutsk

KAZAKHSTAN

• Akmola

• Karaganda

Altai Mountains

MONGOLIA

Lake Balkash

UZBEKISTAN

Dashkhovuz •

TURKMENISTAN

Ashgabat •

• Bukhara

• Samarkand

Tashkent •

Bishkek •

• Almaty

Dushanbe •

KYRGYZSTAN

IRAN

AFGHANISTAN

TAJIKISTAN

KEY

Russian Federation

Former USSR

Collapse of the USSR
After the collapse of the USSR, the former empire split into 15 new states. The independent governments formed a loose union: the Commonwealth of Independent States (CIS).

BEFORE Communist regimes could be found across the world at the high point of communist influence. After Soviet triumph in World War II, communism was embraced by one-third of the world's population. Fear that it would spread further dominated the conduct of the Cold War.

AFTER Today, there are only five communist countries in the world. China is the most prominent, while Laos, Vietnam, North Korea, and Cuba also have communist regimes. Communist parties still exist in many democratic nations.

Magadan

O N

akutsk

Sea of Okhotsk

Svobodnyy

Blagoveshchensk

Vladivostok

CHINA

Sea of Japan (East China Sea)

COLLAPSE OF THE
SOVIET UNION

THE RAPID DISINTEGRATION OF THE SOVIET STATE SHOCKED THE WORLD

In March 1985, Mikhail Gorbachev became leader of a stagnating Soviet Union. He realized that the Soviet Bloc needed radical reforms, and tried to modernize socialism. The result was the total disintegration of the USSR, which transformed the map of Europe and brought about a new world order.

Mikhail Gorbachev was a popular choice for leader. He introduced two new concepts, *glasnost* and *perestroika*—"openness" and "restructuring"— and championed a more liberal, dynamic society. Although Gorbachev's popularity was affirmed when he withdrew troops from Afghanistan, non-Russian minority groups throughout the USSR agitated for independence. In July 1989, Gorbachev announced that countries within the Warsaw Pact (see 1955) could determine their own futures in openly contested elections.

East and Central Europe responded to Gorbachev's greater freedoms: in 1989 Poland elected to end communist rule; Hungary opened its borders with the West; and the Berlin Wall was torn down. When Gorbachev did not respond with force, Czechoslovakia and Romania broke free, followed by Ukraine and Armenia in 1990, and then Turkmenistan and Tajikistan in 1991.

To outsiders, Gorbachev was a hero. He won a Nobel Peace Prize and was feted by foreign leaders. But at home, living standards fell and he wrestled with deep economic problems. Gorbachev struggled to hold the federation together as his ministers deserted him and the clamor for independence in the Baltic States became overwhelming. In July 1991, Boris Yeltsin was elected president of Russia and emerged as a champion of reform when he saved Gorbachev from a coup by hard-line opponents in August. That same month, Yeltsin ordered the Soviet Communist Party to cease its activities in Russia. The Soviet Union faced oblivion when Ukraine, Russia, and Belarus secretly planned to form a new union. His position untenable, on Christmas Day 1991, Gorbachev resigned as Soviet president. Of the 15 remaining Soviet republics, 12 became sovereign states, and the USSR passed into history.

THE RISE AND FALL OF COMMUNISM

Communism was one of the most powerful political movements of the modern world, inspiring great thinkers and guerrilla fighters alike. It was supposed to offer ordinary people freedom from want and oppression, and it united Western critics of the capitalist system.

The great experiment, which began with the seizure of the Winter Palace in Petrograd in 1917, ended in 1989–91, as the Berlin Wall was torn down and the empire of the USSR came apart. China, Cuba, Vietnam, and North Korea still call themselves communist, yet the consensus is that, without the Soviet Union to hold it together, communism is at a dead end.

> ❝ **UPON THE SUCCESS OF PERESTROIKA** DEPENDS THE FUTURE OF **PEACE.** ❞
>
> **Mikhail Gorbachev, Soviet statesman,** 1987

Lithuania 25,174 mi²	Estonia 17,463 mi² Azerbaijan 33,437 mi² Armenia 11,484 mi²
Latvia 333,820 mi²	Moldova 13,068 mi²
Georgia 26,911 mi²	**KAZAKHSTAN** **1,055,950 mi²**
Ukraine 233,062 mi²	Belarus 80,153 mi²
	Turkmenistan 188,456 mi² Tajikistan 55,251 mi²
Uzbekistan 172,742 mi²	Kyrgyzstan 77,182 mi²

RUSSIAN FEDERATION
6,592,850 mi²

Soviet dissolution
Territory that once belonged to the Soviet Union now forms a number of new states. By far the largest is the Russian Federation.

500 BILLION DOLLARS
THE **DECLINE** IN THE **VALUE** OF QUOTED **SHARES** ON **BLACK MONDAY**

The New York Stock Exchange crash on "Black Monday" saw the Dow Jones drop more than 500 points.

5 BILLION
THE **WORLD POPULATION** IN **1987**

IN JULY, THE WORLD POPULATION REACHED FIVE BILLION. This was double what it was in 1950, and a **billion higher** than in 1974. The population of the world was growing at a rate of **220,000 people a day**. Much of the growth was seen in parts of the world least able to sustain it. The concern about the social and economic impact of population growth led to July 11 being known as the **Day of Five Billion**. Thereafter, July 11 became **World Population Day**.

Terry Waite (b. 1939), special envoy to the Archbishop of Canterbury, traveled to Lebanon, in January, to seek the **release of hostages** from Western countries, including the journalist **John McCarthy** (see 1986). However, he himself was **captured by militants** and held in Beirut (see 1991).

In May, **France** was forced to pay $8.6 million to **Greenpeace** for the sinking of their flagship, *Rainbow Warrior*. The vessel, which was to lead a Greenpeace flotilla protesting against **French nuclear testing** in the Pacific, had been sunk by an explosion on July 10, 1985, in **Auckland** harbor, New Zealand. A photographer, Fernando Pereira, was killed in the blast. The incident provoked an **international scandal** and led to the cooling of relations between New Zealand and France. Two **French secret agents**, implicated in the bombing, were imprisoned. France paid $6.5 million to New Zealand as **compensation** and for returning its agents to French jurisdiction.

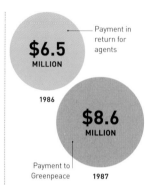

$6.5 MILLION — Payment in return for agents

1986

$8.6 MILLION

Payment to Greenpeace — **1987**

French compensation
France paid New Zealand $6.5 million to return its agents. It also paid $8.6 million to Greenpeace for the sinking of its ship, Rainbow Warrior.

On March 20, the drug azidothymidine (**AZT**) was approved by the US Food and Drug Administration. It was the first antiretroviral drug made specifically to combat **HIV/AIDS**. While AZT could not cure AIDS, it proved that the disease could be managed, and that HIV was not a death sentence.

On October 19, the **Dow-Jones average** in the US declined by 22.6 percent—the **largest single-day percentage drop** in its history. The next day, the London Stock Exchange saw £50 billion wiped off its share values.

Negotiating freedom
Terry Waite became a familiar figure in Lebanon. As a church envoy, he made many missions to negotiate the release of hostages held by Islamic militant organizations.

Stock markets around the globe also **plummeted**. The crash was triggered by fears about the weak dollar and the **US trade deficit**. It was aggravated by news of the US retaliating against Iranian attacks in the Persian Gulf by bombing an oil rig. "Black Monday," as it came to be known, was almost twice as bad as the crash of October 29, 1929.

Margaret Thatcher (1925–2013) **visited Moscow** in March. It was the first official visit by a British prime minister in 12 years, and marked the **normalization of British–Soviet ties**. During the talks, **Mikhail Gorbachev** (b. 1931), the Soviet premier, condemned the Brezhnev doctrine and called the "**Iron Curtain**" archaic, suggesting more liberal policies toward Eastern Europe. The next month, Gorbachev visited Prague, Czechoslovakia, and implied that the Eastern Bloc countries could be **independent**.

In December, the leaders of the **USSR and US signed a treaty** to reduce the size of their ground-based nuclear arsenal. Known as the **Intermediate-range Nuclear Forces (INF) Treaty**, its aim was to reverse the nuclear arms race by destroying all medium- and short-range nuclear weapons in Europe, capable of hitting targets at ranges of 300–3,000 miles (500–5,500 km). This was the first time the superpowers had agreed to **reduce** their massive **nuclear arsenals**.

January 1 Thousands of students march in Tiananmen Square, Beijing, China

January 20 Terry Waite, hostage negotiator, **disappears** in Beirut

March 20 AZT drug introduced to combat AIDS

April 21 Tamil Tigers blamed for Colombo bomb attack, which killed over 100

June 22 Death of American dancer and actor **Fred Astaire** (b. 1893)

August 17 Death of **Rudolf Hess** (b. 1894), Hitler's deputy

August 19 Michael Ryan shoots 14 dead in Hungerford, England

October 16 Hurricane rocks Britain; 13 die

November 8 IRA bomb Remembrance Day parade in Enniskillen, Northern Ireland

December 8 Superpowers sign INF Treaty to reduce nuclear arsenal

January 15 Israeli soldiers clash with Palestinians outside Temple Mount, East Jerusalem

January 15 Death of Sean McBride (b. 1904), Amnesty International cofounder

March 6 The English Channel ferry Herald of Free Enterprise **capsizes**, killing nearly 200

April 19 *The Simpsons* cartoon show launched on Tracey Ullman Show

May 2 France pays Greenpeace compensation for sinking *Rainbow Warrior*

July 3 "Butcher of Lyon," Klaus Barbie, found guilty of wartime atrocities

July 11 World population reaches 5 billion

August 28 Death of American film director John Huston (b. 1906)

October 19 "Black Monday"; stocks around the world tumble

November 18 Fire at King's Cross Station, London; 30 die

December 15 Digging begins in Britain for Channel Tunnel to France

March 6 IRA gang shot dead in Gibraltar by SAS

March 16 Iraq drops chemical bombs on Kurdish town of Halabja

April 1 Stephen Hawking publishes *A Brief History of Time*

1988

" READ MY LIPS: NO NEW TAXES. "

George Bush, accepting the Republican presidential nomination in New Orleans, August 18, 1988

THREE MEMBERS OF THE IRISH REPUBLICAN ARMY (IRA) were shot dead by the Secret Air Service (**SAS**) in Gibraltar, on 6 March. The IRA was planning to **detonate a bomb** during a "change of guard" ceremony in the British territory. The event was to be attended by the 1st Battalion Royal Anglian Regiment, following a tour of Northern Ireland. The incident led to a **wave of violence** in Belfast.

This year saw the first documented use of **chemical weapons** in the Iran–Iraq war, when Iraq dropped bombs containing **mustard gas and nerve agents** on the Kurdish city of **Halabja** in Iraq, in March. Between 3,000 and 5,000 civilians died, and many more suffered long-term health problems. The massacre is known as "**Bloody Friday**" (see 2010).

On 8 August, a UN-arranged **ceasefire** ended the **Iran–Iraq war** (see 1980). Lasting eight years, the war resulted in more than **1 million casualties**.

Throughout 1988, Palestinian Arabs of the **Gaza Strip** and **West Bank** continued a mass uprising against Israeli occupation of Palestinian territories. Known as "**intifada**", it took the form of general strikes, boycott of Israeli products, demonstrations, and use of **petrol bombs**. On 14 November, the Palestine

Liberation Organization (**PLO**) accepted the "**two-state solution**" (see 1947), officially recognizing Israel's right to exist.

On 2 December, **Benazir Bhutto** (see panel, below) was sworn in as **Pakistan's first female prime minister**. At 35, she also became the youngest leader of a world nation (see 2007).

Mikhail Gorbachev's **perestroika** (economic and political reforms), and **glasnost** (open debate), played a key role in ending the Cold War (see 1948). In a dramatic speech to the UN, on 7 December, Gorbachev announced unilateral **arms and troop reductions**, and withdrawal of forces from Eastern Europe.

On 21 December, **Pan Am flight 103** crashed at **Lockerbie**, Scotland, killing all 259 passengers and crew, and 11 on the ground. Evidence of a **bomb** instigated a huge investigation. Two **Libyan intelligence agents** were linked to the bombing, although it took over 11 years to bring them to trial.

George Bush (b.1924) became the first US vice president since 1836 to win the **presidential election**. On 8 November, he claimed a comfortable victory over democrat **Michael Dukakis**.

South Africa's border war with Namibia and Angola had been ongoing since 1966. South Africa was under intense pressure from the international community to **grant Namibia independence**. They agreed to do this, but only if **Cuba** removed its troops from **Angola**. Initially the UN rejected this proposal, but on 22 December the participants met in New York where a **bilateral agreement** was signed by Cuba and Angola, and a **tripartite accord**, by Angola, Cuba, and South Africa.

In April, Stephen Hawking (b.1942) published **A Brief History of Time**, a story of the Universe from the "**Big Bang**". The most popular science book ever, it was translated into 40 languages and sold more than **10 million copies**.

Horsehead nebula
The resumption of shuttle flights, in 1988, meant that NASA's Hubble Space Telescope programme was back on track. Hubble would produce stunning images of the universe.

BENAZIR BHUTTO (1953–2007)

Benazir Bhutto set up the Pakistan People's Party (PPP) in London after her father, Zulfikar Ali Bhutto, was assassinated in 1979. She returned to Pakistan in 1986 and served as prime minister from 1988–90 and 1993–96. Benazir was exiled in 1999 on corruption charges, but returned in 2007 for fresh elections. Two months later, she was assassinated in a suicide attack.

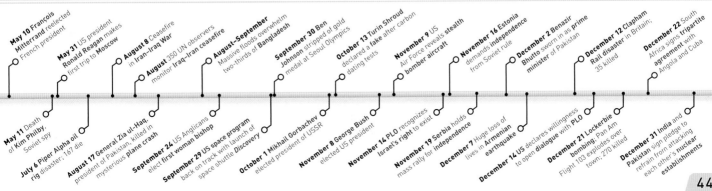

May 10 Francois Mitterrand reelected French president

May 31 US president **Ronald Reagan** makes first trip to Moscow

August 8 Ceasefire in Iran–Iraq War

August 350 UN observers monitor Iraq-Iran ceasefire

August–September Massive floods overwhelm two-thirds of Bangladesh

September 30 Ben Johnson stripped of gold medal at Seoul Olympics

October 13 Turin Shroud declared a fake after carbon dating tests

November 9 US Air Force reveals **stealth bomber aircraft**

November 16 Estonia demands independence from Soviet rule

December 2 Benazir Bhutto sworn in as prime minister of Pakistan

December 12 Clapham Rail disaster in Britain; 35 killed

December 22 South Africa signs **tripartite agreement** with Angola and Cuba

May 11 Death of Kim Philby, Soviet spy

July 6 Piper Alpha oil rig disaster; 167 die

August 17 General Zia ul-Haq, president of Pakistan, killed in mysterious plane crash

September 24 US Anglicans elect first woman bishop

September 29 US space program back on track with launch of space shuttle *Discovery*

October 1 Mikhail Gorbachev elected president of USSR

November 8 George Bush elected US president

November 14 PLO recognizes Israel's right to exist

November 19 Serbia holds mass rally for independence

December 7 Huge loss of lives in Armenian earthquake

December 14 US declares willingness to open dialogue with PLO

December 21 Lockerbie bombing; Pan Am Flight 103 explodes over town; 270 killed

December 31 India and Pakistan sign pledge to refrain from attacking each other's nuclear establishments

Thousands gather during the Velvet Revolution in Czechoslovakia, a bloodless uprising that saw the overthrow of the communist government on December 29.

IN SOUTH AFRICA, F.W. DE KLERK (B. 1936) WAS ELECTED LEADER of the **National Party** on February 2. The party had governed the country since 1948 on the principle of **apartheid**. However, De Klerk was more willing than his predecessors to modernize the political system. On August 15, the incumbent president, P.W. Botha (1916–2006) suffered a stroke and **De Klerk took over**. Klerk began **releasing prominent black leaders** who had been imprisoned, including Walter Sisulu, a close friend of Nelson Mandela (1918–2013), one of the the leaders of the African National Congress (ANC).

On February 14, **Ayatollah Khomeini** (1902–89), the spiritual leader of Iran, issued a *fatwa*, or decree, calling for the death of author **Salman Rushdie** (b. 1947) and the publishers of his book, *The Satanic Verses*. The book was considered to be a **blasphemy against Islam**. Rushdie was forced into hiding, under armed guard, to protect his life (see 1998).

Later in the year, on June 3, **Khomeini died** in Tehran. His death was **mourned by millions**. Eight people were killed in the stampede and hundreds more injured while approaching the body to pay obeisance. The incumbent president, Ali Khamenei became Supreme Leader of Iran.

Vietnam promised to withdraw its troops from Cambodia by the end of September, a decade after invading the country (see 1979). In a declaration made on April 5, Vietnam also urged the world to

Making a stand
The figure of a lone man in front of army tanks in Tiananmen Square, China, became a poignant symbol of the protests.

ensure that the **Cambodian civil war** was truly over and that Khmer Rouge leader **Pol Pot** (see 1973) would never be allowed to return to power again.

In China, a **demonstration** held in **Tiananmen Square**, Beijing, ended in **bloodshed** on June 4, after civilians were killed by the People's Liberation Army. Tanks were lined up in the streets to confront protestors, mainly students, who had been stationed there for seven weeks. The crowds, which swelled to more than 100,000, called for economic and political reform in the country.

Almost a decade after they had stormed the country, **Soviet troops withdrew** from Afghanistan in February. They left the economy

in ruins. Many Afghans had fled, and **civil war continued** as the Mujahideen (Persian for "warriors") pushed to overthrow President Najibullah's Soviet-backed government (see 1992).

On April 17, **Solidarity**, Poland's free trade union movement, was **legalized** after a ban of seven years. It grew into a political movement, and in elections held on June 5, **Solidarity won** an overwhelming majority. After 45 years, **communist rule in Poland ended**. Solidarity formed a new noncommunist government

100,000
PROTEST

— 3,000 killed

Tiananmen Square massacre
The Chinese Army shot dead nearly 3,000 of the 100,000 demonstrators who protested in Tiananmen Square in Beijing.

in the former Eastern Bloc. On September 12, Tadeusz Mazowiecki became prime minister.

By the start of 1989, communist regimes had ruled Eastern Europe for 45 years. By the end of the year they had all been routed by extraordinary **public uprisings**. Following the election of Solidarity in Poland, Hungary's rulers published a **plan for independence**. A **coup in Bulgaria** brought down

party leader Todor Zhivkov. On November 28, the **Czechoslovak communist regime surrendered** to the people. A month later, Václav Havel became President of the Czechoslovak Republic in the nonviolent **Velvet Revolution**. In Romania, the incumbent president, **Nicolae Ceausescu,** was removed from office and **shot** in December.

Erich Honecker, leader of the German Democratic Republic, entered 1989 confident that the reforms in neighboring countries would not affect his country, but protests grew. The Hungarian government demolished the electric fence along the Austrian frontier, part of the **Iron Curtain**—the heavily guarded border between the countries of the Eastern Bloc and the rest of Europe. By September, when the **border controls were lifted**, 60,000 East Germans were in Hungary waiting to pour through to the West. On October 2, a **huge protest calling for reform**

COLD WAR ESPIONAGE

Espionage epitomized the Cold War. Intelligence gathered by electronic devices, satellites, and spies was used for military information and technology. The US Central Intelligence Agency (CIA), the Soviet KGB, and East German secret police, or *Stasi* (see badge, right), spent decades spying on the enemy and undermining rivals through covert action.

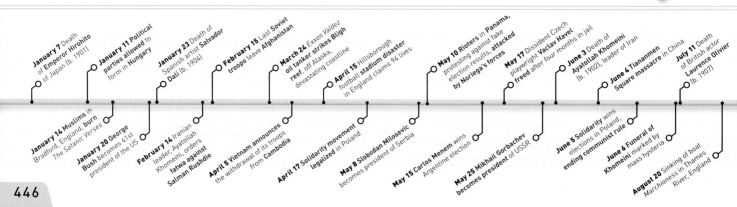

January 7 Death of Emperor Hirohito of Japan (b. 1901)

January 11 Political parties allowed to form in Hungary

January 14 Muslims in Bradford, England, **burn** *The Satanic Verses*

January 20 George Bush becomes 41st president of the US

January 23 Death of Spanish artist Salvador Dali (b. 1904)

February 14 Iranian leader, Ayatollah Khomeini, orders **fatwa against Salman Rushdie**

February 15 Last Soviet troops leave Afghanistan

March 24 *Exxon Valdez* oil tanker strikes Bligh reef, off Alaska, devastating coastline

April 5 Vietnam announces the withdrawal of its troops from Cambodia

April 15 Hillsborough football **stadium disaster** in England claims 94 lives

April 17 Solidarity movement legalized in Poland

May 8 Slobodan Milosevic becomes president of Serbia

May 10 Rioters in Panama, protesting against fake election results, **attacked by Noriega's forces**

May 15 Carlos Menen wins Argentine election

May 17 Dissident Czech playwright **Václav Havel freed** after four months in jail

May 25 Mikhail Gorbachev becomes president of USSR

June 3 Death of Ayatollah Khomeini (b. 1902), leader of Iran

June 4 Tiananmen Square massacre in China

June 5 Solidarity wins elections in Poland, **ending communist rule**

June 6 Funeral of Khomeini marked by mass hysteria

July 11 Death of British actor Laurence Olivier (b. 1907)

August 20 Sinking of boat *Marchioness* in Thames River, England

> ❝ WE HAVE BEEN **TOO LONG IN DARKNESS.** ONCE ALREADY WE HAVE **BEEN IN THE LIGHT,** AND WE **WANT IT AGAIN.** ❞

Alexander Dubcek, Czechoslovakian leader, 1989

Huge crowds demonstrate for the end of communist rule in Hungary. The Republic of Hungary was proclaimed on October 23, marking a new era in Europe.

The Wall falls
An East German border guard peers through a hole in the Berlin Wall, brought down in 1989, a potent symbol of the end of communism.

gathered in Leipzig, and decided to keep meeting every Monday until their demands were met. On October 9, the army refused to fire on the crowds. Honecker was ousted from office on October 18.

After the fall of Honecker's regime, the leader of the East Berlin communist party, Günter Schabowski, announced on November 9 that the **border with West Berlin would be opened** for "private trips abroad." That night, 50,000 East Berliners rushed to the Berlin Wall (see 1961). The guards let them pass. The crowds were met by ecstatic West Berliners on the other side. The next morning, they started **bringing the wall down.**

On December 3, the US and the USSR met in Malta and declared the **end of the Cold War.** At a joint news conference held on board the Soviet cruise ship, *Maxim Gorky*, President George Bush (b. 1924) and President Mikhail Gorbachev (b. 1931) announced plans for **substantial reductions in weapons** in Europe. Praised by those outside the USSR, internally it placed Gorbachev's position as Soviet leader at risk (see pp.442–43).

Kosovo, an autonomous province of Serbia, had been clamoring for independence since the death of Josip Tito

(see 1980). There was increasing **ethnic tension between Serbs and Albanians** for control of the province. Serbs argued that they were being persecuted by the majority Albanians. When **Slobodan Milosevic** became president of Serbia on May 8, he used this alleged persecution as a justification for **stripping Kosovo of its autonomy** and became a champion of Serbian nationalism.

On December 20, **US troops invaded Panama** in a bid to oust dictator Manuel Noriega. Over 200 civilians died in the fighting. A new government, headed by Guillermo Endara, was installed.

In New York, **Wall Street suffered a crash** on Friday October, as a failed buyout of United Airlines caused share values to plummet. It was the

low-gain antenna

radioisotope thermoelectric generator (RTG)

Jupiter atmospheric probe

high-gain antenna

Galileo space probe
Named after astronomer Galilei Galileo, the probe traveled a distance of nearly 3 billion miles (more than 4.5 billion km), circling Jupiter 34 times.

second largest drop of the Dow Jones industrial average, a stock market index, in history, and became known as the **"Friday-the-13th mini-crash."**

The US launched *Galileo*, an **unmanned probe to Jupiter** and its moons, aboard the space shuttle *Atlantis* on October 18. At a cost of $1.5 billion, *Galileo* reached its final destination in 1994 after taking detailed images of Venus and the asteroid belt on the way.

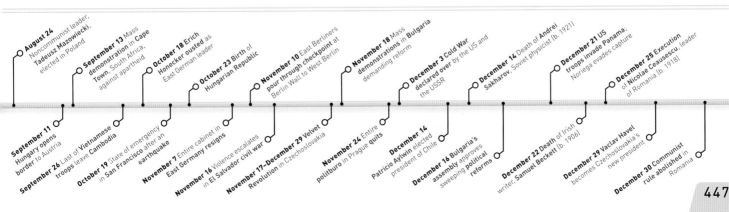

August 24 Noncommunist leader, Tadeusz Mazowiecki, elected in Poland

September 13 Mass demonstration in Cape Town, South Africa, against apartheid

October 18 Erich Honecker ousted as East German leader

October 23 Birth of Hungarian Republic

November 10 East Berliners pour through checkpoint at Berlin Wall to West Berlin

November 18 Mass demonstrations in Bulgaria demanding reform

December 3 Cold War declared over by the US and the USSR

December 14 Death of Andrei Sakharov, Soviet physicist (b. 1921)

December 21 US troops invade Panama; Noriega evades capture

December 25 Execution of Nicolae Ceausescu, leader of Romania (b. 1918)

September 11 Hungary opens border to Austria

September 26 Last of Vietnamese troops leave Cambodia

October 19 State of emergency in San Francisco after an earthquake

November 7 Entire cabinet in East Germany resigns

November 16 Violence escalates in El Salvador civil war

November 17–December 29 Velvet Revolution in Czechoslovakia

November 24 Entire politburo in Prague quits

December 14 Patricio Aylwin elected president of Chile

December 16 Bulgaria's assembly approves sweeping political reforms

December 22 Death of Irish writer, Samuel Beckett (b. 1906)

December 29 Vaclav Havel becomes Czechoslovakia's new president

December 30 Communist rule abolished in Romania

1990

Nelson Mandela and his wife Winnie punch the air in a victory salute after his release from Victor Verster prison. He was held in captivity for 27 years.

THE 30-YEAR BAN ON THE AFRICAN NATIONAL CONGRESS (ANC) in South Africa was lifted by President De Klerk on February 2. This started the long process of **dismantling the apartheid system**. In sweeping reforms, De Klerk also announced that the outlawed South African Communist Party and the Pan-Africanist Congress would be allowed to resume legal political activities.

Nine days later, **Nelson Mandela** (1918–2013), the leader of the ANC, **walked free** after spending **27 years in jail**.

Neighboring **Namibia** became the 47th African country to **gain independence** after 25 years of struggle against South African rule. Sam Nujoma was elected as the first president in March.

In Central America, **free elections** were held **in Nicaragua** on February 25. National Opposition Union, a coalition of political parties backed by US funding, defeated the left-wing Sandinistas. Violeta Chamorro

(b. 1929) became the first female president of Nicaragua.

In the Persian Gulf, **Iraq invaded Kuwait** on August 2. The invasion was preceded by border disputes between the two countries, and Iraq's inability to repay money borrowed from Kuwait during the Iraq–Iran War (1980–88). On August 8, Iraqi leader **Saddam Hussein** (1937–2006) announced that **Kuwait had become a part of Iraq**. World leaders condemned the invasion. Soon after, allied forces led by the US were sent to the Gulf (see 1991).

On August 23, Saddam Hussein appeared on television with **Western hostages**, mostly of British origin, captured in Iraq. He denied accusations that he was using these hostages as "human shields" against a potential US-led coalition attack.

Farther north, Soviet troops were ordered into Baku, Azerbaijan, on the evening of January 19 to put down a separatist movement by **Azerbaijani nationalists**. The

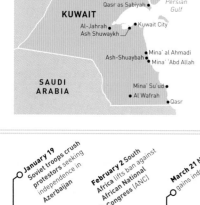

War zone
Kuwait, a small oil-rich Arab nation, was annexed by neighboring Iraq. The seven-month-long occupation ended after military intervention by US-led forces in Operation Desert Storm, a largely air offensive.

LECH WALESA (1943–)

One of the founding members of Poland's Solidarity trade union movement, Lech Walesa was awarded the Nobel Peace Prize in 1983. In 1990, he became Poland's first post-communist president. He failed to gain a second term in office, as he had alienated voters with his erratic leadership style.

next day, thousands of Azerbaijanis set fire to their Communist Party membership cards.

Germany was reunited on October 3, nearly a year after the fall of the Berlin Wall (see 1989). Helmut Kohl (b. 1930) was elected as the first chancellor of the reunified nation.

On December 1, the **Channel Tunnel**, the world's longest undersea railroad tunnel linking Britain with France, came a step closer to completion. The construction workers drilled through the final section of rock to join the two halves of the tunnel.

1991

A man tries to put out a fire at an oil well in Burhan, Kuwait. Iraqi troops had set alight more than 600 oil fields during their occupation of the country.

ON JANUARY 13, SOVIET TROOPS STORMED INTO LITHUANIA to suppress dissident nationalists. In the crackdown, 14 people were killed and more than 500 injured. Protestors had gathered to protect a TV station after a broadcast called for people to defend government buildings from the Soviet troops.

On June 13, **Boris Yeltsin** (1931–2007) became the first popularly elected president of Russia, inflicting a heavy defeat on the Communist Party. The win gave him a power base to challenge the incumbent leader of the Soviet Union, Mikhail Gorbachev (b. 1931).

A **military coup** attempted to remove Gorbachev from power when he was on holiday in August. Yeltsin organized a resistance and the coup collapsed on August 21. Subsequently, Yeltsin ordered the

Iraq–Kuwait war casualties
The superiority of coalition forces is starkly illustrated by the disproportionately heavy losses inflicted on the Iraqi military.

Communist Party of the Soviet Union to end its rule in Russia.

The **USSR disintegrated** into **15 separate countries** as the world looked on in amazement. On December 8, heads of three of the Soviet Union's 15 republics, Russia, Ukraine, and Belarus, met to disband the Soviet Union and form a new union, the **Commonwealth of Independent States**. On December 21, eight others joined it. After four days, Mikhail Gorbachev announced he was resigning as Soviet president; **the USSR was no more**.

Yugoslavia was also breaking up—**Slovenia and Croatia declared independence** in June. Serban president Slobodan Milosevic sent troops to both regions to stop them from seceding. The city of Vukovar in eastern Croatia was devastated after a three-month siege by Serbs, which ended in November.

In **Northern Ireland**, the main political parties held an **historic meeting** on June 18 to discuss the future of the province. Northern Ireland had suffered years of sectarian violence and there was an overwhelming public desire to end bloodshed.

Peace talks were also held on the **Middle East** between Arabs and Israelis in Spain, on October 30. It was the first time in over 40 years that Israel had sat down with all its Arab neighbours to discuss peace.

Elsewhere, the **United Nations** (UN) **issued an ultimatum** to Saddam Hussein to withdraw Iraqi troops from Kuwait by January 15

Residents of Sarajevo, Bosnia, duck sniper shots at a peace march during the Bosnian War as radical Serbs open fire on them.

The division of Yugoslavia
After 72 years, Yugoslavia disappeared from the map of Europe after war and political upheaval led to the formation of six independent countries.

KEY
New Countries

THE IDEA OF A UNITED EUROPE CAME CLOSER TO REALIZATION when leaders of 12 European countries signed the **treaty on European Union** and the **Maastricht Final Act** on February 7. It heralded common citizenship, and common economic and defence policies.

The break up of Yugoslavia continued as **Bosnia and Herzegovina declared independence** on March 3. Serbs living in Bosnia, however, resisted the move. **War broke out** and the

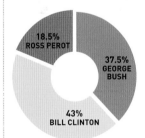

UN PEACEKEEPING

United Nations Peacekeeping emerged out of World War II as a way to place military personnel between warring countries or communities to stop fighting. UN forces were first used as an observer to monitor the armistice between Israel and the Arab states in 1948. Its role has grown substantially since then: supervising elections, checking human rights, clearing land mines, and intervening in failed states. By 1992, UN Peacekeeping forces had made 26 interventions worldwide.

6,000

THE NUMBER OF **BOSNIANS** AND **CROATS HELD IN** OMARSKA **DEATH CAMP**

Yugoslav army under Slobodan Milosevic attacked the Muslim population of Bosnia. The capital, Sarajevo, came under siege from Bosnian Serbs. Supplies became short and people struggled for survival (see 1996).

In August, footage of **Serbian prison camps**, showing starving men behind barbed-wire fences, sparked outrage around the world. The camps, mostly in Bosnia, were part of Serbia's "**ethnic cleansing policy**" that called for the removal of other ethnic groups from Serb-dominated communities.

On December 20, **Slobodan Milosevic was reelected** as Serbian president. Prime minister Milan Panic called for fresh elections, citing fraud. After nine days, Panic lost a parliamentary vote of no confidence.

Algerian president **Mohammed Boudiaf** was **assassinated** on June 29 at a rally in Annaba. Boudiaf had been instrumental in the Algerian uprising against France (see 1958). He had recently returned from exile to help the government combat the Islamic

Salvation Front, a fundamentalist party, whom many believed was responsible for the assassination.

US Marines waded onto the shores of **Somalia** on December 9. Somalia was **stricken by famine**, but extortion and looting prevented foreign aid from getting through. The US-led operation aimed to hold Mogadishu's airport to enable supplies to be airlifted to starving locals.

The **Los Angeles police department** was accused of **racism and excessive force** after a video of four policemen savagely beating a black man, **Rodney King**, was broadcast in 1991. The officers were acquitted in a trial, triggering **race riots** on April 29, which led to 55 casualties.

On November 4, Democrat **Bill Clinton** (b. 1946) **beat George Bush** (b. 1924) in the US presidential elections. Clinton promised to lift the US out of economic stagnation.

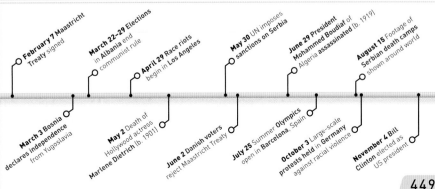

18.5% ROSS PEROT

37.5% GEORGE BUSH

43% BILL CLINTON

Clinton's victory
Bill Clinton became the 42nd president of the US by beating opponents Ross Perot and George Bush.

(see 1990). He refused to comply, and on January 17, the US and coalition forces launched "**Operation Desert Storm**," also known as the **First Gulf War** (1990–91). Kuwait was liberated after five weeks.

The First Gulf War left Saddam Hussein vulnerable in Iraq. There were **antigovernment uprisings by Shi'ite Muslims** in the south of the country and by **Kurds** in the north. During March and April, thousands of people were killed as Saddam crushed the revolts.

In India, **Rajiv Gandhi** (b. 1944), the former prime minister, was **assassinated** on May 21. He was

killed by a bomb in the town of Sriperumbudur while campaigning with his party for the forthcoming elections. A female suicide bomber from Liberation Tigers of Tamil Eelam (LTTE), a guerilla group in Sri Lanka also known as the "**Tamil Tigers**," was later found to have been responsible.

On August 8, **John McCarthy**, a British journalist held hostage by an Islamic extremist group in Lebanon, was **released after five years in captivity** (see 1986). Later in the year, fellow British hostage Terry Waite, and Americans Terry Anderson and Tom Sutherland were also freed.

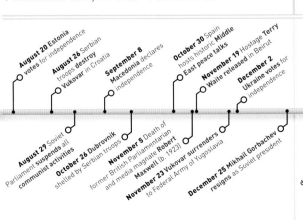

August 20 Estonia votes for independence

August 26 Serbian troops destroy Vukovar in Croatia

September 8 Macedonia declares independence

October 30 Spain hosts historic Middle East peace talks

November 19 Hostage Terry Waite released in Beirut

December 2 Ukraine votes for independence

August 29 Soviet Parliament suspends all communist activities

October 26 Dubrovnik shelled by Serbian troops

November 5 Death of former British Parliamentarian and media magnate Robert Maxwell (b. 1923)

November 23 Vukovar surrenders to Federal Army of Yugoslavia

December 25 Mikhail Gorbachev resigns as Soviet president

February 7 Maastricht Treaty signed

March 22–29 Elections in Albania end communist rule

April 29 Race riots begin in Los Angeles

May 30 UN imposes sanctions on Serbia

June 29 President Mohammed Boudiaf of Algeria assassinated (b. 1919)

August 15 Footage of Serbian death camps shown around world

March 3 Bosnia declares independence from Yugoslavia

May 2 Death of Hollywood actress Marlene Dietrich (b. 1901)

June 2 Danish voters reject Maastricht Treaty

July 25 Summer Olympics open in Barcelona, Spain

October 3 Large-scale protests held in Germany against racial violence

November 4 Bill Clinton elected as US president

449

Prague, famed for its architecturally diverse castle district shown above, became the capital of the newly formed Czech Republic. The castle is the official seat of the Czech head of state.

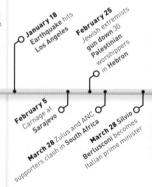

Refugees flee the civil war in Rwanda and head for refugee camps in Zaire.

THE SINGLE MARKET CAME INTO FORCE across European Union (EU) countries in January. It gave greater freedom to citizens of member states to live and work in other EU countries and paved the way for a single currency, **the Euro**.

On January 1, **Czechoslovakia was split into Slovakia and the Czech Republic**, dissolving the 74-year-old federation. The creation of the Czech Republic, with its capital in Prague, and Slovakia, with its capital in Bratislava, became known as the "Velvet Divorce" following the Velvet Revolution (see 1989).

Russian president **Boris Yeltsin** (1931–2007) faced mounting opposition to his "**shock therapy**" program of reforms, which he had initiated in 1992. The measures were aimed at loosening the state's grip on the economy and moving towards a market-driven model, but they were widely regarded as being capitalist and "Western." The Russian parliament tried to impeach Yeltsin, who responded with a decree **dissolving the parliament** on September 21.

Under increasing pressure from his political opponents, Yeltsin ordered parliamentarians to vacate the parliament building. When they refused, Yeltsin ordered the army to seize the building.

A series of **bomb blasts rocked** India's financial capital **Mumbai** (formerly Bombay) on March 12, killing 257 people and injuring 713 others. They were carried out by an underworld crime syndicate.

The **Irish Republican Army** (IRA) exploded a **massive bomb** in the **City of London**, the economic heart of the English capital, on 24 April. This came a month after an IRA blast in Warrington, which killed two children. Later in the year, on December 15, the leaders of Northern Ireland and Britain signed a peace declaration, aiming to end violence in the province.

Moves toward peace were also underway between **Israel** and the

187 KILLED

437 WOUNDED

Coup casualties
Russian president Boris Yeltsin seized absolute authority by storming the parliament in Moscow, ending a rebellion by hardline opponents.

Palestine Liberation Organization (**PLO**). They signed the **Oslo Accords** in Washington, DC in the presence of the US president Bill Clinton in September. Aimed at mutual recognition, the accords were preceded by secret talks between the two parties, encouraged by the Norwegian government.

On April 19, a **siege** at the headquarters of a US religious sect, the Branch Davidian, near Waco, Texas killed at least 70 people, including its leader, **David Koresh**, when it ended in a fire. The Federal Bureau of Investigation (FBI) had surrounded the building since February, when four agents with the Bureau of Alcohol, Tobacco, and Firearms (ATF) were killed while trying to arrest Koresh for illegally possessing firearms.

Mostar Bridge
A 16th-century bridge spanned the Neretva River for 427 years before it was destroyed during the fighting between Croats and Muslims.

IN SOUTH AFRICA, ZULUS AND AFRICAN NATIONAL CONGRESS (ANC) supporters clashed on March 28—more than 18 people were killed. The Zulus were responding to calls by their leaders to boycott the forthcoming national elections. The elections went ahead, and on May 10, **Nelson Mandela** became **South Africa's first black president** after more than three centuries of white rule. His party, the ANC (see panel, opposite), won 252 of the 400 seats in the **first democratic elections** in South Africa's history.

Elsewhere in Africa, the president of Rwanda, **Juvenal Habyarimana** (b.1937), a Hutu, was killed when his **plane was shot down** above Kigali airport on April 6. The incident catalyzed a **mass genocide**. Between April and June, about **800,000 Rwandans were killed**, most of them Tutsis killed by Hutus.

On July 1, PLO chairman **Yasser Arafat** (1929–2004) returned to the **Gaza Strip** after **27 years in exile**. It marked the start of the enactment of the Declaration of Principles agreed at the Oslo Accords, signed in Washington, DC the previous year (see 1993).

Israel and **Jordan** signed a historic peace deal on October 26, **ending 46 years of war**. US president Bill Clinton witnessed the treaty between Israeli prime minister Yitzhak Rabin (1922–95) and King Hussein at a ceremony in Wadi Araba, on the Israel–Jordan border.

On August 31, the **IRA declared a ceasefire** after 25 years of

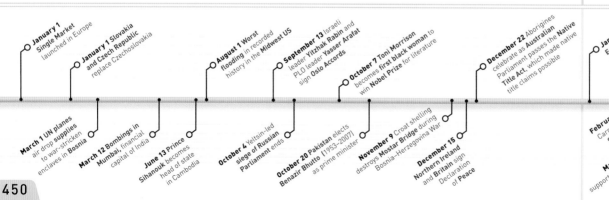

January 1 Single Market launched in Europe

January 1 Slovakia and Czech Republic replace Czechoslovakia

March 1 UN planes air drop supplies to war-stricken enclaves in Bosnia

March 12 Bombings in Mumbai, financial capital of India

June 13 Prince Sihanouk becomes head of state in Cambodia

August 1 Worst flooding in recorded history in the Midwest US

September 13 Israeli leader Yitzhak Rabin and PLO leader Yasser Arafat sign Oslo Accords

October 4 Yeltsin-led siege of Russian Parliament ends

October 7 Toni Morrison becomes first black woman to win Nobel Prize for literature

October 20 Pakistan elects Benazir Bhutto (1953–2007) as prime minister

November 9 Croat shelling destroys Mostar Bridge during Bosnia–Herzegovina War

December 15 Northern Ireland and Britain sign Declaration of Peace

December 22 Aborigines celebrate as Australian Parliament passes the Native Title Act, which made native title claims possible

January 18 Earthquake hits Los Angeles

February 5 Carnage at Sarajevo

February 25 Jewish extremists gun down 30 Palestinian worshippers in Hebron

March 28 Zulus and ANC supporters clash in South Africa

March 28 Silvio Berlusconi becomes Italian prime minister

> **...THE GREATEST FAILURE OF THE WEST SINCE THE 1930s.**
>
> Richard Holbrooke, US Assistant Secretary of State, on the Bosnian crisis

armed struggle against British rule in Northern Ireland. The ceasefire indicated the IRA's willingness to enter into **peace talks** on the political future of the province. The Irish prime minister, Albert Reynolds, asked loyalist paramilitaries to toe the same line. However, loyalists were suspicious of this declaration and feared that Northern Ireland's position in Great Britain would be threatened, but in the end, on October 13, they announced their own ceasefire.

War continued in Bosnia and Herzegovina, and on February 5, a marketplace in downtown **Sarajevo was devastated** by a mortar bomb, killing 68 people and injuring a further 200. The international community condemned the atrocity, which

Eurostar's maiden run
The high-speed rail service, Eurostar, which travels through the Channel Tunnel, linking England and France, made its maiden voyage in 1994.

was believed to have been carried out by Serbians.

On December 11, Russian president Boris Yeltsin ordered troops into the **rebel region of Chechnya** to prevent it from breaking away from the country. This Muslim-dominated region had **declared its independence** from Moscow three years before under the leadership of General Dzhokhar Dudayev.

On September 19, the **US led an invasion force in Haiti** to bring the military junta to an end and restore democracy under President Aristide, exiled three years earlier. No shots were fired.

On May 6, **Queen Elizabeth** of Britain and **President Francois Mitterand** (1916–96) of France formally **opened the Channel Tunnel**. Linking England and France, the tunnel took eight years to build.

MS Estonia, a car and passenger ferry, **sank in the Baltic Sea** on September 28—852 passengers died, half of whom were Swedes.

Brazil's Samba Boys
Marcio Santos of Brazil holds the FIFA World Cup trophy to celebrate victory. Brazil, known as the Samba Boys, beat Italy in the final.

An investigation into the accident found that stormy weather, poor maintenance, and high speed contributed to the disaster.

Millions watched in horror as the Formula One racing champion, **Ayrton Senna**, plowed off the track at the San Marino Grand Prix on May 1, in a **fatal crash**. A state funeral was held in his home city of São Paulo. Senna was a national hero in Brazil and had given millions to help the country's underprivileged children.

AFRICAN NATIONAL CONGRESS

Founded in 1912 with the aim of increasing the rights of black South Africans, the African National Congress (ANC) came to power in 1994, when Nelson Mandela was elected president of South Africa. The ANC still enjoys majority support, but has been troubled by internal power struggles between the successors of Mandela, corruption scandals, and the challenges of poverty and AIDS in the country.

THE CITY OF KOBE IN JAPAN WAS DEVASTATED BY AN EARTHQUAKE on January 17. Measuring 7.2 on the Richter scale, it resulted in hundreds of deaths and over 13,000 injuries.

Barings, a British investment bank, was **declared bankrupt** after an employee, Nick Leeson, risked huge amounts of money on the Nikkei, the Japanese stock market index. The index collapsed after the Kobe earthquake.

On March 20, **Turkey launched a major military offensive**, involving 35,000 troops, against the **Kurds** in northern Iraq. This was an attempt to pursue rebel Turkish Kurds who had fled into the region and prevent them from setting up permanent bases there. The Kurds had been engaged in an armed struggle for a separate homeland since 1984 and had grievances over the lack of rights for Kurds within Turkey.

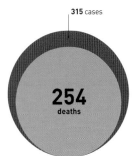

315 cases

254 deaths

The Ebola scare
An outbreak of Ebola occurred in 1995 in Zaire. Of the 315 cases identified, 254 died, giving a fatality rate of 81 percent.

Oklahoma City bombing
A massive truck bomb exploded in front of the Alfred P. Murrah Federal Building in Oklahoma City on April 19. It was felt 30 miles (48 km) away.

The Turkish government hold the separatist **Kurdistan Worker's Party (PKK)** responsible for more than 30,000 deaths over the course of the conflict. Repeated military operations by Turkey against the PKK have not proved effective and the conflict continues.

A powerful **bomb exploded in Oklahoma City** on April 19, killing 168 people. Timothy McVeigh, a Gulf War veteran, was convicted of the attack. The bombing was in reaction to the government's handling of the **Waco siege** (see 1993).

Srebrenica, a Muslim enclave and UN-designated safe haven, was **overrun by Bosnian Serbs** on July 10 and "ethnically cleansed." In December, the leaders of Bosnia, Serbia, and Croatia signed the **Dayton Peace Accord** in Paris, bringing three years of war in Bosnia to an end.

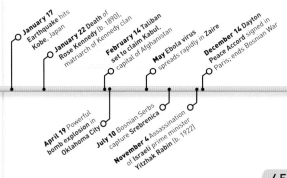

March 28 Death of Eugene Ionesco (b. 1912), playwright of the theater of the absurd

April 21 Red Cross estimates 100,000 dead in Rwandan genocide

May 1 Formula One champion Ayrton Senna (b. 1960) has fatal crash in Italy

May 10 Mandela becomes South Africa's first black president

July 1 Yasser Arafat ends exile and returns to the Gaza Strip

August 31 IRA announces ceasefire

September 28 Estonia ferry disaster in Baltic Sea

December 11 Russian troops storm Chechnya

April 22 Death of Richard Nixon (b. 1913), former US president

May 6 President Mitterand and Queen Elizabeth inaugurate Channel Tunnel

May 27 Russian writer Alexander Solzhenitsyn's exile ends

August 14 World's most wanted terrorist, Carlos the Jackal, held

September 19 US Marines seize Haiti without gunfire

November 29 Death of Ayatollah Mohammed Ali Araki (b. 1884)

December 19 Ceasefire announced in Bosnia

January 17 Earthquake hits Kobe, Japan

January 22 Death of Rose Kennedy (b. 1890), matriarch of Kennedy clan

February 14 Taliban set to claim Kabul, capital of Afghanistan

May Ebola virus spreads rapidly in Zaire

December 14 Dayton Peace Accord signed in Paris; ends Bosnian War

April 19 Powerful bomb explosion in Oklahoma City

July 10 Bosnian Serbs capture Srebrenica

November 4 Assassination of Israeli prime minister Yitzhak Rabin (b. 1922)

THE GROWTH OF THE EU

1957 The Treaty of Rome is signed, establishing the European Economic Community (EEC), with six members.

1973 The Treaty of Accession: Denmark, Ireland, and the United Kingdom join the EU, giving nine member states.

1981 Greece becomes the 10th member of the EU. It had applied to join in 1975, after the restoration of its democracy.

1986 Spain and Portugal join the EU. The Single European Act is signed in 1987, aiming to create a single market.

1995 Austria, Finland, and Sweden join the EU, bringing membership of the EU up to 15 countries.

THE EUROPEAN
UNION

FROM THE RUINS OF WAR, A CONTINENT UNITED

Europe emerged from World War II impoverished and politically unstable. Born of a desire for peace and unity that would make another European war unthinkable, in 1957 six European countries joined in economic union. Since then, the European Union has grown substantially, but growth brings added challenges.

The modern age of the European Union (EU) began in 1987 with the Single European Act, an attempt to unify Europe further and create a "single market" for trade. The EU works toward increased cooperation in areas such as the environment, transportation, and employment. European citizenship and the introduction of the euro, a common currency, have made it easier to work, travel, and to do business with other member states, and the EU has become one of the largest economies in the world. Supporters of enlargement of the EU highlight this, and the benefits of political stability. Critics increasingly worry about immigration, the economic burden of supporting poorer countries, and the huge bureaucracy needed to run the organization.

19

THE NUMBER OF **COUNTRIES** WITH **THE EURO** AS THEIR OFFICIAL CURRENCY

Ireland
GDP: $324.9 billion
Population: 5,011,102

Portugal
GDP: $298.7 billion
Population: 10,839,514

People of Europe
The EU has over half a billion people, which is 6.7 percent of the world's population. It is less than half the size of the US, but its population is almost 50 percent larger.

EU population

6.7%

93.3%

World population

3:4

City living
The EU has a mainly urban population, with 75 percent living in cities rather than in the countryside. By contrast, only around 45 percent of Africa's population lives in cities.

Population comparison
The population of the EU is the world's third largest, after China and India.

CHINA
1,403,500,000

INDIA
1,324,000,000

EU

510,000,000

❝ EUROPE IS THE FORCE THAT PREVENTS HATE FROM **BEING ETERNAL.** WE MUST OPEN OUR **HEARTS** TO THIS NEW **EUROPE. ❞**

Jean-Pierre Raffarin, French prime minister, 2004

2007–2017 *Bulgaria and Romania join the EU in 2007, bringing the total membership to 27; in 2013, Croatia becomes the 28th member. On June 23, 2016, a referendum is held in the UK asking voters if they wish to leave or stay in the EU. The result is a vote to leave. Negotiations on the terms of the exit begin in 2017.*

004 On May 1, the EU takes in 0 new members, most of them rmer communist countries, in s biggest enlargement.

European parliament
The European Parliament is the only part of the EU that is directly elected by the citizens of its member states. It manages the budget and drafts legislation. It has 751 seats, which are divided between member states in proportion to their population.

NUMBER OF SEATS PER COUNTRY FROM 2014

100   80   60   40   20   0

Germany
France
Italy
United Kingdom
Spain
Poland
Romania
Netherlands
Belgium
Greece
Hungary
Czech Republic
Portugal
Sweden
Austria
Bulgaria
Slovakia
Denmark
Finland
Ireland
Croatia
Lithuania
Latvia
Slovenia
Luxembourg
Estonia
Cyprus
Malta

Finland
GDP: $231.4 billion
Population: 5,518,371

Sweden
GDP: $498.1 billion
Population: 9,960,487

Estonia
GDP: $38.45 billion
Population: 1,251,581

Latvia
GDP: $50.62 billion
Population: 1,944,643

Denmark
GDP: $273.9 billion
Population: 5,605,948

Lithuania
GDP: $86.05 billion
Population: 2,823,859

Netherlands
GDP: $869.4 billion
Population: 17,084,719

Germany
GDP: $3.98 trillion
Population: 80,594,017

Poland
GDP: $1.054 trillion
Population: 38,476,269

Czech Republic
GDP: $350.7 billion
Population: 10,674,723

UK
GDP: $2.786 trillion
Population: 64,769,452

Luxembourg
GDP: $59.93 billion
Population: 594,130

Slovakia
GDP: $170.1 billion
Population: 5,445,829

Belgium
GDP: $509.5 billion
Population: 11,491,346

France
GDP: $2.73 trillion
Population: 67,106,161

Hungary
GDP: $270.3 billion
Population: 9,850,845

Romania
GDP: $441.6 billion
Population: 21,529,967

Austria
GDP: $417.2 billion
Population: 8,754,413

Slovenia
GDP: $66.23 billion
Population: 1,972,126

KEY
EU Member
Leaving EU

Spain
GDP: $1.687 trillion
Population: 48,958,159

Croatia
GDP: $95.06 billion
Population: 4,292,095

Bulgaria
GDP: $144.6 billion
Population: 7,101,510

Italy
GDP: $2.235 trillion
Population: 62,137,802

Malta
GDP: $17.3 billion
Population: 416,338

Greece
GDP: $289.4 billion
Population: 10,768,477

Cyprus
GDP: $29.67 billion
Population: 1,221,549

$1,835,300,000

THE GROSS **REVENUE EARNED** AT THE BOX OFFICE BY THE FILM *TITANIC*

Dolly the sheep, the first mammal to be cloned from an adult animal's DNA, in her pen at the Roslin Institute in Edinburgh, Scotland.

CHECHNYAN REBEL LEADER Salman Raduyev was shot on March 6 and reported dead (he had in fact disappeared abroad for medical treatment). A **ceasefire** was signed between Russia and Chechnya (see 1994) on August 31.

Romanian elections were won by the Romanian Democratic Convention, bringing 48 years of communist rule to an end.

Civil war began in **Afghanistan**, when Taliban rebels seized Kabul on September 27, forcing hundreds to flee the war-torn city.

The Kurdish civil war continued, and Iraq seized a city inside the Kurdish "safe haven" protected by

1,353
Ireland

900
France

183,841
UK

BSE cases
Bovine spongiform encephalopathy, or "mad-cow disease," caused a major health scare in Europe. Most cases of BSE occurred in the UK.

sides to find a solution to Northern Ireland's political problems.

US president **Bill Clinton** won another term in office on November 6. When Clinton reshuffled his cabinet on December 12, **Madeleine Albright** became the first female American Secretary of State.

Science fact met science fiction when **Dolly**, a sheep, was born on July 5 in Edinburgh, Scotland. Dolly was the first mammal to be **cloned** from an adult cell.

17

THE NUMBER OF **MONTHS** THE **IRA CEASEFIRE LASTED**

US-led troops on August 31. In response, America launched **Operation Desert Strike**, firing missiles at Iraqi military targets.

The **IRA** (Irish Republican Army) exploded a bomb in the Docklands area of East London on February 10, ending a 17-month ceasefire (see 1994), which had tried to enable both

Online shopping
The online auction site eBay boomed in 1996 with clever technology and a forum for rating buyers and sellers. It is now a global phenomenon.

VIOLENCE IN ZAIRE ESCALATED in February, intensifying the misery of Rwandan–Hutu refugees who had fled there to escape the civil war in Rwanda. In April, rebel soldiers, mainly Tutsis, sealed off camps in eastern Zaire, where refugees were trapped in appalling conditions. Thousands were massacred. The government of Zaire collapsed on April 3, and **Etienne Tshisekedi** (b. 1932) became prime minister of the new government. As the violence escalated 56,000 Zaireans fled into Tanzania.

Albania collapsed into a brief civil war in March and April as protestors and insurgents

Guggenheim museum
This museum in Bilbao, Spain, designed by US architect Frank Gehry, was opened on October 18.

attacked government buildings and looted weapon stores. Southern Albanian insurgents demanded autonomy and seized control of towns and ports. Order was only restored when 7,000 United Nations troops, mainly Italian, arrived in April.

Hong Kong was handed back to the Chinese authorities on July 1 after 150 years of British rule. The new chief executive, **Tung Chee Hwa**, formulated a policy based on "one country, two systems," to preserve Hong Kong's role as a capitalist center in Asia.

Diana, Princess of Wales, died in a car crash on August 31 in a Paris underpass. The news of her death was greeted with unprecedented scenes of mourning around the world.

Iraq refused to allow UN **weapons inspectors** entry in

October. The inspectors had been sent in the aftermath of the 1991 Gulf War with a remit to destroy Iraq's nuclear, biological, and chemical weapons arsenal. This action provoked a **diplomatic crisis** which was defused by a Russian-brokered compromise.

In Japan, the **Kyoto Protocol** was signed on December 11. It committed industrialized nations to reducing emissions of greenhouse gases, principally carbon dioxide, in an attempt to combat **global warming**.

The film *Titanic*, about the ill-fated voyage of the famous passenger liner that sank in 1912, was premiered in December. At the time, it was the most expensive film ever made, but also the most successful, grossing over $1.8 billion. It also won 11 Academy Awards (Oscars).

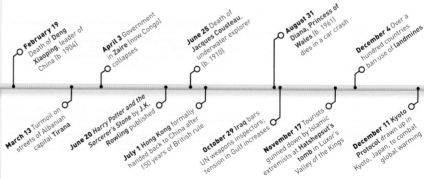

January 2 US troops enter **Bosnia** as part of UN peacekeeping mission

February 10 Docklands bomb blast in London by **IRA** shatters ceasefire

July 19–August 4 **Atlanta**, Georgia: US hosts Summer Olympics

June 23 Death of Greek statesman Andreas **Papandreou** (b. 1919)

July 5 Scientific breakthrough made with birth of **Dolly**, a sheep cloned from an adult DNA

September 27 Taliban capture Afghan capital of Kabul

November 3 Communist rule ends in Romania

February 19 Death of **Deng Xiaoping**, leader of China (b. 1904)

March 13 Turmoil on the streets of Albanian capital **Tirana**

April 3 Government in **Zaire** (now Congo) collapses

June 20 *Harry Potter and the Sorcerer's Stone* by J.K. **Rowling** published

June 25 Death of Jacques **Cousteau**, underwater explorer (b. 1910)

July 1 Hong Kong formally handed back to China after 150 years of British rule

August 31 **Diana, Princess of Wales** (b. 1961) dies in a car crash

October 29 **Iraq** bars UN weapons inspectors; tension in Gulf increases

November 17 Tourists gunned down by Islamic extremists at Hatshepsut's tomb in Luxor's Valley of the Kings

December 4 Over a hundred countries ban use of **landmines**

December 11 Kyoto **Protocol** drawn up in Kyoto, Japan, to combat global warming

Bill Clinton hugs White House intern Monica Lewinsky the day after his reelection in 1996. The image was later said to be evidence of their relationship.

Police confront demonstrators at the WTO conference in Seattle, northwest US. The protests were against large corporations and globalization.

IN JANUARY, US PRESIDENT BILL CLINTON became the center of a scandal involving his relationship with a former White House intern, **Monica Lewinsky**. Clinton was already implicated in a sexual harassment case and was being investigated by independent counsel Kenneth Starr. The president denied the relationship. In December, he became only the second president in US history to

6.1
THE **MAGNITUDE** OF THE **AFGHANISTAN EARTHQUAKE**

be **impeached** (Andrew Johnson was the first, in 1868). Clinton was charged with committing perjury in front of a grand jury, but acquitted the following year.

A devastating **earthquake** hit northern **Afghanistan** on February 4. It killed an estimated 4,000 people, and left around 30,000 homeless.

The **Good Friday Agreement** was signed on April 10. It marked a major breakthrough in the Northern Ireland **peace process**. A referendum held in Northern Ireland and the Republic of Ireland on May 22 was overwhelmingly in favour of the accord.

Pol Pot, former Khmer Rouge ruler of Cambodia (see 1978), died on April 15. The Khmer Rouge had deposed him as leader and sentenced him to life imprisonment in 1997.

Eritrean and **Ethiopian** border clashes turned into a full-scale war in May. Both countries, among the poorest in the world, spent millions on sophisticated weaponry.

India and **Pakistan** went nuclear this year. India performed underground nuclear explosions on May 12 near the Pakistani border; Pakistan responded by carrying out its own tests on May 28.

Japan officially entered a **recession** on June 12. It was the first time its economy had shrunk in 12 years. The news caused global stock markets to slump.

US missiles pounded targets in **Afghanistan** and **Sudan** on August 20, in retaliation for the bombing of US Embassies in

Tanzania and Kenya earlier in the month. America said one target was a base for **Osama Bin Laden**, founder of the Islamic extremist organization **al-Qaeda**.

General Pinochet, former Chilean dictator (see 1973), was arrested in London on October 16 by police acting on behalf of Spain, who alleged Pinochet had committed atrocities against Spanish citizens. Pinochet was deemed too ill for extradition and released in 2000.

On May 1, Saddam Hussein wrote an open letter to the UN Security Council threatening "grave consequences" if sanctions against Iraq were not lifted. The attempts by **UN weapons inspectors** to verify the weapons arsenal in Iraq ended on December 16, when the Iraqis refused to co-operate. US and British air strikes on Iraq, known as **Operation Desert Fox**, began hours later.

Recession in Japan

Japan's recession was at its worst in 1998. It was caused by a drop in exports, weak domestic demand, and a fall in property prices.

A SINGLE EUROPEAN CURRENCY, the **Euro**, was launched on January 1. Eleven European Union member states decided to adopt the Euro, which became a full economic currency in 2002.

The international community accused President Slobodan Milosevic of "**ethnic cleansing**" when 45 ethnic Albanians were found dead, apparently executed by Serbs. Kosovo peace talks ended without agreement on February 23 and a week later NATO forces announced they would escalate their **bombardment of Yugoslavia**. The purging of Albanians by Serbian troops increased, and half a million Albanians fled Kosovo. Milosevic agreed to withdraw his troops on June 9, in response to unrelenting NATO bombing.

Thabo Mbeki won the South African presidential elections on June 2, succeeding Nelson Mandela. He faced huge economic and social challenges, including the terrible impact of HIV/AIDS.

East Timor, in Southeast Asia, asked for intervention from international troops after a complete breakdown in law and order in September. This followed a referendum, which voted for independence from Indonesia. Anti-independence Timorese rebels, supported by the Indonesian military, killed an estimated 1,400 Timorese, and 300,000 people fled to neighboring West Timor.

A military coup in **Pakistan** on October 12 brought to power **General Pervez Musharraf**

Solar eclipse
A total solar eclipse occurred on August 11, 1999. It was watched by over 350 million people in Asia and Europe.

(b. 1943), who took the role of "chief executive." The international community condemned the coup and many nations imposed sanctions against Pakistan.

The **World Trade Organization** (WTO) held a **conference** in Seattle, US, late in the year, which was delayed by protesters campaigning for environmental issues and against globalization. Demonstrators clashed with police before being dispersed.

NASA lost contact with its **Mars Polar Lander** shortly before its planned entry into the Martian atmosphere. The failure of the mission was blamed on a software error.

Macau reverted from Portuguese to Chinese rule on December 20, after 442 years of Portuguese control. Macau was the last remaining colonial state in Asia. **Edmond Ho Hau-wah** (b. 1955), a banker, became leader of the new government.

A trader despairs at the fall of the Nasdaq Stock Market and the New York Stock Exchange when the dot-com bubble burst. The Nasdaq never fully recovered.

George W. Bush was elected president of the US in 2001. Here he shakes hands wi Al Gore, the defeated Democrat candidate, outside the US Capitol in Washington.

Millennium celebrations
Fireworks explode in a spectacular display over Sydney Harbor Bridge and Opera House as Australia welcomed in the new millennium.

$11 BILLION
THE AMOUNT
OF **MONEY LOST**
BY **ENRON**
SHAREHOLDERS

Israel announced its withdrawal from South Lebanon in May, 22 years after occupying it. The occupation had become unpopular with the Israeli electorate.
North and **South Korea** held a summit in June, the first since the peninsula was divided in 1945. The South Korean president Kim Dae-jung received the **Nobel Peace Prize** for his efforts.
More than 800 followers of a **Ugandan cult** known as the Restoration of the Ten Commandments of God died in their churches in March. It is uncertain whether they committed mass suicide or were murdered by the leaders of the cult.
The year ended in bloodshed as a series of terrorist bombs went off on December 30 in the **Philippines**. They became known as the **Rizal Day bombings** because of the national holiday celebrated on this day.

IN JANUARY, THE UN WAR CRIMES TRIBUNAL in The Hague sentenced five Bosnian Croat militiamen to 25 years in prison for a 1993 murder spree that emptied a Bosnian village of all its Muslim inhabitants during the Bosnian War (1992–95).
Opposition supporters from Serbia stormed the Yugoslav parliament building in Belgrade on October 5 using a **bulldozer**, proclaiming **Vojislav Kostunica** as the new Yugoslav president after discrepancies in September elections caused outrage. President **Milosevic** announced his resignation the next day.
In 1991, **Denmark** and **Sweden** agreed to build a bridge connecting the two countries. The 10-mile (16-km) long **Oresund Link**—

running between the Danish capital, Copenhagen, and the Swedish port of Malmo—was opened to traffic this year.
In March, stock markets around the world crashed when internet companies began to fail and the **dot-com bubble**, caused by speculative investment into internet-based companies, **burst**.
Antiglobalization **protestors** descended on Prague in September during meetings between the **World Bank** and the **International Monetary Fund**. The police presence was huge, and more than 600 people were injured in riots.
The first crew arrived at the **International Space Station** in November, with NASA astronaut Bill Shepherd as commander.

2:1 First crew of ISS
The International Space Station received its first crew in 2000. The crew was composed of three men: two Russians and one American.

THE REPUBLIC OF MACEDONIA WAS ON THE BRINK OF WAR in March, as ethnic Albanian rebels demanding equal rights clashed with government forces. In August, NATO announced it would send a **peacekeeping force** to this former Yugoslavian republic.
The **US** experienced an unprecedented day of terror on **September 11**, when 19 al-Qaeda terrorists hijacked four passenger airlines. Two flew into the twin towers of the **World Trade Center**, another into the **Pentagon**. The fourth crashed into a field near Pittsburgh. Nearly 3,000 people were killed. These events left America, and the world, in a profound state of shock. The devastating impact of what became known simply as "**9/11**," September 11, prompted President Bush to declare a "**war on terror**." NATO met the day after the attacks, offering full support and invoking a Cold War-era treaty clause that stated when one member is attacked; all members are attacked.
Only a week after 9/11, letters containing **anthrax** spores were mailed to several news offices and two Democratic US Senators. Five people died and a further

17 were infected. The suspect committed suicide.
In October, the US and Britain launched attacks on targets in **Afghanistan**, where **Osama Bin Laden** (1957–2011), head of the militant Islamic organization al-Qaeda, was believed to be hiding. Operation "**Enduring Freedom**" aimed to remove the Taliban regime and replace it with a democratic government.
Large parts of the world were tipped into **recession** after the 9/11 terror attacks, and many in the business community were mourning deceased colleagues. Economic problems worsened when **Enron**, an American power-trading company, went bust in December in the world's biggest corporate collapse.
In December, **Argentina** plunged into financial ruin. The government announced that its foreign debt could not be paid back and billions of dollars in government spending would be cut.
Another attempted terrorist attack occurred toward the end of the year. **Richard Reid**, a British passenger flying from Paris to Miami, was caught trying to light a fuse protruding from his **shoe**. Reid, an Islamic fundamentalist

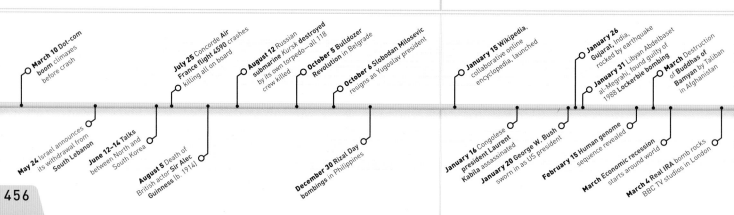

March 10 Dot-com boom climaxes before crash

July 25 Concorde **Air France flight 4590** crashes killing all on board

August 12 Russian submarine **Kursk destroyed** by its own torpedo—all 118 crew killed

October 5 Bulldozer Revolution in Belgrade

October 6 Slobodan Milosevic resigns as Yugoslav president

May 24 Israel announces its withdrawal from **South Lebanon**

June 12–14 Talks between North and South Korea

August 5 Death of British actor **Sir Alec Guinness** (b. 1914)

December 30 Rizal Day bombings in Philippines

January 15 Wikipedia, collaborative online encyclopedia, launched

January 26 Gujarat, India, rocked by earthquake

January 31 Libyan Abdelbaset al-Megrahi, found guilty of 1988 **Lockerbie bombing**

March Destruction of **Buddhas of Bamyan** by Taliban in Afghanistan

January 16 Congolese president Laurent **Kabila** assassinated

January 20 George W. Bush sworn in as US president

February 15 Human genome sequence revealed

March Economic recession starts around world

March 4 Real IRA bomb rocks BBC TV studios in London

and supporter of al-Qaeda, was sentenced to life imprisonment.

As the terrorist threat from al-Qaeda took center stage, the **Irish Republican Army** (IRA) made an historic announcement. On October 23, it stated that it had begun to **disarm** and had put some of its weapons "beyond use."

In India, the state of **Gujarat** was rocked by an **earthquake** on January 26, which registered 7.9 on the Richter scale. More than 20,000 people died and 400,000 homes were destroyed.

The free online encyclopedia "**Wikipedia**" was launched on January 15 by Jimmy Wales and Larry Sanger. By the end of the year, it held more than 20,000 articles in 18 languages. Articles are written by volunteers and can be edited by anyone.

The **Human Genome Project** (HGP) aimed to identify all the genes in the human body. In February, the HGP published its first draft: a 90-percent complete sequence of all three billion base pairs in the human genome.

US technology company, **Apple**, had high hopes for its new digital music player, the **iPod**, which was launched on October 23. The device could store hundreds of music tracks, yet was around the same size as a pack of cards.

Terror attack
Hijacked United Airlines Flight 175 crashed into the South Tower of the World Trade Center and exploded, killing hundreds of people.

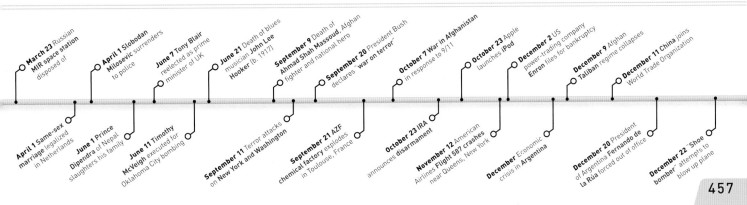

March 23 Russian MIR space station disposed of

April 1 Slobodan Milosevic surrenders to police

June 7 Tony Blair reelected as prime minister of UK

June 21 Death of blues musician John Lee Hooker (b. 1917)

September 9 Death of Ahmad Shah Massoud, Afghan fighter and national hero

September 20 President Bush declares "war on terror"

October 7 War in Afghanistan in response to 9/11

October 23 Apple launches iPod

December 2 US power-trading company Enron files for bankruptcy

December 9 Afghan Taliban regime collapses

December 11 China joins World Trade Organization

April 1 Same-sex marriage legalized in Netherlands

June 1 Prince Dipendra of Nepal slaughters his family

June 11 Timothy McVeigh executed for Oklahoma City bombing

September 11 Terror attacks on New York and Washington

September 21 AZF chemical factory explodes in Toulouse, France

October 23 IRA announces disarmament

November 12 American Airlines Flight 587 crashes near Queens, New York

December Economic crisis in Argentina

December 20 President of Argentina Fernando de la Rúa forced out of office

December 22 "Shoe bomber" attempts to blow up plane

Members of a Chechen militant group speak to journalists inside a theater in Moscow, during a standoff with Russian troops.

THE EURO BECAME LEGAL TENDER

at the start of the year when 12 countries in the **Eurozone** (see 1999) abolished their individual currencies.

Slobodan Milosevic, the former Yugoslav president, went on **trial** on February 12, charged with **crimes against humanity**. He chose to defend himself, and the trial faced many delays due to his ill-health. Milosevic died in 2006, before the trial was completed.

President George W. Bush of **America** and President Vladimir Putin of **Russia** agreed to cut numbers of nuclear warheads by two-thirds each in the **Treaty of Moscow**, signed on May 24.

In Moscow, a gang of heavily armed **Chechen militants** besieged a theater on October 23,

and threatened those inside if Russia did not withdraw from Chechnya. Russian special forces pumped gas into the building before engaging the rebels in a gun battle—118 people were killed.

A **nightclub** on the Indonesian island of **Bali** became the target of a terrorist attack in which more than 200 people died.

Meltdown
A massive chunk of Antarctica's Larsen ice shelf broke up in 2002— it lost a total of about 1,255 sq miles (3,250 sq km).

Common currency
A new currency for 12 members of the European Union, the Euro, was launched in January 2002. It has since become secure as global tender.

Members of a violent Islamist group, **Jemaah Islamiyah**, were convicted of the attack.

US-led forces began the first large-scale campaign against the **Taliban** in Afghanistan—**Operation Anaconda** began in March.

The US journalist **Daniel Pearl** was kidnapped in January in Karachi, Pakistan. Pearl was investigating extremist Muslim groups. His ransom demanded the release and return to Pakistan of prisoners from Guantanamo Bay, a US prison camp in Cuba. Pearl's body was found in May.

India and **Pakistan** came close to war in May, following a major terrorist attack on the Indian parliament in 2001, which India claimed was carried out by Pakistan-based militant groups fighting Indian rule in **Kashmir**, north India. Both countries positioned troops either side of the international border with Kashmir.

Tamil rebels signed a **ceasefire** with the Sri Lankan government in February as part of a Norwegian-led initiative that ended 19 years of civil war.

Sierra Leone in West Africa emerged from a decade of civil war with the help of a strong diplomatic and military presence from Britain, its former colonial ruler.

The 26-year civil war in **Angola** ended in April when a **ceasefire** was agreed between the Angolan Army and UNITA (National Union for the Total Independence of Angola). The civil war had been ongoing since independence from Portugal in 1975.

The **African Union** replaced the Organization of African Unity in July. The new union was intended to reflect the different challenges facing the continent.

> ## WE, …TRUE OWNERS OF THIS LAND, SHALL NOT BUDGE, THE LAND IS OURS.
>
> **Robert Mugabe, president of Zimbabwe**, December 2002

Robert Mugabe, president of Zimbabwe, ordered white farmers to leave as part of his policy on land redistribution to the black populace. The declaration was defied by many farmers.

US millionaire **Steve Fossett** became the first person to fly a balloon solo nonstop around the world. He completed the journey on July 2 in 13 days and 12 hours.

THE BEGINNING OF THE YEAR

was marred by tragedy when the US space shuttle *Columbia* **disintegrated** as it reentered the Earth's atmosphere. All seven crew members were killed. An investigation confirmed that a heat shield had malfunctioned on takeoff, causing it to break up upon reentry.

The last commercial flight of **Concorde**, the supersonic aircraft, was made in October. Concorde was given an emotional farewell at Heathrow airport in London, England. It had flown for 27 years but spiraling costs and dwindling ticket sales led to its demise.

Yugoslavia voted to end its existence in February, becoming **Serbia** and **Montenegro**. The Yugoslavian Federation had existed for 74 years, but had lost its other four republics in

Speedy exit
The supersonic airliner Concorde retired in 2002. Concorde was an international icon and epitomized the advance of modern technology.

January 1 Euro launched as full currency

January 16 UN Security Council establishes an arms embargo against Osama Bin Laden

January 18 End of civil war in Sierra Leone

February 12 Trial begins in The Hague for Slobodan Milosevic

February 22 Separatist group Tamil Tigers and Sri Lanka sign **ceasefire**

March 1 Operation Anaconda launched by US troops in Afghanistan

April 1 The Netherlands becomes the first nation to legalize **euthanasia**

April 4 Civil War ends in Angola

April 11 Attempted coup against President Hugo Chavez of Venezuela

May 20 Independence of East Timor recognized by Portugal

July 9 Launch of the African Union

July 10 Peter Paul Rubens' painting *The Massacre of the Innocents* sold for £49.5 million in London

October 12 Hundreds killed in Bali nightclub bombing

October 23–27 Siege of Moscow Theater by Chechen militants

November 14 Argentina defaults on an $805 million World Bank payment

December 22 Death of Joe Strummer, lead singer of British rock band The Clash (b. 1952)

February Civil war breaks out in Darfur, Sudan

February 4 Serbia and Montenegro emerge from the former Yugoslavian Federation

February 1 US space shuttle Columbia disintegrates upon reentry to Earth's atmosphere

March 20 Invasion of Iraq by US- and British-led forces

> ## " WE HAVE **CONQUERED** THE **SARS EPIDEMIC** IN 2003. "
>
> Wen Jiabao, Premier of China

Doctors and healthcare workers attend a symposium on Severe Acute Respiratory Syndrome (SARS) in Hong Kong.

Star power
Arnold Schwarzenegger, former movie star, greets supporters during his election campaign for governor of California in the US in 2003.

a series of bloody conflicts throughout the 1990s.

The treaty establishing a Constitution for Europe was approved in June. It aimed to create a consolidated **constitution** for the **European Union** (EU). It was to replace the existing European Union treaties with a simplified single text, and would create an EU president and foreign minister.

Arnold Schwarzenegger, a former actor famous for playing the "Terminator" in Hollywood movies, became **governor of California** in October.

Istanbul, Turkey, was rocked by two **bombs** on November 20, which targeted the British consulate and the headquarters of the British-owned HSBC bank. The explosions claimed 60 lives and were linked to **al-Qaeda**.

Iraq's regime crumbled on March 20 when US-led troops invaded and toppled Saddam Hussein's government. They argued that Iraq was hiding **weapons of mass destruction** (WMD). This triggered years of civil conflict in Iraq between rival religious factions. The war was hugely controversial and many questioned its legality. As Western troops began losing their lives, extensive media coverage fanned the flames of public

Fall from grace
A statue of Saddam Hussein in Baghdad, Iraq is toppled from its plinth by Iraqi civilians, aided by US marines.

discontent. **Mass protests** were held all over the world.

Neighboring Iran ended the year with an **earthquake** in the southeast, which devastated the ancient city of **Bam**. On the UNESCO list of World Heritage Sites, the city was more than 2,000 years old. The earthquake killed more than 26,000 people. The US offer of aid helped improve relations between the two nations.

Civil war erupted in the western region of **Darfur**, Sudan, as rebels rose up against the government, claiming the region was being neglected by the authorities in the capital, Khartoum. So far in this civil war, an estimated 200,000 people have died, and 2.5 million have fled to refugee camps.

A virus made headlines around the world and caused considerable panic. **Severe Acute Respiratory**

Syndrome (SARS) is a disease found in humans, which is highly infectious and can be fatal. In 2003, an outbreak spread from China to 37 other countries. Governments took rigorous measures to contain the virus.

Camera phones, which can make calls and take photographs, came into their own this year. They had a profound social impact. Used for surveillance, news gathering, but also enabling voyeurism, they ignited debates about privacy. Some countries banned their use.

2.5 MILLION
THE NUMBER OF **PEOPLE** WHO FLEW WITH **CONCORDE**

Afghan citizens in Kabul wait in line to vote at the Jaffaria Mosque, in the first presidential elections since the overthrow of the Taliban government.

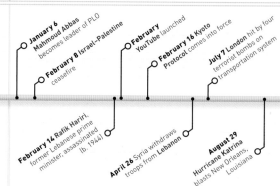

An aerial view of New Orleans in the aftermath of Hurricane Katrina, in which 80 percent of the city was flooded.

THE NEW AFGHAN CONSTITUTION was signed in the capital Kabul on January 26. **Hamid Karzai**, leader of the transitional government, was officially declared the winner of Afghanistan's presidential election on November 3. The result of the election had been delayed due to an investigation into voting irregularities.

In April, the CBS news program "Sixty Minutes" broadcast shocking images in the US showing abuse of prisoners at **Abu Ghraib** in Iraq by members of the US military police. President George W. Bush issued an apology. **Bush was reelected** for a second term as US president on November 2. He portrayed himself as a strong leader in a time of war.

On October 29, Arabic TV station **al-Jazeera** aired a video in which **Osama Bin Laden** threatened fresh attacks on the US. The video was Bin Laden's clearest statement of responsibility for the terror attacks of 9/11.

US and Iraqi forces stormed into western areas of Fallujah, **Iraq**, a rebel stronghold, early on November 8. The aim was to put an end to guerrilla control of the Sunni Muslim city.

The **European Union** (EU) grew on May 1, as ten more countries joined. It was the largest single enlargement in its history. Many of the new member states were former Eastern Bloc countries.

Chechen president **Akhmad Kadyrov** died in an explosion at a stadium in Grozny, the capital of Chechnya, on May 9. The assassination, during a parade, was thought to be the work of Islamic militants.

Trouble continued in Chechnya when **separatists** stormed a school in **Beslan**, North Ossetia, on September 1. They held children and staff hostage for

1,100
TAKEN HOSTAGE

331
KILLED

Beslan crisis
A group of armed Chechen separatists took more than 1,000 people hostage at a Russian school —331 died, many of them children.

three days—hundreds of hostages died in the subsequent shootout, including 186 children.

Spain also experienced terrorist attacks when explosions tore through three **Madrid** train stations on March 11, killing 191. **Al-Qaeda** claimed responsibility.

The Summer **Olympic Games** were held in **Athens**, Greece, birthplace of the ancient games, for the first time since 1896. The US won the most medals—103 in total.

An **earthquake** under the Indian Ocean near the Indonesian island of Sumatra on December 26 unleashed a series of killer waves, **tsunami**, that sped across the sea. More than 200,000 people died and millions made homeless in 11 countries, making this the most destructive tsunami in history.

Wave of destruction
Tsunami waves traveled 1,000 miles (1,600 km) across the Indian Ocean in only 90 minutes. They caused a massive amount of damage.

YASSIR ARAFAT DIED IN 2004, and the leader of the Palestine Liberation Army, **Rawhi Fattouh**, became interim president of the Palestinian Authority. Under Palestinian law he held the post for 60 days until elections were held. **Mahmoud Abbas** became the new president on January 6. Abbas and the Israeli prime minister, Ariel Sharon, announced a **ceasefire** on February 8. It was seen as the best chance for peace in the region in many years.

The former Lebanese prime minister **Rafik Hariri** was killed by a suicide bomb in west Beirut on February 14. Hariri had been planning to make a comeback in forthcoming elections. He had called on Syria to cease its involvement in Lebanese affairs—Syria denied any involvement in his death. The assassination put further

pressure on **Syria** to remove their troops from Lebanon. On 26 April, they announced that they had withdrawn. This was regarded as an historic day in the Middle East.

Former leader of Iraq, **Saddam Hussein**, went on **trial** in October, nearly two years after his capture, for atrocities he carried out during his rule. He refused to acknowledge the authority of the court trying him, and claimed that he was not guilty. Hussein was sentenced to death and executed in 2006.

Four explosions ripped across

> **IT'S TOTALLY WIPED OUT.**
>
> **George W. Bush, US president,** surveying the damage to New Orleans, August 31, 2005

EXTREME WEATHER

Weather became increasingly wild in the 2000s. Hurricane Katrina (pictured) in 2005 was only one of an unprecedented series of hurricanes and tropical storms. Other weather phenomena included record levels of rainfall, melting icecaps, and severe drought, all contributing to increased concerns about the prospect of global warming. The forecast is for more extreme weather, disrupting lifestyles, making animal species extinct, and threatening human lives.

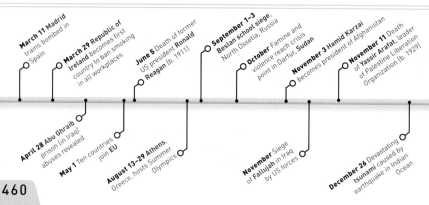

March 11 Madrid trains bombed in Spain

March 29 Republic of Ireland becomes first country to ban smoking in all workplaces

June 5 Death of former US president **Ronald Reagan** (b. 1911)

September 1–3 Beslan school siege, North Ossetia, Russia

October Famine and violence reach crisis point in Darfur, **Sudan**

November 3 Hamid Karzai becomes president of Afghanistan

November 11 Death of Yassir Arafat, leader of Palestine Liberation Organization (b. 1929)

April 28 Abu Ghraib prison (in Iraq) abuses revealed

May 1 Ten countries join EU

August 13–29 Athens, Greece, hosts Summer Olympics

November Siege of Fallujah in Iraq by US forces

December 26 Devastating tsunami caused by earthquake in Indian Ocean

January 6 Mahmoud Abbas becomes leader of PLO

February 8 Israel–Palestine ceasefire

February YouTube launched

February 16 Kyoto Protocol comes into force

July 7 London hit by four terrorist bombs on transportation system

February 14 Rafik Hariri, former Lebanese prime minister, assassinated (b. 1944)

April 26 Syria withdraws troops from Lebanon

August 29 Hurricane Katrina blasts New Orleans, Louisiana

2006

" FUTURE GENERATIONS MAY WELL ASK THEMSELVES, WHAT WERE OUR PARENTS THINKING? "

Al Gore, US politician, *An Inconvenient Truth*, 2006

2007

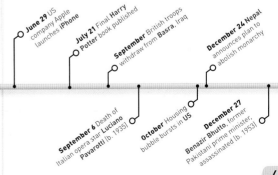

Former prime minister of Pakistan, Benazir Bhutto, campaigning in Karachi before elections.

London on July 7. Coordinated **terrorist attacks** struck three underground trains and a double-decker bus, killing 52 people, and injuring several hundred more. The four suicide bombers, all British men, were backed by **al-Qaeda**.

Weeks after the al-Qaeda attack on the London transport system, the **provisional IRA**— the paramilitary wing of the Irish Republican Army—announced it was **ceasing its armed campaign** on July 28. Two months later there was a verification statement from the independent arms decommissioning body that the IRA had put all its weapons beyond use.

The **Kyoto accord** came into force seven years after it was first agreed (see 1997). It aimed to curb the air pollution blamed for global warming. The US, the world's top polluter, did not sign up, as the protocol was not thought to be in the best interest of the American economy.

Hurricane Katrina hit New Orleans in the US, on August 29 causing unprecedented damage. The hurricane also battered large swathes of the Louisiana and Mississippi coastlines, leaving two oil rigs adrift in the Gulf of Mexico and causing destruction estimated at $26 billion.

YouTube, a video-sharing website, was launched in February and soon grew into one of the most popular websites on the internet. After only a year 100 million videos were being viewed every day.

THE BASQUE SEPARATIST GROUP ETA declared a permanent **ceasefire** on March 22. They aimed to pursue independence for the Basque region through a **democratic process**.

Montenegro became a sovereign state on June 3 after a **referendum** in which just over 55 percent of the populace voted for **independence**. It meant the end of the former Union of Serbia and Montenegro, created only three years earlier from the former Yugoslavia (see 2003).

Iran announced that it had produced the **enriched uranium** needed to make nuclear fuel. It insisted this was for generating nuclear power, but the West was concerned that Iran was making a nuclear bomb.

Power generator
The building of the world's largest hydroelectric installation, the Three Gorges Dam, was completed in 2006, in China.

Another nuclear power, **North Korea**, announced it had tested a **nuclear weapon** on October 9, provoking severe international condemnation.

Construction began on the **Freedom Tower** in New York on April 26. The skyscraper was to replace the twin towers destroyed in the 9/11 attacks (see 2001).

Seven **bombs** exploded on the suburban railway of **Mumbai**, India, on July 11. Over 200 lost their lives. Tension between India and Pakistan increased when evidence suggested that the Pakistani intelligence agency was involved in the attacks.

The **Three Gorges Dam** in China was completed on May 20. At 1.4 miles (2.3km) long, it is one of the world's largest dams, and one of the most controversial public works in modern times. The dam was engineered to prevent flooding along the **Yangtze River**, but had a huge social and ecological impact.

BULGARIA AND ROMANIA joined the **European Union** on January 1. They took the membership of the group from 25 to 27 member states.

Direct rule over **Northern Ireland** by London officially ended on May 8. Democratic Unionist Party leader **Ian Paisley** and Sinn Fein's **Martin McGuinness** were sworn in as first and deputy first ministers of the new executive.

Iranian forces captured 15 British sailors on March 23. The sailors were accused of entering Iranian waters and were held prisoner for 11 days.

Nawaz Sharif, former prime minister of Pakistan, returned home from exile in August, vowing

iPhone
A new type of multimedia phone, the iPhone connects to the internet via a touch screen. It was launched in January by US technology company Apple.

to end the "dictatorship" of President Musharraf. Within weeks he was deported to Saudi Arabia.

Another former leader of Pakistan, **Benazir Bhutto**, was assassinated on December 27 during a political rally. Islamist militants were thought to be responsible.

On December 24, **Nepal** announced that it would abolish its monarchy after elections, which were to be held in 2008. Some parties had refused to serve in government until Nepal became a republic.

A major scientific breakthough was made when the first **artificial sperm** was created in April. It was grown from human bone marrow samples in a laboratory in Newcastle, England.

The mysterious **dark matter** that makes up a quarter of the universe was revealed in May by a 3D map made by the **Hubble telescope**. It helped explain how the universe was formed.

The final book in the **Harry Potter** series by J.K. Rowling was released on July. *Harry Potter and the Deathly Hallows* became the fastest selling book of all time.

" I PUT **MY LIFE** IN **DANGER** AND CAME HERE BECAUSE I **BELIEVE MY COUNTRY** TO BE IN DANGER. "

Benazir Bhutto, Pakistani politician, in a speech shortly before her assassination

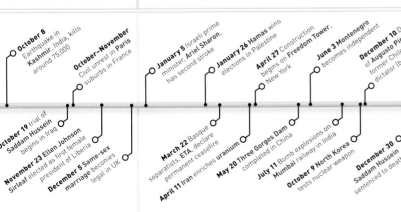

October 8 Earthquake in Kashmir, India, kills around 75,000

October–November Civil unrest in Paris suburbs in France

October 19 trial of Saddam Hussein begins in Iraq

November 23 Ellen Johnson Sirleaf elected as first female president of Liberia

December 5 Same-sex marriage becomes legal in UK

January 5 Israeli prime minister, Ariel Sharon, has second stroke

January 26 Hamas wins elections in Palestine

March 22 Basque separatists, ETA, declare permanent ceasefire

April 11 Iran enriches uranium

April 27 Construction begins on Freedom Tower, New York

May 20 Three Gorges Dam completed in China

June 3 Montenegro becomes independent

July 11 Bomb explosions on Mumbai railway in India

October 9 North Korea tests nuclear weapon

December 10 Death of Augusto Pinochet, former Chilean dictator (b. 1915)

December 30 Saddam Hussein sentenced to death

June 29 US company Apple launches iPhone

July 21 Final Harry Potter book published

September British troops withdraw from Basra, Iraq

September 6 Death of Italian opera star Luciano Pavarotti (b. 1935)

October Housing bubble bursts in US

December 24 Nepal announces plan to abolish monarchy

December 27 Benazir Bhutto, former Pakistani prime minister, assassinated (b. 1953)

Usain Bolt became the fastest man on Earth when he completed the 100m sprint in only 9.69 seconds, setting a world record, at the Summer Olympic Games in Beijing.

173
THE NUMBER OF **DEATHS** IN THE VICTORIA **BUSH FIRES**

A boom is laid to limit damage from the Deepwater Horizon oil spill.

The Hadron collider at CERN
The most intricate machine ever built, it is hoped that the Large Hadron Collider will unravel the mystery of how the Universe began.

THE WORST FINANCIAL CRISIS SINCE THE GREAT DEPRESSION of the 1930s brought the world economy perilously close to collapse, requiring government intervention to keep the capitalist system afloat. Unwise lending on a massive scale had **ruined banks** and other financial institutions, including American mortgage lenders Fannie Mae and Freddie Mac, Northern Rock and the Royal Bank of Scotland in Britain, and the banking sector of Iceland. Some were saved by prompt and costly government actions, but others, including major American investment bank **Lehman Brothers**, went under. The crisis had worldwide effects, with failing businesses and rising unemployment. The developing world also witnessed food riots.

Against this backdrop, Democrat **Barack Obama** was elected president of the US in November, recording a clear victory over Republican John McCain.

There was also a leadership change in Cuba, where **Fidel Castro** (see 1959) retired after almost half a century in power, handing over leadership to his younger brother **Raúl** (b.1931).

In August, **South Ossetia** became the focus of a war between Russia and Georgia when the pro-Russian territory tried to break away from Georgia. A rapid ceasefire averted a more serious international crisis.

In November, **terrorists** attacked targets in **Mumbai, India**, killing 167 people. The attacks severely damaged India's relations with **Pakistan**, whose intelligence services were accused of planning the onslaughts.

On a more peaceful note, the Summer **Olympic Games** were held in **Beijing** in August. Starting with the most lavish opening display ever staged, the games were a major success, with outstanding performances by sprinter Usain Bolt and swimmer Michael Phelps.

The world's largest "atom smasher," the **Large Hadron Collider** built near Geneva, Switzerland, was started on September 10, promising new knowledge of subatomic particles.

THE WORLD ECONOMY WENT INTO RECESSION, shrinking for the first time in 60 years. Among the casualties of the crisis were American car giants **General Motors** and **Chrysler,** who both filed for bankruptcy this year.

On February 7, **Australia** witnessed possibly the worst natural disaster in the country's history, as **bush fires** destroyed communities across the state of Victoria after a prolonged drought. Many linked the severity of the drought to global warming.

A summit meeting in Copenhagen in December reached only a limited and imperfect international agreement between the countries of China, the US, India, Brazil, and South Africa to counter **climate change**.

In tennis, **Roger Federer's** victory in the men's singles at Wimbledon made him the most successful male player in history, with a total of **15 Grand Slam** titles.

BARACK OBAMA (1961–)

Democrat Barack Hussein Obama made history when he was elected to the White House as the 44th President of the US. Born in Hawaii, he became the first African American to hold the office, and gained admirers for his relaxed charm and stirring oratory. However, his first year met with fierce opposition, as he tried to change the US healthcare system, tackle climate change, and reach new agreements on nuclear disarmament.

> ❝ THE **WORST** ENVIRONMENTAL **DISASTER AMERICA** HAS EVER FACED. ❞

President Obama on the Deepwater Horizon oil spill, June 15, 2010

ON JANUARY 12, A DEVASTATING EARTHQUAKE struck a densely populated area in the Caribbean **Republic of Haiti**. One of the world's poorest countries, Haiti was ill-equipped to respond to the widespread destruction. An international relief effort was mounted, but at least 100,000 people were estimated to have died in the disaster.

Human vulnerability to natural forces was witnessed again in April, when the **eruption** of an **Icelandic volcano**, Eyjafjallajökull, spewed fine ash into the air. The **ash cloud** disrupted air travel over a wide area around the British Isles and northern Europe.

The worst disaster in the US this year was manmade. On April 20, an **explosion** at the **Deepwater Horizon drilling rig** in the Gulf of Mexico killed 11 workers and released oil into the ocean, polluting the coasts of Florida, Louisiana, and Mississippi.

But one disaster story had a happy ending. In **Chile, 33 miners** were rescued after being trapped 2,300ft (700m) underground in a mine in the Atacama desert for more than two months.

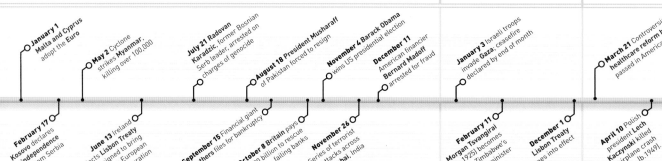

January 1 Malta and Cyprus adopt the Euro

May 2 Cyclone strikes Myanmar, killing over 100,000

July 21 Radovan Karadzic, former Bosnian Serb leader, arrested on charges of genocide

August 18 President Musharraf of Pakistan forced to resign

November 4 Barack Obama wins US presidential election

December 11 American financier **Bernard Madoff** arrested for fraud

January 3 Israeli troops invade Gaza; ceasefire declared by end of month

March 21 Controversial healthcare reform bill passed in America

May 12 In Britain, a coalition government takes power

February 17 Kosovo declares independence from Serbia

June 13 Ireland rejects Lisbon Treaty designed to bring more European integration

September 15 Financial giant Lehman Brothers files for bankruptcy

October 8 Britain pays £500 billion to rescue failing banks

November 26 Series of terrorist attacks across Mumbai, India

February 11 Morgan Tsvangirai (b.1925) becomes Zimbabwe's prime minister

December 1 Lisbon Treaty comes into effect

April 10 Polish president Lech Kaczynski killed in airplane crash (b.1949).

August 19 US troops withdraw from Iraq

Prince William kisses his bride, Catherine Middleton, on the balcony of Buckingham Palace following their wedding at Westminster Abbey on April 29.

> **EVEN IF THEY COME TO KILL ME, I WILL TELL THEM** WHAT THEY ARE TRYING TO DO IS WRONG, THAT **EDUCATION IS OUR BASIC RIGHT.**

Malala Yousafzai, *2012*

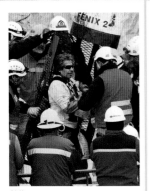

Chilean rescue
A Chilean miner is helped to the surface after being trapped underground for 10 weeks following the collapse of the San Jose mine.

The reverberations of the **economic crisis** continued. The finances of some European states, including Ireland and Greece, became precarious and they had to be bailed out by the International Monetary Fund (IMF).

In Asia, the last American troops were withdrawn from **Iraq**, but in **Afghanistan**, the security situation worsened, with losses of Western forces reaching a new peak. A total of 496 US soldiers died in Afghanistan in 2010.

In **Myanmar**, pro-democracy leader **Aung San Suu Kyi** (b.1945) was released after 21 years of intermittent house arrest.

South Africa became the first African country to host the soccer **World Cup** in June, with Spain emerging as the winner for the very first time.

THE ARAB WORLD WAS SHAKEN up by a series of popular uprisings early in the year, which unsettled or overthrew authoritarian political regimes that had ruled for decades. Dubbed "**the Arab Spring,**" the protests spread from Tunisia across North Africa and the Middle East. In Egypt, **President Hosni Mubarak** (b.1928) was forced to resign and democratic elections were held. In Libya, however, **Muammar Gaddafi** (1942–2011) refused to step down and a civil war ensued. Supported by NATO air forces, the rebels defeated and **killed Gaddafi** in October, but the country remained in turmoil. In **Syria**, **pro-democracy protesters** failed to achieve a change of regime, and by July the country was embroiled in an armed conflict between

supporters and opponents of **President Bashar al-Assad** (b.1965).

In comparison, anti-capitalist protests by the radical **Occupy movement** in Western cities, although attracting considerable support, were relatively minor.

In **Japan**, a massive offshore **earthquake** on March 11 resulted in a devastating **tsunami**. More than 16,000 people were killed, and the **Fukushima** nuclear plant went into meltdown. However, a major nuclear disaster was prevented and officials announced a complete cold shutdown of the plant by the end of the year.

On February 22, **Christchurch** in New Zealand was also hit by an **earthquake**. Around 185 people were killed in the country's **worst natural disaster** in 80 years.

In Pakistan, **Osama Bin Laden** (1957–2011), the leader of al-Qaeda, was tracked down and **killed** by **US special forces** in May, after a decade-long manhunt.

A shaken world
The earthquake in Japan was the fifth largest since records began – this graph shows the magnitude of the ten biggest earthquakes in history.

		MAGNITUDE (RICHTER SCALE)
2011	Japan	
2010	Chile	
2004	Indian Ocean	
1964	Alaska	
1960	Valdivia	
1952	Kamchatka	
1906	Ecuador–Colombia	
1833	Sumatra	
1730	Valparaiso	
1700	Cascadia	

THE TROUBLES OF THE MUSLIM WORLD continued to dominate the headlines. In Syria, armed rebellion escalated into a **full-scale civil war**. In Libya, chaos reigned as rival armed groups vied for power, a situation underlined on September 11 when the US Ambassador to Libya, **John Christopher Stevens**, was **killed** by Islamic militants attacking the American embassy in Benghazi.

Meanwhile, in Egypt, democratic elections were won by **Mohamed Morsi** (b.1951), the candidate of the Islamist **Muslim Brotherhood**. This result was deeply unpopular with the liberals in the country, who had agitated for democracy during the Arab Spring in 2011, and the protesters were soon back on the streets of Cairo.

In February, the casual **burning** of Qu'rans by US personnel at the **Bagram Air Base** in Afghanistan offended Muslims of all political persuasions and led to widespread disturbances.

The most poignant incident occurred in Pakistan's Swat Valley, in October, when 15-year-old **Malala Yousafzai** (b.1997) was **shot**

On the road to recovery
Malala Yousafzai recovers after surviving an assassination attempt. In 2014, she became the youngest recipient of the Nobel Peace Prize.

by a **Taliban** gunman. Her crime had been to campaign for women's education. Fortunately, the murder attempt failed and Malala recovered in a British hospital.

Elsewhere, incumbents **Barack Obama** and **Vladimir Putin** won presidential elections in the US and Russia respectively.

In Britain, judges ruled that **Julian Assange**, the head of the controversial **WikiLeaks** organization dedicated to publishing state secrets, should be **extradited** to Sweden to face allegations of rape. To avoid extradition, Assange took permanent refuge in the Ecuadorian embassy in London.

In July, scientists claimed the discovery of a new particle, the **Higgs boson**, in the Large Hadron Collider.

Probably the most remarkable feat of the year happened on October 14, when **Austrian Felix Baumgartner**, skydiving from the edge of space, **broke** the sound barrier in a free fall.

2,083

THE NUMBER OF **US SERVICEMEN** WHO **DIED** IN **AFGHANISTAN** BY THE END OF **2012**

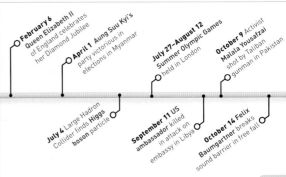

October 8 Jailed Chinese dissident Liu Xiaobo wins Nobel Peace Prize

November 13 In Myanmar, activist **Aung San Suu Kyi** released from house arrest

October 14 Chilean miners emerge from 10-week ordeal underground

January 25 Mass protests in Cairo demand overthrow of Egyptian **President Mubarak**

March 19 NATO forces begin intervention in support of rebels in Libya

May 1 US forces kill Osama Bin Laden

February 11 President Mubarak of Egypt steps down

March 25 Thousands of **Syrians protest** against the government of Bashar al-Assad

October 20 Libyan leader Muammar **Gaddafi** captured and killed by rebels

February 6 Queen Elizabeth II of England celebrates her Diamond Jubilee

April 1 Aung Suu Kyi's party victorious in elections in Myanmar

July 27–August 12 Summer Olympic Games held in London

October 9 Activist Malala Yousafzai shot by Taliban gunman in Pakistan

July 4 Large Hadron Collider finds **Higgs boson** particle

September 11 US ambassador killed in attack on embassy in Libya

October 14 Felix Baumgartner breaks sound barrier in free fall

Pope Francis waves to the crowd during his visit to Florence, Italy.

5 TIMES
THE NUMBER OF DEATHS BY EBOLA IN 2014 COMPARED WITH ALL OTHER KNOWN OUTBREAKS

The Ebola virus causes serious, often fatal, illness to humans.

Syrian refugees arrive in Greece aboard rubber rafts.

ON FEBRUARY 28, POPE BENEDICT XVI RETIRED, the first pope to do so in almost 600 years. Elected in March, Argentinean Cardinal Jorge Mario Bergoglio (b.1936) became **Pope Francis.** He opened the door for a more **liberal Catholicism,** with an emphasis on countering social inequality and climate change.

In Egypt, a military **coup** overthrew **President Morsi** (b.1951) in July and restored army rule. Pro-Morsi protests were suppressed, while Islamist terrorists targeted Egyptian government forces.

Islamist terrorist actions ranged from Mali and Kenya in Africa to the US, where people at the **Boston Marathon** in April were attacked with homemade bombs.

In August, the use of the nerve gas **sarin** on the rebel-held Ghouta suburb of Damascus, **Syria,** came close to triggering a retaliatory Western bombing campaign against the Syrian government.

The former US-government contractor **Edward Snowden** released classified documents revealing the existence of American global mass surveillance programs. Charged with espionage, he fled to Russia in June.

The **airburst** of a **meteor** near Chelyabinsk, in the Russian Urals, in February, drew attention to the risk of natural **strikes from space,** although there were no deaths.

In South Africa, the **death** of **Nelson Mandela** (b.1918) brought together heads of state, royalty, and celebrities to pay homage at a **memorial service** in December.

MALAYSIA AIRLINES FLIGHT 17, en route to Kuala Lumpur, was **shot down** by a **missile** over eastern Ukraine on July 17, killing all **298 people** on board. They were the innocent casualties of the ongoing conflict between Russia and Ukraine. The **overthrow** of **pro-Russian** Ukrainian president **Viktor Yanukovych** (b.1950) in February, after mass protests by pro-Western Ukrainians, was followed by Russian annexation of **Crimea** and the seizure of areas of eastern Ukraine by ethnic Russian militia backed by Moscow—a move resisted by the Ukrainian forces.

Meanwhile, in Iraq, the heavily armed **Islamic State of Iraq and Syria**

(ISIS) movement launched an offensive and captured the city of **Mosul.** With ISIS fighters threatening Syria as well as Iraq, Western air forces vainly attempted to block their progress.

More evidence of the spread of Islamist extremism came from Nigeria, where the **Boko Haram** insurgency against the government attracted world attention when they **kidnapped** more than 200 Christian schoolgirls at Chibok in April.

West Africa witnessed the largest ever **Ebola** epidemic in February. It wreaked havoc in Guinea, Liberia, and Sierra Leone.

Mystery surrounded the fate of **Malaysia Airlines Flight 370,** which **disappeared** without a trace in March, after deviating from its planned route to China.

In the US, 18-year-old African American **Michael Brown** was shot by a white police officer on August 9 in St. Louis, Missouri, triggering violent protests that led to the popularization of the slogan "**Black Lives Matter.**"

From June to July, the **FIFA World Cup** was held in **Brazil.** The event was marred by protests against government corruption.

In November, the **Rosetta mission** was the first to successfully land a probe on a comet's surface. The mission was launched in 2004, making it a ten-year journey.

Rise of ISIS
Islamic State fighters used heavy military equipment in their occupation of the northern provinces of Iraq in summer 2014.

THE MEDITERRANEAN AREA FACED A MASSIVE REFUGEE CRISIS as vast numbers of mostly Muslim migrants **fled wars** in Asia and Africa. Arriving by sea in Greece and Italy, a stream of desperate people headed north, with many finding refuge in **Germany.** Thousands drowned in shipwrecks. The humanitarian response was muted by fears that Islamist terrorists might **infiltrate Europe** disguised as refugees.

France suffered grievously from **Islamist attacks.** On January 7, the attack on the office of the satirical weekly *Charlie Hebdo* for publishing controversial cartoons of the Prophet Muhammad left 12 dead. On November 13, terrorists **killed 130 people** in coordinated attacks on targets in **Paris,** including a rock concert at the **Bataclan theater.**

Other Islamist terrorist acts in the year ranged from shootings at **San Bernardino,** California, to the downing of a Russian airliner over Sinai, in Egypt, and killing of tourists on a Tunisian beach.

873,000
THE NUMBER OF REFUGEES WHO ARRIVED IN GREECE BY SEA IN 2015

March 13 Cardinal Bergoglio elected Pope Francis

July 3 In Egypt, President Morsi is deposed in a military coup

January 1 Latvia joins Eurozone

March 8 Malaysia Airlines jet, carrying 239 people, disappears

April 14 Boko Haram insurgents abduct women and girls from Nigerian school

July 17 Airliner shot down by missile over eastern Ukraine

December 16 Pakistani Taliban massacre 145 people at an army school

January 26 Radical Syriza party forms government in Greece

April 15 Islamists bomb the Boston Marathon

August 21 Syrian government uses chemical weapons in civil war

February Outbreak of Ebola virus epidemic in West Africa

March 21 Russia annexes Crimea, part of Ukraine

June 5 ISIS militants launch an offensive in northern Iraq

November 12 The Rosetta spacecraft lands a probe on the comet 67P/Churyumov–Gerasimenko

December 17 President Obama normalizes relations with Cuba

April More than 1,000 migrants drown in the Mediterranean

> ## " WE CANNOT AFFORD TO BE SO **POLITICALLY CORRECT** ANYMORE "

Donald Trump, Republican National Convention, July 21, 2016

Hurricane Irma strikes Miami, Florida, in September. It was the fiercest hurricane to hit the US since 2005.

ISIS was **condemned** for destroying ancient monuments, mistreating Christian communities, and sadistic killing of prisoners in areas of Iraq and Syria.

Apart from the migrant crisis, European politics were dominated by a reaction **against austerity**, which brought the left-wing **Syriza party** to power in Greece in January and made the radical **Podemos party** a major force in Spain.

In June, **Sepp Blatter**, the head of **FIFA**, was forced to **resign** after corruption revelations.

JUSTIN TRUDEAU (1971–)

Elected prime minister of Canada in 2015, Liberal Party leader Justin Trudeau excited popular enthusiasm through a glamorous image and a message of hope and social inclusiveness. Ousting Conservative Stephen Harper, he increased the number of Liberal seats in parliament from 36 to 184. Justin is the son of Pierre Trudeau (1919–2000), who was the Canadian prime minister for 15 years, from the 1960s to the 1980s.

THIS WAS A YEAR WHEN ELECTORATES DEFIED THE PREDICTIONS of political experts. In the US, most commentators had anticipated that the presidential elections in November would give the country its first woman president in the experienced **Hillary Clinton** (b.1947). Instead, billionaire Republican candidate **Donald Trump** (b.1946) won by a narrow margin, despite being opposed by much of his own party and a campaign marred by some outlandish statements and damaging revelations about his attitude toward women.

In Britain, Prime Minister **David Cameron** (b.1966) called a **referendum** on the country's membership of the **European Union** (EU), confident the vote would uphold the status quo. Instead, after a virulent campaign by advocates of "**Brexit**," the British voted by a small majority to **leave Europe**. This decision led to an upheaval in government, with **Theresa May** (b.1956) taking over as prime minister and "Brexiteers" given key cabinet posts.

Islamist terrorist attacks continued to take their toll on civilians. On June 11, gunman **Omar Mateen** killed 49 people at the **Pulse gay nightclub** in Orlando, Florida. In France, on July 14, a truck was driven into the midst of families celebrating **Bastille Day** in Nice, **killing 86 people**. The perpetrators of this and other such attacks declared allegiance to the **ISIS movement**, which was using the **internet** to incite Muslims to acts of violence. ISIS was also

2016 US Electoral College
Clinton won more of the popular vote, but Trump had a majority in the electoral college.

involved in the Syrian **civil war** (see 2012), where fighting continued to rage with increasing Western and Russian military involvement. The fall of **Aleppo** to Russian-backed government troops in December was a major setback for the anti-government forces and ISIS. Half a million people were believed to have died in the ongoing conflict.

In Colombia, a ceasefire in June ended the long and destructive guerrilla campaign by the **Revolutionary Armed Forces of Colombia (FARC) movement,** begun in 1964. A peace deal was signed between FARC and the Colombian government on November 24.

The **Summer Olympic Games** were held in **Rio de Janeiro**, Brazil, despite concerns about a **Zika** virus epidemic and an ongoing Brazilian political crisis.

The year also witnessed the loss of three popular music gaints **Leonard Cohen, Prince,** and **David Bowie.**

THE START OF DONALD TRUMP'S TERM in office as US President proved predictably **controversial**. His orders to **block visitors** from specific countries were challenged in the courts, and repeal of his predecessor's "**Obamacare**" health legislation ran into difficulty in Congress. Trump faced accusations of eliciting covert **Russian support** during the election campaign and accusations of **racism** over his response to violence at the Unite the Right rally in Charlottesville, Virginia, in August.

As the North Korean leader **Kim Jong-un** indulged in ever more aggressive posturing, threatening to strike US territory with **nuclear missiles**, President Trump countered with his own threat to "**totally destroy**" North Korea.

In June, the US government stated its intention to withdraw from the 2015 **Paris Climate Accord**. In response, some US states formed the United States Climate Alliance, determined to advance the objectives of the Paris Agreement.

Possibly confirming scientific predictions of greenhouse gases worsening extreme weather, the 2017 **Atlantic hurricane** season was one of the most severe on record. The **Caribbean islands** experienced widespread devastation. **Texas** witnessed heavy **flooding** in August as a result of **Hurricane Harvey**.

In Europe, anti-European Union movements consistently lost elections in 2017, most notably in France, where **Emmanuel Macron** (b.1977), a pro-EU centrist, defeated

North Korean threats
North Korea test launches an intercontinental ballistic missile, part of its programme to mount a nuclear threat to the US.

the anti-EU right-wing Front National. Even in Britain, Prime Minister **Theresa May**, who had positioned herself as the leader who could deliver Brexit, suffered a severe **electoral setback**, losing her overall majority in parliament in a general election in June.

In Spain, the Government of Catalonia called an illegal independence referendum, resulting in Spain's central government taking direct control of the region.

In Iraq, ISIS suffered **defeats** and was driven out of **Mosul** in July, but ISIS-inspired terrorism continued. In Britain, a bomb blast at a concert in Manchester, which **killed 23 people** on May 22, was the worst of several mass attacks.

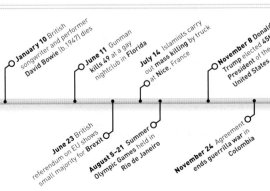

THE GLOBAL
ECONOMY

AN INCREASING DIVIDE BETWEEN RICH AND POOR

The world is richer than ever, strengthened by international alliances and technology, but there is still widespread poverty. Wars continue to be fought, and even developed nations can be devastated by natural disasters.

There are currently more than 7.5 billion people living on the planet, three times the population of 1900. The fate of each person depends on where they live, and the distribution of the world's wealth has changed little since World War II. Many high-income countries are in the northern hemisphere, with the world's poorest in sub-Saharan Africa. The six wealthiest countries account for more than half the world's Gross Domestic Product (GDP)—the value of all the goods and services a country produces—while over half the world's population lives on less than $2.50 a day.

The countries of Western Europe and North America have well-established business sectors, with multinational corporations selling products globally. The nations of Africa and Central America have a smaller range of industries, and many depend on trading a single commodity. But this is slowly changing, and the economies of countries such as Mexico, Brazil, and India are growing rapidly.

Although the US is the wealthiest country in the world, it is home to only 5.2 percent of the world's population. Forty-one percent of the world's millionaires live in the US, but it also has the highest level of total household debt.

POPULATION (IN MILLIONS)

ATLANTIC OCEAN

NORTH AMERICA

Interdependent world
The economies of the world are based on a vast range of industries, and populations range from 800 (Vatican City) to over a billion (India and China). No countries are fully self-supporting, however, and they all depend on trade with other countries to meet their needs fully.

GDP PER CAPITA PPP (INT. $)

Qatar
Luxembourg
Macao
Singapore
Brunei Darussalam
Kuwait
Ireland
Norway
United Arab Emirates
San Marino

In the money
When a country's wealth is divided by the number of people who live in it, Qatar emerges as the richest nation in the world.

On the up
The fastest-growing economies are mainly in developing countries.

GROWTH RATE

Ethiopia
Uzbekistan
Nepal
India
Tanzania
Djibouti
Laos
Cambodia
Myanmar
Philippines

GDP PER CAPITA PPP (INT. $)

Out of pocket
The poorest countries in the world are all in sub-Saharan Africa.

South Sudan
Eritrea
Guinea
Mozambique
Malawi
Niger
Liberia
Burundi
D R Congo
C African Rep

PACIFIC OCEAN

SOUTH AMERICA

Brazil has the largest economy in South America, and the eighth largest in the world. Well-established agriculture, mining, and service sectors have helped create a healthy economy, and Brazil is also rich in natural resources. Huge gaps remain between rich and poor, however.

POPULATION (IN MILLIONS)

ATLANTIC OCEAN

GERMANY

Germany reacted to the union of East and West Germany by becoming the largest economy on the European continent, and the fourth wealthiest in the world by GDP. Germany is the world's third-largest trader in imports and exports.

RUSSIA

The world's largest country, Russia, has seen huge changes since the fall of the Soviet Union. It has vast natural resources, such as oil and gas, and is the world's largest oil producer, but many Russian people still live in poverty.

CHINA

China, the world's most populated country, has one of the fastest-growing economies and is the top exporter. Factories and mines produce most of China's wealth, but in the future this may be slowed by an aging population.

INDIA

It is estimated that India's economy will grow faster than any other country's over the next two decades. It has a young and growing workforce, has opened up foreign trade, and hosts millions of entrepreneurs running small, but successful, businesses.

SOUTH AFRICA

South Africa has one of the largest economies on the African continent, but poverty is widespread. One in eight people is infected with HIV/AIDS, high crime and land redistribution remain an issue, and unemployment is high.

AUSTRALIA

Australia's economy stands out because it survived the global downturn without going into recession. It has a strong service-providing economy as well as healthy exports of agriculture and mining products. Natural gas deposits are evenly spread throughout the continent.

DIRECTORY

RULERS AND LEADERS

Whether leadership is achieved through heredity, democracy, or sheer brute force, leaders make decisions that determine how history will judge their time in power. Great leaders have been the salvation of their people, while weak leaders have been responsible for bringing mighty empires to their knees.

■ EGYPTIAN PHARAOHS

Ancient Egyptian history is divided up into a number of major periods: the Old Kingdom (2649–2150 BCE); the Middle Kingdom (2040–1640 BCE); and the New Kingdom (1550–1070 BCE), with "Intermediate" periods between them and a Late Period (712–332 BCE) at the end. Within these time periods, a large number of dynasties ruled Egypt, from the 1st Dynasty (2920–2880 BCE) even before the Old Period, reaching the 26th Dynasty (672–525 BCE), which ended with Egypt's conquest by the Persian ruler Cambyses. Aside from a brief period when native Egyptian rulers regained power, Egypt remained part of the Persian Empire until 332 BCE, when it was conquered by Alexander the Great. In 30 BCE, it became part of the Roman Empire.

PERIOD	DYNASTY	NOTABLE PHARAOHS
Early Dynastic Period (3100–2686 BCE)	1st Dynasty (3100–2890 BCE)	Narmer (c.3100 BCE) Menes (c.3000 BCE) Den (c.2950 BCE)
	2nd Dynasty (2890–2686 BCE)	Peribsen (c.2700 BCE)
Old Kingdom (2686–2181 BCE)	3rd Dynasty (2686–2613 BCE)	Djoser (2667–2648 BCE)
	4th Dynasty (2613–2494 BCE)	Snefru (2613–2589 BCE) Khufu (Cheops) (2589–2566 BCE) Menkaure (Mycinerus) (2532–2503 BCE) Shepseskaf (2503–2498 BCE)
	5th Dynasty (2494–2345 BCE)	Userkaf (2494–2487 BCE) Sahure (2487–2475 BCE) Nyuserre (2445–2421 BCE) Djedkare (2414–2375 BCE) Unas (2375–2345 BCE)
	6th Dynasty (2345–2181 BCE)	Teti (2345–2323 BCE) Pepi I (2321–2287 BCE) Merenre (2287–2278 BCE) Pepi II (2278–2184 BCE)
First Intermediate Period (2181–2040 BCE)	7th and 8th Dynasties (2181–2125 BCE)	Numerous ephemeral kings, as central authority collapsed
	9th and 10th Dynasties (at Kerakleopolis) (2160–2025 BCE)	Power struggle between minor rulers of Upper and Lower Egypt
	11th Dynasty (at Thebes) (2125–2040 BCE)	Intef II (2112–2063 BCE)
Middle Kingdom (2040–1650 BCE)	11th Dynasty (all Egypt) (2040–1985 BCE)	Mentuhotep II (2040–2004 BCE) Mentuhotep III (2004–1992 BCE) Mentuhotep IV (1992–1985 BCE)
	12th Dynasty (1985–1795 BCE)	Amenemhet I (1985–1955 BCE) Senwosret I (1965–1920 BCE) Amenemhet II (1922–1878 BCE) Senwosret III (1874–1855 BCE) Amenemhet IV (1808–1799 BCE)
	13th Dynasty (1795–c.1650 BCE)	Minor rulers
	14th Dynasty (c.1750–c.1650 BCE)	Minor rulers
Second Intermediate Period (1650–1550 BCE)	15th Dynasty (Hyksos) (1650–1550 BCE)	Apophis (c.1585–c.1542 BCE)
	16th Dynasty (1650–1550 BCE)	Minor Hyksos rulers contemporary with the 15th Dynasty

PERIOD	DYNASTY	NOTABLE PHARAOHS
	17th Dynasty (at Thebes) (1650–1550 BCE)	Kamose (1555–1550 BCE)
New Kingdom (1550–1069 BCE)	18th Dynasty (1550–1295 BCE)	Ahmose (1550–1525 BCE) Amenhotep I (1525–1504 BCE) Tuthmosis I (1504–1492 BCE) Tuthmosis II (1492–1479 BCE) Tuthmosis III (1479–1425 BCE) Hatshepsut (1473–1458 BCE) Amenhotep II (1427–1400 BCE) Tuthmosis IV (1400–1390 BCE) Amenhotep III (1390–1352 BCE) Amenhotep IV/Akhenaten (c.1352–1336 BCE) Smenkhare (1338–1336 BCE) Tutankhamun (1336–1327 BCE) Ay (1327–1323 BCE) Horemheb (1323–1295 BCE)
	19th Dynasty (1295–1186 BCE)	Ramesses I (1295–1294 BCE) Seti I (1294–1279 BCE) Ramesses II (1279–1213 BCE) Merneptah (1213–1203 BCE)
	20th Dynasty (1186–1070 BCE)	Ramesses III (1184–1153 BCE) Ramesses V (1147–1143 BCE) Ramesses XI (1099–1069 BCE)
Third Intermediate Period (1069–747 BCE)	21st Dynasty (1069–945 BCE)	Smendes (1069–1043 BCE) Psusennes I (1039–991 BCE) Osorkon I (984–978 BCE) Psusennes II (959–945 BCE)
	22nd Dynasty (945–715 BCE)	Shoshenq I (945–924 BCE) Osorkon II (874–850 BCE) Shoshenq III (825–773 BCE) Osorkon V (730–715 BCE)
	23rd Dynasty (c.818–715 BCE) 24th Dynasty (727–715 BCE)	Competing lines of lesser rulers at Hermopolis Magna, Leontopolis, and Tanis
Late Period (747–332 BCE)	25th Dynasty (Nubia and all of Egypt) (747–656 BCE)	Piye (747–716 BCE) Shabaqa (716–702 BCE) Taharqa (690–664 BCE)
	26th Dynasty (664–525 BCE)	Psammetichus I (664–610 BCE) Apries (589–570 BCE) Amasis (570–526 BCE) Psammetichus III (526–525 BCE)

■ ROMAN EMPERORS

In 27 BCE, Octavian, on becoming Rome's first emperor, renamed himself Gaius Julius Caesar Augustus. From then on, emperors took the honorific title Augustus for the duration of their reign. Until 286, this was normally a title unique to one person, but there were periods of joint rule, usually when the succession was disputed or the nominated heir was too young to rule alone. However, the emperor Diocletian instigated a different system, the Tetrarchy, under which four individuals ruled the empire, two as Augustus and two as Caesar—a kind of "junior emperor." This persisted (with some variations) until 395, when the eastern and western portions of the empire split from each other.

NAME	REIGN	NAME	REIGN
Augustus	27 BCE–14 CE	**Trajan**	98–117
Tiberius	14–37	**Hadrian**	117–38
Gaius Caligula	37–41	**Antoninus Pius**	138–61
Claudius	41–54	**Marcus Aurelius**	161–80
Nero	54–68	**Lucius Verus** (co-Augustus)	161–69
Galba	68–69	**Commodus**	180–92
Otho	69	**Pertinax**	193
Vitellius	69	**Didius Julianus**	193
Vespasian	69–79	**Septimius Severus**	193–211
Titus	79–81	**Caracalla** (co-Augustus 198–211)	198–217
Domitian	81–96	**Geta** (co-Augustus)	209–11
Nerva	96–98		

NAME	REIGN
Macrinus	217–18
Diadumenianus (co-Augustus)	218
Elagabalus	218–22
Alexander Severus	222–35
Maximinus Thrax	235–38
Gordian I and Gordian II	238
Pupienus and Balbinus	238
Gordian III	238–44
Philip I	244–49
Philip II (co-Augustus)	247–49
Decius	249–51
Herennius Etruscus (co-Augustus)	251
Trebonianus Gallus	251–53
Hostilianus (co-Augustus)	251
Volusianus (co-Augustus)	251–53
Aemilianus	253
Valerian	253–60
Gallienus (co-Augustus 253–60)	253–68
Claudius Gothicus	268–70
Quintillus	270
Aurelian	270–75
Tacitus	275–76
Florian	276
Probus	276–82
Carus	282–83
Numerian	283–84
Carinus (co-Augustus 283–84)	283–85
Diocletian	284–305

WESTERN EMPIRE

NAME	REIGN
Honorius	395–423
Constantius III (co-Augustus)	421
Valentinian III	424–55
Petronius Maximus	455
Avitus	455–56
Majorian	457–61
Libius Severus	461–65
Anthemius	467–72
Olybrius	472
Glycerius	473–74
Julius Nepos	474–75
Romulus Augustulus	475–76

NAME	REIGN
Maximian (Caesar 285–86, co-Augustus 286–305)	286–305
Constantius I Chlorus (Caesar 293–305, co-Augustus 305–06)	305–06
Galerius (Caesar 293–305, co-Augustus 305–11)	305–11
Severus (Caesar 305–06, co-Augustus 306–07)	306–07
Licinius	308–24
Maximinus Daia (Caesar 305–10, co-Augustus 310–13)	310–13
Constantine I (Augustus 306, Caesar 306–07, co-Augustus 307–24)	306–37
Constantine II (Caesar 317–37, co-Augustus 337–40)	337–40
Constantius II (Caesar 324–37, co-Augustus 337–50)	337–61
Constans (Caesar 333–37, co-Augustus 337–50)	337–50
Julian (Caesar 355–60)	360–63
Jovian	363–64
Valentinian I (co-Augustus)	364–75
Valens (co-Augustus)	364–78
Gratian (co-Augustus)	367–83
Valentinian II (co-Augustus)	375–92
Theodosius I (co-Augustus 379–92)	379–95

EASTERN EMPIRE

NAME	REIGN
Arcadius	395–408
Theodosius II (co-Augustus 405–08)	405–50
Marcian	450–57
Leo I	457–74
Zeno (deposed)	474–75
Basiliscus	475–77

BYZANTINE EMPERORS

After 395, the eastern half of the Roman Empire was never ruled by the same emperor as the western portion. The eastern emperors continued to rule from Constantinople after the fall of the western Roman empire in 476, and are referred to after that date as Byzantine emperors (from "Byzantium", the ancient Greek name for a town on the site of Constantinople).

NAME	REIGN
Zeno	477–91
Anastasius	491–518
Justin	518–27
Justinian	527–65
Justin II	565–78
Tiberius II	578–82
Maurice	582–602
Phocas	602–10
Heraclius	610–41
Heraclonas	641
Constantine III	641
Constans II	641–68
Constantine IV	668–85
Justinian II (deposed)	685–95
Leontius	695–98
Tiberius III	698–705
Justinian II (restored)	705–11
Philippicus	711–13
Anastasius II	713–15
Theodosius III	715–17
Leo III the Isaurian	717–41
Constantine V Copronymos	741–75
Leo IV	775–80
Constantine VI	780–97
Irene (Empress)	797–802
Nicephorus I	802–11

NAME	REIGN
Stauracius	811
Michael I	811–13
Leo V the Armenian	813–20
Michael II	820–29
Theophilus	829–42
Michael III	842–67
Macedonian Dynasty	
Basil I the Macedonian	867–86
Leo VI ("the Wise")	887–912
Alexander	912–13
Constantine VII Porphyrogenitus	912–59
Romanus I Lecapenus (co-Emperor)	919–44
Romanus II	959–63
Nicephorus II Phocas	963–69
John I Tzimisces	969–76
Basil II "the Bulgar Slayer"	976–1025
Constantine VIII (co-emperor to 1025)	976–1028
Romanus III Argyrus	1028–34
Michael IV the Paphlagonian	1034–41
Michael V Calaphates	1041–42
Constantine IX Monomachus	1042–55
Zoe (co-ruler as Empress)	1042–50

NAME	REIGN
Theodora (sole ruler as Empress)	1055–56
Michael VI Stratioticus	1056–57
Comnenid Dynasty	
Isaac I Comenus	1057–59
Ducid Dynasty	
Constantine X Ducas	1059–67
Romanus IV Diogenes	1068–71
Michael VII Ducas	1071–78
Nicephorus III Botaniates	1078–81
Comnenid Dynasty	
Alexius I Comnenus	1081–1118
John II	1118–43
Manuel I	1143–80
Alexius II	1180–83
Andronicus I	1183–85
Angelid Dynasty	
Isaac II Angelus	1185–95
Alexius III	1195–1203
Isaac II (restored)	1203–04

NAME	REIGN
Alexius IV (co-Emperor)	1203–04
Alexius V Mourzouphlos	1204
Lascarid Dynasty	
Theodore I Lascaris	1204–22
John III Vatatzes	1222–54
Theodore II	1254–58
John IV	1258–61
Palaeologid Dynasty	
Michael VIII (to 1261 as Emperor of Nicaea)	1259–82
Andronicus II	1282–1328
Michael IX (co-Emperor)	1293–1320
Andronicus III	1328–41
John V	1341–76
John VI (co-Emperor)	1347–54
Andronicus IV	1376–79
John V (restored)	1379–91
Manuel II	1391–1425
John VII (regent)	1399–1402
John VIII	1425–48
Constantine XI	1448–53

OTTOMAN EMPERORS

NAME	REIGN
Osman I	1299–1326
Orkhan	1326–59
Murad I	1359–89
Bayezid I	1389–1403
Suleiman (rival claimant)	1403–10
Mehmed I (rival claimant to 1410)	1403–21
Murad II	1421–44
Mehmed II	1444
Murad II (restored)	1444–51
Mehmed II (restored)	1451–81
Bayezid II	1481–1512
Selim I the Grim	1512–20
Suleiman I the Magnificent	1520–66
Selim II	1566–74
Murad III	1574–95
Mehmed III	1595–1603
Ahmad I	1603–17
Mustafa I	1617–18
Osman II	1618–22
Mustafa I (restored)	1622–23

NAME	REIGN
Murad IV	1623–40
Ibrahim	1640–48
Mehmed IV	1648–87
Suleiman III	1687–91
Ahmad II	1691–95
Mustafa II	1695–1703
Ahmad III	1703–30
Mahmud I	1730–54
Osman III	1754–57
Mustafa III	1757–74
'Abdul Hamid I	1774–89
Selim III	1789–1807
Mustafa IV	1807–08
Mahmud II	1808–39
'Abdul–Majid I	1839–61
'Abdul–'Aziz	1861–76
Murad V	1876
'Abdul–Hamid II	1876–1909
Mehmed V	1909–18
Mehmed VI	1918–22
'Abdul–Majid II (caliph)	1922–24

RULERS OF THE HOLY ROMAN EMPIRE

NAME	REIGN
Charlemagne	800–14
Louis I	814–40
Lothair I	840–55
Louis II	855–75
Charles II	875–77
Charles III	884–87
Guy of Spoleto	891–94
Lambert of Spoleto	894–96
Arnulf	896–99
Louis III	899–911
Berengar I	915–24
Ottonian Saxon Dynasty	
Conrad I of Franconia	911–18
Henry I the Fowler	919–36
Otto I the Great	962–73
Otto II	973–83
Otto III	996–1002
Henry II of Saxony	1014–24
Salian Frankish Dynasty	
Conrad II of Franconia	1027–39
Henry III	1046–56
Henry IV	1084–1105
Henry V	1111–25

NAME	REIGN
Supplingburger Dynasty	
Lothair III	1133–37
Hohenstaufen Dynasty	
Conrad III	1138–52
Frederick I Barbarossa	1155–90
Henry VI	1191–97
Philip of Swabia	1198–1208
Guelph Dynasty	
Otto IV of Saxony	1209–15
Hohenstaufen Dynasty	
Frederick II	1215–50
Conrad IV	1250–54
William of Holland	1254–56
Alfonso X of Castile	1267–73
Rudolf I of Habsburg	1273–91
Adolf of Nassau	1292–98
Albert I of Austria	1298–1308
Henry VII	1312–13
Louis IV of Wittelsbach	1328–47
Charles IV of Luxemburg	1347–78
Wenzel of Luxemburg	1378–1400
Rupert II of the Palatinate	1400–10
Sigismund of Luxemburg	1433–37

RULERS OF THE HOLY ROMAN EMPIRE (CONTINUED)

NAME	REIGN
Habsburg Dynasty	
Albert II	1437–39
Frederick II of Styria	1440–93
Maximilian I	1493–1519
Charles V	1519–56
Ferdinand I	1556–64
Maximilian II	1564–76
Rudolf II	1576–1612
Matthias	1612–19
Ferdinand II of Styria	1619–37
Ferdinand III	1637–58

NAME	REIGN
Leopold I	1658–1705
Charles VI	1711–40
Wittelsbach Dynasty	
Charles VII of Bavaria	1742–45
Habsburg–Lorraine Dynasty	
Francis I	1745–65
Joseph II	1765–90
Leopold II	1790–92
Francis II	1792–1806

EMPERORS OF AUSTRIA

NAME	REIGN
Francis (Holy Roman Emperor Francis II)	1804–35
Ferdinand	1835–48

NAME	REIGN
Franz Joseph	1848–1916
Charles	1916–18

KINGS OF PRUSSIA

NAME	REIGN
Frederick I	1701–13
Frederick William I	1714–40
Frederick II the Great	1740–86
Frederick William II	1786–97

NAME	REIGN
Frederick William III	1797–1840
Frederick William IV	1840–61
William I (from 1871 German Emperor)	1861–71

EMPERORS OF GERMANY

NAME	REIGN
William I (King of Prussia)	1871–88
Frederick	1888

NAME	REIGN
William II (Kaiser Wilhelm)	1888–1918

PRESIDENTS AND CHANCELLORS OF GERMANY

CP Center Party, **CDU** Christian Democratic Union, **FDP** Free Democratic Party, **GPP** German People's Party, **MSDP** Majority Social Democratic Party of Germany, **NSP** National Socialist Party (Nazi), **SDP** Social Democratic Party

UNITED GERMANY (1919–45)

NAME	TERM
PRESIDENTS (FROM 1919)	
Friedrich Ebert (MSDP)	1919–25
Walter Simons	1925
Paul von Hindenburg	1925–34
(Führer) Adolf Hitler (NSP)	1934–45
(Führer) Karl Dönitz (NSP)	1945
CHANCELLORS	
Otto von Bismarck	1871–90
Leo von Caprivi	1890–92
Chlodwig Hohenlohe-Schillingfurst	1894–1900
Bernhard von Bülow	1900–09
Theobald von Bethman-Hollweg	1909–17
Georg Michaelis	1917
Georg von Hertling	1917–18
Prince Max von Baden	1918

NAME	TERM
Friedrich Ebert (MSDP)	1918–19
Philipp Scheidemann (MSDP)	1919
Gustav Bauer (MSDP)	1919–20
Hermann Müller (MSDP)	1920
Konstantin Fehrenbach (CP)	1920–21
Karl Wirth (CP)	1921–22
Wilhelm Cunto	1922–23
Gustav Streseman (GPP)	1923
Wilhelm Marx (CP)	1923–25
Hans Luther	1925–26
Wilhelm Marx (CP)	1926–28
Hermann Müller (SDP)	1928–30
Heinrich Brüning (CP)	1930–32
Franz von Papen (CP)	1932
Kurt von Schleicher	1932–33
Adolf Hitler (NSP)	1933–45
Joseph Goebbels (NSP)	1945

GERMAN DEMOCRATIC REPUBLIC (DDR, 1949–90)

NAME	TERM
PRESIDENTS	
Wilhelm Pieck	1949–60
Walter Ulbricht	1960–73
Willi Stoph	1973–76
Erich Honecker	1976–89
Egon Krenz	1989
Manfred Gerlach	1989–90
Sabine Bergmann-Pohl	1990
PRIME MINISTERS	
Otto Grotewohl	1949–64
Willi Stoph	1964–73
Horst Sindermann	1973–76

NAME	TERM
Willi Stoph	1976–89
Hans Modrow	1989–90
Lother de Maiziere (CDU)	1990
GENERAL SECRETARIES OF COMMUNIST PARTY (SUP)	
Walter Ulbricht	1950–71
Erich Honecker	1971–89
Egon Krenz	1989

FEDERAL REPUBLIC OF GERMANY (1945–1990, REUNITED WITH DDR FROM 1990)

NAME	TERM
PRESIDENTS	
Theodor Heuss (FDP)	1949–59
Heinrich Lübke (CDU)	1959–69
Gustav Heinemann (SDP)	1969–74
Walter Scheel (FDP)	1974–79
Karl Carstens (CDU)	1979–84
Richard von Weizsäcker (CDU)	1984–94
Roman Herzog (CDU)	1994–99
Johannes Rau (SDP)	1999–2004
Horst Köhler (CDU)	2004–10
Christian Wulff (CDU)	2010–12
Joachim Gauck (Independent)	2012–17

NAME	TERM
Frank-Walter Steinmeir (SDP)	2017–
CHANCELLORS	
Konrad Adenauer (CDU)	1949–63
Ludwiq Erhard (CDU)	1963–66
Kurt-Georg Kiesinger (CDU)	1966–69
Willy Brandt (SDP)	1969–74
Walter Scheel (FDP)	1974
Helmut Schmidt (SDP)	1974–82
Helmut Kohl (CDU)	1982–98
Gerhard Schröder (SDP)	1998–2005
Angela Merkel (CDU)	2005–

KINGS OF FRANCE

After the fall of Rome, a number of barbarian groups vied for power in Gaul. The Franks, led by the Merovingian ruler Childeric, emerged victorious, uniting France under Childeric's son Clovis. On Clovis's death, his kingdom was partitioned between his four sons and their descendants until Pepin, the first of the Carolingians, was anointed king of all the Franks by Pope Zachary in 751.

NAME	REIGN
Merovingian Dynasty	
Childeric I	c. 457–81
Clovis I	481–511
Theoderic I (Rheims)	511–34
Chlodomir (Orléans)	511–24
Childebert (Paris)	511–58
Chlotar I (Soissons)	511–61
Theudebert I (Austrasia)	534–48
Theodebald (Austrasia)	548–55
Charibert I (Paris)	561–67
Guntram (Burgundy)	561–92
Sigebert (Metz)	561–75
Chilperic I (Soissons)	561–84
Childebert II (Austrasia)	575–95
Chlotar II (Soissons; sole king 613–23)	584–629
Theudebert II (Austrasia)	595–612
Theoderic II (Burgundy; Austrasia 612–13)	595–613
Dagobert I (Austrasia 623–34, Neustria 629–39)	623–39
Charibert II (Aquitaine)	629–32
Sigebert II (Austrasia)	634–59
Clovis II (Neustria and Burgundy)	639–57
Dagobert II (Austrasia)	659–61
Chlotar III (Neustria)	657–73
Childeric II (Austrasia)	661–75
Theoderic III (Neustria; Austrasia)	673–90
Dagobert II (Austrasia)	676–79
Clovis III	690–954
Childebert III	685–711
Dagobert III	711–15
Chilperic II (Neustria)	715–21
Chlotar IV (Austrasia)	718–19
Theoderic IV	721–37
Childeric III	743–51
Carolingian Dynasty	
Pepin the Short	751–68
Charlemagne (Charles I)	768–814
Carloman (co-ruler)	768–71
Louis I the Pious	814–40
Charles II the Bald	840–77
Louis II the Stammerer	877–79
Louis III	879–82
Carloman II	879–84
Charles the Fat	884–87
Odo	887–98
Charles III the Simple	898–923
Robert I	922–23
Raoul	923–36
Louis IV	936–54
Lothair	954–86
Louis V	986–87
Capetian Dynasty	
Hugh Capet	987–96

NAME	REIGN
Robert II the Pious	996–1031
Henry I	1031–60
Philip I	1060–1108
Louis VI the Fat	1108–37
Louis VII the Young	1137–80
Philip II Augustus	1180–1223
Louis VIII	1223–26
Louis IX the Saint	1226–70
Philip III the Bold	1270–85
Philip IV the Fair	1285–1314
Louis X	1314–16
John I	1316
Philip V	1316–22
Charles IV the Fair	1322–28
House of Valois	
Philip VI the Fortunate	1328–50
John II the Good	1350–64
Charles V the Wise	1364–80
Charles VI	1380–1422
Charles VII	1422–61
Louis XI	1461–83
Charles VIII	1483–98
House of Valois-Orléans	
Louis XII	1498–1515
House of Valois-Angoulême	
Francis I	1515–47
Henry II	1547–59
Francis II	1559–60
Charles IX	1560–74
Henry III	1574–89
House of Bourbon	
Henry IV of Navarre	1589–1610
Louis XIII	1610–43
Louis XIV	1643–1715
Louis XV	1715–74
Louis XVI	1774–92
French Republic	1792–1804
First Empire	
Napoleon I (Bonaparte)	1804–14, 1815
House of Bourbon	
Louis XVII	1814–15, 1815–24
Charles X	1824–30
House of Bourbon–Orléans	
Louis-Philippe	1830–48
Second French Republic	1848–52
Second Empire	
Napoleon III	1852–70

DUKES OF NORMANDY

After the 9th century, much of France was controlled by rulers independent of French kings, notably the Dukes of Normandy, who ruled an area of northwestern France from 911 until the 13th century.

NAME	REIGN	NAME	REIGN
Rolf Ganger	911–32	Robert II	1087–1106
William I	932–42	Henry I (of England)	1106–35
Richard I	942–96	Stephen	1135–44
Richard II	996–1027	Geoffrey of Anjou	1144–50
Richard III	1027–28	Henry II (of England)	1150–89
Robert I	1028–35	Richard IV (I of England)	1189–99
William II (I of England)	1035–87	John (of England)	1199–1204

PRESIDENTS AND PRIME MINISTERS OF FRANCE

CP Center Party, **DA** Democratic Alliance, **DR** Democratic Resistance, **DUR** Democratic Union for the Fifth Republic, **IRP** Independent Republican Party, **PRM** People's Revolutionary Movement, **RA** Republican Alliance, **REM** Republic on the Move, **RFR** Rally for the Republic, **RSP** Radical Socialist Party, **SP** Socialist Party, **RSU** Radical Socialist Union, **UMP** Union for a Popular Movement, **UNR** Union for the New Republic

PRESIDENTS (SINCE 1871)

NAME	TERM	NAME	TERM
Adolphe Thiers	1871–73	Albert Le Brun	1932–40
Patrice MacMahon	1873–79	Philippe Pétain	1940–44
Jules Grevy	1879–87	Vincent Auriol (SP)	1947–54
François Sadi-Carnot	1887–94	René Coty (IRP)	1954–59
Jean Casimir-Périer	1894–95	Charles de Gaulle (UNR, DUR)	1959–69
François Faure	1895–99	Alain Poher (CP)	1969
Emile Loubet	1899–1906	Georges Pompidou (DUR)	1969–74
Armand Fallières	1906–13	Valérie Giscard d'Estaing (IRP)	1974–81
Raymond Poincaré	1913–20	François Mitterand (SP)	1981–95
Paul Deschanel	1920	Jacques Chirac (RFR/UMP)	1995–2007
Alexandre Millerand	1920–24	Nicholas Sarkozy (UMP)	2007–12
Gaston Doumergue	1924–31	Francois Hollande (SP)	2012–17
Paul Doumer	1931–32	Emmanuel Macron (REM)	2017–

PRIME MINISTERS

NAME	TERM	NAME	TERM
Adolphe Thiers	1871–73	Joseph Caillaux	1911–12
Patrice MacMahon	1873–74	Raymond Poincaré	1912–13
Ernest de Cissey	1874–75	Aristide Briand (SP)	1913
Louis Buffet	1875–76	Louis Barthou	1913
Jules Dufaure	1876	Gaston Doumergue (RSP)	1913–14
Jules Simon	1876–77	René Viviani	1914–15
Albert de Broglie	1877	Aristide Briand (SP)	1915–17
Gaëtan de Rochebouet	1877	Alexandre Ribot	1917
Jules Dufaure	1877–79	Paul Painlevé	1917
William Waddington	1879	Georges Clemenceau	1917–20
Charles de Freycinet	1879–80	Alexandre Millerand	1920
Jules Ferry	1880–81	Georges Leygues	1920–21
Léon Gambetta	1881–82	Aristide Briand (SP)	1921–22
Charles de Freycinet	1882	Raymond Poincaré	1922–24
Charles Duclerc	1882–83	Frédéric François-Marsal	1924
Armand Fallières	1883	Edouard Herriot (RSP)	1924–25
Jules Ferry	1883–85	Paul Painlevé	1925
Henri Brisson	1885–86	Aristide Briand (SP)	1925–26
Charles de Freycinet	1886	Edouard Herriot (RSP)	1926
René Goblet	1886–87	Raymond Poincaré	1926–29
Maurice Rouvier	1887	Aristide Briand (SP)	1929
Pierre Tirard	1887–88	André Tardieu	1929–30
Charles Floquet	1888–89	Camille Chautemps (RSP)	1930
Pierre Tirard	1889–90	André Tardieu	1930
Charles de Freycinet	1890–92	Théodore Steeg (RSP)	1930–31
Emile Loubet	1892	Pierre Laval	1931–32
Alexandre Ribot	1892–93	André Tardieu	1932
Charles Dupuy	1893	Edouard Herriot (RSP)	1932
Jean Casimir-Périer	1893–94	Joseph Paul-Boncour (RSU)	1932–33
Charles Dupuy	1894–95	Edouard Daladier (RSP)	1933
Alexandre Ribot	1895	Albert Sarraut (RSP)	1933
Léon Bourgeois	1895–96	Camille Chautemps (RSP)	1933–34
Jules Meline	1896–98	Edouard Daladier (RSP)	1934
Henri Brisson	1898	Gaston Doumergue (RSP)	1934
Charles Dupuy	1898–99	Pierre Flandin (DA)	1934–35
René Waldeck-Rousseau	1899–1902	Ferdinand Bouisson (SP)	1935
Émile Combes	1902–05	Pierre Laval	1935–36
Maurice Rouvier	1905–06	Albert Sarraut (RSP)	1936
Ferdinand Sarrien	1906	Léon Blum (SP)	1936–37
Georges Clemenceau	1906–09	Camille Chautemps (RSP)	1937–38
Aristide Briand (SP)	1909–11	Léon Blum (SP)	1938
Ernest Monis	1911	Edouard Daladier (RSP)	1938–40

NAME	TERM	NAME	TERM
Paul Reynaud (RA)	1940	Félix Gaillard (RSP)	1957–58
Philippe Pétain	1940–42	Pierre Pflimlin (PRM)	1958
Pierre Laval	1942–44	Charles de Gaulle (UNR)	1958–59
Charles de Gaulle	1944–46	Michel Debré (UNR)	1959–62
Félix Gouin (SP)	1946	Georges Pompidou (UNR)	1962–68
Georges Bidault (PRM)	1946	Maurice Couve de Murville (UNR)	1968–69
Léon Blum (SP)	1946–47	Jacques Chaban-Delmas (DUR)	1969–72
Paul Ramadier (SP)	1947	Pierre Messmer (DUR)	1972–74
Robert Schuman (PRM)	1947–48	Jacques Chirac (DUR)	1974–76
André Marie (RSP)	1948	Raymond Barre	1976–81
Robert Schuman (PRM)	1948	Pierre Mauroy (SP)	1981–84
Henry Queuille (RSP)	1948	Laurent Fabius (SP)	1984–86
Georges Bidault (PRM)	1948–50	Jacques Chirac (RFR)	1986–88
Henri Queuille (RSP)	1950	Michel Rocard (SP)	1988–91
René Pleven (DR)	1950–51	Edith Cresson (SP)	1991–92
Henri Queuille (RSP)	1951	Pierre Bérégovoy (SP)	1992–93
René Pleven (DR)	1951–52	Edouard Balladur (RFR)	1993–95
Edgar Faure (RSP)	1952	Alain Juppé (RFR)	1995–97
Antoine Pinay (IRP)	1952–53	Lionel Jospin (SP)	1997–2002
René Mayer (RSP)	1953	Jean-Pierre Raffarin (UMP)	2002–05
Joseph Laniel (IRP)	1953–54	Dominique de Villepin (UMP)	2005–07
Pierre Mendès-France (RSP)	1954–55	François Fillon (UMP)	2007–12
Christian Pineau (SP)	1955	Jean-Marc Ayrault (SP)	2012–14
Edgar Faure (RSP)	1955–56	Manuel Valls (SP)	2014–16
Guy Mollet (SP)	1956–57	Bernard Cazeneuve (SP)	2016–17
Maurice Bourges-Maunoury (RSP)	1957	Édouard Phillippe (LR)	2017–

KINGS AND QUEENS OF SPAIN

The northern Spanish kingdoms of Castile and Leon were joined by marriage in 1037 and were formally united in 1230. In 1469, Isabella of Castile married Ferdinand of Aragon, and when both succeeded to their respective thrones, they united their domains to form the kingdom of Spain.

KINGS AND QUEENS OF CASTILE-LEON

NAME	REIGN	NAME	REIGN
Ferdinand I	1037–65	Ferdinand IV	1295–1312
Sancho II	1065–72	Alfonso XI	1312–50
Alfonso VI	1065–1109	Peter the Cruel	1350–66
Urraca	1109–26	Henry II	1366–67
Alfonso VII	1126–57	Peter the Cruel (restored)	1367–69
Sancho III (Castile)	1157–58	Henry II (restored)	1369–79
Ferdinand II (Leon)	1157–88	John I	1379–90
Alfonso VIII (Castile)	1158–1214	Henry III	1390–1406
Alfonso IX (Leon)	1188–1230	John II	1406–54
Henry I (Castile)	1214–17	Henry IV	1454–74
Ferdinand III (Castile, Leon from 1230)	1217–52	Isabella	1474–1504
		Joanna	1504–16
Alfonso X the Wise	1252–84	Philip I	1504–06
Sancho IV	1284–95	Ferdinand V (II Of Aragon)	1506–16

KINGS OF ARAGON

NAME	REIGN	NAME	REIGN
Ramiro I	1035–63	Alfonso III	1285–91
Sancho	1063–94	James II	1291–1327
Peter I	1094–1104	Alfonso IV	1327–36
Alfonso I	1104–34	Peter IV	1336–87
Ramiro II	1134–37	John I	1387–95
Petronilla	1137–62	Martin	1395–1410
Alfonso II	1162–96	Ferdinand	1412–16
Peter II	1196–1213	Alfonso V	1416–58
James I the Conqueror	1213–76	John II	1458–79
Peter III	1276–85	Ferdinand II (V of Castile)	1479–1516

KINGS AND QUEENS OF UNITED SPAIN

NAME	REIGN	NAME	REIGN
Habsburg Dynasty		Charles IV	1788–1808
Charles I	1516–56	Ferdinand VII	1808
Philip II	1556–98		
Philip III	1598–1621	**House of Bonaparte**	
Philip IV	1621–65	Joseph Bonaparte	1808–13
Charles II	1665–1700		
		Bourbon Dynasty	
Bourbon Dynasty		Ferdinand VII (restored)	1813–33
Philip V	1700–24	Isabella II	1833–68
Luis	1724		
Philip V (restored)	1724–46	**House of Savoy**	
Ferdinand VI	1746–59	Amadeus of Savoy	1870–73
Charles III (of Naples)	1759–88	**First Spanish Republic**	1873–74

KINGS AND QUEENS OF SPAIN (CONTINUED)

NAME	REIGN
Bourbon Dynasty	
Alfonso XII	1874–85
Alfonso XIII	1886–1931
Second Spanish Republic	1931–39

NAME	REIGN
Francoist Spain	1939–75
Bourbon Dynasty	
Juan Carlos I	1975–2014
Felipe VI	2014–

NAME	TERM
Manuel Azaña y Díéz (LRP)	1936
Santiago Cásares Quiroga	1936
Diego Martínez Barrio	1936
José Giral y Pereira	1936
Francisco Largo Caballero (SP)	1936–37
Juan Negrín (SP)	1937–39
Francisco Franco Bahamonde	1939–73
Luis Carrero Blanco	1973
Torcuato Fernández Miranda	1973–74
Carlos Arias Navarro	1974–76

NAME	TERM
Fernando de Santiago y Díaz	1976
Adolfo Suárez González (UDC)	1976–81
Leopoldo Calvo-Sotelo y Bustelo (UDP)	1981–82
Felipe González Marquez (PSOE)	1982–96
José María Aznar López (PP)	1996–2004
José Luis Rodríguez Zapatero (PSOE)	2004–11
Mariano Rajoy Broy (PD)	2011–

PRIME MINISTERS OF SPAIN

CP Conservative Party, **LP** Liberal Party, **LRP** Left Republican Party, **PP** Popular Party, **RP** Radical Party, **SP** Socialist Party, **PSOE** Spanish Socialist Workers' Party, **UDC** Union for the Democratic Center

NAME	TERM
Francisco Cea Bermudez	1833–34
Francisco Martínez de la Rosa	1834–35
Conde de Toreno	1835
Juan Alvarez Mendizábal	1835–36
Manuel Isturiz y Montero	1836
José Calatrava	1836–37
Eusebio Bardaji y Azara	1837
Conde de Ofalia	1837–38
Duc de Frias	1838
Evaristo Pérez de Castro	1838
Isidro Alaix	1838–40
Antonio González y González	1840
Valentin Ferraz	1840
Modesto Cortazar	1840
Duc de Vitoria	1840–41
Antonio González y González	1841–42
José Rodil y Gallaso	1842–43
Joaquín López	1843
Alvaro Gómez Becera	1843
Joaquín López	1843
Salustiano de Olozaga	1843
Luiz González Bravo	1843–44
Duc de Valencia	1844–46
Marqués de Miraflores	1846
Francisco Isturiz y Montero	1846–47
Duc de Sotomayor	1847
Joaquín Pacheco y Gutiérrez	1847
Florencio García Gómez	1847
Duc de Valencia	1847–50
Juan Bravo Murillo	1850–52
Federico Roncali	1852–53
Francisco de Lersundi Ormaechea	1853
Luiz Sartorius	1853–54
Fernando Fernández de Córdoba	1854
Angel de Saavedra	1854–55
Duc de Victoria	1855–56
Leopoldo O'Donnell y Joria	1856
Duc de Valencia	1856–57
Francisco Armero y Peñaranda	1857–58
Francisco Isturiz y Montero	1858
Leopoldo O'Donnell y Joria	1858–63
Marqués de Miraflores	1863–64
Lorenzo Arrazola	1864
Alejandro Mon	1864
Duc de Valencia	1864–65
Leopoldo O'Donnell y Joria	1865–66
Duc de Valencia	1866–68
Luiz González Bravo	1868
José Gutiérrez de la Ocncha	1868
Francisco Serrano y Dominguez	1868–69
Juan Prim y Prets	1869–70
Juan Topete y Carballa	1870–71
Serrano y Dominguez	1871
Manuel Ruiz Zorilla	1871
José Malcampo y Monge	1871
Praxedes Sagasta	1871–72
Juan Topete y Carballa	1872
Manuel Ruiz Zorilla	1872–73
Marqués de Sierra Bullones	1874
Praxedes Sagasta	1874
Antonio Cánovas del Castillo	1874–75
Joaquín Jovellar	1875
Antonio Cánovas del Castillo	1875–79
Arsenio Martínez-Campos	1879
Antonio Cánovas del Castillo	1879–81

NAME	TERM
Praxedes Sagasta	1881–83
José de Posada Herrera	1883–84
Antonio Cánovas del Castillo	1884–85
Praxedes Sagasta	1885–90
Antonio Cánovas del Castillo	1890–92
Praxedes Sagasta	1892–95
Antonio Cánovas del Castillo	1895–97
Marcelo de Azcarraga y Palmero	1897
Praxedes Sagasta	1897–99
Francisco Silvela y Le-Vielleuze	1899–1900
Marcello de Azcarraga y Palmero	1900–01
Praxedes Sagasta	1901–02
Francisco Silvela y Le-Vielleuze	1902–03
Raimundo Fernández de Villaverde (CP)	1903
Antonio Maura y Montaner (CP)	1903–04
Marcello de Azcarraga y Palmero (CP)	1904–05
Raimundo Fernández de Villaverde (CP)	1905
Eugene Montero Ríos	1905
Segismundo Moret y Prendergast (LP)	1905–06
José López Dominguez (LP)	1906
Segismundo Moret y Prendergast (LP)	1906
Marqués de la Vega de Armijo (LP)	1906–07
Antonio Maura y Montaner (CP)	1907–09
Segismundo Moret y Prendergast (LP)	1909–10
José Canalejas y Mendez (LP)	1910–12
Conde de Romanones (LP)	1912
Marqués de Alhucemas (LP)	1912–13
Eduardo Dato y Iradier (CP)	1913–15
Conde de Romanones (LP)	1915–16
Marqués de Alhucemas (LP)	1916–17
Eduardo Dato y Iradier (CP)	1917
Marqués de Alhucemas (LP)	1917–18
Antonio Maura y Montaner (CP)	1918
Marqués de Alhucemas (LP)	1918
Conde de Romanones (LP)	1918–19
Antonio Maura y Montaner (CP)	1919
Joaquín Sánchez de Toca	1919
Manuel Allende Salazar	1919–20
Eduardo Dato y Iradier (CP)	1920–21
Gabino Bugallal Araújo	1921
Manuel Allende Salazar	1921
Antonio Maura y Montaner (CP)	1921–22
José Sánchez Guerra (CP)	1922
Marqués de Alhucemas (LP)	1922–23
Miguel Primo de Rivera y Orbaneja	1923–30
Damaso Berenguer y Fuste	1920–31
Juan Bautista Azmar-Cabanas	1931
Niceto Alcala Zamora	1931
Manuel Azaña y Díéz (LRP)	1931–33
Alejandro Lerroux y García (RP)	1933
Diego Martínez Barrio (RP)	1933
Alejandro Lerroux y García (RP)	1933–34
Ricardo Samper Ibáñez	1934
Alejandro Lerroux y García (RP)	1934–35
Joaquín Chapaprieta y Terragosa	1935
Manuel Portela Valladares	1935–36

KINGS OF SARDINIA

NAME	REIGN
Victor Amadeus II	1718–30
Charles Emmanuel III	1730–73
Victor Amadeus III	1773–96
Charles Emmanuel IV	1796–1802
Victor Emmanuel I	1802–21

NAME	REIGN
Charles Felix	1821–31
Charles Albert	1831–49
Victor Emmanuel II (from 1861 King of Italy)	1849–61

KINGS OF ITALY

NAME	REIGN
Victor Emmanuel II (of Sardinia)	1861–78
Umberto I	1878–1900

NAME	REIGN
Victor Emmanuel III	1900–46
Umberto II	1946

PRESIDENTS AND PRIME MINISTERS OF ITALY

AP Action Party, **FI** Forza Italia, **DC** Christian Democratic Party, **PRI** Italian Republican Party, **PSI** Italian Socialist Party, **PLI** Italian Liberal Party, **Ulivo** Olive Tree, **DS** Left Democrats, **PP** Popular Party, **PL** People of Freedom, **DP** Democratic Party, **I** Independent

PRESIDENTS

NAME	TERM
Enrico de Nicola	1947–48
Luigi Einaudi	1948–55
Giovanni Gronchi (DC)	1955–62
Antonio Segni (DC)	1962–64
Cesare Merzagora	1964
Giuseppe Saragat (DC)	1964–71
Giovanni Leone (DC)	1971–78

NAME	TERM
Amintore Fanfani	1978
Alessandro Pertini (DC)	1978–85
Francesco Cossiga (DC)	1985–92
Oscar Scalfaro (DC, PP)	1992–99
Nicola Mancino	1999
Carlo Azeglio Ciampi	1999–2006
Giorgio Napolitano (DS)/(I)	2006–15
Sergio Mattarella (I)	2015–

PRIME MINISTERS

NAME	TERM
Camille Cavour	1861
Bettino Ricasoli	1861–62
Urbano Rattazzi	1862
Luigi Farina	1862–63
Marco Minghetti	1863–64
Alfonso la Marmora	1864–66
Bettino Ricasoli	1866–67
Urbano Rattazzi	1867
Luigi Menabrea	1867–69
Giovanni Lanza	1869–73
Marco Minghetti	1873–76
Agostini Depretis	1876–78
Benedetto Cairoli	1878
Agostini Depretis	1878–79
Benedetto Cairoli	1879–81
Agostini Depretis	1881–87
Francesco Crispi	1887–91
Marchese di Rudini	1891–92
Giovanni Giolitti	1892–93
Francesco Crispi	1893–96
Marchese di Rudini	1896–98
Luigi Pelloux	1898–1900
Giuseppe Saracco	1900–01
Giuseppe Zanardelli	1901–03
Giovanni Giolitti	1903–05
Alessandro Fortis	1905–06
Sidney Sonnino	1906
Giovanni Giolitti	1906–09
Sidney Sonnino	1909–10
Luigi Luzzatti	1910–11
Giovanni Giolitti	1911–14
Antonio Salandra	1914–16
Paolo Boselli	1916–17
Vittorio Orlando	1917–19

NAME	TERM
Francesco Nitti	1919–20
Giovanni Giolitti	1920–21
Ivanoe Bonomi	1921–22
Luigi Facta	1922
Benito Mussolini	1922–43
Pietro Badoglio	1943–44
Ivanoe Bonomi (PLI)	1944–45
Ferrucio Parri (AP)	1945
Alfredo de Gasperi (DC)	1945–53
Giuseppe Pella (DC)	1953–54
Amintore Fanfani (DC)	1954
Mario Scelba (DC)	1954–55
Antonio Segni (DC)	1955–57
Adone Zoli (DC)	1957–58
Amintore Fanfani (DC)	1958–59
Antonio Segni (DC)	1959–60
Fernando Tambroni (DC)	1960
Amintore Fanfani (DC)	1960–63
Giovanni Leone (DC)	1963
Aldo Moro (DC)	1963–68
Giovanni Leone (DC)	1968
Mariano Rumor (DC)	1968–70
Emilio Colombo (DC)	1970–72
Giulio Andreotti (DC)	1972–73
Mariano Rumor (DC)	1973–74
Aldo Moro (DC)	1974–76
Giulio Andreotti (DC)	1976–79
Francesco Cossiga (DC)	1979–80
Arnaldo Forlani (DC)	1980–81
Giovanni Spadolini (DC)	1981–82
Amintore Fanfani (DC)	1982–83
Benedetto Craxi (PSI)	1983–87
Amintore Fanfani (DC)	1987
Giovanni Goria (DC)	1987–88

NAME	TERM
Ciriaco de Mita (DC)	1988–89
Giulio Andreotti (DC)	1989–92
Giuliano Amato (PSI)	1992–93
Carlo Azeglio Ciampi	1993–94
Silvio Berlusconi (FI)	1994–95
Lamberto Dini	1995–96
Romano Prodi (PP)	1996–98
Massimo D'Alema (DS)	1998–2000

NAME	TERM
Giuliano Amato (Ulivo)	2000–01
Silvio Berlusconi (FI)	2001–06
Romano Prodi (Ulivo)	2006–08
Silvio Berlusconi (PL)	2008– 11
Mario Monti (I)	2011–13
Enrico Letta (DP)	2013–14
Matteo Renzi (DP)	2014–16
Paolo Gentiloni (DP)	2016–

KINGS AND QUEENS OF ENGLAND

NAME	REIGN
House of Wessex	
Egbert	802–39
Ethelwulf	839–55
Ethelbald	855–60
Ethelbert	860–66
Ethelred I	866–71
Alfred the Great	871–99
Edward the Elder	899–925
Athelstan	925–39
Edmund	939–46
Edred	946–55
Edwy	955–59
Edgar	959–75
Edward the Martyr	975–78
Ethelred II the Unready	978–1013
House of Denmark	
Sweyn Forkbeard	1013–14
House of Wessex	
Ethelred II (restored)	1014–16
Edmund Ironside	1016
House of Denmark	
Canute	1016–35
Harold I Harefoot	1035–40
Harthacnut	1040–42
House of Wessex	
Edward the Confessor	1042–66
Harold II Godwinson	1066
House of Normandy	
William I the Conqueror	1066–87
William II Rufus	1087–1100
Henry I	1100–35
Stephen	1135–41
Matilda	1141
Stephen (restored)	1141–54
House of Plantagenet	
Henry II of Anjou	1154–89
Richard I the Lionheart	1189–99

NAME	REIGN
John	1199–1216
Henry III	1216–72
Edward I	1272–1307
Edward II	1307–27
Edward III	1327–77
Richard II	1377–99
House of Lancaster	
Henry IV Bolingbroke	1399–1413
Henry V	1413–22
Henry VI	1422–61
House of York	
Edward IV	1461–70
House of Lancaster	
Henry VI (restored)	1470–71
House of York	
Edward IV (restored)	1471–83
Edward V	1483
Richard III	1483–85
House of Tudor	
Henry VII	1485–1509
Henry VIII	1509–47
Edward VI	1547–53
Mary I	1553–58
Elizabeth I	1558–1603
House of Stuart	
James I (VI of Scotland)	1603–25
Charles I	1625–49
Commonwealth (Republic)	1649–60
House of Stuart	
Charles II	1660–85
James II	1685–88
William III	1689–1702
Mary II (co-ruler)	1689–94
Anne (of Great Britain from 1707)	1702–14

KINGS AND QUEENS OF SCOTLAND

NAME	REIGN
House of Alpin	
Kenneth MacAlpin (of Dalriada)	843–58
Donald I	858–62
Constantine I	862–77
Aed	877–78
Eochaid	878–89
Donald II	889–900
Constantine II	900–42
Malcolm I	942–54
Indulf	954–62
Dubh	962–66
Culen	966–71
Kenneth II	971–95
Constantine III	995–97
Kenneth III	997–1005
Malcolm II	1005–34
House of Dunkeld	
Duncan I	1034–40
Macbeth	1040–57

NAME	REIGN
Lulach	1057–58
Malcolm III Canmore	1058–93
Donald III Bane	1093–94
Duncan II	1094
Donald III Bane (restored)	1094–97
Edgar	1097–1107
Alexander I	1107–24
David I	1124–53
Malcolm IV	1153–65
William the Lion	1165–1214
Alexander II	1214–49
Alexander III	1249–86
Margaret of Norway	1286–1300
House of Balliol	
John Balliol	1292–90
House of Bruce	
Robert I the Bruce	1306–29
David II	1329–71

NAME	REIGN
House of Stuart	
Robert II	1371–90
Robert III	1390–1406
James I	1406–37
James II	1437–60

NAME	REIGN
James III	1460–88
James IV	1488–1513
James V	1513–42
Mary I (Queen of Scots)	1542–67
James VI	1567–1625
(I of England from 1603)	

KINGS AND QUEENS OF GREAT BRITAIN

NAME	REIGN
House of Hanover	
George I	1714–27
George II	1727–60
George III	1760–1820
George IV	1820–30
William IV	1830–37
Victoria	1837–1901

NAME	REIGN
House of Saxe–Coburg–Gotha	
Edward VII	1901–10
House of Windsor	
George V	1910–36
Edward VIII	1936
George VI	1936–52
Elizabeth II	1952–

PRIME MINISTERS OF THE UNITED KINGDOM

C Conservative, **Lib** Liberal, **Lab** Labour, **W** Whig

NAME	TERM
Robert Walpole	1721–42
Earl of Wilmington (Spencer Compton)	1742–43
Henry Pelham	1743–46
Earl of Bath (William Pulteney)	1746
Henry Pelham	1746–54
Duke of Newcastle (Thomas Pelham-Holles)	1754–56
Duke of Devonshire (William Cavendish)	1756–57
Earl of Waldegrave (James Waldegrave)	1757
Duke of Newcastle	1757–62
Earl of Bute (John Stuart)	1762–63
George Grenville	1763–65
Marquis of Rockingham (Charles Wentworth)	1765–66
Earl of Chatham (William Pitt the Elder)	1766–68
Duke of Grafton (Augustus Fitzroy)	1768–70
Baron North (Frederick North)	1770–82
Marquis of Rockingham	1782–82
Earl of Shelburne (William Petty-Fitzmaurice)	1782–83
Duke of Portland (William Cavendish-Bentinck)	1783–83
William Pitt (the Younger)	1783–1801
Henry Addington	1801–04
William Pitt (the Younger)	1804–06
Lord Grenville (William Grenville)	1806–07
Duke of Portland	1807–09
Spencer Perceval	1809–12
Earl of Liverpool (Robert Jenkinson)	1812–27
George Canning	1827–27
Viscount Goderich (Frederick Robinson)	1827–28
Duke of Wellington (Arthur Wellesley) (C)	1828–30
Lord Grey (Charles Grey) (W)	1830–34
Viscount Melbourne (William Lamb) (W)	1834
Duke of Wellington (C)	1834–34
Robert Peel (C)	1834–35
Viscount Melbourne (W)	1835–41
Robert Peel (C)	1841–46
Lord John Russell (W)	1846–52
Earl of Derby (Edward Stanley) (C)	1852
Earl of Aberdeen (George Hamilton-Gordon) (W)	1852–55
Viscount Palmerston (Henry Temple) (W)	1855–58

NAME	TERM
Earl of Derby (C)	1858–59
Viscount Palmerston (W)	1859–65
Lord John Russell (W)	1865–66
Earl of Derby (C)	1866–68
Benjamin Disraeli (C)	1868
William Gladstone (Lib)	1868–74
Benjamin Disraeli (C)	1874–80
William Gladstone (Lib)	1880–85
Marquis of Salisbury (Robert Cecil) (C)	1885–86
William Gladstone (Lib)	1886
Marquis of Salisbury (C)	1886–92
William Gladstone (Lib)	1892–94
Earl of Rosebery (Archibald Primrose) (Lib)	1894–95
Marquis of Salisbury (C)	1895–1902
Arthur Balfour (C)	1902–05
Henry Campbell-Bannerman (Lib)	1905–08
Herbert Asquith (Lib)	1908–16
David Lloyd George (Lib)	1916–22
Andrew Bonar Law (C)	1922–23
Stanley Baldwin (C)	1923–24
Ramsay MacDonald (Lab)	1924
Stanley Baldwin (C)	1924–29
Ramsay MacDonald (Lab)	1929–35
Stanley Baldwin (C)	1935–37
Neville Chamberlain (C)	1937–40
Winston Churchill (C)	1940–45
Clement Attlee (Lab)	1945–51
Winston Churchill (C)	1951–55
Anthony Eden (C)	1955–57
Harold MacMillan (C)	1957–63
Alexander Douglas-Home (C)	1963–64
Harold Wilson (Lab)	1964–70
Edward Heath (C)	1970–74
Harold Wilson (Lab)	1974–76
James Callaghan (Lab)	1976–79
Margaret Thatcher (C)	1979–90
John Major (C)	1990–97
Anthony Blair (Lab)	1997–2007
Gordon Brown (Lab)	2007–10
David Cameron (C)	2010–16
Theresa May (C)	2016–

RULERS OF RUSSIA

NAME	REIGN
RURIKID DYNASTY	
Princes of Moscow	
Daniel	1283–1303
Yuri	1303–25
Ivan I	1325–40
Simeon the Proud	1340–53
Ivan II	1353–59
Grand Princes of	
Moscow–Vladimir	
Dmitri Donskoi	1359–89
Vasili I	1389–1425
Vasili II the Blind	1425–62
Ivan III the Great	1462–1505
Vasili III	1505–33
Czars of Russia	
Ivan IV the Terrible	1533–84
(Czar from 1547)	
Feodor I	1584–98
GODUNOV DYNASTY	
Boris Godunov	1598–1605
Feodor II	1605
Dimitri II	1605–06

NAME	REIGN
SHUISKII DYNASTY	
Vasili IV	1606–10
ROMANOV DYNASTY	
Michael	1613–45
Alexei	1645–76
Feodor III	1676–82
Ivan V	1682–96
Peter I the Great	1696–1725
(Emperor from 1721)	
Catherine I	1725–27
Peter II	1727–30
Anna	1730–40
Ivan VI	1740–41
Elizabeth	1741–62
Peter III	1762
Catherine II the Great	1762–96
Paul I	1796–1801
Alexander I	1801–25
Nicholas I	1825–55
Alexander II	1855–81
Alexander III	1881–94
Nicholas II	1894–1917

LEADERS OF THE SOVIET UNION AND RUSSIAN FEDERATION

After the establishment of the USSR in 1923, the country had heads of state and heads of government, but real power resided in the leadership of the Soviet Communist Party. Some Soviet leaders combined several roles, but their powerbases always lay within the Communist Party.

OHR Our Home is Russia, **UR** United Russia

SOVIET UNION (USSR, 1923–91)

HEADS OF STATE

NAME	TERM
Mikhail Kalinin	1922–46
Nikolai Svernik	1946–53
Marshal Kliment Voroshilov	1953–60
Leonid Brezhnev	1960–64
Anastas Mikoyan	1964–65
Nikolai Podgorny	1965–77
Leonid Breznhev	1977–82

NAME	TERM
Vasili Kuznetsov	1982–83
Yuri Andropov	1983–84
Konstantin Chernenko	1984–85
Vasili Kuznetsov	1985
Andrei Gromyko	1985–88
Mikhail Gorbachev	1988–91

HEADS OF COMMUNIST PARTY

NAME	TERM
Vladimir Lenin	1923–24
Joseph Stalin	1924–53
Georgi Malenkov	1953
Nikita Khrushchev	1953–64

NAME	TERM
Leonid Brezhnev	1964–82
Yuri Andropov	1982–84
Konstanin Chernenko	1984–85
Mikhail Gorbachev	1985–91

HEADS OF GOVERNMENT

NAME	TERM
Vladimir Lenin	1923–24
Alexi Rykov	1924–30
Vyacheslav Molotov	1930–41
Joseph Stalin	1941–53
Georgi Malenkov	1953–55
Nikolai Bulganin	1955–58

NAME	TERM
Nikita Khrushchev	1958–64
Alexi Kosygin	1964–80
Nikolai Tikhonov	1980–85
Nikolai Ryzkov	1985–91
Valentin Pavlov	1991

RUSSIAN FEDERATION (SINCE 1991)

PRESIDENTS

NAME	TERM
Boris Yeltsin	1990–99
Vladimir Putin	1999–2008

NAME	TERM
Dmitry Medvedev	2008–

PRIME MINISTERS

NAME	TERM
Ivan Silayev	1990–91
Boris Yeltsin	1991–92
Yegor Gaidar	1992
Dr. Viktor Chernomyrdin (OHR)	1992–98
Sergei Kiriyenko	1998
Dr. Viktor Chernomyrdin (OHR)	1998
Yevgeni Primakov	1998–99

NAME	TERM
Sergei Stepashin	1999
Vladimir Putin	1999–2000
Mikhail Kasyanov	2000–04
Viktor Khristenko	2004
Mikhail Fradkov	2004–07
Viktor Zubkov	2007–08
Vladimir Putin (UR)	2008–

EMPERORS OF CHINA

China was united by Qin Shi Huangdi, the First Emperor, in 221 BCE. However, the collapse of the Han Dynasty in 220 CE was followed by three centuries of disunity during which the country was sometimes split into as many as 17 kingdoms. China was reunited by the Sui in 589, but after the collapse of their successors, the Tang, in 907, the country was once more divided during the Five Dynasties and Ten Kingdoms period (907–60). The Song reunited China in 960, but they lost control of the north of the country in 1126. Final reunification came under the Mongol Yuan dynasty in 1279.

NAME	REIGN
Qin Dynasty	
Qin Shi Huangdi	221–210 BCE
Er Shi	210–207 BCE
Western Han Dynasty	
Gaodi	206–195 BCE
Huidi	195–188 BCE
Lu Hou (Regent)	188–180 BCE
Wendi	180–157 BCE
Jingdi	157–141 BCE
Wudi	141–87 BCE
Zhaodi	87–74 BCE
Xuandi	74–49 BCE
Yuandi	48–33 BCE
Chengdi	33–7 BCE
Aidi	7–1 BCE
Pingdi	1 BCE–6 CE
Ruzi	7–9
Hsin Dynasty	
Wang Mang	9–23
Eastern Han Dynasty	
Guang Wudi	25–57
Mingdi	57–75
Zhangdi	75–88
Hedi	88–106
Shangdi	106
Andi	106–25
Shundi	125–44
Chongdi	144–45
Zhidi	145–46
Huandi	146–68
Lingdi	169–89
Xiandi	189–220
Period of Disunity	220–581
Sui Dynasty	
Wendi	581–604
Yangdi	604–17
Gongdi	617–18
Tang Dynasty	
Gaozu	618–26
Taizong	626–49
Gaozong	649–83
Zhongzong	684
Ruizong	684–90
Wu Zetian	690–705
Zhongzong (restored)	705–10
Ruizong (restored)	710–12
Xuangzong	712–56
Suzong	756–62
Daizong	762–79
Dezong	779–805
Shunzong	805
Xianzong	805–20
Muzong	820–24

NAME	REIGN
Jingzong	824–27
Wenzong	827–40
Wuzong	840–46
Xuanzong	846–59
Yizong	859–73
Xizong	873–88
Zhaozong	888–904
Aidi	904–07
Five Dynasties and Ten Kingdoms Period	907–60
Northern Song Dynasty	
Taizu	960–76
Taizong	976–97
Zhenzong	998–1022
Renzong	1022–63
Yingzong	1064–67
Shenzong	1068–85
Zhezong	1086–1101
Huizong	1101–25
Qinzong	1126
Southern Song Dynasty	
Gaozong	1127–62
Xiazong	1163–90
Guangzong	1190–94
Ningzong	1195–1224
Lizong	1225–64
Duzong	1265–74
Gongzong	1275
Duanzong	1276–78
Bing Di	1279
Yuan Dynasty	
Shizu (Kublai Khan)	1279–94
Chengzong (Temur Oljeitu)	1294–1307
Wuzong (Khaishan)	1308–11
Renzong (Ayrbarwada)	1311–20
Yingzong (Shidebala)	1321–23
Taiding (Yesun Temur)	1323–28
Wenzong (Tugh Temur)	1328–29
Mingzong (Khoshila)	1329
Wenzong (restored)	1329–32
Shundi (Toghon Temur)	1332–68
Ming Dynasty	
Hongwu	1368–98
Jianwen	1399–1402
Yongle	1403–24
Hongxi	1425
Xuande	1426–35
Zhengtong	1436–49
Jingtai	1449–57
Zhengtong (restored)	1457–64
Chenghua	1464–87
Hongzhi	1487–1505
Zhengde	1505–21
Jiajing	1521–67

NAME	REIGN
Longqing	1567–72
Wanli	1572–1620
Taichang	1620
Tianqi	1620–27
Chongzhen	1628–44
Qing Dynasty	
Shunzhi	1644–61
Kangxi	1661–1722

NAME	REIGN
Yongzheng	1722–35
Qianlong	1735–96
Jiajing	1796–1820
Daoguang	1820–50
Xianfeng	1850–61
Tongzhi	1861–75
Guangxu	1875–1908
Puyi	1908–11

LEADERS OF THE PEOPLE'S REPUBLIC OF CHINA

After the victory of Mao Zedong's Communist Party in the Chinese Civil War in 1949, the leader of the Party occupied the preeminent role in China's government. China retained a president with largely ceremonial powers, and a prime minister who in theory headed the government, but these officials were firmly subordinate to the will of the Communist Party leadership.

HEADS OF STATE

NAME	TERM
Mao Zedong	1949–59
Liu Shaoqi	1959–68
Dong Biwu	1968–75
Position vacant	1975–83
Li Xiannian	1983–87
Yang Shangkun	1987–93
Jiang Zemin	1992–2003
Hu Jintao	2003–13
Xi Jinping	2013–

HEADS OF COMMUNIST PARTY

NAME	TERM
Mao Zedong	1945–79
Hua Guofeng	1979–81
Hu Yaobang	1981–87
Zhao Ziyang	1987–89
Jiang Zemin	1989–2002
Hu Jintao	2002–12
Xi Jinping	2012–

PRIME MINISTERS

NAME	TERM
Zhou Enlai	1949–76
Hua Guofeng	1976–80
Zhao Ziyang	1980–87
Li Peng	1987–98
Zhu Rongji	1998–2003
Wen Jiaobao	2003–13
Li Keqiang	2013–

RULERS OF INDIA

The Indian subcontinent has seen the rise and fall of many kingdoms and empires. The Mauryan Empire encompassed almost all of South Asia; the Gupta Empire formed a wide band across northern India; and the Chola Empire stretched across Southeast Asia. At their heights, the Muslim Delhi Sultanate and Mughal Empire controlled virtually all of modern India and Pakistan.

MAURYA EMPIRE (321–180 BCE)

NAME	REIGN
Chandragupta Maurya	321–297 BCE
Bindusara	297–272 BCE
Ashoka	272–232 BCE
Dasaratha	232–224 BCE
Samprati	224–215 BCE
Salisuka	215–202 BCE
Devadharma	202–195 BCE
Satamdhanu	195–187 BCE
Brihadratha	187–180 BCE

GUPTA INDIA (c. 275–550)

NAME	REIGN
Gupta	c. 275–300
Ghatotkacha	c. 300–20
Chandragupta I	c. 320–50
Samudragupta	c. 350–76
Chandragupta II	c. 376–415
Kumaragupta	c. 415–55
Skandagupta	c. 455–67
Kumaragupta II	c. 467–77
Budhagupta	c. 477–95
Chandragupta III	c. 495–500
Vainyagupta	c. 500–15
Narasimhagupta	c. 515–30
Kumaragupta III	c. 530–40
Vishnugupta	c. 540–50

CHOLA INDIA (c. 846–1279)

NAME	REIGN
Viyayalaya	c. 846–71
Aditya I	c. 871–907
Parantaka I	907–53
Rajaditya I (co-ruler)	947–49
Gandaraditya	953–57
Arinjaya (co-ruler)	956–57
Parantaka II	957–73
Aditya II (co-ruler)	957–69
Madurantaka Uttama	973–85
Rajaraja I	985–1016
Rajendra I	1016–44
Rajadhiraja I	1044–54
Rajendra II	1054–64
Raja Mahendra (co-ruler)	1060–63
Virarajendra	1064–69
Adirajendra	1069–70
Rajendra III Kulottunga Chola	1070–1122
Vikrama Chola	1122–35
Kulottunga Chola II	1135–50
Rajaraja II	1150–73
Rajadhiraja II	1173–79
Kulottunga III	1179–1218
Rajaraja III	1218–46
Rajendra IV	1246–79

DELHI SULTANATE (1206–1526)

NAME	REIGN
Slave Mamluk Dynasty	
Aibak	1206–10
Aran Shan	1210–11
Iltutmish	1211–36
Firuz Shah	1236
Radiyya Begum	1236–40
Bahram Shah	1240–42
Mas'ud Shah	1242–46
Mahmud Shah	1246–66
Balban	1266–87
Kai-Qubadh	1287–90
Kayumarth	1290
Khalji Dynasty	
Firuz Shah II	1290–96
Ibrahim I	1296
Muhammad I	1296–1316
'Umar	1316
Mubarak I	1316–20
Khusraw	1320
Tughluqid Dynasty	
Tughluq I	1321–25
Muhammad II	1325–51
Firuz Shah III	1351–88
Tughluq II	1388–89
Abu Bakr	1389–90
Muhammad III	1390–94
Sikandar I	1394
Mahmud II	1394–13
Daulat Khan Lodi	1413–14
Sayyid Dynasty	
Khidr Khan	1414–21
Mubarak II	1421–34
Muhammad IV	1434–45
Alam Shah	1445–51

NAME	REIGN
Lodi Dynasty	
Bahlul Lodi	1451–89
Sikandar II	1489–17
Ibrahim II	1517–26
Mughal Dynasty	
Babur	1526–30
Humayun	1530–40
Surid Dynasty	
Shir Shah Sur	1540–45
Islam Shah	1545–53
Muhammad 'Adil	1553–55
Ibrahim III	1555
Sikandar III	1555–56
Mughal Emperors	
Humayun (restored)	1555–56
Akbar I the Great	1556–1605
Jahangir	1605–27
Shah Jahan I	1628–58
Aurangzeb	1658–1707
Azam Shah	1707
Bahadur Shah I	1707–12
'Azim-ush-Sha'n	1712
Jahandar Shah	1712–13
Farrukhsiyar	1713–19
Rafi' ud-Darajat	1719
Shah Jahan II	1719
Nikusiyar	1719
Muhammad Ibrahim	1719–48
Ahmad Shah	1748–54
Alamgir II	1754–59
Shah Alam II	1759–88
Baidar Bakht	1788
Shah Alam II (restored)	1788–1806
Akbar II	1806–37
Bahadur Shah II	1837–58

PRESIDENTS AND PRIME MINISTERS OF INDIA

BJP Bharatiya Janata Party, **CP** Congress Party, **CIP** Congress I (Indira) Party, **LD** Lok Dal, **JD** Janata Dal, **JDS** Janata Dal (Secular), **JP** Janata Party, **JSP** Janata Secular Party

PRESIDENTS

NAME	TERM
Dr. Rajendra Prasad	1950–62
Dr. Sarvapali Radhakrishnan	1962–67
Dr. Zakir Husain	1967–69
Sri Vaharagiri Venkata Giri	1969
Muhammad Hidayat Ullah	1969
Sri Vaharagiri Venkata Giri	1969–74
Fakhruddin' 'Ali Ahmad	1974–77
Basappa Danappa Jatti	1977
Neelam Sanjiva Reddy	1977–82

NAME	TERM
Gian Zail Singh	1982–87
Rameswar Venkataraman	1987–92
Dr. Shankar Dayal Sharma	1992–97
Sri Kocheril Raman Narayanan	1997–2002
Dr. Awul Abdul Kalam	2002–07
Pratibha Patil	2007–12
Pranab Mukherjee	2012–17
Ram Nath Kovind	2017–

PRIME MINISTERS

NAME	TERM
Jawaharlal Nehru (CP)	1947–64
Gulzarilal Nanda (CP)	1964
Lal Bahadur Shastri (CP)	1964–66
Gulzarilal Nanda (CP)	1966
Srimati Indira Gandhi (CP)	1966–77
Morarji Ranchhodji Desai (JP)	1977–79
Charan Singh (JSP)	1979–80
Srimati Indira Gandhi (CIP)	1980–84
Rajiv Gandhi (CIP)	1984–89

NAME	TERM
Vishvant Pratap Singh (JD)	1989–90
Sadanand Singh Shekhar (JDS)	1990–91
Pamulaparpi Narasimha Rao (CIP)	1991–96
Atal Bihari Vajpayee (BJP)	1996
Haradanhalli Dewe Gowda (JD)	1996–97
Inder Kumar Gujral (JD)	1997–98
Atal Bihari Vajpayee (BJP)	1998–2004
Dr. Manmohan Singh (CIP)	2004–14
Narendra Modi (BJP)	2014–

RULERS OF JAPAN

Japanese tradition dates the accession of the country's first emperor, Jimmu Tenno, to 660 BCE, but archaeological discoveries have indicated he is more likely to have ruled around 40 CE. Over time, Japan's emperors lost power to influential military families, and from 1185 to the 19th century real power was wielded by a series of military warlords (shoguns), including the Tokugawa family, which held the post of shogun for over 250 years until the restoration of the emperor's powers in 1867.

EMPERORS

NAME	REIGN
Yamato Period	
(c. 40 BCE–710 CE)	
Jimmu	40–10 BCE
Suizei	10 BCE–20 CE
Annei	20–50
Itoki	50–80
Kōshō	80–110
Kōan	110–40
Kōrei	140–70
Kōgen	170–200
Kaika	200–30
Sujin	230–58
Suinin	258–90
Keikō	290–322
Seimu	322–55
Chūai	355–62
Ojin	362–94
Nintoku	394–427
Richū	427–32
Hanzei	432–37
Ingyō	437–54
Ankō	454–57
Yūryaku	457–89
Seinei	489–94
Kenzō	494–97
Ninken	497–504
Buretsu	504–510
Keitai	510–27
Ankan	527–35
Senka	535–39
Kimmei	539–71
Bidatsu	572–85
Yōmei	585–87
Sushun	587–92
Suiko (Empress)	593–628
Jomei	629–41
Kōgyoku (Empress)	642–45
Kōtoku	645–54
Saimei (Kōgyku restored)	655–61
Tenji	661–72
Kobun	672
Temmu	672–86
Jitō (Empress)	686–97
Mommu	697–707
Nara Period	
(710–784)	
Gemmei (Empress)	707–15
Genshō (Empress)	715–24
Shōmu	724–49
Kōken (Empress)	749–58
Junnin	758–64
Shōtoku (Kōken restored)	764–70
Kōnin	770–81
Heian Period	
(784–1185)	
Kammu	781–806
Heizei	806–09
Saga	809–23
Junna	823–33
Nimmyō	833–50
Montoku	850–58
Seiwa	858–76
Yōzei	876–84
Kōkō	884–87
Uda	887–97
Daigo	897–930
Suzaku	930–46
Murakami	946–67
Reizei	967–69

NAME	REIGN
En'yū	969–84
Kazan	984–86
Ichijō	986–1011
Sanjō	1011–16
Go-Ichijō	1016–36
Go-Suzaku	1036–45
Go-Reizei	1045–68
Go-Sanjō	1068–73
Shirakawa	1073–87
Horikawa	1087–1107
Toba	1107–23
Sutoku	1123–42
Konoe	1142–55
Go-Shirakawa	1155–58
Nijō	1158–65
Rokujō	1165–68
Takakura	1168–80
Antoku	1180–85
Kamakura Period	
(1186–1333)	
Go-Toba	1183–98
Tsuchimikado	1198–1210
Juntoku	1210–21
Chūkyō	1221
Go-Horikaw	1221–32
Shij	1232–42
Go-Saga	1242–46
Go-Fukakusa	1246–60
Kameyama	1260–74
Go-Uda	1274–87
Fushimi	1287–98
Go-Fushimi	1298–1301
Go-Nijō	1301–08
Hanazono	1308–18
Southern Court	
(1336–92)	
Go-Daigo	1318–39
Go-Murakami	1339–68
Chōkei	1368–83
Go-Kameyama	1383–92
Northern Court	
(1336–92)	
Kōgon	1331–33
Kōmyō	1336–48
Sukō	1348–51
Go-Kōgon	1352–71
Go-En'yū	1371–82
Muromachi Period	
(1392–1573)	
Go-Komatsu	1382–1412
Shōkō	1412–28
Go-Hanazono	1428–64
Go-Tsuchimikado	1464–1500
Go-Kashiwabara	1500–26
Go-Nara	1526–57
Ōgimachi	1557–86
Tokugawa Period	
(1603–1867)	
Go-Yōzei	1586–1611
Go-Mizunoo	1611–29
Meishō	1629–43
Go-Kōmyō	1643–54
Go-Sai	1655–63
Reigen	1663–87
Higashiyama	1687–1709
Nakamikado	1709–35

NAME	REIGN
Sakuramachi	1735–47
Momozono	1747–62
Go-Sakuramachi (Empress)	1735–47
Go-Momozono	1771–79
Kōkaku	1780–1817
Ninkō	1817–46
Kōmei	1846–67

SHOGUNS

NAME	REIGN
Kamakura Shogunate	
Minamoto Yoritomo	1192–95
Yoriie	1202–03
Sanemoto	1203–19
Kujō Yoritsune	1226–44
Yoritsugu	1244–52
Munetaka	1252–66
Koreyasu	1266–89
Hisaaki	1289–1308
Morikuni	1308–33
Ashikaga Shogunate	
Ashikaga Takauji	1338–58
Yoshiakira	1359–67
Yoshimitsu	1369–95
Yoshimochi	1395–1423
Yoshikazu	1423–25
Yoshinori	1429–41
Yoshikatsu	1442–43
Yoshimasa	1449–74
Yoshihisa	1474–89
Yoshitane	1490–93
Yoshizumi	1495–1508
Yoshitane (restored)	1508–22

NAME	REIGN
Modern Japan	
(1867–)	
Meiji	1867–1912
Taishō	1912–26
Shōwa (Hirohito)	1926–89
Akihito	1989–

NAME	REIGN
Yoshiharu	1522–47
Yoshiteru	1547–65
Yoshihide	1568
Yoshiaki	1568–73
Tokugawa Shogunate	
Tokugawa Ieyasu	1603–05
Hidetada	1605–23
Iemitsu	1623–51
Ietsuna	1651–80
Tsunayoshi	1680–1709
Ienobu	1709–12
Ietsugu	1713–16
Yoshimune	1716–45
Ieshige	1745–60
Ieharu	1760–86
Ienari	1787–1837
Ieyoshi	1837–53
Iesada	1853–58
Iemochi	1858–66
Yoshinobi	1867–68

PRIME MINISTERS OF JAPAN

DP Democratic Party, **JNP** Japan New Party, **JRP** Japan Renewal Party, **LDP** Liberal Democratic Party, **LP** Liberal Party, **SP** Socialist Party

NAME	TERM
Ito Hirobumi	1885–88
Kuroda Kiyotaka	1888–89
Yamagata Aritomo	1889–91
Matsukata Masayoshi	1891–92
Ito Hirobumi	1892–96
Matsukata Masayoshi	1896–97
Kuroda Kiyotaka	1897
Matsukata Masayoshi	1897–98
Ito Hirobumi	1898
Okuma Shigenobu	1898
Yamagata Aritomo	1898–1900
Ito Hirobumi	1900–01
Saionji Kimmochi	1901
Katsura Taro	1901–06
Saionji Kimmochi	1906–08
Katsura Taro	1908–11
Saionji Kimmochi	1911–12
Katsura Taro	1912–13
Yamamoto Gonnohyoe	1913–14
Okuma Shigenobu	1914–16
Terauchi Matsakate	1916–18
Hara Takashi	1918–21
Uchida Yasuya	1921
Takahashi Korekiyo	1921–22
Kato Tomosabura	1922–23
Yamamoto Gonnohyoe	1923–24
Kiyoura Keigo	1924
Kato Takaaki	1924–26
Wakatsuki Reijiro	1926–27
Tanaka Giichi	1927–29
Hamaguchi Osachi	1929–31
Wakatsuki Reijiro	1931
Inukai Takashi	1931–32
Takahashi Korekiyo	1932
Saito Makoto	1932–34
Okada Keisuke	1934–36
Goto Fumio	1936
Hirota Koki	1936–37

NAME	TERM
Hayashi Senjuro	1937
Konoye Fumimaro	1937–1939
Hironuma Kiichiro	1939
Abe Nobyaki	1939–40
Yonai Mitsumasa	1940
Konoye Fumimaro	1940–41
Tojo Hideki	1941–44
Koiso Kuniaki	1944–45
Suzuki Kantaro	1945
Naruhiko Higashikini	1945
Shidehara Kiuro	1945
Yoshida Shigeru (LP)	1946–47
Katayama Tetsu (SP)	1947–48
Ashida Hitoshi (DP)	1948
Yoshida Shigeru (LP)	1948–54
Hatoyama Ichiro (LDP)	1954–56
Ishibashi Tanzan (LDP)	1956–57
Kishi Nobusuke (LDP)	1957–60
Ikeda Hayato (LDP)	1960–64
Sato Eisaku (LDP)	1964–72
Tanaka Kakuei (LDP)	1972–74
Miki Takeo (LDP)	1974–76
Fukuda Takeo (LDP)	1976–78
Ohira Masayoshi (LDP)	1978–80
Ito Masayoshi (LDP)	1980
Suzuki Zenko (LDP)	1980–82
Nakasone Yasuhiro (LDP)	1982–87
Takeshita Nobaru (LDP)	1987–89
Uno Sosuke (LDP)	1989
Kaifu Toshiki (LDP)	1989–91
Miyazawa Kiichi (LDP)	1991–93
Hata Tsutomu (JNP)	1993–94
Murayama Tomiichi (JNP)	1994–96
Hashimoto Ryutaro (LDP)	1996–98
Obuchi Keizo (LDP)	1998–2000
Mori Yoshiro (LDP)	2000–01
Koizumi Jun'ichiro (LDP)	2001–06
Abe Shinzo (LDP)	2006–07

NAME	REIGN	NAME	REIGN
Fukuda Yasuo (LDP)	2007–08	Kan Naoto (DP)	2010–11
Aso Taro (LDP)	2008–09	Noda Yoshihiko (DP)	2011–12
Hatoyama Yukio (DP)	2009–2010	Shinzo Abe (LDP)	2012–

INCA EMPERORS

NAME	REIGN	NAME	REIGN
Manco Capac	c. 1100	Tupac Yupanqui	1471–93
Sinchi Roca	unknown	Huayna Capac	1493–1526
Lloque Yupanqui	unknown	Huascar	1526–32
Mayta Capac	unknown	Atahuallpa	1530–33
Capac Yupanqui	c. 1200	Tupac Hualpa	1533
Inca Roca	unknown	Manco Inca Yupanqui	1533–45
Inca Yupanqui	unknown	Sayri Tupac	1545–60
Viracocha	unknown	Titu Cusi Yupanqui	1560–71
Inca Urco	1438	Tupac Amaru	1571–72
Pachacuti	1438–71		

AZTEC EMPERORS

NAME	REIGN	NAME	REIGN
Acampichtli	1372–91	Tizoc	1481–86
Huitzilihuitl	1391–1415	Ahuitzotl	1486–1502
Chimalpopoca	1415–26	Moctezuma II Xocoyotzin	1502–20
Itzcoatl	1426–40	Cuitlahuac	1520
Moctezuma I Ilhuicamina	1440–68	Cuauhtemoc	1520–21
Axayacatl	1468–81		

PRESIDENTS OF THE UNITED STATES

F Federalist, DR Democratic Republican, D Democratic, R Republican, W Whig, NU National Union

NAME	TERM	NAME	TERM
George Washington	1789–97	Grover Cleveland (D)	1893–97
John Adams (F)	1797–1801	William McKinley (R)	1897–1901
Thomas Jefferson (DR)	1801–09	Theodore Roosevelt (R)	1901–09
James Madison (DR)	1809–17	William Howard Taft (R)	1909–13
James Monroe (DR)	1817–25	Woodrow Wilson (D)	1913–21
John Quincy Adams (DR)	1825–29	Warren G. Harding (R)	1921–23
Andrew Jackson (D)	1829–37	Calvin Coolidge (R)	1923–29
Martin Van Buren (D)	1837–41	Herbert Hoover (R)	1929–33
William Henry Harrison (W)	1841	Franklin D. Roosevelt (D)	1933–45
John Tyler (W)	1841–45	Harry S. Truman (D)	1945–53
James Knox Polk (D)	1845–49	Dwight D. Eisenhower (R)	1953–61
Zachary Taylor (W)	1849–50	John F. Kennedy (D)	1961–63
Millard Fillmore (W)	1850–53	Lyndon B. Johnson (D)	1963–69
Franklin Pierce (D)	1853–57	Richard Nixon (R)	1969–74
James Buchanan (D)	1857–61	Gerald Ford (R)	1974–77
Abraham Lincoln (R)	1861–65	James ("Jimmy") Carter (D)	1977–81
Andrew Johnson (D/NU)	1865–69	Ronald Reagan (R)	1981–89
Ulysses S. Grant (R)	1869–77	George H. W. Bush (R)	1989–93
Rutherford B. Hayes (R)	1877–81	William ("Bill") Clinton (D)	1993–2001
James A. Garfield (R)	1881	George W. Bush (R)	2001–09
Chester A. Arthur (R)	1881–85	Barack Obama (D)	2009–17
Grover Cleveland (D)	1885–89	Donald Trump (R)	2017–
Benjamin Harrison (R)	1889–93		

PRIME MINISTERS OF CANADA

CP Conservative Party, LP Liberal Party, PCP Progressive Conservative Party, UP Unionist Party

NAME	TERM	NAME	TERM
John Alexander MacDonald (LP)	1867–73	Louis St Laurent (LP)	1948–57
Alexander MacKenzie (LP)	1873–78	John Diefenbaker (PCP)	1957–63
John Alexander MacDonald (CP)	1878–91	Lester Pearson (LP)	1963–68
John Abbott (CP)	1891–92	Pierre Trudeau (LP)	1968–79
John Thompson (CP)	1892–94	Joseph Clark (PCP)	1979–80
MacKenzie Bowell (CP)	1894–96	Pierre Trudeau (LP)	1980–84
Charles Tupper (CP)	1896	John Turner (LP)	1984
Wilfred Laurier (LP)	1896–1911	Brian Mulroney (PCP)	1984–93
Robert Borden (CP, UP)	1911–20	Kim Campbell (PCP)	1993
Arthur Meighen (UP)	1920–21	Jean Chrétien (LP)	1993–2003
W. Mackenzie King (LP)	1921–26	Paul Martin (LP)	2003–06
Arthur Meighen (UP)	1926	Stephen Harper (CP)	2006–15
W. MacKenzie King (LP)	1926–30	Justin Trudeau (LP)	2015–
Richard Bennett (CP)	1930–35		
W. MacKenzie King (LP)	1935–48		

PRESIDENTS AND PRIME MINISTERS OF SOUTH AFRICA

ANC African National Congress, LP Labour Party, NP National Party, NPP National People's Party, SAP South African Party, S Solidarity, UP United Party

PRESIDENTS

NAME	TERM	NAME	TERM
Charles Swart	1961–67	Marais Viljoen	1979–84
Jozua Naudé	1967–68	Pieter Botha	1984–89
Jacobus Fouché	1968–75	Frederik de Klerk	1989–94
Jan de Clerk	1975	Nelson Mandela (ANC)	1994–99
Nicolaas Diederich	1975–78	Thabo Mbeki (ANC)	1999–2008
Marais Viljoen	1978	Kgalema Motlanthe (ANC)	2008–09
B. Johannes Vorster	1978–79	Jacob Zuma (ANC)	2009–

PRIME MINISTERS

NAME	TERM	NAME	TERM
Louis Botha (SAP)	1910–19	Charles Swart	1958
Jan Smuts (SAP)	1919–24	Hendrik Verwoerd (NP)	1958–66
James Barry Herzog (NP/UP)	1924–39	Ebenhezer Dönges	1966
Jan Smuts (UP)	1939–48	B. Johannes Vorster (NP)	1966–78
Daniel Malan (NP)	1948–54	Pieter Botha (NP)	1978–84
Johannes Strijdom (NP)	1954–58		

PRIME MINISTERS OF AUSTRALIA (SINCE 1901)

ALP Australian Labour Party, CP Country Party, LPA Liberal Party of Australia, NP National Party, UAP United Australia Party

NAME	TERM	NAME	TERM
Edmund Barton	1901–03	Francis Forde	1945
Alfred Deakin (LPA)	1903–04	Joseph Chifley (ALP)	1945–49
John Watson	1903	Robert Menzies (LPA)	1949–66
George Reid	1904–05	Harold Holt (LPA)	1966–67
Alfred Deakin (LPA)	1905–08	John McEwan (CP)	1967 68
Andrew Fisher (ALP)	1908–09	John Gorton (LPA)	1968–71
Alfred Deakin (LPA)	1909–10	William MacMahon (LPA)	1971–72
Andrew Fisher (ALP)	1910–13	E. Gough Whitlam (ALP)	1972–75
Joseph Cook	1913–14	Malcolm Fraser (LPA)	1975–83
Andrew Fisher (ALP)	1914–15	Robert Hawke (ALP)	1983–91
William Hughes (ALP, NP)	1915–23	Paul Keating (ALP)	1991–96
Stanley Bruce (NP)	1923–29	John Howard (LPA)	1996–2007
James Scullin (ALP)	1929–32	Kevin Rudd (ALP)	2007–10
Joseph Lyons (UAP)	1932–39	Julia Gillard (ALP)	2010–13
Earl Page (CP)	1939	Kevin Rudd (ALP)	2013–13
Robert Menzies (UAP)	1939–41	Tony Abbott (LPA)	2013–15
Arthur Fadden (CP)	1941	Malcolm Turnbull (LPA)	2015–
John Curtin (ALP)	1941–45		

PRIME MINISTERS OF NEW ZEALAND

Lab Labour Party, Lib Liberal Party, NP National party, RP Reform Party, UP United Party

NAME	TERM	NAME	TERM
Henry Sewell	1856	Joseph Ward (Lib)	1906–12
William Fox	1856	Thomas MacKenzie (Lib)	1912
Edward Stafford	1856–61	William Massey (RP)	1912–25
William Fox	1861–62	Francis Bell (RP)	1925
Alfred Domett	1862–63	Joseph Coates (RP)	1925–28
Frederick Whitaker	1863–64	Joseph Ward (UP)	1928–30
Frederick Weld	1864–65	George Forbes (UP)	1930–35
Edward Stafford	1865–69	Michael Savage (Lab)	1935–40
William Fox	1869–72	Peter Fraser (Lab)	1940–49
Edward Stafford	1872	Sidney Holland (NP)	1949–57
George Waterhouse	1872–73	Keith Holyoake (NP)	1957
William Fox	1873	Walter Nash (Lab)	1957–60
Julius Vogel	1873–75	Keith Holyoake (NP)	1960–72
Daniel Pollen	1875–76	John Marshall (NP)	1972
Julius Vogel	1876	Norman Kirk (Lab)	1972–74
Harry Atkinson	1876–77	Hugh Watt (Lab)	1974
George Grey	1877–79	Wallace Rowling (Lab)	1974–75
John Hall	1879–82	Robert Muldoon (NP)	1975–84
Frederick Whitaker	1882–83	David Lange (Lab)	1984–89
Harry Atkinson	1883–84	Geoffrey Palmer (Lab)	1989–90
Robert Stout	1884	Michael Moore (Lab)	1990
Harry Atkinson	1884	James Bolger (NP)	1990–97
Robert Stout	1884–87	Jenny Shipley (NP)	1997–99
Harry Atkinson	1887–91	Helen Clark (Lab)	1999–2008
John Balance (Lib)	1891–93	John Key (NP)	2008–16
Richard Seddon (Lib)	1893–1906	Bill English (NP)	2016–17
William Hall-Jones (Lib)	1906	Jacinda Ardern (Lab)	2017–

HISTORY IN FIGURES

HOMININS

Modern humanity's most distant ancestors were apelike creatures living in Africa millions of years ago. Our own species, Homo sapiens, only appeared 300,000–200,000 years ago.

AUSTRALOPITHECUS ANAMENSIS (4.2–3.9 MYA)
SAHELANTHROPUS TCHADENSIS (7–6 MYA)
ARDIPITHECUS KADABBA (5.8–5.2 MYA)
ORRORIN TUGENENSIS (6.2–5.6 MYA)
ARDIPITHECUS RAMIDUS (4.5–4.3 MYA)

6 MYA   5 MYA   4 MYA

LARGEST CITIES

The greatest cities of the ancient world still had comparatively small populations. The development of more effective sanitation systems then allowed cities such as Rome to grow to almost 500,000 in the 1st century BCE, a figure scarcely matched until after the Industrial Revolution of the 19th century.

Thebes (Greece) Xian (China) 50,000
Babylon (Persia) 200,000
Rome 450,000
Constantinople 400,000
Baghdad (Abbasid caliphate) 700,000
Nineveh (Assyria) 120,000
Chang'an (China) 400,000
Constantinople 300,000
Ctesiphon (Persia) 500,000
Córdoba (Spain) 450,000

800 BCE   650 BCE   400 BCE   200 BCE   100   350   500   625   800   1000

WORST WARS BY CASUALTY FIGURES

Although World War II was the world's worst war in terms of casualties, many older conflicts were astonishingly bloody considering the smaller armies of the time and the lower populations of the countries in which they were fought.

 1 million casualties

World War II 1939–45 — **63** MILLION

Mongol Conquests 1207–1472 — **40** MILLION

An-Shi Rebellion 755–63 — **35** MILLION

Qing-Ming War 1616–62 — **25** MILLION

Taiping Rebellion 1851–64 — **20** MILLION

Conquests of Timur 1369–1405 — **17** MILLION

World War I 1914–18 — **15** MILLION

Russian Civil War 1917–21 — **9** MILLION

Thirty Years' War 1618–48 — **7** MILLION

Napoleonic Wars 1804–15 — **5** MILLION

Yellow Turban Revolt 184–205 — **5** MILLION

Time of Troubles 1589–1613 — **4** MILLION

The Deluge (Poland–Lithuania) 1655–60 — **3** MILLION

Korean War 1950–53 — **3** MILLION

Vietnam War 1955–75 — **3** MILLION

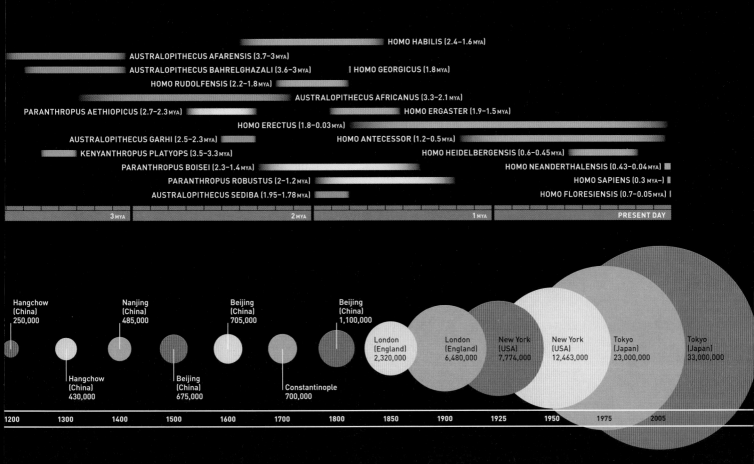

HOMO HABILIS (2.4–1.6 MYA)

AUSTRALOPITHECUS AFARENSIS (3.7–3 MYA)

AUSTRALOPITHECUS BAHRELGHAZALI (3.6–3 BCE) | HOMO GEORGICUS (1.8 MYA)

HOMO RUDOLFENSIS (2.2–1.8 MYA)

AUSTRALOPITHECUS AFRICANUS (3.3–2.1 MYA)

PARANTHROPUS AETHIOPICUS (2.7–2.3 MYA) | HOMO ERGASTER (1.9–1.5 MYA)

HOMO ERECTUS (1.8–0.03 MYA)

AUSTRALOPITHECUS GARHI (2.5–2.3 MYA) | HOMO ANTECESSOR (1.2–0.5 MYA)

KENYANTHROPUS PLATYOPS (3.5–3.3 MYA) | HOMO HEIDELBERGENSIS (0.6–0.45 MYA)

PARANTHROPUS BOISEI (2.3–1.4 MYA) | HOMO NEANDERTHALENSIS (0.43–0.04 MYA)

PARANTHROPUS ROBUSTUS (2–1.2 MYA) | HOMO SAPIENS (0.3 MYA–)

AUSTRALOPITHECUS SEDIBA (1.95–1.78 MYA) | HOMO FLORESIENSIS (0.7–0.05 MYA)

3 MYA   2 MYA   1 MYA   PRESENT DAY

Hangchow (China) 250,000
Nanjing (China) 485,000
Beijing (China) 705,000
Beijing (China) 1,100,000
London (England) 2,320,000
London (England) 6,480,000
New York (USA) 7,774,000
New York (USA) 12,463,000
Tokyo (Japan) 23,000,000
Tokyo (Japan) 33,000,000

Hangchow (China) 430,000
Beijing (China) 675,000
Constantinople 700,000

1200   1300   1400   1500   1600   1700   1800   1850   1900   1925   1950   1975   2005

LONGEST-REIGNING DYNASTIES

Although the life-span of a ruling dynasty has seldom been more than a few hundred years, in exceptional cases a ruling house has held power for more than a thousand, while in Japan the Yamato dynasty has survived for more than 2,500 and still rules today.

Dynasty	
Yamato (Japan)	660 BCE–present (2,671 years)
Hong Bang (Vietnam)	2897–258 BCE (2,639 years)
Gojoseon (Korea)	2333–108 BCE (2,225 years)
Pandyas (South India)	c. 350 BCE–c. 1550 CE (1,900 years)
Sisodia (India)	191–present (1,820 years)
Cham (Vietnam)	192–1832 (1,640 years)
Bagrationi (Georgia)	813–1810 (997 years)
Tu'i Tonga (Tonga)	c. 900–1865 (965 years)
Shilla (Korea)	57 BCE–935 CE (878 years)
Zhou (China)	1046–256 BCE (790 years)
Grimaldi (Monaco)	1297–pres. (714 years)

0   500   1000   1500   2000   2500

YEARS

LONGEST-REIGNING MONARCHS

Some monarchs have had astonishingly long reigns. Although in general this meant they came to the throne as small children and initially exercised little power, those who enjoyed a long reign often brought a period of power and prosperity to their country.

Monarch	
Min hti (Burma)	1279–1374 (95 years)
Pepi II (Egypt)	c. 2278–c. 2184 BCE (94 years)
Taejo (Goguryeo, Korea)	53–146 (93 years)
Sobhuza II (Swaziland)	1899–1982 (82 years)
Jangsu (Goguryeo, Korea)	413–92 (79 years)
Heinrich XI (Reuss-Greiz, Germany)	1723–1800 (77 years)
Christian Augustus (Sulzbach, Germany)	1632–1708 (76 years)
Georg Wilhelm (Schaumburg-Lippe, Germany)	1787–1860 (73 years)
Karl Friedrich (Baden, Germany)	1738–1811 (73 years)
King Louis XIV (France)	1643–1715 (72 years)
Trieu Vieu Vuong (Nanyueh, Vietnam)	207–136 BCE (71 years)

0   25   50   75   100

YEARS

WARS

The human story is one of conflict. Disputes over territory, religion, and governance have escalated into war throughout history, and while the stories of great battles and great commanders make compelling reading, the tragic consequences of war should never be forgotten.

■ MAJOR WARS

WAR	DATE	OPPOSING FORCES
Greek–Persian Wars	490–448 BCE	Coalition of Greek city-states including Athens and Sparta v. Persia
Peloponnesian War	431–404 BCE	Athens and allies v. Sparta and allies
Alexander the Great's Conquests	334–323 BCE	Macedonia v. Persian Empire
First Punic War	264–241 BCE	Rome and allies v. Carthage and allies
Second Punic War	218–202 BCE	Rome and allies v. Carthage and allies
Third Punic War	149–146 BCE	Rome and allies v. Carthage and allies
First Roman Civil War	49–44 BCE	Julius Caesar v. Pompey the Great
Second Roman Civil War	33–31 BCE	Octavian (Augustus) v. Mark Antony
Byzantine–Seljuk Wars	1064–71, 1110–17, 1158–76	Byzantines v. Seljuk Turks
The Crusades	1095–1272	Various Western European Christian armies v. Muslim states of the eastern Mediterranean and Egypt
Mongol Conquests	1206–1405	Mongols v. various European and Asian peoples
Hundred Years' War	1337–1453	English (and Burgundians) v. French
Onin War	1467–77	Yamana clan v. Hosokawa clan
The Italian Wars	1494–95, 1521–25, 1526–30, 1535–38, 1542–44	Italian city-states and Holy Roman Empire v. French and Italian allies
Wars of Japanese Unification	1560–1603	Oda Nobunaga, Toyotomi Hideyoshi, Tokugawa Ieyasu and allies v. opposing *daimyo* (warlord) clans
Eighty Years' War (The Dutch Revolt)	1568–1648	Dutch v. Philip II of Spain and allies in southern Netherlands
War of the Three Kingdoms (The English Civil War)	1642–51	Charles I and Royalists v. Parliamentarians
The Thirty Years' War	1618–48	Imperial Catholic alliance v. mainly Protestant powers plus France
The Great Northern War	1700–21	Sweden v. Denmark, Saxony, Poland–Lithuania, Russia
The Seven Years' War	1756–63	Britain and Prussia v. France, Austria, Russia, Saxony, Sweden
American Revolutionary War	1775–83	Britain v. American colonists (and French allies)
French Revolutionary Wars	1792–1802	France v. varying coalitions including Britain, Austria, Prussia, Russia
The Napoleonic Wars	1803–15	France v. varying coalitions including Britain, Austria, Prussia, Russia
Crimean War	1853–56	Russia v. Ottoman Turkey, Britain, France
The Indian Mutiny	1857–58	British v. native Indian forces
American Civil War	1861–65	The Union v. the Confederacy
Franco–Prussian War	1870–71	France v. Prussia

WAR	DATE	OPPOSING FORCES
Taiping Rebellion	1850–64	Chinese central (Qing) government v. Taiping rebels
Boer Wars (South African Wars)	1880–81, 1899–1902	British v. Boers (Afrikaners)
Balkan Wars	1912–13	(First) Bulgaria, Greece, Serbia, Montenegro v. Ottoman Turkey (Second) Bulgaria v. Turkey, Serbia, Greece, Romania
World War I	1914–18	Entente (Britain, France, Italy, Russia, US and others) v. Central Powers (Germany, Austro-Hungary, and others)
Russian Civil War	1918–21	Bolsheviks v. "White" Russians
Spanish Civil War	1936–39	Nationalists v. Republicans
World War II	1939–45	Allies (British, French, and others) v. Axis (German, Japanese, Italians to 1943, and others)
Chinese Civil War	1945–49	Communists v. Nationalists (Kuomintang)
Korean War	1950–53	North Koreans and Chinese v. South Koreans and UN force (including Americans, Australians, and British)
French Indochina War	1946–54	French v. Vietnamese nationalists (Viet Minh)
Arab–Israeli Wars	1948–73	Israel v. Egypt, Syria, Jordan, Lebanon, Iraq, and Palestinians
Vietnam War	1961–75	South Vietnamese, Americans, and Australians v. North Vietnamese (Viet Cong)
Iran–Iraq War	1980–88	Iraq v. Iran
Gulf Wars	1990–91, 2003	Iraq v. international coalition led by US
Afghanistan War	2001–	US-led coalition v. Taliban
Boko Haram Insurgency	2009–	Nigerian government v. Boko Haram
Syrian Civil War	2011–	The government of President Bashar al-Assad, along with its allies, v. various forces opposing the government

EXPLORERS

The "discoveries" of many early explorers were actually of lands that had thriving indigenous societies, which often led to disastrous results. Yet we can still admire the imagination and tenacity of those who risked their lives journeying into territory completely unknown to them.

■ NOTABLE EXPLORERS

NAME	LIVED	ORIGIN	EXPEDITIONS/DISCOVERIES
Hanno	Active 5th century BCE	Carthage	Sailed down the west coast of Africa (c. 470 BCE)
Erik the Red	c. 950–1002	Norway	Explored the coast of Greenland (985)
Leif Eriksson	Active 11th century	Norway	Discovered Vinland, part of North America (c. 1000)
Marco Polo	1254–1324	Italy	Traveled extensively in China and along the Silk Road (1275–92)
Ibn Battuta	c. 1304–68	Morocco	Explored the Sahara, Arabia, India, Central Asia, China, and Southeast Asia
Dinís Diaz	Active mid-15th century	Portugal	Discovered the Cape Verde islands off the west coast of Africa (1445)
Bartolomeu Dias	c. 1450–1500	Portugal	Rounded Africa's Cape of Good Hope (1488)
Vasco da Gama	c. 1469–1524	Portugal	Sailed around Africa's Cape of Good Hope and reached India (1497–98)

NAME	LIVED	ORIGIN	EXPEDITIONS/DISCOVERIES
Christopher Columbus	1451–1506	Italy	Discovered the Americas, landing in the Bahamas (1492); discovered the mainland of South America (1498)
John Cabot	c. 1450–99	Italy	Discovered mainland North America (1497)
Pedro Alvarez Cabral	c. 1467–1520	Portugal	Discovered Brazil (1500)
Amerigo Vespucci	1454–1512	Italy	Explored the coastline of South America (1501)
Afonso de Albuquerque	1453–1515	Portugal	Reached India via Zanzibar (1503–04)
Vasco Núñez de Balboa	1475–1519	Spain	First European to navigate the South Sea (Pacific Ocean), from Panama (1513)
Juan Ponce de Leon	c. 1460–1521	Spain	Discovered Florida (1513)
Hernán Cortes	1485–1547	Spain	Led the conquest of the Aztec Empire in Mexico (1518–22)
Ferdinand Magellan	c. 1480–1521	Portugal	Explored the Philippines; partially circumnavigated the globe (1520–21)
Francisco Pizarro	1475–1541	Spain	Led the conquest of the Inca Empire in Peru (1530–33)
Jacques Cartier	1491–1557	France	Explored the Gulf of St. Lawrence and St. Lawrence River (1535–36)
Francisco Vásquez de Coronado	1510–54	Spain	Reached the Grand Canyon in 1540
García López de Cárdenas	Active 1540s	Spain	Voyaged to Russia via the North Cape (1553–56)
Martin Frobisher	c. 1535–94	England	Reached the Frobisher Strait (Canada) while searching for the Northwest Passage (1576)
Francis Drake	c. 1540–96	England	Circumnavigated the globe (1580)
John Davis	c. 1550–1605	England	Explored Greenland, discovered the Davis Strait (1585) while searching for the Northwest Passage
Willem Barents	1550–97	Netherlands	Searched for the Northeast Passage (1594–97)
Walter Raleigh	1552–1618	England	Undertook numerous voyages to America; attempted, unsuccessfully, to found a colony in Virginia (1584)
Cornelis de Houtman	1565–99	Netherlands	Led first Dutch expedition to the East Indies; sailed the south coast of Java (1598)
Samuel de Champlain	1567–1635	France	Explored the St. Lawrence River (1603); founded Quebec (1608)
Henry Hudson	c. 1565–1611	England	Discovered Hudson Bay (Canada) (1610)
William Baffin	1584–1622	England	Explored Baffin Bay, part of the Northwest Passage (1616)
Abel Tasman	1603–c.1659	Netherlands	Reached New Zealand and Tasmania (1642)
William Dampier	1651–1715	England	Crossed the Pacific Ocean (1683)
Vitus Bering	1681–1741	Denmark	Explored Siberia (1733–41)
James Bruce	1730–94	Britain	Explored the Blue Nile; claimed to have found the source of the Nile (1768–74)
James Cook	1728–79	Britain	Mapped the New Zealand and Australian coasts (1769); made first Australian landfall, at Botany Bay, New South Wales (1770)
Antoine Bruni d'Entrecasteaux	1739–93	France	Surveyed the South Pacific (1791–93)
Mungo Park	1771–1806	Britain	Explored the Niger River (1795–96)
George Bass	1771–1803	Britain	Explored the coastline of southeastern Australia (1795–98)
Friedrich Alexander von Humboldt	1769–1859	Germany	Explored modern Venezuela and the Orinoco River (1799–1800)

NAME	LIVED	ORIGIN	EXPEDITIONS/DISCOVERIES
Matthew Flinders	1774–1814	Britain	Circumnavigated Australia (1801–03)
Meriwether Lewis	1774–1809	US	Led the first transcontinental expedition across the US (1804–05)
William Clark	1770–1838	US	Co-leader of expedition with Lewis (above)
Fabian von Bellingshausen	1778–1852	Estonia	Early explorer of the Antarctic (1819–21)
Alexander Gordon Laing	1793–1826	Britain	First European to reach Timbuktu, in Mali (1826)
William Edward Parry	1790–1855	Britain	Made an early attempt to reach the North Pole overland (1827)
James Clark Ross	1800–62	US	Made an extensive exploration of the Antarctic, discovering the Ross Sea and Ross Ice Shelf (1841)
John Franklin	1786–1847	Britain	Searched for the Northwest Passage; never returned from his expedition (1847)
Richard Francis Burton	1821–90	Britain	Traveled in Arabia and reached Medina and Mecca (1853)
David Livingstone	1813–73	Britain	Discovered the Victoria Falls on the Zambezi River (1855)
Robert O'Hara Burke	1820–61	Ireland	Led an ill-fated expedition to explore the Australian interior (1860–61)
Henry Morton Stanley	1841–1904	Britain	Undertook voyages down the Congo (1874)
Fridtjof Nansen	1861–1930	Norway	Crossed Greenland (1888)
Sven Hedin	1865–1962	Sweden	Explored Central Asia and discovered lost cities in the Taklamakan desert (1893–97)
Salomon Andrée	1854–97	Sweden	Attempted to balloon over the Arctic; disappeared during the flight (1897)
Otto Nordenskjöld	1869–1928	Sweden	Spent the winter in Antarctica (1901–03)
Francis Younghusband	1863–1942	Britain	Led an expedition that reached Lhasa in Tibet (1903–04)
Aurel Stein	1862–1943	Hungary	Explored Central Asia and located an ancient complex at Dunhuang (1906–08)
Robert Peary	1856–1920	US	Claimed to have reached North Pole (1909)
Roald Amundsen	1872–1928	Norway	First man to reach the South Pole (1911)
Robert Falcon Scott	1868–1912	Britain	Lost out to Roald Amundsen in the race to reach the South Pole (1911–12)
Ernest Shackleton	1874–1922	Britain	Led an expedition to cross Antarctica, but became stranded for four months on Elephant Island (1914)
Richard Byrd	1888–1957	US	Completed the first overflight of the North Pole (1926)
Vivian Fuchs	1908–99	Britain	Completed the first land crossing of the Antarctic continent (1958)
Wilfred Thesiger	1910–2003	Britain	Intrepid traveler who twice crossed the Empty Quarter of Arabia
Jacques-Yves Cousteau	1910–97	France	Marine ecologist who dedicated his life to deep-water oceanic exploration
Thor Heyerdahl	1914–2002	Norway	Sought to prove theories of prehistoric migration by sea with long voyages using rafts built from natural materials
Edmund Hillary	1919–2008	New Zealand	Completed the first ascent of Mount Everest in the Himalayas (1953)
Yuri Gagarin	1934–68	USSR	Vostok 1 (April 12, 1961); first man in space, and first to orbit the Earth
Alan Shepard	1923–98	US	Freedom 7 (May 5, 1961); first American in space, and later fifth man to walk on Moon
Gherman Titov	1935–2000	USSR	Vostok 2 (August 6, 1961); youngest person in space at 25 years old, and second man to orbit the Earth
Valentina Tereshkova	b.1937	USSR	Vostok 6 (June 16, 1963); first woman in space
Alexei Leonov	b.1943	USSR	Voskhod 2 (March 18, 1965); first tethered spacewalk

NOTABLE EXPLORERS (CONTINUED)

NAME	LIVED	ORIGIN	EXPEDITIONS/DISCOVERIES
Neil Armstrong	b. 1930	US	Apollo 11 (July 20, 1969); first man to walk on the Moon
Vladimír Remek	b. 1948	Czechoslovakia	Soyuz 28 (March 2, 1978); first person in space from a country other than the US or USSR
Sigmund Jähn	b. 1937	German Democratic Republic	Soyuz 31 (August 26, 1978); first German in space
Jean-Loup Chrétien	b. 1938	France	Soyuz T-11 (June 24, 1982); first French person in space
Ulf Merbold	b. 1941	Germany	STS-9 28 (November 1983); first ESA astronaut, second German in space
Rakesh Sharma	b. 1949	India	Soyuz T-11 (April 3, 1984); first Indian in space
Sultan Salman al Saud	b. 1956	Saudi Arabia	STS-56 (June 17, 1985); first Arab (and first Muslim) in space
Mamoru Mori	b. 1948	Japan	STS-47 (September 12, 1992); first Japanese person in space
Valeri Polyakov	b. 1942	Russia	Soyuz TM-18 (January 8, 1998); longest space flight at 437 days
John Glenn	b. 1921	US	STS-95 (October 29, 1998); oldest person in space at 77 years old—previously flew on Friendship 7 in 1962
Dennis Tito	b. 1940	US	Soyuz TM 32 (April 28, 2001); first "space tourist"
Yang Liwei	b. 1965	China	Shenzhou 5 (October 15, 2003); first Chinese person in space
Sergei Krikalev	b. 1958	Russia	Soyuz TMA-6 (October 11, 2005); reached most time spent in space (803 days 9 hours 39 minutes)

INVENTIONS AND DISCOVERIES

The modern world is very different from the world of our ancestors. Over the course of human existence, basic human needs—from the need to survive to the urge to obtain knowledge—have produced tens of thousands of inventions and discoveries. These have transformed both the way we function and the way we think, and have made us distinct from the rest of the animal kingdom.

NOTABLE INVENTIONS AND DISCOVERIES

INVENTION/DISCOVERY	DATE	ORIGINATOR	PLACE OF ORIGIN
Stone tools	c. 2.75 MYA	Early humans	Africa
Control of fire	c. 400,000 YA	Early humans	Africa
Boat	c. 50,000 YA	Early migrants	Australasia
Mining	c. 40,000 YA	Paleolithic humans	Europe
Permanent shelters	c. 28,000 YA	Paleolithic humans	Eastern Europe
Pottery vessels	c. 14,000 BCE	Jomon people	Ancient Japan
Farming	c. 10,000 BCE	West Asian peoples	Mesopotamia
Irrigation	c. 5000 BCE	West Asian peoples	Mesopotamia
Horse domestication	c. 4500 BCE	Andronovo culture	Europe/Asia
Plough	c. 4000 BCE	Sumerian people	Mesopotamia
Wheeled transport	c. 3500 BCE	Sumerian people	Sumer
Silk weaving	c. 3500 BCE	Chinese peoples	Ancient China
Writing	c. 3300 BCE	Sumerian people	Sumer/Egypt
Calendar	c. 3000 BCE	Babylonians	Babylonia

INVENTION/DISCOVERY	DATE	ORIGINATOR	PLACE OF ORIGIN
Papyrus scroll	c. 2600 BCE	Imhotep (attributed)	Ancient Egypt
Plumbing	c. 2500 BCE	Indus Valley civilization	Indus (Pakistan)
Law code	c. 1755 BCE	King Hammurabi	Babylonia
Alphabet	14th century BCE	Semitic people (slaves of the Egyptians)	Ancient Egypt
Magnetism	c. 1000 BCE	Thales of Miletus (attributed)	Ancient Greece
Coinage	c. 600 BCE	Lydian people	Ancient Turkey
World map	6th century BCE	Babylonians	Babylonia
Planetary models	c. 360 BCE	Eudoxus of Cnidus	Ancient Greece
Rotation of the Earth	c. 350 BCE	Heraclides Ponticus	Ancient Greece
Steel production	c. 200 BCE	Han dynasty	India/China
Compound pulley	c. 200 BCE	Archimedes	Ancient Greece
Encyclopaedia	77	Pliny the Elder	Roman Empire
Paper	c. 105	Cai Lun	Ancient China
Compass	250	Chinese peoples	Ancient China
Concept of zero/decimal system	c. 590–650	Brahmagupta	India
Astrolabe	c. 800	Muhammad al-Fazari	Arabia
University	859	Fatimah al-Fihri	Morocco
Star chart	c. 1000–50	Abu Rayhan Biruni	Persia
Pendulum	c. 000	Ibn Yunus	Egypt
Magnifying glass	c. 1021	Ibn al-Haytham	Persia
Moveable type	c. 1045	Bi Sheng	China
Mechanical clock	1088	Su Song	China
Algebra	1202	Fibonacci	Italy
The scientific method	c. 1220–35	Robert Grosseteste	England
Printing press	c. 1445	Johannes Gutenburg	Germany
Terrestrial globe	c. 1490	Martin Behaim	Bohemia
Sun-centred Universe	1503–43	Copernicus	Italy
Compound microscope	c. 1595	Hans Lippershey, Zacharias Janssen	Netherlands
Laws of planetary motion	1609–19	Johannes Kepler	Germany
Newspaper	1609	Johann Carolus	Germany
Refracting telescope	1609	Galileo Galilei	Italy
Mechanical calculator	1642	Wilhelm Schickard	Germany
Barometer	1643	Evangelista Torricelli	Italy
Atmospheric pressure	1647–48	Blaise Pascal	France
Microscopic life	1673	Antoni van Leeuwenhoek	Netherlands
Laws of motion	1687	Sir Isaac Newton	England
Seed drill	1701	Jethro Tull	England
Steam piston engine	1712	Thomas Newcomen	Britain
Marine chronometer	1735	John Harrison	Britain
Lightning rod	1752	Benjamin Franklin	US
Watt steam engine	1776	James Watt	Britain
Oxygen	1777	Antoine Lavoisier	France
Hot air balloon	1783	Montgolfier brothers	France
Threshing machine	1786	Andrew Meikle	Britain
Battery	1800	Alessandro Volta	Italy
Bicycle	1818	Karl Drais	Germany
Permanent photography	c. 1820	Joseph Nicéphore Niépce	France
Braille alphabet	1821	Louis Braille	France
Electric motor	1821	Michael Faraday	Britain

INVENTION/DISCOVERY	DATE	ORIGINATOR	PLACE OF ORIGIN
Programmable computer	1822	Charles Babbage	Britain
Electromagnet	1823	William Sturgeon	Britain
Internal combustion engine	1826	Samuel Morey	US
Water turbine	1827	Claude Burdin, Benoît Fourneyron	France
Steam locomotive	1829	George Stephenson	Britain
Electrical generator	1831	Michael Faraday	Britain
Refrigerator	1834	Jacob Perkins	US/Britain
Vulcanization of rubber	1837	Charles Goodyear	US
Polystyrene	1839	Eduard Simon	Germany
Undersea telegraph cable	1858	Charles Wheatstone	Britain
Theory of evolution	1859	Charles Darwin	Britain
Pasteurization	1862	Louis Pasteur, Claude Bernard	France
Laws of heredity	1866	Gregor Mendel	Austria
Dynamite	1867	Alfred Nobel	Sweden
Periodic table	1869	Dmitri Mendeleev	Russia
Telephone	1876	Alexander Graham Bell	Britain
Phonograph	1877	Thomas Edison	US
Incandescent light bulb	1878	Joseph Wilson Swan	Britain
Automobile	1885	Karl Benz	Germany
Petrol engine	1886	Gottlieb Daimler	Germany
Wireless communication	1893	Nikolai Tesla	Austria-Hungary
Radio telegraph	1895	Guglielmo Marconi	Italy
Cinematography	1895	Auguste & Louis Lumière	France
Radium	1898	Marie & Pierre Curie	Poland/France
Quantum theory	1900	Max Planck	Germany
Rigid dirigible airship	1900	Ferdinand Graf von Zeppelin	Germany
Airplane (controlled powered flight)	1903	Wright brothers	US
Conditioned reflexes	1904	Ivan Pavlov	Russia
Theory of relativity	1905	Albert Einstein	Switzerland
Bakelite plastic	1909	Leo Baekeland	Belgium
Stainless steel	1913	Harry Brearley	Britain
Structure of the atom	1913	Niels Bohr	Denmark
Television	1925	John Logie Baird	Britain
Law of the expanding universe	1929	Edwin Hubble	US
Nylon	1935	Wallace Carothers	US
RADAR	1935	Robert Watson-Watt	Britain
Jet engine	1937	Frank Whittle	Britain
Ball-point pen	1938	László Bíró	Hungary
Nuclear reactor	1942	Enrico Fermi	Italy /US
Aqualung	1943	Jacques Cousteau, Emile Gagnan	France
Atomic bomb	1945	J. Robert Oppenheimer	US
Photosynthesis	1946	Melvin Calvin	US
Commercial jet airliner	1948	Vickers	Britain
Radiocarbon dating	1949	Willard Libby	US
Big Bang theory	1949	George Gamow, Ralph Alpher, Robert Herman	US
Structure of DNA	1953	Francis Crick, Rosalind Franklin, James D. Watson	Britain/US

INVENTION/DISCOVERY	DATE	ORIGINATOR	PLACE OF ORIGIN
Communications satellite	1958	Kenneth Masterman-Smith	US
LASER	1960	Theodore H. Maiman	US
Plate tectonics	1967	Dan McKenzie	Britain
Microprocessor	1969	Intel	US
Email	1971	Ray Tomlinson	US
Genetic modification	1973	Stanley Norman Cohen, Herbert Boyer	US
Personal computer	1973	Xerox PARC	US
Cellphone	1973	Martin Cooper (Motorola)	US
Compact disc	1980	Philips Electronic/ Sony Corporation	Netherlands/ Japan
World Wide Web	1990	Tim Berners-Lee	Britain
Global Positioning System	1995	US Department of Defense	US
Genetic cloning	1996	Ian Wilmut, Keith Campbell	Britain
Portable media player	2001	Apple	US
Higgs boson	2012	CERN	Switzerland
Gravitational waves (observed)	2015	LIGO	US

PHILOSOPHY AND RELIGION

The earliest inquiries into the nature and meaning of life come from the founders of the great Eastern religions. Since their time, Western philosophers have journeyed to the outer limits of thought and understanding, posing questions that challenge our most fundamental beliefs.

Originating from almost every corner of the globe, the world's great faiths are as diverse as its cultures. Some have their origin in prehistoric times, yet the 20th century saw the emergence of several new religions that have attracted followers in their millions.

GREAT THINKERS

NAME	LIVED	ORIGIN	IDEAS/KEY WORK
Siddhartha Gautama (Buddha)	c. 563–483 BCE	India	Founder of Buddhism as a path to achieving nirvana (spiritual enlightenment) and thus release from the earthly cycle of reincarnation.
Laozi	Active 6th century BCE	China	Founder of Daoism, concerning an individual's approach to life. *Dao De Jing*.
Confucius	551–479 BCE	China	Founder of Confucianism: social harmony is promoted via social conventions and practices.
Pythagoras	c. 550– c. 500 BCE	Greece	Polymath interested in esoteric knowledge (that he made available to only a few initiates) and the mystical power of numbers.
Socrates	c. 469–399 BCE	Greece	One of the founders of Western philosophy, to whom this quote is attributed: "A life unexamined is not worth living." No surviving writings.
Plato	c. 427–347 BCE	Greece	A pupil of Socrates; argued that everything we perceive is a mere shadow of its abstract, ideal Form. *The Republic* (c. 360 BCE).
Aristotle	384–322 BCE	Greece	Wide-ranging philosopher with a special interest in logical classification. *Metaphysics* (350 BCE).
Plotinus	205–270	Greece / Roman Empire	Founder of Neoplatonism, a development of Plato's original ideas. *Enneads* (c. 253–70).
St. Augustine of Hippo	354–430	North Africa/ Roman Empire	Transmitted Platonism through Christian theology. *The City of God* (413–26).

GREAT THINKERS (CONTINUED)

NAME	LIVED	ORIGIN	IDEAS/KEY WORK
St. Thomas Aquinas	1225–74	Italy	Greatest Medieval religious philosopher. *Summa Theologiae* (1259–69).
Niccolò Machiavelli	1469–1527	Italy	Argued that the state should promote the common good, irrespective of any moral evaluation of its acts. *The Prince* (1513).
Francis Bacon	1561–1626	England	Recognized that scientific knowledge could procure power over nature. *Novum Organum* (1620).
Thomas Hobbes	1588–1679	England	Father of English political philosophy, the study of how societies are organized. *Leviathan* (1651).
René Descartes	1596–1650	France	Overturned Medieval and Renaissance scholasticism. *Meditations* (1641).
Baruch Spinoza	1632–77	Netherlands	One of the most important 17th-century Rationalists, arguing that knowledge of the world can be gained through reason. *Tractatus Theologico-Politicus* (1670).
John Locke	1632–1704	England	Proponent of empiricism, the view that all knowledge of anything that actually exists must be derived from experience. *Treatises of Government* (1690).
Gottfried Wilhelm Leibniz	1646–1716	Germany	Mathematican and rationalist philosopher. *Monadology* (1714).
George Berkeley	1685–1753	England	Great empiricist who developed an idealist metaphysical system, maintaining that reality ultimately consists of something nonmaterial. *Principles of Human Knowledge* (1710).
David Hume	1711–76	Britain	Leading sceptic of metaphysics, the philosophy concerned with the ultimate nature of what exists. *Treatise of Human Nature* (1734–37).
Jean-Jacques Rousseau	1712–78	Switzerland	Proponent of the sovereignty of the citizen body. *The Social Contract, or Principles of Political Right* (1762).
Immanuel Kant	1724–1804	Germany	Sought to establish the authority of reason by critical examination. *Critique of Pure Reason* (1781).
Thomas Paine	1737–1809	Britain	Governments must respect the natural rights of their citizens. *The Rights of Man* (1791–92).
G. W. F. Hegel	1770–1831	Germany	Most influential of the German Idealists. *The Phenomenology of Spirit* (1807).
Karl Marx	1818–83	Germany	Radical social theorist and philosopher of Communism. *Das Kapital* (1867).
Arthur Schopenhauer	1788–1860	Germany	Espoused transcendental idealism, the belief that human experience of things consists of how they appear to us. *The World as Will and Representation* (1818).
Søren Kierkegaard	1813–55	Denmark	A forerunner of Existentialism, stressing the individual's unique position as a self-determining agent. *Concluding Unscientific Postscript to Philosophical Fragments* (1846).
Friedrich Nietzsche	1844–1900	Germany	Rejected religious and metaphysical interpretations of the human condition in favor of the principle of the "Superman." *Thus Spake Zarathustra* (1883–85).
Bertrand Russell	1872–1970	Britain	Founder of analytic philosophy, emphasizing clarity and argument. *Principia Mathematica* (1910–13).
Ludwig Wittgenstein	1889–1951	Austria	Most prominent analytical philosopher. *Tractatus Logico-Philosophicus* (1921).
Jean-Paul Sartre	1905–80	France	Leader of the Existentialist movement, which focused on the totality of human freedom. *Being and Nothingness* (1943).

MAJOR WORLD FAITHS

NAME	PLACE/DATE	ADHERENTS	FOUNDER	TEXT
Chinese traditional religion	Unknown, prehistoric	400 million	Indigenous	n/a
Hinduism	India, prehistoric	900 million	Indigenous	The Vedas, Upanishads, and Sanskrit epics
Shinto	Japan, prehistoric	3–4 million	Indigenous	*Kojiki, Nihon-gi*
Voodoo	West Africa, unknown	8 million	Indigenous	n/a
Judaism	Israel, c. 1300 BCE	15 million	Abraham; Moses	Hebrew Bible; Talmud
Zoroastrianism	Iran, 6th century BCE	200,000	Zoroaster	The Avesta
Daoism	China, c. 550 BCE	20 million	Laozi	*Dao De Jing*
Jainism	India, c. 550 BCE	4 million	Mahavira	Mahavira's teachings
Buddhism	Northeast India, c. 520 BCE	375 million	Siddhartha Gautama (Buddha)	Pali canon, Mahayana sutras
Confucianism	China, 6th/5th centuries BCE	5–6 million	Confucius	The Four Books and Five Classics
Christianity	Israel, c. 30	2,000 million	Jesus Christ	The Bible (Old and New Testaments)
Islam	Saudi Arabia, revealed in 7th century	1,500 million	n/a; Muhammad is Prophet	The Qu'ran (scripture); Hadith (tradition)
Sikhism	Punjab, India, c. 1500	23 million	Guru Nanak	Adi Granth (Guru Granth Sahib)
Church of Jesus Christ of Latter-Day Saints (Mormons)	New York, 1830	13 million	Joseph Smith	The Bible; *Book of Mormon*
Tenrikyo	Japan, 1838	1 million	Nakayama Miki	*Mikigaurata, Ofudesaki, Osashizu*
Baha'i Faith	Tehran, Iran, 1863	5–7 million	Baha'u'llah	Writings of Baha'u'llah
Church of Christ (Scientist)	New York, USA, 1879	Up to 400,000	Mary Baker Eddy	The Bible; *Science and Health with Key to the Scriptures*
Cao Dai	Vietnam, 1926	8 million	Ngo Van Chieu	Cao Dai Canon
Rastafari	Jamaica, 1930s	1 million	Haile Selassie I	*Holy Piby*
Family Federation for World Peace and Unification	South Korea, 1954	3 million (official figure)	Sun Myung Moon	*Sun Myung Moon, the Divine Principle*
Wicca	1950s, but based on ancient beliefs	1–3 million	Gerald Gardner	n/a
Falun Gong	China, 1992	10 million	Li Hongzhi	Writings of master Li, including *Zhuan Falun*

CULTURE AND LEARNING

From the poets, sculptors, and painters of the ancient world to the commentators and conceptual artists of the 21st century, the work of writers and artists provides an invaluable insight into the thoughts and aspirations of these the great civilizations of the past. In Europe, from the 11th century, and in the succeeding centuries on other continents, the talents of many of these people were nurtured in the universities that sprang up as conduits for the transmission of learning.

POETS, PLAYWRIGHTS, AND NOVELISTS

Literature gives us a special insight into the past. Though the plots of novels and plays may be invented, the characters speak and behave in ways that reflect the preoccupations, social mores, and artistic conventions of their time, and in many works, a fictional chain of events plays out against a rich background of verifiable historical happenings.

NAME	LIVED	ORIGIN	GENRE	NOTABLE WORKS
Homer	8th century BCE	Ancient Greece	Poet	Odyssey (8th century BCE)
Aeschylus	c. 525–456 BCE	Ancient Greece	Playwright	Seven Against Thebes (c.467 BCE)
Sophocles	c. 496–406 BCE	Ancient Greece	Playwright	Antigone (c.442 BCE)
Euripides	c. 484–406 BCE	Ancient Greece	Playwright	Medea (c.431 BCE)
Aristophanes	c. 448–388 BCE	Ancient Greece	Playwright	The Frogs (c.405 BCE)
Valmiki	c. 400–200 BCE	Ancient India	Poet	Ramayana (c.400–200 BCE)
Virgil	70–19 BCE	Roman Empire	Poet	Aeneid (c.29–19 BCE)
Ovid	43 BCE–c.17 CE	Roman Empire	Poet	Metamorphoses (8 CE)
Murasaki Shikibu	c. 978–1014	Japan	Novelist	The Tale of Genji (c.1001–10)
Dante Alighieri	1265–1321	Italy	Poet	Divine Comedy (c.1321)
Petrarch	1304–74	Italy	Poet	Canzoniere (1327–68)
Geoffrey Chaucer	1343–1400	England	Poet	The Canterbury Tales (1387–1400)
Miguel de Cervantes	1547–1616	Spain	Novelist/poet/playwright	Don Quixote (1605)
William Shakespeare	1564–1616	England	Playwright/poet	Romeo and Juliet (c.1591–95)
John Milton	1608–74	England	Poet	Paradise Lost (1667)
Molière	1622–73	France	Playwright	Le Misanthrope (1666)
Jean Racine	1639–99	France	Playwright	Phèdre (1677)
Jonathan Swift	1667–1745	Ireland	Novelist/essayist	Gulliver's Travels (1726)
Xueqin Cao	c. 1715–63	China	Novelist	Dream of the Red Chamber (1791)
Johann Wolfgang von Goethe	1749–1832	Germany	Novelist/playwright	Faust (1808)
William Wordsworth	1770–1850	Britain	Poet	The Prelude (1799)
Jane Austen	1775–1817	Britain	Novelist	Pride and Prejudice (1813)
John Keats	1795–1821	Britain	Poet	Endymion (1818)
Alexander Pushkin	1799–1837	Russia	Poet/novelist	Eugene Onegin (1828)
Honoré de Balzac	1799–1850	France	Novelist	La Comédie Humaine (1827–47)
Alexandre Dumas	1802–70	France	Novelist	The Three Musketeers (1844)
Victor Hugo	1802–85	France	Novelist	Les Misérables (1862)
Ralph Waldo Emerson	1803–82	US	Essayist/poet	The Conduct of Life (1860)

NAME	LIVED	ORIGIN	GENRE	NOTABLE WORKS
Hans Christian Andersen	1805–75	Denmark	Novelist	Fairy Tales (1835–37)
Henry Longfellow	1807–82	US	Poet	Hiawatha (1855)
Charles Dickens	1812–70	Britain	Novelist	Great Expectations (1860–61)
Ivan Turgenev	1818–83	Russia	Novelist/playwright	Fathers and Sons (1862)
George Eliot	1819–80	Britain	Novelist	The Mill on the Floss (1860)
Fyodor Dostoyevsky	1821–81	Russia	Novelist	Crime and Punishment (1866)
Walt Whitman	1819–92	US	Poet	Leaves of Grass (1855–89)
Gustave Flaubert	1821–80	France	Novelist	Madame Bovary (1857)
Henrik Ibsen	1828–1906	Norway	Playwright	Peer Gynt (1867)
Leo Tolstoy	1828–1910	Russia	Novelist	War and Peace (1865–69)
Mark Twain	1835–1910	US	Novelist	Huckleberry Finn (1885)
Thomas Hardy	1840–1928	Britain	Novelist	Tess of the d'Urbervilles (1891)
Henry James	1843–1916	US	Novelist	The Bostonians (1886)
August Strindberg	1849–1912	Sweden	Playwright	The Dance of Death (1901)
George Bernard Shaw	1856–1950	Ireland	Playwright	Man and Superman (1903)
Joseph Conrad	1857–1924	Poland	Novelist	Heart of Darkness (1902)
Anton Chekhov	1860–1904	Russia	Playwright	The Cherry Orchard (1904)
Rabindranath Tagore	1861–1941	India	Poet/playwright	Gitanjali, Song Offerings (1912)
Edith Wharton	1862–1937	US	Novelist	The Age of Innocence (1920)
William Butler Yeats	1865–1939	Ireland	Poet	The Wild Swans at Coole (1917)
Marcel Proust	1871–1922	France	Novelist	Remembrance of Things Past (1912–27)
Robert Frost	1874–1963	US	Poet	Mountain Interval (1916)
Thomas Mann	1875–1955	Gemany	Novelist	Death in Venice (1913)
Hermann Hesse	1877–1962	Germany	Novelist	The Glass Bead Game (1945)
James Joyce	1882–1941	Ireland	Novelist	Ulysses (1922)
Virginia Woolf	1882–1941	Britain	Novelist	Mrs Dalloway (1925)
Franz Kafka	1883–1924	Czech Republic	Novelist	The Metamorphosis (1916)
D.H. Lawrence	1885–1930	Britain	Novelist/poet	Sons and Lovers (1913)
Ezra Pound	1885–1972	US	Poet	The Cantos (1915–62)
T.S. Eliot	1888–1965	US/Britain	Poet/playwright	The Waste Land (1922)
Karel Capek	1890–1938	Czech Republic	Playwright	R.U.R. (1920)
Boris Pasternak	1890–1960	Russia	Novelist	Doctor Zhivago (1957)
Mikhail Bulgakov	1891–1940	Russia	Novelist	The Master and Margarita (1928)
William Faulkner	1897–1962	US	Novelist	The Sound and the Fury (1929)
Bertolt Brecht	1898–1956	Germany	Playwright	Mother Courage (1938)
Federico García Lorca	1898–1936	Spain	Playwright	The House of Bernarda Alba (1936)
Ernest Hemingway	1899–1961	US	Novelist	The Old Man and the Sea (1952)
Jorge Luis Borges	1899–1986	Argentina	Novelist	Labyrinths (1953)
Vladimir Nabokov	1899–1977	Russia/US	Novelist	Lolita (1958)
John Steinbeck	1902–68	US	Novelist	The Grapes of Wrath (1939)
George Orwell	1903–50	Britain	Novelist	Nineteen Eighty-Four (1949)
Samuel Beckett	1906–89	Ireland	Playwright/novelist	Waiting for Godot (1954)

POETS, PLAYWRIGHTS, AND NOVELISTS (CONTINUED)

NAME	LIVED	ORIGIN	GENRE	NOTABLE WORKS
W. H. Auden	1907–73	Britain	Poet	The Sea and the Mirror (1944)
Naguib Mahfouz	1911–2006	Egypt	Novelist	The Cairo Trilogy (1956–57)
Albert Camus	1913–60	France	Novelist	The Plague (1947)
Saul Bellow	1915–2005	Canada	Novelist	Humboldt's Gift (1975)
Arthur Miller	1915–2005	US	Playwright	Death of a Salesman (1949)
Alexander Solzhenitsyn	1918–2008	Russia	Novelist	One Day in the Life of Ivan Denisovich (1962)
Iris Murdoch	1919–99	Britain	Novelist	The Sea, The Sea (1978)
Yukio Mishima	1925–70	Japan	Novelist	The Sea of Fertility (1965–70)
Dario Fo	1926–2016	Italy	Playwright	Accidental Death of an Anarchist (1970)
Gabriel Garcia Marquez	1928–2014	Colombia	Novelist	One Hundred Years of Solitude (1967)
Milan Kundera	1929–	Czech Republic	Novelist	The Unbearable Lightness of Being (1984)
Harold Pinter	1930–2008	Britain	Playwright	The Birthday Party (1958)
Toni Morrison	1931–	US	Novelist	Beloved (1987)
V. S. Naipaul	1932–	Trinidad	Novelist	A House for Mr. Biswas (1971)
Philip Roth	1933–	US	Novelist	Portnoy's Complaint (1972)
Wole Soyinka	1934–	Nigeria	Playwright/poet	A Dance of the Forests (1960)
Seamus Heaney	1939–2013	Ireland	Poet	Door into the Dark (1969)
Margaret Atwood	1939–	Canada	Novelist/poet	The Handmaid's Tale (1985)
Peter Carey	1943–	Australia	Novelist	Oscar and Lucinda (1988)

PAINTERS AND SCULPTORS

All of the great civilizations, from Egypt to Greece and Rome, from ancient China to India and Medieval Europe, have produced works of art of great power. It is only later, around the 9th century CE, that we begin to know the names of some of these artists. In almost all societies, religious scenes were an important part of the output, as well as portraits that flattered the rulers and the aristocracy. Landscapes and rural scenes have also delighted artistic patrons through the ages. In the modern era, artists, free from patronage, have pursued their own, often shocking, agendas.

NAME	LIVED	ORIGIN	NOTABLE WORKS
Exekias	c. 550–525 BCE	Greece	Achilles and Ajax Playing in a Game
Phidias	c. 480–420 BCE	Greece	Frieze of the Parthenon
Praxiteles	Active c. 350 BCE	Greece	Cnidian Aphrodite
Gu Kaizhi	c. 345–406	China	Admonitions of the Instructress to the Court Ladies
Yan Liben	c. 600–73	China	Imperial Sedan Chair
Wu Daozi	c. 710–c. 760	China	Flying Demon
Han Gan	c. 720–c. 780	China	Shining Night of Light
Lu Hong	Active early 8th century	China	Ten Views from a Thatched Lodge
Zhang Xuan	Active 714–42	China	Ladies Preparing Newly Woven Silk
Guanxiu	832–912	China	The Arhat Pindola
Huang Quan	903–65	China	Sketches of Birds and Insects
Li Cheng	919–67	China	A Solitary Temple amid Clearing Peaks
Huang Jucai	933–c. 93	China	Pheasant and Small Birds by a Jujube Shrub
Dong Yuan	d. 962	China	Summer Mountains
Juran	Active c. 960–85	China	Distant Mountain Forests
Zhang Zeduan	Mid–11th century	China	Peace Reigns over the River
Guo Xi	c. 1020–90	China	Early Spring

NAME	LIVED	ORIGIN	NOTABLE WORKS
Li Gonglin	1049–1106	China	Pasturing Horses
Wang Shen	Late 12th century	China	Serried Hills over a Misty River
Li Di	c. 1100–c.97	China	Shrike on a Winter Tree
Ma Yuan	c. 1190–1224	China	Bare Willows and Distant Mountains
Lian Kai	13th century	China	The Sixth Ch'an Patriarch Chopping Bamboo
Qian Zuan	c. 1235–1307	China	Dwelling in the Floating Jade Mountains
Cimabue	c. 1250–1302	Italy	Madonna Enthroned
Zhao Mengfu	1254–1322	China	Autumn Colours on the Qiao and Hua Mountains
Nicola Pisano	c. 1258–84	Italy	Pulpit of the Baptistry of Pisa Cathedral
Giotto di Bondone	c. 1267–1337	Italy	Life of St Francis
Huang Gongwang	1269–1354	China	Dwelling in the Fuchun Mountains
Wu Zhen	1280–1354	China	Stalks of Bamboo by a Rock
Ni Zan	1301–74	China	Six Gentlemen
Wang Meng	1308–74	China	Dwelling in the Qinghai Mountains
Muto Shi	14th century	Japan	Portrait of Muso Soseki
Taiku Josetzu	Active 1405–23	Japan	Hyonen-zu
Donato de Niccolo (Donatello)	1386–1466	Italy	David
Fra Angelico	1387–1455	Italy	Annunciation
Jan van Eyck	c. 1395–1441	Belgium	Wedding Portrait
Paolo Uccello	1397–1475	Italy	The Battle of San Romano
Rogier van der Weyden	c. 1400–64	Flemish	Deposition
Fra Filippo Lippi	c. 1406–69	Italy	Tarquinia Madonna
Piero della Francesca	c. 1415–92	Italy	Nativity
Sesshu Toyo	1420–1506	Japan	Autumn Landscape
Shen Zhou	1427–1509	China	Lofty Mount
Giovanni Bellini	c. 1430–1516	Italy	Agony in the Garden
Hans Memling	c. 1430–1494	Netherlands	Mystic Marriage of St Catherine
Andrea Mantegna	1431–1506	Italy	The Triumph of Caesar
Sandro Botticelli	1445–1510	Italy	Mystic Nativity
Hieronymus Bosch	c. 1450–1516	Netherlands	Christ Crowned with Thorns
Leonardo da Vinci	1452–1519	Italy	Mona Lisa
Lu Ji	Active c. 1500	China	Egret, Eagle, and Falling Lotus Flowers
Mathias Grünewald	c. 1460–1528	Germany	Isenheim Altarpiece
Wen Zhengming	1470–1559	China	The Peach Blossom Spring
Albrecht Dürer	1471–1528	Germany	The Four Apostles
Michelangelo Buonarotti	1475–1564	Italy	David
Lucas Cranach (the Elder)	1472–1553	Germany	Rest on the Flight into Egypt
Jan Gossaert	c. 1478–1533	Belgium	Adoration of the Magi
Kano Montonobu	1476–1559	Japan	Landscape with Waterfall and Crane
Raffaello Sanzio da Urbino (Raphael)	1483–1520	Italy	Sistine Madonna
Tiziano Vecelli (Titian)	c. 1487–1576	Italy	The Tribute Money
Hans Holbein (the Younger)	c. 1497–1543	Germany	The Ambassadors

NAME	LIVED	ORIGIN	NOTABLE WORKS
Jacobo Robusti Tintoretto	c. 1487–1576	Italy	Last Supper
Sukei Sesson	c. 1504–1589	Japan	Landscape and Boat in Stormy Weather
Pieter Bruegel (the Elder)	c. 1525–69	Flemish	The Peasant Dance
Kaiho Yushio	1533–1615	Japan	Peonies
Pieter Paul Rubens	1577–1640	Belgium	Adoration of the Magi
Hasegawa Tohaku	1539–1610	Japan	Pine Trees
El Greco	1541–1614	Spain	The Burial of Count Orgaz
Kano Eitoku	1543–1590	Japan	Crane and Pine Tree
Dong Qichang	1555–1636	China	Autumn Mountains
Hon-Ami Koetsu	1558–1637	Japan	Flowers of the Four Seasons
Kano Sanraku	1559–1635	Japan	Plum Tree and Pheasant
Michelangelo Merisi da Caravaggio	1573–1610	Italy	Deposition
Tawaraya Sotatsu	1576–1643	Japan	Deer and Calligraphy
Frans Hals	1580–1666	Netherlands	Laughing Cavalier
José Ribera	1591–1652	Spain	The Martyrdom of St Bartholomew
Nicolas Poussin	1593–1665	France	Worship of the Golden Calf
Gianlorenzo Bernini	1598–1680	Italy	The Ecstasy of St Teresa
Diego Velasquez	1599–1660	Spain	The Water Carrier
Anthony van Dyck	1599–1641	Belgium	Charles I of England
Claude Lorrain	1600–82	France	Embarkation of St Ursula
Harmensz Rembrandt van Rijn	1606–69	Netherlands	The Night Watch
Hongren	1610–64	China	Monumental Landscape
Bartolomé Esteban Murillo	1617–82	Spain	Virgin and Child
Jan Vermeer	1632–75	Netherlands	Woman with a Water Jug
Wang Hui	1632–1717	China	The Kangxi Emperor's Southern Inspection Tour
Tao-Chi	1641–c.1717	China	Landscape
Ogata Korin	1658–1716	Japan	White Plum Blossoms in the Spring
Antoine Watteau	1684–1721	France	The Pilgrimage to Cythera
Giovanni Battista Tiepolo	1696–1770	Italy	The Finding of Moses
William Hogarth	1697–1764	England	Rake's Progress
Giovanni Antonio Canal (Canaletto)	1697–1768	Italy	A Regatta on the Grand Canal
Joshua Reynolds	1723–92	Great Britain	The Three Graces
Ikeno Taiga and Yosa Buson	1723–76, 1716–83	Japan	The Ten Conveniences and the Ten Pleasures
Thomas Gainsborough	1727–88	Britain	The Blue Boy
Maruyama Okyo	1733–95	Japan	Nature Studies
Francisco de Goya	1746–1828	Spain	The Naked Maja
Jacques-Louis David	1748–1825	France	The Rape of the Sabines
Utamaro Kitagawa	1753–1806	Japan	Book of Insects
William Blake	1757–1827	Britain	Divine Comedy
Katsuhika Hokusai	1760–1849	Japan	The Great Wave
Caspar David Friedrich	1774–1840	Germany	The Cross in the Mountains

NAME	LIVED	ORIGIN	NOTABLE WORKS
Joseph Mallord William Turner	1775–1851	Britain	Juliet and her Nurse
John Constable	1776–1837	Britain	The Haywain
Jean-August-Dominique Ingres	1780–1867	France	Odalisque
John James Audubon	1785–1851	US	Birds of America
Theodore Gericault	1791–1824	France	The Raft of the Medusa
Ichiyu-sai (Ando) Hiroshige	1797–1858	Japan	Landscape at Shono
Eugène Delacroix	1798–1863	France	Liberty Leading the People
Edwin Landseer	1802–73	Britain	Monarch of the Glen
Gustave Courbet	1819–77	France	Burial at Ornans
Edouard Manet	1823–83	France	Déjeuner sur l'Herbe
William Holman Hunt	1827–1910	Britain	Light of the World
Dante Gabriel Rosetti	1828–82	Great Britain	Beata Beatrix
John Everett Millais	1829–96	Britain	Order of Release
Camille Pissarro	1830–1903	France	The Harvest
James Abbott McNeill Whistler	1834–1903	US	The Artist's Mother
Hilaire-Germain-Edgar Degas	1834–1917	France	La Danseuse au Bouquet
Alfred Sisley	1839–99	Britain	Flood at Port Marly
Paul Cézanne	1839–1906	France	Bathers
Auguste Rodin	1840–1917	France	The Kiss
Claude Monet	1840–1926	France	Waterlilies
Pierre-Auguste Renoir	1841–1919	France	Luncheon of the Boating Party
Paul Gauguin	1848–1903	France	Ta Matete
Vincent van Gogh	1853–90	Netherlands	Road with Cypresses
John Singer Sargent	1856–1925	US	Carnation, Lily, Lily, Rose
Georges Seurat	1859–91	France	Sunday Afternoon on the Grande Jatte
Walter Richard Sickert	1860–1942	Britain	Ennui
Gustav Klimt	1862–1928	Austria	Mosaic mural for the Palais Stoclet in Brussels
Edvard Munch	1863–1944	Norway	The Scream
Henri de Toulouse-Lautrec	1864–1901	France	At the Moulin Rouge
Akseli Gallen-Kallela	1865–1931	Finland	Lake Keitele
Wassily Kandinsky	1866–1944	Russia	Improvisations with Colour
Henri Matisse	1869–1954	France	Odalisque
Piet Mondrian	1872–1944	Netherlands	Composition
Paul Klee	1879–1940	Switzerland	Twittering Machine
Jacob Epstein	1880–1959	Britain	Memorial for Oscar Wilde
Ernst Ludwig Kirchner	1880–1938	Germany	Street Scene
Pablo Picasso	1881–1973	Spain	Guernica
Georges Braque	1882–1963	France	Vase of Anemones
Edward Hopper	1882–1967	US	Nighthawks
Max Beckmann	1884–1905	Germany	The Night
Amedeo Modigliani	1884–1920	Italy	Portrait of Madame Zborowski Green on Blue

PAINTERS AND SCULPTORS (CONTINUED)

NAME	LIVED	ORIGIN	NOTABLE WORKS
Diego Rivera	1886–1957	Mexico	Creation
Oskar Kokoschka	1886–1980	Austria	View of the Thames
Georgia O'Keeffe	1887–1986	USA	Cityscapes of New York
Marcel Duchamp	1887–1968	France	Fountain
Marc Chagall	1887–1985	France	Calvary
Giorgio de Chirico	1888–1978	Italy	Nostalgia of the Infinite
Paul Nash	1889–1946	Britain	Dead Sea
Egon Schiele	1890–1918	Austria	The Artist's Mother Sleeping
Giorgio Morandi	1890–1964	Italy	Still Life
Man Ray	1890–1978	US	The Rope Dancer Accompanies Herself with her Shadows
Max Ernst	1891–1976	Germany	The Elephant Celebes
George Grosz	1893–1959	Germany	Suicide
Joan Miró	1893–1983	Spain	Harlequin's Carnival
Henry Moore	1898–1986	Britain	Recumbent Figure
René Magritte	1898–1967	Belgium	This is not a Pipe
Alberto Giacometti	1901–66	Switzerland	Tall Figures
Mark Rothtko	1903–70	US	Green on Blue
Salvador Dali	1904–89	Spain	The Persistence of Memory
Willem de Kooning	1904–97	US	Woman Series
Frida Kahlo	1907–54	Mexico	The Frame
Francis Bacon	1909–92	Britain	Three Studies at the Base of a Crucifixion
Jackson Pollock	1912–56	USA	Autumn Rhythm
Sidney Nolan	1917–92	Australia	Themes from the Career of Ned Kelly
Roy Lichtenstein	1923–97	US	Whaam!
Andy Warhol	1930–87	US	Campbell's Soupcans
David Hockney	b. 1937	Britain	Mr and Mrs Clark and Percy
Antony Gormley	b. 1950	Britain	Angel of the North
Ai Weiwei	b. 1957	China	Sunflower Seeds
Liu Xiadong	b. 1963	China	Three Gorges: Newly Displaced Population

THE WORLD'S OLDEST UNIVERSITIES

UNIVERSITY	COUNTRY	DATE OF FOUNDATION
Bologna	Italy	1088
Oxford	England	c. 1167
Modena	Italy	1175
Vicenza	Italy	1204
Cambridge	England	1209
Salamanca	Spain	1218
Padua	Italy	1222
Naples	Italy	1224
Siena	Italy	1246
Lisbon	Portugal	1290
Madrid	Spain	1293
Lérida	Spain	1297
La Sapienza	Rome, Italy	1303
Coimbra	Portugal	1308
Perugia	Italy	1308
Pisa	Italy	1343
Charles	Prague, Czech Republic	1347
Perpignan	France	1350
Pavia	Italy	1361
Jagiellonian	Poland	1364
Vienna	Austria	1365
Heidelberg	Germany	1385
Universidad Michoacana de San Nicolás de Hidalgo	Mexico	1540
Harvard	Masachusetts, US	1636
Fourah Bay College	Sierra Leone	1827
Calcutta	India	1857
Sydney	Australia	1850

DISASTERS

Few civilizations have been immune to the effects of natural disasters, which have sometimes killed hundreds of thousands, or even, in the case of plagues, many millions of people. Disasters such as the eruption of Pompeii, the Antioch earthquake of 526 CE, and the Black Death caused huge losses of life, but modern societies are no less vulnerable, as evidenced by the loss of life in the 2004 Indian Ocean and 2011 Japanese tsunamis.

EARTHQUAKES

PLACE	DATE	MAGNITUDE	DEATHS	DESCRIPTION
Sparta, Greece	464 BCE	7.2	c. 20,000	Led to revolt of helots and contributed to the outbreak of the Peloponnesian War
Rhodes, Greece	226 BCE	Unknown	Unknown	Destroyed the Colossus of Rhodes
Crete and Eastern Mediterranean	365	9.0	Unknown	Widespread destruction in Crete and North Africa
Antioch (Turkey)	526	8.0	250,000	Partial destruction of the city
Lebanese coast	551	7.5	30–50,000	Widespread destruction in Beirut, Tyre, Tripoli, and other coastal cities
Aleppo, Syria	1138	9.0	200–250,000	Partial destruction of city
Eastern Mediterranean	1201	7.6	Unknown	Caused famines in which more than a million people died
Shaanxi, China	1556	8.3	830,000	Most destructive earthquake in China's history
Peru	1687	8.7	5,000	Severely damaged Lima, destroyed port of Pisco
Lisbon, Portugal	1755	8.7 and tsunami	80,000	Destroyed most of city
Ecuador and Peru	1797	7.3	40,000	Widespread destruction in Quito and Cuzco
Arica, Chile	1868	8.5	25,000	Destroyed a number of towns, including Arica and Arequipa
San Francisco	1906	7.9	3,000	Widespread destruction in San Francisco, partly caused by fire
Valparaiso, Chile	1906	8.2	4,000	Destruction of most of Valparaiso
Ningxia, China	1920	7.8	250,000	Total destruction in Haiyuan County
Kanto, Japan	1923	7.9	125,000	Most deadly earthquake in Japanese history
Ancash, Peru	1970	7.9	75,000	Worst natural disaster in Peruvian history
Tangshan, China	1976	7.5	240,000–255,000	Largest 20th-century earthquake by death toll
Armenia	1988	6.9	240,000	Destruction of city of Spitak (many deaths caused by substandard building design)
Western Turkey	1999	7.6	18,000	Partial destruction of city of Izmit; many substandard buildings collapsed
Bam, Iran	2003	6.6	27,000	Ancient mud-brick city of Bam destroyed
Indian Ocean	2004	9.2 and tsunami	230,000	Widespread devastation along Indian Ocean coastlines
Kashmir, Pakistan	2005	7.6	75,000	Widespread damage around Muzaffarabad
Sichuan, China	2008	8.0	70,000	Deadliest Chinese earthquake since Tangshan (1976)
Haiti	2010	7.0	316,000	Widespread damage in Port-au-Prince; worst death toll in western hemisphere
Northeast Japan	2011	9.0 and tsunami	c. 18,0000	Widespread damage around Sendai; caused emergency at Fukushima Nuclear Power Plant

VOLCANIC ERUPTIONS

VOLCANO NAME	DATE	DESCRIPTION
Vesuvius (southern Italy)	79	Destroyed cities of Pompeii and Herculaneum
Oraefajökull (Iceland)	1362	"Glacier burst" devastated coastal communities and covered northern Iceland in ash
Mount Etna (Sicily)	1669	Worst eruption in modern times, destroying a dozen villages
Lanzarote (Canary Islands)	1730–36	Longest recorded eruption in the Canary Islands, burying communities in the west
Laki (Iceland)	1783	Produced largest flow of lava ever recorded
Tambora, Sumbawa, (Indonesia)	1815	Effects of volcanic ash aerosol caused the "year without a summer" and crop failures and famines in many countries
Krakatoa (Indonesia)	1883	Caused much of island of Krakatoa to sink, killing 35,000 people, The volcanic aerosol produced beautiful sunsets worldwide for several months
Montagne Pelée (Martinique)	1902	Destroyed the town of Saint-Pierre.
Mount St. Helens (Washington State)	1980	Destroyed 185 miles (300 km) of roads.
Nevada del Ruiz (Colombia)	1985	Mud flow destroyed town of Magdalena, killing 23,000 people.
Pinatubo (Philippines)	1991	Expelled 10 times as much material as Mount St. Helens, but mass evacuations meant only 200–300 people died
Eyjafjallajökull (Iceland)	2010	Volcanic ash cloud grounded aviation in much of Europe
Puyehue-Cordón Caulle (Chile)	2011	Air traffic disrupted across most of Southern hemisphere

FLOODS

COUNTRY	DATE	DESCRIPTION
England	48	Flooding of Thames River caused 10,000 deaths
England and Netherlands coastline	1099	Severe winter storm caused floods that killed 100,000 and created the Goodwin Sands
Netherlands and Germany	1218	North Sea storm surge killed 100,000
Belgium, Netherlands, Denmark	1287	Severe storms caused floods, killing 50–80,000
Denmark, Netherlands, northern Germany	1362	Widespread coastal floods killed 100,000
Western England	1606	Tsunami in the Bristol Channel killed 3,000
China	1887	Floods along the Yellow River broke dikes, drowning 900,000
Central China	1931	Flooding of Yellow, Yangtze, and Huai rivers killed up to 3,000,000
Guatemala	1949	Hurricane caused floods, killing 40,000
Bangladesh	1974	Heavy monsoon rains caused floods, killing 29,000
China	1975	Failure of the Banqiao Dam, Henan Province, led to floods and deaths of 86,000; worst dam failure in history
Pakistan	2010	Floods submerged one-fifth of the country, killing 2,000
Australia	2010–11	River surges killed 35 and devastated several towns in Queensland
Southeast Asia	2011	Widespread flood across several countries in the region, killing almost 3,000 people
Uttarakhand, North India	2013	Flash floods and landslides, killing more than 5,700 people

FAMINES

PLACE	DATE	DESCRIPTION
Central America	c. 800–900	Drought and famine caused collapse of Classic Maya civilization
China	875–884	Famine sparked the Huang Zhao rebellion, which fatally undermined the Tang dynasty
Japan	1229–32	The Kangi famine, worst in Japanese history
Northern Europe	1315–17	"The Great Famine" killed up to 10 percent of the population (partly through effects of disease on a weakened population)
India	1406–17	The Durga Devi famine in Maharashtra killed many thousands over a 12-year period
Russia	1601–03	Worst famine in Russian history, killed up to 2 million – one third of the population
India	1630–32	Severe famine in the Deccan led to around 2 million deaths
Prussia	1708–11	Famine killed 250,000 (around two-fifths of the population)
Bengal, India	1769–73	Worst famine in Indian history killed 10 million
Ireland	1845–49	Potato blight caused severe famine and death of 1 million
Iran	1870–71	"The Great Persian Famine" killed 1.5 million and led to many nomadic tribes becoming sedentary
Ethiopia	1888–92	"The Great Ethiopian Famine"; pest killed 90 percent of cattle; locust and caterpillar plagues ate most crops; one-third of population perished
Ukraine	1932–33	The "Holodomor"; Soviet collectivization and industrialization policies caused famine that killed 4 million
China	1959–61	"The Great China Famine", the worst in Chinese history, killed 30 million
Ethiopia	1984–85	Failure of rains caused famine, killing up to 1 million
Niger	2005	Desert locust damage to crops, acute poverty, and high food prices led to a widespread food crisis in the area, affecting almost 3.6 million people
Somalia	2011	Drought in East Africa caused a widespread food crisis, affecting the livelihood of more than 6.2 million people
South Sudan	2017	Food crisis caused by economic instability due to war and drought, starving almost 100,000 people and leaving 100,000 on the brink of famine
Yemen	2017	Severe food crisis and cholera affecting over 7 million people

EPIDEMICS AND PLAGUES

PLACE	DATE	DESCRIPTION
Greece	430–427 BCE	Early description of plague symptoms during epidemic at Athens
Mediterranean world	165–180	The Antonine Plague killed up to 5 million, one-third of the population of the Roman Empire, severely weakening the military might of the Roman army
Mediterranean world	541–542	Plague of Justinian killed 40 percent or more of population
Worldwide	1348–50	The Black Death killed around 30 million people
India	1817	First recorded outbreak of cholera in Bengal
India	1907	Outbreak of bubonic plague killed 1.5 million
India	1630–32	Severe famine in the Deccan led to around 2 million deaths
Worldwide	1918–19	Spanish influenza killed 50 million, the worst recorded natural disaster

GLOSSARY

Terms defined elsewhere in the glossary are in *italics*.

abolitionism
Advocacy of the abolition of slavery.

absolutism
A theory of the state where a country's ruler or government is regarded as possessing an **absolute authority**: that is, an authority that is not dependent on the consent of the people being governed.

accession
The point at which a monarch begins his or her reign.

agrarian
Relating to land and its cultivation. The term **agrarianism** relates to political movements aimed at promoting the interests of agriculture and rural life.

allies/Allied
People or countries working together. In World War I and World War II, the Allies or Allied forces were the countries fighting against Germany.

anarchy
In its original meaning, absence of government; also used for a condition of public disorder. Politically, **anarchism** is a movement or ideology that believes in the abolition of government as an ideal for society.

anticlericalism
Opposition to the influence of churches and other religious organizations in society. In some (mainly *Catholic*) countries such as France, Spain, and Italy it has been an important political force.

anti-Semitism
Antagonism and hostility toward Jewish people.

apartheid
The policy of racial *segregation* formerly followed in the Republic of South Africa, or policies elsewhere that resemble this.

armistice
A truce or cessation of hostilities.

authoritarian
Term applied to leaders or governments who exercise power with little or no regard for *democracy* or other constraints.

autocracy
A form of political rule where all power is concentrated in one person (the **autocrat**). Unlike the similar term *dictator*, the word autocrat is often applied to a powerful king or emperor.

Axis
The alliance between Germany and Italy (and later Japan) before and during World War II; also these countries considered collectively (Axis forces or Axis domination).

bilateral
Involving two governments (or other organizations), especially with reference to treaties and agreements. Compare *multilateral*.

bloc
A group of countries that act together in matters of international relations.

bourgeois
Originally a member of the French middle classes, now often used disparagingly for a supporter of the capitalist system (see *capitalism*), or simply for a person with conventional views. In *Marxist* theory, the **bourgeoisie** are the class of capitalists.

buffer state
A smaller country lying between two more powerful rival countries. The presence of a buffer state is considered useful in decreasing tension between the rival countries.

Byzantine Empire
The mainly Greek-speaking Christian Empire that was a continuation of the eastern Roman Empire and lasted for around 1,000 years, until its conquest by the Ottoman Turks in 1453.

Caliphate
In Islamic (see *Islam*) culture this is a political/religious institution in which a chosen individual, the **caliph**, is regarded as a successor to the Prophet Muhammad, and thus able to confer political legitimacy on individual rulers across the Islamic world. Once powerful rulers themselves, caliphs later became mainly figureheads, although the Ottoman rulers of Turkey continued to claim the title until the 20th century.

Calvinism
A strict form of Protestantism named after the 16th-century religious reformer John Calvin. **Calvinist churches** are usually *Presbyterian* in organization.

capitalism
A way of organizing society that favors the activity of **capitalists**: private individuals or organizations who accumulate wealth (**capital**), especially in the form of the buildings and equipment that are necessary to produce goods and services. These businesses generate employment, while also providing profits for the capitalists.

Catholic
A term that originally meant inclusive or all-embracing, so that the **Catholic Church** originally meant the whole of the Christian Church. After various splits over the centuries, the Catholic Church is now the organization of churches that owes its allegiance to the pope in Rome, thus it is also called the Roman Catholic Church.

charter
A written grant of rights or similar legal document.

city-state
A self-governing, independent city.

classical/Classical
Relating to the civilizations of ancient Greece and Rome and their achievements (the **Classical Period**) or to later artistic and cultural movements that emulated the values of this period. The term classical can also be applied to the high point of any civilization or culture, and can be used with other shades of meaning, such as "possessing timeless value."

client state
A country that is dependent on another larger country for trade, protection, etc.

coalition
A formal arrangement in which two or more different groups agree to act together, such as when different political parties come together to form a government.

Cold War
The period of hostility between the West and the communist countries dominated by the former USSR. The Cold War lasted from shortly after World War II until the collapse of *communism* in Eastern Europe in 1989.

collective
Organized in common; taken together as a whole.

colonialism
The practice and policy of acquiring foreign colonies, often with the implication that this involves cultural domination and exploitation.

commonwealth/Commonwealth
The term commonwealth originally meant "the common good." With an initial capital, Commonwealth refers either to the government of Britain in the years following the execution of Charles I, or to the (British) Commonwealth of Nations, the association set up to maintain links between countries of the former British Empire. The word also occurs in the full official names of several countries and US states.

commune
A community of people who aim at sharing everything in common.

communism
(1) Any society based on the principles of mutual help, in which property is not owned by individuals, but is held in common. (2) More specifically, political movements or governments inspired by or claiming to act in the name of the political and philosophical doctrines of Karl Marx (see *Marxist*).

Congress
In the US Constitution, the body forming the legislative arm of the federal government (see *federal system*). It comprises two elected assemblies, the House of Representatives (or Lower House) and the Senate (or Upper House).

conservative/Conservative
Various social and political meanings, including: caution in accepting change; respect for traditional values and authority; support for free-market *capitalism* and opposition to government intervention; membership of a particular political party, such as the Conservative Party in the United Kingdom.

consul
One of the two highest officials in the Roman republic, who each held power for only one year.

Counter-Reformation
The period of revival in the *Catholic* Church following the Protestant *Reformation*, involving both internal reforms and active opposition to *Protestantism*.

coup
Short for coup d'etat, the sudden illegal seizing of power by a small group.

Crusades
Military expeditions organized by the papacy in the *Medieval period*, initially with the goal of gaining control of the "Holy Land" (Palestine) from Islamic powers (see *Islam*).

czar
The title of the former emperors of Russia. A female czar, or a czar's wife, is a **czarina**.

Danegeld
A tax raised in Anglo-Saxon England to pay off and defend against Danish invaders. It later became a general land tax.

decimal system (army)
The principle of organization of Genghis Khan's Mongol army, with a hierarchy of military units that contained between 10 and 10,000 men.

demagogue
A politician whose power base relies on stirring up the emotions of the people of a country through charismatic and emotional speeches, often in opposition to established authority.

democracy
A political system in which the people of a country control their government. **Direct democracy**, which operated in ancient Athens, allowed citizens to decide policy by direct votes. Most democracy is **representative democracy**, with the people electing politicians to represent them. Democracy has often been popular with groups that are excluded from voting, such as women and non-property owners.

denomination
A body of religious believers sharing a common faith and organization and having a recognized name; most commonly applied to sections within the Christian Church—for example, Baptists and Methodists.

dependency
A subordinate territory that does not form an integral part of the country which has overall control of it.

despotism
An *autocracy*, especially one that is headed by a king or emperor. An **enlightened despot** is one who is seen as ruling for the benefit of the people rather than for him/herself. Also refers to the exercise of power itself by the ruler.

detente
The lessening of tension between two countries; used especially for the time when tension was decreasing between the US and the former USSR.

devaluation
The lowering in value of one country's currency compared with other currencies.

diaspora
The members of a particular ethnic group (see *ethnicity*) who are living away from their land of origin. It was originally used with reference to the Jews.

dictator
Originally an official in ancient Rome who was given sweeping powers for a short period during a time of national emergency. Now used for any person who rules a country alone and with no effective restrictions on their individual power. The word is not normally applied to hereditary kings or emperors, unlike the similar terms autocrat and despot (see *autocracy* and *despotism*).

dissolution
In general, this means the process of dissolving or separating into constituent parts. The **Dissolution of Parliament** is the official end of a parliament before a general election is held to elect new representatives. The **Dissolution of the Monasteries** was the disbanding of monasteries and other religious institutions in 16th-century England during the reign of Henry VIII.

dominion/Dominions
(**1**) The right to govern or control. (**2**) Any territory owing allegiance to a particular ruler or government. (**3**) A term formerly used, especially the plural (Dominions), for the larger self-governing territories within the British Empire, especially Canada and Australia.

dynasty
A royal family that rules over a country for several generations.

Eastern Bloc
The communist (see *communism*) countries of eastern Europe during the *Cold War* period.

ecclesiastical
Relating to the Church or to the clergy.

ecumenical
Relating to: (**1**) the whole of the Christian Church; (**2**) movements aimed at reuniting different branches of the Church.

ethnicity
Characteristics and features associated with belonging to a particular ethnic group, which may be defined purely by culture or with reference to biological or racial characteristics.

evangelical
Relating to: (**1**) the Christian Gospels; (**2**) Protestant (see *Protestantism*) doctrines that emphasize personal salvation by faith; (**3**) religious movements that actively go out to preach to and convert others (to **evangelize**).

excommunication
The action taken by a religious organization of cutting off an individual from communication or membership of the organization, and/or from taking part in its rites.

fascism
Originally, the ideology of the political movement led by Benito Mussolini, who was in power in Italy between 1922 and 1943. Fascist doctrines were *authoritarian*, antidemocratic (see *democracy*), and anticommunist (see *communism*); they emphasized subjection of the individual to the state and tended to glorify war and *nationalism*. The term **fascist** is now used loosely for any ideology or attitude seen as authoritarian or intolerant.

fatwa
In *Islam*, a pronouncement, especially by a cleric, that gives an opinion and/or seeks to direct an action.

federal system
Any political system where there is an overall central government (**federal government**), but with many areas of decision-making being carried out by regional governments—for example, governments of provinces or states; the division of powers between the federal and regional governments is normally guaranteed by a constitution.

feudalism
The elaborate social system that grew up in *Medieval* Europe, where each nation was conceived of as a "pyramid," with a monarch at the top. Each level of society was entitled to claim rights from, but also obliged to undertake duties to, those "above" and "below" in the hierarchy.

fiefs
Lands held on condition of service offered to a superior lord under the feudal system (see *feudalism*).

free trade
Trading of goods and services between countries without restrictions, such as quota limits or taxes on imported goods. See also *protectionism*.

fundamentalism
A strict belief in all the traditional teachings of a given religion.

genocide
The systematic extermination of a racial or ethnic group (see *ethnicity*).

globalization
The process by which improved communications and international links have resulted in ideas, cultures, labor markets, and ways of life becoming increasingly widespread and/or interconnected globally.

gnosticism
Any of various religious ideologies and movements that emphasize the acquiring of secret or mystical knowledge as a way to salvation. Gnosticism was widespread in early Christianity, but came to be regarded as heretical (see *heresy*) by the Church.

Gothic
(**1**) Relating to the Goths, a Germanic tribe that invaded the Roman Empire in the 3rd and 4th centuries CE; (**2**) A style of European architecture that flourished from the 13th to 16th centuries, and was characterized by distinctive pointed windows and other features. Most of the great *Medieval* cathedrals were built in this style.

Greek Church
The branch of the Christian Church associated with the (Greek-speaking) *Byzantine Empire*, in which church services were conducted in Greek. See also *Orthodox Church*.

guerrilla warfare
Warfare where the fighters operate in small irregular units, often without uniforms or an official army structure.

guild
A *Medieval* mutual-aid association. Craftsmen and merchants in towns were often organized into guilds, and individuals were often only allowed to practise their trade if they belonged to the guild of that particular trade.

hegemony
A situation in which a powerful country exerts a significant influence over its less powerful neighbors.

heresy
Usually a minority belief or tendency within a given religion that is regarded as unacceptable or even evil by other adherents to the religion. A **heretic** is a person regarded as heretical.

Holy Roman Empire
An empire set up in Western Europe in *Medieval* times, whose territory was centred on modern-day Germany. Both connected to and forming a rival to the papacy, it increasingly took the form of a loose collection of states. The emperor of the Holy Roman Empire held little power by the time it was formally abolished by Napoleon in 1806.

hominin
A member of the biological group that includes humans and their extinct ancestors and relatives, back to the point at which they split from the line leading to chimpanzees.

Huguenots
Historical term for French Protestants (see *Protestantism*), whose history of persecution led many to emigrate and settle in other countries.

humanist
(**1**) A Latin or Greek scholar, especially of the *Renaissance* period. The work of Renaissance humanists involved the rediscovery of classical texts and their human-centered values, as opposed to the emphasis on God and theology of the *Medieval period*. (**2**) A person who advocates an ethical approach to human life that does not involve belief in a god or gods.

imperialism
Originally the system of government or rule in an empire. Now, more particularly, the attitudes of mind that supported the acquisition of distant territories by 19th-century Western powers.

Iron Curtain
Term for the barrier between the USSR-dominated communist countries (see *communism*) of Eastern Europe and the capitalist West during the *Cold War*.

Islam
A monotheistic (single-god) religion established in the 7th century CE in Arabia by the Prophet Muhammad. Islam means "submission" (to God). The two main branches of Islam, **Sunni** and **Shi'ite**, differ in the authority and legitimacy they ascribe to different members of the Prophet's family after his death.

Islamism
A tendency within *Islam* that aims to establish Islamic law and values in societies worldwide.

isolationism
A policy of isolating a country from international disputes, especially by not taking part in alliances. The term is particularly associated with certain periods of Chinese, Japanese, and US history.

Jacobin
A member of the extreme revolutionary group during the French Revolution.

Jacobite
In British history, a supporter of the claims of the Stuart monarchs to regain the throne, after James II (Jacobus in Latin) was forced to flee and abdicate the British throne in 1689.

Jesuit
A member of the Society of Jesus, an organization founded in 1534 within the *Catholic* Church, which played a leading role in the *Counter-Reformation*. It continues to be active in education and in the spreading of Catholic doctrine.

jihad
A struggle or war undertaken on behalf of the Islamic faith (see *Islam*).

judiciary
A collective term for the judges holding office in a particular country.

khedive
A title used mainly by the rulers of Egypt from 1867 to 1914, who were nominally subject to the authority of the Ottoman (Turkish) Empire, but in practice were largely independent.

knight
A feudal rank (see *feudalism*) that combined a high status in society with obligations to undertake military service.

league
An association between individuals or states for mutual protection, or for furthering common interests.

legion
A fighting unit of the Roman army consisting of 3,000–6,000 men.

legislature
The institution(s) of government that are responsible for passing laws.

Levant
The region of the eastern Mediterranean and the territories bordering it.

liberalism
A political movement or philosophy that emphasizes individual freedom, as well as supporting forms of government that are answerable to the people (contrast *absolutism*). The term **economic liberalism** means support for free-market *capitalism*. In the US, **liberal** often implies a left-wing stance that supports increased governmental intervention and spending on social welfare.

mandate
A legal command or commission, especially a commission in which a country was authorized by the former League of Nations to govern a particular territory in the interests of its inhabitants. See also *trusteeship*.

manifesto
A written declaration of policy and goals, especially one issued by a political party or movement.

Marxist
Term applied to a variety of doctrines that trace their origin to the German-born philosopher and social thinker Karl Marx. Marx himself believed that he had discovered laws of history that proved that eventually *capitalism* would collapse and be replaced by *communism*.

Medieval period
The period from approximately 600 to 1450 CE in Europe, from the end of the western Roman Empire to the *Renaissance*.

mercenary
A soldier who fights for other nations for money.

missionary
A representative of a particular religion who travels to another country, region, or culture with the goal of converting people to his or her religion.

Monophysitism
The belief that Jesus Christ has only one nature (with his divine nature absorbing his human nature), rather than having two separate natures. A minority view in the Christian Church, it is upheld mainly by the Coptic Church and other churches with their roots in the ancient Near East.

multilateral
Involving three or more governments (or other organizations), especially with reference to treaties and agreements. Compare *bilateral*.

nation
(1) An independent country. (2) A people defined by shared historical, cultural, and linguistic ties, whether constituting a single independent country or not.

nationalism
A political attitude of strong support for the interests and future of one's nation.

nationalization
The taking of private property into public ownership by the state, especially on a large scale, such as an entire industry.

NATO
North Atlantic Treaty Organization, an international military alliance of Western powers established in 1949.

Nazism
The doctrines of the National Socialist (Nazi) party, in power in Germany under Adolf Hitler 1933–45. Nazism was similar to *fascism*, but in addition was racist, believing in the supremacy of a supposed "Aryan" race of which the German people were allegedly the "purest" representatives. See also *totalitarianism*.

neoclassicism
Any cultural movement in which styles or ideals of a *classical* period are revived. More specifically, an 18th-century movement in European art and literature that was inspired by renewed interest in the values of ancient Greek and Roman art.

neocolonialism
The situation in which a powerful, developed country has influence over a less developed country (especially a former colony) in ways that are seen as similar to aspects of actual *colonialism*.

oligarchy
A political system where a few powerful, and often rich, individuals combine to rule a country. The former Republic of Venice is a historic example. Many former communist countries (see *communism*) were also effectively oligarchies, with communist party officials monopolizing power.

order (religious)
In the Christian Church, a body of people adhering to a particular rule or way of life that is often set down by an individual founder—orders of monks, for example. The phrase "**in orders**" means occupying a clerical position, such as priest or bishop.

Orthodox Church
A major group of Christian Churches that descend from a split with the Western (*Catholic*) Church that occurred in 1054 CE. Prominent in Eastern and southeastern Europe, it includes several different traditions and national Churches.

Outremer
The *Medieval* French states set up in the Near East after the *Crusades*.

overlord
A lord who is superior to other lords or rulers, especially within the feudal system (see *feudalism*).

pacifism
Opposition to all war.

papal bull
An order or edict issued by a pope on a matter of importance.

peasant
A worker on the land, especially an agricultural laborer or small farmer.

pharaoh
Title of the ruler of ancient Egypt, who was traditionally seen as both a king and a god.

pilgrimage
A journey undertaken for religious reasons to a shrine or other sacred site.

plebiscite
A referendum, especially on a major constitutional issue.

pogrom
An organized massacre, especially one carried out against the Jews in Eastern Europe in the late 19th and early 20th centuries.

polity
A form of government and political organization.

populist
Generally a critical term for a politician whose power base comes from successfully appealing to the general public, without necessarily being respected by other politicians. It is often implied that a populist simply tells people what they want to hear.

Praetorian prefect
A high administrative office in the Roman Republic and Empire, deriving originally from the headship of the state bodyguards—the Praetorian Guard.

pre-Colombian
Relating to the cultures of the Americas before their contact with European explorers and conquerors.

Presbyterians
Members of various *Protestant* Churches that do not have a hierarchy of bishops, but are run by **presbyters** (elders) elected by church congregations.

proletariat
A collective term for working-class wage earners who do not possess their own capital (see *capitalism*); often contrasted with *bourgeoisie* (see *bourgeois*) in *Marxist* theory.

protectionism
The policy of defending the industries of a country by creating barriers to foreign competition, for example, restricting imports.

protectorate
A colony in which the emphasis is on the colonizing power being responsible for defense and foreign affairs for the benefit of the people of the territory.

Protestantism
Any of the forms of Christianity resulting from the *Reformation* of the 16th century and afterward, in which allegiance is no longer offered to the pope in Rome.

puppet state
A country that, though nominally independent, is actually under the control of another country.

purge
A term, usually associated with totalitarian systems (see *totalitarianism*), for the expulsion of people from an organization who are regarded as undesirable by the organization's leadership.

Puritanism
Originally a movement within the Church of England in the 16th and 17th centuries that pressed for further changes to Church organization and doctrine, going beyond the split from the *Catholic* Church that had occurred under Henry VIII. The term was later applied to religious groups with similar views outside the Church of England, and then eventually to any way of thinking that was seen as disapproving of pleasure and indulgence.

putsch
A violent attempt to overthrow a government.

recession
A reduction in the economic activity of a country, though less serious than a depression. A recession is often defined as having occurred when economic output has declined for two successive three-month periods.

Reformation
The Christian reform movement of the 16th century, in which many churches and individuals broke from the Western (*Catholic*) Church headed by the pope in Rome.

Renaissance
A cultural phase of European history, centered on Italy in the 15th and early 16th centuries, that involved the rediscovery of the cultural achievements of ancient Greece and Rome. This in turn became the inspiration for new ideas in literature and the creation of new artworks.

reparations
A term that came into use after World War I for payments made by the defeated countries to the victors, regarded as being in recompense for their aggression. An older term for the same thing is **indemnity**.

republic
Any country not headed by a hereditary king, prince, or emperor. Modern republics are usually headed by presidents and range from democratic regimes to dictatorships.

republicanism
(**1**) Support for a *republic* as the preferred form of government. (**2**) Beliefs and values associated with the Republican Party in the US. (**3**) In Irish contexts, support for the complete independence of Ireland from the UK.

restoration/Restoration
The restoring of a previous state of affairs. In British history, the Restoration refers to the return of the British monarchy in 1660, after the English Civil War and *Commonwealth*, and the years following this.

Roman Church
The Western branch of the Christian Church, which developed under the leadership of the pope in Rome, and in which church services are, or were, conducted in Latin. See also *Catholic*, *Greek Church*.

Romantic Movement
A many-sided cultural and artistic movement in Europe that reached its peak in the early 19th century. It included an increased appreciation of nature and an emphasis on feelings and emotions in contrast to reason.

royal minority
The period when the monarch of a country is still a child (a minor).

satrap
A provincial governor in the ancient Persian Empire; also, a subordinate ruler generally.

scholasticism
The approach to reasoning and knowledge that is characteristic of centres of higher education during the Christian *Medieval period*.

sect
A religious group or organization that holds distinctive or nonstandard beliefs. The term is often used to imply that the views held are doubtful, or even heretical.

sectarian
Displaying hostile attitudes to people from a different social grouping, especially those adhering to a different denomination of the same religion.

secular
Nonreligious.

segregation
Separation, in particular separation of one race from another within a racist or *apartheid* social system.

self-determination
Situation in which a people or nation are able to choose their own government, or to govern themselves.

Senate
(**1**) The assembly that acted as the main ruling body in ancient Rome (eventually losing most of its powers to the emperors). (**2**) The upper legislative house of the US *Congress*, or of other legislatures that are similarly organized.

serf
A *peasant* living in a condition of semi-slavery, with no right to leave the land of the landowner for whom he or she works.

shogun
A hereditary commander-in-chief in Japan. For various periods in Japanese history, shoguns, rather than the emperor, held the real power.

social democracy
Formerly another term for *socialism* or *communism*. In modern usage it refers to a moderate form of socialism that is compatible with democracy and *liberalism*.

socialism
Term used for a variety of left-wing ideologies and movements that all involve some government intervention in society and the economy, with the goal of redistributing wealth for the common good. Socialist movements have ranged from the moderate and democratic to revolutionary communist movements (see *democracy* and *communism*).

sovereignty
Complete legitimate authority over a given territory.

soviet
One of the many elected councils that operated at all levels of society in the former USSR. **Soviet Union** is another name for the USSR.

Soviet Bloc
Another name for the *Eastern Bloc*.

speculation
An economic term for the buying and selling of shares, or other tradeable assets, for the purpose of making a profit if the price rises or falls in the way that the speculator predicts.

state
(**1**) An independent country. (**2**) A self-governing region within a country. (**3**) The governmental apparatus of a country.

stock exchange
An organization that allows trading in shares of companies, government bonds, and other financial assets.

suffrage
The right to vote, especially in a public election. A **suffragist** is an advocate of the right to vote; especially, in many cases, the rights of women.

sultan
A title, equivalent to king or emperor in some *Islamic* contexts and cultures (see *Islam*).

suzerainty
Feudal overlordship (see *overlord*). Also, the supremacy of one state over a less powerful one.

synod
A church council or assembly.

technocrat
(**1**) A member of a technical elite. (**2**) Someone who regards political problems as being best approached by seeking technical solutions, rather than via ideologies or value judgments.

tetrarchy
A governing arrangement in parts of the Roman Empire whereby a region was divided into four subdivisions, each with its own ruler (**tetrarch**). Also the name for the district ruled by a particular tetrarch.

theocracy
Rule by a priest or a priesthood.

tithe
A tax imposed for the upkeep of the Church, especially in the *medieval period*, usually consisting of one-tenth of the agricultural produce of a given piece of land.

totalitarianism
A form of *authoritarian* rule in which the government aims to control the details of individual people's lives and thoughts, treating individual freedom as unimportant compared with the state.

trade union
An association of workers, formed to advance their economic interests and to provide mutual support.

tribune
A title for various officials in ancient Rome. A tribune of the people was one of two (later more) officials appointed to protect the rights of the common people against the nobility. A military tribune was an officer attached to a *legion*.

triumph
An official victory procession in ancient Rome.

trusteeship
Situation in which a territory is administered by a particular country on behalf of the United Nations, for the benefit of the territory's inhabitants. See also *mandate*.

usurp
To seize power from another in a manner regarded as wrongful.

Utopia
An imaginary, ideal world. The name, meaning "nowhere," comes from the title of a book by Sir Thomas More, published in 1516. The word **Utopian** has come to be applied to any impractically idealistic plan.

vassal In the feudal system (see *feudalism*), a person holding land from a superior, in return for offering them allegiance; also used more generally for a servant or subordinate.

viceroy
A person who governs as the deputy of a monarch in a colony, region, or province.

Viet Cong
The political and military organization that carried out guerrilla warfare and other activities during the Vietnam War. Although it claimed to be an independent rebel movement within the then non-communist South Vietnam, in fact, it was largely controlled by communist North Vietnam (see *communist*).

Zionist
A supporter of the creation of an independent state for the Jewish people. Also, following the creation of Israel in 1948, a strong supporter of Israel's continued existence as a Jewish state.

INDEX

ACKNOWLEDGMENTS

The publisher would like to thank the following people at the **Smithsonian** for their kind assistance: Kealy Gordon, Product Development Manager; Ellen Nanney, Licensing Manager; Brigid Ferraro, Vice President, Education and Consumer Products; Carol LeBlanc, Senior Vice President, Education and Consumer Products; President, Chris Liedel.

Dorling Kindersley would like to thank the following people: Irene Lyford for proof reading; Jonny Burrows, Philip Fitzgerald, Spencer Holbrook, Clare Joyce, Maxine Pedliham, Hugh Schermuly, and Jackie Swan for design assistance; Steve Crozier for colour work; Amy Smith and Jen Allison at the Ure Museum, Reading University; Rachel Grocke and Helen Armstrong at Durham University Oriental Museum; Catherine Harvey at Hastings Museum; Gary Ombler for photography.

**New Photography:
Durham University Oriental Museum**

The Oriental Museum is the only museum in the North of England devoted entirely to the art and archaeology of the Orient. The world class collections include more than 23,000 objects relating to Egypt, China, Japan, India and the other great cultures of Asia and the Near and Middle East. Founded in 1960 to support teaching and research at Durham University, the museum is now open to everyone.

DK India would like to thank Dharini, Sreshtha Bhattacharya, Archana Ramachandran, Anita Kakar, Aisvarya Misra, and Vineetha Mokkil for editorial assistance; Ira Sharma, Priyabrata Roy Chowdhury, and Niyati Gosain for design assistance; Neeraj Bhatia, Nityanand Kumar, and Mohd Rizwan for hires assistance; Aditya Katyal for additional picture research.

The publisher would like to thank the following for their kind permission to reproduce their photographs:

(Key: a-above; b-below/bottom; c-centre; f-far; l-left; r-right; t-top)

© 1982 MJJ Productions, Inc.: Used by permission. Photographer: Dick Zimmerman 439ca.

Courtesy of 3M: 282cr.
akg-images: British Library, London 222bl, 232tr; CDA / Guillemot 188-189t, 192cl, 206tc, 218cr; DEA Picture Library 188cl; François Guénet 77t; Joseph Martin 200tl; Nimatallah 208 209b, 223b, North Wind Picture Archives 292tc; Russian Picture Service 319tl, 351tl; Sotheby's 233tr; Yvan Travert 137tr; Tretjakov Gallery 235r, 309tr, 318t; Ullstein Bild 334br; World History Archive / IAM 28cr, 154cb, 186bl; Erich Lessing 40cl, 108tc, 182fbr, 183t.
Alamy Stock Photo: AAA Photostock 193cl; Nir Alon 301cr; Ayhan Altun 94-95t, Ancient Art & Architecture Collection 41t, 70c, 146c; Antiques & Collectables 240br, 244bc; Arco Images GmbH 25t; Art Directors & TRIP 36-37t, 78l, 213tr; The Art Archive 30bl, 34tl, 35br, 36c, 41cr, 48tl, 64bc, 65c, 72b, 92t, 112c, 114tc, 116tc, 138cl, 142tc, 143cl, 156cl, 160cl, 170bl, 171b, 182cb, 192b, 193c, 194-195t, 195tr, 195cl, 196tl, 201tr, 201c, 206-207t, 211cl, 216crb, 218tl, 220tc, 226cr, 234tr, 242tr, 259tl, 272cl, 273tr, 284tc, 288tl, 292tr, 294ca, 296tl, 302-303tc, 304tr, 313tc, 332clb, 335tl, 358bl, 402ftr, 410crb, 411cra; The Art Gallery Collection 7tl, 18cra, 50tl, 68tr, 80cl, 102cl, 114cl, 114c, 129cr, 143c, 159c, 179tr, 181tc, 196ca, 201tl, 202tc, 212tl, 238cl, 265cr, 285c; ASP Religion 131tl; Authors Image 142bl; Greg Balfour Evans 114tl; Peter Barritt 137tl; Paul Bevitt 282clb; Anders Blomqvist 35tr; BrazilPhotos.com 224-225t; Vlad Breazu 80b; CBW 65bl; Charistoone-Images 149tr; B. Christopher 41cl; Classic Image 329tr; Dennis Cox 153tr; Stephen Coyne 116cl; Craig Joiner Photography 26-27t; CuboImages srl 76b; Gianni Dagli Orti / The Art Archive 312br, 318cra; DBI Studio 326cra; Dinodia Photos 225b; Michael Doolittle 333br; EmmePi Travel 177tr; Eye Ubiquitous 19cra; Stuart Forster 149b; Robert Fried 169cr; GL Archive 334tl; Globuss Images 26tl; Tim Graham 153tc; Spencer Grant 332ca; Mike Greenslade 284-285t; Handout 464cb; Sonia Halliday Photographs 116-117t; Mark Harmel FAP 283crb; Hemis 27tr; Peter Horree 34ca, 52c; Imagebroker 132tl; ImageClick, Inc. 127tr; Images and Stories 195c; Interfoto 27bl, 55bl, 94cr, 99t, 147b, 153b, 159tr, 167ca, 170-171b, 211b, 212tr, 220tl, 229bl, 267tr, 323tl; Hanan Isachar 139tl; F. Jack Jackson 248tl; Martin Jenkinson 70-71t; Jon Arnold Images / Demetrio

Carrasco 7ftr; Wolfgang Kaehler 34-35t; LatitudeStock 151br; Lebrecht Music and Arts Photo Library 185c, 207tr, 225tr, 234br, 289ca, 364cb; David Lyons 88cl; Celia Mannings 288tc; Mary Evans Picture Library 51b, 98c, 99t, 157tl, 163cr, 181tl, 232tl, 240bl, 259tc, 261tc, 306t, 318br, 323cr, 330tc, 364ctlb; Steven May 330br; John Mitchell 305tr; Carver Mostardi 136tl; Niday Picture Library 222tc, 303tr; North Wind Picture Archives 126tc, 150c, 211tr, 224br, 244cr, 270tr, 277tl, 285tc, 301tc, 321tr, 322tl, 329ca; B O'Kane 147tl; Oasis / Photos 12 332br; Olivier Parent 73c; David Paterson 245t; PhotoEdit 454clb; Photos-12 150tr, 329tl; Pictorial Press Ltd. 197tl, 220-221t, 295cra, 296tc, 414clb; Pictures Colour Library 118c; Paris Pierce 320tr; Mark Pink 140-141tl; Pink Sun Media 215tr; PjrStudio 88tc; Niels Poulsen DK 239br; The Print Collector 31br, 112tr, 151tr, 162tl, 166c, 175ca, 194bl, 251bc, 289crb, 305b, 313cra; Prisma Archivo 319br; Prisma Bildagentur AG 249tr; Ria Novosti 143tl, 207bl; Rolf Richardson 163tc; Robert Estall Photo Agency 109tc; Robert Harding World Imagery 108-109t; Robert Preston Photography 92bl; Russ Images 146b; Kumar Sriskandan 365bl; Stock Montage, Inc. 206c; Homer Sykes Archive 434-435t; Vintage Power and Transport / Mark Sykes 187cr; Giovanni Tagini 194tc; TAO Images Limited 120t; The Natural History Museum 216fclb; TTL Images 152c; V&A Images 136cr, 280tc; Ivan Vdovin 323bl; Visions of America, LLC 220bl; Janine Wiedel Photolibrary 425tl; Pete M. Wilson 296tr; World History 4-5, 65tr, 113tl, 176tl, 252t, 278tl, 309tc, 320tl, 326tr, 327bl, 415cra.
www.BibleLandPictures.com 21tr, 40tl, 64c.
Ancient Art & Architecture Collection: 148b; Prisma 100tl.
The Art Archive: Bibliothèque Nationale Paris 62cl, British Library 196bl, Cathedral of Santiago de Compostela / Gianni Dagli Orti 127c; Edinburgh University Library 146tr, Galleria d'Arte Moderna Rome / Alfredo Dagli Orti 71br; Genius of China Exhibition 27cr; Musée du Louvre Paris / Gianni Dagli Orti 94cl; Musée Guimet Paris / Gianni Dagli Orti 99b; Museum of the City of New York, Gift of Rita and Murray Hartstein (inv 96.13.1) 210tr; Naval Museum Genoa / Alfredo Dagli Orti 205tr; Royal Horticultural Society / Eileen Tweedy 257tl; V&A Images 259crb.

Bibliothèque Nationale De France, Paris: 154crb;
The Bridgeman Art Library: 103r, 143tr, 184tr, 253tr, 264cra, 269cr, 271tr, 374bc; Archives Charmet 157tr, 167tr, 208bl 236cr, 253cl, 277tr, 288tr, 328tr; Art Gallery of New South Wales, Sydney 319tr; Ashmolean Museum, University of Oxford, UK 40cr, 243t; Bibliothèque de l'Institut de France 205bc; Bibliothèque Nationale, Paris 6ftr, 129tl, 130cl, 140tl, 152tc, 156tr; Bildarchiv Steffens Henri Stierlin 40tr; Bonhams, London 314tl; William Bradley 273cr; Bristol City Museum and Art Gallery, UK 297ca; © British Library Board. All Rights Reserved 118tc, 132tc, 141cla, 200tr, 272tr, 301tl; Brooklyn Museum of Art, New York, USA 169cb; Brooklyn Museum of Art, New York, USA/Gift of K. Thomas amd Sharon Elghanayan 110-111t; Burgos Cathedral, Burgos, Spain 175tr; Byzantine / Prado, Madrid, Spain 112tc; Chester Beatty Library, Dublin 220br; Chicago History Museum 312bl; Chiostro dei Morti, Santissima Annunziata, Florence 149tl; Christie's Images 243tl; City of Edinburgh Museums and Art Galleries, Scotland 264tr; English Heritage Photo Library 72tl; Giraudon 50-51t, 102tl, 102-103t, 115cl, 187r; Harappan 26bl; Index 88tr; Indian School 68cl; Patrick Lorette Giraudon 295tl; Louvre, Paris 189b; Massachusetts Historical Society, Boston, MA, USA 236c; Ministere des Affaires Etrangeres, Paris, France / Flammarion Giraudon 218bl; Mucha Trust 119cr; Musée de la Presse, Paris / Giraudon 337tl; Museo Histórico Nacional, Buenos Aires, Argentina / Index 312tl; National Gallery, London 205br; National Museums of Scotland 316tr; Palacio del Senado, Madrid, Spain 141tc; Palazzo Ducale, Venice, Italy, Cameraphoto Arte Venezia 156tl; Peabody Essex Museum, Salem, Massachusetts 300tc; Peter Newark Historical Pictures 151tl; Peter Newark Military Pictures 196tr; Private Collection 257crb; Private Collection / Heini Schneebeli 203br; Private Collection / The Stapleton Collection 204bl; RIA Novosti 224c; The Royal Collection © 2011 Her Majesty Queen Elizabeth II 229t; Science Museum, London, UK 154br; Sumy Art Museum, Sumy, Ukraine 168tl; The Board of Trinity College, Dublin, Ireland 29bl; Professor Ernest Tristram 67tl; Universitetskaya Naberezhnaya, St. Petersburg, Russia / Bernard Cox 244tl;

Victoria & Albert Museum, London 198bl; Wallace Collection, London 214bl; Courtesy of the Warden and Scholars of New College, Oxford 131b; © Trustees of the Watts Gallery, Compton, Surrey 301tr.
The Trustees of the British Museum: 2, 6tc, 8h, 25c, 27t, 54bl, 64t, 67c, 87bl, 93c, 108tl, 149cr, 176-177b, 257clb.
ChinaFotoPress: 30cr.
Corbis: 7tc, 7r, 89cl, 186br, 205bl, 222tl, 238bl, 252br, 256tc, 278clb, 282bl, 284ca, 330tl, 348cla, 350tr, 373cla, 393cra, 404c, 414ca, 426t, 439cra, 441tr, 444-445, 450t, 456cla, 457c, 459tl, 459cla, 460clb; Mike Agliolo 238crb, Albright-Knox Art Gallery / © Successió Miró 2011, 366bl; Alinari Archives 357cla; Paul Almasy 88bc, 128bl, 213c; Amanaimages 192tl; Mladen Antonov, 455cra; H. Armstrong Roberts / ClassicStock 433crb; Tony Arruza 161cr; Arte & Immagini 205tc; 237cl; Asian Art & Archaeology, Inc. 105br, 138tl; Atlantide Phototravel 87cr; Maher Attar / Sygma 444clb; Nathan Benn 21cb, 21bc; Bettmann 29bc, 47c, 65br, 68c, 87t, 139tr, 175cr, 176cl, 201cr, 208tc, 210cr, 225tl, 229br, 264tl, 266tr, 267clb, 278tr, 278crb, 289tl, 289tr, 300tl, 306cra, 308b, 309bc, 315tl, 328bl, 329tc, 329cla, 334tc, 340clb, 342tl, 343br, 350bc, 358tr, 360tl, 362bl, 363tl, 365clb, 366tr, 369tl, 370-371t, 371crb, 375br, 377tr, 378bl, 381tr, 391cra, 393tl, 397t, 399t, 400tl, 404bl, 407t, 412tr, 419t, 421crb, 428cb, 430, 433cl, 446ca; Stefano Bianchetti 228tr, 374cr; Bernard Bisson / Sygma 447tr; Brooklyn Museum 30-31t, 126cr, 241bl; Henri Bureau, 437cb; Alexander Burkatovski 41bl; Burstein Collection 66t, 127cl, 180c, 191c, 227cr; Car Culture 333bl; Charles Caratini 450-451b, Jacques M. Chenet, 440-441t; Christie's Images 163tr, 240tl; Elio Ciol 95ca, 105bl; Pierre Colombel 46-47t, 105t; Christopher Cormack 266tc; Marco Cristofori 152tl; Gianni Dagli Orti 28bl, 45b, 46cr, 49tc, 50c, 53cr, 57cr, 61tl, 62-63t, 259tr, 314b; Keith Dannemiller 158tl; David J. & Janice L. Frent Collection 337clb; Araldo de Luca 73bl, 77b, 81bl, 86cr, 89cr, 91cr, 374bl; Leonard de Selva 374br; Destinations 207tc; Dennis di Cicco 183bl; DPA / Agentur Voller Ernst / Yevgeny Khaldei 404-405; Richard Dudman / Sygma 435r; EFE 386t, 400t, 462cla; Anatoly Maltsev / EPA 118bl, EPA 226b, 462cla; Waltraud Grubitzsch / EPA 29cl; Patrick Escudero / Hemis 67tr; Dominique Faget,